AVIATION LAW AFTER SEPTEMBER 11TH

CASES AND MATERIALS

Second Edition

AVIATION LAW AFTER SEPTEMBER 11TH

CASES AND MATERIALS

Second Edition

TIMOTHY M. RAVICH

VANDEPLAS PUBLISHING LLC

United States of America

Aviation law after September 11th: cases and materials
Second Edition

Ravich, Timothy M.

Published by:

Vandeplas Publishing – January 2016

801 International Parkway, 5th Floor
Lake Mary, FL. 32746
USA

www.vandeplaspublishing.com

ISBN: 978-1-60042-274-4

For Carl Ravich

PREFACE

Publishing a book whose title identifies a specific day in history risks being discounted as dated. In this case, however, the events and lessons of September 11, 2001 are as relevant now as they were when this book was first published five years ago.

As this second edition goes to press, America and the world are again—or still—recovering from terror attacks by Islamic extremists. In November 2015, several terrorists associated with the Islamic State of Iraq and the Levant—ISIL or ISIS—detonated explosive belts and killed at least at 129 people in attacks at a rock concert, café, and other venues in and around Paris. A few weeks earlier, a homemade bomb brought down a Russian airliner over Egypt's Sinai desert. And, in December 2015, a religious Muslim and U.S. citizen, and his wife, a Pakistani from Saudi Arabia, massacred 14 people and wounded 21 in a shooting at a holiday party at a center for the disabled in San Bernardino, California, before they died in a shootout with authorities. "Terrorists have quickly adapted and evolved in order to carry out heinous plots since 9/11, and this tragedy reinforces the need for law enforcement to evolve its intelligence-gathering and investigative techniques," the chairman of the House Judiciary Committee said in reaction. Meanwhile, a leading U.S. presidential candidate proposed temporarily banning Muslims from entering the United States. To say that the issues in this book—including the Constitution, the right to travel, aviation security, passenger profiling, "no fly" lists, and accident litigation—are still relevant and important in this context is self-evident.

Additionally, studying the aviation business environment is as compelling today as it was five years ago. Southwest Airlines, United Airlines, and American Airlines acquired AirTran, Continental, and U.S. Airways, respectively. Interestingly, then, fewer airlines exist now than five years ago, raising new questions about the legacy of deregulation and quality of airline passenger consumer rights and protections. Meanwhile, the emergence of unmanned aerial systems—"drones"—and the reaction of lawmakers to new aviation technologies introduces fresh content into this book.

Finally, of 87 primary sources, this second edition features 24 new legal authorities. This book also now includes introductory remarks before each chapter and 150 detailed notes and commentary after each section, 20 of which are new. And, the book now provides expanded margins, larger font, and a detailed table of authorities and index—substantive and structural enhancements invited by students and colleagues who have enjoyed the first edition of this text and who made possible this second installment.

INTRODUCTION

This book introduces the topic of aviation law, focusing on the subject matter since the terrorism of September 11, 2001—no less an aviation than a national security event.

AVIATION LAW AFTER SEPTEMBER 11TH is a traditional law course book that presents the main legal, business, and political aspects of the nation's air transportation system. While a definite set of laws and regulations exists to govern the ownership and use of aircraft, airports and airspace, "aviation law" is contextual, requiring the study of other areas of substantive and doctrinal law, including administrative, bankruptcy, constitutional, contract, labor, procedural, property, and tort law, as applied in a specific industry.

Significantly, issues in the general and commercial aviation industries reflect the major tensions in the global marketplace: consumer protection and the corporate bottom-line; regulation versus deregulation; private enterprise and positive government; price versus convenience; labor and management; balancing liberty and privacy interests against national security; internationalism versus nationalism; democracy versus terror; and fundamentally, life and death.

Today, though airline travel has become a routine part of life, modern airline passengers—among whom are members of Congress—fume at airline automation, overbooking practices, delays, and congestion at airports. They continue to demand more rights in the form of "Airline Passengers' Bill of Rights." Meanwhile, the terrorist attacks of September 11th jolted the nation's focus from issues of comfort and convenience to safety and security. Air travelers are subjected to—and in some cases welcome—invasive security protocols such as "No-Fly" lists and profiling. AVIATION LAW AFTER SEPTEMBER 11TH explores the inverse relationship between private rights and government power in this atmosphere.

In all, AVIATION LAW AFTER SEPTEMBER 11TH presents more than just legal precedent for judges, lawyers and students of aviation law. It features primary data detailing how the rule of law was applied (or not) to unprecedented threats. AVIATION LAW AFTER SEPTEMBER 11TH offers a historical narrative of the ongoing "war on terror" through court opinions, regulations, and statutory law; the circumstances in which air passengers travel today; and the policies that lawmakers are implementing to optimize and protect the mobility of its citizens.

ACKNOWLEDGMENTS

I am very grateful to the many people who made this book possible. Professionally, I am grateful to the faculty and administrators at the University of Miami School of Law and Florida International University's College of Law for the opportunity to introduce and teach the topic of aviation law for the last decade. Thanks, too, to the University of Central Florida, and particularly James D. Beckman, Chair of the Department of Legal Studies, and Professor David Slaughter, for their friendship and support of my scholarship and aviation law course. Finally, personally, I am grateful to my family: Sara, Steve, Linda, Matt, Carli, Melissa, Heather, Haley, David, Carol, and Mark for their love, support, and encouragement.

ABOUT THE AUTHOR

Timothy M. Ravich, Assistant Professor at the University of Central Florida, is an internationally recognized authority in aviation law and one of only thirty-seven lawyers in the State of Florida who is a Board Certified Specialist in Aviation Law. His scholarship focuses on administrative law, civil litigation, and national security law through the lens of civil, commercial, and military aviation.

Professor Ravich has written extensively in connection with aviation issues, including airline deregulation and passenger rights, aviation security and terrorism, and unmanned aerial vehicles ("UAVs" or "drones").

He has published numerous articles in peer-reviewed journals and is widely cited and has appeared in publications such as the *Columbia Journal of Law and Social Problems*, *William and Mary Business Law Review*, *American Business Law Journal*, *Washington University Journal of Law and Policy*, *Georgetown Journal of International Law*, and *U.C. Davis Journal of International Law and Policy*.

In addition, national and international media outlets regularly feature Professor Ravich in television and radio programming, podcasts, and articles featuring aviation and aerospace issues, including BLOOMBERGNEWS, *Christian Science Monitor*, NBC Universal, MSNTravel, FOX, China Central Television, HUFFPost, Mercatus Center at George Mason University, National Public Radio, the *Atlantic*, *Daily Business Review*, NTV (Russia), *Asia Times*, and Scientific American. He blogs at *droninglawyer.com* and is followed on Twitter @ravichaviation.

Prior to joining the University of Central Florida, Professor Ravich practiced as a commercial trial lawyer with McDermott, Will & Emery and Hunton & Williams LLP. He also served as President and CEO of the Dade County Bar Association, the largest voluntary bar association in the State of Florida. He has received an AV rating from Martindale-Hubbell, the highest possible rating, based on legal ability and general ethical standards. In addition, Professor Ravich was named as a "Leading Lawyer" by the South Florida Legal Guide and consistently selected by his colleagues as a Florida "Super Lawyer."

A *cum laude* graduate of the University of Miami School of Law, where he was the Editor-in-Chief of the *University of Miami Business Law Review* and tapped as a member of the Iron Arrow Honor Society, Professor Ravich also earned an M.B.A. in Aviation Policy and Planning from Embry-Riddle Aeronautical University.

TABLE OF CONTENTS

CHAPTER 1
THE RIGHT TO TRAVEL

A. LIBERTY VERSUS NATIONAL SECURITY—CONSTITUTIONAL AND COMMON LAW PRINCIPLES

AUTHORITY TO GRANT AND RESTRICT TRAVEL RIGHTS

INTERNATIONAL TRAVEL AND NATIONAL SECURITY

B. AIRLINE PASSENGER RIGHTS

DOMESTIC AIR TRAVEL

INTERNATIONAL TRAVEL: EUROPEAN UNION

C. AIRPORTS AND AIRSPACE

AIRPORTS

AIRSPACE

CHAPTER 2
DEREGULATION AND PREEMPTION

A. AVIATION FEDERALISM AND SUPREMACY

B. AIRLINE BUSINESS TORTS—PRICES, ROUTES, AND SERVICES

C. CONTRACTS OF CARRIAGE

CHAPTER 3
AIRLINE ECONOMICS

A. ANTITRUST AND LOW COST CARRIERS

B. BANKRUPTCY AND POST-9/11 INSURANCE

CHAPTER 4
AIRMEN

A. ENFORCEMENT AND TRANSPORTATION SECURITY

B. LABOR RELATIONS— COLLECTIVE BARGAINING AND THE RAILWAY LABOR ACT

C. UNMANNED AVIATION: "DRONES"

LAW AND TECHNOLOGY

AVIATION SURVEILLANCE AND SECURITY

CHAPTER 5
AVIATION SECURITY

A. AIR PIRACY AND TERRORISM

B. INTERFERENCE WITH FLIGHT CREW

C. FOURTH AMENDMENT ISSUES: PROFILING AND "NO-FLY"

CHAPTER 6
ACCIDENT SAFETY

A. SAFETY AND PREEMPTION

B. CHOICE OF AVIATION LAW ADMIRALTY, DOHSA, FTCA, GARA

C. INTERNATIONAL LIABILITY TREATIES

TABLE OF AUTHORITIES

CHAPTER 1

THE RIGHT TO TRAVEL

A. LIBERTY VERSUS NATIONAL SECURITY—CONSTITUTIONAL AND COMMON LAW PRINCIPLES

In studying aviation law, you will be reading primarily federal court decisions addressing the constitutionality of national regulations and international treaties with respect to travel rights. The judicial power to say whether a citizen can move across borders is significant, raising important questions about the limitations on such judicial power specifically, the role of sovereign powers and governmental authorities in defining and enforcing travel rights generally, and the opportunity for individuals to petition governmental authorities to safeguard the freedom of mobility broadly.

The contemporary relevance of the right to travel, both domestically and internationally, is apparent. On November 13, 2015, several terrorists associated with the Islamic State of Iraq and the Levant—ISIL or ISIS—detonated explosive belts and killed at least at 129 people in attacks at a rock concert, café, and other venues in and around Paris. One of suspects in the attack may have entered into France as a refugee from years-long civil war in Syria. As a consequence, at least two dozen Republican governors announced their opposition to President Barack Obama's commitment to accepting 100,000 Syrian refuges in 2016. In France, meanwhile, President François Hollande announced heightened and immediate security initiatives implicating travel rights:

> Created during the Algerian war in 1955, the state of emergency gives authorities far-reaching powers, including banning travel in certain areas, shutting shops and concert halls. The interior minister can ban people from leaving their homes, and the state can take "all measures" to control the press and radio. Searches can be undertaken without a judge's approval, and those who refuse to comply can be fined and held in custody for as long as two months.

William Horobin et al., *Hollande Outlines Tougher Security Policies*, WALL. ST. J., Nov. 17, 2015, at A9. Travel and movement rights are central to national and international security obviously and critical to the subject of aviation law given the integral role commercial and general airplanes play in animating these rights. The origin of the right to travel—essentially the right of free ingress into and egress from a state—dates back more than 800 years to the Magna Carta, excerpted below, and *Corfield v. Coryell*, an 1823 decision in which the United States Supreme Court recognized the freedom of movement as a fundamental right. The authorities below detail the evolution of this freedom, including modern limitations driven by the events of September 11th.

Authority to Grant and Restrict Travel Rights

Article 42 of the Magna Carta reads:

> It shall be lawful to any person, for the future, to go out of our kingdom, and to return, safely and securely, by land or by water, saving his allegiance to us, unless it be in time of war, for some short space, for the common good of the kingdom: excepting prisoners and outlaws, according to the laws of the land, and of the people of the nation at war against us, and Merchants who shall be treated as it is said above.

SAENZ v. ROE

526 U.S. 428 (1999)

Justice STEVENS delivered the opinion of the Court.

The word "travel" is not found in the text of the Constitution. Yet the "constitutional right to travel from one State to another" is firmly embedded in our jurisprudence. Indeed, as Justice Stewart reminded us in *Shapiro v. Thompson* (1969), the right is so important that it is "assertable against private interference as well as governmental action ... a virtually unconditional personal right, guaranteed by the Constitution to us all."

In *Shapiro*, we reviewed the constitutionality of three statutory provisions that denied welfare assistance to residents of Connecticut, the District of Columbia, and Pennsylvania, who had resided within those respective jurisdictions less than one year immediately preceding their applications for assistance. Without pausing to identify the specific source of the right, we began by noting that the Court had long "recognized that the nature of our Federal Union and our constitutional concepts of personal liberty unite to require that all citizens be free to travel throughout the length and breadth of our land uninhibited by statutes, rules, or regulations which unreasonably burden or restrict this movement." We squarely held that it was "constitutionally impermissible" for a State to enact durational residency requirements for the purpose of inhibiting the migration by needy persons into the State. We further held that a classification that had the effect of imposing a penalty on the exercise of the right to travel violated the Equal Protection Clause "unless shown to be necessary to promote a compelling governmental interest," and that no such showing had been made.

The "right to travel" discussed in our cases embraces at least three different components. It protects the right of a citizen of one State to enter and to leave another State, the right to be treated as a welcome visitor rather than an unfriendly alien when temporarily present in the second State, and, for those travelers who elect to become permanent residents, the right to be treated like other citizens of that State.

It was the right to go from one place to another, including the right to cross state borders while enroute, that was vindicated in *Edwards v. California* (1941), which invalidated a state law that impeded the free interstate passage of the indigent. We reaffirmed that right in *United States v. Guest* (1966), which afforded protection to the "'right to travel freely to and from the State of Georgia and to use highway facilities and other instrumentalities of interstate commerce within the State of Georgia.'" The right of "free ingress and regress to and from" neighboring States, which was expressly mentioned in the Articles of Confederation, may simply have been "conceived from the beginning to be a necessary concomitant of the stronger Union the Constitution created."

The second component of the right to travel is, however, expressly protected by the text of the Constitution. The first sentence of Article IV, § 2, provides: "The Citizens of each State shall be entitled to all Privileges and Immunities of Citizens in the several States." Thus, by virtue of a person's state citizenship, a citizen of one State who travels in other States, intending to return home at the end of his journey, is entitled to enjoy the "Privileges and Immunities of Citizens in the several States" that he visits. This provision removes "from the citizens of each State the disabilities of alienage in the other States." Those protections are not "absolute," but the Clause "does bar discrimination against citizens of other States where there is no substantial reason for the discrimination beyond the mere fact that they are citizens of other States."

At issue in this case is this third aspect of the right to travel—the right of the newly arrived citizen to the same privileges and immunities enjoyed by other citizens of the same State. That right is protected not only by the new arrival's status as a state citizen, but also by her status as a citizen of the United States. That additional source of protection is plainly identified in the opening words of the Fourteenth Amendment: "All persons born or naturalized in the United States, and subject to the jurisdiction thereof, are citizens of the United States and of the State wherein they reside. No State shall make or enforce any law which shall abridge the privileges or immunities of citizens of the United States." Despite fundamentally differing views concerning the coverage of the Privileges or Immunities Clause of the Fourteenth Amendment, most notably expressed in the the *Slaughter–House Cases* (1872), it has always been common ground that this Clause protects the third component of the right to travel.

That newly arrived citizens "have two political capacities, one state and one federal," adds special force to their claim that they have the same rights as others who share their citizenship. Neither mere rationality nor some intermediate standard of review should be used to judge the constitutionality of a state rule that discriminates against some of its citizens because they have been domiciled in the State for less than a year. The appropriate standard may be more categorical than that articulated in *Shapiro*, but it is surely no less strict.

Because this case involves discrimination against citizens who have completed their interstate travel, the State's argument that its welfare scheme affects the right to travel only "incidentally" is beside the point. Were we concerned solely with actual deterrence to migration, we might be persuaded that a partial withholding of benefits constitutes a lesser incursion on the right to travel than an outright denial of all benefits. But since the right to travel embraces the citizen's right to be treated equally in her new State of residence, the discriminatory classification is itself a penalty.

Chief Justice REHNQUIST, with Justice THOMAS joining, dissenting.

The Court today breathes new life into the previously dormant Privileges or Immunities Clause of the Fourteenth Amendment—a Clause relied upon by this Court in only one other decision, *Colgate v. Harvey* (1935), overruled five years later by *Madden v. Kentucky* (1940). It uses this Clause to strike down what I believe is a reasonable measure falling under the head of a "good-faith residency requirement." Because I do not think any provision of the Constitution—and surely not a provision relied upon for only the second time since its enactment 130 years ago—requires this result, I dissent.

Much of the Court's opinion is unremarkable and sound. The right to travel clearly embraces the right to go from one place to another, and prohibits States from impeding the free interstate passage of citizens. The state law in *Edwards v. California* (1941), which prohibited the transport of any indigent person into California, was a classic barrier to travel or migration and the Court rightly struck it down. Indeed, for most of this country's history, what the Court today calls the first "component" of the right to travel, was the entirety of this right.

But I cannot see how the right to become a citizen of another State is a necessary "component" of the right to travel, or why the Court tries to marry these separate and distinct rights. A person is no longer "traveling" in any sense of the word when he finishes his journey to a State which he plans to make his home. Indeed, under the Court's logic, the protections of the Privileges or Immunities Clause recognized in this case come into play only when an individual stops traveling with the intent to remain and become a citizen of a new State. The right to travel and the right to become a citizen are distinct, their relationship is not reciprocal, and one is not a "component" of the other.

KENT v. DULLES

357 U.S. 116 (1958)

Justice DOUGLAS delivered the opinion of the Court.

This case concerns two applications for passports, denied by the Secretary of State. One was by Rockwell Kent who desired to visit England and attend a meeting of an organization known as the "World Council of Peace" in Helsinki, Finland. The

Director of the Passport Office informed Kent that issuance of a passport was precluded by the Regulations promulgated by the Secretary of State on two grounds: (1) that he was a Communist and (2) that he had had "a consistent and prolonged adherence to the Communist Party line." Kent was told that, before a passport would be issued, he would need to submit an affidavit as to whether he was then or ever had been a Communist.

Kent took the position that the requirement of an affidavit concerning Communist Party membership "is unlawful and that for that reason and as a matter of conscience," he would not supply one. He did, however, have a hearing at which the principal evidence against him was from his book "It's Me O Lord," which Kent agreed was accurate.

* * *

The right to travel is a part of the "liberty" of which the citizen cannot be deprived without the due process of law under the Fifth Amendment. So much is conceded by the Solicitor General. In Anglo-Saxon law that right was emerging at least as early as the Magna Carta. Freedom of movement across frontiers in either direction, and inside frontiers as well, was a part of our heritage.

Travel abroad, like travel within the country, may be necessary for a livelihood. It may be as close to the heart of the individual as the choice of what he eats, or wears, or reads. Freedom of movement is basic in our scheme of values. "Our nation," wrote Chafee, "has thrived on the principle that, outside areas of plainly harmful conduct, every American is left to shape his own life as he thinks best, do what he pleases, go where he pleases." Freedom of movement also has large social values. As Chafee put it:

> Foreign correspondents and lecturers on public affairs need first-hand information. Scientists and scholars gain greatly from consultations with colleagues in other countries. Students equip themselves for more fruitful careers in the United States by instruction in foreign universities. Then there are reasons close to the core of personal life—marriage, reuniting families, spending hours with old friends. Finally, travel abroad enables American citizens to understand that people like themselves live in Europe and helps them to be well-informed on public issues. An American who has crossed the ocean is not obliged to form his opinions about our foreign policy merely from what he is told by officials of our government or by a few correspondents of American newspapers. Moreover, his views on domestic questions are enriched by seeing how foreigners are trying to solve similar problems. In many different ways direct contact with other countries contributes to sounder decisions at home.

Freedom to travel is, indeed, an important aspect of the citizen's "liberty." We need not decide the extent to which it can be curtailed. We are first concerned with the extent, if any, to which Congress has authorized its curtailment. The difficulty is that while the power of the Secretary of State over the issuance of passports is expressed in broad terms, it was apparently long exercised quite narrowly. So far as material here, the cases of refusal of passports generally fell into two categories. First, questions pertinent to the citizenship of the applicant and his allegiance to the United States had to be resolved by the Secretary, for the command of Congress was that "No passport shall be granted or issued to or verified for any other persons than those owing allegiance, whether citizens or not, to the United States." Second, was the question whether the applicant was participating in illegal conduct, trying to escape the toils of the law, promoting passport frauds, or otherwise engaging in conduct which would violate the laws of the United States. The grounds for refusal asserted here do not relate to citizenship or allegiance on the one hand or to criminal or unlawful conduct on the other. We, therefore, hesitate to impute to Congress, when in 1952 it made a passport necessary for foreign travel and left its issuance to the discretion of the Secretary of State, a purpose to give him unbridled discretion to grant or withhold a passport from a citizen for any substantive reason he may choose.

More restrictive regulations were applied in 1918 and in 1941 as war measures. In a case of comparable magnitude, *Korematsu v. United States* (1944), we allowed the Government in time of war to exclude citizens from their homes and restrict their freedom of movement only on a showing of "the gravest imminent danger to the public safety." There the Congress and the Chief Executive moved in coordinated action; and, as we said, the Nation was then at war. No such condition presently exists. No such showing of extremity, no such showing of joint action by the Chief Executive and the Congress to curtail a constitutional right of the citizen has been made here.

Thus we do not reach the question of constitutionality. We only conclude that the law does not delegate to the Secretary the kind of authority exercised here. We deal with beliefs, with associations, with ideological matters. We must remember that we are dealing here with citizens who have neither been accused of crimes nor found guilty. They are being denied their freedom of movement solely because of their refusal to be subjected to inquiry into their beliefs and associations. They do not seek to escape the law nor to violate it. They may or may not be Communists. But assuming they are, the only law which Congress has passed expressly curtailing the movement of Communists across our borders has not yet become effective. It would therefore be strange to infer that pending the effectiveness of that law, the Secretary has been silently granted by Congress the larger, the more pervasive power to curtail in his discretion the free movement of citizens in order to satisfy himself about their beliefs or associations. We would be faced with important constitutional questions were we to hold that Congress had given the Secretary authority to withhold passports to citizens because of their beliefs or associations. Congress has made no such provision in explicit terms; and absent one, the Secretary may not employ that standard to restrict the citizens' right of free movement.

Mr. Justice CLARK, with whom Mr. Justice BURTON, Mr. Justice HARLAN, and Mr. Justice WHITTAKER concur, dissenting.

The Secretary's action clearly must be held authorized by Congress if the requested information is relevant to any ground upon which the Secretary might properly refuse to issue a passport. The Court purports today to preclude the existence of such a ground by holding that the Secretary has not been authorized to deny a passport to a Communist whose travel abroad would be inimical to our national security. In thus construing the authority of the Secretary, the Court recognizes that all during our history he has had discretion to grant or withhold passports. This discretionary authority, which we previously acknowledged in *Perkins v. Elg* (1939), was exercised both in times of peace and in periods of war. During war and other periods of national emergency, however, the importance of the Secretary's passport power was tremendously magnified by a succession of "travel-control statutes" making possession of a passport a legal necessity to leaving or entering this country.

The first of these was enacted in 1815 just prior to the end of the War of 1812, when it was made illegal for any citizen to "cross the frontier" into enemy territory without a passport. After the same result was accomplished during the Civil War without congressional sanction, World War I prompted passage in 1918 of the second travel-control statute. The 1918 statute, directly antecedent to presently controlling legislation, provided that in time of war and upon public proclamation by the President that the public safety required additional travel restrictions, no citizen could depart from or enter into the country without a passport. Shortly thereafter, President Wilson made the required proclamation of public necessity, and provided that no citizen should be granted a passport unless it affirmatively appeared that his "departure or entry is not prejudicial to the interests of the United States."

Orders promulgated by the Passport Office periodically have required denial of passports to "political adventurers" and "revolutionary radicals," the latter phrase being defined to include "those who wish to go abroad to take part in the political or military affairs of foreign countries in ways which would be contrary to the policy or inimical to the welfare of the United States."

Were this a time of peace, there might very well be no problem for us to decide, since petitioners then would not need a passport to leave the country. Either war or national emergency is prerequisite to imposition of its restrictions. Indeed, rather than being irrelevant, the wartime practice may be the only relevant one, for the discretion with which we are concerned is a discretionary control over international travel. Yet only in times of war and national emergency has a passport been required to leave or enter this country, and hence only in such times has passport power necessarily meant power to control travel.

SHACHTMAN v. DULLES

225 F. 2d 938 (D.C. 1955)

FAHY, Circuit Judge.

Appellant sued in the District Court to enjoin the Secretary of State from denying, for the reason assigned by the Secretary, his application for a passport to visit Europe, and for a declaratory judgment. His complaint was dismissed on motion, the court holding that it failed to state a claim upon which relief could be granted and that since the denial was in the proper exercise of the Secretary's discretion the court lacked jurisdiction. Appellant does not ask that the Secretary be required by the court to issue the passport. He seeks in this court only a ruling to the effect that the denial thus far has been on a ground that is legally insufficient. This position assumes that the discretion residing in the Secretary is subject in its exercise to some judicial scrutiny. We agree. The courts by reason of the Constitution have a responsibility in the matter although a limited one.

Congress has placed the issuance of passports in the hands of the Secretary under rules prescribed by the President. These provide, "The Secretary of State is authorized in his discretion to refuse to issue a passport." However, in *Perkins v. Elg*, the Supreme Court, while stating that the Court's action would not interfere with the Secretary's discretion, precluded denial of a passport for the asserted reason that the applicant had lost her American citizenship, when she had not done so. Though that case factually is not like this one, it nevertheless shows that the subject of passports is not entirely beyond judicial assistance. And this is to notwithstanding the relation of the subject to the Executive's power over the conduct of foreign affairs, for it too, "like every other governmental power, must be exercised in subordination to the applicable provisions of the Constitution."

Is there a provision of the Constitution applicable to the present situation? In answering this we bear in mind that the issuance of a passport is not a purely political matter. If it were it would be a non-justiciable one. In other words, a passport is no longer a document "purporting only to be a request, that the bearer of it may pass safely and freely'; it is no longer 'to be considered rather in the character of a political document, by which the bearer is recognized, in foreign countries, as an American citizen.'" This description parallels early rulings of Secretaries of State, opinions of Attorneys General, texts and other court decisions, which have recognized a great breadth of Executive authority and discretion.

We do not suggest that a passport is no longer a political document, or that its issuance is not allied to, and at times a part of, the conduct of foreign affairs, but only that it is not merely of this character. For it is now, in addition, a document which is essential to the lawful departure of an American citizen for Europe. Regulations now in effect and authorized by Congress so provide. Earlier in our history, except, *e.g.*, during the War between the Sections, this was not the case. It was then a desirable incident to travel, not a necessity, and was granted more or less at the pleasure of the Executive. Now it is unlawful for a citizen to travel to Europe and impossible to enter European countries without a passport.

The denial of a passport accordingly causes a deprivation of liberty that a citizen otherwise would have. The right to travel, to go from place to place as the means of transportation permit, is a natural right subject to the rights of others and to reasonable regulation under law. A restraint imposed by the Government of the United States upon this liberty, therefore, must conform with the provision of the Fifth Amendment that "No person shall be ... deprived of ... liberty ... without due process of law."

It is not procedural due process that is involved in the case as now presented. There is no complaint the Secretary has failed to disclose the reason for his denial of the passport. Furthermore, a hearing of a sort was granted appellant He was at least given an opportunity to state informally to an official of the Department the matters on which he relied in rebuttal of the reason given by the Department for refusing him a passport.

What is involved at the present stage is a question of substantive due process—whether the refusal for the reason given, as alleged in the complaint and undisputed thus far by the Secretary, was arbitrary. If so, it is not a valid foundation for the denial, for the Government may not arbitrarily restrain the liberty of a citizen to travel to Europe. Discretionary power does not carry with it the right to its arbitrary exercise. Otherwise the existence of the power itself would encounter grave constitutional doubts.

What is arbitrary, however, in the sense of constituting a denial of due process, depends upon circumstances. Restraint upon travel abroad might be reasonable during an emergency though in normal times it would be arbitrary. World conditions, and those in particular areas, as to which the Executive has special information and on the basis of which he is especially qualified to make decisions, bear upon the question. For reasons thus suggested the issuance of passports throughout our history has been left to the judgment of the Secretary of State under Presidential regulation, and is subject only to constitutional safeguards. And even these must be defined with cautious regard for the responsibility of the Executive in the conduct of foreign affairs.

The appellant's own statement in the complaint of the reason he was refused a passport must be taken as true in the present posture of the case, for the Secretary has not answered the complaint. We must take it as true, then, that appellant was first notified of tentative disapproval because of information he was Chairman of the Independent Socialist League, which the Secretary understood had been classified by the Attorney General as both subversive and Communistic, although it appeared to the Secretary the organization had no direct connection with the Communist International.

The Secretary also notified appellant that the Department had been advised that the League's publication described the organization as an "organ of revolutionary

Marxism." At the hearing granted appellant by the Department of State, he testified the League was anti-Stalinist, anti-totalitarian, opposed to violence as a means of solving political, social and economic problems, and that he and the League believed in and strove for the establishment of a socialist economic system by democratic means. He explained that the description of the organ above referred to meant only that the League and he stood for a thorough-going reorganization of the economic and social foundations of society but used the term "revolutionary" with reference to the result rather than the means of achieving it. At the hearing he said the League advocated the formation by the labor movement of a labor party similar to the Labor Party of Great Britain. The complaint further alleges that the League has never had any international affiliations; that appellant desired a passport solely for the purpose of consulting people in Europe whose knowledge of political conditions he respected, and observing those conditions in order to acquired material for his work of writing and lecturing; that he had no intention of engaging in any political activity abroad, and would not engage there in activities which would violate the laws of, reflect upon or embarrass, the United States.

The complaint then alleges that the passport was subsequently denied in a letter to appellant in which the Department stated that despite the fact that the League had no connection with the Communist International and was hostile thereto, the Department felt that it would be contrary to the best interests of the United States to grant passport facilities to the actual head of an organization which had been classified by the Attorney General as subversive, especially when he desired to travel abroad on behalf of the organization, adding that should there be a change in the classification by the Attorney General the Department would then give further consideration to the question. The wording of the Department's letter indicates that the listing of the League as Communistic was no longer relied upon. The hearing appears to have convinced the Department that the League was hostile to the Communist International.

Appellant in the end alleges that the passport was denied "solely because of the inclusion of the Independent Socialist League on the Attorney General's List," that this listing was without notice or hearing or presentation of evidence or opportunity to answer, and that appellant, as National Chairman of the League, for nearly six years and on at least fifteen separate occasions, without avail, had attempted to persuade the Attorney General to grant a hearing to the League so that it could prove the injustice of the designation.

We think the complaint fairly read shows that the listing of the League by the Attorney General as subversive was the reason for the Secretary's refusal to issue the passport, that is to say, that except for such listing the fact that appellant was head of the organization and wished to go to Europe on its business would not have been considered by the Secretary as ground for rejection of his application. Therefore, with no answer by the Department, we must decide whether this listing, followed by nearly six years of effort by appellant to obtain a hearing thereon, is sufficient basis for the Secretary's refusal, when considered with the undenied allegations of the complaint that the listing is erroneous.

We do not here characterize as invalid, for its own purposes, the listing by the Attorney General. He is not a party, and, in any event, his listing is not subject to collateral attack in these proceedings. We are called upon only to consider the use made by the Secretary of the listing. Reliance by the Secretary on action by the Attorney General is not precluded. Warning given by the Nation's chief law officer can at least lead to investigation, and in a proper case be an element in decision. But in the present state of the pleadings we must take it as a fact that the League is non-subversive as well as non-Communistic, and has sought for nearly six years the opportunity to demonstrate the former to the Attorney General as it appears to have demonstrated the latter to the Secretary.

It is not for us to determine, in this case at least, that a passport should or should not be granted, but only whether the reason given by the Secretary for its denial is sufficient. As to this, we think the law must consider to be arbitrary, regardless of good faith, refusal of appellant's application only because the League was listed by the Attorney General as subversive when appellant in detail denies the correctness of this characterization, alleges lack of opportunity so to demonstrate, and when these allegations are not challenged by the Secretary.

For us to hold that the restraint thus imposed upon appellant is not arbitrary would amount to judicial approval of a deprivation of liberty without a reasonable relation to the conduct of foreign affairs. Unless some additional reason is supplied for the denial, a citizen is prevented indefinitely from traveling to Europe while at the same time it is impossible for him to remove the cause, even though we must assume in the present state of the pleadings that he would be able to do so if afforded the opportunity. If there is something which justifies this it should be set forth by an answer to the complaint. Otherwise the denial, judged on the basis alone of the appellant's allegations, creates a situation which the law cannot reconcile with due process. It is worth noting in this connection that when the Attorney General lists an organization for purposes of standards of Federal employment prescribed by the President, which was the occasion for the listing of the League, a separate judgment by the employing agency of the fitness of the individual employee who is a member of the organization is required before removing him from public service. The listing alone is not enough.

We must not confuse the problem of appellant's application for a passport with the conduct of foreign affairs in the political sense, which is entirely removed from judicial competence. For even though his application might be said to come within the scope of foreign affairs in a broad sense, it is also within the scope of the due process clause, which is concerned with the liberty of the individual free of arbitrary administrative restraint. There must be some reconciliation of these interests where only the right of a particular individual to travel is involved and not a question of foreign affairs on a political level.

International Travel and National Security

LEE v. CHINA AIRLINES, LTD.
669 F. Supp. 979 (C.D. Cal. 1987)

WILSON, District Judge.

This case is one of several involving China Airlines Flight 006 (a Boeing 747) on February 19, 1985. The Lees were injured on that flight when the 747 made an unexpected and uncontrolled 31,000 foot descent off the coast of California.

The Lees are permanent residents of California. Mr. Lee is in the international garment manufacturing business, so he makes frequent trips to Asia. They purchased the tickets which allowed them to travel on Flight 006 in Hong Kong. These tickets were for round trip travel from Hong Kong to San Francisco. The date and flight number on the return portion of the ticket were left open.

Article 28 of the Warsaw Convention will not allow the Lees' case against China Airlines to be heard in the United States. The Lees argue that the Warsaw Convention does not apply in this case because their ill-fated flight did not depart from a country that is a party to the Convention. They are incorrect. The Convention applies to "international transportation." This term is defined in Article 1, Paragraph (2) of the Convention as:

> [A]ny transportation in which, according to the contract made by the parties, the place of departure and the place of destination, whether or not there be a break in the transportation or a transshipment, are situated either in the territories of two High Contracting Parties, or within the territory of a single High Contracting Party, if there is an agreed stopping place in a territory subject to the sovereignty, suzerainty, mandate or authority of another power, even though that power is not a party to this Convention.

According to this language, the Convention will apply in two situations. First, it applies, if according to the contract of transportation (*e.g.*, a plane ticket), travel will be from one High Contracting Party to another. Second, if the contract of transportation provides for travel from a High Contracting Party, for stops abroad, and then for a return to that same High Contracting Party, then the Convention also applies. The ticket in this case provided for transportation from Hong Kong to Taipei to San Francisco to Hong Kong. Because the Convention only allows for one destination, the departure point and the destination of the Lees must officially be considered Hong Kong. Thus, the Convention will not apply here unless Hong Kong is a High Contracting Party. And, Hong Kong qualifies as a High Contracting Party to the Convention. The United Kingdom is a High Contracting party, and its adherence to the Convention covers Hong Kong.

The Lees argue that even if the court finds that Article 28 requires dismissal of China Airlines, the court should still not dismiss them because the Warsaw Convention is unconstitutional. The Lees make three different arguments on the constitutionality issue. First, they argue that the Convention constitutes a substantive due process violation because it impairs the allegedly fundamental right to international travel. Second, they argue that the Convention constitutes an equal protection violation because it treats passengers on the same airplane differently depending upon the content of their tickets. Finally, they argue, at the suggestion of the court, that the Convention is a procedural due process violation because it deprives them of the opportunity to have their tort claim heard in the United States. The court finds all three arguments to be without merit.

A. Substantive Due Process

The Lees argue that the Convention violates the Fifth Amendment because it impairs a fundamental right. They assert that they have a fundamental right to travel internationally and that the liability limitation of the Convention infringes upon this right. If such a right is impaired, then the court must examine the Convention with strict scrutiny to see if the Convention furthers a compelling governmental interest. The strict scrutiny analysis need not be reached, however, because the court finds that while the right to travel interstate is fundamental, the right to international travel is not. Therefore, the court need only evaluate the Convention under a rational basis test, and under that test, the Convention passes muster.

In support of their argument that international travel is a fundamental right, the Lees cite *In re Aircrash in Bali, Indonesia* (9th Cir.1982) ("International travel, like interstate travel, is a fundamental right."). This case, however, does not appear in accordance with prior Supreme Court authority. *See Califano v. Aznavorian* (1978) ("[L]egislation which is said to infringe the freedom to travel abroad is not to be judged by the same standard applied to laws that penalize the right of interstate travel, such as durational residency requirements imposed by the States.") The Court added:

> [T]his court has often pointed out the crucial difference between the freedom to travel internationally and the right of interstate travel. The constitutional right of interstate travel is virtually unqualified. ... by contrast, the "right" of international travel has been considered to be no more than an aspect of the "liberty" protected by the Due Process Clause of the Fifth Amendment. As such, this "right" the Court has held, can be regulated within the bounds of due process.

Aznavorian makes clear that limitations upon international travel are to be evaluated under a rational basis test. *Aznavorian* dealt with legislation that provided that a person could not receive SSI benefits during a month when that individual was out of the country. The Court upheld this legislation, saying that it only had an "incidental" effect on international travel. Given this incidental impact, the Court said that the limitation should be upheld unless it is "wholly irrational." This court turns, then, to an evaluation of the Lees' contention that the Convention impairs their right to travel and holds that the Convention has only an incidental impact on international travel and that this limitation is not wholly irrational.

First, the court notes that the impact of the Convention upon international travel is *de minimus*. While the liability and jurisdictional limitations in the Convention may have a slight chilling effect upon some people considering a trip abroad, the Convention does not prevent anyone from taking such a journey. The court notes that the Convention does not prevent someone who is concerned about the liability limitation from obtaining additional insurance before embarking on a journey abroad. Whatever limitation there is, however, is justifiable. The Convention was designed to establish uniformity in the law regarding international aviation. It recognizes that aviation links many countries with different languages, customs, and legal systems, and this goal is achieved somewhat through standard documentation, procedures for claims, and jurisdictional requirements. Because the Warsaw Convention helps to achieve the goal of uniformity in the law regarding international air travel, the court finds the treaty passes the rational basis test.

B. Equal Protection

The Lees also suggest that Article 28 violates the equal protection clause of the Fifth Amendment because it makes distinctions among passengers on the same plane depending upon their tickets. They note that while the journeys of some passengers on a particular plane may be governed by the Convention, other journeys may not be so covered. Furthermore, even when the Convention applies to two passengers on the same plane, the Convention may allow one passenger to sue in the United States, but prohibit the other passenger from doing so. This differentiation among passengers, however, does not amount to an equal protection violation because no fundamental right is impaired by the distinction, and the distinction has a rational basis.

Treating similarly situated people differently is not always unconstitutional. *See, e.g., Williamson v. Lee Optical of Oklahoma* (1955). Usually, making such distinctions is acceptable if a rational basis exists for the distinction. If, however, the classification created is suspect or impinges upon a fundamental right, then a court should apply strict scrutiny in reviewing the law creating the classification. *See, e.g., Korematsu v. United States* (1944) (suspect class); *Shapiro v. Thompson* (1969) (fundamental right). In this case, the court must apply a rational basis test. First, as set forth above, the Convention does not impinge on any fundamental rights. Second, the classifications created are not suspect.

The court finds that the distinctions made between passengers on the same plane because of the provisions of the Convention are rational. The goal of the Convention is to bring uniformity to the law governing international air travel. This goal is fostered by the method set up by the Convention to determine whether it is applicable to a particular journey. The Convention dictates that applicability is determined by the place of departure and the place of destination as listed upon a passenger's ticket. This mechanism insures that the Convention will only apply to journeys with a clear nexus to High Contracting Parties, and it also ensures that passengers will have had some notice and an opportunity to choose whether they are willing to subject themselves to the dictates of the Convention. Thus the Convention does create a rational system for bringing some uniformity to the law regarding international air travel in a world in which every nation has not agreed to abide by its terms. In light of this analysis, the court cannot say that distinctions created by the Convention among passengers on the same plane are irrational.

C. Procedural Due Process

The Lees argue that the jurisdictional limitation violates due process because it prevents American residents who were injured in or near the United States from bringing a tort action here. This argument also fails. When engaging in due process analysis, the court must first examine if a governmental action is infringing upon a life, liberty, or property interest. If the court finds that such an interest is affected, then the next question is what process is due. To determine what process is due, the court must go through a three part analysis:

> First, the private interest that will be affected by the official action; second, the risk of an erroneous deprivation of such interest through the procedures used, and the probable value, if any, of additional or substitute procedural safeguards; and finally, the Government's interest, including the function involved and the fiscal and administrative burdens that the additional or substitute procedural requirement would entail.

Assuming for the sake of argument, then, that the Lees have a property interest in their claim, the next question is what process is due.

Turning to the *Mathews v. Eldridge* test quoted above, the court finds that dismissal here would not be a due process violation. The Lees assert that if their claim against China Airlines is dismissed, they will not be able to receive an adequate hearing of their claims abroad in either Taiwan or Hong Kong. The Lees have not shown, however, that having their claims heard abroad will create a substantial risk of "erroneous deprivation." They have come forward with almost no evidence regarding the nature of judicial proceedings in either Hong Kong or Taiwan. The Lees' only contention regarding the unfairness of potential proceedings in either Taiwan or Hong Kong is that it would be unfair to subject them to the uncertainty regarding what law will apply to this case in those countries. At least in this case, however, some of the usual mystery regarding what law a foreign forum will apply disappears.

The court surmises that the Warsaw Convention will figure prominently in the decision making process over there since both Hong Kong and Taiwan adhere to it. The Ninth Circuit recently noted that "the cardinal purpose of the [Convention] is to ensure the existence of a uniform and universal system of recovery for losses incurred in the course of international air transportation." Because the plaintiffs have not met their burden of showing the proceedings abroad are likely to be erroneous, the court cannot act further on the Lees' due process contentions. In conclusion, then, the court disagrees with the Lees' contention that the Warsaw Convention is unconstitutional and dismisses their claims in accordance with the Convention's mandate.

ABC CHARTERS, INC. v. BRONSON

2009 WL 1010435 (S.D. Fla. 2009)

ALAN S. GOLD, District Judge.

Travel agencies and charter companies providing services to individuals traveling to Cuba or who wish to send humanitarian aid or family remittances to Cuba advanced a facial challenge to the constitutionality of the amendments to the Florida Sellers of Travel Act effective July 1, 2008 ("Travel Act Amendments").

The Travel Act Amendments: (1) require companies providing lawful travel related services to Cuba to post a bond in an amount of $100,000 or $250,000 while requiring those companies not offering travel to Cuba or other "terrorist states" to post a bond of $25,000; (2) allow the state of Florida to use the bond to pay its own investigatory expenses without any limits to the exposure under the bond and prioritize the payment of the bond funds to the state over compensation to consumers; (3) permit the imposition of higher registration fees and fines on travel providers offering travel to Cuba; (4) automatically make any violation of federal law by Plaintiffs a third-degree felony under Florida law; and (5) require disclosure and identification by Plaintiffs of each company with whom each Plaintiff does any Cuba-related business or commerce, and make that information publicly available.

In my Preliminary Injunction Order, I concluded that:

(1) The Travel Act Amendments are designed and structured to end or seriously hamper federally licensed travel from Florida to Cuba, and that such a law is more than just a state consumer protection decision but also a political statement of condemnation of Cuba;

(2) The significant burdens on travel and charter service providers impair the ability of this Nation to choose between a range of policy options in developing its foreign relations with Cuba;

(3) The Airline Deregulation Act, which extends to indirect air carriers such as Plaintiffs, expressly preempts the Travel Act Amendments because they would have a significant effect on rates, routes or services;

(4) The Travel Act Amendments conflict with, and are therefore preempted by, federal laws and regulations including the Trading with the Enemy Act and the Office of Foreign Assets Control's ("OFAC") Cuba Asset Control Regulations;

(5) Federal laws and regulations occupy the field as to regulation interactions and transactions with Cuba by persons and businesses in the United States;

(6) The Travel Act Amendments impermissibly discriminate against the flow of foreign commerce and regulate conduct outside the borders of the United States; and

(7) Under the interstate commerce clause, the extensive web of federal laws regulating business with and travel to Cuba displaces state laws such as the Travel Act Amendments.

The United States is in substantial agreement with these conclusions. According to its Statement of Interest, the State of Florida enacted the Travel Act Amendments "in an attempt to conduct its own foreign policy," and "the very existence of the legislation ... impairs the federal government's ability to present a single, unified foreign policy on behalf of the United States when dealing with other countries."

Recent developments further indicate our nation's changing foreign policy objectives with respect to Cuba, further counseling against permitting the Travel Act Amendments from going into effect. I take judicial notice that Office of Foreign Assets Control has recently issued, in response to the Omnibus Appropriations Act, 2009, a general license permitting an expanded range of family travel to permit visiting close relatives in Cuba from once every three years to once every year. Even more recently, President Barack Obama announced on April 13, 2009 that the restrictions on family travel, and remittances and gifts to Cuba will be lifted and Cuban Americans will now be permitted to travel freely to the island and send as much money as they want to their family members, in a marked reversal of the United States' prior policy. Such changes in foreign policy with respect to Cuba further demonstrate that the Travel Act Amendments interfere with this country's foreign policy objectives. As the United States represented at oral argument, these recent changes aptly demonstrate that the Travel Act Amendments would undermine the power of the federal government to act on behalf of the entire nation with respect to our relations with Cuba.

The State of Florida is not entitled to adopt a foreign policy under our Constitution or interfere with the exclusive prerogative of the United States to establish a carefully balanced approach to relations with foreign countries, including Cuba. The Travel Act Amendments are unconstitutional insofar as they are preempted by federal law and violate the foreign affairs power, the Foreign Commerce Clause, and the Interstate Commerce Clause.

GILMORE v. GONZALES

435 F.3d 1125 (9th Cir. 2006)

PAEZ, Circuit Judge.

On July 4, 2002, John Gilmore ("Gilmore"), a California resident and United States citizen, attempted to fly from Oakland International Airport to Baltimore-Washington International Airport on a Southwest Airlines flight. Gilmore intended to travel to Washington, D.C. to "petition the government for redress of grievances and to associate with others for that purpose." He was not allowed to fly, however, because he refused to present identification to Southwest Airlines when asked to do so.

Gilmore approached the Southwest ticketing counter with paper tickets that he already had purchased. When a Southwest ticketing clerk asked to see his identification, Gilmore refused. Although the clerk informed Gilmore that identification was required, he refused again. Gilmore asked whether the requirement was a government or Southwest rule, and whether there was any way that he could board the plane without presenting his identification. The clerk was unsure, but posited that the rule was an "FAA security requirement." The clerk informed Gilmore that he could opt to be screened at the gate in lieu of presenting the requisite identification. The clerk then issued Gilmore a new boarding pass, which indicated that he was to be searched before boarding the airplane. At the gate, Gilmore again refused to show identification. In response to his question about the source of the identification rule, a Southwest employee stated that it was a government law. Gilmore then met with a Southwest customer service supervisor, who told him that the identification requirement was an airline policy. Gilmore left the airport, without being searched at the gate.

That same day, Gilmore went to San Francisco International Airport and attempted to buy a ticket for a United Airlines flight to Washington, D.C. While at the ticket counter, Gilmore saw a sign that read: "PASSENGERS MUST PRESENT IDENTIFICATION UPON INITIAL CHECK-IN." Gilmore again refused to present identification when asked by the ticketing agent. The agent told him that he had to show identification at the ticket counter, security checkpoint, and before boarding; and that there was no way to circumvent the identification policy.

A United Airlines Service Director told Gilmore that a United traveler without identification is subject to secondary screening, but did not disclose the source of the identification policy. United's Ground Security Chief reiterated the need for identification, but also did not cite the source of the policy. The Security Chief informed Gilmore that he could fly without presenting identification by undergoing a more intensive search, *i.e.* by being a "selectee." A "selectee" search includes walking through a magnetometer, being subjected to a handheld magnetometer scan, having a light body patdown, removing one's shoes, and having one's carry-on baggage searched by hand and a CAT-scan machine. Gilmore refused to allow his bag to be searched by hand and was therefore barred from flying.

The Security Chief told Gilmore that he did not know the law or government regulation that required airlines to enforce the identification policy. Another member of United's security force later told Gilmore that the policy was set out in government Security Directives, which he was not permitted to disclose. He also told Gilmore that the Security Directives were revised frequently, as often as weekly; were transmitted orally; and differed according to airport. The airline security personnel could not, according to the Government, disclose to Gilmore the Security Directive that imposed the identification policy because the Directive was classified as "sensitive security information" ("SSI"). Gilmore left the airport and has not flown since September 11, 2001 because he is unwilling to show identification or be subjected to the "selectee" screening process.

Gilmore filed a complaint against Southwest Airlines and the United State Attorney General, challenging the constitutionality of several security measures, which he collectively referred to as "the Scheme," including the identification policy, CAPPS and CAPPS II, and No-Fly and Selectee lists. Gilmore alleged that these government security policies and provisions violated his right to due process, right to travel, right to be free from unreasonable searches and seizures, right to freely associate, and right to petition the government for redress of grievances. Gilmore also alleged that "similar requirements have been placed on travelers who use government-regulated passenger trains, and that similar requirements are being instituted for interstate bus travel."

Gilmore also alleged that the identification policy violates his constitutional right to travel because he cannot travel by commercial airlines without presenting identification, which is an impermissible federal condition. We reject Gilmore's right to travel argument because the Constitution does not guarantee the right to travel by any particular form of transportation.

Identification Request

Gilmore next alleges that both options under the identification policy—presenting identification or undergoing a more intrusive search—are subject to Fourth Amendment limitations and violated his right to be free from unreasonable searches and seizures.

Gilmore argues that the request for identification implicates the Fourth Amendment because "the government imposes a severe penalty on citizens who do not comply." Gilmore highlights the fact that he was once arrested at an airport for refusing to show identification and argues that the request for identification "[i]mposes the severe penalty of arrest." Gilmore further argues that the request for identification violates the Fourth Amendment because it constitutes "a warrantless general search for identification" that is unrelated to the goals of detecting weapons or explosives.

The request for identification, however, does not implicate the Fourth Amendment. "[A] request for identification by the police does not, by itself, constitute a Fourth Amendment seizure." Rather, "[a]n individual is seized within the meaning of the Fourth Amendment only if, in view of all of the circumstances surrounding the incident, a reasonable person would have believed that he was not free to leave." Similarly, an airline personnel's request for Gilmore's identification was not a seizure within the meaning of the Fourth Amendment.

Gilmore's experiences at the Oakland and San Francisco airports provide the best rebuttal to his argument that the requests for identification imposed a risk of arrest and were therefore seizures. Gilmore twice tried to board a plane without presenting identification, and twice left the airport when he was unsuccessful. He was not threatened with arrest or some other form of punishment; rather he simply was told that unless he complied with the policy, he would not be permitted to board the plane. There was no penalty for noncompliance.

Request to Search

Gilmore argues that the selectee option is also unconstitutional because the degree of intrusion is unreasonable. We reject this argument because it is foreclosed by our decisions in *United States v. Davis* (9th Cir. 1973) and *Torbet v. United Airlines, Inc.* (9th Cir. 2002). The identification policy's search option implicates the Fourth Amendment. *See Davis* (holding that the government's participation in airport search programs brings any search conducted pursuant to those programs within the reach of the Fourth Amendment). Airport screening searches, however, do not *per se* violate a traveler's Fourth Amendment rights, and therefore must be analyzed for reasonableness. As we explained in *Davis*:

> To meet the test of reasonableness, an administrative screening search must be as limited in its intrusiveness as is consistent with satisfaction of the administrative need that justifies it. It follows that airport screening searches are valid only if they recognize the right of a person to avoid search by electing not to board the aircraft.

Gilmore was free to reject either option under the identification policy, and leave the airport. In fact, Gilmore did just that. United Airlines presented him with the "selectee" option, which included walking through a magnetometer screening device, being subjected to a handheld magnetometer scan, having a light body patdown, removing his shoes, and having his bags hand searched and put through a CAT-scan machine. Gilmore declined and instead left the airport.

Additionally, the search option "is no more extensive or intensive than necessary, in light of current technology, to detect weapons or explosives ... [and] is confined in good faith to [prevent the carrying of weapons or explosives aboard aircrafts]; and ... passengers may avoid the search by electing not to fly." Therefore, the search option was reasonable and did not violate Gilmore's Fourth Amendment rights.

Gilmore also suggests that the identification policy did not present a meaningful choice, but rather a "Hobson's Choice," in violation of the unconstitutional conditions doctrine. We have held, as a matter of constitutional law, that an airline passenger has a choice regarding searches:

> [H]e may submit to a search of his person and immediate possessions as a condition to boarding; or he may turn around and leave. If he chooses to proceed, that choice, whether viewed as a relinquishment of an option to leave or an election to submit to the search, is essentially a "consent," granting the government a license to do what it would otherwise be barred from doing by the Fourth Amendment.

Gilmore had a meaningful choice. He could have presented identification, submitted to a search, or left the airport. That he chose the latter does not detract from the fact that he could have boarded the airplane had he chosen one of the other two options. Thus, we reject Gilmore's Fourth Amendment arguments.

Right to Associate and Right to Petition the Government

Finally, Gilmore argues that because the identification policy violates his right to travel, it follows that it also violates his right to petition the government and freely associate. These claims, as Gilmore argued in his appellate brief, are based on the notion that "[f]reedom to physically travel and the free exercise of First Amendment rights are inextricably intertwined." Here, this logic works to Gilmore's detriment. That is, even accepting Gilmore's assertion that there is a connection between the right to travel and First Amendment freedoms, his argument fails because, as we explained, his right to travel was not unreasonably impaired.

Gilmore argues that the identification requirement impinges his First Amendment right to associate anonymously. In support of this argument he relies principally on *Thomas v. Collins* (1945), in which the Supreme Court concluded that a registration requirement for public speeches is "generally incompatible with an exercise of the rights of free speech and free assembly." Unlike the regulation in *Thomas*, the identification policy is not a direct restriction on public association; rather it is an airline security measure.

Further, Gilmore did not allege that he was exercising his right to freely associate in the airport, but rather that he was attempting to fly to Washington, D.C. so that he could exercise his right to associate there. The enforcement of the identification policy did not prevent him from associating anonymously in Washington, D.C. because he could have abided by the policy, or taken a different mode of transport. Although the policy did inconvenience Gilmore, this inconvenience did not rise to the level of a constitutional violation. In the end, Gilmore's free association claim fails because there was no direct and substantial action impairing this right.

Gilmore's right to petition claim similarly fails. Although Gilmore did not fly to Washington, D.C., where he planned to petition the government for redress of grievances, the identification policy did not prevent him from doing so. The identification policy is not a direct regulation of any First Amendment expressive activity, nor does it impermissibly inhibit such activity. Gilmore's claims that Defendants violated his rights to associate anonymously and petition the government are without merit.

NOTES

1. The right to travel was encapsulated in a former marketing slogan of Southwest Airlines: "You are Now Free to Move about the Country." Historically, however, such a right did not apply equally to all America citizens. "[T]he right of "free ingress and regress to and from" neighboring states traces back at least to the express text of the Articles of Confederation, 3 RECORDS OF THE FEDERAL CONVENTION OF 1787, at 112 (M. Farrand ed. 1966), and examples of restrictions of the freedom of movement and travel are replete in the annals of American History, particularly on the basis of race. Indeed, "Americans have enjoyed the freedom to walk the streets and move about the country free from unreasonable government intrusion for many years[, but] not all Americans have been able to move freely about the country. In many parts of colonial America, both North and South, Negroes were required to carry 'passes.'" Tracy Maclin, *The Decline of the Right of Locomotion: The Fourth Amendment on* the *Streets*, 75 CORNELL L. REV. 1258, 1260, 1337 n.4 (1990). *See also* Note, *State Parochialism, and Right to Travel, and the Privileges and Immunities Clause of Article IV*, 41 STAN. L. REV. 1557 (1989).

2. While *Kent v. Dulles* (1958), *supra*, discusses a right to travel as emanating from the liberty interest protected by the Fifth Amendment of the United States Constitution, the Supreme Court's decision itself makes no ruling on the constitutionality of a right to travel and is more narrow in scope—at most, a First Amendment case or an opinion merely that Congress had not authorized the Secretary of State to deny certain passports.

In any event, a right to interstate travel is well-established and its origins appear to reflect a concern over state discrimination against outsiders rather than concerns over the general ability to move about, *i.e.*, a right to movement. *See Saenz v. Roe* (1999) (grounding at least one component of the right to interstate travel in the Privileges and Immunities Clause of the Fourteenth Amendment); *Shapiro v. Thompson* (1969) (describing the right as deriving from general principles of federalism); *United States v. Guest* (1966) (describing the right to interstate travel as originating in the Articles of Confederation and as being a "necessary concomitant of the stronger Union the Constitution created"); *Zobel v. Williams* (1982) (O'Connor, J., concurring) (describing the right as originating in the Privileges and Immunities Clause of Art. IV); *Edwards v. California* (1941) (describing the right as being grounded in the Commerce Clause).

Apart from a right to *travel*, federal law has recognized a generalized freedom or right of *movement*:

> Freedom of movement, at home and abroad, is important for job and business opportunities—for cultural, political, and social activities—for all the commingling which gregarious man enjoys. Those with the right of free movement use it at times for mischievous purposes. But that is true of many liberties we enjoy. We nevertheless place our faith in them, and against restraint, knowing that the risk of abusing liberty so as to give rise to punishable conduct is part of the price we pay for this free society.

Aptheker v. Sec. of State (1964) (Douglas, J., concurring). *See also Kent v. Dulles* (1958), *supra* ("Freedom of movement is basic in our scheme of values"); *United States v. Guest* (1966) (proclaiming that citizens of the United States "must have the right to pass and repass through every part of [the country] without interruption, as freely as in [their] own states"); *Williams v. Fears* (1900) (indicating that the "right of locomotion," like the "right to contract," is protected by substantive due process). *But see Memorial Hospital v. Maricopa County* (1974) ("[e]ven a bona fide residence requirement would burden the right to travel if travel meant merely movement").

The right to travel involved in *Kent* and *Aptheker* may be distinct from the recognized right to interstate travel as courts have opined that *international* travel is no more than an aspect of liberty that is subject to reasonable government regulation within the bounds of due process, whereas *interstate* travel is a fundamental right subject to a more exacting standard. *See Haig v. Agee* (1981) (upholding constitutionality of regulation authorizing the revocation of passport on the ground that the regulation authorized revocation only where the holder's activities in foreign countries are causing or are likely to cause serious damage to national security).

3. With the advent of profiling, screening devices, and evermore intrusive security measures at airports, does Dr. Walter Briehl's argument in *Kent v. Dulles* (1958), *supra*, that "every American has the right to travel regardless of politics," ring true after September 11th? What is the state of the "right to travel" or "freedom of movement" today? *See* Heather E. Reser, Comment, *Airline Terrorism: The Effect of Tightened Security on the Right to Travel*, 63 J. AIR L. & COM. 819 (1998).

4. *Kent v. Dulles* (1958), *supra*, illustrates the potential, if not actual, influence of time and circumstance on judges themselves. Consider that the *Kent* decision did not arise in a vacuum, but occurred in the midst of the "Second Red Scare." In 1958, Nikita Khruschev had become the Premier of the Soviet Union, which had launched Sputnik to begin the "Space Race." Fidel Castro's Revolutionary Army began its attacks on Havana, Cuba. The fear of Communists—typified by McCarthysim politics—reached a crescendo in 1958, when it was estimated that roughly one out of every five employees in the United States was required to pass some sort of loyalty review. RALPH S. BROWN, LOYALTY AND SECURITY: EMPLOYMENT TESTS IN THE UNITED STATES (Yale University Press 1958). *See generally* Daniel A. Farber, *National Security, the Right to Travel, and the Court*, 1981 SUPREME COURT REV. 263 (1981).

5. The court in *Gilmore v. Gonzales* (9th Cir. 2006), *supra*, "reject[ted] Gilmore's right to travel argument because the Constitution does not guarantee the right to travel by any particular form of transportation … Gilmore does not possess a fundamental right to travel by airplane even though it is the most convenient mode of travel for him." Should the scope of the right to travel depend upon the type of transportation being used? *See, e.g.*, Katherine Warner, *You Can't Get There from Here: Travel Restrictions and the Airlines*, 58 J. AIR L. & COM. 345 (1992). For example, should the right to travel be more restrictive in the context of commercial aviation than highway travel? *See Miller v. Reed* (9th Cir. 1999) (determining that there is no fundamental right to drive).

6. The Ninth Circuit in *Gilmore v. Gonzales* (9th Cir. 2006), *supra*, reasoned that airline passengers have meaningful alternatives when balancing security mandates with personal privacy: They can present identification, submit to a search, or leave the airport. Are these choices false options, however? Flying commercially is less of a privilege or sign of social status than it was historically and airlines may be akin to a public utility. Given the almost essential character of airline travel, should a right to fly be recognized and enforceable under federal or state law? Would that right be sustained

under *ABC Charters, Inc. v. Bronson, Inc.* (S.D. Fla. 2009), *supra*, under applicable principles of federalism and state power in the aviation and travel contexts?

7. Taxes can be a significant burden on aviation interests and may potentially interfere with the fundamental right to travel to an unacceptable extent. For example, in *Evansville-Vanderburgh Airport Authority Dist. v. Delta Airlines, Inc.* (1972), the Supreme Court of the United States held that the Commerce Clause does not prohibit states or municipalities from charging commercial airlines a "head tax" on passengers boarding flights at airports within their jurisdiction, to defray the costs of airport construction and maintenance: "At least so long as the toll is based on some fair approximation of use or privilege for use, ... and is neither discriminatory against interstate commerce nor excessive in comparison with the governmental benefit conferred, it will pass constitutional muster, even though some other formula might reflect more exactly the relative use of the state facilities by individual users."

Congress enacted the Anti-Head Tax Act ("AHTA") to address a concern that the *Evansville-Vanderburgh Airport Authority Dist.* case would prompt a proliferation of local taxes burdensome to interstate air transportation. *See Aloha Airlines, Inc. v. Director of Taxation of Haw.* (1983) ("The head tax ... cuts against the grain of the traditional American right to travel among the States."). *See also* S. Rep. No. 93-12, p. 4 (1973) (Congress intended AHTA to "ensure … that local 'head' taxes will not be permitted to inhibit the flow of interstate commerce."). The AHTA provides in pertinent part:

> (a) *Prohibition; exemption*
> No State shall levy or collect a tax, fee, head charge, or other charge, directly or indirectly, on persons traveling in air commerce or on the carriage of persons traveling in air commerce or on the sale of air transportation or on the gross receipts derived therefrom
>
> (b) *Permissible State taxes and fees*
> [N]othing in this section shall prohibit a State) from the levy or collection of taxes other than those enumerated in subsection (a) of this section, including property taxes, net income taxes, franchise taxes, and sales or use taxes on the sale of goods or services; and nothing in this section shall prohibit a State (or political subdivision thereof ...) owning or operating an airport from levying or collecting reasonable rental charges, landing fees, and other service charges from aircraft operators for the use of airport facilities.

49 U.S.C. § 1513. *See, e.g., Northwest Airlines, Inc. v. County of Kent, Michigan* (1994) (evaluating the claim of seven commercial airlines that certain airport user fees charged to them were unreasonable and discriminatory in violation of the AHTA and the Commerce Clause). For further discussion of the taxation of aviation commerce see generally *Wardair Canada Inc. v. Florida Dep't of Revenue* (1986) and *Massachusetts v. United States* (1978).

For further discussion of taxes of aviation operations see generally Anthony Ryan, *How Airline Security Fees in a Post September 11, 2001 Environment are Spiraling Out of Control*, 29 TRANSP. L.J. 253 (2002); Carolyn P. Meade, Note, *Aviation Taxes: Can We Leave FAA Funding on Auto-Pilot?*, 20 VA. TAX. REV. 191 (2000).

8. Passports arise from a sovereign's need for evidence of citizenship. That need is no less important today than it was during the 1960s in *Kent*, *supra*. Consider:

> Western security officials are struggling to respond to the threat that Islamic State can make authentic-looking Syrian and Iraqi passports, which could be used to hide operative planning attacks in Europe or the U.S. among refugees.
>
> The Nov. 13 Paris attacks have shown that the proliferation of Syrian passports amid the chaos of war poses a serious security threat to the West. At least one of the suicide bombers who attacked Paris had been registered as a refugee at the Greek island of Leros using a fraudulent Syrian passport. ***
>
> European governments now grant asylum to almost all Syrians, creating a thriving black market for authentic-looking fake Syrian passports.

Matthew Dalton, *Passport Forgery Poses Terror Threat*, WALL. ST. J., Dec. 24, 2015. What limits, if any, should be imposed upon government requirements of citizens to demonstrate nationality? For example, would a passport containing a citizen's biometric information synch with constitutionally protected civil liberties? *See generally* Arnold Henson, *Constitutional Law: Right to Travel: Authority of Secretary of State to Deny Passports*, 57 MICH. L. REV. 119 (1958). *See also* James D. Barnett, *Passport Administration and the Courts*, 32 ORE. L. REV. 193 (1953); Leonard B. Boudin, *The Constitutional Right to Travel*, 56 COLUM. L. REV. 47 (1956); Reginald Parker, *The Right to Go Abroad: To Have and to Hold a Passport*, 40 VA. L. REV. 853 (1954).

9. The author of the *Kent v. Dulles* (1958), *supra*,—Justice William Orville Douglas—was nominated by President Franklin D. Roosevelt to succeed Justice Louis D. Brandeis. *See* Samuel D. Warren and Louis D. Brandeis, *The Right to Privacy*, 4 HARV.

L. REV. 193 (1890). Both jurists were champions of a constitutional right to privacy. For example, in *Griswold v. Connecticut* (1965), Justice Douglas recognized a "right to privacy" in the "penumbras" of the first eight amendments of the Bill of Rights. He believed that

> [t]he privacy and dignity of our citizens [are] being whittled away by sometimes imperceptible steps. Taken individually, each step may be of little consequence. But when viewed as a whole, there begins to emerge a society quite unlike any we have seen—a society in which government may intrude into the secret regions of a [person's] life.
>
> Big Brother in the form of an increasingly powerful government and in an increasingly powerful private sector will pile the records high with reasons why privacy should give way to national security, to law and order, to efficiency of operation, to scientific advancement and the like.

See BRUCE ALLEN MURPHY, WILD BILL: THE LEGEND AND LIFE OF WILLIAM O. DOUGLAS (Random House 2003). Given *Gilmore v. Gonzales* (9th Cir. 2006), *supra*, which interest should be greater in the context of commercial air travel: privacy or security? *See* Chapter 5.C, *infra*.

10. Arab- and Muslim-Americans clearly do not enjoy the same right to airline travel as other Americans today. A Louisiana Congressman who favors airline passenger profiling stated that "any person who has a 'diaper on his head and fan belt around the diaper' needs to be singled out for questioning." Dennis Camire, *Muslim Council Seeks Action against Cooksey for Slur*, GANNETT NEWS SERV., Sept. 21, 2001, at 2001 WL 5112923.

PROBLEM

Two passengers boarded a commercial domestic flight. Seated separately, they "talk[ed] to each other, over the heads of the other passengers, in a mixture of Arabic and English." As the plane took off, and throughout the flight, one of the passengers appeared to be "timing" various events, such as takeoff, attainment of flight level, and the commencement of the meal service.

Counterterrorism agents aboard the airplane believed the passengers might have been "conducting [terrorist] surveillance or probing operations" and should be detained after landing. The passengers were seized, detained, and interrogated upon landing. They later sued the United States for violation of their Fourth Amendment rights and for false arrest and false imprisonment. In defense, the Government argued that the plaintiffs' Arab ethnicity and use of the Arabic language are relevant factors in the probable-cause and reasonable-suspicion determination because "all of the persons who participated in the 9/11 terrorist attacks were Middle Eastern … the United States continues to face a very real threat of domestic terrorism from Islamic terrorists."

The passengers move for summary judgment on their claims. What should the court decide? *See Farag v. United States* (E.D.N.Y. 2008).

B. AIRLINE PASSENGER RIGHTS

Before—and since—September 11th, commercial airline passengers have been unhappy with the quality of airline service, from delays and cancellations to lost bags and ancillary pricing policies seemingly nickel-and-diming consumers.

Meanwhile, airlines themselves are dissatisfied with the regulatory headwinds impacting their operations and bottom-line. Consider that nearly 20 percent of a domestic airline ticket in the United States—$61 of a typical $300 roundtrip fare—goes to the federal government to satisfy 17 different aviation fees and taxes. On top of this, Congress enacted the Bipartisan Budget Act of 2013, increasing Transportation Security Administration fees at an annual cost of over $1 billion to the airline industry. And, on July 21, 2014, regulators increased a "September 11th Security Fee," costing passengers $5.60 per one-way trip. Denouncing these and other facts and figures, the self-described industry trade organization for the leading airlines in the country, Airlines for America ("A4A") has called for a National Airline Policy.

Yet, while the airline industry calls for regulatory relief for its own sake, individual carriers are the beneficiary of federal regulations that largely make them impervious to legal liability arising from poor service. Indeed, customer service issues that rarely if ever presented before enactment of the Airline Deregulation Act of 1978 have dominated the legal and policy landscape in the three decades since enactment of that historic law.

The topic of airline passenger rights can thus be viewed as a subcategory of the broader right to travel. Overbookings, "bumping," and limitations of liability inhibit consumer mobility and travel choices. In fact, airline passengers (among whom are federal legislators themselves) have become frustrated to the point of demanding new legal rights in the form of an airline passenger bill of rights. (*See* Chapter 2, *infra*). This impulse receded after September 11th as airline passengers and lawmakers necessarily focused on matters of life and death rather than pillows and peanuts.

The cases and materials in this section track the shift in policy and consumer preferences from convenience to safety and back again, and reveal the distrust among carriers, airline passengers, and governmental authorities. This section also spotlights how lawmakers and jurists in America and Europe have worked to delineate rights and responsibilities of passengers and carriers along a broad spectrum of commercial airline travel rights, including delays, denied boardings, and flight cancellations.

Domestic Air Travel

IN RE JETBLUE AIRWAYS CORP. PRIVACY LITIGATION
379 F. Supp. 2d 299 (E.D.N.Y. 2005)

AMON, District Judge.

In the wake of September 11, 2001, Torch, a data mining company similar to Acxiom, presented the Department of Defense ("DOD") with a data pattern analysis proposal geared toward improving the security of military installations in the United States and possibly abroad. Torch suggested that a rigorous analysis of personal characteristics of persons who sought access to military installations might be used to predict which individuals pose a risk to the security of those installations. DOD showed interest in Torch's proposal and added Torch as a subcontractor to an existing contract, which was amended to include airline PNRs as a possible data source in connection with Torch's study.

Because Torch needed access to a large national-level database of personal information and because no federal agencies approached by Torch would grant access to their own governmental databases, Torch independently contacted a number of airlines in search of private databases that might contain adequate information to serve its requirements. These airlines declined to share their passengers' personal information unless the Department of Transportation ("DOT") and/or the Transportation Security Administration ("TSA") were involved and approved of such data sharing.

Unable to obtain the data through its own devices, Torch asked members of Congress to intervene on its behalf with the airlines or federal agencies. Torch also contacted the DOT directly. Following a series of meetings, the DOT and the TSA agreed to assist Torch in obtaining consent from a national airline to share its passenger information. The TSA sent JetBlue a written request to supply its data to the DOD, and JetBlue agreed to cooperate. In September 2002, JetBlue and Acxiom collectively transferred approximately five million electronically-stored PNRs to Torch in connection with the contract. Then, Torch separately purchased additional data from Acxiom for use in connection with contract. This data was merged with the September 2002 data to create a single database of JetBlue passenger information including each passenger's name, address, gender, home ownership or rental status, economic status, social security number, occupation, and the number of adults and children in the passenger's family as well as the number of vehicles owned or leased. Using this data, Torch began its data analysis and created a customer profiling scheme designed to identify high-risk passengers among those traveling on JetBlue.

In or about September 2003, government disclosures and ensuing public investigations concerning the data transfer to Torch prompted JetBlue Chief Executive Officer David Neeleman to acknowledge that the transfer had been a violation of JetBlue's privacy policy. A class of plaintiffs whose personal information was among that transferred now brings this action against JetBlue, Torch, and Acxiom seeking monetary damages, including punitive damages, and injunctive relief.

Plaintiffs assert five causes of action against all defendants: (1) violation of the Electronic Communications Privacy Act of 1986, 18 U.S.C. § 2701 *et seq*., (2) violation of the New York General Business Law and other similar state consumer protection statutes, (3) trespass to property, (4) unjust enrichment, and (5) declaratory judgment. In addition, plaintiffs bring a sixth claim for breach of contract against JetBlue.

DISCUSSION

A. Electronic Communications Privacy Act

Plaintiffs allege that all defendants violated the ECPA by divulging stored passenger communications without the passengers' authorization or consent. JetBlue, supported by a Statement of Interest filed by the federal government, counters that plaintiffs have failed to state a viable claim under the ECPA, because § 2702 applies only to persons or entities providing a remote computing service or electronic communication service to the public and, as a commercial airline, it provides neither of these. This Court finds as a matter of law that JetBlue is not an electronic communication service provider within the meaning of the ECPA.

B. Express Preemption of State and Common Law Claims

1. *New York General Business Law*

Plaintiffs claim that, in violation of the New York General Business Law and other consumer protection statutes, all defendants engaged in unfair or deceptive acts and practices by knowingly and surreptitiously conspiring to obtain and by obtaining, maintaining, and manipulating class members' personal data that was received in direct violation of JetBlue's privacy policy. This claim fits squarely within the range of state law actions that the Supreme Court concluded are expressly preempted by the Airline Deregulation Act of 1978, because it represents a direct effort to regulate the manner in which JetBlue communicates with its customers in connection with reservations and ticket sales, both of which are services provided by the airline to its customers.

Where a state law claim is said to relate to an airline service, courts in this and other circuits apply a tripartite test for preemption set forth in *Rombom v. United Air Lines, Inc.*, (S.D.N.Y. 1994). *See Donkor v. British Airways, Corp.*, (E.D.N.Y. 1999) (collecting federal district court and appellate cases that cite the *Rombom* test). First, a court must determine "whether the activity at issue in the claim is an airline service." Second, "[i]f the activity implicates a service, the court must then determine whether the claim affects the airline service directly or tenuously, remotely, or peripherally." If the effect is only incidental, the state law claim is not preempted. Where the activity in question directly implicates a service, the court should proceed to the third prong of the preemption inquiry, "whether the underlying tortious conduct was reasonably necessary to the provision of the service." If the challenged conduct did not occur during the course of the service in question or did not further the provision of the service in a reasonable manner, then there is no express preemption and the state court action should continue. The *Rombom* court observed that this three-factor analysis is important because "[c]onfining the question of whether the tasks implicated in the complaint ... are services under the [ADA] is inadequate." "The manner in which an activity is conducted also bears on the question of preemption."

Applying the *Rombom* test to the facts of this case, the first prong is clearly satisfied. As this claim concerns the lawfulness of representations made by JetBlue in the course of communicating with potential passengers, the relevant activity for purposes of preemption analysis is the provision of reservations and the sale of tickets to travel with JetBlue. In arguing that the service in question is the disclosure of passenger data for use in a military base security study, plaintiffs misconstrue the issue. The second prong is also met, as an attempt to regulate the representations and commitments that JetBlue makes in connection with reservations and ticket sales directly affects the airline's provision of those services. Finally, the third prong is satisfied because the communication of company policy concerning data collection and disclosure is reasonably necessary to the facilitation of reservations and ticket sales. In this regard, it is important to note that although the unauthorized disclosure of plaintiffs' personal information is at issue in this claim, the principal focus of the claim is the allegedly deceptive steps taken to obtain that information. Thus, the complained-of conduct did occur in the course of the provision of the service of reservations and ticket sales, and as stated, the communication of company policy with respect to collection and use of data obtained in the course of that service is reasonably related to the provision of the service.

2. *Common Law Claims*

In addition to the state statutory claims, plaintiffs bring a claim for breach of contract against JetBlue and claims for trespass to property and unjust enrichment against all defendants. None of these claims is preempted. The breach of contract claim falls within the exception for the enforcement of self-imposed contractual undertakings. Neither of the tort claims relates to JetBlue's rates, routes, or services in the same way that the state statutory claim does.

a. *Breach of Contract*

The basis for plaintiffs' breach of contract claim is the allegation that JetBlue's published privacy policy constitutes a self-imposed contractual obligation by and between the airline and the consumers with whom it transacted business, including plaintiffs and the members of the class. Plaintiffs further allege that JetBlue breached this contract when it disclosed its passengers' personal information, without their consent, in violation of its privacy policy.

JetBlue argues that this claim is preempted because the Court will have to resort to external sources of law, including federal regulations, to determine if the privacy policy became a term in the Contract of Carriage. JetBlue also argues that, if that the privacy statement is determined to constitute a contract, the Court will have to look outside the "terms" of that contract, to state law damages schemes, to determine recoverable damages. In JetBlue's view, "even a self-imposed undertaking that requires resort to state law to address its breach is, by that resort to state law, preempted."

These arguments are misplaced. In *American Airlines v. Wolens*, The Supreme Court sought to preclude states from undoing federal deregulation of the airline industry. In carving out an exception for the enforcement of contracts, the Court recognized that the application of state law to honor private bargains does not threaten to undermine federal deregulation in the same way that enforcement of state public policy would. JetBlue's suggestion that courts may never look to generalized canons of contract interpretation to determine the parameters of private agreements without implicating the doctrine of preemption is unsupportable. If JetBlue's position were correct, there would be very little left of the *Wolens* exception, as most contractual arrangements that become the subject of litigation present some question that requires resort to general principles of state contract law. The critical distinction between principles of contract law that fall within and without the *Wolens* exception is whether they "seek to effectuate the intent of the parties rather than the State's public policies." *See In re EVIC Class Action Litigation, Inc.* (S.D.N.Y. 2002).

The relief plaintiffs seek in connection with the breach of contract claim is limited to actual damages. Resolution of this claim will require the Court to determine whether the privacy policy gave rise to a contractual obligation and, if so, what damages rules apply. These determinations must be made with reference to state law, but that state law does not impose any substantive standards with respect to airline rates, routes, or services. *See Wolens* (holding that the ADA preemption clause "stops States from imposing their own substantive standards with respect to rates, routes, or services, but not from affording relief to a party who claims and proves that an airline dishonored a term the airline itself stipulated"). Accordingly, plaintiffs' breach of contract claim is not expressly preempted by the Airline Deregulation Act, and JetBlue's motion to dismiss this claim as preempted is therefore denied.

b. *Trespass to Property*

Plaintiffs allege that the transfer by JetBlue of data containing passengers' personal information amounts to trespass to property. To date, no federal court has specifically addressed the preemptive effect of the Airline Deregulation Act clause on state law claims for trespass to property. Defendants argue that "[t]he manner in which an airline handles and utilizes passenger information is intimately intertwined with its rates, routes, and services and is, in fact, regulated by federal law."

The thrust of defendants' argument with regard to rates and routes is that prevention of future terrorist attacks on military installations will protect the integrity of routes and avoid negative impacts on the financial prospects of air carriers. More specifically, defendants claim that a successful military base security study could ultimately improve the safety of commercial air travel and possibly reduce rates to the extent that JetBlue is able to transfer the costs of certain security improvements to the federal government. Defendants further urge that "[i]n order for Plaintiffs to succeed in stating any common law claim, they must ... scrub historical context from all of JetBlue's actions ..." The historical context to which defendants allude begins, of course, with the events of September 11, 2001.

Although defendants raise emotionally compelling concerns about the potential of state tort liability to chill airline participation in security studies, they fail to establish how a claim for trespass to property that pertains to the dissemination of plaintiffs' information directly relates to airline rates or routes. In pointing to the potential economic and safety benefits of a successful security study, the connection that plaintiffs suggest to rates and routes is attenuated at best. The Second Circuit has held that indirect effects on an airline's competitive position do not meet the test for preemption of state law claims. *See Abdu-Brisson v. Delta Airlines, Inc.* (2d Cir. 1997) (indirect effects of state law claims on an airline's competitive position do not warrant preemption). Here, it is nothing more than conjecture that the security study could actually have an effect on the integrity of routes or result in any reduction of JetBlue's rates. Accordingly, the impact of plaintiffs' claim on JetBlue's rates and routes is "too tenuous, remote or peripheral ... to have pre-emptive effect."

Defendants' argument based on airline services also fails the *Rombom* test. With regard to the first prong of that test, whether the activity at issue is an airline service, defendants claim that the assembly and use of passenger information supplied during the purchase of air transportation constitutes an integral part of an airline's services. Defendants further claim that compiling the data into a PNR for the airline's use relates to services because the PNR reflects the airline's copy of the passenger's travel arrangements and enables the airline to determine flight capacity and schedules and to define routes.

The problem with this argument is that plaintiffs' trespass to property claim concerns the unauthorized disclosure of PNR data to a third party which has no role in determining flight capacity, schedules, or routes. Moreover, the disclosure of this information is not alleged to have any relation to JetBlue's manipulation or use of the data to determine flight capacity, schedules, or routes. Thus, to the extent that use of PNR data for these purposes constitutes an airline service within the meaning of the Airline Deregulation Act, the trespass to property claim at issue in this case does not implicate that service. As defendants have not proffered any other basis upon which the Court might conclude that the trespass to property claim implicates a service, they have not met their burden of establishing that the claim is preempted by the Airline Deregulation Act. Accordingly, as understandable as defendants' motivations may have been, it is not relevant for purposes of express preemption analysis that defendants disclosed the PNR data in response to changed market conditions and security concerns occasioned by the events of September 11, 2001.

c. *Unjust Enrichment*

Plaintiffs allege that all defendants in this case were unjustly enriched by the disclosure of confidential information concerning JetBlue passengers. Specifically, they claim that JetBlue received remuneration from Torch or another party in exchange for disclosing PNR data, and that the other defendants profited as contractors or subcontractors on the Department of Defense study as a result of JetBlue's contribution of the data. Defendants make the very same preemption argument in connection with this claim as they make in connection with the trespass to property claim, that a successful military base security study could affect routes by improving the safety of commercial air travel and rates by transferring the cost of certain security improvements to the federal government.

Few federal courts have considered the preemptive effect of the ADA clause on claims for unjust enrichment. Of those that have, most found that the claims at issue directly related to air carrier rates or services and held those claims preempted. *See, e.g.*, *Lehman v. USAir Group, Inc.* (S.D.N.Y. 1996) (claim expressly referred to the collection of air transportation excise tax, which relates to rates because it directly impacts the ticket price); *All World Professional Travel Services, Inc. v. American Airlines, Inc.* (C.D. Cal. 2003) (claim premised on airline's imposition of a fee for processing refunds for tickets that could not be used in the days immediately following September 11, 2001); *Dugan v. FedEx Corp.* (C.D. Cal. 2002) (claim challenged air carrier's contractual limitation of liability for damage to contents of packages that occurred during shipment); *Deerskin Trading Post, Inc. v. United Parcel Service of America, Inc.* (N.D. Ga. 1997) (plaintiff alleged defendant inappropriately based prices on the dimensional weight of packages rather than the actual weight).

But the nature of the claims at issue in those cases had quite a different relation to airline rates, routes, and services than the unjust enrichment claim in this case. Unjust enrichment claims premised on the imposition of fees or collection of taxes quite obviously relate to airline rates. In this case, the unjust enrichment claim, like the trespass to property claim, seeks to remedy conduct without any cognizable relation to JetBlue's rates, routes, or services. Accordingly, it is not preempted under the deregulation act.

C. Implied Preemption of State and Common Law Claims

Because the information at issue in this case was turned over for a security study at the behest of a federal agency, defendants argue that plaintiffs' claims are impliedly preempted by the federal government's pervasive occupation of the field of aviation security. Field preemption occurs "if federal law so thoroughly occupies a legislative field as to make reasonable the inference that Congress left no room for the States to supplement it." *Cipollone v. Liggett Group, Inc.* (1992). Although in this case the state laws at issue are not specific to aviation security, and therefore in a strict sense do not fall within that field, the Supreme Court has recognized that field preemption analysis may be understood as a species of conflict preemption, which exists where a state law "stands as an obstacle to the accomplishment and execution of the full purposes and objectives of Congress." *English v. General Elec. Co.* (1990). Thus, to the extent that plaintiffs' state law claims would have the effect of undermining federal efforts in the field, field preemption analysis is properly implicated.

Defendants contend that a "mosaic of federal laws and regulations" evince an intent on the part of Congress for the federal government to completely occupy the field of aviation security and national security as it relates to the dissemination of passenger information by commercial airlines for the prevention of terrorist attacks. This mosaic begins with the creation of the Federal Aviation Agency, later renamed the Federal Aviation Administration ("FAA"), as an agency within the Department of Transportation. The FAA was created in the wake of a "series of fatal air crashes between civilian and military aircraft operating under separate flight rules," *United States v. Christensen* (9th Cir. 1969). The Administrator was charged *inter alia* to prescribe rules and regulations "necessary to provide adequately for national security and safety in air commerce." Federal Aviation Act of 1958 ("FAA Act"), Pub. L. No. 85-726 (1958). It is undisputed that FAA regulations have preemptive effect in certain discrete fields such as pilot certification, aircraft noise, airspace management and flight operations.

Defendants posit that federal regulatory control is particularly dominant in the area of aviation security. In support, they cite several legislative enactments beginning with the 1961 passage of a statute criminalizing air piracy. Enacted immediately after the first hijacking of a U.S. commercial aircraft, this statute, combined with "related rules issued under the regulatory authority of the Administrator, provide[s] the basis for the antihijacking program." *United States v. Davis* (9th Cir. 1973). This authority was supplemented by the Antihijacking Act of 1974 (1974), which included the Air

Transportation Security Act of 1974, (1974), and thus provided ongoing authority for the FAA Administrator to regulate passenger screening as well as research and development of systems, procedures, and facilities designed to guard against acts of aircraft piracy. The FAA Act was subsequently amended by the International Security and Development Cooperation Act of 1985, Pub. L. No. 99-83, 99 Stat. 190 (1985), which prescribes measures for improving security standards in foreign air transportation.

After the bombing of Pan Am Flight 103 over Lockerbie, Scotland, Congress again amended the FAA Act by enacting the Aviation Security Improvement Act of 1990, Pub. L. No. 101-604, 104 Stat. 3066 (1990). This Act established a Director of Intelligence and Security in the office of the Secretary of Transportation and provided *inter alia* for security improvements at airports. The Act also called for the FAA Administrator to "establish and carry out a program to accelerate and expand the research, development, and implementation of technologies and procedures to counteract terrorist acts against civil aviation."

Following the terrorist attacks of September 11, 2001, Congress passed two free-standing statutes: the Aviation and Transportation Security Act, Pub. L. No. 101-71, 115 Stat. 597 (2001), and the Homeland Security Act of 2002, Pub. L. No. 107-296, 116 Stat. 2135 (2002). In addition to broadening authority for aviation security measures, the Aviation and Transportation Security Act transferred responsibility that previously fell upon the FAA to a newly created administrative body, the Transportation Security Administration ("TSA"). *See* 49 U.S.C. § 114. The Homeland Security Act removed the TSA from the Department of Transportation and placed it under the jurisdiction of the Department of Homeland Security, which in defendants' view emphasizes the role of the commercial airline industry in the realm of national security. The TSA is the entity that requested JetBlue provide its PNR data for use in the security study.

The TSA is specifically charged with management of security information. Among its enumerated powers and responsibilities, it is tasked to "identify and undertake research and development activities necessary to enhance transportation security," and to establish policies and procedures requiring air carriers to use information supplied by government agencies to identify high-risk passengers. Notably, it also has specific Congressional authorization to "consider [in consultation with the Transportation Security Oversight Board] requiring passenger air carriers to share passenger lists with appropriate Federal agencies for the purpose of identifying individuals who may pose a threat to aviation safety or national security." Presumably, after undertaking the appropriate consultative process, the TSA would have had authority to require JetBlue to share its passenger lists for use in the Torch security study. It bears noting that the TSA did not exercise that authority prior to the events at issue in this case and instead issued a request with which JetBlue voluntarily complied. The data transfer by JetBlue is therefore not insulated from state law liability as a result of any direct conflict with federal regulatory action on this issue.

Regulations issued pursuant to Congressional authorization after litigation is commenced are also relevant to preemption analysis because they bear upon the issue of Congressional intent to occupy a field. In that regard, the Court notes that on November 15, 2004, the TSA issued a final order requiring aircraft operators to provide certain specified PNR data for use in testing the "Secure Flight" system, an aviation passenger pre-screening program designed to identify passengers known or reasonably suspected to be engaged in terrorist activity. The final order specifically mentions 49 U.S.C. § 114(f)(8) as one of the bases for the TSA's authority for requiring the PNR data.

Defendants cite a host of additional functions entrusted to the TSA and other federal entities, as well as a litany of security-related regulations enacted by the TSA, to round out the argument that the field of aviation security—particularly as it relates to information sharing among air carriers and federal agencies—is entirely preempted by federal law. Though only a small subset relates specifically to the collection and dissemination of passenger information, the breadth of these regulations and responsibilities is extensive.

Even if field preemption could be established in the area of aviation security—a question on which the Court expresses no final opinion at this time—it is at least an issue of fact, on the record now before the Court, whether or not the actions complained of in this case properly implicate the field of aviation security. Plaintiffs allege, and defendants do not dispute, that the purpose of the JetBlue data transfer was to support a study designed to prevent attacks on military installations following the September 11, 2001 attack on the Pentagon. According to plaintiffs' Amended Complaint, Torch considered that data pattern analysis of personal characteristics of persons who sought access to military installations might help predict which persons pose a risk to the security of those installations. Although defendants suggest that the study specifically aimed to identify potential terrorists arriving by air in areas near military bases, the facts pled only establish that a large, national level database was needed to assess the efficacy of Torch's data analysis tool for predicting terrorist behavior, not that the database had to concern commercial airline passengers in particular.

Indeed, according both to plaintiffs' Amended Complaint and to an official report of the Department of Homeland Security ("DHS") Privacy Office, Torch initially approached a number of federal agencies unrelated to aviation that operate governmental databases containing personal information suitable for use in testing its program. When each of those agencies refused to participate in the study, Torch turned its attention to commercial sources of personal information, including airlines and data aggregators which were thought to maintain databases containing adequate cross-sections of personal characteristics.

Unable to obtain the necessary personal information, Torch then turned to members of Congress, asking them to intervene on the company's behalf with airlines or federal agencies. Although the agency that ultimately became involved on Torch's behalf was the TSA, and although the supplier of the database used happened to be JetBlue, the record before the Court does not establish that the study was inherently or necessarily focused on aviation-based threats to military base security or that data concerning commercial airline passengers was essential to advance the study's purposes. Indeed, the official DHS Report found that "[w]hile one form of base security may have included preventing terrorist attacks by air directed at military installations, the overarching purpose was the prevention of unauthorized or unwanted entry onto military bases via a variety of forms of entry." The primary purpose of the study thus was something "other than transportation security."

The Court appreciates that JetBlue's decision to cooperate with Torch was likely motivated, at least in part, by a legitimate interest in advancing efforts to reduce threats to aviation security. The fact that the TSA encouraged JetBlue's involvement could well have been persuasive, and in the wake of September 11, 2001, the potential for hijacked commercial airliners to be used as instruments of attack on military bases can hardly be denied. Nonetheless, even if defendants were acting with the best of intentions and an eye to aviation security concerns, the record before the Court does not establish as a matter of law that the data transfer at issue in this case properly implicates the field of aviation security. At the very least, there is a question of fact about whether the complained of conduct implicates that field. And as plaintiffs argue, the Court simply cannot assume that Congress intended to relieve airlines of the state law consequences of everything an airline might believe it does for national security reasons, particularly where such conduct is neither mandated nor even permitted by any federal law.

Discovery would be needed to establish whether aviation security is the relevant field in which to ground implied preemption analysis. Accordingly, the issue of implied preemption cannot be resolved on a Rule 12(b)(6) motion to dismiss, and all state and common law claims other than that arising under the New York General Business Law will be addressed on their merits.

D. Failure to State a Claim under State or Common Law

In addition to arguing that plaintiffs' state and common law claims are preempted, defendants argue that plaintiffs have failed to state a cause of action for any claim under state law. The Court need not address the merits of the claim raised under the New York General Business Law and similar state statutes, as that claim is expressly preempted by the ADA. Each of the claims that survives preemption analysis is addressed in turn below. For purposes of resolving this motion, all parties agree that New York law applies.

1. Breach of Contract

Plaintiffs allege that they made reservations to fly with JetBlue in reliance on express promises made by JetBlue in the company's privacy policy. The substance of the contract alleged is therefore a promise by JetBlue not to disclose passengers' personal information to third parties. Plaintiffs allege that JetBlue breached that promise, thereby causing injury. With regard to the existence of a contract, plaintiffs contend that JetBlue undertook a "self-imposed contractual obligation by and between [itself] and the consumers with whom it transacted business" by publishing privacy policies on its website or otherwise disclosing such policies to its consumers. Plaintiffs maintain that "these self-imposed public assurances created an obligation under the contract-of-carriage and a duty on the part of JetBlue and the persons with whom it did business not to act in derogation of JetBlue's privacy policy ..."

JetBlue counters that its "stand-alone privacy statement"—which "could only be accessed and viewed by clicking on a separate stand-alone link" on the bottom of JetBlue's website—is not a term in the contract of carriage. It further notes in this connection that "the entire transaction of purchasing transportation can be done on JetBlue's website (or by phone or in person) without ever viewing, reading, or relying on JetBlue's website privacy statement." Although plaintiffs do allege that the privacy policy constituted a term in the contract of carriage, they argue alternatively that a stand-alone contract was formed at the moment they made flight reservations in reliance on express promises contained in JetBlue's privacy policy. JetBlue posits no persuasive argument why this alternative formulation does not form the basis of a contract.

JetBlue further argues that failure to allege that plaintiffs read the privacy policy defeats any claim of reliance. Although plaintiffs do not explicitly allege that the class members actually read or saw the privacy policy, they do allege that they and other class members relied on the representations and assurances contained in the privacy policy when choosing to purchase air transportation from JetBlue. Reliance presupposes familiarity with the policy. It may well be that some members of the class did not read the privacy policy and thus could not have relied on it, but the issue of who actually read and relied on the policy would be addressed more properly at the class certification stage. For purposes of this motion, the Court considers an allegation of reliance to encompass an allegation that some putative members of the class read or viewed the privacy policy. Accordingly, failure to specifically allege that all plaintiffs and class members read the policy does not defeat the existence of a contract for purposes of this motion to dismiss.

JetBlue also argues that plaintiffs have failed to meet their pleading requirement with respect to damages, citing an absence of any facts in the Amended Complaint to support this element of the claim. Plaintiffs' sole allegation on the element of contract damages consists of the statement that JetBlue's breach of the company privacy policy injured plaintiffs and members of the class and that JetBlue is therefore liable for "actual damages in an amount to be determined at trial." In response to JetBlue's opposition on this point, plaintiffs contend that the Amended Complaint is "replete" with facts demonstrating how plaintiffs were damaged, but cite to nothing more than the boilerplate allegation referenced above and another allegation in the Amended Complaint that they were "injured."

When pressed to identify the "injuries" or damages referred to in their complaint, counsel for plaintiffs stated that the "contract damage could be the loss of privacy," acknowledging that loss of privacy "may" be a contract damage. It is apparent based on the briefing and oral argument held in this case that the sparseness of the damages allegations is a direct result of plaintiffs' inability to plead or prove any actual contract damages. As plaintiffs' counsel concedes, the only damage that can be read into the present complaint is a loss of privacy. At least one recent case has specifically held that this is not a damage available in a breach of contract action. This holding naturally follows from the well-settled principle that "recovery in contract, unlike recovery in tort, allows only for economic losses flowing directly from the breach."

Plaintiffs allege that in a second amended complaint, they could assert as a contract damage the loss of the economic value of their information, but while that claim sounds in economic loss, the argument ignores the nature of the contract asserted. Citing the hoary case of *Hadley v. Baxendale*, the Second Circuit reminded the parties to the case before it that "damages in contract actions are limited to those that 'may reasonably be supposed to have been in the contemplation of both parties, at the time they made the contract, as the probable result of the breach of it.'"

A similarly basic principle of contract law is that the "purpose of contract damages is to put a plaintiff in the same economic position he or she would have occupied had the contract been fully performed." Plaintiffs may well have expected that in return for providing their personal information to JetBlue and paying the purchase price, they would obtain a ticket for air travel and the promise that their personal information would be safeguarded consistent with the terms of the privacy policy. They had no reason to expect that they would be compensated for the "value" of their personal information. In addition, there is absolutely no support for the proposition that the personal information of an individual JetBlue passenger had any value for which that passenger could have expected to be compensated.

It strains credulity to believe that, had JetBlue not provided the PNR data *en masse* to Torch, Torch would have gone to each individual JetBlue passenger and compensated him or her for access to his or her personal information. There is likewise no support for the proposition that an individual passenger's personal information has or had any compensable value in the economy at large. Accordingly, plaintiffs having claimed no other form of damages apart from those discussed herein and having sought no other form of relief in connection with the breach of contract claim, JetBlue's motion to dismiss the claim is granted.

2. *Trespass to Property*

Plaintiffs allege that defendants committed trespass to property by participating in the transfer of data containing their personal and private information. Because their claim concerns an alleged trespass to something other than real property, it is most accurately treated as a claim for trespass to chattels. To state a claim for trespass to chattels under New York law, plaintiffs must establish that defendants "intentionally, and without justification or consent, physically interfered with the use and enjoyment of personal property in [plaintiffs'] possession," and that plaintiffs were thereby harmed. Where the trespass alleged is to an intangible property right arising under a contract, actual injury to the claimed property interest must be shown.

Preliminarily, in order to sustain this cause of action, plaintiffs must establish that they were in possession of the PNR data that was transferred to Torch. *Kelman v. Wilen* (2d Dep't. 1954) (possession is an essential element of a cause of action in trespass). Plaintiffs argue that the limitations placed on the use of PNR data by the JetBlue privacy policy granted them continued possessory interests over their personal information, entitling them to pursue legal action if ever those limits are exceeded. Plaintiffs provide no legal support for this argument, and the Court has serious doubts as to its validity. Although defendants raise several arguments in response, none is directly responsive to plaintiffs' position. In any event, the Court need not determine whether plaintiffs enjoy a continued possessory interest in their personal data, because even assuming *arguendo* that they do, plaintiffs have not established an actual injury sufficient to sustain a claim for trespass to chattels.

Under New York law, liability only obtains on this cause of action if a defendant causes harm to "the [owner's] materially valuable interest in the physical condition, quality, or value of the chattel, or if the [owner] is deprived of the use of the chattel for a substantial time." In addition, "the defendant must act with the intention of interfering with the property or with knowledge that such interference is substantially certain to result."

In this case, plaintiffs allege rather generically that they have suffered "actual damages" or, in the alternate, "an irreparable injury for which there is no adequate remedy at law" as a result of the data transfer. They do not, however, allege that the quality or value of their personal information was in any way diminished as a result of defendants' actions, nor do they allege any facts that could sustain such a showing. The only type of harm plaintiffs allege anywhere is harm to their privacy interests, and even if their privacy interests were indeed infringed by the data transfer, such a harm does not amount to a diminishment of the quality or value of a materially valuable interest in their personal information. Plaintiffs also have not been deprived of the use of their personal information at any point, let alone for a substantial period of time.

3. *Unjust Enrichment*

Plaintiffs claim that "[e]ach defendant was unjustly enriched by the disclosure of confidential information concerning JetBlue passengers." In order to state a claim for unjust enrichment under New York law, a plaintiff must prove that (1) the defendant was enriched, (2) the enrichment was at plaintiff's expense, and (3) the circumstances were such that equity and good conscience require the defendant to make restitution.

As to the first element in the claim against JetBlue, plaintiffs argue that defendants in this case engaged in the complained-of conduct for their own commercial benefit. Plaintiffs speculate that JetBlue "received some form of remuneration from Torch or another party as a result of its disclosure of information." However, according to JetBlue, the data was made available to Torch for no consideration at the request of the Transportation Security Administration, and the only benefit JetBlue derived was "the potential for increased safety on its flights and the potential to prevent the use of commercial airlines as weapons that target military bases." Plaintiffs do not allege any facts to the contrary, and as JetBlue contends, plaintiffs may not create an issue of fact for purposes of surviving a motion to dismiss simply "by asserting a 'belief' that is supported by no reasonable inquiry, information or fact." Thus, plaintiffs have failed to establish that JetBlue was enriched by the complained-of conduct.

In addition, the circumstances of this case are not such that equity and good conscience require JetBlue to make restitution to this class of plaintiffs. Under New York law, the granting of equitable relief on a theory of unjust enrichment requires the "indispensable ingredient" of an injustice as between the two parties involved. Plaintiffs have not alleged facts to suggest that JetBlue obtained any benefit that rightfully belonged to them or that they were otherwise subjected to any injustice by virtue of JetBlue's conveyance of their personal data to Torch.

To the contrary, as plaintiffs themselves acknowledge, the purpose of the data transfer was to advance a project that "arose out of a desire to prevent attacks on military installations." Thus, even assuming *arguendo* that JetBlue was enriched at plaintiffs' expense, plaintiffs have failed to demonstrate that equity and good conscience require restitution by JetBlue. For these reasons, the unjust enrichment claim as against all defendants is dismissed.

4. *Declaratory Relief*

Plaintiffs seek a declaratory judgment stating that defendants violated the Electronic Communications Privacy Act, the New York General Business Law and other similar statutes listed in connection with the deceptive practices claims, as well as plaintiffs' common law rights against trespass to property, invasion of privacy, breach of contract, and unjust enrichment. As plaintiffs have failed to state viable claims against any defendant, this application is denied.

NADER v. ALLEGHENY AIRLINES, INC.
426 U.S. 290 (1976)

Mr. Justice POWELL delivered the opinion of the Court.

On April 25, petitioner reserved a seat on respondent's flight 864 for April 28. The flight was scheduled to leave Washington, D.C., at 10:15 A.M. and to arrive in Hartford at 11:15 A.M. Petitioner's ticket was purchased from a travel agency on the morning of the flight. It indicated, by the standard "OK" notation, that the reservation was confirmed.

Petitioner arrived at the boarding and check-in area approximately five minutes before the scheduled departure time. He was informed that all seats on the flight were occupied and that he, like several other passengers who had arrived shortly before him, could not be accommodated. Explaining that he had to arrive in Hartford in time for the noon rally, petitioner asked respondent's agent to determine whether any standby passengers had been allowed to board by mistake or whether anyone already on board would voluntarily give up his or her seat. Both requests were refused. In accordance with respondent's practice, petitioner was offered alternative transportation by air taxi to Philadelphia, where connections could be made with an Allegheny flight scheduled to arrive in Hartford at 12:15 P.M. Fearing that the Philadelphia connection, which allowed only 10 minutes between planes, was too close, petitioner rejected this offer and elected to fly to Boston. Both parties agree that petitioner's reservation was not honored because respondent had accepted more reservations for Flight 864 than it could in fact accommodate. One hour prior to the flight, 107 reservations had been confirmed for the 100 seats actually available.

Such overbooking is a common industry practice, designed to ensure that each flight leaves with as few empty seats as possible despite the large number of "no-shows" reservation-holding passengers who do not appear at flight time. By the use of statistical studies of no-show patterns on specific flights, the airlines attempt to predict the appropriate number of reservations necessary to fill each flight. In this way, they attempt to ensure the most efficient use of aircraft while preserving a flexible booking system that permits passengers to cancel and change reservations without notice or penalty. At times the practice of overbooking results in oversales, which occur when more reservation-holding passengers than can be accommodated actually appear to board the flight. When this occurs, some passengers must be denied boarding ("bumped").

The chance that any particular passenger will be bumped is so negligible that few prospective passengers aware of the possibility would give it a second thought. In April 1972, the month in which petitioner's reservation was dishonored, 6.7 confirmed passengers per 10,000 enplanements were denied boarding on domestic flights. For all domestic airlines, oversales resulted in bumping an average of 5.4 passengers per 10,000 enplanements in 1972, and 4.6 per 10,000 enplanements in 1973. In domestic operations respondent oversold 6.3 seats per 10,000 enplanements in 1972 and 4.5 seats per 10,000 enplanements in 1973. Thus, based on the 1972 experience of all domestic airlines, there was only slightly more than one chance in 2,000 that any particular passenger would be bumped on a given flight. Nevertheless, the total number of confirmed ticket holders denied seats is quite substantial, numbering over 82,000 passengers in 1972 and about 76,000 in 1973.

Board regulations require each airline to establish priority rules for boarding passengers and to offer "denied boarding compensation" to bumped passengers. These "liquidated damages" are equal to the value of the passenger's ticket with a $25 minimum and a $200 maximum. *See* 14 C.F.R. § 250.5 (1975). Passengers are free to reject the compensation offered in favor of a common-law suit for damages suffered as a result of the bumping.

Petitioner refused the tender of denied boarding compensation ($32.41 in his case) and filed this suit for compensatory and punitive damages. His suit did not seek compensation for the bumping *per se* but asserted two other bases of liability: a common-law action based on fraudulent misrepresentation arising from respondent's alleged failure to inform petitioner in advance of its deliberate overbooking practices, and a statutory action under § 404(b) of the Act, 49 U.S.C. § 1374(b), arising from respondent's alleged failure to afford petitioner the boarding priority specified in its rules filed with the Board under 14 C.F.R. § 250.3 (1975).

Section 404(b) provides:

> No air carrier or foreign air carrier shall make, give, or cause any undue or unreasonable preference or advantage to any particular person, port, locality, or description of traffic in air transportation in any respect whatsoever or subject any particular person, port, locality, or description of traffic in air transportation to any unjust discrimination or any undue or unreasonable prejudice or disadvantage in any respect whatsoever.

The District Court entered a judgment for petitioner on both claims, awarding him a total of $10 in compensatory damages and $25,000 in punitive damages. The Court of Appeals for the District of Columbia Circuit reversed. The merits of petitioner's statutory claim were remanded for further findings. The award of punitive damages to petitioner on the statutory claim was reversed on the ground that respondent's conduct contained no "elements of intentional wrongdoing or conscious disregard for" petitioner's rights.

* * *

BUCK v. AMERICAN AIRLINES, INC.

476 F.3d 29 (1st Cir. 2007)

SELYA, Senior Circuit Judge.

On November 4, 2004, fifteen individuals filed suit against a number of airlines and related entities in a Massachusetts state court. The plaintiffs alleged that the defendants had wrongfully retained fees and taxes collected at the time of their purchase of nonrefundable tickets. This retention of funds was wrongful, the plaintiffs maintained, because they never used the tickets and, thus, the fees and taxes, which did not become due until the commencement of air travel, should have been returned.

The defendants removed the case to the federal district court. The plaintiffs, now reduced to nine in number, served an amended complaint that named six domestic and seven international airlines as the culprits. Of the domestic airlines, American Airlines, Alaska Airlines, Continental Airlines, and Southwest Airlines remain as defendants. Two other domestic carriers (Northwest and Delta) have been dismissed due to ongoing bankruptcy proceedings. The international airlines named in the suit are Aer Lingus, Alitalia, British Airways, China Eastern Airlines, China Southern Airlines, Lufthansa, and Olympic Airways. Of these, six remain (Olympic Airways appears to have been dropped as a party). The Federal Aviation Administration ("FAA") also was named, but the district court dismissed all claims against the FAA on grounds wholly unrelated to the issues raised on appeal.

The fees and taxes said to have been wrongly withheld include passenger facility charges, see 14 C.F.R. § 158.5; customs fees, see 19 C.F.R. § 24.22(g)(1); immigration fees, see 8 C.F.R. § 286.2; agricultural quarantine fees, see 7 C.F.R. § 354.3(f); security fees, see 49 C.F.R. § 1510.5; and charges on behalf of foreign sovereigns (collectively, the "fees"). The plaintiffs averred that, in keeping the fees, the defendants violated a host of federal regulations, most notably a regulation that provides:

> A passenger shall not be bound by any terms restricting refunds of the ticket price, imposing monetary penalties on passengers, or permitting the carrier to raise the price, unless the passenger receives conspicuous written notice of the salient features of those terms on or with the ticket.

14 C.F.R. § 253.7. The plaintiffs claim that the retained fees constitute a forbidden monetary penalty, imposed without due notice. In this connection, they admit having had adequate notice that their tickets were nonrefundable; in their view, however, this only alerted them to the fact that they could not recover the base ticket price. They had no notice that the fees would be forfeit as well.

The plaintiffs cloaked this theory in pleochroic raiment; their multitudinous statements of claim included counts for declaratory judgment, rescission, breach of contract, unjust enrichment, breach of a covenant of good faith and fair dealing, breach of fiduciary duty, and civil conspiracy. In addition, the plaintiffs purposed to sue pursuant to an implied right of action arising under a federal regulation. Their prayer for relief requested certification of a class; a declaration that (i) the airlines had failed to provide adequate notice of an intention to withhold the fees and (ii) the airlines' retention of the fees was wrongful; treble damages; injunctive and other equitable remediation; and attorneys' fees.

A majority of the defendants moved to dismiss on the ground, *inter alia*, that all the claims were preempted by section 105(a) of the Airline Deregulation Act ("ADA"), 49 U.S.C. § 41713(b)(1). The district court granted the motion to dismiss. This timely appeal followed.

DISCUSSION

We begin our analysis with the plaintiffs' lone federal-law claim: their claim of an implied right of action under 14 C.F.R. § 253.4 and § 253.7. These provisions govern the disclosure of terms in contracts for air travel. Among other things, they prevent airlines from claiming the benefit of contract terms not incorporated by reference in a specified manner. *See* 14 C.F.R. § 253.4(a). They go on to restrict the authority of airlines to impose monetary penalties on passengers without clear notice. *See id.* § 253.7. In this instance, the plaintiffs argue that they were denied notice that they would forfeit the fees (in addition to the base fares) in the event that they did not use their nonrefundable tickets.

In support of this argument, the plaintiffs invoke the test formulated in *Cort v. Ash*, 422 U.S. 66 (1975), which they insist controls whether a private right of action is to be implied in connection with a federal statute. Under that test, courts are to ask four questions:

> [I]s the plaintiff a member of the class for whose "especial benefit" the statute was passed? Is there any cogent indication of legislative intent to create or deny the remedy sought? Would recognition of the remedy be "consistent with the underlying purposes' of the statutory scheme? Would it be inappropriate to infer a federal remedy because 'the cause of action [is] one traditionally relegated to state law?'"

Royal Business Group., Inc. v. Realist, Inc. (1st Cir. 1991). The plaintiffs maintain that the regulations' goal is to protect consumers and, thus, that it is appropriate to imply a private right of action.

This argument cannot withstand scrutiny. In the first place, the plaintiffs misapprehend the relevant unit of analysis. Regulations alone cannot create private rights of action; the source of the right must be a statute. *See Alexander v. Sandoval* (2001). The regulations upon which the plaintiffs rely were promulgated pursuant to 49 U.S.C. § 41707—a statute that has its roots in the CAB Sunset Act, Pub. L. No. 98-443, § 7 (1984). The CAB Sunset Act embodies a series of amendments to the ADA, which six years earlier had significantly revamped the Federal Aviation Act.

We recently rejected an entreaty to imply a private cause of action pursuant to other regulations implementing the ADA. In the process, we made clear that, for the purpose of implying private rights of action, the Federal Aviation Act (and, hence, the ADA) is barren soil. There is nothing about the case at bar that shakes our confidence in that assessment.

To cinch matters, "[e]very court faced with the question of whether a consumer protection provision of the ADA allows the implication of a private right of action against an airline has answered the question in the negative." *Casas v. American Airlines, Inc.* (5th Cir. 2002). We see no justification for creating a circuit split. Thus, we hold that the consumer protection provisions of the ADA do not permit the imputation of a private right of action against an airline and that, therefore, the plaintiffs do not have an implied right of action under 14 C.F.R. § 253.4 or § 253.7. Lacking a federal-law cause of action, the plaintiffs are relegated to their array of state-law claims. Yet, even though Massachusetts law offers them a cornucopia of vehicles for their theory that the fees should have been refunded, this bounty avails them naught; state-law claims premised on that theory cannot survive the ADA's broad preemptive sweep. We explain briefly.

Pertinently, the ADA declares that no state may "enact or enforce a law, regulation, or other provision having the force and effect of law related to a price, route, or service of an air carrier." 49 U.S.C. § 41713(b)(1). The Supreme Court has offered considerable guidance as to how this preemption provision should be construed. In *Morales v. Trans World Airlines, Inc.* (1992), the Court referred to the "sweeping nature" of the preemption provision, emphasizing the reach of the provision's "relationship" language. The *Morales* Court held that the provision should be construed broadly. This court has explained that, under *Morales*, the ADA preempts both laws that explicitly refer to an airline's prices and those that have a significant effect upon prices.

Three years after *Morales*, the Supreme Court reaffirmed the breadth of the ADA's preemption provision. *See American Airlines, Inc. v. Wolens* (1995). However, the Court carved out an exception for "suits alleging no violation of state-imposed obligations, but seeking recovery solely for the airline's alleged breach of its own, self-imposed undertakings." It follows that, in order to avoid preemption, the plaintiffs in this case must demonstrate either that their state-law claims do not constitute state enforcement related to airline prices or services, or that they can navigate the straits of the *Wolens* exception.

The plaintiffs' doctrinal starting point is the assertion that their claims are outside the ambit of ADA preemption because they seek to enforce federal, not state, regulatory requirements. At the heart of this assertion lies the dubious premise that since federal rules govern the airlines' collection of the fees and provide certain forms of passenger protection in the contracting process, only federal policies are being advanced by this litigation. On this telling, "[s]tate court enforcement of Federal law is not the same as enforcement of a State-imposed requirement," and the fact that the causes of action themselves spring from state law is less important than the source of the underlying policies. This is so, the plaintiffs asseverate, because federal preemption should not disrupt federal policies; after all, nationwide uniformity is the driver for preemption, see *Morales*, and that uniformity is not offended by enforcement of federal policies.

This sleight of hand will not work. While the plaintiffs strive to characterize their suit as one that invokes state remedies to right a federal wrong, that characterization does not ring true. More accurately, they are attempting to invoke state remedies to further a state policy: that those who are wronged should have individualized access to the courts in order to remediate that wrong. It is the imposition of this state policy that would constitute forbidden state enforcement, in violation of the ADA's preemption provision, because the ADA itself provides no private right of action.

As an alternative, the plaintiffs posit that allowing their suit to proceed "does not—and in fact cannot—affect the prices (or rates), routes, or services [of airlines], since the redress occurs only after the prices (or rates), routes, and services have been determined by the Air Industry." In their view, "[a]irline ticket prices (or rates) are composed of two separate components: (1) the fare prices (or rates) set by the airlines, which comprise the base cost of a ticket, and (2) the taxes, fees, and, charges imposed by the Government or other fee-levying authorities."

This dichotomy blurs when contextualized within the contours of the "significant effect" doctrine. Although the fees are in one sense separate from the base fare, the two are inextricably intertwined. In all events, an air traveler's concern is with the overall cost of his or her ticket. Thus, when an airline establishes the base fare, it must take cognizance of any surcharges that will be imposed by operation of law.

It is freshman-year economics that higher prices mean lower demand, and that consumers are sensitive to the full price that they must pay, not just the portion of the price that will stay in the seller's coffers. For that reason, an airline must account for the fees when setting its own rates. It follows that a finding for the plaintiffs in this case would impact base fares—and since past judgments affect future behavior, this is as true of the retrospective relief requested by the plaintiffs as it is of the prospective relief that they request. In view of these practical realities, it is not surprising that most of the courts to have considered suits for refunds of government fees associated with air travel have found those suits preempted. We say "most" because at least one court has found to the contrary. *See In re Air Transp. Excise Tax. Litig.*, (D. Minn. 1999). We regard that decision as mistaken.

The plaintiffs next argue that their suit was improvidently dismissed because their contract-based claims fit within the *Wolens* exception. But the plaintiffs' amended complaint identifies only a single word—"nonrefundable"—as common to their contracts of carriage with a multitude of airlines. It seems fanciful to suggest, in the circumstances of this case, that the word "nonrefundable" alone can anchor a breach of contract claim. The same result would follow even if, as plaintiffs insist, the word "nonrefundable" is ambiguous. At best, an ambiguity would furnish a rejoinder to a claim that the airlines gave clear notice about fees being forfeit. It could not, without more, support a claim that the defendants have breached their duty to treat the tickets as "nonrefundable" by withholding both the fare and the fees.

The plaintiffs attempt to circumvent this conspicuous obstacle by latching onto the federal regulatory guidelines relating to the disclosure of terms in airline contracts. These guidelines, they suggest, are "federally mandated terms of their air travel contracts." In making this point, the plaintiffs again emphasize 14 C.F.R. § 253.7, the provision prohibiting the imposition of monetary penalties without clear notice. The plaintiffs allege that this regulation is written implicitly into every airline contract of carriage and thus, by retaining the fees, the airlines have breached their contractual duty not to levy an unwarned monetary penalty. The plaintiffs have not directed us to a single case holding that a federal regulation incapable of spawning an implied private right of action may be enforced between private parties as an implicit contract term. The precedent that they most loudly trumpet—the Texas Supreme Court's decision in *Delta Air Lines, Inc. v. Black* (Tex. 2003)—is inapposite. The contract at issue there explicitly incorporated federal regulations.

We conclude, without serious question, that the proposition asserted by the plaintiffs is untenable. As they conceded at oral argument, construing all federal regulations touching upon air travel as automatically incorporated into every airline's contracts of carriage would allow litigants freely to skirt the implied right of action doctrine. There is nothing to distinguish the regulation at issue here from the mine-run of federal regulations touching upon air travel, and we will not countenance the flagrant undermining of Supreme Court doctrine that the plaintiffs invite.

Our reluctance is evidently shared by the Fifth Circuit, which confronted a similar problem in *Casas*. There, the plaintiff argued for a remedy under federal common law with respect to violations of regulations prescribed by the federal Department of Transportation. The court rejected this argument, observing that a contrary holding "would be, in substance, to craft a private right of action for violations of [the regulation]—and thus to circumvent the conclusion that the ADA, and therefore the regulations enacted pursuant to it, creates no private right of action." Like the Fifth Circuit, we refuse to abet a blatant evasion of the implied right of action doctrine.

To say more on this point would be supererogatory. At bottom, the plaintiffs would have us believe that the implied right of action doctrine contains a gaping aperture that allows federal regulations, promulgated pursuant to a statute that creates no right of private enforcement, to be privately enforced through state-law mechanisms. We cannot imagine that the Supreme Court, which has devoted nearly three decades to cabining the implied right of action doctrine would approve so vagarious a course. We hold instead that, because no implied right of action exists under the ADA and the regulation at issue here, the regulation cannot be read as an implied contract provision. Next, the plaintiffs launch a naked appeal to public policy. They tell us that if state-law causes of action are denied them, there will be a wrong (the airlines' withholding of the fees) without a remedy. Put in more hyperbolic terms, a rejection of the plaintiffs' claims would render "almost all airline contracts and certain provisions of Federal law" meaningless.

The first half of this lament—that a finding for the defendants will jeopardize the enforceability of all airline contracts of carriage—is empty rhetoric. A finding for the defendants merely retains the configuration of the *Wolens* exception crafted by the Supreme Court, which limited that exception to "self-imposed undertakings." The second half of this lament—that a finding for the defendants will undercut the federal regulatory scheme—is equally baseless. Refusing to treat federal regulations as implied contract terms does not in any way diminish the efficacy of the regulatory scheme itself. Contrary to the plaintiffs' importunings, we do not think it "inexplicabl[e]" that Congress might view certain regulations as sufficiently important to warrant their promulgation, yet "not sufficiently important to permit [private] enforcement in any court."

What the plaintiffs fail to grasp is that the unavailability of private enforcement is not the same as the unavailability of any enforcement at all. We made that point in another case where we remarked upon the power of the Secretary of Transportation to conduct investigations and issue orders with respect to the airline industry. This led us to the conclusion that Congress's preference in this area is for public, rather than private, enforcement. In other words, Congress reasonably expected the regulations to be enforced by the Secretary.

DELTA AIR LINES, INC. v. BARNARD

799 So. 2d 208 (Ala. Civ. 2001)

YATES, Judge.

Dr. Henry H. Barnard II and his wife purchased two Delta round-trip tickets from All Seasons Travel in Dothan, to fly on August 7, 1997, from Mobile to Brunswick, Georgia, with a return trip on August 10, 1997. The return trip required the Barnards to fly through Atlanta. The ticket Dr. Barnard purchased indicated that the return flight would be on Delta flight 7264; however, the Brunswick-to-Atlanta leg of the flight was to be operated by ASA. ASA flights from Brunswick fly only to Atlanta.

On the day of the return trip, Dr. Barnard and his wife arrived at the Brunswick airport between 5:00 P.M. and 5:30 P.M. for their flight, which was scheduled to depart Brunswick at 6:45 P.M. Upon arriving at the airport, Dr. Barnard checked two pieces of luggage to Mobile, and his wife checked her luggage to Dothan. This flight was the last scheduled flight of the day from Brunswick to Atlanta and was the only flight on which Dr. Barnard's luggage could be placed, because the previous flight had departed Brunswick for Atlanta at 2:45 P.M. Dr. Barnard's luggage consisted of a suitcase that contained clothing, and a hard-plastic carrying case that contained golf clubs and other golf equipment. He testified that each golf club carried a sticker showing his name, address, and telephone number. The clubs were first placed inside a soft carry bag, which had two attached tags bearing Dr. Barnard's name. He testified that the soft bag was then placed inside the hard case. He stated that he had placed a sticker and an identification tag on the hard case. Additionally, Dr. Barnard testified that he had watched the ASA representative affix the baggage seal to the case.

The airport in Brunswick is a small facility. Dr. Barnard testified that he actually watched the ticket agent push the hard-case carrier into the luggage chute that opened directly onto the tarmac. This was the last time Dr. Barnard saw the hard case. He boarded the plane and flew to Atlanta. He had a one-and-one-half hour layover in Atlanta and then flew to Mobile. When Dr. Barnard arrived in Mobile, he proceeded to the baggage-claim area, where he retrieved his suitcase from the baggage carousel. His carrying case containing his golf clubs did not arrive. He then filed a "Lost Bag Claim" with a Delta agent in Mobile and was told that he had been on the day's last flight to Mobile from Atlanta and therefore there was no chance that the carrying case would arrive that night. He was given a telephone number and told to call back the following morning to check the status of his claim.

Dr. Barnard called the following morning and was informed by Delta that the carrying case had not arrived and that Delta was attempting to locate it. He was given Delta's lost-baggage department's toll-free telephone number to follow up on his claim. He called, to no avail. Dr. Barnard testified that two days later he was told by someone at Delta, "[I]f we haven't found [the case] yet, we are not going to find it." He then spoke to a Delta manager, who informed him that after three days "[the case] is probably not going to show up, it's probably gone." The manager informed him that Delta's liability was limited to $1,250 and he offered to send Dr. Barnard a check for that amount. Dr. Barnard testified that the value of the clubs and equipment was $3,292.50. Dr. Barnard received a check for $1,250 two days later, but he returned it to Delta.

Beau Goss, a Delta customer-service agent, testified that Delta's baggage-tracking system is sophisticated. He stated that a "bag tag" containing an identification number, a three-letter abbreviation of the destination, and a bar-code number is attached to a passenger's luggage when it is checked. He said that Delta can track luggage nationwide by the "bag tag" number and the bar code, through its computer system. He also testified that the destination of any luggage is easily ascertainable by looking at the three-letter abbreviation on the "bag tag." Goss further testified that the baggage handling area is a Federal Aviation Administration ("FAA") restricted area, accessible by Delta employees with a security clearance. He had no explanation as to how the carrying case containing numerous pieces of identification could get lost on a flight from Brunswick to Mobile with a layover in Atlanta. The record indicates that at no time was Dr. Barnard referred to ASA regarding the missing case. Ronnie Edwards, an ASA representative, testified that only ASA employees would have access to the baggage-handling area in Brunswick, and that only ASA and Delta employees would have access to the baggage-handling area in Atlanta. Edwards also had no explanation as to how the carrying case could have been lost during the trip.

Delta argues that the trial court erred as a matter of law in refusing to enforce its baggage-liability limitation of $1,250, which it alleges was made part of the contract of carriage entered into between Dr. Barnard and Delta. *In Ex parte Delta Air Lines, supra*, the plaintiff sued Delta in the district court, alleging negligence and a breach of contract. The plaintiff contended that Delta had negligently handled her luggage and that as a result she had suffered damage, including the loss of her family jewelry. The district court entered a judgment in favor of the plaintiff, awarding her damages of $5,000. Delta appealed to the circuit court.

The rules applicable to the carriage of baggage in interstate and overseas air transportation are found at 14 C.F.R. § 254. Section 254 sets permissible limitations of air-carrier liability for loss, damage, or delay in the carriage of a passenger's baggage and requires an air carrier to provide certain kinds of notice to passengers regarding its limitation of liability. 14 C.F.R. § 254.4 provides:

> In any flight segment using large aircraft, or on any flight segment that is included on the same ticket as another flight segment that uses large aircraft, an air carrier shall not limit its liability for provable direct or consequential damages resulting from the disappearance of, damage to, or delay in delivery of a passenger's personal property, including baggage, in its custody to an amount less than $1,250 for each passenger.

Section 254.5 provides:

> In any flight segment using large aircraft, or on any flight segment that is included on the same ticket as another flight segment that uses large aircraft, an air carrier shall provide to passengers, by conspicuous written material included on or with its ticket, either: (a) notice of any monetary limitation on its baggage liability to passengers; or (b) the following notice: "Federal rules require any limit on an

> airline's baggage liability to be at least $1,250 per passenger."

The notice requirement that governs the incorporation of terms by reference into a contract of carriage and that makes such incorporation of terms effective is found at 14 C.F.R. § 253. Section 253.1 provides: "The purpose of this rule is to set uniform disclosure requirements, which preempt any State requirements on the same subject, for terms incorporated by reference into contracts of carriage for scheduled service in interstate and overseas passenger air transportation." Section 253.4 provides:

> A ticket or other written instrument that embodies the contract of carriage may incorporate contract terms by reference (*i.e.*, without stating their full text), and if it does so shall contain or be accompanied by notice to the passenger as required by this part. In addition to other remedies at law, an air carrier may not claim the benefit as against the passenger of, and the passenger shall not be bound by, any contract term incorporated by reference if notice of the term has not been provided to that passenger in accordance with this part.
>
> Each air carrier shall make the full text of each term that it incorporates by reference in a contract of carriage available for public inspection at each of its airport and city ticket offices. Each air carrier shall provide free of charge by mail or other delivery service to passengers, upon their request, a copy of the full text of its terms incorporated by reference in the contract. Each carrier shall keep available at all times, free of charge, at all locations where its tickets are sold within the United States information sufficient to enable passengers to order the full text of such terms.

Section 253.5 provides, in part:

> Except as provided in § 253.8, each air carrier shall include on or with a ticket, or other written instrument given to a passenger, that embodies the contract of carriage and incorporates terms by reference in that contract, a conspicuous notice that:
>
> Any terms incorporated by reference are part of the contract, passengers may inspect the full text of each term incorporated by reference at the carrier's airport or city ticket offices, and passengers have the right, upon request

> at any location where the carrier's tickets are sold within the United States, to receive free of charge by mail or other delivery service the full text of each such incorporated term.
>
> The incorporated terms may include and passengers may obtain from any location where the carrier's tickets are sold within the United States further information concerning: Limits on the air carrier's liability for personal injury or death of passengers, and for loss, damage, or delay of goods and baggage, including fragile or perishable goods.

As stated previously, Dr. Barnard and his wife had purchased their airline tickets from All Seasons Travel in Dothan. Dr. Barnard's ticket was prepared by Janet Lattime, the branch manager of All Seasons Travel. The back of the airline ticket issued to Dr. Barnard contained the following language:

> Air transportation to be provided between points in the U.S. (including its overseas territories and possessions) is subject to the individual contract terms (including rules, regulations, tariffs and conditions) of the transporting air carriers, which are herein incorporated by reference and made part of the contract of carriage.

Delta introduced into evidence a copy of its conditions of contract that are incorporated by reference into the terms of the contract of carriage. Section V pertains to baggage and contains language limiting to $1,250 Delta's liability for the loss of, or damage to, a passenger's baggage, unless a higher value is declared by the passenger.

> Where this coupon is issued for transportation, or services other than air travel, specific terms and conditions may apply. These terms and conditions may be included in the ticket set or may be obtained from this issuing company or agent. Please make sure you have received the important legal notices entitled "Conditions of Contract," "Notice of Incorporated Terms," "Notice of Baggage Liability Limitations," and "Notice of Overbooking," or the specific terms and conditions relating to non-air transportation or services. If not, contact the nearest office of the company or agent to obtain copies.

Dr. Barnard testified that he never read the wording on the back of the ticket and did not obtain the legal notices referenced therein. Lattime testified that a two-page insert had accompanied Dr. Barnard's ticket when it was issued to him. Page one of the insert contained the following language:

> NOTICE OF BAGGAGE
> LIABILITY LIMITATIONS
>
> Liability for loss, delay, or damage to baggage is limited unless a higher value is declared in advance and additional charges are paid ... For travel wholly between U.S. points federal rules require any limit on an airline's baggage liability to be at least $1,250 per passenger. Excess valuation may be declared on certain types of articles. Some carriers assume no liability for fragile, valuable or perishable articles. Further information may be obtained from the carrier.

Page two of the insert contained the following language:

> NOTICE OF INCORPORATED TERMS
>
> Effective January 1, 1983, this notice forms part of the conditions of contract between the airline and the passenger. If there is any inconsistency between the incorporated terms described below and the terms and conditions in the passenger's ticket, these incorporated terms govern.
>
> Air transportation to be provided between points in the U.S. (including its overseas territories and possessions) is subject to the individual terms of the transporting air carriers, which are herein incorporated by reference and made part of the contract of carriage. Incorporated terms may include, but are not restricted to: *Limits on liability for baggage, including fragile or perishable goods, and availability of excess valuation coverage.*
>
> You can obtain additional information on items 1 through 6 above at any U.S. location where the transporting air carrier's tickets are sold. You have the right to inspect the full text of each transporting air carrier's terms at its airport and city ticket offices. You also have the right upon request, to receive free of charge the full text of the applicable terms incorporated by reference from each of the transporting air carriers. Information on ordering the full

> text of each air carrier's terms is available at any U.S. location where the air carrier's tickets are sold.

Lattime testified that attached to every airline ticket issued by All Seasons is a copy of the above-mentioned insert, and she testified that she specifically recalls including the insert in the ticket packet issued to Dr. Barnard. Dr. Barnard testified that he did not recall seeing the insert in the ticket packet, but that he did not look at all of the information contained in the packet. He did state that it was possible that he had seen the insert before August 10, 1997. Additionally, Dr. Barnard stated that he had flown commercially approximately 30 to 40 times and that he was generally aware that airlines contractually limit their liability for passenger baggage.

Based on our supreme court's holding in *Ex parte Delta Air Lines*, we conclude that Dr. Barnard's conversion claim in this case relates to an airline's service and therefore must be determined in accordance with federal law. We further note that Delta conceded at trial that a contract of carriage existed between the parties and that it had breached that contract; however, it argued that its liability was limited to $1,250, because, it contended, it had satisfied the notice requirements contained in 14 C.F.R. §§ 253 and 254. Following the denial of its motion for a JML on Dr. Barnard's conversion claim, Delta argued that the limitation of liability also applied to any compensatory damages that Dr. Barnard might recover under his conversion claim for the loss of the case containing the golf clubs. The trial court gave Delta's requested jury charge regarding the limitation of liability and instructed the jury that if it found that Delta had properly delivered notice of the limitation of liability to Dr. Barnard, then the amount of compensatory damages under either the conversion claim or the breach-of-contract claim, was limited to $1,250. We conclude, from the evidence presented, that Delta complied with the notice requirements set forth in 14 C.F.R. §§ 253 and 254 and it was entitled, as a matter of law, to have its $1,250 limitation of liability enforced.

International Air Travel: European Union

REGULATION (EC) NO 261/2004 OF THE EUROPEAN PARLIAMENT AND OF THE COUNCIL

Official Journal L 046, 17/02/2004 P. 0001 - 0008

THE EUROPEAN PARLIAMENT AND THE COUNCIL OF THE EUROPEAN UNION, having regard to the Treaty establishing the European Community, and in particular Article 80(2) thereof; having regard to the proposal from the Commission(1); having regard to the opinion of the European Economic and Social Committee(2); after consulting the Committee of the Regions; acting in accordance with the procedure laid down in Article 251 of the Treaty(3), in the light of the joint text approved by the Conciliation Committee on 1 December 2003, Whereas:

(1) Action by the Community in the field of air transport should aim, among other things, at ensuring a high level of protection for passengers. Moreover, full account should be taken of the requirements of consumer protection in general.

(2) Denied boarding and cancellation or long delay of flights cause serious trouble and inconvenience to passengers.

(3) While Council Regulation (EEC) No 295/91 of 4 February 1991 establishing common rules for a denied boarding compensation system in scheduled air transport(4) created basic protection for passengers, the number of passengers denied boarding against their will remains too high, as does that affected by cancellations without prior warning and that affected by long delays.

(4) The Community should therefore raise the standards of protection set by that Regulation both to strengthen the rights of passengers and to ensure that air carriers operate under harmonised conditions in a liberalised market.

(5) Since the distinction between scheduled and non-scheduled air services is weakening, such protection should apply to passengers not only on scheduled but also on non-scheduled flights, including those forming part of package tours.

(6) The protection accorded to passengers departing from an airport located in a Member State should be extended to those leaving an airport located in a third country for one situated in a Member State, when a Community carrier operates the flight.

(7) In order to ensure the effective application of this Regulation, the obligations that it creates should rest with the operating air carrier who performs or intends to perform a flight, whether with owned aircraft, under dry or wet lease, or on any other basis.

(8) This Regulation should not restrict the rights of the operating air carrier to seek compensation from any person, including third parties, in accordance with the law applicable.

(9) The number of passengers denied boarding against their will should be reduced by requiring air carriers to call for volunteers to surrender their reservations, in exchange for benefits, instead of denying passengers boarding, and by fully compensating those finally denied boarding.

(10) Passengers denied boarding against their will should be able either to cancel their flights, with reimbursement of their tickets, or to continue them under satisfactory conditions, and should be adequately cared for while awaiting a later flight.

(11) Volunteers should also be able to cancel their flights, with reimbursement of their tickets, or continue them under satisfactory conditions, since they face difficulties of travel similar to those experienced by passengers denied boarding against their will.

(12) The trouble and inconvenience to passengers caused by cancellation of flights should also be reduced. This should be achieved by inducing carriers to inform passengers of cancellations before the scheduled time of departure and in addition to offer them reasonable re-routing, so that the passengers can make other arrangements. Air carriers should compensate passengers if they fail to do this, except when the cancellation occurs in extraordinary circumstances which could not have been avoided even if all reasonable measures had been taken.

(13) Passengers whose flights are cancelled should be able either to obtain reimbursement of their tickets or to obtain re-routing under satisfactory conditions, and should be adequately cared for while awaiting a later flight.

(14) As under the Montreal Convention, obligations on operating air carriers should be limited or excluded in cases where an event has been caused by extraordinary circumstances which could not have been avoided even if all reasonable measures had been taken. Such circumstances may, in particular, occur in cases of political instability, meteorological conditions incompatible with the operation of the flight concerned, security risks, unexpected flight safety shortcomings and strikes that affect the operation of an operating air carrier.

(15) Extraordinary circumstances should be deemed to exist where the impact of an air traffic management decision in relation to a particular aircraft on a particular day gives rise to a long delay, an overnight delay, or the cancellation of one or more flights by that aircraft, even though all reasonable measures had been taken by the air carrier concerned to avoid the delays or cancellations.

(16) In cases where a package tour is cancelled for reasons other than the flight being cancelled, this Regulation should not apply.

(17) Passengers whose flights are delayed for a specified time should be adequately cared for and should be able to cancel their flights with reimbursement of their tickets or to continue them under satisfactory conditions.

(18) Care for passengers awaiting an alternative or a delayed flight may be limited or declined if the provision of the care would itself cause further delay.

(19) Operating air carriers should meet the special needs of persons with reduced mobility and any persons accompanying them.

(20) Passengers should be fully informed of their rights in the event of denied boarding and of cancellation or long delay of flights, so that they can effectively exercise their rights.

(21) Member States should lay down rules on sanctions applicable to infringements of the provisions of this Regulation and ensure that these sanctions are applied. The sanctions should be effective, proportionate and dissuasive.

(22) Member States should ensure and supervise general compliance by their air carriers with this Regulation and designate an appropriate body to carry out such enforcement tasks. The supervision should not affect the rights of passengers and air carriers to seek legal redress from courts under procedures of national law.

(23) The Commission should analyse the application of this Regulation and should assess in particular the opportunity of extending its scope to all passengers having a contract with a tour operator or with a Community carrier, when departing from a third country airport to an airport in a Member State.

(24) Arrangements for greater cooperation over the use of Gibraltar airport were agreed in London on 2 December 1987 by the Kingdom of Spain and the United Kingdom in a joint declaration by the Ministers of Foreign Affairs of the two countries. Such arrangements have yet to enter into operation.

(25) Regulation (EEC) No 295/91 should accordingly be repealed,

HAVE ADOPTED THIS REGULATION:

Article 1
Subject

1. This Regulation establishes, under the conditions specified herein, minimum rights for passengers when: (a) they are denied boarding against their will; (b) their flight is cancelled; (c) their flight is delayed.

2. Application of this Regulation to Gibraltar airport is understood to be without prejudice to the respective legal positions of the Kingdom of Spain and the United Kingdom with regard to the dispute over sovereignty over the territory in which the airport is situated.

3. Application of this Regulation to Gibraltar airport shall be suspended until the arrangements in the Joint Declaration made by the Foreign Ministers of the Kingdom of Spain and the United Kingdom on 2 December 1987 enter into operation. The Governments of Spain and the United Kingdom will inform the Council of such date of entry into operation.

Article 2
Definitions

For the purposes of this Regulation:

(a) "air carrier" means an air transport undertaking with a valid operating licence;

(b) "operating air carrier" means an air carrier that performs or intends to perform a flight under a contract with a passenger or on behalf of another person, legal or natural, having a contract with that passenger;

(c) "Community carrier" means an air carrier with a valid operating licence granted by a Member State in accordance with the provisions of Council Regulation (EEC) No 2407/92 of 23 July 1992 on licensing of air carriers(5);

(d) "tour operator" means, with the exception of an air carrier, an organiser within the meaning of Article 2, point 2, of Council Directive 90/314/EEC of 13 June 1990 on package travel, package holidays and package tours(6);

(e) "package" means those services defined in Article 2, point 1, of Directive 90/314/EEC;

(f) "ticket" means a valid document giving entitlement to transport, or something equivalent in paperless form, including electronic form, issued or authorised by the air carrier or its authorised agent;

(g) "reservation" means the fact that the passenger has a ticket, or other proof, which indicates that the reservation has been accepted and registered by the air carrier or tour operator;

(h) "final destination" means the destination on the ticket presented at the check-in counter or, in the case of directly connecting flights, the destination of the last flight; alternative connecting flights available shall not be taken into account if the original planned arrival time is respected;

(i) "person with reduced mobility" means any person whose mobility is reduced when using transport because of any physical disability (sensory or locomotory, permanent or temporary), intellectual impairment, age or any other cause of disability, and whose situation needs special attention and adaptation to the person's needs of the services made available to all passengers;

(j) "denied boarding" means a refusal to carry passengers on a flight, although they have presented themselves for boarding under the conditions laid down in

Article 3(2), except where there are reasonable grounds to deny them boarding, such as reasons of health, safety or security, or inadequate travel documentation;

(k) "volunteer" means a person who has presented himself for boarding under the conditions laid down in Article 3(2) and responds positively to the air carrier's call for passengers prepared to surrender their reservation in exchange for benefits.

(l) "cancellation" means the non-operation of a flight which was previously planned and on which at least one place was reserved.

Article 3
Scope

1. This Regulation shall apply: (a) to passengers departing from an airport located in the territory of a Member State to which the Treaty applies; (b) to passengers departing from an airport located in a third country to an airport situated in the territory of a Member State to which the Treaty applies, unless they received benefits or compensation and were given assistance in that third country, if the operating air carrier of the flight concerned is a Community carrier.

2. Paragraph 1 shall apply on the condition that passengers: (a) have a confirmed reservation on the flight concerned and, except in the case of cancellation referred to in Article 5, present themselves for check-in: (i) as stipulated and at the time indicated in advance and in writing (including by electronic means) by the air carrier, the tour operator or an authorised travel agent, (ii) or, if no time is indicated,—not later than 45 minutes before the published departure time; or (b) have been transferred by an air carrier or tour operator from the flight for which they held a reservation to another flight, irrespective of the reason.

3. This Regulation shall not apply to passengers travelling free of charge or at a reduced fare not available directly or indirectly to the public. However, it shall apply to passengers having tickets issued under a frequent flyer programme or other commercial programme by an air carrier or tour operator.

4. This Regulation shall only apply to passengers transported by motorised fixed wing aircraft.

5. This Regulation shall apply to any operating air carrier providing transport to passengers covered by paragraphs 1 and 2. Where an operating air carrier which has no contract with the passenger performs obligations under this Regulation, it shall be regarded as doing so on behalf of the person having a contract with that passenger.

6. This Regulation shall not affect the rights of passengers under Directive 90/314/EEC. This Regulation shall not apply in cases where a package tour is cancelled for reasons other than cancellation of the flight.

Article 4
Denied boarding

1. When an operating air carrier reasonably expects to deny boarding on a flight, it shall first call for volunteers to surrender their reservations in exchange for benefits under conditions to be agreed between the passenger concerned and the operating air carrier. Volunteers shall be assisted in accordance with Article 8, such assistance being additional to the benefits mentioned in this paragraph.

2. If an insufficient number of volunteers comes forward to allow the remaining passengers with reservations to board the flight, the operating air carrier may then deny boarding to passengers against their will.

3. If boarding is denied to passengers against their will, the operating air carrier shall immediately compensate them in accordance with Article 7 and assist them in accordance with Articles 8 and 9.

Article 5
Cancellation

1. In case of cancellation of a flight, the passengers concerned shall: (a) be offered assistance by the operating air carrier in accordance with Article 8; and (b) be offered assistance by the operating air carrier in accordance with Article 9(1)(a) and 9(2), as well as, in event of re-routing when the reasonably expected time of departure of the new flight is at least the day after the departure as it was planned for the cancelled flight, the assistance specified in Article 9(1)(b) and 9(1)(c); and (c) have the right to compensation by the operating air carrier in accordance with Article 7, unless:

(i) they are informed of the cancellation at least two weeks before the scheduled time of departure; or

(ii) they are informed of the cancellation between two weeks and seven days before the scheduled time of departure and are offered re-routing, allowing them to depart no more than two hours before the scheduled time of departure and to reach their final destination less than four hours after the scheduled time of arrival; or

(iii) they are informed of the cancellation less than seven days before the scheduled time of departure and are offered re-routing, allowing them to depart no more than one hour before the scheduled time of departure and to reach their final destination less than two hours after the scheduled time of arrival.

2. When passengers are informed of the cancellation, an explanation shall be given concerning possible alternative transport.

3. An operating air carrier shall not be obliged to pay compensation in accordance with Article 7, if it can prove that the cancellation is caused by extraordinary circumstances which could not have been avoided even if all reasonable measures had been taken.

4. The burden of proof concerning the questions as to whether and when the passenger has been informed of the cancellation of the flight shall rest with the operating air carrier.

Article 6
Delay

1. When an operating air carrier reasonably expects a flight to be delayed beyond its scheduled time of departure: (a) for two hours or more in the case of flights of 1500 kilometres or less; or (b) for three hours or more in the case of all intra-Community flights of more than 1500 kilometres and of all other flights between 1500 and 3500 kilometres; or (c) for four hours or more in the case of all flights not falling under (a) or (b), passengers shall be offered by the operating air carrier: (i) the assistance specified in Article 9(1)(a) and 9(2); and (ii) when the reasonably expected time of departure is at least the day after the time of departure previously announced, the assistance specified in Article 9(1)(b) and 9(1)(c); and (iii) when the delay is at least five hours, the assistance specified in Article 8(1)(a).

2. In any event, the assistance shall be offered within the time limits set out above with respect to each distance bracket.

Article 7
Right to compensation

1. Where reference is made to this Article, passengers shall receive compensation amounting to: (a) EUR 250 for all flights of 1500 kilometres or less; (b) EUR 400 for all intra-Community flights of more than 1500 kilometres, and for all other flights between 1500 and 3500 kilometres; (c) EUR 600 for all flights not falling under (a) or (b).

In determining the distance, the basis shall be the last destination at which the denial of boarding or cancellation will delay the passenger's arrival after the scheduled time.

2. When passengers are offered re-routing to their final destination on an alternative flight pursuant to Article 8, the arrival time of which does not exceed the scheduled arrival time of the flight originally booked (a) by two hours, in respect of all flights of 1500 kilometres or less; or (b) by three hours, in respect of all intra-Community flights of more than 1500 kilometres and for all other flights between 1500 and 3500 kilometres; or (c) by four hours, in respect of all flights not falling under (a) or (b), the operating air carrier may reduce the compensation provided for in paragraph 1 by 50%.

3. The compensation referred to in paragraph 1 shall be paid in cash, by electronic bank transfer, bank orders or bank cheques or, with the signed agreement of the passenger, in travel vouchers and/or other services.

4. The distances given in paragraphs 1 and 2 shall be measured by the great circle route method.

Article 8
Right to reimbursement or re-routing

1. Where reference is made to this Article, passengers shall be offered the choice between: (a) reimbursement within seven days, by the means provided for in Article 7(3), of the full cost of the ticket at the price at which it was bought, for the part or parts of the journey not made, and for the part or parts already made if the flight is no longer serving any purpose in relation to the passenger's original travel plan, together with, when relevant, a return flight to the first point of departure, at the earliest opportunity; (b) re-routing, under comparable transport conditions, to their final destination at the earliest opportunity; or (c) re-routing, under comparable transport conditions, to their final destination at a later date at the passenger's convenience, subject to availability of seats.

2. Paragraph 1(a) shall also apply to passengers whose flights form part of a package, except for the right to reimbursement where such right arises under Directive 90/314/EEC.

3. When, in the case where a town, city or region is served by several airports, an operating air carrier offers a passenger a flight to an airport alternative to that for which the booking was made, the operating air carrier shall bear the cost of transferring the passenger from that alternative airport either to that for which the booking was made, or to another close-by destination agreed with the passenger.

Article 9
Right to care

1. Where reference is made to this Article, passengers shall be offered free of charge: (a) meals and refreshments in a reasonable relation to the waiting time; (b) hotel

accommodation in cases where a stay of one or more nights becomes necessary, or where a stay additional to that intended by the passenger becomes necessary; (c) transport between the airport and place of accommodation (hotel or other).

2. In addition, passengers shall be offered free of charge two telephone calls, telex or fax messages, or e-mails.

3. In applying this Article, the operating air carrier shall pay particular attention to the needs of persons with reduced mobility and any persons accompanying them, as well as to the needs of unaccompanied children.

Article 10
Upgrading and downgrading

1. If an operating air carrier places a passenger in a class higher than that for which the ticket was purchased, it may not request any supplementary payment.

2. If an operating air carrier places a passenger in a class lower than that for which the ticket was purchased, it shall within seven days, by the means provided for in Article 7(3), reimburse (a) 30 % of the price of the ticket for all flights of 1500 kilometres or less, or (b) 50 % of the price of the ticket for all intra-Community flights of more than 1500 kilometres, except flights between the European territory of the Member States and the French overseas departments, and for all other flights between 1500 and 3500 kilometres, or (c) 75 % of the price of the ticket for all flights not falling under (a) or (b), including flights between the European territory of the Member States and the French overseas departments.

Article 11
Persons with reduced mobility or special needs

1. Operating air carriers shall give priority to carrying persons with reduced mobility and any persons or certified service dogs accompanying them, as well as unaccompanied children.

2. In cases of denied boarding, cancellation and delays of any length, persons with reduced mobility and any persons accompanying them, as well as unaccompanied children, shall have the right to care in accordance with Article 9 as soon as possible.

Article 12
Further compensation

1. This Regulation shall apply without prejudice to a passenger's rights to further compensation. The compensation granted under this Regulation may be deducted from such compensation.

2. Without prejudice to relevant principles and rules of national law, including case-law, paragraph 1 shall not apply to passengers who have voluntarily surrendered a reservation under Article 4(1).

Article 13
Right of redress

In cases where an operating air carrier pays compensation or meets the other obligations incumbent on it under this Regulation, no provision of this Regulation may be interpreted as restricting its right to seek compensation from any person, including third parties, in accordance with the law applicable. In particular, this Regulation shall in no way restrict the operating air carrier's right to seek reimbursement from a tour operator or another person with whom the operating air carrier has a contract. Similarly, no provision of this Regulation may be interpreted as restricting the right of a tour operator or a third party, other than a passenger, with whom an operating air carrier has a contract, to seek reimbursement or compensation from the operating air carrier in accordance with applicable relevant laws.

Article 14
Obligation to inform passengers of their rights

1. The operating air carrier shall ensure that at check-in a clearly legible notice containing the following text is displayed in a manner clearly visible to passengers: "If you are denied boarding or if your flight is cancelled or delayed for at least two hours, ask at the check-in counter or boarding gate for the text stating your rights, particularly with regard to compensation and assistance".

2. An operating air carrier denying boarding or cancelling a flight shall provide each passenger affected with a written notice setting out the rules for compensation and assistance in line with this Regulation. It shall also provide each passenger affected by a delay of at least two hours with an equivalent notice. The contact details of the national designated body referred to in Article 16 shall also be given to the passenger in written form.

3. In respect of blind and visually impaired persons, the provisions of this Article shall be applied using appropriate alternative means.

Article 15
Exclusion of waiver

1. Obligations vis-à-vis passengers pursuant to this Regulation may not be limited or waived, notably by a derogation or restrictive clause in the contract of carriage.

2. If, nevertheless, such a derogation or restrictive clause is applied in respect of a passenger, or if the passenger is not correctly informed of his rights and for that reason has accepted compensation which is inferior to that provided for in this Regulation, the passenger shall still be entitled to take the necessary proceedings before the competent courts or bodies in order to obtain additional compensation.

Article 16
Infringements

1. Each Member State shall designate a body responsible for the enforcement of this Regulation as regards flights from airports situated on its territory and flights from a third country to such airports. Where appropriate, this body shall take the measures necessary to ensure that the rights of passengers are respected. The Member States shall inform the Commission of the body that has been designated in accordance with this paragraph.

2. Without prejudice to Article 12, each passenger may complain to any body designated under paragraph 1, or to any other competent body designated by a Member State, about an alleged infringement of this Regulation at any airport situated on the territory of a Member State or concerning any flight from a third country to an airport situated on that territory.

3. The sanctions laid down by Member States for infringements of this Regulation shall be effective, proportionate and dissuasive.

Article 17
Report

The Commission shall report to the European Parliament and the Council by 1 January 2007 on the operation and the results of this Regulation, in particular regarding: the incidence of denied boarding and of cancellation of flights; the possible extension of the scope of this Regulation to passengers having a contract with a Community carrier or holding a flight reservation which forms part of a "package tour" to which Directive 90/314/EEC applies and who depart from a third-country airport to an airport in a Member State, on flights not operated by Community air carriers; the possible revision of the amounts of compensation referred to in Article 7(1). The report shall be accompanied where necessary by legislative proposals.

This Regulation shall enter into force on 17 February 2005. This Regulation shall be binding in its entirety and directly applicable in all Member States. Done at Strasbourg, 11 February 2004.

STURGEON v. CONDOR FLUGDIENST GMBH (C-402/07 (2009))

These references for a preliminary ruling concern the interpretation of Articles 2(l), 5, 6 and 7 of Regulation (EC) No 261/2004 of the European Parliament and of the Council of 11 February 2004 establishing common rules on compensation and assistance to passengers in the event of denied boarding and of cancellation or long delay of flights, and repealing Regulation (EEC) No 295/91.

The references were made in proceedings between (i) Mr Sturgeon and his family and Condor Flugdienst GmbH and (ii) Mr. Bock and Ms. Lepuschitz and Air France SA, concerning the refusal of those airlines to pay compensation to the passengers concerned, whose arrival at the airport of destination was delayed by 25 and 22 hours respectively in relation to the scheduled arrival time.

The Sturgeons booked return tickets with Condor from Frankfurt am Main (Germany) to Toronto (Canada). The return flight from Toronto to Frankfurt was due to depart at 16.20 on 9 July 2005. Following check-in, passengers on that flight were informed that the flight was cancelled, as was indicated on the airport departures board. Their luggage was returned to them and they were then driven to a hotel where they spent the night. The following day, the passengers were checked in at another airline's counter for a flight with the same number as that on their booking. Condor did not schedule another flight with the same number for the day concerned. The passengers were given different seats from those they had been allocated on the previous day. The booking was not converted into a booking for a flight scheduled by another airline. The flight concerned arrived in Frankfurt at around 07.00 on 11 July 2005, some 25 hours after its scheduled arrival time.

The Sturgeons took the view that, in light of all the abovementioned circumstances, in particular the delay of more than 25 hours, the flight had been not delayed but cancelled. The Sturgeons brought an action against Condor before the Amtsgericht Rüsselsheim (Local Court, Rüsselsheim) (Germany), claiming compensation of EUR 600 per person plus damages, since, in their view, the damage sustained was the result not of a flight delay but of a cancellation.

Condor contended that the action as framed should be dismissed on the ground that the flight in question was delayed and not cancelled. Prior to the proceedings before the national court, Condor claimed that the flight had been delayed as the result of a hurricane in the Caribbean but during the proceedings it attributed the delay to technical faults on the plane and illness among the crew.

The Amtsgericht Rüsselsheim concluded that the flight had been delayed not cancelled and, consequently, dismissed the Sturgeons' claim for compensation. The Sturgeons appealed to the Landgericht Darmstadt (Regional Court, Darmstadt) which upheld the decision of the lower court. The Sturgeons then appealed on a point of law

('Revision') to the Bundesgerichtshof (Federal Court of Justice). Taking the view that the outcome of the appeal depended on the interpretation of Articles 2(l) and 5(1)(c) of Regulation No 261/2004, the Bundesgerichtshof decided to stay the proceedings and to refer the following questions to the Court for a preliminary ruling:

1. Is it decisive for the interpretation of the term "cancellation" whether the original flight planning is abandoned, with the result that a delay, regardless of how long, does not constitute a cancellation if the air carrier does not actually abandon the planning for the original flight?

2. If Question 1 is answered in the negative: in what circumstances is a delay of the planned flight no longer to be regarded as a delay but as a cancellation? Is the answer to this question dependent on the length of the delay?

Mr. Böck and Ms. Lepuschitz booked return tickets with Air France from Vienna (Austria) to Mexico City (Mexico) via Paris (France). The Mexico City-Paris flight which Mr. Böck and Ms. Lepuschitz were due to take was scheduled to depart at 21.30 on 7 March 2005. When they came to check in, they were immediately informed, without the check-in taking place, that their flight was cancelled. The cancellation resulted from a change in the flight planning between Mexico City and Paris, which arose because of a technical breakdown on the aircraft due to fly from Paris to Mexico City and on account of the need to observe the rest period prescribed by law for the crew.

In order to get back earlier, Mr. Böck and Ms. Lepuschitz accepted Air France's offer of seats on a flight operated by Continental Airlines, which was scheduled to leave the following day, 8 March 2005, at 12.20. Their tickets were first cancelled and then new tickets were issued to them at the Continental Airlines counter. The other passengers on the Mexico City-Paris flight, who did not take the Continental Airlines flight, left Mexico City, with a number of additional passengers, on 8 March 2005 at 19.35. That flight, whose original number was followed by the letter "A," was operated in addition to the regular flight scheduled by Air France on the same day.

Mr. Böck and Ms. Lepuschitz arrived in Vienna almost 22 hours after the scheduled arrival time. Mr. Böck and Ms. Lepuschitz brought an action against Air France before the Bezirksgericht für Handelssachen Wien (District Commercial Court, Vienna) (Austria), claiming EUR 600 compensation per person for cancellation of their flight, on the basis of Articles 5 and 7(1)(c) of Regulation No 261/2004. That court dismissed their claim on the ground that, despite the evident flight delay, Regulation No 261/2004 did not support the conclusion that there was a flight cancellation. Mr. Böck and Ms. Lepuschitz appealed against that decision to the Handelsgericht Wien (Commercial Court, Vienna).

Before the national courts, the applicants in the main actions claim from Condor and Air France respectively the compensation provided for in Article 7 of Regulation No 261/2004 on the ground that with those airlines they reached their airports of destination, in the first case, 25 and, in the second case, 22 hours after the scheduled arrival times. Condor and Air France assert that the applicants are not entitled to any compensation, since the flights concerned were not cancelled but delayed and Regulation No 261/2004 provides for a right to compensation only in the case of flight cancellation. Furthermore, the airlines maintain that the late arrival of the flights was attributable to technical faults on the aircraft, which are covered by the concept of 'extraordinary circumstances' within the meaning of Article 5(3) of Regulation No 261/2004, and that they are thus released from the obligation to pay compensation. In those circumstances, in order to give the national courts a useful answer, the questions referred should be understood as seeking, in essence, to ascertain:

1. Whether a flight delay must be regarded as a flight cancellation for the purposes of Articles 2(l) and 5 of Regulation No 261/2004 where the delay is long;

2. Whether Articles 5, 6 and 7 of Regulation No 261/2004 must be interpreted as meaning that passengers whose flights are delayed may, for the purpose of the application of the right to compensation laid down in Article 7 of that regulation, be treated as passengers whose flights are cancelled, and

3. Whether a technical problem in an aircraft is covered by the concept of 'extraordinary circumstances' within the meaning of Article 5(3) of Regulation No 261/2004.

I. *Concept of "Delay"*

Regulation No 261/2004 does not contain a definition of "flight delay." That concept may, however, be clarified in the light of the context in which it occurs. In that regard, it should be recalled, first, that a "flight" within the meaning of Regulation No 261/2004 consists in an air transport operation, performed by an air carrier which fixes its itinerary. Thus, the itinerary is an essential element of the flight, as the flight is operated in accordance with the carrier's pre-arranged planning.

It is clear furthermore from Article 6 of Regulation No 261/2004 that the Community legislature adopted a notion of "flight delay" which is considered only by reference to the scheduled departure time and which implies as a consequence that, after the departure time, the other elements pertaining to the flight must remain unchanged. Thus, a flight is "delayed" for the purposes of Article 6 of Regulation No 261/2004 if it is operated in accordance with the original planning and its actual departure time is later than the scheduled departure time.

Second, according to Article 2(l) of Regulation No 261/2004, flight cancellation, unlike delay, is the result of non-operation of a flight which was previously planned. It follows that, in that regard, cancelled flights and delayed flights are two quite distinct categories of flights. It cannot therefore be inferred from Regulation No 261/2004 that a flight which is delayed may be classified as a "cancelled flight" merely on the ground that the delay is extended, even substantially. Consequently, a flight which is delayed, irrespective of the duration of the delay, even if it is long, cannot be regarded as cancelled where there is a departure in accordance with the original planning.

In those circumstances, where passengers are carried on a flight whose departure time is later than the departure time originally scheduled, the flight can be classified as 'cancelled' only if the air carrier arranges for the passengers to be carried on another flight whose original planning is different from that of the flight for which the booking was made. Thus, it is possible, as a rule, to conclude that there is a cancellation where the delayed flight for which the booking was made is 'rolled over' onto another flight, that is to say, where the planning for the original flight is abandoned and the passengers from that flight join passengers on a flight which was also planned – but independently of the flight for which the passengers so transferred had made their bookings.

By contrast, it cannot, as a rule, be concluded that there is a flight delay or cancellation on the basis of a "delay" or a "cancellation" being shown on the airport departures board or announced by the air carrier's staff. Similarly, the fact that passengers recover their luggage or obtain new boarding cards is not, as a rule, a deciding factor. Those circumstances are not connected with the objective characteristics of the flight as such. They can be attributable to inaccurate classifications or to factors obtaining in the airport concerned or, yet again, they may be unavoidable given the waiting time and the fact that it is necessary for the passengers concerned to spend the night in a hotel.

Nor, as a rule, is it conclusive that the composition of the group of passengers who initially held reservations is essentially identical to that of the group subsequently transported. Indeed, as the delay grows longer by reference to the departure time originally scheduled, the number of passengers in the first of those groups may decrease because some passengers have been offered re-routing on another flight and others, for personal reasons, have decided not to take the delayed flight. Conversely, to the extent that seats have become available on the flight for which the booking was made, there is nothing to prevent the carrier accepting, before departure of the plane which is delayed, additional passengers.

In view of the foregoing, the answer to the first part of the questions referred is that Articles 2(l), 5 and 6 of Regulation No 261/2004 must be interpreted as meaning that a flight which is delayed, irrespective of the duration of the delay, even if it is long, cannot be regarded as cancelled where the flight is operated in accordance with the air carrier's original planning.

II. *Right to Compensation in the Event of Delay*

Article 5(1) of Regulation No 261/2004 provides that in the event of cancellation of a flight, the passengers concerned are to have the right to compensation by the operating air carrier in accordance with Article 7 of the regulation. By contrast, it does not expressly follow from the wording of Regulation No 261/2004 that passengers whose flights are delayed have such a right. Nevertheless, as the Court has made clear in its case-law, it is necessary, in interpreting a provision of Community law, to consider not only its wording, but also the context in which it occurs and the objectives pursued by the rules of which it is part. In that regard, the operative part of a Community act is indissociably linked to the statement of reasons for it, so that, when it has to be interpreted, account must be taken of the reasons which led to its adoption.

It must be stated that, even though the possibility of relying on "extraordinary circumstances," allowing air carriers to be released from the obligation to pay compensation under Article 7 of Regulation No 261/2004, is provided for only in Article 5(3) thereof, which concerns flight cancellation, Recital 15 in the preamble to the regulation nevertheless states that that ground may also be relied on where an air traffic management decision in relation to a particular aircraft on a particular day gives rise to "a long delay [or] an overnight delay." As the notion of long delay is mentioned in the context of extraordinary circumstances, it must be held that the legislature also linked that notion to the right to compensation.

That is implicitly borne out by the objective of Regulation No 261/2004, since it is apparent from Recitals 1 to 4 in the preamble, in particular from Recital 2, that the regulation seeks to ensure a high level of protection for air passengers regardless of whether they are denied boarding or whether their flight is cancelled or delayed, since they are all caused similar serious trouble and inconvenience connected with air transport. That is *a fortiori* the case since the provisions conferring rights on air passengers, including those conferring a right to compensation, must be interpreted broadly. In those circumstances it cannot automatically be presumed that passengers whose flights are delayed do not have a right to compensation and cannot, for the purposes of recognition of such a right, be treated as passengers whose flights are cancelled.

Next, it must be stated that, according to a general principle of interpretation, a Community act must be interpreted, as far as possible, in such a way as not to affect its validity. Likewise, where a provision of Community law is open to several interpretations, preference must be given to that interpretation which ensures that the provision retains its effectiveness. In that regard, all Community acts must be interpreted in accordance with primary law as a whole, including the principle of equal treatment, which requires that comparable situations must not be treated differently and that different situations must not be treated in the same way unless such treatment is objectively justified.

In view of the objective of Regulation No 261/2004, which is to strengthen protection for air passengers by redressing damage suffered by them during air travel, situations covered by the regulation must be compared, in particular by reference to the type and extent of the various types of inconvenience and damage suffered by the passengers concerned. In this instance, the situation of passengers whose flights are delayed should be compared with that of passengers whose flights are cancelled.

In that connection, Regulation No 261/2004 seeks to redress damage in an immediate and standardised manner and to do so by various forms of intervention which are the subject of rules relating to denied boarding, cancellation and long flight delay. Regulation No 261/2004 has, in those measures, the objective of repairing, inter alia, damage consisting, for the passengers concerned, in a loss of time which, given that it is irreversible, can be redressed only by compensation. In that regard, it must be stated that that damage is suffered both by passengers whose flights are cancelled and by passengers whose flights are delayed if, prior to reaching their destinations, the latter's journey time is longer than the time which had originally been scheduled by the air carrier. Consequently, passengers whose flights have been cancelled and passengers affected by a flight delay suffer similar damage, consisting in a loss of time, and thus find themselves in comparable situations for the purposes of the application of the right to compensation laid down in Article 7 of Regulation No 261/2004.

More specifically, the situation of passengers whose flights are delayed is scarcely distinguishable from that of passengers whose flights are cancelled, who are re-routed in accordance with Article 5(1)(c)(iii) of Regulation No 261/2004 and who may be informed of the flight cancellation at the very last moment, when they actually arrive at the airport. First, both categories of passengers are informed, as a rule, at the same time of the incident which will make their journey by air more difficult. Second, even if they are transported to their final destination, they reach it after the time originally scheduled and, as a consequence, they suffer a similar loss of time.

That said, passengers who are re-routed under Article 5(1)(c)(iii) of Regulation No 261/2004 are afforded the right to compensation laid down in Article 7 of the regulation where the carrier fails to re-route them on a flight which departs no more than one hour before the scheduled time of departure and reaches their final destination less than two hours after the scheduled time of arrival. Those passengers thus acquire a right to compensation when they suffer a loss of time equal to or in excess of three hours in relation to the duration originally planned by the air carrier.

If, by contrast, passengers whose flights are delayed did not acquire any right to compensation, they would be treated less favourably even though, depending on the circumstances, they suffer a similar loss of time, of three hours or more, in the course of their journey. There appears, however, to be no objective ground capable of justifying such a difference in treatment.

Given that the damage sustained by air passengers in cases of cancellation or long delay is comparable, passengers whose flights are delayed and passengers whose flights are cancelled cannot be treated differently without the principle of equal treatment being infringed. That is *a fortiori* the case in view of the aim sought by Regulation No 261/2004, which is to increase protection for all air passengers. In those circumstances, the Court finds that passengers whose flights are delayed may rely on the right to compensation laid down in Article 7 of Regulation No 261/2004 where they suffer, on account of such flights, a loss of time equal to or in excess of three hours, that is to say when they reach their final destination three hours or more after the arrival time originally scheduled by the air carrier. That solution is, moreover, consistent with Recital 15 in the preamble to Regulation No 261/2004. As stated in this judgment, it must be held that the legislature, in that recital, also linked the notion of "long delay" to the right to compensation. That notion corresponds to a delay to which the legislature attaches certain legal consequences. As Article 6 of the regulation already accepts such legal consequences in the case of certain flights which are delayed for two hours, Recital 15 necessarily covers delays of three hours or more.

It is important to point out that the compensation payable to a passenger under Article 7(1) of Regulation No 261/2004 may be reduced by 50% if the conditions laid down in Article 7(2) of the regulation are met. Even though the latter provision refers only to the case of re-routing of passengers, the Court finds that the reduction in the compensation provided for is dependent solely on the delay to which passengers are subject, so that nothing precludes the application mutatis mutandis of that provision to compensation paid to passengers whose flights are delayed. It follows that the compensation payable to a passenger whose flight is delayed, who reaches his final destination three hours or more after the arrival time originally scheduled, may be reduced by 50%, in accordance with Article 7(2)(c) of Regulation No 261/2004, where the delay is—in the case of a flight not falling under points (a) or (b) of Article 7(2)—less than four hours.

The conclusion set out in paragraph 61 of this judgment is not undermined by the fact that Article 6 of Regulation No 261/2004 provides for different forms of assistance under Articles 8 and 9 thereof for passengers whose flights are delayed. As the Court has already stated, Regulation No 261/2004 provides for various forms of intervention in order to redress, in a standardised and immediate manner, the different types of damage constituted by the inconvenience that delay in the carriage of passengers by air causes. Those measures are autonomous in the sense that they address different aims and seek to make up for various types of damage caused by such delay.

That said, it should be recalled that, with the adoption of Regulation No 261/2004, the legislature was also seeking to strike a balance between the interests of air passengers and those of air carriers. Having laid down certain rights for those passengers, it provided at the same time, in Recital 15 and Article 5(3) of the regulation, that air carriers are not obliged to pay compensation if they can prove that the cancellation or long delay is caused by extraordinary circumstances which could not have been avoided even if all reasonable measures had been taken, namely circumstances which are beyond the air carrier's actual control.

Moreover, the discharge of obligations pursuant to Regulation No 261/2004 is without prejudice to air carriers' rights to seek compensation from any person who caused the delay, including third parties, as Article 13 of the regulation provides. Such compensation may accordingly reduce or even remove the financial burden borne by carriers in consequence of those obligations. Nor does it appear unreasonable for those obligations initially to be borne, subject to the abovementioned right to compensation, by the air carriers with which the passengers concerned have a contract of carriage that entitles them to a flight that should be neither cancelled nor delayed.

In the light of the foregoing, the answer to the second part of the questions referred is that Articles 5, 6 and 7 of Regulation No 261/2004 must be interpreted as meaning that passengers whose flights are delayed may be treated, for the purposes of the application of the right to compensation, as passengers whose flights are cancelled and they may thus rely on the right to compensation laid down in Article 7 of the regulation where they suffer, on account of a flight delay, a loss of time equal to or in excess of three hours, that is, where they reach their final destination three hours or more after the arrival time originally scheduled by the air carrier. Such a delay does not, however, entitle passengers to compensation if the air carrier can prove that the long delay was caused by extraordinary circumstances which could not have been avoided even if all reasonable measures had been taken, namely circumstances beyond the actual control of the air carrier.

III. *Extraordinary Circumstances resulting from Technical Problem*

The Court has already held that Article 5(3) of Regulation No 261/2004 must be interpreted as meaning that a technical problem in an aircraft which leads to the cancellation of a flight is not covered by the concept of 'extraordinary circumstances' within the meaning of that provision, unless that problem stems from events which, by their nature or origin, are not inherent in the normal exercise of the activity of the air carrier concerned and are beyond its actual control. The same conclusion applies when Article 5(3) of Regulation No 261/2004 is pleaded in the case of flight delay.

Thus, the answer to the third question in Case C-432/07 is that Article 5(3) of Regulation No 261/2004 must be interpreted as meaning that a technical problem in an aircraft which leads to the cancellation or delay of a flight is not covered by the concept of 'extraordinary circumstances' within the meaning of that provision, unless that problem stems from events which, by their nature or origin, are not inherent in the normal exercise of the activity of the air carrier concerned and are beyond its actual control. On those grounds, the Court (Fourth Chamber) hereby rules:

1. Articles 2(l), 5 and 6 of Regulation (EC) No 261/2004 of the European Parliament and of the Council of 11 February 2004 establishing common rules on compensation and assistance to passengers in the event of denied boarding and of cancellation or long delay of flights, and repealing Regulation (EEC) No 295/91, must be interpreted as meaning that a flight which is delayed, irrespective of the duration of the delay, even if it is long, cannot be regarded as cancelled where the flight is operated in accordance with the air carrier's original planning.

2. Articles 5, 6 and 7 of Regulation No 261/2004 must be interpreted as meaning that passengers whose flights are delayed may be treated, for the purposes of the application of the right to compensation, as passengers whose flights are cancelled and they may thus rely on the right to compensation laid down in Article 7 of the regulation where they suffer, on account of a flight delay, a loss of time equal to or in excess of three hours, that is, where they reach their final destination three hours or more after the arrival time originally scheduled by the air carrier. Such a delay does not, however, entitle passengers to compensation if the air carrier can prove that the long delay was caused by extraordinary circumstances which could not have been avoided even if all reasonable measures had been taken, namely circumstances beyond the actual control of the air carrier.

3. Article 5(3) of Regulation No 261/2004 must be interpreted as meaning that a technical problem in an aircraft which leads to the cancellation or delay of a flight is not covered by the concept of 'extraordinary circumstances' within the meaning of that provision, unless that problem stems from events which, by their nature or origin, are not inherent in the normal exercise of the activity of the air carrier concerned and are beyond its actual control.

GERMANWINGS GMBH v. HENNING (C-452/13 (2014))

This request for a preliminary ruling concerns the interpretation of the concept of "arrival time" within the meaning of Articles 2, 5 and 7 of Regulation (EC) No 261/2004 of the European Parliament and of the Council of 11 February 2004 establishing common rules on compensation and assistance to passengers in the event of denied boarding and of cancellation or long delay of flights, and repealing Regulation (EEC) No 295/91 (OJ 2004 L 46, p. 1). The request has been made in proceedings between Germanwings GmbH ("Germanwings"), an air carrier, and Mr. Henning concerning that carrier's refusal to compensate Mr. Henning for the alleged delay with which his flight arrived at Cologne/Bonn airport (Germany).

Mr. Henning purchased an aeroplane ticket from Germanwings in order to go from Salzburg (Austria) to Cologne/Bonn. That ticket specified a take-off from Salzburg airport at 13.30 on 11 May 2012 and an arrival at Cologne/Bonn airport at 14.40 on the same day. The flight distance between those two airports is, according to the great circle route method, less than 1 500 kilometres.

On 11 May 2012, Mr. Henning's aircraft was delayed in taking off from Salzburg airport. On arrival, the aircraft touched down on the tarmac of the runway at Cologne/Bonn airport at 17.38. The aircraft did not, however, reach its parking position until 17.43, that is to say three hours and three minutes after the scheduled arrival time. The doors of the aircraft were opened shortly afterwards.

Mr. Henning takes the view that the final destination was reached with a delay of more than three hours in relation to the scheduled arrival time. He thus considers that he has the right to compensation of EUR 250 on the basis of Articles 5 to 7 of Regulation No 261/2004. Germanwings submits that, as the actual arrival time was the time at which the plane touched down on the tarmac at Cologne/Bonn airport, the delay in relation to the scheduled arrival time is only two hours and 58 minutes, with the result that no compensation is payable.

The first-instance court held that the actual arrival time to be taken into account was the time at which the first door of the aircraft was opened to enable the passengers to leave. Consequently, that court ordered Germanwings to pay compensation of EUR 250 to Mr. Henning. That company lodged an appeal against that judgment before the referring court. In those circumstances the Landesgericht Salzburg (Regional Court, Salzburg) decided to stay the proceedings and to refer the following question to the Court of Justice for a preliminary ruling:

What time is relevant for the term "time of arrival" used in Articles 2, 5 and 7 of Regulation [No 261/2004]: (a) the time that the aircraft lands on the runway ("touchdown"); (b) the time that the aircraft reaches its parking position and the parking brakes are engaged or the chocks have been applied ("in-block time"); (c) the time that the aircraft door is opened; or (d) a time defined by the parties in the context of party autonomy?

By its question the referring court asks, in essence, whether Articles 2, 5 and 7 of Regulation No 261/2004 are to be interpreted as meaning that the concept of "arrival time," which is used to determine the length of the delay to which passengers on a flight have been subject, refers to (a) the time at which the aircraft touches down on the runway of the destination airport; (b) the time at which the aircraft reaches its parking position and the parking brakes are engaged or the chocks have been applied; (c) the time at which the aircraft door is opened or (d) a time defined by the parties by common accord.

It must be pointed out at the outset that that regulation envisages two different types of flight delay. First, in some cases, such as the flight delay described in Article 6 of Regulation No 261/2004, that regulation refers to a flight's being delayed beyond its scheduled departure time. Secondly, in other cases, such as those referred to in Articles 5 and 7 of that regulation, the regulation refers to the situation where arrival has been delayed. It is apparent from those articles that, in order to establish the length of such a delay, it is necessary to compare the scheduled arrival time of the aircraft with the time at which it actually arrived at its destination.

Regulation No 261/2004 does not define the actual arrival time. That being the case, the need for a uniform application of EU law and the principle of equal treatment require that the terms of a provision of EU law which makes no express reference to the law of the Member States for the purpose of determining its meaning and scope must normally be given an independent interpretation throughout the European Union. It follows that that concept of "actual arrival time" must be interpreted in such a way as to apply uniformly throughout the European Union. In those circumstances, one of the possibilities envisaged by the referring court, namely that according to which that concept is defined by the parties concerned on a contractual basis, must, in the absence of any indication to that effect in Regulation No 261/2004, be rejected at the outset.

It must also be noted that the Court has held that when their flights are subject to long delay, that is delay equal to or in excess of three hours, passengers of such flights are entitled to compensation on the basis of Article 7 of Regulation No 261/2004, like those passengers whose original flights have been cancelled and whom an air carrier is not able to offer re-routing in accordance with the conditions laid down in Article 5(1)(c)(iii) of that regulation, given that they also suffer an irreversible loss of time. During a flight, passengers remain confined in an enclosed space, under the instructions and control of the air carrier, in which, for technical and safety reasons, their possibilities of communicating with the outside world are considerably restricted. In such circumstances, passengers are unable to carry on, without interruption, their personal, domestic, social or business activities. It is only once the flight has ended that they are able to resume their normal activities.

Although such inconveniences must be regarded as unavoidable as long as a flight does not exceed the scheduled duration, the same is not true if there is a delay, since the time by which, in the circumstances described in the preceding paragraph, the scheduled duration of the flight has been exceeded, represents 'lost time' in the light of the fact that the passengers concerned cannot use it to achieve the objectives which led them to go at the desired time to the destinations of their choice. It follows that the concept of "actual arrival time" must be understood, in the context of Regulation No 261/2004, as corresponding to the time at which the situation described in paragraph 20 of the present judgment comes to an end.

In that regard, it must be stated that, in principle, the situation of passengers on a flight does not change substantially when their aircraft touches down on the runway at the destination airport, when that aircraft reaches its parking position and the parking brakes are engaged or when the chocks are applied, as the passengers continue to be subject, in the enclosed space in which they are sitting, to various constraints. It is only when the passengers are permitted to leave the aircraft and the order is given to that effect to open the doors of the aircraft that the passengers may in principle resume their normal activities without being subject to those constraints.

It is apparent from the foregoing considerations that Articles 2, 5 and 7 of Regulation No 261/2004 must be interpreted as meaning that the concept of "arrival time," which is used to determine the length of the delay to which passengers on a flight have been subject, corresponds to the time at which at least one of the doors of the aircraft is opened, the assumption being that, at that moment, the passengers are permitted to leave the aircraft. That finding is not invalidated by the fact that a number of European Regulations and also certain International Air Transport Association (IATA) documents refer to the concept of "actual arrival time" as the time at which an aircraft reaches its parking position. Those regulations and documents pursue objectives relating to air navigation rules and, in particular, to the allocation of slots, which are different from those of Regulation No 261/2004. Consequently, the definitions that they give cannot be regarded as relevant for the interpretation of corresponding terms in the context of Regulation No 261/2004, which is aimed exclusively at conferring minimum rights on passengers who are subject to various inconveniences because they are denied boarding against their will or have their flights cancelled or delayed.

In the light of all of the foregoing considerations, the answer to the referring court's question is that Articles 2, 5 and 7 of Regulation No 261/2004 must be interpreted as meaning that the concept of "arrival time," which is used to determine the length of the delay to which passengers on a flight have been subject, refers to the time at which at least one of the doors of the aircraft is opened, the assumption being that, at that moment, the passengers are permitted to leave the aircraft.

On those grounds, the Court (Ninth Chamber) hereby rules: Articles 2, 5 and 7 of Regulation (EC) No 261/2004 of the European Parliament and of the Council of 11 February 2004 establishing common rules on compensation and assistance to passengers in the event of denied boarding and of cancellation or long delay of flights, and repealing Regulation (EEC) No 295/91, must be interpreted as meaning that the concept of 'arrival time', which is used to determine the length of the delay to which passengers on a flight have been subject, refers to the time at which at least one of the doors of the aircraft is opened, the assumption being that, at that moment, the passengers are permitted to leave the aircraft.

WALLENTIN-HERMANN v. ALITALIA—LINEE AEREE ITALIANE, SPA (C549/07 (2008))

This reference for a preliminary ruling concerns the interpretation of Article 5(3) of Regulation (EC) No 261/2004 of the European Parliament and of the Council of 11 February 2004 establishing common rules on compensation and assistance to passengers in the event of denied boarding and of cancellation or long delay of flights, and repealing Regulation (EEC) No 295/91. The reference was made in the course of proceedings between Mrs. Wallentin-Hermann and Alitalia Linee Aree Italiane SpA ("Alitalia") following Alitalia's refusal to pay compensation to the applicant in the main proceedings whose flight had been cancelled.

It is apparent from the order for reference that Mrs. Wallentin-Hermann booked three seats on a flight with Alitalia from Vienna (Austria) to Brindisi (Italy) via Rome (Italy) for herself, her husband and her daughter. The flight was scheduled to depart from Vienna on 28 June 2005 at 6.45 a.m. and to arrive at Brindisi on the same day at 10.35 a.m. After checking in, the three passengers were informed, five minutes before the scheduled departure time, that their flight had been cancelled. They were subsequently transferred to an Austrian Airlines flight to Rome, where they arrived at 9.40 a.m., that is 20 minutes after the time of departure of their connecting flight to Brindisi, which they therefore missed. Mrs. Wallentin-Hermann and her family arrived at Brindisi at 2.15 p.m.

The cancellation of the Alitalia flight from Vienna resulted from a complex engine defect in the turbine which had been discovered the day before during a check. Alitalia had been informed of the defect during the night preceding that flight, at 1.00 a.m. The repair of the aircraft, which necessitated the dispatch of spare parts and engineers, was completed on 8 July 2005.

Mrs. Wallentin-Hermann requested that Alitalia pay her EUR 250 compensation pursuant to Articles 5(1)(c) and 7(1) of Regulation No 261/2004 due to the cancellation of her flight and also EUR 10 for telephone charges. Alitalia rejected that request. In the judicial proceedings that Mrs. Wallentin-Hermann then brought, the Bezirksgericht für Handelssachen Wien (District Commercial Court, Vienna) upheld her application for compensation, in particular on the ground that the technical defects which affected the aircraft concerned were not covered by the 'extraordinary circumstances' provided for in Article 5(3) of Regulation No 261/2004 which exempt from the obligation to pay compensation. Alitalia lodged an appeal against that decision before the Handelsgericht Wien (Commercial Court, Vienna), which decided to stay the proceedings and to refer the following questions to the Court for a preliminary ruling:

(1) Are there extraordinary circumstances within the meaning of Article 5(3) of Regulation ... No 261/2004, having regard to recital 14 in the preamble to the regulation, if a technical defect in the aeroplane, in particular damage to the engine, results in the cancellation of the flight, and must the grounds of excuse under Article 5(3) of [that] regulation be interpreted in accordance with the provisions of Article 19 of the Montreal Convention?

(2) If the answer to the first question is in the affirmative, are there extraordinary circumstances within the meaning of Article 5(3) of Regulation [No 261/2004] where air

carriers cite technical defects as a reason for flight cancellations with above average frequency, solely on the basis of their frequency?

(3) If the answer to the first question is in the affirmative, has an air carrier taken all "reasonable measures" in accordance with Article 5(3) of Regulation [No 261/2004] if it establishes that the minimum legal requirements with regard to maintenance work on the aeroplane have been met and is that sufficient to relieve the air carrier of the obligation to pay compensation provided for by Article 5 in conjunction with Article 7 of [that] regulation?

(4) If the answer to the first question is in the negative, are extraordinary circumstances within the meaning of Article 5(3) of Regulation [No 261/2004] cases of force majeure or natural disasters, which were not due to a technical defect and are thus unconnected with the air carrier?

Article 5(3) of Regulation (EC) No 261/2004 of the European Parliament and of the Council of 11 February 2004 establishing common rules on compensation and assistance to passengers in the event of denied boarding and of cancellation or long delay of flights, and repealing Regulation (EEC) No 295/91, must be interpreted as meaning that a technical problem in an aircraft which leads to the cancellation of a flight is not covered by the concept of 'extraordinary circumstances' within the meaning of that provision, unless that problem stems from events which, by their nature or origin, are not inherent in the normal exercise of the activity of the air carrier concerned and are beyond its actual control.

The Convention for the Unification of Certain Rules for International Carriage by Air, concluded in Montreal on 28 May 1999, is not decisive for the interpretation of the grounds of exemption under Article 5(3) of Regulation No 261/2004. Additionally, the frequency of the technical problems experienced by an air carrier is not in itself a factor from which the presence or absence of 'extraordinary circumstances' within the meaning of Article 5(3) of Regulation No 261/2004 can be concluded.

Finally, the fact that an air carrier has complied with the minimum rules on maintenance of an aircraft cannot in itself suffice to establish that that carrier has taken 'all reasonable measures' within the meaning of Article 5(3) of Regulation No 261/2004 and, therefore, to relieve that carrier of its obligation to pay compensation.

MCDONAGH v. RYANAIR, LTD. (C-12/11 (2013))

This request for a preliminary ruling concerns the interpretation and assessment of the validity of Articles 5(1)(b) and 9 of Regulation (EC) No 261/2004 of the European Parliament and of the Council of 11 February 2004 establishing common rules on compensation and assistance to passengers in the event of denied boarding and of cancellation or long delay of flights, and repealing Regulation (EEC) No 295/91.The request has been made in proceedings between Ms. McDonagh and Ryanair Ltd ("Ryanair") regarding the airline company's refusal to give Ms. McDonagh the care provided for in Article 5(1)(b) of Regulation No 261/2004 after the eruption of the Icelandic volcano Eyjafjallajökull had caused the cancellation of her flight and, more generally, closure of part of European airspace.

On 11 February 2010, Ms. McDonagh booked a flight with Ryanair from Faro (Portugal) to Dublin (Ireland) scheduled for 17 April 2010, for EUR 98. On 20 March 2010, the Eyjafjallajökull volcano in Iceland began to erupt. On 14 April 2010, it entered an explosive phase, casting a cloud of volcanic ash into the skies over Europe. On 15 April 2010, the competent air traffic authorities closed the airspace over a number of Member States because of the risks to aircraft. On 17 April 2010, Ms. McDonagh's flight was cancelled following the closure of Irish airspace. Ryanair flights between continental Europe and Ireland resumed on 22 April 2010 and Ms. McDonagh was not able to return to Dublin until 24 April 2010. During the period between 17 and 24 April 2010, Ryanair did not provide Ms. McDonagh with care in accordance with the detailed rules laid down in Article 9 of Regulation No 261/2004.

Ms. McDonagh brought an action against Ryanair before the referring court for compensation in the amount of EUR 1 129.41, corresponding to the costs which she had incurred during that period on meals, refreshments, accommodation and transport. Ryanair claims that the closure of part of European airspace following the eruption of the Eyjafjallajökull volcano does not constitute "extraordinary circumstances" within the meaning of Regulation No 261/2004 but "super extraordinary circumstances," releasing it not only from its obligation to pay compensation but also from its obligations to provide care under Articles 5 and 9 of that regulation.

In light of its doubts as to whether the obligation to provide that care may be subject to limitations in circumstances such as those at issue in the main proceedings and taking the view that the Court of Justice has not yet ruled on that matter, the Dublin Metropolitan District Court decided to stay the proceedings and to refer the following questions to the Court of Justice for a preliminary ruling:

(1) Do circumstances such as the closures of European airspace as a result of the eruption of the Eyjafjallajökull volcano in Iceland, which caused widespread and prolonged disruption to air travel, go beyond "extraordinary circumstances" within the meaning of Regulation No 261/2004?

(2) If the answer to Question 1 is yes, is liability for the duty to provide care excluded under Articles 5 and 9 [of Regulation No 261/2004] in such circumstances?

(3) If the answer to Question 2 is no, are Articles 5 and 9 [of Regulation No 261/2004] invalid in so far as they violate the principles of proportionality and non-discrimination, the principle of an "equitable balance of interests" enshrined in the

Montreal Convention, and Articles 16 and 17 of the Charter of Fundamental Rights of the European Union ["the Charter"]?

(4) Is the obligation in Articles 5 and 9 [of Regulation No 261/2004] to be interpreted as containing an implied limitation, such as a temporal and/or a monetary limit, to provide care in cases where cancellation is caused by "extraordinary circumstances"?

(5) If the answer to Question 4 is no, are Articles 5 and 9 [of Regulation No 261/2004] invalid in so far as they violate the principles of proportionality and non-discrimination, the principle of an "equitable balance of interests" enshrined in the Montreal Convention, and Articles 16 and 17 of the [Charter]?'

I. *"Extraordinary Circumstances"*

By its first question the referring court asks, in essence, whether Article 5 of Regulation No 261/2004 must be interpreted as meaning that circumstances such as the closure of part of European airspace as a result of the eruption of the Eyjafjallajökull volcano constitute "extraordinary circumstances" within the meaning of that regulation which do not release air carriers from their obligation laid down in Articles 5(1)(b) and 9 of the regulation to provide care or, on the contrary and because of their particular scale, go beyond the scope of that notion, thus releasing air carriers from that obligation.

At the outset, it should be noted that the term "extraordinary circumstances" is not defined in Article 2 of Regulation No 261/2004 or in the other provisions of that regulation, even though a non-exhaustive list of those circumstances can be derived from recitals 14 and 15 in the preamble to the regulation. European Union law provides no definition must be determined by considering their usual meaning in everyday language, while also taking into account the context in which they occur and the purposes of the rules of which they are part. In accordance with everyday language, the words "extraordinary circumstances" literally refer to circumstances which are "out of the ordinary."

In the context of air transport, they refer to an event which is not inherent in the normal exercise of the activity of the carrier concerned and is beyond the actual control of that carrier on account of its nature or origin. In other words, they relate to all circumstances which are beyond the control of the air carrier, whatever the nature of those circumstances or their gravity. Regulation No 261/2004 contains nothing that would allow the conclusion to be drawn that it recognises a separate category of "particularly extraordinary" events, beyond 'extraordinary circumstances' referred to in Article 5(3) of that regulation, which would lead to the air carrier being exempted from all its obligations, including those under Article 9 of the regulation.

Next, as for the context of and the aims pursued by Article 5 of Regulation No 261/2004, which prescribes the obligations of an air carrier in the event of cancellation of a flight, it must be noted, first, that when exceptional circumstances arise, Article 5(3) exempts the air carrier only from its obligation to pay compensation under Article 7 of that regulation. The European Union legislature thus took the view that the obligation on the air carrier to provide care under Article 9 of that regulation is necessary whatever the event which has given rise to the cancellation of the flight. Second, it is clear from recitals 1 and 2 of Regulation No 261/2004 that the regulation aims at ensuring a high level of protection for passengers and takes account of the requirements of consumer protection in general, inasmuch as cancellation of flights causes serious inconvenience to passengers.

If circumstances such as those at issue in the main proceedings went beyond the scope of "extraordinary circumstances" within the meaning of Regulation No 261/2004 due in particular to their origin and scale, such an interpretation would go against not only the meaning of that notion in everyday language but also the objectives of that regulation. Such an interpretation would in fact mean that air carriers would be required to provide care pursuant to Article 9 of Regulation No 261/2004 to air passengers who find themselves, due to cancellation of a flight, in a situation causing limited inconvenience, whereas passengers, such as the plaintiff in the main proceedings, who find themselves in a particularly vulnerable state in that they are forced to remain at an airport for several days would be denied that care.

In the light of the foregoing, the answer to the first question is that Article 5 of Regulation No 261/2004 must be interpreted as meaning that circumstances such as the closure of part of European airspace as a result of the eruption of the Eyjafjallajökull volcano constitute "extraordinary circumstances" within the meaning of that regulation which do not release air carriers from their obligation laid down in Articles 5(1)(b) and 9 of the regulation to provide care. It follows from the answer given to the first question that there is no need to answer the second and third questions.

II. *Limitations on Obligation to Provide Passenger Care*

By its fourth and fifth questions, which should be examined together, the referring court asks, in essence, whether Articles 5(1)(b) and 9 of Regulation No 261/2004 must be interpreted as meaning that, in the event of cancellation of a flight due to "extraordinary circumstances" such as those at issue in the main proceedings, the obligation to provide care to passengers laid down in those provisions is limited in temporal or monetary terms and, if not, whether those provisions thus interpreted are invalid in the light of the principles of proportionality and non-discrimination, the principle of an "equitable balance of interests" referred to in the Montreal Convention or Articles 16 and 17 of the Charter.

It should be noted that, in the case of cancellation of a flight on account of "extraordinary circumstances," the European Union legislature sought to modify the obligations of air carriers laid down in Article 5(1) of Regulation No 261/2004. Under recital 15 and Article 5(3) of Regulation No 261/2004, by way of derogation from the provisions of Article 5(1), the air carrier is thus exempted from its obligation to compensate passengers under Article 7 of that regulation if it can prove that the cancellation is caused by extraordinary circumstances which could not have been avoided even if all reasonable measures had been taken, namely circumstances which are beyond the air carrier's actual control (Nelson and Others, paragraph 39). In that regard, the Court has held that, in such circumstances, the air carrier is only released from its obligation to provide compensation under Article 7 of Regulation No 261/2004 and that, consequently, its obligation to provide care in accordance with Article 9 of that regulation remains. Furthermore, no limitation, whether temporal or monetary, of the obligation to provide care to passengers in extraordinary circumstances such as those at issue in the main proceedings is apparent from the wording of Regulation No 261/2004.

It follows from Article 9 of Regulation No 261/2004 that all the obligations to provide care to passengers whose flight is cancelled are imposed, in their entirety, on the air carrier for the whole period during which the passengers concerned must await their re-routing. To that effect, it is clear from Article 9(1)(b) that hotel accommodation is to be offered free of charge by the air carrier during the "necessary" period. Moreover, any interpretation seeking the recognition of limits, whether temporal or monetary, on the obligation of the air carrier to provide care to passengers whose flight has been cancelled would have the effect of jeopardising the aims pursued by Regulation No 261/2004 recalled in paragraph 31 of this judgment, in that, beyond the limitation adopted, passengers would be deprived of all care and thus left to themselves.

As the Advocate General noted in his Opinion, the provision of care to such passengers is particularly important in the case of extraordinary circumstances which persist over a long time and it is precisely in situations where the waiting period occasioned by the cancellation of a flight is particularly lengthy that it is necessary to ensure that an air passenger whose flight has been cancelled can have access to essential goods and services throughout that period. Consequently, and contrary to what Ryanair claims, it cannot be deduced from Regulation No 261/2004 that, in circumstances such as those at issue in the main proceedings, the obligation referred to in Articles 5 and 9 of that regulation to provide care to passengers must be subject to a temporal or monetary limitation.

However, it is necessary to ensure that the interpretation in the preceding paragraph does not conflict with the principles of proportionality, of an "equitable balance of interests" referred to in the Montreal Convention and of non-discrimination, or with Articles 16 and 17 of the Charter. Under a general principle of interpretation, a European Union measure must be interpreted, as far as possible, in such a way as not to affect its validity and in conformity with primary law as a whole.

As regards, first, the principle of proportionality, it must be noted that the Court has already had occasion to find that Articles 5 to 7 of Regulation 543No 261/2004 are not invalid by reason of infringement of the principle of proportionality. There is nothing to justify, even on the basis of the lack of a temporal or monetary limit on the obligation to provide care in circumstances such as those at issue in the main proceedings, the finding of validity made by the Court in that case being called into question.

The fact that the obligation defined in Article 9 of Regulation No 261/2004 to provide care entails, as Ryanair claims, undoubted financial consequences for air carriers is not such as to invalidate that finding, since those consequences cannot be considered disproportionate to the aim of ensuring a high level of protection for passengers. The importance of the objective of consumer protection, which includes the protection of air passengers, may justify even substantial negative economic consequences for certain economic operators. In addition, as the Advocate General noted, air carriers should, as experienced operators, foresee costs linked to the fulfilment, where relevant, of their obligation to provide care and, furthermore, may pass on the costs incurred as a result of that obligation to airline ticket prices. It follows that Articles 5(1)(b) and 9 of Regulation No 261/2004 are not contrary to the principle of proportionality.

None the less, an air passenger may only obtain, by way of compensation for the failure of the air carrier to comply with its obligation referred to in Articles 5(1)(b) and 9 of Regulation No 261/2004 to provide care, reimbursement of the amounts which, in the light of the specific circumstances of each case, proved necessary, appropriate and reasonable to make up for the shortcomings of the air carrier in the provision of care to that passenger, a matter which is for the national court to assess.

As regards, second, the principle of an "equitable balance of interests" referred to in the last paragraph of the preamble to the Montreal Convention, suffice it to note that the standardised and immediate compensatory measures laid down by Regulation No 261/2004, which include the obligation to provide care to passengers whose flight has been cancelled, are not among those whose institution is governed by the Montreal Convention. Therefore, there is no need to assess the validity of the aforesaid provisions in the light of the principle of an 'equitable balance of interests' referred to in that Convention.

As regards, third, the general principle of non-discrimination or equal treatment, Ryanair claims that the obligation laid down in Articles 5(1)(b) and 9 of Regulation No 261/2004 to provide care in a situation such as that as issue in the main proceedings imposes obligations on air carriers which, in circumstances similar to those at issue in the main proceedings, do not fall upon other modes of transport governed by Regulation (EC) No 1371/2007 of the European Parliament and of the Council of 23 October 2007 on rail passengers' rights and obligations, Regulation (EU) No 1177/2010 of the European Parliament and of the Council of 24 November 2010 concerning the rights of passengers when travelling by sea and inland waterway and amending Regulation (EC) No 2006/2004 and Regulation (EU) No 181/2011 of the European Parliament and of the Council of 16 February 2011 concerning the rights of passengers in bus and coach transport and amending Regulation (EC) No 2006/2004, even though passengers stranded by widespread and prolonged disruption of transport find themselves in an identical situation whatever their mode of transport. In that respect, it should be noted that the Court has already held in IATA and ELFAA, paragraphs 93 to 99, that Articles 5 to 7 of Regulation No 261/2004 do not infringe the principle of equal treatment.

The situation of undertakings operating in the different transport sectors is not comparable since the different modes of transport, having regard to the manner in which they operate, the conditions governing their accessibility and the distribution of their networks, are not interchangeable as regards the conditions of their use. In those circumstances, the European Union legislature was able to establish rules providing for a level of customer protection that varied according to the transport sector concerned. It follows that Articles 5(1)(b) and 9 of Regulation No 261/2004 do not infringe the principle of non-discrimination.

As regards, fourth, Articles 16 and 17 of the Charter, guaranteeing freedom to conduct a business and the right to property respectively, Ryanair claims that the obligation to provide care to passengers imposed on air carriers in circumstances such as those at issue in the main proceedings has the effect of depriving air carriers of part of the fruits of their labour and of their investments. In that regard, it must be noted, first, that freedom to conduct a business and the right to property are not absolute rights but must be considered in relation to their social function. Next, Article 52(1) of the Charter accepts that limitations may be imposed on the exercise of rights enshrined by it as long as the limitations are provided for by law, respect the essence of those rights and freedoms, and, subject to the principle of proportionality, are necessary and genuinely meet objectives of general interest recognised by the European Union or the need to protect the rights and freedoms of others. Lastly, when several rights protected by the European Union legal order clash, such an assessment must be carried out in accordance with the need to reconcile the requirements of the protection of those various rights and striking a fair balance between them.

In this case, the referring court mentions Articles 16 and 17 of the Charter. However, it is also necessary to take account of Article 38 thereof which, like Article 169 TFEU, seeks to ensure a high level of protection for consumers, including air passengers, in European Union policies. As has been noted in paragraph 31 of this judgment, protection of those passengers is among the principal aims of Regulation No 261/2004. It follows from paragraphs 45 to 49 of this judgment relating to the principle of proportionality that Articles 5(1)(b) and 9 of Regulation No 261/2004, as interpreted in paragraph 43 of this judgment, must be considered to comply with the requirement intended to reconcile the various fundamental rights involved and strike a fair balance between them. Therefore, those provisions do not breach Articles 16 and 17 of the Charter.

Consequently, the answer to the fourth and fifth questions is that Articles 5(1)(b) and 9 of Regulation No 261/2004 must be interpreted as meaning that, in the event of cancellation of a flight due to "extraordinary circumstances" of a duration such as that in the main proceedings, the obligation to provide care to air passengers laid down in those provisions must be complied with, and the validity of those provisions is not affected. However, an air passenger may only obtain, by way of compensation for the failure of the air carrier to comply with its obligation referred to in Articles 5(1)(b) and 9 of Regulation No 261/2004 to provide care, reimbursement of the amounts which, in the light of the specific circumstances of each case, proved necessary, appropriate and reasonable to make up for the shortcomings of the air carrier in the provision of care to that passenger, a matter which is for the national court to assess.

NOTES

1. The facts in *Nader v. Allegheny Airlines, Inc.* (1976) *supra*, underscore the significant discord between what the general public views as unfair and deceptive practice, on the one hand, and what airlines reason is sound business policy, on the other hand. Meanwhile, *Buck v. American Airlines, Inc.* (1st Cir. 2007), *supra*, previews the frustration passengers often experience upon learning whether they can privately enforce their aviation travel right in a court of law. United States Senator Ron Wyden (D-Or.) has said that, "[m]ovie theatres can't cancel a show if only a few people show up for the movie, but airlines can cancel flights when they determine they don't have enough passengers ... That's patently unfair." *See, e.g.*, Paul Mann, *Passenger Rights Movement Expected to Bounce Back*, AVIATION WEEK & SPACE TECH., Oct. 25, 1999, at 54, 58. What alternatives to overbooking might airlines consider? Would issuance of non-refundable tickets be a solution?

2. What should be done to improve airline service? *See, e.g.*, Adam Bryant, *7 Ways to Fix Air Travel*, NEWSWEEK, Apr. 23, 2001, at 38 ((1) construct more runways at existing airports; (2) use an auction to set the rates for landing fees at major airports; (3) improve customer service, *i.e.*, "customers before cargo;" (4) improve air traffic navigation with modern technology such as Global Positioning Satellite; (5) create an independent, nonprofit corporation to operate air traffic control in place of the FAA; (6) "stop the merger madness;" and (7) encourage passengers to choose a carrier based on quality of service not just fare or frequent flyer accounts).

3. Query whether the inconvenience caused by airline delays, bumping, and cancellations can ever adequately be monetized or translated into dollars-and-cents as court-awarded damages. *See, e.g.*, *Smith v. Piedmont Aviation, Inc.* (5th Cir. 1978) (affirming $1,000 award to plaintiff-groomsman "for inconvenience, inability to reach wedding rehearsal on time, missing part of the rehearsal dinner, being required to drive an automobile in mountainous territory, and the cost of automobile rent"). For example, compensation for damaged, delayed, or lost baggage currently is subject to a liability

ceiling of $3,300 per passenger—a figure that is adjusted every two years. *Compare* 14 C.F.R. § 254.4 (2010) *with Delta Air Lines, Inc. v. Barnard* (Ala. Civ. 2001), *supra* ($1,250 per passenger). For European Commission rules governing "bumping" in overseas aviation travel see *http://ec.europa.eu/transport/passengers/air/air_en.htm.*

4. Are courts of law (or equity) the best place for airline complaints to be resolved and travel rights to be vindicated—as opposed to the ticket counter or customer service department? *See, e.g.*, Jayne O'Donnell, *Airline Chiefs Vow Customer-Service Plans Will Improve*, USA TODAY, June 8, 2001, at 2B (quoting travel industry lawyer, "The judge is going to say 'What are your damages? ... You had a long-distance phone-call to relatives, dinner in the airport—your damages are about $15.'"); Keith L. Alexander, *Passenger Rights Expanded*, WASH. POST, June 8, 2001, at E01 (quoting United States Senator Ron Wyden (D-Or.), "[t]he airlines are saying the passengers can try to protect themselves in court. But it's going to be a long time before they get a remedy.").

5. Airline passengers tell "horror stories" about air travel, but they are not themselves blameless. Consider:

> Dear Ann Landers: A lot of people are traveling this summer, and my friends and I came up with a list of suggestions that we would like to call "Airline Etiquette."
>
> 1. Be courteous to the crew and fellow passengers. One rude person in a small area makes for a very unpleasant trip for everyone.
> 2. If there is no room in the overhead for your carry-on luggage, put your bag in the foot space in front of your legs. If you have a hang-up bag, ask the flight attendant where it should go.
> 3. Do not bring an overstuffed carry-on bag that won't fit in the assigned space. Bring only important, necessary items with your.
> 4. Do not lean your back seat any farther than absolutely necessary. Most airlines have so little leg room that your head will be on another passenger's lap.
> 5. If you must recline your seat, be sure to put it in the upright position when food is served. The person behind you will appreciate it.

> 6. If the person next to you spills a drink, offer them your napkin, and press the call button for the flight attendant. Your seatmate will have his hands full.
>
> 7. Be considerate of the passenger in front of you. Do not bump or kick the seat. Don't slam the tray table. Use care when removing items from the seat pocket.
>
> 8. On long flights, be quiet when the cabin lights are dimmed. You may want to have a loud conversation, but other people are trying to sleep.
>
> 9. Keep the volume down on personal entertainment devices such as CD players and videogame players, or use headphones.
>
> 10. Please demonstrate good hygiene. Airplanes are stuffy. Take a shower, and put on clean clothes before getting on board. The person next to you will be grateful.

Letter, Fellow Travelers in Queen Creek, Ariz. to Ann Landers, MIAMI HERALD, July 27, 2002, at 9E.

6. *In re JetBlue Airways Corp. Privacy Litigation*, (E.D.N.Y. 2005), *supra*, showcases the new reality or normalcy of airline travel after September 11th. Consider, in 1998, counsel for the American Civil Liberties Union ("ACLU") suggested:

> [a] passenger "Bill of Rights" should be posted at ticket counters to inform passengers of their rights; such as the right to refuse to present identification if they choose to travel anonymously, their right to refrain from answering intrusive questions or to be subjected to intrusive security measures; the consequences, if any, of exercising these rights; and the way to contact the entity to which complaints of security-related abuses should be directed.

Gregory T. Nojeim, *Aviation Security Profiling and Passengers' Civil Liberties*, 13 AIR & SPACE LAW. 3, 9 (1998).

7. Given preemption of state customer service initiatives governing commercial aviation, there is a public cry for federal legislation aimed at improving airline service. But, is any law really necessary toward this end or is airline customer service strictly a business matter? As one television commentator said in 2001 while assessing the remarks of a United Airlines CEO:

> He says, "We're in the service business. And if we don't find ways to provide that level of service, passengers will obviously find other airlines that can." Now, that's not just spin; that's a pretty good point. Why in the world would the airlines intentionally aggravate their customers? Congress doesn't need to tell restaurants to serve tasty food. Restaurants that serve bad food go out of business.
>
> This is all about members of Congress and how they're treated by the airlines ... This is about them. This is about their inconveniences, and they're taking it out on the country—not the first time.

CNN Crossfire, *Is It Time for Congress to Give Airline Passengers More Rights?* (CNN television broadcast, Feb. 15, 2001). Alternatively, "the problem isn't that airlines have an incentive to antagonize their customers, but that the airlines *lack* an incentive *not* to antagonize their customers." *See* James Higgins, *The Industry You Love to Hate*, WKLY. STANDARD, Mar. 19, 2001, at 24. (Emphasis added.)

8. The terrorism of September 11, 2001 shifted the nation's focus from deficiencies in airline service to problems with aviation security. Should the impetus to regulate airline service be renewed? United States Representative Peter DeFazio (D-Or.) noted the commercial aviation industry

> was tremendously mismanaged before 9/11 ... Remember the big subject before 9/11 was passenger rights because people felt so abused ... We need to begin to think about whether we're going to have to regulate this industry again.

NBC News' Meet the Press (NBC television broadcast, Aug. 18, 2002). *See also* Michael E. Levine, *Why Weren't the Airlines Reregulated?*, 23 YALE J. ON REG. 269 (2006).

9. Has commercial airline transportation become sufficiently inconvenient that consumers will find alternative modes of transportation? One commentator opines:

> Because of Sept. 11, passengers are being treated worse now than before—the lines are longer, the demands on customers are more intrusive, no-frills service has taken on new meaning. But the passengers can't complain—to do so would sound unpatriotic. In the name of safety—and for good reason—the airports are being run in a way that would have been unrecognizable before Sept. 11.

> Because of this, the airlines are probably safer today than they were back in August [2001]. Which is why safety will not be the underlying reason people continue to stay away from airports.
>
> The real reason comes down to something that has been building for years, and that has been reported upon here even before Sept. 11—something that can be summed up in a slogan protestors used to write on signs they waived at Dwight D. Eisenhower's secretary of state before he went off on far-flung foreign travels: "Is this trip necessary?"

Bob Greene, *Safety Isn't the Airlines' Only Worry*, CHI. TRIB., Dec. 4, 2001, at 1C. If so, is traveling other than by airplane a viable option in today's global marketplace?

10. In the aftermath of September 11, 2001, a former airline executive presented an ultimatum: "You want to travel on the airline system? You give up your privacy. You don't want to give up your privacy? Don't fly. Your privacy isn't equal to the rest of the safety of the rest of us." Robert L. Crandall, *Security for the Future: Let's Get Our Airlines Flying* in Symposium, *Airline Security and Economic* Symposium—*Freedom versus Fear: The Future of Air Travel,* 67 J. AIR L. & COM. 19 (2002). In assessing airline passengers' rights, is the trade-off between personal privacy and national security necessary or appropriate? *See, e.g., In re American Airlines, Inc., Privacy Litig.* (N.D. Tex. 2005); *Privacy Rights Clearinghouse v. JetBlue Airways Corp.* (Cal. 2005); *In re Northwest Airlines Privacy Litig.* (D. Minn. 2004).

PROBLEM

A passenger traveling from Kansas City to Philadelphia arrived at the airport two hours before departure, but was told the "the flight is full" and there was no seat on the airplane for him. The airline did not provide him with a written statement of the Department of Transportation's regulations compensating passengers bumped off of oversold flights as required by 14 C.F.R. § 250.9. He was booked on a different airline, yet did not arrive at his destination until almost twenty-four full hours later. The passenger sues for compensatory and punitive damages in federal court. Does he have a private right of action under applicable regulations governing oversold flights? What rights, if any, does he have to claim punitive damages? *See Kalick v. Northwest Airlines, Corp.* (3d Cir. 2010).

C. AIRPORTS AND AIRSPACE

This chapter, originally entitled "Environment and Property Rights" in the first edition of this book, has been renamed to more explicitly feature where authorities permit and restrict aviation operations and transactions to take place. Traditionally, key areas of airport law include airport governance and control such as financing, funding and taxation; zoning and airside obligations (*e.g.*, road, runway, and taxi-way construction); tenant rights, including food and beverage concessions and parking fees; and airport and community improvement. Environmental concerns generally focus on safety and noise pollution and abatement.

Unmistakably, the subject matter of airports has taken on a heightened security-driven dimension since September 11th. The events of September 11th led to the creation of new agencies such as the Department of Homeland Security and Transportation Security Administration ("TSA"), and changed relationships among airport operators, owners, and users. Registered and "trusted traveler" programs and invasive search and seizure protocols also are new and regular features of airports, impacting important speech, associational, and property rights under the First, Fourth, and Fifth Amendments.

The airspace above and around airports has also changed. Historically, ownership of land extended to the periphery of the universe as expressed in the ancient doctrine *cujus est solum ejus usque ad coelom*— "whoever owns the soil, it is theirs up to Heaven." This doctrine was a part of the American common law until it was abandoned in the case of *United States v. Causby*, *infra*. Modernly, since enactment of the Air Commerce Act of 1926, the United States has "complete and exclusive national sovereignty in the air space" over the United States while its citizens enjoy "a public right of freedom of transit in air commerce through the navigable air space of the United States." In this context, "navigable air space" includes "airspace above the minimum safe altitudes of flight prescribed by the [FAA]." But, this definition may need to be revisited and revised given technological innovations such as unmanned aerial vehicles—"drones," as discussed in Chapter 7, *supra*.

In all, the cases in this section introduce the seminal legal authorities respecting airport and airspace. In reading these materials, consider what airports and airspace laws say about the health of democracy and the Constitution in the United States. Do the *post*-September 11th security protocols and restrictions on airport and airspace reflect a police state or a free society? Alternatively, consider what *pre*-September 11th airport and airspace laws require modification and fortification in light of ubiquitous global terror threats.

Airports

INT'L SOC. FOR KRISHNA CONSCIOUSNESS, INC. v. LEE
505 U.S. 672 (1992)

Chief Justice REHNQUIST delivered the opinion of the Court.

In this case we consider whether an airport terminal operated by a public authority is a public forum and whether a regulation prohibiting solicitation in the interior of an airport terminal violates the First Amendment.

The relevant facts in this case are not in dispute. Petitioner International Society for Krishna Consciousness, Inc. ("ISKCON"), is a not-for-profit religious corporation whose members perform a ritual known as *sankirtan*. The ritual consists of "'going into public places, disseminating religious literature and soliciting funds to support the religion.'" The primary purpose of this ritual is raising funds for the movement.

Respondent Walter Lee, now deceased, was the police superintendent of the Port Authority of New York and New Jersey and was charged with enforcing the regulation at issue. The Port Authority owns and operates three major airports in the greater New York City area: John F. Kennedy International Airport ("Kennedy"), La Guardia Airport ("La Guardia"), and Newark International Airport ("Newark"). The three airports collectively form one of the world's busiest metropolitan airport complexes. They serve approximately 8% of this country's domestic airline market and more than 50% of the trans-Atlantic market. By decade's end they are expected to serve at least 110 million passengers annually.

The airports are funded by user fees and operated to make a regulated profit. Most space at the three airports is leased to commercial airlines, which bear primary responsibility for the leasehold. The Port Authority retains control over unleased portions, including La Guardia's Central Terminal Building, portions of Kennedy's International Arrivals Building, and Newark's North Terminal Building (we refer to these areas collectively as the "terminals"). The terminals are generally accessible to the general public and contain various commercial establishments such as restaurants, snack stands, bars, newsstands, and stores of various types. Virtually all who visit the terminals do so for purposes related to air travel. These visitors principally include passengers, those meeting or seeing off passengers, flight crews, and terminal employees.

The Port Authority has adopted a regulation forbidding within the terminals the repetitive solicitation of money or distribution of literature. The regulation states:

> The following conduct is prohibited within the interior areas of buildings or structures at an air terminal if conducted by a person to or with passers-by in a continuous

> or repetitive manner: (a) the sale or distribution of any merchandise, including but not limited to jewelry, food stuffs, candles, flowers, badges and clothing; (b) the sale or distribution of flyers, brochures, pamphlets, books or any other printed or written material; (c) the solicitation and receipt of funds.

The regulation governs only the terminals; the Port Authority permits solicitation and distribution on the sidewalks outside the terminal buildings. The regulation effectively prohibits ISKCON from performing *sankirtan* in the terminals. As a result, ISKCON brought suit seeking declaratory and injunctive relief under 42 U.S.C. § 1983, alleging that the regulation worked to deprive its members of rights guaranteed under the First Amendment.

The suit was filed in 1975. ISKCON originally sought access to both the airline controlled areas and to the terminals and as a result sued both respondent and various private airlines. The suit worked a meandering course, with the private airlines eventually being dismissed and leaving, as the sole remaining issue, ISKCON's claim against respondent seeking a declaration and injunction against the regulation. The regulation at issue was not formally promulgated until 1988 although it represents a codification of presuit policy. Respondent concedes that sankirtan may be performed on the sidewalks outside the terminals.

The District Court analyzed the claim under the "traditional public forum" doctrine. It concluded that the terminals were akin to public streets, the quintessential traditional public *fora*. This conclusion in turn meant that the Port Authority's terminal regulation could be sustained only if it was narrowly tailored to support a compelling state interest. In the absence of any argument that the blanket prohibition constituted such narrow tailoring, the District Court granted ISKCON summary judgment. The Court of Appeals affirmed in part and reversed in part. Relying on our recent decision in *United States v. Kokinda* (1990), a divided panel concluded that the terminals are not public *fora*. As a result, the restrictions were required only to satisfy a standard of reasonableness. The Court of Appeals then concluded that, presented with the issue, this Court would find that the ban on solicitation was reasonable, but the ban on distribution was not.

ISKCON and one of its members, also a petitioner here, sought *certiorari* respecting the Court of Appeals' decision that the terminals are not public *fora* and upholding the solicitation ban. Respondent cross-petitioned respecting the court's holding striking down the distribution ban. We granted both petitions to resolve whether airport terminals are public *fora*, a question on which the Circuits have split and on which we once before granted *certiorari* but ultimately failed to reach.

It is uncontested that the solicitation at issue in this case is a form of speech protected under the First Amendment. But it is also well settled that the government need not permit all forms of speech on property that it owns and controls. Where the government is acting as a proprietor, managing its internal operations, rather than acting as lawmaker with the power to regulate or license, its action will not be subjected to the heightened review to which its actions as a lawmaker may be subject. Thus, we have upheld a ban on political advertisements in city-operated transit vehicles even though the city permitted other types of advertising on those vehicles. Similarly, we have permitted a school district to limit access to an internal mail system used to communicate with teachers employed by the district.

These cases reflect, either implicitly or explicitly, a "forum based" approach for assessing restrictions that the government seeks to place on the use of its property. Under this approach, regulation of speech on government property that has traditionally been available for public expression is subject to the highest scrutiny. Such regulations survive only if they are narrowly drawn to achieve a compelling state interest.

The second category of public property is the designated public forum, whether of a limited or unlimited character—property that the State has opened for expressive activity by part or all of the public. Regulation of such property is subject to the same limitations as that governing a traditional public forum. Finally, there is all remaining public property. Limitations on expressive activity conducted on this last category of property must survive only a much more limited review. The challenged regulation need only be reasonable, as long as the regulation is not an effort to suppress the speaker's activity due to disagreement with the speaker's view.

The parties do not disagree that this is the proper framework. Rather, they disagree whether the airport terminals are public *fora* or nonpublic *fora*. They also disagree whether the regulation survives the "reasonableness" review governing nonpublic *fora*, should that prove the appropriate category. Like the Court of Appeals, we conclude that the terminals are nonpublic *fora* and that the regulation reasonably limits solicitation.

The suggestion that the government has a high burden in justifying speech restrictions relating to traditional public *fora* made its first appearance in *Hague v. Committee for Industrial Organization* (1939). Justice Roberts, concluding that individuals have a right to use "streets and parks for communication of views," reasoned that such a right flowed from the fact that "streets and parks ... have immemorially been held in trust for the use of the public and, time out of mind, have been used for purposes of assembly, communicating thoughts between citizens, and discussing public questions." We confirmed this observation in *Frisby v. Schultz* (1988), where we held that a residential street was a public forum.

Our recent cases provide additional guidance on the characteristics of a public forum. In *Cornelius v. NAACP Legal Defense & Ed. Fund, Inc.* (1985), we noted that a traditional public forum is property that has as "a principal purpose ... the free exchange of ideas." Moreover, consistent with the notion that the government—like other property owners—"has power to preserve the property under its control for the use to which it is lawfully dedicated," the government does not create a public forum by inaction. Nor is a public forum created "whenever members of the public are permitted freely to visit a place owned or operated by the Government." The decision to create a public forum must instead be made "by intentionally opening a nontraditional forum for public discourse." Finally, we have recognized that the location of property also has bearing because separation from acknowledged public areas may serve to indicate that the separated property is a special enclave, subject to greater restriction.

These precedents foreclose the conclusion that airport terminals are public *fora*. Reflecting the general growth of the air travel industry, airport terminals have only recently achieved their contemporary size and character. *See* H. HUBBARD, M. MCCLINTOCK, & F. WILLIAMS, AIRPORTS: THEIR LOCATION, ADMINISTRATION AND LEGAL BASIS 8 (1930) (noting that the United States had only 807 airports in 1930). But given the lateness with which the modern air terminal has made its appearance, it hardly qualifies for the description of having "immemorially ... time out of mind" been held in the public trust and used for purposes of expressive activity.

Moreover, even within the rather short history of air transport, it is only "[i]n recent years [that] it has become a common practice for various religious and non-profit organizations to use commercial airports as a forum for the distribution of literature, the solicitation of funds, the proselytizing of new members, and other similar activities." 45 Fed. Reg. 35,314 (1980). Thus, the tradition of airport activity does not demonstrate that airports have historically been made available for speech activity. Nor can we say that these particular terminals, or airport terminals generally, have been intentionally opened by their operators to such activity; the frequent and continuing litigation evidencing the operators' objections belies any such claim. In short, there can be no argument that society's time-tested judgment, expressed through acquiescence in a continuing practice, has resolved the issue in petitioners' favor.

Petitioners attempt to circumvent the history and practice governing airport activity by pointing our attention to the variety of speech activity that they claim historically occurred at various "transportation nodes" such as rail stations, bus stations, wharves, and Ellis Island. Even if we were inclined to accept petitioner's historical account describing speech activity at these locations, an account respondent contests, we think that such evidence is of little import for two reasons.

First, much of the evidence is irrelevant to public *fora* analysis, because sites such as bus and rail terminals traditionally have had private ownership. *See United Transportation Union v. Long Island R. Co.* (1982). The development of privately owned parks that ban speech activity would not change the public *fora* status of publicly held parks. But the reverse is also true. The practices of privately held transportation centers do not bear on the government's regulatory authority over a publicly owned airport.

Second, the relevant unit for our inquiry is an airport, not "transportation nodes" generally. When new methods of transportation develop, new methods for accommodating that transportation are also likely to be needed. And with each new step, it therefore will be a new inquiry whether the transportation necessities are compatible with various kinds of expressive activity. To make a category of "transportation nodes," therefore, would unjustifiably elide what may prove to be critical differences of which we should rightfully take account. The "security magnet," for example, is an airport commonplace that lacks a counterpart in bus terminals and train stations. And public access to air terminals is also not infrequently restricted—just last year the Federal Aviation Administration required airports for a 4-month period to limit access to areas normally publicly accessible. To blithely equate airports with other transportation centers, therefore, would be a mistake.

The differences among such facilities are unsurprising since, as the Court of Appeals noted, airports are commercial establishments funded by users fees and designed to make a regulated profit, and where nearly all who visit do so for some travel related purpose. As commercial enterprises, airports must provide services attractive to the marketplace. In light of this, it cannot fairly be said that an airport terminal has as a principal purpose promoting "the free exchange of ideas." To the contrary, the record demonstrates that Port Authority management considers the purpose of the terminals to be the facilitation of passenger air travel, not the promotion of expression. Even if we look beyond the intent of the Port Authority to the manner in which the terminals have been operated, the terminals have never been dedicated (except under the threat of court order) to expression in the form sought to be exercised here: *i.e.*, the solicitation of contributions and the distribution of literature.

The terminals here are far from atypical. Airport builders and managers focus their efforts on providing terminals that will contribute to efficient air travel. *See, e.g.*, R. HORONJEFF & F. MCKELVEY, PLANNING AND DESIGN OF AIRPORTS 326 (3d ed. 1983) ("The terminal is used to process passengers and baggage for the interface with aircraft and the ground transportation modes."). The Federal Government is in accord; the Secretary of Transportation has been directed to publish a plan for airport development necessary "to anticipate and meet the needs of civil aeronautics, to meet requirements in support of the national defense ... and to meet identified needs of the Postal Service." 49 U.S.C. § 2203(a)(1); *see also* 45 Fed. Reg. 35,317 (1980) ("The purpose for which the [Dulles and National airport] terminal[s] [were] built and maintained is to process and serve air travelers efficiently").

Although many airports have expanded their function beyond merely contributing to efficient air travel, few have included among their purposes the designation of a forum for solicitation and distribution activities. Thus, we think that neither by tradition nor purpose can the terminals be described as satisfying the standards we have previously set out for identifying a public forum. The restrictions here challenged, therefore, need only satisfy a requirement of reasonableness. We reiterate what we stated in *Kokinda*: The restriction "'need only be reasonable; it need not be the most reasonable or the only reasonable limitation.'" We have no doubt that under this standard the prohibition on solicitation passes muster.

We have on many prior occasions noted the disruptive effect that solicitation may have on business. "Solicitation requires action by those who would respond: The individual solicited must decide whether or not to contribute (which itself might involve reading the solicitor's literature or hearing his pitch), and then, having decided to do so, reach for a wallet, search it for money, write a check, or produce a credit card." Passengers who wish to avoid the solicitor may have to alter their paths, slowing both themselves and those around them. The result is that the normal flow of traffic is impeded. This is especially so in an airport, where "[a]ir travelers, who are often weighted down by cumbersome baggage ... may be hurrying to catch a plane or to arrange ground transportation." Delays may be particularly costly in this setting, as a flight missed by only a few minutes can result in hours' worth of subsequent inconvenience.

In addition, face-to-face solicitation presents risks of duress that are an appropriate target of regulation. The skillful, and unprincipled, solicitor can target the most vulnerable, including those accompanying children or those suffering physical impairment and who cannot easily avoid the solicitation. The unsavory solicitor can also commit fraud through concealment of his affiliation or through deliberate efforts to shortchange those who agree to purchase. Compounding this problem is the fact that, in an airport, the targets of such activity frequently are on tight schedules. This in turn makes such visitors unlikely to stop and formally complain to airport authorities. As a result, the airport faces considerable difficulty in achieving its legitimate interest in monitoring solicitation activity to assure that travelers are not interfered with unduly.

The Port Authority has concluded that its interest in monitoring the activities can best be accomplished by limiting solicitation and distribution to the sidewalk areas outside the terminals. This sidewalk area is frequented by an overwhelming percentage of airport users [no more than 3% of air travelers passing through the terminals are doing so on intraterminal flights, *i.e.*, transferring planes]. Thus the resulting access of those who would solicit the general public is quite complete. In turn we think it would be odd to conclude that the Port Authority's terminal regulation is unreasonable despite the Port Authority having otherwise assured access to an area universally traveled.

The inconveniences to passengers and the burdens on Port Authority officials flowing from solicitation activity may seem small, but viewed against the fact that "pedestrian congestion is one of the greatest problems facing the three terminals," the Port Authority could reasonably worry that even such incremental effects would prove quite disruptive. The congestion problem is not unique to these airports. Moreover, "[t]he justification for the Rule should not be measured by the disorder that would result from granting an exemption solely to ISKCON." For if ISKCON is given access, so too must other groups. "Obviously, there would be a much larger threat to the State's interest in crowd control if all other religious, nonreligious, and noncommercial organizations could likewise move freely. As a result, we conclude that the solicitation ban is reasonable [and] for the foregoing reasons, the judgment of the Court of Appeals sustaining the ban on solicitation in Port Authority terminals is affirmed.

UNITED STATES v. HARTWELL

436 F.3d 174 (3d Cir. 2005)

ALITO, Circuit Judge.

Christian Hartwell set off a metal detector at a security checkpoint in an airport. Transportation Security Administration ("TSA") agents then used a magnetic wand to pinpoint any metal on his person. They detected something in Hartwell's pocket and asked to see it. Ultimately, they discovered that the object was crack cocaine and placed Hartwell under arrest. Hartwell argues that the drugs should have been suppressed because the search offended the Fourth Amendment. We hold that it did not.

Hartwell arrived at the Philadelphia International Airport on Saturday, May 17, 2003, intending to catch a flight to Phoenix. He reached the security checkpoint, placed his hand luggage on a conveyor belt to be X-rayed, and approached the metal detector. Hartwell's luggage was scanned without incident, but he set off the magnetometer when he walked through. He was told to remove all items from his pockets and try again. Hartwell removed several items—including a large quantity of cash—from his pocket, and passed through again. Transportation Security Administration agent Carlos Padua took Hartwell aside after he passed through the metal detector a second time. Padua used a handheld wand-like magnetometer to discover what set off the metal detector. The wand revealed a solid object in Hartwell's cargo pants pocket. Padua asked what it was, but Hartwell did not respond.

What occurred next is the subject of some dispute. Hartwell claims that he was escorted to a private screening room near the checkpoint, where he refused Padua's repeated requests to reveal the contents of his pocket. Frustrated by Hartwell's unresponsiveness, Padua eventually reached into Hartwell's pocket and pulled out a package of drugs. He immediately called the Philadelphia police, who searched Hartwell, found two additional packages of drugs and about $3000 in cash, and promptly arrested him. The government claims that neither Padua nor the police officer ever reached into Hartwell's pocket without his consent. According to Agent Padua, the following occurred. After requesting private screening, Hartwell refused several requests to empty his pocket, nervously backed away from Agent Padua while he was being questioned, and suddenly dropped his pants. This suspicious behavior prompted Padua to call for backup. A police officer arrived and asked Hartwell to remove any items from his pocket, and Hartwell complied by handing over one package of drugs. He then feigned falling to the floor and dropped a second package of drugs.

The District Court found it unnecessary to resolve these conflicting accounts, finding that the search was justified based on undisputed facts. In particular, the Court observed that "[t]here is no dispute that defendant triggered the magnetometer at least once and that Padua attempted to resolve the alarm through the use of the wand." The Court also noted that Hartwell "does not dispute that he was instructed to remove all metal objects from his person prior to each screening and that he was specifically requested to remove the items in his lower pocket several times." In the District Court's view, these circumstances justified the officers' behavior, regardless of whose version of the rest of the story was true. "Whether defendant voluntarily produced the drugs or whether defendant was frisked," the Court stated, "the search was reasonable under the Fourth Amendment."

Although the District Court had no difficulty reaching this result, it recognized that courts have not settled on a single framework for analyzing warrantless searches at airport checkpoints. The Court therefore considered three separate justifications for Hartwell's search, and found each sufficient. The Court first held that the search passed muster under the Fourth Amendment's "general proscription against unreasonable searches and seizures." The Court next sustained the search under the theory that it was a "consensual administrative search." Finally, the Court stated that "by submitting to the screening process, defendant impliedly consented to the search and was lawfully required to complete the search to determine the cause of the alarm." On appeal, Hartwell argues that all three rationales are unfounded. We disagree.

We hold that the search was permissible under the administrative search doctrine. *Cf. United States v. Marquez* (9th Cir. 2005) ("Airport screenings of passengers and their baggage constitute administrative searches and are subject to the limitations of the Fourth Amendment."). Finding this rationale sufficient, we deem it unnecessary to evaluate the District Court's alternative holdings on generalized reasonableness and implied consent.

The Fourth Amendment provides:

> The right of the people to be secure in their persons, houses, papers, and effects, against unreasonable searches and seizures, shall not be violated, and no Warrants shall issue, but upon probable cause, supported by Oath or affirmation, and particularly describing the place to be searched, and the persons or things to be seized.

This provision limits government action in two ways. First, it requires that searches and seizures be reasonable, and second, it states that when a warrant is required—in circumstances not explicitly defined by the text—it must have certain characteristics. The

Supreme Court has read the Amendment's twin commands in tandem, holding that when people have a reasonable expectation of privacy in their persons or effects, all searches and seizures must be supported by a warrant, unless they fall into one of the exceptions to that requirement.

The first step in Fourth Amendment analysis is to identify whether a search or seizure has taken place. The Government concedes that an airport pre-boarding security screening is a search. But this concession obscures the difficult issue of whether Hartwell experienced one prolonged search, or several individual searches. The District Court considered this question and found authority on both sides.

Cases like *United States v. Skipwith* (5th Cir.1973), appear to analyze an entire checkpoint search, including "[m]etal detectors, visual inspection, and rare but potential physical searches," as a single search. By contrast, cases like *United States v. Albarado* (2d Cir. 1974), treat a magnetometer screening and a "frisk" as two separate searches. The District Court concluded that the procedure would be permissible under either view, and therefore did not decide which mode of analysis was appropriate. We will employ *Skipwith's* method of analyzing Hartwell's entire experience as a single search under the administrative search doctrine, and—finding this approach sufficient to resolve the case—do not pass judgment on the *Albarado* approach.

Thus, we find that Hartwell experienced a single, warrantless search, which was initiated without individualized suspicion. Since it was not conducted pursuant to a warrant, the search must be grounded in an exception to the warrant requirement.

Next, Hartwell's search at the airport checkpoint was justified by the administrative search doctrine. "A search or seizure is ordinarily unreasonable in the absence of individualized suspicion of wrongdoing. While such suspicion is not an 'irreducible' component of reasonableness, [the Supreme Court has] recognized only limited circumstances in which the usual rule does not apply." These circumstances typically involve administrative searches of "closely regulated" businesses, other so-called "special needs" cases, and suspicionless "checkpoint" searches. Suspicionless checkpoint searches are permissible under the Fourth Amendment when a court finds a favorable balance between "the gravity of the public concerns served by the seizure, the degree to which the seizure advances the public interest, and the severity of the interference with individual liberty." *Illinois v. Lidster* (2004) (quoting *Brown v. Texas* (1979)).

Michigan Dept. of State Police v. Sitz (1990) provides an illustrative example of a permissible suspicionless checkpoint procedure. In that case, Michigan established a sobriety checkpoint along a state road, stopping every vehicle that passed by in order to question the driver and look for signs of intoxication. If the police observed indicia of impairment, they would pull drivers aside to conduct additional tests. Applying the *Brown* balancing test, the Court found the system permissible because "the balance of the

State's interest in preventing drunken driving, the extent to which this system can reasonably be said to advance that interest, and the degree of intrusion upon individual motorists who are briefly stopped, weighs in favor of the state program." As to the State's interest, the Court wrote that "[n]o one can seriously dispute the magnitude of the drunken driving problem or the States' interest in eradicating it." The stop was deemed effective because some quantum of evidence showed that it furthered the purpose for which it was created. "Conversely," the Court stated, "the weight bearing on the other scale—the measure of the intrusion on motorists stopped briefly at sobriety checkpoints—is slight," because the stop lasted for only a short time and the investigation was of minimal intensity.

In this case, the airport checkpoint passes the *Brown* test. First, there can be no doubt that preventing terrorist attacks on airplanes is of paramount importance. *See United States v. Marquez* (9th Cir.2005) ("It is hard to overestimate the need to search air travelers for weapons and explosives before they are allowed to board the aircraft. As illustrated over the last three decades, the potential damage and destruction from air terrorism is horrifically enormous."); *United States v. Yang* (7th Cir. 2002) ("the events of September 11, 2001, only emphasize the heightened need to conduct searches at this nation's international airports"); *Singleton v. Comm'r of Internal Revenue* (3d Cir.1979) ("The government unquestionably has the most compelling reasons[—]the safety of hundreds of lives and millions of dollars' worth of private property for subjecting airline passengers to a search for weapons or explosives that could be used to hijack an airplane.").

Second, airport checkpoints also "advance the public interest," as *Brown* requires. As this Court has held, "absent a search, there is no effective means of detecting which airline passengers are reasonably likely to hijack an airplane." Additionally, it is apparent that airport checkpoints have been effective.

Third, the procedures involved in Hartwell's search were minimally intrusive. They were well-tailored to protect personal privacy, escalating in invasiveness only after a lower level of screening disclosed a reason to conduct a more probing search. The search began when Hartwell simply passed through a magnetometer and had his bag x-rayed, two screenings that involved no physical touching. Only after Hartwell set off the metal detector was he screened with a wand—yet another less intrusive substitute for a physical pat-down. And only after the wand detected something solid on his person, and after repeated requests that he produce the item, did the TSA agents (according to Hartwell) reach into his pocket.

In addition to being tailored to protect personal privacy, other factors make airport screening procedures minimally intrusive in comparison to other kinds of searches. Since every air passenger is subjected to a search, there is virtually no "stigma attached to being subjected to search at a known, designated airport search point." Moreover, the possibility for abuse is minimized by the public nature of the search. "Unlike searches conducted on dark and lonely streets at night where often the officer and the subject are the only witnesses, these searches are made under supervision and not far from the scrutiny of the traveling public." And the airlines themselves have a strong interest in protecting passengers from unnecessary annoyance and harassment.

Lastly, the entire procedure is rendered less offensive—if not less intrusive—because air passengers are on notice that they will be searched. *Cf. Singleton* (approving a search where passengers "were given advance notice that the search was to be conducted, and could elect not to be searched by deciding not to board the aircraft"). Air passengers choose to fly, and screening procedures of this kind have existed in every airport in the country since at least 1974. The events of September 11, 2001, have only increased their prominence in the public's consciousness. It is inconceivable that Hartwell was unaware that he had to be searched before he could board a plane. Indeed, he admitted that he had previously been searched before flying. *Cf. United States v. Pulido–Baquerizo* (9th Cir.1986) ("in light of the circumstances surrounding today's airport checkpoints," travelers who put their belongings on a conveyor belt "impliedly consent to a visual inspection and limited hand search of their luggage if the x-ray scan is inconclusive")

In conclusion, Hartwell's search does not offend the Fourth Amendment even though it was initiated without individualized suspicion and was conducted without a warrant. It is permissible under the administrative search doctrine because the State has an overwhelming interest in preserving air travel safety, and the procedure is tailored to advance that interest while proving to be only minimally invasive, as that term is understood in *Brown*.

GOODSPEED AIRPORT, LLC v.
EAST HADDAM INLAND WETLANDS & WATERCOURSES COMM'N.

681 F. Supp. 2d 182 (D. Conn. 2010)

MARK R. KRAVITZ, District Judge.

This case raises important questions regarding the extent to which Congress intended federal regulation of aviation safety to preempt generally applicable state and local environmental laws. Plaintiff Goodspeed Airport, LLC, the owner and operator of Goodspeed Airport in East Haddam, Connecticut, seeks a declaration that two Connecticut environmental laws—the Inland Wetlands and Watercourses Act and the Connecticut Environmental Protection Act ("CEPA")—are preempted by federal aviation law insofar as the state statutes require Goodspeed to obtain a permit before removing certain trees located at the Airport.

Goodspeed claims that the trees are "obstructions to air navigation" under Federal Aviation Administration regulations, making them potential hazards to aeronautical safety that the Airport is obligated to remediate. However, because the trees are located in wetlands protected by the Wetlands Act and the CEPA, Goodspeed is required to obtain permission of the Town of East Haddam's Inland Wetlands and Watercourses Commission before trimming or removing the trees. If Goodspeed undertakes the trimming or removal of these trees without the required permit, the Airport could be subjected to civil liability and substantial fines under the Wetlands Act and the CEPA.

After considering evidence presented at a bench trial, and as explained below, the Court concludes that in the particular circumstances of this case, federal regulation of airport safety does not preempt state and local environmental laws in the manner in which Goodspeed asserts. The Court emphasizes that it does not take the Airport's safety concerns lightly, and it does not mean to suggest that the obstructing trees ought to be ignored—there do appear to be a number of trees that pose legitimate safety concerns. But if Goodspeed wishes to remove the trees that it believes are obstructions, it will need to seek a permit to do so from the Wetlands Commission, which may, consistent with state law, impose conditions designed to mitigate degradation of the wetlands.

PROCEDURAL HISTORY

Goodspeed sought a declaratory judgment that once trees at the Airport constitute "obstructions to air navigation," local and state agencies are prohibited from interfering with whatever action Goodspeed wishes to take to remediate those obstructions. It asked further that the Defendants be enjoined from bringing any future action related to the removal of any tree that would qualify as an "obstruction to air navigation" under FAA regulations.

The Court suggested that it would seek the opinion of the FAA on Goodspeed's preemption claims. The [parties] agreed that the FAA's views could be useful. The parties were therefore asked to collaborate on producing a set of stipulated facts and proposed questions that the Court could submit and the Court sent a letter to the U.S. Attorney's Office for the District of Connecticut requesting that the FAA and/or the U.S. Government answer a series of questions related to Goodspeed's claims. Those questions were:

1. Does 49 U.S.C. § 40103(a)(1) of the Federal Aviation Act completely preempt Conn. Gen. Stat. §§ 22a-42a(a) and (c)(1) and the regulations promulgated thereunder regulating wetlands in the State of Connecticut?

2. Does 49 U.S.C. § 40103(a) of the Federal Aviation Act completely preempt Connecticut's Environmental Protection Act, Conn. Gen. Stat. § 22a-16?

3. Does 49 U.S.C. § 41713(b)(1) of the Airline Deregulation Act completely preempt Conn. Gen. Stat. §§ 22a-42a(a) and (c)(1) and the regulations promulgated thereunder regulating wetlands in the State of Connecticut?

4. Does 49 U.S.C. § 41713(b)(1) of the Airline Deregulation Act completely preempt Connecticut's Environmental Protection Act, Conn. Gen. Stat. § 22a16?

5. Does 49 U.S.C. § 41713(b)(1) of the Airline Deregulation Act apply to Goodspeed Airport?

6. To what extent is a licensed, privately-owned and operated commercial airport receive[ing] no federal funds or aid bound by or subject to the FAA regulations set forth in 14 C.F.R. Part 77?

7. To what extent is the FAA interested in issues concerning terrain growth into navigable airspace at a licensed, privately-owned and operated commercial airport that receives no federal funds or aid?

A few days before a bench trial, the United States submitted a Statement of Interest that addressed the Court's questions. The Statement of Interest stated that while "[t]he FAA has a strong interest in monitoring terrain growth on airport property as it relates to air safety," the Federal Aviation Act "does not facially preempt generally applicable state environmental laws," including the Wetlands Act and the CEPA. The United States also confirmed that Part 77 of the FAA regulations does apply to Goodspeed Airport, but that those regulations do not authorize the FAA to order the removal of an obstruction. Finally, the Statement of Interest opined that the Airline Deregulation Act does not expressly preempt the state laws at issue because they "do not have a significant effect on the operations of air carriers at Goodspeed Airport."

The Court held a one-day bench trial. At trial, Goodspeed submitted some thirty exhibits and the live testimony of five witnesses. First to testify was Timothy Mellon, the sole member of Plaintiff Goodspeed Airport, LLC, which purchased the Airport in 1999. Mr. Mellon is also a pilot licensed by the FAA, the owner of two aircraft, and the former owner and operator of an air carrier. Mr. Mellon testified that at least since he has owned the Airport, it has not received any federal funding, and that while Goodspeed does not have any regularly-scheduled passenger service, the Airport is utilized by privately-owned aircraft and an air charter (or "air taxi") operation, Action Airlines.

Mr. Mellon said that the Airport has between 25 and 30 daily departures and arrivals in the summer and approximately 5 to 6 per day in the winter. Goodspeed charges $5 per-landing and a $10 fee for storing a plane overnight. Mr. Mellon stated that as the owner, he is responsible for the Airport's upkeep, which includes maintaining the integrity of the runway surface; keeping wildlife off the runway; ensuring that the Airport is properly lit; and monitoring the security of its hangars, fences, and gates. The Airport does not have a control tower, and does not have prescribed instrument procedures. Therefore, arrivals and departures are typically accomplished pursuant to visual flight rules. The Airport is self-controlled by those using it; there is no employee located at the airport on a regular basis.

Mr. Mellon explained that pilots are permitted to land and depart in either direction of the Airport's single paved runway, which runs in a general north-south orientation. Goodspeed Airport has what is defined as a "utility runway," accommodating propeller-driven aircraft weighing 12,500 pounds or less. No matter which direction an aircraft is flying, the pilot must navigate certain "obstructions"—primarily trees and other vegetation, but also, in regards to a northern approach, a bridge.

Goodspeed Airport is situated on the eastern bank of the Connecticut River, and is surrounded by marshland. The Airport also serves as a seaplane base for aircraft arriving and departing on the river. Mr. Mellon said that the trees that primarily concern him are located on either side of the runway near its southern end. The trees at issue in this lawsuit are only those situated on the Airport's property.

Mr. Mellon stated his belief that these trees constitute threats to the safe operation of the Airport, and that he has both a legal and moral obligation to make the Airport as safe as possible. He acknowledged that the trees have been growing on the Airport property for decades—long before he purchased the Airport—and have long constituted "obstructions" under FAA regulations. Some of the trees are in excess of 50-60 feet in height. But Mr. Mellon said that because he believes the trees make the Airport unsafe, he feels compelled to remove them entirely; or, at the very least, to cut them down to the point where they would no longer be considered obstructions—which, in many cases, would require cutting the trees to the ground. Moreover, he does not wish to seek permission from the Wetlands Commission, which may require him to undertake mitigation efforts to minimize damage to the wetlands. Rather, Mr. Mellon wants to remove the trees at whatever time and in whatever manner he deems appropriate.

Mr. Mellon also explained that the Airport is licensed by the State of Connecticut, which issues such licenses every three years. And although he acknowledged that Goodspeed's license was most recently renewed by the State in June 2009 after an inspection by the Connecticut Department of Transportation in late 2008 or early 2009, Mr. Mellon testified that the State has implicitly threatened to revoke Goodspeed's license if the tree obstructions are not remedied. This implicit threat, according to Mr. Mellon, is contained in letters sent by DOT to a prior owner of the Airport in the late 1970s and early 1980s. Mr. Mellon conceded, however, that neither the DOT nor the FAA has ordered him to lower the trees or given him any indication that it intends to take any action to close the Airport if the trees are not removed or trimmed.

Mr. Mellon also confirmed that he has not applied to the Wetlands Commission for a permit to trim or remove the trees, but stated that if he were to apply, and were his application denied, one option that he would consider would be closing the Airport. If he took that option, the aircraft that currently use Goodspeed Airport would be forced to use other area airports. On cross-examination, however, Mr. Mellon stated that another alternative to removing the trees would be to use what is known as a "displaced threshold." Instead of utilizing the entire length of the runway, aircraft would treat a line painted across the runway some distance from its paved end as the effective end of the runway. This line—the "displaced threshold"—would effectively shorten the usable portion of the runway, but it would permit aircraft sufficient clearance over the obstructing trees. According to Mr. Mellon, however, shortening the runway in this manner would make the runway less safe for arriving and departing aircraft; he therefore stated that he would use a displaced threshold only "reluctantly and hopefully temporarily." Mr. Mellon also confirmed that even were he to remove the obstructing trees located on the Airport property, other trees on the property of adjacent homeowners would still be considered "obstructions" due to their height and location, but Mr. Mellon disavowed any authority to remove or trim the trees located on his neighbors' properties.

Next to testify was Donald L. Gesick, Jr., a professional land surveyor. Mr. Gesick's testimony introduced a survey that he conducted of the Airport. His report plotted the location, girth, and height of the trees and shrubbery on the Airport property, as well as the precise locations of its runway and hangars. After Mr. Gesick completed the Airport Survey, it was then used by James B. Downar, Jr., an expert on airport design and safety, to calculate which of the trees constituted "obstructions to air navigation." Mr. Downar's analysis applied the definitions contained in Part 77 of the Federal Aviation Regulation ("FAR"), 14 C.F.R. Part 77, which are explained in more detail below.

Applying the measurements in FAR 77 to Mr. Gesick's survey, Mr. Downar calculated that a great number of trees (including an entire tree line) on Goodspeed's property are indeed "obstructions to air navigation"—some by more than 50 feet. Mr. Downar and Mr. Gesick also suggested that, although they did not explicitly consider the Airport's hangars in their respective analyses, the hangars may also technically count as "obstructions," depending on their height (which is not in the record). Mr. Downar confirmed that lowering the trees to the point at which they would no longer be considered obstructions would involve, at least in many situations, effectively cutting them to the ground. However, Mr. Downar, who has conducted obstruction analyses at a number of area airports, and who said that he has worked with wetlands commissions in other states on removing trees as obstructions, also testified that tree obstructions are a "fact of life" with most airports, including utility airports, and that they are tolerated to varying degrees depending on their relative impact on the safety of the airport.

As to Goodspeed Airport, Mr. Downar testified that in his expert opinion, the tree obstructions do not pose such a risk to its safety that the Airport should be shut down. In fact, he testified that he was not aware of the FAA ever shutting down an airport because of tree obstructions. He emphasized, though, that the obstructions should not simply be ignored, especially a few particularly inconveniently-located trees. Mr. Downar also noted two alternatives to removing the trees. First, the airport could use a displaced threshold. Second, the airport could light the trees so that they would be more visible to pilots in low-light situations. To date, Mr. Mellon has not lit the trees that he considers obstructions.

Mr. Downar also confirmed that simply because a tree or other object constitutes an "obstruction to air navigation" does not automatically render it a "hazard to air navigation" under FAA regulations. In his experience, an "obstruction" only becomes a "hazard" after the FAA has made that determination; to his knowledge, the FAA has made no hazard determination as to any obstruction located at Goodspeed Airport. Mr. Downar further confirmed that the FAA has no authority to order the removal of trees or other obstructions from airports, though they may, in appropriate circumstances, condition licensing or funding on removal or the trees or obstructions.

Goodspeed's final witness was John A. Rutledge, Jr. Mr. Rutledge is the owner of JIB, Inc., which does business as Action Airlines. JIB, Inc. is an air carrier licensed by the FAA under Part 135 of the Federal Aviation Regulations, 14 C.F.R. Part 135. Action Airlines currently has one airplane with the capacity to carry six individuals (including the pilot). The airplane is stored at Goodspeed Airport, and Action Airlines has operated out of Goodspeed Airport as a Part 135 air carrier since 1979. Currently, Mr. Rutledge is Action Airlines' only full-time employee. In addition to being a licensed pilot for more than 50 years, Mr. Rutledge is a pilot instructor and previously served for a number of years as a pilot examiner on behalf of the FAA. He has the further distinction of being one of the relatively few pilots to receive the Wright Brothers Award, an award that the FAA gives to pilots who have flown for at least 50 years without an accident or regulatory violation.

Mr. Rutledge, whose home and office are adjacent to Goodspeed, has been flying into and out of the Airport since shortly after it opened in the mid-1960s. He described Action Airlines as essentially an "airborne limousine service," providing point-to-point transportation to and from airports in the region. Fees for this service are set either on a per-mile or per-hour basis. Mr. Rutledge estimated that in the first 11 months of 2009, Action Airlines had transported approximately 300 to 400 individuals.

Mr. Rutledge said that, given his experience with the Airport, he does not consider the tree obstructions to be a safety concern; indeed, he testified that he did not believe Goodspeed Airport to be unsafe at all, and that he has every intention of continuing to operate Action Airlines out of the Airport in the future regardless of whether the trees are trimmed or removed. He did note, however, that the trees could pose a concern for less experienced pilots while they are landing, because the trees—especially those that line the Connecticut River—block the wind that typically blows in from the west and southwest, perpendicular to the Airport's runway. Mr. Rutledge explained that once a landing aircraft drops below the trees, the intensity of the crosswind is significantly lessened, which inexperienced pilots may not anticipate and which could contribute to an airplane landing short of the runway's edge. Mr. Rutledge testified that he believed that this was a cause of the last accident that occurred at Goodspeed Airport, in 1999. Mr. Rutledge noted, however, that trees and buildings create the same issue at other Connecticut airports, and that in his substantial experience at Goodspeed Airport, there have been very few accidents.

Mr. Rutledge also testified that lighting the trees could alleviate at least some of the safety concerns with using the Airport at night, but that a displaced threshold could impact the operation of Action Airlines, depending on how much shorter it made the runway. Were the runway shortened too much, he may have to limit the weight of his airplane's cargo (be it passengers, luggage, or fuel) in order for the airplane to be able to clear any obstacles during takeoff or for it to stop on the shortened runway. Finally, Mr. Rutledge said that in the event that Goodspeed Airport closed, he would relocate his air taxi service to any number of different airports in the area. Relocation would affect the fees Action Airlines charges for its services, since its clients would have to pay for the additional time Mr. Rutledge spent commuting to and from this alternate location.

Following Mr. Rutledge, the Defendants called Defendant James Ventres as their only witness. Mr. Ventres is the land use administrator for the Town of East Haddam, and his duties include serving as the enforcement officer for Defendant Wetlands Commission. Mr. Ventres has held that position since 1995; prior to that, he served as a member of the Wetlands Commission from approximately 1983. Mr. Ventres testified that Goodspeed Airport has two types of wetlands regulated by the Wetlands Act. The entire Goodspeed Airport sits on a designated flood plain, and is sometimes completely under water. Additional portions of the airport are also considered the more traditional "wetlands" due to the soil's typical moisture level. Mr. Ventres said that while Goodspeed did submit an application to the Wetlands Commission for permission to extend the Airport's runway in 2002 or 2003, that application was withdrawn without an official explanation and before the Wetlands Commission had made a final determination. Goodspeed Airport has not submitted a permit application to the Wetlands Commission since.

Mr. Ventres testified that in recent years the Wetlands Commission has approved applications to remove and/or trim trees and other vegetation in regulated wetlands; he gave as an example a developer that was permitted to construct a golf course that traversed regulated wetlands. Upon consideration of the application, the Wetlands Commission permitted the construction to take place under certain conditions meant to minimize and mitigate its environmental impact, including refraining from using large equipment; leaving stumps of felled trees in place; and undertaking the regulated activity when the ground was frozen. Mr. Ventres explained that the Wetlands Commission regulations set forth various requirements for applications and certain criteria that the Commission must take into account when considering applications. In considering an application, the Wetlands Commission considers whether there are "reasonable and prudent alternatives" to the proposed activity that would cause "less or no environmental impact to the wetlands or watercourse."

In applying this standard, the Wetlands Commission will frequently attach conditions to its approval of an application, such as requiring that the activity take place in specific times of the year, using certain methods designed to minimize impact, replacing the removed vegetation with other trees or shrubs that will continue to hold the soil in place, and/or utilizing other mitigation techniques. On cross-examination, Mr. Ventres acknowledged that since Goodspeed has not submitted an application, he cannot speculate what it would be permitted to do regarding the trees it wishes to remove and/or trim. Mr. Ventres also agreed that the application process can last several months.

FINDINGS OF FACT

Goodspeed Airport, located in East Haddam, Connecticut, is a small, privately-owned airport open for public use , as defined by 14 C.F.R. § 77.2. The Airport was established in 1964 and maintains a "utility runway," which is intended to accommodate propeller-driven aircraft weighing 12,500 pounds or less. Approaches to the Airport are governed solely by visual (as opposed to instrument) flight rules. The Airport does not provide regularly-scheduled passenger service and does not receive any federal funds or aid. As a consequence, the Airport does not have (and is not required to have) a certificate issued by the FAA under Part 139 of the Federal Aviation Regulations.

In fact, because Goodspeed does not serve scheduled air carrier operations, the FAA apparently does not have the statutory authority to directly license or certify Goodspeed Airport at all. *See* 49 U.S.C. § 44706(a)(2) (granting the FAA the authority to certificate airports serving scheduled air carrier operations using aircraft of at least 10 passenger seats, except in Alaska); *see also* § 44706(a)(3) ("Nothing in this title may be construed as requiring a person to obtain an airport operating certificate if such person does not desire to operate an airport [serving scheduled air carrier operations].").

Instead, Goodspeed Airport is licensed and regulated by the State of Connecticut. Within Connecticut, jurisdiction over and responsibility for airports have been entrusted to the Commissioner of the Department of Transportation (hereinafter, "the Commissioner"). The Commissioner is given the authority to issue and renew airport licenses, which are effective for three years and to revoke licenses upon a determination that an airport "is not being maintained or used in accordance with" Connecticut's statutes and regulations regarding aviation. Any air navigation facility at which more than 36 takeoffs and landings are expected to be made in any year must obtain a license. Pursuant to specific statutory authority, the Commissioner has promulgated various regulations related to the safety of Connecticut's airports. The record suggests that Goodspeed has remained licensed and operational without interruption since opening in 1964, despite the continual presence of trees that constitute "obstructions."

The Connecticut General Assembly has also given the Commissioner the authority to require landowners to remove obstacles that "constitute a hazard to aerial navigation or to the efficient or safe use of any airport." An "airport hazard" is defined as "any structure, object of natural growth or use of land which obstructs the air space required for the flight of aircraft in landing or taking off at any airport, heliport or restricted landing area or is otherwise hazardous to such landing or taking-off." The Commissioner also may condition the approval of an airport license on the removal of an obstacle "at or near the landing area." If such a condition is imposed, the applicant for the airport license is required to compensate the owner of the obstacle for its removal. Goodspeed has not provided any evidence that the Commissioner has ever required Goodspeed or any nearby landowner to remove any obstacle or airport hazard.

Although not licensed by the FAA, Goodspeed Airport must participate in the "Airport Safety Data Program." This program was established in 1981 by FAA Order 5010-4, which describes it as "the primary means for collection, maintenance and dissemination of information related to public-use airports." State agencies throughout the country collect this information through "5010 Inspections." In Connecticut, according to Mr. Stannard, the DOT conducts the inspections approximately once every three years. During the inspection, the DOT inspector collects basic technical information about the airport (runway length, services offered, etc.), as well as safety-related information, including data on obstructions, as defined in Part 77 of the FAA regulations. This information is submitted to the National Flight Data Center, which then updates the "Airport Master Record" for every public-use airport in the country. The Airport Master Records are published in the FAA's "Airport/Facilities Directory," as well as in other FAA publications and on the Internet. The information in the Directory is used primarily by pilots flying into an unfamiliar airport for the first time.

The definitions and standards for determining what constitutes an "obstruction to air navigation" are found in Part 77 of the Federal Aviation Regulations ("FAR"), 14 C.F.R. Part 77. The FAA promulgated these regulations pursuant to a Congressional directive. *See* 49 U.S.C. § 44718(a). The Part 77 regulations—which explicitly apply to "objects of natural growth," 14 C.F.R. §§ 77.5(a), 77.21—state in relevant part that an object is considered "an obstruction to air navigation" if it is of greater height than any one of several imaginary surfaces.

One of those imaginary surfaces is called the "primary surface." The length of the primary surface extends 200 feet beyond each end of the runway. For utility airports with only visual approaches such as Goodspeed, the primary surface is 250 feet wide, longitudinally centered on the center of the runway (that is, extending 125 feet on either side of the center line of the runway). Since the runway at Goodspeed is 50 feet wide, this means that the primary surface is 75 feet wider on each side of the paved portion of Goodspeed's runway.

Also relevant here are the "approach surface" and the "transitional surface." The "approach surface" is applied to each end of the primary surface, and for an airport such as Goodspeed, it is 1250 feet wide and extends for a horizontal distance of 5,000 feet at a slope of 20-to-1 (that is, 20 feet up for every 1 foot out). *See* 14 C.F.R. § 77.25(d). The "transitional surface" is shaped like a trapezoid; it flares upwards and outwards at right-angles from the edge of the primary surface to 1250 horizontal feet at a slope of 7-to-1. *See id.* § 77.25(e). Together, the primary surface, approach surface, and the transitional surface create what is, in essence, a "bowl" of airspace, and any object—including a tree—that penetrates any of these imaginary surfaces is considered, by definition, an "obstruction to air navigation." *See id.* § 77.23(a)(5).

The parties have stipulated that certain of the trees at Goodspeed penetrate both the "primary surface" and the "transitional surface" such that they are "obstructions to air navigation" under Part 77. The testimony of Mr. Gesick and Mr. Downar supports this stipulation, as well as the conclusion that the trees also penetrate the "approach surface." A review of the DOT inspections of Goodspeed over the past 30 years reveals that the Airport has long experienced substantial tree obstructions. However, Goodspeed is not unique in this regard, even within Connecticut; in fact, the vast majority of airports in the State have obstructions (mostly trees), which appear to be a chronic problem for all airports. *See Conn. Statewide Airport System Plan* (2006), (discussing obstructions at each of Connecticut's public-use airports).

The crux of this case turns in large part on the import of the determination that the trees at Goodspeed are "obstructions" under Part 77. Significantly, nothing in either Part 77 or its authorizing statute, 49 U.S.C. § 44718, grants the FAA the power to regulate how land is used insofar as structures that may penetrate navigable airspace are concerned. In other words, the FAA cannot require that a structure or object be altered or removed, even if it is an obstruction; instead, the regulations focus on studying potential hazards and giving notice to interested individuals.

Thus, for example, Part 77 requires notice to be given to the FAA of any proposed structure that would be more than 200 feet above ground level at its site, see 14 C.F.R. § 77.13(a)(1), as well as any proposed construction or alteration that would be of greater height than an imaginary surface extending outward and upward from any public use airport's runway at certain slopes (depending on the length of the runway). Similarly, any proposed construction or alteration of an airport itself requires notice to be given to the FAA, either under § 77.13(a)(5) or Part 157. The notice provisions of Part 77 and Part 157 do overlap some, but notice is never required to be given under both Parts. *See* 14 C.F.R. § 77.15(d) ("No person is required to notify the Administrator for any ... construction or alteration for which notice is required by any other FAA regulation.").

Once the FAA has been given notice under Part 77, the FAA's Obstruction Evaluation Service has the responsibility for conducting an "obstruction evaluation" to determine the effect, if any, that the proposed construction or alteration would have on navigable airspace. *See* FAA Order JO 7400.2G, "Procedures for Handling Airspace Matters" The result of a study under Part 77 "is normally a determination as to whether the specific proposal studied would be a hazard to air navigation."

But even when the Obstruction Evaluation Service determines that the proposed construction or alteration would result in a "hazard to air navigation," the FAA has no authority to require the proposal to be altered. Rather, the hazard is noted in FAA publications (including, if applicable, the relevant Airport Master Record) so that pilots and other affected individuals are made aware of it. *See Aircraft Owners and Pilots Ass'n v. Fed. Aviation Admin.* (D.C. Cir. 1979) ("Once issued, a hazard/no-hazard determination has no enforceable legal effect. The FAA is not empowered to prohibit or limit proposed construction it deems dangerous to air navigation.").

Other agencies may condition their own actions on the outcome of an obstruction evaluation. For example, 49 U.S.C. § 44718(c) requires the FCC to consult with the FAA when considering whether to approve a new radio broadcast tower. Accordingly, the FCC requires that the FAA be given notice of any proposed broadcast towers over a certain height, see 47 C.F.R. § 17.7, and the FCC generally only authorizes construction if the FAA makes a "no hazard" determination. Likewise, when the FAA is given notice, the FAA's Airports Division conducts an "airport airspace analysis." This analysis considers:

> [T]the effects the proposed action would have on existing or contemplated traffic patterns of neighboring airports; the effects the proposed action would have on the existing airspace structure and projected programs of the FAA; and the effects that existing or proposed manmade objects and natural objects within the affected area would have on the airport proposal.

The airport airspace analysis results in a "determination" of the proposal—either "no objection," "conditional," or "objectionable"—but no matter the outcome of the analysis, the regulation is explicit that "[a] determination does not relieve the proponent of responsibility for compliance with any local law, ordinance or regulation, or state or other Federal regulation. Aeronautical studies and determinations will not consider environmental or land use compatibility impacts."

Finally, the FAA also has issued an order that deals with obstruction-related issues with even more specificity. *See* FAA Order JO 7400.2G, "Procedures for Handling Airspace Matters." And while Parts 77 and 157 and their authorizing statute, 49 U.S.C. § 44718, seem to apply just to proposals for alterations or new construction projects (as described above), Section 6-1-3 of the FAA Order explains that the FAA does conduct studies of existing structures, including trees, "when deemed necessary by the FAA." The FAA Order lists several situations "that may require obstruction evaluation of existing structures."

Such circumstances include "[d]etermining whether the FAA should recommend that an existing structure be altered or removed" and "[p]roviding technical assistance or information to a person, or government organization (Federal, state or local) expressing an interest in the structure and the FAA's responsibility associated with the structure's effect on the safe and efficient use of navigable airspace." In addition to the procedures outlined in Part 77 and Part 157, a study of an existing structure may be initiated as a result of "information received or a situation observed"; a "request for study from ... a person with a valid interest in the matter"; and "[o]ther situations for which an aeronautical study would be appropriate." *See also* FAA, Obstruction Evaluation/Airport Airspace Analysis, *http://oeaaa.faa.gov* (providing more information on the FAA's "obstruction evaluation" and "airport airspace analysis" procedures).

It is undisputed that the FAA has not conducted any study of the trees at Goodspeed, much less determined that they are "hazards to air navigation." But even if the FAA had done so, the FAA has no authority to order that obstructions or hazards be remediated. And unlike airports licensed by the FAA under Part 139, Goodspeed is licensed only by the State of Connecticut, meaning that the FAA could not even condition Goodspeed's license on the removal of obstructions or hazards. Nor could the FAA place such a condition on the receipt of federal funds, for Goodspeed does not receive any. Thus, any potential threat to Goodspeed's continued licensed operation must come from the DOT's exercise of its authority to revoke licenses for the failure to "maintain or use" the Airport "in accordance with" Connecticut's laws and regulations regarding aviation.

From the record, it appears that the closest that DOT has come to revoking Goodspeed's license was in the late 1970s and early 1980s. In a letter dated May 2, 1977, which was sent to a former manager of Goodspeed, the DOT made four "recommendations" for the continued safe operation of the Airport. Chief among them was to "[r]epair or resurface [the] runway and ramp pavement." Also of concern were broken runway lights and an aircraft that was parked in a location that made it an obstruction to the primary surface. The final recommendation was to "[r]emove or lower trees to the south," which the DOT had determined constituted obstructions to the approach surface. As to this recommendation, however, the letter noted that "[i]f [removing or lowering the trees] is a problem, you may want to consider a displaced threshold. If you choose this alternative, we would be glad to work with you in determining the proper distance and markings." The letter concluded by warning Goodspeed that if the recommendations were not carried out by the subsequent inspection, the Airport's license would be revoked.

A letter sent the following year, after another inspection of the Airport, reveals that while the problems with the runway surface had been addressed (albeit inadequately), the trees remained the same height. The 1978 letter also ended with the admonition that "if these substandard conditions are allowed to continue, you may jeopardize the license to operate the Goodspeed Airport." The record is silent as to the next few years, but in a letter dated June 20, 1983, the DOT again warned Goodspeed that the condition of its runway surface, in particular, could jeopardize the Airport's license. As with the 1977 letter, both the 1978 and the 1983 letters suggested that Goodspeed consider a displaced threshold if it could not lower or remove obstructing trees.

Although not discussed during the testimony, sometime prior to an inspection on April 11, 1984, Goodspeed did, in fact, adopt a displaced threshold of 340 feet at its runway's southern end. With the displaced threshold installed, the approach ratio was returned to a 20-to-1 ratio. DOT Landing Area Inspection Reports from 1985 and 1988-1991 also state that the threshold of the southern runway was displaced.

In the ordinary case, of course, an airport owner is generally free to remove or lower trees that are on airport property without an order from DOT. In this case, however, the parties have stipulated that the trees at Goodspeed Airport, including those that constitute Part 77 obstructions, are located within wetlands protected by the State of Connecticut through the Wetlands Act, Conn. Gen. Stat. §§ 22a-36 through 22a-45, and the CEPA, Conn. Gen. Stat. §§ 22a-14 through 22a-20. Under Conn. Gen. Stat. § 22a-42, the East Haddam Wetlands Commission is charged with administering the Wetlands Act within East Haddam. As a consequence, before undertaking any "regulated activity" within the wetlands—including removing trees and other vegetation, see Conn. Gen. Stat. §§ 22a-38(13)—Goodspeed is required to obtain a permit from the East Haddam Wetlands Commission. *See* Conn. Gen. Stat. § 22a-42a. The failure to secure a permit before undertaking regulated activity is punishable by a fine. Additionally, removing trees or other vegetation from protected wetlands can constitute "pollution" and/or "destruction" of the wetlands under the CEPA, which grants standing to a variety of individuals to bring claims for equitable relief against the responsible individual(s).

It is undisputed that no one affiliated with Goodspeed has applied to the Wetlands Commission for a permit to remove any trees or vegetation on Airport property. Therefore, it is not possible to speculate as to how the Wetlands Commission would treat such an application. However, Mr. Ventres testified that the Wetlands Commission has granted permits to applicants wishing to cut or trim certain trees within protected wetlands in the past. Goodspeed has not produced any examples of the Wetlands Commission denying a permit request outright, and Mr. Ventres testified that, in his experience, the Wetlands Commission has never done so. That is to say, by its history, the Wetlands Commission does not have a flat prohibition on all trimming or cutting of trees in protected wetlands. In fact, the record suggests that the Wetlands Commission (through its enforcement officer, Mr. Ventres) allowed Goodspeed to trim trees and vegetation in the protected wetlands on numerous occasions in the past, apparently without a permit and without consequence (at least until Goodspeed went beyond merely trimming). Based on the record presented, the Court finds no evidence that the Wetlands Commission would prohibit all trimming or removal of the obstructing trees, although it may impose conditions on such activity to ameliorate damage to the protected wetlands.

While Mr. Mellon testified that he believes that the Airport's license remains under an implicit threat—that either he lower the obstructing trees or the DOT would revoke the license—the record does not support this supposition. The results of all of the many inspections of Goodspeed after 1983 do not contain any suggestion whatsoever that the Airport's license is in danger of revocation, even while the trees have continued growing and have reduced the approach to the runway's southern end to a 7-to-1 ratio. Moreover, the DOT letters from 1977, 1978 and 1983 are all explicit that the primary threat to Goodspeed's license was the poor condition of its runway, and not any Part 77 obstructions. To be sure, many of the more recent DOT Landing Area Inspection Reports recommend that Goodspeed continue to trim the surrounding vegetation—as it clearly had been doing, and which it could potentially resume with the permission of the Wetlands Commission—but none of the Inspection Reports suggests that the Airport's license is in any danger if it did not do so, even as the trees continued to encroach further and further into the imaginary surfaces established by Part 77.

Finally, and not insignificantly, both Goodspeed's expert on airport safety, Mr. Downar, and the pilot with presumably the most experience flying into and out of Goodspeed Airport, Mr. Rutledge, testified that the Airport is not unsafe. Indeed, Mr. Rutledge testified that he has every intention of continuing to base the operation of Action Airlines—the only "air carrier" currently operating out of Goodspeed—at the Airport into the foreseeable future. On the basis of the evidence presented, the Court finds that the obstructing trees that Goodspeed wishes to lower or remove do not pose a present-day threat to its continued operation as an airport.

CONCLUSIONS OF LAW

Goodspeed has brought claims of field preemption and express preemption only. First, it argues that because the Wetlands Act and the CEPA regulate the removal of obstructions in navigable airspace, they are facially preempted by the Federal Aviation Act and the Part 77 regulations promulgated thereunder. Second, Goodspeed argues that the express preemption clause of the federal Airline Deregulation Act ("ADA") applies to invalidate the two state statutes because they have an impermissible effect on air carriers utilizing the airport. Goodspeed is not pursuing any claim of conflict preemption in this case, and therefore the Court expresses no view on that subject. However, as is explained below, the Court disagrees with Goodspeed, and holds that the neither the Wetlands Act nor the CEPA is either field preempted or expressly preempted.

A. Implied (Field) Preemption

The Supremacy Clause of the United States Constitution, article VI, clause 2, declares that "the laws of the United States ... shall be the supreme law of the land," thereby "invalidat[ing] state laws that interfere with, or are contrary to, federal law." When considering a claim of federal preemption, a court's principal focus is discerning whether Congress intended to displace an area of state law.

Congressional intent to preempt state law can be either express or implied. Express preemption, discussed in the next section, is present when "a federal statute expressly directs that state law be ousted." Implied preemption comes in two varieties, known as field preemption and conflict preemption. Conflict preemption arises when state law "actually conflicts with federal law," such that it is not possible to comply with both and "state law stands as an obstacle to the accomplishment" of the congressional objective. Field preemption, on the other hand, is present under circumstances where it is clear that Congress intended for its regulation of a particular area (or "field") to be the only regulation, to which states and localities may not add or detract. Courts infer the presence of this congressional intent when "the pervasiveness of the federal regulation precludes supplementation by the States, where the federal interest in the field is sufficiently dominant, or where the object sought to be obtained by the federal law and the character of obligations imposed by it ... reveal the same purpose."

Goodspeed's field preemption argument is based on the Federal Aviation Act, 49 U.S.C. § 40101 *et seq.*, and the FAA's regulations on obstructions, codified at 14 C.F.R. Part 77. The task of this Court, then, is two-fold: first, to determine whether Congress intended to occupy the entire field of aviation safety, as Goodspeed argues; and, if so, to determine whether the Wetlands Act and the CEPA are within the scope of the preempted field. As explained below, the Court answers the former question in the affirmative, but reaches the opposite conclusion with regard to the latter.

With these principles in mind, and mindful of the Supreme Court's warning that "prior cases on preemption are not precise guidelines ..., for each case turns on the peculiarities and specific features of the federal regulatory scheme in question," the Court now turns to consideration of the laws at issue. To begin, the Court agrees that the Federal Aviation Act evidences a clear congressional intent to occupy the entire field of aviation safety to the exclusion of state law. The Federal Aviation Act declares that "[t]he United States Government has exclusive sovereignty of airspace of the United States," and directs the FAA Administrator to "develop plans and policy for the use of the navigable airspace and assign by regulation or order the use of the airspace necessary to ensure the safety of aircraft and the efficient use of airspace."

"'Navigable airspace' is defined broadly as 'airspace above the minimum altitudes of flight prescribed by regulations ..., including airspace needed to ensure safety in the takeoff and landing of aircraft.'" 49 U.S.C. § 40102(a)(32). The primary purpose of the Federal Aviation Act is safety through the "creat[ion] and enforce[ment of] one unified system of flight rules." As Congress explained in passing the Federal Aviation Act in 1958:

> [A]viation is unique among transportation industries in its relation to the federal government—it is the only one whose operations are conducted almost wholly within federal jurisdiction, and are subject to little or no regulation by States or local authorities. Thus, the federal government bears virtually complete responsibility for the promotion and supervision of this industry in the public interest.

Accordingly, the Secretary of Transportation is charged with "assigning and maintaining safety as the highest priority in air commerce." In response to this congressional mandate, the FAA has established a comprehensive regulatory scheme "addressing virtually all areas of air safety," including the certification of aircraft, most airports, pilots and mechanics; air traffic control systems; air navigation and communication; and airspace classifications.

However, while the conclusion that Congress intended to occupy the entire field of aviation safety is a necessary condition for the success of Goodspeed's field preemption argument, it is not sufficient. The essence of Goodspeed's argument is that since the trees it wishes to remove penetrate "navigable airspace," over which the federal government has exclusive dominion, Connecticut is powerless to interfere in any way with whatever the Airport wishes to do to remove or lower the trees. The scope of Congress's preemption of state law does not necessarily sweep this broadly. Courts have long distinguished between state laws that directly affect aeronautical safety, on the one hand, and facially neutral laws of general application that have merely an incidental impact on aviation safety.

Logically, there must be a limit to the preemptive effect of federal law, even in an area, like aeronautical safety, where Congress has expressed an intention to occupy the "entire" field. Otherwise, a virtually unlimited number of state and local laws and regulations that might conceivably touch upon the operation of airports, even to a negligible degree, could be said to have some impact on aviation safety, assuming one is willing to retreat far enough up the chain of causation. As the Supreme Court has repeatedly emphasized, the limiting principle is the intent of Congress. Consideration of the issues raised by this case, and application of the presumption against finding federal preemption of state laws on health and safety, leads inexorably to the conclusion that neither the Wetlands Act nor the CEPA fall within the preemptive scope of federal law regulating aviation safety.

The state laws challenged by Goodspeed—environmental laws that make no reference whatsoever to aviation or aviation safety—are certainly deserving of the presumption against preemption. Neither statute expresses any intent to directly regulate airport operations or aeronautical safety. Instead, the Wetlands Act was passed to prevent a variety of deleterious effects brought about by the unregulated use of Connecticut's wetlands and watercourses—"an indispensable and irreplaceable but fragile natural resource with which the citizens of the state have been endowed"—that were occurring through the "deposition, filling or removal of material, the diversion or obstruction of water flow, the erection of structures and other uses, all of which have despoiled, polluted and eliminated wetlands and watercourses." The CEPA evidences a complementary intent to protect the "public trust in the air, water and other natural resources of the state of Connecticut."

Goodspeed has not argued, and nor could it, that Congress's intent in enacting the Federal Aviation Act was to preempt all state laws, such as these, whose express purpose are environmental protection. Rather, Goodspeed argues that, in this case, "[t]he relevant inquiry is whether the effect of the state law is such that it impacts the field of air safety and aircraft operations." The crux of Goodspeed's argument is that "state environmental laws that prohibit the removal of obstructions to air navigation, obstructions which are situated directly at the end of a runway, surely have an effect on air safety and aircraft operations, two areas solely within the province of the federal government," and are thereby preempted.

While Goodspeed is no doubt correct that, in the abstract, state laws that prohibit the removal of such obstructions would "have an effect on air safety and aircraft operations," Goodspeed's argument suffers a fatal flaw. The argument is misleadingly premised on "state environmental laws that prohibit the removal of obstructions to air navigation." But neither the Wetlands Act nor the CEPA contains such a prohibition. Rather, the Wetlands Act merely requires that Goodspeed obtain a permit before attempting to remove or trim the trees in question. The statute contains no outright prohibition on undertaking regulated activity, and as Mr. Ventres testified, the East Haddam Wetlands Commission has never applied the law in that manner. Similarly, the CEPA simply prohibits the Airport from "unreasonabl[y] pollut[ing], impair[ing] or destr[oying]" the "air, water and other natural resources of the state."

Thus, the "relevant inquiry" is not as Goodspeed presents it, but rather, whether state environmental laws that impose a permitting requirement on the removal of trees in protected wetlands and prohibit unreasonable environmental degradation are field preempted by federal law that is meant to ensure aviation safety. Presented appropriately, the answer to this question is certainly "no." There is nothing in the text or legislative history of the Federal Aviation Act that even hints at the congressional intent that Goodspeed asserts can be found therein.

For sure, Congress intended that safety be "the highest priority in air commerce." But accepting Goodspeed's field preemption argument would require the conclusion that Congress intended to completely eviscerate all attempts by states to protect their own environmental integrity whenever those attempts would have an indirect, incidental, or even speculative impact on the operations of an airport within its boundaries. In this case, it would mean Congress intended to preempt state wetlands protections regardless of whether, for example, the protected trees pose an actual threat to air safety and/or the Airport's continued operation, and regardless of the impact Goodspeed's actions may have on the surrounding environment. There is absolutely no indication that this is what Congress intended when it passed the Federal Aviation Act—and nor would Congress have needed to intend such a dramatic alteration of the federal/state balance of power to effectuate its purpose in passing the Act.

Rather, it is much more consistent with the values inherent in our federal system for Congress to have intended for its regulation of aviation safety to preempt only those state laws that either a) have the purpose or effect of directly regulating an aspect of air safety; or b) are actually shown, on an as-applied basis, to impact the unified regulation of air safety. The Court has already explained that the state laws at issue here do not have the purpose of directly regulating any aspect of air safety, and Goodspeed has not shown that the permitting requirement of the Wetlands Act or the CEPA's prohibition on environmental degradation have that impermissible effect, either. Therefore, since Goodspeed has chosen not to bring an as-applied challenge, there is no basis for concluding that either state law is preempted.

This holding is supported by the conclusions other courts have reached in adjudicating similar cases. For example, in *City of Burbank v. Lockheed Air Terminal, Inc.*, the Supreme Court held that with the passage of the Federal Aviation Act and the Noise Control Act, 49 U.S.C. § 1431 *et seq.*, Congress occupied the entire field of aircraft noise regulation, thereby invalidating the City of Burbank's attempt to curtail aircraft noise by placing curfews on aircraft flights at the Holloway-Burbank Airport. The Court found that "the pervasive nature of the scheme of federal regulation of aircraft noise ... leads us to conclude that there is pre-emption" of the City's ordinance—which was an unabashed attempt to directly regulate in the very same field addressed by Congress. The Supreme Court explained that "[i]f we were to uphold the Burbank ordinance and a significant number of municipalities followed suit, it is obvious that fractionalized control of the timing of takeoffs and landings would severely limit the flexibility of FAA in controlling air traffic flow."

While ultimately deciding the case only on express preemption grounds, the Second Circuit expressed a similar concern over "fractionalized control," noting that were it to uphold the State of New York's Passenger Bill of Rights—which required airlines to provide food, water, electricity, and restrooms to passengers during lengthy ground delays—that would mean that "another state could be free to enact a law prohibiting the service of soda on flights departing from its airports, while another could require allergen-free food options on its outbound flights, unraveling the centralized federal framework for air travel." The Ninth Circuit used the same logic to find preempted a state law claim that would have required airlines to warn passengers about the dangers of deep-vein thrombosis during long flights, explaining that "[i]f the FAA did not impliedly preempt state requirements for passenger warnings, each state would be free to require any announcement it wished on all planes arriving in, or departing from, its soil."

Upholding the state laws challenged here, by contrast, would risk no such "fractionalized control" of any aspect of air safety by the FAA, particularly since airport operators are free to bring as-applied challenges based on an actual conflict between the state laws and the objectives of the Federal Aviation Act. On this point, the Court finds instructive the actions of the FAA in dealing with the evidently common challenge posed by tree obstructions at airports. Rather than ordering that trees be removed—even at airports that it is statutorily-authorized to license—the FAA only requires that the obstructions be noted and/or studied so that pilots can be given appropriate notice. To be sure, the FAA does occasionally condition federal funds or licenses on an airport taking steps to remediate obstructions, but it generally relies on the notice provisions, together with "moral suasion," to bring about compliance with its guidelines on obstructions.

Although the Court does not doubt that trees as obstructions do pose a risk to aircraft, the FAA's relatively restrained attempts at regulating the presence of trees supports the conclusion that requiring airport owners to get a permit to remove trees does not unduly undermine the federal government's regulation of airport safety. To put it another way, were other states to adopt laws identical to the Wetlands Act and the CEPA, there is no evidence that the result would be "fractionalized control" of air safety that concerned the Supreme Court in *Burbank*. In fact, a number of states do have laws quite similar to those at issue here, and Mr. Downar testified that he has worked with local bodies like the Wetlands Commission to obtain permission to undertake regulated activity at other airports in the region.

Nonetheless, and as a testament to the flexibility of our federal system, examining courts have generally found that these laws regulating land use can co-exist with federal aviation law—at least in regards to principles of field preemption—so long as neither their purpose nor their effect encroaches into the field of airspace management or safety. *See, e.g., Gustafson v. City of Lake Angelus*, (6th Cir. 1996) (finding the Federal Aviation Act did not preempt a municipality exercising its authority to regulate the creation of new airports because "the designation of plane landing ... is a matter left primarily to local control," and noting that "[t]he FAA has acknowledged that land use matters within the federal aviation framework are intrinsically local"); *Condor Corp. v. City of St. Paul*, (8th Cir. 1990) (same holding); *Hoagland v. Town of Clear Lake*, (N.D. Ind. 2004) (same); *Faux-Burhans v. County Comm'rs of Frederick County*, (D. Md. 1987) (holding that county zoning regulations that affect private airfield management are not preempted by federal law because they do not affect flight operations within navigable airspace, and noting that "no federal law gives a citizen the right to operate an airport free of local zoning control"); *Dallas/Fort Worth Int'l Airport Bd. v. City of Irving*, (Tex. Ct. App. 1993) (holding that local zoning laws were not preempted by an established airport's attempt to expand by acquiring adjacent land).

B. Express Preemption

Goodspeed's argument that the Wetlands Act and the CEPA are expressly preempted, at least insofar as they regulate the removal of trees that are "obstructions," is based on the Airline Deregulation Act ("ADA"). Prior to passage of the ADA, the Civil Aeronautics Board, a federal agency, exercised exclusive control over pricing in the airline industry. With passage of the ADA in 1978, Congress sought to improve the service and efficiency of the airline industry through deregulation and increased market competition amongst air carriers. *See Morales v. Trans World Airlines, Inc.* (1992). The ADA's express preemption clause was included "[t]o ensure that the States would not undo [this] deregulation with regulation of their own." The ADA's express preemption clause, found at 49 U.S.C. § 41713(b)(1), states in relevant part:

> Except as provided in this subsection, a State, political subdivision of a State, or political authority of at least 2 States may not enact or enforce a law, regulation, or other provision having the force and effect of law related to a price, route, or service of an air carrier that may provide air transportation ...

It is worth emphasizing that it is the effect on the "price, route or service" of an air carrier—not an airport—that is prohibited by the ADA. The act defines an "air carrier" as "a citizen of the United States undertaking by any means, directly or indirectly, to provide air transportation" as a common carrier for compensation. The only "air carrier" that Goodspeed has identified as utilizing the Airport at present is Mr. Rutledge's company, JIB, Inc., which does business as Action Airlines.

Express preemption arises when "a federal statute expressly directs that state law be ousted," which the ADA no doubt does. The inclusion of the "related to" language in the express preemption clause has been interpreted expansively to preempt even state laws that have an "indirect" effect on rates, routes, or services. In *Morales*, the Supreme Court construed the ADA's preemption clause *in pari materia* with the preemption provision of the Employee Retirement Income Security Act ("ERISA"), 29 U.S.C. § 1144(a), and concluded that "[s]tate enforcement actions having a connection with, or reference to airline 'rates, routes, or services' are pre-empted." In applying this interpretation to invalidate the state consumer fraud statute at issue, the Court held that the requisite connection exists where the law has a "forbidden significant effect" upon the price, route or services of an air carrier. The Court emphasized, however, that while merely "indirect" effects of a state law can be enough to find express preemption, there are limits: the impact of some state actions would have an effect that is "too tenuous, remote, or peripheral to have pre-emptive effect.:

Goodspeed does not claim that either the Wetlands Act or the CEPA directly "relate to" or "reference" the "rates, routes, or services" of an air carrier. Nor could it. Rather, Goodspeed argues that by regulating the removal of obstructions at the Airport (trees), the state laws have a sufficient "connection" to—and have a "significant and adverse impact" on—the "rates, routes, or services" of air carriers. Goodspeed, citing Mr. Stannard's testimony, argues that the DOT could revoke its license if obstructions make the airport unsafe. Goodspeed then relies on Mr. Rutledge's testimony to argue that if the Airport is closed, Action Airlines would have to utilize other area airports instead, which would increase the rates it charges customers. Finally, the Airport argues that Mr. Rutledge's testimony suggested that at least one alternative to lowering the trees—

installing a displaced threshold—could affect his operations as well, depending on the how much the threshold was displaced. Either outcome—closing the Airport or using a displaced threshold—Goodspeed argues, would have the requisite "significant and adverse impact" on the "rates, routes, or services" of an air carrier necessary to find express preemption.

The Court disagrees. Not only would the state laws' impact on Mr. Rutledge's operations be indirect, but they are entirely speculative and, in fact, unsupported by the evidentiary record. Although it is no doubt true that the loss of Goodspeed's operating license would have an impact on Action Airlines, the Airport has presented no evidence to suggest that the obstructing trees are actually jeopardizing its operating license. First and most critically, the Airport has yet to seek a permit from the East Haddam Wetlands Commission to remove or trim the trees in question. If, for example, the Wetlands Commission permits Goodspeed to remove or lower the trees such that they are no longer "obstructions" under Part 77, then obviously the state law would have no impact on the Airport's continued operation. While Goodspeed may think this possibility remote, the Court credits Mr. Ventres' testimony in finding it probable that the Wetlands Commission would permit the Airport to undertake at least some of the trimming and cutting that it wishes to undertake, albeit under conditions that minimize harm to the environment. This possibility alone is sufficient for the Court to hold that the state law is not preempted, at least on the record.

Second, even if the Wetlands Commission were to forbid completely the Airport from undertaking any "regulated activity"—speculation that, again, is not supported by the evidentiary record—there is nothing in the record to support Goodspeed's claim that the obstructing trees have put its license in danger of revocation. For example, Mr. Stannard merely reaffirmed the uncontroverted fact that the DOT has the authority to revoke an airport license if the airport is unsafe for continued operation. And while Mr. Stannard did testify that "obstructions to approach slopes to airport runways" are "a safety issue," he did not testify that the trees that constitute "obstructions" at Goodspeed are sufficiently serious to threaten the Airport's license. In fact, Mr. Stannard conducted the 1999 inspection of Goodspeed Airport, during which he noted that obstructing trees at the Airport had reduced the approach slope to the runway to 7-to-1 (whereas 20-to-1 is the preferred slope), but he said nothing to suggest that this jeopardized Goodspeed's license. He did recommend that the trees be removed to maximize the Airport safety, *see id.*, but in his deposition, he explicitly disavowed any authority for the DOT or the FAA to "trump the local regulatory boards with respect to work that needs to be done at an airport."

Moreover, the trees that Mr. Stannard recommended be removed in 1999 are still standing today, and the approach slope to Goodspeed's Airport remains at a 7-to-1 ratio. And yet, the Airport's license was renewed by the DOT within the last eight months, which necessarily reflects the DOT's judgment that the Airport remains safe in its present condition—a judgment that was echoed by the testimony of both Mr. Rutledge and

Goodspeed's expert on airport safety, Mr. Downar. And, as discussed previously, the DOT letters from 1977, 1978, and 1983, all of which threatened the Airport's license for substandard conditions, are both far too remote in time and in subject matter to create a present-day threat to Goodspeed's license. Therefore, Goodspeed has not presented sufficient evidence to find that the state laws regulating the removal of obstructing trees at the Airport create any impact on the "rates, routes, or services" of an air carrier—much less an "adverse and significant" one.

Finally, Goodspeed's argument that the use of a displaced threshold in lieu of removing the trees would have a significant and prohibited effect on the "rates, routes, or services" of air carriers is similarly unpersuasive. Goodspeed submitted no evidence regarding the degree to which the threshold would have to be displaced to accommodate the presence of the trees, and therefore Mr. Rutledge's testimony that a displaced threshold could affect his operations, depending on how much shorter it made the runway, is simply too speculative to find that the impact would be significant. The record reflects that Goodspeed utilized a displaced threshold of as much as 340 feet for a number of years in the late 1980s and 1990s, and yet there is no evidence that this had an adverse effect on the "rates, routes, or services" of an air carrier (and Mr. Rutledge's company has operated out of the Airport since 1979).

Mr. Mellon's testimony that he believes a displaced threshold may make the Airport unsafe is also not supported by the record. The fact that the Airport remained operational throughout the time period in which it had a displaced threshold necessary reflects the judgment of DOT that shortening the runway to that extent did not make the Airport unsafe, and there is no reason to think that DOT would not reach the same conclusion should Goodspeed reinstate the displaced threshold today. Moreover, Goodspeed has not even attempted to light the trees, which the testimony established would be another way of addressing the safety concerns created by the obstructing trees.

Again, the Court emphasizes that it is not advocating that Goodspeed or the East Haddam Wetlands Commission ignore the safety risks associated with the tree obstructions located at the Airport; indeed, the Court thinks it prudent for Goodspeed to work in a cooperative manner with the Wetlands Commission to address that subset of the obstructing trees that present the greatest threats to aircraft safety. The Court merely holds that Goodspeed has not demonstrated that going through the Wetlands Commission's permitting process—or adhering to the state laws more generally—would have an adverse and significant impact on the "rates, routes, or prices" of an air carrier. Accordingly, the state laws are not expressly preempted by the ADA.

CONCLUSION

Based on the foregoing, the Court concludes that the Defendants' actions in regulating the removal of trees at Goodspeed Airport that are within the protected wetlands are neither field preempted by federal aviation law nor expressly preempted.

Airspace

SOVEREIGNTY AND USE OF AIRSPACE
49 U.S.C. § 40103

(a) ***Sovereignty and public right of transit.***

(1) The U.S. Government has exclusive sovereignty of airspace of the United States.

(2) A United States citizen has a public right of transit through the navigable airspace.

(b) ***Use of airspace.***

(1) The Administrator of the FAA Federal Aviation Administration shall develop plans and policy for the use of the navigable airspace and assign by regulation or order the use of the airspace necessary to ensure the safety of aircraft and the efficient use of airspace. The Administrator may modify or revoke an assignment when required in the public interest.

(2) The Administrator shall prescribe air traffic regulations on the flight of aircraft (including regulations on safe altitudes) for (a) navigating, protecting, and identifying aircraft; (b) protecting individuals and property on the ground; (c) using the navigable airspace efficiently; and (d) preventing collision between aircraft, between aircraft and land or water vehicles, and between aircraft and airborne objects.

(3) To establish security provisions that will encourage and allow maximum use of the navigable airspace by civil aircraft consistent with national security, the Administrator, in consultation with the Secretary of Defense, shall (a) establish areas in the airspace the Administrator decides are necessary in the interest of national defense; and (b) by regulation or order, restrict or prohibit flight of civil aircraft that the Administrator cannot identify, locate, and control with available facilities in those areas.

(c) ***Foreign aircraft***. A foreign aircraft, not part of the armed forces of a foreign country, may be navigated in the United States as provided in section 41703 of this title.

(d) ***Aircraft of armed forces of foreign countries***. Aircraft of a foreign armed forces may be navigated in the United States only when authorized by the Secretary of State.

UNITED STATES v. CAUSBY

328 U.S. 256 (1946)

Mr. Justice DOUGLAS delivered the opinion of the Court.

This is a case of first impression. The problem presented is whether respondents' property was taken within the meaning of the Fifth Amendment by frequent and regular flights of army and navy aircraft over respondents' land at low altitudes.

Respondents own 2.8 acres near an airport outside of Greensboro, North Carolina. It has on it a dwelling house, and also various outbuildings which were mainly used for raising chickens. The end of the airport's northwest-southeast runway is 2,220 feet from respondents' barn and 2,275 feet from their house. The path of glide to this runway passes directly over the property, which is 100 feet wide and 1,200 feet long. The 30 to 1 safe glide angle approved by the Civil Aeronautics Authority passes over this property at 83 feet, which is 67 feet above the house, 63 feet above the barn and 18 feet above the highest tree. The use by the United States of this airport is pursuant to a lease executed in May, 1942, for a term commencing June 1, 1942 and ending June 30, 1942, with a provision for renewals until June 30, 1967, or six months after the end of the national emergency, whichever is the earlier.

Various aircraft of the United States use this airport—bombers, transports and fighters. The direction of the prevailing wind determines when a particular runway is used. The north-west-southeast runway in question is used about four per cent of the time in taking off and about seven per cent of the time in landing. Since the United States began operations in May, 1942, its four-motored heavy bombers, other planes of the heavier type, and its fighter planes have frequently passed over respondents' land buildings in considerable numbers and rather close together. They come close enough at times to appear barely to miss the tops of the trees and at times so close to the tops of the trees as to blow the old leaves off. The noise is startling. And at night the glare from the planes brightly lights up the place.

As a result of the noise, respondents had to give up their chicken business. As many as six to ten of their chickens were killed in one day by flying into the walls from fright. The total chickens lost in that manner was about 150. Production also fell off. The result was the destruction of the use of the property as a commercial chicken farm. Respondents are frequently deprived of their sleep and the family has become nervous and frightened. Although there have been no airplane accidents on respondents' property, there have been several accidents near the airport and close to respondents' place. These are the essential facts found by the Court of Claims. On the basis of these facts, it found that respondents' property had depreciated in value. It held that the United States had taken an easement over the property on June 1, 1942, and that the value of the property destroyed and the easement taken was $2,000.

The United States relies on the Air Commerce Act of 1926, as amended by the Civil Aeronautics Act of 1938. Under those statutes the United States has "complete and exclusive national sovereignty in the air space" over this country. They grant any citizen of the United States "a public right of freedom of transit in air commerce through the navigable air space of the United States." And "navigable air space" is defined as "airspace above the minimum safe altitudes of flight prescribed by the Civil Aeronautics Authority." And it is provided that "such navigable airspace shall be subject to a public right of freedom of interstate and foreign air navigation." It is, therefore, argued that since these flights were within the minimum safe altitudes of flight which had been prescribed, they were an exercise of the declared right of travel through the airspace.

The United States concludes that when flights are made within the navigable airspace without any physical invasion of the property of the landowners, there has been no taking of property. It says that at most there was merely incidental damage occurring as a consequence of authorized air navigation. It also argues that the landowner does not own superadjacent airspace which he has not subjected to possession by the erection of structures or other occupancy. Moreover, it is argued that even if the United States took airspace owned by respondents, no compensable damage was shown. Any damages are said to be merely consequential for which no compensation may be obtained under the Fifth Amendment.

It is ancient doctrine that at common law ownership of the land extended to the periphery of the universe—*Cujus est solum ejus est usque ad coelum*. But that doctrine has no place in the modern world. The air is a public highway, as Congress has declared. Were that not true, every transcontinental flight would subject the operator to countless trespass suits. Common sense revolts at the idea. To recognize such private claims to the airspace would clog these highways, seriously interfere with their control and development in the public interest, and transfer into private ownership that to which only the public has a just claim.

But that general principle does not control the present case. For the government conceded that if the flights over respondents' property rendered it uninhabitable, there would be a taking compensable under the Fifth Amendment. It is the owner's loss, not the taker's gain, which is the measure of the value of the property taken. Market value fairly determined is the normal measure of the recovery. And that value may reflect the use to which the land could readily be converted, as well as the existing use. If, by reason of the frequency and altitude of the flights, respondents could not use this land for any purpose, their loss would be complete. It would be as complete as if the United States had entered upon the surface of the land and taken exclusive possession of it.

We agree that in those circumstances there would be a taking. Though it would be only an easement of flight which was taken, that easement, if permanent and not merely temporary, normally would be the equivalent of a fee interest. It would be a definite exercise of complete dominion and control over the surface of the land. The fact that the planes never touched the surface would be as irrelevant as the absence in this day of the feudal livery of seisin on the transfer of real estate. The owner's right to possess and exploit the land—that is to say, his beneficial ownership of it—would be destroyed. It would not be a case of incidental damages arising from a legalized nuisance such as was involved in *Richards v. Washington Terminal Co.* (1914). In that case property owners whose lands adjoined a railroad line were denied recovery for damages resulting from the noise, vibrations, smoke and the like, incidental to the operations of the trains. In the supposed case the line of flight is over the land. And the land is appropriated as directly and completely as if it were used for the runways themselves.

There is no material difference between the supposed case and the present one, except that here enjoyment and use of the land are not completely destroyed. But that does not seem to us to be controlling. The path of glide for airplanes might reduce a valuable factory site to grazing land, an orchard to a vegetable patch, a residential section to a wheat field. Some value would remain. But the use of the airspace immediately above the land would limit the utility of the land and cause a diminution in its value. That was the philosophy of *Portsmouth Harbor Land & Hotel Co. v. United States* (1922). In that case the petition alleged that the United States erected a fort on nearby land, established a battery and a fire control station there, and fired guns over petitioner's land. The Court, speaking through Mr. Justice Holmes, reversed the Court of Claims which dismissed the petition on a demurrer, holding that "the specific facts set forth would warrant a finding that a servitude has been imposed."

The fact that the path of glide taken by the planes was that approved by the Civil Aeronautics Authority does not change the result. The navigable airspace which Congress has placed in the public domain is "airspace above the minimum safe altitudes of flight prescribed by the Civil Aeronautics Authority." If that agency prescribed 83 feet as the minimum safe altitude, then we would have presented the question of the validity of the regulation. But nothing of the sort has been done. The path of glide governs the method of operating—of landing or taking off. The altitude required for that operation is not the minimum safe altitude of flight which is the downward reach of the navigable airspace. The minimum prescribed by the authority is 500 feet during the day and 1000 feet at night for air carriers (Civil Air Regulations, Pt. 61, §§ 61.7400, 61.7401) and from 300 to 1000 feet for other aircraft depending on the type of plane and the character of the terrain.

Hence, the flights in question were not within the navigable airspace which Congress placed within the public domain. If any airspace needed for landing or taking off were included, flights which were so close to the land as to render it uninhabitable would be immune. But the United States concedes, as we have said, that in that event there would be a taking. Thus, it is apparent that the path of glide is not the minimum safe altitude of flight within the meaning of the statute. The Civil Aeronautics Authority has, of course, the power to prescribe air traffic rules. But Congress has defined navigable airspace only in terms of one of them—the minimum safe altitudes of flight.

We have said that the airspace is a public highway. Yet it is obvious that if the landowner is to have full enjoyment of the land, he must have exclusive control of the immediate reaches of the enveloping atmosphere. Otherwise buildings could not be erected, trees could not be planted, and even fences could not be run. The principle is recognized when the law gives a remedy in case overhanging structures are erected on adjoining land. The landowner owns at least as much of the space above the ground as the can occupy or use in connection with the land. The fact that he does not occupy it in a physical sense—by the erection of buildings and the like—is not material. As we have said, the flight of airplanes, which skim the surface but do not touch it, is as much an appropriation of the use of the land as a more conventional entry upon it.

We would not doubt that if the United States erected an elevated railway over respondents' land at the precise altitude where its planes now fly, there would be a partial taking, even though none of the supports of the structure rested on the land. The reason is that there would be an intrusion so immediate and direct as to subtract from the owner's full enjoyment of the property and to limit his exploitation of it. While the owner does not in any physical manner occupy that stratum of airspace or make use of it in the conventional sense, he does use it in somewhat the same sense that space left between buildings for the purpose of light and air is used. The superadjacent airspace at this low altitude is so close to the land that continuous invasions of it affect the use of the surface of the land itself. We think that the landowner, as an incident to his ownership, has a claim to it and that invasions of it are in the same category as invasions of the surface.

In this case, as in *Portsmouth Harbor Land & Hotel Co*., the damages were not merely consequential. They were the product of a direct invasion of respondents' domain. As stated in *United States v. Cress* (1917), "it is the character of the invasion, not the amount of damage resulting from it, so long as the damage is substantial, that determines the question whether it is a taking." We said in *United States v. Powelson* (1943), that while the meaning of "property" as used in the Fifth Amendment was a federal question, "it will normally obtain its content by reference to local law." If we look to North Carolina law, we reach the same result. Sovereignty in the airspace rests in the State "except where granted to and assumed by the United States."

The flight of aircraft is lawful "unless at such a low altitude as to interfere with the then existing use to which the land or water, or the space over the land or water, is put by the owner, or unless so conducted as to be imminently dangerous to persons or property lawfully on the land or water beneath." Subject to that right of flight, "ownership of the space above the lands and waters of this State is declared to be vested in the several owners of the surface beneath." Our holding that there was an invasion of respondents' property is thus not inconsistent with the local law governing a landowner's claim to the immediate reaches of the superadjacent airspace.

The airplane is part of the modern environment of life, and the inconveniences which it causes are normally not compensable under the Fifth Amendment. The airspace, apart from the immediate reaches above the land, is part of the public domain. We need not determine at this time what those precise limits are. Flights over private land are not a taking, unless they are so low and so frequent as to be a direct and immediate interference with the enjoyment and use of the land. We need not speculate on that phase of the present case. For the findings of the Court of Claims plainly establish that there was a diminution in value of the property and that the frequent, low-level flights were the direct and immediate cause. We agree with the Court of Claims that a servitude has been imposed upon the land.

The Court of Claims held, as we have noted, that an easement was taken. But the findings of fact contain no precise description as to its nature. It is not described in terms of frequency of flight, permissible altitude, or type of airplane. Nor is there a finding as to whether the easement taken was temporary or permanent. Yet an accurate description of the property taken is essential, since that interest vests in the United States. Since on this record it is not clear whether the easement taken is a permanent or a temporary one, it would be premature for us to consider whether the amount of the award made by the Court of Claims was proper. The judgment is reversed and the cause is remanded to the Court of Claims so that it may make the necessary findings in conformity with this opinion. Reversed.

Mr. Justice BLACK, dissenting.

The Fifth Amendment provides that "private property" shall not "be taken for public use, without just compensation."The Court holds today that the Government has "taken" respondents' property by repeatedly flying Army bombers directly above respondents' land at a height of eighty-three feet where the light and noise from these planes caused respondents to lose sleep and their chickens to be killed. Since the effect of the Court's decision is to limit, by the imposition of relatively absolute Constitutional barriers, possible future adjustments through legislation and regulation which might become necessary with the growth of air transportation, and since in my view the Constitution does not contain such barriers, I dissent.

The following is a brief statement of the background and of the events that the Court's opinion terms a "taking" within the meaning of the Fifth Amendment: Since 1928 there has been an airfield some eight miles from Greensboro, North Carolina. In April, 1942, this airport was taken over by the Greensboro-High Point Municipal Airport Authority and it has since then operated as a municipal airport. In 1942 the Government, by contract, obtained the right to use the field "concurrently, jointly, and in common" with other users.

Years before, in 1934, respondents had bought their property, located more than one-third of a mile from the airport. Private planes from the airport flew over their land and farm buildings from 1934 to 1942 and are still doing so. But though these planes disturbed respondents to some extent, Army bombers, which started to fly over the land in 1942 at a height of eighty-three feet, disturbed them more because they were larger, came over more frequently, made a louder noise, and at night a greater glare was caused by their lights. This noise and glare disturbed respondents' sleep, frightened them, and made them nervous. The noise and light also frightened respondents' chickens so much that many of them flew against buildings and were killed.

The Court's opinion seems to indicate that the mere flying of planes through the column of air directly above respondents' land does not constitute a "taking." Consequently, it appears to be noise and glare, to the extent and under the circumstances shown here, which make the government a seizer of private property. But the allegation of noise and glare resulting in damages, constitutes at best an action in tort where there might be recovery if the noise and light constituted a nuisance, a violation of a statute, or were the result of negligence. But the Government has not consented to be sued in the Court of Claims except in actions based on express or implied contract. And there is no implied contract here, unless by reason of the noise and glare caused by the bombers the Government can be said to have "taken" respondents' property in a Constitutional sense.

The concept of taking property as used in the Constitution has heretofore never been given so sweeping a meaning. The Court's opinion presents no case where a man who makes noise or shines light onto his neighbor's property has been ejected from that property for wrongfully taking possession of it. Nor would anyone take seriously a claim that noisy automobiles passing on a highway are taking wrongful possession of the homes located thereon, or that a city elevated train which greatly interferes with the sleep of those who live next to it wrongfully takes their property.

Even the one case in this Court which in considering the sufficiency of a complaint gave the most elastic meaning to the phrase "private property be taken" as used in the Fifth Amendment, did not go so far. *Portsmouth Harbor Land & Hotel Co.* I am not willing, nor do I think the Constitution and the decisions authorize me, to extend that phrase so as to guarantee an absolute Constitutional right to relief not subject to legislative change, which is based on averments that at best show mere torts committed by Government agents while flying over land. The future adjustment of the rights and remedies of property owners, which might be found necessary because of the flight of planes at safe altitudes, should, especially in view of the imminent expansion of air navigation, be left where I think the Constitution left it, with Congress.

Nor do I reach a different conclusion because of the fact that the particular circumstance which under the Court's opinion makes the tort here absolutely actionable, is the passing of planes through a column of air at an elevation of eighty-three feet directly over respondents' property. It is inconceivable to me that the Constitution guarantees that the airspace of this Nation needed for air navigation, is owned by the particular persons who happen to own the land beneath to the same degree as they own the surface below. No rigid Constitutional rule, in my judgment, commands that the air must be considered as marked off into separate compartments by imaginary metes and bounds in order to synchronize air ownership with land ownership.

I think that the Constitution entrusts Congress with full power to control all navigable airspace. Congress has already acted under that power. It has by statute provided that "the United States of America is to possess and exercise complete and exclusive national sovereignty in the air space (over) the United States." This was done under the assumption that the Commerce Clause of the Constitution gave Congress the same plenary power to control navigable airspace as its plenary power over navigable waters. To make sure that the airspace used for air navigation would remain free, Congress further declared that "navigable airspace shall be subject to a public right of freedom of interstate and foreign air navigation," and finally stated emphatically that there exists "a public right of freedom of transit through the navigable airspace of the United States." Congress thus declared that the air is free, not subject to private ownership, and not subject to delimitation by the courts. Congress and those acting under its authority were the only ones who had power to control and regulate the flight of planes. "Navigable air-space" was defined as "airspace above the minimum safe altitudes of flight prescribed by the Civil Aeronautics Authority."

Thus, Congress has given the Civil Aeronautics Authority exclusive power to determine what is navigable airspace subject to its exclusive control. This power derives specifically from the Section which authorizes the Authority to prescribe "air traffic rules governing the flight of, and for the navigation, protection, and identification of, aircraft, including rules as to safe altitudes of flight and rules for the prevention of collisions between aircraft, and between aircraft and land or water vehicles." Here there was no showing that the bombers flying over respondents' land violated any rule or regulation of the Civil Aeronautics Authority. Yet, unless we hold the Act unconstitutional, at least such a showing would be necessary before the courts could act without interfering with the exclusive authority which Congress gave to the administrative agency. Not even a showing that the Authority has not acted at all would be sufficient. For in that event, were the courts to have any authority to act in this case at all, they should stay their hand till the Authority has acted.

The broad provisions of the Congressional statute cannot properly be circumscribed by making a distinction as the Court's opinion does between rules of safe altitude of flight while on the level of cross-country flight and rules of safe altitude during landing and taking off. First, such a distinction cannot be maintained from the practical standpoint. It is unlikely that Congress intended that the Authority prescribe safe altitudes for planes making cross-country flights, while at the same time it left the more hazardous landing and take-off operations unregulated. The legislative history, moreover, clearly shows that the Authority's power to prescribe air traffic rules includes the power to make rules governing landing and take-off.

Nor is the Court justified in ignoring that history by labeling rules of safe altitude while on the level of cross-country flight as rules prescribing the safe altitude proper and rules governing take-off and landing as rules of operation. For the Conference Report explicitly states that such distinctions were purposely eliminated from the original House Bill in order that the Section on air traffic rules "might be given the broadest construction by the (Civil Aeronautics Authority) and the courts." In construing the statute narrowly the Court thwarts the intent of Congress. A proper broad construction, such as Congress commanded, would not permit the Court to decide what it has today without declaring the Act of Congress unconstitutional. I think the Act given the broad construction intended is constitutional.

That the rules for landing and take-off are rules prescribing "minimum safe altitudes of flight" is shown by the following further statement in the House Report: "the minimum safe altitudes of flight ... would vary with the terrain and location of cities and would coincide with the surface of the land or water at airports."

No greater confusion could be brought about in the coming age of air transportation than that which would result were courts by Constitutional interpretation to hamper Congress in its efforts to keep the air free. Old concepts of private ownership of land should not be introduced into the field of air regulation. I have no doubt that Congress will, if not handicapped by judicial interpretations of the Constitution, preserve the freedom of the air, and at the same time, satisfy the just claims of aggrieved persons. The noise of newer, larger, and more powerful planes may grow louder and louder and disturb people more and more. But the solution of the problems precipitated by these technological advances and new ways of living cannot come about through the application of rigid Constitutional restraints formulated and enforced by the courts.

What adjustments may have to be made, only the future can reveal. It seems certain, however, the courts do not possess the techniques or the personnel to consider and act upon the complex combinations of factors entering into the problems. The contribution of courts must be made through the awarding of damages for injuries suffered from the flying of planes, or by the granting of injunctions to prohibit their flying. When these two simple remedial devices are elevated to a Constitutional level under the Fifth Amendment, as the Court today seems to have done, they can stand as obstacles to better adapted techniques that might be offered by experienced experts and accepted by Congress. Today's opinion is, I fear, an opening wedge for an unwarranted judicial interference with the power of Congress to develop solutions for new and vital and national problems. In my opinion this case should be reversed on the ground that there has been no "taking" in the Constitutional sense.

CITY OF BURBANK v. LOCKHEED AIR TERMINAL, INC.

411 U.S. 624 (1973)

Mr. Justice DOUGLAS delivered the opinion of the Court.

This suit brought by appellees asked for an injunction against the enforcement of an ordinance adopted by the City Council of Burbank, California, which made it unlawful for a so-called pure jet aircraft to take off from the Hollywood-Burbank Airport between 11 P.M. of one day and 7 A.M. the next day, and making it unlawful for the operator of that airport to allow any such aircraft to take off from that airport during such periods. The only regularly scheduled flight affected by the ordinance was an intrastate flight of Pacific Southwest Airlines originating in Oakland, California, and departing from Hollywood-Burbank Airport for San Diego every Sunday night at 11:30.

The Federal Aviation Act of 1958, as amended by the Noise Control Act of 1972, and the regulations under it are central to the question of pre-emption. Section 1108(a) of the Federal Aviation Act provides in part, "[t]he United States of America is declared to possess and exercise complete and exclusive national sovereignty in the airspace of the United States ..." By law, the Administrator of the Federal Aviation Administration ("FAA") has been given broad authority to regulate the use of the navigable airspace, "in order to insure the safety of aircraft and the efficient utilization of such airspace ..." and "for the protection of persons and property on the ground ...

The Solicitor General, though arguing against pre-emption, concedes that as respects "airspace management" there is pre-emption. That, however, is a fatal concession, for as the District Court found: "The imposition of curfew ordinances on a nationwide basis would result in a bunching of flights in those hours immediately preceding the curfew. This bunching of flights during these hours would have the twofold effect of increasing an already serious congestion problem and actually increasing, rather than relieving, the noise problem by increasing flights in the period of greatest annoyance to surrounding communities. Such a result is totally inconsistent with the objectives of the federal statutory and regulatory scheme." It also found "(t)he imposition of curfew ordinances on a nationwide basis would cause a serious loss of efficiency in the use of the navigable airspace."

Curfews such as Burbank has imposed would, according to the testimony at the trial and the District Court's findings, increase congestion, cause a loss of efficiency, and aggravate the noise problem. The FAA has occasionally enforced curfews. *See Virginians for Dulles v. Volpe, D.C.* (1972). But the record shows that FAA has consistently opposed curfews, unless managed by it, in the interests of its management of the "navigable airspace." As stated by Judge Dooling in *American Airlines v. Hempstead, D.C.* (2d Cir. 1968):

> The aircraft and its noise are indivisible; the noise of the aircraft extends outward from it with the same inseparability as its wings and tail assembly; to exclude the aircraft noise from the Town is to exclude the aircraft; to set a ground level decibel limit for the aircraft is directly to exclude it from the lower air that it cannot use without exceeding the decibel limit.

The Noise Control Act of 1972, which was approved October 27, 1972, also involves the Environmental Protection Agency ("EPA") in the comprehensive scheme of federal control of the aircraft noise problem. There is, to be sure, no express provision of pre-emption in the 1972 Act. That, however, is not decisive. As we stated in *Rice v. Santa Fe Elevator Corp.*:

> Congress legislated here in a field which the States have traditionally occupied. So we start with the assumption that the historic police powers of the States were not to be superseded by the Federal Act unless that was the clear and manifest purpose of Congress. Such a purpose may be evidenced in several ways.
>
> The scheme of federal regulation may be so pervasive as to make reasonable the inference that Congress left no room for the States to supplement it. Or the Act of Congress may touch a field in which the federal interest is so dominant that the federal system will be assumed to preclude enforcement of state laws on the same subject. Likewise, the object sought to be obtained by the federal law and the character of obligations imposed by it may reveal the same purpose. Or the state policy may produce a result inconsistent with the objective of the federal statute.

It is the pervasive nature of the scheme of federal regulation of aircraft noise that leads us to conclude that there is pre-emption. As Mr. Justice Jackson stated, concurring in *Northwest Airlines, Inc. v. Minnesota* (1944): "Federal control is intensive and exclusive. Planes do not wander about in the sky like vagrant clouds. They move only by federal permission, subject to federal inspection, in the hands of federally certified personnel and under an intricate system of federal commands. The moment a ship taxis onto a runway it is caught up in an elaborate and detailed system of controls."

Both the Senate and House Committees included in their Reports clear statements that the bills would not change the existing pre-emption rule. The House Report stated: "No provision of the bill is intended to alter in any way the relationship between the authority of the Federal Government and that of the State and local governments that existed with respect to matters covered by section 611 of the Federal Aviation Act of 1958 prior to the enactment of the bill." The Senate Report stated: "States and local governments are preempted from establishing or enforcing noise emission standards for aircraft unless such standards are identical to standards prescribed under this bill. This does not address responsibilities or powers of airport operators, and no provision of the bill is intended to alter in any way the relationship between the authority of the Federal government and that of State and local governments that existed with respect to matters covered by section 611 of the Federal Aviation Act of 1958 prior to the enactment of the bill."

These statements do not avail appellants. Prior to the 1972 Act, § 611(a) provided that the Administrator "shall prescribe and amend such rules and regulations as he may find necessary to provide for the control and abatement of aircraft noise and sonic boom." Under § 611(b)(3) the Administrator was required to "consider whether any proposed standard, rule, or regulation is consistent with the highest degree of safety in air commerce or air transportation in the public interest." When the legislation which added this section to the Federal Aviation Act was considered at Senate hearings, Senator Monroney (the author of the 1958 Act) asked Secretary of Transportation Boyd whether the proposed legislation would "to any degree preempt State and local government regulation of aircraft noise and sonic boom." The Secretary requested leave to submit a written opinion, and in a letter dated June 22, 1968, he stated:

> The courts have held that the Federal Government presently preempts the field of noise regulation insofar as it involves controlling the flight of aircraft ... R. 3400 would merely expand the Federal Government's role in a field already preempted. It would not change this preemption. State and local governments will remain unable to use their police powers to control aircraft noise by regulating the flight of aircraft.

According to the Senate Report, it was "not the intent of the committee in recommending this legislation to effect any change in the existing apportionment of powers between the Federal and State and local governments," and the Report concurred in the views set forth by the Secretary in his letter. The letter from the Secretary of Transportation also expressed the view that "the proposed legislation will not affect the rights of a State or local public agency, as the proprietor of an airport, from issuing regulations or establishing requirements as to the permissible level of noise which can be created by aircraft using the airport. Airport owners acting as proprietors can presently deny the use of their airports to aircraft on the basis of noise considerations so long as such exclusion is nondiscriminatory." This portion as well was quoted with approval in the Senate Report.

Appellants and the Solicitor General submit that this indicates that a municipality with jurisdiction over an airport has the power to impose a curfew on the airport, notwithstanding federal responsibility in the area. But, we are concerned here not with an ordinance imposed by the City of Burbank as "proprietor" of the airport, but with the exercise of police power. While the Hollywood-Burbank Airport may be the only major airport which is privately owned, many airports are owned by one municipality yet physically located in another. For example, the principal airport serving Cincinnati is located in Kentucky. Thus, authority that a municipality may have as a landlord is not necessarily congruent with its police power. We do not consider here what limits, if any, apply to a municipality as a proprietor.

The Senate version of the 1972 Act as it passed the Senate contained an express pre-emption section. But the Senate version never was presented to the House. Instead, the Senate passed, with amendments, the House version; the House, also with amendments, then concurred in the Senate amendments. The Act as passed combined provisions of both the House and Senate bills on the subject that each had earlier approved. When the blended provisions of the present Act were before the House, Congressman Staggers, Chairman of the House Committee on Interstate and Foreign Commerce, in urging the House to accept the amended version, said:

> I cannot say what industry's intention may be, but I can say to the gentleman what my intention is in trying to get this bill passed. We have evidence that across America some cities and States are trying to pass noise regulations. Certainly we do not want that to happen. It would harass industry and progress in America. That is the reason why I want to get this bill passed during this session.

When the House approved the blended provisions of the bill, Senator Tunney moved that the Senate concur. He made clear that the regulations to be considered by EPA for recommendation to FAA would include

> proposed means of reducing noise in airport environments through the application of emission controls on aircraft, the regulation of flight patterns and aircraft and airport operations, and modifications in the number, frequency, or scheduling of flights (as well as) ... the imposition of curfews on noisy airports, the imposition of flight path alternations in areas where noise was a problem, the imposition of noise emission standards on new and existing aircraft—with the expectation of a retrofit schedule to abate noise emissions from existing aircraft—the imposition of controls to increase the load factor on commercial flights, or other reductions in the joint use of airports, and such

> other procedures as may be determined useful and necessary to protect public health and welfare.

The statements by Congressman Stagers and Senator Tunney are weighty ones. For Congressman Staggers was Chairman of the House Committee on Interstate and Foreign Commerce which submitted the Noise Control Act and Report; and Senator Tunney was a member of the Senate Committee on Public Works, which submitted the Act and Report. When the President signed the bill he stated that "many of the most significant sources of noise move in interstate commerce and can be effectively regulated only at the federal level."

Our prior cases on pre-emption are not precise guidelines in the present controversy, for each case turns on the peculiarities and special features of the federal regulatory scheme in question. Control of noise is of course deep-seated in the police power of the States. Yet the pervasive control vested in EPA and in FAA under the 1972 Act seems to us to leave no room for local curfews or other local controls. What the ultimate remedy may be for aircraft noise which plagues many communities and tens of thousands of people is not known. The procedures under the 1972 Act are under way.

The Administrator has adopted regulations prescribing noise standards which must be met as a condition to type certification for all new subsonic turbojet-powered aircraft. On January 30, 1973, the FAA gave advance notice of proposed rulemaking for the control of fleet noise levels ("FNL") of airplanes operating in interstate commerce. 38 Fed. Reg. 2769. (The regulations would not pertain to carriers also operating in foreign commerce.) The proposed rules are designed to limit FNL prior to July 1, 1978, when the covered aircraft become subject to the requirements of 14 C.F.R. pt. 36. The FNL would be determined as a function of the takeoff and approach noise levels of each airplane in the fleet and the number of takeoffs and landings of the fleet. Until July 1, 1976, the cumulative noise level of any fleet subject to regulation could not exceed the FNL during the previous 90-day base period. In 1976 each fleet would be required to reduce its FNL by 50% of the difference between the original base-period level and the level ultimately required by 14 C.F.R. pt. 36.

In addition the Administrator has imposed a variety of regulations relating to takeoff and landing procedures and runway preferences. The Federal Aviation Act requires a delicate balance between safety and efficiency and the protection of persons on the ground. Any regulations adopted by the Administrator to control noise pollution must be consistent with the "highest degree of safety." The interdependence of these factors requires a uniform and exclusive system of federal regulation if the congressional objectives underlying the Federal Aviation Act are to be fulfilled.

If we were to uphold the Burbank ordinance and a significant number of municipalities followed suit, it is obvious that fractionalized control of the timing of takeoffs and landings would severely limit the flexibility of FAA in controlling air traffic flow. In order to insure efficient and safe use of the navigable airspace, FAA uses centralized "flow control," regulating the number of aircraft that will be accepted in a given area and restricting altitudes and routes that may be flown. Flow control has resulted in the Los Angeles Air Route Traffic Control Center holding aircraft on the ground at the Hollywood-Burbank Airport. Prior to April 1970, 21 regional Air Route Traffic Control Centers exercised independent control over traffic flow in their areas. In April 1970 FAA established a Central Flow Facility to coordinate flow control throughout the Air Traffic Control system. This change was necessitated because no regional center "had enough information to make a judgment based on the overall condition of the ATC system ..." FOURTH ANNUAL REPORT OF THE SECRETARY OF TRANSPORTATION FOR FISCAL YEAR 1970.

The difficulties of scheduling flights to avoid congestion and the concomitant decrease in safety would be compounded. In 1960 FAA rejected a proposed restriction on jet operations at the Los Angeles airport between 10 P.M. and 7 A.M. because such restrictions could "create critically serious problems to all air transportation patterns." The complete FAA statement said:

> The proposed restriction on the use of the airport by jet aircraft between the hours of 10 P.M. and 7 A.M. under certain surface wind conditions has also been reevaluated and this provision has been omitted from the rule. The practice of prohibiting the use of various airports during certain specific hours could create critically serious problems to all air transportation patterns.
>
> The network of airports throughout the United States and the constant availability of these airports are essential to the maintenance of a sound air transportation system. The continuing growth of public acceptance of aviation as a major force in passenger transportation and the increasingly significant role of commercial aviation in the nation's economy are accomplishments which cannot be inhibited if the best interest of the public is to be served. It was concluded therefore that the extent of relief from the noise problem which this provision might have achieved would not have compensated the degree of restriction it would have imposed on domestic and foreign Air Commerce.

This decision, announced in 1960, remains peculiarly within the competence of FAA, supplemented now by the input of EPA. We are not at liberty to diffuse the powers given by Congress to FAA and EPA by letting the States or municipalities in on the planning. If that change is to be made, Congress alone must do it.

Mr. Justice REHNQUIST, with whom Mr. Justice STEWART, Mr. Justice WHITE, and Mr. Justice MARSHALL join, dissenting.

The Court concludes that congressional legislation dealing with aircraft noise has so "pervaded" that field that Congress has impliedly pre-empted it, and therefore the ordinance of the city of Burbank here challenged is invalid under the Supremacy Clause of the Constitution. The Court says that the 1972 "Act reaffirms and reinforces the conclusion that FAA, now in conjunction with EPA, has full control over aircraft noise, pre-empting state and local control." Yet the House and Senate committee reports explicitly state that the 1972 Act to which the Court refers was not intended to alter the balance between state and federal regulation which had been struck by earlier congressional legislation in this area.

The House Report in discussing the general pre-emptive effect of the entire bill, stated: "The authority of State and local government to regulate use, operation, or movement of products is not affected at all by the bill. (The preemption provision discussed in this paragraph does not apply to aircraft. See discussion of aircraft noise below.)." The report went on to state specifically: "No provision of the bill is intended to alter in any way the relationship between the authority of the Federal Government and that of State and local governments that existed with respect to matters covered by section 611 of the Federal Aviation Act of 1958 prior to the enactment of the bill."

The report of the Senate Public Works Committee expressed the identical intent with respect to pre-emption:

> States and local governments are preempted from establishing or enforcing noise emission standards for aircraft, unless such standards are identical to standards prescribed under this bill. This does not address responsibilities or powers of airport operators, and no provision of the bill is intended to alter in any way the relationship between the authority of the Federal government and that of State and local governments that existed with respect to matters covered by section 611 of the Federal Aviation Act of 1958 prior to the enactment of the bill.

The Burbank ordinance prohibited jet takeoffs from the Hollywood-Burbank Airport during the late evening and early morning hours. Its purpose was to afford local residents at least partial relief, during normal sleeping hours, from the noise associated with jet airplanes. The ordinance in no way dealt with flights over the city nor did it categorically prohibit all jet takeoffs during those hours.

Appellees do not contend that the noise produced by jet engines could not reasonably be deemed to affect adversely the health and welfare of persons constantly exposed to it; control of noise, sufficiently loud to be classified as a public nuisance at common law, would be a type of regulation well within the traditional scope of the police power possessed by States and local governing bodies.

Because noise regulation has traditionally been an area of local, not national, concern, in determining whether congressional legislation has, by implication, foreclosed remedial local enactments "we start with the assumption that the historic police powers of the States were not to be superseded by the Federal Act unless that was the clear and manifest purpose of Congress." *Rice v. Santa Fe Elevator Corp.* (1947). This assumption derives from our basic constitutional division of legislative competence between the States and Congress; from "due regard for the presuppositions of our embracing federal system, including the principle of diffusion of power not as a matter of doctrinaire localism but as a promoter of democracy ..." *San Diego Building Trades Council v. Garmon* (1959). Unless the requisite pre-emptive intent is abundantly clear, we should hesitate to invalidate state and local legislation for the added reason that "the state is powerless to remove the ill effects of our decision, while the national government, which has the ultimate power, remains free to remove the burden."

Since Congress' intent in enacting the 1972 Act was clearly to retain the *status quo* between the federal regulation and local regulation, a holding of implied pre-emption of the field depends upon whether two earlier congressional enactments, the Federal Aviation Act of 1958 and the 1968 noise abatement amendment to that Act manifested the clear intent to preclude local regulations, that our prior decisions require.

The 1958 Act was intended to consolidate in one agency in the Executive Branch the control over aviation that had previously been diffused within that branch. The paramount substantive concerns of Congress were to regulate federally all aspects of air safety, and, once aircraft were in "flight," airspace management. While the Act might be broad enough to permit the Administrator to promulgate takeoff and landing rules to avoid excessive noise at certain hours of the day, Congress was not concerned with the problem of noise created by aircraft and did not intend to preempt its regulation. Furthermore, while Congress clearly intended to pre-empt the States from regulating aircraft in flight, the author of the bill, Senator Monroney, specifically stated that FAA would not have control "over the ground space" of airports.

The development and increasing use of civilian jet aircraft resulted in congressional concern over the noise associated with those aircraft. Hearings were held over a period of several years, resulting in a report but no legislation. The report of the House Committee on Interstate and Foreign Commerce, H.R. Rep. No.36, 88th Cong., 1st Sess., shows clearly that the 1958 Act was thought by at least some in Congress neither to pre-empt local legislative action to alleviate the growing noise problem, nor to prohibit local curfews:

> Until Federal action is taken, the local governmental authorities must be deemed to possess the police power necessary to protect their citizens and property from the unreasonable invasion of aircraft noise. The wisdom of exercising such power or the manner of the exercise is a problem to be resolved on the local governmental level.
>
> Airports in the United States, as a general rule, are operated by a local governmental authority, either a municipality, a county, or some independent unit. These airport operators are closer, both geographically and politically, to the problem of the conflict of interests between those citizens who have been adversely affected by the aircraft noise and the needs of the community for air commerce. Some airport operators have exercised the proprietary right to restrict in a reasonable manner, the use of any runway by limiting either the hours during which it may be used or the types of civil transport aircraft that may use it.

Several years after the conclusion of these hearings, Congress enacted the 1968 noise abatement amendment, which added § 611 to the 1958 Act, and which was the first congressional legislation dealing with the problem of aircraft noise.

On its face, § 611 as added by the 1968 amendment neither pre-empted the general field of regulation of aircraft noise nor dealt specifically with the more limited question of curfews. The House Committee on Interstate and Foreign Commerce, after reciting the serious proportions of the problem, outlined the type of federal regulation that the Act sought to impose:

> The noise problem is basically a conflict between two groups or interests. On the one hand, there is a group who provide various air transportation services. On the other hand there is a group who live, work, and go to schools and churches in communities near airports. The latter group is frequently burdened to the point where they can neither enjoy nor reasonably use their land because of noise resulting from aircraft operations. Many of them derive no direct benefit from the aircraft operations which create the unwanted noise.
>
> Therefore, it is easy to understand why they complain, and complain most vehemently. The possible solutions to this demanding and vexing problem which appear to offer the most promise are (1) new or modified engine and airframe

> designs, (2) special flight operating techniques and procedures, and (3) planning for land use in areas adjacent to airports so that such land use will be most compatible with aircraft operations. This legislation is directed toward the primary problem; namely, reduction of noise at its source.

Far from indicating any total pre-emptive intent, the House Committee observed: "Rather, the committee expects manufacturers, air carriers, all other segments of the aviation community, and State and local civic and governmental entities to continue and increase their contributions toward the common goal of quiet." The Senate Commerce Committee's view of the House bill followed a similar vein:

> This investment by the industry is representative of one of the avenues of approach to aircraft noise reduction, that is, the development of aircraft which generate less noise. Another approach to noise reduction is through the establishment of special flight operating techniques and procedures. The third principal control technique which merits serious consideration is the planning for land use in areas near airports so as to make such use compatible with aircraft operations. This is a matter largely within the province of State and local governments.
>
> While all of these techniques must be thoroughly studied and employed, the first order of business is to stop the escalation of aircraft noise by imposing standards which require the full application of noise reduction technology. A completely quiet airplane will not be developed within the foreseeable future. However, with the technological and regulatory means now at hand, it is possible to reduce both the level and the impact of aircraft noise. Within the limits of technology and economic feasibility, it is the view of the committee that the Federal Government must assure that the potential reductions are in fact realized.

With specific emphasis on pre-emption, the Senate Committee observed:

> The bill is an amendment to a statute describing the powers and duties of the Federal Government with respect to air commerce. As indicated earlier in this report, certain actions by State and local public agencies, such as zoning to assure compatible land use, are a necessary part of the total attack on aircraft noise.

In this connection, the question is raised whether this bill adds or subtracts anything from the powers of State or local governments. It is not the intent of the committee in recommending this legislation to effect any change in the existing apportionment of powers between the Federal and State and local governments.

In this regard, we concur in the following views set forth by the Secretary in his letter to the committee of June 22, 1968:

> The courts have held that the Federal Government presently preempts the field of noise regulation insofar as it involves controlling the flight of aircraft.
>
> Local noise control legislation limiting the permissible noise level of all overflying aircraft has recently been struck down because it conflicted with Federal regulation of air traffic. The court said, "[t]he legislation operates in an area committed to Federal care, and noise limiting rules operating as do those of the ordinance must come from a Federal source."
>
> H.R. 3400 would merely expand the Federal Government's role in a field already preempted. It would not change this preemption. State and local governments will remain unable to use their police powers to control aircraft noise by regulating the flight of aircraft.

However, the proposed legislation will not affect the rights of a State or local public agency, as the proprietor of an airport, from issuing regulations or establishing requirements as to the permissible level of noise which can be created by aircraft using the airport. Airport owners acting as proprietors can presently deny the use of their airports to aircraft on the basis of noise considerations so long as such exclusion is nondiscriminatory.

> Just as an airport owner is responsible for deciding how long the runways will be, so is the owner responsible for obtaining noise easements necessary to permit the landing and takeoff of the aircraft. The Federal Government is in no position to require an airport to accept service by larger aircraft and, for that purpose, to obtain longer runways. Likewise, the Federal Government is in no position to require an airport to accept service by noisier aircraft, and for that purpose to obtain additional noise easements.
>
> The issue is the service desired by the airport owner and the steps it is willing to take to obtain the service. In dealing with this issue, the Federal Government should not substitute its judgment for that of the States or elements of local government who, for the most part, own and operate our Nation's airports. The proposed legislation is not designed to do this and will not prevent airport proprietors from excluding any aircraft on the basis of noise considerations. Of course, the authority of units of local government to control the effects of aircraft noise through the exercise of land use planning and zoning powers is not diminished by the bill.
>
> Finally, since the flight of aircraft has been preempted by the Federal Government, State and local governments can presently exercise no control over sonic boom. The bill makes no change in this regard.

In terms of pre-emption analysis, the most reasonable reading of § 611 appears to be that it was enacted to enable the Federal Government to deal with the noise problem created by jet aircraft through study and regulation of the "source" of the problem—the mechanical and structural aspects of jet and turbine aircraft design. The authority to "prescribe and amend such rules and regulations as he may find necessary to provide for the control and abatement of aircraft noise and sonic boom," while a broad grant of authority to the Administrator, cannot fairly be read as prohibiting the States from enacting every type of measure, which might have the effect of reducing aircraft noise, in the absence of a regulation to that effect under this section. The statute established exclusive federal control of the technological methods for reducing the output of noise by jet aircraft, but that is a far cry from saying that it prohibited any local regulation of the times at which the local airport might be available for the use of jet aircraft.

Considering the language Congress enacted into law, the available legislative history, and the light shed by these on the congressional purpose, Congress did not intend either by the 1958 Act or the 1968 Amendment to oust local governments from the enactment of regulations such as that of the city of Burbank. The 1972 Act quite clearly intended to maintain the *status quo* between federal and local authorities.

The legislative history of the 1972 Act, quite apart from its concern with avoiding additional pre-emption, discloses a primary focus on the alteration of procedures within the Federal Government for dealing with problems of aircraft noise already entrusted by Congress to federal competence. The 1972 Act set up procedures by which the Administrator of EPA would have a role to play in the formulation and review of standards promulgated by FAA dealing with noise emissions of jet aircraft. But because these agencies have exclusive authority to reduce noise by promulgating regulations and implementing standards directed at one or several of the causes of the level of noise, local governmental bodies are not thereby foreclosed from dealing with the noise problem by every other conceivable method.

A local governing body that owns and operates an airport is certainly not, by the Court's opinion, prohibited from permanently closing down its facilities. A local governing body could likewise use its traditional police power to prevent the establishment of a new airport or the expansion of an existing one within its territorial jurisdiction by declining to grant the necessary zoning for such a facility. Even though the local government's decision in each case were motivated entirely because of the noise associated with airports, I do not read the Court's opinion as indicating that such action would be prohibited by the Supremacy Clause merely because the Federal Government has undertaken the responsibility for some aspects of aircraft noise control. Yet if this may be done, the Court's opinion surely does not satisfactorily explain why a local governing body may not enact a far less "intrusive" ordinance such as the city of Burbank's.

The history of congressional action in this field demonstrates, I believe, an affirmative congressional intent to allow local regulation. But even if it did not go that far, that history surely does not reflect "the clear and manifest purpose of Congress" to prohibit the exercise of "the historic police powers of the States" which our decisions require before a conclusion of implied preemption is reached. Clearly Congress could pre-empt the field to local regulation if it chose, and very likely the authority conferred on the Administrator of FAA by 49 U.S.C. § 1431 is sufficient to authorize him to promulgate regulations effectively pre-empting local action. But neither Congress nor the Administrator has chosen to go that route. Until one of them does, the ordinance of the city of Burbank is a valid exercise of its police power.

The District Court found that the Burbank ordinance would impose an undue burden on interstate commerce, and held it invalid under the Commerce Clause for that reason. Neither the Court of Appeals nor this Court's opinion, in view of their determination as to pre-emption, reached that question. The District Court's conclusion appears to be based, at least in part, on a consideration of the effect on interstate commerce that would result if all municipal airports in the country enacted ordinances such as that of Burbank. Since the proper determination of the question turns on an evaluation of the facts of each case and not on a predicted proliferation of possibilities, the District Court's conclusion is of doubtful validity. The Burbank ordinance did not affect emergency flights, and had the total effect of prohibiting one scheduled commercial flight each week and several additional private flights by corporate executives; such a result can hardly be held to be an unreasonable burden on commerce.

AIR PEGASUS OF D.C., INC. v. UNITED STATES

424 F.3d 1206 (Fed. Cir. 2005)

Opinion for the court filed by Circuit Judge SCHALL.

From February of 1992 to September 30, 2002, Air Pegasus owned and operated a heliport business at 1724 South Capitol Street, S.E., Washington, D.C. Air Pegasus did not own the South Capitol Street property, but leased it from Steuart Investment Company ("Steuart Investment"). The lease specified that Air Pegasus agreed to use the property

> solely in the conduct of a private use and/or public use heliport/vertiport ... and for any uses related thereto, including but not limited to fuel sales, maintenance and repair of helicopters and other vertical takeoff and landing air craft and sea planes, commercial, chartered, corporate and sightseeing services and general administrative offices, and for no other purpose without the prior written consent of Landlord, which consent shall not be unreasonably withheld or delayed.

Air Pegasus entered the lease in February of 1992 and in due course renewed it through October 31, 2010. As agreed in the lease, Air Pegasus only used the South Capitol Street property for the operation of its heliport. Air Pegasus did not actually operate any of the helicopters serviced by its heliport. Rather, its business was limited to providing, in return for a fee, a location from which helicopters could land and take off (and, perhaps, also obtain needed fueling and mechanical services). Air Pegasus's heliport therefore functioned much like an airport, only it serviced helicopters instead of airplanes (fixed-wing aircraft).

Air Pegasus's heliport business was greatly affected by events following the terrorist attacks of September 11, 2001. In particular, immediately following the attacks—in which four commercial airplanes were hijacked and three were used as weapons to attack the World Trade Center and Pentagon—the Federal Aviation Administration used its emergency powers to shut down virtually all commercial air traffic throughout the United States. The FAA did this by issuing "Notices to Airmen," or

"NOTAMs," pursuant to 14 C.F.R. § 91.139 (2001) ("Emergency Air Traffic Rules") and 14 C.F.R. § 91.137 (2001) ("Temporary Flight Restrictions in the Vicinity of Disaster/Hazard Areas"). The FAA's flight ban applied to both helicopters and airplanes. Therefore, by issuing the NOTAMs, the FAA essentially grounded operations at all commercial aviation ports in the days immediately following September 11, 2001.

For most aviation ports, the FAA's flight ban merely amounted to a temporary grounding of aircraft. In fact, the FAA permitted most commercial aviation ports to resume flights as early as September 13, 2001. However, this was not the case for Air Pegasus's heliport, as the FAA's decision allowing resumption of commercial air travel specifically excluded the area within twenty-five nautical miles of Washington, D.C. Although some of the flight restrictions in the Washington, D.C. area were subsequently relaxed, much of the area's airspace is still off limits to commercial aircrafts. This includes the airspace over 1724 South Capitol Street, S.E.

Therefore, unlike most other commercial aviation ports, Air Pegasus was not able to resume flight operations after the FAA issued its initial flight ban on September 11, 2001. This caused obvious economic hardships for Air Pegasus's heliport and, on September 30, 2002, Air Pegasus abandoned its lease and ceased business operations at the South Capitol Street Heliport.

* * *

Air Pegasus filed this lawsuit against the United States in the Court of Federal Claims, alleging that the various NOTAMs issued by the FAA after September 11, 2001, resulted in a regulatory taking of its heliport business located at 1724 South Capitol Street, S.E., Washington, D.C. More specifically, Air Pegasus alleged that it acquired through its lease with Steuart Investment, "the legal right to operate a Heliport ... through October 31, 2010," and that "[t]he NOTAMs had the immediate and intended effect of shutting down virtually all air traffic at the Heliport ... [which,] in turn, made it economically nonviable to continue to operate the business under the Lease." Therefore, "[s]olely as a result of the NOTAMs," Air Pegasus alleged that "the economic value of [its] business and its leasehold interest in the Property ha[d] been destroyed."

In response, the government conceded that the flight restrictions issued by the FAA had the effect of prohibiting helicopters from flying into and out of Air Pegasus's heliport. However, the government denied that the restrictions resulted in a compensable taking of any property interest of Air Pegasus. In particular, the government averred that "[t]he property interest that [Air Pegasus] allege[d][to] have been taken is not compensable under the Fifth Amendment."

The parties subsequently stipulated to the facts of the case and filed cross-motions for summary judgment. Air Pegasus argued that the undisputed facts showed that the FAA's flight restrictions had the effect of eliminating all economic value in its heliport and, therefore, amounted to either a categorical or non-categorical regulatory taking of its leasehold. The government, in turn, argued that the FAA's restrictions did not deprive Air Pegasus's lease of all economic value, and that even if they did have such an effect, the restrictions did not take any property that the government did not already have authority to regulate. The Court of Federal Claims ultimately sided with the government and granted summary judgment based on Air Pegasus's failure to show the taking of a cognizable property interest.

The court started from the principle that, in evaluating a takings claim, a court must first "inquire into the nature of the landowner's estate to determine whether the use interest proscribed by the governmental action was part of the owner's title to begin with, *i.e.*, whether the land use interest was a stick in the bundle of property rights acquired by the owner." The court stated that, under this inquiry, when "a party voluntarily enters into an area that is subject to pervasive government control, then a property right that would justify compensation under the Takings Clause may not exist." The court further stated that background principles of common law nuisance and property law can also provide the government with a defense to what would otherwise amount to a taking of private property. That, according to the court, is because such "background principles" may place pre-existing limitations on the property owner's title.

With respect to the facts of the case, the court first noted that Air Pegasus did not dispute the federal government's sovereignty over the navigable airspace. The court further noted that the airspace over Washington, D.C., was subject to regulations when Air Pegasus entered its lease in 1992, and that "the FAA [also] retain[ed] broad authority to instantly alter air flight requirements through NOTAMs." Therefore, the court concluded, "Air Pegasus entered this highly regulated area, in Washington, D.C., with the knowledge that the government reserved the power, and indeed regularly exercised its power, to restrict air flight patterns and procedures."

Next, the court turned to background principles of property law to determine whether any pre-existing limitations inhered in Air Pegasus's leasehold interest. The court first concluded that the federal government's dominant servitude over navigable waterways "may constitute part of the 'background principles' to which a property owner's rights are subject and, thus, may provide the Government with a defense to a takings claim." The court then reasoned that the government's similar exercise of exclusive sovereignty over the navigable airways indicated that it also had a dominant avigational servitude. Therefore, the court found that Air Pegasus acquired its leasehold subject to the government's dominant servitude to regulate the surrounding navigable airspace.

The Court of Federal Claims rejected Air Pegasus's argument that under the Supreme Court's decision in *United States v. Causby* (1946), the government's use of navigable airspace can still result in a taking despite the existence of an avigational servitude. The court stated that the private property right the Court found in *Causby* was the right to habitable land, not the right to navigable airspace. The court also rejected Air Pegasus's argument that under *Palazzolo v. Rhode Island* (2001), a takings claim cannot be barred simply because the plaintiff acquired its property interest with knowledge of an existing regulatory program. The court acknowledged that *Palazzolo* does not bar a claim where the federal regulation "is so unreasonable or onerous as to compel compensation," but in this case, the court continued, "the regulatory scheme certainly is not unreasonable." On the contrary, citing the grave risks to national security following the terrorist attacks of September 11, 2001, the court found that the FAA's flight restrictions were "not only reasonable, but also appropriate and responsible."

Accordingly, having found that Air Pegasus voluntarily chose to operate a business in a highly regulated industry, and having further found that the government has a pre-existing servitude over the navigable airspace, the Court of Federal Claims held that "[n]o [private] property right exists to public navigable airspace," and that "no property right over the navigable airspace above the leased area at the South Capitol Street Heliport [could therefore] attach to the lessee, Air Pegasus." As a result, the court concluded that "although the FAA's regulatory activity may have had an adverse impact on [Air Pegasus's] heliport business," there was not a taking of any cognizable property interest of Air Pegasus. The court therefore granted summary judgment to the government and dismissed Air Pegasus's complaint.

Air Pegasus timely appealed the final judgment of the Court of Federal Claims. We have jurisdiction over the appeal pursuant to 28 U.S.C. § 1295(a)(3).

DISCUSSION

The issue of whether a taking has occurred is a question of law based on factual underpinnings. The Takings Clause of the Fifth Amendment of the U.S. Constitution states that "private property [shall not] be taken for public use, without just compensation." The purpose of the Takings Clause is to prevent "Government from forcing some people alone to bear public burdens which, in all fairness and justice, should be borne by the public as a whole." *Penn Cent. Transp. Co. v. City of New York* (1978). We have developed a two-part test for determining whether "fairness and justice" require compensation for burdens imposed by a particular government action.

"First, as a threshold matter, the court must determine whether the claimant has established a property interest for purposes of the Fifth Amendment." That is because "only persons with a valid property interest at the time of the taking are entitled to compensation." The protections of the Takings Clause apply to real property, personal property, and intangible property. However, the Constitution does not itself create or define the scope of "property" interests protected by the Fifth Amendment. "Instead, 'existing rules and understandings' and 'background principles' derived from an independent source, such as state, federal, or common law, define the dimensions of the requisite property rights for purposes of establishing a cognizable taking."

"Second, after having identified a valid property interest, the court must determine whether the governmental action at issue amounted to a compensable taking of that property interest." A compensable taking can occur not only through the government's physical invasion or appropriation of private property, but also by government regulations that unduly burden private property interests. Again, we do not reach this second step without first identifying a cognizable property interest. Therefore, we now turn to the Court of Federal Claims' decision finding that Air Pegasus lacked a cognizable interest in the airspace over the South Capitol Street Heliport.

* * *

Air Pegasus contends the Court of Federal Claims erred in finding that Air Pegasus did not acquire a constitutionally protected property interest through its leasehold. Air Pegasus asserts that it acquired from the lease the express right to operate a heliport, and that this property right was taken as a result of the FAA's flight restrictions. At oral argument, counsel for Air Pegasus more clearly defined the asserted property right as "the right to operate a heliport, which includes the right to have a helicopter leave the ground and hit the ground," *i.e.*, the right to have helicopters land and take off at the heliport. Air Pegasus's counsel further stated that, contrary to the Court of Federal Claims' finding, Air Pegasus does "not claim a property right in the public airspace." Rather, Air Pegasus merely claims that it acquired a leasehold interest, which explicitly included the right to operate a heliport, which "properly assumed the ability for the helicopters to use [the] airspace."

Air Pegasus further contends that, in finding no cognizable property right, the Court of Federal Claims took "a sweeping, absolutist view of the federal government's power under the Commerce Clause [which] if allowed to stand, would seriously erode if not obliterate the value of private property in relation to government authority." In particular, Air Pegasus asserts that "[p]roperty subject to 'pervasive regulation' may still be property," and that "the federal government's navigational servitude does not provide an absolute defense to a takings claim."

First, with respect to the scope of the government's avigational servitude, Air Pegasus argues the servitude only extends to government actions taken to both promote interstate commerce and improve public avigation. In this case, Air Pegasus continues, the FAA's restrictions did not improve public aviation because, instead of promoting or improving air travel, they completely banned air travel. (Air Pegasus recognizes the FAA issued the flight restrictions in the interest of national security. However, Air Pegasus contends that national security interests are not included within the scope of the avigational servitude and that the government must consequently compensate individuals for property taken for such purposes.)

Second, with respect to the regulated nature of the aviation industry, Air Pegasus asserts that the level of government regulation in a given industry goes to the issue of whether a taking actually occurred, not to the issue of whether the plaintiff asserted a cognizable property interest. Finally, noting that other airports in the region were allowed to open shortly after September 11, 2001, Air Pegasus contends it was singled out to bear a disproportionate burden for the sake of alleged public benefits, and that it is therefore entitled to compensation.

In response, the government argues that the Court of Federal Claims properly concluded that Air Pegasus failed to assert the taking of a cognizable property interest. The government further argues that Air Pegasus's arguments on appeal confuse the difference between simply not being disturbed in a particular use of property and having an affirmative right to that use. Specifically, the government argues that while Air Pegasus's lease may have given it the right to use the land at 1724 South Capitol Street as a heliport, it did not, and could not, give Air Pegasus the right to actually operate the heliport, *i.e.* the right to have helicopters enter and exit the navigable airspace from the South Capitol Street site. According to the government, that is because the navigable airspace has always been subject to the exclusive and complete control of the federal government and is consequently not available for private ownership. In other words, the government's pervasive regulation of the public airways serves as one of the background principles limiting private property interests. Therefore, the government contends, Air Pegasus only had a right to operate helicopters from its heliport to the extent the FAA did not find it necessary to restrict air travel in the vicinity of Washington, D.C.

We agree with the Court of Federal Claims that Air Pegasus failed to assert a cognizable property interest for purposes of the Fifth Amendment. However, we reach that conclusion in a slightly different manner.

As an initial matter, a claimant seeking compensation from the government for an alleged taking of private property must, at a minimum, assert that its property interest was actually taken by the government action. In this case, however, Air Pegasus does not appear to assert that its property was actually taken by the FAA's regulations. In particular, at oral argument, Air Pegasus's counsel conceded that Air Pegasus's takings claim was really for compensation resulting from a "derivative injury." Counsel characterized the injury as derivative because, while the FAA's regulations prohibit the operation of helicopters (and other aircraft) in the airspace around Washington, D.C. Air Pegasus does not actually own or operate any helicopters. Therefore, Air Pegasus's economic injury is not the result of the government taking Air Pegasus's property, but is the more attenuated result of the government's purported taking of other people's property. This circumstance does not form the basis for a viable takings claim.

Similarly, in this case, Air Pegasus owns a property interest in its leasehold. However, Air Pegasus, which did not itself own or operate any helicopters, does not allege that the FAA's restrictions regulated its operations under the lease. Instead, Air Pegasus basically alleges that the FAA, by regulating helicopters owned by third parties, frustrated its business expectations at the South Capitol Street heliport. Therefore, like the appellant in *Omnia*, Air Pegasus, while no doubt injured by reason of the government's actions, has not alleged a taking of private property under the Fifth Amendment.

Although we have concluded that Air Pegasus's alleged derivative injury does not present a cognizable takings claim, our analysis is not quite complete. That is because, despite its noted concession at oral argument (specifically, counsel stated that Air Pegasus does "not claim a property right in the public airspace") Air Pegasus nevertheless seems to claim a right of access to the navigable airspace from its heliport. This use of the airspace is at least implicitly proscribed by the FAA's flight restrictions over Washington, D.C. Therefore, if Air Pegasus has a private right to access the navigable airspace from its heliport, then Air Pegasus has, at a minimum, asserted a cognizable property interest allegedly taken by the FAA regulations. However, for the reasons that follow, we do not think that Air Pegasus has such a private property right for purposes of the Fifth Amendment.

We first note that Air Pegasus's claimed property interest is not merely a right to access the airspace over its heliport, but a right to access the navigable airspace from its heliport. This means that we need not consider the extent to which Air Pegasus, as a lessee of the South Capitol Street property, has the right to use the non-navigable airspace immediately above its leasehold. Our review is therefore limited to the specific issue of whether Air Pegasus has a private property right of access to the navigable airspace from the South Capitol Street Heliport.

Turning to that issue, the text of the Fifth Amendment expressly states that compensation is due for government takings of "private property." However, it is well established under federal law that the navigable airspace is public property not subject to private ownership. *See* 49 U.S.C. § 40103(a)(2) (2000) ("A citizen of the United States has a public right of transit through the navigable airspace."); Air Commerce Act of 1926 ("[T]he term 'navigable airspace' means airspace above the minimum safe altitudes of flight prescribed by the Secretary of Commerce ..., and such navigable airspace shall be subject to a public right of freedom of interstate and foreign air navigation in conformity with the requirements of this Act."). As the Supreme Court aptly stated over a half-century ago:

> The air is a public highway, as Congress declared. Were that not true, every transcontinental flight would subject the operator to countless trespass suits. Common sense revolts at the idea. To recognize such private claims to the airspace would clog these highways, seriously interfere with their control and development in the public interest, and transfer into private ownership that to which only the public has a just claim.

In addition, the government has long exercised dominant control over the navigable airspace in regulating the public right of transit. *See* 49 U.S.C. § 40103(a)(1) (2000) ("The United States Government has exclusive sovereignty of airspace of the United States."); Air Commerce Act of 1926 ("The Congress hereby declares that the Government of the United States has, to the exclusion of all foreign nations, complete sovereignty of the airspace over the lands and waters of the United States, including the Canal Zone."). Therefore, "background principles" of long-standing federal property law indicate that there is no private property right in the navigable airspace of the United States. For that reason, we hold that Air Pegasus does not have a cognizable property interest in its alleged right to access the navigable airspace from the South Capitol Street Heliport.

In reaching our conclusion, we are also mindful of Air Pegasus's contention that the FAA acted outside of the government's navigational servitude. However, our conclusion is not grounded in the government's navigational servitude. The navigational servitude is a dominant servitude. This means that, when properly invoked, the government's servitude takes priority over the underlying property interests of private parties. Rather, our conclusion in this case is that Air Pegasus simply does not have a private property interest in what is public airspace, regardless of whether the government is acting to promote aviation. Therefore, because there is no private property interest here to which the government's servitude could attach, we do not see how the principles underlying the servitude are relevant to this case.

Air Pegasus also argues that voluntarily choosing to enter a regulated industry does not, by itself, deprive a person of a Fifth Amendment property interest. We agree. However, this case does not involve a typical claim to property in a regulated area. Rather, Air Pegasus claims the right to property that, since at least 1929, has been committed to the public domain. The fact that Air Pegasus was able to operate the heliport prior to September 11, 2001, is irrelevant. Private property interests simply do not, as a general matter, exist in the navigable airspace of the United States.

Finally, we do not share Air Pegasus's concern that upholding the Court of Federal Claims' decision will provide the government with a complete "blanket" defense to takings claims involving air commerce. In our decision today, we simply hold that Air Pegasus does not have a private property right to access the navigable airspace from the South Capitol Street Heliport. We hold that Air Pegasus failed to assert a cognizable property interest sufficient to support a takings claim under the Fifth Amendment. We base our decision on two separate grounds. First, Air Pegasus appears to assert a claim based on a perceived taking of property owned by other parties. The Fifth Amendment does not provide a remedy for such a derivative claim. Air Pegasus also appears to assert a right to access the navigable airspace from the South Capitol Street Heliport, access which was no doubt restricted by the FAA's regulations. We do not think this right of access is a cognizable property interest under the Fifth Amendment. Accordingly, we affirm the judgment of the Court of Federal Claims.

PAULINE NEWMAN, Circuit Judge, dissenting.

The panel majority holds that because an airport operator knowingly enters a highly regulated industry, he bears the risk of regulatory action by government. I agree. However, the act of closing the airspace around the National Capitol to helicopter traffic is not routine regulation, and it is not disputed that this action was not reasonably foreseeable. The sudden and total prohibition of Air Pegasus' business was not an ordinary regulatory act in ordinary times, but an extraordinary response to a catastrophic event. This unforeseeable governmental action rendered Air Pegasus' leasehold valueless.

Air Pegasus argues that compensation is prescribed by the Fifth Amendment policy, that the Amendment is designed "to bar Government from forcing some people alone to bear public burdens which, in all fairness and justice, should be borne by the public as a whole." The courts are charged to consider this fundamental question: the placement of the economic burden of the government's actions in the national interest. That is, does Air Pegasus alone bear the financial consequences of enhanced security in the National Capitol, or does the nation share this burden. My colleagues on this panel do not discuss this question, and although they agree that "Air Pegasus owns a property interest in its leasehold," they conclude that the extinction of that property interest raises no issue under the Fifth Amendment. It is established that leaseholds are compensable property interests under the takings clause. And it is not disputed that the closing of the airspace to helicopter traffic deprived the leasehold of its value, raising the "clear principle of national equity that the individual whose property is thus sacrificed must be indemnified." Thus the court's holding that Air Pegasus had no compensable property right is contrary to long-established precedent.

Even an environment of "pervasive" regulation does not mean that all regulatory changes will be reasonably foreseeable in that environment. Air Pegasus cannot reasonably be charged with accepting the commercial risk of the 9/11 terrorist attacks and the immediate government response by closing the airspace, which clearly were different in kind as well as degree from any reasonable regulatory limitation before 9/11.

The Court of Federal Claims and my colleagues appear to have been diverted by the government's concentration on the concept of who "owns" the air, thus ignoring the effect of the government action on the heliport leasehold. The result negates the basic rights and protections secured by the Fifth Amendment, and places the financial burden of emergency government action for national security, on the property owner whose property became valueless. Precedent makes clear that Air Pegasus indeed possessed a compensable property interest in Fifth Amendment terms. From my colleagues' contrary decision, I respectfully dissent.

HUNTLEIGH USA CORP. v. UNITED STATES

75 Fed. Cl. 642 (Fed. Cl. 2007)

MARGOLIS, Senior Judge.

The U.S. Congress passed the Aviation and Transportation Security Act in response to the terrorist attacks of September 11, 2001, and the President signed the Act into law on November 19, 2001. *See* Aviation and Transportation Security Act (2001), ("ATSA" or "Act"). It created the new Transportation Security Administration to oversee civil aviation security. The Act required virtually all passenger and baggage screening to be conducted by federal employees within one year. In the interim, ATSA required the new Under Secretary of Transportation for Security (and head of TSA) to take over responsibility for security screening within three months.

Since 1973, the airlines had been responsible for passenger and baggage screening, pursuant to regulations and guidelines established by the Federal Aviation Administration. Most airlines met their security responsibilities by contracting with private companies to conduct screening. Huntleigh USA Corp. ("Huntleigh") had been providing passenger screening services since at least 1989 and checked baggage screening since 1999. By November 2001, Huntleigh had screening contracts with approximately 75 airlines in about 35 cities. As a result of ATSA, the airlines terminated their screening contracts with Huntleigh on or about February 17, 2002, and Huntleigh signed interim letter contracts with the TSA to continue providing passenger and baggage screening at locations where Huntleigh already operated until federal employees took over the function. Huntleigh earned $235,112,000 from screening revenues in 2002, a significant increase from its $68,983,000 in screening revenues in 2001.

DISCUSSION

I. TAKINGS CLAIM

The Takings Clause of the Fifth Amendment states, "nor shall private property be taken for public use, without just compensation." U.S. Const. Amend. V. The Supreme Court has expanded on these 12 words to declare that the "Fifth Amendment's guarantee ... [is] designed to bar Government from forcing some people alone to bear public burdens which, in all fairness and justice, should be borne by the public as a whole." Beyond this simple principle, however, there is no formula for determining when a taking has occurred, only "ad hoc, factual inquiries" for each case.

With regard to regulatory takings, the framework for these inquiries has been defined by the analysis in *Loretto v. Teleprompter Manhattan CATV Corp.* (1982). Before a court can reach any of these analyses as to whether a compensable taking of private property occurred, however, it must first address the threshold issue of whether the claimant possessed a legally protected property interest at the time of the alleged taking. *Air Pegasus of D.C., Inc. v. United States* (Fed. Cir. 2005). Although Huntleigh may have been injured, it has not alleged a taking of private property under the Fifth Amendment.

Huntleigh's claim is similar to that in *NL Industries, Inc. v. United States*. In that case, the plaintiff did not have a compensable property interest in the physical plant and systems it had developed for transporting spent nuclear fuel, which were rendered valueless when a change in U.S. policy resulted in a moratorium on the license application of the reprocessing plant with which the plaintiff had contracted. The Court found in *NL Industries* that the regulatory scheme that allowed the agency to deny the license to the reprocessing plant was in place before the plaintiff entered the market. Whether the plaintiff could have or should have anticipated the particular regulatory decisions at issue was irrelevant.

Likewise, when Huntleigh entered the security screening business, it contracted with the airlines pursuant to security regulations issued by the government. Plaintiff's own aviation security expert admitted at trial that the federal government retained the right to change those regulations. Before the Fall of 2001, both the Congress and executive branch entities had publicly discussed the possibility of changing the aviation screening paradigm, to include federalizing the screening functions and workforce. It is immaterial that Huntleigh did not anticipate the specific policy shifts that occurred after the terrorist attacks of September 11, 2001, or deem federalization likely, because the regulatory scheme allowing those changes was already in place.

With regard to Huntleigh's screening contracts, the government's actions amount, at most, to frustration of purpose rather than a taking. Lawful government action that renders a contract impossible to perform does not amount to a taking of the contract. *Omnia Commercial Co. v. United States* (1923) (government requisition of steel, preventing the steel producer from honoring its contract, frustrated customer's contract with the steel producer, but was not a taking).

Huntleigh's former and current presidents and Chief Executive Officers testified at trial that all of Huntleigh's screening contracts with the airlines contained a clause that gave either party the right to terminate the contract in compliance with its specified notice provisions. They testified that the notice requirements were usually 30, 60, or 90 days, with the vast majority requiring 30 days' notice. The airlines terminated these contracts with Huntleigh as a result of ATSA, but Huntleigh did not consider the terminations to be a breach and did not sue any of the air carriers for breach of contract. The airlines were within their rights to terminate the screening contracts at any time, for any reason or no reason. The government did not interfere with these contracts.

The airlines terminated the contracts because they no longer needed Huntleigh's services when the federal government took over the screening functions covered by the contracts. Huntleigh no longer had a customer for its services. Relying on *Omnia*, the

Federal Circuit has declared that "frustration of a business by loss of a customer was not a taking" of private contracts. Like the airlines in Huntleigh, a contracting party in *NL Industries* was unable to fulfill its contract obligations because of a government policy decision.

The Federal Circuit also found frustration of purpose rather than a taking when aviation restrictions in response to the terrorist attacks of September 11, 2001, interfered with the operation of a business. Specifically, a heliport operator in Washington, D.C., was forced to close the only business permitted under its lease when the Federal Aviation Administration banned commercial aircraft from the area that included the heliport. The regulations merely frustrated the plaintiff's business because they did not apply to the heliport itself, but to the third parties who sought to fly in and out of the facility. Likewise, ATSA did not address Huntleigh or the other screening companies; it merely moved the responsibility for aviation security from the airlines to the newly-created TSA.

In summary, Huntleigh did not possess a compensable property interest under the Fifth Amendment, and the Court's analysis ends there. Without a property interest, there can be no taking, and the Court need not address the *Lucas* or *Penn Central* requirements.

II. STATUTORY CLAIM

Huntleigh also asserts that, aside from its takings claim, it is entitled to "adequate compensation" under the Aviation and Transportation Security Act. It argues that "adequate compensation" in the Act can be interchangeable with "just compensation" in the Fifth Amendment context, and Congress therefore intended the phrase "adequate compensation" to create a statutory right to takings compensation without the traditional, common law takings requirements. The Court turns to traditional rules of statutory interpretation to determine if Huntleigh is entitled to compensation under § 101(g) of ATSA.

Section 101(g)(1), "Schedule for assumption of civil aviation security functions," states that the new Under Secretary for Transportation Security "shall assume civil aviation security functions and responsibilities" within three months of the Act's November 19, 2001, enactment date. The next section, "Assumption of contracts," declares that "the Under Secretary may assume the rights and responsibilities of an air carrier or foreign air carrier contract for provision of passenger screening services at airports." This assumption could occur "as of" the date in section 101(g)(1), meaning at or on February 19, 2002. Finally, "not later than 90 days" after the November 19, 2001 enactment date, § 101(g)(3), "Assignment of Contracts," states that an air carrier may, at the request of the Under Secretary, make an agreement to transfer to the Under Secretary any contract for passenger and baggage screening. By using both "shall" and "may," the clear implication of these provisions is that the Under Secretary was required to take over responsibility for passenger and baggage screening within three months, but the assumption or assignment of contracts was discretionary—*i.e.*, it was a possible means for accomplishing the mandate of the Act. The Act's language is clear and unambiguous. As such, examination of legislative history is unnecessary and inappropriate, and the Court will not stray from the plain language of the statute.

The TSA did not assume Huntleigh's contracts by taking on the airlines' obligations because, among other reasons, the contracts differed greatly and contained provisions that were inappropriate for federal government contracts. Instead, the airlines terminated their contracts with Huntleigh and the other screening companies on or about February 17, 2002, and the TSA entered into new contracts with the screening companies for the interim period before complete federalization occurred.

However, Huntleigh argues that the TSA's eventual takeover of Huntleigh's screening responsibilities amounts to an assumption of its contracts under the Act, even though the government did not assume Huntleigh's contracts with the airlines in the strict, legal sense. The language of the Act undermines this assertion. Section 101(g)(1) requires the assumption of "civil aviation security functions and responsibilities." In contrast, § 101(g)(2), "Assumption of Contracts," allows the Under Secretary to "assume the rights and responsibilities of an air carrier ... contract for provision of passenger screening services ... subject to payment of adequate compensation to parties to the contract, if any."

In interpreting a statute, a court must attempt to give effect to every word and clause. The court also must avoid interpretations that make a word or clause "inconsistent, meaningless, or superfluous." Following these tenets, this Court must give significance to the Congress' use of the word "contract" in § 101(g)(2), and the absence of that word in § 101(g)(1). In the first section, the Act requires assumption of "functions and responsibilities," but not necessarily contracts. In the second, it specifically permits assumption of contracts for adequate compensation of the contract parties. To adopt Huntleigh's interpretation would ignore the Congress' deliberate insertion of "contract" in § 101(g)(2) and render the word superfluous.

As a result, this Court must conclude that the Congress intended § 101(g)(2) to apply only if the government chose to assume screening company contracts as defined by BLACK'S LAW DICTIONARY—taking the airlines' contract obligations onto itself. That did not happen, and Huntleigh has not asserted that it did. Plaintiff's counsel even admitted at the post-trial hearing that the government "did not directly assume those contracts." The language of § 101(g)(3) also does not apply because the airlines never entered into any agreements to transfer contracts to the government. The government did not assume Huntleigh's contracts under the Act, and Huntleigh therefore is not entitled to compensation.

NOTES

1. In terms of aviation law, "environment" connotes at least four different, but intertwined, settings for aviation operations: the actual physical environment; the legal context; local, state, national, and global business realities; and the post-September 11th security climate.

United States v. Causby (1946) and *City of Burbank v. Lockheed Air Terminal, Inc.* (1973), *supra*, introduce a basic feature of modern aviation that has been and continues to be a significant environmental consideration for people on the ground: Noise pollution. Indeed, "NIMBY"—"Not In My Back Yard"—frequently characterizes the attitudes of citizens who live or work nearby airports and airfields, particularly those airports and airfields seeking to expand runways, facilities, or operations. In contrast, in the general aviation environment, some "small" communities welcome the investment and development of businesses and commercial infrastructure that are ancillary to aviation operations, including "air taxis." In any case, many airports are obligated to comply with the Airport Noise and Capacity Act of 1990. *See* 49 U.S.C. § 40101 *et seq.*; 14 C.F.R. Pt. 36, 161.

See generally Jay M. Zitter, Annotation, *Airport Operations or Flight of Aircraft as Constituting Taking or Damaging of Property*, 22 A.L.R.4th 863 (1983 & 2005 Supp.); Jay M. Zitter, Annotation, *Zoning Regulations Limiting Use of Property Near Airport as Taking of Property*, 18 A.L.R.4th 542 (1982 & 2005 Supp.); Paul Stephen Dempsey, *Local Airport Regulation: The Constitutional Tension between Police Power, Preemption & Takings*, 11 PENN. ST. ENVTL. L. REV. 1 (2002); Luis G. Zambrano, Comment, *Balancing the Rights of Landowners with the Needs of Airports: The Continuing Battle over Noise,* 66 J. AIR L. & COM. 445 (2000); Jack L. Litwin, Annotation, *Airport Operations or Flight Aircraft as Nuisance*, 79 A.L.R.3d 253 (1977 & 2004 Supp.).

2. With respect to the natural environment, climatologists have long wondered whether contrails (*e.g.*, condensation or vapor trails) from the thousands of jetliners airborne over the United States each day cool or heat the atmosphere. When all airline activity in the nation was grounded on September 11, 2001, climatologists had an unprecedented opportunity to study that issue. Several studies now suggest that "contrails can suppress both daytime highs (by reflecting sunlight back to space) and nighttime lows (by trapping radiated heat). That is, they can be both cooling and warming clouds." *See* Peter Tyson, *Diming the Sun—Inquiry: The Contrail Effect*, NOVA ONLINE, Apr. 2006, *http://www.pbs.org/wgbh/nova/sun/contrail.html.*

Meanwhile, in April 2010, all commercial aviation to-and-from Europe was shut down for six days as the Eyjafjallajokull volcano in Iceland erupted, throwing volcanic ash several kilometers into the atmosphere, creating a humongous ash cloud over Europe, and causing the biggest closure of airspace in peacetime. Pierre Sparaco, *Europe's*

Volcanic Failure, AVIATION WEEK & SPACE TECH., May 3, 2010, at 53 (noting that "individual [European] countries still 'own' their airspace and no cross-border agreement is required to implement local decisions, including the temporary creation of a no-fly zone. Individual decisions resulting from volcano fears [ ] were coordinated, but the EU's 27 member states nevertheless could not speak with a single voice for nearly a week."). Once operations normalized, airlines and passengers alike demanded compensation for the extensive delay and disruption caused by the air space ban (estimated to have cost the industry more than £1 billion).

Where weather is a contributing factor to an aviation accident, litigation frequently centers on issues of weather reporting, air traffic control, and responsibility for weather forecasting. *See, e.g.*, *United States Aviation Underwriters, Inc. v. United States* (11th Cir. 2009) (concluding that the National Weather Service must issue Significant Meteorological Information ("SIGMENT") warnings to pilots, whenever moderate to severe clear air turbulence ("CAT") is forecast, but the underlying determination of whether severe CAT is occurring is discretionary, insulating the federal government from liability under the discretionary function exception of the Federal Tort Claims Act, 28 U.S.C. § 2680(a).)

3. Airlines are a natural target of public concern about the emission of carbon dioxide (CO_2) and other greenhouse gases. Some officials report that the transportation sector contributes 32 percent of all CO_2 emissions, 12 percent of which (*e.g.*, 3 to 4 percent of total CO_2) are attributable to aviation. UNITED STATES ENVIRONMENTAL PROTECTION AGENCY, INVENTORY OF U.S. GREENHOUSE GAS EMISSIONS AND SINKS: 1990-2005 (2007). *See also* Daniel H. Conrad, Note, *into the Wild Green Yonder: Applying the Clean Air Act to Regulate Emissions of Greenhouse Gases from Aircraft*, 34 N.C. J. INT'L L. & COM. REG. 919 (2009).

To address climate change and reduce aviation's "footprint," European Union ("EU") regulators have instituted a market-based cap-and-trade and emissions trading scheme ("ETS"). *See generally* Ruwantissa Abeyratne, *The Authority of the European Union to Unilaterally Impose an Emissions Trading Scheme*, 21 AIR & SPACE LAW. 5 (2008).

> Consider two companies, A and B, both of which emit significant quantities of a given pollutant. Their emissions may damage air quality, and the relevant authorities may decide that emissions should be reduced by a given amount, say by 10 per cent.
>
> At first glance, the solution seems simple: both A and B cut their emissions by 10 per cent. But in the real world, this may impose very different burdens on the two companies.

> For example, company A may, by the nature of its activities, be able to reduce its emissions by 10 per cent or even more at relatively low cost. Company B, on the other hand, may find this a difficult and costly process. It is this potential difference in reduction cost between A and B that creates a market opportunity.

UNITED NATIONS ENVIRONMENT PROGRAM, AN EMERGING MARKET FOR THE ENVIRONMENT: A GUIDE TO EMISSIONS TRADING; UNITED NATIONS ENVIRONMENT PROGRAMME DIVISION OF TECHNOLOGY, INDUSTRY AND ECONOMICS 4 (2002). *See generally* Carl Burleson, *The EU Emissions Trading System Proposal*, 21 AIR & SPACE LAW. 1 (2007); Allen Pei-Jan Tsai & Annie Petsonk, *The Skies: An Airline-Based System for Limiting Greenhouse Gas Emissions from International Civil Aviation*, 6 ENVT. LAW. 763 (2000).

Application of the EU's ETS globally is controversial, raising issues of extraterritorial jurisdiction. For example, under ETS, if a U.S.-operated airliner travels from Los Angeles, California, across the entire United States, over the Atlantic Ocean, over Great Britain, and through the airspace over mainland Europe, to its final destination in Ankara, Turkey, should the carrier be taxed over the entire journey or for those emissions discharged over Europe only?

4. Microsoft Chief Executive Bill Gates articulated the freedom that flight has represented from its earliest stage: "The Wright brothers created the single greatest cultural force since the invention of writing. The airplane became the first world wide web, bringing people of different languages, ideas and values together." *See* Gregory P. Sreenan, *Aviation Law*, JUN. FLA. B.J. 44, 47-48 (2003). While commercial jets regularly traverse state boundaries (*i.e.*, "transcontinental"), the notion of truly "Open Skies" is an emerging and challenging issue internationally.

For example, when Continental Airlines Flight 28 from New York arrived at London's Heathrow Terminal 4 on March 30, 2008, at 6:45 A.M., it was decades overdue in the minds of some airline executives. Until that time, several pacts between the United States and Great Britain controlled which foreign airlines could serve the that airport. Continental Airlines was excluded from one of the world's busiest aviation gateways. Only four airlines—British Airways, Virgin Atlantic, American Airlines, and United Airlines—operated between London's Heathrow Airport and the United States pursuant to the "Bermuda II" accord, a 1977 agreement between Great Britain and the United States that permitted only two airlines from each country to serve London Heathrow Airport, prohibited U.S. carriers from serving inter-European routes originating from the United Kingdom, and restricted British carriers from servicing points between U.S. cities. *See* Agreement Between the Government of the United States of America and the Government of the United Kingdom of Great Britain Relating to Air Services Between

Their Respective Territories, Feb. 11, 1946. U.S.-U.K., 60 Stat. 1499 ["Bermuda I"], and 23 July 1977, 28 U.S.T. 5367, T.I.A.S. No. 8641 ["Bermuda II"].

This restriction eased on April 30, 2007, when the United States and European Union Member States completed the first phase of a new era of "Open Skies" agreement that would increase international flight routes and landing rights for transatlantic commercial airlines. *See* 2007 O.J. (L 134) 4-41, 46 I.L.M. 470 (2007). *See generally Open Skies Causes a Continental Shift*, TRAVEL TRADE GAZETTE (United Kingdom), Mar. 21, 2008, at 2008 WLNR 5741461 (quoting Continental Airlines Senior Director for the United Kingdom and Ireland: "The world's premier airport was permanently written out of our brief by the most anti-competitive air service agreement, which has protected the incumbents wonderfully."). *See also* Michelle Higgins, *Open-Skies Promises More Flights to Europe*, CHI. TRIB., Mar. 30, 2008, at 2.

Are Open Skies sensible in the aftermath of September 11th? For further discussion of Open Skies initiatives across European and Asian markets see Allan P. Dobson & Joseph A. McKinney, *Sovereignty, Politics, and U.S. International Airline Policy*, 74 J. AIR L. & COM. 527 (2009); Miron Mushkat & Roda Mushkat, *The Political Economy of Hong Kong's "Open Skies" Legal Regime: An Empirical and Theoretical Exploration*, 10 SAN DIEGO INT'L L.J. 381 (2009); Robert M. Hardaway, *Of Cabbages and Cabotage: The Case for Opening Up the U.S. Airline Industry to International Competition*, 34 TRANSP. L.J. 1 (2007); Ruwantissa Abeyratne, *US/EU Open Skies Agreement—Some Issues*, 75 J. AIR L. & COM. 21 (2007); Bruce Stockfish, *Opening Closed Skies: The Prospects for Further Liberalization of Trade in International Air Transport Services*, 57 J. AIR L. & COM. 599 (1992). *See also* A.J. THOMAS, JR., ECONOMIC REGULATION OF SCHEDULED AIR TRANSPORT 174 (1955).

5. In *United States v. Causby* (1946), *supra*, Justice Douglas wrote that the "ancient doctrine that at common law ownership of the land extended to the periphery of the universe—*Cujus est solum ejus est usque ad coelum* ... has no place in the modern world. The air is a public highway, as Congress has declared. Were that not true, every transcontinental flight would subject the operator to countless trespass suits. Common sense revolts at the idea." *See also Air Pegasus of D.C., Inc. v. United States* (Fed. Cir. 2005), *supra*. Commentary respecting "Open Skies" reveals that this rationale has gained traction internationally only slowly.

In terms of international aviation property law rights, airline operations are bound by legal boundaries and barriers intended to fortify national security, economic, and protectionist concerns. Dating back at least to the Paris Convention of 1919, the evolution of international aviation necessarily has been tied to the principle that nation states enjoy and should safeguard exclusive sovereignty over their airspace. In 1944, more than fifty nations gathered near the conclusion of World War II to create and implement a global civil aviation marketplace that respected national sovereignty without also hamstringing the development of international aviation. Convention on International Civil Aviation, *opened for signature*, Dec. 7, 1944, 61 Stat. 1180, T.I.A.S. No. 1951 ("Chicago Convention"). At the "Chicago Convention," delegates announced their objectives:

> WHEREAS, the development of international civil aviation can greatly help to create and preserve friendship and understanding among the nations and peoples of the world, yet its abuse can become a threat to the general security; and
>
> WHEREAS, it is desirable to avoid friction and to promote that cooperation between nations and peoples which the peace of the world depends;
>
> THEREFORE, the undersigned governments have agreed on certain principles and arrangements in order that international civil aviation may be developed in a safe and orderly manner and that international air transport services may be established on the basis of equal opportunity and operating soundly and economically[.]

Int'l Civ. Aviation Org., International Civil Aviation Conference: Chicago, Ill., 1 Nov. to 7 Dec. 1994.

The Chicago Convention delegates formed the International Civil Aviation Organization ("ICAO"), a United Nations agency that has successfully created international technical standards for global aviation (*e.g.*, requiring communications with air traffic facilities worldwide in the English language and establishing international standards for aircraft airworthiness, flight crew certification, and radio aids to navigation). *See www.icao.int/*. Over 190 nations are signatories to the Chicago Convention and the success of ICAO in establishing international technical standards for aircraft (*e.g.*, a series of published Annexes known as International Standards and Recommended Practices ("SARPs")) is widely recognized.

6. The Chicago Convention delegates (see Note 5, *supra*) sought to develop principles and procedures for the economic regulation of rates, fares, frequency, and capacity in international commercial aviation and overcome restrictions on foreign competition in domestic airline markets. That objective is elusive.

Chicago Convention delegates were successful in affirming "that every State has complete and exclusive sovereignty over the air space above its territory" and defining "five freedoms of the air." Those freedoms included:

(1) the right to fly over the territory of another country without landing;

(2) the right to land in another country for technical, non-traffic reasons such as refueling or maintenance;

(3) the right to discharge traffic from the home country in a foreign country, for example, international airline travel between the United States and destinations in particular European nations;

(4) the right to pick up traffic in a foreign country bound for the home country; and

(5) "beyond rights" or the right to pick up traffic in a foreign country and convey them to a different foreign country, provided that the flight originated or terminated in the home country.

Only the first two freedoms were annexed to the Chicago Convention, leaving the remaining "freedoms"—including the right of "cabotage" (*i.e.*, the right of a foreign-flagged carrier to serve domestic passenger and cargo routes between points *within* a foreign nation)—to be negotiated individually between states as restrictive bilateral or multilateral agreements.

A liberal aviation treaty between the United States and Mexico reached in December 2015, after two years of talks, is an example of such a bilateral aviation treaty:

> The U.S. and Mexico reached a liberal air treaty that would clear the way for airlines on both sides of the border to set their own prices and fly any routes between the two nations with unlimited frequency.
>
> * * *
>
> Mexico was one of the largest countries with which the U.S. lacked a modernized air accord. Others include Russia and China. The U.S. currently has 118 Open Skies air treaties with foreign governments.

See Susan Carey & Laurence Iliff, *U.S., Mexico Forge Air Pact*, WALL ST. J., Dec. 21, 2015, at B3. *See also* FED. AVIATION ADMIN, BILATERAL AGREEMENT LISTING, *http://www.faa.gov/aircraft/air_cert/international/bilateral_agreements/baa_basa_listing/*.

7. Ownership and control of airlines is strictly limited by operation of law. Only American citizens may own and control an American airline—a requirement traditionally defended on grounds of national security and safety (*i.e.*, to prevent airlines from flying under "flags of convenience" in countries with lax safety regulations). In 1926, Congress enacted the Air Commerce Act to restrict foreign ownership of United States airlines. *See* Air Commerce Act of 1926, Pub. L. No. 69-254 (1926) (formerly 49 U.S.C. §§ 171-184 (1951) (repealed 1958). *See generally* ISABELLE LELIEUR, LAW AND POLICY OF SUBSTANTIAL OWNERSHIP AND CONTROL OF AIRLINES 32 (Ashgate 2003). Through a Bureau of Air Commerce and the Civil Aeronautics Administration—precursors of today's Federal Aviation Administration—Congress authorized the development of regulations, enforceable by civil penalties, respecting the registration and licensing of aircraft, together with the certification and medical examination of pilots.

By enacting the Civil Aeronautics Act of 1928, Congress mandated that aircraft in the United States could be registered only by citizens (or partnerships of U.S. citizens) or by corporations of which the president and at least two-thirds of its board members were citizens and at least 75 percent of the voting shares were controlled by U.S. citizens. *See* 49 U.S.C. § 40102(a)(15). The United States Department of Transportation has proposed increasing the stake foreigners might hold in U.S. airlines to 49 percent, thereby providing access to U.S. carriers to international capital markets, encouraging U.S. airlines to develop more efficient, market driven-networks, creating opportunities for airlines to enter into new markets, and achieving consistency with the European Union and other bilateral partners' foreign investment restrictions. That objective has not been reached to date, however. *See generally* L.F.E. Goldie, *Environmental Catastrophes and Flags of Convenience—Does the Present Law Pose Special Liability Issues?*, 3 PACE Y.B. INT'L L. 53, 64 n.5 (1991); Howard Kass, *Cabotage and Control: Bringing 1938 U.S. Aviation Policy into the Jet Age*, 26 CASE W. RES. J. INT'L L. 143, 150 (1994); Ved P. Nanda, *Substantial Ownership and Control of International Airlines in the United States*, 50 AM. J. COMP. L. 357, 359 (2002); Moritz Ferdinand Scharpenseel, *Consequences of E.U. Airline Deregulation in the Context of the Global Aviation Market*, 22 NW. J. INT'L BUS. 91, 110 (2001).

8. In the late 1960's several of the nation's airports experienced severe congestion, resulting in numerous and substantial delays. In 1968 the Federal Aviation Administration ("FAA") issued the High Density Traffic Airports Rule ("HDAR"), 14 C.F.R. §§ 93.121 to .133 (1980) (effective April 27, 1969), in order to reduce delays in takeoffs and landings at five crowded airports (Kennedy International Airport and LaGuardia Airport in New York, Newark Airport in New Jersey, O'Hare Airport in Chicago, and National (Reagan) in Washington, D.C.) and thus promote efficient utilization of the navigable airspace. More specifically, the FAA assigned slots—essentially a reservation for arriving and departing. Such slots are in fact alienable property and, to this day, significant amounts of litigation have centered on the federal government's allocation and auctioning of such slots among airlines and the airlines' own possession and attempted exchange of such slots. *See generally* Andrew Compart, Who

Owns Slots?, AVIATION WK. & SPACE TECH., May 10, 2010, at 48-49. *See also Eastern Airlines, Inc. v. Fed. Aviation Admin.* (11th Cir. 1985); *Northwest Airlines, Inc. v. Goldschmidt* (8th Cir. 1981); *Laker Airways, Inc. v. British Airways, PLC* (11th Cir. 1999).

By the early 1990s, the HDAR was perceived as a barrier to improved service, in part because new air carriers were unable to establish service due to the lack of slot availability. *See* H.R. Rep. No. 106-167, at 225-26, *reprinted at* 1999 WL 355951 (1999). As a result, in 1994, Congress enacted a provision giving the United States Secretary of Transportation discretion to grant exemptions from the slot requirement where the Secretary "finds it to be in the public interest and the circumstances to be exceptional." *See* Pub. L. No. 103-305, § 206(c)(1) (prior to 2000 amendment). By the late 1990s, however, Congress, dissatisfied with the number of exemptions granted, concluded that "[e]xpanding the current exemptions or adding new exemptions no longer seems to be the best approach," H.R. Rep. No. 106-167, at 226, and decided to eliminate the HDAR at LaGuardia, Kennedy, and O'Hare, while retaining some limits at Reagan National. *See* Ken Belson, *Ending a Limit on Kennedy Flights Increases Passengers and Delays*, N.Y. TIMES, July 12, 2007, at B3.

The new law, the Wendell H. Ford Aviation Investment and Reform Act for the 21st Century ("AIR21"), Pub. L. No. 106-181 (2000) (codified in scattered sections of 49 U.S.C.), phased out the HDAR at LaGuardia and Kennedy as of January 1, 2007 (and O'Hare, after July 1, 2002), *see* 49 U.S.C. § 41715(a)(2) (2000). AIR21 provided interim slot rules for new entrants to offer services at the two airports until that date. The legislation is generally intended to increase the number both of carriers offering services and of non-stop flights from the two airports to small hub or non-hub airports through the use of regional jets. *E.g.*, *City of New York v. Minetta* (2d Cir. 2001). *See also* Michael E. Levine, *Airport Congestion: When Theory Meets Reality*, 26 YALE J. ON REG. 37 (2009).

9. The Federal Aviation Administration has extensive and plenary authority concerning the use and management of the navigable airspace, air traffic control, and air navigation facilities. 49 U.S.C. §§ 40103(b), 44502, and 44721. How "unmanned aerial vehicles"—UAVs—are incorporated into the national airspace, if at all, will present a significant practical and regulatory challenge for lawmakers in the decade ahead. FED. AVIATION ADMIN., AFS-400 UAS Policy 05-01, UNMANNED AIRCRAFT SYSTEMS OPERATIONS IN THE U.S. NATIONAL AIRSPACE SYSTEM—INTERIM OPERATIONAL APPROVAL GUIDANCE (2005). *See also* Timothy M. Ravich, *The Integration of Unmanned Aerial Vehicles into the National Airspace*, 85 N.D. L. REV. 597 (2009); Douglas Marshall, *Unmanned Aerial Systems and International Civil Aviation Organization Regulations*, 85 N.D. L. REV. 693 (2009); Mark E. Peterson, *The UAV and the Current and Future Regulatory Construct for Integration into the National Airspace System*, 71 J. AIR L. & COM. 521 (2006).

10. As introduced in *Goodspeed Airport, LLC v. East Haddam Inland Wetlands and Watercourses Comm'n* (D. Conn. 2010), *supra*, airports—their operations, land use, finances, and safety—are regulated extensively. Public or private agencies that control airports (*e.g.*, "sponsors") assume certain obligations in exchange for accepting airport development assistance from the federal government. Such obligations are undertaken either by contract or by restrictive covenants in property deeds, to maintain and operate airport facilities safely and efficiently in accordance with specified conditions. Some grant programs include the Federal Aid to Airports Program ("FAAP"), the National Plan of Integrated Airport Systems ("NPIAS"), the Airport Development Aid Program ("ADAP"), and the Airport Improvement Program ("AIP) (49 U.S.C. § 47101 *et seq.*) *See generally* FED. AVIATION ADMIN., AIRPORT COMPLIANCE MANUAL, ORDER 5190.6B (Sept. 30, 2009):
http://www.faa.gov/airports/resources/publications/orders/compliance_5190_6/.

Sponsors are obligated to make "grant assurances" as part of their grant agreement with the government. One such assurance involves "economic nondiscrimination," *i.e.* the promise to make an airport available for public use to any entity for aeronautical use on reasonable terms and without unjust discrimination. *See Lange v. Fed. Aviation Admin.* (2d Cir. 2000); *Penobscot Air Svcs. Ltd. v. Fed. Aviation Admin.* (1st Cir. 1999). *See also* 49 U.S.C. § 47107 (2010).

PROBLEM

Frequent Flyer Depot, Inc. ("Frequent Flyer") brokers the purchase and sale of airline frequent flyer miles and awards, including AAdvantage® rewards points issued by American Airlines to its AAdvantage® members. American Airlines sued Frequent Flyer and similar brokers and their principals, contending that the brokering, purchase, bartering, and sale of AAdvantage® rewards is improper. Among its claims against Frequent Flyer were claims for tortious interference with contract, tortious interference with prospective relations, misappropriation, and fraud. After filing suit, American Airlines sought a temporary injunction prohibiting Frequent Flyer from buying, selling, bartering, or soliciting AAdvantage® rewards during pendency of the suit.

What property rights, if any, does Frequent Flyer have in the rewards points issued by American Airlines? *See Frequent Flyer Depot, Inc. v. American Airlines, Inc.* (Tex. App. 2010).

CHAPTER 2

DEREGULATION AND PREEMPTION

A. AVIATION FEDERALISM AND SUPREMACY

In *Northwest Airlines, Inc. v. Minnesota*, a 1944 case of first impression about the constitutional limitations upon state power to tax airplanes, Justice Robert H. Jackson wrote in a concurring opinion that "[p]lanes do not wander about in the sky like vagrant clouds." Rather, "[t]hey move only by federal permission, subject to federal inspection, in the hands of federally certified personnel and under an intricate system of federal commands." The "moment a ship taxies onto a runway it is caught up in an elaborate and detailed system of controls. It takes off only by instruction from the control tower, it travels on prescribed beams, it may be diverted from its intended landing, and it obeys signals and orders. Its privileges, rights, and protection, so far as transit is concerned, it owes to the Federal Government alone and not to any state government."

Justice Jackson's concurrence touches on how pervasively aviation operations are regulated by the federal government. Indeed, at the heart of the *Northwest Airlines, Inc. v. Minnesota* is the concept of federalism—the constitutional relationship between state governments and the central federal government.

Understanding the dynamics of federalism and the breadth of the Supremacy Clause in the Constitution is critical in the context of aviation law in the United States. Each state has jurisdiction over local and intrastate aviation issues, including licensing airports, channeling federal funds to airports, imposing local taxes, legislating land use, and even enacting laws allowing or disallowing guns in airport terminals. But, the national and international nature of air travel invites, if not requires, extensive federal oversight (particularly when safety is concerns, as discussed in Chapter 6, *supra*). In fact, as detailed below, whether there is any room for state law in an industry prevalently controlled by the federal government is a frequent issue that continues to be litigated regularly in courts around the nation.

ROWE v. NEW HAMPSHIRE MOTOR TRANSPORT ASS'N

552 U.S. 364 (2008)

Justice BREYER delivered the opinion of the Court.

We here consider whether a federal statute that prohibits States from enacting any law "related to" a motor carrier "price, route, or service" pre-empts two provisions of a Maine tobacco law, which regulate the delivery of tobacco to customers within the State. We hold that the federal law pre-empts both provisions.

In 1978, Congress "determin[ed] that 'maximum reliance on competitive market forces' " would favor lower airline fares and better airline service, and it enacted the Airline Deregulation Act. *Morales v. Trans World Airlines, Inc.* (1992). In order to "ensure that the States would not undo federal deregulation with regulation of their own," that Act "included a pre-emption provision" that said "no State ... shall enact or enforce any law ... relating to rates, routes, or services of any air carrier."

In 1980, Congress deregulated trucking. *See* Motor Carrier Act of 1980, 94 Stat. 793. And a little over a decade later, in 1994, Congress similarly sought to pre-empt state trucking regulation. *See* Federal Aviation Administration Authorization Act of 1994, 108 Stat. 1605–1606; *see also* ICC Termination Act of 1995, 109 Stat. 899. In doing so, it borrowed language from the Airline Deregulation Act of 1978 and wrote into its 1994 law language that says: "[A] State ... may not enact or enforce a law ... related to a price, route, or service of any motor carrier ... with respect to the transportation of property." *See* 49 U.S.C. § 14501(c)(1); § 41713(b)(4)(A) (similar provision for combined motor-air carriers).

The State of Maine subsequently adopted An Act to Regulate the Delivery and Sales of Tobacco Products and To Prevent the Sale of Tobacco Products to Minors, two sections of which are relevant here. The first section forbids anyone other than a Maine-licensed tobacco retailer to accept an order for delivery of tobacco. It then adds that, when a licensed retailer accepts an order and ships tobacco, the retailer must "utilize a delivery service" that provides a special kind of recipient-verification service. The delivery service must make certain that (1) the person who bought the tobacco is the person to whom the package is addressed; (2) the person to whom the package is addressed is of legal age to purchase tobacco; (3) the person to whom the package is addressed has himself or herself signed for the package; and (4) the person to whom the package is addressed, if under the age of 27, has produced a valid government-issued photo identification with proof of age. Violations are punishable by civil penalties (first offense up to $1,500; subsequent offenses up to $5,000).

The second section forbids any person "knowingly" to "transport" a "tobacco product" to "a person" in Maine unless either the sender or the receiver has a Maine license. It then adds that a "person is deemed to know that a package contains a tobacco product" (1) if the package is marked as containing tobacco and displays the name and license number of a Maine-licensed tobacco retailer; or (2) if the person receives the package from someone whose name appears on a list of un-licensed tobacco retailers that Maine's Attorney General distributes to various package-delivery companies. Violations are again punishable by civil penalties (up to $1,500 per violation against violator and/or violator's employer).

Respondents, several transport carrier associations, brought this lawsuit in federal court, claiming that federal law pre-empts several sections of Maine's statute. The District Court held (among other things) that federal law pre-empts the portions of the two sections we have described, namely the "recipient-verification" provision and the "deemed to know" provision. On appeal, the Court of Appeals for the First Circuit agreed that federal law pre-empted the two provisions. We granted *certiorari* to review these determinations.

II.

In *Morales*, this Court interpreted the pre-emption provision in the Airline Deregulation Act of 1978. And we follow *Morales* in interpreting similar language in the 1994 Act before us here. We have said that "when judicial interpretations have settled the meaning of an existing statutory provision, repetition of the same language in a new statute indicates, as a general matter, the intent to incorporate its judicial interpretations as well." Here, the Congress that wrote the language before us copied the language of the air-carrier pre-emption provision of the Airline Deregulation Act of 1978. And it did so fully aware of this Court's interpretation of that language as set forth in *Morales*. *See* H.R. Conf. Rep., at 83, U.S. CODE CONG. & ADMIN. NEWS 1994, pp. 1676, 1755 (motor carriers will enjoy "the identical intrastate preemption of prices, routes and services as that originally contained in" the Airline Deregulation Act).

In *Morales*, the Court determined: (1) that "[s]tate enforcement actions having a connection with, or reference to" carrier "'rates, routes, or services' are pre-empted," (2) that such pre-emption may occur even if a state law's effect on rates, routes or services "is only indirect," (3) that, in respect to pre-emption, it makes no difference whether a state law is "consistent" or "inconsistent" with federal regulation, and (4) that pre-emption occurs at least where state laws have a "significant impact" related to Congress' deregulatory and pre-emption-related objectives. The Court described Congress' overarching goal as helping assure transportation rates, routes, and services that reflect "maximum reliance on competitive market forces," thereby stimulating "efficiency, innovation, and low prices," as well as "variety" and "quality." *Morales* held that, given these principles, federal law pre-empts States from enforcing their consumer-fraud statutes against deceptive airline-fare advertisements. *See American Airlines, Inc. v. Wolens* (1995) (federal law pre-empts application of a State's general consumer-protection statute to an airline's frequent flyer program).

Finally, *Morales* said that federal law might not pre-empt state laws that affect fares in only a "tenuous, remote, or peripheral ... manner," such as state laws forbidding gambling. But the Court did not say where, or how, "it would be appropriate to draw the line," for the state law before it did not "present a borderline question."

In light of *Morales*, we find that federal law pre-empts the Maine laws at issue here. Section 1555–C(3)(C) of the Maine statute forbids licensed tobacco retailers to employ a "delivery service" unless that service follows particular delivery procedures. In doing so, it focuses on trucking and other motor carrier services (which make up a substantial portion of all "delivery services," thereby creating a direct "connection with" motor carrier services.

At the same time, the provision has a "significant" and adverse "impact" in respect to the federal Act's ability to achieve its pre-emption-related objectives. The Solicitor General and the carrier associations claim (and Maine does not deny) that the law will require carriers to offer a system of services that the market does not now provide (and which the carriers would prefer not to offer). And even were that not so, the law would freeze into place services that carriers might prefer to discontinue in the future. The Maine law thereby produces the very effect that the federal law sought to avoid, namely, a State's direct substitution of its own governmental commands for "competitive market forces" in determining (to a significant degree) the services that motor carriers will provide.

We concede that the regulation here is less "direct" than it might be, for it tells shippers what to choose rather than carriers what to do. Nonetheless, the effect of the regulation is that carriers will have to offer tobacco delivery services that differ significantly from those that, in the absence of the regulation, the market might dictate. And that being so, "treating sales restrictions and purchase restrictions differently for pre-emption purposes would make no sense." If federal law pre-empts state efforts to regulate, and consequently to affect, the advertising about carrier rates and services at issue in *Morales*, it must pre-empt Maine's efforts to regulate carrier delivery services themselves.

Section 1555–D's "deemed to know" provision applies yet more directly to motor carrier services. The provision creates a conclusive presumption of carrier knowledge that a shipment contains tobacco when it is marked as originating from a Maine-licensed tobacco retailer or is sent by anyone Maine has specifically identified as an unlicensed tobacco retailer. That presumption means that the Maine law imposes civil liability upon the carrier, not simply for its knowing transport of (unlicensed) tobacco, but for the carrier's failure sufficiently to examine every package. The provision thus requires the carrier to check each shipment for certain markings and to compare it against the Maine attorney general's list of proscribed shippers. And it thereby directly regulates a significant aspect of the motor carrier's package pickup and delivery service. In this way it creates the kind of state-mandated regulation that the federal Act pre-empts.

Maine replies that the regulation will impose no significant additional costs upon carriers. But even were that so (and the carriers deny it), Maine's reply is off the mark. As with the recipient-verification provision, the "deemed to know" provision would freeze in place and immunize from competition a service-related system that carriers do not (or in the future might not) wish to provide.

To allow Maine to insist that the carriers provide a special checking system would allow other States to do the same. And to interpret the federal law to permit these, and similar, state requirements could easily lead to a patchwork of state service-determining laws, rules, and regulations. That state regulatory patchwork is inconsistent with Congress' major legislative effort to leave such decisions, where federally unregulated, to the competitive marketplace. If federal law pre-empts state regulation of the details of an air carrier's frequent flyer program, a program that primarily promotes carriage, *see Wolens*, it must pre-empt state regulation of the essential details of a motor carrier's system for picking-up, sorting, and carrying goods—essential details of the carriage itself.

* * *

Maine's primary arguments focus upon the reason why it has enacted the provisions in question. Maine argues for an exception from pre-emption on the ground that its laws help it prevent minors from obtaining cigarettes. In Maine's view, federal law does not pre-empt a State's efforts to protect its citizens' public health, particularly when those laws regulate so dangerous an activity as underage smoking.

Despite the importance of the public health objective, we cannot agree with Maine that the federal law creates an exception on that basis, exempting state laws that it would otherwise pre-empt. The Act says nothing about a public health exception. To the contrary, it explicitly lists a set of exceptions (governing motor vehicle safety, certain local route controls, and the like), but the list says nothing about public health.

Maine suggests that the provision's history indicates that Congress' primary concern was not with the sort of law it has enacted, but instead with state "economic" regulation. But it is frequently difficult to distinguish between a State's "economic"-related and "health"-related motivations, and, indeed, the parties vigorously dispute Maine's actual motivation for the laws at issue here. Consequently, it is not surprising that Congress declined to insert the term "economic" into the operative language now before us, despite having at one time considered doing so.

* * *

In this case, the state law is not general, it does not affect truckers solely in their capacity as members of the general public, the impact is significant, and the connection with trucking is not tenuous, remote, or peripheral. The state statutes aim directly at the carriage of goods, a commercial field where carriage by commercial motor vehicles plays a major role. The state statutes require motor carrier operators to perform certain services, thereby limiting their ability to provide incompatible alternative services; and they do so simply because the State seeks to enlist the motor carrier operators as allies in its enforcement efforts.

Given these circumstances, from the perspective of pre-emption, this case is no more "borderline" than was *Morales*. Given *Morales*, where the Court held that federal law pre-empts state consumer-protection laws, we find that federal law must also pre-empt Maine's efforts directly to regulate carrier services.

Justice GINSBURG, concurring.

Today's decision declares key portions of Maine's Tobacco Delivery Law incompatible with the Federal Aviation Administration Authorization Act of 1994 (FAAAA). The breadth of FAAAA's preemption language, coupled with our decisions closely in point, *Morales v. Trans World Airlines, Inc.* and *American Airlines, Inc. v. Wolens*, impel that conclusion. I write separately to emphasize the large regulatory gap left by an application of the FAAAA perhaps overlooked by Congress, and the urgent need for the National Legislature to fill that gap.

Tobacco use by children and adolescents, we have recognized, may be "the single most significant threat to public health in the United States." But no comprehensive federal law currently exists to prevent tobacco sellers from exploiting the underage market. Instead, Congress has encouraged state efforts. Congress has done so by providing funding incentives for the States to pass legislation making it unlawful to "sell or distribute any [tobacco] product to any individual under the age of 18."

State measures to prevent youth access to tobacco, however, are increasingly thwarted by the ease with which tobacco products can be purchased through the Internet. "As cyberspace acts as a risk-free zone where minors can anonymously purchase tobacco, unrestricted online tobacco sales create a major barrier to comprehensive youth tobacco control."

Maine and its *amici* maintain that, to guard against delivery of tobacco products to children, "the same sort of age verification safeguards [must be] used when tobacco is handed over-the-doorstep as ... when it is handed over-the-counter." The FAAAA's broad preemption provisions, the Court holds, bar States from adopting this sensible enforcement strategy. While I join the Court's opinion, I doubt that the drafters of the FAAAA, a statute designed to deregulate the carriage of goods, anticipated the measure's facilitation of minors' access to tobacco. Now alerted to the problem, Congress has the capacity to act with care and dispatch to provide an effective solution.

Justice SCALIA, concurring in part.

I join the opinion of the Court, except those portions that rely on the reports of committees of one House of Congress to show the intent of that full House and of the other—with regard to propositions that are apparent from the text of the law, unnecessary to the disposition of the case, or both.

* * *

BAILEY v. ROCKY MOUNTAIN HOLDINGS, LLC

2015 WL 5885379 (S.D. Fla. 2015)

WILLIAM J. ZLOCH, United States District Judge.

Defendant Air Methods Corporation ("AMC") is authorized by the Federal Aviation Act ("FAA"), 49 U.S.C. §§ 40101 *et seq.*, to operate as a Part 135 air carrier providing on-demand and air ambulance services. AMC is registered with the Department of Transportation ("DOT") to operate as a Part 298 air taxi operator providing on-demand air ambulance services. Pursuant to their Part 135 certificate and their Part 298 registration, AMC doing business in the state of Florida as Rocky Mountain Holdings, LLC, ("RMH") is authorized to operate interstate flights as a common carrier for compensation. The DOT has expressly recognized AMC d/b/a RMH as an "air carrier" that is authorized to provide interstate transportation. As a Part 135 air carrier, AMC d/b/a RMH is pervasively regulated on safety and economic matters by the FAA.

On March 17, 2013, Plaintiff's son, Lemar Bailey, sustained fatal injuries in a motor vehicle accident in Martin County, Florida. He was ejected from the vehicle and transported by Defendants by helicopter from the accident scene to St. Mary's Medical Center in West Palm Beach, Florida. Plaintiff was thereafter invoiced for the air ambulance service provided by Defendants in an amount totaling $27,975.90.

Defendants also submitted an invoice to State Farm Insurance, the insurer for the motor vehicle involved in the accident. State Farm, pursuant to Florida's Personal Injury Protection statute ("PIP"), paid 80% of what it considered to be the allowable amount, or $6,911.54, which is 200% of the Medicare Part B fee. Thereafter, Defendants submitted a claim for payment to Mr. Lemar Bailey's health insurer, Aetna, which was secondary to the PIP coverage. Aetna then paid Defendants the sum of $3,681.60. Defendants applied the amounts paid by both State Farm and Aetna to Plaintiff's outstanding balance. Plaintiff did not make any payments to Defendants, and the remaining balance of $17,382.76 for air ambulance services was ultimately written off as a bad debt.

Lenworth Bailey, as Personal Representative of the Estate of Lemar Bailey, seeks a declaratory judgment that Defendants' billing practices violate the Florida PIP Statute and that Defendants' actions violate Florida's Deceptive and Unfair Trade Practices Act. Additionally, Plaintiff seeks damages for Defendants' alleged violations of FDUPTA. Plaintiff further alleges violations of the Florida Consumer Collection and Practices Act, and unjust enrichment.

ANALYSIS

The Supremacy Clause of the United States Constitution invalidates state and local laws that interfere with or are contrary to the laws of Congress. "[W]here Congress has legislated concerning a subject, on which it is authorized to act, all State legislation which interferes with it, is absolutely void." *Gibbons v. Ogden* (1824). Federal law can preempt state and local laws either expressly or impliedly.

Congress manifested its intent "to rest sole responsibility for supervising the aviation industry with the federal government" when it enacted the FAA:

> [A]viation is unique among transportation industries in its relation to the federal government—it is the only one whose operations are conducted almost wholly within federal jurisdiction, and are subject to little or no regulation by States or local authorities. Thus, the federal government bears virtually complete responsibility for the promotion and supervision of this industry in the public interest.

S. Rep. No. 1811 (85th Cong., 2d Sess. 5) (1985). In 1978, Congress amended the FAA and enacted the ADA. "To ensure that the States would not undo federal deregulation with regulation of their own," the ADA included an express preemption clause, codified at 49 U.S.C. § 41713(b). This clause states, in pertinent part, that:

> a State, political subdivision of a State, or political authority of at least 2 States may not enact or enforce a law, regulation, or other provision having the force and effect of law *related to a price, route, or service* of an air carrier that may provide air transportation under this subpart.

Thus, States are expressly prohibited from enacting or enforcing any law, regulation, or other provision which relates to an air carrier's price, route, or service. "The purpose of the ADA's preemption provision was to increase 'reliance on competitive market forces rather than pervasive federal regulation.'" *Koutsouradis v. Delta Air Lines, Inc.* (11th Cir. 2005). In *Rowe v. N.H. Motor Transport Ass'n*, the Supreme Court described the goal of Congress in the ADA's preemption provision "as helping ensure transportation rates, routes, and services that reflect 'maximum reliance on competitive market forces,' thereby stimulating 'efficiency, innovation, and low prices,' as well as 'variety' and 'quality.'"

Notwithstanding the ADA's express preemption provision, Plaintiff contends that Florida's PIP Statute "reverse preempts" federal law in this case, pursuant to the McCarran–Ferguson Act ("MFA"). The MFA is a federal statute directed at insulating state insurance regulation from implied preemption by federal domestic commerce legislation. The MFA initially declares that "*silence* on the part of the Congress shall not be construed to impose any barrier" to state regulation or taxation of the business of insurance. It further provides that "[n]o Act of Congress shall be construed to invalidate, impair, or supersede any law enacted by any State for the purpose of regulating the business of insurance, or which imposes a fee or tax upon such business, unless such Act specifically relates to the business of insurance." Accordingly, the McCarran–Ferguson Act authorizes "reverse preemption" of federal statutes by state laws enacted to regulate the business of insurance. However, the Court finds that Congress has not been silent here, and the MFA therefore does not apply to reverse-preempt the ADA.

In enacting the ADA and including in it an express preemption provision, Congress made plain its intent to altogether preempt state laws that regulate an air carrier's prices, routes, or services. The MFA was intended only to protect state insurance regulation from inadvertent intrusion by the federal government, and not to insulate the same from every federal law. *See Humana Inc. v. Forsyth* (1999) ("We reject any suggestion that Congress intended to cede the field of insurance regulation to the states, saving only instances in which Congress expressly orders otherwise. If Congress had meant generally to preempt the field for the States, Congress could have said ... '[n]o federal statute that does not say so explicitly shall be construed to apply to the business of insurance.'*"); Barnett Bank of Marion Cnty., N.A. v. Nelson* (1996) ("Particularly the word 'silence,' indicates that the Act does not seek to insulate state insurance regulation from the reach of all federal law. Rather, it seeks to protect state regulation primarily against inadvertent federal intrusion-say, through enactment of a federal statute that describes an affected activity in broad, general terms, of which the insurance business happens to constitute one part."). Indeed "when the intended effect of a federal statute is to displace state regulations, [the court] must give effect to this intent, regardless of whether an insurance company is involved." *Lander v. Hartford Life & Annuity Ins. Co.* (2d Cir. 2001).

As stated above, the Parties agree that Defendant AMC is an "air carrier" within the meaning of the statute. Further, the Court finds that each of Plaintiff's state and common law claims can only be fairly characterized as directly challenging Defendants' rates for its air ambulance services. These claims, if permitted to proceed, would naturally affect the provision of Defendants' services in addition to the prices of and payment for those services. Consequently, the above-styled cause is essentially a state enforcement action having a very strong connection with or reference to a price, route, or service of an air carrier. And the Court finds that this state and common law challenge is expressly disallowed by the ADA's express preemption provision, which intentionally leaves the price of such services to the competitive market. *See Crane v. Native Am. Ambulance, Inc.*, No. (D. Ariz. Feb. 23, 2007) (finding class action regarding air ambulance fees was preempted by the ADA). Accordingly, the above-styled cause is altogether preempted as a matter of law and cannot proceed. Because the Court finds that the above-styled cause is expressly preempted by the ADA, it does not reach the alternative bases for summary judgment raised in Defendants' Motion.

U.S. AIRWAYS, INC v. O'DONNELL

627 F.3d 1318 (10th Cir. 2010)

BRISCOE, Chief Judge.

The New Mexico Liquor Control Act ("NMLCA"), N.M. Stat. § 60–3A–1 *et seq.*, regulates the sale, service and public consumption of alcoholic beverages in the State of New Mexico. NMLCA states, in relevant part, that "[e]very person selling alcoholic beverages to travelers on ... airplanes within the state shall secure a public service license." Further, NMLCA prohibits any person from being "employed as a server on a licensed premises unless that person obtains within thirty days of employment alcohol server training."

US Airways, an interstate airline carrier regulated by the Federal Aviation Administration of the United States Department of Transportation, operates flights that travel to and from the State of New Mexico at the Albuquerque International Sunport Airport. These flights generally originate from or arrive at locations outside New Mexico. US Airways serves alcoholic beverages during its flights, including those that arrive in and depart from New Mexico. However, passengers are not permitted to remove from the aircraft the alcoholic beverages served during flight. Further, the U.S. Airways beverage carts containing the alcoholic beverages are not removed from the aircraft in New Mexico. US Airways does not stock its aircraft with alcoholic beverages and does not purchase or store such beverages in New Mexico. Prior to 2007, U.S. Airways provided alcoholic beverage service to passengers on flights departing from and arriving in New Mexico without possessing a public service license as required by NMLCA.

In November 2006, Dana Papst was a passenger on a U.S. Airways flight departing from Phoenix, Arizona and arriving in Albuquerque, New Mexico. He allegedly purchased and consumed alcoholic beverages during his U.S. Airways flight. During his drive home from the Albuquerque airport and approximately three hours after deplaning, he caused an automobile accident that resulted in his death and the death of five others. An analysis of Papst's blood drawn after the accident revealed that Papst's blood alcohol content was approximately 0.329. After conducting an investigation of the incident, the Federal Aviation Administration declined to take any action against U.S. Airways or its employees.

In January 2007, the Alcohol and Gaming Division ("AGD") of the New Mexico Regulation and Licensing Department served U.S. Airways with a citation asserting that U.S. Airways had served alcohol to an intoxicated person, namely Dana Papst. The AGD also served U.S. Airways with a cease-and-desist order directing U.S. Airways to "refrain from selling, serving and otherwise dispensing, storing or possessing alcoholic beverages of any kind in the State of New Mexico" without properly complying with the requirements of the New Mexico Liquor Control Act ("NMLCA"), N.M. Stat. § 60–3A–1 *et seq.*

In February 2007, while noting its belief that federal law preempted the application of NMLCA to an airline, U.S. Airways applied for a public service license to serve alcoholic beverages to passengers on aircraft in New Mexico. In response to the application, AGD issued U.S. Airways a ninety-day temporary license. However, in June 2007, AGD declined to extend U.S. Airways' temporary license explaining that U.S. Airways' alcohol server training did not comply with NMLCA's requirements. AGD ultimately rejected U.S. Airways' application for a license in November 2007 citing as reasons for the denial the Dana Papst incident and another incident which involved a passenger who had been served alcoholic beverages on a U.S. Airways flight and was apprehended for driving while intoxicated approximately an hour after he had deplaned at Albuquerque.

US Airways filed this action seeking to "enjoin New Mexico state officials [in the AGD and the New Mexico Regulation and Licensing Department] from enforcing laws that purport to govern U.S. Airways' alcoholic beverage service on flights departing from or arriving into New Mexico." US Airways asserted both express and implied preemption in support of its request for injunction.

Specifically, U.S. Airways argued that the enforcement of NMLCA against an airline violated the Supremacy Clause of the United States Constitution as the ADA expressly preempts state regulation of airline services, including the alcoholic beverage service provided to passengers on flights. Alternatively, U.S. Airways contended that federal law impliedly preempts the application of NMLCA to airlines as the application of NMLCA to an airline implicates the field of aviation safety, which federal law regulates to the exclusion of state regulation. Further, U.S. Airways asserted that New Mexico's regulatory efforts could not be otherwise authorized pursuant to the Twenty-first Amendment to the United States Constitution.

The parties filed cross-motions for summary judgment and the district court concluded that federal law neither expressly nor impliedly preempts New Mexico's regulation of the alcoholic beverage service that airlines provide. Specifically, the district court narrowly construed the explicit preemption provision in the ADA, concluding that the provision's reference to "service" did not include an airline's alcoholic beverage service. The district court reasoned that the narrow interpretation necessarily avoided rendering the ADA preemption provision violative of § 2 of the Twenty-first Amendment. Further, the district court addressed field preemption and concluded that federal law did not preempt the field of alcohol service on airlines. In reaching this decision, the district court reasoned that, when enacting the FAA, "Congress was addressing the need for exclusive and complete rules for the physical and mechanical operation of aircraft." The district court then denied U.S. Airways' motion for summary judgment and granted New Mexico's motion.

On appeal, U.S. Airways argues that the Airline Deregulation Act of 1978 ("ADA") expressly preempts state regulation of airlines' alcoholic beverage services provided to passengers. In addition to express preemption, U.S. Airways argues that federal law impliedly preempts the application of the NMLCA to U.S. Airways. Specifically, U.S. Airways contends that the Federal Aviation Act of 1958 ("FAA") and the federal regulations promulgated pursuant to the FAA occupy the field of aviation safety to the exclusion of state regulation and that NMLCA's application to an airline implicates the field of aviation safety. Exercising jurisdiction under 28 U.S.C. § 1291, we conclude that New Mexico's regulatory scheme is impliedly preempted as it falls within the field of aviation safety that Congress intended federal law to occupy exclusively, but that the Twenty-first Amendment of the United States Constitution requires a balancing of New Mexico's core powers and the federal interests underlying the FAA. Accordingly, we reverse and remand for the district court to conduct a Twenty-first Amendment balancing.

A. Preemption

The Supremacy Clause provides that the laws of the United States "shall be the supreme Law of the Land; ... any Thing in the Constitution or Laws of any State to the Contrary notwithstanding." U.S. CONST. art. VI, cl. 2. Pursuant to this provision, Congress has the power to enact statutes that preempt state law. Thus, preemption is ultimately a question of congressional intent.

There are three types of preemption: (1) "express preemption, which occurs when the language of the federal statute reveals an express congressional intent to preempt state law;" (2) "field preemption, which occurs when the federal scheme of regulation is so pervasive that Congress must have intended to leave no room for a State to supplement it;" and (3) "conflict preemption, which occurs either when compliance with both the federal and state laws is a physical impossibility, or when the state law stands as an obstacle to the accomplishment and execution of the full purposes and objectives of Congress."

In this case, U.S. Airways asserts that federal law expressly preempts NMLCA's application to an airline. Additionally, U.S. Airways asserts that the FAA, 49 U.S.C. § 40101 *et seq*., and the federal regulations promulgated pursuant to the FAA occupy the field of aviation safety to the exclusion of state regulation, including the NMLCA. Because we conclude that applying New Mexico's regulatory scheme to U.S. Airways implicates the field of aviation safety that Congress intended federal law to regulate exclusively, we need not reach the question of express preemption.

1. *Field Preemption*

Field preemption occurs when a "state law ... regulates conduct in a field that Congress intended the Federal Government to occupy exclusively." Congress's intent for federal law to occupy a field exclusively "may be inferred from a scheme of federal regulation so pervasive as to make reasonable the inference that Congress left no room for the States to supplement it, or where an Act of Congress touches a field in which the interest is so dominant that the federal system will be assumed to preclude enforcement of state laws on the same subject."

When conducting a field preemption analysis, we must first identify the legislative field that the state law at issue implicates. In this case, the district court narrowly construed NMLCA as regulating the field of alcoholic beverage service provided on airplanes. In our view, however, the regulation of an airline's alcoholic beverage service necessarily implicates the field of airline safety. The FAA similarly recognized the safety considerations implicated when promulgating 14 C.F.R. § 121.575 to regulate the alcoholic beverage services provided on airplanes. *See* Drinking and Serving of Alcoholic Beverages, 25 Fed. Reg. 168, 168–69 (Jan. 9, 1960) (discussing the safety concerns associated with an airline's alcoholic beverage service). Additionally, NMLCA's regulatory scheme extends beyond the field of airline alcoholic beverage services. Specifically, NMLCA prescribes training and certification requirements for flight attendants and other airline crew members serving alcoholic beverages on aircraft. Thus, we conclude that New Mexico's regulatory scheme as applied to an airline generally implicates the field of aviation safety.

Having identified the legislative field at issue, we must next evaluate whether Congress intended to occupy the field to the exclusion of the states. Thus, in this case, we must determine whether Congress intended to occupy the field of aviation safety to the exclusion of the states. While recognizing that the purpose of Congress must be clear as we presume that "Congress does not cavalierly pre-empt state-law causes of action," the field of aviation safety "has long been dominated by federal interests." *Montalvo v. Spirit Airlines* (9th Cir. 2007). Thus, the presumption against preemption does not apply in this case.

Based on the FAA's purpose to centralize aviation safety regulation and the comprehensive regulatory scheme promulgated pursuant to the FAA, we conclude that federal regulation occupies the field of aviation safety to the exclusion of state regulations. The FAA was enacted to create a "uniform and exclusive system of federal regulation" in the field of air safety. Specifically, Congress enacted the FAA in response to a series of "fatal air crashes between civil and military aircraft operating under separate flight rules." H.R. Rep. No. 85–2360, at 2 (1958), *reprinted in* 1958 U.S.C.C.A.N. 3741, 3742 (noting that "[t]he magnitude and critical nature of [airspace use and air-safety problems] came ... to general public notice ... as a result of" a series of airplane crashes). In response to the air safety concerns, the House Report discussing the FAA indicated that the "Administrator of the new Federal Aviation Agency ... would be given full responsibility and authority for the ... promulgation and enforcement of safety regulations." Further, as documented in the House Report, a letter from a representative of the Executive Branch to the House Committee on International and Foreign Commerce explained that "[i]t is essential that one agency of government, and one agency alone, be responsible for issuing safety regulations."

The language of the FAA explicitly directs the Administrator of the Federal Aviation Administration to promulgate regulations for the "safe flight of civil aircraft in air commerce." Beyond the types of regulations specifically enumerated, the FAA directs the Administrator to regulate any "other practices, methods, and procedure the Administrator finds necessary for safety in air commerce and national security." The Federal Aviation Administration has exercised its authority pursuant to the FAA to promulgate regulations addressing "virtually all areas of air safety." *Air Transp. Ass'n of Am., Inc. v. Cuomo* (2d Cir. 2008); *see, e.g.*, 14 C.F.R. § 91.13(a) (identifying the general standard of care for operating an aircraft); 14 C.F.R. § 121.571 (specifying the mandatory briefings that must be provided to all passengers on aircraft); 14 C.F.R. pt. 121, app. A (identifying the minimum number of first-aid kits that must be stored on aircraft and the items that each first-aid kit must contain). Significantly, as relevant to the present case, the Federal Aviation Administration has promulgated a regulation pursuant to the FAA specifically addressing airlines' alcoholic beverage services. See 14 C.F.R. § 121.575.

We conclude that the comprehensive regulatory scheme promulgated pursuant to the FAA evidences the intent for federal law to occupy the field of aviation safety exclusively.

2. *NMLCA Related to Air Safety*

Having addressed the field of aviation safety generally, we must consider whether the NMLCA implicates the field as occupied by federal law. Even if we narrowly define the field of aviation safety, we conclude that NMLCA's regulation of an airline's alcoholic beverage service directly implicates the field of aviation safety regulated by federal law. As noted, the Federal Aviation Administration has promulgated a federal regulation specifically addressing airlines' alcoholic beverage services.

Section 121.575 provides in full:

> (a) No person may drink any alcoholic beverage aboard an aircraft unless the certificate holder operating the aircraft has served that beverage to him.
>
> (b) No certificate holder may serve any alcoholic beverage to any person aboard any of its aircraft who— (1) appears to be intoxicated; (2) is escorting a person or being escorted; or (3) has a deadly or dangerous weapon accessible to him while aboard the aircraft.

(c) No certificate holder may allow any person to board any of its aircraft if that person appears to be intoxicated.

(d) Each certificate holder shall, within five days after the incident, report to the Administrator the refusal of any person to comply with paragraph (a) of this section, or of any disturbance caused by a person who appears to be intoxicated aboard any of its aircraft.

Notably, the Federal Aviation Administration promulgated this regulation to promote aviation safety. Specifically, the Federal Aviation Administration balanced the safety concerns inherent in regulating airline alcoholic beverage service against the imposition of additional responsibilities on flight crew members by explaining that airline flight crew members would not have the responsibility to "restrain physically a passenger who wished to consume drinks that were not served to him by the carrier."

Additionally, the Federal Aviation Administration considered whether the proposed provision adequately addressed safety concerns, noting that "flat prohibition [of alcohol on aircraft] has not proven successful" and "it might even work adversely, since passengers who wish to drink might ... do so to excess in advance of the flight, knowing that they could not obtain a drink aboard an aircraft." Thus, NMLCA implicates the field of aviation safety as occupied by federal law.

Further, New Mexico's regulatory efforts extend beyond the alcoholic beverage service that airlines provide on flights. By requiring airlines to comply with NMLCA, New Mexico is seeking to impose additional training requirements on flight attendants and crew members serving alcoholic beverages on airplanes. *See* N.M. Stat. § 60–6E–4 ("No person shall be employed as a server on a licensed premises unless that person obtains within thirty days of employment alcohol server training pursuant to the provisions of [N.M. Stat. § 60–6E–1 *et seq.*]."); N.M. Stat. § 60–6E–5(B) (delineating the subjects that the training program for employees serving alcoholic beverages must cover). In fact, when New Mexico denied the renewal of U.S. Airways' temporary public service license, New Mexico noted that U.S. Airways "ha[d] done little if anything to consider implementing applicable portions of [New Mexico's] required alcohol server training."

However, federal law extensively regulates flight attendant and crew member training programs and certification requirements due to the aviation safety considerations involved. *See* 49 U.S.C. § 44728(a)(1) ("No person may serve as a flight attendant aboard an aircraft of an air carrier unless that person holds a certificate of demonstrated proficiency from the Administrator of the Federal Aviation Administration...."); 14 C.F.R. §§ 121.404 (requiring that flight attendants and aircraft dispatchers "complete[ ] approved crew resource management ... or dispatcher resource management ... initial training"), 121.405 (explaining the approval process for training programs or revisions to existing training programs), 121.415 (delineating the training program requirements),

121.421 (describing the initial and transition ground training requirements for flight attendants), 121.427 (explaining the recurrent training requirements for crew members and dispatchers), 121.433 (describing the mandatory crew member training requirements). Thus, NMLCA's regulatory scheme implicates the field occupied by federal law.

Based on the pervasive federal regulations concerning flight attendant and crew member training and the aviation safety concerns involved when regulating an airline's alcoholic beverage service, we conclude that NMLCA's application to an airline implicates the field of airline safety that Congress intended federal law to regulate exclusively. Thus, New Mexico's regulatory efforts are impliedly preempted.

B. Twenty-first Amendment

While we conclude that federal law preempts NMLCA's regulation of the alcoholic beverage service on aircraft, our analysis does not end there. We must next evaluate whether § 2 of the Twenty-first Amendment permits New Mexico's regulatory scheme, as applied to an airline's alcoholic beverage service, to override federal policy.

Section 2 of the Twenty-first Amendment provides: "The transportation or importation into any State, ... for delivery or use therein of intoxicating liquors, in violation of the laws thereof, is hereby prohibited." U.S. Const. amend. XXI, § 2. "Notwithstanding the [Twenty-first] Amendment's broad grant of power to the States, ... the Federal Government plainly retains authority under the Commerce Clause to regulate even interstate commerce in liquor."

The Supreme Court has recognized that "there is no bright line between federal and state powers over liquor." Instead, "[b]oth the Twenty-first Amendment and the Commerce Clause are parts of the same Constitution. Like other provisions of the Constitution, each must be considered in light of the other, and in the context of the issues and interests at stake in any concrete case." When resolving conflicts between different provisions of the Constitution, courts must undertake a "pragmatic effort to harmonize state and federal powers." Thus, as Congress enacted the FAA pursuant to the Commerce Clause, the state interests protected under the Twenty-first Amendment must be balanced against the federal interests.

While we defer to the district court to conduct the balancing of state and federal interests in the first instance, we offer some guidance for this analysis. The key inquiry in balancing state and federal interests is "whether the interests implicated by a state regulation are so closely related to the powers reserved by the Twenty-first Amendment that the regulation may prevail, notwithstanding that its requirements directly conflict with express federal policies." In conducting this balancing, the court should be guided by the following three-step framework:

> First, the court should examine the expressed state interest and the closeness of that interest to those protected by the Twenty-first Amendment.... Second, the court should examine whether, and to what extent, the regulatory scheme serves its stated purpose.... Simply put, is the scheme effective? ... [T]he answer to this question may ultimately rest upon findings and conclusions having a large factual component. Finally, the court should balance the state's interest ... (to the extent that interest is actually furthered by the regulatory scheme) against the federal interest.

TFWS, Inc. v. Schaefer (4th Cir. 2001).

In this case, the district court never conducted any balancing of state and federal interests. Thus, the district court did not have the opportunity to evaluate the effectiveness of New Mexico's regulatory scheme in furtherance of its interests protected under the Twenty-first Amendment. As this inquiry may ultimately depend upon factual findings and conclusions, we remand this case to the district court to conduct the balancing of state and federal interests.

RAY v. SPIRIT AIRLINES, INC.

767 F.3d 1220 (11th Cir. 2014)

MARCUS, Circuit Judge.

Plaintiffs commenced this civil suit against Spirit Airlines, Inc. ("Spirit") under the Racketeer Influenced and Corrupt Organizations Act ("RICO"), 18 U.S.C. §§ 1961–68, alleging that Spirit conducted an enterprise by means of racketeering activity—here, two or more predicate acts of mail and wire fraud involving the concealment and misrepresentation of airfares and user fees. The district court dismissed the action, ruling that comprehensive federal regulation of the airline industry precluded Plaintiffs' civil RICO claims. We disagree.

Because federal laws do not preempt other federal laws, subsequent legislation could preclude Plaintiffs' claims only if Congress had repealed the provisions of RICO, at least insofar as they authorized Plaintiffs' actions. Congress did not do so expressly through the Airline Deregulation Act of 1978 ("ADA"). And we find no "repeal by implication" because Congress has not exhibited the requisite clear and manifest intent. *E.g.*, *Posadas v. Nat'l City Bank of N.Y.* (1936). The ADA explicitly preempted state laws but, notably, said nothing about any federal cause of action. Moreover, a saving clause found in the ADA did not disturb any other remedies provided by law. Quite simply, the two laws are not irreconcilably in conflict, nor was the ADA clearly intended as a substitute for RICO. Applying the strong presumption against implied repeals, we are constrained to conclude that RICO supplements, rather than subverts, federal regulation of air carriers.

Our decision in no way addresses whether Plaintiffs adequately alleged the elements of their civil RICO claim. Thus, we have no occasion today to pass any judgment on whether fraud is pled with particularity, or whether Plaintiffs adequately pled the elements of mail and wire fraud, or indeed whether Plaintiffs sufficiently pled a RICO injury. All we hold today is that the federal regulatory scheme governing the airline industry does not preclude a claim founded on the civil provisions of RICO.

BACKGROUND

Spirit holds itself out as an "Ultra Low Cost Carrier" offering airfares at rates far lower than other providers. These cheap fares disguise the total cost of travel because Spirit forces consumers to pay unbundled charges traditionally included in the price of an airline ticket. Specifically, Spirit charges a Passenger Usage Fee to all consumers who buy tickets through its website or call center. When searching for flights on Spirit's website, a consumer sees only the base fares. Once he has selected a flight, a webpage directs him to "confirm" the flight on a page that displays both the base fare and an undifferentiated amount labeled "Taxes & Fees." For a breakdown of these charges, the consumer then must click on an additional link, "more information," which lists "Passenger Usage Fee" alongside government taxes and fees.

Plaintiffs filed a class action complaint in the United States District Court for the Southern District of Florida, alleging that Spirit concealed the existence and purpose of the Passenger Usage Fee between approximately 2008 and 2011 and used the mails and wires to execute the scheme or artifice to defraud, thereby yielding civil RICO liability. Spirit moved to dismiss the action pursuant to Federal Rule of Civil Procedure 12(b)(6) for failure to state a claim upon which relief could be granted. Spirit argued that permitting Plaintiffs' RICO action would thwart Congress's intent to delegate entirely the regulation of airline ticket prices and price advertising to the Department of Transportation (DOT). Spirit also argued that Plaintiffs' RICO claims were precluded by the ADA's preemption provision. Alternatively, Spirit urged that Plaintiffs had failed to adequately plead RICO mail and wire fraud related to the Passenger Usage Fee.

The district court granted Spirit's motion to dismiss, finding that Congress intended the DOT to be the sole legal control on deceptive airfare, fees, and deceptive fee and fare advertising. Therefore, the broad federal remedial scheme precluded Plaintiffs from challenging the Passenger Usage Fee through a civil RICO action. The district court had no occasion to address whether the complaint adequately and with sufficient particularity pled the elements of wire and mail fraud and civil RICO on this claim. The district court, however, did find that Plaintiffs alleged a separate misrepresentation or scheme to defraud not related to fees, fares, or advertising that was not precluded by federal regulations: Spirit's marketing materials encouraged consumers to book tickets online but failed to disclose that online purchases carried an additional fee. Still, the district court dismissed that RICO claim because Plaintiffs had failed to properly allege a predicate act and injury. The court granted leave to file a third amended complaint setting forth a RICO claim related to the buy-online marketing. Plaintiffs, however, filed notice of their intention not to amend the complaint, and the district court entered final judgment. Plaintiffs timely appealed, raising a single issue: whether the district court erred in determining that a civil RICO action related to the Passenger Usage Fee was precluded by the federal scheme of airline regulation. We review *de novo* the grant of a Rule 12(b)(6) motion to dismiss for failure to state a claim.

The Federal Aviation Act ("FAA"), Pub. L. No. 85–726 (1958), gives the DOT the power to "investigate and decide whether an air carrier ... has been or is engaged in an unfair or deceptive practice or an unfair method of competition in air transportation or the sale of air transportation." The DOT may order an air carrier to stop an unfair or deceptive practice or method and may impose civil penalties of no more than $25,000 for each day of these violations. *See* § 46301(a)(1) ("A person is liable to the United States Government for a civil penalty of not more than $25,000 for violating [§ 41712]"); § 46301(a)(2) ("A separate violation occurs under this subsection for each day the violation ... continues ...").

The DOT's "full-fare advertising rule" deems unfair and deceptive any price advertising for air transportation that does not state the "entire price to be paid by the customer." 14 C.F.R. § 399.84(a) ("Although charges included within the single total price listed (*e.g.*, government taxes) may be stated separately or through links or 'pop ups' on websites that display the total price, such charges may not be false or misleading, may not be displayed prominently, may not be presented in the same or larger size as the total price, and must provide cost information on a per passenger basis that accurately reflects the cost of the item covered by the charge.").

When first enacted, the FAA provided that it did not "in any way abridge or alter the remedies now existing at common law or by statute." Instead, Congress wrote, its provisions "are in addition to such remedies." The 1978 ADA, however, contained a preemption provision expressly prohibiting "a State" from "enact[ing] or enforc [ing] a law, regulation, or other provision having the force and effect of law related to a price, route, or service of an air carrier that may provide air transportation under this subpart." At the same time, the ADA included a saving clause to the effect that "[a] remedy under this part is in addition to any other remedies provided by law."

Meanwhile, in 1970 Congress enacted RICO, which created both criminal and civil liability for "racketeering activity" connected to interstate commerce. Section 1961(1) of RICO defines racketeering activity to include acts indictable as mail fraud and wire fraud. RICO provides criminal penalties, but also allows "[a]ny person injured in his business or property" by a RICO violation to sue to recover treble damages, as well as fees and costs. To recover, a civil plaintiff must establish that a defendant (1) operated or managed (2) an enterprise (3) through a pattern (4) of racketeering activity that included at least two racketeering acts. In addition, "the plaintiff only has standing if, and can only recover to the extent that, he has been injured in his business or property by the conduct constituting the violation."

Though the FAA and ADA do not provide a private right of action, RICO created a separate statutory action that allows plaintiffs to recover for injuries caused by the operation of an enterprise through a pattern of racketeering activity. In this case, Plaintiffs do not attempt to enforce FAA restrictions on unfair and deceptive practices or methods of competition, nor do they seek relief on the ground that Spirit violated the DOT's full-fare advertising rule. Instead, their claim depends on RICO's independent federal prohibition on mail and wire fraud.

This is not a preemption case. Federal preemption of state laws is a creature of the Supremacy Clause. *See* U.S. CONST. art. VI, cl. 2 ("This Constitution, and the Laws of the United States which shall be made in Pursuance thereof ... shall be the supreme Law of the Land...."). But federal statutes do not preempt other federal statutes. Rather, this case involves the interplay between two statutory schemes created by Congress for different reasons and at different times. Nevertheless, Spirit claims to find a profound conflict between federal air regulation and the application of civil RICO. If Spirit is right, "[t]he term for this dynamic is *repeal*—whether and how a later act of Congress modifies an earlier one." *Miccosukee Tribe of Indians of Fla. v. U.S. Army Corps of Eng'rs*, (11th Cir. 2010).

The essential problem here is that Spirit does not—and cannot—argue that Congress has expressly repealed the application of the civil provisions of RICO by codifying the ADA. Thus, Plaintiffs' RICO claims would be precluded only if the ADA implicitly repealed RICO's authorization of civil claims related to airline prices and fees. But "[t]he cardinal rule is that repeals by implication are not favored." We apply a strong presumption against finding repeals by implication precisely because they involve so much speculation about congressional intent. Thus, when Congress passes two statutes that may touch on the same subject, we give effect to both unless doing so would be impossible. We must "assiduously attempt" to construe two statutes in harmony before concluding that one impliedly repeals the other.

The Supreme Court has instructed that repeals by implication may only be found when Congress's intent to repeal is "clear and manifest." We may infer clear and manifest intent from the existence of an "irreconcilable conflict." We also may find an implied repeal when "the later act covers the whole subject of the earlier one and is clearly intended as a substitute." Still, it is not enough to establish that a later law covers some or even all of the cases provided for by an earlier law, because the subsequent statute "may be merely affirmative, or cumulative or auxiliary."

As a matter of chronological necessity, the 1958 FAA could not have repealed any part of the yet-to-be-born 1970 RICO statute. Regardless of whether the FAA established a "comprehensive federal regulatory scheme governing air carriers," *Musson Theatrical, Inc. v. Fed. Express Corp.* (6th Cir. 1996), Spirit cannot claim implied repeal through the FAA because Congress enacted RICO on top of its framework.

Nor did Congress give any indication that the 1978 ADA repealed the portion of RICO authorizing civil claims predicated on mail and wire fraud. In the first place, there is no irreconcilable conflict between the two laws. The ADA substantially deregulated the airline industry in an effort to place "maximum reliance on competitive market forces." To ensure its work was not undone by state regulation, the ADA amended the FAA to expressly preempt state laws relating to an air carrier's price, route, or service. The statutory text and legislative history indicate that the preemption provision was included to delineate areas of federal and state responsibility in a way that would avoid conflicting demands on air carriers. The ADA said nothing about federal laws in this area, which strongly signals that Congress meant not to disturb them. *Cf., e.g., Cipollone v. Liggett Grp., Inc.* (1992) ("Congress' enactment of a provision defining the preemptive reach of a statute implies that matters beyond that reach are not preempted.")

Congress even more clearly indicated that the ADA did not interrupt federal RICO actions by including a saving clause, which expressly stated that remedies provided by federal air commerce and safety regulations are in addition to other remedies provided by law. The legislative history indicates no "unambiguous congressional perception" that the ADA was designed to exempt a civil RICO claim predicated on acts of mail and wire fraud somehow involving airline fees, prices, or advertising. Nor does the legislative history signal that Congress gave the slightest consideration to the partial repeal of RICO, let alone to suggest "that Congress consciously abandoned its (prior) policy." Simply put, nothing in the statute nor the legislative history indicates an intent on the part of Congress to create an exemption from federal RICO when it divided federal and state responsibility for airline regulation.

Moreover, we recognize the two federal remedial schemes as "capable of co-existence" because they feature different requirements and offer different protections. DOT's administrative process provides for a lower level of culpability but less severe sanctions. DOT need not find deceptive intent, fraud, or injury before levying penalties or ordering a carrier to alter an unfair or deceptive practice or an unfair method of competition. But these penalties do not compensate consumers for their injuries; instead, fines are paid to the United States Treasury and are capped at comparatively modest levels.

In sharp contrast, in order to sustain a private civil RICO action, the plaintiffs must plead far more than the existence of an unfair or deceptive practice or an unfair method of competition. RICO requires proof that the defendant operated or managed an enterprise through a pattern of racketeering activity that injured the plaintiff. For civil

RICO claims predicated on acts of mail and wire fraud, the plaintiff must establish that the defendant devised or intended to devise a scheme or artifice to defraud, and that the defendant used the mail or interstate wire, radio, or television communication for the purpose of executing that scheme or artifice.

Unlike with the DOT regulations, then, mail and wire fraud require "that a defendant actually intended to create a scheme to defraud." Mail and wire fraud are specific intent crimes, requiring that a defendant acted with bad purpose either to disobey or disregard the law. *See United States v. Maxwell* (11th Cir. 2009) ("[T]he specific intent required under the mail and wire fraud statutes is the intent to defraud."). If defendants are culpable under this more demanding standard, civil RICO's treble damages provision compensates plaintiffs, and at a far greater cost to defendants than DOT's limited penalties. There is no inconsistency in a federal system that creates tiered levels of liability by providing stiffer sanctions when an air carrier is involved in criminal fraud, not merely engaged in an unfair or deceptive act.

Similarly, the ADA does not cover the whole subject of, and is not clearly intended as a substitute for, RICO. The different remedial means we've described serve different legislative purposes. DOT's regulation of unfair and deceptive practices seek to promote fair competition among carriers, while civil RICO targets a broad category of criminally fraudulent acts not restricted to air carriers, pricing, or advertising. The ADA was a wholly different animal from RICO, which "was an aggressive initiative to supplement old remedies and develop new methods for fighting crime." *Sedima, S.P.R.L v. Imrex Co., Inc.* (1985). "When we consider the different objects which it is reasonably clear the legislature had in view in the passage of these two acts, it is a fair construction to hold that it was not the intention of the legislature, by the passage of the later act, to repeal the older act, either totally or partially." *Red Rock v. Henry* (1883).

While Spirit may prefer a narrow interpretation of RICO, Congress expressly admonished that the statute is to "be liberally construed to effectuate its remedial purposes." RICO, Pub. L. No. 91–452, § 904(a). When confronted with "extraordinary" uses of civil RICO that "appear to be primarily the result of the breadth of the predicate offenses, in particular the inclusion of wire, mail, and securities fraud," the Supreme Court has refused to engage in "statutory amendment": "correction must lie with Congress." We can divine no clear and manifest congressional intent for the ADA to have made such an alteration to RICO.

Spirit relies on *Ayres v. General Motors Corp.* (11th Cir. 2000), but that precedent offers little guidance in this case. The *Ayres* plaintiffs claimed that the defendants had breached a duty to disclose alleged safety defects as required by the National Traffic and Motor Vehicle Safety Act ("Safety Act"), and that this breach necessarily gave rise to the predicate acts of mail and wire fraud under Georgia's RICO statute. We found "it clear that Congress did not intend to equate a violation of the Safety Act's notification requirements in and of itself with the felony of mail or wire fraud." In other words, plaintiffs could not use the Safety Act's regulatory scheme, which featured "its own extensive array of administrative remedies for a violation of its notification obligations," to establish a RICO predicate act of mail or wire fraud where none could otherwise be shown. But under Ayres a plaintiff still "can show a scheme to defraud if he proves that some type of deceptive conduct occurred." He simply cannot use the Safety Act to establish that the defendant pursued a fraudulent scheme and used the mails or wires to execute that scheme, all in violation of RICO.

In this case, however, the Plaintiffs have not alleged that the FAA, the ADA, or DOT regulations expand the scope of RICO by spawning new predicate acts. Plaintiffs do not argue that a previous DOT ruling on unfair or deceptive advertising proves the existence of a predicate act of mail or wire fraud. Simply put, the district court was concerned that the federal statutes overlap. But that is how Congress wrote them. Sometimes a defendant's actions may qualify both as unfair and deceptive advertising under the FAA and as mail or wire fraud under federal criminal statutes. So long as Plaintiffs do not argue that violation of the first establishes the second, our precedent does not restrict their RICO action.

The only other federal court to confront a RICO action like Plaintiffs' found no preclusion from the ADA. *See All World Prof'l Travel Servs., Inc. v. Am. Airlines, Inc.* (C.D. Cal. 2003). In *All World*, a travel agency sued an airline in a dispute over cancellation fees charged for flights in the months following September 11, 2001. The court recognized that the plaintiffs could have complained to the DOT, but held that "Congress did not intend to require the type of conduct alleged in the Complaint"—including mail and wire fraud—"to be submitted to the DOT." Just as in this case, the airline insisted that the comprehensiveness of the ADA precluded the travel agency from challenging airline fees "in the guise of a RICO claim." The court was unmoved because the RICO claims were based on mail and wire fraud instead of ADA violations, because the ADA was not intended to completely subsume the field of airline liability, and because no provision in the ADA conflicted with RICO.

For the reasons we've explained, we agree with the *All World* court that civil RICO claims predicated on mail and wire fraud are not precluded by the ADA simply because they involve fraud arising out of pricing, fees, and advertising in the airline industry. We vacate the dismissal of Plaintiffs' claim tied to Spirit's Personal Usage Fee because Congress did not expressly or impliedly repeal RICO's authorization of civil suits based on acts of mail and wire fraud. Again, we pass no judgment on whether Plaintiffs have adequately pled a RICO claim, and remand to allow the district court to make that determination.

NOTES

1. Why is preemption analysis so complicated and varied? It is a matter of interpretation. As the first part of the analysis in *Baily v. Rocky Mountain Holdings, LLC* (S.D. Fla. 2015), *supra*, states, "[t]he Supremacy Clause of the United States Constitution invalidates state and local laws that interfere with or are contrary to the laws of Congress. '[W]here Congress has legislated concerning a subject, on which it is authorized to act, all State legislation which interferes with it, is absolutely void.' *Gibbons v. Ogden* (1824)." Notwithstanding this apparently unambiguous precedent, courts are routinely asked to address the tension between broad federal laws purporting to regulate the airline industry and laws enacted at the local level. *Amerijet Int'l v. Miami-Dade County* (11th Cir. 2015) is a recent example. There, the Eleventh Circuit Court of Appeals was asked to decide whether a section of Miami-Dade County's Living Wage Ordinance, as applied to air carriers, was preempted by the Airline Deregulation Act of 1978. (*See generally* Chapter 4, "Airmen.")

Passed in 1999, the ordinance was one of the first of its kind, and required that "certain individuals or entities that conduct business with the County or that use the facilities of Miami International Airport" pay a "living wage" to workers providing "covered services," which was defined as:

> Guiding aircraft in and out of Airport; aircraft loading and unloading positions, designated by the Aviation Department; placing in position and operating passenger, baggage and cargo loading and unloading devices, as required for the safe and efficient loading and unloading of passengers, baggage and cargo to and from aircraft; performing such loading and unloading; providing aircraft utility services, such as air start and cabin air; fueling; catering; towing aircraft; cleaning of aircraft; delivering cargo, baggage and mail to and from aircraft to and from locations at any Miami-Dade County Aviation Department facility; and providing such other ramp services approved in writing by the Aviation Department.

An all-cargo airlines (*i.e.* an airline that only carries property and mail) argued that the ordinance was preempted as an inappropriate attempt by the county to regulate the preempted field of air carrier regulation.

In a *per curiam* opinion, the Eleventh Circuit disagreed, ruling that "the ordinance resembles a law of general application, as opposed to a law that is designed to regulate the airline industry." As such, the ordinance was "not targeted at, and does not single out, airlines or carriers." In addition, the court reasoned that the "services" at issue—the provision of cargo handling services for other airlines—"are not the type that implicate the [Airline Deregulation Act's] preemption provision." Given *U.S. Airways, Inc. v. O'Donnell* (10th Cir. 2010), *supra*, would this result hold uniformly in other appellate circuits around the nation?

2. Notice that the court in *U.S. Airways, Inc. v. O'Donnell* (10th Cir. 2010), *supra*, expressed its opinion in terms of field preemption, a subcategory of implied preemption. The court did not address whether the Airline Deregulation Act of 1978 expressly preempts New Mexico's efforts to regulate airlines' onboard service of alcohol. As such, *O'Donnell* represents a continuing trend of courts taking an expansive view of implied preemption of commercial aviation. On the one hand, the Third and Ninth Circuit Courts of Appeal narrowly define the term "service" in the Airline Deregulation Act of 1978, the consequence of which is to find that most activities are not preempted. On the other hand, the Second, Fourth, Fifth, and Seventh Circuits have interpreted "service" broadly to encompass activities such as boarding procedures to food and drink provisions, resulting in preemption of most aviation passenger complaints. As one commentator associated with the law firm that represented U.S. Airways suggests that, "[a] desire to avoid taking sides in this circuit conflict may have prompted the Tenth Circuit in *O'Donnell* to begin (and end) with implied preemption, rather than express preemption." David S. Volchok, U.S. Airways v. O'Donnell: *The Tenth Circuit Upholds Broad Federal Preemption of State Regulation of Airlines*, 23 No. 4. AIR & SPACE L. 1, 21 n. 20 (2012).

3. *Ray v. Spirit Airlines, Inc.* (11th Cir. 2014), *supra*, demonstrates that courts frequently make critical and dispositive preemption determinations that permit or bar a claim from proceeding to the merits, the Racketeer Influenced and Corrupt Organizations Act in that case. To some extent, this is an example of procedure driving substance, where claims rise and fall with strategic motion practice—usually a motion to dismiss or a motion for summary judgment. In *Tobin v. Federal Express Corp.* (1st Cir. 2014), for example, a federal court considered whether the Airline Deregulation Act of 1978 preempted common law claims of general negligence and intentional and negligent infliction of emotional distress at the summary judgment phase of trial.

The case arose from the incorrect delivery of a package containing marijuana, which was opened by an eleven-year-old girl. The girl's mother called the police, who in turn asked FedEx to flag the shipment and refrain from disclosing any information regarding the delivery address to anyone who might inquire about the package. On the same day, the intended recipient called FedEx to inquire about the status of the package. FedEx initiated a "trace." Meanwhile, a man came to the unintended recipient's door asked whether she had received a package. The visitor's car was parked in the plaintiff's driveway with two men seated inside. Terrified, the plaintiff slammed the door shut and again contacted the police. In the aftermath of these events, the plaintiff and her minor daughter suffered fear and anxiety and manifested a range of symptoms. She bought suit, alleging that FedEx was responsible not only for mislabeling and misdelivering the package but also for wrongfully disclosing her address to the sender or intended recipient.

FedEx, classified as a regulated air carrier under law, moved for summary judgment on grounds of preemption.

The First Circuit Court of Appeals agreed, framing the litigation in terms of two questions: (1) a "mechanism question," *i.e.*, whether the claim was predicated on a law, regulation, or other provision having the force and effect of law; and if so, (2) a "linkage question," whether the claim is sufficiently "related to" an air carrier's prices, routes, or services to warrant preemption. The court found the "mechanism question" was "easily answered. The Supreme Court has made it pellucid that state common-law causes of action are provisions that have the force and effect of law for purposes of preemption under the Airline Deregulation Act.

Next, turning to the "linkage question," the court determined that FedEx's "services" were implicated and that the plaintiff's claims "related to" such services. Accordingly, they were barred as a matter of law:

> Stripped of rhetorical flourishes, the plaintiff's common-law claims all depend on FedEx's mislabeling and misdelivery of the package. In other words, they are claims about FedEx's package handling, address verification, and delivery procedures. Package handling, address verification, and package delivery plainly concern the contractual arrangement between FedEx and the users of its services (those who send packages). Thus, they are necessary appurtenances of the contract of carriage. Seen in this light, *Rowe* leads inexorably to the conclusion that the plaintiff's claims implicate FedEx's services.
>
> * * *
>
> Having established that the plaintiff's claims implicate FedEx's services, we next must consider whether the plaintiff's claims are sufficiently "related to" those services to warrant preemption under the [Airline Deregulation Act ("ADA")]. The Supreme Court has instructed that the "related to" language of the ADA is meant to be construed broadly, consistent with Congress's intention that ADA preemption should have an expansive reach.
>
> Thus, a state-law claim having "connection with, or reference to," an airline's prices, routes, or services is preempted. That connection, however, cannot be *de minimis*—the challenged law must have a "forbidden significant effect" on prices, routes, or services in order to

> fall under the ADA's protective carapace. If the connection to an airline's prices, routes, and services is "tenuous, remote, or peripheral," preemption will not attach.
>
> * * *
>
> For the plaintiff to prevail on her common-law claims, she would have to prove either that FedEx's procedures were inadequate or that those procedures, though adequate, were carried out carelessly by FedEx's employees.
>
> A finding that FedEx's procedures were inadequate would have the significant effect of requiring new and enhanced procedures for labeling, verification, and delivery of packages (FedEx's main business). That effect would not be tenuous, remote, or peripheral.
>
> In the latter circumstance, a finding that the actions of FedEx's employees breached a state-law duty of care would also produce a significant forbidden effect. Such a finding would effectively supplant market forces with Massachusetts common-law definitions of reasonableness and, thus, create the very patchwork of state-based regulations that ADA preemption is meant to preclude. And the risk of a patchwork effect is heightened where, as here, the claims are of the sort typically tried to a jury.

Against this background, is preemption just insofar as it might deprive private litigants of the proverbial day in court? Is preemption just insofar as it might require corporate litigants to defend themselves against creative, but ultimately unsuccessful lawsuits?

4. The concept of preemption is not limited to garden variety suits relating to lost bags or cancelled flights. As one practitioner noted, an increase in child abduction via international air transportation portends litigation:

> From 1998 to the present, there have been five court cases involving claims by left-behind parents against air carriers alleged to have transported the abducting parent and child(ren). The obvious question is: If there have only been five cases involving parental child abduction over the past sixteen years, why is this an issue with which air carriers should be concerned? The answer is straight forward: According to the State Department, approximately 64% of

> abductions are to non-border countries, almost all of which likely are accomplished by international flight.
>
> * * *
>
> In light of the increasing number of abductions each year, a majority of which are accomplished through international transportation by air, claims against air carriers in these abductions can be expected to arise more frequently. As the verdicts of $15 million and $27 million in the two cases to reach verdict against carrier[s] evidence, airline exposure for these claims is substantial. Because of the high stakes and sympathy for the plaintiffs, carriers do not want to rely on the application of state tort law to the facts of a particular case. Accordingly, it is essential that carriers vigorously pursue all available defenses, especially the defense of preemption. While the results to date have been mixed, the law is on the side of the carriers.

See Barry S. Alexander, *"Not without My Daughter": Preemption of Claims against an Airline for Parental Child Abduction*, 79 J. AIR L. & COM. 255 (2014). Should national and international lawmakers create an exception? If so, what standard of intent or liability would suffice, *e.g.*, negligence, strict liability?

5. Recognize that the national character of aviation laws and regulations essentially may—and frequently does—divest state courts of jurisdiction over claims ordinarily tried there as well as deprive claimants of claims traditionally cognizable under state law. *Baugh v. Delta Air Lines, Inc.* (N.D. Ga. 2015) presents a rare exception. There, a blind passenger who needed assistance boarding an aircraft bound for Boston, Massachusetts was required to board without assistance, which led to her tripping and falling and sustaining serious injuries and medical expenses. She sued the airline in state court based upon state-law negligence. The airline removed her case to federal court, arguing that the Air Carrier Access Act of 1986 ("ACAA") applied, providing that a carrier

> must promptly provide or ensure the provision of assistance requested by or on behalf of passengers with a disability, or offered by carrier or airport operator personnel and accepted by passengers with a disability, in enplaning and deplaning.

The airline argued that the ACAA both preempted the passenger's claim and supplied no private right or remedy of action that she could otherwise enforce. The Eleventh Circuit Court of Appeals found that the ACAA did not preclude or preempt state-law negligence claims in their entirety, however, even though the ACAA did preempt state-law standards of care:

> Four of Plaintiff's allegations of negligence are inexplicably tied to Defendant's alleged failure to assist Plaintiff in boarding the aircraft, a duty of care that is regulated by the ACAA Regulations. The Court concludes that the ACAA and the ACAA Regulations establish the standard of care Defendant owed to Plaintiff when she was boarding Defendant's aircraft, and thus preempt any different standard of care that may exist under Massachusetts tort law. Massachusetts law, however, still governs the other elements of negligence, as well as the choice and availabilities of remedies.

How does this decision square with *U.S. Airways, Inc. v. O'Donnell* (10th Cir. 2010) and *Ray v. Spirit Airlines, Inc.* (11th Cir. 2014), *supra*?

6. Despite the variation in outcomes, preemption jurisprudence is guided by two well-established and uniformly accepted cornerstones. First, "the purpose of Congress is the ultimate touchstone in every pre-emption case," and "[s]econd, [i]n all pre-emption cases, and particularly those in which Congress has 'legislated in a field which the States have traditionally occupied' … we start with the assumption that the historic police powers of the States were not to be superseded by the Federal Act unless that was the clear and manifest purpose of Congress." *See Wyeth v. Levine* (2009). In other words, there exists a "presumption against preemption" in litigation arising under the Airline Deregulation Act. Recognize how often this presumption is overcome in favor of carriers and against passengers, or in favor of passengers and against carriers, throughout the opinion in this course book.

7. As explored in detail in Chapter 6, Part C, *infra*, preemption defenses regularly arise under the Warsaw Convention and Montreal Convention in the context of *international* air transportation. Those treaties apply exclusively to all international carriage of persons, baggage or cargo performed by aircraft for reward, together with gratuitous carriage by aircraft performed by an air transport undertaking. *See generally* Christopher E. Cotter, *Recent Developments in Montreal Convention Litigation*, 79 J. AIR L. & COM. 291 (2014). Do the exclusivity of remedy provisions of these international fairly balance the rights of passengers and carriers or is one party favored over the other?

8. While not strictly an issue of federal preemption, the question of whether foreign airline consumer protection laws may be enforced in the United States has confronted some courts. In *Volodarskiy v. Delta Airlines, Inc.* (7th Cir. 2015), for example, several air travelers sued Delta Airlines, Inc. under the Class Action Fairness Act, 28 U.S.C. § 1332(d), seeking compensation for themselves and a nationwide class of persons who were inconvenienced when their flights from airports located in the

European Union were delayed for more than three hours or cancelled on short notice. The claims specifically arose under a consumer-protection regulation promulgated by the European Parliament setting standardized compensation rates ranging from € 250 to € 600 (depending on flight distance) for cancellations and long delays of flights departing from airports located within EU Member States. See Regulation 261/2004, 2004 O.J. (L 46) 1(EC). *See also* Chapter 1, Part B, *supra.*

Affirming the district court's opinion, the Seventh Circuit Court of Appeals ruled that no cognizable breach of claim was asserted as EU 261 was not incorporated into Delta's contract of carriage; additionally, a direct claim for compensation under EU 261 is actionable only as provided in the regulation itself, which requires that each EU Member State designate an appropriate administrative body to handle enforcement responsibility and implicitly limits judicial redress to courts in Member States under the procedures of their own national law. In other words, passenger may only seek direct statutory redress in the European Union.

9. No less important than its application to consumer issues considered in this Chapter is the role preemption jurisprudence plays in the area of aviation product liability. As of late 2015, in *Sikkelee v. Precision Automotive Corp.*, the United States Court of Appeal for the Third Circuit is considering the Federal Aviation Administration's stance on preemption of state law standards in design defect cases, including:

- What is the scope of field preemption under the Federal Aviation Act of 1958? Specifically, does the preempted field include tort claims based on alleged defective design or manufacturing?
- If such tort claims fall within the preempted field, may they proceed using a federal standard of care? If so, what is that standard and where is it found within the Act or its regulations?
- What weight, if any, should be accorded to the issuance of a type certificate in determining whether the relevant standard of care has been met?

See generally Jane M. Sigda & Andrew J. Nadel, *A New Standard of Care: The Third Circuit Considers FAA's Stance on Preemption of State Law Standards in Design Defect Cases*, Nov. 20, 2015, *available at http://www.condonlaw.com/2015/11/andrew-j-nadel-2/.*

10. An open question exists as to whether federal law preempts state law with respect to the private use of unmanned aerial systems—"drones." Consider that the Idaho legislature enacted a statute that prohibits citizens from using "an unmanned aircraft system to intentionally conduct surveillance of, gather evidence or collect information about, or photographically or electronically record specifically targeted persons or

specifically targeted private property." *See* IDAHO CODE ANN. § 21-213(2)(a) (2013). Similarly, Oregon prohibits the "operat[ion] of a drone that is flown at a height of less than 400 feet" over private property without the consent of the property owner. *See* OREGON LAWS CH. 686 § 15(1). Florida and Texas, in turn, prohibit citizens from using drones to capture the image of an individual or privately owned real property with the intent to conduct surveillance on the individual or property captured in the image. *See* TEX. GOV'T CODE ANN. § 423.003(a) (2013) and FLA. STAT. § 934.50 (2015). *See generally* Jol A. Silversmith, *You Can't Regulate This: State Regulation of the Private Use of Unmanned Aircraft*, 26 No. 3 AIR AND SPACE L. (2013), *http://www.americanbar.org/content/dam/aba/publications/air_space_lawyer/2013_december/ASL_V26N3_WINTER13_Silversmith.authcheckdam.pdf.* *See also* Margot E. Kaminski, *Drone Federalism: Civilian Drones and the Things They Carry*, 4 CAL. L. REV. 57 (2013). *See also* Chapter 4, Part C.

PROBLEM

Ayman Abdel–Karim, flew from New York City to Cairo with several weapon-like items in his checked baggage. When he arrived in Cairo, he was detained, arrested, and charged for bringing weapons into Egypt. The charges were eventually dismissed. He subsequently brought suit in New York state court against EgyptAir Airlines, the airline in which he flew to Egypt, and EgyptAir Holding Company, a related company, claiming that their negligence, among other things, led to his arrest and detention in Egypt. He specifically alleged thirteen different state law claims, including breach of contract, negligence, fraud, and discrimination claims. The defendants, who removed the case to federal court, move for summary judgment, contending that the passenger's claims are preempted by the Airline Deregulation Act. What result should obtain? *See Abdel-Karim v. Egypt Airlines* (S.D.N.Y. 2015).

B. AIRLINE BUSINESS TORTS—PRICES, ROUTES, AND SERVICES

In 1938, Congress created the Civil Aeronautics Board ("CAB") to regulate interstate air transportation as a public utility. This meant that the CAB—not carriers themselves—established the rates airlines could charge and the routes airlines could fly. This framework was thought necessary to insulate the fledgling airline industry from the competitive forces at work in mature sectors of the national economy. As a result, from 1938 to 1978, the U.S. airline industry essentially consisted of an oligopoly or cartel of four carriers.

In the 1970s, however, deregulatory impulses overtook regulatory schemes as the modern era of mass airline transportation evolved. And, on October 24, 1978, President Jimmy Carter signed into law the Airline Deregulation Act. Originally introduced by Senator Howard W. Cannon (D. Nev.), the act, by amending the Federal Aviation Act of

1958, facilitated a market-driven commercial aviation system. Consumers benefitted. New airlines now set their own prices, routes, and services. Airline travel became routine and inexpensive. But so did poor customer service, as recounted in 2011 by U.S. Supreme Court Justice Stephen Breyer, who worked as an aide to the late Senator Edward Kennedy (D. Mass) on airline deregulation in the 1970s:

> Thirty-five years ago this month, Senator Edward Kennedy (D-Mass.) held hearings on the federal government's regulation of the airlines. His primary focus was on fares. Why were they so high? Officials at the Federal Trade Commission believed that regulation itself was the primary reason. The Civil Aeronautics Board had forbidden price competition. The result was service competition instead: empty seats, steak sandwiches, Aloha bars near the galley, and sky-high prices.
>
> * * *
>
> The hearings brought together a Democratic senator and a Republican President in Gerald Ford. They created alliances among consumer groups, pro-competition business groups, economists, and regulatory reformers. They helped make the "regulatory reform" issue politically visible. They showed that government regulation, being administered not by angels but by human beings, was itself imperfect. And they gave content to the notion of reform … reform would mean increased reliance on competition, sometimes to the point where government could abandon the effort to control prices.
>
> Pressure from these broad alliances eventually brought change to the airline industry. President Jimmy Carter took up the theme and appointed as chairman of the Civil Aeronautics Board a Cornell economist, Alfred E. Kahn. Kahn knew regulation; he understood government; and he understood human nature. He began to dismantle fare and route controls and he supported deregulatory legislation, which, with the support of Kennedy and Senators Orrin Hatch (R-Utah) and Strom Thurmond (R-S.C.), became law in 1978.
>
> What does the industry's history tell us? Was this effort worthwhile? Certainly it shows that every major reform brings about new, sometimes unforeseen, problems. No one

> foresaw the industry's spectacular growth, with the number of air passengers increasing from 207.5 million in 1974 to 721.1 million [in 2011]. As a result, no one foresaw the extent to which new bottlenecks would develop: a flight-choked Northeast corridor, overcrowded airports, delays, and terrorist risks consequently making air travel increasingly difficult. Nor did anyone foresee the extent to which change might unfairly harm workers in the industry.
>
> Still, fares have come down. Airline revenue per passenger mile has declined from an inflation-adjusted 33.3 cents in 1974, to 13 cents in the first half of 2010. In 1974 the cheapest round-trip New York-Los Angeles flight (in inflation-adjusted dollars) that regulators would allow: $1,442. Today one can fly that same route for $268. That is why the number of travelers has gone way up.
>
> So we sit in crowded planes, munch potato chips, flare up when the loudspeaker announces yet another flight delay. But how many now will vote to go back to the "good old days" of paying high, regulated prices for better service? Even among business travelers, who wants to pay "full fare for the briefcase?"

Stephen Breyer, *Airline Deregulation, Revisited*, BLOOMBERG BUS., Jan. 20, 2011, *http://www.bloomberg.com/bw/stories/2011-01-20/airline-deregulation-revisitedbusinessweek-business-news-stock-market-and-financial-advice*.

In reading *Morales v. Trans World Airlines, Inc.* and the cases that follow, consider whether the legacy of deregulation is positive, and if so, for whom (*e.g.* carrier or passengers); consider, too, how to reconcile the interpretive splits of authority as to what airline "prices, routes, and services" legislators intended to prohibit states from regulating.

MORALES v. TRANS WORLD AIRLINES, INC.

504 U.S. 374 (1992)

Justice SCALIA delivered the opinion of the Court.

The issue in this case is whether the Airline Deregulation Act of 1978, 49 U.S.C. § 1301 *et seq.*, pre-empts the States from prohibiting allegedly deceptive airline fare advertisements through enforcement of their general consumer protection statutes.

Prior to 1978, the Federal Aviation Act of 1958 ("FAA"), gave the Civil Aeronautics Board ("CAB") authority to regulate interstate airfares and to take administrative action against certain deceptive trade practices. It did not, however, expressly pre-empt state regulation, and contained a "saving clause" providing that "[n]othing ... in this chapter shall in any way abridge or alter the remedies now existing at common law or by statute, but the provisions of this chapter are in addition to such remedies." As a result, the States were able to regulate intrastate airfares (including those offered by interstate air carriers), and to enforce their own laws against deceptive trade practices.

In 1978, however, Congress, determining that "maximum reliance on competitive market forces" would best further "efficiency, innovation, and low prices" as well as "variety [and] quality ... of air transportation services," enacted the Airline Deregulation Act ("ADA"). To ensure that the States would not undo federal deregulation with regulation of their own, the ADA included a pre-emption provision, prohibiting the States from enforcing any law "relating to rates, routes, or services" of any air carrier. The ADA retained the CAB's previous enforcement authority regarding deceptive trade practices (which was transferred to the Department of Transportation ("DOT") when the CAB was abolished in 1985), and it also did not repeal or alter the saving clause in the prior law.

In 1987, the National Association of Attorneys General ("NAAG"), an organization whose membership includes the attorneys general of all 50 States, various Territories, and the District of Columbia, adopted Air Travel Industry Enforcement Guidelines (set forth in an Appendix to this opinion) containing detailed standards governing the content and format of airline advertising, the awarding of premiums to regular customers (so-called "frequent flyers"), and the payment of compensation to passengers who voluntarily yield their seats on overbooked flights. These guidelines do not purport to "create any new laws or regulations" applying to the airline industry; rather, they claim to "explain in detail how existing state laws apply to air fare advertising and frequent flyer programs." NAAG GUIDELINES, INTRODUCTION (1988).

Despite objections to the guidelines by the DOT and the Federal Trade Commission ("FTC") on pre-emption and policy grounds, the attorneys general of seven States, including petitioner's predecessor as attorney general of Texas, sent a memorandum to the major airlines announcing that "it has come to our attention that although most airlines are making a concerted effort to bring their advertisements into compliance with the standards delineated in the ... guidelines for fare advertising, many carriers are still [not disclosing all surcharges]" in violation of § 2.5 of the guidelines.

The memorandum said it was the signatories "'purpose ... to clarify for the industry as a whole that [this practice] is a violation of our respective state laws on deceptive advertising and trade practices"; warned that this was an "advisory memorandum before [the] initiati[on of] any immediate enforcement actions"; and expressed the hope that "protracted litigation over this issue will not be necessary and that airlines will discontinue the practice ... immediately." Several months later, petitioner's office sent letters to several respondents serving "as formal notice[s] of intent to sue."

Those respondents then filed suit in federal district court claiming that state regulation of fare advertisements is pre-empted by [the ADA]; seeking a declaratory judgment that, *inter alia*, § 2.5 of the guidelines is pre-empted; and requesting an injunction restraining Texas from taking any action under its law in conjunction with the guidelines that would regulate respondents' rates, routes, or services, or their advertising and marketing of the same. The District Court entered a preliminary injunction to that effect, determining that respondents were likely to prevail on their pre-emption claim. The Court of Appeals affirmed. Subsequently, the District Court, in an unreported order, permanently enjoined the States from taking "any enforcement action" which would restrict "any aspect" of respondents' fare advertising or operations relating to rates, routes, or services. The Court of Appeals once again affirmed. We granted *certiorari.*

* * *

We now turn to the question whether enforcement of the NAAG guidelines on fare advertising through a State's general consumer protection laws is pre-empted by the ADA. As we have often observed, "[p]re-emption may be either express or implied, and is compelled whether Congress' command is explicitly stated in the statute's language or implicitly contained in its structure and purpose." The question, at bottom, is one of statutory intent, and we accordingly "'begin with the language employed by Congress and the assumption that the ordinary meaning of that language accurately expresses the legislative purpose.'" *Park 'N Fly, Inc. v. Dollar Park & Fly, Inc.* (1985).

A.

Section 1305(a)(1) expressly pre-empts the States from "enact[ing] or enforc[ing] any law, rule, regulation, standard, or other provision having the force and effect of law relating to rates, routes, or services of any air carrier ..." For purposes of the present case, the key phrase, obviously, is "relating to." The ordinary meaning of these words is a broad one—"to stand in some relation; to have bearing or concern; to pertain; refer; to bring into association with or connection with," BLACK'S LANGUAGE DICTIONARY 1158 (5th ed. 1979)—and the words thus express a broad pre-emptive purpose. We have repeatedly recognized that in addressing the similarly worded pre-emption provision of the Employee Retirement Income Security Act of 1974 ("ERISA"), which pre-empts all state laws "insofar as they ... relate to any employee benefit plan."

We have said, for example, that the "breadth of [that provision's] pre-emptive reach is apparent from [its] language," that it has a "broad scope," and an "expansive sweep"; and that it is "broadly worded," "deliberately expansive," and "conspicuous for its breadth." True to our word, we have held that a state law "relates to" an employee benefit plan, and is pre-empted by ERISA, "if it has a connection with, or reference to, such a plan." Since the relevant language of the ADA is identical, we think it appropriate to adopt the same standard here: State enforcement actions having a connection with or reference to airline "rates, routes, or services" are pre-empted under 49 U.S.C. § 1305(a)(1).

Petitioner raises a number of objections to this reading, none of which we think is well taken. First, he claims that we may not use our interpretation of identical language in ERISA as a guide, because the sweeping nature of ERISA pre-emption derives not from the "relates to" language, but from "the wide and inclusive sweep of the comprehensive ERISA scheme," which he asserts the ADA does not have. This argument is flatly contradicted by our ERISA cases, which clearly and unmistakably rely on express pre-emption principles and a construction of the phrase "relates to."

Petitioner also stresses that the FAA "saving" clause, which preserves "the remedies now existing at common law or by statute," 49 U.S.C. § 1506, is broader than its ERISA counterpart. But it is a commonplace of statutory construction that the specific governs the general, a canon particularly pertinent here, where the "saving" clause is a relic of the pre-ADA/no pre-emption regime. A general "remedies" saving clause cannot be allowed to supersede the specific substantive pre-emption provision—unless it be thought that a State having a statute requiring "reasonable rates," and providing remedies against "unreasonable" ones, could actually set air fares. As in *Int'l Paper Co. v. Ouellette* (1987), "we do not believe Congress intended to undermine this carefully drawn statute through a general saving clause."

Petitioner contends that §1305(a)(1) only pre-empts the States from actually prescribing rates, routes, or services. This simply reads the words "relating to" out of the statute. Had the statute been designed to pre-empt state law in such a limited fashion, it would have forbidden the States to "regulate rates, routes, and services." Moreover, if the pre-emption effected by section 1305(a)(1) were such a limited one, no purpose would be served by the very next subsection, which preserves to the States certain proprietary rights over airports. It also bears mention that the rejected Senate bill did contain language that would have produced precisely the result the dissent desires: "No State shall enact any law ... determining routes, schedules, or rates, fares, or charges in tariffs of ..."

The dissent is unperturbed by the full Congress' preference for "relating to" over "determining," because the Conference Report gave "no indication that the conferees thought the House's 'relating to' language would have a broader pre-emptive scope than the Senate's language,"—which is to say because the Conference Report failed to specify the completely obvious, that "relating to" is broader than "determining." The dissent evidently believes not only that plain statutory language cannot be credited unless specifically explained in legislative history, but also that the apparent import of legislative history cannot be credited unless specifically explained in legislative history.

Next, petitioner advances the notion that only state laws specifically addressed to the airline industry are pre-empted, whereas the ADA imposes no constraints on laws of general applicability. Besides creating an utterly irrational loophole (there is little reason why state impairment of the federal scheme should be deemed acceptable so long as it is effected by the particularized application of a general statute), this notion similarly ignores the sweep of the "relating to" language. We have consistently rejected this precise argument in our ERISA cases: "[A] state law may 'relate to' a benefit plan, and thereby be pre-empted, even if the law is not specifically designed to affect such plans, or the effect is only indirect."

Last, the State suggests that pre-emption is inappropriate when state and federal law are consistent. State and federal law are in fact inconsistent here—the DOT opposes the obligations contained in the guidelines, and Texas law imposes greater liability—but that is beside the point. Nothing in the language of § 1305(a)(1) suggests that its "relating to" pre-emption is limited to inconsistent state regulation; and once again our ERISA cases have settled the matter: "'The pre-emption provision ... displace[s] all state laws that fall within its sphere, even including state laws that are consistent with ERISA's substantive requirements.'"

B.

It is hardly surprising that petitioner rests most of his case on such strained readings of § 1305(a)(1), rather than contesting whether the NAAG guidelines really "relat[e] to" fares. They quite obviously do. Taking them seriatim: Section 2.1, governing print advertisements of fares, requires "clear and conspicuous disclosure [defined as the lesser of one-third the size of the largest typeface in the ad or ten-point type] of restrictions such as" limited time availability, limitations on refund or exchange rights, time-of-day or day-of-week restrictions, length-of-stay requirements, advance-purchase and round-trip-purchase requirements, variations in fares from or to different airports in the same metropolitan area, limitations on breaks or changes in itinerary, limits on fare availability, and "[a]ny other material restriction on the fare."

Section 2.2 imposes similar, though somewhat less onerous, restrictions on broadcast advertisements of fares; and § 2.3 requires billboard fare ads to state clearly and conspicuously "'Substantial restrictions apply'" if there are any material restrictions on the fares' availability. The guidelines further mandate that an advertised fare be available in sufficient quantities to "meet reasonably foreseeable demand" on every flight on every day in every market in which the fare is advertised; if the fare will not be available on this basis, the ad must contain a "clear and conspicuous statement of the extent of unavailability." *See* § 2.4.

Section 2.5 requires that the advertised fare include all taxes and surcharges; round-trip fares, under § 2.6, must be disclosed at least as prominently as the one-way fare when the fare is only available on round trips; and § 2.7 prohibits use of the words "'sale,' 'discount,' [or] 'reduced'" unless the advertised fare is available only for a limited time and is "substantially below the usual price for the same fare with the same restrictions."

One cannot avoid the conclusion that these aspects of the guidelines "relate to" airline rates. In its terms, every one of the guidelines enumerated above bears a "reference to" airfares. And, collectively, the guidelines establish binding requirements as to how tickets may be marketed if they are to be sold at given prices. Under Texas law, many violations of these requirements would give consumers a cause of action for an airline's failure to provide a particular advertised fare—effectively creating an enforceable right to that fare when the advertisement fails to include the mandated explanations and disclaimers. This case therefore appears to us much like *Pilot Life Ins. Co. v. Dedeaux* (1987), in which we held that a common-law tort and contract action seeking damages for the failure of an employee benefit plan to pay benefits "related to" employee benefit plans and was pre-empted by ERISA.

In any event, beyond the guidelines' express reference to fares, it is clear as an economic matter that state restrictions on fare advertising have the forbidden significant effect upon fares. Advertising "serves to inform the public of the … prices of products and services, and thus performs an indispensable role in the allocation of resources." *Bates v. State Bar of Arizona* (1977). Restrictions on advertising "serve to increase the difficulty of discovering the lowest cost seller ... and [reduce] the incentive to price competitively." Accordingly, "where consumers have the benefit of price advertising, retail prices often are dramatically lower than they would be without advertising." As Judge Easterbrook succinctly put it, compelling or restricting "[p]rice advertising surely 'relates to' price." *Illinois Corporate Travel v. American Airlines, Inc.* (7th Cir. 1989).

Although the State insists that it is not compelling or restricting advertising, but is instead merely preventing the market distortion caused by "false" advertising, in fact the dynamics of the air transportation industry cause the guidelines to curtail the airlines' ability to communicate fares to their customers. The expenses involved in operating an airline flight are almost entirely fixed costs; they increase very little with each additional passenger. The market for these flights is divided between consumers whose volume of purchases is relatively insensitive to price (primarily business travelers) and consumers whose demand is very price sensitive indeed (primarily pleasure travelers). Accordingly, airlines try to sell as many seats per flight as possible at higher prices to the first group, and then to fill up the flight by selling seats at much lower prices to the second group (since almost all the costs are fixed, even a passenger paying far below average cost is preferable to an empty seat). In order for this marketing process to work, and for it ultimately to redound to the benefit of price-conscious travelers, the airlines must be able to place substantial restrictions on the availability of the lower priced seats (so as to sell as many seats as possible at the higher rate), and must be able to advertise the lower fares.

The guidelines severely burden their ability to do both at the same time: The sections requiring "clear and conspicuous disclosure" of each restriction make it impossible to take out small or short ads, as does (to a lesser extent) the provision requiring itemization of both the one-way and round-trip fares. Since taxes and surcharges vary from State to State, the requirement that advertised fares include those charges forces the airlines to create different ads in each market. The section restricting the use of "sale," "discount," or "reduced" effectively prevents the airlines from using those terms to call attention to the fares normally offered to price-conscious travelers. As the FTC observed, "[r]equiring too much information in advertisements can have the paradoxical effect of stifling the information that consumers receive." Further, § 2.4, by allowing fares to be advertised only if sufficient seats are available to meet demand or if the extent of unavailability is disclosed, may make it impossible to use this marketing process at all.

All in all, the obligations imposed by the guidelines would have a significant impact upon the airlines' ability to market their product, and hence a significant impact upon the fares they charge. In concluding that the NAAG fare advertising guidelines are pre-empted, we do not, as Texas contends, set out on a road that leads to pre-emption of state laws against gambling and prostitution as applied to airlines. Nor need we address whether state regulation of the nonprice aspects of fare advertising (for example, state laws preventing obscene depictions) would similarly "relat[e] to" rates; the connection would obviously be far more tenuous.

Finally, we note that our decision does not give the airlines carte blanche to lie to and deceive consumers; the DOT retains the power to prohibit advertisements which in its opinion do not further competitive pricing, see 49 U.S.C. § 1381. We hold that the fare advertising provisions of the NAAG guidelines are pre-empted by the ADA, and affirm the judgment of the Court of Appeals insofar as it awarded injunctive and declaratory relief with respect to those provisions. Insofar as that judgment awarded injunctive relief directed at other matters, it is reversed and the injunction vacated.

Justice STEVENS, with whom THE CHIEF JUSTICE and Justice BLACKMUN join, dissenting.

Although I agree that the plain language of § 105(a) pre-empts any state law that relates directly to rates, routes, or services, the presumption against pre-emption of traditional state regulation counsels that we not interpret § 105(a) to pre-empt every traditional state regulation that might have some indirect connection with, or relationship to, airline rates, routes, or services unless there is some indication that Congress intended that result. To determine whether Congress had such an intent, I believe that a consideration of the history and structure of the ADA is more illuminating than a narrow focus on the words "relating to."

In 1938 Congress enacted two statutes that are relevant to today's inquiry. In March it broadened § 5 of the Federal Trade Commission Act by giving the Commission the power to prohibit "unfair or deceptive acts or practices in commerce" as well as "[u]nfair methods of competition in commerce." Three months later it enacted the Civil Aeronautics Act of 1938. That statute created the Civil Aeronautics Board and mandated that it regulate entry into the interstate airline industry, the routes that airlines could fly, and the fares that they could charge consumers. Moreover, the statute contained a provision, patterned after § 5 of the FTCA, giving the Civil Aeronautics Board the power to prohibit "unfair or deceptive practices or unfair methods of competition in air transportation." But the Board's power in this regard was not exclusive, for the statute also contained a "saving clause" that preserved existing common-law and statutory remedies for deceptive practices.

Although the 1938 Act was replaced by a similar regulatory scheme in 1958, the principal provisions of the statute remained in effect until 1978. In that year, Congress decided to withdraw economic regulation of interstate airline rates, routes, and services. Congress therefore enacted the ADA "to encourage, develop, and attain an air transportation system which relies on competitive market forces to determine the quality, variety, and price of air services." Because that goal would obviously have been frustrated if state regulations were substituted for the recently removed federal regulations, Congress thought it necessary to pre-empt such state regulation. Consequently, Congress enacted § 105(a) of the Act, which pre-empts any state regulation "relating to rates, routes, or services of any air carrier having authority under subchapter IV of this chapter to provide air transportation."

At the same time, Congress retained § 411, which gave the Civil Aeronautics Board the power to prohibit "unfair or deceptive practices or unfair methods of competition in air transportation." Congress also retained the saving clause that preserved common-law and statutory remedies for fraudulent and deceptive practices. Moreover, the state prohibitions against deceptive practices that had coexisted with federal regulation in the airline industry for 40 years, and had coexisted with federal regulation of unfair trade practices in other areas of the economy since 1914, were not mentioned in either the ADA or its legislative history.

Because the Department of Transportation has authority to prohibit unfair or deceptive practices and unfair methods of competition in air transportation, 49 U.S.C. § 1381, it, too, could promulgate regulations that would pre-empt inconsistent state laws and regulations. But the Court does not rest its holding on the fact that the state prohibitions of unfair and deceptive advertising conflict with federal regulations; instead, it relies on the much broader holding that the ADA itself pre-empts state prohibitions of deceptive advertising.

In short, there is no indication that Congress intended to exempt airlines from state prohibitions of deceptive advertising. Instead, this history suggests that the scope of the prohibition of state regulation should be measured by the scope of the federal regulation that was being withdrawn. This is essentially the position adopted by the Civil Aeronautics Board, which interpreted the scope of § 105 in light of its two underlying policies—to prevent state economic regulation from frustrating the benefits of federal deregulation, and to clarify the confusion under the prior law which permitted some dual state and federal regulation of the rates and routes of the same carrier. The Board thus explained:

> Section 105 forbids state regulation of a federally authorized carrier's routes, rates, or services. Clearly, states may not interfere with a federal carrier's decision on how much to charge or which markets to serve … Similarly, a state may not interfere with the services that carriers offer in exchange for their rates.
>
> Accordingly, we conclude that preemption extends to all of the economic factors that go into the provision of the *quid pro quo* for passenger's fare, including flight frequency and timing, liability limits, reservation and boarding practices, insurance, smoking rules, meal service, entertainment, bonding and corporate financing.

See also John W. Freeman, *State Regulation of Airlines and the Airline Deregulation Act of 1978*, 44 J. AIR L. & COM. 747, 766-67 (1979).

Because Congress did not eliminate federal regulation of unfair or deceptive practices, and because state and federal prohibitions of unfair or deceptive practices had coexisted during the period of federal regulation, there is no reason to believe that Congress intended § 105(a) to immunize the airlines from state liability for engaging in deceptive or misleading advertising.

* * *

The Court finds in Congress' choice of the words "relating to" an intent to adopt a broad pre-emption provision, analogous to the broad ERISA pre-emption provision. The legislative history does not support that assumption, however.

The bill proposed by the Civil Aeronautics Board provided that "[n]o State ... shall enact any law ... relating to rates, routes, or services in air transportation." *Hearings on H.R. 8813 before the Subcommittee on Aviation of the House Committee on Public Works and Transportation*, 95th Cong., 1st Sess., pt. 1, p. 200 (1977). Yet the Board's accompanying prepared testimony neither focused on the "relating to" language nor suggested that those words were intended to effect a broad scope of pre-emption; instead, the testimony explained that the pre-emption section was "added to make clear that no state or political subdivision may defeat the purposes of the bill by regulating interstate air transportation. This provision represents simply a codification of existing law and leaves unimpaired the states' authority over intrastate matters."

The "relating to" language in the bill that was finally enacted by Congress came from the House bill. But the House Committee Report—like the Civil Aeronautics Board—did not describe the pre-emption provision in the broad terms adopted by the Court today; instead, the Report described the scope of the pre-emption provision more narrowly, saying that it "provid[ed] that when a carrier operates under authority granted pursuant to title IV of the Federal Aviation Act, no State may regulate that carrier's routes, rates or services." U.S. CODE CONG. & ADMIN. NEWS, p. 3752. The pre-emption section in the Senate bill, on the other hand, did not contain the "relating to" language. That bill provided, "[n]o State shall enact any law, establish any standard determining routes, schedules, or rates, fares, or charges in tariffs of, or otherwise promulgate economic regulations for, any air carrier ..." S. 2493, § 423(a)(1), *reprinted in* S. Rep. No. 95-631, p. 39 (1978). The Senate Report explained that this section "prohibits States from exercising economic regulatory control over interstate airlines."

The Conference Report explained that the Conference adopted the House bill (with an exception not relevant here), which it described in the more narrow terms used in the House Report. H.R. Conf. Rep. No. 95-1779, pp. 94-95 (1978). There is, therefore, no indication that the conferees thought the House's "relating to" language would have a broader pre-emptive scope than the Senate's "determining ... or otherwise promulgate economic regulation" language. Nor is there any indication that the House and conferees thought that the pre-emption of state laws "relating to rates, routes, or services" pre-empted substantially more than state laws "regulating rates, routes, or services."

* * *

Even if I were to agree with the Court that state regulation of deceptive advertising could "relat[e] to rates" within the meaning of § 105(a) if it had a "significant impact" upon rates, I would still dissent.

The airlines' theoretical arguments have not persuaded me that the NAAG guidelines will have a significant impact upon the price of airline tickets. The airlines' argument (which the Court adopts) is essentially that (1) airlines must engage in price discrimination in order to compete and operate efficiently; (2) a modest amount of misleading price advertising may facilitate that practice; (3) thus compliance with the NAAG guidelines might increase the cost of price advertising or reduce the sales generated by the advertisements; (4) as the costs increase and revenues decrease, the airlines might purchase less price advertising; and (5) a reduction in price advertising might cause a reduction in price competition, which, in turn, might result in higher airline rates. This argument is not supported by any legislative or judicial findings.

Even on the assumption that the Court's economic reasoning is sound and restrictions on price advertising could affect rates in this manner, the airlines have not sustained their burden of proving that compliance with the NAAG guidelines would have a "significant" effect on their ability to market their product and, therefore, on their rates. Surely Congress could not have intended to pre-empt every state and local law and regulation that similarly increases the airlines' costs of doing business and, consequently, has a similar "significant impact" upon their rates. For these reasons, I respectfully dissent.

APPENDIX TO OPINION OF THE COURT

National Association of Attorneys General
Task Force on the Air Travel Industry
Revised Guidelines

INTRODUCTION

In June, 1987, the National Association of Attorneys General ("NAAG") directed the appointment of a Task Force of states to study the advertising and marketing practices of the airline industry in the United States. In addition to the study, the Task Force was directed to determine the nature and extent of existing unfair and deceptive airline advertising practices and to report a recommended course of action to NAAG at its meeting in December 1987.

The Task Force Report and Recommendations were adopted by NAAG at its winter meeting on December 12, 1987, with a continuing direction to the Task Force (1) to receive and examine any comments from industry, consumer groups, federal agencies, and other interested parties; (2) to evaluate these comments; and (3) to report to NAAG at its Spring 1988 meeting on the advisability of any modifications of the Guidelines.

The Task Force received written comments from the Air Transport Association, the American Association of Advertising Agencies, American Airlines, the Association of National Advertisers, the Council of Better Business Bureaus, the Federal Trade Commission, the National Association of Broadcasters, Southwest Airlines, United Airlines, USAir, and the U.S. Department of Transportation. Assistant attorneys general of the Task Force states evaluated these comments, and reported their recommendations to NAAG. It is important to note that these Guidelines do not create any new laws or regulations regarding the advertising practices or other business practices of the airline industry. They merely explain in detail how existing state laws apply to air fare advertising and frequent flyer programs.

Section 1—Definitions

1.0 Advertisement means any oral, written, graphic or pictorial statement made in the course of solicitation of business. Advertisement includes, without limitation, any statement or representation made in a newspaper, magazine or other public publication, or contained in any notice, sign, billboard, poster, display, circular, pamphlet, or letter (collectively called "print advertisements"), or on radio or television ("broadcast commercials").

Comment: This definition *encompasses those materials and media covered by most states' false advertising statutes. "Print advertisements" and "broadcast commercial" are separated into different categories because they are afforded slightly different treatment under these Guidelines. This represents a change from an earlier draft of the Guidelines and is an attempt to address some of the airlines' concerns regarding the difficulties of lengthy disclosures in broadcast commercials.*

1.1 Award means any coupon, certificate, voucher, benefit or tangible thing which is promised, given, sold or otherwise transferred by an airline or program partner to a program member in exchange for mileage, credits, bonuses, segments or other units of value credited to a consumer as an incentive to fly on any airline or to do business with any program partner.

*Comment: This definition, [and] definitions 1.2, 1.3, 1.4, 1.6, 1.9, and 1.10, is self-*explanatory.

1.2 Award level means a specified amount of mileage or number of credits, bonuses, segments or other units which a program member must accumulate in order to receive an award.

1.3 Blackout date means any date on which travel or use of other program benefits is not permitted for program members seeking to redeem their award levels. This is a form of capacity control.

1.4 Capacity control means the practice by which an airline or program partner restricts or otherwise limits the opportunity of program members to redeem their award levels for travel or other benefits offered in the program.

1.5 Clear and conspicuous means that the statement, representation or term ("statement") being disclosed is of such size, color contrast, and audibility and is so presented as to be readily noticed and understood by the person to whom it is being disclosed. All language and terms should be used in accordance with their common or ordinary usage and meaning. For example, "companion" should be used only when it means any companion (*i.e.*, any person traveling with the program member), not solely family members. Without limiting the requirements of the preceding sentences:

(a) A statement in a print advertisement is considered clear and conspicuous if a type size is used which is at least one-third the size of the largest type size used in the advertising. However, it need not be larger than: 10-point type in advertisements that are 200 square inches or smaller, and 12-point type in advertisements that are larger than 200 square inches.

If the statement is in the body copy of the advertisement, it may be in the same size type as the largest type used in the body copy, and does not have to meet these type-size requirements.

(b) A statement in a broadcast commercial is considered clear and conspicuous if it is made orally and is as clear and understandable in place and volume as the fare information.

(c) A statement on any billboard is considered clear and conspicuous if a type is used which is at least one-third the size of the largest one size used on the billboard.

(d) A statement required by Section 3, relating to frequent flyer programs, is considered clear and conspicuous if it is prominently located directly adjacent to the materials to which it applies. Type size should be no smaller than the most commonly-used print size in the document, but in no event smaller than 10-point type. Any reservation of any right to make future changes in the program or award levels should be located prominently at the beginning of printed materials.

Comment: One of the most deceptive aspects of current air fare advertisements is the completely inadequate manner in which those advertisements disclose the restrictions and limitations which apply to the advertised fares. The restrictions disclosed in print advertisements are rarely located near the fare advertised and often appear only in extremely small type at the bottom of the advertisement. In broadcast commercials, such disclosures are generally absent from radio advertisements, and if included at all in television commercials appear as written disclosures flashed on the screen much too quickly for the average person to read. On billboards any mention of restrictions on advertised fares is unusual.

Given this background, NAAG believes that it is necessary to define clearly for the airlines what constitutes clear and adequate disclosure in all advertising media. The type-size minima for print advertisements are aimed at making the disclosures both easy to read and noticeable. Consequently, a slightly larger size print is suggested in larger size advertisements. These type-size minima are not absolute. That is, print disclosures do not in every instance have to be in at least 10-point type, as long as they are clear and conspicuous regardless of the size of the type. The type size suggestions are merely examples of advertising practices which give an airline a reasonable expectation that it will not be sued if it follows the Guidelines. In the Task Force's meetings with the airlines last summer, one common note expressed was that the airlines could abide by disclosure guidelines, as long as they were clear and enforced uniformly. If an airline does not choose this safe harbor and instead ventures into untested waters, it may run aground and it may not. But it is free to do so.

The comments to this Guideline were critical largely because NAAG singled out airline advertisements *for this treatment. However, on the whole, the airlines indicated they could meet the type size standard relatively easily in print advertisements.*

NAAG elected to encourage *oral disclosures in broadcast media, because written disclosures are difficult if not impossible to read and because many people listen to, rather than watch television commercials. We continue to believe that oral disclosure is the best method of conveying information in a television commercial. However, the converse of this Guideline is not true—a disclosure in a television commercial is not necessarily deceptive if it is instead made in a video super or crawl, as long as it is still clear and conspicuous. For safety reasons, very large type is provided for billboards.*

1.6 Frequent flyer program means any program offered by an airline or program partner in which awards are offered to program members.

1.7 Limited-time availability means that the fare is only available for a specific period of time or that the fare is not available during certain blackout periods.

Comment: This definition applies to air fares that are only available certain times of the year *(e.g., available December 15 through April 15), are not available at certain times at all (not available December 23 through January 5), or are only available until a date certain (available only until January 15). It does not apply to fares that are unavailable only on certain days of the week or times of the day.*

1.8 Material restriction means a restriction, limitation, or other requirement which affects the use or refundability of a ticket, and which is not generally applicable to all classes of fares or tickets (such as standard conditions of carriage).

Comment: Due to the numerous standard conditions applicable to most airline tickets, NAAG has confined the definition of "material restrictions" to those restrictions and limitations that are specific and unique to certain fare categories (i.e., those that are different from the restrictions and limitations that apply to a standard coach ticket).

1.9 Program member means any consumer who has applied and been accepted for membership in an airline's frequent flyer program, regardless of whether he or she has accrued mileage, credits, bonuses, segments or other units of value on an airline or with any program partner.

1.10 Program partner means any business entity which provides awards as part of an airline's frequent flyer program.

1.11 Vested member means a member of a frequent flyer program who is enrolled in an existing program and has provided consideration to the airline or its partners, and who has not received adequate notice of program changes such as set forth in Sections 3.2 and 3.9. For example, consideration includes purchasing tickets on an airline, renting a car or using a specific credit card.

Comment: This definition separates out those consumers who joined a frequent flyer program without receiving adequate notice of how that program could change prospectively. The Guidelines afford some special protections to vested members and miles. There is sound reason for this.

After reviewing the travel reward promotional materials for most of the major airlines, NAAG concluded that currently vested members have not received adequate disclosure of the potential for significant increases in award levels or imposition of other restrictions which may result in the airlines' unilateral devaluation of awards. Therefore, the Guidelines treat vested members and the miles which members accrued before receiving adequate notice of prospective changes differently.

1.12 Vested mile means program mileage (or other credits) accumulated by a vested member before that person receives adequate notice of program changes, as set forth in Sections 3.2 and 3.9.

Comment: This definition identifies any mileage or credit accrued by a vested member before he or she received adequate notice regarding the possibility of future detrimental changes in the program. See the comments to the definition of vested member.

Section 2—Fare Advertisements

2.0 General guideline

Any advertisement which provides air fares or other price information must be in plain language, clear and conspicuous, and non-deceptive. Deception may result not only from a direct statement in the advertisement and from reasonable inferences therefrom, but also omitting or obscuring a material restriction.

Comment: This Guideline and the following Guidelines restate individual states' false advertising and deceptive practices statutes as they apply to air fare and price advertising.

2.1 Disclosure in print advertisements

Print advertisements for fares must make clear and conspicuous disclosure of restrictions such as:

- **Limited-time availability.**
- **Limitations on right to refund or exchange of ticket.**
- **Time of day or day of week restrictions.**
- **Length of stay requirements.**
- **Advance purchase requirements.**
- **Round trip purchase requirements.**
- **Variations in fares to or from two or more airports serving the same metropolitan area.**
- **Limitations on, or extra charges for, breaks or changes in itinerary, such as failure to travel on every leg as scheduled.**
- **The statement, if any, required by Guideline 2.4.**
- **Any other material restriction on the fare.**

Comment: The advantage to consumers of print advertisements over television or radio advertisements is that they give consumers something tangible to use as a reference when shopping for low cost air fares. Because consumers can take their time and carefully read a print advertisement it is especially important that this type of advertisement contain the most accurate and complete information possible regarding any advertised air fares. The restrictions singled out by NAAG in this Guideline for disclosure are those NAAG believes are the most significant to a consumer contemplating purchasing a ticket. An advertisement that complies with this Guideline will give a consumer three crucial pieces of information:

1. Eligibility—consumers will know if they are eligible for the fare (i.e., can a consumer meet advance purchase requirements or other restrictions affecting time or date of travel?);

2. Availability—consumers can accurately gauge the likelihood that they will be able to obtain a ticket at the advertised price; and

3. Risk—consumers will know the risks associated with purchasing a ticket at the advertised price (i.e., is the ticket non-refundable or do other penalties apply upon cancellation or changes in itinerary?).

This particular Guideline received a great deal of negative comment because the airlines and government agencies misunderstood it to mean that it required full disclosure of all of the restrictions that apply to each specific flight. This is not correct. The Guideline only requires that if any of the restrictions listed in the Guideline apply to any of the air fares advertised then the advertisement must disclose the existence of that restriction and the fact that the restriction applies to one or more of the air fares advertised. To clear up this misunderstanding, NAAG included specific examples of the disclosures required by the revised Guidelines. There was also some misunderstanding that disclosure in a box was required. As the Guideline states, this is just one option.

The comments made to the December Guidelines evidenced another misconception about the wording of the disclosures on fare restrictions. This Guideline provides suggested wording, again to assist the airlines in determining how to meet the disclosures, but the language is by no means sacrosanct. The best creative minds in the advertising business are available to the airlines through their advertising agencies. The airlines are free to avail themselves of these talents, who are certainly adept at phrasing a message the advertiser wants to get across to the consumer.

The essence of the Guidelines is that consumers must be advised of the limits which the airlines has [sic] chosen to impose on consumers' ability to buy tickets at the advertised price.

2.2 Disclosure in broadcast commercials

Broadcast commercials for fares must make clear and conspicuous disclosure of limited-time availability; limitations on right to refund or exchange of ticket; the statement, if any, required by Guideline 2.4.

In addition, if the following seven disclosures are not made in a clear and conspicuous manner in the commercial, any that are applicable must be disclosed orally to the passenger before reservations are actually made:

- **Time of day or day of week restrictions.**
- **Length of stay requirements.**
- **Advance purchase requirements.**
- **Round trip purchase requirements.**
- **Variations in fares to or from two or more airports serving the same metropolitan area.**

- **Limitations on, or extra charges for, breaks or changes in itinerary, such as failure to travel on every leg as scheduled.**
- **Any other material restriction in the fare.**

As to these seven types of disclosure, the airline may include any or all in the commercial or may choose to defer disclosure until the time reservations are actually made.

If any of these seven disclosures applies to the fare advertised and the airline chooses to defer disclosure until the time the reservations are actually made, the commercial must give clear and conspicuous disclosure that "Other substantial restrictions apply," or similar language. The statement "Restrictions apply" is not sufficient.

Comment: In an earlier draft, the Guidelines required that radio and television advertisements include all the same disclosures required in print advertisements. The airline industry unanimously responded that such detailed disclosures would be impossible to include in the 15 and 30 second advertising spots generally purchased for radio and television ads, and argued that, even if time allowed this much oral disclosure, the resulting commercial would provide too much information for a consumer to absorb usefully. They concluded that such a requirement would eliminate airline price advertising on television and radio.

The provision of fare information, without stating the most significant restrictions that apply to the fare advertised, is deceptive and ultimately harmful to consumers and the airline industry alike.

The Guideline as revised provides a compromise. It suggests disclosure of the three most serious restrictions that can apply to an airline ticket—limited time availability, nonrefundability or exchangeability and limitations on fare availability. Disclosure of all of these restrictions can be accomplished by something as simple as the following statement: "Tickets are nonrefundable, are not available on all flights, and must be purchased by December 15. Other significant restrictions apply." These 20 words can easily be read in a 30 second commercial. In addition, some or all of this information may be clearly and conspicuously disclosed in a video super or crawl in television commercials. Of course, this option is not available for radio commercials. However, commenting airlines confirmed that the typical radio spot is 60 seconds, making the concern about time less crucial.

Airlines then have the option of disclosing any additional material restrictions in the advertisement itself or deferring such disclosure until a consumer makes a reservation. Of course, if an airline does not choose to restrict its fare severely, fewer words (and thus, less air time) is needed.

This compromise position also recognizes that print advertising lends itself more readily to detailed information in a form which the consumer can retain and refer to at his own pace. For this reason, NAAG has chosen to require less disclosure in broadcast, allowing print to be the medium for full disclosure.

2.3 Disclosure on billboards

Any billboard which provides air fare or other price information on a fare to which any material restrictions apply must have clear and conspicuous language such as "Substantial restrictions apply." The statement "Restrictions apply" is not sufficient.

Comment: For safety reasons, NAAG concluded that lengthy written disclosures on billboards are inappropriate and potentially hazardous to drivers. We disagree with the DOT that this special treatment of price advertising on billboards will result in a proliferation of billboards on our nation's highways.

2.4 Fare availability

Any advertised fare must be available in sufficient quantity so as to meet reasonably foreseeable demand on *every* flight each day for the market in which the advertisement appears, beginning on the day on which the advertisement appears and continuing for at least three days after the advertisement terminates. However, if the advertised fare is not thus available, the advertisement must contain a clear and conspicuous statement to the extent of unavailability of the advertised fare.

Statements such as "Seats limited" and "Restrictions apply" do not meet this Guideline. These examples do meet this Guideline:

- **This fare may not be available when you call.**
- **This fare is not available on all flights.**
- **This fare is only available on some Saturday and Sunday flights.**

Comment: This Guideline elicited the greatest amount of negative comments from the airline industry, the ATA, FTC and the DOT. They argue that this Guideline is impossible to implement because, due to the complexity of airline pricing systems, the number of seats available at a particular low fare on a particular flight is not a fixed number. It is continuously modified up to the point of departure. They suggest that it is acceptable for the airlines to communicate a general invitation to the public to buy low fare seats, but then reduce the number of seats available to zero or close to zero for the most popular flights, because the possibility that a consumer can purchase a seat at the advertised price exists at the time the advertisement is placed.

The complexity of the airlines' system cannot justify the unfairness of such an approach. No other retailer would be allowed to justify a failure to stock an advertised item on the grounds that, at the last minute the retailer decided it was less costly not to stock the item it had just advertised. The availability of an item advertised, at the price advertised, goes to the very heart of truthful advertising. If an airline advertises an air fare that is not available on each and every flight to the destination advertised, and this fact is not disclosed, then the advertisement is deceptive on its face.

While NAAG appreciates the difficulty of disclosing the specific number of seats available on each flight advertised, a disclosure that "This fare is not available on all flights" or "This fare may not be available when you call" is not particularly onerous. Absent such disclosure, airlines, as all other retailers, should be required to have sufficient stock available to meet reasonable demand for any fare advertised.

2.5 Surcharges

Any fuel, tax, or other surcharge to a fare must be included in the total advertised price of the fare.

Comment: Recently, several airlines considered the possibility of passing along an increase in the cost of fuel to consumers by imposing a "fuel surcharge" rather than simply raising air fares to reflect their increased costs. The air fare advertised was to remain the same, but a footnote would be added to the advertisement in the "mice type" disclosing that, for instance, a \$16 fuel surcharge would be tacked on to the advertised fare. The potential for abuse, if this type of price advertising is permitted, is obvious. It would only be a matter of time before \$19 air fares from New York to California could be advertised with \$300 meal, fuel, labor, and baggage surcharges added in a footnote. The total advertised price of the fare must include all such charges in order to avoid these potential abuses. However, this Guideline should not be construed to require an airline to do the impossible. We do not believe that such minimal tour-related charges fall within the meaning of "fare" and therefore do not believe that unknown charges must be disclosed as a surcharge (if the amounts are not in fact known). This of course does not mean that charges which are known—either as an exact amount or as a percentage—do not have to be disclosed in advertisements.

2.6 Round-trip fare advertising

If an airline elects to advertise the one-way portion of a fare that is only available as a round-trip purchase, this restriction, together with the full round-trip fare, must be advertised in a clear and conspicuous manner, at least as prominently as the one-way fare.

Comment: Airlines routinely advertise one-half of the price (i.e., the alleged "one-way" price) for tickets that are only available if a consumer makes a round-trip purchase. Under this Guideline, if an airline elects to continue this advertising practice, it must also disclose that the fare is only available if a consumer purchases a round trip ticket and the actual price of the full round trip ticket. The disclosure must be made in a type size and location as prominent as the fare advertised.

The airlines have, for the most part, stated a willingness to advertise the full round trip air fare if all of the airlines do the same. This Guideline is intended to encourage all airlines to adopt this practice.

2.7 Deceptive use of "sale," "discount," "reduced," or similar terms. A fare may be advertised by use of the words "sale," "discount," "reduced," or other such words that suggest that the fare advertised is a temporarily reduced fare and is not a regularly-available fare only if that fare is: available only for a specified, limited period of time, and substantially below the usual price for the same fare with the same restrictions.

Comment: The majority of airline tickets sold each year sell at prices significantly lower than the full "Y" or standard regular coach fare. These lower fares are offered year round and airlines in theory allocate a certain amount of seats to each fare "bucket." As a result, the regular coach fare has ceased to have any meaning as a starting point for determining whether or not a ticket is being offered for a "sale" price as consumers have come to understand that term.

In this Guideline NAAG has attempted to prevent consumer confusion by limiting the use of such words as "sale," "discount," or "reduced," to describe only those fares that represent a true savings over regularly available air fares—those that are available only for short periods of time and are substantially below any regularly offered fare for a ticket carrying identical restrictions.

Section 3—Frequent Flyer Programs

General Comments to Section 3

Frequent flyer programs have been widely acknowledged as the most successful marketing programs in airline industry history. The bargain struck between customers and the airlines has proven to be very costly to many of the airlines. Customers who have accrued the necessary mileage are expecting to collect the awards which led them to join and fly in the programs in the first place. Some airlines are now disturbed by the cost of keeping their side of the bargain and the real possibility that they may lose revenue because passengers flying on frequent flyer awards may begin displacing paying customers. The solution contemplated by some carriers has been to raise award thresholds and implement restrictions to decrease the cost to them of the award program. The effect of these actual and/or potential changes is to significantly devalue vested members' accrued mileage or other credits in the program. Although various frequent flyer program awards materials have contained some obscure mention of the possibility of future program changes, these disclosures have been wholly inadequate to inform program members of the potentially major negative changes which are contemplated by *many* airlines.

These Guidelines cover frequent flyer programs including any partner airlines or other providers of goods or services such as rental cars and hotel rooms. They are intended to protect those consumers who have participated in these programs in good faith, without adequate notice that the programs could change, and to advise the airlines of how they can reserve this right in the future by adequately providing this information to all members in a nondeceptive manner consistent with state law.

3.0 Capacity controls

1. If an airline or its program partners employ capacity controls, the airline must clearly and conspicuously disclose in its frequent flyer program solicitations, newsletters, rules and other bulletins the specific techniques used by the airline or program partner to control capacity in any solicitation which states a specific award. This includes blackout dates, limits on percentage of seats (for example, "the number of seats on any flight allocated to award recipients is limited"), maximum number of seats or rooms allocated or any other mechanism whereby the airline or program partner limits the opportunities of program members redeeming frequent flyer award levels. To meet this Guideline, all blackout dates must be specifically disclosed.

2. As to awards for vested miles, the airline or program partner must provide the award to the vested member without capacity controls or provide the award with capacity controls within a reasonable period of time. A reasonable period would be within 15 days before or after the date originally requested. If all seats within this 31-day period were sold at the time the vested member requested a reservation, so that the member could not be accommodated without displacing a passenger to whom a seat has been sold, then a reasonable period would be the period to the first available date on which every seat was not sold to the requested destination at the time the program member requests a reservation.

Comment: All of the airlines that met with the Task Force stated that they intended to retain the right to impose capacity controls, in the future, to limit the number of seats available to consumers purchasing tickets with frequent flyer award certificates. The imposition of capacity controls, including blackout dates, has the potential for unreasonably restricting the supply of seats or other benefits in such a way as to significantly devalue the awards due vested program members. NAAG found that this potential limitation has not been adequately disclosed to program members in the frequent flyer promotional materials we reviewed. This Guideline puts the airlines on notice as to what information they should provide to consumers if they want to impose capacity controls on the use of frequent flyer awards at some future date.

In earlier drafts of the Guidelines the Task Force took the position that capacity controls could not be applied to awards based on any mileage or credits accrued by vested members before they received adequate notice that capacity controls could be imposed. However, as a compromise, and to permit the airlines reasonable flexibility around holiday or other peak travel times, the revised Guideline provides for a reasonable time to accommodate passengers with award tickets: a 31-day "time window"—15 days before and 15 days after the date requested for ticketing. This "time window" allows the airlines to allocate capacity to meet demand over a reasonable, yet defined period of time. In the event all flights to a certain destination are sold out during the entire 31-day time window, ticketing on the next available seat would be reasonable. This approach has the additional benefit of being simple and straightforward to implement with less possibility of customer confusion and frustration.

3.1 Program changes affecting vested members

1. Any airline or program partner that has not reserved the right to make future changes in the manner required by Sections 3.2 and 3.9 of these Guidelines and that changes any aspect of its program (for example, imposition of capacity controls, increases in award levels, or any other mechanism whereby a vested member's ability to redeem any award will be adversely affected) must protect vested program members. Examples which meet this Guideline are:

(a) All vested members may not be adversely affected by that change for a reasonable period. A reasonable period would be one year following mailing of notice of that change.

(b) The airline or program partner may allow vested members to lock in any award level which is in effect immediately preceding any change in the program. That award level would be guaranteed for a period of one year after mailing notice of any increase in award levels. A vested member would also be permitted to change his or her selection to lock in a different award in existence at any time prior to an increase in award levels.

(c) The airline or program partner may credit vested program members with miles or other units sufficient to assume that, at the time of any change in the program, the member will be able to claim the same awards he or she could have claimed under the old program.

Comment: This Guideline institutes corrective measures to protect vested members and the mileage they accrued before receiving adequate notice that a program could change to their detriment at some point in the future. The Guideline sets forth three acceptable alternative approaches to allow airlines to change existing programs without unreasonably altering the rights and expectations of vested members. For example, an airline may wish to create a new program with higher award levels for persons who join in the future. Guideline 3.1.1(a) grandfathers in vested members for a one-year period after notice. Guideline 3.1.1(b) grandfathers only a specified locked-in award for a one-year period after the effective date of the change and thereby gives the member an additional year to accrue mileage or units toward a specific award. Guideline 3.1.1(c) allows the program to avoid the administrative problems of distinguishing between old and new members and old and new award levels by equitably adjusting the award levels of the vested members. These examples are not the only ways in which airlines can reasonably protect vested members when changing existing programs. They are intended to delineate minimum acceptable standards.

3.2 Notice of changes

1. Adequate notice of changes in current frequent flyer program award levels must be provided to vested program members by the airline or program partner to allow a reasonable time for the vested member to obtain and use an award. For example, a notice no less than one year prior to the effective date of such change would be reasonable. Reduction in award levels would not require such notice.

2. Any airline which has a policy of deleting program members from its mailing list for notices and statements must clearly and conspicuously disclose that policy in plain language in its rules and regulations.

3. To reserve the right to make future changes in the award levels and program conditions or restrictions in a manner providing reasonable notice consistent with state law, which notice is less than the notice set forth in Guideline 3.2.1, an airline must first clearly and conspicuously disclose that reservation and the nature of such future changes, in plain language. This disclosure should include examples which make clear the outer limits within which program awards may be changed. For example, the following is not adequate disclosure: "Program rules, regulations and mileage levels are subject to change without notice."

This example is adequate disclosure: "(Airline) reserves the right to terminate the program with six months' notice. This means that regardless of the amount you participate in this program, your right to accumulate mileage and claim awards can be terminated six months after we give you notice."

Or: "(Airline) reserves the right to change the program rules, regulations, and mileage level. This means that (Airline) may raise mileage levels, add an unlimited number of blackout days, or limit the number of seats available to any or all destinations with notice. Program members may not be able to use awards to

certain destinations, or may not be able to obtain certain types of awards such as cruises."

Or, if the airline so intends, the disclosure might also say: "In any case, (Airline) will make award travel available within—days of a program member's requested date, except for blackout dates listed here."

The airline's right to make future changes, in a manner other than that provided in Guideline 3.1, shall apply only to mileage accrued after members receive the notice required by this Guideline.

Comment: In the past, airlines have attempted to reserve the right to make radical future changes in their programs by using such vague and uncertain blanket language as "Subject to additions, deletions, or revisions at any time." The consumer outrage that ensued when several of the major airlines attempted unilaterally to change their programs in the winter of 1986-87 makes it clear that consumers were not adequately told, when they joined and participated in frequent flyer programs, that they were taking a gamble that the award they were striving for would still be available, at the mileage level originally advertised by the time they accrued the necessary miles.

To avoid a recurrence of this same problem in the future, this Guideline provides that the potential for such extensive program changes must be clearly and conspicuously disclosed to the public by specific example. It also puts the airlines on notice that (1) their previous attempts to disclose this critical information have been inadequate, (2) if they intend to reserve the right to make such changes in the future, they must give members new and different notice, and (3) as to vested members, airlines cannot implement any adverse changes until one year after notice is given. One year is deemed reasonable because many consumers can only travel during particular periods of the year due to work or family constraints, and therefore notice of less than a year may impact unduly harshly on a particular class of program members.

If an airline wants to reserve the rights to change the terms of its program without giving its members one year's notice (1) it can do so only after clear and adequate notice has been given to the program members and (2) this reduced standard can apply only to mileage accrued after clear and adequate notice has been given.

NAAG discovered that many airlines delete program members from their mailing lists if they are determined to be "inactive." Inactive is defined differently by each airline, but generally includes some formula requiring active participation in the program within a six to ten month period prior to any given mailing. Because crucial information regarding changes is included in program mailings, the Guidelines require that any airline with a policy of deleting program members from its mailing list clearly and conspicuously disclose that policy in the rules and regulations distributed to all program members when they join.

3.3 Fare or passenger class limitations

Any limitation upon the type or class of fare with which an upgrade certificate, discount flight coupon, or free companion coupon may be used must be clearly and conspicuously disclosed before the program member claims the award. Disclosure of the fare by airline terminology (for example, "Y Class") is not deemed sufficient.

Comment: Many airlines are encouraging consumers to use their accrued mileage or credits to obtain upgrade certificates or free campaign coupons, rather than free tickets because this is more cost effective for the airlines. Many of these coupons and certificates can be used only in conjunction with a regular coach fare ticket. Because of the high cost of a full coach ticket (often disclosed only as "Y Class") many of these coupons and certificates represent no real savings and therefore are useless to consumers. This Guideline requires that any such restriction be clearly disclosed to consumers before the award is claimed.

3.4 Certificates issued for vested miles

Certificates, coupons, vouchers, or tickets issued by an airline for awards redeemed for vested miles must be valid for a reasonable period of time. One year is deemed to be reasonable. Any restrictions on use, redeposit, extension, or re-issuance of certificates must be clearly and conspicuously disclosed on the certificate and in any rules, regulations, newsletter or other program materials.

Comment: Again, because many consumers may only travel during certain periods of the year, fairness requires that awards be valid for at least a full twelve month cycle.

3.5 Fees

Any airline which charges a fee for enrollment in its frequent flyer program must fully disclose at airline ticket counters and in all advertisements, solicitations or other materials distributed to prospective members prior to enrollment all terms and conditions of the frequent flyer program. Such disclosure must be made prior to accepting payment for enrollment in the airline's program.

Comment: Some airlines have required that consumers fill out a membership application and pay a membership fee before obtaining a copy of the program rules and regulations. Because of the serious restrictions that can apply to a travel reward program, it is essential that all consumers have an opportunity to review all of the program rules and regulations before paying an enrollment fee.

3.6 Redemption time

All airlines must disclose clearly and conspicuously the actual time necessary for processing award redemption requests where such requests are not normally processed promptly. An example of prompt processing would be within 14 days of processing the request. An example of a disclosure would be "processing of awards may take up to 30 days."

Comment: The airlines indicated that full disclosure of redemption time will not be a problem.

3.7 Termination of program affecting vested members

In the event a frequent flyer program is terminated, adequate notice of termination must be sent to all vested members so that vested members have a reasonable time to obtain awards and use them. Adequate notice would be notice at least one year prior to the termination of the program. Award levels in existence prior to such notice should remain in effect for one year. Program members should then have one year to use certificates, coupons, vouchers or tickets. Any applicable capacity controls should be modified as necessary to meet the demand for all award benefits due program members.

Comment: The airlines uniformly take the position that because participation in travel reward programs is "free," an airline should be able to terminate a travel reward program at any time without notice. NAAG strenuously disagrees. Consumers pay significant consideration for the airlines' promise to award them "free tickets" and other awards. Program members fly on a particular airline to accrue mileage in a travel reward program often foregoing a more convenient departure time, a more direct flight, and even a less expensive ticket. Those consumers who kept their part of the bargain have a right to expect the airlines to keep theirs, regardless of the cost. This Guideline affords consumers reasonable protection against unilateral changes. It gives consumers one year to accrue the mileage to reach a desired award level and one year to use the award.

This Guideline is intended to apply to programs that are terminated due to mergers or for any other reason. It would be unconscionable to permit airlines, which have reaped the rewards of these travel incentive programs, to walk away from their obligations to consumers under any circumstances.

3.8 Restrictions

All material restrictions on frequent flyer programs must be clearly and conspicuously disclosed to current program members and to prospective members at the time of enrollment.

Comment: This Guideline is intended as a corrective measure. Any airline that has not clearly and conspicuously disclosed material program restrictions to vested members should do so now. New members are entitled to full disclosure at the time of enrollment.

3.9 Method of disclosure

Disclosures referred to in these Guidelines should be made in frequent flyer program solicitations, newsletters, rules, and other bulletins in a clear and conspicuous manner so as to assure that all program members receive adequate notice. As used in these Guidelines, disclosure also refers to information on program partners.

Comment: The brochures containing the rules and regulations for airlines' frequent flyer programs have been as long as 52 pages. Extremely important restrictions are often buried under inappropriate topic headings or hidden on the back of the last inside pages of the brochure. This Guideline requires that restrictions be disclosed in reasonable print size in a location that will be most helpful and informative to consumers.

Any reservation of the right to make future changes in a program is so significant to consumers that it should be disclosed prominently to insure that the maximum number of people see and read this restriction. The Guideline permits the airlines flexibility to determine when and how often a disclosure must be made so long as the airline discloses the information in a manner which gives meaningful notice to all affected members.

One airline complained that Guideline 3.9 is unreasonable because it proposes that all the restrictions be disclosed at the beginning of the program brochure. In fact, the only disclosure the Guidelines suggested listing at the beginning of a brochure is the reservation of the right to change the program prospectively. The significance of such a restriction—that the terms and conditions of the program can change at any moment—is so critical that potential members should be made aware of it immediately. All other disclosures can be made in the text of the brochure.

Section 4—Compensation for Voluntary Denied Boarding

4.0 Disclosure of policies

If an airline chooses to offer ticketed passengers incentives to surrender their tickets on overbooked flights, the airline must clearly and conspicuously disclose all terms and conditions of the proposal—including any restrictions on offers of future air travel—to the person to whom the offer is made, and in the same manner in which the offer is made, before the person accepts the offer.

Comment: Federal regulations offer specific protections and certain rights to individuals who are involuntarily bumped from a flight. Airlines, however, are free to offer whatever compensation they want to people who voluntarily give up their seat on an airplane because of overbooking. For economic reasons, airlines prefer to offer vouchers good for free tickets on future flights, instead of cash compensation to these passengers. While these vouchers may seem very attractive to a consumer who has the flexibility to wait for a later flight, many carry serious restrictions on their use or are subject to lengthy blackout periods when they cannot be used.

This Guideline requires that airlines fully disclose any and all restrictions on offers for future air travel, before a consumer agrees to give up his or her seat. It does not, as several airlines and government agencies argued in their responsive comments, set any standards for the type of compensation that airlines must offer to these passengers.

CONCLUSION

Consumer dissatisfaction with the airline industry has reached crisis proportions. Federal agencies have focused their attention on airline scheduling problems, on-time performance, safety, and other related issues, but have not addressed airline advertising and frequent flyer programs. Unchecked, the airlines have engaged in practices in these areas that are unfair and deceptive under state law. The individual states through NAAG can play an important role in eliminating such practices through these Guidelines.

HODGES v. DELTA AIRLINES, INC.

44 F.3d 334 (5th Cir. 1995)

EDITH H. JONES, Circuit Judge.

During a flight from the Caribbean to Miami, Frances Hodges was injured when a fellow passenger opened an overhead compartment and dislodged a case containing several bottles of rum. The box fell and cut her arm and wrist. In her lawsuit against Delta Airlines, Hodges alleged that the airline's negligence caused her injury and medical expenses.

The question before this court *en banc* is whether her state law tort claim for physical injury based on alleged negligent operation of the aircraft is preempted by § 1305(a)(1) of the Airline Deregulation Act of 1978 ("ADA"). We hold that it is not and therefore overrule *Baugh v. Trans World Airlines, Inc.* (5th Cir. 1990), an originally unpublished opinion that, as circuit precedent, compelled the opposite result in the panel opinion herein.

DISCUSSION

Section 1305(a)(1) provides in pertinent part:

> [N]o state ... shall enact or enforce any law, rule, regulation, standard, or other provision having the force and effect of law relating to rates, routes or services of any air carrier having authority under Title IV of this Act to provide air transportation.

This provision originated in the ADA, an economic deregulation statute. The Federal Aviation Act of 1958 ("FAA"), 49 U.S.C. § 1301 *et seq*. (as amended), conferred on the Civil Aeronautics Board economic regulatory authority over interstate air transportation. The FAA did not expressly preempt state regulation of intrastate air transportation. In 1978, Congress amended the FAA after determining that efficiency, innovation, low prices, variety, and quality would be promoted by reliance on competitive market forces rather than pervasive federal regulation. Congress enacted the ADA to dismantle federal economic regulation. To prevent the states from frustrating the goals of deregulation by establishing or maintaining economic regulations of their own, Congress enacted § 1305(a)(1), which preempts the states from enforcing any law "relating to rates, routes or services" of any carrier.

The question in this case is the breadth of that express preemption of state law. State law is displaced by federal law where (1) Congress expressly preempts state law; (2) Congressional intent to preempt is inferred from the existence of a pervasive regulatory scheme; or (3) state law conflicts with federal law or interferes with the achievement of federal objectives. Interpretation of the statutory language is the key to construing its preemptive force.

The Supreme Court has twice broached the subject of ADA preemption in a way that informs but does not squarely resolve this case. In the first decision the question was whether section 1305(a)(1), in providing that no state may enforce any law "relating to rates," overcame the attempts of several state attorneys general to apply state deceptive advertising laws against the airlines. *Morales* held that it did. *Morales* drew upon the broad construction of the phrase "relating to" in the ERISA cases. Thus, the phrase "relating to" means "to stand in some relation; to have bearing or concern; to pertain; refer; to bring to association with or connection with." Consequently, "[s]tate enforcement actions having a connection with or reference to airline 'rates, routes or services' are preempted" under § 1305(a)(1).

As a necessary consequence of its broad interpretation, the Court rejected the argument that § 1305(a)(1) preempts the states only from actually prescribing rates, routes, or services. The Court also rejected the notions that "only state laws specifically addressed to the airline industry are preempted" and that "preemption is inappropriate when state and federal law are consistent." Laws of general applicability, even those consistent with federal law, are preempted if they have the "forbidden significant effect" on rates, routes or services. The Court acknowledged, however, that "[s]ome state actions may affect [airline services] in too tenuous, remote or peripheral a manner" to be preempted. Refusing to state exactly where the line would be drawn in a close case, the Court observed that the facts before it presented no close question of the connection between the attempted regulation and air fares.

Morales commands that whatever state laws "relate to rates, routes or services" are broadly preempted, but it does not define "services." The panel opinion in this case concluded that:

> "Services" generally represent a bargained—for or anticipated provision of labor from one party to another. If the element of bargain or agreement is incorporated in our understanding of services, it leads to a concern with the contractual arrangement between the airline and the user of the service.
>
> Elements of the air carrier service bargain include items such as ticketing, boarding procedures, provision of food and drink, and baggage handling, in addition to the transportation itself. These matters are all appurtenant and necessarily included with the contract of carriage between the passenger or shipper and the airline. It is these [contractual] features of air transportation that we believe Congress intended to de-regulate as "services" and broadly to protect from state regulation.

Hodges v. Delta Airlines, Inc. (5th Cir. 1993). The court adheres to this definition of services *en banc*, a definition inferentially reinforced by the Court's decision in *American Airlines, Inc. v. Wolens* (1995) (describing claims concerning American Airlines' frequent flyer program as related to rates and "services," *i.e.*, access to flights and class-of-service upgrades.").

Thus, federal preemption of state laws, even certain common law actions "related to services" of an air carrier, does not displace state tort actions for personal physical injuries or property damage caused by the operation and maintenance of aircraft. This definition harmonizes § 1305(a)(1) with other sections of airline regulatory law, with Congressional intent underlying the ADA, with the regulatory agencies' understanding of the statute, and with general principles of federal preemption.

Under the regulatory framework established by the FAA, the term "service" or "services" had an established definition, consistent with dictionary usage. Webster's Third New International Dictionary (1976) includes some of the following definitions:

> An action or use that furthers some purpose; supply of needs [*e.g.*, a vending machine for the service of passersby]; railroads and telephone companies produce services—useful labor that does not produce a good; provision for conducting a public utility [*e.g.*, air freight service]; regularly scheduled trip on public transportation ([free air services]).

A vestige of this definition remains in what is left of the federal airline regulatory statutes: "All-cargo air service" means the carriage by aircraft in interstate or overseas air transportation of only property or mail, or both. 49 U.S.C. § 1301(11) ("Definitions"). "Air service" referred at the time of passage of the ADA to the point-to-point transportation of passengers, cargo or mail, and it encompassed the business of transportation as well as the schedules and type of contract (common carriage or charter). This court interpreted "service" to embody the airlines' quality of service in such a fashion as to authorize federal regulation of smoking on commercial flights. *Diefenthal v. Civil Aeronautics Bd.* (1982).

Following deregulation, the CAB's statements implementing the ADA strongly support the view that the ADA was concerned solely with economic deregulation, not with displacing state tort law. The Board concluded that:

> preemption extends to all of the economic factors that go into the provision of the *quid pro quo* for passenger's [sic] fare, including flight frequency and timing, liability limits, reservation and boarding practices, insurance, smoking rules, meal service, entertainment, [and] bonding and corporate financing.

44 Fed. Reg. 9948, 9951 (Feb. 15, 1979). The CAB also opined:

> [A] state may not interfere with the services that carriers offer in exchange for their rates and fares. For example, liquidated damages for bumping (denial of boarding), segregation of smoking passengers, minimum liability for loss, damages and delayed baggage, and ancillary charges for headsets, alcoholic beverages, entertainment, and excess baggage would clearly be "service" regulation within the meaning of section 105.

The Federal Aviation Agency, to which some of the Civil Aeronautics Board's powers were transferred by the ADA, *see* 49 U.S.C. § 1551(b), continues to identify "service" or "services" in its regulations to incorporate the accoutrements of the passenger- or shipper- and carrier contract. Specific references to the words "service" or "services" in the Code of Federal Regulations governing airlines are too numerous to incorporate here. Some examples include (all within 14 C.F.R.): § 201.1 (domestic all-cargo air service); § 201.4(d) (the type of service-passengers, property or mail to be rendered and whether such services are to be rendered on scheduled or charter operations); § 204.3(t) (a description of the service to be operated if an application is granted); § 207.1 (defining special "services"); § 207.13(b) (terms of service for charter trips); § 207.71(a) (terms of service for charter trips include those for ground accommodations and services); § 217.4(b) (listing classes of service including scheduled passengers/cargo; scheduled all-cargo, ... non-scheduled services).

A facile analogy to *Morales* and the ERISA pre-emption cases could suggest that "services" includes all aspects of the air carrier's "utility" to its customers, hence, any state tort claim may "relate to" services as a result of its indirect regulatory impact on the airline's practices. Taken to its logical extreme, this argument would suggest that a lawsuit following a fatal airplane crash could relate to "services."

That Congress did not, however, intend § 1305(a)(1) to preempt all state claims for personal injury is evident from at least one other provision of the remaining airline regulatory statutes. Air carriers are required to maintain insurance or self-insurance as prescribed by the Federal Aviation Administration that covers "amounts for which ... air carriers may become liable for bodily injuries to or the death of any person, or for loss of or damage to property of others, resulting from the operation or maintenance of aircraft." 49 U.S.C. § 1371(q) (1994); *see also*, 14 C.F.R. § 205.5(a) (1992) (insurance regulations.). The importance of § 1371(q) cannot be understated, for it can only be understood to qualify the scope of "services" removed from state regulation by § 1305(a)(1). A complete preemption of state law in this area would have rendered any requirement of insurance coverage nugatory.

The FAA further defines "operation of aircraft" as "the use of aircraft for the purpose of air navigation ... includ[ing] the navigation of aircraft." 49 U.S.C. § 1301(31) (1988). One uses the overhead luggage racks or the food and beverages provided in aircraft operation just as one uses the cigarette lighter or built-in cooler compartment in an automobile, and all these devices are available to support the general purpose of navigation.

Significantly, too, neither the ADA nor its legislative history indicates that Congress intended to displace the application of state tort law to personal physical injury inflicted by aircraft operations, or that Congress even considered such preemption. "This silence takes on added significance in light of Congress's failure to provide any federal remedy for persons injured by such conduct. It is difficult to believe that Congress would, without comment, remove all means of judicial recourse for those injured by illegal conduct." The Supreme Court has repeatedly cautioned that federal courts should not displace state police powers by federal law unless that was the "clear and manifest purpose of Congress." [Meanwhile], the Seventh Circuit noted that "[s]tate courts award damages every day in air crash cases, notwithstanding that federal law preempts the regulation of safety in air travel," confidently adding that "[t]he Federal Aviation Act does not expressly preempt state damages remedies."

Delta Airlines agrees that among the "services" deregulated under the ADA and covered by its preemption clause are the economic or contractual features of air transportation. Delta argues, however, that Mrs. Hodges' accident arose out of the "services" of baggage handling and boarding, not out of the "operation and maintenance of aircraft" covered by § 1371(q). The "services" that the state may not regulate under § 1305(a)(1) are distinct from the "operation and maintenance of aircraft," and all claims related to "services" are preempted.

This argument fails on two levels. First, if the statutory provisions created a strict dichotomy between services and operation or maintenance of aircraft, Hodges' injury more properly is laid at the door of operations. Whether certain luggage may be placed in overhead bins and whether the flight attendants properly monitor compliance with overhead rack regulations are matters that pertain to the safe operation of a flight. "Baggage handling" and "boarding," as referred to in the above-quoted CAB statement, concern the airline's policy for permitting baggage to be carried or passengers to be permitted to board. These are aspects of the "service" offered; they do not refer directly to the way in which the aircraft is operated.

Delta confuses its argument by contending that this state tort suit should not be permitted to proceed because it could impose duties that conflict with Federal Aviation Administration regulations governing carry-on baggage. There are no facts in the record that intimate the basis for such a conflict. Moreover, in *Cipollone v. Liggett Group, Inc.* (1992), the Supreme Court held that when Congress has enacted an explicit preemption provision, courts should not usually imply broader preemption of state law. Therefore, this decision of our court does not address the possible preemptive effect of Federal Aviation Administration safety regulations governing aircraft and carriers. *See Public Health Trust of Dade Cty., Fla. v. Luke Aircraft, Inc.* (11th Cir. 1993).

Second, as this example shows, the provinces of "services" and "operation and maintenance of aircraft" overlap somewhat conceptually; no strict dichotomy exists. There is not, however, a fundamental inconsistency between the two provisions. By means of § 1305(a)(1), Congress intended to prevent the states from regressing on economic deregulation by applying their own laws or rules concerning "services," but in § 1371(q), Congress explicitly preserved airlines' duty to respond to tort actions, inferentially state law actions, for physical injury or property damage.

Finally, unlike the NAAG Guidelines in *Morales*, enforcement of tort remedies for personal physical injury ordinarily has no "express reference" to services as defined above. Enforcement of such tort duties normally will not have "the forbidden significant effect" on airlines' services. *Morales* relied in part on the fact that the state restrictions on airfare advertising had a significant economic effect on fares. Generally, however, state tort laws concerning the operation and maintenance of aircraft can be enforced consistently with and distinctly from the services that Congress deregulated. Most cases will not pose as close a question as this one. But this general vindication of state tort claims arising from the maintenance or operation of aircraft does not extend to all conceivable state tort claims. Two examples of the continued scope of preemption are illustrative.

In *O'Carroll v. American Airlines, Inc.* (5th Cir.1989), the plaintiff and his cousin were removed from a commercial airline flight because they were loud, boisterous, and intoxicated. O'Carroll sued, alleging that he was wrongfully evicted from the flight. This court vacated O'Carroll's sizeable jury verdict, holding that his state law claims were preempted by § 1305(a)(1). *O'Carroll* did not discuss the scope of § 1305(a)(1) because the state law claims arising from the alleged wrongful exclusion undeniably related only to the services provided by the airline. No claim was made that the airline breached any safety-related tort duty by bumping O'Carroll. Enforcement of O'Carroll's state law claims would result in significant *de facto* regulation of the airlines' boarding practices and, moreover, would interfere with federal law granting the airlines substantial discretion to refuse to carry passengers.

Similarly, the claims asserted by the plaintiff in *West v. Northwest Airlines* (9th Cir. 1993), would be preempted under our interpretation of "services." Plaintiff West sued because he was "bumped" from the overbooked airline flight for which he had reserved a seat. After remand for reconsideration in light of *Morales*, the Ninth Circuit held, over a dissent, that West's state law claims were too tenuously connected to "rates, routes and services" to be preempted by § 1305(a)(1). The majority did find West's punitive damage claim preempted. Under either *Morales* or the analysis advanced here, it is difficult to see how a lawsuit for overbooking would not "relate to" the airline's contract for "services" with its passenger.

Hodges' Claims

Hodges alleged that Delta was negligent in allowing the case of rum to be stowed in an overhead storage bin. This tort claim for personal injury has no specific "reference to" airline services, although it does derive from the operation of the aircraft. Nor would enforcement of her claim significantly affect Delta's services, as defined above. As other cases have recently held, this type of claim does not relate to Delta's services and is not preempted.

E. GRADY JOLLY, specially concurring.

I concur in the judgment in this case and its companion, *Smith v. America West Airlines* (5th Cir. 1995). I cannot approve, however, of the rationale used to decide these cases. The majority and the dissent agree on the principle that a claim is preempted by the ADA express preemption provision if the claim relates to services that are not a part of the maintenance or operation of an airline; only the application of this rule prompts the dissent. The fact that the majority and the dissent disagree only on the application of this principle reveals that it promises uncertainty and inconsistent results.

I would have preferred that we give effect to the plain language of the ADA preemption provision. Plainly, it preempts only claims "related to a price, route, or service" that involve an instance of a "state ... enact[ing] or enforc[ing] a law, regulation, or other provision having the force and effect of law." In my view, while these claims are unquestionably related to a service, they simply do not run afoul of the provision's prohibition of state-adopted legislation or regulation, or state enforcement of legislation or regulation. I would hold that claims by private individuals to obtain remedies for an asserted breach of the duty of reasonable care—traditional, well-settled common law tort remedies, in short—are not preempted by the ADA preemption provision either.

I view as a mistake the majority's ascribing a broader sweep to the preemption provision than its language will admit, and then engrafting upon its own broad interpretation a series of narrowing distinctions that lack a basis in the words of the statute and are not susceptible of clear meaning or certain application. I would prefer, instead of erecting these tenuous and uncertain judge-made distinctions, to rely upon the plain language of the provision as Congress intended and enacted it and our other, well-settled, federal preemption principles.

The House Report accompanying the enactment of Section 1305 states that the lack of a clear delineation of state and federal jurisdiction over airlines had created "uncertainties and conflicts, including situations in which carriers have been required to charge different fares for passengers traveling between two cities, depending on whether these passengers were interstate passengers whose fares are regulated by the CAB, or intrastate passengers, whose fare is regulated by a state." 1978 U.S. CODE CONG. & ADMIN. NEWS. 3751-52. To that end, § 1305 would "prevent conflicts and inconsistent regulations by providing that when a carrier operates under authority granted pursuant to ... the Federal Aviation Act, no state may regulate that carrier's routes, rates or services. The bill also eliminates Federal jurisdiction over certain service which is essentially intrastate in nature."

Similarly, the House Conference Report explains that § 1305 "prohibits a state from enacting any law, establishing any standard determining routes, schedules, or rates, fares, or charges in tariffs of, or otherwise promulgating economic regulations for, any air carrier certified by the Board." Nowhere, however, does Congress evidence an intent to relieve air carriers of their obligation to exercise reasonable care for the safety of their passengers.

A consideration of two cases referred to by the majority reveals the difficulties created by its departure from the plain language of the preemption provision. The majority today overrules *Baugh v. Trans World Airlines* (5th Cir. 1990), and reaffirms *O'Carroll v. American Airlines* (5th Cir.1989), but as far as I understand the majority's approach, it seems to compel an overruling of *O'Carroll* and a reaffirmance of *Baugh*. These cases bear out my expectation that confusion and uncertainty will ensue from the approach outlined in the majority's opinions.

In *Baugh*, a flight attendant stomped on a passenger's foot while engaged in some unspecified activity. We held that the passenger's claim was preempted because it related to the services afforded to the passengers on an airline. In *Hodges*, the majority specifically includes "provision of food and drink" in its open-ended definition of services that are preempted. As far as the majority knows, the flight attendant in *Baugh* was engaged in the provision of food and drink when the injury occurred, which means that one would assume under the majority's opinion that the cause of action in *Baugh* remains preempted. Why, then, does the majority assume that *Baugh* must be reversed?

Baugh relied upon *O'Carroll.* Although both this case and *Smith* reaffirm *O'Carroll*, I am convinced that under the majority's approach, *O'Carroll* would be overruled. In that case, the majority explains, we held that state claims stemming from an assertedly wrongful exclusion from an airplane were preempted. The majority states today that O'Carroll's claims are preempted by the express preemption provision because they "undeniably relate to services." Under *Smith*, however, the majority's explanation is not sufficient because the probability exists that, although the claim did relate to services, it implicated safety concerns, and thus would fall outside the preemption provision. *Smith* answers, in an oblique way, that O'Carroll's claims implicated economic practices as opposed to the safety of the flight. That answer, however, belies the fact that O'Carroll and his companion were excluded from the flight, and later jailed for disorderly conduct, because they were intoxicated and had been behaving so boisterously that at one point one of them offered his assistance to the pilot in flying the plane. O'Carroll's claims plainly implicated the safety of the flight. As a consequence, O'Carroll's suit should not be preempted under the approach announced by the majority today.

The result in *O'Carroll* can be reconciled with the plain language approach suggested by this concurring opinion. In *O'Carroll*, we determined that the claims were preempted for two reasons. First, 49 U.S.C. § 1511(a) granted broad discretion to refuse to transport any passenger if it "would or might be inimical to safety of flight." Clearly, transporting O'Carroll in his condition threatened the safety of the flight. O'Carroll's claims thus were impliedly preempted by the separate federal statute. A wholly convincing reason independent of the express preemption provision thus justified our determination that O'Carroll's claim was preempted. Seen in this light, our conclusory statement in *O'Carroll* that "[T]here is no need to rely upon inference alone as section 1305 ... expressly preempts state law," and that "[i]n view of this explicit manifestation of congressional intent, we conclude that O'Carroll's common law claims are preempted under § 1305," is properly regarded as obiter dictum.

PATRICK E. HIGGINBOTHAM, Circuit Judge, with whom EMILIO M. GARZA, Circuit Judge, joins, dissenting.

While the term services must be given its ordinary meaning, it is clear that Congress did not intend operation or maintenance of an aircraft to fall within the statute's definition of services, despite its common sense relationship to provision of services. Section 1371(q)(1) requires each air carrier to maintain insurance to cover "amounts for which ... such air carrier may become liable for bodily injuries to or the death of any person, or for loss of or damage to property of others, resulting from the operation or maintenance of aircraft." We cannot read § 1305(a)(1)'s use of the term services to include operation or maintenance of an aircraft and give meaning to § 1371(q)(1). If the claim relates to services, then it is preempted unless it also results from "the operation or maintenance of aircraft." If there is doubt as to whether the claim results from the operation or maintenance of the aircraft, that doubt is to be resolved in favor of the operation or maintenance category. Thus, preemption turns on whether judicial enforcement of a claim would regulate and whether the regulation was of the operation or maintenance of an aircraft.

Reflecting upon the practical reach of a tort claim sheds light on both inquiries. A mine run tort case from Louisiana makes the point. In *Schwamb v. Delta Air Lines, Inc.* (La. Ct. 1987), Schwamb was injured when a briefcase fell out of an overhead bin and struck him on the head. Schwamb introduced the testimony of Miller, an expert in aeronautical engineering, aviation accident investigation and reconstruction, human factors, crash survivability, safety engineering, and safety management. Miller testified that the following steps could have been taken to minimize a passenger's risk of being struck by objects falling from overhead bins:

(1) A pre-boarding announcement to passengers about how to load the baggage; *e.g.*, "Put the heavy things on the bottom, the lighter things on top."

(2) A pre-boarding announcement to passengers to stow their baggage but not to close the doors. If the doors were open, flight attendants could come down the aisle before takeoff and check each and every one of the bins without having to take the time to open closed bins.

(3) A pre-boarding inspection of carry-on baggage, in which flight attendants check the volume of the luggage as well as its weight.

(4) An on-board announcement by the flight attendant to passengers, *e.g.*, in conjunction with the safety briefing concerning oxygen masks and emergency exits.

(5) A warning on the plastic safety card which says something such as: "Be careful; don't overload bins and use caution when you use them."

(6) A warning or illustration depicting the proper way to pack an overhead bin.

(7) A pre-landing announcement to passengers concerning the removal of baggage from the overhead bins.

(8) An announcement or warning while taxiing to the arrival gate when the vast majority of passengers are still seated, to the effect that passengers need to be cautious when opening the bins.

The placement of baggage in an overhead compartment plainly relates to airline services. State enforcement of the claim plainly regulates. Hodges' claim is then preempted unless the activity she complains of constitutes operation or maintenance of an aircraft. "Operation of aircraft" means "the use of aircraft, for the purpose of air navigation and includes the navigation of aircraft." *See* 49 U.S.C. § 1301(31). The statute does not define "maintenance of aircraft." Nonetheless, I have little difficulty in concluding that stowing carry-on items in an overhead compartment is a service airlines provide for passengers who do not wish to check their baggage. It does not in any way relate to the navigation or maintenance of aircraft. Hodges' claim is preempted, and the judgment of the district court should be affirmed.

WITTY v. DELTA AIR LINES, INC.

366 F.3d 380 (5th Cir. 2004)

REAVLEY, Circuit Judge.

Milton Witty brought this diversity suit in Louisiana federal district court against Delta Air Lines, Inc. ("Delta"). He claims that he developed Deep Vein Thrombosis ("DVT") while on a Delta flight from Monroe, Louisiana to Hartford, Connecticut.

DVT occurs when a blood clot develops in a deep vein, usually in the leg. It can cause serious complications if the clot breaks off and travels to the lungs or brain. Witty alleged that Delta was negligent in failing to warn passengers about the risks of DVT. He asserts in his appellate brief that "[t]he warning should be that there is a high risk of developing [DVT] in pressurized cabins that exceed a certain length of time." The complaint also alleged that Delta was negligent in failing to provide adequate leg room to prevent DVT and in "failing to allow [passengers] to exercise their legs."

Delta filed a motion to dismiss, arguing that the state law claims were preempted. The district court denied the motion. The court reasoned that under *Hodges v. Delta Airlines, Inc.* (5th Cir. 1995) (*en banc*), state regulation of airline "services" is preempted but that "state tort actions for personal physical injuries caused by the operation and maintenance of aircraft are not preempted by federal law." The court concluded that Witty's claim arose from the operation of Delta's aircraft and therefore was not preempted. The district court found that the order was appropriate for interlocutory appeal under 28 U.S.C. § 1292(b), and we permitted the appeal.

DISCUSSION

We review *de novo* the district court's ruling on preemption. Sitting *en banc* in *Hodges*, we held that a passenger's personal injury claim under state law was not preempted. The passenger "was injured when a fellow passenger opened an overhead compartment and dislodged a case containing several bottles of rum." We analyzed the effect of the preemption provision of Airline Deregulation Act of 1978 ("ADA"), which states that, subject to certain exceptions not relevant here, "a State ... may not enact or enforce a law, regulation, or other provision having the force and effect of law related to a price, route or service of any air carrier that may provide air transportation under this subpart."

In *Hodges*, we held that the preemptive effect of § 41713(b)(1) is limited by a provision of the Federal Aviation Act of 1958 ("FAA"), which provides that air carriers must maintain insurance or self-insurance that covers liability "for bodily injury to, or death of, an individual … resulting from the operation or maintenance of the aircraft …" We reasoned that § 41112(a) "can only be understood to qualify the scope of 'services' removed from state regulation by [§ 41713(b)(1)]. A complete preemption of state law in this area would have rendered any requirement of insurance coverage nugatory … Thus, federal preemption of state laws, even certain common law actions 'related to services' of an air carrier, does not displace state tort actions for personal physical injuries or property damage caused by the operation and maintenance of aircraft."

We recognized in *Hodges* that there is no "strict dichotomy" between "services" and "operation or maintenance of aircraft," concluding instead that the terms "overlap somewhat conceptually," and thereby suggesting a case by case resolution of preemption questions. We ultimately concluded that the state personal injury claim was not related to the provision of airline services and did "derive from the operation of the aircraft," and accordingly was not preempted. Merely describing our analysis in *Hodges* demonstrates that preemption questions in this arena do not always submit to a simple analysis. Insofar as plaintiff Witty in the pending case alleges that Delta should have provided more leg room, we hold that such a requirement would inexorably relate to prices charged by airlines, and Witty does not seriously contend otherwise.

Since requiring more leg room would necessarily reduce the number of seats on the aircraft, such a requirement would impose a standard "relating to a price" under § 41713(b)(1), and is accordingly preempted by the ADA. Section 41713(b)(1) not only preempts the direct regulation of prices by states, but also preempts indirect regulation "relating to" prices that have "the forbidden significant effect" on such prices. *Morales v. Trans World Airlines, Inc.* (1992). While the state regulation of leg room might not relate to prices as obviously as the state regulation of fare advertising at issue in *Morales*, the economic effect on prices would in our view be significant, perhaps much more so than the advertising rules at issue in *Morales*.

The failure to warn claim presents a closer question, but we conclude under implied preemption doctrines that Congress intended to preempt state standards for the warnings that must be given airline passengers. The complaint, by alleging that Delta was negligent in "failing to allow [passengers] to exercise their legs," might be construed as asserting a separate "failure to instruct" claim that passengers were not advised to move about the cabin or were instructed verbally or by the seat belt sign to remain in their seats. We conclude however that the preemption analysis of such a claim is essentially identical to the analysis of a failure to warn claim, and our discussion of the latter is intended to cover both claims.

At the outset, we note that *Hodges* described the ADA as "an economic deregulation statute," suggesting that the express preemption provision of that Act is not necessarily the only conceivable basis for finding preemption in a personal injury case based on inadequate safety warnings. There is a separate federal act, the FAA, which addresses air safety. The Supreme Court, after *Hodges*, has recognized that preemption under ordinary implied preemption principles is not necessarily foreclosed by the existence of an express preemption provision. Moreover, *Hodges* expressly did not reach the issue of "the possible preemptive effect of Federal Aviation Administration safety regulations governing aircraft and carriers." This issue is squarely raised in the pending case.

Preemption ultimately turns on congressional intent. Preemption may be express or implied. In the pending case, field preemption and conflict preemption are both applicable, because there exists a comprehensive scheme of federal regulation, and the imposition of state standards would conflict with federal law and interfere with federal objectives.

The FAA not only authorizes but affirmatively directs the Administrator of the Federal Aviation Administration to promulgate air safety standards and regulations, including standards and regulations relating to aircraft design, aircraft maintenance and inspections, "the maximum hours or periods of service of airmen and other employees of air carriers," and as a catchall provision, "other practices, methods, and procedure the Administrator finds necessary for safety in air commerce and national security." The administrator is generally charged with carrying out the FAA "in a way that best tends to reduce or eliminate the possibility or recurrence of accidents in air transportation."

Pursuant to its congressional charge to regulate air safety, the Federal Aviation Administration has issued a broad array of safety-related regulations codified in Title 14 of the Code of Federal Regulations. These regulations cover airworthiness standards, crew certification and medical standards, and aircraft operating requirements. The regulations include a general federal standard of care for aircraft operators, requiring that "[n]o person may operate an aircraft in a careless or reckless manner so as to endanger the life or property of another." 14 C.F.R. § 91.13(a) (2003).

There are a number of federal regulations governing the warnings and instructions which must be given to airline passengers. These regulations require, for example, that "no smoking" placards be placed in lavatories, that "no smoking" signs be illuminated during the entire flight on non-smoking flights, and that the "fasten seat belt" sign "shall be turned on during any movement on the surface, for each takeoff, for each landing, and at any other time considered necessary by the pilot in command." In addition, the Federal Aviation Administration has published regulations, 14 C.F.R. §§ 121.571 & 121.585, and an advisory circular setting out in detail the oral briefings, familiar to all domestic air travelers, which flight attendants or other flight personnel must give passengers, as well the information that must be included in passenger safety briefing cards.

We hold that federal regulatory requirements for passenger safety warnings and instructions are exclusive and preempt all state standards and requirements.

Congress enacted a pervasive regulatory scheme covering air safety concerns that includes regulation of the warnings and instructions that must be given airline passengers. The Supreme Court has observed that the FAA "requires a delicate balance between safety and efficiency, and the protection of persons on the ground ... The interdependence of these factors requires a uniform and exclusive system of federal regulation if the congressional objectives underlying the Federal Aviation Act are to be fulfilled." *City of Burbank v. Lockheed Air Terminal Inc.* (1973).

Allowing courts and juries to decide under state law that warnings should be given in addition to those required by the Federal Aviation Administration would necessarily conflict with the federal regulations. In this case, the conflict is more than theoretical, since Witty claims that a DVT warning should have been given, while federal regulations do not require such a warning. And any warning that passengers should not stay in their seats, but should instead move about to prevent DVT, would necessarily conflict with any federal determination that, all things considered, passengers are safer in their seats. Warnings by their nature conflict, in the sense that the import of one warning is diluted by additional warnings that might be imposed under state law.

Ultimately, we need not decide whether a state claim for failure to warn passengers of air travel risks is entirely preempted, or, as another circuit has held, is preempted to the extent that a federal standard must be used but that state remedies are available. We hold that, at a minimum, any such claim must be based on a violation of federally mandated warnings. In this case, federal regulations do not require warnings to passengers about the risks of DVT or methods for preventing this condition. Delta therefore cannot be held liable for failing to provide warnings or instructions to Witty.

We hold that the leg room claim is preempted by the ADA. We further hold that federal law exclusively provides the safety warnings that airlines must give passengers, and that state law regarding air safety warnings is preempted. Since there is no federal requirement that airlines give DVT warnings, Witty's state claim for failure to warn fails. Accordingly, the order denying the motion to dismiss is reversed, and we render judgment in favor of Delta.

CHARAS v. TRANS WORLD AIRLINES, INC.

160 F.3d 1259 (9th Cir. 1998)

SILVERMAN, Circuit Judge.

These consolidated cases cause us to consider once again the circumstances under which the Airline Deregulation Act of 1978 ("ADA") preempts certain state law claims. We have taken these cases *en banc sua sponte* to rethink our previous decisions.

We now hold that in enacting the ADA, Congress intended to preempt only state laws and lawsuits that would adversely affect the economic deregulation of the airlines and the forces of competition within the airline industry. Congress did not intend to preempt passengers' run-of-the-mill personal injury claims. Accordingly, we hold that Congress used the word "service" in the phrase "rates, routes, or service" in the ADA's preemption clause to refer to the prices, schedules, origins and destinations of the point-to-point transportation of passengers, cargo, or mail. In the context in which it was used in the Act, "service" was not intended to include an airline's provision of in-flight beverages, personal assistance to passengers, the handling of luggage, and similar amenities.

We expressly overrule our decisions in *Harris v. American Airlines, Inc.* (9th Cir. 1995), and *Gee v. Southwest Airlines* (9th Cir. 1997), to the extent that they are inconsistent with this interpretation.

FACTUAL AND PROCEDURAL BACKGROUND

I. *Beverage v. Continental Airlines*

Robert A. Beverage was a passenger on a Continental Airlines flight. He claims that a flight attendant hit his shoulder with a service cart and caused him serious injuries, including a dislocated shoulder and a cracked and detached scapular prosthesis. Beverage filed a state tort claim against Continental for negligence and breach of contract. The district court concluded that the ADA preempted Beverage's claims and granted Continental's motion to dismiss. Beverage timely appealed the district court's ruling.

II. *Jacoby v. Trans World Airlines*

Mildred Jacoby was a passenger on Trans World Airlines. After the plane landed, another passenger opened an overhead bin and a large piece of luggage fell on Jacoby's head, causing her injuries. Jacoby filed suit in state court against TWA; the airline removed the case and filed a motion to dismiss. Finding that the ADA preempted Jacoby's claims against TWA, the district court granted the motion to dismiss. Jacoby appealed.

III. *Charas v. Trans World Airlines*

Cherie Charas, a passenger on a TWA flight, tripped over a piece of luggage allegedly left in the aisle by a flight attendant. Due to the fall, Charas claims that she suffered a fractured humerus and required a shoulder joint replacement. Charas sued TWA for negligence. In granting TWA's motion for summary judgment, the district court concluded that Charas's claims were preempted by the ADA. Charas timely appealed the district court's ruling.

IV. *Gulley v. American Airlines*

Bernice Gulley was a passenger aboard a small commuter airplane operated by American Airlines. Gulley has a bone condition that makes her susceptible to bone fractures. She claims that she advised American of her condition and informed the airline that she needed assistance in disembarking, but that American employees provided no help. Gulley exited the plane, unassisted, on a stairway with only a single, movable chain handhold. She alleges that she fell and sustained injuries. Gulley brought a state negligence action against American. The district court held that although Gulley's claim for negligent failure to provide safe equipment involved the "maintenance and operation" of the aircraft and was not preempted, Gulley's claim for negligent failure to assist her down the stairs involved the rendering of "service" and was preempted by the ADA. Gulley appealed the district court's order granting American's motion for summary judgment.

V. *Newman v. American Airlines, Inc.*

Elizabeth Newman's complaint stems from her attempt to fly from San Diego to Long Island on an American Airlines flight. Newman claims that in making her reservations, she informed American that she was blind, suffered from a heart condition, and required assistance in boarding the plane. She flew from Long Island to San Diego without incident. However, it is alleged that on her return flight to Long Island, a flight attendant attempted to check Newman's carry-on bags due to space constraints.

At that time, the flight attendant learned that the bags contained Newman's medications. The flight attendant then informed the captain that Newman might have a disability that would preclude her from flying. The captain asked the flight attendant to ask Newman about her medication and to ascertain the phone number of Newman's doctor to verify whether or not Newman was at risk for a heart attack during flight. When Newman could not remember her doctor's number, American denied her passage until she could provide a letter from her doctor certifying that it was safe for her to fly. Prior to obtaining the required certificate, Newman was required to stay overnight at a motel and suffered injuries when she fell upon boarding the shuttle bus transporting her there. She filed various claims, including state tort claims and federal statutory claims, against American. The district court granted American's motion for summary judgment, concluding that Newman's state law claims were preempted by the ADA and that American had "permissibly refused" boarding to Newman for the purposes of her federal claims. Newman timely appealed.

DISCUSSION

In 1978, Congress determined that efficiency, low prices, variety, and quality would be furthered by reliance on competitive market forces rather than pervasive federal regulation. To prevent states from "undo[ing] federal deregulation with regulation of their own," *Morales v. Trans World Airlines* (1992), Congress enacted § 1305(a)(1) which preempts state laws "relating to the rates, routes, or service of any air carrier." However, the scope of this preemption has been a source of considerable dispute since its enactment.

In our own circuit, we have addressed the issue on several occasions. Prior to *Harris*, we held that the ADA did not preempt state law tort claims that were only "tenuously connected" with airline deregulation. *See Lathigra v. British Airways PLC* (9th Cir. 1994) (looking to congressional intent, the panel concluded that the ADA did not preempt state tort actions for negligent reconfirmation because they did not undermine the goals of airline deregulation.); *West v. Northwest Airlines, Inc.* (9th Cir. 1993) (holding that state law tort claim for compensatory damages was "too tenuously connected to airline regulation to trigger preemption under the ADA"). However, in 1995, we took a different approach.

Harris brought a tort suit against American Airlines for continuing to serve alcohol to an intoxicated passenger who was harassing her. In declining to look beyond the bare preemption language to congressional intent, the majority, over Judge Norris's dissent, concluded that the ADA preempted *Harris's* claim because it "relate[d] to [a] service" that the airline rendered, namely the provision of a drink. The panel did not discuss or distinguish *West* or *Lathigra.*

Two years later, we wrestled with this problem again in *Gee*. There, we expressed doubts about *Harris* and the validity of its analysis. However, in an attempt to mitigate the impact of *Harris*, we expressly adopted the Fifth Circuit's approach in *Hodges v. Delta Airlines, Inc.* (5th Cir. 1995) (*en banc*). Under *Hodges*, claims related to an airline's "operations and maintenance" are not preempted by the ADA while claims related to a "service" provided by the airline are preempted. As Judges O'Scannlain and Jolly predicted in their respective concurrences in *Gee* and *Hodges*, the distinction between an airline's operations and its service turned out to be as elusive as it is unworkable.

Judge O'Scannlain noted that the operations-versus-service dichotomy invites nonsensical, inequitable, and inconsistent results, and in any event has nothing to do with the purpose of airline deregulation. For example, under the rule announced in *Gee*, a plaintiff injured when struck by a beverage cart door would be able to bring a tort action if the door swung open because a bolt was missing (because the injury arises out of the "operations and maintenance" of the aircraft), but not if the flight attendant negligently failed to latch the door properly (because the flight attendant's conduct relates to "service"). Judge O'Scannlain demonstrated the folly of the distinction between "operations and maintenance" and "service," and suggested instead that the court examine whether the state laws underlying the claims frustrate the goal of economic deregulation by interfering with the forces of competition. If they do, the claims would be preempted; otherwise, they would not.

In reconsidering our view of the scope of the ADA's preemption, we conclude that Judge Norris and Judge O'Scannlain got it right and that *Harris* is contrary to congressional intent. Further, although we recognize that we were bound by *Harris* when we decided *Gee*, we now believe that the rule we adopted in *Gee* was imprecise, difficult to apply, and inadequately reflective of the ADA's goal of economic deregulation. Accordingly, in defining the "service" that the ADA preempts, we adopt Judge O'Scannlain's approach, an approach consistent with Supreme Court precedent and the ADA's plain language and legislative history.

The Supreme Court twice has addressed the scope of § 1305(a)(1). In both decisions, the Supreme Court took great pains to articulate the boundaries of the preemption, indicating that the ADA would not preempt most state law tort claims. Although neither cases directly resolved whether the § 1305(a)(1) preemption encompasses state law tort claims, they certainly suggest that such claims are not within the intended reach of the preemption. Moreover, in its decisions interpreting § 1305(a)(1), the Supreme Court has not had occasion to define the term "service." In attempting to deduce its meaning, we are mindful that principles of statutory construction require us to consider the term within its context. Airlines' "rates" and "routes" generally refer to the point-to-point transport of passengers. "Rates" indicates price; "routes" refers to courses of travel. It therefore follows that "service," when juxtaposed to "rates" and "routes," refers to such things as the frequency and scheduling of transportation, and to the selection of markets to or from which transportation is provided (as in, "This airline provides service from Tucson to New York twice a day.")

To interpret "service" more broadly is to ignore the context of its use; and, it effectively would result in the preemption of virtually everything an airline does. It seems clear to us that that is not what Congress intended. Nowhere in the legislative history, or in what remains of the federal airline regulatory statutes, does Congress intimate that "service," in the context of deregulation, includes the dispensing of food and drinks, flight attendant assistance, or the like.

We conclude that when Congress enacted federal economic deregulation of the airlines, it intended to insulate the industry from possible state economic regulation as well. It intended to encourage the forces of competition. It did not intend to immunize the airlines from liability for personal injuries caused by their tortious conduct. Like "rates" and "routes," Congress used "service" in § 1305(a)(1) in the public utility sense—*i.e.*, the provision of air transportation to and from various markets at various times. In that context, "service" does not refer to the pushing of beverage carts, keeping the aisles clear of stumbling blocks, the safe handling and storage of luggage, assistance to passengers in need, or like functions.

We expressly overrule our decisions in *Harris* and *Gee* to the extent that they are inconsistent with this interpretation. Accordingly, we remand these cases to the panel for resolution consistent with this decision.

AIR TRANSPORT ASS'N OF AMERICA v. CUOMO

520 F.3d 218 (2d Cir. 2008)

PER CURIAM.

Appellant Air Transport Association of America ("Air Transport"), the principal trade and service organization of the United States airline industry, appeals from an order of the United States District Court for the Northern District of New York granting summary judgment to Appellees and dismissing its complaint seeking declaratory and injunctive relief against enforcement of the New York State Passenger Bill of Rights (the "PBR"). We hold that the PBR is preempted by the express preemption provision of the Airline Deregulation Act of 1978 (the "ADA") and therefore reverse.

BACKGROUND

Following a series of well-publicized incidents during the winter of 2006-'07 in which airline passengers endured lengthy delays grounded on New York runways, some without being provided water or food, the New York legislature enacted the PBR. The substantive provisions of the PBR state as follows:

> Whenever airline passengers have boarded an aircraft and are delayed more than three hours on the aircraft prior to takeoff, the carrier shall ensure that passengers are provided as needed with: (a) electric generation service to provide temporary power for fresh air and lights; (b) waste removal service in order to service the holding tanks for on-board restrooms; and (c) adequate food and drinking water and other refreshments.

N.Y. Gen. Bus. Law § 251-g(1). Taking effect on January 1, 2008, the law also requires all carriers to display consumer complaint contact information and an explanation of these rights.

Air Transport filed suit in the United States District Court for the Northern District of New York seeking declaratory and injunctive relief on the grounds that the PBR is preempted by the ADA and violates the Commerce Clause of the U.S. Constitution. Appellant Air Transport moved for summary judgment, and the district court granted summary judgment *sua sponte* to the appellees, holding that the PBR was not expressly preempted by the ADA because it is not "related to a price, route, or service of an air carrier" and was not impliedly preempted because Congress did not intend for the ADA to occupy the field of airplane safety. We granted Air Transport's motion for an expedited appeal.

DISCUSSION

Air Transport's complaint asserts a claim under the Supremacy Clause and a claim that the PBR violates § 41713(b)(1). Importantly, Section 41713(b)(1) does not provide an express private right of action, and we have held with regard to its predecessor statute, which is substantively identical, that no private right of action can be implied. *Western Air Lines, Inc. v. Port Auth. of N.Y. & N.J.* (2d Cir. 1987). Air Transport therefore cannot sue for a violation of the statute.

Nevertheless, Air Transport is entitled to pursue its preemption challenge through its Supremacy Clause claim. The distinction between a statutory claim and a Supremacy Clause claim, although seemingly without a difference in this particular context, is important and is not a trifling formalism:

> A claim under the Supremacy Clause that a federal law preempts a state regulation is distinct from a claim for enforcement of that federal law … A claim under the Supremacy Clause simply asserts that a federal statute has taken away local authority to regulate a certain activity. In contrast, an implied private right of action is a means of enforcing the substantive provisions of a federal law. It provides remedies, frequently including damages, for violations of federal law by a government entity or by a private party. The mere coincidence that the federal law in question in this case contains its own preemption language does not affect this distinction.

Congress enacted the ADA in 1978, loosening its economic regulation of the airline industry after determining that "'maximum reliance on competitive market forces' would best further 'efficiency, innovation, and low prices' as well as 'variety [and] quality ... of air transportation.'" Recognizing this goal, the Supreme Court has repeatedly emphasized the breadth of the ADA's preemption provision. *See American Airlines, Inc. v. Wolens* (1995).

Although this Court has not yet defined "service" as it is used in the ADA, we have little difficulty concluding that requiring airlines to provide food, water, electricity, and restrooms to passengers during lengthy ground delays relates to the service of an air carrier.

A majority of the circuits to have construed "service" have held that the term refers to the provision or anticipated provision of labor from the airline to its passengers and encompasses matters such as boarding procedures, baggage handling, and food and drink—matters incidental to and distinct from the actual transportation of passengers. The Third and Ninth Circuits, in contrast, have construed service to refer more narrowly to "the prices, schedules, origins and destinations of the point-to-point transportation of passengers, cargo, or mail," but not to "include an airline's provision of in-flight beverages, personal assistance to passengers, the handling of luggage, and similar amenities." *Charas v. Trans World Airlines, Inc.* (9th Cir. 1998) (*en banc*).

Charas's approach, we believe, is inconsistent with the Supreme Court's recent decision in *Rowe*. There, the Court necessarily defined "service" to extend beyond prices, schedules, origins, and destinations. Indeed, in determining that the ADA's preemption provision reached, among other things, the imposition of recipient verification requirements on tobacco shipments, the Court stated expressly that "federal law must ... preempt Maine's efforts directly to regulate carrier *services*." It noted further that to interpret the federal preemption provision not to reach such regulation "could easily lead to a patchwork of state service-determining laws, rules, and regulations," which would be "inconsistent with Congress' major legislative effort to leave such decisions, where federally unregulated, to the competitive marketplace."

We hold that requiring airlines to provide food, water, electricity, and restrooms to passengers during lengthy ground delays does relate to the service of an air carrier and therefore falls within the express terms of the ADA's preemption provision. As a result, the substantive provisions of the PBR, codified at section 251-g(1) of the New York General Business Law, are preempted.

The unanimous *Rowe* opinion held that Maine's law resulted in Maine's "direct substitution of its own governmental commands for 'competitive market forces'" in determining "the services that motor carriers will provide" to their customers. In this respect, the PBR is indistinguishable. It substitutes New York's commands for competitive market forces, requiring airlines to provide the services that New York specifies during lengthy ground delays and threatening the same "patchwork of state service-determining laws, rules, and regulations" that concerned the Court in *Rowe*.

At least nine other states have proposed legislation regarding lengthy ground delays. *See* H.R. 2149, 48th Leg., 2d Reg. Sess. (Ariz. 2008); Assem. 1943, 2007-2008 Reg. Sess. (Cal. 2008); S. 2062, 110th Reg. Sess. (Fla. 2008); S. 161, 115th Gen. Assem., 2d Reg. Sess. (Ind. 2008); H.R. 5475, 94th Legis., 2007 Reg. Sess. (Mich. 2007); Assem. 967, 213th Leg., 1st Ann. Sess. (N.J. 2008); H.R.2055, 190th Gen. Assem., 2007 Sess. (Pa. 2007); S.2088, 2008 Legis. Sess. (R.I. 2008); S. 6269, 60th Legis., 2008 Reg. Sess. (Wash. 2008). These proposed laws would impose obligations ranging from a requirement that the airline accommodate passengers on the next available route, see Mich. H.R. 5475 § 5(2), to a requirement that passengers be permitted to disembark, see Pa. H.R. 2055 § 3(b).

It is irrelevant that these bills all seek to impose the same principal service obligations as the PBR—requiring airlines to provide food, water, electric generation, and waste removal after a three-hour ground delay—for state laws related to airline service are preempted regardless of whether they are consistent with each other and regardless of whether they are consistent with the ADA's objective. We note that the Department of Transportation has proposed and sought comment on several similar passenger protection measures that could provide uniform standards to deal with lengthy ground delays. *See* Enhancing Airline Passenger Protections, 72 Fed. Reg. 65,233 (Nov. 20, 2007) (to be codified at 14 C.F.R. pts. 234, 253, 259, 399).

Additionally, we note that *Rowe* declined to read into Section 14501(c)(1)'s preemption provision an exception that preserves state laws protecting the public health. *Rowe* accordingly forecloses New York's argument and the district court's conclusion that classifying the PBR as a health and safety regulation or a matter of basic human necessities somehow shields it from the preemptive force of Section 41713(b)(1). Onboard amenities, regardless of whether they are luxuries or necessities, still relate to airline service and fall within the express terms of the preemption provision—a conclusion, we note, that even the drafters of the PBR appear to have been unable to escape. *See* N.Y. Gen. Bus. Law § 251-g(1)(a) (referring to "electric generation service"); *id.* § 251-g(1)(b) (referring to "waste removal service").

Finally, insofar as the PBR is intended to prescribe standards of airline safety, we note that it may also be impliedly preempted by the FAA and regulations promulgated thereunder. The FAA was enacted to create a "uniform and exclusive system of federal regulation" in the field of air safety. Shortly after it became law, we noted that the FAA "was passed by Congress for the purpose of centralizing in a single authority—indeed, in one administrator—the power to frame rules for the safe and efficient use of the nation's airspace." Congress and the Federal Aviation Administration have used this authority to enact rules addressing virtually all areas of air safety. These regulations range from a general standard of care for operating requirements, see 14 C.F.R. § 91.13(a) ("No person may operate an aircraft in a careless or reckless manner so as to endanger the life or property of another"), to the details of the contents of mandatory onboard first-aid kits, to the maximum concentration of carbon monoxide permitted in "suitably vented" compartments, § 125.117. This power extends to grounded planes and airport runways. *See* § 91.123 (requiring pilots to comply with all orders and instructions of air traffic control); § 139.329 (requiring airlines to restrict movement of pedestrians and ground vehicles on runways).

The intent to centralize air safety authority and the comprehensiveness of these regulations pursuant to that authority have led several other circuits (and several courts within this Circuit) to conclude that Congress intended to occupy the entire field and thereby preempt state regulation of air safety. *See, e.g., Montalvo v. Spirit Airlines* (9th Cir. 2007) ("[T]he FAA preempts the entire field of aviation safety through implied field preemption. The FAA and regulations promulgated pursuant to it establish complete and thorough safety standards for air travel, which are not subject to supplementation by ... state laws."). Although we have not addressed this precise issue, we have acknowledged that the FAA does not preempt all state law tort actions. *See In re Air Crash Disaster at John F. Kennedy Int'l Airport on June 24, 1975* (2d Cir. 1980). However, the FAA has a savings clause that specifically preserves these actions. *See* 49 U.S.C. § 40120(c).

If New York's view regarding the scope of its regulatory authority carried the day, another state could be free to enact a law prohibiting the service of soda on flights departing from its airports, while another could require allergen-free food options on its outbound flights, unraveling the centralized federal framework for air travel. On this point, the decisions of the Fifth and Ninth Circuits finding preemption of state common law claims for failure to warn of the risk of deep vein thrombosis are instructive. *See Montalvo* ("[A] state [is not] free to require any announcement it wishe[s] on all planes arriving in, or departing from, its soil.").

In light of our determination that the PBR is preempted by the ADA, however, we need not address the scope of any FAA preemption, and we decline to do so here. Although the goals of the PBR are laudable and the circumstances motivating its enactment deplorable, only the federal government has the authority to enact such a law. We conclude, then, by reiterating our holding that the PBR's substantive provisions, codified at section 251-g(1) of the New York General Business Law, are preempted.

MARTIN v. MIDWEST EXPRESS HOLDINGS, INC.

555 F.3d 806 (9th Cir. 2009)

KOZINSKI, Chief Judge.

We consider whether, and to what extent, the Federal Aviation Act, 49 U.S.C. §§ 40101 *et seq*., preempts an airline passenger's personal injury claims.

A pregnant woman fell from an airplane's stairs, injuring herself and her fetus. She sued the airline, Midwest Express, and the airplane's manufacturer, Fairchild Dornier and related companies, alleging that the stairs were defectively designed because they had only one handrail. Midwest Express settled the claim for $8 million, and now seeks indemnity from the manufacturer. Relying on *Montalvo v. Spirit Airlines* (9th Cir. 2007), the manufacturer argues that the Federal Aviation Act preempts the passenger's personal injury claims and, consequently, Midwest Express' indemnity claim.

ANALYSIS

The Federal Aviation Act has no express preemption clause. The personal injury claim here conflicts with no provision of the act or regulation promulgated under it. The manufacturer's argument thus rests on implied field preemption.

The touchstone of preemption is congressional intent. *Cipollone v. Liggett Group, Inc.* (1992). To find field preemption here, we must infer that Congress intended to exclude all state law personal injury suits from the area of air travel, even though it didn't say so. The FAA betrays no such intention. It expressly preserves state remedies, declaring "[a] remedy under this part is in addition to any other remedies provided by law." 49 U.S.C. § 40120(c). Moreover, it requires airlines to maintain liability insurance "sufficient to pay ... for bodily injury to, or death of, an individual or for loss of, or damage to, property of others, resulting from the operation or maintenance of the aircraft." 49 U.S.C. § 41112. As the FAA doesn't create a federal cause of action for personal injury suits, this clause can only contemplate tort suits brought under state law.

Two amendments to the FAA added limited preemption provisions, neither of which applies here. The Airline Deregulation Act preempts laws and regulations "related to a price, route, or service" of airlines. The General Aviation Revitalization Act provides an eighteen-year statute of repose for product liability claims against airplane manufacturers. 49 U.S.C. § 40101. As we explained in *Charas v. Trans World Airlines, Inc.*, the airline regulatory acts "evidence congressional intent to prohibit states from regulating the airlines while preserving state tort remedies that already existed at common law." *See also American Airlines v. Wolens* (1995) (suggesting that the airline regulatory statutes "leave room for personal injury claims").

While the FAA did not displace all state tort law touching air travel, neither did it leave states free to impose tort liability on all aspects of airplane operations. Citing "the pervasive nature of the scheme of federal regulation of aircraft noise," *City of Burbank v. Lockheed Air Terminal* (1973), held that the FAA and the Noise Control Act preempted a noise ordinance prohibiting planes from taking off between 11 P.M. and 7 A.M. Aircraft noise, the Court reasoned, is inextricably linked to the movement of aircraft, which is under exclusive federal control. As Justice Jackson had earlier remarked, "[p]lanes do not wander about in the sky like vagrant clouds. They move only by federal permission ... under an intricate system of federal commands." *Northwest Airlines, Inc. v. Minnesota* (1944) (Jackson, J., concurring).

Following *Burbank*, the circuits have generally analyzed FAA preemption by looking to the pervasiveness of federal regulations in the specific area covered by the tort claim or state law at issue. Claims regarding airspace management, pilot qualifications and failure to warn have been declared preempted. *French v. Pan American Express, Inc.* (1st Cir. 1989); *Kohr v. Allegheny Airlines, Inc.* (7th Cir. 1974); *Witty v. Delta Air Lines, Inc.* (5th Cir. 2004). But several defective product claims, such as the claim here, have not. *Cleveland v. Piper Aircraft Corp.* (10th Cir. 1993); *Public Health Trust of Dade Cty, Fla. v. Lake Aircraft, Inc.* (11th Cir. 1993). *See also Air Transp. Ass'n of Am. v. Cuomo* (2d Cir. 2008) ("we have acknowledged that the FAA does not preempt all state law tort actions").

The Third Circuit, considering a failure to warn claim, took a different approach. Rather than limiting its analysis to regulations on warnings, the court decided that "federal law establishes the applicable standards of care in the field of air safety, generally, thus preempting the entire field from state and territorial regulation." *Abdullah v. American Airlines, Inc.* (3d Cir. 1999). The savings and insurance clauses, the court reasoned, only preserve state remedies, while excluding all state standards of care. In *Montalvo*, citing *Abdullah*, we stated that the FAA "demonstrate[s] an intent to occupy exclusively the entire field of aviation safety and ... preempt all state law in this field."

Considered as a whole, however, *Montalvo* cuts against the manufacturer's argument for broad FAA preemption. *Montalvo* dealt with three state tort claims against an airline, all based on passengers getting dangerous blood clots from long flights in cramped seating. First, passengers claimed that the airline was negligent because the crew didn't warn them about blood clots, or tell them how to lessen their risk. The FAA, we held, preempts this claim, and "all state law on the subject of air safety."

Our analysis rested heavily on the Federal Aviation Administration's "pervasive regulations" of warnings to passengers. The familiar litany of warnings—seatbelts should be worn low and tight around the hips; the seat cushion can be used as a flotation device—is federally required. *See* 14 C.F.R. § 121.571. The agency intended its list of warnings to be comprehensive. If every state could supplement this list through tort law or legislation, there would be so many warnings that the ones the agency prescribed would be drowned out by the others.

As the Fifth Circuit explained in *Witty*, "warnings by their nature conflict, in the sense that the import of one warning is diluted by additional warnings that might be imposed under state law." Therefore, the FAA preempts any state tort claim based on a theory that the warnings required by the agency are insufficient.

Relying on this section of *Montalvo*, the manufacturer argues that the FAA preempts all personal injury claims by airline passengers, except claims based on violations of specific federal regulations. However, this argument conflicts with the second part of *Montalvo* which considered a claim that the seating configuration was too cramped, putting passengers at risk of blood clots. The passengers didn't allege that the seating violated a federal regulation, see 14 C.F.R. § 23.785, and yet we didn't hold that the FAA preempted the claim, which would follow from a broad reading of the first section. Indeed, we didn't consider FAA preemption at all. Instead, we reversed the district court's holding that the Airline Deregulation Act preempted the claim and remanded for consideration whether providing roomier seating would significantly affect ticket prices or competition between airlines—a required element for ADA preemption.

In a third claim, the *Montalvo* plaintiffs alleged that the airplane seats were defectively designed. The district court held that the FAA impliedly preempted the claim because seat designs were pervasively regulated, noting that "the FAA Administrator has enacted a wealth of federal regulations governing the design, maintenance, structure and position of aircraft seats." *In re Deep Vein Thrombosis Litig.* (N.D. Cal. 2005). The plaintiffs did not appeal that holding. Our analysis of *Montalvo* does not depend, as the concurrence argues, on any analogy between the seating design and configuration claims. Rather, it springs from *Montalvo's* different treatment of the seating configuration and failure to warn claims. If *Montalvo* had held that the FAA preempts all state law personal injury claims, it would have been unnecessary to reverse the district court's dismissal of the seating configuration claim and remand for further consideration of ADA preemption.

Furthermore, the manufacturer's broad reading of *Montalvo* precluding any claim not based on a violation of a specific federal regulation, is in tension with our *en banc* decision in *Charas*. *Charas* considered several state law personal injury claims based on aircrews' negligent actions, such as leaving luggage in the aisles and hitting passengers with the beverage cart. *Charas* even considered a claim similar to the one here, that the aircrew negligently allowed a passenger to fall from a stairway with only one handrail. That passenger also brought the exact claim at issue here, that the stair design was defective, but the district court held that the claim was not preempted and the airline did not appeal. Reading the ADA's preemption provision narrowly, we overruled several district courts, and two of our own decisions, and held that Congress "did not intend to preempt passengers' run-of-the-mill personal injury claims," drawing no distinction between state remedies and state standards of care. Although *Charas* did not consider FAA preemption, it reversed several district court and panel decisions for interpreting ADA preemption too broadly. This holding would be moot if all the claims at issue were preempted anyway by the FAA.

The concurrence argues there is a federal standard of care in all airplane personal injury cases, but that it is not exclusively set by federal regulations. Instead, in areas without pervasive and relevant regulations, the federal standard should be set by expert testimony on standard industry practices. But neither *Montalvo* nor *Abdullah*, nor any language in the FAA, contemplates such a rule; *Montalvo* does not mention expert testimony at all, and *Abdullah* suggests that it could be used only for interpreting the relevant federal regulations, not for setting a federal standard independent from the regulations. The FAA itself makes no mention of federal courts developing a federal common law standard of care for airplane personal injury actions, and "[t]here is no federal general common law." *Erie R.R. v. Tompkins* (1938); *see generally* Suzanna Sherry, *Overruling Erie: Nationwide Class Action and National Common Law*, 156 U. PA. L. REV. 2135, 2138 (2008) (advocating the demise of the Erie doctrine for tort actions that impact national markets).

Montalvo, then, neither precludes all claims except those based on violations of specific federal regulations, nor requires federal courts to independently develop a standard of care when there are no relevant federal regulations. Instead, it means that when the agency issues "pervasive regulations" in an area, like passenger warnings, the FAA preempts all state law claims in that area. In areas without pervasive regulations or other grounds for preemption, the state standard of care remains applicable.

This conclusion accords with the decisions of other circuits, refusing to find various defective product claims impliedly preempted by the FAA in the absence of relevant and pervasive regulations on the allegedly defective part. The Tenth Circuit, in *Cleveland*, held that a claim that a plane was defectively designed because the pilot had inadequate visibility was not preempted, although the design violated no federal regulations and was approved by the agency. And in *Lake Aircraft, Inc.*, the Eleventh Circuit held that the FAA didn't preempt a defective seat design claim. *See also Greene v. B.F. Goodrich Avionics Sys., Inc.* (6th Cir. 2005) (citing *Abdullah* to find FAA preemption of a failure to warn claim, but applying a state law analysis to a claim that a navigational instrument was defectively manufactured).

The manufacturer further argues that defective product claims are preempted by the federal certification process required for every plane design. To certify a plane design, the manufacturer must show that it meets the agency's regulations, and "that no feature or characteristic makes it unsafe." *See* 14 C.F.R. § 21.21. The regulations contain numerous specific requirements for the designs, largely focused on preventing crashes and limiting the seriousness of those that occur. *See, e.g.*, 14 C.F.R. § 25.341, 25.561. They also include a prohibition on "design features or details that experience has shown to be hazardous or unreliable." 14 C.F.R. § 25.601.

The agency generally uses sections 25.601 and 21.21 when implementing "special conditions," alternative requirements for plane designs with "novel or unusual" components "not envisioned" by the other regulations. *See* 73 Fed. Reg. 389-01; 72 Fed. Reg. 57,842-01; *see* 14 C.F.R. § 21.16; *but see* 70 Fed. Reg. 76,728-01 (declaring that a seat belt design does not comply with section 25.601). When a design does not include novel components, the certification process simply implements the specific regulations. There's no indication that the agency has interpreted section 25.601 and 21.21 as directing it to pervasively regulate every aspect of plane design.

Airstairs are not pervasively regulated; the only regulation on airstairs is that they can't be designed in a way that might block the emergency exits. *See* 14 C.F.R. § 25.810. The regulations have nothing to say about handrails, or even stairs at all, except in emergency landings. No federal regulation prohibits airstairs that are prone to ice over, or that tend to collapse under passengers' weight. The regulations say nothing about maintaining the stairs free of slippery substances, or fixing loose steps before passengers catch their heels and trip. It's hard to imagine that any and all state tort claims involving airplane stairs are preempted by federal law. Because the agency has not comprehensively regulated airstairs, the FAA has not preempted state law claims that the stairs are defective.

BEA, Circuit Judge, concurring.

I agree the district court's order dismissing the complaint should be reversed, but I part with the majority as to *Montalvo* at two points.

First, in the majority's major premise: that airline seat configuration and seat design are analogous for purposes of determining whether federal preemption exists. Second, that *Montalvo* directs an implication that absent "pervasive" federal regulations on seat design, no federal standard of care exists.

First, that airline seat configuration and seat design are not analogous and should be subject to different liability rules makes some sense. Airline seat configuration is determined by the airline; seat design is determined by the manufacturer. The airlines have different business locations; they fly intrastate as well as interstate. They can expect to be subject to local notions of passenger safety. On the other hand, airplane manufacturers design and manufacture similar seats for airplanes sold throughout the country and overseas; they lack knowledge of precisely where the airplane will end up or how the airline buyer will configure the seats' placement. Airplane manufacturers should be able to rely on a uniform rule for proper seat design and construction.

Second, in *Montalvo* the plaintiffs brought not only a claim for negligent configuration, but also one for negligent design of the seats themselves. The district court dismissed the negligent design claim as preempted by the FAA—and that ruling was not appealed. Accordingly, contrary to the majority's view that *Montalvo* implicitly decided there was no federal preemption of the negligent seat design claim, the lesson of *Montalvo* is that the plaintiffs thought so little of the idea that federal law did not preempt state theories of negligent design liability that they chose to let dead dogs lie by not even attempting to resuscitate that claim by appeal. But note, there was no more "pervasive" federal regulation of seat design than there is of stairway bannister design.

Even if it did not decide the precise issue before us, however, *Montalvo* still provides the framework by which we analyze preemption of state law tort actions against airlines, and I think the solution to this case lies in *Montalvo's* plain text: "[w]e adopt the Third Circuit's broad, historical approach [in *Abdullah*]." Thus, the question here is whether the *Abdullah* rule, which establishes federal preemption of state standards of care in state law personal injury actions against airlines, applies to negligent design actions in which the FAA has not promulgated relevant regulations describing the particular obligations of the airline.

The majority holds the *Abdullah* rule does not apply to such a situation, and that state law standards of care govern. Contrary to the majority's position, neither *Abdullah* nor *Montalvo* contemplated state standards of care would apply in any circumstance. As I read *Abdullah*, expressly adopted by *Montalvo*, the court contemplated district courts would allow a factfinder to consider relevant FAA regulations and, to the extent those regulations are unclear or nonexistent, expert testimony of common industry practices, as relevant evidence of reasonable care under the circumstances, so the factfinder might determine the applicable standard of care. Indeed, in *Abdullah* the FAA had issued regulations relevant to the standard of care—but the court nevertheless found "expert testimony on various aspects of aircraft safety may be helpful to the jury" in identifying and applying the correct standard of care created by those federal regulations.

The majority cites Erie, for the proposition there cannot be a federal standard of care for airline personal injury torts because, in diversity cases, "[t]here is no federal general common law." *Erie* was a railroad accident case that involved only state common law negligence; it involved no claim of preemption based on any Interstate Commerce Commission regulations regarding the design of railcar door latches or how to keep railcar doors from swinging open and hitting nearby pedestrians. Here, on the other hand, we have a federal statute (the FAA) that we have held partly displaces state law through preemption of personal injury tort standards of care. In other words, the majority is incorrect to assume the crucial question is simply whether our jurisdiction lies in diversity.

Here, although this action was originally brought by the injured plaintiff under a strict liability theory, our case stems from a third party complaint by Midwest Express seeking indemnity against Fairchild Dornier for negligent design of the aircraft. Midwest Express's theory is that Fairchild Dornier failed to employ reasonable care in designing the aircraft staircase because, according to the allegations of the complaint, unlike most other airplanes, the staircase here has one handrail instead of two. [Thus,] we have a negligence case in which there are no regulations that dictate whether an airplane staircase must have one or two handrails. As a negligence case, reasonable care applies, and expert testimony (or FAA regulations, if there were any) should be admitted so a factfinder might determine what reasonable care means in airplane design at a nationwide level. For instance, an expert may testify all other commercial passenger airplane staircases designed in the United States use two handrails; based on this testimony, a factfinder might well conclude that using only one handrail was unreasonable and, thus, negligent.

This reading of *Montalvo* and *Abdullah* makes more sense to me than the majority's. Without federal preemption of the standard of care in personal injury tort actions, airlines and airplane manufacturers would be subject to the standard of care in whichever state their planes happen to be in (or over) when the injury occurs; the majority's rule essentially means airlines and airplane manufacturers must prepare for fifty kinds of liability.

With federal preemption of the standard of care, both airlines and airplane manufacturers, on the one hand, and passengers, on the other, would have some manageable guidance regarding duties owed. Further, by allowing the states to determine the elements of breach (*i.e.*, whether the failure properly to design is excusable under the circumstances), causation (*i.e.*, whether the damages plaintiff claims may be offset totally or partially by the plaintiff's contributory or comparative fault), and, most importantly, damages (*i.e.*, whether damages caps should be imposed for particular non-economic claims and whether punitive damages should be allowed), the *Abdullah* approach allows states to maintain individual policy priorities in line with Congress's intent to preserve state law remedies.

Accordingly, I would hold *Montalvo* requires us to remand this case to the district court to allow a factfinder to consider evidence to determine the federal standard of care for negligent stairway design, and state standards for breach, causation, and damages.

NOTES

1. With respect to airline deregulation, it should not go unnoticed that "[t]he impetus for change came almost entirely from the academics and politicians; the public never did call for deregulation of the airline industry. Various public opinion polls had shown that the airlines consistently ranked at the very top among all industries in terms of

consumer satisfaction and confidence." James W. Callison, *Airline Deregulation—Only Partially a Hoax: The Current Status of the Airline Deregulation Movement*, 45 J. AIR L. & COM. 961, 964 n.4 (1980). *See also* Michele McDonald, *Trouble on the Hill; Congress Considers Possible Airline Regulations*, AIR TRANSP. WORLD, June 1, 2001, at 95 (noting that some industry observers question "whether the industry isn't secretly hoping for reregulation" by resisting passengers' rights legislation: "It was, after all, the airlines themselves who invited the government to impose regulation in order to save them from competition, and only United among the then trunk carriers supported deregulation in 1978.").

2. In January 1999, Marti Sousanis was among thousands of post-holiday travelers at a crowded airport ready to go home. After waiting several hours in lines at Detroit Metropolitan Airport, she boarded Northwest Airlines flight 992 to San Francisco. Despite an announcement reporting that the flight was on time, the airplane sat on the tarmac for a seemingly interminable period. A blizzard covered the Detroit airport with over a foot of snow and stranded Sousanis's flight and more than two dozen other airplanes for up to eleven hours. Conditions on the planes became nightmarish as the hours passed. Food and water ran out and toilets overflowed. Passengers "became physically ill [and were] exposed to the growing odor of [a] concentrated number of humans in an enclosed small space." *See Ex Parte* Amended Class Action Complaint, *Koczara et al. v. Wayne County et al.*, No. 99-900422 (MI Cir. Ct. Wayne County 1999), ¶ 19. The crew of flight 992 was rude. Each time Sousanis tried to stand to relieve her chronically-pained back, the flight crew threatened her with arrest and told her to obey an unrelenting "fasten seatbelt" sign.

In January, 2001, Northwest Airlines agreed to a settlement, paying $5 million among 700 class action plaintiffs based on the length of time each person was delayed. Plaintiffs' counsel remarked, "We've been working on this for two years and they were on the plane for 11 hours. That's the nature of our legal system." Michael Katz, *Airline Peanuts*, FORBES, Feb. 19, 2001, at 53.

3. The 1999 Detroit Blizzard prompted members of Congress—themselves commercial airline passengers—to propose various legislation under the title "Airline Passengers' Bill of Rights." One bill, for example, proposed the imposition of financial liability on airlines for "excessive departure or arrival delay," *i.e.*, a period of time excess of two hours —

> (A) in the case of departure, beginning when the door of an aircraft is closed at an airport and ending when the aircraft takes off from the airport or when the door of the aircraft is open for deplaning of passengers at the airport; and

> (B) in the case of arrival delay, beginning upon touchdown of an aircraft at an airport and ending when the door of the aircraft is open for deplaning of passengers at the airport.

Airline Passenger Bill of Rights, H.R. 700, 106th Cong. (1999). The penalty for a delay between two and three hours would have been 200 percent of the ticket purchase price, plus another 100 percent for each additional hour (or portion thereof) beyond a three hour delay. *See also* Biztravel.com, *Your Flight Arrives on Time or We Pay You Back*, WALL. ST. J., June 5, 2000, at A9 (advertising $100 refund if flight arrives thirty minutes late, $200 if one hour late, and the full ticket price if two hours late or cancelled).

4. Presuming that states cannot enact their own airline customer service laws, *inter alia*, pursuant to the precedent established in *Cuomo v. Air Transport Ass'n of Am.* (2d Cir. 2008), and *Morales v. Trans World Airlines, Inc.* (1992), *supra*, should Congress enact a federal "Airline Passengers' Bill of Rights" to ensure a positive flying experience for the traveling public as a matter of law? *See, e.g.*, Timothy M. Ravich, *Re-Regulation and Airline Passengers' Rights*, 67 J. AIR L. & COM. 935 (2002); Daniel H. Rosenthal, Notes, *Legal Turbulence: The Courts's Miscontrual of the Airline Deregulation Act's Preemption Clause and the Effect on Passengers' Rights*, 51 DUKE L.J. 1857 (2002); Zachary Garsek, *Giving Power Back to the Passengers: The Airline Passengers' Bill of Rights*, 66 J. AIR L. & COM. 1187 (2001); Audrey Johnson, *Consumers and Congress Lobby for Airline Customer Service Improvements: Voluntary Action of Legislation*, 13 LOY. CONSUMER L. REV. 402 (2001). *See also Airline Passengers' Bill of Rights: Is It Time to Re-Regulate the Airline Industry with New Customer Protections?,* National Public Radio ("The Conversation" KUOW), Seattle, WA (2007).

Other transportation businesses afford their passengers specific rights. For example:

> As a [New York] taxi rider, you have the right to: (1) direct the destination and route used; (2) travel to any destination in the five boroughs of the City of New York; (3) a courteous, English-speaking driver who knows the streets of Manhattan and the way to major destinations in other boroughs; (4) a driver who knows and obeys all traffic laws; (5) air-conditioning on demand; (6) a radio-free (silent) trip; (7) smoke and incense-free air; (8) a clean passenger seat area; (9) a clean trunk; (10) a driver who uses the horn only when necessary to warn of danger; and (11) refuse to tip, if the above are not complied with.

NEW YORK CITY TAXI & LIMOUSINE COMM'N TAXICAB RIDER'S BILL OF RIGHTS, at *http://www.nyc.gov/html/tlc/html/rights.html*. *See also* Raphael Lewis, *T Puts Punctuality to the Test with Free-Ride Promise*, BOSTON GLOBE, Feb. 21, 2001, at A1 (discussing

"MBTA Rider's Bill of Rights" governing travel on city trolleys, buses, ferries, and commuter trains).

5. Increasingly, airline passengers feel neglected or purposefully mistreated by the deregulated airlines, which appear unable or unwilling to both manage dense traffic patterns and provide quality service. Brent D. Bowen & Dean E. Headley, THE AIRLINE QUALITY RATING 2001, at 6, 7 ("Qualitative assessment of consumer experiences indicates an increasing frequency of consumer/employee confrontations that clearly stem from management policies and practices that encourage misinformation regarding flight status information and flight delays ... Given the complexity of the problem, lack of desire by the airlines to help themselves and the consumer, and the need to better utilize public resources, government intervention seems necessary and appropriate."). "Passengers do not trust airlines. In fact, many frequent fliers assume the airline is lying to them, no matter what an airline employee says." Don Phillips, *21 Days, 18 Flights: A Journey of Discovery Finds Miles of Discontent in the Coach Cabin*, WASH. POST, June 13, 1999, at H01. *See also* Andrew Downer Crane, *Ford, Carter, and Deregulation in the 1970s,* 5 J. TELECOMM. & HIGH TECH. L. 413 (2007).

Passengers sometimes analogize their air travel experiences to hostage situations while, reciprocally, flight crews regard passengers as "the enemy." *See, e.g.*, Doug Gamble, *Remember the "Friendly Skies?"*, SACRAMENTO BEE, Aug. 15, 1999, at I2 (stating that "there is no private-sector business with more open hostility between server and customer than that which exists with the airline industry."). *See also* David Butwin, *Have We Got a Deal for You! (Just Don't Read the Small Print)*, AIRLINERS, Mar./Apr. 2010, at 6 ("Spirit [Airlines] has taken the no-frills notion to a new level, charging for all amenities, drinks, snacks, baggage, even hidden online items ...[their CEO] goes so far as to say that if Spirit passengers are unhappy, 'They should fly someone else. That's the way the free market works.'"). What role, if any, should the law play in addressing or resolving customer service issues?

6. An important aspect of airline passenger rights is a federal statutory regime—the Air Carrier Access Act ("ACAA"), 49 U.S.C. § 41705 *et seq.*, which prohibits discrimination against handicapped individuals:

> In general.—In providing air transportation, an air carrier, including (subject to section 40105(b)) any foreign air carrier, may not discriminate against an otherwise qualified individual on the following grounds: (1) the individual has a physical or mental impairment that substantially limits one or more major life activities; (2) the individual has a record of such an impairment; (3) the individual is regarded as having such an impairment.

See also 14 C.F.R. § 382.7. One federal district court has interpreted the ACAA as follows:

> The ACAA prohibits air carriers from discriminating against an individual because they have, or are regarded as having, a disability. The regulations promulgated in connection with the ACAA explain that the Act requires air carriers: (1) to provide services and benefits without discrimination on the basis of disability; and (2) to provide disabled individuals with certain services, equipment or assistance. 14 C.F.R. §§ 382.7, 382.39 (1996). In other words, all persons are entitled to be treated equally, but "qualified handicapped individuals" are further entitled to certain services.

Rivera v. Delta Air Lines, Inc. (E.D. Pa. 1997).

In addition to these general prohibitions, there are a series of specific regulations in Title 14 of the Code of Federal Regulations relating to discrimination vis-à-vis aircraft accessibility: (i) a carrier's "refusal" of transportation; (ii) a requirement of advance notice of travel by a handicapped person; (iii) a requirement (with certain special exceptions) that a handicapped person travel with his or her own "attendant," (iv) seating assignments, seating accommodation, provision of certain services and equipment (*e.g.*, wheelchairs, etc.); (v) boarding assistance on small and large aircrafts; (vi) assistance in stowage of personal equipment, treatment of mobility aids and assistive devices, passenger information (*e.g.*, seating locations, lavatory information, etc.); (vii) accommodations for those with hearing impairments; (viii) security screening; (ix) refusal to provide transportation to those with communicable diseases (except where the health and safety of others would be endangered); (x) a requirement that handicapped persons have medical certificates; and (xi) prohibiting the charging of a fee to accommodate handicapped persons. *See*, *e.g.*, *Deterra v. America West Airlines, Inc.* (D. Mass. 2002). *See also Elassaad v. Independence Air, Inc.* (3d Cir. 2010) ("the ACAA does not preempt any standard of care in a negligence action, *even if* federal law applies through preemption.").

7. Face-to-face interaction between passengers and airline customer agents may produce conflict, but ironically technologies intended to improve airline service also contribute to passenger frustration by reducing the amount of personal contact between passengers and carriers. *E.g.*, Ruwantissa Abeyratne, *E-Commerce and the Airline Passenger*, 66 J. AIR L. & COM. 1345 (2001); Marilyn Adams, *Tech Takes Bigger Role in Air Service*, USA TODAY, July 18, 2001, at 1B (observing that "[t]oday, you can book a domestic flight, check in, upgrade from coach to business class, reserve a window or aisle seat, get a boarding pass and check luggage—all without speaking to a human."). Should airlines be required to advise airline passengers of their rights? Or, should passengers

bear the burden of learning about travel rights and restrictions applicable to them given readily-available resources such as the Internet?

8. The Air Cargo Deregulation Act of 1977, Pub. L. No. 95-163 (1977), was the precursor to the Airline Deregulation Act of 1978, Pub. L. No. 95-504, 92 Stat. 1705-54 (1978). *See generally* Jill E. Fisch, *How Do Corporations Play Politics? The FedEx Story*, 58 VAND. L. REV. 1495 (2005); Stephen A. Alterman, *Safety in the All-Cargo Air Carrier Industry*, 25 TRANSP. L.J. (1998); Paul Stephen Dempsey, *Transportation Deregulation—On a Collision Course?*, 13 TRANSP. L.J. 239 (1984). Like commercial airlines, air cargo companies were significantly impacted by the events of September 11th. *See, e.g., Air Line Pilots Ass'n v. Fed. Express Corp.* (D.C. Cir. 2005); *Fed. Express Corp. v. Mineta* (D.C. Cir. 2004).

9. Since its first days of operation in 1971, Federal Express ("FedEx") has been classified as an air express carrier for purposes of the Railway and Labor Act of 1926 ("RLA") on the basis that it operates an integrated air-ground network. *See generally* Chapter 4.B, *supra*. That is,

> Federal Express is exactly the kind of an expedited all-cargo service that Congress specified and the kind of integrated transportation system that was federally desired. Because it is an integrated system, it is a hybrid, an air carrier employing trucks. Those trucks do not destroy its status as an air carrier. They are an essential part of the all-cargo air service that Federal Express innovatively developed to meet the demands of an increasingly interlinked nation.

Fed. Express Corp. v. California Public Utilities Comm'n (9th Cir. 1991).

FedEx-archrival United Parcel Service ("UPS") and the Teamsters have lobbied Congress to pass legislation as part of the Federal Aviation Association's Reauthorization bill to change FedEx's status under the RLA and effectively permit FedEx employees to unionize under the National Labor Relations Act ("NLRA"). Employees under the RLA can unionize, if at all, only across nationwide classes of employees and must participate in mandatory government-led mediation of contract disputes supervised by the National Mediation Board before they can strike or an employer can replace employees or impose contract terms.

In contrast, the NLRA permits employees to unionize in small localized groups, and government led mediation is not a required step in the negotiation process. *See* FAA Reauthorization Act of 2009, H.R. 915, 111th Cong. § 806 (2010). *See also* Frank N. Wilner, *RLA or NLRA? FedEx and UPS Follow the Money Trail*, 57-JAN. FED. LAW. 40 (2010).

10. In 2010, Congress enacted "Enhancing Airliner Passenger Protections," 14 C.F.R. Pt. 259. Effective April 29, 2010, air carriers must adopt contingency plans for hours-long tarmac delays; develop and publish customer service plans, and respond to consumer problems. Through the new regulation, the United States Department of Transportation will consider continued delays on flights that are chronically late to be unfair and deceptive in violation of federal law. The regulation provides:

> **§ 259.1 Purpose.**
>
> The purpose of this part is to mitigate hardships for airline passengers during lengthy tarmac delays and otherwise to bolster air carriers' accountability to consumers.
>
> **§ 259.2 Applicability.**
>
> This rule applies to all the flights of a certificated or commuter air carrier if the carrier operates scheduled passenger service or public charter service using any aircraft originally designed to have a passenger capacity of 30 or more seats, except as provided in this part. This part does not apply to foreign carrier charters that operate to and from the United States if no new passengers are picked up in the United States.
>
> **§ 259.3. Definitions.**
>
> *Certificated air carrier* means a U.S. carrier holding a certificate to conduct passenger service or holding an exemption to conduct passenger operations.
>
> *Commuter air carrier* means a U.S. carrier that has been found fit and is authorized to carry passengers on at least five round trips per week on at least one route between two or more points according to a published flight schedule using small aircraft.
>
> *Covered carrier* means a certificated carrier, a commuter carrier, or a foreign air carrier operating to, from or within the United States, conducting scheduled passenger service or public charter service with at least one aircraft having a designed seating capacity of 30 or more seats.
>
> *Foreign air carrier* means a carrier that is not a citizen of the United States that holds a foreign air carrier permit or an exemption authorizing direct foreign air transportation.
>
> *Large hub airport* means an airport that accounts for at least 1.00 percent of the total enplanements in the United States.

Medium hub airport means an airport accounting for at least 0.25 percent but less than 1.00 percent of the total enplanements in the United States.

Non-hub airport means an airport with 10,000 or more annual enplanements but less than 0.05 percent of the country's annual passenger boardings.

Small hub airport means an airport accounting for at least 0.05 percent but less than 0.25 percent of the total enplanements in the United States.

Tarmac delay means the holding of an aircraft on the ground either before taking off or after landing with no opportunity for its passengers to deplane.

§ 259.4 Contingency plan lengthy tarmac delays.

Adoption of Plan. Each covered carrier shall adopt a Contingency Plan for Lengthy Tarmac Delays for its scheduled and public charter flights at each large and medium hub U.S. airport at which it operates such air service and shall adhere to its plan's terms.

Contents of Plan. Each Contingency Plan for Lengthy Tarmac Delays shall include, at a minimum, the following:

(1) For domestic flights, assurance that the air carrier will not permit an aircraft to remain on the tarmac for more than three hours unless:

(i) Pilot-in-command determines there is a safety-related or security-related reason (*e.g.*, weather, a directive from an appropriate government agency) why the aircraft cannot leave its position on the tarmac to deplane passengers; or

(ii) Air traffic control advises the pilot-in-command that returning to the gate or another disembarkation point elsewhere in order to deplane passengers would significantly disrupt airport operations.

(2) For international flights that depart from or arrive at a U.S. airport, assurance that the air carrier will not permit an aircraft to remain on the tarmac at a large or medium hub U.S. airport for more than a set number of hours, as

determined by the carrier and set out in its contingency plan, before allowing passengers to deplane, unless:

(i) Pilot-in-command determines there is a safety-related or security-related reason why the aircraft cannot leave its position on the tarmac to deplane passengers; or

(ii) Air traffic control advises the pilot-in-command that returning to the gate or another disembarkation point elsewhere in order to deplane passengers would significantly disrupt airport operations.

(3) For all flights, assurance that the air carrier will provide adequate food and potable water no later than two hours after the aircraft leaves the gate (in the case of departure) or touches down (in the case of an arrival) if the aircraft remains on the tarmac, unless the pilot-in-command determines that safety or security considerations preclude such service;

(4) For all flights, assurance of operable lavatory facilities, as well as adequate medical attention if needed, while the aircraft remains on the tarmac;

(5) Assurance of sufficient resources to implement the plan; and

(6) Assurance that the plan has been coordinated with airport authorities at all medium and large hub airports that the carrier serves, including medium and large hub diversion airports.

Code-Share Responsibility. The tarmac delay contingency plan of the carrier under whose code the service is marketed governs, if different from the operating carrier, unless the marketing carrier specifies in its contract of carriage that the operating carrier's plan governs.

Amendment of plan. At any time, an air carrier may amend its Contingency Plan for Lengthy Tarmac Delays to decrease the time for aircraft to remain on the tarmac for domestic flights covered in paragraph (b)(1) of this section, for aircraft to remain on the tarmac for international flights covered in paragraph (b)(2) of this section, and for the trigger point for food and water covered in paragraph (b)(3) of this section. An air carrier may also amend its plan to increase these intervals (up to the limits in this rule), in which case the amended plan shall apply only to those flights that are first offered for sale after the plan's amendment.

Retention of records. Each air carrier that is required to adopt a Contingency Plan for Lengthy Tarmac Delays shall retain for two years the following information about any tarmac delay that lasts at least three hours:

(1) The length of the delay;

(2) the precise cause of the delay;

(3) The actions taken to minimize hardships for passengers, including the provision of food and water, the maintenance and servicing of lavatories, and medical assistance;

(4) Whether the flight ultimately took off (in the case of a departure delay or diversion) or returned to the gate; and

(5) An explanation for any tarmac delay that exceeded 3 hours (*i.e.*, why the aircraft did not return to the gate by the 3-hour mark).

Unfair and Deceptive Practice. An air carrier's failure to comply with the assurances required by this rule and as contained in its Contingency Plan for Lengthy Tarmac Delays will be considered an unfair and deceptive practice within the meaning of 49 U.S.C. § 41712 that is subject to enforcement action by the Department.

§ 259.5 Customer Service Plan.

Adoption of Plan. Each covered carrier shall adopt a Customer Service Plan applicable to its scheduled flights and shall adhere to this plan's terms.

Contents of Plan. Each Customer Service Plan shall, at a minimum, address the following subjects:

(1) Offering the lowest fare available;

(2) Notifying consumers of known delays, cancellations, and diversions;

(3) Delivering baggage on time;

(4) Allowing reservations to be held without payment or cancelled without penalty for a defined amount of time;

(5) Providing prompt ticket refunds;

(6) Properly accommodating passengers with disabilities and other special-needs, including during tarmac delays;

(7) Meeting customers' essential needs during lengthy tarmac delays;

(8) Handling "bumped" passengers with fairness and consistency in the case of oversales;

(9) Disclosing travel itinerary, cancellation policies, frequent flyer rules, and aircraft configuration;

(10) Ensuring good customer service from code-share partners;

(11) Ensuring responsiveness to customer complaints; and

(12) Identifying the services it provides to mitigate passenger inconveniences resulting from cancellations and misconnects.

Self-auditing of Plan and Retention of Records. Each air carrier that is required to adopt a Customer Service Plan shall audit its own adherence to its plan annually. Carriers shall make the results of their audits available for the Department's review upon request for two years following the date any audit is completed.

§ 259.6 Posting of Contracts of Carriage, Tarmac Delay Contingency Plans and Customer Service Plans on websites.

(a) Each U.S. air carrier that has a website and each foreign air carrier that has a website marketed to U.S. consumers, and that is required to adopt a contingency plan for lengthy tarmac delays, shall post its current contingency plan on its website in easily accessible form.

(b) Each U.S. air carrier that has a website and each foreign air carrier that has a website marketed to U.S. consumers, and that is required to adopt a customer service plan, shall post its current customer service plan on its website in easily accessible form.

(c) Each U.S. air carrier that has a website and each foreign air carrier that has a website marketed to U.S. consumers shall post its current contract of carriage on its website in easily accessible form.

§ 259.7 Response to consumer problems.

Designated Advocates for Passengers' Interests. Each covered carrier shall designate for its scheduled flights an employee who shall be responsible for monitoring the effects of flight delays, flight cancellations, and lengthy tarmac delays on passengers. This employee shall have input into decisions on which flights to cancel and which will be delayed the longest.

Informing consumers how to complain. Each covered carrier shall make available the mailing address and e-mail or Web address of the designated department in the airline with which to file a complaint about its scheduled service. This information shall be provided on the carrier's Web site (if any), on all e-ticket confirmations and, upon request, at each ticket counter and boarding gate staffed by the carrier.

Response to complaints. Each covered carrier shall acknowledge receipt of each complaint regarding its scheduled service to the complainant within 30 days of receiving it and shall send a substantive response to each complainant within 60 days of receiving the complaint. A complaint is a specific written expression of dissatisfaction concerning a difficulty or problem which the person experienced when using or attempting to use an airline's services.

Social networking sites. Each covered carrier that uses a social networking site (e.g. Facebook, Twitter) and that does not intend for that site to be a vehicle for receipt of written consumer complaints subject to this section shall clearly indicate on the carrier's primary page on that social networking site that it will not reply to consumer complaints on that site and shall direct consumers to the carrier's mailing address and e-mail or website location for filing written complaints.

§ 259.8 Notify passengers of known delays, cancellations, and diversions.

(a) Each covered carrier for its scheduled flights to, from or within the U.S. must promptly provide to passengers who are ticketed or hold reservations, and to the public, information about a change in the status of a flight within 30 minutes after the carrier becomes aware of such a change in the status of a flight. A change in the status of a flight means, at

> a minimum, cancellation of a flight, a delay of 30 minutes or more in the planned operation of a flight, or a diversion. The flight status information must at a minimum be provided in the boarding gate area for the flight at a U.S. airport, on the carrier's website, and via the carrier's telephone reservation system upon inquiry by any person.
>
> (1) With respect to any U.S. carrier or foreign air carrier that permits passengers to subscribe to flight status notification services, the carrier must deliver such notification to such passengers, by whatever means is available to the carrier and of the passenger's choice, within 30 minutes after the carrier becomes aware of such a change in the status of a flight.
>
> (2) The U.S. carrier or foreign air carrier shall incorporate such notification service commitment into its Customer Service Plan as specified in section 259.5 of this chapter.
>
> (b) For its scheduled flights to, from or within the U.S, within 30 minutes after the carrier becomes aware of a flight cancellation, a flight delay of 30 minutes or more, or a flight diversion, each covered carrier must update all flight status displays and other sources of flight information that are under the carrier's control at U.S. airports with information on that flight irregularity.
>
> (c) If an airport-controlled display system at a U.S. airport accepts flight status updates from carriers, covered carriers must provide flight irregularity information to that airport for the carrier's scheduled flights to, from or within the U.S. within 30 minutes after the carrier becomes aware of such a change in the status of a flight. Flight irregularity refers to flight cancellations, flight delays of 30 minutes or more, and diversions.

Will this new rule achieve its objectives? *See, e.g.*, Kelly Yamanouchi, *Critics: Tarmac-Delay Rule Won't Fly*, ATLANTA J.-CONST., Apr. 28, 2010, at A1; Susan Stellin, *Wider Protections for Travelers*, N.Y. TIMES, Mar. 23, 2010, at B6; David Koenig, *Continental Asks Tarmac Rules Exemption: Carrier Says It May Have to Speed Up Cancellations*, HOUS. CHRON., Mar. 19, 2010, at 3.

PROBLEM

On December 29, 2006, the Dallas-Fort Worth area experienced unseasonably severe weather that generated successive waves of massive lightning storms and a tornado warning, all of which caused the airport to shut down. As a result, American Airlines cancelled, diverted, or delayed over 1,100 of its 1,600 scheduled flights (*i.e.*, 69 percent), disrupting holiday travel plans for over 13,000 passengers system-wide. Many passengers were stranded on the tarmac for a period of two to twelve hours. Only September 11, 2001 recorded more diversions than December 29, 2006.

Some of the diverted passengers sued American Airlines in connection with the delays under theories of false imprisonment, intentional infliction of emotional distress, negligence, intentional misrepresentation, conversion, civil conspiracy, violation of the Racketeer Influenced and Corrupt Organizations Act ("RICO"), and breach of contract. The passengers moved for class certification of their claims. Should the court grant the request and certify the dispute for a class-wide determination? If so, how should the class be defined? *See, e.g., Hanni v. American Airlines, Inc.* (N.D. Cal. Jan. 15, 2010). *See also Ray v. American Airlines* (W.D. Ark. Apr. 2, 2010).

C. CONTRACTS OF CARRIAGE

While the cases in Chapter 2, Part A, *supra*, show the broad preemptive effect of the "prices, routes, and services" clause of the Airline Deregulation Act of 1978 as applied to state consumer protection laws, the Supreme Court has rejected the claim that preemption serves to "shelter airlines from suits alleging no violations of state-imposed obligations, but seeking recovery for the airline's alleged breach of its own self-imposed undertakings." The Court articulated this rule in *American Airlines, Inc. v. Wolens*, and most recently in *Northwest, Inc. v Ginsberg, supra*.

AMERICAN AIRLINES, INC. v. WOLENS

513 U.S. 219 (1995)

Justice GINSBURG delivered the opinion of the Court.

The Airline Deregulation Act of 1978 ("ADA") prohibits States from "enact[ing] or enforc[ing] any law ... relating to [air carrier] rates, routes, or services." This case concerns the scope of that preemptive provision, specifically, its application to a state-court suit, brought by participants in an airline's frequent flyer program, challenging the airline's retroactive changes in terms and conditions of the program. We hold that the ADA's preemption prescription bars state-imposed regulation of air carriers, but allows room for court enforcement of contract terms set by the parties themselves.

Plaintiffs (respondents here) are participants in American Airlines' frequent flyer program, AAdvantage. AAdvantage enrollees earn mileage credits when they fly on American. They can exchange those credits for flight tickets or class-of-service upgrades. Plaintiffs complained that AAdvantage program modifications, instituted by American in 1988, devalued credits AAdvantage members had already earned. Plaintiffs featured American's imposition of capacity controls (limits on seats available to passengers obtaining tickets with AAdvantage credits) and blackout dates (restrictions on dates credits could be used). Conceding that American had reserved the right to change AAdvantage terms and conditions, plaintiffs challenged only the retroactive application of modifications, *i.e.*, cutbacks on the utility of credits previously accumulated. These cutbacks, plaintiffs maintained, violated the Illinois Consumer Fraud and Deceptive Business Practices Act (Consumer Fraud Act or Act), and constituted a breach of contract. Plaintiffs currently seek only monetary relief.

In March 1992, the Illinois Supreme Court rejected plaintiffs' prayer for an injunction. Such a decree, the Illinois court reasoned, would involve regulation of an airline's current rendition of services, a matter preempted by the ADA. That court, however, allowed the breach-of-contract and Consumer Fraud Act monetary relief claims to survive. The ADA's preemption clause, the Illinois court said, ruled out "only those State laws and regulations that specifically relate to and have more than a tangential connection with an airline's rates, routes or services."

American petitioned for *certiorari*. The airline charged that the Illinois court, in a decision out of sync with had narrowly construed the ADA's broadly preemptive § 1305(a)(1). We granted the petition, vacated the judgment of the Supreme Court of Illinois, and remanded for further consideration in light of *Morales*. On remand, the Illinois Supreme Court, with one dissent, adhered to its prior judgment. Describing frequent flyer programs as not "essential," but merely "peripheral to the operation of an airline," the Illinois court typed plaintiffs' state-law claims for money damages as "relat[ed] to American's rates, routes, and services" only "tangential[ly]" or "tenuous[ly]." We granted American's second petition for *certiorari*, and we now reverse the Illinois Supreme Court's judgment to the extent that it allowed survival of plaintiffs' Consumer Fraud Act claims; we affirm that judgment, however, to the extent that it permits plaintiffs' breach-of-contract action to proceed. In both respects, we adopt the position of the DOT, as advanced in this Court by the United States.

I.

We need not dwell on the question whether plaintiffs' complaints state claims "relating to [air carrier] rates, routes, or services." *Morales*, we are satisfied, does not countenance the Illinois Supreme Court's separation of matters "essential" from matters unessential to airline operations. Plaintiffs' claims relate to "rates," *i.e.*, American's charges in the form of mileage credits for free tickets and upgrades, and to "services," *i.e.*, access to flights and class-of-service upgrades unlimited by retrospectively applied capacity controls and blackout dates. But the ADA's preemption clause contains other words in need of interpretation, specifically, the words "enact or enforce any law" in the instruction: "[N]o State ... shall enact or enforce any law ... relating to [air carrier] rates, routes, or services." Taking into account all the words Congress placed in § 1305(a)(1), we first consider whether plaintiffs' claims under the Consumer Fraud Act are preempted, and then turn to plaintiffs' breach-of-contract claims.

A.

The Consumer Fraud Act declares unlawful

> [u]nfair methods of competition and unfair or deceptive acts or practices, including but not limited to the use or employment of any deception, fraud, false pretense, false promise, misrepresentation or the concealment, suppression or omission of any material fact, with intent that others rely upon the concealment, suppression or omission of such material fact, or the use or employment of any practice described in Section 2 of the 'Uniform Deceptive Trade Practices Act' ... in the conduct of any trade or commerce ... whether any person has in fact been misled, deceived or damaged thereby.

Ill. Comp. Stat., ch. 815, § 505/2 (1992).

The Act is prescriptive; it controls the primary conduct of those falling within its governance. It serves as a means to guide and police the marketing practices of the airlines; the Act does not simply give effect to bargains offered by the airlines and accepted by airline customers. In light of the full text of the preemption clause, and of the ADA's purpose to leave largely to the airlines themselves, and not at all to States, the selection and design of marketing mechanisms appropriate to the furnishing of air transportation services, we conclude that § 1305(a)(1) preempts plaintiffs' claims under the Consumer Fraud Act.

B.

American maintains, and we agree, that "Congress could hardly have intended to allow the States to hobble [competition for airline passengers] through the application of restrictive state laws." We do not read the ADA's preemption clause, however, to shelter airlines from suits alleging no violation of state-imposed obligations, but seeking recovery solely for the airline's alleged breach of its own, self-imposed undertakings. As persuasively argued by the United States, terms and conditions airlines offer and passengers accept are privately ordered obligations and thus do not amount to a State's enactment or enforcement of any law, rule, regulation, standard, or other provision having the force and effect of law within the meaning of the ADA. A remedy confined to a contract's terms simply holds parties to their agreements—in this instance, to business judgments an airline made public about its rates and services.

The ADA, as we recognized in *Morales* was designed to promote "maximum reliance on competitive market forces." Market efficiency requires effective means to enforce private agreements. *See* Daniel Farber, *Contract Law and Modern Economic*

Theory, 78 NW. U. L. REV. 303, 315 (1983) (remedy for breach of contract "is necessary in order to ensure economic efficiency"); RICHARD POSNER, ECONOMIC ANALYSIS OF LAW 90-91 (4th ed. 1992) (legal enforcement of contracts is more efficient than a purely voluntary system). As stated by the United States: "The stability and efficiency of the market depend fundamentally on the enforcement of agreements freely made, based on needs perceived by the contracting parties at the time." That reality is key to sensible construction of the ADA.

The FAA's text, we note, presupposes the vitality of contracts governing transportation by air carriers. Section 411(b), 49 U.S.C. § 1381(b), thus authorizes airlines to "incorporate by reference in any ticket or other written instrument any of the terms of the contract of carriage" to the extent authorized by the DOT. And the DOT's regulations contemplate that, upon the January 1, 1983, termination of domestic tariffs, "ticket contracts" ordinarily would be enforceable under "the contract law of the States." Correspondingly, the DOT requires carriers to give passengers written notice of the time period within which they may "bring an action against the carrier for its acts."

American does not suggest that its contracts lack legal force. American sees the DOT, however, as the exclusively competent monitor of the airline's undertakings. American points to the Department's authority to require any airline, in conjunction with its certification, to file a performance bond conditioned on the airline's "making appropriate compensation ..., as prescribed by the [Department], for failure ... to perform air transportation services in accordance with agreements therefor."

But neither the DOT nor its predecessor, the CAB, has ever construed or applied this provision to displace courts as adjudicators in air carrier contract disputes. Instead, these agencies have read the provision to charge them with a less taxing task: In passing on air carrier fitness, the DOT and the CAB have used their performance bond authority to ensure that, when a carrier's financial fitness is marginal, funds will be available to compensate customers if the carrier goes under before providing already-paid-for services. *See, e.g.*, U.S. Bahamas Service Investigation, CAB Order 79-11-116, p. 3, 84 CAB Reports 73, 75 (1979) ("We ... find that Southeast [Airlines] is fit to provide scheduled foreign air transportation. However, because of Southeast's current financial condition its operations present an unacceptable risk of financial loss to consumers. Therefore, we shall require the carrier ... to procure and maintain a bond for the protection of passengers who have paid for transportation not yet performed.").

The United States maintains that the DOT has neither the authority nor the apparatus required to superintend a contract dispute resolution regime. Prior to airline deregulation, the CAB set rates, routes, and services through a cumbersome administrative process of applications and approvals. When Congress dismantled that regime, the United States emphasizes, the lawmakers indicated no intention to establish, simultaneously, a new administrative process for DOT adjudication of private contract disputes. We agree.

Nor is it plausible that Congress meant to channel into federal courts the business of resolving, pursuant to judicially fashioned federal common law, the range of contract claims relating to airline rates, routes, or services. The ADA contains no hint of such a role for the federal courts. In this regard, the ADA contrasts markedly with the ERISA, which does channel civil actions into federal courts, under a comprehensive scheme, detailed in the legislation, designed to promote "prompt and fair claims settlement." The conclusion that the ADA permits state-law-based court adjudication of routine breach-of-contract claims also makes sense of Congress' retention of the FAA's saving clause, 49 U.S.C. § 1506 (preserving "the remedies now existing at common law or by statute"). The ADA's preemption clause, § 1305(a)(1), read together with the FAA's saving clause, stops States from imposing their own substantive standards with respect to rates, routes, or services, but not from affording relief to a party who claims and proves that an airline dishonored a term the airline itself stipulated.

This distinction between what the state dictates and what the airline itself undertakes confines courts, in breach-of-contract actions, to the parties' bargain, with no enlargement or enhancement based on state laws or policies external to the agreement. American suggests that plaintiffs' breach-of-contract and Consumer Fraud Act claims differ only in their labels, so that if Fraud Act claims are preempted, contract claims must be preempted as well. But a breach of contract, without more, "does not amount to a cause of action cognizable under the [Consumer Fraud] Act and the Act should not apply to simple breach of contract claims." *Golembiewski v. Hallberg Ins. Agency, Inc.* (Ill. App. Ct. 1994). The basis for a contract action is the parties' agreement; to succeed under the consumer protection law, one must show not necessarily an agreement, but in all cases, an unfair or deceptive practice.

II.

American ultimately argues that even under the position on preemption advanced by the United States—the one we adopt—plaintiffs' claims must fail because they "inescapably depend on state policies that are independent of the intent of the parties ... The state court cannot reach the merits," American contends, "unless it first invalidates or limits [American's] express reservation of the right to change AAdvantage Program rules contained in AAdvantage contracts."

American's argument is unpersuasive, for it assumes the answer to the very contract construction issue on which plaintiffs' claims turn: Did American, by contract, reserve the right to change the value of already accumulated mileage credits, or only to change the rules governing credits earned from and after the date of the change? That question of contract interpretation has not yet had a full airing, and we intimate no view on its resolution.

Responding to our colleagues' diverse opinions dissenting in part, we add a final note. This case presents two issues that run all through the law. First, who decides (here, courts or the DOT, the latter lacking contract dispute resolution resources for the task)? On this question, all agree to this extent: None of the opinions in this case would foist on the DOT work Congress has neither instructed nor funded the Department to do.

Second, where is it proper to draw the line (here, between what the ADA preempts, and what it leaves to private ordering, backed by judicial enforcement)? Justice Stevens reads our *Morales* decision to demand only minimal preemption; in contrast, Justice O'Connor reads the same case to mandate total preemption. The middle course we adopt seems to us best calculated to carry out the congressional design; it also bears the approval of the statute's experienced administrator, the DOT. And while we adhere to our holding in *Morales*, we do not overlook that in our system of adjudication, principles seldom can be settled "on the basis of one or two cases, but require a closer working out." Roscoe Pound, *Survey of the Conference Problems*, 14 U. CIN. L. REV. 324, 339 (1940) (Conference on the Status of the Rule of Judicial Precedent).

For the reasons stated, the judgment of the Illinois Supreme Court is affirmed in part and reversed in part, and the case is remanded for proceedings not inconsistent with this opinion.

Justice SCALIA took no part in the decision of the case.

Justice STEVENS, concurring in part and dissenting in part.

Although I agree with the majority that the Airline Deregulation Act of 1978 ("ADA") does not pre-empt respondents' breach-of-contract claims, I do not agree with the Court's disposition of their consumer-fraud claims. In my opinion, private tort actions based on common-law negligence or fraud, or on a statutory prohibition against fraud, are not pre-empted. Under the broad (and in my opinion incorrect) interpretation of the words "law ... relating to rates, routes, or services" that the Court adopted in *Morales*, direct state regulation of airline advertising is pre-empted; but I would not extend the holding of that case to embrace the private claims that respondents assert in this case.

Unlike the National Association of Attorneys General ("NAAG") guidelines reviewed in *Morales*, the Illinois Consumer Fraud and Deceptive Business Practices Act ("Consumer Fraud Act") does not instruct the airlines about how they can market their services. Instead, it merely requires all commercial enterprises—airlines included—to refrain from defrauding their customers. The *Morales* opinion said nothing about pre-empting general state laws prohibiting fraud. The majority's extension of the ADA's pre-emptive reach from airline-specific advertising standards to a general background rule of private conduct represents an alarming enlargement of *Morales'* holding.

I see no reason why a state law requiring an airline to honor its contractual commitments is any less a law relating to its rates and services than is a state law imposing a "duty not to make false statements of material fact or to conceal such facts." *Cipollone v. Liggett Group, Inc.* (1992) (finding similar claim not to be pre-empted under Federal Cigarette Labeling and Advertising Act). In this case, the two claims are grounded upon the exact same conduct and would presumably have an identical impact upon American's rates, routes, and services. I see no reason why the ADA should pre-empt a claim that the airline defrauded its customers in the making and performance of that very same agreement.

I would analogize the Consumer Fraud Act to a codification of common-law negligence rules. Under ordinary tort principles, every person has a duty to exercise reasonable care toward all other persons with whom he comes into contact. Presumably, if an airline were negligent in a way that somehow affected its rates, routes, or services, and the victim of the airline's negligence were to sue in state court, the majority would not hold all common-law negligence rules to be pre-empted by the ADA.

Like contract principles, the standard of ordinary care is a general background rule against which all individuals order their affairs. Surely Congress did not intend to give airlines free rein to commit negligent acts subject only to the supervision of the Department of Transportation, any more than it meant to allow airlines to breach contracts with impunity. And, if judge-made duties are not pre-empted, it would make little sense to find pre-emption of identical rules codified by the state legislature. The duty imposed by the Consumer Fraud Act is to refrain from committing fraud in commercial dealings—it is "the duty not to deceive." This is neither a novel nor a controversial proscription. It falls no more heavily upon airlines than upon any other business. It is no more or less a state-imposed "public policy" than a negligence rule. In sum, I see no difference between the duty to refrain from deception and the duty of reasonable care, and I see no meaningful difference between the enforcement of either duty and the enforcement of a private agreement.

The majority's extension of *Morales* is particularly untenable in light of the interpretive presumption against pre-emption. As in *Cipollone*, I believe there is insufficient evidence of congressional intent to supersede laws of general applicability to justify a finding that the ADA pre-empts either the contract or the fraud claim. Indeed, the presumption against pre-emption is especially appropriate to the ADA because Congress retained the "saving clause" preserving state "remedies now existing at common law or by statute." 49 U.S.C. § 1506.

Justice O'CONNOR, with whom Justice THOMAS joins, in part, concurring in the judgment in part and dissenting in part.

In permitting respondents' contract action to go forward, the Court arrives at what might be a reasonable policy judgment as to when state law actions against airlines should be pre-empted if we were free to legislate it. It is not, however, consistent with our controlling precedents, and it requires some questionable assumptions about the nature of contract law. I would hold that none of respondents' actions may proceed.

Applying *Morales* to this case, I agree with the Court that respondents' consumer fraud and contract claims are "related to" airline "rates" and "services." The Court says, however, that judicial enforcement of a contract's terms, in accordance with state contract law, does not amount to a "State ... enforc[ing] any law," but instead is simply a State "hold[ing] parties to their agreemen[t]." It therefore concludes that § 1305 does not apply to respondents' contract actions. I cannot agree with that conclusion.

I do not understand the Court to say that a State only "enforces" its "law" when some state employee (*e.g.*, an attorney general, or a judge) orders someone to do something. If that were the meaning of "enforce" in this context, then a diversity action brought by a private party under state law in federal court would never be subject to § 1305 pre-emption, because no state employee is involved, whereas the same action might be pre-empted in state court. That would make little sense, and federal courts have routinely considered § 1305 in determining whether a particular state law claim is pre-empted. Consequently, one must read "no State ... shall ... enforce any law" to mean that no one may enforce state law against an airline when the "enforcement actio[n] ha[s] a connection with, or reference to, airline 'rates, routes, or services.'" This explains the Court's conclusion, with which I agree, that private parties such as respondents may not enforce the Illinois consumer fraud law against petitioner in an action whose subject matter relates to airline rates and services.

As I read § 1305 and *Morales*, however, respondents' contract claims also must be preempted. The Court recognizes that the "guidelines" at issue in *Morales* did not "'create any new laws or regulations' applying to the airline industry; rather, they claim[ed] to 'explain in detail how existing state laws apply to air fare advertising and frequent flyer programs.'" Nonetheless, we stated our holding quite clearly: "We hold that the fare advertising provisions of the NAAG guidelines are pre-empted by [§ 1305]."

How can it be that the guidelines, which did not themselves constitute "law," were nonetheless pre-empted by a statute whose coverage is limited to "laws" or other "provision[s] having the force and effect of law"? The answer is that in *Morales* we held that an action to invoke the State's coercive power against an airline, by means of a generally applicable law, when the subject matter of the action related to airline rates, would constitute "Stat[e] ... enforce[ment]" of a "law ... relating to rates, routes, or services." Accordingly, we held that § 1305 pre-empted the action. It is not the case, as Justice STEVENS urges, that *Morales* was limited to "airline-specific advertising standards." We examined the content of those standards—which had no binding force on their own—only to ascertain whether they "related to" airline rates (and we thought they "quite obviously" did). The only "laws" at issue in *Morales* were generally applicable consumer fraud statutes, not facially related to airlines, much like the law at issue in respondents' consumer fraud claims here.

The Court concludes, however, that § 1305 does not preempt enforcement, by means of generally applicable state law, of a private agreement relating to airline rates and services. I cannot distinguish this case from *Morales*. In both, the subject matter of the action (the guidelines in *Morales*, the contract here) relates to airline rates and services. In both, that subject matter has no legal force, except insofar as a generally applicable state law (a consumer fraud law in *Morales*, state contract law here) permits an aggrieved party to invoke the State's coercive power against someone refusing to comply with the subject matter's terms (the requirements of the guidelines in *Morales*, the terms of the contract here). *Morales'* conclusion that § 1305 pre-empts such an invocation is dispositive here, both of respondents' consumer fraud claims, and of their contract claims. The lower courts seem to agree; as far as I know, no court to have considered ADA pre-emption since we decided *Morales* has suggested that enforcement of state contract law does not fall within § 1305 if the necessary relation to airline rates, routes, or services exists.

The Court argues that the words "law, rule, regulation, standard, or other provision" in § 1305 refer only to "'official, government-imposed policies, not the terms of a private contract.'" To be sure, the terms of private contracts are not "laws," any more than the guidelines at issue in *Morales* were "laws." But contract law, and generally applicable consumer fraud statutes, are laws, and *Morales* held that section 1305 prevents enforcement of "any [state] law" against the airlines when the subject matter of the action "relates" to airline rates, routes, or services. Thus, where the terms of a private contract relate to airline rates and services, and those terms can only be enforced through state law, *Morales* is indistinguishable. As Justice Stevens persuasively argues, there is "no reason why a state law requiring an airline to honor its contractual commitments is any less a law relating to its rates and services than is a state law imposing a 'duty not to make false statements of material fact or to conceal such facts.'"

As the Court recognizes, my view of *Morales* does not mean that personal injury claims against airlines are always pre-empted. Many cases decided since *Morales* have allowed personal injury claims to proceed, even though none has said that a State is not "enforcing" its "law" when it imposes tort liability on an airline. In those cases, courts have found the particular tort claims at issue not to "relate" to airline "services," much as we suggested in *Morales* that state laws against gambling and prostitution would be too tenuously related to airline services to be preempted. *E.g., Hodges v. Delta Airlines, Inc.* (5th Cir. 1993) (arguing that "'services' is not coextensive with airline 'safety,'" so safety-related tort claim should not be preempted; urging *en banc* review to bring Circuit precedent into conformity with that view).

Our recent decision in *Norfolk & Western R. Co. v. Train Dispatchers* (1991), is relevant. The question in that case was whether a rail carrier's statutory exemption from "all other law," which we read to mean "all law as necessary to carry out an ICC-approved transaction," exempted the carrier from contractually imposed obligations. We held that it did. We noted that "[a] contract depends on a regime of common and statutory law for its effectiveness and enforcement," that "[a] contract has no legal force apart from the law that acknowledges its binding character," and that "'[l]aws which subsist at the time and place of the making of a contract, and where it is to be performed, enter into and form a part of it, as fully as if they had been expressly referred to or incorporated in its terms." Accordingly, we concluded that "the exemption ... from 'all other law' effects an override of contractual obligations ... by suspending application of the law that makes the contract binding." In so concluding, we specifically rejected the Court of Appeals' views that the "all other law" exemption "[n]owhere ... sa[id] that the ICC may also override contracts," and that it did not exempt the carrier from "'all legal obstacles.'"

The Court does not dispute this reading of *Norfolk & Western*, which in my view makes clear that a State is enforcing its "law" when it brings its coercive power to bear on a party who has violated a contractual obligation. We reiterated in *Norfolk & Western* that "[t]he obligation of a contract is the law which binds the parties to perform their agreement." We therefore read the words "all other law" in the statutory exemption broadly enough to "suspen[d] application of the law that makes the contract binding." I would give the words "any law" in § 1305 a similar reading.

As support for its theory, the Court cites only a statement in the plurality opinion in *Cipollone v. Liggett Group, Inc.* The *Cipollone* plurality said that "a common-law remedy for a contractual commitment voluntarily undertaken should not be regarded as a 'requirement ... imposed under State law 'within the meaning of § 5(b)." But the plurality elaborated on this point in a footnote. In rejecting the argument that specific warranty obligations are "imposed under State law," the plurality agreed that pre-emption might be required "if the Act pre-empted 'liability 'imposed under state law ...; but instead the Act expressly pre-empts only a 'requirement or prohibition' imposed under state law." It agreed that contractual requirements are "only enforceable under state law," but argued that those requirements are "'imposed' by the contracting party upon itself."

The plurality thus distinguished the situation where substantive requirements contained in a contract are enforceable only under state law from the situation where state law itself imposes substantive requirements, and concluded that the statute before it pre-empted only the latter kind of state law. Here, as in *Cipollone*, the requirements at issue are contained in a contract, and have no legal force except insofar as state law makes them enforceable. But we concluded in *Morales* that § 1305 does pre-empt state law in those circumstances, unlike the statute in *Cipollone*. The difference between this case and *Cipollone* is the very different language in the two pre-emption statutes.

The Court also concludes that § 1305 only "stops States from imposing their own substantive standards with respect to rates, routes, or services." In *Morales*, however, we specifically rejected an interpretation of § 1305 that would have rewritten it to read: "'No State shall regulate rates, routes, and services.'" There is little distinction between "regulating rates, routes, and services" and "imposing substantive standards with respect to rates, routes, and services" and the Court does not explain how *Morales'* rejection of the former allows it now to adopt the latter. The Court relies on the statute's "saving clause," 49 U.S.C. § 1506 but we said in *Morales* that "[a] general 'remedies' saving clause cannot be allowed to supersede the specific substantive pre-emption provision," particularly where, as here, "the 'saving' clause is a relic of the pre-ADA/no pre-emption regime."

Without question, *Morales* gave § 1305 a broad pre-emptive sweep. The dissent in that case argued that such a broad interpretation went too far by pre-empting areas of traditional state regulation without a clear expression of congressional intent to do so. But the Court rejected the dissent's reading, holding instead that § 1305's language demonstrated a clear "statutory intent" to expressly preempt generally applicable state law as long as the "particularized application" of that law relates to airline rates, routes, or services.

* * *

Congress has recently revisited § 1305, and said that it "d[id] not intend to alter the broad pre-emption interpretation adopted by the United States Supreme Court in *Morales*," H.R. Conf. Rep. No. 103-677, p. 83 (1994). If the Court nonetheless believes that *Morales* misread § 1305, the proper course of action would be to overrule that case, despite Congress' apparent approval of it. The Court's reading of § 1305 is not, in my view, a "'closer working out'" of ADA pre-emption; rather, it is a new approach that does not square with our decisions in *Morales* and *Norfolk & Western.*

Stare decisis has "special force" in the area of statutory interpretation. It sometimes requires adherence to a wrongly decided precedent. Here, however, Congress apparently does not think that our decision in *Morales* was wrong, nor do I. In the absence of any "'special justification,'" for departing from *Morales*, I would recognize the import of *Morales* and *Norfolk & Western* here, and render the decision that the language of § 1305, in light of those cases, compels. If, at the end of the day, Congress believes we have erred in interpreting § 1305, it remains free to correct our mistake.

* * *

Our decisions in *Morales* and *Norfolk & Western* suffice to decide this case along the lines I have described. In addition, however, I disagree with the Court's view that courts can realistically be confined, "in breach-of-contract actions, to the parties' bargain, with no enlargement or enhancement based on state laws or policies external to the agreement." When they are so confined, the Court says, courts are "simply hold[ing] parties to their agreements," and are not "enforcing" any "law." The Court also says that "'[s]ome state-law principles of contract law might well be preempted to the extent they seek to effectuate the State's public policies, rather than the intent of the parties.'"

The doctrinal underpinnings of the notion that judicial enforcement of the "intent of the parties" can be divorced from a State's "public policy" have been in serious question for many years. As one author wrote some time ago:

> A contract, therefore, between two or more individuals cannot be said to be generally devoid of all public interest. If it be of no interest, why enforce it? For note that in enforcing contracts, the government does not merely allow two individuals to do what they have found pleasant in their eyes.
>
> Enforcement, in fact, puts the machinery of the law in the service of one party against the other. When that is worthwhile and how that should be done are important questions of public policy.
>
> [T]he notion that in enforcing contracts the state is only giving effect to the will of the parties rests upon an ... untenable theory as to what the enforcement of contracts involves.

Morris Cohen, *The Basis of Contract*, 46 HARV. L. REV. 553, 562 (1933).

More recent authors have expressed similar views. *See, e.g.*, Jean Braucher, *Contract Versus Contractarianism: The Regulatory Role of Contract Law*, 47 WASH. & LEE L. REV. 697, 699 (1990) ("Mediating between private ordering and social concerns, contract is a socioeconomic institution that requires an array of normative choices ... The questions addressed by contract law concern what social norms to use in the enforcement of contracts, not whether social norms will be used at all").

Contract law is a set of policy judgments concerning how to decide the meaning of private agreements, which private agreements should be legally enforceable, and what remedy to afford for their breach. The Court fails to recognize that when a State decides to force parties to comply with a contract, it does so only because it is satisfied that state policy, as expressed in its contract law, will be advanced by that decision. Thus, the Court's allowance that "'[s]ome state-law principles of contract law ... might well be preempted to the extent they seek to effectuate the State's public policies, rather than the intent of the parties,'" threatens to swallow all of contract law.

For example, the Court observes that on remand, the state court will be required to decide whether petitioner reserved the right to alter the terms of its frequent flyer program retroactively, or instead only prospectively. The court will presumably decide that question by looking to the usual "rules" of contract interpretation to decide what the contract's language means. If the court finds the language to be ambiguous, it might invoke the familiar rule that the contract should be construed against its drafter, and thus that respondents should receive the benefit of the doubt. That rule of contract construction is not essential to a functional contract system. It is a policy choice that our contract system has made. Other such policy choices are that courts should not enforce agreements unsupported by consideration; that courts should supply "reasonable" terms to fill "gaps" in incomplete contracts; the method by which courts should decide what terms to supply; and that a breach of contract entitles the aggrieved party to expectation damages most of the time, but specific performance only rarely. If courts are not permitted to look to these aspects of contract law in airline-related actions, they will find the cases difficult to decide.

Even the doctrine of unconscionability, which the United States suggests as an aspect of contract law that "might well be preempted" because it "seek[s] to effectuate the State's public policies, rather than the intent of the parties" cannot be so neatly categorized. On the one hand, refusing to enforce a contract because it is "unfair" seems quintessentially policy oriented. But on the other, "[p]rocedural unconscionability is broadly conceived to encompass not only the employment of sharp practices and the use of fine print and convoluted language, but a lack of understanding and an inequality of bargaining power." 1 FARNSWORTH § 4.28, at 506-07. In other words, a determination that a contract is "unconscionable" may in fact be a determination that one party did not intend to agree to the terms of the contract. Thus, the unconscionability doctrine, far from being a purely "policy-oriented" doctrine that courts impose over the will of the parties, instead demonstrates that state public policy cannot easily be separated from the methods by which courts are to decide what the parties "intended."

"[T]he law itself imposes contractual liability on the basis of a complex of moral, political, and social judgments." The rules laid down by contract law for determining what the parties intended an agreement to mean, whether that agreement is legally enforceable, and what relief an aggrieved party should receive, are the end result of those judgments. Our legal system has decided to allow private parties to invoke the coercive power of the State in the effort to enforce those (and only those) private agreements that conform to rules set by those state policies known collectively as "contract law." Courts cannot enforce private agreements without reference to those policies, because those policies define the role of courts in deciding disputes concerning private agreements. For these reasons, I would reverse the judgment of the Illinois Supreme Court.

NORTHWEST, INC. v. GINSBERG

134 S. Ct. 1422 (2014)

ALITO, J., delivered the opinion for a unanimous Court.

We must decide in this case whether the Airline Deregulation Act pre-empts a state-law claim for breach of the implied covenant of good faith and fair dealing. Following our interpretation of the Act in *American Airlines, Inc. v. Wolens*, we hold that such a claim is pre-empted if it seeks to enlarge the contractual obligations that the parties voluntarily adopt. And because the doctrine is invoked in the present case in an attempt to expand those obligations, we reverse the judgment of the Court of Appeals.

Like many airlines, petitioner Northwest, Inc. (Northwest), established a frequent flyer program, its WorldPerks Airline Partners Program, to attract loyal customers. Under this program, members are able to earn "miles" by taking flights operated by Northwest and other "partner" airlines. Members can then redeem these miles for tickets and service upgrades with Northwest or its airline partners. Respondent became a member of Northwest's WorldPerks program in 1999, and as a result of extensive travel on Northwest flights, he achieved "Platinum Elite" status (the highest level) in 2005. In 2008, however, Northwest terminated respondent's membership, apparently in reliance on a provision of the WorldPerks agreement that provided that "[a]buse of the ... program (including ... improper conduct as determined by [Northwest] in its sole judgment)] ... may result in cancellation of the member's account." According to respondent, a Northwest representative telephoned him in June 2008 and informed him that his "Platinum Elite" status was being revoked because he had "'abused'" the program. In a letter sent about two weeks later, Northwest wrote:

> You have contacted our office 24 times since December 3, 2007 regarding travel problems, including 9 incidents of your bag arriving late at the luggage carousel. Since December 3, 2007, you have continually asked for compensation over and above our guidelines. We have awarded you $1,925.00 in travel credit vouchers, 78,500 WorldPerks bonus miles, a voucher extension for your son, and $491.00 in cash reimbursements. Due to our past generosity, we must respectfully advise that we will no longer be awarding you compensation each time you contact us.

Respondent requested clarification of his status, but a Northwest representative sent him an e-mail stating that "[a]fter numerous conversations with not only the Legal Department, but with members of the WorldPerks department, I believe your status with the program should be very clear."

Alleging that Northwest had ended his membership as a cost-cutting measure tied to Northwest's merger with Delta Air Lines, respondent filed a class action in the United States District Court for the Southern District of California on behalf of himself and all other similarly situated WorldPerks members. Respondent's complaint asserted four separate claims. Applying California choice-of-law rules, the District Court held that Minnesota law applies because respondent "was a resident of Minneapolis, appears to fly in and out of Minnesota, and Northwest's principal place of business is Minnesota." That determination was not challenged on appeal.

First, his complaint alleged that Northwest had breached its contract by revoking his "Platinum Elite" status without valid cause. Second, the complaint claimed that Northwest violated the duty of good faith and fair dealing because it terminated his membership in a way that contravened his reasonable expectations with respect to the manner in which Northwest would exercise its discretion. Third, the complaint asserted a claim for negligent misrepresentation, and fourth, the complaint alleged intentional misrepresentation. Respondent sought damages in excess of $5 million, as well as injunctive relief requiring Northwest to restore the class members' WorldPerks status and prohibiting Northwest from future revocations of membership.

The District Court held that respondent's claims for breach of the covenant of good faith and fair dealing, negligent misrepresentation, and intentional misrepresentation were pre-empted by the Airline Deregulation Act of 1978, as amended, 49 U.S.C. § 41713. These claims, the court concluded, were "relate[d] to" Northwest's rates and services and thus fell within the ADA's express pre-emption clause. Respondent's remaining claim—for breach of contract—was dismissed without prejudice for failure to identify any material breach where the frequent flyer agreement gave Northwest sole discretion to determine whether a participant had abused the program. Respondent appealed the dismissal of his breach of the duty of good faith and fair dealing claim. The Ninth Circuit reversed. Relying on pre-*Wolens* Circuit precedent, the Ninth Circuit first held that a breach of implied covenant claim is "'too tenuously connected to airline regulation to trigger preemption under the ADA.'" Such a claim, the Ninth Circuit wrote, "does not interfere with the [Act's] deregulatory mandate" and does not "'force the Airlines to adopt or change their prices, routes or services—the prerequisite for ... preemption.'" In addition, the Court held that the covenant of good faith and fair dealing does not fall within the terms of the Act's pre-emption provision because it does not have a "direct effect" on either "prices" or "services." We granted *certiorari*.

DISCUSSION

I. *Preemption of Common Law Rules*

The first question we address is whether, as respondent now maintains, the ADA's pre-emption provision applies only to legislation enacted by a state legislature and regulations issued by a state administrative agency but not to a common-law rule like the implied covenant of good faith and fair dealing. We have little difficulty rejecting this argument. To begin, state common-law rules fall comfortably within the language of the ADA pre-emption provision. As noted above, the current version of this provision applies to state "law[s], regulation[s], or other provision[s] having the force and effect of law," 49 U.S.C. § 41713(b)(1). It is routine to call common-law rules "provisions." And a common-law rule clearly has "the force and effect of law." In *Wolens*, we noted that this phrase is most naturally read to "'refe[r] to binding standards of conduct that operate irrespective of any private agreement,'" and we see no basis for holding that such standards must be based on a statute or regulation as opposed to the common law.

This understanding becomes even clearer when the original wording of the pre-emption provision is taken into account. When first enacted in 1978, this provision also applied to "rule[s]" and "standard[s]," and there surely can be no doubt that this formulation encompassed common-law rules. Indeed, we held in *CSX Transp., Inc. v. Easterwood* (1993) that virtually identical language in the Federal Railroad Safety Act of 1970 includes "[l]egal duties imposed ... by the common law." While "rule[s]" and "standard[s]" are not mentioned in the current version of the statute, this omission is the result of a recodification that was not meant to affect the provision's meaning. Those additional terms were deleted as part of a wholesale recodification of Title 49 in 1994, but Congress made it clear that this recodification did not effect any "substantive change."

In arguing that common-law rules fall outside the scope of the ADA pre-emption provision, respondent relies on our decision in *Sprietsma v. Mercury Marine* (2002), which held that the Federal Boat Safety Act of 1971 did not pre-empt a common-law tort claim, but there are critical differences between the pre-emption provisions in the Boat Safety Act and the ADA. The Boat Safety Act provision applies only to "a law or regulation," whereas the ADA provision, as just explained, is much more broadly worded.

In addition, the relationship between the ADA's pre-emption provision and the saving provision carried over from the prior law is also quite different. The *Sprietsma* decision placed substantial weight on the Boat Safety Act's saving provision, which was enacted at the same time as the pre-emption provision, but we have described the Federal Aviation Act saving clause as "a relic of the pre-ADA/no pre-emption regime." That provision applies to the entire, sprawling Federal Aviation Act, and not just to the ADA, and as we held in *Morales*, this "general 'remedies' saving clause cannot be allowed to supersede the specific substantive pre-emption provision." *See also Wolens* (O'Connor, J., concurring in judgment in part and dissenting in part). For these reasons, respondent's interpretation of the ADA pre-emption provision cannot be squared with the provision's terms.

Exempting common-law claims would also disserve the central purpose of the ADA. The Act eliminated federal regulation of rates, routes, and services in order to allow those aspects of air transportation to be set by market forces, and the pre-emption provision was included to prevent the States from undoing what the Act was meant to accomplish. What is important, therefore, is the effect of a state law, regulation, or provision, not its form, and the ADA's deregulatory aim can be undermined just as surely by a state common-law rule as it can by a state statute or regulation. As the First Circuit has recognized, "[i]t defies logic to think that Congress would disregard real-world consequences and give dispositive effect to the form of a clear intrusion into a federally regulated industry." Finally, if all state common-law rules fell outside the ambit of the ADA's pre-emption provision, we would have had no need in *Wolens* to single out a subcategory of common-law claims, i.e., those based on the parties' voluntary undertaking, as falling outside that provision's coverage. Accordingly, we conclude that the phrase "other provision having the force and effect of law" includes common-law claims.

II. *Whether Implied Covenant "Relates To" Rates, Routes or Services*

We must next determine whether respondent's breach of implied covenant claim "relates to" "rates, routes, or services." A claim satisfies this requirement if it has "a connection with, or reference to, airline" prices, routes, or services, and the claim at issue here clearly has such a connection. That claim seeks respondent's reinstatement in Northwest's frequent flyer program so that he can access the program's "valuable ... benefits," including "flight upgrades, accumulated mileage, loyalty program status or benefits on other airlines, and other advantages."

Like the frequent flyer program in *Wolens*, the Northwest program is connected to the airline's "rates" because the program awards mileage credits that can be redeemed for tickets and upgrades. When miles are used in this way, the rate that a customer pays, *i.e.*, the price of a particular ticket, is either eliminated or reduced. The program is also connected to "services," *i.e.*, access to flights and to higher service categories. Respondent argues that his claim differs from the claims in *Wolens* because he "does not challenge access to flights and upgrades or the number of miles needed to obtain air tickets" but instead contests "the termination of his WorldPerks elite membership," but this argument ignores respondent's reason for seeking reinstatement of his membership, *i.e.*, to obtain reduced rates and enhanced services.

Respondent and *amici* suggest that *Wolens* is not controlling because frequent flyer programs have fundamentally changed since the time of that decision. We are told that "most miles [are now] earned without consuming airline services" and are "spent without consuming airline services." But whether or not this alleged change might have some impact in a future case, it is not implicated here. In this case, respondent did not assert that he earned his miles from any activity other than taking flights or that he attempted to redeem miles for anything other than tickets and upgrades.

III. *Implied Covenant: Legal Obligation or Voluntary Undertaking?*

With these preliminary issues behind us, we turn to the central issue in this case, *i.e.*, whether respondent's implied covenant claim is based on a state-imposed obligation or simply one that the parties voluntarily undertook. Petitioners urge us to hold that implied covenant claims are always pre-empted, and respondent suggests that such claims are generally not pre-empted, but the reasoning of *Wolens* neither dooms nor spares all such claims.

While most States recognize some form of the good faith and fair dealing doctrine, it does not appear that there is any uniform understanding of the doctrine's precise meaning. "[T]he concept of good faith in the performance of contracts 'is a phrase without general meaning (or meanings) of its own.'" *Tymshare, Inc. v. Covell*, (D.C. Cir. 1984) (Scalia, J.) (quoting Summers, "Good Faith" in *General Contract Law and the Sales Provisions of the Uniform Commercial Code*, 54 VA. L. REV. 195, 201 (1968)). Of particular importance here, while some States are said to use the doctrine "to effectuate the intentions of parties or to protect their reasonable expectations," other States clearly employ the doctrine to ensure that a party does not "'violate community standards of decency, fairness, or reasonableness.'"

Whatever may be the case under the law of other jurisdictions, it seems clear that under Minnesota law, which is controlling here, the implied covenant must be regarded as a state-imposed obligation. Respondent concedes that under Minnesota law parties cannot contract out of the covenant. And as a leading commentator has explained, a State's "unwillingness to allow people to disclaim the obligation of good faith ... shows that the obligation cannot be implied, but is law imposed." 3A A. CORBIN, CORBIN ON CONTRACTS § 654A, p. 88 (L. Cunningham & A. Jacobsen eds. Supp. 1994). When the law of a State does not authorize parties to free themselves from the covenant, a breach of covenant claim is pre-empted under the reasoning of *Wolens*.

Another feature of Minnesota law provides an additional, independent basis for our conclusion. Minnesota law holds that the implied covenant applies to "every contract," with the notable exception of employment contracts. The exception for employment contracts is based, in significant part, on "policy reasons," and therefore the decision not to exempt other types of contracts must be based on a policy determination, namely, that the "policy reasons" that support the rule for employment contracts do not apply (at least with the same force) in other contexts. When the application of the implied covenant depends on state policy, a breach of implied covenant claim cannot be viewed as simply an attempt to vindicate the parties' implicit understanding of the contract.

For these reasons, the breach of implied covenant claim in this case cannot stand, but petitioners exhort us to go further and hold that all such claims, no matter the content of the law of the relevant jurisdiction, are pre-empted. If pre-emption depends on state law, petitioners warn, airlines will be faced with a baffling patchwork of rules, and the deregulatory aim of the ADA will be frustrated. But the airlines have means to avoid such a result. A State's implied covenant rules will escape pre-emption only if the law of the relevant State permits an airline to contract around those rules in its frequent flyer program agreement, and if an airline's agreement is governed by the law of such a State, the airline can specify that the agreement does not incorporate the covenant. While the inclusion of such a provision may impose transaction costs and presumably would not enhance the attractiveness of the program, an airline can decide whether the benefits of such a provision are worth the potential costs.

Our holding also does not leave participants in frequent flyer programs without protection. The ADA is based on the view that the best interests of airline passengers are most effectively promoted, in the main, by allowing the free market to operate. If an airline acquires a reputation for mistreating the participants in its frequent flyer program (who are generally the airline's most loyal and valuable customers), customers can avoid that program and may be able to enroll in a more favorable rival program.

Federal law also provides protection for frequent flyer program participants. Congress has given the Department of Transportation (DOT) the general authority to prohibit and punish unfair and deceptive practices in air transportation and in the sale of air transportation, 49 U.S.C. § 41712(a), and Congress has specifically authorized the DOT to investigate complaints relating to frequent flyer programs. See FAA Modernization and Reform Act of 2012, § 408(6), 126 Stat. 87. Pursuant to these provisions, the DOT regularly entertains and acts on such complaints.

We note, finally, that respondent's claim of ill treatment by Northwest might have been vindicated if he had pursued his breach-of-contract claim after its dismissal by the District Court. Respondent argues that, contrary to the holding of the District Court, the frequent flyer agreement did not actually give Northwest unfettered discretion to terminate his membership in the program, and the United States makes a related argument, namely, that even if the agreement gave Northwest complete discretion with respect to a determination regarding abuse of the program, the agreement did not necessarily bar a claim asserting that membership was ended for an ulterior reason, such as an effort to cut costs. If respondent had appealed the dismissal of his breach-of-contract claim, he could have presented these arguments to the Court of Appeals, but he chose not to press that claim. He voluntarily dismissed the breach-of-contract claim and instead appealed only the breach of implied covenant claim, which we hold to be pre-empted.

Because respondent's implied covenant of good faith and fair dealing claim seeks to enlarge his contractual agreement with petitioners, we hold that 49 U.S.C. § 41713(b)(1) pre-empts the claim. The judgment of the Court of Appeals for the Ninth Circuit is reversed, and the case is remanded for further proceedings consistent with this opinion.

WEISS v. EL AL ISRAEL AIRLINES, LTD.
433 F. Supp. 2d 361 (S.D.N.Y. 2006)

LYNCH, District Judge.

Plaintiffs Tobias and Gertrude Weiss bring this action against El Al Israel Airlines ("El Al") to recover losses that they incurred as a result of their being involuntarily denied boarding, or "bumped," from a flight from New York to Jerusalem. They bring this action under regulations promulgated under the Federal Aviation Act, 14 C.F.R. § 250.1 *et seq*. ("Federal Regulations"), and under state tort and contract law.

El Al has moved to dismiss the complaint, contending that plaintiffs' claims are preempted by the Montreal Convention and the Airline Deregulation Act ("ADA"), and that plaintiffs have no cause of action under the Federal Regulations. Plaintiffs in response have submitted a motion to strike, which for the most part simply opposes El Al's motion to dismiss, but also raises certain issues of service and jurisdiction that the Court separately addresses. For the reasons set forth below, El Al's motion to dismiss will be denied in part and granted in part, and plaintiffs' motion to strike will be denied.

BACKGROUND

The facts as alleged in the Complaint are as follows: Plaintiffs purchased tickets at a combined price of $2,434 from El Al for round-trip transportation between New York Kennedy airport and Jerusalem Ben-Gurion airport, departing New York on March 31, 2004, at 6:30 P.M. They arrived at Kennedy airport on the scheduled date of departure a little more than one hour before the flight and were cleared by airline security, but were involuntarily denied boarding because the flight had been oversold by the airline and, as a result, their reserved seats given to other passengers. Plaintiffs, in a manner familiar to any regular flyer, had been "bumped." Bumping is an airline industry practice whereby passengers are denied seats due to intentional overselling, which is intended to minimize the number of empty seats due to cancellations. *Nader v. Allegheny* (1976); *see also* Elliott Blanchard, *Terminal 250: Federal Regulation of Airline Overbooking*, 79 N.Y.U. L. REV. 1799 (2004) (discussing economic incentives that gave rise to industry practice of overselling).

El Al subsequently placed the bumped passengers, including plaintiffs, on a standby list to enable them to obtain seats on future El Al flights in the coming days in the event that seats opened up. El Al also took an extra $100 from plaintiffs in order to upgrade their seats, should they get seats, to business class.

As a result of their standby status, plaintiffs were induced to remain at the airport for two days in the hope of obtaining seats on a subsequent flight. They spent the time moving about the airport attempting to comply with the airline's procedures for standby passengers. During that period, plaintiffs allege that they suffered physical fatigue and exhaustion from all the activity. Plaintiffs also allege that they were treated in a "wanton, oppressive, indifferent, and uncaring" manner by the airline's employees, who "shunt[ed] the passengers around from place to place." Finally, plaintiffs allege that they suffered "emotional stress, and worry and anxiety, and great inconvenience in being denied the transportation on which they depended." To date, plaintiffs have not received a refund for the cost of these tickets nor have they received any compensation for being "bumped" from their reserved seats on the March 31 flight.

DISCUSSION

A. The Montreal Convention

El Al's first contention is that the Montreal Convention preempts plaintiffs' federal and state law claims. In determining whether the Montreal Convention preempts plaintiffs' claims, the Court faces two questions: First, does the Montreal Convention apply to plaintiffs' flight to Israel, even though Israel is not a party to the Convention? Second, is a claim for bumping a claim for "delay" under Article 19 of the Convention, and therefore preempted? Ultimately, the Court need not determine whether the Convention applies to plaintiffs' travel because it concludes that bumping, at least under the circumstances alleged in the Complaint, is not covered by the Convention.

Defendant argues that plaintiffs' bumping claims are claims for damages occasioned by delay, which are covered by Article 19 of the Convention and therefore are preempted by Article 29. Plaintiffs respond that the Montreal Convention does not apply because bumping is more accurately described as complete non-performance of contract than as delay. The drafting history indicates that the drafters of the Montreal Convention intended that the national courts would determine the meaning of "delay," and national courts have almost universally accepted the interpretation of bumping as contractual non-performance and not delay. Consequently, in light of the interest in international uniformity and the greater focus on consumer protection intended in the Montreal Convention, plaintiffs' bumping claims should be read as grounded in a cause of action for non-performance of contract and not delay. They are, therefore, not preempted by the Montreal Convention.

B. The ADA

El Al next contends that even if plaintiffs' claims are not preempted by the Montreal Convention, they are preempted by the ADA, which amended the FAA to place exclusive legislative and regulatory authority in the aviation context in the hands of the federal government.

In this case, plaintiffs' state law claims sound both in tort and contract. Their breach of contract claim for bumping is clearly not preempted by the ADA. On the other hand, claims tort damages for physical and emotional suffering, and for "great inconvenience," based on the airline's treatment of plaintiffs during the two days they remained at JFK airport and the airline's "failure to furnish the transportation represented by the tickets it sold to them." This claim is clearly preempted by the ADA, and is dismissed.

C. The Federal Regulations

Finally, El Al contends, in its reply memorandum, that even if plaintiffs' claims are not preempted by the Montreal Convention or the ADA, Count I of the Complaint, which alleges that El Al violated provisions of the regulations at 14 C.F.R. § 250.1 *et seq*., relating to overselling practices, fails to state a claim because no right of action is either expressly or impliedly provided for in the governing statutes or in the regulations themselves.

As an initial matter, El Al does not argue that the regulations preempt plaintiffs' remaining contract claim, and such an argument would be meritless. The regulations themselves, their legislative history, and the courts to have interpreted them, all make clear that they indeed permit such an action. *See* 14 C.F.R. § 250.9(b) (stating bumped passenger shall be informed that he or she "may decline the payment [mandated under the regulations] and seek to recover damages in a court of law or in some other manner"); 47 Fed. Reg. 52,980, 52,982, 52,987 (Civil Aeronautics Bd. Nov. 24, 1982) (noting that "[i]n the exceptional case where the regulatory ... payment is not adequate compensation, the passenger is free to refuse it and bring private legal action," and that "[t]he passenger may ... insist on the cash payment, or refuse all compensation and bring private legal action"); *West v. Northwest Airlines* (9th Cir. 1993) ("The plain language of the regulation indicates that passengers retain the option ... of pursuing compensatory damages in state court."); *Stone v. Continental Airlines*, (N.Y. Civ. Ct. 2005) (noting section 250.9(b) "is universally regarded as permitting a claim for contract damages which may exceed the amount of compensation offered by an airline").

The Court recognizes that the "right of action" argument was first raised in El Al's reply memorandum, after plaintiffs had submitted their opposition papers. Thus, it might be argued that plaintiffs should be given a formal opportunity to respond to El Al's argument before the Court dismisses this claim. However, plaintiffs did not seek leave to file a sur-reply. As to whether El Al waived the argument altogether, the law is clear, and El Al cannot, by failing to raise the argument in a timely manner, vest in plaintiffs a right of action that Congress has declined to create.

NOTES

1. Concerns about delays, cancellations, and other airline customer service issues ceded to the larger issue of aviation security after September 11, 2001. *See, e.g.*, AIR TRANSP. ASSN., STATE OF THE AIRLINE INDUSTRY: A REPORT ON RECENT TRENDS FOR U.S. AIR CARRIERS 8 (2002) ("The delay problem has temporarily receded since September 11, due to the reduction in flights. However, as airlines return to their pre-September 11 schedules, the number and duration of flight delays will increase."). *See also* Al Frank, *American Airlines CEO: Don't Forget Old Problems*, STAR-LEDGER (New Jersey), Feb. 20, 2002 ("We will find ourselves headed for gridlock once again if we don't keep pushing to modernize and expand the capacity of our nation's aviation system in the air and on the ground.").

2. In 2007, hundreds of airline passengers were stranded aboard nine JetBlue Airways airplanes on the snow-covered tarmac of New York's JFK International Airport for almost 10 hours. To stave off Congressional action and repair its public image, JetBlue subsequently announced its own "Customer Bill of Rights," setting out self-imposed penalties and "major" rewards for passengers if that are inconvenienced beyond a "reasonable" amount of time. *See, e.g.*, Jeff Bailey, *Chief "Mortified" by JetBlue Crisis*, N.Y. TIMES, Feb. 19, 2007, at A1. Subject to its own Contract of Carriage, JetBlue's "Customer Bill of Rights" (*http://www.jetblue.com/about/ourcompany/promise/index.html*) provides:

> Above all else, JetBlue Airways is dedicated to bringing humanity back to air travel. We strive to make every part of your experience as simple and as pleasant as possible. Unfortunately, there are times when things do not go as planned. If you're inconvenienced as a result, we think it is important that you know exactly what you can expect from us. That's why we created our Customer Bill of Rights
>
> These Rights will always be subject to the highest level of safety and security for our customers and crewmembers.
>
> ***INFORMATION***
>
> JetBlue will notify customers of the following:
>
> - Delays prior to scheduled departure
> - Cancellations and their cause
> - Diversions and their cause

CANCELLATIONS

All customers whose flight is cancelled by JetBlue will, at the customer's option, receive a full refund or re-accommodation on the next available JetBlue flight at no additional charge or fare. If JetBlue cancels a flight within 4 hours of scheduled departure and the cancellation is due to a Controllable Irregularity, JetBlue will also provide the customer with a $50 Credit good for future travel on JetBlue.

DEPARTURE DELAYS

Customers whose flight is delayed for 1-1:59 hours after scheduled departure time due to a *Controllable Irregularity* are entitled to a $25 Credit good for future travel on JetBlue.

Customers whose flight is delayed for 2-4:59 hours after scheduled departure time due to a *Controllable Irregularity* are entitled to a $50 Credit good for future travel on JetBlue.

Customers whose flight is delayed for 5-5:59 hours after scheduled departure time due to a *Controllable Irregularity* are entitled to a Credit good for future travel on JetBlue in the amount paid by the customer for the oneway trip less taxes and fees (or $50, whichever is greater).

Customers whose flight is delayed for 6 or more hours after scheduled departure time due to a *Controllable Irregularity* are entitled to a Credit good for future travel on JetBlue in the amount paid by the customer for the roundtrip (or the oneway trip, doubled) less taxes and fees.

DELAYS (DEPARTURE DELAYS AND ONBOARD GROUND DELAYS ON DEPARTURE)

For customers whose flight is delayed 3 hours or more after scheduled departure, JetBlue will provide free movies on flights that are 2 hours or longer.

OVERBOOKINGS

(As defined in JetBlue's [39-page] Contract of Carriage) Customers who are involuntarily denied boarding shall receive $1,000.

ONBOARD GROUND DELAYS

JetBlue will provide customers experiencing an Onboard Ground Delay with 36 channels of DIRECTV®, food and drink, access to clean restrooms and, as necessary, medical treatment. For customers who experience an Onboard Ground Delay for more than 5 hours, JetBlue will take necessary action so that customers may deplane.

Arrivals:
Customers who experience an Onboard Ground Delay on Arrival for 1-1:59 hours after scheduled arrival time are entitled to a $50 Credit good for future travel on JetBlue.

Customers who experience an Onboard Ground Delay on Arrival for 2 or more hours after scheduled arrival time are entitled to a Credit good for future travel on JetBlue in the amount paid by the customer for the roundtrip (or the oneway trip, doubled) less taxes and fees.

Departures:
Customers who experience an Onboard Ground Delay on Departure for 3-3:59 hours after scheduled departure time are entitled to a $50 Credit good for future travel on JetBlue.

Customers who experience an Onboard Ground Delay on Departure for 4-4:59 hours after scheduled departure time are entitled to a Credit good for future travel on JetBlue in the amount paid by the customer for the oneway trip less taxes and fees (or $50, whichever is greater).

Customers who experience an Onboard Ground Delay on Departure for 5 or more hours after scheduled departure time are entitled to a Credit good for future travel on JetBlue in the amount paid by the customer for the roundtrip (or the oneway trip, doubled) less taxes and fees.

IN-FLIGHT ENTERTAINMENT

> JetBlue offers 36 channels of DIRECTV® service on its flights in the Continental U.S. If our LiveTV™ system is inoperable on flights in the Continental U.S, customers are entitled to a $15 Credit good for future travel on JetBlue.

3. The objective of any contract is performance, but many of the defenses to a breach of contract claim—including impossibility of performance, impracticability, or *force majeure*—are a routine part of aviation travel. In this context, how effective are contract rights in the airline industry likely to be when "breaches" are not merely possible, but probable depending upon the region and season in which any particular flight is delayed, cancelled, or diverted? Are airlines more likely to preemptively cancel more flights in order to avoid any self- or government-imposed penalties for delay?

4. Pursuant to the Supreme Court's decision in *American Airlines v. Wolens, Inc.* (1995), *supra*, the full range of state-law claims against air carriers—all statutory and common law claims other than breach-of-contract claims seeking solely to enforce the obligations that air carriers placed on themselves—are preempted when they relate to air carrier prices, routes, or services. *See United Airlines, Inc. v. Mesa Airlines, Inc.* (7th Cir. 2000) (finding the ADA "defeats external rules" of fiduciary obligations); *Statland v. American Airlines, Inc.* (7th Cir. 1993) (holding state law claim for breach of fiduciary duty was preempted where plaintiff based claims on allegations that the airline collected and withheld taxes for tickets that were then cancelled); *Buck v. American Airlines, Inc.* (1st Cir. 2007) (holding ticket purchasers' claims, including breach of fiduciary duty and breach of the covenant of good faith and fair dealing, were preempted where claims were based on airlines' refusal to refund fees and taxes paid in the purchase of non-refundable tickets that were subsequently not used); *Cerdant, Inc. v. DHL Express (USA), Inc.* (S.D. Ohio 2009) (dismissing plaintiff's non-contract claims including breach of good faith and fair dealing for allegations of improper shipping charges as preempted by the Federal Aviation Administration Authorization Act of 1994 ("FAAA") because they "would constitute an enlargement or enhancement of the parties' bargain"); *McMullen v. Delta Air Lines, Inc.* (N.D. Cal. 2008) (holding plaintiff's claim that Delta breached an implied covenant of good faith and fair dealing by collecting a Mexican nonimmigrant tax for each passenger was preempted by the ADA); *Ray v. American Airlines, Inc.* (W.D. Ark. 2008) (holding passenger's claims of breach of implied covenant of good faith and fair dealing for allegations stemming from a delayed trip were preempted to the extent they claimed relief beyond any specific terms in the airline's conditions of carriage contract).

5. In the wake of *American Airlines, Inc. v. Wolens* (1995), *supra*, claims for equitable estoppel, promissory estoppel, constructive fraud/fraudulent concealment, and attorney's fees are preempted because they seek relief outside the scope of the parties' agreements. *See A.J.'s Wrecker Serv. of Dallas, Inc. v. Salazar* (Tex. Ct. App. 2005) (finding state law claims including equitable estoppel and promissory estoppel preempted

by federal law where plaintiff sued towing company for wrongfully towing her car); *see also Cerdant, Inc. v. DHL Express (USA), Inc.* (S.D. Ohio 2009) (dismissing plaintiff's non-contract claims, including promissory estoppel, for allegations of improper shipping charges as preempted by Federal Aviation Administration Authorization Act of 1994 because they "would constitute an enlargement or enhancement of the parties' bargain."); *Osband v. United Airlines, Inc.* (Colo. Ct. App. 1998) (finding employees' promissory estoppel claim to reinstate prior travel benefits preempted); *Deerskin Trading Post, Inc. v. United Parcel Serv. of Am., Inc.* (N.D. Ga. 1997) (finding ADA preempts equitable relief); *In re Korean Air Lines Co., Ltd. Antitrust Lit.* (C.D. Cal. 2008) (finding state law claims including fraudulent concealment preempted in case alleging violations of antitrust and consumer protection laws as a result of an alleged price-fixing conspiracy); *Wagman v. Fed. Exp. Corp.* (7th Cir. 1995) (affirming dismissal on preemption grounds of constructive fraud and other claims based on allegations of misleading advertising arising from the late delivery of plaintiff's package); *See United Airlines, Inc. v. Mesa Airlines, Inc.* (7th Cir. 2000) (noting air carriers are not free to engage in "unscrupulous" or fraudulent practices because the Secretary of Transportation has responsibility to investigate claims of deceit and to issue remedial orders); *Statland v. American Airlines, Inc.* (7th Cir. 1993) (finding statutory fraud claims preempted where passenger sued regarding non-refunded taxes and fees on a canceled ticket).

6. Claims for punitive damages arising from a breach of contract may be preempted even under the holding of *American Airlines, Inc. v. Wolens* (1995), *supra*, as such damages awards are instruments of state public policy. *See Travel All Over the World, Inc. v. Saudi Arabia* (7th Cir. 1996) (holding punitive damages preempted because "[r]ather than merely holding parties to the terms of a bargain, punitive damages represent an 'enlargement or enhancement [of the bargain] based on state laws or policies external to the agreement.'" (quoting *Wolens*)); *see also, e.g., Galieo Int'l, L.L.C. v. Ryanair, Ltd.*, (N.D. Ill. 2002) (holding claim for punitive damages to deter allegedly deceptive and misleading conduct related to a consumer reservation system agreement and other claims preempted); *Deerskin Trading Post, Inc. v. United Parcel Serv. of Am., Inc.* (N.D. Ga. 1997) ("[T]he Supreme Court did state explicitly that the parties should be held to their bargain, with no enlargement or enhancement based on state policy. An award of punitive damages would constitute such an enhancement.").

7. The modern Supreme Court of the United States generally is considered "split" between conservative and liberal jurists. Note the authors of the *Morales v. Trans World Airlines, Inc.* (Scalia, J.) and *American Airlines, Inc. v. Wolens* (Ginsburg, J.) opinions (Justice Scalia "took no part in the decision of the (*Wolens*) case."). Note, too, the appearance of Chief Justice William Rehnquist in the dissent to *Morales*, *supra*. What insight, if any, does this offer about the politics of aviation law? Taken together, what do *Wolens* and *Morales* say about the current view of federalism? For further discussion of federal preemption see Kyle Volluz, Comment, *The Aftermath of* Morales *and* Wolens*: A Review of the Current State of Federal Preemption of State Law Claims under the Airline Deregulation Act of 1978*, 62 J. AIR L. & COM. 1195 (1997).

8. Are the airlines solely blameworthy for delays and congestion? In 2000 weather caused approximately 70 percent of all airline delays, whereas traffic contributed nearly 14 percent. Yet, one industry observer noted:

> Even clear skies and functioning airports can cause fits. One day, Newark's [air traffic controllers'] request for a five-to-ten minute hold on 15 arrivals from the west mushroomed into an airborne gridlock. This rolling-snowball-turned-avalanche began with airplanes holding in Cleveland Center's airspace.
>
> To ease the strain, over-worked Cleveland controllers turned to Chicago and Indianapolis Centers, asking them to also hold Newark-bound flights. Now some 70 airplanes were affected. Then Chicago Center asked Minneapolis Center to hold Newark flights. All of these orbiting airplanes forced controllers to re-route flights headed to or from Atlanta, Boston, Chicago and Philadelphia. Within a mere 20 minutes some 250 airplanes were facing delays of one sort or another.

Stan Solomon, *'D' is for Delay*, AIRWAYS, July 2001, at 21.

9. Only six of the nations' largest airports completed new runway projects between 1995 and 2001. Deficiencies in airport infrastructure contribute significantly to airline delays:

> Congestion at major airports at peak travel times (and the consequent inability of passengers to whom time is very valuable to get the delay-free travel they would willingly pay for) obviously means to an economist that the pertinent government authorities have on the one hand failed efficiently to expand airport and air traffic control capacity, and, on the other, to price those scarce facilities at their marginal opportunity costs. No wonder there are shortages.

Alfred E. Kahn, *Surprises of Airline Deregulation*, 78 AM. ECON. REV. 316, 321. Is the solution as simple and "concrete" as building new runways? *See, e.g.*, Mark Sappenfield, *The Unfinished Story of a Runway*, CHRISTIAN SCI. MONITOR, Feb. 12, 2001, at 1.

10. One market-based approach to reducing air traffic and delays is "congestion pricing" or "peak hour pricing." This regulatory framework would mean that airlines would be charged higher landing fees at the busiest times at the major hub airports. Such costs likely would be borne by airline passengers ultimately. Is this a

sensible policy solution? Consider the reaction of Don Carty, American Airlines Chief Executive Officer during an interview in 2003:

> Q: Why are you opposed to this idea of congestion pricing, which is a very businesslike, marketplace way of getting people who want to travel at peak times to pay for it and to bring down the number of people traveling at peak times?
>
> A: I don't think it would have any impact on people traveling at peak times. We already revenue-manage that equation. For example, at LaGuardia at 5 P.M., we're not selling any $69 leisure fares. All you're talking about doing is raising the costs further, which we'll pass along to the consumer. If you're a businessman going to New York and you need to put in a productive business day, you're going to leave New York at 5 A.M. or 6 A.M. whether the fare is $10 or $15 higher, because if you waste 3 hours of your day in New York you haven't accomplished anything. We think it would be simply the raising of the costs of doing business rather than effectively changing the patterns of the use of the air traffic control system.

Air Delays Will Ease, but Not Before 2003, USA TODAY, June 21, 2001, at 15A. *See also* David Bond, *Justice Dept. Backs Slot Auctions at LGA*, AVIATION WK. & SPACE TECH., July 15, 2002, at 37 (reporting that the Justice Department views congestion pricing as an inferior market-based option because "if the fee were increased too much, operations would be reduced unnecessarily; if too little, they would not be reduced enough."). Overseas, commercial aviation traffic has so outpaced infrastructure that, for example, the government-controlled civil authority in China refused to approve new airlines before 2010, in order to slow down growth. *See, e.g.*, Bradly Perrett, *Throttling Back*, AVIATION WK. & SPACE TECH., Aug. 20/27, 2007, at 30; Edward Russell, *China Blocks Takeoff of New Airlines*, ASIA ONLINE, Aug. 31, 2007, *http://www.atimes.com/atimes/China_Business/IH31Cb01.html.*

PROBLEM

In the aftermath of September 11th, national security officials strictly limited whether passengers could check their baggage at the airport terminal curb. As airline travel normalized, baggage-curb check-has resumed, in part. "Skycaps" are airline employees who help passengers check in luggage at the curbs of airport terminals. In a national class action suit against United Air Lines, all skycaps who worked at United terminals sued the airline in connection with the carrier's imposition of a $2 fee per bag for curbside check-in, a service that used to be a source of tips for baggage handlers. The skycaps presented two theories: first, passengers intend the cash payments to be "tips" that belong to the employees; second, the charges interfere with the skycaps' wages because passengers are unlikely to tip in addition to airline bag fees. Based on these theories, the skycaps assert claims on behalf of the entire class for tortious interference with advantageous relations and unjust enrichment and violation of the Massachusetts Tips Law, Mass. Gen. Laws ch. 149 § 152A, which requires payments intended as tips to be remitted to service employees.

Applying *Morales v. Trans World Airlines, Inc.* (1992), and *American Airlines, Inc. v. Wolens* (1992), *supra*, should the skycaps prevail as a matter of law? *See Brown v. United Air Lines, Inc.* (D. Mass. 2009).

CHAPTER 3

AIRLINE ECONOMICS

A. ANTITRUST AND LOW COST CARRIERS

The emergence of low cost or "no frills" carriers such as Frontier Airlines and Spirit Airlines suggests robust competition in the commercial airline industry. But, in fact, just four airlines—Delta, American, United, and Southwest—account for nearly 80% of all domestic air travel in the United States. Is this consistent with the intent and policy underpinnings of the Airline Deregulation Act of 1978?

Consider, too, that on November 10, 2015, the United States Department of Justice filed a lawsuit against United Continental Holdings Inc. to block a deal allowing the company to gain 24 takeoff-and-landing slots at Newark International Airport from Delta Air Lines, Inc. *See* Brent Kendall & Susan Carey, *U.S. Targets Deal over United's Hub*, WALL ST. J., Nov. 11, 2015, at B3. Several months earlier, the Department of Justice launched an investigation into alleged collusion between major airlines to keep ticket prices high. Meanwhile, as of August 2015, consumers had filed 75 lawsuits against airlines around the United States, alleging that the four major airlines conspired to hold down capacity in order to make airfares higher than they would otherwise be. *See* Terry Maxon, *Guess How Many Antitrust Lawsuits Have Been Filed against the Big 4 Airlines (No, More than That—Guess Again)*, DALLAS MORNING NEWS, Aug. 12, 2015. These cases—and collusive and predatory behavior by airlines generally—are, and have been, surprisingly difficult to prove in courts of law, as detailed in the materials below. *See generally* Chris Sagers, *"Rarely Tried, And ... Rarely Successful": Theoretically Impossible Price Predation among the Airlines*, 74 J. AIR L. & COM. 919 (2009).

PREDATION IN THE AIRLINE INDUSTRY
1997 WL 1187715

Remarks of Roger W. Fones
Chief Transportation, Energy, and Agricultural Section, Antitrust Division

Before the American Bar Association Forum on Air and Space Law

There has been in recent years a noticeable growth in the number and size of "upstart" (low cost) airlines. Southwest is the classic example, but more recent entrants such as Kiwi, Reno, Valujet and others also come readily to mind. Most upstarts have average seat mile costs in the 7 cent range, compared to the 10 cent range of traditional carriers. Upstarts maintain their low costs by a number of strategies, including lower labor costs, direct marketing and "no frills" service.

Even casual observers of the airline industry are familiar with the significant consumer benefits that can result when an upstart airline enters a market—fares drop and capacity and frequencies increase, sometimes dramatically. It is not unusual for a deep fare cut to double the demand for airline service on a city pair. This not only confirms that competition is good for consumers, but also demonstrates that actual competition enhances consumer welfare far more than the threat of potential entry. Because of its beneficial effect on competition and consumer welfare, the Antitrust Division has a strong interest in assuring that new entry is not thwarted by anticompetitive behavior by incumbent airlines.

It is not surprising that incumbent carriers respond to new entry. The combination of low fares and increased demand may prompt an Incumbent to increase its own service. If it matches the entrant's fares across the board, Incumbent may increase its capacity to handle profitable new traffic generated by the lower fares; and if Incumbent only lowers fares selectively, Upstart may grow, perhaps eventually building a competing hub and spoke network of its own. Either way, the consumer is better off. This is the essence of the competitive process.

In some cases, Upstart's lower operating costs and high load factors allow it to survive and even prosper; in other cases, too many passengers decide that the new lower fares offered by Incumbent, combined with other amenities such as better schedules, frequent flier programs, passenger lounges and in-flight service, are a better value than Upstart offers. The higher frequencies and network efficiencies of Incumbent sometimes more than counterbalance the lower operating costs of Upstart; Upstart fails to maintain profitability and must exit. After Upstart's exit, Incumbent's fares and service offerings quickly move back toward pre-entry levels, much to the chagrin of passengers.

If Upstart is forced to exit a route, it often believes that it has been the victim of "predation"—that is, Upstart suspects Incumbent lowered its fares in order to drive Upstart from the route, and then raise fares back to the previous, highly profitable level. Although an encouraging number of new low cost airlines have begun service, some have foundered or failed in the face of intense competition. It is important that the antitrust enforcement agencies and the courts correctly identify and prevent any instances where Upstart's exit or failure is the result of illegal predation.

Accordingly, the Division has over the years investigated a number of what we considered meritorious claims of possible predation. The claims of predation that we find most credible involve not only price cuts, but also significant capacity expansion by incumbents. Our starting presumption is that Incumbent's pre-entry schedules are optimal for efficiently operating its network. And if the existing network is optimal, the added cost of carrying an additional passenger on the existing network can be quite small. Thus, in the absence of additional reasons to be suspicious, we are unlikely to pursue a predation complaint where Incumbent made few or no changes to its network operations post-entry, even if it cut fares significantly.

Claims of predation are more credible when they involve not only price cuts, but also significant capacity increases or other changes in network operations by Incumbent. Entry by Incumbent into a route it was not currently serving would seldom be a normal competitive response to a rival. If the route were not profitable for Incumbent before Upstart entered, why would it be profitable afterwards? On the other hand, expansion of capacity by Incumbent on a route it already serves might be a normal response if the new entrant forced prices down enough to greatly increase demand.

Probably our best-known airline predation investigation involved Northwest's response to Reno Air's entry into the Reno-Minneapolis city-pair in 1993. Not only did Northwest institute service of its own on this route that it had previously abandoned, it also opened a new mini-hub in Reno that overlaid much of Reno Air's own operation. Our investigation was well under way when the matter was resolved because, with the intervention of the Department of Transportation, Northwest decided to abandon its overlay of Reno Air's hub operation.

The Reno Air case is perhaps an extreme example of increased capacity by an incumbent, but we have investigated a number of other possible predation situations. Let me emphasize that there is nothing inherently wrong with Incumbent responding to new entry by cutting fares or increasing service. To the contrary, lowering fares in the face of new competition is desirable, and increasing service may be an appropriate adjustment by Incumbent to the higher level of demand stimulated by the new low fares in the market. Although in such situations the route will not be as profitable as it was before there was competition, Incumbent may be able to maximize its post-entry profits by increasing service. But a capacity response to Upstart can under some circumstances cross the line between legitimate competition and unlawful predation.

Because we are committed to examine claims of predation where they appear to have potential merit, it is useful for the industry to understand how we approach the issue. In order to distinguish illegal predation from legitimate price and service competition, we focus on a handful of fundamental principles. This isn't to say that the nuts and bolts details of a predation analysis are not crucial—they are. But the first step is always to have a clear understanding of the basic principles.

Principle No. 1: It's not illegal predation unless Consumers are worse off in the long run as a result.

What consumer doesn't enjoy, even relish, a good price war? Everyone agrees that consumers benefit in the short run from predation in exactly the same way they benefit from vigorous competition. Prices are lower, service and quality are better. In the airline industry, steep fare discounts inevitably result in a traffic surge—consumers, both business and leisure passengers, take trips they otherwise would not, resulting in tangible benefits to the traveling public.

It is important to keep in mind that our concern is not with the financial health of Upstart as such, but rather with whether Upstart's survival benefits the consumer. As is often said, the antitrust laws protect competition, not competitors. So it is not without considerable care and trepidation that an antitrust enforcer contemplates a lawsuit, or even an investigation, that sends the message that prices might be too low, and service too good or plentiful. We want to be certain that consumers really would be, on balance, better off in the long run if short run prices were higher. How do we go about determining where the overall consumer welfare lies?

Principle No. 2: A pricing strategy by a suspected predator harms consumers when the strategy is rational only if the victim exits the market.

I used the word "rational" instead of "profitable" because I want to sidestep for a moment the issue of whether Incumbent's short-term pricing strategy is "below cost," and instead focus entirely on the long-term effect of the strategy on passengers. A strategy could be profitable, but still harm consumers. But to be "rational," a strategy must be more profitable than alternate strategies. If a particular strategy is more profitable than alternate (less aggressive) strategies only because it causes Upstart to exit, then the strategy harms consumers. Restated, the strategy satisfies Principle No. 2 if the predator's conduct involves a short-term sacrifice that it more than recovers (or anticipates recovering) once Upstart has exited. This is starting to sound like the "recoupment" element that a plaintiff must prove under the Supreme Court's two-part legal test for predatory pricing.

If there is no prospect of recoupment, then we can be confident that Incumbent's pricing strategy benefits consumers, not only in the short run, but in the long run as well. If, on the other hand, Incumbent charges consumers "irrationally" low prices in the short run, but can more than make up for it with higher prices in the long run, illegal predation may be occurring.

Many if not most predatory pricing cases fail on the recoupment element. Indeed, the *Brooke Group* case resulted in summary judgment for the defendants on this element. A number of commentators have suggested always looking at the recoupment issue first, and proceeding to a cost analysis only if the conduct in question satisfies the recoupment requirement. This is a sensible approach and it is the one we use.

Recoupment can come to Incumbent in different forms. The most direct recoupment comes when Incumbent raises fares and reduces capacity on a specific city-pair after Upstart has exited that city-pair. We are also mindful, however, that the "demonstration effect" of predation on one city-pair can protect or enhance Incumbent's profits on other city-pairs it serves. Thus, it is not necessary that all recoupment occur in the market where the predation occurs. Our experience in the airline industry, however, suggests that recoupment on a city-pair by Incumbent after Upstart's exit is not only possible, but in many cases quite likely. Indeed, we have seen examples where short term drops in profitability during a post-entry fare war are more than recovered within a few weeks or months following exit. But it is not enough to prove that recoupment is likely.

Principle No. 3: The incumbent's prices must be "below an appropriate measure" of its own costs.

Corollary A: An appropriate measure of costs should not establish a price umbrella for inefficient firms.

Corollary B: An appropriate measure of costs should minimize the risks of condemning legitimate competitive behavior.

Corollary C: An appropriate measure of cost should be reasonably measurable with a high degree of confidence and predictability.

One might reasonably ask, "Why does the law insist that the prices in question be below cost?" After all, the fundamental purpose of the antitrust laws is to protect consumers from the creation and exercise of market power. If we could be certain that a pricing strategy has the purpose and effect of enhancing or sustaining market power and consumers are harmed, why worry about Incumbent's costs?

There are two reasons identified by the Supreme Court: First, the "below cost" element helps assure that the law protects Upstart if it is at least as efficient as Incumbent. Although a number of commentators have correctly pointed out that even competition from inefficient firms can benefit consumers and improve overall efficiency, particularly where Incumbent is exercising considerable market power, the loss to society is greatest when firms that are more efficient than Incumbent are artificially excluded from the market. Second, the "below cost" element reduces the risk of chilling legitimate, hard-nosed competition, which often involves aggressive price-cutting. The "below cost" element acknowledges that it is difficult for courts to distinguish competition from predation, especially where the prices charged by the alleged predator are profitable, even in the short run.

While the Supreme Court has made it clear that prices are illegal only when below cost, the Court has not yet spoken on exactly what "an appropriate measure of costs" is. There are a number of alternatives that have garnered support from the lower courts and in the academic literature. Most of the alternatives exhibit some common themes, but with different advantages and disadvantages. The cost structure of the airline industry makes it one of the most interesting industries in which to address the issue.

The cost tests most widely accepted by the courts, if not by economic theoreticians, are based on price-cost calculations that can be derived from a firm's accounting records. Price-cost tests are based on the notion that firms normally do not price below their short run marginal cost because they could reduce their losses by cutting output. The most frequently cited price-cost measure is the Areeda-Turner Average Variable Cost ("AVC") test, which was first proposed in 1975 and used AVC as a more measurable surrogate for marginal cost. The major criticism of price-cost tests is that they are theoretically flawed—they do not necessarily test for long run consumer welfare (Principle 2), and thus produce both "false positives" and "false negatives." (Principle 3B). More theoretically-based approaches test better for consumer welfare by focusing on economic or opportunity costs rather than accounting data. A major criticism of economic or opportunity cost tests is practical: they are difficult to apply because they often require speculative calculations about the profitability of hypothetical alternative business strategies. (Principle 3C).

While I cannot tell you the "right" answer or predict what the Supreme Court ultimately will say, I can describe how the Antitrust Division analyzes the "below cost" issue in the airline industry. Our general approach is to identify and measure only those costs that Incumbent could have avoided had it not embarked on the pricing/capacity strategy under scrutiny. We then compare those costs to the revenue attributable to the strategy. Not surprisingly, this approach is easier to describe in general than to apply in specific situations. A number of questions have to be answered before we can proceed to the difficult process of measuring the relevant costs (and their associated revenues). For example, should costs be measured seat-by-seat, flight-by-flight, route-by-route, or with some broader grouping? What is the appropriate time period over which to measure costs and revenues? How should the costs and revenues attributable to connecting passengers be allocated to the flight segments involved?

We seldom if ever limit our analysis to the "marginal seats." There is a popular misconception that predation cannot occur in the airline industry because the avoidable cost of filling an empty seat is so low—as little as the cost of issuing the ticket and providing a bag of peanuts. If this were true, there would be little reason for us to open predation investigations. We would of course be concerned in the unlikely event that fares were below even avoidable seat costs. But we would also be concerned if the avoidable costs of any unit of output exceeded the revenues it generates. In the airline industry, capacity is readily increased and decreased by adding and subtracting flights. Therefore, we normally examine the revenue and avoidable costs of individual flights and groupings of flights on a city-pair. And as I suggested earlier, we consider responses by Incumbents that involve significant increases in capacity or changes in operations to be more suspicious, and we look first at the profitability of any flights added on a city pair in response to new entry.

We also must determine the relevant time period(s) over which to measure costs and revenues. The shorter the time period, the fewer the avoidable costs. But given enough time, most if not all costs of a flight are avoidable. For a scheduled flight leaving this afternoon, avoidable costs are very low. But given six months or a year, an entire hub could be pulled down or even closed—gates and ticket counters could be returned to airport authorities or sublet, aircraft could be redeployed or sold, and employees could be transferred or let go. The longer Incumbent anticipated its low-pricing strategy would be necessary, the more the costs of maintaining that strategy become avoidable, and the less likely it is that a consistent level of passenger revenues from that time period will cover the "appropriate measure of costs."

A key issue in any airline predation analysis is the correct treatment of aircraft costs. In the very short run, a carrier's fleet is fixed, and its costs of leasing or owning its aircraft are fixed and unavoidable. On the other hand, aircraft are not like rail lines or electric power lines—they are mobile assets that are reasonably marketable, at least up to a point. Therefore, we treat aircraft costs as avoidable within a relatively short to medium time frame. The time period can be even shorter if a carrier can profitably redeploy an aircraft from the route in question to another route. On the other hand, we do not automatically assume that Incumbent can easily abandon any city pair it served pre-entry without harming its network operations to some extent.

The reasons for including aircraft costs are easiest to demonstrate by example. Incumbent airline provides a morning and evening flight on city-pair AB, when Upstart enters with one midday flight, charging half of Incumbent's fares. Incumbent quickly matches Upstart's fares, at least for some seats, but also adds two flights that bracket Upstart's midday flight. Unlike a manufacturer operating at half capacity that can double its output without building a new plant, aircraft for Incumbent's midday flights must come from somewhere.

If Incumbent had quickly arranged a short-term lease from another carrier to initiate the mid-day flights, it would be easy to see why the lease costs are avoidable costs of the strategy Incumbent is pursuing. It is less obvious, but no less valid, when Incumbent simply redeploys two of its own airplanes from other routes it serves—in essence leasing the aircraft from itself. In either case, Incumbent is incurring avoidable aircraft costs to pursue its responsive strategy to Upstart.

When measuring aircraft costs, we must decide whether to use actual historical costs or some other measure. The answer is again dictated by examining what aircraft costs are avoidable, and over what time period. At a minimum, Incumbent has avoidable aircraft costs to the extent it could sublease the planes to others. Thus, as a first approximation, we include the fair market lease value as an avoidable cost.

We might also adjust avoidable costs upward if there is a clear basis for doing so. One reason we might do this is because the asset has a specific opportunity cost to Incumbent in excess of the market value of the asset itself. For example, assume Incumbent leases an aircraft for $200,000 per month, and is flying it on city pair XY where its profits are $20,000 per month. After Upstart enters city-pair AB, Incumbent shifts the plane to city pair AB in competition with Upstart, where the plane incurs losses of $5,000 per month (with lease costs taken into account). Should the $20,000 in foregone monthly profits of operating the aircraft on city pair XY be included in the costs of operating on city pair AB? Professors Areeda and Hovenkamp have argued that the answer is "yes," although some court decisions can be read to suggest the answer is "no."

Another issue we face is whether to look at the costs of Incumbent's two midday flights separately, or together with the morning and evening flights. What if the four flights taken together are covering costs, but one or both midday flights are not? While we are very cautious in drawing legal inferences from individual flights, it is also relevant that the money-losing flight(s) were not operating in the market until after Upstart had entered. That the flights were added suggests both that many of the costs of adding them were avoidable, and that there was no pre-existing business justification to operate below cost flights, such as repositioning or promotional purposes.

Finally, we must decide how to account for the costs and revenues attributable to connecting passengers on a flight. Like many multi-product firms, airlines incur a significant number of joint costs that must be properly allocated. Returning to our example, if Incumbent has a hub at City B, its flights between A and B carry not only local passengers in competition with Upstart, but also carry connecting passengers in city pairs AC, AD and AE where Upstart has no service. Suppose on average, half of the passengers on Incumbent's AB flights are local, and half are connecting to other flights. Incumbent cannot cancel all of its flights on city-pair AB without also exiting from city-pairs AC, AD and AE. Any allocation of joint costs, such as aircraft operating costs or overhead, to local AB traffic rather than AC, AD and AE traffic will be arbitrary. Consequently, we compare all revenue (local and attributable connecting) with all avoidable costs of the flight. Because there is a mix of local and connecting revenue on most flights, a strategy that harms consumers in the local market may not require pricing below cost for the flight as a whole. Pricing below cost for the flight as a whole is more likely where Incumbent increases its capacity in response to Upstart's entry on AB. The new flights may not conveniently meet Incumbent's connecting banks at B, causing a large proportion of the passengers on the new flights to be local. Moreover, the low fares stimulate traffic on city pair AB, but not on other city pairs where Upstart does not serve. So there may be relatively fewer connecting passengers on the incremental flights. If so, there is an increased likelihood that Incumbent is failing to cover "an appropriate measure of costs" for the added flights, even where connecting passenger revenues are added in.

In closing, I want to emphasize two thoughts. First, our experience has led us to conclude that the structure of the airline industry is conducive to successful predation strategies, so we will remain alert to the possibility and investigate suspicious conduct. Second, we are most likely to investigate conduct that includes significant capacity increases by an incumbent. If Upstart complains only that Incumbent has cut its fares so much that they must be below cost, we will be skeptical that predation is occurring. On the other hand, if Incumbent is contemplating a competitive response that includes shifting significant capacity to a route Upstart entered, Incumbent should review its strategy carefully to be certain it is within legal bounds.

UNITED STATES v. AMR CORP.

335 F.3d 1109 (10th Cir. 2003)

LUCERO, Circuit Judge.

This case involves the nature of permissible competitive practices in the airline industry under the antitrust laws of this country, centered around the hub-and-spoke system of American Airlines. The United States brought this suit against AMR Corporation, American Airlines, Inc., and American Eagle Holding Corporation ("American"), alleging monopolization and attempted monopolization through predatory pricing in violation of § 2 of the Sherman Act.

In essence, the government alleges that American engaged in multiple episodes of price predation in four city-pair airline markets, all connected to American's hub at Dallas/Fort Worth International Airport ("DFW"), with the ultimate purpose of using the reputation for predatory pricing it earned in those four markets to defend a monopoly at its DFW hub. The four "core" routes are: DFW-Kansas City, DFW-Wichita; DFW-Colorado Springs; and DFW-Long Beach.

At its root, the government's complaint alleges that American: (1) priced its product on the routes in question below cost; and (2) intended to recoup these losses by charging supracompetitive prices either on the four core routes themselves, or on those routes where it stands to exclude competition by means of its "reputation for predation." Finding that the government failed to demonstrate the existence of a genuine issue of material fact as to either of these allegations, the district court granted summary judgment in favor of American, from which the government now appeals.

I.

Airlines are predominantly organized in a hub-and-spoke system, with traffic routed such that passengers leave their origin city for an intermediate hub airport. Passengers traveling to a concentrated hub tend to pay higher average fares than those traveling on comparable routes that do not include a concentrated hub as an endpoint. This is known as the "hub premium" and a major airline's hub is often an important profit center. Entry of low cost carriers ("LCCs") into a hub market tends to drive down the fares charged by major carriers. Consequently, major carriers generally enjoy higher margins on routes where they do not face LCC competition.

Both American and Delta Airlines ("Delta") maintain hubs at DFW, though Delta's presence is considerably smaller than American's. As of May 2000, American's share of passengers boarded at DFW was 70.2%, Delta's share was roughly 18%, and LCC share was 2.4%. As of mid-2000, there were seven low-cost airlines serving DFW. In the period between 1997 to 2000, five new low-cost airlines entered DFW: American Trans Air, Frontier, National, Sun Country, and Ozark. DFW has more low-fare airlines than any other hub airport and the number of passengers carried by low-fare airlines increased by over 30% from May 1999 to May 2000.

Nevertheless, LCCs have a significantly higher market share in some other major U.S. hubs. The district court noted that in the third quarter of 2000:

- New York, including LaGuardia, JFK, and Newark, was served by nine LCCs with a 9.7% market share.
- Chicago, including Chicago O'Hare and Midway, was served by six LCCs and Southwest, for a total market share of 12.3%.
- Denver had an LCC market share of 15.3%. Atlanta had an LCC market share of 16.8%.

LCCs generally enjoy the advantage of having lower costs than major carriers, allowing them to offer lower fares than their major-airline competitors. For example, in 1994, American calculated ValuJet's stage-length adjusted cost per available seat mile to be 4.32 cents, and American's to be 8.54 cents. Southwest has costs that are 30% lower than American's. During the period between 1995 and 1997, a number of LCCs, including Vanguard, Western Pacific, and Sunjet, began to take advantage of these lower costs by entering certain city-pair routes serving DFW and charging lower fares than American. The instant case primarily involves DFW-Kansas City, DFW-Wichita, DFW-Colorado Springs, and DFW-Long Beach.

American responded to lower LCC fares on these routes with changes in: (1) pricing (matching LCC prices); (2) capacity (adding flights or switching to larger planes); and (3) yield management (making more seats available at the new, lower prices). By increasing capacity, American overrode its own internal capacity-planning models for each route, which had previously indicated that such increases would be unprofitable. In each instance, American's response produced the same result: the competing LCC failed to establish a presence, moved its operations, or ceased its separate existence entirely.

Once the LCC ceased or moved its operations, American generally resumed its prior marketing strategy, reducing flights and raising prices to levels roughly comparable to those prior to the period of low-fare competition. Capacity was reduced after LCC exit, but usually remained higher than prior to the alleged episode of predatory activity.

This pattern is illustrated by the average fares and passengers on the DFW-Wichita route before, during, and after one of the alleged episodes of predation:

Pre-"Predation" 6/94 – 5/95	*"Predatory" Period* 10/96 - 12/96	*Post-"Predation"* 7/97 - 6/98	*Post-"Predation"* 7/98 - 6/99
Average Fare $99-108	$58 - 61	$88 - 102	$100 - 123
Avg. Passengers/Month 3,932-5,557	10,076 - 11,041	7,019 - 8,373	5,744 - 8,257
Avg. Seats/Month 21,314-32,109	44,798 - 47,588	29,939 - 33,790	25,891 - 33,790

The government filed suit on May 13, 1999, alleging that American participated in a scheme of predatory pricing in violation of § 2 of the Sherman Act. In the government's view, American's combined response of lowering prices, increasing capacity, and altering yield management in response to LCC competition constituted an unlawful, anticompetitive response. After reviewing a voluminous record and receiving extensive briefs the district court granted American's motion for summary judgment on all antitrust claims, concluding that the government failed to demonstrate the existence of a genuine issue of material fact as to (1) whether American had priced below cost and (2) whether American had a dangerous probability of recouping its alleged investment in below-cost prices.

II.

Monopolization claims under § 2 of the Sherman Act require proof: (1) that a firm has monopoly power in a properly defined relevant market; and (2) that it willfully acquired or maintained this power by means of anticompetitive conduct. This is to be distinguished from a business that acquired monopoly power by greater skill, efficiency, or by "building a better mousetrap." Claims of attempted monopolization under § 2 of the Sherman Act require four elements of proof: (1) a relevant geographic and product market; (2) specific intent to monopolize the market; (3) anticompetitive conduct in furtherance of the attempt; and (4) a dangerous probability that the firm will succeed in the attempt.

In the instant case, the anticompetitive conduct at issue is predatory pricing. The crux of the government's argument is that the "incremental" revenues and costs specifically associated with American's capacity additions show a loss. Because American spent more to add capacity than the revenues generated by the capacity additions, such capacity additions made no economic sense unless American intended to drive LCCs out of the market. Under the government's theory, American attempted to monopolize the four city-pair routes in question in order to develop a reputation as an exceedingly aggressive competitor and set an example to all potential competitors. Fearing American's predatory response, the theory goes, future potential competitors will decline to enter other DFW market routes and compete. If American succeeds in preventing or at least forestalling the formation of an LCC hub at DFW, it will then be able to charge higher prices on other DFW routes and thereby recoup the losses it incurred from its "capacity dumping" on the four core routes.

III.

Scholars from the Chicago School of economic thought have long labeled predatory pricing as implausible and irrational. Frank Easterbrook, a leader of the Chicago School, once concluded "there is no sufficient reason for antitrust law or the courts to take predation seriously." Frank H. Easterbrook, *Predatory Strategies & Counterstrategies*, 48 U. CHI. L. REV. 263, 264 (1981). Chicago scholars argued that lowering prices could only be pro-competitive and any prohibition on such conduct could ultimately deter firms from engaging in conduct that is socially beneficial. Commentators viewed below-cost pricing as irrational largely because of the uncertainty of recouping losses through later price increases. In order for a predatory pricing scheme to be successful, two future events had to take place: first, the victim of the alleged predation would have to exit and second, the predator would have to generate profits in excess of its initial losses.

In two seminal antitrust opinions, the Supreme Court adopted the skepticism of Chicago scholars, observing, "there is a consensus among commentators that predatory pricing schemes are rarely tried, and even more rarely successful." *Matsushita Elec. Indus. Co. v. Zenith Radio Corp.* (1986); *Brooke Group Ltd. v. Brown & Williamson Tobacco Corp.* (1993). Implausibility of predatory pricing schemes was said to flow from the fact that their success is inherently uncertain. While "the short-run loss is definite ... the long-run gain depends on successfully neutralizing the competition." Moreover, "[t]he success of any predatory scheme depends on maintaining monopoly power for long enough both to recoup the predator's losses and to harvest some additional gain." Furthermore, caution in predatory pricing cases is the watchword as "the costs of an erroneous finding are high."

Recent scholarship has challenged the notion that predatory pricing schemes are implausible and irrational. *See, e.g.*, Patrick Bolton et al., *Predatory Pricing: Strategic Theory and Legal Policy*, 88 GEO. L.J. 2239, 2241 (2000). Post-Chicago economists have theorized that price predation is not only plausible, but profitable, especially in a multi-market context where predation can occur in one market and recoupment can occur rapidly in other markets. Although this court approaches the matter with caution, we do not do so with the incredulity that once prevailed.

IV.

The Supreme Court has formulated two prerequisites to recovery on a predatory pricing claim, conditions that "are not easy to establish." First, the government must prove that "the prices complained of are below an appropriate measure of [American's] costs." While the first element is crucial, "[t]hat below-cost pricing may impose painful losses on its target is of no moment to the antitrust laws if competition is not injured." Thus, the second prerequisite to recovery on a predatory pricing claim, a demonstration that American had "a dangerous probability of recouping its investment in below-cost prices," must also be met. Without a dangerous probability of recoupment, competition remains unharmed even if individual competitors suffer. As frequently noted, "the antitrust laws were passed for the protection of competition, not competitors."

Speaking to the first prerequisite to recovery, the Supreme Court stated that "[p]redatory pricing means pricing below some appropriate measure of cost." The government notes in its brief that the "gravamen of the complaint is not limited to American's pricing." Rather, the complained of behavior includes American's capacity additions. However, as the district court correctly noted, prices and productive output are "two sides of the same coin." While the specific behavior complained of in the instant case is an increase in output or frequency, these actions must be analyzed in terms of their effect on price and cost. Thus, in order to succeed in the present action, the government must meet the standards of proof for predatory pricing cases established in *Brooke Group*.

Despite a great deal of debate on the subject, no consensus has emerged as to what the most "appropriate" measure of cost is in predatory pricing cases. Costs can generally be divided into those that are "fixed" and do not vary with the level of output (management expenses, interest on bonded debt, property taxes, depreciation, and other irreducible overhead) and those that are "variable" and do vary with the level of output (materials, fuel, labor used to produce the product). Marginal cost, the cost that results from producing an additional increment of output, is primarily a function of variable cost because fixed costs, as the name would imply, are largely unaffected by changes in output.

For predatory pricing cases, especially those involving allegedly predatory production increases, the ideal measure of cost would be marginal cost because "[a]s long as a firm's prices exceed its marginal cost, each additional sale decreases losses or increases profits." However, marginal cost, an economic abstraction, is notoriously difficult to measure and "cannot be determined from conventional accounting methods."

Economists, therefore, must resort to proxies for marginal cost. A commonly accepted proxy for marginal cost in predatory pricing cases is Average Variable Cost ("AVC"), the average of those costs that vary with the level of output. In a seminal law review article, Professors Areeda and Turner argue that pricing below a firm's short-run marginal cost should be deemed unlawful, and that prices above that level should be deemed lawful. While they acknowledge that there may be situations where AVC will differ from marginal cost, they nevertheless advocate the use of AVC as a proxy in predatory pricing cases. Philip E. Areeda & Donald F. Turner, *Predatory Pricing and Related Practices under Section 2 of The Sherman Act*, 88 HARV. L. REV. 697, 718 (1975).

The Supreme Court has declined to state which of the various cost measures is definitive. Because there may be times when courts need the flexibility to examine both AVC as well as other proxies for marginal cost in order to evaluate an alleged predatory pricing scheme, we again decline to dictate a definitive cost measure for all cases. Sole reliance on AVC as the appropriate measure of cost may obscure the nature of a particular predatory scheme and, thus, contrary to what is suggested by the district court, we do not favor AVC to the exclusion of other proxies for marginal cost. Whatever the proxy used to measure marginal cost, it must be accurate and reliable in the specific circumstances of the case at bar.

Conceding that AVC is a good proxy for marginal cost in most cases, the government nevertheless argues that there may be times when looking only to a market-wide AVC test will disguise the nature of the predatory conduct at issue. Where there is a challenge to well-defined incremental conduct, and where incremental costs may be directly and confidently measured utilizing alternative proxies to AVC, argues the government, the market-wide AVC test is inappropriate. Considering this to be the situation in the instant case, the government proffers four tests that purport to measure reliably incremental costs—the precise costs associated with the capacity additions at issue.

Rather than creating independent measures of the costs associated with American's capacity additions, the government's experts rely on cost measures used in AAIMSPAN, American's internal decisional-accounting system (accounting measures that are used for internal decision making, not financial reporting). The government notes that a range of tests is necessary to rule out false positives and assure confidence in the results. Thus, the tests operate as crosschecks to each other to avoid misleading indications of predation. (Not all of the government's tests are applicable to all of the routes. For example, Test Four cannot be applied to DFW-Long Beach.) Due to similarities among the four tests, the district court grouped them as Tests Two and Three, and Tests One and Four for purposes of analysis. We proceed to consider each test to determine whether it is valid as a matter of law.

Two of the tests grouped together by the district court, Tests Two and Three, purport to measure incremental cost by looking to whether certain of American's internal cost-accounting measures became negative following the allegedly predatory capacity additions. Both tests rely on an internal accounting measure known as FAUDNC, or "Fully Allocated earnings plus Upline/Downline contribution Net of Costs." As the name would imply, FAUDNC is a fully allocated earnings measure, meaning that general operating expenses are arbitrarily allocated by American's decision accounting system to the flight or route level, and do not necessarily represent the exact costs associated with a particular flight or route. FAUDNC reflects 97-99% of American's total costs, which include fixed costs not affected by the capacity additions at issue. Thus, while FAUDNC includes some costs directly caused by a particular flight or operations on a particular route (such as fuel and landing fees), it also includes many costs that are not related to the operation of a particular flight or route (dispatch, city ticket offices, certain station expenses, certain maintenance expenses, American's flight academy, flight simulator maintenance, general sales and advertising). In other words, FAUDNC includes costs that are not entirely avoidable even if American were to abandon an entire route.

Because Tests Two and Three rely on fully allocated costs and include many fixed costs, the district court held that utilizing these cost measures would be the equivalent of applying an average total cost test, implicitly ruled out by *Brooke Group's* mention of incremental costs only. The district court therefore concluded that, by relying on FAUDNC, Tests Two and Three were, by definition, not measures of marginal or incremental cost. We agree with this conclusion.

While we will accept alternative proxies to marginal cost beyond AVC, Tests Two and Three are simply not proxies for marginal or incremental cost. Moreover, because these tests rely on "arbitrary allocation of costs among different classes of service," they "cannot purport to identify those costs which are caused by a product or service, and this is fundamental to economic cost determination." Thus, given that Tests Two and Three rely on cost measures that are not, in large part, variable or avoidable with respect to capacity increases, we conclude that they are invalid as a matter of law as a measure of allegedly predatory capacity increases.

In holding that Tests Two and Three are invalid as a matter of law, we consider the uncontested fact that these tests, by relying on FAUDNC, measure a significant amount of American's fixed costs. As such, Tests Two and Three are inappropriate measures of incremental costs under *Brooke Group*, as they cannot demonstrate that American priced below an "appropriate measure of cost" with respect to the challenged capacity additions.

As to Tests One and Four, the district court grouped them together, labeling them as short-run profit-maximization tests. Test One examines changes in profitability. It employs FAUDNC, discussed above, and an internal measure of American's variable costs known as VAUDNC ["Variable earnings plus Upline/Downline contribution Net of

Costs"] as well as a version of VAUDNC that has been modified by the government, VAUDNC-AC. Unlike the other costs measures, which are taken straight out of American's internal accounting system, VAUDNC-AC is a government creation. It represents VAUDNC costs plus the cost of aircraft ownership, which is traditionally considered a fixed cost in the airline industry, not an avoidable cost of changes in capacity on a route. By treating aircraft ownership as a variable expense, this measure reduces the apparent performance of the routes by increasing the costs attributed to operations on a particular flight or route. VAUDNC-AC represents over 79% of the total costs in American's decision accounting system. The district court concluded that VAUDNC-AC overstates short-run cost because it includes fixed, unavoidable aircraft-ownership costs.

If these measures declined following a capacity addition, this test allegedly demonstrates that adding capacity forced American to forgo better profit performance elsewhere. Test Four relies on VAUDNC-AC to compare the supposed revenue from incremental passengers with the average avoidable cost of adding capacity. Under Test Four, if incremental revenues are below incremental costs, this is "evidence of sacrifice."

In rejecting tests One and Four, the district court concluded that they were, in essence, short-run profit-maximization tests that focus on whether a company has sacrificed some level of profit to compete more effectively. Courts and scholars have observed that such a sacrifice test would necessarily involve a great deal of speculation and often result in injury to the consumer and a chilling of competition. *See* 3 PHILLIP E. ARREDA & HERBERT HOVENKAMP. ANTITURST LAW ¶ 736c2 (2d ed. 2002). Upon closer examination, it is clear that rather than determining whether the added capacity itself was priced below an appropriate measure of cost, Test One effectively treats forgone or "sacrificed" profits as costs, and condemns activity that may have been profitable as predatory.

For example, if an airline earned $20.6 million on a route that cost $18 million to operate, it would have $2.6 million in profit. If the airline then added a flight to the route that would cost $500,000 to operate, but brought in an additional $1 million in revenue from passengers, the airline would make $500,000 profit. If adding this extra capacity to the route reduced the profitability of other flights on that route, reducing revenue for the rest of the route by $600,000 down to $20 million, under Test One, this conduct would be considered predatory because rather than comparing the additional flight's $1 million in revenue to its $500,000 in costs, Test One looks only to the reduction in profits on the route as a whole from $2.6 million to $2.5 million. Thus, this conduct would be labeled predatory because the profits for the route as a whole declined, even though the capacity additions themselves were profitable and the route as a whole was still profitable. It is clear, therefore, that, in proffering Test One, the government has not "attempted to identify the actual costs associated with the capacity additions."

Rather than isolating the costs actually associated with the capacity additions the government purports to measure directly, Test One simply performs a "before-and-after" comparison of the route as a whole, looking to whether profits on the route as a whole decline after capacity was added, not to whether the challenged capacity additions were done below cost. In the end, Test One indicates only that a company has failed to maximize short-run profits on the route as a whole. Such a pricing standard could lead to a strangling of competition, as it would condemn nearly all output expansions, and harm to consumers. We conclude that Test One is invalid as a matter of law.

Test Four does not appear to suffer from this flaw, and we do not reject it for being a short-run profit-maximization test. As with Test One, the district court noted that, in proffering Test Four, the government has not "identif[ied] the actual costs associated with the capacity additions." We agree with this conclusion as well.

Test Four attempts to reveal American's predatory conduct by measuring and comparing the incremental costs incurred by American when it added capacity to the city-pair routes in question to the incremental revenue it received from the additional capacity. The government's expert who developed Test Four, Steven Berry, characterized it as a comparison of the "average revenue from incremental passengers who traveled after the capacity addition with the average avoidable cost of the capacity addition." Berry further stated that, when considering an increase in capacity, an avoidable cost test compares, "the incremental revenue generated by the increment of capacity to the avoidable cost of the increment of capacity." Therefore, the only appropriate costs included in Test Four are those costs that American could have avoided by not adding the challenged capacity to the city-pair routes.

Test Four utilizes VAUDNC-AC, the cost component of which includes both aircraft ownership costs and costs characterized as variable over an eighteen-month planning period by AAIMSPAN. The costs included in VAUDNC-AC include variable costs American incurs with respect to all of its operations at DFW. Because some of those variable costs do not vary proportionately with the level of flight activity, they are allocated arbitrarily to a flight or route by AAIMSPAN. American identifies these variable, non-proportional common costs as: (1) airport ticket agents, (2) arrival agents, (3) ramp workers, and (4) security. Therefore, American argues that because VAUDNC-AC is an allocated variable cost measure, it cannot be used to calculate the avoidable cost of the added capacity.

The government first responds to American's criticism by arguing that cost allocation is a key component of managerial accounting and a relevant and sensible method by which to assign costs for decision-making purposes. While the government may be correct, this court is not presented with the question of whether cost allocation is a reasonable accounting method or a technique that provides businesses with reliable data to evaluate business decisions. Because the government asserts that Test Four measures average avoidable cost, this court must instead determine whether that assertion is correct. Thus, the government's first response is wholly irrelevant.

The government also alleges that there exists a genuine issue of material fact because its expert reworked Test Four so as to omit the contested costs and the results still indicated predation. The government's expert, however, states that when he reworked the numbers in response to criticism from American's expert, he eliminated the following costs from the test: (1) CTO ticketing, (2) direct reservations, (3) reservation communications, (4) cargo reservations, (5) and dispatch. Although the propriety of including these costs in Test Four was also disputed by American, they are not the costs that American disputed on the grounds that they are allocated arbitrarily to a route or flight by AAIMSPAN. Consequently, the expert's revisions to Test Four are not responsive to American's criticism and no genuine issue of material fact exists.

Because the cost component of Test Four includes arbitrarily allocated variable costs, it does not compare incremental revenue to average avoidable cost. Instead, it compares incremental revenue to a measure of both average variable cost and average avoidable cost. Therefore, Test Four does not measure only the avoidable or incremental cost of the capacity additions and cannot be used to satisfy the government's burden in this case.

We conclude that all four proxies are invalid as a matter of law, fatally flawed in their application, and fundamentally unreliable. Because it is uncontested that American did not price below AVC for any route as a whole, we agree with the district court's conclusion that the government has not succeeded in establishing the first element of *Brooke Group*, pricing below an appropriate measure of cost. Our conclusion that the government has not succeeded in establishing a genuine issue of material fact as to the first prong of *Brooke Group*, pricing below an appropriate measure of cost, renders an examination of whether the government has succeeded in creating a genuine issue of material fact as to the second prong of *Brooke Group*, dangerous probability of recoupment, unnecessary. Given the exceedingly thin line between vigorous price competition and predatory pricing, the balance the Supreme Court has struck in *Brooke Group*, and the fatally flawed nature of the alternative pricing proxies proffered by the government, we conclude that summary judgment in favor of American was appropriate.

SPIRIT AIRLINES, INC. v. NORTHWEST AIRLINES, INC.

431 F.3d 917 (6th Cir. 2004)

HAYNES, District Judge.

Plaintiff Spirit Airlines, Inc. appeals from the district court's final order granting summary judgment to the Defendant Northwest Airlines, Inc. on Plaintiff's claims of monopolization and attempted monopolization under Section 2 of the Sherman Antitrust

Act, 15 U.S.C. § 2. Spirit alleged that Northwest engaged in predatory pricing and other predatory tactics in the leisure passenger airline markets for the Detroit-Boston and Detroit-Philadelphia routes. In sum, the district court found that Spirit's proof had not established predatory pricing by Northwest in these markets. Specifically, the district court rejected Spirit's definition of the relevant market as limited to low fare or leisure passengers and adopted Northwest's market definition of all passengers on these routes. With this conclusion, the district court found that Northwest's total revenues exceeded its total costs for these routes. Moreover, the district court opined that even if the low fare or leisure passenger market were the appropriate market, Northwest's expert proof demonstrated that Northwest's total revenues still exceeded its relevant costs. The district court deemed Spirit's expert proof and analysis of Northwest's costs and revenue to be implausible. Given these conclusions, the district court deemed it unnecessary to decide Spirit's other predatory practices claims.

From our review of the record, when the evidence is considered in a light most favorable to Spirit, as is required in this context, we conclude that a reasonable trier of fact could find that a separate and distinct low-fare or leisure-passenger market existed. The evidence presented by Spirit in support of such a market includes Northwest's own marketing data, the testimony of its marketing officials, the findings of government regulators and Spirit's experts. Moreover, based on the evidence presented, a reasonable trier of fact could find that at the time of predation, the market in the two relevant geographic routes was highly concentrated, Northwest possessed overwhelming market share, and the barriers to entry were high. Accordingly, a reasonable trier of fact could conclude that Northwest engaged in predatory pricing in the leisure passenger markets on these two geographic routes in order to force Spirit out of the business. Finally, based on the evidence presented by Spirit's experts, a reasonable trier of fact could find that once Spirit exited the market, Northwest raised its prices to recoup the losses it incurred during the predation period. Accordingly, we reverse the grant of summary judgment in favor of Northwest and remand the case to the district court for further proceedings consistent with this opinion.

A. FACTUAL BACKGROUND

1. The Parties

Spirit obtained its certificate for a scheduled passenger service in Michigan in 1990 as Charter One. In 1992, Charter One changed its name to Spirit, a low fare carrier with its base of operations in Detroit. In 1992, Spirit had four airplanes servicing four cities with 140,931 passengers, approximately 125 employees and annual revenues of approximately $60 million. Spirit's primary routes were point-to-point flights between Detroit-Atlantic City and, for a time, Detroit-Boston. By the end of 1993, Spirit had added service to cities in Florida and in 1995, Spirit expanded to other cities. Spirit targeted local leisure or price-sensitive passengers whose travel is generally discretionary, such as passengers visiting friends and relatives, and tourists or vacationers who might not otherwise fly. Spirit's pricing strategy provided a price incentive to such leisure travelers with unrestricted, but non-refundable fares. Spirit's services lacked first class service, frequent flyer benefits, and connecting service. Leisure or low price-sensitive passengers purchase tickets with restrictions on their use, *e.g.*, an advance purchase or stay-over requirement, in exchange for low prices for a particular route.

In 1992, Spirit approached the Detroit Metropolitan airport's management about access to additional ticket counters and gates. Because "Northwest had a stranglehold on the gates at Detroit Metro," Spirit's efforts "were futile." Northwest controlled the majority of the gates at the Detroit airport either by lease or secondary rights from other airlines. Spirit cited an internal Northwest memorandum advocating that when Detroit built its new airport, the existing Detroit concourses should be destroyed, so that other carriers would not "benefit from the vacuum which is created once [Northwest] vacates its existing gates" at the old Detroit airport.

Spirit was allowed to use gates formerly used by Trump Shuttle and Charter, but could not secure a permanent gate arrangement. Spirit was unsuccessful in its negotiations with U.S. Airways to use two gates that Northwest subsequently acquired. The district court found that Spirit did secure short-term leases from United Airlines and Continental Airlines, but that Spirit expended $100,000 to add its Detroit-Philadelphia flight. Spirit also paid a 25% higher landing fee than airlines that had leases with the Detroit airport authority.

In 1995, Spirit explored expansion of its service between Detroit and other cities, including Boston and Philadelphia. Mark Kahan, Spirit's general counsel, explained that these two major cities have business and leisure travelers. With this model, Spirit expected to attract primarily the price conscious or leisure traveler. Spirit's management considered the Detroit-Philadelphia route a particularly attractive market given its other flights from the Philadelphia airport and the route's potential base of price-sensitive and leisure travelers.

On December 15, 1995, Spirit commenced a single daily non-stop round trip flight between Detroit-Philadelphia on an 87-seat DC-9 airplane at a $49 fare with a load factor of 74.3 percent. Spirit soon experienced a higher load factor on the Detroit-Philadelphia route in June, 1996, rising to 88.5 percent from 64.1 percent in January, 1996. On June 28, 1996, Spirit added a second non-stop round trip flight for the Detroit-Philadelphia route. On April 15, 1996, Spirit started its Detroit-Boston route with one daily non-stop round trip, initially at fares of $69, $89 and $109.

By 1995, Spirit operated 10 aircraft and serviced 13 travel routes carrying 583,969 passengers and employing approximately 450 people. By 1996, Spirit increased its capacity to 11 aircraft, with 15 routes. In June 1996, Spirit had 71,364,828 seat miles with annual revenues of $62.9 million and approximately 455 employees.

Northwest was founded in 1926 as an air mail carrier for the Minneapolis to Chicago route. The firm's operations at Minneapolis grew and Northwest developed a hub there. By 1986, Northwest merged with Republic Airlines, which had hubs at Detroit and Memphis. In 1995, Northwest was the fourth largest air passenger carrier in the United States with annual revenues of $9.1 billion from its domestic and international operations. At the Detroit Metro airport, Northwest "controlled" 64 of the airport's 86 gates and had 78 percent of all passenger travel from the Detroit-Metro airport.

Northwest operates a hub-and-spoke network with hubs at Detroit, Minneapolis-St. Paul and Memphis. In the hub system, the hub serves as the connecting point for flights between other cities that serve as the "spokes." In a word, in this system passengers do not begin or end their journey on a single flight. The initial flight is from a spoke airport to the hub and after deplaning, the passenger boards a second flight to the passenger's ultimate destination, another spoke airport. Northwest offers restricted and unrestricted tickets, airport clubs, frequent flyer benefits, advanced seat selection, first and other classes of service, and on-board meals. Northwest utilizes the yield management policy, which, in essence, seeks "to maximize the revenue that we earn for our domestic network ... and ... try to sell every seat at its highest possible fare."

Prior to Spirit's entry, Northwest offered non-stop service on the Detroit-Boston and Detroit-Philadelphia routes. For the Detroit-Philadelphia route, Northwest had a 72% market share. For the Detroit-Boston route, Northwest had an 89% market share. Northwest's only competitor for the service to Philadelphia was U.S. Airways, which was the highest cost service provider in the market, and Spirit's expert characterized U.S. Airways as a "compliant" competitor of Northwest. Northwest had six daily non-stop round trip flights on the Detroit-Philadelphia route and U.S. Airways had four.

2. Northwest Response to Spirit's Entry

Northwest adopted its "New Competitive Equilibrium Analysis" for its response to any new competitor on its routes. In step one of this analysis, Northwest considers the impact of the new entrant's service on Northwest's revenue. In step two, Northwest studies whether to add capacity on the route. Northwest executive Paul Dailey admits that this analysis is more "art" than "science."

At the time of Spirit's entry, Northwest's lowest unrestricted fare for Detroit-Philadelphia flight was $355 and its lowest restricted fare was $125 each way. U.S. Airways' fares were comparable to Northwest's fares. Initially, neither Northwest nor U.S. Airways reduced its fares nor added capacity after Spirit's entry into the Detroit-Philadelphia route, until Spirit achieved high load factors, *e.g.*, as high as 88% in April 1996. Before Spirit's entry into the Detroit-Boston route, Northwest provided non-stop air passenger service on the Detroit-Boston route with 8.5 daily round trips; its lowest unrestricted fare was $411, and its lowest restricted fare was $189 each way. Prior to

Spirit's entry, Northwest intended to reduce its capacity for the Detroit-Boston route in the summer of 1996 by 13.7% to 3,238 seats from 3,753 seats.

Effective April 15, 1996, Northwest dramatically reduced its fare on the Detroit-Boston route to $69, offering this lowest fare on all of its flights. Northwest also increased its daily non-stop round trip flights on the Detroit-Boston route to 10.5. Northwest added a 289-seat DC-10 airplane that had three times Spirit's entire daily capacity on the Detroit-Boston route.

Prior to Spirit's entry into the market, Northwest's fare had been in excess of $300. On the Detroit-Boston route, 74.5% of Northwest's passengers flew on fares at or below $69. For this route, Northwest passenger fares were less than Spirit's lowest fare on 93.9% of the days during which Spirit flew this route. In July 1996, 74% of Northwest's passengers on the Detroit-Boston route flew on fares at or below $69, but that percentage fell in September 1996 to 67%. Spirit's monthly average load factors on the Detroit-Boston route during Northwest's price response were 18% (April 1996), 21% (May), 24% (June), 31% (July), 29% (August), 17% (September). Spirit never flew more than 1,700 passengers per month, while Northwest averaged well over 30,000 passengers per month during the same period.

On June 19, 1996, Northwest reduced its lowest fares (including unrestricted) to $49 on all Northwest flights on the Detroit-Philadelphia route. By August 20, 1996, Spirit discontinued its second flight on the Detroit-Philadelphia route. On September 30, 1996, Spirit abandoned its Detroit-Philadelphia route. Northwest resumed its status as the only provider of non-stop service on the route. After Spirit's exit on this route, Northwest increased its fare initially to $271 and later to $461 as its lowest unrestricted fare. From July to September 1996, 40.5% of Northwest's passengers flew on fares at or below $49. By September 1996, 70% of Northwest's passengers flew on fares above $49 on the Detroit-Philadelphia route and equal to or below $69. In sum, Northwest transported passengers at fares less than Spirit's lowest fare for 92.5% of the days during the predation period.

Spirit's monthly load factors on the Detroit-Philadelphia route were 43% (July 1996), 36% (Aug.), 31% (Sept.). As a result, Spirit abandoned its Detroit-Philadelphia route on September 29, 1996. On October 28, 1996, Northwest increased its lowest unrestricted fare on the Detroit-Philadelphia route to $279 and by April 20, 1998, increased that fare to $416.

B. PROCEDURAL HISTORY

Spirit filed its Section 2 claims against Northwest for anti-competitive and exclusionary practices, including, but not limited to, predatory pricing. Spirit's complaint alleged, in pertinent part:

> As part of its unlawful scheme, Northwest hampered Spirit's ability to compete at Detroit by denying Spirit access to unused gates controlled by Northwest and/or charging Spirit unreasonable and discriminatory prices to use those gates, and upon information and belief, threatening to eliminate or eliminating discounts, promotions or other benefits to companies in the greater Detroit metropolitan area if those companies designated a carrier other than Northwest for service to or from Detroit. The combination of very low prices and very high capacity on the Detroit-Boston route caused Northwest's revenues on that city pair to go into a free fall.
>
> At that time, Northwest dramatically lowered its fares, matching Spirit's $49 one-way fare, and increased capacity on the city pair. Northwest's one-two punch against Spirit in the Detroit-Boston and Detroit-Philadelphia markets produced the result Northwest intended when, by that start of the fourth quarter of 1996, Spirit was forced to abandon service in both city pairs.

Upon completion of discovery, Northwest moved for summary judgment, contending, in sum, that the evidence showed: (1) that the relevant service or product market included local and connecting passengers through the Detroit airport on the Detroit-Boston and Detroit-Philadelphia routes; (2) that at all relevant times, Northwest's revenues exceeded its average variable costs on these routes; (3) that even if Spirit's proposed market of price-sensitive or leisure travelers market were appropriate, Northwest's total revenues on these routes still exceeded its relevant costs; and (4) that Northwest's low price strategy was a pro-competitive response to Spirit's entry into these geographic markets.

In its response, Spirit relied upon its experts, who opined on the definitions of the relevant geographic and service markets, the anticompetitive characteristics of this market, the determination of the appropriate measure of Northwest's costs and the likelihood of recoupment based upon the factual record. In essence, Spirit's proof was that the relevant product or service market is the low price or price-sensitive or leisure fare travelers for the Detroit-Boston and Detroit-Philadelphia routes, the undisputed geographic markets. In Spirit's experts' opinions, the appropriate measure of costs is Northwest's incremental costs for providing the additional capacity to divert these passengers from Spirit on these routes. By these standards, Spirit's experts opined that Northwest's prices on these routes were below its average variable costs. Spirit's expert proof was that within months after Spirit's exit from these markets, Northwest successfully and completely recouped its losses with substantially higher fares and reduced capacity on these routes.

In addition, Spirit cited Northwest's high market share of enplanements at the Detroit airport, Northwest's expansion of its capacity on these routes in response to Spirit's entry, and the significant barriers to entry in this market, as enabling Northwest to engage in a successful predatory campaign to drive Spirit from this market and to recoup its lost revenues from its predatory pricing on these routes. As the competitive injury from Northwest's predation, Spirit cited the significant reduction in the number of leisure travelers on these routes who lost the competitive option of low price travel from the Detroit airport to these cities and who paid substantially higher prices to travel these routes after Spirit's exit from this market.

In its ruling, the district court adopted Northwest's definition of the relevant product or services market and found that Northwest's revenues exceeded its costs on these routes. The district court rejected Spirit's definition of the relevant service market, but concluded that even in that market, Northwest's revenues exceeded its costs on these routes. As the district court summarized:

> [T]he brute market facts established that Northwest's fares did not fall below the airline's average variable costs, and Spirit has not produced sufficient facts or identified pertinent legal authority to validate its experts' opinion that below-cost pricing occurred in some alternative, legally relevant "lowest fare" or "price-sensitive" market.
>
> The law governing claims of predatory pricing and endorsed by scholars including Spirit's own experts, deliberately eschews any qualitative judgments about the competitive desirability of one business practice verses another.
>
> The sole and objective benchmark is whether the alleged predator's prices exceed its costs, by reference to the products it actually sells and the markets in which it actually competes with the alleged victim of predation. Under this standard, the record compels the conclusion that Northwest's prices were not predatory, because the airline operated profitably on both the Detroit-Boston and Detroit-Philadelphia routes during the entire period of alleged predation.

As to Spirit's remaining Section 2 claims, the district court deemed consideration of them unnecessary given its conclusion about predatory pricing, as Spirit conceded. Given this conclusion, the Court need not address Northwest's two remaining arguments in support of its motion. This leaves only the question whether anything remains of Spirit's claims in this case.

C. THE SUMMARY JUDGMENT RECORD

1. Market Characteristics of the Passenger Airline Industry

The proof before the district court included a Department of Transportation study finding that "low-fare air carriers provide important service and competitive benefits: fare levels are much lower and traffic levels are higher, on routes served by low-fare airlines." Spirit's expert's analysis revealed that low fare carriers significantly reduce the fares of major carriers: "[i]n markets that do involve dominated hubs, low-cost service results in average one way fare savings of $70 per passenger, or 40 percent."

The record also includes a study, "Predatory Pricing in the U.S. Airline Industry" by Clinton V. Oster of Indiana University and John S. Strong of the College of William and Mary. The Oster-Strong study notes that in 1590 markets "the number of passengers traveling increased dramatically in response to the large number of seats offered at low fares." The Oster-Strong study also reflects that there are "Multiple Competitive Tools" in this industry that provide price and non-price bases for competition among airlines.

> While the fare a passenger pays is an important element of competition, airlines don't compete solely on the basis of the price of the ticket. Instead, they compete over multiple dimensions including: the ticket price; the number of flights a day and the timing of those flights; the characteristics of the flight itinerary such as whether the flight is nonstop, continuing single-plane service, or connecting service; rebates to the traveler in the form of frequent flier programs or corporate discounts; in-flight amenities including food service and how closely the seats are spaced together; ground amenities including club lounges; and so forth.
>
> Airlines can also compete by paying travel agent commission overrides ("TACOs"), to encourage travel agents to book passengers on their flights rather than those of a competitor. To focus only on a single dimension may miss the full range of the ways in which airlines can compete with one another, particularly if price and cost are narrowly defined.
>
> Airlines can offer different fares on a given flight, attaching restrictions or conditions of travel to some fares and, most importantly, offering only a limited number of seats in some fare categories. [A]n example of the coach/economy class fares with associated types of restrictions [is] offered by United Airlines for its flights 1956 from Denver to

> Miami for travel in January 2001. For this travel, United offered 6 different coach fares ranging from the lowest fare of $483 to the highest fare of $1,045.
>
> These multiple fares give an airline considerable flexibility in how to price seats on its flights. The airline could, for example, offer service at low average fares by simply making a large number of seats available in the lower fare categories, as Northwest did in the third quarter of 1996 in the Detroit to Philadelphia market.
>
> Conversely, if there is sufficient demand and no meaningful competition, the airline can offer most of its service at high average fares by making few or no seats available in the lower fare categories. However, the presence of a low-fare carrier such as Southwest reduces an airline's ability to extract high fares from travelers.
>
> The entry of a low-fare carrier dramatically shifts the distribution of fares away from the higher fare classes toward the lower fare classes. The result is that the average fare fell from about $173 to about $115. Some high fares still remain after low-fare entry, but a much smaller proportion of travelers pay them. There are still tickets sold in all of the fare categories after low-fare entry, as was the case before entry, but the proportion of tickets sold in each of these categories has changed dramatically.

In the airline industry, access to gates is critical, but access is not determined by open competition and, for a new entrant, gate access is a substantial barrier to entry. Professor Kenneth Elzinga, one of Spirit's experts quoted one analyst who summarized this aspect of the market.

> While route schedules and pricing for the airline industry have been largely deregulated for over 20 years, many other aspects of the industry are still highly regulated. Perhaps the most important regulation comes from local governments, which own and manage the airports in their region and therefore control key bottlenecks to airport service: access to boarding gates and runways. Most local airport commissions allocate gates without a formal market mechanism.

Professor Elzinga's report shows that the majority of airport gates are controlled by long-term exclusive-use leases with the local airport authority. In 1996, the GAO found that 76 of the 86 gates at the Detroit airport were covered by long term leases until 2008 and Northwest had 64 of such leases.

Michael Levine, one of Northwest's experts in Northwest's action against American Airlines for predatory pricing opined that, "the barriers to entry in those relevant hub, hub-network, regional and national markets are very high; the barriers to entry in hub-to-hub city pairs are also very high; barriers to entry in certain city pairs are also high." In that action, Levine also stated that "[n]ew entrants are facing a higher cost of entry than even existing competitors have incurred. Existing [airlines] obtained their initial awareness and facilities base pursuant to government regulations that protected them from competition."

Professor Keith B. Leffler, another Spirit expert, is an Associate Professor of Economics at the University of Washington who teaches and researches in the areas of industrial organization, antitrust economics and the economics of contracts. Professor Leffler analyzed Northwest's experts' reports in Northwest's action against American Airlines for predatory pricing. Professor Leffler found that in those reports, Northwest's experts opined that:

- air travel between city-pairs are relevant economic markets in the airline industry;
- predatory pricing can be a rational economic strategy in the airline industry;
- recoupment from predatory pricing is likely for an airline dominant in a relevant economic market in the airline industry;
- there are substantial barriers to entry into the airline industry;
- business travelers constitute a distinct market segment in the airline industry;
- the measure of the average variable cost in the airline industry should include the cost of changing capacity.

2. Market Power

At the time of Spirit's entry into these geographic routes in 1995, Northwest had 78% of all passengers traveling from the Detroit Metro airport and 64 of 78 gates at the Detroit airport. During 1996, Northwest's share of the air passenger traveler market at its Minneapolis hub was 75 to 80% of all enplanements and about 65 to 70% at its Memphis hub. Northwest's share of local passengers on the Detroit-Philadelphia route was between

60-75% of flown seats. Prior to Spirit's entry into the Detroit-Philadelphia market, Northwest carried about 70% of the non-stop traffic on this route, and offered six daily flights; U.S. Airways was a distant second with a market share of about 27%. Prior to Spirit's entry, Northwest was the prime carrier on the Detroit-Boston route and had an 89% market share for that route. After Spirit's exit, Northwest resumed its status as the only supplier of local passenger service on the Detroit-Boston route.

After his review of these markets, Professor Elzinga concluded that Northwest possessed sufficient market power on the Detroit-Boston and Detroit-Philadelphia routes "to make predatory pricing plausible." In Professor Elzinga's view, Northwest's match of Spirit's fares for a large number of its passengers who are price sensitive reflected Northwest's ability to engage in price discrimination by charging higher fares to passengers who are unlikely to travel on Spirit, *e.g.*, businesses travelers, even at substantially lower prices.

3. The Relevant Market

The factual record reflects that Northwest's internal documents and its marketing representatives recognize the "low price or price sensitive traveler" or "leisure traveler" as a distinct and relevant market in the air passenger travel market. After a review of this market, Spirit's experts found that a leisure travel passenger or price-sensitive market exists and cited this market as the focus of the actual competition between Spirit and Northwest. Two federal regulators studied this market and also found a distinct market for low fare or price sensitive or leisure travelers.

4. Northwest's Strategy

Aside from the market issues, Spirit's proof reflects that Northwest's Chief Executive Officer deemed the Detroit Metro Airport to be Northwest's "most unique strategic asset" that must be protected "at almost all cost." Northwest studied low fare carriers and estimated that competing with such airlines could cost Northwest $250-$375 million in annual revenue at its hubs. This study expressly identified Spirit as one such low cost carrier.

In addition, Michael Levine, Northwest's executive vice president, published an article, *Airline Competition In Deregulated Markets*, 4 YALE J. ON REG. 393, 476-78 (1987), describing a two-fold strategy to respond to low fare carriers. This strategy, entitled the "new competitive equilibrium analysis," addresses the impact of a new entrant's service in this market. "The essence of the strategy is simple. Match, or better yet, beat the new entrant's lowest restricted fare to confine its attractiveness to the leisure oriented price-sensitive sector of the market ... Make sure enough seats are available on your flights in the market to accommodate increases in traffic caused by the fare war. In short, leave no traveler with either a price or a schedule incentive to fly the new entrant." Significantly, Levine states: "The incumbent will not operate profitably under such conditions especially, if, as is usually the case, it is a higher-cost airline than its competitor." In its comprehensive study of the industry, the United States Department of Transportation concluded, "Northwest's response forced Spirit's exit from this market and was designed to do so."

5. Recoupment

On the issue of recoupment, Professor David Mills, a Spirit expert, describes the predator's view of below cost pricing as "an investment strategy" that is the core of Elzinga-Mills recoupment test for predatory pricing. Under this test "[t]he proper benchmark to use in calculating the predator's reasonably expected gains and losses is the profit the firm would earn if the target remained in the market." To determine predation, "[t]he first task is to compare Northwest's average fares during the months when Spirit operated its flights on the [Detroit-Boston] route to the average fares that would have prevailed on the route, but for Northwest's alleged predation."

This factor "measure[s] the monthly financial sacrifice the airline shouldered by charging prices below the otherwise prevailing level ... The second task ... compares the average fares Northwest would expect to charge, during the months immediately after Spirit exited the market, to the average fares that otherwise would have prevailed in the market." This second factor "measure[s] the monthly financial return Northwest could achieve by driving Spirit from the market with its predatory pricing." The third factor "compare[s] the anticipated monthly sacrifice during predation with the anticipated monthly return during recoupment to understand whether predatory pricing plausibly would have been a profitable option for Northwest to exercise." Considering the evidence on market characteristics in this industry, and applying a number of mathematical formulae to these facts, Professor Mills concluded, in sum, that Northwest had successfully recouped its lost revenue within months after Spirit's departure from these routes.

6. Northwest's Non-Price Predatory Practices

Professor Elzinga also deemed Northwest's combination of its matching Spirit's lower prices and its expansion of its flight capacity on these routes as the keys to Northwest's successful predation against Spirit. Dr. Daniel Kaplan, a Spirit expert, also challenged Northwest's strategy for the Detroit-Boston route. For example, to justify the addition of the DC-10, Northwest's analysts arbitrarily assumed a 362% increase in passenger traffic in Detroit-Boston upon Spirit's entry that is wholly contrary to Northwest's price-out model forecast for these flights.

D. STANDARD OF REVIEW

As discussed in more detail *infra*, we conclude that when the evidence is considered in a light most favorable to Spirit, a reasonable trier of fact could find that in the relevant geographic and service markets, the markets were highly concentrated, Northwest possessed overwhelming market share, and the barriers to entry were very high. As a result, a reasonable trier of fact could conclude that by dropping its prices below its costs as well as by quickly expanding capacity, Northwest engaged in anti-competitive conduct aimed at driving Spirit out of the relevant markets. Moreover, based on the evidence presented by Spirit's experts, a reasonable trier of fact could conclude that following Spirit's exit, Northwest recouped its losses incurred during the predation period. Accordingly, we conclude that Spirit has presented sufficient evidence of predatory pricing to withstand summary judgment in this case.

E. LEGAL ANALYSIS

Section 2 of the Sherman Act, in pertinent part, makes it unlawful to "monopolize, or attempt to monopolize any part of the trade or commerce among the several States ..." 15 U.S.C. § 2. "[Section] 2 addresses the actions of single firms that monopolize or attempt to monopolize ... The purpose of the Act is not to protect businesses from the working of the market; it is to protect the public from the failure of the market." Under this statute, the defendant must "use ... monopoly power 'to foreclose competition, to gain a competitive advantage, or to destroy a competitor.'"

We must decide whether Spirit has presented sufficient evidence that Northwest engaged in predatory pricing to withstand summary judgment in this case. Within that general question are several issues of what a reasonable trier of fact could find, such as whether leisure travelers constitute a distinct market in this industry; whether Northwest possessed sufficient market power to engage in predatory pricing; whether Northwest's prices in response to Spirit's entry were below an appropriate measure of its costs; whether Northwest recouped its lost profits from its reduced prices; and whether the characteristics of this market would facilitate and render economically plausible Spirit's assertion of Northwest's predatory pricing. On each issue, summary judgment principles require us to view the evidence in a light most favorable to Spirit.

1. Relevant Markets

a. Geographic Market

The threshold issue under Section 2 is the definition of "the relevant product and geographic markets in which [plaintiff] competes with the alleged monopolizer, and with respect to the monopolization claim, to show that the defendant, in fact, possesses monopoly power … A geographic market is defined as an area of effective competition" or "the locale in which consumers of a product or service can turn for alternative sources of supply." The Sherman Act governs "localized geographic area(s)" and "the relevant geographic submarkets [based upon] commercially significant areas in which the defendant operated and in which [the defendant's] customers could turn to other suppliers."

The district court's opinion, the parties' agreement and the proof reflect that the relevant geographic markets are the Detroit-Boston and Detroit Philadelphia routes. Spirit's expert cited an industry study to the effect that in the passenger airline industry, "[a]t its most basic level, the unit of output of a passenger airline is transportation of passengers between cities … [T]he airline industry is a multiple-product industry producing and selling thousands of different product-travel between city pairs ... It is at the route level, after all, that airlines actually compete with one another." According to the Transportation Research Board of the National Research Council, "[a]irlines compete for passengers at the city-pair level. There are thousands of combinations of origin and destination (O-D) points that constitute the market for our transportation system ..." In its report, the General Accounting Office stated "that city-pairs can also be used to analyze various air markets."

b. Relevant Service Market

As to product or service market, the Supreme Court emphasized that a product market may have submarkets and the definition of a market or submarket focuses on economic realities and industry practice. "The boundaries of ... a (product) submarket may be determined by examining such practical indicia as industry or public recognition of the submarket as a separate economic entity, the products' peculiar characteristics and uses, unique production facilities, distinct customers, distinct prices, sensitivity to price changes, and specialized vendors."

The district court adopted Northwest's position that the relevant product or service market includes "local" passengers who travel from Detroit on these non-stop flights to either Philadelphia or Boston and "connecting" passengers from other Northwest flights who travel to these cities from the Detroit airport. Based on the proof here, a reasonable trier of fact could find that Spirit and Northwest both recognize "leisure" or "discretionary" or "price-sensitive" passengers as a distinct market in the air passenger travel market.

For example, during the relevant period, Northwest had separate fares for business travelers and leisure travelers. Northwest's internal documents on pricing and passenger fares reflect Northwest's distinction between business and leisure travel. A Northwest internal document states that its "FARE RESTRICTIONS ATTEMPT SEGMENTATION" and that "Restrictions are designed to make passengers reveal their own demand."

Michael Gerend, Northwest's manager for domestic pricing, responded to the following question: "Q: Did the Pricing Department make distinctions between business and leisure products? A. Yes." "Q. Do you view the business market and the leisure market as separate markets? A. Yes." Kenneth Pomerantz, Northwest's director of sales, development and analysis, answered a similar question: "Q: Are they considered two different markets, business travel and leisure travel? A: I believe they are considered different products."

Northwest filed an action against American Airlines for predatory pricing and in that action Northwest's experts recognized that "business travelers constitute a distinct market segment in the airline industry." In his expert report for that action, Michael Levine, a Northwest executive, opined "that there were at least two relevant product market segments in which airlines compete: business and discretionary and leisure travel." John T. Griffin, another witness in Northwest's action against American Airlines, stated: "There's nothing that necessarily links business fares and leisure fares. We really have treated those as distinct. And within the objective of attempting to maximize my business revenue and the leisure revenue separately."

In Northwest's comment on the proposed enforcement policy of the United States Transportation Department, Dr. Laura D'Andrea Tyson presented a paper for Northwest entitled, "Competition in the Airline Industry: A Response to the Department of Transportation's Proposed Enforcement Policy." In pertinent part, Dr. Tyson stated: "Airlines have different products on the same airplane that offer customers different characteristics and thus cover a wide range of prices ... All airline seats on a particular flight provide transportation between the two airports served by that flight, but it is not accurate to say, even within a specific class, that these seats provide the same service or have the same cost."

To study this market, Spirit retained Professor Kenneth G. Elzinga, a highly regarded economist. Professor Elzinga is a Professor of Economics at the University of Virginia. Among his prior experiences are as an economist in the United States Department of Justice and as consultant to the Federal Trade Commission. Professor Elzinga's publications on antitrust economics, include writings on predatory pricing, and as noted below, his writings have been cited by the United States Supreme Court in its predatory pricing opinions. Professor Elzinga also served as a special consultant to the Honorable Lewis D. Kaplan in a complex antitrust action.

After his study, Professor Elzinga opined that a distinct product or service market existed. "The relevant market for air travel consists of all local passengers whose itineraries originate in a particular city and terminate in another; in other words, relevant markets consist of passenger service between city-pairs. In this litigation, the two markets are the city pairs of Detroit and Boston and Detroit and Philadelphia." Although Professor Elzinga's market definition is not expressly limited to price-sensitive passengers, clearly Professor Elzinga's cost-comparison is so limited. In Professor Elzinga's analysis of the cost-revenue comparison, the relevant passengers in this market are low fare passengers. Based on the evidence presented by Spirit, including Northwest's own documents, the testimony of its officials, and the opinions of Spirit's experts, we conclude that a reasonable trier of fact could find that leisure or price-sensitive passengers represent a separate and distinct market in this industry for Section 2 purposes.

2. Monopoly Power

As to whether Northwest possessed monopoly power in this market, the Supreme Court's formulations of monopoly power are "the ability of a single seller to raise price and restrict output," or the power to "control prices or exclude competition."

"[A]s an economic matter, market power exists whenever prices can be raised above the levels that would be charged in a competitive market." We described monopoly power as the defendant's power "to raise prices or to exclude competition when it is desired to do so." Judge Learned Hand enunciated what has become the classic explanation of when market share becomes large enough to constitute a monopoly: "over ninety ... percentage is enough to constitute a monopoly; it is doubtful whether sixty or sixty-four percent would be enough; and certainly thirty-three percent is not."

As applied here, when Spirit entered the Detroit-Boston and Detroit-Philadelphia markets, Northwest was the dominant carrier in each market. At the time of Spirit's entry, Northwest had an 89% market share and became the sole provider on the Detroit-Boston route. Northwest had more than a 70% market share on the Detroit-Philadelphia route. Prior to Spirit's entry, Northwest competed with only one other carrier, U.S. Airways, for non-stop service on the Detroit-Philadelphia route. Northwest had 78% of all passengers traveling from the Detroit airport and controlled 64 of the 78 gates at the Detroit airport under long-term leases. Once Spirit left this market, Northwest reduced the number of flights on these routes, restricting output, and increased its fares on these routes significantly. These two measures could reasonably be interpreted as a clear exercise of monopoly power. Professor Elzinga deemed the facts here to establish that Northwest had the requisite market power to render its predatory pricing plausible and successful. We conclude that a reasonable trier of fact could find that Professor Elzinga's opinion is a reasonable economic conclusion based upon the proof.

In evaluating the economic reasonableness of Professor Elzinga's conclusion, we note commentators' views, as the Supreme Court commonly does, and as the district court did below. As to requisite power to engage in successful predatory pricing, Jonathan Baker, a former Senior Economist at the Council of Economic Advisers and an economist in the United States Department of Justice, opined that "[i]f imperfections in the market for capital cause the prey to have less access to financial capital than the predator, then the predator may reasonably expect to use its 'deep pockets' in the traditional way to drive the prey to exit. In addition, if high prices following the exit of the prey are unlikely to be eroded by new competition (because of entry barriers), predatory pricing with single market recoupment may no longer be an irrational strategy ... A firm can deter aggressive competition with a low price, even if the low price exceeds the price-cutter's average cost, so long as the price is sufficiently low relative to its rivals' cost. Hence, it is possible that competition can be harmed by low prices even if those prices are not below the price-cutter's cost." Jonathan Baker, *Predatory Pricing after* Brooke Group*; An Economic Perspective*, 62 ANTITRUST L.J. 585, 591 (1994).

In his article, *Predation, Competition & Antitrust Law: Turbulence in the Airline Industry*," 67 J. AIR L. & COM. 685, 702 (2002), Professor Paul Stephen Dempsey, a former airline executive and Professor of Law and Director of the Air and Space Law Institute at McGill University noted that: "new entry cannot be sustained where the incumbent airline is willing to endure significant short-term losses in a below-cost predatory pricing strategy designed to force the new entrant out of the market (or into bankruptcy) so that after the new entrant leaves, the incumbent can resume its monopoly price gouging well above competitive levels." According to Professor Dempsey, "[w]hen a less-well-capitalized, younger, low-cost, new entrant airline attempts to enter, the competitive response is predatory, with the intent of driving the new entrant out of the market."

Chronologically, the predation process is as follows:

1. Major airline establishes dominance at airport serving competitive levels.

2. Dominance allows major airline to price well above competitive levels.

3. When a new entrant attempts to enter a major airline's hub, dominant airline responds with below-cost pricing, capacity dumping, and/or a number of other predatory practices until the new entrant is driven out.

4. Once the new entrant is driven out of the market, dominant airlines raises prices to levels sometimes higher than those prevailing before the new entrant attempted entry.

These commentators' views of this market and Northwest's conduct within it are consistent with the opinions of Spirit's economic experts and further confirm our conclusion that a reasonable trier of fact could find that Northwest possessed the requisite market power to engage in its predatory conduct and that Northwest successfully used it.

3. The Appropriate Measure of Costs

The next step is to determine the appropriate measure of Northwest's costs to determine if Northwest's response to Spirit's entry pricing were predatory. Under § 2 of the Sherman Act, "a plaintiff seeking to establish competitive injury resulting from a rival's low prices must prove that the prices complained of are below an appropriate measure of its rival's costs." The Supreme Court declined to resolve the conflict among the circuits over the appropriate measure of costs, but utilized the average variable cost standard "[b]ecause the parties in this case agree the relevant measure is average variable cost."

In addition to providing his opinions on the relevant markets and their characteristics, Professor Elzinga was also retained to provide the methodology to determine Northwest's relevant prices and costs. Dr. Daniel Kaplan, an economist who specializes in airline economics and is the former director of the Office of Economic Analysis for the Civil Aeronautics Board, performed that analysis. Professor David Mills, an economist and co-author with Professor Elzinga in the earlier cited articles, analyzed Northwest's recoupment of its lost profits from its earlier predatory pricing after Spirit's exit from this market. Professor Mills employed the predation and recoupment test developed with Professor Elzinga and cited by the United States Supreme Court.

After defining the relevant markets, Professor Elzinga established the following methodology for determining Northwest's costs.

> To apply the price-cost part of a predation analysis for this case involved examining the marginal or incremental costs associated with Northwest's response to Spirit compared with the additional revenues the company received from that response. That is, by incurring the costs of the campaign that Spirit claims is predatory, what revenues did Northwest receive as a result? Is the difference between these numbers positive or negative?
>
> The analysis, in other words, focuses on revenue from the additional flights (*i.e.*, the extra capacity) that Northwest added (at discounted fares) because the alleged predation was executed through those additional flights. Therefore, the assessment of predation compares the revenues (the price) Northwest received from this tactic versus the incremental (or average variable) cost Northwest incurred from carrying those passengers.

In sum, Professor Elzinga's methodology would determine as the appropriate measure of Northwest's costs, its average variable costs to transport the non-connecting passengers on the Detroit-Boston and Detroit-Philadelphia routes. As Professor Elzinga explained, in the alleged predation, "Northwest only ... match[ed] Spirit's fares for those passengers who might choose Spirit instead of Northwest." Professor Elzinga noted that these standards for the appropriate measure of average variable costs are consistent with the classic antitrust treatise of Professors Areeda and Hovenkamp in which the scholars posit that "[i]n such a case involving excess capacity and lower prices to marginal customers, the theocratic ally correct benchmark is short-run marginal costs with respect to the low price customers."

Utilizing Professor Elzinga's methodology, Dr. Kaplan determined Northwest's actual average variable costs for the price-sensitive passengers on these routes. Dr. Kaplan utilized Northwest's Flight Profitability System ("FPS") that collects the monthly revenues and costs of each Northwest flight and then aggregates those numbers to determine the profitability of each hub and the relevant spoke. To calculate costs for the routes at issue, Dr. Kaplan determined Northwest's average variable costs to be "equal to the total variable costs that Northwest incurs serving that city pair during a given time period divided by the number of passengers traveling in that city pair during that time period." Dr. Kaplan studied the fares for various months for both city-pairs during 1996. Utilizing Professor Elzinga's definition of the market, Dr. Kaplan deemed a fare of $225 as a reasonable dividing line between the price sensitive travelers and other travelers in both city-pairs. In Dr. Kaplan's analysis, all those passengers traveling below $225 in both Philadelphia-Detroit and Boston-Detroit were deemed price-sensitive passengers.

Dr. Kaplan included within average variable costs: flight costs, passenger costs, and gate and ticket counter costs, the latter reflected in depreciation and amortization expenses. In his report on variable costs, Professor Elzinga also found that

> In the airline industry, there are several layers of marginal (*i.e.,* variable) costs ... Think of these as passenger variable costs ... and include ... the cost of processing the ticket, the cost of processing the passenger through the gate, the cost of in-flight food and beverages, insurance and other liability related expenses, and the cost of the extra fuel burned because of the passenger's additional weight ... [F]light variable costs ... include the single-passenger variable costs described above, plus takeoff or landing fees, the fuel costs of flying the empty aircraft, and some additional maintenance and crew costs incurred from the operation of the aircraft.
>
> The third are the costs [that] include the opportunity cost associated with the use of that aircraft ... Finally ... route variable costs ... include all of the costs listed above plus costs incurred in setting the new "station" with ticket counters, maintenance facilities, and other service expenses.

Dr. Kaplan opined that in relation to its response to Spirit, Northwest's flight costs included fuel and labor as well as the cost of the additional aircraft in each market that represented the incremental capacity in Northwest's response to Spirit's presence.

The economic cost of using an airplane was based on the market lease rate for the airplane. Passenger variable costs for each route were the costs of processing a passenger's ticket and boarding, the cost of in-flight food and beverages, the expense of liability insurance, and the incremental cost of the fuel needed to carry each passenger. Other relevant variables costs are for pilots, flight attendants, gate, and counter space.

Dr. Kaplan then calculated Northwest's average variable costs for Boston-Detroit and Philadelphia-Detroit "by dividing the various cost factors for each route in each month that Northwest's Flight Profit System ("FPS") identifies as variable, as well as aircraft market value, by the total number of passengers traveling on that segment during the relevant time period. The monthly average variable cost in Boston-Detroit ranged between $65.87 and $85.24 during April though September 1996. The monthly average variable cost ranged between $53.47 and $60.17 in Philadelphia-Detroit during July through September 1996. The price range is a function of the variations in the load factor of the flight."

In comparing Northwest's average variable costs and Northwest's average net revenue from "the all passenger service market" on these routes, Dr. Kaplan found, in sum:

Boston-Detroit

> From April through September 1996, 74.5 percent of Northwest's Boston-Detroit passengers traveled on fares of $69 or less. (Northwest established the $69 fare in response to Spirit's April 1996 entry into Boston-Detroit). Northwest's $69 fare on Boston-Detroit on average generated per passenger net revenue of $61.98 after deducting commissions and adding certain other ancillary revenues. This per passenger net revenue was $10.75 below Northwest's average variable cost. Thus, between April and September 1996 the $69 fare being used by passengers traveling on Northwest's Boston-Detroit service was $10.75 below Northwest's average variable cost.

Philadelphia-Detroit

> From July through September 1996, 40.5 percent of Northwest's Philadelphia-Detroit passengers traveled on fares of $49 or less. (Northwest established the $49 fare in response to Spirit's addition of a second flight between Philadelphia and Detroit at the end of June 1996). Northwest's $49 fare on Philadelphia-Detroit on average generated per passenger net revenue of $44.29 during this

> period after deducting commissions and adding certain other ancillary revenues. This per passenger net revenue was $11.86 below Northwest's average variable cost on Philadelphia-Detroit in the period from July to September 1996. In September 1996, 70 percent of Northwest's Philadelphia-Detroit passengers flew on fares above $49 but equal to or below $69. The $69 fare in September 1996 generated average net revenue to Northwest of $58.31, which was $1.86 below its average variable cost of serving Philadelphia-Detroit in that month. Consequently, 65 percent of Northwest's Philadelphia-Detroit passengers flew on fares that were less than Northwest's average variable cost in July through September 1996.

For the "price-sensitive airline passengers" market on the Boston-Detroit and Philadelphia-Detroit routes, Dr. Kaplan performed the same methodology using Northwest's data and found as follows:

Boston-Detroit

> [Northwest's] average net revenue from the price-sensitive passengers on this city-pair was $64.82 between April and September 1996. This figure was $8.07 below Northwest's average variable cost during that time period.

Philadelphia-Detroit

> [Northwest's] average net revenue from the price-sensitive passengers on this city-pair was $50.35 from July to September 1996. This figure was $6.53 below Northwest's average variable cost during that time period.

As noted earlier, both parties' experts calculated Northwest's average variable costs based upon data from Northwest's FPS data system, but Northwest's expert reached different results in his calculation of Northwest's costs and revenues.

Northwest's expert, Professor Janusz A. Ordover, is a Professor of Economics at New York University and former Deputy Assistant Attorney General for the Antitrust Division of the United States Department of Justice. Professor Ordover identified his four step test to determine whether Northwest engaged in predatory pricing and monopolization:

1. A structural analysis of the relevant market;

2. An assessment of the likelihood of anticompetitive (exclusionary) effects resulting from the alleged conduct;

3. An analysis of pertinent prices (or revenues) and costs to assess whether the competitive response made business sense only because of its adverse impact on competition and would not have made sense if the rival remained viable; and

4. An evaluation of whether the firm is able to recoup the profits foregone during the period of the predatory behavior.

Yet, for his initial analysis, Professor Ordover deemed only an analysis of Step 3 necessary. In a rebuttal report, Professor Ordover addressed the other three factors. In a word, Professor Ordover concluded that by comparing Northwest's average variable costs on each route to Northwest's revenue from all passengers traveling on that route, including connecting passengers, it became clear that Northwest had an incremental profit on each route.

In his analysis, Professor Ordover considered the total revenue from all passengers, leisure travelers as well as connecting passengers, earned from these routes and compared those revenues to Northwest's variable costs for those flights. Revenues from fares of all airline passengers business were totaled and divided to yield an average fare. Professor Ordover then compared Northwest's average prices with its average variable costs on the Detroit-Philadelphia and Detroit-Boston routes during the months when Spirit operated on these routes. For his determination of "route level costs and resources," entitled the "competitive response package," Professor Ordover included "total onboard revenue plus the allocated segmented revenue from the connecting passengers on a flight, plus a beyond contribution from the flow connecting passengers."

As to variable costs, Professor Ordover included several of the same cost elements as Dr. Kaplan, but for the costs of the aircraft, Professor Ordover declined to use the commercial lease rates for the aircraft and instead chose "the opportunity costs of the aircraft and its least attractive alternative deployment within the airline's system." Utilizing the components of Northwest's FPS, Professor Ordover found, in sum, as follows:

> As seen there, both VABS and VABSO were positive during the time period when Northwest was matching, or partially matching, Spirit's fares (April through September 1996). For example, in June 1996 the VABS measure was approximately $5.8 million for the route and the VABSO measure was approximately $5.0 million. These June 1996 amounts are equivalent to about $68 and $58 per one-way

> segment passenger, respectively. The positive VABS and VABSO results for April through September indicate that the average fare plus the beyond contribution from passengers traveling between Detroit and Boston exceeded average variable cost.

Professor Ordover explained, "VABS is equal to total onboard revenue (for the route segment) plus net beyond revenue contribution, minus variable expenses. VABSO is equal to VABS minus the cost of aircraft ownership. These measures which include the beyond contribution are used by Northwest in order to assess the profitability of individual routes as part of the overall network. VABS is often used for relatively short-term tactical marketing decisions and VABSO is frequently used to determine whether a route is successful over time."

Further, even the measures that do not take account of the beyond contribution, the VAC and VACO measures, were positive in every month (*i.e.*, Northwest's average Detroit-Boston segment fare exceeded its average variable cost). Indeed, the only negative profitability measure is the May 1996 fully allocated contribution ("FAC"), which excludes the beyond contribution and is equal to total revenue minus fully allocated expenses. When the beyond contribution is included, in the fully allocated with beyond contribution ("FABS"), this cost measure was positive for May 1996. As discussed above, variable rather than fully allocated costs are the pertinent standard; yet the fact that Northwest was profitable even based on the much higher fully allocated cost standard during this period provides further support for the conclusion that its conduct was not predatory.

> [According to] FPS data for the Detroit-Philadelphia route for 1995 and 1996[,][b]oth VABS and VABSO were positive during the entire time period when Northwest was matching Spirit's fares on this route (July through September). The July 1996 amounts of approximately $2.8 million for VABS and $2.5 million for VABSO, for example, are equivalent to about $67 and $60 per one-way segment passenger, respectively. In addition, both the variable cost-based measures that do not take account of the beyond contribution (VAC and VACO) and the measures based on fully allocated costs (FAC and FABS) were positive in every month.
>
> In summary, the positive FPS profitability measures based on variable costs clearly demonstrate that predation did not occur on the Detroit-Boston and Detroit-Philadelphia routes. In addition, with revenues exceeding the pertinent measure of total cost, each route clearly makes economic

> sense. Put another way, an airline would not deliberately lose money on the routes by offering the schedule of flights that it did. This means that the competitive response makes sense even if the competitor continues to be viable.

Based on his comparison, Professor Ordover concluded that Northwest's average fares on the routes exceeded its average variable costs. From these findings, Professor Ordover inferred that Northwest's pricing response to Spirit's entry on these routes would have been profitable even if Spirit had continued to serve these cities.

Professor Ordover criticizes Dr. Kaplan's segmentation of Northwest's average variable costs for local passengers on those routes because all passengers, including connecting passengers, contribute to the revenue of the flight as part of the hub network. Moreover, Professor Ordover notes that added capacity affects more than revenue, including enhancement to the overall schedule to connecting flights, reduction in crowding and increasing the availability of attractive fares. Hence, Professor Ordover views any contribution of revenues from connecting passengers as necessary to assess whether Northwest's response was predatory.

In his rebuttal report, Professor Elzinga supported Dr. Kaplan's comparison of Northwest's prices and costs in the leisure traveler market as the more appropriate measure of average variable costs. In Professor Elzinga's view, Professor Ordover improperly calculated all passengers revenue on each of those routes, including connecting passengers. Professor Elzinga explains that the relevant market is the local passengers because those are the passengers whom Northwest sought to divert from Spirit.

As to Professor Ordover's statement that: "each route (and flight) is part of a network; if the route or flight were removed there would be a reduction in revenues not only from that route or flight but also on other routes in the network," citing a Northwest document called "Boston-Detroit STIMULATION ANALYSIS." Dr. Kaplan responded that this document actually "demonstrates that Northwest had flexibility to adjust capacity to accommodate changes in local and connecting passenger demands independently of one another."

In Dr. Kaplan's view, this document "also demonstrates that additional connecting passengers in Boston-Detroit provided little value to Northwest." Dr. Kaplan also cited Northwest's plan to reduce its scheduled capacity in the summer of 1996 before Spirit's entry and opined that this decision "suggest[s] that revenue generated by the added passengers would not cover the opportunity cost of serving them." Spirit also noted that Northwest executive vice-president Michael E. Levine acknowledged that: "All connecting passengers are not of equal value. The least valuable connecting passengers who go through a hub are purely price driven and not-not a very interesting source of revenue; it's just that you use them to fill seats."

To be sure, Professor Leffler, a Spirit expert, cited the opinion of Northwest's expert, Robert S. Pindyck, on the appropriate measure of average variable costs in Northwest's action against American Airlines for predatory pricing. Professor Pindyck is the Mitsubishi Bank Professor of Applied Economics at the Sloan School of Management at the Massachusetts Institute of Technology. Professor Pindyck's research and teaching are in the areas of industrial organization and antitrust economics, and his writings include articles on monopoly power and pricing that have been published in leading economics journals. Professor Pindyck is an author or co-author of six books, including two leading textbooks, Microeconomic and Econometric Models and Economic Forecasts. In Northwest's action against American Airlines for predatory pricing, Professor Pindyck opined: "Although costs have been measured for all domestic national airline passenger service, it may be useful to determine costs separately for "business" service and "leisure" service." Moreover, in the action against American Airlines, another Northwest expert stated: "All airline seats on a particular flight provide transportation between the two airports served by that flight, but it is not accurate to say, even within a specific class, that these seats provide the same service or have the same cost."

Professor Elzinga noted that his standards for the appropriate measure of average variable costs are consistent with the classic antitrust treatise of Professors Areeda and Hovenkamp, in which the scholars assert that "[i]n such a case involving excess capacity and lower prices to marginal customers, the theoretically correct benchmark is short-run marginal costs with respect to the low price customers."

As we stated earlier, we conclude that a reasonable trier of fact could find that the underlying cost data from Northwest's data systems, which Professor Elzinga and Dr. Kaplan used in their analyses, is reasonably accurate and that this data supports their cost calculations for the price-sensitive market. Northwest's expert used the same cost data in his cost-revenue analysis. If a reasonable trier of fact could accept Professor Ordover's cost determinations as reasonably accurate, it stands to reason that Spirit's experts' determinations, which are based on the same cost data, must be deemed reasonably accurate as well.

To be sure, the district court found that Spirit failed "to explain why it is not necessary to isolate the costs of serving price-sensitive passengers from those incurred in serving Northwest's remaining passengers." Spirit's cost analysis included cost measures that were not specifically linked to price-sensitive passengers, but common to all passengers. Spirit's experts explained their rationale for using this metric rather than a figure more narrowly defined to the price-sensitive market. We hold that a reasonable trier of fact could find Spirit's rationale convincing and therefore conclude that the costs attributable to all customers is a reasonably accurate proxy for the costs associated with price-sensitive passengers only.

The evidence reflects that in its data system, Northwest did not consider any meaningful differences to exist in the average variable costs for different passengers. Northwest's FPS data system that both Dr. Kaplan and Professor Ordover utilized to calculate Northwest's costs for these routes, does not distinguish among passengers in its allocations of costs. Northwest's "Price-Out Model," for its flight profitability analysis likewise does not distinguish between passengers in computing costs. If a reasonable trier of fact could find Northwest's FPS data system and "Price-Out-Model" are accurate and reliable for cost allocations, then Dr. Kaplan's use of that same data must be reasonably accurate as well.

Moreover, as Dr. Kaplan explained, non-passenger variable costs such as crew, fuel and possibly aircraft do not vary with passengers because the same service is provided to both sets of passengers. As Dr. Kaplan stated:

> I assumed ... the cost of providing service ... on a route such as [Detroit-Boston/Philadelphia] had roughly constant returns to scale and that consequently ... looking at the average variable cost was a reasonable representation of what their cost would be if they expanded capacity, expanded output on the route.
>
> My view is that ... there are reasonably constant returns to scale. And, the reason that I believe that is ... airlines have a variety of mix of aircraft of ... different ages and different sizes and different configuration. And as consequences, when you are looking at ... the operation in any given route, ... it's perfectly reasonable to assume that ... when they expand capacity it will roughly be at the cost at which they ... had provided the capacity that [had] existed prior to that.

Professor Ordover, Northwest's expert, considered his dispute with Spirit's economic experts on the determination of the appropriate measure of average variable costs to be an "intellectual disagreement."

For summary judgment purposes, we think this evidence supports the reasonable inference that average variable costs did not vary among passengers and thus, Spirit's experts' cost determinations could be found by the trier of fact to be reasonable. In our view, a trier of fact could reasonably accept Spirit's experts' definition and calculation of Northwest's incremental costs to attract the leisure travel passengers on these routes as the appropriate measure of Northwest's average variable costs for deciding Spirit's Section 2 claim against Northwest.

We conclude that this "intellectual disagreement" among the parties' experts creates material factual disputes on the relevant market and the appropriate measure of costs for the service at issue so as to preclude an award of summary judgment. Although the district court found that Spirit's expert-opinion testimony made no economic sense, we conclude that a reasonable trier of fact could find that the testimony of Spirit's experts is reasonable based upon facts in the record and relevant economic principles.

In support of its summary judgment motion, Northwest relies upon the Tenth Circuit's decision in *United States v. AMR Corp.* (10th Cir. 2003), in which the Government alleged that American Airlines engaged in predatory pricing on routes from its hub at Dallas-Fort Worth airport in an attempt to drive emerging low-cost carriers out of the market. At issue in the case was the viability of the four price-cost tests that the Government claimed demonstrated that American Airlines was pricing below its costs. In granting summary judgment in favor of American Airlines, the Tenth Circuit held that none of the four tests the Government had utilized was a true measure of the incremental cost of adding additional passengers on the challenged routes. Therefore, the court held that the Government's evidence of alleged predatory conduct made no economic sense. Relying on this holding, Northwest argues that Spirit's price-cost analysis is similarly flawed. We disagree.

First, unlike three of the tests in *AMR*, Northwest does not contend that Spirit's price-cost test is flawed because it includes a portion of fixed costs or measures reduced profitability. Instead, Northwest relies on the Tenth Circuit's rejection of a price-cost test that included arbitrarily allocated common costs that do not vary proportionately with changes in American Airlines' capacity. The Tenth Circuit held that it was inappropriate to evaluate incremental passenger revenue against these more general administrative and overhead costs.

By contrast, in this case, Spirit's price-cost analysis is based on Northwest's FPS system that specifically distinguishes between fixed and variable costs, defining the latter term as costs that do vary with flight activity. Northwest's expert conceded that the FPS system calculates a reasonable approximation of the average variable costs for a route and is the proper measure to use in evaluating allegations of predatory pricing. Accordingly, we conclude that a reasonable trier of fact could find that Spirit's price-cost analysis is accurate and reliable, and therefore distinguishable from the analysis put forth in *AMR*.

4. Significant Barriers to Entry

In this Circuit, another factor in determining predatory pricing is "whether ... barriers to entry are high" because "[t]he existence of high entry barriers is significant in determining the existence of predatory intent, inasmuch as only where such barriers exist will there be incentive to price predatorily."

Here, the record reveals that Northwest controlled sixty-four of the seventy-eight gates at the Detroit airport under long-term leases. Levine, a Northwest executive, testified that these leases created a "very high" barrier to entry into the Detroit market for any competitor. To provide service from Detroit, Spirit had to pay $100,000 to access a gate as well as 25% higher landing fees than airlines with long-term leases, like Northwest. Relying on this evidence in the record, a reasonable trier of fact could certainly conclude that significant barriers to entry existed in the Detroit market which made predatory pricing possible. Moreover, a law review note collecting economic studies of this market reported as follows:

> [T]he linear point-to-point structure that predominated under regulation was replaced by a nearly pervasive hub-and-spoke system. While some have praised the hub-and-spoke system for its efficiency, many others have also described its utility as an entry-deterrence strategy. Legacy airlines remain dominant in the industry, and their hub-and-spoke route structure is still the industry's single most important structural characteristic.
>
> Economists studying networks have demonstrated that ... adopting a hub-and-spoke structure is an effective means of entry deterrence. Part of this deterrence stems from the market power that hubbing creates on flights that originate or terminate at the hub. Since the hubbing airline typically controls a large proportion of the flights in and out of its hub airport, it can raise fares on those flights without fear of competitive entry. Furthermore, an airline's dominant presence at its hub may allow it to exert veto power over any plans to expand the airport's capacity, which further limits the possibility of competitive entry and its attendant check on market power.
>
> According to some scholars, having a large network also enables legacy airlines to price predatorily on routes served by entrants, thereby causing the entrant to expend cash reserves and exit the market while the incumbent "experiences an economy of scope in the value of reputation for fierceness as a deterrent to other entrants in other markets or in the future.

Note, *Compatibility and Interconnection Pricing in the Airline Industry: A Proposal for Reform*, 114 YALE L.J. 405, 423, 424, and 425 (2004). Another law review note describes the market power that this barrier creates in this industry: "When an airline controls a substantial percentage of enplanements at an airport, it wields significant power over its competitors' access to airport space." Note, *The Antitrust Implications of Airport Lease Restrictions*, 104 HARV. L. REV. 548, 567 (1990).

In sum, the facts and the economics of this industry could reasonably be found to establish significant barriers to entry. Further, a reasonable fact-finder could conclude that these barriers enabled Northwest's predatory pricing to be plausible and successful.

5. Recoupment

The second prerequisite under § 2 of the Sherman Act is proof that the competitor recovered or had a reasonable prospect or a dangerous probability of recouping its investment in below-cost prices. "For the investment to be rational, the [predator] must have a reasonable expectation of recovering, in the form of later monopoly profits, more than the losses suffered." It must be remembered that: "Recoupment is the ultimate object of an unlawful predatory pricing scheme; it is the means by which a predator profits from predation. Without it, predatory pricing produces lower aggregate prices in the market, and consumer welfare is enhanced. Although unsuccessful predatory pricing may encourage some inefficient substitution toward the product being sold at less than its cost, unsuccessful predation is in general a boon to consumers."

As the Supreme Court explained, proof of sales below the defendant's appropriate measure of costs and the likelihood of recoupment are "prerequisites to recovery [that] are not easy to establish, but they are not artificial obstacles to recovery; rather, they are essential components of real market injury."

> For recoupment to occur, below-cost pricing must be capable, as a threshold matter, of producing the intended effects on the firm's rivals, whether driving them from the market, or, as was alleged to be the goal here, causing them to raise their prices to supracompetitive levels within a disciplined oligopoly. This requires an understanding of the extent and duration of the alleged predation, the relative financial strength of the predator and its intended victim, and their respective incentives and will. *See* 3 AREEDA & TURNER ¶ 711b. The inquiry is whether, given the aggregate losses caused by the below-cost pricing, the intended target would likely succumb.
>
> If circumstances indicate that below-cost pricing could likely produce its intended effect on the target, there is still the further question whether it would likely injure competition in the relevant market. The plaintiff must demonstrate that there is a likelihood that the predatory scheme alleged would cause a rise in prices above a

> competitive level that would be sufficient to compensate for the amounts expended on the predation, including the time value of the money invested in it.
>
> As we have observed on a prior occasion, "[i]n order to recoup their losses, [predators] must obtain enough market power to set higher than competitive prices, and then must sustain those prices long enough to earn in excess profits what they earlier gave up in below-cost prices."

Matsushita. Likewise, we have required proof of an injury to competition by a firm's predatory pricing, to sustain a Section 2 claim of monopolization.

Professor Mills, one of Spirit's experts, calculated Northwest's recoupment from its predatory pricing within months after Spirit's exit from these routes. Professor Mills concluded:

> A. *Northwest Monthly Sacrifice during Predation in the DTW-PTL*
>
> Northwest did not cut its fares in response to Spirit's entry on the Detroit-Philadelphia route until Spirit added a second flight in late June 1996. Once underway, Northwest sustained its low fares until Spirit halted both of its flights on the route and withdrew from the Detroit-Philadelphia market in late September 1996 (the same month Spirit withdrew from the Detroit-Boston market).
>
> I apply the same methodology used in the Detroit-Boston market to calculate the average monthly sacrifice Northwest would expect to incur by charging predatory prices in the Detroit-Philadelphia market. To get this quantity, I calculate and average the monthly sacrifice for each of the months July, August, September 1996. This quantity measures the sacrifice Northwest would expect during every month it charged predatory prices.
>
> Values for Northwest's anticipated average monthly sacrifice are shown in ... estimates of E the elasticity of Northwest's residual demand, in the range of 0.3-1.0 ... [F]or instance, ... if the price elasticity of Northwest's residual demand were 0.65, Northwest's average monthly sacrifice during predation, using cost based estimates for the otherwise prevailing price, would have been $241,126.

B. *Northwest's Monthly Returns: After Predation in the Detroit-Philadelphia Market*

As before, the second task is to calculate the average monthly return Northwest expected to receive immediately after Spirit exited the Detroit-Philadelphia market. Applying the same methodology used in the Detroit-Boston market, I calculate and average the monthly return Northwest anticipated on both a looking forward basis and a looking backward basis. I do this for the three months of November 1996-January 1997 for the looking forward scenario and for the same three months in 1995-1996 for the looking backward scenario.

Values for Northwest's anticipated average monthly return are shown in ... alternative estimates of E ranging from 0.3 to 1.0. For instance, if the price elasticity of Northwest's residual demand were 0.65, Northwest's average monthly return during recoupment would have been $756,845, evaluated on a looking forward basis, and $570,769 evaluated on a looking backward basis.

C. *How Long Does Recoupment Take in Detroit-Philadelphia?*

To judge whether Northwest would have anticipated that predatory pricing in the Detroit-Philadelphia market would be profitable, one must compare Northwest's anticipated monthly sacrifice during predation with the airline's anticipated monthly return during recoupment. If Northwest expected that it would take two-four months of predation to drive Spirit out of the market (in fact, it took three months), how many months of recoupment would the company have needed to recoup its predatory investment? The answer to that question is found using the same approach as before in the Detroit-Boston market.

Based on the values of M and R ..., an annual hurdle rate of 15% and the residual price elasticity measures used before, and substituting values and six for p, the number of months of predation anticipated, I find how long Northwest would expect it to take to recoup its investment in predatory pricing ...

> For instance, if Northwest's otherwise prevailing prices were those predicated by the cost-based approach, and if it anticipated two months of predation, Northwest would recoup its investment during the first month of recoupment. If the airline anticipated four months of predation, Northwest would recoup its investment during the second month of recoupment. Recoupment is not as immediate using the comparable market-based otherwise prevailing prices. But even if Northwest's otherwise prevailing prices were those predicted by the comparable market approach, and if it anticipated two months of predation, Northwest would recoup its investment between the second and fourth month of recoupment, depending on the elasticity of its residual demand. And if it anticipated four months of predation, Northwest would recoup its investment between the third and seventh month of recoupment, depending on its elasticity of residual demand. Just as in the Detroit-Boston market, Northwest could not expect to be back "in the black" in the Detroit-Philadelphia market as quickly as if otherwise prevailing prices were lower.
>
> D. *Is Recoupment Plausible in the Detroit-Philadelphia Market?*
>
> Given entry conditions, and especially the gate-constrained conditions Northwest's potential competitors faced at Detroit, as Professor Elzinga emphasized, Northwest certainly would have expected its renewed high prices to last long enough for the airline to recoup its investment in predatory pricing. Barriers to entry were sufficiently high that Northwest would not have expected Spirit to re-enter, or another entrant to arrive, for a period substantially longer than the necessary recoupment period. This conclusion is supported by the fact that, in retrospect, the first and only significant entry event in Detroit-Philadelphia since Spirit withdrew from the market occurred in May 1998 when Pro Air introduced service between Detroit City Airport (DET) and PHL. This happened nineteen months after Spirit's withdrawal; there was ample time for Northwest to recoup its investment in predatory pricing before Pro Air challenged Northwest's dominance in the market.

The trier of fact could reasonably find that Northwest recouped any losses from its predatory pricing quickly after Spirit left these routes. Here, Spirit's expert proof shows that Northwest recovered its losses within months of Spirit's exit from the market. In addition, upon Spirit's exit, Northwest increased its prices on these routes to a multiple of seven from its prices during Spirit's presence. These facts could also lead a reasonable juror to conclude that a competitive injury occurred in this market, namely, air travelers' payment of higher prices by consumers for air travel on these routes.

After Spirit's exit, Northwest also dropped flights notwithstanding the increased customer demand of "price-sensitive travelers" for those routes. The significant adverse competitive impact from Northwest's conduct could reasonably be found to be those Detroit consumers who were leisure travelers to Boston and Philadelphia and who lost a choice of airlines. These consumers suffered not only a reduction in the supply of flights to these cities, but to travel these routes, had to pay an almost seven-fold price increase. With the "very high" barriers to entry, the consumers for this route likely would not have any viable alternatives to Northwest airlines for the foreseeable future. To be sure, the antitrust laws are for "the protection of competition, not competitors." *Brooke Group*, 509 U.S. at 224. Yet, in a concentrated market with very high barriers to entry, competition will not exist without competitors. *See* Andrew I. Gavil, *Exclusionary Distribution Strategies by Dominant Firms: Striking a Better Balance*, 72 ANTITRUST L.J. 3, 81 (2004).

6. Spirit's Non-Price Predation Claims

As stated earlier, Spirit also maintained that a key component of its monopolization claim and Northwest's predatory strategy was Northwest's expansion of its capacity on these routes. Professor Elzinga identified this response as critical to Northwest's successful predation. Michael Levine, a Northwest executive, had authored an article espousing this strategy for responding to new low fare carriers. The district court deemed its finding on the cost issue to be determinative. We respectfully disagree.

Contrary to the district court's conclusion that proof of Northwest's revenues exceeding its average variable costs effectively ends the inquiry, *Brooke Group* emphasized that even where theory suggests that predatory pricing is rare, "[h]owever unlikely that possibility may be as a general matter, when the realities of the market and the record facts indicate that [a predatory pricing scheme] has occurred and was likely to have succeeded, theory will not stand in the way of liability."

Spirit's experts provided a reasonable economic explanation of the anticompetitive effects of Northwest's two-prong response to Spirit's entry on these routes, that included a rapid expansion of Northwest's capacity on these routes. As Professor Elzinga explained:

> The goal of predation in this case is for the incumbent firm, Northwest, to drive the entrant, Spirit, from the market. The most effective way for Northwest to do this is to divert

passengers that would have otherwise flown on Spirit to Northwest, thereby lowering Spirit's revenues below its costs. This is in fact what happened. Spirit's load factor plummeted after Northwest lowered prices to match Spirit's and added capacity. Spirit's per passenger costs for serving its remaining customer base rose.

If Northwest simply lowered its price on its extant flights and did not add capacity, it is unlikely that a sufficiently large number of Spirits's passengers would be diverted and as a consequence drive Spirit from the market. The reason is because Northwest presumably had optimized its capacity utilization before Spirit entered and so Northwest could not add a large number of additional passengers even at lower prices unless it also increased capacity.

Thus, a critical element of predation in the markets at issues here is not only whether Northwest lowered its prices, but whether Northwest added capacity as part of a predatory strategy in order to drive Spirit's load factor so low that Spirit could no longer remain in the market.

The lowering of price on Northwest's extant capacity would seldom if ever be judged predatory under the price-cost test suggested by Areeda and Turner. This is an artifact of the cost structure in the airline industry compared to conventional manufacturing plants envisioned by Areeda and Turner. In the airline industry, the marginal cost of additional passengers on extant flights with excess capacity is very low, and below almost any imaginable fare. But even very low prices on extant flights are unlikely to drive a low-price entrant from the market because such low prices on extant flights would not divert sufficient passengers to cause the entrant to exit.

In contrast, when a major carrier like Northwest drops prices radically and adds capacity and output, it incurs all of the variable costs associated with additional capacity described earlier. Thus, if the incremental costs of capacity additions (aimed at serving the new lower-fare passengers that Northwest hopes to divert from Spirit) are more that the incremental revenues, then the addition of capacity is predatory because it entails losses that can be explained only as an investment to drive Spirit from the market.

> These incremental costs can be avoided by not adding capacity. Consequently, the revenues and costs of additional capacity are (or at least should be) the focus of the analysis of predation in the airline industry.
>
> For a firm with market power, such as Northwest on the routes in question, economic analysis teaches that it is not optimal to add capacity whose costs exceed revenues in response to entry unless the incumbent can hope to drive the entrant from the market.
>
> The reason is that a firm with market power sets its output (or selects its market capacity) so that marginal revenue equals marginal cost. When a new firm enters the market, the (residual) demand curve for the incumbent firm decreases (shifts to the left), thereby decreasing the incumbent firm's marginal revenue and making it optimal to lower price and reduce capacity and output, not increase it as did Northwest.

This explanation is wholly consistent with the strategy described by Levine, Northwest's executive, and is corroborated by the Oster-Strong economic study on the "Multiple Competitive Tools" in this industry.

In sum, even if the jury were to find that Northwest's prices exceeded an appropriate measure of average variable costs, the jury must also consider the market structure in this controversy to determine if Northwest's deep price discounts in response to Spirit's entry and the accompanying expansion of its capacity on these routes injured competition by causing Spirit's departure from this market and allowing Northwest to recoup its losses and to enjoy monopoly power as a result. For these collective reasons, we reverse and remand this action for further proceedings in accordance with this opinion.

MOORE, Circuit Judge, concurring in the judgment.

While I agree with the majority's holding, I write separately to express my own views on this complicated case.

Inquiring into whether Northwest Airlines charged prices below an appropriate measure of costs implicates several peculiarities of the airline industry. Professors Areeda and Turner, the first commentators to propose a specific cost-based standard for predatory pricing, argued that pricing below short-term marginal cost should be deemed unlawful. Given the real-world difficulty in ascertaining a firm's marginal cost, however, Professors Areeda and Turner suggested using a firm's average variable cost, defined as total variable costs divided by total units produced, as a proxy for marginal cost. Thus, in a traditional industry, if a manufacturer prices its product, a widget, below the average variable cost of producing widgets, the Areeda-Turner model would find the price to be predatory.

Unlike a traditional manufacturer, however, the airline industry presents a more complicated scenario because the bulk of its variable costs are common costs shared among all passengers on a flight. Once an airline commits to flying a plane along a specific route, the airline must incur the costs of the pilots, flight attendants, fuel to fly the empty plane, ownership of the plane, and servicing, without regard to the actual number of passengers on the plane. Despite the common nature of these costs, they are still treated as variable costs of the route because the airline could avoid incurring all of them by exiting the route and redeploying the plane to an alternative route. In addition to these common-variable costs, the airline incurs incremental costs for each additional passenger added on the plane. These passenger-variable costs include the costs associated with processing the ticket, beverage and food service (if any), incremental fuel required to carry the passenger, and baggage service. Thus, the passenger-variable costs are quite minimal compared to the common-variable costs, or non-passenger variable costs of the route.

This disproportional nature between the passenger-variable costs and the common-variable costs has significant implications with regard to evaluating a predatory-pricing claim. For example, suppose on a given route the common-variable costs were $1,000 and the passenger-variable costs were $10 per passenger, and only two passengers were flown, the total variable costs would be approximately $1,020, and the average variable cost would be $510. A fare charged below that amount would be considered predatory pricing under the Areeda-Turner analysis. With each additional passenger added to the plane, however, the average variable cost declines because the common-variable costs are the bulk of the airline's expense and the incremental cost of each additional passenger is so minimal. Thus, if twenty passengers flew on the plane, the total variable costs would be approximately $1,200, and the average variable cost would be $60. Thus, in this scenario, under the Areeda-Turner model, a fare must be below $60 to be considered predatory.

The analysis of the airline market takes on an additional level of complexity when price discrimination is taken into account. Anyone who has ever flown on short notice can attest to the fact that similar seats on the same plane are not priced identically. Indeed, once an airline has committed to flying a plane on a certain route and the common-variable costs have already been incurred, it is in the airline's interest to fill the capacity on the plane given the fact that the incremental cost of each additional passenger is so low and each passenger further reduces the average variable cost. Thus, airlines often sell deeply discounted fares to utilize the unused seats. As Professors Areeda and Hovenkamp have stated, "[i]n the airplane case the seat is going out anyway, full or empty, and any price above the cost of serving the additional passenger will make the additional sale profitable." III PHILLIP E. ARREDA & HERBERT HOVENKAMP, ANTITRUST LAW ¶ 742c, at 466 (2d ed. 2002).

The question before a court in evaluating an antitrust claim becomes whether predatory pricing should be evaluated based on each individual fare or on a larger route-wide basis. For example, under the scenario laid out above, if ten passengers paid a fare of $120 each and thereby covered the total variable costs, while the remaining ten passengers paid a discounted fare of $50 each, the route itself would be profitable, generating $500 more than the total variable costs. The $50 discounted fare, however, would be below the average variable cost, and therefore, the question before the court would be whether pricing on that fare should be considered predatory. This is precisely the issue at the heart of Spirit Airlines's § 2 claim against Northwest.

V. LEGAL ANALYSIS

Having studied the expert reports submitted in this case, I believe both sides have presented credible opinions, which are supported by evidence presented in the record. Specifically, a reasonable trier of fact could find that Spirit's experts have put forth a compelling argument that Northwest did engage in predatory pricing in the limited market in which Spirit competed that eventually forced Spirit out of the market. In addition, a reasonable trier of fact could conclude instead that the relevant market must be viewed as the route itself and that predation cannot be measured by just one type of fare. As we have stated, however, determination of the relevant product market is an issue for the jury to decide. *See Lewis v. Philip Morris Inc.* (6th Cir. 2004) (holding that the definition of the relevant product market "is a factual inquiry for the jury; the court may not weigh evidence or judge witness credibility").

Moreover, even if the relevant market is found to be price-sensitive leisure passengers, disputes exist regarding whether Northwest priced its fares in that market below average variable cost and whether recoupment was a plausible strategy. Thus, a reasonable trier of fact could find either that Dr. Kaplan demonstrated that Northwest's matching fares were below its average variable cost or instead could agree with Dr. Ordover's opinion as to the correct formulation of variable costs. In addition, a reasonable trier of fact could find that Professor Mills had persuasively explained that recoupment was plausible or instead could adopt Dr. Ordover's reasoning that the assumptions upon which Spirit relied were flawed.

In sum, because I find that both parties' expert opinions were reasonable, supported by evidence in the record, and could each be found persuasive by a reasonable trier of fact, I conclude the district court erred in granting Northwest summary judgment in this case. Specifically, the district court erred in adopting Northwest's expert analysis over the one presented by Spirit. Like the majority opinion, I believe that the parties'" competing expert opinions present the 'classic battle of the experts' and it [is] up to a jury to evaluate what weight and credibility each expert opinion deserves."

UNITED STATES DISTRICT COURT
FOR THE DISTRICT OF NEW JERSEY

UNITED STATES OF AMERICA, 450 Fifth Street, NW, Suite 8000 Washington, DC 20530 *Plaintiff,* v. UNITED CONTINENTAL HOLDINGS, INC., 233 S. Wacker Drive Chicago, IL 60606 and DELTA AIR LINES, INC., 1030 Delta Boulevard Atlanta, GA 30354 *Defendants.*	Case No.

VERIFIED COMPLAINT

The United States of America, acting under the direction of the Attorney General of the United States, brings this civil antitrust action to enjoin the proposed acquisition of additional airport takeoff and landing slots at Newark Liberty International Airport ("Newark") by the dominant airline at that airport, United Continental Holdings, Inc. ("United").

I. INTRODUCTION

1. Over 35 million passengers fly in and out of Newark each year to destinations across the United States and around the world. Newark serves the New York-New Jersey metropolitan area and is the most convenient airport for passengers

1

traveling to or from locations in populous Northern New Jersey and portions of Manhattan. To serve Newark, an airline must have "slots," which are takeoff and landing authorizations issued by the Federal Aviation Administration ("FAA") to manage airport congestion and delay.

2. Air passengers flying out of Newark pay among the highest fares in the country. United is the monopoly nonstop provider to 139 of the 206 destinations served nonstop from Newark, and already controls 902 (or 73%) of the 1,233 slots the FAA has allocated to airlines at the airport—over 10 times more slots than the next largest airline. No other airline controls more than 70 slots.

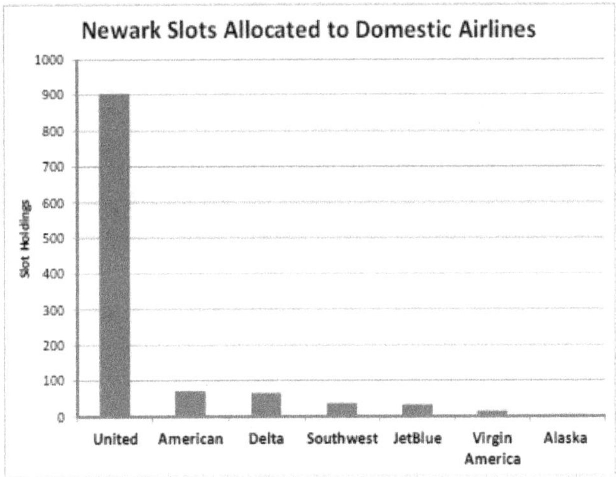

3. United does not use all of the slots it controls at Newark. Each day, it "grounds" as many as 82 slots at Newark—more slots than any of its competitors have the option to fly. United's failure to use the slots it already controls deprives Newark passengers of flight options that would exist if the slots were flown.

4. Yet United wants more. It is now attempting to acquire 24 slots from one of its largest competitors at Newark, Delta Air Lines, Inc. ("Delta"). But with each additional slot it acquires, United reduces competition and forecloses entry or expansion of a rival that would otherwise use the slot to compete. In doing so, United strengthens an already formidable barrier to competition at Newark. In short, permitting United to acquire more slots would further entrench United's dominance at Newark and foreclose competition that is already in critically short supply. As a result, passengers at Newark would face even higher fares and fewer choices.

II. DEFENDANTS AND THE TRANSACTION

5. Defendant United Continental Holdings, Inc., the parent company of United Airlines, is a Delaware corporation headquartered in Chicago, Illinois. United is the third largest airline in the world in terms of revenues. Last year United flew over 138 million passengers to over 352 destinations throughout the world. United has hubs in Newark, Chicago, Denver, Dulles Airport, Houston, Los Angeles, and San Francisco.

6. Defendant Delta Air Lines, Inc., is a Delaware corporation headquartered in Atlanta, Georgia. Delta is the second largest airline in the world in terms of revenues. Last year Delta flew over 170 million passengers to over 316 destinations throughout the world. Delta has hubs in Atlanta, Cincinnati, Detroit, John F. Kennedy International Airport ("JFK"), LaGuardia Airport, Los Angeles, Minneapolis-St. Paul, and Salt Lake City.

7. On June 16, 2015, United and Delta entered into the transaction challenged here: a so-called "slot lease agreement" pursuant to which Delta would lease to United 22 Newark slots that are usable year-round, and two Newark slots that are

usable during the March to October summer season, for $14 million. The lease is long term and automatically renewable and, despite FAA regulation prohibiting the sale of Newark slots, is intended to effectuate a permanent transfer of the slots to United. This slot lease agreement gives United control over these Newark slots.

8. Also on June 16, 2015, United and Delta entered into a separate slot lease agreement pursuant to which United leased to Delta 24 year-round, three summer, and three winter slots at JFK Airport (October to March), also for $14 million. The lease is long term and automatically renewable, and is intended to effectuate a permanent transfer of the slots to Delta. This slot lease agreement gives Delta control over these JFK slots. That transaction closed in June 2015.

III. JURISDICTION, INTERSTATE COMMERCE, AND VENUE

9. The United States brings this action, and this Court has subject-matter jurisdiction over this action, under Section 4 of the Sherman Act, 15 U.S.C. § 4, to prevent and restrain United and Delta from violating Section 1 of the Sherman Act, and United from violating Section 2 of the Sherman Act, 15 U.S.C. §§ 1 and 2.

10. The defendants are engaged in, and their activities substantially affect, interstate commerce. United and Delta each annually transport millions of passengers across state lines throughout this country, generating billions of dollars while doing so.

11. Venue is proper under Section 12 of the Clayton Act, 15 U.S.C. § 22. This Court also has personal jurisdiction over each defendant. Both defendants are found and transact business in this judicial district.

IV. BACKGROUND

A. Slots Are a Barrier to Entry and Expansion at Newark

12. Lack of access to slots constitutes a barrier to entry and expansion at Newark. To serve Newark, the FAA requires that an airline have slots—operational authorizations allowing the carrier to take off and land during designated times of the day. Newark is one of four airports in the United States on which the FAA has imposed slot restraints. The FAA uses slot restraints to manage congestion and delay caused by the fact that demand for service exceeds the airport's capacity during certain times of day.

13. At Newark, the FAA has imposed slot restraints from 6:00 A.M. to 10:59 P.M. Each slot is associated with a particular half-hour window during which the carrier may perform either a takeoff or landing. The FAA has limited Newark to 81 operations, or slots, per hour. Not all of the 81 slots per hour have been allocated to carriers. Some slots are available from the FAA, but undesirable because they are for time periods or days of the week that would not support a commercially viable service pattern without additional slots at time periods when slots are unavailable.

14. Carriers may use their slots to serve any route out of Newark with aircraft of any size. Thus, an airline can choose the destinations it will serve with its slots, and the capacity and frequency with which it will serve them. Airlines continually reassess how to deploy their assets, and enter and exit routes as they seek to take advantage of profit opportunities. Airlines at slot-controlled airports such as Newark deploy slots in different ways over time to respond to changes in consumer demand and competitive moves by their rivals.

15. At slot-controlled airports, slots at times of peak demand are particularly scarce assets and have historically been concentrated in the hands of large airlines that have little incentive to sell or lease slots to carriers that are most likely to compete aggressively against them. This is particularly true at Newark where United holds 73% of all allocated slots, the big three carriers (United, Delta, and American) together control 84%, and the significantly smaller slot holdings of low cost carriers and other domestic competitors at the airport are almost entirely the result of government intervention.

16. Over the years, carriers other than the big three largely have been unable to secure the slots necessary to enter or expand. For example, Virgin America tried to obtain Newark slots from the FAA for years before finally obtaining 15 slots in 2013. As Virgin Group's founder, Richard Branson, explained: "It took us four years to get into Newark. The slots were locked into the legacy carriers. . . . It was only when American went bankrupt that we actually managed to get some slots there." JetBlue and Alaska Airlines have made similar attempts to add to their slim portfolios, but have been unable to obtain additional slots at commercially viable times.

17. In the same vein, Alaska Airlines, Allegiant Air, Frontier Airlines, Spirit Airlines, and Virgin America have jointly advocated for reforms of the existing slot regimes at Newark and other airports, saying in a recent letter to the Department of Transportation and the FAA that they "have been frustrated in their attempts to obtain slots at commercially viable times of the day to provide this needed new service and competition at the NYC Airports."

B. United is the Dominant Slot Holder at Newark

18. United controls 902 of the 1,233 allocated slots at Newark, flies to 189 destinations on a nonstop basis using those slots, and is the monopoly nonstop carrier to 139 of those destinations. United's slot holdings dwarf those of its competitors. Delta, the third largest slot holder at Newark, has only 64 slots and provides nonstop service to just eight destinations. American has 70 slots and serves six destinations on a nonstop basis. Low cost carriers Southwest and JetBlue are limited to 36 and 33 slots, respectively, and each serves eight destinations on a nonstop basis. The remaining carriers provide even more limited service. None has more than 25 slots or 2% of all slots allocated at the airport; for example, Virgin America has just 15 slots, and Alaska Airlines only four.

19. The bulk of United's current slot portfolio was inherited from Continental Airlines when it merged with United in 2010. Before the merger, the two airlines competed on nonstop service on four large domestic routes out of Newark. At that time, Continental held 894 slots at Newark and United held 36 slots.

20. In response to the Department of Justice's concerns expressed during its review of the United/Continental merger, United divested all of its 36 slots at Newark to Southwest. United's then-CEO, Jeff Smisek, touted the settlement: "We think this would be a fair solution that would allow Continental and United to create an airline that will provide customers with an unparalleled global network and top-quality products and services, while enhancing domestic competition at Newark."

21. Nevertheless, United has attempted three times in the intervening years to reverse the benefits to consumers of that divestiture by increasing its slot dominance at

Newark. In July 2014, United presented to the Justice Department a proposal under which it would reacquire from Southwest the very 36 slots it had divested as a condition of its merger. When the Department of Justice objected, United abandoned the transaction. Several months later, in March 2015, United returned with a proposal to acquire 18 Newark slots from American in exchange for 26 slots at JFK. When the Department of Justice again expressed competitive concerns about United's acquisition of additional slots at Newark, negotiations between United and American broke down and the deal was abandoned. In June 2015, United returned once again with the current proposal to acquire 24 Newark slots, this time from Delta.

22. The present transaction is the latest of United's efforts to buy up any additional slots that become available at Newark, despite United already owning more than it is willing to use. Just before its merger with United, Continental acquired 13 slots from AirTran, and after it, the merged firm acquired an additional eight slots from Republic in two separate transactions.

C. <u>United Does Not Use Many of the Slots it Already Controls at Newark</u>

23. Even as United seeks to enhance its dominance at Newark with the acquisition of 24 additional slots, United holds many slots that it does not use. Indeed, United "grounds" as many as 82 slots each day. As illustrated in the chart below, United's unused slots exceed the slots, both used and unused, of each of its competitors:

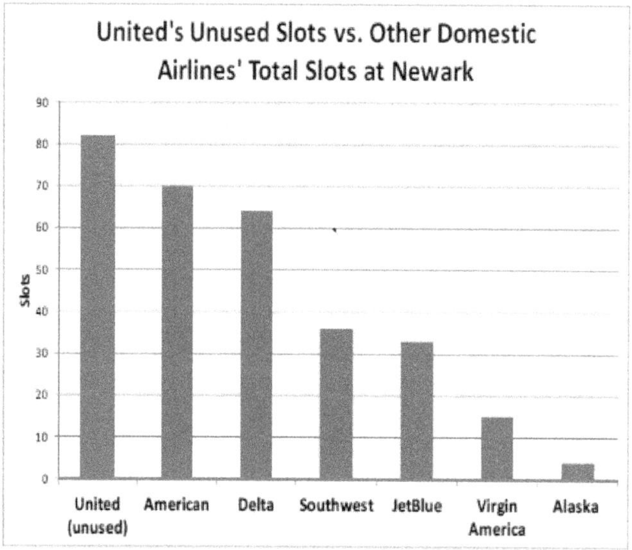

24. Despite its dominance of slots and stockpile of unused slots, United persists in its efforts to buy up more slots at Newark. United has suggested the slots it proposes to acquire from Delta could allow it to provide service to a handful of new destinations and add frequencies to existing routes, though it has yet to commit to specific service plans. But United's existing cache of excess slots would allow it to add flights at Newark if that were its true goal.

D. Slots in the Hands of Rivals Force United to Compete

25. When new entrants have acquired slots at Newark, they have forced United to compete on the merits, resulting in measurable benefits for consumers. For example, when United divested 36 slots to Southwest in 2010 to address the Department of Justice's concerns with the United/Continental merger, Southwest initiated low fare service out of Newark. United was forced to compete and fares dropped significantly. Southwest used the slots to enter the five nonstop routes from Newark listed below. The

9

introduction of head-to-head competition against the merged United/Continental on these routes resulted in substantially lower fares to consumers and increased seats available to travelers:

Route	Year-over-year Percentage Decrease in Average Fare	Year-over-year Percentage Increase in Number of Passengers
Newark-St. Louis	-27%	66%
Newark-Houston	-15%	53%
Newark-Phoenix	-14%	57%
Newark-Chicago	-11%	35%
Newark-Denver	-5%	49%

Passengers flying on these five nonstop routes after Southwest began service saved about $75 million annually compared to what they would have paid under United's substantially higher fares before Southwest's entry.

26. Similarly, when Virgin America acquired slots from American in 2012 and launched service to Los Angeles and San Francisco in direct competition with United, United was forced to respond. It substantially increased capacity and reduced fares on those routes. Virgin Group's founder described the benefits of this fierce competition in a public interview: "They've [United] slashed the fares by 40 percent to try to damage us. Obviously, we've matched the fares. . . . The public is going to be very, very happy with that." United later calculated that its pricing concessions on these two routes in response to Virgin's entry cost it approximately $66 million in annual revenue.

27. By buying up additional slots at Newark, United strengthens an already substantial barrier to entry and expansion and forecloses competition from its rivals. As past experience at Newark shows, such entry and expansion produces significant benefits for consumers.

V. RELEVANT MARKETS

28. If permitted to proceed, anticompetitive effects from the proposed transaction would arise in at least two relevant antitrust markets: the market for Newark slots, and the market for scheduled air passenger service between Newark and other destinations.

A. Takeoff and Landing Slots at Newark Airport

29. Slots at Newark, particularly in peak hours, are difficult to obtain and only rarely change hands between airlines. Even rarer are instances in which slots pass from one of the big three airlines to a low cost carrier or other competitor. There are no alternatives to slots for airlines seeking to enter or expand service at Newark.

30. Airlines do not view service at other airports as reasonable substitutes for service offered at Newark, and thus they are unlikely to switch away from slots at Newark in response to a small but significant increase in the price of slots. Thus, slots at Newark constitute a relevant market under the antitrust laws.

B. Scheduled Air Passenger Service Between Newark and Other Destinations

31. Air passenger service to and from Newark constitutes a relevant antitrust market. The Department in the context of its reviews of airline mergers would typically examine each route from Newark to another airport as a relevant market itself or as part of a broader relevant market involving flights between two cities. We analyze competition at the route level because we are able to see where competition between the two merging firms exists and analyze directly on which route harm is likely to occur.

32. However, in this transaction, the asset that is being acquired is a package of slots, and those slots can be used on any route that the carrier holding the slots

chooses. As a consequence, the impact of a slot transaction on particular routes will differ depending upon how the slots acquired will be used, which can and does change over time. In other words, a slot is simply a form of capacity that can be shifted as needed to and from routes within the Newark airport as a whole. Given that slots can be used to serve any route to or from Newark, it is appropriate to aggregate all routes that either originate or terminate in Newark for the purpose of defining a relevant market in which the transaction will cause anticompetitive harm.

33. In addition, while LaGuardia and JFK offer service to many of the same cities served out of Newark, Newark is the most convenient airport for passengers traveling to or from locations in Northern New Jersey and portions of Manhattan. Many passengers who live or work in these areas have a strong preference for Newark over LaGuardia and JFK, do not consider those other airports to be meaningful alternatives, and would not turn to them even if fares at Newark were to increase by a modest amount.

34. A hypothetical monopolist over all scheduled air passenger service at Newark likely would increase fares on routes to and from Newark by, on average, at least a small but significant and non-transitory amount. Thus, scheduled air passenger service to and from Newark is a relevant market under the antitrust laws.

VI. ANTICOMPETITIVE EFFECTS OF THE TRANSACTION

A. The Market for Scheduled Air Passenger Service Between Newark and Other Destinations and the Market for Slots at Newark Airport are Highly Concentrated and Would Become More So as a Result of the Proposed Transaction

35. Market concentration is one useful indicator of the level of competitive vigor in a market, and of the likely competitive effects of a transaction involving competitors. The more concentrated a market, and the more a transaction would increase

concentration in a market, the more likely it is that a transaction would result in a meaningful reduction in competition. Concentration in relevant markets is typically measured by the Herfindahl-Hirschman Index ("HHI"). The Horizontal Merger Guidelines consider markets in which the HHI exceeds 2,500 points to be "highly concentrated." Horizontal Merger Guidelines, § 5.3. The Guidelines further consider post-acquisition increases in HHI of more than 200 points to be significant increases in concentration that are "presumed to be likely to enhance market power." *Id.*

36. Slots are in essence units of capacity that can be deployed by carriers to serve any destination to or from Newark. Lack of access to slots constitutes a barrier to an airline's ability to provide air passenger service between Newark and other destinations in competition with United. A carrier's Newark slot holdings therefore provide a measure of its ability to compete for passengers at Newark, and each firm's share of Newark slots reflects its competitive significance in the air passenger service market.

37. United's proposed acquisition of 24 slots from Delta would give United a market share of approximately 75% in the already highly concentrated Newark slots market, and a correspondingly high share in the Newark air passenger service market. United would be by far the largest holder of slots, dwarfing the second largest carrier, American, which controls just under 6%. The pre-acquisition HHI is 5440—double the level considered to be highly concentrated under the Horizontal Merger Guidelines. *Id.* The post-acquisition HHI would increase to 5710. The resulting change in concentration of 270 represents a significant increase in concentration. These facts create a strong

presumption that the transaction would enhance United's market power and harm competition at Newark.

38. United's 73% share of Newark slots is consistent with other measures of concentration at the airport. For example, United accounts for 73% of scheduled flights at Newark and 68% of seats.

B. The Proposed Transaction Would Diminish Delta's Competitive Significance at Newark, Foreclose Other Airlines from Obtaining Slots Needed to Compete Against United, and Reduce Service at Newark

39. As the largest airline at Newark by a substantial margin, United already enjoys market power, which its competitors, with their significantly smaller slot holdings, have limited ability to discipline. United's large pool of Newark slots affords it tremendous flexibility to defend its dominance at Newark. It can neutralize rivals' efforts to enter or expand by adding flights to the route or routes that are threatened, making it difficult for rivals to attract enough passengers to operate profitably. By contrast, United's existing competitors and new entrants with very few slots are limited in their ability to add service or shift flights to other Newark routes to counter United's initiatives.

40. If the proposed transaction is not enjoined, one immediate impact is that it would diminish Delta's ability to compete on routes served by United out of Newark, leaving Delta with only 40 slots to compete against United's 926. Delta and United currently compete on domestic nonstop service to Delta's hubs in Atlanta, Cincinnati Detroit, and Minneapolis, and consumers have benefitted from this competition. But with one-third fewer slots, Delta would need to cut back service to one or more of these cities or reschedule flights at less convenient times. Moreover, with no slots to spare,

Delta would have no ability to add frequencies to counter initiatives by United, its only nonstop competitor on these routes. Nor would Delta have slots available to launch new service or reinstate service to markets it once served in response to changes in consumer demand.

41. The proposed transaction would also substantially reduce the likelihood of entry or expansion by other airlines at Newark. As the third largest slot holder at Newark, Delta is one of the most promising sources of slots for new entrants seeking to serve the airport. By agreeing to transfer these slots to United—the dominant firm—for $14 million, Delta has signaled its willingness to part with these valuable competitive assets. In the hands of anyone other than United, these slots would result in more competition for United at Newark. By contrast, if the slots are acquired by United, such competition is foreclosed.

42. As the dominant carrier with 73% of the slots and 73% of the flights at Newark, United has a strong incentive to pursue a foreclosure strategy. It stands to lose more than any other airline from entry or expansion by rivals because any new service is likely to introduce competition on one of its routes. As a result, United has a greater incentive than any other Newark carrier, including Delta, to keep slots out of the hands of its competitors. Delta is unlikely to face new entry or expansion on routes serving its hubs. United's incentive and ability to engage in foreclosure strategies at Newark would increase with an increase in the number of slots it controls.

43. The transaction likely would also result in reduced service at Newark, pushing up fares and leaving passengers with less choice. United's portfolio of 902 Newark slots permits the operation of as many as 451 roundtrip flights each day. On

average, however, United only operates 386 roundtrip flights each day at Newark. By consciously limiting its Newark capacity, United is able to raise fares to and from the airport. And with significantly fewer slots, United's competitors have little ability to adjust frequencies to respond to United's capacity reductions. Thus, United can reduce service on a route without fear that its rivals will enter or expand and steal business. The proposed transaction would make this dynamic worse since it would reduce the number of slots that could be deployed to compete against United.

VII. MONOPOLY MAINTENENCE

44. United's control of 73% of the slots at Newark gives it monopoly power over the markets for Newark slots and Newark scheduled air passenger service. United is already exercising this monopoly power, and has long been able to extract a "Newark premium" for its service. Indeed, airfares at Newark are among the highest in the country and service ranks among the worst.

45. United now seeks to maintain and enhance its monopoly power by acquiring 24 additional slots from one of its largest competitors at Newark, Delta. The addition of 24 slots to United's existing cache would further enhance its existing monopoly power as well as its ability to maintain and reinforce the high entry barriers faced by competitors seeking to enter or expand at Newark.

VIII. ABSENCE OF COUNTERVAILING FACTORS

46. New entry or expansion by existing competitors is unlikely to prevent or remedy the transaction's likely anticompetitive effects. United's rivals cannot easily enter or expand service at Newark due to the limited availability of slots as well as other barriers to entry.

47. There are no transaction-specific efficiencies that outweigh the likely competitive harms of the proposed transaction. United claims it will use the 24 slots it proposes to acquire from Delta to serve a handful of new destinations and add frequencies to existing routes. On this basis, United asserts that the transaction would result in network efficiencies and benefits to consumers. But United has yet to commit to a specific service plan, and it already has dozens of extra slots at its disposal should it wish to add new service. Passengers at Newark will be better off if United is forced to compete on the merits for their business.

IX. VIOLATIONS ALLEGED

48. The proposed transaction is a contract that would unreasonably restrain interstate trade and commerce in violation of Section 1 of the Sherman Act, 15 U.S.C. § 1.

49. Through the proposed transaction and other actions, United is monopolizing and/or maintaining and enhancing its current monopoly over the markets for Newark slots and for scheduled air transportation in Newark in violation of Section 2 of the Sherman Act, 15 U.S.C. § 2.

50. Unless enjoined, the proposed transaction would impose a permanent structural change at Newark that is likely to have the following effects, among others:

(a) The elimination of actual and potential competition between United and Delta at Newark;

(b) The substantial reduction of Delta's competitive presence at Newark;

(c) The removal of an additional 24 slots from competition with United, thereby further enhancing United's market power;

(d) The further extension of barriers to entry and expansion at Newark by United's rivals;

(e) The increase in United's ability to remove capacity from the Newark markets; and

(f) The further entrenchment and enhancement of United's already dominant position at Newark.

X. REQUEST FOR RELIEF

51. Plaintiff, the United States of America, requests:

(a) That the proposed Newark slot lease agreement between United and Delta be adjudged to violate Sections 1 and 2 of the Sherman Act, 15 U.S.C. §§ 1 and 2;

(b) That Defendants be permanently enjoined from and restrained from carrying out the proposed acquisition or any similar acquisition that would result in United acquiring control of slots from Delta at Newark;

(c) That United be required to notify the Antitrust Division of the U.S. Department of Justice at least 90 days in advance of any acquisition, lease, or agreement whereby United assumes long-term control of slots at Newark within the next five years;

(d) That Plaintiff be awarded its costs of this action; and

(e) That Plaintiff be awarded such other relief as the Court may deem just and proper.

NOTES

1. "[N]o mass transportation system in the history of mankind has been profitable over time." Kevin P. Mitchell, *The U.S. Airline Industry Fate*, 15 KNOWLEDGE, TECH. & POL'Y 3, 5 (2002). Are airlines destined for the same fate? *See* Richard D. Cudahy, *The Airlines: Destined to Fail?*, 71 J. AIR L. & COM. 3 (2006). *Compare* Paul Stephen Dempsey, *The Financial Performance of the Airline Industry Post-Deregulation*, 45 HOUS. L. REV. 421, 423 (2008) (after thirty years of deregulation policy "the airline industry is in far worse financial condition after deregulation than before it.") *with* Peter C. Carstensen, *The Poor Financial Performance of Deregulated Airlines: Competition as Causation or Only Correlation? Reflections on Professor Dempsey's Article*, 45 HOUS. L. REV. 487, 488 (2008) ("The problem is that, in the absence of legal standards that meaningfully constrain the discretion of airlines, individually rational competitors can, and apparently have, engaged in destructive competition.").

2. "Deregulation" is a bit of a misnomer. While the airline industry was deregulated economically in 1978, the airline industry itself remains among the most regulated industries in the United States. Indeed, the "dichotomization [between regulation and deregulation] is false ... 'Deregulation' has in fact meant eliminating a few, specific controls while retaining all others. Air travel today, [for example,] as in the past, is totally dependent on the existence and effective operation of such industry specific controls as the FAA's air traffic system." Peter C. Carstensen, *Evaluating "Deregulation" of Commercial Air Travel: False Dichotomization, Untenable Theories, and Unimplemented Premises*, 46 WASH. & LEE L. REV. 109, 116 (1989).

Travelers have benefitted or were intended to benefit by airline deregulation policy vis-à-vis competition, discount fares, democratization of air travel, and frequent flyer programs. *See, e.g.*, Herbert D. Kelleher, *Deregulation and the Troglodytes—How the Airlines Met Adam Smith*, 50 J. AIR L. & COM. 299, 304 (1985) ("Deregulation has produced substantial societal benefits in the form of lower fares, increased service, diversity of service and price alternatives, reduced industry concentration, more efficient allocation of resources and, in the long run, a more healthy, efficient and innovative airline industry.")

"Hub premiums," airline bankruptcies, complex fare structures, and yield management have cast doubt on the policy decision to economically deregulate airlines in the United States, however. *See, e.g.*, Wesley G. Kaldahl, *Let the Process of Deregulation Continue*, 50 J. AIR L. & COM M. 285, 295 (1985) ("The *public* has not benefited. There is less nonstop service, most lengthy trips require stops at intermediate hubs, and fares are widely inconsistent and tend to favor the few chosen markets."). *See also* LAURENCE E. GESELL, AIRLINE RE-REGULATION 17 (Coast Aire Publications 1990) (hypothesizing that "there has been an increase in finance-oriented managers during the airline deregulatory process ... that ... results in negative welfare interests."). Additionally, from a passenger's viewpoint, airlines may be charging low fares, but they otherwise are nickel-and-diming consumers for additional fees and surcharges, including upwards of $45 for checked luggage, fees for carry-on baggage, $8 for pillows, fees for "advanced boarding," different costs for window, middle and aisle seats, and so on. *E.g.*, Glorida Goodale, *First It Was the Baggage Fees. What's Next? Pay Toilets?*, CHRISTIAN SCIENCE MONITOR, Apr. 26, 2010, at 2010 WL 8635095.

Commentary discussing the benefits and drawbacks of Airline Deregulation Act, Pub. L. 95-504 (codified as amended in scattered sections of 49 U.S.C.), is substantial. *See generally* Ann K. Wooster, Annotation, *Construction and Application of § 105 Airline Deregulation Act (49 U.S.C. § 41713), Pertaining to Preemption of Authority over Prices, Routes, and Services*, 149 A.L.R. FED. 299 (1998); GEORGE WILLIAMS, AIRLINE COMPETITION: DEREGULATION'S MIXED LEGACY (Ashgate 2002); KENNETH BUTTON & ROGER STOUGH, AIR TRANSPORT NETWORKS (2000); GEORGE WILLIAMS, THE AIRLINE INDUSTRY AND THE IMPACT OF DEREGULATION (1993); PAUL STEPHEN DEMPSEY & ANDREW R. GOETZ, AIRLINE DEREGULATION AND LAISSEZ-FAIRE MYTHOLOGY (1992); Laurence E. Gesell & Martin T. Farris, *Airline Deregulation: An Evaluation of Goals and Objectives*, 21 TRANSP. L.J. 105 (1992); Theodore P. Harris, *The Disaster of Deregulation*, 20 TRANSP. L.J. 87 (1991); Alfred E. Kahn, *Deregulation: Looking Backward and Looking Forward*, 7 YALE J. ON REG. 325 (1990); Andrew R. Goetz & Paul Stephen Dempsey, *Airline Deregulation Ten Years After: Something Foul in the Air*, 54 J. AIR L. & COM. 927 (1989); Melvin A. Brenner, *Airline Deregulation—A Case Study in Public Policy Failure*, 16 TRANSP. L.J. 179 (1988); Alfred E. Kahn, *Airline Deregulation—A Mixed Bag, But a Clear Success Nevertheless*, 16 TRANSP. L.J. 229 (1988); Thomas G. Moore, *U.S. Airline Deregulation: Its Effects on Passengers, Capital and Labor*, 29 J.L. & ECON. 1 (1986); Edward A. Morash, *Airline Deregulation: Another Look*, 50 J. AIR L. & COM. 253 (1985); Michael E. Levine, *Revisionism Revised? Airline Deregulation and the Public Interest*, 44 L. & CONTEMP. PROBS. 179 (1981); C. Vincent Olson & John M. Trapani, III, *Who Has Benefited from Regulation of the Airline Industry?*, 24 J.L. & ECON. 75 (1981); *The Impact of Government Regulation on Air Transportation*, 9 AKRON L. REV. 629 (1976); Richard D. Gritta, *Profitability and Risk in Air Transport: A Case for Deregulation*, 7 TRANSP. L.J. 197 (1975); WILLIAM A. JORDAN, AIRLINE REGULATION IN AMERICA: EFFECTS AND IMPERFECTIONS (The Johns Hopkins Press 1970).

3. The deregulated airline market was heralded as one that would be "perfectly contestable." *See* Elizabeth E. Bailey & William J. Baumol, *Deregulation and the Theory of Contestable Markets*, 1 YALE J. ON REG. 111, 113 (1984). Has this been achieved? One commentator notes that "[t]he vision of the deregulated airline industry as effectively competitive suggested that merger policies developed under antitrust laws would suffice for whatever mergers and acquisitions might transpire. In this the proponents [of airline deregulation] were wrong." Almarin Philips, *Airline Mergers in the New Regulatory Environment*, 129 U. PA. L. REV. 856, 857 (1981) ("The nation may be left with a really small number of large, quasi-monopolistic and not necessarily efficient carriers"). *See also* Yochi J. Dreazen et al., *Why the Sudden Rise in the Urge to Merge*

and Form Oligopolies?, WALL. ST. J., Feb. 25, 2002, at A10 (quoting economist Carl Shapiro, "Twenty [competitors] to four is good. It's four to two that is much more dubious.").

4. Ten years after the Airline Deregulation Act of 1978 was enacted, Alfred Kahn—a Cornell University economist widely referred to as the "father of airline deregulation"—remarked:

> Just as one of the most pleasant surprises of the early deregulation experience was the large-scale entry of new, highly competitive carriers, so probably the most unpleasant one has been the reversal of that trend—the departures of almost all of them, the reconcentration of the industry both nationally and at the major hubs, the diminishing disciplinary effectiveness of potential entry by totally new firms, and the increased likelihood, in consequence, of monopolistic exploitation.
>
> * * *
>
> Were these developments surprises? Yes, to a large extent.

Alfred E. Kahn, *Surprises of Airline Deregulation*, 78 AM. ECON. REV. 316, 318 (1988) ("Most of us probably did not foresee the deterioration in the average quality of the flying experience, and in particular the congestion and delays that have plagued air travelers in recent years.").

Indeed, the number of major airlines shrunk considerably in 1986 alone, from 18 to 8. Over the years since deregulation, Air California, Air Florida, Braniff, Eastern, National, New York Air, PEOPLExpress, Pan Am, Piedmont, Ozark, Republic, and Western Air Lines, among others, either stopped operations or were merged into American, Delta, Northwest, TWA, and/or Texas Air. *See generally* L. Milton Glisson, *Is U.S. Domestic Airline Competition on a Flight to Oblivion?*, 58 TRANSP. PRAC. J. 217, 218 (1991); Robert L. Thornton, *Airlines and Agents: Conflict and the Public Welfare*, 52 J. AIR L. & COM. 371, 396 (1986) (concluding "if [the DOT] fails to act soon, the number of effective competitors in the airline industry may fall below the point from which deconcentration is possible without a major crisis"); Paul Stephen Dempsey, *Antitrust Law and Policy in Transportation: Monopoly I$ the Name of the Game*, 21 GA. L. REV. 505, 514 (1987).

In 2008, Northwest Airlines merged into Delta Airlines to create the world's largest airline, and in 2010, United Airlines and Continental Airlines announced a merger between the two carriers that will become the world's largest airline. *See, e.g.*, Darren Shannon, *Fit to be Tied?*, AVIATION WK. & SPACE TECH., May 10, 2010, at 20. Such mergers have raised the possibility of re-regulation of the airline industry. Representative

James Oberstar (D-Minn.), for example, voted for the Airline Deregulation Act of 1978, but threatened financial re-regulation of commercial airlines should the United States Department of Justice approve the United-Continental merger:

> Deregulation has been credited with making airline travel affordable for the average American. But Oberstar pointed to the $2.7 billion the airlines earned in baggage fees in 2009 as evidence that consumers are no longer benefiting from the system. He said he believes there's support in the House for re-regulation.
>
> "Hardly a day passes where I don't walk out on the [House] floor that someone asks me, 'When are we going to re-regulate the airlines?'" Oberstar told reporters after the hearing.
> The legislation would impose federal regulation of airline pricing and re-establish a government gatekeeper role similar to that played by the old Civil Aeronautics Board before deregulation in 1978, Oberstar said.
>
> * * *
>
> Airlines have suffered repeated shocks in recent years, including 9-11, the SARS virus, volatile oil prices and the recession. They have shed more than 158,000 full-time jobs since employment peaked in 2001 and lost an estimated $30 billion to $60 billion in recent years. At least 13 airlines have filed for bankruptcy in the past several years.

Congress to Revisit Airline Re-Regulation if Merger Goes Through, FORT WORTH-STAR TELEGRAM, June 17, 2010, at 2010 WLNR 12256952. *See also* Timothy M. Ravich, *Re-Regulation and Airline Passengers' Rights*, 67 J. AIR L. & COM. 935 (2002); Robert L. Crandall, *Bring Back Airline Regulation*, AVIATION WK. & SPACE TECH., June 16, 2008, at 62 ("Our airlines are now laggards in every category. Their financial health is precarious. … The solution is not consolidation. Mergers will not lower fuel prices. They will require major capital expenditures, are likely to increase labor costs and will disadvantage many employees."; Adrian Schofield, *Free to Fail*, AVIATION WK. & SPACE TECH., Oct. 27, 2008, at 48 (reporting concern by lawmakers that airline mergers will reduce consumer choice too much, which the very opposite of what deregulation was supposed to achieve).

5. The court in *Spirit Airlines, Inc. v. Northwest Airlines, Inc.*, *supra*, focused intently on determining the relevant "market" (*i.e.*, low-fare or leisure-passenger) and the relative power exercised in that market by the incumbent airline for purposes of assessing

claims of monopolization and attempted monopolization. What is the relevant market for determining whether economic deregulation of commercial air travel in the United States is an effective policy? Some economists posit that industry consolidation may bring beneficial density gains that offset the effect of lost competition:

> [I]f fewer effective competitors exist at the national level, deregulation has not necessarily decreased airline competition: for it is at the *route* level that airlines compete head to head. For example, four effective competitors at the national level can operate in two very different ways: with each having a monopoly share on one-quarter of the routes or with each having a one-quarter share on all routes. Although the number of airlines is the same either way, the second situation is obviously more competitive because more airlines serve each route. Thus fewer effective competitors at the national level does not necessarily mean that the industry is less competitive.

STEVEN A. MORRISON & CLIFFORD WINSTON, THE EVOLUTION OF THE AIRLINE INDUSTRY 9 (The Brookings Institute 1995).

6. Predatory tactics are difficult to distinguish from allowable competition. Indeed, "[a] plaintiff charging predation will classify a reduction in price, an expansion in output, the building of a new plant, and so on as proof of the defendant's villainy. Unless we have some powerful tools to separate predation from its cousin, hard competition, any legal inquiry is apt to lead to more harm than good." Frank H. Easterbrook, *Predatory Strategies and Counterstrategies*, 48 U. CHI. L. REV. 263, 266-67 (1981). *See also* Phillip Areeda & Donald F. Turner, *Predatory Pricing and Related Practices under Section 2 of the Sherman Act*, 88 HARV. L. REV. 697, 698 (1975). *See generally* Chris Sagers, *"Rarely Tried ... and Rarely Successful": Theoretically Impossible Price Predation among the Airlines*, 74 J. AIR L. & COM. 919 (2009) (noting that *Spirit Airlines, Inc. v. Northwest Airlines, Inc.*, 431 F.3d 917 (6th Cir. 2004) never reached the merits as the parties entered a confidential settlement after summary judgment was entered); Shubha Ghosh & Darren Bush, *Predatory Conduct and Predatory Legislation: Exclusionary Tactics in Airline Markets*, 45 HOUS. L. REV. 343 (2008).

7. Significantly, *United States v. AMR Corp.* (10th Cir. 2003) and *Spirit Airlines, Inc. v. Northwest Airlines, Inc.* (6th Cir. 2004), *supra*, were disposed of via summary judgment. Is this surprising? Predatory tactics conceivably are employed in the airline industry:

> There is sufficient market power in the airline industry, as shown by the persistence of hub premiums at many airports, to allow recoupment of losses incurred in driving a

> competitor from a market [despite] that the antitrust laws, as they have been applied in other industries, may not be sufficient to identify some types of predatory practices in the airline industry.

Clinton V. Oster & John S. Strong, *Predatory Practices in the U.S. Airline Industry*, Jan. 15, 2001, at 3, *http://ostpxweb.dot.gov/aviation/domestic-competition/predpractices.pdf.*

Congress has tried to address the issue of predation in the airline industry at various times. For example, in 1993, Congress proposed the "Airline Predatory Pricing Prevention Act of 1993," S. 770, 103d Cong. 2(c)(4) (1993), which offered two indicators of predatory pricing:

> (A) The pricing by the air carrier for air transportation in the city-pair market at issue is below the direct operating costs of the air carrier in providing such transportation.
>
> (B) Decreases in the pricing by the air carrier for such air transportation are occurring when market forces have led to sustained downward development of air fares deviating significantly from ordinary seasonal pricing movements and resulting in widespread losses among all air carriers for providing such air transportation.

See generally Patrick Bolton et al., *Predatory Pricing: Strategic Theory and Legal Policy*, 89 GEO. L.J. 2239 (2000); Russell A. Klingaman, *Predatory Pricing and Other Exclusionary Conduct in the Airline Industry: Is Antitrust Law the Solution?*, 4 DEPAUL BUS. L.J. 281 (1992); Janusz A. Ordover & Robert D. Willig, *An Economic Definition of Predation: Pricing and Product Innovation*, 91 YALE L.J. 8 (1981).

8. The actual impact of consolidation in the commercial airline marketplace "may be less harmful than is generally expected" as

> [c]onsolidation lowers competition, which tends to reduce welfare. At the same time, consolidation increases traffic densities in the networks of the surviving carriers. Since higher densities reduce costs, this effect tends to raise welfare. If the economies of density are sufficiently strong, the cost effect will overshadow the effect of lost competition, leading to a welfare gain. This outcome is in fact familiar from standard oligopoly models, which show that industry consolidation in the presence of increasing returns can be welfare-improving.

Jan K. Brueckner & Pablo T. Spiller, *Economies of Traffic Density in the Deregulated Airline Industry*, 37 J.L. & ECON. 379, 408 (1994). *Contra* Melanie Trottman & Scott McCartney, *The Age of 'Wal-Mart' Airlines Crunches the Biggest Carriers*, WALL ST. J., June 18, 2002, at A1.

9. In the early 1980s, American Airlines and Braniff Airlines were competing fiercely for passengers flying to, from and through Dallas-Ft. Worth, by offering lower fares and better service. During a telephone conversation between Robert Crandall, American's president, and Howard Putnam, Braniff's president, the following exchange occurred:

> Crandall: I think it's dumb as hell, for Christ's sake all right, to sit here and pound the shit out of each other and neither one of us making a fucking dime.
>
> Putnam: Well –
>
> Crandall: I mean, goddamn! What the fuck is the point of it? Nobody asked American to serve Harlingen. Nobody asked American to serve Kansas City, and there were low fares in there, you know, before. So
>
> Putnam: If you're going to overlay every route of American's on top of every route that Braniff has, I can't just sit here and allow you to bury us without giving you our best effort.
>
> Crandall: Oh sure, but Eastern and Delta do the same thing in Atlanta and have for years.
>
> Putnam: Do you have a suggestion for me?
>
> Crandall: Yes, I have a suggestion for you. Raise your goddamn fares twenty percent. I'll raise mine the next morning.
>
> Putnam: Robert, we can't talk about pricing.
>
> Crandall: Oh, bullshit Howard. We can talk about any goddamn thing we want to talk about.

Putnam did not raise Braniff's fares in response to Crandall's proposal; he presented the government with a tape recording of the conversation instead. *See United States v. American Airlines, Inc.* (5th Cir. 1984). *See also In reAir Passenger Computer Reservations Systems Antitrust Litigation* (C.D. Cal. 1988).

10. *American Airlines v. Dep't of Transp.* (5th Cir. 2000), *supra*, and a related case, *Legend Airlines, Inc. v. City of Fort Worth* (Tx. Ct. App. 2000), show the extent to which "legacy" carriers went to derail the emergence of low cost carriers.In fact, Southwest Airliners—founded by lawyer Herbert D. Kelleher—continues to market itself in terms of a running narrative of us-versus-them, a veritable David-versus-Goliath battle for the right to fly. KEVIN FREIBERG & JACKIE FRIEBERG, NUTS! SOUTHWEST AIRLINES' CRAZY RECIPE FOR BUSINESS AND PERSONAL SUCCESS 10 (Broadway Books 1996) ("The people of Southwest Airlines are crusaders with an egalitarian spirit who truly believe they are in the business of freedom."). John Grantham, *A Free Bird Sings the Song of the Caged: Southwest Airlines' Fight to Repeal the Wright Amendment*, 72 J. AIR L. & COM. 429 (2007); Robert B. Gilbreath & Paul C. Watler, *Perimeter Rules, Proprietary Powers, and the Airline Deregulation Act: A Tale of Two Cities ... and Two Airports*, 66 J. AIR L. & COM. 223 (2000).

PROBLEM

Virgin Atlantic Airways, Ltd. ("Virgin Atlantic") alleges that British Airways, while marketing its global network of airline services, engaged in predatory business practices, pointing specifically to British Airways' use of incentive agreements with corporate clients and travel agencies. Virgin Atlantic theorizes that these agreements offered below-cost pricing and thus attracted passengers to British Airways' transatlantic flights. Losses from pricing tickets below cost, Virgin continues, were recouped by coupling these flights with other routes on which British Airways exercised monopoly power and could charge higher fares. The net effect, according to Virgin Atlantic, was to impede Virgin Atlantic's efforts to expand service from London's Heathrow Airport to five markets in the United States: New York (John F. Kennedy airport); Los Angeles; Chicago; San Francisco; and Washington, D.C. Virgin Atlantic further claims British Airways offset its losses from the incentive agreements by charging higher fares on these five transatlantic routes, until Virgin Atlantic emerged as a competitor. British Airways moves for summary judgment. Should Virgin Atlantic's claim survive as a matter of law? Is the alleged conduct by British Airways anti-competitive in violation of applicable U.S. antitrust law? *See Virgin Atlantic Airways, Ltd. v. British Airways PLC* (2d Cir. 2001).

B. BANKRUPTCY AND POST-9/11 INSURANCE

Airline deregulation (*see* Chapter 2)—borne out of the very same policy impulse that perhaps contributed to energy deregulation and corporate frauds like Enron, banking deregulation, and the Great Recession of 2008—invite serious reconsideration. As aviator and United States Bankruptcy Judge (Southern District of Florida) A.J. Cristol has observed:

> Yes, we have lower fares on certain routes [but it is] because the airline industry, like the United States Congress, is unable to understand that if you sell your product for less than it costs you, you have a deficit. At the same time, we have astronomical airfares on other routes.
>
> Robert Crandall, the former president and CEO of American Airlines, used to make a speech where he opened up by asking his audience "How much did a Hershey Bar cost in 1945?" Members of the audience would volunteer, "a quarter," "a dime." Crandall would then point out that in 1945 you could buy a Hershey Bar for a nickel. A new Chevrolet could be purchased for $900. Roundtrip airfare from New York to Paris was $700.
>
> Today a Hershey bar is as much as a buck. A new Chevy Camero is listed out as Chevy $33,600, and roundtrip airfare? New York to Paris can be $500 to $600, sometime less.
>
> Crandall's point is simple ... Most airfares are too low. Airlines charge too much for first and business class and far too little for coach or economy ... Each year they continue to lose more and more money and they try to make it up with charges for your suitcase or your seat assignment.
>
> In the irrational airline industry of today, the doctrine is sell your seats at a loss and make it up on volume. A few quarters ago, Delta announced a huge loss. Their solution: Reduce fares ... and Pricing: It goes from the sublime to the ridiculous.

Hon. A.J. Cristol, United States Bankruptcy Judge, Southern District of Florida, Guest Lecture at the University of Miami School of Law (Sept. 12, 2013) (recording available at *http:// www.law.miami.edu/webcast/video.php?location=Departments&stream=Aviation_ Economics_(Judge_Cristol_Guest_Lecture)_September_12_ 2013.mp4&width=480&height=270&page=*). Not only did the Airline

Deregulation Act of 1978 deteriorate the relationship among airlines and their passengers and employees, but also left airlines financially vulnerable to the terrorism of September 11th, as explored below.

IN RE IONOSPHERE CLUBS, INC.

922 F.2d 984 (2d Cir. 1990)

TIMBERS, Circuit Judge.

This appeal involves two issues in a labor dispute between Eastern Airlines, Inc. ("Eastern") and the Air Line Pilots Association, International ("ALPA"). At all times relevant to this appeal, the relationship between the two parties was governed by a collective bargaining agreement dated February 23, 1986 and entered into pursuant to the Railway Labor Act ("RLA"), 45 U.S.C. § 151 *et seq*. (1988).

BACKGROUND

On March 4, 1989, the International Association of Machinists and Aerospace Workers ("IAM") began a primary strike against Eastern. Soon thereafter, ALPA and the Transportation Workers Union of America struck Eastern in sympathy with the IAM. On March 9, 1989, Eastern filed a petition for reorganization under Chapter 11 of the Bankruptcy Code in the Southern District of New York. On June 21, 1989, Eastern filed a motion in the bankruptcy court to reject the collective bargaining agreement pursuant to Section 1113. Eastern later withdrew that motion. At the time the bankruptcy court reached the decisions under review on the instant appeal, no application under § 1113 to terminate or modify the collective bargaining agreement was pending before it. Martin R. Shugrue, Jr. was appointed Trustee for Eastern on April 19, 1990.

The collective bargaining agreement contained labor protective provisions ("LPPs") designed to protect ALPA members in the event of a merger. The collective bargaining agreement provided that disputes arising from it would be submitted to arbitration and it set forth a procedure governing that process. Eastern was sold to Texas Air Corporation ("Texas Air") within days after the collective bargaining agreement became operative. After Eastern's acquisition by Texas Air, a dispute arose as to the operation of the LPPs. On June 10, 1986, Eastern commenced an action in the Southern District of Florida, seeking a declaration that the collective bargaining agreement was invalid. That contention was rejected and Eastern was ordered to arbitrate the dispute.

On August 6, 1986, pursuant to the provisions of the collective bargaining agreement, ALPA filed a grievance with the System Board of Adjustments, the body established to hear and determine grievances based on disputes concerning the collective bargaining agreement. On March 8, 1989, the arbitration panel ruled in favor of ALPA. It concluded that the LPPs provided that, in the event of a merger, seniority lists were to be merged. The panel did not decide whether a merger had taken place that would have triggered the LPPs. The decision was not signed by all the panel members until the next day, approximately seven minutes after Eastern filed its bankruptcy petition.

On July 21, 1989, ALPA filed a motion in the bankruptcy court, seeking a determination that the arbitration decision became effective prior to Eastern's Chapter 11 filing and, thus, was not affected by the automatic stay, or, in the alternative, it sought relief from the automatic stay to implement the arbitration decision. ALPA supplemented its motion requesting relief from the automatic stay with a request to commence a second arbitration to determine whether Eastern and Continental had merged, thus triggering the LPPs. Eastern did not oppose the request for relief from the stay to implement the first arbitration decision, but did oppose the supplemental request to commence a second arbitration.

The bankruptcy court lifted the stay for the limited purpose of formally issuing the arbitration decision interpreting the LPPs, but declined to lift the stay for the purpose of allowing ALPA to initiate an arbitration to determine whether a merger had taken place. *In re Ionosphere Clubs, Inc., supra.* The court reasoned that issues raised in the arbitration would duplicate efforts being made by the examiner it had appointed.

* * *

Wet-leasing refers to the practice of one airline leasing aircraft and crews from another airline. The collective bargaining agreement prohibited Eastern from engaging in this practice. It required Eastern to employ ALPA pilots on the Eastern pilot's system seniority list to perform its flying. In August 1989, since its pilots were on strike and replacement pilots were still being trained, Eastern entered into wet-lease contracts with Continental.

On September 1, 1989, ALPA commenced an action in the Southern District of Florida ("Florida Action"), seeking to enjoin the wet-leasing as violative of the collective bargaining agreement and of the RLA. The district court set the case on an expedited discovery schedule. On September 25, 1989, Eastern commenced an adversary proceeding in the bankruptcy court, seeking to enjoin ALPA from prosecuting the Florida Action. In its complaint, Eastern alleged that its wet-lease contracts were reasonably necessary to its continued operation during the strike.

The bankruptcy court held that the Florida Action violated the provisions of the automatic stay, specifically, 11 U.S.C. § 362(a)(3) (1988), which provides for a stay of "any act to exercise control over property of the estate." *In re Ionosphere Clubs, supra.* The court determined that Eastern's actions were "reasonably necessary" to its continued operation during the strike and were protected under the doctrine announced in *Brotherhood of Ry. & S.S. Clerks v. Florida East Coast Ry.* (1966). Finally, the bankruptcy court enjoined further prosecution of the Florida Action pursuant to its powers under § 105(a). ALPA appealed both bankruptcy court orders to the district court pursuant to 28 U.S.C. § 158(a) (1988). The appeal from the LPP decision was assigned to Judge Sweet. The appeal from the Wet-Lease Decision was assigned to Judge Leval. Subsequently, the two appeals were consolidated before Judge Sweet.

On April 10, 1990, the district court entered its opinion and order, reversing the orders of the bankruptcy court in both cases. *In re Ionosphere Clubs, Inc.* (S.D.N.Y. 1990). The district court reasoned that § 1113 of the Bankruptcy Code was intended to be the "exclusive ... means in the Bankruptcy Code by which a debtor could modify or reject its collective bargaining contract obligations." The court concluded that application of the automatic stay to bar enforcement of a collective bargaining agreement outside the bankruptcy court was precluded by § 1113(f), which provides that no provision of the Bankruptcy Code other than § 1113 should be construed to permit a trustee unilaterally to alter or terminate a collective bargaining agreement. This appeal followed.

This appeal raises the question of the effect of § 1113 of the Bankruptcy Code on the application of the automatic stay provisions of § 362 of the Bankruptcy Code to non-bankruptcy proceedings to enforce a collective bargaining agreement. Resolution of this dispute requires us to consider the intent of Congress in enacting these sections.

Section 362 of the Bankruptcy Code provides that the filing of a petition in bankruptcy automatically stays certain actions directed against the debtor or against the debtor's property. The automatic stay provisions promote two principal purposes of the Bankruptcy Code. First, the automatic stay "provides the debtor with 'a breathing spell from his creditors.'" *In re Petrusch* (2d Cir. 1981). In addition, the automatic stay allows the bankruptcy court to centralize all disputes concerning property of the debtor's estate in the bankruptcy court so that reorganization can proceed efficiently, unimpeded by uncoordinated proceedings in other arenas. The Bankruptcy Code "provide[s] for centralized jurisdiction and administration of the debtor, its estate and its reorganization in the Bankruptcy Court, and [this policy] is effectuated by Sections 362 and 105 of the Code."

* * *

We turn next to § 1113 of the Bankruptcy Code. Our discussion of that section must begin with the Supreme Court's decision in *National Labor Relations Bd. v. Bildisco & Bildisco* (1984). In *Bildisco*, the Court held, in part, that the filing of a petition in bankruptcy rendered collective bargaining agreements unenforceable. The debtor, therefore, could terminate unilaterally the collective bargaining agreement or alter its provisions prior to seeking bankruptcy court approval for rejection of an executory contract under § 365(a).

In response to *Bildisco*, Congress enacted § 1113 of the Bankruptcy Code as part of the Bankruptcy Amendments and Federal Judgeship Act of 1984 ("BAFJA") (1984). Section 1113 governs the means by which a debtor may assume, reject or modify its collective bargaining agreement. It ensures that the debtor attempt to negotiate with the union prior to seeking to terminate a collective bargaining agreement. § 1113(b). In the event such negotiations fail, it delineates the standard by which an application by the debtor to terminate the collective bargaining agreement is to be judged by the bankruptcy court and establishes a time frame in which this determination is to be made. Subsection (f) provides:

> No provision of [the Bankruptcy Code] shall be construed to permit a trustee to unilaterally terminate or alter any provisions of a collective bargaining agreement prior to compliance with the provisions of [section 1113].

Subsection 1113(a) provides that a debtor "may assume or reject a collective bargaining agreement only in accordance with the provisions of [section 1113]." Subsection 1113(f) evinces an intent that other provisions of the Bankruptcy Code are inoperable to the extent that they allow a debtor to bypass the requirements of § 1113. The language of the statute indicates that Congress intended § 1113 to be the sole method by which a debtor could terminate or modify a collective bargaining agreement and that application of other provisions of the Bankruptcy Code that allow a debtor to bypass the requirements of § 1113 are prohibited.

In *Bildisco*, a debtor ignored "its obligations under the collective-bargaining agreement, including the payment of health and pension benefits and the remittance to the Union of dues collected under the agreement ... [and] refused to pay wage increases called for in the collective-bargaining agreement." Those alterations were made prior to seeking relief from those obligations in the bankruptcy court and absent negotiation with the union.

> Section 1113(f) reverses that part of *Bildisco & Bildisco* which held that a trustee or debtor in possession was not legally bound to a collective bargaining agreement subsequent to the filing date and prior to the court determination of the application for authority to reject such agreement. The trustee or debtor in possession must adhere to the terms of the collective bargaining agreement unless the court approves the application for rejection pursuant to section 1113(c) or grants interim relief under section 1113(e).

5 COLLIER ON BANKRUPTCY, ¶ 1113.01 at 1113-11 (15th ed. 1990). We conclude, from the language of the statute, statements made by the sponsors of the legislation, and the context in which it was enacted, that Congress intended that a collective bargaining agreement remain in effect and that the collective bargaining process continue after the filing of a bankruptcy petition unless and until the debtor complies with the provisions of § 1113. We construe subsection 1113(f) quite literally. We hold that it was meant to prohibit the application of any other provision of the Bankruptcy Code when such application would permit a debtor to achieve a unilateral termination or modification of a collective bargaining agreement without meeting the requirements of § 1113.

* * *

We consider, on the instant appeal, a very specific question, *i.e.*, whether Congress intended in enacting § 1113(f) to preclude the application of the automatic stay provisions of § 362 to any dispute concerning a collective bargaining agreement absent compliance with the provisions of § 1113. We find no evidence that Congress had that specific intent.

Section 1113(f) is circumstance specific rather than section specific. Congress did not choose to direct § 1113(f) at any specific provision whose application it deemed would always permit a debtor unilaterally to alter a collective bargaining agreement. Rather, § 1113(f) presumes a particularized determination in any circumstance as to whether the application of another provision of the Bankruptcy Code will permit a debtor unilaterally to terminate or alter a collective bargaining agreement. If Congress had intended to preclude application of the automatic stay to any dispute involving a collective bargaining agreement, it could have excepted explicitly proceedings to enforce a collective bargaining agreement from the automatic stay provisions. Indeed, in enacting the legislation that included § 1113, Congress added two exceptions to the automatic stay. Moreover, other sections of the Bankruptcy Code explicitly state that § 362 is inapplicable. *E.g.*, 11 U.S.C. § 1110(a) (1988) (right of secured creditor with purchase money security interest in aircraft or its parts not subject to § 362); 11 U.S.C. § 1168 (1988) (right of secured creditor with purchase money security interest in rolling stock equipment or accessories used on such equipment not subject to § 362).

Since we discern no congressional intent on the specific issue before us, our analysis is governed by two rules of statutory construction. The first encourages consistent interpretations of statutes so as to give the fullest effect to congressional intent. "'[W]hen two statutes are capable of co-existence, it is the duty of the courts to regard each as effective.'" *Radzanower v. Touche Ross & Co.* (1976). The second instructs us that, when two statutes are in irreconcilable conflict, we must give effect to the most recently enacted statute since it is the most recent indication of congressional intent. We agree with the district court's conclusion that, to the extent the purpose of the automatic stay is to give the debtor a "breathing spell," it cannot be reconciled with § 1113, which provides the sole method by which a debtor may obtain a "breathing spell" from its obligations under a collective bargaining agreement. Were that the only purpose of the automatic stay, we would be inclined to affirm the district court's thorough opinion in its entirety.

The automatic stay, however, also allows the bankruptcy court to protect its jurisdiction over property of the debtor's estate by ruling on the appropriate manner and forum in which such disputes should be resolved. We previously have recognized the importance of that policy in reorganization proceedings. In view of the importance of that policy, we conclude that a bright line rule precluding the application of the automatic stay to any situation involving a collective bargaining agreement was not intended by

Congress. Rather, we believe that a case by case adjudication is preferable. We will give effect to the automatic stay to the extent that its application is not in irreconcilable conflict with § 1113. We hold, therefore, that § 1113(f) precludes application of the automatic stay to disputes involving a collective bargaining agreement only when its application allows a debtor unilaterally to terminate or alter any provision of a collective bargaining agreement.

* * *

We turn now to the application of the foregoing principles to the disputes at issue in the instant case. We consider the LPP decision first. Eastern contends that the district court erred in determining that § 1113(f) precluded application of the automatic stay to the arbitration that ALPA sought to commence to determine whether the LPPs in the collective bargaining agreement had been triggered. We disagree.

Eastern contends that a stay of arbitration does not deprive a union of a forum in which to enforce the collective bargaining agreement. That argument ignores the fact that adjudication of this dispute in the bankruptcy court would nullify effectively the arbitration clause in the collective bargaining agreement and would substitute the court's judgment for that of the arbitrator.

The collective bargaining agreement expressly provides for arbitration as the method of dispute resolution. "[S]ection 1113 unequivocally prohibits the employer from *unilaterally* modifying *any provision* of the collective bargaining agreement." This prohibition applies to arbitration clauses.

Application of the automatic stay to ALPA's attempt to invoke that provision of the collective bargaining agreement would allow Eastern unilaterally to alter the collective bargaining agreement by avoiding its obligation to arbitrate. In this context, application of the automatic stay is in irreconcilable conflict with § 1113(f), which requires that Eastern seek relief under the provisions of § 1113 if it wishes to avoid its obligation to arbitrate labor disputes. We must give effect to § 1113(f) as the later expression of congressional intent.

Our holding is consistent with the purpose underlying § 1113 to the extent that it ensures that the collective bargaining process continue unless and until the bankruptcy court grants the debtor relief under § 1113. The federal judiciary and Congress both have recognized the importance to the collective bargaining process of arbitration. We hold that an arbitration brought pursuant to a provision in a collective bargaining agreement is not subject to the automatic stay since its application would allow a debtor unilaterally to avoid its obligation to arbitrate. The district court properly reversed the bankruptcy court's LPP decision.

This brings us to the Wet-Lease Decision. Eastern contends that the district court erred in reversing the bankruptcy court's determination that the Florida Action was subject to the automatic stay. We agree.

Unlike the LPP decision, application of the automatic stay to the action commenced by ALPA in the Southern District of Florida did not relieve Eastern of the obligation to participate in the method of dispute resolution provided for in the collective bargaining agreement. Adjudication in the bankruptcy court itself does not violate § 1113(f). When a union seeks judicial enforcement of a collective bargaining agreement, the purposes behind §§ 362 and 1113(f) both can be promoted if the dispute can be adjudicated in the bankruptcy court. We agree with ALPA's contention that precluding it from enforcing the collective bargaining agreement would render § 1113 illusory since a debtor would have no need to invoke it. If enforcement is foreclosed, then a union has no recourse against unilateral modifications imposed by a debtor.

The application of § 362 to a non-bankruptcy judicial proceeding only forecloses enforcement of the collective bargaining agreement if it cannot be enforced in the bankruptcy court. Accordingly, if a union has a procedural mechanism to place the dispute before the bankruptcy court and the bankruptcy court has jurisdiction to resolve the dispute, enforcement of the collective bargaining agreement is not foreclosed and application of the automatic stay does not permit a debtor unilaterally to alter its collective bargaining agreement.

We are not persuaded by ALPA's fear that the automatic stay may be interpreted to stay all proceedings against the debtor, even those commenced in the bankruptcy court. The only appropriate purpose that the stay promotes with respect to collective bargaining agreements is allowing the bankruptcy court to protect its jurisdiction so that it can proceed efficiently with reorganization. Therefore, § 1113(f) compels the bankruptcy court to provide relief from the stay pursuant to § 362(d) to hear the dispute itself, to the extent that is necessary, or, in the event that the bankruptcy court determines that it is not the appropriate forum for the resolution of such a dispute, to allow the resolution of the dispute to proceed in a non-bankruptcy forum.

Moreover, the fact that the bankruptcy court may not have jurisdiction to hear every conceivable claim that might arise from the collective bargaining agreement does not invalidate our analysis. The relevant inquiry is whether the bankruptcy court has jurisdiction to hear the particular dispute at issue. If the bankruptcy court does have jurisdiction to hear a dispute, it has the power to take the necessary steps to enforce its resolution. Finally, our concern with a procedural mechanism by which the union can present the dispute to the bankruptcy court does not foreclose debtor-initiated resolutions of disputes. A situation in which the union could not bring the dispute before the bankruptcy court and the debtor chose not to, however, would render the collective bargaining agreement unenforceable. That result is prohibited by § 1113(f).

It follows from our preceding analysis that, if the wet-lease dispute was properly presented to the bankruptcy court, or could have been, and the bankruptcy court could exercise jurisdiction over it, application of the automatic stay was not precluded by § 1113(f). We hold that the bankruptcy court had jurisdiction to resolve the issues presented by the Florida Action.

* * *

We turn next to the propriety of the bankruptcy court's exercise of its powers under § 105 to enjoin ALPA from prosecuting the wet-lease action. Eastern contends that the district court erred in holding that the bankruptcy court was precluded by § 1113(f) from issuing an injunction against prosecution of the Florida lawsuit. We agree.

Section 105(a) of the Bankruptcy Code provides that: "The court may issue any order, process or judgment that is necessary or appropriate to carry out the provisions of this title." This power "must and can only be exercised within the confines of the Bankruptcy Code." The bankruptcy court's equitable powers cannot be exercised in derogation of other sections of the Bankruptcy Code. The district court reasoned that an injunction issued to bar enforcement of a collective bargaining agreement outside the bankruptcy court would violate § 1113. It followed, from the district court's analysis, that the bankruptcy court's equitable powers could not be used to that end.

Since § 105, like § 362, is a means by which the bankruptcy court can protect its jurisdiction, we hold that its application is not always inconsistent with § 1113. We hold that the bankruptcy court's exercise of its equitable powers pursuant to § 105 to enjoin enforcement of a collective bargaining agreement is subject to the same considerations set forth above for the application of § 362.

* * *

We hold that application of the automatic stay provisions of § 362 of the Bankruptcy Code is precluded by § 1113(f) only to the extent that they permit a debtor unilaterally to terminate or alter a collective bargaining agreement. With respect to the LPP decision, we hold that application of the automatic stay to the arbitration brought pursuant to the collective bargaining agreement violated § 1113(f) since it allowed Eastern unilaterally to avoid its obligation to arbitrate. We hold that the bankruptcy court may stay a non-bankruptcy judicial proceeding to enforce a collective bargaining agreement if the union can bring the dispute before the bankruptcy court and the bankruptcy court has jurisdiction to resolve it. With respect to the Wet-Lease Decision, we hold that the bankruptcy court had jurisdiction to resolve the issues raised by the Florida Action and, therefore, the stay of that action was not precluded by § 1113(f). Finally, we hold that section 1113(f) did not prohibit the bankruptcy court from issuing an injunction against prosecution of the Florida Action. We remand the case to the district court for further consideration of the Wet-Lease Decision.

MINER, Circuit Judge, concurring in part and dissenting in part.

I agree with my colleagues insofar as they conclude that application of the automatic stay provided by § 362 of the Bankruptcy Code to the arbitration of the labor protective provisions of the collective bargaining agreement is violative of § 1113(f) of the Code. I respectfully disagree with my colleagues insofar as they conclude that § 1113(f) does not bar an automatic stay of the Florida Action, the injunction issued by the Bankruptcy Court against further prosecution of that action, and the Bankruptcy Court's resolution of the wet-leasing dispute.

Section 1 of the Collective Bargaining Agreement between Eastern and ALPA provides:

> that all present or future flying including flight training (except for initial factory-conducted training in newly purchased equipment), revenue flying, ferry flights, charters and wet-leases performed in or for the service of Eastern Air Lines, Inc., shall be performed by pilots whose names appear on the then-current Eastern Air Lines' System Seniority List.

In apparent violation of the foregoing provision, Eastern entered into wet-leasing agreements whereby it leased aircraft with crews from Continental while Eastern pilots were on strike. As a debtor in a Chapter 11 reorganization, however, Eastern may not "unilaterally alter any provisions of a collective bargaining agreement" prior to court approval in the manner specified by § 1113(f) of the Code.

Rather than first seeking the requisite court approval authorizing rejection of the collective bargaining agreement upon a showing that modifications in the agreement "are necessary to permit the reorganization of the debtor," 11 U.S.C. § 1113(b)(1)(A), Eastern proceeded to lease aircraft and crews for its normal business operations. Eastern made no effort to negotiate with ALPA before making its arrangements with Continental. As a consequence, ALPA sought in the district court in Florida to compel expedited arbitration of its wet-leasing grievance, to procure the issuance of an injunction in aid of arbitration and to obtain other relief as well. Arbitration of the wet-leasing grievance is required by the labor agreement, which also requires arbitration of the labor protective provisions issue and of any other dispute that may arise out of the performance or non-performance of the agreement.

My colleagues "hold that application of the automatic stay to the arbitration brought pursuant to the collective bargaining agreement violated § 1113(f) since it allowed Eastern unilaterally to avoid the obligation to arbitrate." In their opinion, this holding serves only to bar the application of the stay to the labor protective provisions arbitration proceeding. To the extent that § 1113(f) is implicated, however, it seems to me that there is no difference between rejecting the automatic stay as a bar to that arbitration proceeding and rejecting it as a bar to an action to compel arbitration of the wet-leasing issue.

By obtaining its relief in the Bankruptcy Court in the context of an action to enforce an automatic stay, Eastern is able to avoid compliance with a carefully-drawn statute enacted by Congress to govern labor-management relations in a bankruptcy reorganization. As noted by my colleagues, the statute was designed to overcome the Supreme Court's decision in *National Labor Relations Board v. Bildisco & Bildisco* (1984), which allowed a debtor unilaterally to terminate or alter a collective bargaining agreement prior to seeking bankruptcy court approval under § 365(a) for rejection of an executory contract. The statute specifically forbids termination in the manner permitted by *Bildisco* and promotes the long-established national labor policy of encouraging collective bargaining.

Eastern simply cannot be relieved of its obligation to avoid wet-leasing unless it follows the step-by-step procedure established by Congress. Since it contends that the modification in employee benefits and protection it seeks is necessary to permit its reorganization, it first must make a proposal to ALPA. Eastern must provide ALPA with information relevant to an evaluation of the proposal. It must hold meetings with ALPA in a good faith effort to reach a mutually satisfactory modification. It may file an application for rejection only after the modification proposal has been made, discussed and rejected. The court then will decide, after a hearing on notice to interested parties, whether to reject the agreement.

Eastern cannot prevail, even after a hearing, unless the court finds that a proposal of the sort contemplated by the statute was made prior to the hearing, ALPA has refused without good cause to accept the proposal and "the balance of the equities clearly favors rejection of [the collective bargaining] agreement." In making its decision, "the court must consider whether rejection would increase the likelihood of successful reorganization." It is only after all the preliminary steps have been completed, and the court fails to rule on the application within thirty days after the hearing is commenced, that the debtor unilaterally "may terminate or alter any provisions of the collective bargaining agreement pending the ruling of the court on such application."

Eastern took this one-sided action without bothering with the preliminaries. We should not countenance this conduct, for it precludes resolution of the wet leasing dispute through the preferred process of collective bargaining.

I have no quarrel with the notion that the Bankruptcy Court has jurisdiction to perform the court functions described in § 1113. That jurisdiction was not invoked here, however, and there was accordingly an evasion of congressional purpose. My colleagues say that if a collective bargaining agreement can somehow be enforced in a bankruptcy court, then the automatic stay provisions of § 362 may be applied to enforcement of the agreement in a non-bankruptcy court; that the wet-leasing dispute properly was placed before the Bankruptcy Court here; and that the Bankruptcy Court's exercise of its equitable powers under § 105 to enjoin enforcement of the collective bargaining agreement is a means that may be used for the protection of bankruptcy court jurisdiction. I say that application of the automatic stay provisions of § 362 to an action brought to compel compliance with the arbitration provisions of a collective bargaining agreement is inconsistent with the broad purposes and specific language of § 1113; that the wet-leasing dispute was not properly placed before the Bankruptcy Court here; and that the equitable powers of a bankruptcy court under § 105 may not be used to enjoin enforcement of a collective bargaining agreement in any manner inconsistent with § 1113. Accordingly, I would affirm the judgment of the district court in all respects.

WEINBERGER v. LORENZO

16 Del. J. Corp. L. 1647 (1991)

Court of Chancery of the State of Delaware, New Castle

CHANDLER, Vice-Chancellor.

Plaintiff William B. Weinberger ("Weinberger") brought this action on his own behalf and as a class action on behalf of all persons who hold or held preferred stock of Eastern Air Lines, Inc. ("Eastern"). Weinberger alleges that he and the Eastern preferred shareholders (the "class") have suffered injury through the acts and conduct of defendant Texas Air Corporation ("Texas Air"), which owns all the common stock of Eastern, and Texas Air's chairman Frank A. Lorenzo ("Lorenzo").

Defendant Continental Airlines, Inc. ("Continental"), of which Lorenzo is also chairman, is alleged to have aided and abetted Texas Air. Eastern, which is in Chapter 11 bankruptcy, is not, due to the automatic bankruptcy stay under 11 U.S.C. § 362(a), a named defendant. Defendant Lorenzo moves to dismiss the complaint on the ground that it is a purely derivative action belonging to Eastern, which is therefore an indispensable party. Defendants also assert that Weinberger has not made the allegations required by Rule 23.1, and that Weinberger cannot prosecute Eastern's claims because all such claims are the sole property of Eastern's bankruptcy estate. Weinberger, of course, maintains that his complaint states direct (non-derivative) claims. Whether Weinberger's claims are direct or derivative is the central issue of this motion.

I.

Eastern and Continental are national airlines, both of which are incorporated in Delaware. Continental is headquartered in Houston, Texas, Eastern in Miami Beach, Florida. The common stock of Eastern and Continental is wholly owned by Texas Air, which is also a Delaware corporation. Weinberger alleges that Texas Air controls the operations of Eastern and Continental by virtue of its stock ownership and common management. The only alleged manifestation of such common management is defendant Lorenzo, who is chairman of the board of directors of Eastern as well as Texas Air and Continental.

The central theme of Weinberger's complaint is that defendants have injured the class through a plan and scheme "to strip Eastern of its best assets, its most profitable operations and routes, and to unfairly use it to finance the operations of Texas Air and Continental." Defendant's objective, Weinberger theorizes, was to divert assets and resources from Eastern, which has a strong union, to Continental and Texas Air which, because they are non-union, promise to yield defendants more profit. Texas Air, as the sole common stockholder of Eastern and Continental, the argument goes, has engaged in a scheme whereby it has simply taken assets out of its right pocket (Eastern) and put them into its left pocket (Continental). Texas Air, therefore, suffered no injury by repositioning these assets among its entities. Weinberger presents the following factual background in support of his theory.

In 1981, Texas Air acquired control of Continental. In the process, Weinberger contends, Texas Air ousted Continental's union, the absence of which has contributed to Continental's profitability. On November 26, 1986, Eastern became a wholly owned subsidiary of Texas Air. Lorenzo allegedly assumed the management responsibilities of Eastern following its acquisition. Sometime thereafter, Weinberger claims, Texas Air and Lorenzo, with the help of Continental, "embarked on a program to strip Eastern of its valuable assets, saddle it with costs ... and otherwise divert Eastern's assets to its common shareholder in derogation of the duties owed to the preferred shareholders." The results of this program, states Weinberger, are indicated by Eastern's declining operating income and increased net deficits in the face of increasing revenues. Weinberger points to the following acts as part of this alleged program to strip Eastern.

Weinberger alleges that defendants caused Eastern to lease and sell aircraft to Continental on terms unfair to Eastern. Defendants are also accused of having caused Eastern to sell its profitable computer reservation system ("System One Direct Access") to Texas Air at an unfair price. In addition, defendants are alleged to have caused Eastern to transfer valuable gates, routes and pilot training facilities to defendants for inadequate compensation. Finally, Weinberger claims that defendants caused Eastern to enter into other agreements with Texas Air and Continental which were disadvantageous to Eastern and which caused Eastern to pay excessive management and other fees to defendants or their affiliates. As noted, the pending motion turns on whether these allegations support direct or derivative claims.

II.

This Court has long acknowledged a sharp distinction between derivative and individual actions in corporate litigation. In the former, the alleged wrongdoing harms the corporation and therefore—because they own the corporation—the shareholders derivatively. Individual actions, on the other hand, involve direct harm to the shareholder in his or her individual capacity. The distinction is important because derivative actions are deemed to belong to the subject corporation, whereas individual actions do not. For this reason, shareholders may not freely bring derivative actions and in turn must satisfy certain requirements when doing so. The applicability of these requirements depends, therefore, on whether the present action is derivative or individual.

To determine whether Weinberger states a derivative or an individual cause of action, I must look to the nature of the wrongs alleged in the complaint rather than plaintiff's designations or stated intention. For an action to be individual, the plaintiff must be injured directly or independently of the subject corporation. Stated another way, the question of whether an action is individual comes down to whether "the plaintiff has alleged 'special' injury, in whatever form." The so-called "special injury" test has evolved into the two-pronged test of *Moran v. Household International, Inc.* (Del. Ch. 1985). Under *Moran*, to set out an individual, as opposed to a derivative action, a plaintiff must allege either: (1) an injury which is separate and distinct from that suffered by other shareholders, or (2) a wrong involving a contractual right of a shareholder, which exists independent of any right of the corporation. The *Moran* test is, however, only a guide with the ultimate determination being whether the "plaintiff has alleged 'special' injury in whatever form."

Weinberger alleges injury as a result of defendants' having "caused" Eastern to mismanage itself. Each specific act of mismanagement alleged in the complaint states that "[d]efendants caused Eastern to …" In other words, Texas Air, through its control of Eastern, caused Eastern to commit acts characterized by plaintiff as mismanagement. These acts, the argument goes, have rendered the preferred stock, owned by the class, virtually worthless. Texas Air, in turn, through its purported practices and course of conduct, has breached the fiduciary duties of care and loyalty owed to plaintiff and members of the class.

From these allegations, Weinberger concludes that Eastern's preferred shareholders have suffered a "special injury. This injury is "special," the argument goes, because Texas Air, as the sole common stockholder of Eastern, has suffered no injury by repositioning its assets from Eastern to its other wholly owned airline—Continental. The repositioning of assets, therefore, only "really" diminishes the value of plaintiff's preferred shares. Weinberger goes on to argue that the special injury suffered by the Eastern preferred is like that suffered by the minority shareholders in *Rabkin v. Phillip A. Hunt Chemical Corp.* (Del. Ch. 1986).

The injury alleged in *Rabkin* is, however, wholly distinguishable from the injury presently alleged by Weinberger. *Rabkin* involved a cash out of minority shareholders by a majority shareholder. The minority shareholders challenged the transaction, alleging that the majority was treating them unfairly. Inherent in such an action, it goes without saying, is that the minority suffers some special injury not suffered by the majority. Indeed, such was the case in *Rabkin.*

In the present case, unlike *Rabkin*, there are no allegations that any class or group of Eastern stockholders are being directly singled out and treated disparately. The Eastern preferred shareholders have not been singled out and treated differently from other Eastern shareholders. The essence of Weinberger's claim is that the value of his stock has been reduced due to defendants' having caused Eastern's management to deplete or destroy Eastern's corporate assets. Such alleged mismanagement, in fact, reduces the value of Eastern's stock *in toto* regardless of Weinberger's contention that Texas Air (Eastern's common stockholder) suffers no real injury by shifting its own assets. For this reason, Delaware courts have long recognized that mismanagement is the type of potential action belonging to the corporation or the corporation's shareholders derivatively. As stated in another case, "[a] claim of mismanagement resulting in corporate waste, if proven, represents a direct wrong to the corporation that is directly experienced by all shareholders." The injury to plaintiff's stock falls equally upon all stockholders, thereby precluding individual recovery by Weinberger and requiring that he seek recovery derivatively. This finding necessitates that Weinberger's complaint be dismissed for several reasons.

The most obvious reason for dismissal is that in a stockholder's derivative suit the beneficiary corporation is an indispensable party. It is undisputed that Eastern, the beneficiary corporation, is precluded by the automatic bankruptcy stay from being part of this litigation. An additional reason, if the bankruptcy stay did not exist, is that Weinberger has not made demand on Eastern or made the allegations required by Chancery Court Rule 23.1. For these reasons, plaintiff's complaint is dismissed.

IN RE SEPTEMBER 11 LITIGATION

280 F. Supp. 2d 279 (S.D.N.Y. 2003)

HELLERSTEIN, District Judge.

The injured, and the representatives of the thousands who died from the terrorist-related aircraft crashes of September 11, 2001, are entitled to seek compensation. By act of Congress, they may seek compensation by filing claims with a Special Master established pursuant to the Air Transportation Safety and System Stabilization Act of 2001, 49 U.S.C. § 40101.

Or they may seek compensation in the traditional manner, by alleging and proving their claims in lawsuits, with the aggregate of their damages capped at the limits of defendants' liability insurance. If they choose the former alternative, their claims will be paid through a Victim Compensation Fund from money appropriated by Congress, within a relatively short period after filing. Claimants will not have to prove fault or show a duty to pay on the part of any defendant. The amount of their compensation, however, may be less than their possible recovery from lawsuits, for non-economic damages are limited to $250,000, economic damages are subject to formulas that are likely to be less generous than those often allowable in lawsuits, and punitive damages are unavailable.

Approximately seventy of the injured and representatives of those who died, and ten entities which sustained property damage, have chosen to bring lawsuits against defendants whom they claim are legally responsible to compensate them: the airlines, the airport security companies, the airport operators, the airplane manufacturer, and the operators and owners of the World Trade Center.

The motions before me challenge the legal sufficiency of these lawsuits, and ask me to dismiss the complaints because no duty to the plaintiffs existed and because the defendants could not reasonably have anticipated that terrorists would hijack several jumbo jet airplanes and crash them, killing passengers, crew, thousands on the ground, and themselves. I discuss in this opinion the legal duties owed by the air carriers, United and American Airlines, and other airlines and airport security companies affiliated with the air carriers to the plaintiffs who were killed and damaged on the ground in and around the Twin Towers and the Pentagon; by the Port Authority of New York and New Jersey ("Port Authority") and World Trade Center Properties LLC ("WTC Properties") to those killed and injured in and around the Twin Towers; and by the Boeing Company, the manufacturer of the "757" jets that were flown into the Pentagon and the field near Shanksville, Pennsylvania, to those killed and injured in the two crashes. I hold in this opinion that each of these defendants owed duties to the plaintiffs who sued them, and I reject as well defendants' alternative arguments for dismissal.

I. BACKGROUND

A. Exclusive Jurisdiction and the Governing Law

The Air Transportation Safety and System Stabilization Act of 2001, passed in the weeks following the September 11 attacks, provides that those who bring suit "for damages arising out of the hijacking and subsequent crashes" must bring their suits in the United States District Court for the Southern District of New York. The Southern District has "original and exclusive jurisdiction" "over all actions brought for any claim (including any claim for loss of property, personal injury, or death) resulting from or relating to the terrorist-related aircraft crashes of September 11, 2001," with the exception of claims to recover collateral source obligations and claims against terrorists and their aiders, abettors and conspirators, Act § 408(c). The Act provides that the governing law shall be "derived from the law, including choice of law principles, of the State in which the crash occurred unless such law is inconsistent with or preempted by Federal law." Thus, all cases, whether arising out of the crashes in New York, Virginia, or Pennsylvania, must be brought in the Southern District of New York, to be decided in accordance with the law of the state where the crash occurred.

B. The Complaints

Plaintiffs allege that the airlines, airport security companies, and airport operators negligently failed to fulfill their security responsibilities, and in consequence, the terrorists were able to hijack the airplanes and crash them into the World Trade Center, the Pentagon, and the field in Shanksville, Pennsylvania, killing passengers, crew, and thousands in the World Trade Center and the Pentagon and causing extensive property damage. The complaints allege that the owners and operators of the World Trade Center, World Trade Center Properties LLC and the Port Authority of New York and New Jersey, negligently designed, constructed, maintained, and operated the buildings, failing to provide adequate and effective evacuation routes and plans. Plaintiffs who died in the crashes of American flight 77 and United flight 93 also sue Boeing, the manufacturer of the two "757" airplanes, for strict tort liability, negligent product design, and breach of warranty.

C. Motions to Dismiss

The three motions before the court, and which I now decide are: by the airlines and airport security companies (the "Aviation Defendants"); by the Port Authority and World Trade Center Properties LLC (together, the "WTC Defendants"); and by Boeing.

The Aviation Defendants concede that they owed a duty to the crew and passengers on the planes, but contend that they did not owe any duty to "ground victims." The Port Authority and WTC Properties argue that they did not owe a duty to protect occupants in the towers against injury from hijacked airplanes and, even if they did, the terrorists' actions broke the chain of proximate causation, excusing any negligence by the WTC Defendants. And Boeing argues that it did not owe a duty to ground victims or passengers, and that any negligence on its part was not the proximate cause for the harms suffered by the plaintiffs.

II. DISCUSSION

Existence of Duty to Ground Victims

"The threshold question in any negligence action is: does the defendant owe a legally recognized duty of care to plaintiff?" In New York, the existence of a duty is a "legal, policy-laden declaration reserved for judges." The injured party must show that a defendant owed not merely a general duty to society but a specific duty to the particular claimant, for "without a duty running directly to the injured person there can be no liability in damages, however careless the conduct or foreseeable the harm." Courts traditionally "fix the duty point by balancing factors, including the reasonable expectations of parties and society generally, the proliferation of claims, the likelihood of unlimited or insurer—like liability, disproportionate risk and reparation allocation, and public policies affecting the expansion or limitation of new channels of liability."

New York courts have been cautious in extending liability to defendants for their failure to control the conduct of others, "even where as a practical matter [the] defendant can exercise such control." "This judicial resistance to the expansion of duty grows out of practical concerns both about potentially limitless liability and about the unfairness of imposing liability for the acts of another." However, courts have imposed a duty when the defendant has control over the third party tortfeasor's actions, or the relationship between the defendant and plaintiff requires the defendant to protect the plaintiff from the conduct of others.

As the New York Court of Appeals ruled, "The key in each [situation] is that the defendant's relationship with either the tortfeasor or the plaintiff places the defendant in the best position to protect against the risk of harm." One additional consideration, the Court of Appeals added, is that "the specter of limitless liability is not present because the class of potential plaintiffs to whom the duty is owed is circumscribed by the relationship."

Plaintiffs allege that the Aviation Defendants negligently failed to carry out their duty to secure passenger aircraft against potential terrorists and weapons smuggled aboard, enabling the terrorists to hijack and crash four airplanes. Plaintiffs argue that the Aviation Defendants employed their security measures specifically to guard against hijackings, and knew or should have known that the hijacking of a jumbo jet would create substantial risks of damage to persons and property, not only to passengers and crew, but also to people and property on the ground. Plaintiffs assert also that terrorism was a substantial international concern, and that suicidal acts by terrorists seeking to cause death, injury and havoc to as many innocent people as possible had become a frequently used strategy.

Airplane crashes in residential areas are not unknown. In January 1952, an American Airlines Convair crashed into a residential area of Elizabeth, New Jersey on its approach to Newark airport, killing passengers and crew, as well as seven residents of houses it struck. A month later, another plane out of Newark, a National Airlines DC-6, struck an apartment house in New Jersey, killing 29 passengers and four tenants of the apartment house. Military airplanes have had to make emergency landings on highways, and have collided with automobiles. On July 9, 1982, a Pan American World Airways jet crashed shortly after takeoff, killing all on board and eight individuals on the ground. The airline and the government acknowledged liability for the crash, which was caused by windy conditions. *See Pan Am and U.S. Accept Responsibility for Crash*, N.Y. TIMES, May 13, 1983, at 6. In January 1990, a Columbian passenger airplane exhausted its fuel supply while circling La Guardia Airport waiting for clearance to land, and crashed into a residential backyard in Long Island's populated North shore. On November 12, 2001, two months after the aircraft crashes of September 11, 2001, a jumbo-jet passenger airplane lost its stability in take-off from JFK airport and crashed into a populated area of the Rockaways, causing the deaths of over two hundred passengers and crew members and five people on the ground. Such incidents are inevitable in the context of the sheer number of miles flown daily in the United States. None matches the quantity or quality of tragedy arising from the terrorist-related aircraft crashes of September 11.

Airlines typically recognize responsibility to victims on the ground. As counsel for the Aviation Defendants stated in argument,

> [a]ssuming negligence and assuming there is damage to houses on the ground that is the type of traditional ground damage negligent maintenance cases in which the courts have imposed duty ... [W]e would concede in those circumstances assuming the facts of liability are proven there is a legal duty.

However, counsel did not concede duty in relation to those killed and injured on the ground in the September 11, 2001 aircraft crashes. The "potential for a limitless liability to an indeterminate class of plaintiffs," he argued, made the instant cases distinguishable. The distinction, in his opinion, is "no[t][a] difference in kind," but "the law of extraordinary consequences [which] can sometimes draw a distinction based on degree." He explained: We are in an area of policy and there are lines to be drawn that may occasionally seem arbitrary. But what really distinguishes our case from [the hypothetical example of an airplane crash into Shea Stadium while taking off from, or landing at, La Guardia airport] is the intentional intervening acts of the third party terrorists. As defense counsel commented, "we are in an area of policy," where "the existence and scope of a tortfeasor's duty is ... a legal question for the courts," *532 Madison Ave. Gourmet Foods, Inc. v. Finlandia Center, Inc.* (N.Y. 2001).

It is the court's job to "fix the duty point by balancing factors," including the following:

> the reasonable expectations of parties and society generally, the proliferation of claims, the likelihood of unlimited or insurer-like liability, disproportionate risk and reparation allocation, and public policies affecting the expansion or limitation of new channels of liability.

532 Madison Avenue involved collapses of a high-rise office building and a 48-story construction elevator tower, both in midtown Manhattan and both causing busy areas of the city to be closed for a two-week period. The lawsuits sought recovery of financial losses resulting from the closures; plaintiffs had not suffered personal injury or property damage. Applying the considerations set out above, the Court of Appeals limited the scope of defendants' duty "to those who have, as a result of these events, suffered personal injury or property damage," but held that those who suffered merely financial losses could not recover.

The Court of Appeals acknowledged that "[p]olicy-driven line-drawing is to an extent arbitrary because, wherever the line is drawn, invariably it cuts off liability to persons who foreseeably might be plaintiffs." If those who suffered financial losses were to be allowed to sue, the Court of Appeals held, "an indeterminate group in the affected areas" would be able to recover. If, however, the field of plaintiffs was to be limited to those who "suffered personal injury or property damage" as a result of defendants' negligence, the limitation would "afford a principled basis for reasonably apportioning liability," and be "historically" consistent with New York precedents.

The cases before me involve claims to recover for personal injuries, death, or property damage. They fall within the line drawn by the New York Court of Appeals in *532 Madison Avenue*. There may be more plaintiffs within the ambit of duty at issue here than those contemplated under the rule set forth in *532 Madison Avenue*, but that is not a principled basis of distinction. I therefore hold that the Aviation Defendants owed a duty of care, not only to their passengers to whom they concede they owed this duty, but also to victims on the ground.

In terms of the *532 Madison Avenue* analysis, plaintiffs are favored by the first of the factors set out above, for plaintiffs and society generally could have reasonably expected that the screening performed at airports by the Aviation Defendants would be for the protection of people on the ground as well as for those in airplanes. Ours is a complicated and specialized society. We depend on others charged with special duties to protect the quality of the water we drink and the air we breathe, to bring power to our neighborhoods, and to enable us to travel with a sense of security over bridges, through tunnels and via subways. We live in the vicinity of busy airports, and we work in tall office towers, depending on others to protect us from the willful desire of terrorists to do us harm. Some of those on whom we depend for protection are the police, fire and intelligence departments of local, state and national governments. Others are private companies, like the Aviation Defendants. They perform their screening duties, not only for those boarding airplanes, but also for society generally. It is both their expectation, and ours, that the duty of screening was performed for the benefit of passengers and those on the ground, including those present in the Twin Towers on the morning of September 11, 2001.

Nothing that I hold or say should be considered as any form of ruling on the reasonableness of the Aviation Defendants' conduct. Nor should it be construed as a finding on whether their conduct was the proximate cause of plaintiffs' damages, or whether that of the terrorists' constituted an intervening act breaking the chain of causation. I simply hold that the Aviation Defendants, and plaintiffs and society generally, could reasonably have expected that the screening methods at Logan, Newark, and Dulles airports were for the protection of people on the ground as well as for those on board the airplanes that the terrorists hijacked.

The second factor to consider is "the proliferation of claims." Proliferation, however, should not be mistaken for size of number. As long as the claimants are known and circumscribed by those "who have, as a result of these events, suffered personal injury or property damage," there is not an impermissible proliferation. *See also In re Air Crash Disaster at Cove Neck* (E.D.N.Y. 1995) (allowing claims of emotional injury only for those who also suffered physical injury).

Plaintiffs, the ground victims in the cases before me, complain of directly-caused physical injuries to their persons or property. Their number may be large, tragically large, and the potential liability may be substantial if negligence and cause is proven, but the class is not indefinite and claims at this point cannot proliferate. Furthermore, the defendants will be liable only if plaintiffs sustain their burden of proof, with the aggregate liability of the air carriers, aircraft manufacturers, airport sponsors, and persons with a property interest in the World Trade Center capped by federal statute to the limits of their liability insurance coverage. Thus, "the likelihood of unlimited or insurer-like liability," the third factor of *532 Madison Avenue*, does not weigh heavily against a finding of duty.

The fourth factor of *532 Madison Avenue* is "disproportionate risk and reparation allocation." This inquiry probes who was best able to protect against the risks at issue and weighs the costs and efficacy of imposing such a duty. The airlines, and the airport security companies, could best screen those boarding, and bringing objects onto, airplanes. The same activities reasonably necessary to safeguard passengers and crew are those that would protect the public as well. Hijacking presents a substantial elevation of risks, not only to those aboard the hijacked airplane, but also to those on the ground. This case is thus distinguishable from other cases where courts did not find a duty to protect against third-party conduct.

The Aviation Defendants could best control the boarding of airplanes, and were in the best position to provide reasonable protection against hijackings and the dangers they presented, not only to the crew and passengers, but also to ground victims. Imposing a duty on the Aviation Defendants best allocates the risks to ground victims posed by inadequate screening, given the Aviation Defendants' existing and admitted duty to screen passengers and items carried aboard.

Lastly, recognition of a duty on the part of the Aviation Defendants would not substantially expand or create "new channels of liability," the fifth and last factor of *532 Madison Avenue*. New York courts have found on other occasions that aircraft owners and operators owe a duty to those on the ground who may be harmed or sustain property damage resulting from improper or negligent operation of an aircraft. *See, e.g., Hassanein v. Avianca Airlines* (E.D.N.Y. 1995) (denying defendant's motion for summary judgment where plane crash could have caused a handrail in plaintiff's house to loosen, causing her fall down the stairs); *Rehm v. United States* (E.D.N.Y. 1961) (awarding damages where car occupants were hit by a plane which crashed after engine failure). *Cf. In re Air Crash Disaster at Cove Neck* (ground victims of plane crash could only sustain claim if they suffered personal injury or property damage). Although these cases involved injuries resulting from negligent operation or maintenance of airplanes, rather than negligence in regulating the boarding of airplanes, there is no principled distinction between the modes of negligence. The same general principle governs, that air carriers owe a duty to people on the ground as well as to passengers and crew.

The Second Circuit has recognized that airlines have a duty not only to passengers on the flights they operate, but also to passengers on connecting flights, and thus may be liable when they allow terrorists to board planes. In *Stanford v. Kuwait Airways Corp.* (2d Cir. 1996), the airline failed adequately to screen passengers against terrorists. The hijacking occurred, not on the airplane initially boarded, but on the connecting flight. The Second Circuit, relying on general tort principles including New York law, upheld the air carrier's duty of care as to the passengers on the connecting flight. Clearly, the duty of care extends to cover those embraced by the risk of the terrorists' conduct. Accordingly, I hold on the pleadings that the Aviation Defendants owed a duty of care to the ground victim plaintiffs.

Scope of Duty to Ground Victims: The Issue of Foreseeability

Defendants argue that the ground victims lost their lives and suffered injuries from an event that was not reasonably foreseeable, for terrorists had not previously used a hijacked airplane as a suicidal weapon to destroy buildings and murder thousands. Defendants contend that because the events of September 11 were not within the reasonably foreseeable risks, any duty of care that they would owe to ground victims generally should not extend to the victims of September 11.

The scope of duty to a particular class of plaintiffs depends on the relationship to such plaintiffs, whether plaintiffs were within a zone of foreseeable harm, and whether the harm was within the class of reasonably foreseeable hazards that the duty exists to prevent. *See Palsgraf v. Long Island R.R. Co.* (N.Y. 1928). While foreseeability is generally for the fact finder to resolve, courts may dismiss cases where the risks are unforeseeable as a matter of law. "The nature of the inquiry depends, of course, on the particular facts and circumstances in which the duty question arises."

In order to be considered foreseeable, the precise manner in which the harm was inflicted need not be perfectly predicted. As *Di Ponzio v. Riordan* explained: "Where an individual breaches a legal duty and thereby causes an occurrence that is within the class of foreseeable hazards that the duty exists to prevent, the individual may be held liable, even though the harm may have been brought about in an unexpected way. On the other hand, no liability will result when the occurrence is not one that is normally associated with such hazards. Significantly, the kind and number of hazards encompassed within a particular duty depend on the nature of the duty." However, courts must be careful to draw a line between remote possibilities and those that are reasonably foreseeable in order to prevent the imposition of liability "with the wisdom born of the event."

New York cases emphasize that courts must closely examine the nature of the duty owed and the injury sustained in order to determine if the injury was within a class of foreseeable risks. *Di Ponzio* held that the alleged misconduct of defendant's employees—gas station attendants who failed to require a customer to turn off his engine while getting gas—did not give rise to liability from a risk that was not associated with the duty of care. In that case, a car that had been left running slid backward, striking the plaintiff. The court found that the injuries sustained by the plaintiff were not among the hazards associated with leaving a car engine running during the operation of a gas pump. The duty existed to avoid fire and explosion, not to protect against a vehicle that was not properly braked.

Construing the factual allegations in the light most favorable to the plaintiffs, I conclude that the crash of the airplanes was within the class of foreseeable hazards resulting from negligently performed security screening. While it may be true that terrorists had not before deliberately flown airplanes into buildings, the airlines reasonably could foresee that crashes causing death and destruction on the ground was a hazard that would arise should hijackers take control of a plane. The intrusion by terrorists into the cockpit, coupled with the volatility of a hijacking situation, creates a foreseeable risk that hijacked airplanes might crash, jeopardizing innocent lives on the ground as well as in the airplane. While the crashes into the particular locations of the World Trade Center, Pentagon, and Shanksville field may not have been foreseen, the duty to screen passengers and items brought on board existed to prevent harms not only to passengers and crew, but also to the ground victims resulting from the crashes of hijacked planes, including the four planes hijacked on September 11.

The Aviation Defendants controlled who came onto the planes and what was carried aboard. They had the obligation to take reasonable care in screening precisely because of the risk of terrorist hijackings, and the dangerous consequences that would inevitably follow. The consequences that in fact followed were within the scope of the duty that the Aviation Defendants undertook to carry out. I hold at this stage of the litigation, on the pleadings and before any discovery has taken place, that the injuries suffered by the ground victims arose from risks that were within the scope of the duty undertaken by the Aviation Defendants.

Federal Law Preemption

Defendants argue that federal law preempts plaintiffs' claims and that an imposition of a duty of care on the part of the Aviation Defendants in favor of ground victims would be "inconsistent with" the air safety provisions of federal law. Section 408(b)(2) of the Act provides: "The substantive law for decision in any such suit shall be derived from the law, including choice of law principles, of the state in which the crash occurred unless such law is inconsistent with or preempted by Federal law."

Defendants contend that since federal regulations providing for protection of passengers and property on aircraft in the event of air piracy do not mention people or property on the ground, it would be inconsistent with the regulatory scheme to impose a duty on the Aviation Defendants towards ground victims. *See* 49 U.S.C. § 44903(b) (mandating the promulgation of "regulations to protect passengers and property on an aircraft" against acts of criminal violence or aircraft piracy); 14 C.F.R. § 107.3(a)(1) (2001) (air carrier security programs shall "[p]rovide for the safety of persons and property traveling in air transportation and intrastate air transportation against acts of criminal violence and air privacy").

They also contend that the Federal Aviation Administration's "common strategy" approach of full cooperation with the hijackers demonstrates the policy of protecting those on board. Thus, because federal regulations and the FAA's terrorist countermeasures did not account for the lives of ground victims, the Aviation Defendants believe they did not owe a duty under federal law to the ground victims.

There is no beginning assumption against preemption in those areas of the law "where there has been a history of significant federal presence." In areas in which there has been a history of significant federal control, courts "must ask whether the local laws in question are consistent with the federal statutory structure," rather than assuming that "concurrent regulation by the State is a valid exercise of its police powers." Aviation is clearly an area with a significant history of federal control.

The courts have taken different positions on the scope of preemption in the aviation context. For example, the First and Third Circuits, as well as courts in this district, have held that federal law establishes the applicable standards of care in the field of aviation. *Abdullah v. American Airlines* (3d Cir. 1999) (examining a claim brought by passengers injured during flight as a result of turbulence and concluding that traditional state and territorial law remedies continue to exist for violation of federal standards); *French v. Pan Am Express, Inc.* (1st Cir. 1989) (holding that Federal Aviation Act's prescriptions for the employment of pilots preempted state statute regulating drug testing for employees); *Curtin v. Port Auth. of N.Y. and N.J.* (S.D.N.Y. 2002) (finding proper removal of state law claims accusing an airline of negligent supervision and control of emergency evacuation procedures because the comprehensive federal regulatory scheme covering emergency evacuation procedures preempts state law); *Schaeffer v. Cavallero* (S.D.N.Y. 1998) (federal law, not state law, determines right of air carrier to refuse to transport, and to evict, passenger).

A few courts have taken a different approach, holding that federal law does not always preempt state law tort claims. *See Cleveland v. Piper Aircraft Corp.* (10th Cir. 1993) (holding that Congress has not indicated a "clear and manifest" intent to occupy the field of airplane safety to the exclusion of state common law); *Sakellaridis v. Polar Air Cargo, Inc.* (E.D.N.Y. 2000) (claims by airline mechanic injured while servicing large aircraft may be brought under New York Labor Law and are not preempted by federal statutes relating to safety equipment).

These cases do not involve the issue of duty. Preemption is generally found, not in connection with the existence and scope of duty, but in connection with the standards governing the conduct and procedures relating to aviation—the standard of care, that is, by which an air carrier must carry out its activities. Defendants have not shown any inconsistency between the law of duty provided by New York law and federal statutes or regulations. The FAA may not have predicted a hijacking that had as its purpose crashing the airplane into a heavily occupied office tower, but that says nothing about the extent, or limitation, of the duty of the screening procedures that the Aviation Defendants performed. The federal regulations do not suggest that crashes of hijacked airplanes and death and destruction to people on the ground as well as in the airplanes were unforeseeable as a matter of law.

I therefore hold that New York's law of duty is not inconsistent with, or preempted by, federal law. For the reasons stated, I deny the Aviation Defendants' motion to dismiss the claims of the ground victims.

World Trade Center Defendants' Motions to Dismiss

The Port Authority of New York and New Jersey and WTC Properties LLC move to dismiss all claims brought against them as owners and operators of the World Trade Center for loss of life, personal injury, and damage to nearby property and businesses resulting from the collapse of the Twin Towers. The claims are alleged in two Master Complaints regarding Flights 11 and 175 in the consolidated litigation, and in numerous individual complaints.

Plaintiffs allege that the WTC Defendants: (1) failed to design and construct the World Trade Center buildings according to safe engineering practices and to provide for safe escape routes and adequate sprinkler systems and fireproofing; (2) failed to inspect, discover, and repair unsafe and dangerous conditions, and to maintain fireproofing materials; (3) failed to develop adequate and safe evacuation and emergency management plans; (4) failed to apply, interpret and/or enforce applicable building and fire safety codes, regulations and practices; and (5) instructed Tower Two occupants to return to their offices and remain in the building even while the upper floors of Tower One were being consumed by uncontrolled fires following the airplane crash into Tower One.

The WTC Defendants argue that the complaints against them should be dismissed because they had no duty to anticipate and guard against deliberate and suicidal aircraft crashes into the Towers, and because any alleged negligence on their part was not a proximate cause of the plaintiffs' injuries. The Port Authority argues also that it is entitled to immunity because the complained-of conduct essentially consisted of governmental functions.

Because all these claims arise from crashes into the World Trade Center Towers, New York's choice of law rules apply. *See* Act § 408(b). As discussed earlier, New York has the strongest interest in applying its substantive law to define the issues of duty, proximate causation, and governmental immunity involved in this motion and thus its law will be applied.

Existence and Scope of Duty

The WTC Defendants contend that they owed no duty to "anticipate and guard against crimes unprecedented in human history." Plaintiffs argue that defendants owed a duty, not to foresee the crimes, but to have designed, constructed, repaired and maintained the World Trade Center structures to withstand the effects and spread of fire, to avoid building collapses caused by fire and, in designing and effectuating fire safety and evacuation procedures, to provide for the escape of more people.

The existence of a duty owed by the WTC Defendants to its lessees and business occupants has been clearly set out in New York law. "A landowner has a duty to exercise reasonable care under the circumstances in maintaining its property in a safe condition," including the duty to adopt reasonable fire-safety precautions, regardless of the origin of the fire. What constitutes reasonable fire prevention is dictated by the actual property. Specific fire hazards caused by the actual building's design or by the materials used in the building must be corrected by the owner in a timely fashion, even when the owner has fully complied with all applicable fire and building codes.

The duty of landowners and lessors to adopt fire-safety precautions applies to fires caused by criminals. "[L]andowners have a duty to protect tenants, patrons or invitees from foreseeable harm caused by the criminal conduct of others while they are on the premises." The WTC Defendants owed a duty to the occupants to create and implement adequate fire safety measures, even in the case of a fire caused by criminals such as those who hijacked flights 11 and 175 on 9/11.

Plaintiffs argue that the WTC Defendants had a duty to exercise reasonable care in order to mitigate the effects of fires in the Twin Towers. They allege that defendants knew about the fire safety defects in the Twin Towers, as evident by the *Allied* litigation concerning inadequate fireproofing in the construction of the buildings; that defendants could have reasonably foreseen crashes of airplanes into the Towers, given the near miss in 1981 of an Aerolineas Argentinas Boeing 707 and the studies conducted during the Towers' construction reporting that the Towers would be able to withstand an aircraft crash; that defendants were aware of numerous fires and evacuations that had occurred at the World Trade Center since its creation, including arson fires in 1975 and the 1993 terrorist-caused explosion in the garage under Tower One; and that the World Trade

Center continued to be a prime target of terrorists. A finding of duty does not require a defendant to have been aware of a specific hazard. It is enough to have foreseen the risk of serious fires within the buildings and the goal of terrorists to attack the building.

This is a very early point in the litigation. There has been no discovery, and defendants' motions to dismiss accept, as they must, all allegations of the complaints. I hold that the WTC Defendants owed a duty to the plaintiffs, and that plaintiffs should not be foreclosed from being able to prove that defendants failed to exercise reasonable care to provide a safe environment for its occupants and invitees with respect to reasonably foreseeable risks.

Proximate and Supervening Causation

The WTC Defendants argue that even if they are held to have owed a duty to the plaintiffs and even if a jury ultimately finds that they acted negligently, their negligence was not the proximate cause of plaintiffs' damages. This is because, they claim, the terrorist-related aircraft crashes into the Twin Towers were so extraordinary and unforeseeable as to constitute intervening and superceding causes, severing any link of causation to the WTC Defendants.

When an intervening act "is of such an extraordinary nature or so attenuates defendants' negligence from the ultimate injury that responsibility for the injury may not be reasonably attributed to the defendant," proximate cause is lacking. Thus, "when such an intervening cause 'interrupts the natural sequence of events, turns aside their course, prevents the natural and probable result of the original act or omission, and produces a different result that could not have been reasonably anticipated,' it will prevent a recovery on account of the act or omission of the original wrongdoer." The "negligence complained of must have caused the occurrence of the accident from which the injuries flow."

Generally, an intervening intentional or criminal act severs the liability of the original tort-feasor. But that "doctrine has no application when the intentional or criminal intervention of a third party or parties is reasonably foreseeable."

At this early stage of the case and in the absence of a factual record, I find that plaintiffs have pleaded sufficient facts to allege legal proximate cause. Plaintiffs allege that the WTC Defendants' negligence was a substantial cause of their injuries, because adequate fireproofing and evacuation would have enabled many more escapes. According to plaintiffs, the terrorist acts did not merely "operate upon" the defendants' negligence; rather, the failure to provide certain safeguards caused the entrapment of many more people and the loss of many more lives. Large-scale fire was precisely the risk against which the WTC Defendants had a duty to guard and which they should have reasonably foreseen.

I also decline at this stage to find that the acts of the terrorists qualify as "extraordinary" intervening cause. While the specific acts of the terrorists were certainly horrific, I cannot find that the WTC Defendants should be excused of all liability as a matter of policy and law on the record before me, especially given the plaintiffs' allegations regarding the defendants' knowledge of the possibility of terrorist acts, large-scale fires, and even airplane crashes at the World Trade Center. The defendants may well be able to show at a later stage in this litigation that the conduct of the terrorists "so attenuates defendants' negligence from the ultimate injury that responsibility for the injury may not be reasonably attributed to the defendant."

Discovery will either supply evidence to substantiate or eviscerate the parties' divergent claims about foreseeability. At this point, however, both plaintiffs and defendants should be allowed to proceed to discovery on these issues of causation.

Governmental Immunity

The Port Authority claims that it is immune from liability to the extent that the plaintiffs complain that the Port Authority was negligent in its performance of governmental functions such as planning for public safety and responding to a public emergency. The Port Authority agrees, however, that it does not enjoy a blanket immunity to suit. The allegations and proofs have to be parsed in order to determine whether, and to what extent, the defense of government immunity applies.

The defense of governmental immunity requires a court to scrutinize specific claims." It is the specific act or omission out of which the injury is claimed to have arisen and the capacity in which that act or failure to act occurred which governs [governmental] liability, not whether the agency involved is engaged generally in proprietary activity or is in control of the location in which the injury occurred."

The inquiry is to determine a point "along a continuum of responsibility," one side of which may be considered as proprietary, and the other, governmental. "[The continuum] begins with the simplest matters directly concerning a piece of property for which the entity acting as landlord has a certain duty of care, for example, the repair of steps or the maintenance of doors in an apartment building. The spectrum extends gradually out to more complex measures of safety and security for a greater area and populace, whereupon the actions increasingly, and at a certain point only, involve governmental functions, for example, the maintenance of general police and fire protection." When a public entity acts in a proprietary capacity as a landlord, it is held to the same duty as private landlords.

Plaintiffs allege negligence by the Port Authority in a number of respects: (1) failure to design and construct the World Trade Center buildings according to safe engineering practices and to provide for safe escape routes and adequate sprinkler systems and fireproofing; (2) failure to inspect, discover, and repair unsafe and dangerous conditions, and to maintain fireproofing materials; (3) failure to develop an adequate and safe evacuation plan and emergency management plan; (4) failure to apply, interpret and/or enforce applicable building and fire safety codes, regulations and practices; and (5) instructing Tower Two occupants to remain in the building rather than evacuate.

Based only on the pleadings and before any discovery has occurred, I have been given no basis to determine where, on the continuum between functions that are essentially proprietary and those that are essentially governmental, these various allegations should fall. It would seem, from the pleadings alone, that it would be difficult for the Port Authority to establish its defense with respect to claims of negligent design, construction, inspection, repair, maintenance, and application and enforcement of building codes, for these functions are not likely to differ from those required of private landowners.

The same is true regarding allegations relating to inadequate evacuation and emergency management plans and procedures, but these allegations may touch also upon the functions of the Port Authority police force within the Twin Towers, and come closer to the governmental end of the continuum. This may be even more so for the allegation that occupants of Tower Two were told, before the crash into that Tower, to return to, and remain in, their offices, rather than evacuate. The record does not yet show who gave this instruction, whether a member of the Port Authority's security force or some other employee, and for what reasons the instruction was given.

At this point, the Port Authority has not shown that it will prove its defense of governmental immunity as to the negligence allegations made by WTC occupants.

The Port Authority argues also that it should have immunity in its capacity as operator of Newark Airport, for alleged negligence in permitting terrorists and weapons aboard United Air Lines flight 93, and for the hijacking and deaths that resulted. The Port Authority claims that it was performing a governmental function. Again, however, the Port Authority has not shown that it was performing a governmental function with respect to the "specific act or omission out of which the injury is claimed to have arisen and the capacity in which that act or failure to act occurred." For the reasons stated, I deny the WTC Defendants' motion to dismiss the complaints.

* * *

Boeing's Motions to Dismiss

Some of those who were injured and the successors of those who died in the Pentagon, in American Airlines flight 77 which crashed into the Pentagon, and in United Air Lines flight 93 which crashed into the Shanksville, Pennsylvania field, claim the right to recover against Boeing, the manufacturer of the two "757" jets flown by United and American. Plaintiffs allege that Boeing manufactured inadequate and defective cockpit doors, and thus made it possible for the hijackers to invade the cockpits and take over the aircraft. Boeing moves to dismiss the lawsuits. I hold that plaintiffs have alleged legally sufficient claims for relief under the laws applicable to the claims, Virginia and Pennsylvania, respectively. I therefore deny the motion except for certain claims, as discussed below.

Choice of Law

Section 408(b)(2) of the Act provides that the substantive law "shall be derived from the law, including choice of law principles, of the State in which the crash occurred unless such law is inconsistent with or preempted by Federal law," that is, Virginia as to the claims relating to the crash of American flight 77 into the Pentagon, and Pennsylvania as to the claims relating to the crash of United flight 93 into the Shanksville field.

As discussed above, Virginia conflicts law chooses the substantive law of the "place of the wrong" (*lex loci delicti*), and thus Virginia law must govern the claims arising from the crash of American Airlines flight 77 into the Pentagon. Pennsylvania's conflicts law chooses the substantive law of the state having the most interest in the outcome of the case. The parties agree that the substantive law of Pennsylvania should govern the claims arising from the crash of United flight 93 in Shanksville.

Thus far, three individual complaints have been filed with respect to the flight 77 crash. They charge Boeing with strict tort liability and negligent design based on an unreasonably dangerous design of the cockpit doors. The Plaintiffs' First Amended Flight 77 Master Liability Complaint contains three counts applicable to Boeing. Count Six alleges strict tort liability for an unreasonably dangerous design of the cockpit doors. Count Seven alleges that Boeing breached its duty of care by failing to design the cockpit doors and accompanying locks in a manner that would prevent hijackers and/or passengers from accessing the cockpit. Count Eight alleges that Boeing violated its express or implied warranty that the aircraft structure and frame, with respect to the cockpit doors, were fit for the purposes for which they were designed, intended and used.

Strict liability claims

Virginia does not permit recovery on a strict liability theory in product liability cases. Thus, Count Six in the Flight 77 Master Complaint, and the underlying related claims in the individual complaints-Count Three in Edwards, Count Five in Powell, and Count Five in Gallop-are all dismissed.

Negligent design and breach of warranty claims

Boeing moves to dismiss both the claims of negligent design and breach of warranty, arguing that it did not owe a duty to prevent the use of the plane as a weapon, and that the independent and supervening acts of the terrorists, not Boeing's acts, caused the injuries of the plaintiffs. A plaintiff, to state a claim of negligence, must allege the existence of a legal duty, violation of that duty, and proximate causation which results in injury. In order to state a claim of breach of warranty, plaintiff may invoke the Virginia law of an implied warranty of merchantability, which guarantees that a product "was reasonably safe for its intended use when it was placed in the stream of commerce."

In order to recover under either a negligence or breach of warranty theory against a product manufacturer, "a plaintiff must show (1) that the goods were unreasonably dangerous either for the use to which they would ordinarily be put or for some other reasonably foreseeable purpose, and (2) that the unreasonably dangerous condition existed when the goods left the manufacturer's hands." Thus, a manufacturer owes a duty to supply a product "fit for the ordinary purposes for which it is to be used" and safe notwithstanding a reasonably foreseeable misuse that could cause injury. However, "a manufacturer is not required to supply an accident-proof product."

The existence of duty in the products liability context is a question of law. "[T]he purpose of making the finding of a legal duty as a prerequisite to a finding of negligence, or breach of implied warranty, in products liability is to avoid the extension of liability for every conceivably foreseeable accident, without regard to common sense or good policy." Legal duty may extend to a user of the product, as well as to its purchaser. While the existence of duty is a question of law, whether a product is unreasonably dangerous is generally a question of fact, as is the question whether the misuse was reasonably foreseeable. Courts have emphasized that these determinations require careful examination of the record.

Boeing argues that its design of the cockpit was not unreasonably dangerous in relation to reasonably foreseeable risks, and that the risk of death to passengers and ground victims caused by a terrorist hijacking was not reasonably foreseeable. The record at this point does not support Boeing's argument. There have been many efforts by terrorists to hijack airplanes, and too many have been successful. The practice of terrorists to blow themselves up in order to kill as many people as possible has also been prevalent. Although there have been no incidents before the ones of September 11, 2001 where terrorists combined both an airplane hijacking and a suicidal explosion, I am not able to say that the risk of crashes was not reasonably foreseeable to an airplane manufacturer. Plaintiffs have alleged that it was reasonably foreseeable that a failure to design a secure cockpit could contribute to a breaking and entering into, and a take-over of, a cockpit by hijackers or other unauthorized individuals, substantially increasing the risk of injury and death to people and damage to property. I hold that the allegation is sufficient to establish Boeing's duty.

Boeing also argues that the regulations of the Federal Aviation Administration ("FAA") relating to design of passenger airplanes did not require an impenetrable cockpit door, and thus its designs, which satisfied FAA requirements, could not be defective. However, the only support provided by Boeing for its argument is an after-the-fact FAA policy statement, issued to explain why the FAA, in 2002, was requiring airplane manufacturers to provide such doors even though the FAA previously had not done so.

> Flightcrew compartment doors on transport category airplanes have been designed principally to ensure privacy, so pilots could focus their entire attention to their normal and emergency flight duties. The doors have not been designed to provide an impenetrable barrier between the cabin and the flightcrew compartment. Doors have not been required to meet any significant security threat, such as small arms fire or shrapnel, or the exercise of brute force to enter the flightcrew compartment.

67 Fed. Reg. 12,820-12,824 (Mar. 19, 2002).

Boeing has not proffered the parameters that existed when it manufactured its "757" jumbo-jet airplanes that United and American flew on September 11, 2001. Boeing also has not shown the extent to which FAA regulations determined how passenger airplanes were to be constructed. Although a FAA promulgation of standards for the design and manufacture of passenger aircraft may be entitled to weight in deciding whether Boeing was negligent, statements by the FAA characterizing what its former regulations required does not dictate the totality of the duty owed by aircraft manufacturers. Boeing's argument is not sufficient to support its motion to dismiss the complaints against it.

Proximate Causation

Boeing next argues that its design of the cockpit doors on its "757" passenger aircraft, even if held to constitute an "unreasonably dangerous condition," was not the proximate cause of plaintiffs' injuries. Boeing argues that the criminal acts of the terrorists in hijacking the airplanes and using the airplanes as weapons of mass destruction constituted an "efficient intervening cause" which broke the "natural and continuous sequence" of events flowing from Boeing's allegedly inadequate design. Plaintiffs have the burden to prove proximate cause and, generally, the issue is a question of fact to be resolved by a jury. However, when reasonable people cannot differ, the issue becomes a question of law for the court.

The record at this point does not support Boeing's argument that the invasion and take-over of the cockpit by the terrorists must, as a matter of law, be held to constitute an "efficient intervening act" that breaks the "natural and continuous sequence" flowing from Boeing's allegedly inadequate design. Plaintiffs allege that Boeing should have designed its cockpit door to prevent hijackers from invading the cockpit, that acts of terrorism, including hijackings of airplanes, were reasonably foreseeable, and that the lives of passengers, crew and ground victims would be imminently in danger from such hijackings. Virginia law does not require Boeing to have foreseen precisely how the injuries suffered on September 11, 2001 would be caused, as long as Boeing could reasonably have foreseen that "some injury" from its negligence "might probably result." Given the critical nature of the cockpit area, and the inherent danger of crash when a plane is in flight, one cannot say that Boeing could not reasonably have foreseen the risk flowing from an inadequately constructed cockpit door.

Boeing relies heavily on *Baltimore & Ohio Railroad Co. v. Patterson* (Va. 1963), to support its argument that proximate causation was broken by an "efficient intervening cause." The case, however, is distinguishable.

The railroad had been using a certain type of switch for more than forty years. While a long freight train was stopped, with eight cars having passed over the switch and the balance of 51 freight cars still on the other side, a six-year old boy living at the side of the track surreptitiously came onto the tracks and threw the switch. When the train resumed its movement, a number of cars derailed, causing property damage to adjoining properties. The Virginia Supreme Court reversed the verdict for the plaintiff, holding that the railroad reasonably could not have foreseen the occurrence. The switch was of a standard type in use for more than forty years; it was used throughout the railroad's extensive system, and at the location in issue; it had consistently been operated in an identical manner for the forty years; the switch had never before been tampered with; and the railroad crew had not been negligent in monitoring the child or the tampered switch. The court held that an imposition of liability on the railroad would be unreasonable, for it would require the railroad to station employees at or near all its switches. The court ruled also that the boy's criminal conduct, not reasonably being foreseen by the railroad, constituted an independent and proximate cause of the adjoining property owner's damage. In contrast, the danger that a plane could crash if unauthorized individuals invaded and took over the cockpit was the very risk that Boeing should reasonably have foreseen. "Privacy" within a cockpit means very little if the door intended to provide security is not designed to keep out potential intruders.

Boeing's citation to cases in other jurisdictions are also distinguishable (see *Port Authority of N.Y. and N.J. v. Arcadian Corp.* (3d Cir. 1999) and *Gaines-Tabb v. ICI Explosives USA, Inc.* (10th Cir. 1998)). The courts of appeals in both cases addressed the question of causation and held that defendants' actions or inactions were not the "legal proximate cause" of the injuries suffered by the victims of the 1993 World Trade Center and 1995 Oklahoma City bombings. They ruled that the manufacturers of the fertilizer products utilized in the attacks, having made lawful and economically and socially useful fertilizer products, did not have to anticipate that criminals would misappropriate ingredients, mix them with others, and make bombs to bring down a building. The bomb-making by the terrorists were found to be superseding and intervening events and were not natural or probable consequences of any design defect in defendants' products.

In re Korean Air Lines Disaster of September 1, 1983, (D.D.C. 1985), involved lawsuits by the legal successors of passengers who died when Korean Airlines passenger flight 007 was shot down by Russian fighter planes. The passenger plane had flown off course and over a sensitive military zone in Russia. Russian fighter pilots intercepted the plane and, instead of following international protocol for causing the plane to return to international routes over the high seas or to land at a selected landing field, shot it down. Plaintiffs sued Boeing, the manufacturer of the airplane, alleging that a product defect in its navigation systems caused it to fly off course and over Soviet territory, and that Boeing's improper and unsafe design was therefore the proximate cause of plaintiffs' damages. The court dismissed the complaint, holding that Boeing could not foresee that the Soviet Union would destroy an intruding aircraft in violation of international conventions, and had no ability to guard against such conduct. The court held, consequently, that Boeing did not owe a duty to passengers with respect to such risks, and that the actions of the Russian pilots were independent and supervening causes that broke the chain of causation.

These three cases do not offer Boeing much support in its motion. In each, the acts of the third-parties were held to be superseding causes because they were not reasonably foreseeable to the product manufacturer. In *Gaines-Tabb* and *Arcadian*, the courts of appeals held that the fertilizer manufacturers could not reasonably foresee that terrorists would mix their products with other ingredients to create explosives to cause buildings to collapse and occupants to be killed. In KAL, the court held that the manufacturer of airplane navigational systems could not reasonably foresee that a passenger aircraft that strayed off course would be shot down by hostile military forces in violation of international conventions. In the cases before me, however, plaintiffs allege that Boeing could reasonably have foreseen that terrorists would try to invade the cockpits of airplanes, and that easy success on their part, because cockpit doors were not designed to prevent easy opening, would be imminently dangerous to passengers, crew and ground victims. Plaintiffs' allegations that duty and proximate cause existed cannot be dismissed as a matter of law on the basis of the record now before me. Accordingly, I deny Boeing's motion to dismiss the complaints against it arising from the crash of flight 77 into the Pentagon.

* * *

Motion to Dismiss Claims Arising out Crash of United Air Lines Flight 93

The successors of the passengers who died in the crash of United Air Lines flight 93 in Shanksville have filed four lawsuits. Their allegations are encapsulated in Plaintiffs' Flight 93 Master Liability Complaint, which mirrors the Plaintiffs' First Amended Flight 77 Master Liability Complaint. The Flight 93 Master Complaint alleges claims against Boeing based on strict tort liability, for an unreasonably dangerous design of the cockpit doors; negligence, for failure to design cockpit doors and accompanying locks in a manner that would prevent hijackers and/or passengers from accessing the cockpit; and express or implied warranty, for creating a product that was unfit for the purposes for which it was designed, intended and used.

Strict tort liability and breach of warranty claims

Under Pennsylvania law, following section 402A of the RESTATEMENT (SECOND) OF TORTS, a plaintiff pressing a product liability or strict tort liability claim must allege and prove that the product was defective, that the defect existed when it left the defendant, and that the defect proximately caused the harm. The elements of breach of warranty and strict product liability are the same.

"The question of whether a product is unreasonably dangerous is a question of law. In answering this question a court is essentially making a social policy determination and acting as both a social philosopher and a risk-utility economic analyst." Courts must weigh factors such as "the gravity of the danger posed by the challenged design; the likelihood that such danger would occur; the mechanical feasibility of a safer design; and the adverse consequences to the product and to the consumer that would result from a safer design." Manufacturers are held strictly liable for product defects because they "market their product for use and because they have a better opportunity to control the defect." "The focus is on the nature of the product and the consumer's reasonable expectations with regard to the product."

Within the risk-utility analysis, courts must examine if the product was safe for its intended use. "A product is defective when it is not safe for its intended use ... a manufacturer is entitled to believe that the product will be used in its usual manner, and need not be the insurer for the extraordinary risks an operator might choose to take." The use must also be by one who is an intended user.

Because the decision of whether the product was unreasonably dangerous and unsafe for its intended use is a question of law, Boeing argues that the judge should not be influenced by conclusory allegations of the complaint. The reason, Boeing argues, is that "the trial court is not bound by any party's legal conclusions as to the intended purpose of a product, even if those conclusions are couched as averments of fact or presented as expert evidence. To hold otherwise would force trial courts (and reviewing courts) to accept unrealistic, generalized or distorted views of the product's purpose simply because they are presented as factual evidence."

But this is not the situation in the case before me. The cockpit door, like any door, is intended as a separation, a "movable barrier of wood or other material, consisting either of one piece, or of several pieces framed together, usually turning on hinges or sliding in a groove, and serving to close or open a passage into a building, room, etc." OXFORD ENGLISH DICTIONARY (2d ed. 1999). A door may be fitted with, and without, locks, depending on who may be allowed to enter and in what circumstances. The intended users of a door, and in particular a locked door, are those within, in order to assure their privacy, and possibly those without who may have an interest in allowing those within to perform their jobs without unwanted intrusion.

Boeing asks me to hold that since the terrorists who hijacked the airplanes were not the intended users of the cockpit doors, one cannot say that the doors were unreasonably dangerous or unsafe in relation to the use that terrorists would be expected to make of the doors. Clearly, however, the intended users of the cockpit doors were not the terrorists who broke through them, but the pilots who had the right to protection from unwanted intrusion, and the passengers who had the right to believe that the pilots could continue to guide the plane, free from intrusion, to ensure their safe arrival at their intended destination.

If, as Boeing argues, a person who breaks through a door is considered to be an unintended user, no manufacturer of a door and lock system could ever be liable. The intended user of a door is the person who wishes it to be closed and stay closed, not the person who can easily force it open. The pilots and passengers are not mere "casual bystanders," but people with a vital stake in the door's performing its intended purpose. *See* RESTATEMENT (SECOND) TORTS § 402A, Comments (l) and (o) (intended users include "those who are passively enjoying the benefit of the product, as in the case of passengers in automobiles or airplanes ... casual bystanders, and others who may come in contact with the product, as in the case of employees of the retailer, or a passer-by injured by an exploding bottle, or a pedestrian hit by an automobile have been denied recovery").

Boeing may be able to show that the cockpit doors were not unreasonably dangerous, and that it was not unreasonable to design them to provide privacy without making them impenetrable. At this point, it would be inappropriate for a judge to make this determination. The record will have to be developed to show if the cockpit doors, incapable of keeping out unwanted intruders, were unreasonably dangerous, taking into consideration: (1) the gravity of the danger posed by the design; (2) the likelihood that the danger would occur; (3) the feasibility of a safer design; (4) the adverse consequences to the product and to the consumer that would result from a safer design; (5) the usefulness and desirability of the product; (6) the likelihood that the product will cause injury and the probable seriousness of the injury; (7) the availability of a substitute product which meets the same needs and is not unsafe; (8) the manufacturer's ability to eliminate the unsafe character of the product without impairing usefulness or making the product too expensive; (9) the user's ability to avoid danger by the exercise of care in the use of the product; (10) the user's anticipated awareness of the dangers inherent in the product and their avoidability; and (11) the ability of the manufacturer to spread loss through price-setting or insurance coverage.

In order to prevail on their strict liability and breach of warranty claims, the plaintiffs must also show that the defect was the proximate cause for the injuries; this will be discussed in the negligent design analysis below.

Negligent design claims

Boeing argues that the plaintiffs' negligent design claims must be dismissed because it did not owe a duty of care to the plaintiffs, and because its alleged negligence was not the proximate cause of plaintiffs' damages. The elements of a claim of negligence are: the existence of a duty to plaintiffs; the breach of that duty; a causal relationship between the breach and the resulting injury; and actual loss by the plaintiff. Because Pennsylvania and Virginia law do not appear to differ significantly, the analysis is similar to that for Flight 77.

Duty is "imposed on all persons not to place others at risk of harm through their actions. The scope of this duty is limited, however, to those risks which are reasonably foreseeable by the actor in the circumstances of the case." "In the context of duty, the concept of foreseeability means the likelihood of the occurrence of a general type of risk rather than the likelihood of the occurrence of the precise chain of events leading to the injury." Plaintiffs have alleged that Boeing reasonably should have foreseen that a negligently designed cockpit door, permitting unauthorized individuals to enter the cockpit, would lead to risk of injury or death. For the same reasons as I have discussed previously, Boeing's motion to dismiss based on the absence of a duty of care to plaintiffs is denied.

To determine whether proximate cause exists, "the court must determine whether the injury would have been foreseen by an ordinary person as the natural and probable outcome of the act complained of." The existence of a concurring cause responsible for producing injury does not relieve a defendant of liability, if "a jury could reasonably believe that a defendant's actions were a substantial factor in bringing about the harm." "Among the factors to consider in determining whether a subsequent force is an intervening or superseding cause are whether the force is operating independently of any situation created by the first actor's negligence and whether it is a normal result of that situation." Plaintiffs allege that without defendant's negligence, the hijackers would not have been able to intrude into the cockpit and take over the airplane. Again, for the reasons previously discussed, the terrorists' unauthorized entry into the cockpit was not unforeseeable, and did not constitute an "intervening" or "superseding" cause that could, as a matter of law, break the chain of causation. Accordingly, I deny Boeing's motion to dismiss the complaints against it arising from the crash of flight 93 into Shanksville.

U.S. AIRWAYS, INC. v. COMMONWEALTH INS. CO.

2004 WL 1637139 (Va. Cir. Ct. 2004)

JOANNE F. ALPER, Judge.

This case comes before the Court on U.S. Airways' Motion for Judgment against PMA Capital Insurance Company ("PMA") alleging breach of an insurance contract.

U.S. Airways claims damages as a result of business interruption caused by the nationwide ground stop orders issued by the Federal Aviation Administration and the closure of Reagan National Airport in the wake of the terrorist attacks on September 11, 2001.

U.S. Airways Group, Inc. ("U.S. Airways") entered into an insurance contract with several insurers for property liability insurance. The Policy is a subscription policy, where several insurance providers jointly agree to underwrite a percentage of coverage, with a limit of $25 million. The Policy does not cover aircraft or personal injury liability. This case involves only one of the insurers under the Policy, PMA. PMA is a successor in interest to Caliber One Indemnity Company, who was one of the original subscribers to the Policy.

On May 14, 2004, this Court issued rulings on cross-motions for summary judgment. In denying PMA's motion for summary judgment, the Court found that actual damage to U.S. Airways property is not a condition precedent to recovery for business interruption under the Policy. Rather, the Court found that the Policy was clear and unambiguous on its face and a jury could find, under the facts presented, coverage applied under the civil or military intervention provisions. The Court sustained PMA's motion for summary judgment finding that U.S. Airways could not recover for loss of market share as the Policy explicitly excludes recovery for such a loss. PMA sought summary judgment on the issue of whether U.S. Airways submitted a valid proof of loss for the claim which was denied.

Summary judgment was granted in favor of PMA on the issue of U.S. Airways' claim of breach of the covenant of good faith and fair dealing. The law in Virginia supports the Court's finding that U.S. Airways cannot seek recovery for bad faith in the current litigation. The Court dismissed the claim, without prejudice, as premature.

The final issue raised in the May 14th ruling was whether PMA can offset any damages under the Policy with funds received by U.S. Airways from the Federal government under the Air Transportation Safety and System Stabilization Act. The Court found that U.S. Airways is required to offset any insurance proceeds from any claim under the Stabilization Act, but that does not require U.S. Airways to offset the federal payments from its claims for coverage under the business interruption Policy. Therefore, the Court granted summary judgment in favor of U.S. Airways.

Based on these rulings, the Court heard this matter, without a jury, on the sole issue of whether U.S. Airways' claim was covered under the Policy. Having taken evidence, considered the arguments of counsel, and taken the matter and PMA's Motion to Strike the Plaintiff's Evidence under advisement, the Court issues the following findings of facts and conclusions of law.

FINDINGS OF FACT

U.S. Airways Group, Inc., entered into a property insurance contract with Caliber One Indemnity Company ("Policy") which provides for coverage for the period of December 1, 2000 through December 1, 2001. The Policy states that coverage extends to U.S. Airways Group, Inc. "and any subsidiary, associated, or affiliated company, corporation, firm, organization, partnership, joint venture, or individual as now exist or are hereafter constituted or acquired, and any other party in interest that is required by contract or other agreement to be named, hereafter referred to as the 'Insured.'"

The Policy is a subscription policy which covers damage to property, including business interruption, up to a limit of $25 million. The Policy does not cover loss or damage to aircraft. PMA Capital Insurance Corporation became a party to this action as a successor in interest to Caliber One Indemnity Company.

The relevant sections of the Policy are as follows:

> 7. COVERAGE
>
> Except as hereinafter excluded, this policy covers:
>
> *A. Real and Personal Property*
>
> The interest of the Insured in all real and personal property (including improvements and betterments) owned, used or intended for use by the Insured, or hereafter constructed, erected, installed, or acquired including while in course of construction, erection, installation, and assembly.
>
> *B. Business Interruption*
>
> Loss resulting from necessary interruption of business conducted by the Insured and caused by loss, damage, or destruction to real or personal property by any of the perils covered herein during the term of this policy
>
> * * *
>
> *Resumption of Operations*: It is a condition of this insurance that if the Insured could reduce the loss resulting from the interruption of business ... by a complete or partial resumption of operation of the property insured, whether damaged or not;
>
> * * *

F. Business Interruption

Interruption by Civil or Military Authority: This policy extended to cover the loss sustained during the period of time, not to exceed 30 consecutive days when, as a direct result of a peril insured against, access to real or personal property is prohibited by order of civil or military authority.

8. PERILS INSURED AGAINST

This policy insures against all risk of direct physical loss of or damage to property described herein including general average, salvage, and all other charges on shipments covered hereunder, except as hereinafter excluded ...

9. PERILS EXCLUDED

This policy does not insure … against loss of market, except as provided for elsewhere in this policy.

* * *

28. Notice of Loss

As soon as practicable after any loss or damage occurring under this policy is known to the Insured's home office insurance department, the Insured shall report such loss or damage with full particulars to Aon Risk Services, Inc. of Il.

29. Proof of Loss

It shall be necessary for the Insured to render a signed and sworn proof of loss to the Company or its appointed representative stating: the place, time, and cause of the loss, damage, or expense; the interest of the Insured and of all others; the value of the property involved in the loss; and the amount of loss, damage, or expense.

* * *

34. Assistance and Cooperation of the Insured

The insured shall cooperate with this Company and, upon this Company's request and expense, shall attend hearings and trials and shall assist in effecting settlements, in

> securing and giving evidence, in obtaining the attendance of witnesses, and in conducting suits.
>
> * * *
>
> 38. Suit against the Company
>
> No suit or action on this policy for the recovery of any claim shall be sustainable in any court of law or equity unless the Insured shall have fully complied with all the requirements of this policy. The Company agrees that any action or proceeding against it for recovery of any loss under this policy shall not be barred if commenced within the time prescribed therefor in the statutes of [the] State of New York.

On September 11, 2001, terrorists launched an attack on the United States in which commercial aircraft were hijacked and used as weapons. U.S. Airways sought coverage under the Policy for losses related to the shut down of the national airspace and the closure of Reagan National Airport as a result of the terrorist attacks on the United States on September 11, 2001. U.S. Airways bases its claim for business interruption coverage on the "Interruption by Civil or Military Authority" provision in the Policy.

On September 11, 2001, the Department of Transportation ("DOT"), through the Federal Aviation Administration ("FAA"), issued a national ground stop order which closed the entire national airspace in the United States for the first time. The routine method of communication between the FAA and U.S. Airways is via teletype sent by the FAA from the FAA Command Center located in Herndon, Virginia to the U.S. Airways Operations Command Center ("OCC") located in Pittsburgh, Pennsylvania. Another method of communication between the FAA and U.S. Airways is via telephone conference calls every two hours between the FAA Command Center in Herndon, Virginia and the U.S. Airways OCC. On September 11, 2001, U.S. Airways' OCC received the national ground stop order from the FAA. U.S. Airways' OCC forwarded the FAA national ground stop order to U.S. Airways' operations personnel, including personnel at all subsidiary airlines, at each airport from which U.S. Airways operated flights. The FAA ground stop order prohibited any aircraft from departing from designated airports.

All commercial air traffic ceased in each of U.S. Airways' stations as a direct consequence of the FAA ground stop order. The Metropolitan Washington Airport Authority ("MWAA") ordered Reagan National Airport terminals closed to the public and ordered personnel to exclude public access to the Airport facilities. Reagan National Airport remained close to the public and all airport employees, but for only a select few for security purposes, until October 4, 2001. The national ground stop implemented by the FAA on September 11, 2001 remained in effect through 11:00 A.M. EST on

September 13, 2001. After the landing of its aircraft following the ground stop, U.S. Airways did not operate any commercial flights until the ground stop was lifted on September 13, 2001.

U.S. Airways' only business is the transportation of people and cargo by aircraft. Each airport in the United States remained closed to commercial air traffic until September 13, 2001. U.S. Airways sustained business interruption losses as a result of the FAA ground halt order which closed the national airspace for the period of September 11, 2001 to September 13, 2001.

Reagan National Airport was closed to all commercial air traffic from September 11, 2001 to October 4, 2001, when it partially resumed commercial operations. During the closure of Reagan National Airport, officials for MWAA installed locks on the doors and maintained a security presence to bar not only the public but most airport personnel from the premises. U.S. Airways sustained business interruption losses as a result of the orders of civil and military authority which closed Reagan National Airport for the period of September 11, 2001 to October 4, 2001. The Federal Aviation Administration, the Department of Transportation and the Metropolitan Washington Airport Authority are civil authorities within the meaning of the Policy. On October 26, 2001, U.S. Airways provided Caliber One with notice of its intent to file a business interruption claim under the Policy. On July 30, 2002, U.S. Airways submitted an amended Proof of Loss to Caliber One claiming losses under the policy as the insured "U.S. Airways, Inc."

CONCLUSIONS OF LAW

In Virginia, insurance policies are construed in accordance with traditional principles of contract law. To that end, polices must be read as a whole. In reading an insurance contract, as a whole, each component of the insurance contract must be considered. When the language in a policy is clear and unambiguous, the language will be given its plain and ordinary meaning and enforced as written. Multiple related components of an insurance contract must be construed together and seemingly conflicting provisions harmonized when that can reasonably be done. The agreement entered into between U.S. Airways and Caliber One Insurance Company is a valid contract. The Policy before the Court is plain and unambiguous by its terms.

COVERAGE UNDER THE POLICY

In order for this Court to find coverage under the Policy, U.S. Airways must demonstrate, by a preponderance of the evidence, that a civil or military authority issued an order which caused a denial of access to U.S. Airways' property and that order was issued as a direct result of a peril insured against. "Peril insured against" is defined in the Policy as "all risk of direct physical loss of or damage to property described herein including general average, salvage, and all other charges on shipments covered hereunder, except as hereinafter excluded."

PMA concedes that as a result of the orders of civil and military authorities the national airspace was closed from September 11, 2001 through September 13, 2001, and that Reagan National Airport was closed for the period of September 11, 2001 through October 4, 2001. PMA asserts that the orders were not issued as a direct result of a peril insured against and therefore coverage under the Policy should be denied.

At trial, U.S. Airways put forth evidence that established that Reagan National Airport was closed as a direct result of fear that United Flight 93 was heading for the airport. One computer generation had the aircraft less than 20 minutes away and heading directly for National Airport. At the time of the evacuation, Christopher Brown, airport manager of Reagan National Airport, testified that it was his understanding that Reagan National Airport could be a target of a terrorist attack. In addition to the large number of people on the premises, the fuel storage facility, holding about 4 million gallons of jet fuel, was thought to have been a target. The order to close Reagan National Airport was made specifically out of fear of being a target for further terrorist attacks. Closing the premises acted to protect the property of not only U.S. Airways, but all of the other commercial and private operators at the airport.

The Policy does not require actual damage or loss of property to invoke coverage. It is clear from the evidence that an order by civil or military authority was issued as a direct result of risk of damage or loss to U.S. Airways property. As counsel for PMA acknowledged during closing arguments, coverage would apply if MWAA closed Reagan National Airport, denying access to the premises, during a thunderstorm because lightning struck a building next to the airport and a fire threatened U.S. Airways' property. The same is true here, MWAA closed Reagan National Airport out of a fear that a hazard existed and the remedy was to evacuate the premises and deny access not only to the public but also airline employees. Since MWAA's orders denied access to Reagan National Airport and denied "access to real or personal property" of U.S. Airways the orders qualify under the Civil Authority provision of the Policy. Likewise, the ground stop order issued by the FAA closing the nation's airspace clearly denied U.S. Airways use of its property and prohibited U.S. Airways from operating its business which is the transportation of passengers and cargo by aircraft.

Based upon the evidence presented, the Court finds that the events of September 11, 2001 and the resulting closure of the national airspace until September 13, 2001, and the continued closure of Reagan National Airport until October 4, 2001, are covered events under the Policy. The Court, as a matter of law, must now determine whether U.S. Airways satisfied the conditions precedent to recovery under the Policy or determine whether PMA waived those conditions.

PROOF OF LOSS

The Policy requires that "[a]s soon as practicable after any loss or damage occurring under this policy is known to the Insured's home office insurance department, the Insured shall report such loss or damage with full particulars to Aon Risk Services, Inc. of Il. ..." It is established law in Virginia that "such a requirement of timely notice of an accident or occurrence is a condition precedent to an insurance company's liability coverage requiring 'substantial compliance by the insured.'"

The Supreme Court has held that "if a violation of the notice requirement is substantial and material, the insurance company need not show that it was prejudiced by such a violation," rather, only a showing that notice was not given is sufficient to prove the condition precedent was satisfied. *State Farm Fire & Cas. Co. v. Scott* (Va. 1988). PMA admits that it received notice from U.S. Airways of their intent to file a claim under the Policy on October 26, 2001. This admission provides adequate basis for the Court to rule that U.S. Airways satisfied the notice requirement under the Policy. In addition to submitting a notice of claim, U.S. Airways was required to submit a proof of loss under the Policy.

The Policy provides: "It shall be necessary for the Insured to render a signed and sworn proof of loss to the Company or its appointed representative stating: the place, time, and cause of the loss, damage, or expense; the interest of the Insured and of all others; the value of the property involved in the loss; and the amount of loss, damage, or expense." When determining whether an insured has submitted a valid proof of loss, the settled law of this Commonwealth is that "if an insurance policy makes the furnishing of a proof of loss a condition precedent to an action upon it, performance or waiver of it must be shown before a recovery can be had."

The purpose of the proof of loss is to enable the insurer to investigate the insured's losses, to estimate its rights and liabilities, and to prevent assertion of fraudulent or unjust claims. The burden of proving that a valid proof of loss was submitted rests upon the insured to "[prove] compliance with the necessary requirements of an insurance policy as to proof of loss, or the waiver of such compliance on the party of the company ... if [the insured] fails to establish the same by a preponderance of the evidence his action must fail."

PMA admits that it received a proof of loss from U.S. Airways on July 29, 2002 and an amended proof of loss on July 30, 2002. The proof of loss submitted on July 30, 2002 stated that the Insured, U.S. Airways, Inc., sustained business interruption losses from on September 11, 2001 through September 13, 2001 for its entire fleet and losses associated with the closure of Reagan National Airport from September 11, 2001 through October 4, 2001. The proof of loss estimated damages of $58,199,634. That damage estimate included an asterisk which indicated that the loss figure specifically did not include the losses suffered by the covered subsidiary airlines.

The question before the Court is whether the proof of loss submitted to PMA was for U.S. Airways alone or whether it was for U.S. Airways Group, Inc., the named insured in the Policy, which includes the mainline carrier and its four subsidiaries—

Allegheny Airlines, Inc., Piedmont Airlines, Inc., PSA Airlines, Inc. and MidAtlantic Airways, Inc.

PMA has asserted throughout the litigation that the language in the proof of loss explicitly excludes the subsidiaries within U.S. Airways' claim, while U.S. Airways contends that since the loss exceed the policy limit by two fold the failure to give the dollar amount of the U.S. Airways subsidiaries' losses was neither a substantial nor material omission. The law in Virginia is clear that "liability is determined by the loss itself, the policy's coverage restrictions, and the limits of the policy, not by the dollar amount the insured places on the proof of loss." "Not knowing the dollar amount of the insured's claim does not affect the ability of the insurance company to determine the amount of its liability."

The Policy, clearly and unambiguously, covers not only U.S. Airways but all of its subsidiaries. PMA clearly knew the nature of the claim from the notice submitted on October 26, 2001 and the proof of losses submitted on July 29 and 30, 2002. The proof of loss was filed under the name of the insured, the proof of loss refers to the policy, by number, which covers both the mainline carrier and the subsidiaries, and the proof of loss clearly references the four subsidiaries. Since the damages well exceeded the Policy limits, it would have been a futile effort to require U.S. Airways to extract the exact amount of damages for each subsidiary when PMA was clearly put on notice that subsidiaries also experience losses as a result of business interruption. At trial, PMA did not present any evidence of prejudice based upon the omission of the subsidiaries' losses. It is clear from the record that the notice of claim and proof of loss provides PMA with sufficient information "to investigate the loss, to determine its liability, and to prevent a fraudulent claim."

Based upon the evidence presented, the Court finds that PMA was given sufficient information to investigate the claim, and the proof of loss submitted by U.S. Airways on July 30, 2002 was valid for not only U.S. Airways mainline carrier, but also the four subsidiaries included in the Policy.

COOPERATION CLAUSE

The Policy requires: "The insured shall cooperate with this Company and, upon this Company's request and expense, shall attend hearings and trials and shall assist in effecting settlements, in securing and giving evidence, in obtaining the attendance of witnesses, and in conducting suits." PMA argues that U.S. Airways failed to cooperate with the investigation of its claim and as a result has breached the Policy. If U.S. Airways failed to cooperate in the investigation of the claim, that inaction could constitute breach and relieve PMA of any liability under the Policy. In evaluating an allegation of failure to cooperate with an insurer, the Supreme Court has stated "there must be a lack of cooperation in some substantial and material respect."

During its investigation, Caliber One requested that U.S. Airways provide it with certain factual and documentary information so that Caliber One could render a coverage determination. At trial, PMA did not present any evidence to demonstrate that U.S. Airways failed to cooperate with the investigation of the claim. Based on the evidence, the Court finds that U.S. Airways did not breach its duty to cooperate under the Policy.

UNITED AIR LINES, INC. v. INS. CO. OF STATE OF PA.

439 F.3d 128 (2d Cir. 2006)

SACK, Circuit Judge.

On July 14, 2003, the plaintiff, United Air Lines, Inc., ("United") brought suit in the United States District Court for the Southern District of New York seeking a declaratory judgment and recovery in breach of contract under its $25 million "Property Terrorism & Sabotage" insurance policy with the defendant, Insurance Company of the State of Pennsylvania ("ISOP"). United sought indemnity for losses it suffered as a result of the September 11, 2001, terrorist attacks on the World Trade Center in New York City and the Pentagon in Arlington, Virginia.

United's ticket office located in the World Trade Center was destroyed. It is undisputed that United can recover from ISOP for any lost earnings that are attributable to this physical damage. Its facilities at Ronald Reagan Washington National Airport (the "Airport"), in Arlington, Virginia, suffered no significant physical damage as a result of the attack on the nearby Pentagon. The issue on this appeal is whether United can nonetheless recover for its lost earnings caused by the national disruption of flight service and the government's temporary shutdown of the Airport. (As of August 2002, United had received $782 million in federal aid under the Air Transportation Safety and System Stabilization Act of 2001, 49 U.S.C. § 40101. United's remaining unreimbursed losses allegedly total approximately $400 million.)

We agree with the district court that, because United cannot show that such lost earnings resulted from physical damage to its property or from physical damage to an adjacent property, under the unambiguous language of the insurance policy, the losses are not covered.

BACKGROUND

The first section of United's "Property Terrorism & Sabotage" insurance policy with ISOP states in pertinent part: "[ISOP] will indemnify [United] for property damage, loss of gross earnings, and extra expense in excess of the Deductible [as later defined] ... resulting from [terrorism], and any ensuing fire damage, damage from looting, or other damage caused by an act of a lawfully constituted authority for the purpose of suppressing or minimizing the consequences of [an incident of terrorism]." Property Terrorism & Sabotage Insurance Policy between ISOP and United (the "Policy").

A subsequent section of the Policy provides that the Policy "insures against loss resulting directly from the necessary interruption of business caused by damage to or destruction of [United's] Insured Locations [which include United's facilities at both the World Trade Center and the Airport] resulting from Terrorism." The Policy then states that "[t]his section is specifically extended to cover a situation when access to the Insured Locations is prohibited by order of civil authority as a direct result of damage to adjacent premises."

United seeks a declaratory judgment pursuant to 28 U.S.C. § 2201(a) and an award of damages for breach of contract against ISOP. In this pursuit, it made two principal arguments to the district court to support its position that the cited provisions of the Policy entitle it to compensation for the lost earnings at issue. First, it argued that section I, quoted above, contains within it a free-standing "Suppression Damages Clause," which covers United's lost earnings resulting from the terrorist attacks even in the absence of physical damage to its Airport property: "[ISOP] will indemnify [United] for ... loss of gross earnings ... resulting from [terrorism] ... or other damage caused by an act of a lawfully constituted authority for the purpose of suppressing ... [an incident of terrorism]."

Second, United argued that it is entitled to recover for lost earnings arising from the post-attack shutdown of the Airport under the "Civil Authority Clause" contained in section III.C.1. of the Policy because the closure was a direct result of physical damage to the Pentagon, which was on "adjacent premises." ISOP asserts seven counterclaims and seeks a declaratory judgment that it is not obligated to reimburse United for the disputed portion of its lost earnings.

On March 31, 2005, in a thorough and thoughtful opinion, the district court granted ISOP's motion for summary judgment and denied United's cross-motion for summary judgment. The court concluded that the plain and unambiguous terms of the Policy did not cover the claims that United asserted.

First, the court reasoned, paragraph III.C.1. of the Policy states that the Policy covers losses from business interruption "caused by damage to or destruction of the Insured Locations." United could (as both parties agreed) therefore recover the amount of losses attributable to the destruction of its ticket office in the World Trade Center. But because the other loss of earnings was caused by the nation-wide suspension of air service rather than "damage to or destruction of [a United] Location[ ]," United could not recover under the Policy for earnings lost as a result of the system-wide disruption of air service.

Second, the court noted that under the Policy's "civil authority" clause in paragraph III.C.1., United would not have been required to show physical damage to its property had it been seeking to recover for damages resulting from blocked access to its Airport property as "a direct result of damage to adjacent premises." But the district court rejected United's argument that the Pentagon qualified as an "adjacent premise" to the Airport for purposes of this paragraph. The court further concluded that, even if the Pentagon were "adjacent" to the Airport, the closing of the Airport and consequent lost earnings incurred by United were not direct results of the physical damage to the Pentagon. United appeals.

DISCUSSION

I. *Standard of Review and Governing Law*

"We review a district court's grant of summary judgment *de novo*, construing the evidence in the light most favorable to the nonmoving party and drawing all inferences and resolving all ambiguities in favor of the nonmoving party."

The Policy is, according to its choice-of-law provision, governed by New York law. Neither party disputes the applicability of New York law to this dispute.

II. *Recovering Loss of Gross Earnings under the "Suppression Damages Clause"*

"The purpose of business interruption insurance is to indemnify the insured against losses arising from an inability to continue normal business operations and functions due to damage sustained as a result of the hazard insured against. In other words, the goal is to preserve the continuity of the insured's earnings." Although the Policy's business interruption clause requires that the loss of earnings stem from physical damage to United's property, a "civil authority" clause extends the Policy's coverage to instances in which United is unable to reach its property as a result of physical damage to an adjacent property. The complete provision reads:

> III. VALUATION
>
> C. BUSINESS INTERRUPTION
>
> GROSS EARNINGS
>
> This policy insures against loss resulting directly from the necessary interruption of business caused by damage to or destruction of the Insured Locations resulting from Terrorism, Sabotage, Mutiny, Insurrection, Rebellion, or Coup d'Etat.

> This section is specifically extended to cover a situation when access to the Insured Locations is prohibited by order of civil authority as a direct result of damage to adjacent premises, not exceeding, however, two (2) consecutive weeks.

Policy, § III.C.1.

To recover gross earnings under this language, United would be required to demonstrate that the business interruption at issue resulted from either (1) physical damage to property at the insured location in question, *i.e.*, the Airport, or (2) an order of civil authority as a direct result of physical damage to property adjacent to the insured location in question, *i.e.*, United contends, the Pentagon. As explained in part III of this opinion, United is able to show neither.

United argues, however, that a third provision of the Policy, contained in section I.A.—what it calls the "Suppression Damages Clause"—provides a separate basis upon which it may recover from ISOP its loss of gross earnings without having to establish either of the foregoing prerequisites. United's argument in this respect fails because, simply put, there is no "Suppression Damages Clause."

The first section of the Policy states:

> I. INSURING AGREEMENT
>
> The Company will indemnify the Insured for property damage, loss of gross earnings, and extra expense in excess of the Deductible, but not exceeding the Limit of Liability, resulting from the following incidents, and any ensuing fire damage, damage from looting, or other damage caused by an act of a lawfully constituted authority for the purpose of suppressing or minimizing the consequences of any of the following incidents, during the policy period: Terrorism; sabotage; mutiny, insurrection, rebellion or Coup d'Etat.

Policy, § 1.A. We do not read this language as providing coverage separate and independent from that set forth elsewhere in the Policy.

The function of section I.A., read in the context of the Policy as a whole, is to serve as an introduction to the Policy. It indicates that the Policy covers three categories of damages: (1) "property damage," (2) "loss of gross earnings," and (3) "extra expense." Section III of the Policy, titled "Valuation," describes how these various types of damages should be calculated. For example, section III.B. ("Buildings and Contents") details how to calculate the value of damages to physical property. Section III.C.1.

describes how to calculate "gross earnings." And section III.C.2. explains how to calculate "extra expense."

United argues, however, that section I.A. of the Policy actually provides coverage for four different categories of damage: (1) "property damage," (2) "loss of gross earnings," (3) "extra expense," and (4) "other damage caused by an act of a lawfully constituted authority for the purpose of suppressing or minimizing the consequences of ... Terrorism[,] Sabotage[,] Mutiny, Insurrection, Rebellion or Coup d'Etat." Thus, United contends that when the government closed the Airport in order to thwart possible airborne attacks, United suffered "other damage caused by an act of a lawfully constituted authority for the purpose of suppressing or minimizing the consequences of ... Terrorism," for which it is entitled to indemnification, under section I.A. of the Policy. We disagree.

This introductory section states that ISOP will indemnify United for certain specified types of damages resulting from certain specified causes. It sets forth three types of damages: physical damage, loss of gross earnings, and extra expenses. It then lists a variety of triggering events that may cause one or more of these kinds of damages. They are fire, looting, or acts of a "lawfully constituted authority for the purpose of suppressing or minimizing the consequences of," *inter alia*, "Terrorism." These are triggering events for the three categories of damages—physical damage, loss of gross earnings, and extra expenses—each of which is further explained and limited by subsequent sections III.B and III.C.1., and III.C.2., respectively. The triggering events are not further categories of damages for which United is entitled to indemnity for loss of gross earnings free of the restrictions contained elsewhere in the Policy.

In other words, the Policy states that whenever there is an act of, *inter alia*, terrorism—or terrorism-caused fire, terrorism—caused looting, or an "act of a lawfully constituted authority for the purpose of suppressing or minimizing the consequences of [an incident of terrorism]"- then United will be indemnified for its physical damages, loss of gross earnings, and extra expenses resulting therefrom. It does not provide that if there is an "act of a lawfully constituted authority for the purpose of suppressing or minimizing the consequences of [an incident of terrorism]," United is entitled to indemnity for any and all resulting loss, including loss of gross earnings, however caused and unlimited by the remaining terms of the contract.

Indeed, if the phrase "suppression damages" created a free-standing basis of coverage—one that was not restricted by the subsequent valuation sections—then, by the same logic employed by United here, any fire damage or damage from looting should also create a free standing right to recover loss of gross earnings unconstrained by the remainder of the Policy. The specific limitations contained in Section III of the Policy would then be surplusage. The Policy states that in calculating loss of gross earnings, United can recover for business interruptions caused by orders of civil authority in response to physical damage of an adjacent structure. There would be no need for such a specific provision— providing a two-week maximum duration of coverage—if the separate "suppression damages" clause that United finds in section I.A. covered all losses attributable to orders of civil authority designed to suppress the effects of terrorism for an indefinite period of time.

There is therefore no merit to United's argument that the district court improperly inserted the word "physical" between the words "other damages" in section I.A. According to that provision, United can indeed recover loss of gross earnings, as contrasted with loss of property through physical damage to the property, that it suffers as a result of a government exclusion order. But the scope of the economic damages it can recover for that business interruption must be determined by cross-reference to the section of the Policy that specifically deals with loss of gross earnings. And that section—section III.C.1—provides that, in order for ISOP to have the duty to indemnify United for lost earnings, the government action in question must either have physically damaged United's property or been caused by physical damage to adjacent property. Similarly, if in attempting to suppress or minimize the consequences of terrorism, the government were to order that United's physical property be destroyed, then United would be able to recover for that physical damage by cross referencing to section III.B., which specifies how to valuate loss of buildings and their contents. And if the government's attempt to suppress damages caused by terrorism resulted in "other expenses" as defined by the insurance policy, those other expenses would be calculated by cross-referencing section III.C.2.

There is, in sum, no validity to United's argument that there arises under section I.A. of the Policy a duty for ISOP to indemnify United for any and all damages of any kind whatsoever that result from the government's efforts to suppress terrorism. There is thus no duty on the part of ISOP under the policy to indemnify United for all damages it incurred, including lost earnings, that resulted from the government's decision to shut down nationwide air service for several days, and the Airport for several weeks, in the wake of the September 11 terrorist attacks.

III. *Recovering Loss under the "Gross Earnings" Section of the Policy*

As noted, United's property at the Airport was not physically damaged. United argues—and ISOP disputes—that its "gate property" was physically damaged by the accumulation of ash as a result of the attack on the Pentagon. But, as the district court correctly noted, there is no evidence that this ash in any way caused the Airport's shutdown. *See* Deposition Transcript of Christopher U. Browne dated Apr. 20, 2004, at 88 ("Q: But there was burning debris landing on the airport property? A: S[m]oldering debris. Q: And how was it removed? A: People picked it up.").

It therefore cannot recover, with respect to its Airport location, for "damage to or destruction of the Insured Locations resulting from Terrorism" under section III.C.1. of the Policy. But the airline also seeks to recover under the "civil authority clause" of that section of the Policy for its loss of gross earnings during the government's suspension of flights into and out of the Airport. In order to do so, United must show that it was denied access to its "locations" at the Airport "as a direct result of damage to adjacent premises." The district court determined that the Pentagon does not qualify as an "adjacent premise" under this provision.

"'As with contracts generally, a provision in an insurance policy is ambiguous when it is reasonably susceptible to more than one reading.'" United correctly points out that the term "adjacent" may indeed be ambiguous: two properties can be adjacent, it seems, without necessarily sharing a border, *i.e.*, without "adjoining." *See, e.g.*, *United States v. St. Anthony R.R. Co.* (1904) (noting that the word adjacent has "uncertain meaning" and declaring that "[i]t is very difficult to determine just where twilight ends and night begins, but it is easy enough to distinguish noon from midnight").

On the one hand, United argues persuasively that, under the circumstances, the distance between the two locations should be judged by the air-distance of less than 1 mile instead of the driving distance of 3.4 miles. But on the other hand, as the district court pointed out, even judging the distance from an aerial photograph, the properties are still "separated by the Crystal City apartment complex, three highways, an active railway, fifteen identifiable parcels of property, a waterfowl sanctuary, and a wooded area."

ISOP also notes that, were we to conclude nonetheless that the Airport's outermost runway is adjacent to the Pentagon property line, the airport runway is not an "Insured Location" of United. United's facilities are inside the airport terminal, some 1.25 miles from the nearest boundary of Pentagon property.

Ultimately, though, we need not resolve whether the Pentagon is "adjacent" to United's property. Even if it is, United cannot show that the Airport was shut down "as a direct result of damage to" the Pentagon. There was apparently a temporary halt of flights into and out of the Airport on 9/11 before the Pentagon was struck. The evidence also indicates, not surprisingly, that the government's subsequent decision to halt operations at the Airport indefinitely was based on fears of future attacks. *See* "Memorandum of Understanding between U.S. Department of Transportation and Metropolitan Washington Airports Authority on Assistance for Ronald Reagan Washington National Airport" ("Because of the location of [the Airport] and the airport's flight paths that take aircraft near the White House, Pentagon, Capitol, and other facilities in the Nation's capital, the Federal Government required that [the Airport] remain completely closed until October 4, 2001, when a phased reopening began.").

The Airport was reopened when it was able to comply with more rigorous safety standards; the timetable had nothing to do with repairing, mitigating, or responding to the damage caused by the attack on the Pentagon. *See* ALAN R. MILLER, BUSINESS INTERRUPTION INSURANCE: CURRENT ISSUES, 702 PLI LITIG. & ADMIN. PRACTICE COURSE HANDBOOK SERIES 233, 267 (2004) ("Access may have been prevented to some property, but not because of the physical damage that occurred. For example, access may have been prohibited because of concerns over a possible further attack. In such a case, it cannot be considered due to physical damage of the type insured.").

In other words, suppose American Airlines Flight 77 that day had missed the Pentagon and smashed into a private office building a mile beyond, or some other similar property not very far from the Airport but clearly not "adjacent" to it. In light of the hijacking of the other airplanes that morning and the successful attack on the World Trade Center, it can hardly be doubted that the effect on subsequent flight operations generally, and United operations at the Airport in particular, would have been virtually identical. The interruption to United's business following the attacks was, therefore, not the "direct result" of damage to adjacent premises. For the foregoing reasons, the judgment of the district court is affirmed.

NOTES

1. Eastern Airlines Chief Executive Officer and NASA astronaut Frank Borman famously said, "Capitalism without bankruptcy is like Christianity without Hell." *In re Ionosphere Clubs, Inc.* (2d Cir. 1990), and *Weinberger v. Lorenzo*, 16 DEL. J. CORP. L. 1647 (1991), *supra*, tell a part of the tumultuous story of a fatal battle waged on March 4, 1989, when International Association of Machinists & Aerospace Workers AFL-CIO ("IAM"), led by Charles E. Bryan, began a labor strike that culminated in the collapse of Eastern Airlines—a storied airline and deregulation casualty.

Prior to *In re Ionosphere Clubs, Inc.*, airline executives, including Frank Lorenzo of Texas Air Corp.—a conglomerate airline holding company—utilized the United States Bankruptcy Code as a powerful union-busting weapon to wipe out labor agreements. In 1983, Continental Airlines filed for bankruptcy under Chapter 11, wiped out its existing labor contracts, fired employees who refused a pay cut, and hired a new workforce at half the cost. *See In re Continental Airlines Corp.* (S.D. Tex. 1985). *See also* Katherine Van Wezel Stone, *Labor Relations on the Airlines: The Railway Labor Act in the Era of Deregulation*, 42 STAN. L. REV. 1485, 1491-92 (1990) (mid-1980s airline management "used the threat of bankruptcy, merger, or sale in negotiations to procure concessions"); Agis Salpukas, *A Wrenching Week at Airline*, N.Y. Times, Oct. 8, 1983, at 1 ("leaders of the pilot, flight attendant and machinist unions ... charge that Frank A. Lorenzo, the airline chairman, was using bankruptcy laws to repudiate union contracts and break the power of the union."). Congress subsequently reformed the bankruptcy laws to prevent such action in the future—"a kind of 'Lorenzo Amendment.'" THOMAS PETZINGER, JR., HARD LANDING 274 (Three Rivers Press 1996).

Eastern Airlines was based in Miami, Florida, where Mr. Lorenzo was vilified. The core allegation in *Weinberger v. Lorenzo*, *supra*, was that Mr. Lorenzo was stripping

"Eastern of its best assets, its most profitable operations and routes, and to unfairly use it to finance the operations of Texas Air and Continental." Local media opined:

> When the same person is both the buyer and the seller, both the lender and the borrower, the normal checks and balances of competitive business obviously don't apply. A seller might price his goods very low when he is himself the buyer, and a lender might forget about collecting the payments from himself. So long as no one else is involved, no harm is done. But when there are shareholders, creditors, and employees with a stake in the deals, Federal commerce laws are supposed to govern …

Out of One Pocket ... Lorenzo Bleeds Eastern, Editorial, THE MIAMI HERALD, Mar. 3, 1990. *See also* James L. Linsey, *Labor and Corporate Law Questions at Eastern Airlines*, C501 ALI-ABA 407, Apr. 6, 1990. The venue in which Eastern filed for bankruptcy protection is telling in this context. A subsidiary of Eastern Airlines—Ionosphere Clubs, the airline's passenger lounges—was incorporated in New York (not Miami) and filed a bankruptcy petition in the Southern District of New York. Six minutes later, the airline itself filed for bankruptcy in that venue. AARON BERNSTEIN, GROUNDED: FRANK LORENZO AND THE DESTRUCTION OF EASTERN AIRLINES (1999). Putatively because the forum of a bankruptcy proceeding is for the convenience of the debtor and not creditors, there was no apparent procedural vehicle to re-venue the bankruptcy proceeding in South Florida.

2. Two airlines filed for bankruptcy in the aftermath of September 11th notwithstanding a $15 billion federal bailout for the airline industry. *See, e.g.*, *What $87 Billion Buys*, WALL ST. J. Sept. 11, 2003, at A12. *See also* Margaret M. Blair, *The Economics of Post-September 11 Financial Aid to Airlines*, 36 IND L. REV. 367 (2003); Charles G. Moerdler, *Deregulation—The United States Experience*, 6 HOFSTRA LAB. L.J. 177, 185-86 (1989).

As explored in greater detail in Chapter 4, *infra*, bankruptcy can and has played a defining role in airline labor-management policies, particularly in the context of the Railway Labor Act of 1926. *See In re Northwest Airlines Corp.*, 483 F.3d 160 (2d Cir. 2007). For further discussion of the role of bankruptcy and labor relations see John J. Gallagher et al., *An Unhappy Crossroads: The Interplay of Bankruptcy and Airline Labor Law* SR035 ALI-ABA 773 (2010); Richard M. Seltzer & Thomas N. Ciantra, *The Return of Government by Injunction, in Airline Bankruptcies*, 15 AM. BANKR. INST. L. REV. 499 (2007); Eva M. Dowdell, *The Chapter 11 "Shuttle"—Coincidence or Competitive Strategy?*, 71 J. AIR L. & COM. 669 (2006); Jody Hoffer Gittell, *Mutual Gains or Zero Sum? Labor Relations and Firm Performance in the Airline Industry*, 57 INDUS. & LAB. REL. REV. 163, 169 (2004); Richard M. Seltzer, *The Changed Role of Unions in Chapter 11 Bankruptcies*, 18-FALL AIR & SPACE LAW. 8 (2003); GEORGE E. HOPKINS, THE

AIRLINE PILOTS: A STUDY IN ELITE UNIONIZATION (2000); AIRLINE LABOR RELATIONS IN THE GLOBAL ERA: THE NEW FRONTIER (Peter Cappelli ed., 1995); Laurie Schoder, Note, *Flying the Unfriendly Skies: The Effect of Airline Deregulation on Labor Relations*, 22 TRANSP. L.J. 105 (1994); Herbert R. Northrup, *The Railway Labor Act—Time for Repeal?*, 13 HARV. J.L. & PUB. POL'Y 441, 457-58 (1990); Elizabeth L. Cocanougher, Comment, *Merging the RLA and NLRA for Eastern Air Lines: Can it Fly*, 44 U. MIAMI L. REV. 549 (1989); Beverly Smaby, *Cooperation vs. Competition at Eastern Air Lines*, 23 HARV. C.R.-C.L. L. REV. 29 (1988); CLEARED FOR TAKEOFF: AIRLINE LABOR RELATIONS SINCE DEREGULATION (Jean T. McKelvey ed., 1988); Beth S. Adler, Comment, *Deregulation in the Airline Industry: Toward a New Judicial Interpretation of the Railway Labor Act*, 80 NW. U. L. REV. 1003 (1986).

3. The one-sentence mention of "computer reservations systems" ("CRSs") in *Weinberger v. Lorenzo*, 16 DEL. J. CORP. L. 1647 (1991), *supra*, warrants further discussion—"Defendants are also accused of having caused Eastern to sell its profitable computer reservation system (System One Direct Access) to Texas Air at an unfair price." CRSs are and were a hugely important feature of commercial aviation economics and the subject of rigorous antitrust enforcement from the beginning of airline deregulation until 2004.

> In the infancy of commercial air travel, the manner in which airlines made and tracked reservations was simple, reflecting supply and demand of a not-yet-penetrated, unsaturated market.
>
> Airline management relied on rudimentary and manual document-retention and retrieval systems to orchestrate flight times, seat assignment, and the like. Airline travel agents mechanically created and/or maintained records by, for example, retrieving records around a "Lazy Susan" or using binoculars to read flight availability.
>
> The acute need for quicker, electronic technology presented itself, however, as the number of consumers using airline travel increased exponentially, outpacing infrastructure. Practical needs and chance motivated airline research and development of modern CRSs. As one narrator tells:
>
>> One day in 1953 an IBM sales representative named Blair Smith, finding himself on an American [Airlines] flight sitting next to [American Airlines founder] C.R. Smith, discovered that their surnames were only the first coincidence. Smith of American explained his

> frustration in managing reservations while Smith of IBM betrayed his eagerness to make a sale.
>
> Before long IBM had a contract to apply the war-making technology [of a Cold War computer system] to American's computer reservations problems. IBM called the project SABER, for Semi-Automatic Business Environment Research. For nearly a decade the project engineers toiled. Along the way, in 1959, an American executive flipping through a magazine stopped at an ad for the 1960 Buick LeSabre; he transposed the last two letters of the acronym and called the system Sabre. It would become, in every respect, the weapon that its name implied.

And so, American Airlines had its Sabre. United Airlines countered with Apollo. Worldspan developed as a merger between Northwest Airlines's PARS system and TWA's and Delta's DATAS. Eventually, European interests entered the CRS market (vis-à-vis Amadeus) by purchasing Continental Airlines' "System One" or "SODA," which itself was a critical asset and product of Eastern Airlines.

There were others systems, too. Each such system originally was developed, owned, and marketed by an airline for use by travel agents and travel agencies.

In an early period of CRS development, CRSs were for internal airline use and, therefore "were production tools, rather than systems of demand enhancement; they presented few opportunities for exploitation of principal-agent relationships because employees of the customer airline generally did their own booking and inventory management using the system hardware and software provided by the vendor."

Once developed, CRS technology helped airlines to maximize their revenue and capture important marginal dollars by automating an airline's manipulation of flight inventories, rates, routes, services, restrictions, and the like. Moreover, CRS technology incentivized airlines to provide their CRSs to travel intermediaries (*i.e.*, travel agents and travel agencies).

> The business advantages of CRS technology for a CRS-owning airline against competitors airlines without CRS ownership were obvious. After all, inasmuch as they were originally developed by airlines, CRSs were a proprietary interest and asset of individual airlines, not of the airline industry generally. Consequently, the DOT reasoned that airlines that developed and owned CRSs had an incentive to prejudice distribution channels in their favor.

Timothy M. Ravich, *Deregulation of the Airline Computer Reservation Systems (CRS) Industry*, 69 J. AIR L. & COM. 378 (2004). *See also* Barry C. Smith et al., *E-Commerce and Operations Research in Airline Planning, Marketing, and Distribution*, 31 INTERFACES 37, 38-39 (2001); THOMAS PETZINGER JR., HARD LANDING 60 (Three Rivers Press 1996); Larry G. Locke, *Flying the Unfriendly Skies: The Legal Fallout over the Use of Computerized Reservation Systems as a Competitive Weapon in the Airline Industry*, 2 HARV. J.L. & TECH. 219, 221 (1989) ("CRS technology created more than just enhanced technical efficiency for travel agents and airlines. It also created opportunities for proprietary airlines to exploit the system as a competitive weapon."); Ian E. Pate, Comment, *In re Travel Agency Commission Antitrust Litigation: A Case of Nonprice Predation within the Travel Industry*, 64 J. AIR L. & COM. 941 (1999) (concluding that "airlines were engaging in collusion and conspiracy to eliminate travel agencies"); Michael E. Levine, *Airline Competition in Deregulated Markets: Theory, Firm Strategy, and Public Policy*, 4 YALE J. ON REG. 393, 459 (1987); Marj P. Leaming, Note, *Enlightened Regulation of Computerized Reservations Systems Requires a Balance Between Consumer Protection and Profitable Airline Marketing*, 21 TRANSP. L.J. 469 (1993) ("The burgeoning air transportation market became dependent on the technological innovation of the CRS."); *Airline Reservation Systems: Curse of the Mommy Tomb*, 9 REGULATION 8 (Jan./Feb. 1985). Airlines have been accused of using data on other airlines' fares to reduce competition. *See United States v. Airline Tariff Publ'g Co.* (D.C. 1993).

4. While impactful of millions of travelers daily, airline economics—in terms of customer service, bankruptcies, insurance, and antitrust issues—are only a subpart of the broader topic of aviation economics. Transactions including the purchase and sale and lease of general and commercial aviation aircraft is an extensively regulated area of the law. Domestically, for example, an intricate system of recording and registration rules and priority schemes (*e.g.*, liens, conveyances, security agreements) exists with respect to aircraft and engines. *See* 49 U.S.C. § 44101 *et seq. See also* 14 C.F.R. Pts. 47, 49. The Federal Aviation Act prohibits all transfers of title to aircraft from having validity against innocent third parties unless the transfer has been evidenced by a written instrument, and the instrument has been recorded with the Federal Aviation Administration. *Philko Aviation, Inc. v. Schaket* (1982). The issue of preemption (see Chapter 2, *supra*) has significance in the context of aviation economics, too, as some courts have determined that state and local filing requirements are preempted by applicable federal law. *See, e.g.*,

In re Holiday Airlines Corp. (9th Cir. 1980). *But see In re Tradewinds Airlines, Inc.* (S.D. Fla. Bankr. 2008).

Internationally, delegations from around the globe (including the United States on March 1, 2006) have adopted the Cape Town Convention on International Interests in Mobile Equipment, an international computerized registry for the filing of interests, including prospective interests, in certain airframes, helicopters, and aircraft engines. *E.g., Ireland v. Dotson*, 2007 WL 3232566 (D. Kan. 2007). *See generally* Lorne S. Clark, *The 2001 Cape Town Convention on International Interests in Mobile Equipment and Aircraft Equipment Protocol: Internationalising Asset-Based Financing Principles for the Acquisition of Aircraft and Engines*, 69 J. AIR L. & COM. 3 (2004).

5. The obituary list for bankrupt airlines (U.S. and foreign) in the last ten years of the deregulated era alone is significant (see *http://airconsumer.dot.gov/cessations.htm*), including Zoom Airlines, Eos Airlines Skybus, ATA Airlines, Aloha Airlines, and BigSky in 2008; Maxjet and Traveland in 2007; Florida Coastal Airlines and Independence Air in 2006; TransMeridian Airlines and Westward Airways in 2005; Southeast Airlines in 2004; National Airlines, Vanguard Airlines, and Midway Airlines in 2002; Legend Airlines, Pro Air, and Tower Air in 2000; Access Air, Sunjet International/Myrtle Beach Jet Express, Kiwi International Airlines in 1999; Euram Flight Center, Pan American World Airways, and Western Pacific Airlines in 1998. Are airlines in pending bankruptcies safe to fly? Kenneth A. Clark, *Flying at Risk: How Should Bankruptcy Interact with Aviation Safety Enforcement?*, 12 BANKR. DEV. J. 845 (1996).

6. While *U.S. Airways, Inc. v. Commonwealth Ins. Co.* (Va. Cir. Ct. 2004), and *United Air Lines, Inc. v. Ins. Co. of State of Pa.* (2d Cir. 2006), *supra,* evaluates aviation insurance after September 11th specifically, aviation insurance generally is an extensive and expansive topic arising in myriad contexts, including hull loss, general contract interpretation, reinsurance, and exculpatory policies. *See, e.g., Gonzalez v. Mission American Ins. Co.* (Tex. 1990) (passenger liability endorsement for "bodily injury" did not include death); *Flamingo Express, Inc. v. Federal Aviation Admin.* (6th Cir. 2008) (upholding government's determination that $20-million liability-insurance requirement imposed on commuter airline as precondition to operations); *Avemco Ins. Co. v. Auburn Flying Svc., Inc.* (8th Cir. 2001) (applying commercial purpose "shared expense" exclusion to flights offered for the general public for a fee).

7. Air carriers are required to maintain "minimum" insurance or self-insurance as follows:

> (a) Insurance contracts and self-insurance plans shall provide for payment on behalf of the carrier, within the specific limits of liability in this section, of all sums that the carrier shall become legally obligated to pay as damages,

excluding any deductible in the policy, for bodily injury to or death of a person, or for damage to the property of others, resulting from the carrier's operation or maintenance of aircraft in air transportation provided under its authority from the Department.

(b) U.S. and foreign direct air carriers, including commuter air carriers but excluding U.S. air taxi operators and Canadian charter air taxi operators, shall maintain the following coverage:

(1) Third-party aircraft accident liability coverage for bodily injury to or death of persons, including nonemployee cargo attendants, other than passengers, and for damage to property, with minimum limits of $300,000 for any one person in any one occurrence, and a total of $20,000,000 per involved aircraft for each occurrence, except that for aircraft of not more than 60 seats or 18,000 pounds maximum payload capacity, carriers need only maintain coverage of $2,000,000 per involved aircraft for each occurrence.

(2) Any such carrier providing air transportation for passengers shall, in addition to the coverage required in paragraph (b)(1) of this section, maintain aircraft accident liability insurance coverage for bodily injury to or death of aircraft passengers, with minimum limits of $300,000 for any one passenger, and a total per involved aircraft for each occurrence of $300,000 times 75 percent of the number of passenger seats installed in the aircraft.

* * *

(e) Notwithstanding paragraph (b), the carrier may be insured for a combined single limit of liability for each occurrence. The combined single-limit coverage must be not less than the combined required minimums for bodily injury and property damage coverage plus, if the aircraft is used in passenger service, the required total passenger coverages stipulated in paragraph (b) of this section for U.S. and foreign direct air carriers and commuter carriers. The single-limit liability policy for the required aircraft accident liability coverage may be provided by a single policy or by a combination of primary and excess policies.

> (f) The liability coverage shall not be contingent upon the financial condition, solvency, or freedom from bankruptcy of the carrier. The limits of the liability for the amounts required by this part shall apply separately to each occurrence. Any payment made under the policy or plan because of any one occurrence shall not reduce the coverage for payment of other damages resulting from any other occurrence.

14 C.F.R. § 205.5 (2010).

8. Aviation accidents arising from both general and commercial operations are archetypical "mass torts." *E.g.*, Timothy M. Ravich, *Aviation Litigation and Mass Torts: A Crash Course*, AMERICAN BAR ASS'N, SECTION OF LITIGATION, MASS TORTS (2010). In terms of damages, "there is virtually always someone who is liable for an aviation accident ..." JAMES S. KAKALIK ET AL., COSTS AND COMPENSATION PAID IN AVIATION ACCIDENT LITIGATION 88 (1988). Indeed, where mass tort plaintiffs generally receive about 50 percent of funds expended, that figure reaches 71 percent in aviation torts. *Id.* at 93-94. In 1996-97, the median jury verdicts in aviation cases in federal district court was $937,000, far higher than the median for "product liability" cases, and 43.8 percent of the verdicts were $1 million or more. *See* BUREAU OF JUSTICE STATISTICS, BULLETING: FEDERAL TORT TRIALS AND VERDICTS 1996-97 5 (1999), *available at http://www.ojp.usdoj.gov/bjs/pub/pdf/fttv97.pdf.*

In the context of aviation insurance, the law requires airlines to maintain minimum insurance (see Note 7, *supra*) to further a public policy of compensating survivors and family members of aviation accident victims. Public policy also favors programs that encourage aviators to report misconduct or errors voluntarily for the purpose of improving safety:

> Voluntary Disclosure programs ("VDPs") in aviation are a rich source of safety-related data that are only obtainable from front-line users of the national airspace system. Confidentiality and the absence of retribution are critical components of effective VDPs, such as Flight Operations Quality Assurance ("FOQA") and the Aviation Safety Action Program ("ASAP").
>
> Consequently, if regulatory agencies wish to continue to receive this information (and the substantial safety-related gains resulting from this information), these programs must be encouraged, not stifled. The information derived from such programs must be used primarily for safety purposes, and the front-line users (typically employees of a

> commercial enterprise) reporting such information must have their confidentiality reasonably protected.
>
> However, despite the fact that industry stakeholders, the Federal Aviation Administration ("FAA") and the National Transportation Safety Board ("NTSB"), view the unfettered flow of information from employee reports as integral to producing future improvements in aviation safety, VDPs, in particular the ASAP, are being threatened by attempts to discover the voluntarily disclosed information during civil litigation. Two decisions on this matter, arising out of two fatal crashes, reached diametrically opposed conclusions on whether ASAP information is entitled to a limited qualified privilege.
>
> A federal statute protecting this information, similar to the protection given to cockpit voice recorders, is the only way to bring finality to this issue and avoid expensive and incredibly time-consuming, case-by-case, jurisdiction-by-jurisdiction examination and resolution of this issue.

Christa Meyer Hinckley, *The Argument for Federal Legislation Protecting the Confidentiality of Aviation Safety Action Program Information*, 75 J. AIR L. & COM. 161-162 (2010).

9. On November 19, 2001, Congress enacted the September 11th Victim Compensation Fund of 2001, providing a "[f]ederal cause of action for damages arising out of the hijacking and subsequent crashes of American Airlines flights 11 and 77, and United Airlines flights 93 and 175, on September 11, 2001" and also limiting liability:

> **Sec. 408. Limitation on liability.**
>
> (a) In general. —
>
> (1) *Liability limited to insurance coverage.*— Notwithstanding any other provision of law, liability for all claims, whether for compensatory or punitive damages or for contribution or indemnity, arising from the terrorist-related aircraft crashes of September 11, 2001, against an air carrier, aircraft manufacturer, airport sponsor, or person with a property interest in the World Trade Center, on September 11, 2001, whether fee simple, leasehold or easement, direct or indirect, or their directors, officers, employees, or agents, shall not be in an

> amount greater than the limits of liability insurance coverage maintained by that air carrier, aircraft manufacturer, airport sponsor, or person.
>
> (2) *Willful defaults on rebuilding obligation.*—Paragraph (1) does not apply to any such person with a property interest in the World Trade Center if the Attorney General determines, after notice and an opportunity for a hearing on the record, that the person has defaulted willfully on a contractual obligation to rebuild, or assist in the rebuilding of, the World Trade Center.
>
> (3) *Limitations on liability for New York City.*—Liability for all claims, whether for compensatory or punitive damages or for contribution or indemnity arising from the terrorist-related aircraft crashes of September 11, 2001, against the City of New York shall not exceed the greater of the city's insurance coverage or $350,000,000. If a claimant who is eligible to seek compensation under section 405 of this Act [section 405 of this note], submits a claim under section 405 [of this note], the claimant waives the right to file a civil action (or to be a party to an action) in any Federal or State court for damages sustained as a result of the terrorist-related aircraft crashes of September 11, 2001, including any such action against the City of New York. The preceding sentence does not apply to a civil action to recover collateral source obligations.

49 U.S.C. § 40101.

Are these damages limitations appropriate and defensible as a matter of law and policy? *See*, *e.g.*, George W. Conk, *Will the Post 9/11 World be a Post-Tort World?*, 112 PENN. ST. L. REV. 175, 178 (2007) ("The Act created the Victims Compensation Fund for those who died or were injured that day at the disaster sites in New York, the Pentagon, and Pennsylvania and it brought liability protections for those whose breaches of duty may have enabled the crimes that stunned the nation and the world."). *See also* Richard P. Campbell, *The September 11th Attack on America: Ground Zero in Tort and Insurance Law*, 9 CONN. INS. L.J. 51 (2002).

See generally Erin G. Holt, *The September 11 Victim Compensation Fund: Legislative Justice Sui Generis*, 59 N.Y.U. ANN. SURV. AM. L. 513 (2004). Kent C. Krause and John A. Swiger, *Analysis of the Department of Justice Regulations for the*

September 11th Victim Compensation Fund, 67 J. AIR L. & COM. 117 (2002); Harold Caplan, *Post 9/11-Air Carrier Liability Towards Third Parties on Land or Water as a Consequence of War on Terrorism*, 30 AIR AND SPACE L. 5 (2005); Kenneth P. Nolan & Jeanne M. O'Grady, *The Victim Compensation Fund—Looking a Gift Horse in the Mouth*, 53 DEPAUL L. REV. 231 (2003); Robert S. Peck, *The Victim Compensation Fund: Born from a Unique Confluence of Events not Likely to be Duplicated*, 53 DEPAUL L. REV. 209 (2003); Note, *The Victims Compensation Fund: A Model for Future Mass Casualty Situations*, 29 TRANSP. L.J. 283 (2002); C. Krause & John A. Siger, *Analysis of the Department of Justice Regulations for the September 11th Victim Compensation Fund*, 67 J. AIR L. & COM. 117 (2002).

10. *Federal Express Corp. v. Dep't of Transp.* (D.C. Cir. 2006) presents a thorough narrative of the federal economic legislation enacted following September 11, 2001:

> At 9:25 A.M. on the morning of September 11, 2001, the Federal Aviation Administration issued a ground stop order to bring all aviation in the United States to an immediate halt. *See* NAT'L COMM'N ON THE TERRORIST ATTACKS UPON THE U.S., THE 9/11 COMMISSION REPORT 25 (2004). Eleven days later, in response to that order and the decline in air traffic following September 11, Congress passed the Air Transportation Safety and System Stabilization Act, which the President signed on September 22, 2001. Section 101(a)(2) of the Act provides that the President shall
>
>> [c]ompensate air carriers in an aggregate amount equal to [five billion dollars] for (A) direct losses incurred ... by air carriers as a result of any Federal ground stop order ... and (B) the incremental losses incurred beginning September 11, 2001, and ending December 31, 2001, by air carriers as a direct result of such attacks.
>
> An "'incremental loss' does not include any loss that the President determines would have been incurred if the terrorist attacks ... had not occurred." For any loss to be compensable, it must be "demonstrate[d] to the satisfaction of the President."
>
> The Secretary of the Department of Transportation, in turn, promulgated a series of regulations to carry out the Act. "In order to fulfill Congress' intent to expeditiously provide compensation to eligible air carriers," the Department

would make an initial payment of roughly fifty percent of a carrier's estimated losses, and two later installments to reach full compensation. 66 Fed. Reg. at 54,616-17.

As a starting point in determining the amount of a carriers's compensation, the Department would compare "the difference between pre-September 11 forecasts and the updated forecasts or actual results." The resulting difference would "provide[ ] an approximation of the incremental losses that are a direct result of the attacks, and that approximation, without more, [would] give[ ] effect to the language of the statute."

This methodology was based on two assumptions: (1) the differences between a carrier's forecast and its actual results are primarily due to September 11; and (2) "it is extremely difficult if not impossible to distinguish, on a line item by line item basis, individual revenue and expense items that were affected directly by the terrorist attacks from those that were affected indirectly, or those that were partially affected, or not affected at all."

The regulations left room, however, for adjustments to address items of "significant relative financial impact" that were "extraordinary or non-recurring" and unrelated to September 11. For instance, an adverse $1 million judgment that occurred during the compensation period as a result of operative facts before September 11 could not be included as a compensable net loss. The regulations also contemplated that there would be situations in which carriers experienced "a reduction in actual versus forecast expenses."

To address those situations, the cost savings rule provides:

> The Department generally does not accept claims by air carriers that cost savings should be excluded from the calculation of incurred losses. Consequently, the Department will generally not allow such claims to be used in a way that has the effect of increasing the compensation for which an air carrier is eligible.

> 14 C.F.R. § 330.39(b) (2005). The rule reflected a general presumption against such adjustments because: (1) cost reductions unrelated to September 11 would be expected to have been included in pre-September 11 forecasts; (2) it is "highly likely that expense reduction efforts undertaken after September 11 were attributable, implicitly if not explicitly, to changed expectations regarding revenues after the attacks"; (3) cost savings "in fact reduce an air carrier's losses, and the calculations required under [the] rules may not be manipulated to exclude actual reductions in expenses, thereby generating a basis for increased compensation; and (4) Congress intended that carriers not receive compensation for cost savings, "which they have an independent obligation to their managements and shareholders to achieve, and which it is reasonable to expect them to undertake to mitigate the need for compensation under the Act." 67 Fed. Reg. at 18,473. Carriers were instructed to submit their calculations of revenues and expenses on Department "Form 330" along with sworn financial statements reviewed by an independent public accountant. *See* 14 C.F.R. §§ 330.27, 330.33.

Int'l Art and Antique Dealers Show, Ltd. v. ASU Int'l, Inc. (S.D.N.Y. 2002) further synthesized the Air Transportation Safety and System Stabilization Act, which provided, in part:

> **(1) Availability of action**. There shall exist a Federal cause of action for damages arising out of the hijacking and subsequent crashes of American Airlines flights 11 and 77, and United Airlines flights 93 and 175, on September 11, 2001. Notwithstanding section 40120(c) of title 49, United States Code, this cause of action shall be the exclusive remedy for damages arising out of the hijacking and subsequent crashes of such flights.
>
> **(2) Substantive law**. The substantive law for decision in any such suit shall be derived from the law, including choice of law principles, of the State in which the crash occurred unless such law is inconsistent with or preempted by Federal law.
>
> **(3) Jurisdiction**. The United States District Court for the Southern District of New York shall have original and exclusive jurisdiction over all actions brought for any claim

> (including any claim for loss of property, personal injury, or death) resulting from or relating to the terrorist-related aircraft crashes of September 11, 2001.

Air Transportation Safety Act § 408(b).

> The first three titles of the Act established an airline stabilization plan that includes, *inter alia*, the provision of federal aid to the airlines, the creation of an Air Transportation Stabilization Board to review and decide on applications by the airlines for federal assistance, and the provision of federal reimbursement to the airlines for increased insurance costs. The Act "was meant to bolster an airline industry reeling from the horrific events of September 11th."
>
> Section 408(b) appears in Title IV of the Act, which begins with a description of the purpose of Title IV, "It is the purpose of this title to provide compensation to any individual (or relatives of a deceased individual) who was physically injured or killed as a result of the terrorist-related aircraft crashes of September 11, 2001." Air Transportation Safety Act § 403.
>
> Title IV established a compensation program to be administered by a Special Master that permits eligible individuals to make claims for compensation from a federal fund.
>
> Those individuals who elect to make a claim under Title IV "waive[ ] the right to file a civil action (or to be a party to an action) in any Federal or State court for damages sustained as a result of the terrorist-related aircraft crashes of September 11, 2001." Title IV defined an "eligible individual" as an individual who was on board one of the hijacked airplanes or who was present at the crash site, or their representative. Specifically, it defined an "eligible individual" as
>
> (A) an individual who—(i) was present at the World Trade Center, (New York, New York), the Pentagon (Arlington, Virginia), or the site of the aircraft crash at Shanksville, Pennsylvania at the time, or in the immediate aftermath, of the terrorist-related aircraft

crashes of September 11, 2001; and (ii) suffered physical harm or death as a result of such an air crash;

(B) an individual who was a member of the flight crew or a passenger on American Airlines flight 11 or 77 or United Airlines flight 93 or 175, except that an individual identified by the Attorney General to have been a participant or conspirator in the terrorist-related aircraft crashes of September 11, 2001, or a representative of such individual shall not be eligible to receive compensation under this title; or

(C) in the case of a decedent who is an individual described in subparagraph (A) or (B), the personal representative of the decedent who files a claim on behalf of the decedent.

Air Transportation Safety Act § 405(c)(2).

In addition to creating a program of federal compensation for eligible individuals who elected to file claims, Title IV also created a federal cause of action for damages "arising out of the hijacking and subsequent crashes," establishing the Southern District of New York as the court having jurisdiction to hear all actions brought for any claim "resulting from or relating to the terrorist-related aircraft crashes of September 11," and includes a liability limitation provision. As amended, Section 408, titled "Limitation on Liability," addresses the overall exposure of businesses connected to the four airplanes that were crashed on September 11 and of those persons with a property interest in the World Trade Center as of September 11. Section 408(a) provides in part that

> liability for all claims, whether for compensatory or punitive damages or for contribution or indemnity, arising from the terrorist-related aircraft crashes of September 11, 2001, against an air carrier, aircraft manufacturer, airport sponsor, or person with a property interest in the World Trade Center, on September 11, 2001, whether fee simple, leasehold or easement, direct or indirect, or their directors,

> officers, employees, or agents, shall not be in an amount greater than the limits of liability insurance coverage maintained by that air carrier, aircraft manufacturer, aircraft sponsor, or person.

Aviation and Transportation Security Act § 201(b)(2). Originally, Section 408 was titled "Limitation on Air Carrier Liability," and provided in subsection (a) that "liability for all claims, whether for compensatory or punitive damages, arising from the terrorist-related aircraft crashes of September 11, 2001, against any air carrier shall not be in an amount greater than the limits of the liability coverage maintained by the air carrier." Air Transportation Safety Act § 408(a).

The structure of Title IV demonstrates that Congress intended there to be two avenues for the direct victims of the events of September 11 to seek compensation. Eligible individuals may either elect to file a claim through the Special Master for compensation from a federal fund, or pursue a claim for damages pursuant to Section 408(b)(1) against the air carriers, aircraft manufacturers and sponsors, or persons with property interests in the World Trade Center in court, in which case any recovery will be limited by the insurance coverage of each entity.

Although the references in the legislative record to Title IV are limited, see 147 Cong. Rec. S9589-9606 (Sept. 21, 2001) and 147 Cong. Rec. H5884-5917 (Sept. 21, 2001), the pertinent passages also indicate an objective of providing the direct victims of the terrorist attacks with the option of seeking compensation from the fund established by Title IV or litigating their claims in court. Senator McCain stated that "[t]hese victims and their families may, but are not required to, seek compensation from the Federal fund instead of through the litigation system." 147 Cong. Rec. S9594 (Sept. 21, 2001).

This view was echoed by Senator Nickles, who observed that "victims and/or their family survivors may receive financial assistance or at least have legal recourse either by suing in a Federal district court or through a new system we are now creating in this legislation called the special master," and by Representative Bentsen, who noted that victims may "elect to use this compensation program" but cautioned that "it is important that families ultimately still have the right to seek higher compensation through a legal case."

As Representative Conyers stated,

> The legislation creates a Federal cause of action for damages arising out of the hijacking and subsequent crashes of September 11, 2001. Thus, individuals who elect not to be part of the victim compensation plan under this legislation have recourse of their Federal cause of action to claim damages.

References in the legislative record to Section 408(b)(3) specifically are even more sparse, and they do not discuss the difference in language between Sections 408(b)(1) and (b)(3) nor the precise scope of the provision. They indicate principally that Congress viewed the consolidation of all civil litigation arising from or relating to the events of September 11 in one court as desirable. Arizona Senator John McCain explained that, "[i]n addition to removing the specter of devastating potential liability from the airlines, and guaranteeing that victims and their families will receive compensation regardless of the outcomes of the tangle of lawsuits that will ensue, the bill attempts to provide some sense to the litigation by consolidating all civil litigation arising from the terrorist attacks of September 11 in one court." *Id.* at S9594. Senator Hatch also stated his pleasure with the decision to "consolidate [ ] the causes of action in one Federal court so that there will be some consistency in the judgments awarded," "[f]or those who seek to pursue the litigation route." *Id.* at S9595. At a hearing before the Senate Commerce, Science and Transportation Committee, the jurisdictional language of Section 408(b)(3) was addressed in the following colloquy between Senator McCain and Delta Airlines CEO Leo Mullen:

McCain: Consolidating all suits in one United States District Court.

Mull[e]n: Yes.

McCain: Is that important to you?

Mull[e]n: Yes. Anything that moves the liability, I'm not a lawyer, but, yes, as I understand it, that's a very good move.

> This exchange suggests that the initial motivation for Section 408(b)(3) was to consolidate potential suits against the airlines in the Southern District of New York. In the later debate on the Senate floor, New York Senator Charles Schumer clarified that the provision was not limited to suits against the airlines, stating: "It may be a little unclear to some whether all lawsuits or just lawsuits against the airlines will be situated in the Southern District of New York. The intent here is to put all civil suits arising from the tragic events of September 11 in the Southern District." 147 Cong. Rec. S9592 (Sept. 21, 2001).
>
> Vermont Senator Patrick Leahy also commented that "all legal cases stemming from the[ ] incidents [of September 11] will be consolidated in the United States District court of the Southern District of New York."

For further discussion about the Air Transportation Safety and Stabilization Act see Jonathan Lewinsohn, Note, *Bailing Out Congress: An Assessment and Defense of the Air Transportation Safety and System Stabilization Act of 2001*, 115 YALE L.J. 438 (2005); Robert J. Rhee, *Terrorism Risk in a Post-9/11 Economy: The Convergence of Capital Markets, Insurance, and Government Action*, 37 ARIZ. ST. L. REV. 435 (2005); Robert M. Ackerman, *The September 11th Victim Compensation Fund: An Effective Administrative Response to National Tragedy*, 10 HARV. NEGOT. L. REV. 135 (2005); Aimee Jodoi Lum, Comment *America's Two Days of Infamy: The Immediate and Lasting Effects of Pearl Harbor and September 11th on the Ever-Evolving Insurance Industry*, 27 U. HAW. L. REV. 111 (2004); Saul Levmore & Kyle D. Logue, *Insuring against Terrorism—and Crime*, 102 MICH. L. REV. 268 (2003). *See also* Terrorism Risk Insurance Act, Pub. L. No. 107-291 (2002).

PROBLEM

On September 6, 1970 Pan American Flight 083, while on a regularly scheduled flight from Brussels to New York, was hijacked in the sky over London about 45 minutes after it had taken off from an intermediate stop in Amsterdam. Two men, Diop and Gueye, acting for the Popular Front for the Liberation of Palestine (the "PELP"), forced the crew of the aircraft to fly to Beirut, where a demolitions expert and explosives were put on board. The aircraft, a Boeing 747, was then flown to Egypt still under PFLP control. In Cairo, after the passengers were evacuated, the aircraft was totally destroyed. An operative insurance policy provided the following exclusions:

> This policy does not cover anything herein to the contrary notwithstanding loss or damage due to or resulting from: (1) capture, seizure ... or any taking of the property insured or damage to or destruction thereof … by any military … or usurped power, whether any of the foregoing be done by way of requisition or otherwise and whether in time of peace or war and whether lawful or unlawful …; (2) war, … civil war, revolution, rebellion, insurrection or warlike operations, whether there be a declaration of war or not; (3) … riots, civil commotion.

Does the PELP hijacking fall within one of the specific policy exclusions? *See Pan American World Airways, Inc. v. Aetna Cas. & Surety Co.* (2d Cir. 1974). *See also Sunny South Aircraft Service, Inc. v American Fire & Casualty Co.* (Fla. 3d DCA 1962).

CHAPTER 4

AIRMEN

A. Enforcement and Transportation Security

The term "airmen" refers to pilots, mechanics, and flight attendants. To say that the relationship between airmen and regulators, on the one hand, and airmen and their employers and their employers' customers, on the other hand, is often tense is an understatement (*see* Chapter 3, Part B, *infra*). An early illustration of the degree to which airmen are sometimes distrusted presented in the infamous case of the "Unabomer," a code-name for the University and Airline BOMBing investigation by the Federal Bureau of Investigation ("FBI") and U.S. Postal Inspection Service that would eventually lead to the arrest of serial killer Ted Kaczynski.

On November 15, 1979, the Unabomber attacked American Airlines Flight 444 from Chicago to Washington, D.C. by planting a bomb in the cargo hold of the Boeing 727 jetliner. While the bomb failed to detonate and cause catastrophic damage obliterating the airplane, it released large quantities of smoke and twelve passengers were treated for smoke inhalation.

This was not the first Unabomber attacker, but it led the FBI to become involved because an airliner bombing is a federal crime. Interestingly, an initial theory was that the culprit was a disgruntled airline mechanic. *See generally* FBI 100: The Unabomber, *https://www.fbi.gov/news/stories/2008/april/unabomber_042408*. (FBI "[a]gent John Douglas, the father of "profiling" criminals, disagreed with this assessment, reasoning that the bombs were much too sophisticated and that the bomber was most likely an academic. Profiling was a new investigative tool at the time, and so Douglas's theory was largely ignored." CINDY C. COMBS & MARTIN SLANN, ENCYCLOPEDIA OF TERRORISM (2007), at 342-43. *See also* Chapter 5, Part C, *infra*.)

Fast forward to March 2015, when Andreas Lubitz, a Germanwings copilot, locked himself in the flight deck, set the automated altimeter for the ground, and crashed an airliner into a French mountainside, killing all 150 people onboard.

These events—not to mention the coordinated hijackings on September 11, 2001—are extraordinary, but they introduce and frame the important issues of airmen laws and regulations considered in the cases below.

AIR WISCONSIN AIRLINES CORP. v. HOEPER

134 S. Ct. 852 (2014)

Justice SOTOMAYOR delivered the opinion of the Court.

In 2001, Congress created the Transportation Security Administration ("TSA") to assess and manage threats against air travel. Aviation and Transportation Security Act ("ATSA"), 49 U.S.C. § 44901 *et seq.* To ensure that the TSA would be informed of potential threats, Congress gave airlines and their employees immunity against civil liability for reporting suspicious behavior. But this immunity does not attach to "any disclosure made with actual knowledge that the disclosure was false, inaccurate, or misleading" or "any disclosure made with reckless disregard as to the truth or falsity of that disclosure."

The question before us is whether ATSA immunity may be denied under § 44941(b) without a determination that a disclosure was materially false. We hold that it may not. Because the state courts made no such determination, and because any falsehood in the disclosure here would not have affected a reasonable security officer's assessment of the supposed threat, we reverse the judgment of the Colorado Supreme Court.

BACKGROUND

William Hoeper joined Air Wisconsin Airlines Corporation as a pilot in 1998. But by late 2004, Air Wisconsin had stopped operating flights from Denver, Hoeper's home base, on any type of aircraft for which he was certified. To continue flying for Air Wisconsin out of Denver, Hoeper needed to gain certification on the British Aerospace 146 (BAe–146), an aircraft he had not flown. Hoeper failed in his first three attempts to pass a proficiency test. After the third failure, as he later acknowledged at trial, his employment was "at [Air Wisconsin's] discretion." But he and Air Wisconsin entered into an agreement to afford him "one more opportunity to pass [the] proficiency check." The agreement left little doubt that Hoeper would lose his job if he failed again.

In December 2004, Hoeper flew from Denver to Virginia for simulator training as part of this final test. During the training, Hoeper failed to cope with a challenging scenario created by the instructor, Mark Schuerman, and the simulator showed the engines "flam[ing] out" due to a loss of fuel. As Schuerman began to tell Hoeper that he "should know better," Hoeper responded angrily. He later described what happened:

> At this point, that's it. I take my headset off and I toss it up on the glare shield.... [Schuerman] and I exchanged words at the same elevated decibel level. Mine went something like this: This is a bunch of shit. I'm sorry. You are railroading the situation and it's not realistic.

When Hoeper announced that he wanted to call the legal department of the pilots' union, Schuerman ended the session so that Hoeper could do so. Schuerman then reported Hoeper's behavior to Patrick Doyle, the Wisconsin-based manager of the BAe–146 fleet. Doyle booked Hoeper on a United Airlines flight back to Denver.

Several hours after Schuerman's report, Doyle discussed the situation at Air Wisconsin's headquarters with the airline's Vice President of Operations, Kevin LaWare; its Managing Director of Flight Operations, Scott Orozco; and its Assistant Chief Pilot, Robert Frisch. LaWare later explained the accretion of his concerns about what Hoeper might do next. He regarded Hoeper's behavior in the simulator as "a fairly significant outburst," of a sort that he "hadn't seen ... before." And he knew "it was a given that ... Hoeper's employment was ... going to be terminated" as a result of his failure to complete the simulator training.

Then, LaWare testified, Orozco mentioned that Hoeper was a Federal Flight Deck Officer (FFDO). The FFDO program allows the Government to "deputize volunteer pilots of air carriers ... to defend the flight decks of aircraft ... against acts of criminal violence or air piracy." FFDOs are permitted "to carry a firearm while engaged in providing air transportation." Hoeper had become an FFDO earlier in 2004 and had been issued a firearm. He was not allowed to carry the firearm during his trip to the training facility, because he was not "engaged in providing air transportation." But according to one official at the meeting, the Denver airport's security procedures made it possible for crew members to bypass screening, so that Hoeper could have carried his gun despite the rule. Indeed, Frisch later testified that he was "aware of one" incident in which an Air Wisconsin pilot had come to training with his FFDO weapon. On the basis of this information, LaWare concluded, there was "no way ... to confirm" whether "Hoeper had his weapon with him, even though ... by policy, [he was] not supposed to have it with him."

Finally, LaWare testified, he and the other Air Wisconsin officials discussed two prior episodes in which disgruntled airline employees had lashed out violently. In one incident, a FedEx flight engineer under investigation for misconduct "entered the cockpit" of a FedEx flight "and began attacking the crew with a hammer" before being subdued. *United States v. Calloway* (6th Cir. 1997). In another, a recently fired ticket agent brought a gun onto a Pacific Southwest Airlines flight and shot his former supervisor and the crew, leading to a fatal crash. *Report Confirms That Gunman Caused 1987 Crash of PSA Jet*, L.A. TIMES, Jan. 6, 1989, at 29.

In light of all this—Hoeper's anger, his impending termination, the chance that he might be armed, and the history of assaults by disgruntled airline employees—LaWare decided that the airline "need[ed] to make a call to the TSA," to let the authorities know "the status" of the situation.

Doyle offered to make the call. According to the jury, he made two statements to the TSA: first, that Hoeper "was an FFDO who may be armed" and that the airline was "concerned about his mental stability and the whereabouts of his firearm"; and second, that an "[u]nstable pilot in [the] FFDO program was terminated today." The TSA responded to the call by ordering that Hoeper's plane return to the gate. Officers boarded the plane, removed Hoeper, searched him, and questioned him about the location of his gun. When Hoeper stated that the gun was at his home in Denver, a Denver-based federal agent went there to retrieve it. Later that day, Hoeper boarded a return flight to Denver. Air Wisconsin fired him the following day.

Hoeper sued Air Wisconsin in Colorado state court on several claims, including defamation. Air Wisconsin moved for summary judgment on the basis of ATSA immunity, but the trial court denied it, ruling that the jury was entitled to find the facts pertinent to immunity. The case went to trial, and the court denied Air Wisconsin's motion for a directed verdict on the same basis. It submitted the question of ATSA immunity to the jury, with the instruction—following the language of § 44941(b)—that immunity would not apply if Hoeper had proved that Air Wisconsin "made the disclosure [to the TSA] with actual knowledge that the disclosure was false, inaccurate, or misleading" or "with reckless disregard as to its truth or falsity." The jury instructions did not state that ATSA immunity protects materially true statements.

The jury found for Hoeper on the defamation claim and awarded him $849,625 in compensatory damages and $391,875 in punitive damages. The court reduced the latter award to $350,000, for a total judgment of just under $1.2 million, plus costs. The Colorado Court of Appeals affirmed, as did the Colorado Supreme Court. We granted certiorari to decide "[w]hether ATSA immunity may be denied without a determination that the air carrier's disclosure was materially false."

DISCUSSION

Congress patterned the exception to ATSA immunity after the actual malice standard of *New York Times Co. v. Sullivan* (1964), and we have long held that actual malice requires material falsity. Because we presume that Congress meant to incorporate the settled meaning of actual malice when it incorporated the language of that standard, we hold that a statement otherwise eligible for ATSA immunity may not be denied immunity unless the statement is materially false.

In *New York Times*, we held that under the First Amendment, a public official cannot recover "for a defamatory falsehood relating to his official conduct unless he proves that the statement was made with 'actual malice'—that is, with knowledge that it was false or with reckless disregard of whether it was false or not." Congress borrowed this exact language in denying ATSA immunity to "(1) any disclosure made with actual knowledge that the disclosure was false, inaccurate, or misleading; or (2) any disclosure made with reckless disregard as to the truth or falsity of that disclosure."

One could in principle construe the language of the actual malice standard to cover true statements made recklessly. But we have long held, to the contrary, that actual malice entails falsity. Indeed, we have required more than mere falsity to establish actual malice: The falsity must be "material." *Masson v. New Yorker Magazine, Inc.* (1991). As we explained in *Masson*, "[m]inor inaccuracies do not amount to falsity so long as 'the substance, the gist, the sting, of the libelous charge be justified.'" A "statement is not considered false unless it 'would have a different effect on the mind of the reader from that which the pleaded truth would have produced.'"

These holdings were settled when Congress enacted the ATSA, and we therefore presume that Congress meant to adopt the material falsity requirement when it incorporated the actual malice standard into the ATSA immunity exception. "[I]t is a cardinal rule of statutory construction that, when Congress employs a term of art, it presumably knows and adopts the cluster of ideas that were attached to each borrowed word in the body of learning from which it is taken."

A material falsity requirement also serves the purpose of ATSA immunity. The ATSA shifted from airlines to the TSA the responsibility "for assessing and investigating possible threats to airline security." In directing the TSA to "receive, assess, and distribute intelligence information related to transportation security," Congress wanted to ensure that air carriers and their employees would not hesitate to provide the TSA with the information it needed. This is the purpose of the immunity provision, evident both from its context and from the title of the statutory section that contained it: "encouraging airline employees to report suspicious activities." It would defeat this purpose to deny immunity for substantially true reports, on the theory that the person making the report had not yet gathered enough information to be certain of its truth. Such a rule would restore the pre-ATSA state of affairs, in which air carriers bore the responsibility to investigate and verify potential threats.

We therefore hold that ATSA immunity may not be denied under § 44941(b) to materially true statements. This interpretation of the statute is clear enough that Hoeper effectively concedes it. Hoeper does point out that given Congress' desire to deny immunity to "'bad actors,'" and "given that the vast majority of reckless statements will not turn out to be true[,] ... Congress could have quite reasonably chosen to deny the special privilege of ATSA immunity to all reckless speakers," even those whose statements turned out to be true. But although Congress could have made this choice, nothing about the statute's text or purpose suggests that it actually did. Instead, Congress chose to model the exception to ATSA immunity after a standard we have long construed to require material falsity.

* * *

We are not persuaded by Hoeper's arguments that we should affirm the judgment of the Colorado Supreme Court notwithstanding its misapprehension of the ATSA immunity standard. Hoeper first argues that Air Wisconsin forfeited the claim that it is entitled to immunity because its statements were materially true. His premise is that Air Wisconsin argued the truth of its statements only in challenging the evidentiary basis for the defamation verdict, not in asserting immunity. But Air Wisconsin's brief before the Colorado Supreme Court argued that the exception to ATSA immunity "appears to incorporate the *New York Times* actual malice standard," which—as we have explained—requires material falsity.

Hoeper next argues that the Colorado Supreme Court performed the requisite analysis of material falsity, albeit in the context of finding the record sufficient to support the jury's defamation verdict. For several reasons, however, this analysis does not suffice for us to affirm the denial of ATSA immunity. First, to the extent that the immunity determination belongs to the court—as the Colorado Supreme Court held—a court's deferential review of jury findings cannot substitute for its own analysis of the record. Second, the jury here did not find that any falsity in Air Wisconsin's statements was material, because the trial court instructed it only to determine whether "[o]ne or more of th[e] statements was false," without addressing materiality. Third, applying the material falsity standard to a defamation claim is quite different from applying it to ATSA immunity. In both contexts, a materially false statement is one that "'would have a different effect on the mind of the reader [or listener] from that which the ... truth would have produced.'" *Masson*. But the identity of the relevant reader or listener varies according to the context. In determining whether a falsehood is material to a defamation claim, we care whether it affects the subject's reputation in the community. In the context of determining ATSA immunity, by contrast, we care whether a falsehood affects the authorities' perception of and response to a given threat.

* * *

Finally, the Colorado Supreme Court's analysis of material falsity was erroneous. We turn next to explaining why, by applying the ATSA immunity standard to the facts of this case. We begin by addressing how to determine the materiality of a false statement in the ATSA context. As we noted earlier, a materially false statement is generally one that "'would have a different effect on the mind of the reader [or listener] from that which the ... truth would have produced.'" The parties quibble over whether ATSA immunity requires some special version of this standard, but they more or less agree—as do we—that the usual standard suffices as long as the hypothetical reader or listener is a security officer.

A further question is what it means for a statement to produce "'a different effect on the mind of'" a security officer from that which the truth would have produced. In defamation law, the reputational harm caused by a false statement is its effect on a reader's or listener's mind. But contrary to the position of Hoeper's counsel at oral argument, courts cannot decide whether a false statement produced "'a different effect on the mind of'" a hypothetical TSA officer without considering the effect of that statement on TSA's behavior. After all, the whole reason the TSA considers threat reports is to determine and execute a response.

A plaintiff seeking to defeat ATSA immunity need not show "precisely what a particular official or federal agency would have done in a counterfactual scenario." Such a showing would be "impossible ... given the need to maintain secrecy regarding airline security operations." But any falsehood cannot be material, for purposes of ATSA immunity, absent a substantial likelihood that a reasonable security officer would consider it important in determining a response to the supposed threat. This standard "is an objective one, involving the [hypothetical] significance of an omitted or misrepresented fact to a reasonable" security official, rather than the actual significance of that fact to a particular security official.

* * *

We apply the material falsity standard to the facts of this case. In doing so, we neither embrace nor reject the Colorado Supreme Court's unanimous holding "that immunity under the ATSA is a question of law to be determined by the trial court before trial." Rather, we conclude that even if a jury were to find the historical facts in the manner most favorable to Hoeper, Air Wisconsin is entitled to ATSA immunity as a matter of law.

We begin with Air Wisconsin's statement that Hoeper "was an FFDO who may be armed." Hoeper cannot dispute the literal truth of this statement: He was an FFDO, and because FFDOs possess weapons, any FFDO "may be armed." Hoeper argues only that to avoid any misinterpretation, Air Wisconsin should have qualified the statement by adding that it had no reason to think he was actually carrying his gun during the trip to Virginia, especially because he was not allowed to do so under Section § 44921(f)(1). We agree that Air Wisconsin's statement could have been misinterpreted by some, but we reject Hoeper's argument for two reasons.

First, any confusion of the nature that Hoeper suggests would have been immaterial: A reasonable TSA officer, having been told only that Hoeper was an FFDO and that he was upset about losing his job, would have wanted to investigate whether Hoeper was carrying his gun. Second, to accept Hoeper's demand for such precise wording would vitiate the purpose of ATSA immunity: to encourage air carriers and their employees, often in fast-moving situations and with little time to fine-tune their diction, to provide the TSA immediately with information about potential threats. Baggage handlers, flight attendants, gate agents, and other airline employees who report suspicious behavior to the TSA should not face financial ruin if, in the heat of a potential threat, they fail to choose their words with exacting care.

We next consider Air Wisconsin's statement that Hoeper "was terminated today." When Air Wisconsin made that statement, Hoeper had not yet been fired. But everyone knew the firing was almost certainly imminent. Hoeper acknowledged that his employment was "at [Air Wisconsin's] discretion" after his third failed test, and the agreement between him and Air Wisconsin stated that his "fourth ... attempt" to pass the test would be his "final" one. No reasonable TSA officer would care whether an angry, potentially armed airline employee had just been fired or merely knew he was about to meet that fate.

Finally, we consider Air Wisconsin's statements that Hoeper was "[u]nstable" and that it was "concerned about his mental stability." Although the details of Hoeper's behavior during the simulator session may be disputed, Hoeper himself testified that he had become visibly angry: He decided "that's it," he removed his headset and "toss[ed] it," and he accused the instructor—at an "elevated decibel level," and with an expletive—of "railroading the situation." It would surely have been correct, then, for Air Wisconsin to report that Hoeper "'blew up'" during the test.

The question is whether, from the perspective of a reasonable security officer, there is any material difference between a statement that Hoeper had just "blown up" in a professional setting and a statement that he was "[u]nstable." We think not.

We are no more troubled by Air Wisconsin's related statement that it was "concerned about [Hoeper's] mental stability." Hoeper is correct that many of the Air Wisconsin officials who attended the meeting at headquarters might not have framed their concerns in terms of "mental stability." LaWare, for instance, testified that "[t]hose weren't the words that [he] would have anticipated" when he directed Doyle to call the TSA. But the officials who attended the meeting did harbor concerns about Hoeper's mental state: They knew he had just "blown up," and they worried about what he might do next. It would be inconsistent with the ATSA's text and purpose to expose Air Wisconsin to liability because its employee could have chosen a slightly better phrase than "mental stability" to articulate its concern.

Just as "[m]inor inaccuracies do not amount to falsity" in the defamation context, "so long as 'the substance, the gist, the sting, of the libelous charge be justified,'" a statement that would otherwise qualify for ATSA immunity cannot lose that immunity because of some minor imprecision, so long as "the gist" of the statement is accurate. Doyle's statements to the TSA accurately conveyed "the gist" of the situation; it is irrelevant whether trained lawyers or judges might with the luxury of time have chosen more precise words.

Hoeper's overarching factual theory appears to be that members of the BAe–146 team, including Doyle and Schuerman, harbored personal animosity toward him, which caused them to manipulate the proficiency tests in order to fail him. But even if Hoeper were correct about all this (and we express no view on that question), we do not see why it would have made him any less a threat in the eyes of a reasonable security officer. As between two employees—one who thinks he is being fired because of his inadequate skills, another who thinks he is being fired because his employer hates him—the latter is presumably more, not less, likely to lash out in anger.

The Colorado Supreme Court recognized that even if the facts are viewed in the light most favorable to Hoeper, Air Wisconsin "would likely be immune" had it "reported that Hoeper ... knew he would be terminated soon, that he had acted irrationally at the training three hours earlier and 'blew up' at test administrators, and that he was an FFDO pilot." But the court erred in parsing so finely the distinctions between these hypothetical statements and the ones that Air Wisconsin actually made. The minor differences are, for the reasons we have explained, immaterial as a matter of law in determining Air Wisconsin's ATSA immunity. By incorporating the actual malice standard into § 44941(b), Congress meant to give air carriers the "'breathing space'" to report potential threats to security officials without fear of civil liability for a few inaptly chosen words. To hold Air Wisconsin liable for minor misstatements or loose wording would undermine that purpose and disregard the statutory text. The judgment of the Supreme Court of Colorado is therefore reversed, and the case is remanded for proceedings not inconsistent with this opinion.

Justice SCALIA, with whom Justice THOMAS and Justice KAGAN join, concurring in part and dissenting in part.

I agree with the Court that under the Aviation and Transportation Security Act ("ATSA"), an airline may not be denied immunity for a report it made to the Transportation Security Administration ("TSA") absent a finding that the report was materially false. I also agree that, in this context, materiality means that the falsehood had a natural tendency to influence a reasonable TSA officer's determination of an appropriate response to the report; and that neither the jury nor the courts below considered material falsity in this ATSA-specific way.

Having answered the question we granted certiorari to decide, I would stop there and remand the case for further proceedings. Instead, the Court proceeds to "apply the [ATSA] material falsity standard to the facts of this case" in the first instance and concludes as a matter of law that Air Wisconsin's report to the TSA about William Hoeper was not materially false. In so holding, the Court in my view reaches out to decide a factbound question better left to the lower courts, and then proceeds to give the wrong answer. I therefore respectfully dissent.

We have held that under the First Amendment, a court's role is to determine whether "[a] reasonable jury could find a material difference between" the defendant's statement and the truth. *Masson.* That makes sense, since materiality is the sort of "'mixed question of law and fact'" that "has typically been resolved by juries." The jury has a vital role to play in the materiality inquiry, which entails "'delicate assessments of the inferences a "reasonable decisionmaker" would draw from a given set of facts and the significance of those inferences to him'" and is therefore "'peculiarly one for the trier of fact.'" Such a question cannot be withdrawn from the jury unless "the facts and the law will reasonably support only one conclusion" on which "reasonable persons ... could [not] differ." The same rule applies to a determination of immunity from suit: When a defendant raises qualified immunity on summary judgment, the court must "adop [t] ... the plaintiff's version of the facts" unless "no reasonable jury could believe it."

Therefore, if we are to apply the ATSA materiality standard to the complex record in this case in the first instance, it is proper to view "the historical facts in the manner most favorable to Hoeper," as the Court purports to do. We must of course begin by taking as given the findings that we know the jury already made, including that Air Wisconsin told the TSA that the airline was "concerned about [Hoeper's] mental stability" and that he was an "[u]nstable pilot," Next, we must ask whether a reasonable jury could find the remaining historical facts to be such that those statements were not only false, but materially false from the perspective of a reasonable TSA agent. If not, judgment for Air Wisconsin is proper; but if so, the ATSA materiality question should be tried to a (properly instructed) jury. (Unless, of course, a reasonable jury would be compelled to find facts that would render the statements materially false, in which case judgment for Hoeper would be proper; but that is assuredly not the case here.)

Applying that reasonable-jury standard, I do not see how we can possibly hold as a matter of law that Air Wisconsin's report was not materially false. The Court acknowledges Hoeper's description of the confrontation that spawned the airline's threat report: After failing a flight simulator test, Hoeper "decided 'that's it,' he removed his headset and 'toss[ed] it,' and he accused the instructor—at an 'elevated decibel level,' and with an expletive—of 'railroading the situation.'" A jury could credit Hoeper's account. It could also believe his "overarching factual theory" that his anger was reasonable because the instructor had "manipulate[d]" the test to cause him to fail out of "personal animosity,"—a theory that was not without supporting evidence. Moreover, there was evidence from which a jury could conclude that no one who interacted with Hoeper during or after the confrontation—including the instructor—viewed him as either unstable or threatening, *e.g.*, instructor acknowledging that he "'quickly realized it wasn't a threatening situation;'" instructor testifying he "'never felt that [Hoeper] was going to go do something stupid,'" [and] "'didn't believe that Mr. Hoeper posed a threat in any way to anybody else at all,'" [and] "'did not believe that Mr. Hoeper was engaging in irrational behavior,'" and "'deem[ed] him perfectly safe to get on an airplane'" [and] airline representative who gave Hoeper permission to fly home testifying he "had no concern that [Hoeper] was a physical threat to anybody" and "didn't believe he was mentally unstable."

In short, a jury could find that Hoeper did nothing more than engage in a brief, run-of-the-mill, and arguably justified display of anger that included raising his voice and swearing, but that did not cause anyone, including the person on the receiving end of the outburst, to view him as either irrational or a potential source of violence. Viewing the facts in that light, I cannot agree with the Court that a reasonable TSA official would not "consider ... important," the difference between an individual who engaged in this sort of heated but commonplace display of anger, on the one hand, and on the other, an individual whose colleagues regard him as "mentally unstable." It is the difference between a category that no doubt includes millions of perfectly harmless air travelers and one that, in ordinary parlance, connotes an alarming degree of unpredictability and aggressiveness. Indeed, we have used that term in connection with individuals so "dangerously mentally ill" that they may be subject to civil confinement. The importance of that difference was highlighted by the expert testimony in this case of a former TSA Federal Security Director, who stated—based on a version of the underlying facts the jury was entitled to accept—that Hoeper's behavior did not warrant any report to the TSA.

The association with dangerous mental illness is not merely one "connotation of the phrase 'mental [in]stability'" among many; it is the everyday understanding of that phrase. The Court also suggests that the circumstances of this case—particularly the fact that Hoeper knew his firing was imminent, had reason to be angry with the airline, and was authorized to carry a firearm—distinguish Hoeper's confrontation with the instructor from an ordinary "fit of pique." But if so, it was all the more important for the airline to make an accurate report to the TSA, so that the agency could assess the possible danger and determine an appropriate response. Falsely reporting to the TSA that a young Irishman is an IRA terrorist is much more likely to produce a prompt and erroneous response than reporting that a 70–year–old English grandmother is. The circumstances the Court identifies enhanced, rather than diminished, the likelihood that the false "mentally unstable" designation would have a material effect on the TSA's response.

In sum, it is simply implausible that, taking the facts of this case in the light most favorable to Hoeper, a reasonable jury would have to find that the report of mental instability would have no effect upon the course of action determined by the TSA. The Court's holding to the contrary demonstrates the wisdom of preserving the jury's role in this inquiry, designed to inject a practical sense that judges sometimes lack. I respectfully dissent from that holding.

JIFRY v. FED. AVIATION ADMIN.

370 F.3d 1174 (D.C. Cir. 2004)

ROGERS, Circuit Judge.

Petitions filed by two non-resident alien pilots challenge certain aviation regulations adopted in the wake of the September 11, 2001 terrorist attacks. From the establishment of the Transportation Security Administration ("TSA") in November 2001 to the promulgation of the challenged regulations in January 2003, aviation security has undergone a fundamental transformation. The pilots contend that the new procedures resulting in the revocation of their airman certificates issued by the Federal Aviation Administration ("FAA") violated the Administrative Procedure Act ("APA") and the due process clause of the Fifth Amendment to the United States Constitution. Specifically, they contend that the January 2003 regulations were unlawfully promulgated without notice and comment, that the revocations were not supported by substantial evidence in the record, and that they were denied meaningful notice of the evidence against them and a meaningful opportunity to be heard.

* * *

Congress has delegated broad discretion to the Federal Aviation Administration ("FAA") to prescribe regulations and standards for safety in air commerce and national security. The FAA may "at any time" reexamine the issuance of an airman certificate and issue an order "modifying, suspending, or revoking" a certificate if the Administrator determines that such action is required for "safety in air commerce" and "the public interest." With regard to issuing airman certificates to qualified individuals, Congress distinguished between citizens and aliens, conferring broad discretion to the FAA regarding alien pilots.

After the September 11, 2001 terrorist attacks, Congress established the Transportation Security Administration ("TSA") on November 19, 2001, and transferred much of the responsibility for civil aviation security from the FAA to the TSA.

This case concerns alien pilots only. The two pilots, Jifry and Zarie, are citizens of Saudi Arabia who have used their FAA certificates to pilot flights abroad, but have not operated Saudi Arabian Airlines flights to the United States in the past nine and four years, respectively. On August 14, 2002, the TSA sent letters to the FAA requesting that Captain Jifry and Captain Zarie have their airman certificates revoked, stating that "[b]ased upon information available to us," they presented "a security risk to civil aviation or national security." The FAA notified Jifry and Zarie by letters of August 20, 2002, that their airman certificates would be revoked because the Acting Under Secretary of Transportation for Security, pursuant 49 U.S.C. §§ 44709(b)(1)(A) and 46105(c), had determined that they presented risks to aviation or national security. The FAA revoked the pilots' certificates and the pilots appealed the revocations to the National Transportation Safety Board ("NTSB").

An administrative law judge ("ALJ") held a telephonic pre-hearing conference on January 17, 2003, and ordered that the FAA and the TSA provide a privilege log and that depositions of key witnesses take place by mid-February.

A week later, on January 24, 2003, the FAA dismissed the revocation actions against Jifry and Zarie, and in conjunction with the TSA, published, without notice and comment, new regulations governing the suspension and revocation of airman certificates for security reasons. The new FAA regulation, 14 C.F.R. § 61.18, provides for automatic suspension by the FAA of airman certificates upon written notification from the TSA that the pilot poses a security threat and, therefore, is not eligible to hold an airman certificate.

The TSA simultaneously promulgated 49 C.F.R. § 1540.117, which establishes the procedure by which the TSA initially and finally notifies non-resident aliens who hold or apply for FAA certificates that they pose a security threat, and requires the TSA to notify the FAA once the TSA has determined that a pilot is a security threat.

Upon finding that a pilot poses a "security threat" the TSA Assistant Administrator for Intelligence issues an Initial Notification of Threat Assessment ("Initial Notice") to the individual and serves that determination upon the FAA. The FAA then suspends the pilot's certificate. No later than 15 days after service, the pilot may make a written request for copies of releasable materials upon which the Initial Notice was based. The TSA must respond not later than 30 days after receiving the request, and the pilot may submit a written reply within 15 days of receiving the TSA's response. At that point, the TSA Deputy Administrator must review the entire record *de novo* to determine if the pilot poses a security risk. If the Deputy so determines, the TSA serves a Final Notification of Threat Assessment ("Final Notice") and the FAA revokes the certificate. The pilot may appeal the certificate revocation to the NTSB. Upon exhaustion of these administrative remedies, the pilot may seek review in the court of appeals, which may review the case on the merits.

On January 24, 2003, the TSA also served an Initial Notice of Threat Assessment designating Jifry and Zarie as security threats, and the FAA suspended their certificates. The pilots appealed the Initial Notice, and requested the materials upon which the Initial Notice had been issued. The TSA provided the releasable materials, but did not include the factual basis for TSA's determination, which was based on classified information.

The pilots then appealed the suspension of their certificates to the NTSB. The ALJ granted the TSA's motion for summary judgment, ruling that the only question was procedural—whether the pilots had been duly advised by the TSA, in writing, that they posed a security threat, and finding that they had. Upon the pilots' appeals, the NTSB affirmed the ALJ's order in favor of the TSA. Jifry and Zarie then filed replies to the TSA's Initial Notice, stating that the "lack of evidence and information about the basis for the determination contained in the TSA's response" made it impossible for them to specifically rebut the TSA's allegations, and denying that they were security threats.

On May 8, 2003, the TSA Deputy Administrator, upon *de novo* review of the administrative record, denied the pilots' challenge to the Initial Notice and issued a Final Notice based on finding that Jifry and Zarie posed security threats. *See* 49 C.F.R. § 1540.117(c). The FAA then revoked the pilots' airman certificates. On August 13, 2003, the NTSB denied the pilots' appeal of the revocation of their certificates for the same reasons it had denied their challenges to the suspensions, and affirmed the ALJ's grant of summary judgment to the TSA and the emergency orders of revocation.

* * *

The pilots make three challenges to the revocations of their FAA airman certificates: first, that the January 2003 regulations were unlawfully promulgated without notice and comment; second, that the revocations were not supported by substantial evidence in the record; and third, that the procedures provided by the January 2003 regulations violated their due process rights under the Fifth Amendment to the Constitution. We address each in turn.

Section 553 of the Administrative Procedure Act ("APA") requires an agency to publish a general notice of proposed rulemaking and to afford an opportunity for interested persons to participate in the rulemaking. *See* 5 U.S.C. § 553(b), (c). The "good cause" exception, however, provides that "when the agency for good cause finds ... that notice and public procedure thereon are impracticable, unnecessary, or contrary to the public interest," the agency need not engage in notice and comment.

The pilots contend that the regulations of January 2003 are invalid because they were unlawfully promulgated without notice and comment, and there was no rational basis for eliminating the right to a meaningful appeal before the NTSB. They maintain that the "good cause" exception does not apply because notice and comment had not been "impracticable, unnecessary or contrary to the public interest" inasmuch as the FAA already had the authority to immediately suspend or revoke a certificate upon finding that "safety in air commerce or air transportation and the public interest" required such an action.

Generally, the "good cause" exception to notice and comment rulemaking, is to be "narrowly construed and only reluctantly countenanced." The exception excuses notice and comment in emergency situations or where delay could result in serious harm. The latter circumstance is applicable here in examining the TSA's determination that "[t]he use of notice and comment prior to issuance of th[e] [January 2003 regulations] could delay the ability of TSA and the FAA to take effective action to keep persons found by TSA to pose a security threat from holding an airman certificate," and was "necessary to prevent a possible imminent hazard to aircraft, persons, and property within the United States."

The pilots contend that the "good cause" exception does not apply because the FAA already had unlimited power to revoke a certificate immediately if it believed an airman to be a security risk, and the TSA was already authorized to make security assessments under 49 U.S.C. § 114(f). While true, the pilots fail to acknowledge that at the time the challenged regulations were adopted, the FAA's power to suspend or revoke certificates was permissive only. Congress had not yet enacted 49 U.S.C. § 46111, which formalized the requirement that the FAA shall suspend, modify, or revoke a certificate if notified by the TSA that an individual posed a security risk.

As the respondents explain, the January 2003 regulations mandated a "streamlined process" by which an individual's pilot certificate would be automatically suspended or revoked by the FAA upon notification by the TSA that a pilot posed a security threat. The TSA and FAA deemed such regulations necessary "in order to minimize security threats and potential security vulnerabilities to the fullest extent possible." Given the respondents' legitimate concern over the threat of further terrorist acts involving aircraft in the aftermath of September 11, 2001, the agencies had "good cause" for not offering advance public participation.

On the merits, the pilots' APA challenge fails. The court's review of agency rulemaking is highly deferential, limited to determining "whether the agency has considered the relevant factors and articulated a 'rational connection between the facts found and the choice made.'" Contrary to the pilots' position, the regulations are not arbitrary and capricious for bearing no rational connection to the problem identified by the FAA. It is self-evident that the regulations are related to the TSA's and FAA's goals of improving the safety of air travel. Nor is the court in a position to second-guess the respondents' judgment that imposing stricter procedures for coordinating security risks and restricting individuals who pose security threats from holding airman certificates was necessary to further that goal.

Moreover, the pilots' contention that the risk posed by the certificate holders alleged to be security threats was not remedied by providing fewer procedural protections to the certification holders and narrowing their right to NTSB review is to no avail because 49 U.S.C. § 46111 produces the same result. Section 46111 makes no provision for NTSB review even for citizens, and the Conference Report states that non-resident aliens "have the right to the appeal procedures that [TSA] has already provided for them." In addition, § 46111(a) requires the FAA to respond automatically to TSA threat assessments, providing that the FAA "shall issue an order amending, modifying, suspending, or revoking any part of a certificate issued under this title if the Administrator is notified by ... the Department of Homeland Security that the holder of the certificate poses, or is suspected of posing, a risk of air piracy or terrorism or a threat to airline or passenger safety."

Accordingly, if these pilots retain any right to NTSB review at all, it is no broader than the review for procedural regularity that they have received, and they would therefore garner no benefit from a remand. Indeed, an additional ground for rejecting the pilots' challenge to the promulgation of the FAA regulation without notice and comment exists precisely because § 46111 now provides an express statutory authorization for the automatic revocation that was previously predicated on the regulations alone; even were the court to invalidate the regulations for lack of notice and comment, the statute would compel the FAA to honor the TSA's notification and take immediate action against the pilots' certificates.

* * *

The scope of the court's review of the pilots' challenges to the TSA's actions is limited to determining whether the actions were "arbitrary, capricious, an abuse of discretion, or otherwise not in accordance with law." Under this standard, the court must consider whether those actions were "based on a consideration of the relevant factors and whether there has been a clear error of judgment." The court must affirm the agency's findings of fact if they are supported by "substantial evidence" and there is a "rational connection between the facts found and the choice made." "Substantial evidence" is simply such relevant evidence as a reasonable person might accept as proof of a conclusion.

In contending that the revocations of their airman certificates are unsupported by substantial evidence in the record, the pilots do not challenge the definition of "security threat" under the TSA regulations.

An individual poses a "security threat" if the individual "is suspected of posing, or is known to pose (1) A threat to transportation or national security; (2) A threat to air piracy or terrorism; (3) A threat to airline or passenger security; or (4) A threat to civil aviation security." 49 C.F.R. § 1540.117(c). Consistent with *Camp v. Pitts* (1973), where the Supreme Court stated that when an agency official fails to adequately explain its decision, the agency should submit "either through affidavits or testimony, such additional explanation of the reasons for the agency decision as may prove necessary," the affidavit of TSA Deputy Administrator Stephen McHale provides an adequate basis for the TSA's determination that Jifry and Zarie each posed a "security threat" within the meaning of § 1540.117(c).

The unsealed affidavit recounts that the Deputy Administrator affirmed the TSA's determination on the basis of classified intelligence reports, combined with reports from the intelligence community that aircraft would continue to be used as weapons of terrorism, and consideration of "the ease with which an individual may obtain access to aircraft in the United States once he or she has a pilot license." The Deputy Administrator attested that "because it would be very difficult to avert harm once a terrorist had control of an aircraft, I concluded that it was important to err on the side of caution in determining whether [the two pilots] ... pose a security threat ..."

Viewing as a whole the record evidence before the TSA, including *ex parte* in camera review of the classified intelligence reports, we hold that there was substantial evidence to support the TSA's determination that the pilots were security risks. While we reject the pilots' contention that the court apply a *de novo* standard of review, we have carefully reviewed the classified intelligence reports on which TSA relied. The record is not lengthy and the basis for the TSA's conclusion is obvious.

The pilots' motion to bar the respondents' reliance on classified information in this court is not well-taken. Even assuming the respondents' failure to provide notice of its intention to rely on classified information on appeal until one month after the pilots filed their opening brief prevented the pilots from timely addressing the "classified information" question in their opening brief, the pilots' motion fails on its merits for several reasons. First, because the court reviewed the information designated by the respondents as "classified," the court is in a position to determine whether it was properly classified without the Vaughn Index, see *Vaughn v. Rosen* (D.C. Cir. 1973), that the pilots urge be obtained. Reliance on *Vaughn* is misplaced, in any event, because that case involved the Freedom of Information Act and presented a very different situation than that presented here. Second, the court has inherent authority to review classified material *ex parte*, in camera as part of its judicial review function.

The pilots' focus on the TSA Deputy Administrator's reliance on "sensitive security information," as defined by 49 U.S.C. §§ 114(s), 40119(b)(1), and 49 C.F.R. Part 1520, and "law enforcement sensitive" information, fares no better. Although 49 C.F.R. § 1520.5(b) provides that a person has a "need to know sensitive security information" when the information is necessary to represent an individual in a judicial or administrative proceeding, § 1520.5(b)(5) applies only to individuals representing persons listed in § 1520.5(a), and the pilots are not among the persons listed in subsection (a) who are required to restrict disclosure of and access to sensitive security information to those with a "need to know."

* * *

The court reviews *de novo* the pilots' challenge to the constitutionality of the procedures under the January 2003 regulations. They contend that the TSA and FAA procedures violate the Fifth Amendment of the Constitution by depriving the pilots of their property interest in their airman certificates without due process of law.

The Supreme Court has long held that non-resident aliens who have insufficient contacts with the United States are not entitled to Fifth Amendment protections. Exceptions may arise where aliens have come within the territory of the United States and established "substantial connections" with this country, or "accepted some societal obligations." In such situations, the Court has recognized that aliens may be accorded protections under the Constitution. This court has applied these principles in a series of cases concerning the designation of certain dissident organizations as "foreign terrorist organization[s]." We need not decide whether or not Jifry and Zarie are entitled to constitutional protections because, even assuming that they are, they have received all the process that they are due under our precedent. "The fundamental requirement of due process is the opportunity to be heard 'at a meaningful time and in a meaningful manner.'"

Generally, in determining whether administrative procedures are constitutionally adequate, courts weigh three factors:

> First, the private interest that will be affected by the official action; second, the risk of an erroneous deprivation of such interest through the procedures used, and the probable

> value, if any, of additional or substitute procedural safeguards; and finally, the Government's interest, including the function involved and the fiscal and administrative burdens that the additional or substitute procedural requirement would entail.

The pilots' interests at stake here—their interest in possessing FAA airman certificates to fly foreign aircraft outside of the United States—pales in significance to the government's security interests in preventing pilots from using civil aircraft as instruments of terror. As the Supreme Court has noted, "It is 'obvious and unarguable' that no governmental interest is more compelling than the security of the Nation." *Haig v. Agee* (1981).

Whatever the risk of erroneous deprivation, the pilots had the opportunity to file a written reply to the TSA's initial determination and were afforded independent *de novo* review of the entire administrative record by the Deputy Administrator of the TSA, and *ex parte*, in camera judicial review of the record. In light of the governmental interests at stake and the sensitive security information, substitute procedural safeguards may be impracticable, and in any event, are unnecessary under our precedent.

The TSA Assistant Administrator's Initial Notices informed the pilots that "[b]ased upon materials available to the [TSA], which I have personally reviewed, I have determined that you pose a security threat." The pilots were afforded an opportunity to respond to the designation and both filed written challenges to the TSA's Initial Notice, along with affidavits that they did not pose a threat to aviation or national security. These materials were considered by the TSA Deputy Administrator when he conducted a *de novo* review of the administrative record before issuing the Final Notice. While the pilots protest that without knowledge of the specific evidence on which TSA relied, they are unable to defend against the charge that they are security risks, the court has rejected the same argument in the terrorism listing cases. The due process protections afforded to them parallel those provided under similar circumstances are sufficient here.

HUGHES v. STATE

943 So. 2d 176 (Fla. 3d DCA 2006)

ROTHENBERG, Judge.

Christopher Scott Hughes ("Hughes"), a pilot for a commercial airline, and Thomas Porter Cloyd ("Cloyd"), a copilot for the same airline, were criminally prosecuted as codefendants and convicted of operating an aircraft while intoxicated or in a careless or reckless manner, in violation of section 860.13, Florida Statutes (2002). As Hughes and Cloyd have filed separate appeals, we have reviewed each separately. After a careful review of the record and the issues raised by Hughes, we affirm, and this opinion reflects our findings as to Hughes.

THE EVIDENCE

A brief review of the evidence is as follows. Hughes and Cloyd were scheduled to fly a commercial aircraft with approximately 125 passengers onboard, from Miami International Airport to Phoenix, Arizona, at 10:38 A.M., on July 1, 2002. Less than forty minutes prior to departure, Cloyd attempted to pass through an airport security checkpoint, carrying a cup of coffee. When security personnel stopped him and informed him that he could not pass through with the coffee, Cloyd became belligerent, demanded to see the regulations which prohibited the conduct, and used profanity. He did eventually dispose of the coffee.

Meanwhile, when Hughes passed through the checkpoint, security personnel noticed an odor of an alcoholic beverage coming from Hughes, and asked him if he had been drinking. Hughes denied that he had been drinking. Security personnel allowed the defendants to continue to their gate, but reported their observations to the Transportation Security Administration ("TSA") and the defendants' airline. The TSA notified the Miami-Dade Police Department, and a number of police officers who worked at the airport responded. When they arrived, the defendants were in the cockpit of the aircraft, the jet way had been pulled back from the aircraft, and the aircraft was connected to the tug that pushes it out from the gate. The officers stopped the aircraft by ordering the tug driver to return the aircraft to the gate.

Sergeant Steve Leibowitz, who conducted an examination of the defendants, noticed that each had a flushed face, bloodshot eyes, and the odor of an alcoholic beverage on his breath. Based upon his observations, Sergeant Leibowitz performed a horizontal gaze nystagmus test ("HGN test") on each of the defendants, and testified that the HGN tests indicated that each was impaired, with an estimated breath alcohol level of approximately .10 percent. He, therefore, arranged for the defendants to be transported to the police station for further testing.

Officer Harold Ruffner, who conducted a breath test of the defendants at the station, testified that Cloyd's first breath result was .1091 and his second was .09; while Hughes' readings were .084 and .081. H. Chip Wells, a forensic toxicologist, testified that, based upon the lowest of Cloyd's breathalyzer test results, he calculated through retrograde extrapolation that Cloyd's breath alcohol content was between .121 and .15; and that, based upon Hughes' lowest breathalyzer result, Hughes' breath alcohol content was between .113 and .145, when they were onboard the aircraft.

In addition to the observations of the security personnel and law enforcement, the results of the HGN tests, the breathalyzer results, and the forensic toxicologist's expert opinion regarding the defendants' breath alcohol at the time they were onboard the aircraft, the State introduced the defendants' bar tab from the night before, a videotape of them at the bar being served, and the testimony of witnesses. This evidence corroborated the observations and test results regarding the defendants' consumption of alcohol.

The night before this scheduled flight, the defendants shared a bottle of wine with two crew members at dinner, and each of the defendants also drank a martini. From the restaurant, they proceeded to Mr. Moe's Restaurant and Bar ("Moe's") where they opened a bar tab at approximately 10:49 P.M. From 10:49 at night until after 5:00 the next morning, they drank at Moe's, ordering seven 34-ounce mugs of beer, eight 16-ounce mugs of beer, a martini, and a burger. The two crew members, who were with the defendants, consumed one 16-ounce beer, the martini, and the burger, and left before midnight. The videotape showed the defendants continuously drinking throughout the night, and leaving just after 5:00 A.M., with the remainder of their beers, which they poured into a plastic cup carried by Cloyd. The evidence also established that Cloyd, Hughes, and the crew arrived at the airport late because Hughes had overslept.

Over defense objection, the State elicited testimony regarding the .08 blood alcohol limitation for operating a motor vehicle contained in section 316.193, Florida Statutes, even though the statute Cloyd and Hughes were charged with violating, section 360.13, contains no such limitation. Also, over defense objection, the State's witnesses were permitted to discuss the .04 civil standard contained in the federal aviation regulations, whereas the defense was precluded from introducing the .10 presumption of impairment contained in the federal criminal code, 18 U.S.C. § 343 (1988).

Whether the defendants were operating the aircraft before the police intervened was a matter hotly disputed at trial. The State's commercial aviation expert testified that he considered the pilots to be operating the aircraft when they activated and checked systems prior to departure, and he testified as to the extensive preflight inspections and systems checks that the pilots were required to complete. The pilots must enter critical data into the aircraft's computer, including the flight plan of the route, performance data, takeoff speeds, fuel load, and radio configurations for the navigation radio. The information entered into the computer is then displayed in the cockpit for the pilots to refer to when flying the aircraft. The aviation expert testified that he would consider it careless and reckless to perform any of these functions while under the influence of alcohol because they are critical for safety. He testified that the captain gives permission to the tug to begin the push back of the aircraft, and that, although the driver of the tug is physically controlling the movement of the aircraft at that point, the captain is in actual control of the aircraft.

The driver of the tug testified that once the aircraft is hooked up to the tug, he has control of the aircraft; to his knowledge the pilot cannot steer the aircraft; and its engines are not on. He did admit, however, that, when he is operating the tug, he has to wear a headset to communicate with the pilot and copilot, and cannot begin the push back until the pilot instructs him to do so.

The defendants moved for a judgment of acquittal, arguing that the evidence demonstrated that they did not operate or control the aircraft. The trial court denied their motions. The defendants requested a jury instruction on "inoperability," arguing that the evidence established that the aircraft could not be flown while it was attached to the tug. Cloyd, but not Hughes, additionally requested that the court instruct the jury on attempt. Both requests were denied by the trial court. Over the defendants' objections, the court granted the State's request for an instruction on principals.

In closing argument, the State argued, over defense objection, that the defendants could be found guilty of violating section 860.13 under two separate theories: (1) by being under the influence of an alcoholic beverage or (2) by operating the aircraft in a careless or reckless manner. The State told the jury that it could find the defendants guilty even if it did not have unanimity regarding the specific theory of prosecution. The defendants moved for mistrial or, in the alternative, requested a specific instruction, requiring a unanimous verdict as to the theory upon which their verdict was based, and requested that the jury be given a special verdict form in order to identify its verdict as to each of the two theories of prosecution. The trial court denied these motions. The jury returned a guilty verdict, and the defendants were sentenced.

PREEMPTION

The first issue we address in this appeal is whether the trial court erred in denying Hughes' motion to dismiss for lack of jurisdiction. It is Hughes' position that the federal government has preempted all state action regarding the physical qualifications and capacity of a federally certified pilot.

Hughes argues that his prosecution is expressly preempted by 14 C.F.R. 121 I, § XI, which provides, in part, that any state law covering the subject matter of 14 C.F.R. Parts 65, 121, and 135, including drug testing, is preempted. We find that section 860.13, Florida Statutes, criminalizing the operation of an aircraft while under the influence or in a careless or reckless manner, does not cover the subject matter of the specified Parts. As explained by the Eleventh Circuit Court of Appeals, "[t]hose Parts deal with certification and operating requirements of various designated airline employees," such as the drug testing requirements imposed upon such employees.

However, unlike federal aviation regulations, above, section 860.13 does not impose certification or operating requirements upon airline employees. Rather, it regulates the conduct of persons operating aircrafts. There is no language in 14 C.F.R. § 121 I, § XI or any other federal source stating that state criminal statutes regulating the conduct of those operating aircrafts are preempted. Therefore, 14 C.F.R. § 121 I, § XI does not expressly preempt this action.

Hughes argues that his prosecution is expressly preempted by 49 U.S.C. § 41713(b). This section is a part of the Federal Aviation Act, as amended by the Airline

Deregulation Act. We find that this section does not expressly preempt state action either. The purpose of the Airline Deregulation Act was to deregulate the airline industry, while promoting not only lower prices, but higher quality, efficiency, and innovation. Since Congress did not want the states to interfere with those goals, it expressly preempted state laws or regulations related to price, route, and services of an air carrier. It did not include, however, a preemption of the criminal conduct of the crew.

In fact, the Federal Aviation Act, as amended by the Airline Deregulation Act, does not provide for any criminal penalties for crew members operating an aircraft under the influence. While there are federal statutes criminalizing such conduct, they are not a part of the federal aviation legislation or any statutory scheme dealing specifically with the airline industry. Rather, they are contained in the general criminal section of the Federal Code, and were enacted as a part of the Anti-Drug Abuse Act of 1986. We conclude that if Congress intended for section 41713(b) of the United States Code to preempt state law regarding criminal conduct, it could have expressly stated so as it did in regard to other areas.

In the alternative, Hughes argues that field preemption bars his prosecution because the federal government, through the Federal Aviation Administration ("FAA"), has issued pervasive regulations that preempt interference in the subject area of the qualifications and capacity of airmen to pilot aircraft in interstate commercial air transportation. We disagree.

First, we note that field preemption should not be inferred "simply because [an] agency's regulations are comprehensive." Secondly, we find, as did the Eleventh Circuit Court of Appeals, that the existence of 14 C.F.R. § 91.17(c) "severely undercuts [the] argument that the challenged Florida criminal statutes are preempted." Section 91.17(c) of the Code of Federal Regulations provides:

> A crewmember shall do the following:
>
> On request of a law enforcement officer, submit to a test to indicate the percentage by weight of alcohol in the blood, when —
>
> (i) The law enforcement officer is authorized under State or local law to conduct the test or to have the test conducted; and
>
> (ii) The law enforcement officer is requesting submission to the test to investigate a suspected violation of State or local law governing the same or substantially similar conduct prohibited by paragraph (a)(1) [operating an aircraft within eight hours of consuming alcohol], (a)(2)

> [operating an aircraft while under the influence of alcohol], or (a)(4) [operating an aircraft while having a .04 percent or more blood alcohol level] of this section.

This section clearly allows states to investigate violations of their laws which make it illegal to pilot an aircraft while intoxicated, and may specifically do so when the state law prohibits conduct that is the same or is substantially similar to the conduct that is prohibited by a federal regulation. By allowing the investigation of a state law violation, it also clearly implies that such laws, once violated, may be prosecuted and are, therefore, not preempted.

Hughes' final preemption argument is that his prosecution is barred by conflict preemption. We disagree because a pilot could comply with both the Florida law and the federal law and regulations, and criminalizing the operation of an aircraft while intoxicated does not stand as an obstacle to the federal regulatory scheme.

CONSTITUTIONAL CHALLENGES

Hughes claims that section 860.13, Florida Statutes (2002), is unconstitutional (1) due to vagueness and (2) because it incorporates federal standards.

Vagueness Challenge

Hughes claims that the statute is unconstitutionally vague as it fails to define "under the influence" and "operate." He argues that the failure to define these terms denies a man of ordinary understanding the ability to determine what action is proscribed. By way of example, he argues that a person who consumes one alcoholic beverage and operates an emergency door on the aircraft, could be subject to this statute.

We begin our review and analysis with the presumption that the statute is constitutional and that "courts have the judicial obligation to sustain legislative enactments when possible." A constitutional challenge as to vagueness is based upon procedural due process, whether the statute provides fair notice, measured by common practice and understanding, as to the conduct which is prohibited. To raise a vagueness challenge, the defendant must demonstrate that the statute in question lacks specificity as to his own actions, as opposed to some hypothetical situation or "on the ground that it may conceivably be applied unconstitutionally to others in situations not before the Court."

After reviewing the evidence presented at trial, we conclude that Hughes lacks the requisite standing to challenge the statute on vagueness grounds since his conduct clearly falls within the conduct proscribed in section 860.13, and that Hughes, who is a person of at least ordinary intelligence, should have had no difficulty in knowing that his conduct was violative of section 860.13.

Section 860.13 is entitled "Operation of aircraft while intoxicated or in careless or reckless manner" and provides that it is unlawful to operate an aircraft in the air or on the ground while under the influence of alcoholic beverages or in a careless or reckless manner so as to endanger the life or property of another.

The evidence presented at trial was that Hughes, knowing that he was scheduled to fly a commercial aircraft at 10:38 A.M. and required to board the aircraft forty-five minutes prior to departure (9:53 A.M.), and upon boarding, he was required to conduct a lengthy, detailed preflight procedure critical to the safety of the flight, the crew, and passengers, began drinking the evening before the flight, and continued to drink throughout the night and until 5:00 in the morning. He began with a martini and wine with dinner, and between he and the copilot, Cloyd, drank seven 34-ounce and seven 16-ounce mugs of beer. After drinking all night, Hughes returned to his hotel room at 5:30 A.M., overslept, causing him and the crew to arrive late at the airport. Based upon the HGN test conducted by Sergeant Leibowitz shortly after the aircraft was pushed back from the gate and cleared for departure, Sergeant Leibowitz estimated that Hughes' blood alcohol level was at least .10.

The breath test subsequently performed placed Hughes' blood alcohol level at between .113 and .145 at the time Hughes was onboard the aircraft performing his preflight inspections, and safety checks, entering critical data in the aircraft's computer, computing takeoff speeds, fuel load, and radio configurations, and communicating with the tower and the tug.

We, therefore, agree with the State, that Hughes' conduct is clearly prohibited by section 860.13 and that he "cannot seriously contend that [he] [was] not on notice that [his] conduct was illegal." This is especially true given the fact that commercial airline pilots operate in a highly regulated industry where there is zero tolerance for alcohol in the cockpit. *See Johnson v. Nat'l Transp. Safety Bd.* (7th Cir. 1992) (upholding the revocation of Johnson's commercial pilot certificate for allowing his intoxicated copilot to fly the aircraft); 14 C.F.R § 91.11 (1999) (federal aeronautics safety regulation which prohibits any crewmember from serving as a crewmember with a .04 blood alcohol level or within eight hours of having consumed any alcohol).

While we conclude that the statute, as applied to Hughes and under the facts of this case, is not unconstitutionally vague, and that Hughes, therefore, lacks standing to facially attack the statute on vagueness grounds, we will nevertheless extend our analysis to address the merits of his claim.

Hughes argues that the statute is unconstitutionally vague as it fails to define the terms "operate" and "under the influence." We disagree. The plain and ordinary meaning of a word can be ascertained by reference to a dictionary or one may look to "'case law or related statutory provisions which define the term.'" Section 860.13(2) provides:

> In any prosecution charging careless or reckless operation of aircraft in violation of this section, the court, in determining whether the operation was careless or reckless, shall consider the standards for safe operation of aircraft as prescribed by federal statutes or regulations governing aeronautics.

As the statute itself incorporates the federal regulations and statutes governing aeronautics in determining what constitutes careless or reckless operation of an aircraft, we have reviewed both the dictionary definition of "operate" and the federal definition. "Operate" is defined as "[t]o run or control the functioning of." THE AMERICAN HERITAGE DICTIONARY OF THE ENGLISH LANGUAGE 1233 (4th ed. 2000).

The FAA is charged with the responsibility of promoting air safety and has established various regulations regulating the airline industry and the conduct of pilots. The federal regulations governing aeronautics defines "operate" as follows:

> Operate, with respect to aircraft, means use, cause to use or authorize to use aircraft, for the purpose (except as provided in § 91.13 of this chapter) of air navigation including the piloting of aircraft, with or without the right of legal control (as owner, lessee, or otherwise).

14 C.F.R. § 1.1 (1997).

Although Hughes did not fly the aircraft, the evidence established that he did "control the functioning of" the aircraft, and did "use, cause to use or authorize to use [the] aircraft, for the purpose ... of air navigation." He conducted extensive preflight inspections and systems checks, and inputted critical data into the aircraft computer with the intent ("for the purpose ... of") to fly the passengers and crew from Miami to Phoenix ("air navigation"). As his onboard preflight activities clearly fall within both the dictionary definition and the definition of "operate" contained in the federal regulations, and the jury was provided with the definition of "operate" contained in the Code of Federal Regulations, we reject Hughes' constitutional challenge of the statute based upon the failure of the statute to specifically define "operate."

We likewise reject Hughes' constitutional challenge based upon the statute's failure to define "under the influence," as his conduct, which we have previously addressed, is clearly prohibited under the statute. "The standard for testing vagueness under Florida law is whether the statute gives a person of ordinary intelligence fair notice of what constitutes forbidden conduct." "A person whose conduct clearly falls within [a] statute's prohibition cannot reasonably be said to have been denied adequate notice."

Incorporation Challenge

Hughes additionally argues that section 860.13(2) unconstitutionally incorporates federal regulations that did not exist at the time that the statute was enacted. Article II, section 3 of the Florida Constitution provides that no person belonging to one branch of the government may exercise any power belonging to the other branches.Because the legislature has the sole authority and responsibility to make laws, this provision has been construed to prohibit the legislature from delegating its power to others. Therefore, although the legislature may adopt or incorporate regulatory and statutory standards existing at the time of the adoption, any attempt to adopt or incorporate standards that will arise in the future is unconstitutional as an improper delegation of legislative power.

Section 860.13 was last reenacted without any amendments in 1983. Thus, incorporation of a federal standard that did not come into existence until after 1983, would be unconstitutional. Section 860.13(2) provides:

> In any prosecution charging careless or reckless operation of aircraft in violation of this section, the court, in determining whether the operation was careless or reckless, shall consider the standards for safe operation of aircraft as prescribed by federal statutes or regulations governing aeronautics.

In a different case, we found that section 860.13(2) incorporates federal standards for the safe operations of aircraft. As it was undisputed three that the federal standards relied upon in that case existed at the time of section 860.13's enactment, we concluded there was no improper delegation of legislative power.

In the instant case, however, the parties dispute whether the federal standards relied upon in this case existed at the time that section 860.13 was reenacted in 1983. The federal standards referred to in the instant case are found in 14 C.F.R. § 91.17(a), which prohibit a crewmember from acting in that capacity within eight hours of consuming any alcoholic beverage or with a blood alcohol level of .04 percent or higher. In 1983, the federal regulations clearly prohibited acting as a crewmember within eight hours of consuming alcohol. *See* 14 C.F.R. § 91.11. However, the prohibition against acting as a crewmember with a blood alcohol level of .04 percent or higher, did not exist in 1983.

Thus, for section 860.13(2) to adopt and include the federal regulation prohibiting acting as a crew member with a blood alcohol level of .04 percent or higher, would constitute an unconstitutional delegation of legislative power. Because we must construe statutes in a manner so as to uphold their constitutionality, we interpret section 860.13(2) to incorporate only those federal aeronautic safety regulations that existed in 1983. As we conclude that section 860.13(2) cannot and, therefore, does not incorporate the federal .04 percent blood alcohol standard, we deny Hughes' constitutional challenge on that ground.

EVIDENTIARY ISSUES

Admission at Trial of Federal Aviation Regulations

Over defense objection, the trial court permitted the State to introduce evidence that, pursuant to federal regulations for the safe operation of an aircraft, a crewmember is prohibited from operating an aircraft within eight hours of consuming any alcoholic beverages, or with a blood alcohol level of .04 or above. As section 860.13(2) specifically provides that the court shall consider federal regulations governing aeronautics in determining whether the operation of the aircraft was done in a careless or reckless manner, and the prohibition against operating an aircraft within eight hours of consuming any alcoholic beverage, which is found in 14 C.F.R. § 91.17(a), was in existence when section 860.13(2) was reenacted in 1983, we conclude that the trial court properly allowed the introduction of this evidence.

We, however, agree with Hughes that the trial court erred in allowing the State to introduce evidence that under these same regulations, a crewmember is prohibited from operating an aircraft with a blood alcohol level of .04 percent or above, as this regulation was not in existence when section 860.13 was reenacted. Based upon our review of the evidence and the focus of the State's closing argument, we, however, find that the error was harmless beyond a reasonable doubt.

A review of the record reflects that the State focused on Hughes' actions, not on federal regulations. The State argued that it had proven its case based upon the following. When Hughes arrived for the 10:38 A.M. flight, he was late, smelled of alcoholic beverages, had bloodshot eyes and a flushed face, but denied that he had been drinking. The evidence established that he had consumed a martini and wine with dinner and continued to drink all night with the copilot. Together they consumed seven 34-ounce and seven 16-ounce mugs of beer, drinking until at least 5:00 A.M., despite being required to begin preflight operations before 10:00 that morning for a commercial flight carrying over 100 passengers.

In support of the State's claim that Hughes appeared to be under the influence and that he had in fact consumed as much alcohol and as late as the evidence suggested, the State relied on the results of the HGN test, which placed Hughes' blood alcohol level at, at least, .10; the subsequent breath test results, which placed his blood alcohol level at between .113 and .145 when he was operating the aircraft; Hughes' admission that he had consumed "many" beers throughout the night; and the expert's testimony that Hughes' ability to operate the critical systems of the aircraft would be impaired at these levels. As the State did not place any emphasis on the improperly admitted evidence, and the evidence establishing that Hughes operated the aircraft under the influence of alcoholic beverages and/or in a careless or reckless manner so as to endanger the lives of those aboard the aircraft was overwhelming, we conclude that the improperly introduced evidence was harmless beyond a reasonable doubt.

Failure to Admit the .10 Federal Criminal Presumption

While Hughes claims that the trial court erred when it precluded him from introducing evidence that, under the federal law criminalizing the operation of a common carrier under the influence of alcohol, the presumption of intoxication is .10, we reject this argument on the same basis wherein we concluded that the federal regulation prohibiting operation of an aircraft with a blood alcohol level of .04 was inadmissible.

The federal statutes in question, 18 U.S.C. §§ 342-43 (2000), was not created until 1986. This federal statute, therefore, could not have been adopted by the Florida Legislature when it reenacted section 860.13 in 1983 and, thus, was not admissible. Furthermore, section 860.13(2) requires the court to consider the "standards for safe operation of aircraft as prescribed by federal statutes or regulations governing aeronautics." The .10 presumption of intoxication is not relevant as to whether Hughes was operating the aircraft under the influence or in a careless or reckless manner. They are entirely different standards. The trial court, therefore, did not abuse its discretion in denying the introduction of the federal criminal intoxication presumption.

JURY INSTRUCTIONS

Inoperability

Hughes argues that, because the aircraft was attached to a tug which controlled the movement of the aircraft, the trial court erred in rejecting his request for a jury instruction on inoperability. Inoperability is a defense to driving a motor vehicle under the influence, pursuant to section 316.193, Florida Statutes (2002).

Section 316.193, the driving under the influence statute, provides that, before a person may be found guilty of this offense, the State must prove the following two elements beyond a reasonable doubt:

> 1. That the defendant drove or was in actual physical control of a vehicle, and
>
> 2. While driving or in actual physical control of the vehicle the defendant (a) was under the influence of [alcoholic beverages][a chemical substance][a controlled substance] to the extent that [his][her] normal faculties were impaired, or (b) had a blood-alcohol level of 0.08 or more grams of alcohol per 100 milliliters of blood, or a breath-alcohol level of 0.08 or more grams of alcohol per 210 liters of breath.

> "Actual physical control of a vehicle" means the defendant must be physically in or on the vehicle and have the capability to operate the vehicle, regardless of whether he/she is actually operating the vehicle at the time.

Fla. Std. Jury Instr. (Crim.) 28.1.

A defendant, therefore, may be found guilty of this offense if he/she (1) drove or is driving a vehicle while under the influence or (2) is in actual physical control of a vehicle while under the influence. While the State is not required to prove that the vehicle is capable of operation, inoperability may be a defense to whether the defendant was in actual physical control of the vehicle. The defense of inoperability is based upon the premise that:

> a person ought not be convicted of having a vehicle under his or her control while intoxicated when in fact the vehicle was inoperable, the intoxicated person did not operate the vehicle prior to its becoming disabled, and the vehicle's mechanical problems were such that it could not under any reasonable circumstances have been operated by the person accused.

Hughes, however, was not charged with violating section 316.193, the driving under the influence statute. Rather, he was charged with violating section 860.13, Florida Statutes (2002), "Operation of aircraft while intoxicated or in careless or reckless manner," which provides, in part, that:

> (1) It shall be unlawful for any person to operate an aircraft in the air or on the ground or water while under the influence of alcoholic beverages; or to operate an aircraft in the air or on the ground or water in a careless or reckless manner so as to endanger the life or property of another.
>
> (2) In any prosecution charging careless or reckless operation of aircraft in violation of this section, the court, in determining whether the operation was careless or reckless, shall consider the standards for safe operation of aircraft as prescribed by federal statutes or regulations governing aeronautics.

Since the statute itself requires that the federal statutes and regulations governing aeronautics be considered in determining whether the operation of the aircraft was careless or reckless, the trial court relied on the federal statute which defines what "operates" means with respect to an aircraft: "Operate, with respect to aircraft, means use, cause to use or authorize to use aircraft, for the purpose (except as provided in § 91.13 of this chapter) of air navigation including the piloting of aircraft, with or without the right of legal control (as owner, lessee, or otherwise)." 14 C.F.R. § 1.1 (1997).

As is readily obvious, section 860.13, the statute under which Hughes was charged and convicted, differs from section 316.193, the driving under the influence statute. The elements are not the same, nor is the proof which is required to sustain a conviction. While the driving under the influence statute, section 316.193, requires that the State prove that the accused was driving or in actual physical control of the vehicle while under the influence, the statute Hughes was charged with violating, section 860.13, requires operation of the aircraft while under the influence or in a careless or reckless manner. While operability may be a defense to the driving under the influence statute, it is an element of the crime charged pursuant to section 860.13.

While the trial court must instruct the jury on the applicable law regarding a defense whenever there is evidence introduced at trial which supports that theory of defense operability in this case is an element of the crime charged. As such, the jury was instructed that before it could find the defendant guilty, the State was required to prove beyond a reasonable doubt that the defendant operated the aircraft, and the trial court also instructed the jury as to the definition of "operate" with respect to an aircraft.

Because "operate" is an element of the crime charged and that term was defined, we find that the trial court did not err in failing to instruct the jury on "inoperability." Additionally, as actual physical control only requires that the vehicle, which in this case is an aircraft, be reasonably capable of being rendered operable, not that the defendant have the immediate ability to operate the vehicle, the trial court did not err by failing to provide the requested instruction.

A review of the case law reveals that the "reasonably capable of being rendered operable standard" is applied when a person is charged with driving under the influence and claims either that the vehicle was not operational or that he was not in actual physical control of the vehicle. For example, if a person is found passed out behind the steering wheel of a vehicle with the keys either in the ignition or on the floor of the vehicle, he may be found guilty of violating this statute because he is in actual physical control of a vehicle which can readily be made operational.

In the instant case, there was no evidence introduced which even suggested that the aircraft was experiencing any mechanical difficulties. Although the aircraft was not capable of moving under its own power when it was attached to the tug, the defendants easily could have rendered it capable of moving under its own power at any time by ordering the tug to be detached from the aircraft. But more importantly, whether the defendants could move the aircraft under its own power during the time it was being towed by the tug is irrelevant and, with all due respect to the defense, nothing more than a red herring. The undisputed evidence at trial was that the defendants "operated" the aircraft well before it was attached to the tug and towed away from the gate in preparation for its takeoff. The undisputed evidence was that the defendants, acting as pilot and copilot of this commercial aircraft with over 100 passengers onboard, while sitting in the cockpit of the aircraft and thus in actual physical control of the aircraft, performed extensive preflight duties for the purpose of flying the aircraft.

To "[o]perate, with respect to aircraft, means use, cause to use or authorize to use aircraft, for the purpose ... of air navigation including the piloting of aircraft, with or without the right of legal control ..." 14 C.F.R. § 1.1.

Captain Chronic, an expert in the field of aircraft operations and flight standardization safety, testified that part of operating the aircraft is properly checking the operational systems; imputing the flight plan, takeoff speeds, fuel load, and any special radio configuration for navigation into the computer system; performing the "flow" and systems checks; obtaining permission to fly by radioing the air traffic controller on an assigned frequency and obtaining clearance information, the altitude, and the transponder code; and obtaining the total weight of the aircraft just before departure which is then used to correlate a speed from a speed chart which becomes critical information in the event a takeoff must be aborted. He testified that each of the many required and vital tasks the pilot and copilot must perform before the aircraft can move, is operating the aircraft, and that it is only after all of these functions are concluded that clearance may be obtained to move the aircraft. Once clearance has been obtained, the captain (pilot) releases the brake and orders the tug to push back the aircraft.

Captain Chronic testified that, although the ramp crew is steering the aircraft while it is being towed, the captain (pilot) is actually in charge of the aircraft and is in charge from the time the door is closed. His undisputed testimony was that, by engaging in the extensive preflight procedures, the defendants were "using the aircraft for the purpose of air navigation" and, therefore, operating the aircraft.

The State's case, simply put, was that the defendants operated the aircraft under the influence of alcohol or in a careless or reckless manner during these preflight procedures, not that they flew or drove the aircraft while under the influence or in a careless or reckless manner. If the jury was not persuaded by the evidence that these procedures satisfied the "operate" prong, the defendants would have been not guilty. In summary, since (1) the State was required to prove beyond a reasonable doubt that Hughes did operate the aircraft (an essential element of the crime charged); (2) the State's case was premised on whether the pilot and copilot violated the statute by taking control of the aircraft and performing the preflight functions while under the influence of alcohol; and (3) as there was no evidence of any mechanical or other problem which rendered the aircraft incapable of being operated without substantial mechanical repairs, the trial court did not abuse its discretion by failing to instruct on inoperability.

THE VERDICT

Pursuant to section 860.13, it is unlawful to operate an aircraft (1) while under the influence or (2) in a careless or reckless manner so as to endanger the life or property of another. Hughes claims that the statute, as written, defines two separate unlawful acts. He, therefore, argues that the trial court erred in permitting the State to argue, over his objection, that it was not necessary for the jurors to reach a unanimous verdict as to which unlawful act the defendant had committed, and in denying his request for a unanimity instruction. We agree.

Based upon our review of these cases, we conclude that when a statute sets forth a specific prohibited act and then specifies the various means by which the act can be committed, then, and only then, does it create a single offense. When a statute sets forth various acts, stating that each is prohibited and/or provides for different punishment depending on the act committed, then the statute creates multiple offenses.

The State argues that section 860.13 creates a single offense, the dangerous operation of an aircraft, which can be violated in either of two ways, by operating an aircraft while under the influence or by operating an aircraft in a careless or reckless manner. We disagree, as the statute is simply not worded as the State suggests. The title of the statute is "Operation of aircraft while intoxicated or in careless or reckless manner," while the statute itself specifies that "(1) It shall be unlawful for any person: (a) To operate an aircraft ... while under the influence ... or (b) To operate an aircraft ... in a careless or reckless manner so as to endanger the life or property of another." Thus, we conclude that the statute prohibits two separate acts: one prohibiting the operation of an aircraft while under the influence and, the other, prohibiting the operation of an aircraft in a careless or reckless manner. Because the statute, as worded, creates two separate offenses, we agree with Hughes that unanimity was required. Thus, the trial court erred in permitting the State to argue otherwise and by denying Hughes' request for a curative instruction.

Based on the particular facts of this case and the wording of section 860.13, we, however, conclude that the error constitutes harmless error, as any reasonable person who concluded that Hughes was operating the aircraft while under the influence, would conclude that his conduct was careless or reckless. Thus, the jury by unanimously finding that Hughes was guilty of operating an aircraft either under the influence, or in a careless or reckless manner, necessarily found that he had operated the aircraft in a careless or reckless manner.

BRANCHE v. AIRTRAN AIRWAYS, INC.

342 F.3d 124 (11th Cir. 2003)

MARCUS, Circuit Judge.

This case ultimately requires us to determine whether a claim brought by appellant Michael Branche ("Branche") against his former employer, Airtran Airways, Inc. ("Airtran"), pursuant to Florida's Whistleblower Act, Fla. Stat. § 448.102, is expressly pre-empted by the federal Airline Deregulation Act ("ADA"), 49 U.S.C. § 41713.

This question forces us, in turn, to decide whether Branche's claim significantly affects "air carrier services," as that phrase is used in the ADA's pre-emption clause. This is a close question that is rendered especially difficult by Congress's 1999 amendment of the ADA to include the Whistle blower Protection Program ("WPP"), 49 U.S.C. § 42121, a provision that offers a remedy for plaintiffs in Branche's position that parallels the one available under Florida law. After thoroughly considering the arguments raised by the parties and the applicable caselaw, we conclude that Branche's claim is not pre-empted.

I.

The basic facts are these. Branche was first hired by Airtran on September 2, 1998 as a maintenance controller, and he subsequently was transferred to the position of aircraft inspector at Tampa International Airport ("TIA"). In fact, Branche was appellee's only aircraft inspector at TIA. In this capacity, appellant was required to conduct safety inspections of Airtran's aircraft after they had been serviced by appellee's maintenance crew but prior to takeoff. These inspections were governed by FAA regulations, including 14 C.F.R. § 121.365(c), which provides that this inspection function is to be exercised free from the oversight of the maintenance department whose work the inspector reviews. This subsection provides:

> Each person performing required inspections in addition to other maintenance, preventive maintenance, or alterations, shall organize the performance of those functions so as to separate the required inspection functions from the other maintenance, preventive maintenance, and alteration functions. The separation shall be below the level of administrative control at which overall responsibility for the required inspection functions and other maintenance, preventive maintenance, and alteration functions are exercised.

Branche says that during 2001, Guy Lewis, Airtran's maintenance manager at TIA, began exercising supervisory authority over him in direct contravention of § 121.365(c).

Branche alleges that on June 30, 2001, an Airtran DC-9 airplane landed at TIA with one of its two engines running at a temperature that exceeded Federal Aviation Administration ("FAA") safety guidelines, a condition that could have resulted in engine failure. After perceiving this dangerous condition, Branche recommended to Lewis that the engine be subjected to a detailed physical inspection. Instead, Lewis and two maintenance workers climbed into the aircraft's cockpit and conducted a "high powered run," *i.e.*, began running the engine at high power to ascertain its air-worthiness.

Appellant alleges that none of these individuals were qualified to undertake this diagnostic maneuver, and that as such they violated 14 C.F.R. § 65.81 in performing it. This section provides:

> A certificated mechanic may perform or supervise the maintenance, preventive maintenance or alteration of an aircraft or appliance, or a part thereof, for which he is rated (but excluding major repairs to, and major alterations of, propellers, and any repair to, or alteration of, instruments), and may perform additional duties in accordance with §§ 65.85, 65.87, and 65.95. However, he may not supervise the maintenance, preventive maintenance, or alteration of, or approve and return to service, any aircraft or appliance, or part thereof, for which he is rated unless he has satisfactorily performed the work concerned at an earlier date.
>
> If he has not so performed that work at an earlier date, he may show his ability to do it by performing it to the satisfaction of the Administrator or under the direct supervision of a certificated and appropriately rated mechanic, or a certificated repairman, who has had previous experience in the specific operation concerned.
>
> A certificated mechanic may not exercise the privileges of his certificate and rating unless he understands the current instructions of the manufacturer, and the maintenance manuals, for the specific operation concerned.

Branche further asserts that Paul Picarelli, an employee who was authorized to perform high powered runs, was present at TIA at the time, and that under § 65.81 Picarelli should have been asked to test the engine in question. Branche says that after the plane departed from TIA on June 30, 2001, the engine overheated during its flight to Atlanta and the plane subsequently was taken out of service. Moreover, he alleges that the following day he investigated this particular engine and learned that it had overheated on two separate occasions during the preceding two weeks.

On July 2, 2001, Branche informed the FAA of Airtran's regulatory violations, and both he and Airtran subsequently were contacted regarding his allegations. Airtran soon became aware that Branche was the source of the FAA's knowledge of the incidents in question. On July 6, 2001, appellant filed a formal union grievance in which he asserted that neither Lewis nor the mechanics who accompanied him in the cockpit were authorized to perform a high power engine run. Then, on July 13, 2001, Airtran accused him of falsifying his time card and stealing approximately two hours of pay. Appellant denied the allegation. On July 23, 2001, Branche was terminated based on this alleged time card violation. Appellant posits that the true reason for his discharge was retaliatory, *i.e.*, to punish him for reporting Airtran's violations of FAA regulations.

Based on this pattern of dealing, on August 27, 2001 Branche filed this action in the Circuit Court for the Sixth Judicial Circuit, in Pinellas County, Florida. He advanced a single claim under Florida's Whistleblower Act, *Fla. Stat.* § 448.102. Airtran promptly removed the case on the basis of diversity to the United States District Court for the Middle District of Florida, where discovery proceeded. On June 24, 2002, Airtran moved for final summary judgment denying appellant's claim, arguing that as applied in this case the state Whistleblower Act was explicitly pre-empted by the ADA, 49 U.S.C. § 41713. The district court agreed, and granted Airtran's motion on August 27, 2002. This appeal ensued.

On appeal, Branche argues that the district court erred by holding that the ADA pre-empts Florida's Whistleblower Act, as applied in this case. He says that pre-emption under the ADA exists only where the state law in question purports to regulate airline prices, routes or services. In this case, he argues, the relationship between Florida's prohibition against retaliatory discharges and these facets of air carrier operations is too attenuated to give rise to ADA pre-emption. Airtran responds that the scope of the ADA's express pre-emption provision is extremely broad, and that the connection between the type of conduct prohibited by the Whistleblower Act and air carrier "services" is sufficient to implicate the ADA's pre-emption clause. Moreover, appellee contends, Congress's enactment in 1999 of the WPP, 49 U.S.C. § 42121, supports a finding of pre-emption here, as the WPP provides an exclusive remedy for plaintiffs in Branche's position.

II.

Just as state law personal injury actions generally have been held not to be pre-empted under the ADA, employment discrimination actions typically have been held to fall outside the scope of the ADA's pre-emption clause. It is true that an airline's employment decisions may have an incidental effect on its "services," but as the Second Circuit observed in *Abdu-Brisson*, "[p]ermitting full operation of ... [anti-]discrimination law[s] will not affect competition between airlines—the primary concern underlying the ADA." Indeed, employment standards fall squarely within the traditional police powers of the states, and as such should not be disturbed lightly.

Several courts have considered the specific question presented in this case, *i.e.*, whether a claim for retaliatory discharge is pre-empted under § 41713, and although they have recognized that such employment actions ultimately may affect in some way the transport of passengers or other incidents of "service," the majority of them have concluded that such claims are not pre-empted.

Put as simply as possible-and setting aside for the moment the impact of Congress's enactment of the WPP on our ultimate holding in this case-given the particularities of Branche's claim that he was discharged for his *post hoc* reporting of Airtran's safety violations, we believe that this case is more analogous to the majority of those cases, and hold that appellant's state law claim is not pre-empted by the ADA. This is so essentially because safety is not a basis on which airlines compete for passengers, and as such is not something for which air travelers bargain; it is implicit in every ticket sold by every carrier. Accordingly, it does not serve the purposes of the ADA to pre-empt state law employment claims related to safety. Although some safety-related claims may be tied to air carrier services, the very fact that they concern safety, standing alone, is insufficient to demonstrate this nexus.

Thus, because Branche's state Whistleblower Act claim is fundamentally an employment discrimination claim that does not implicate any arena in which airlines compete, we conclude based on the foregoing analysis that his claim does not relate to the services of an air carrier within the meaning of § 41713, and consequently is not pre-empted under that section. Importantly, however, there is one more issue that we must consider before ultimately resolving this pre-emption question. In 1999, subsequent to the majority of the decisions discussed above, Congress enacted as part of the ADA the WPP, which provides that:

> No air carrier may discharge an employee or otherwise discriminate against an employee with respect to compensation, terms, conditions, or privileges of employment because the employee provided, caused to be provided, or is about to provide (with any knowledge of the employer) ... to the employer or Federal Government information relating to any violation or alleged violation of any order, regulation, or standard of the [FAA] or any other provision of Federal law relating to air carrier safety or any other law of the United States.

This provision represents a federal analog to Florida's Whistleblower Act. In evaluating whether the WPP has any effect on the foregoing analysis, the question we must ask is whether any aspect of that statute explains the proper scope of the ADA's pre-emption clause to a degree sufficient to alter our conclusion that pre-emption is inappropriate here because Branche's claim does not relate to the bargained-for aspects of air carrier operations.

Congress's enactment of the WPP figured prominently in the district court's finding of pre-emption in this case and in *Botz v. Omni Air Int'l* (8th Cir. 2002), the one circuit court decision handed down since the WPP's effective date to address ADA pre-emption in the context of a state whistleblower statute. *Botz* featured a claim brought by a flight attendant pursuant to Minnesota's whistleblower statute, under which employers are prohibited from subjecting employees to any adverse employment action in retaliation for the employee's refusal "to perform an action that the employee has an objective basis in fact to believe violates any state or federal law or rule or regulation..."

Botz alleged that she had been fired in retaliation for refusing a flight assignment that she believed violated federal safety regulations. The airline argued in response that Botz's claim was pre-empted under § 41713. In analyzing this contention, the Eighth Circuit drew a straight line between a flight attendant's refusal to serve, federal regulations that prohibit the operation of a flight with fewer than a minimum number of flight attendants, and a resulting disruption of air service. In essence, the court was especially concerned that the state whistleblower statute functionally ensured the plaintiff's ability to ground a plane, and thereby disrupt the airline's service. It thus categorized Minnesota's statute as "a state law that granted a flight attendant or other air-carrier employee the right to refuse an assignment that is essential to a carrier's ability to provide its scheduled services." Accordingly, it held, this law was related to air carrier services within the meaning of § 41713.

Notably, the court also found support for this holding in Congress's enactment of the WPP. It reasoned that in passing the WPP Congress sought to impose a "more predictable response to public air-safety complaints than would likely be possible if it had granted review in the courts of the fifty States." It then rejected Botz's argument that "the WPP was not intended to pre-empt State whistleblower protections because, if it had been, Congress could easily have made such pre-emption express by including language in the WPP indicating that it was a whistleblowing air-carrier employee's exclusive remedy." It said:

> We think this turns the proper logic on its head. When it fashioned the WPP, Congress was surely aware of the ADA's express pre-emption provision. It was presumably aware, as well, that the Supreme Court had determined that the provision had a broad application and should be given an expansive interpretation. Given this, we would expect Congress to have directed language in the WPP to the issue of federal pre-emption only if it had been Congress's intent that the WPP not exert any pre-emptive effect upon state whistleblower provisions.

Finally, the Eighth Circuit dismissed *Botz*'s reliance on several other cases that had rejected pre-emption arguments under the ADA in the context of retaliatory discharge claims, because "[e]ach of these cases ... relie[d] on the fact—a fact that is no longer true—that the ADA provided no claim or remedy for air-carrier employees discharged in retaliation for their whistleblowing conduct. Such employees now enjoy protection under the WPP."

After carefully considering the reasoning employed in *Botz* and the enactment of the WPP, we remain convinced that Branche's whistleblower claim is not pre-empted. As for the connection between retaliatory discharge claims and airline services, we do not dispute the Eight Circuit's conclusion that the grounding of an airplane is related to airline services, in particular, the transport of passengers from one place to another. However, in this case, the connection—or, indeed, the potential connection—between Branche's actions and air carrier services is far more attenuated than in *Botz*.

As the Eighth Circuit said, if a flight attendant refuses to fly and a replacement cannot be found, FAA regulations prevent the plane from leaving the gate, thereby disrupting service. Here, by contrast, we are not concerned with the withdrawal of clearance for a plane to take off based on mechanical concerns, but instead only with Branche's *post hoc* reporting of a FAA violation. The likely consequence of reporting an unauthorized high powered run (as opposed to the reporting of a malfunctioning engine) is an investigation by FAA officials into the practices of Airtran's TIA mechanics, but not the grounding of the plane, which presumably has either been mechanically cleared and flown away or grounded for mechanical reasons independent of the subsequent report of the improper diagnostic procedure. Had Branche claimed that Airtran fired him in retaliation for refusing to allow a plane to take off due to safety concerns, this would present a situation closer to the one at issue in *Botz*. But that is not the claim before us.

As our employment of this analytical modality indicates, it is the specifics of the retaliation claim, not the whistleblower statute, that appropriately determine pre-emption. Thus, retaliation claims brought under state whistleblower statutes must be evaluated on a case-by-case basis to determine the connection between the action in question and airline services. In Branche's case, this evaluation reveals that this connection is extremely loose at best.

As for the enactment of the WPP, this statute says nothing whatsoever about pre-emption, an omission that is susceptible to more than one interpretation. We could say, as the *Botz* court did, that the absence of any discussion of pre-emption stemmed from a Congressional assumption that the ADA already pre-empted state whistleblower claims and that it was content with maintaining this *status quo*. Although this certainly is plausible, we believe that this interpretation ultimately is incorrect. Indeed, the basis for the Eighth Circuit's holding is simply that (1) at the time of the WPP's enactment Congress knew of the ADA's express pre-emption provision; and (2) it also was aware that the Supreme Court had interpreted this provision broadly.

Although the first premise is undoubtable, it also is not especially helpful. Congress's knowledge of the provision implies nothing about the legislature's view of its scope. As for the second, the Supreme Court has interpreted only the phrase "related to." To date it has not weighed in on the meaning of "air carrier services." Moreover and more significantly, to the extent that Congress can be charged with cognizance of judicial views regarding the scope of § 41713, it must have known that the majority of courts to consider the issue found state law retaliatory discharge claims not to be pre-empted by the ADA.

Against this background, it becomes significantly less clear that in saying nothing about pre-emption in the WPP Congress was somehow indicating that it assumed state whistleblower claims to be pre-empted. Indeed, an equally compelling argument could be made that Congress was indicating its acquiescence in the view that such state law claims are not pre-empted. Because the WPP says nothing about pre-emption and this silence is ambiguous, we find its enactment less probative of Congressional intent regarding the pre-emption of state whistleblower claims than did the Eighth Circuit.

As for the desire to enact a uniform means of resolving whistleblower claims, to infer from the very enactment of a federal remedy that Congress also intended to pre-empt all remotely equivalent state law causes of action—as distinguished from divining Congress's intent regarding the scope of its express pre-emption provision (which, as stated, is ambiguous)—would be a species of implied pre-emption, which we presume is inapplicable where the statute in question features an express pre-emption clause.

Simply stated, it is possible to point to a multitude of substantive contexts in which parallel state and federal remedies exist and the very enactment of a federal remedy, without more, cannot cause us to expand the scope of an express pre-emption provision to encompass and pre-empt all equivalent state remedies.

In deciding pre-emption, whether before or after the enactment of the WPP, the question we must answer remains the same: Is the state law in question "related to" air carrier "services?" Though we do not wish to understate the importance of this legislation, the WPP changed neither the nature of Florida's Whistleblower Act nor the language of the ADA's pre-emption provision in any meaningful way. It simply added an additional remedy for plaintiffs seeking to advance a retaliatory discharge claim.

Because the WPP says nothing about pre-emption, it leaves us in precisely the same position as we occupied before considering this statute; that is, it leaves us with our conclusion that the pre-emption of Branche's retaliatory discharge claim would not advance the pro-competitive goals of the ADA, as outlined by the Supreme Court in *Wolens*. Put differently, the WPP did not render these claims any more related to the bargained-for aspects of air carrier operations over which the airlines compete. As such, although the enactment of this statute renders the question of ADA pre-emption more difficult in this case, we do not believe that the WPP changed the legal landscape-or that it illuminated the intent of Congress to pre-empt state law whistleblower claims-to a degree sufficient to alter the conclusion that prior to its passage such claims were not pre-empted. Because the district court erroneously concluded that Branche's state law whistleblower claim was pre-empted by the ADA, its summary judgment in favor of Airtran is vacated and this case is remanded for further proceedings consistent with this opinion.

NOTES

1. Observe that the airline-employer in *Hughes v. State* (Fla. 3d DCA 2006), *supra*—America West Airlines—is not mentioned by name, but only as "a commercial airline." The carrier's anonymity focuses attention on the fact that, like other licensed professionals, "airmen"—a term that includes pilots, flight instructors, mechanics, and flight attendants—are themselves accountable to federal aviation authorities, independent of any legal obligations borne by their employer.

Indeed, an elaborate administrative scheme—featuring administrative judges, the Federal Aviation Administration, and National Transportation Safety Board—exists to oversee civil penalties and/or the denial, suspension, or revocation of medical and operational certificates through enforcement actions and related formal and informal proceedings involving airmen. *See* 14 C.F.R. Pts. 13, 61, 67, 91; 49 U.S.C. §§ 1101-1155, 44701-44723, 46301; 49 C.F.R. Pt. 821. *See also* Jack Harrington, *The FAA Wants to Suspend Your Airman Certificate*, 10 AIR & SPACE L. 3 (1995); Alan Armstrong, *Pilot Certificate Actions and Civil Penalties*, 52 J. AIR L. & COM. 77 (1986); Colin S. Diver, *The Assessment and Mitigation of Civil Money Penalties by Federal Administrative Agencies*, 79 COLUM. L. REV. 1435 (1979); W. J. Dunn, *Revocation or Suspension of Airman's License or Certificate*, 78 A.L.R.2d 1150 (1968).

2. Though commonly referred to as a "pilot's license," the right to fly is conferred by an appropriate "certificate." Airmen complete stringent training requirements to obtain the appropriate operational certificate (*e.g.*, "student," "sport," "recreational," "private," "commercial," or "air transport" pilot) and rating certificate (*e.g.*, category, class, and type or equipment). *See generally http://www.faa.gov/licenses_certificates/airmen_certification/.*

Certificated airmen must adhere to extensive operational regulations in order to maintain their certificate(s). Mistakes and human error occur, of course, and the Federal Aviation Administration ("FAA") enforces the Federal Aviation Act of 1958 and Federal Aviation Regulations ("FARs") through administrative actions, reexaminations, certificate actions, civil penalties, and criminal investigations. *See* 49 U.S.C. §§ 46308, 46310-13. *See also* 14 C.F.R. § 13.23. There is "no right to demand that the FAA select a statutory enforcement action that encompasses a jury trial option." *E.g., Go Leasing, Inc. v. Nat'l Transp. Safety Bd.*, 800 F.2d 1514, 1519 (9th Cir. 1986).

Administrative actions against airmen are not legal or adjudicative proceedings in nature, therefore the opportunity for notice and hearing is not required. *See* Fed. Aviation Admin., FAA Compliance and Enforcement Program, Order 2150.3B (Oct. 1, 2007). Administrative action may be taken instead of legal enforcement when all of the following elements are present:

- Applicable law does not require legal enforcement action and administrative action would serve as an adequate deterrent to future violations;
- The nature of the violation does not indicate that the certificate holder lacks qualifications to hold a certificate;
- The violation was inadvertent and not deliberate and not the result of purposeful conduct (*see Ferguson v. Nat'l Transp. Safety Bd.* (9th Cir. 1982));
- The violation was not the result of a substantial disregard for safety or security and the circumstances of the violation are not aggravated;
- The alleged violator has a constructive attitude toward complying with regulations; and
- The alleged violator has not been involved previously in similar violations and the apparent violation does not indicate a trend of noncompliance.

In evaluating the fourth criterion, above, two different meanings and applications of the term "substantial disregard" exist. In the case of a certificate holder, "the act or failure to act must involve a substantial deviation from the degree of care, judgment, and responsibility normally expected of a person holding a certificate with that type, quality and level experience, knowledge and proficiency." In the case of a violator who is not a certificate holder, however, "substantial disregard" involves an act or failure to act that represents a substantial deviation from the degree of care and diligence expected of a "reasonable person in those circumstances."

FAA investigative personnel may take enforcement action once they determine that legal enforcement action is necessary. For example, through certificate actions, the FAA may amend, modify, suspend, or revoke a pilot's certificate if it determines "that safety in air commerce or air transportation and the public interest require that action." *See* 49 U.S.C. § 44709(b). *See also* 14 C.F.R. § 13.19(b). If an infraction is operational in nature, the FAA may seek to suspend a pilot's license. On the other hand, the FAA may seek to revoke the license of a pilot who shows a lack of qualification or an attitude that is at odds with compliance with air safety regulations.

In certain cases, the FAA Administrator may make certificate actions effective immediately where an emergency exists and safety in air commerce or air transportation require imminent action. An emergency certificate action immediately deprives the certificate holder of the right to exercise the privileges of that certificate. Order 2150.3B, at 5-16. In this circumstance, the certificate holder may not continue to exercise the privileges of that certificate while an appeal is pending unless the National Transportation Safety Board reverses the emergency nature of the order.

3. To avoid civil penalty actions, airmen may voluntarily disclose violations of federal aviation regulations. *See* Fed. Aviation Admin., FAA Compliance and Enforcement Program, Order 2150.3B, at 5-8 (Oct. 1, 2007). The voluntary disclosure reporting program applies to certificate-holding entities, production approval holders, and other entities subject to regulation under 14 C.F.R. Pts. 21, 119, 125, 129, 133, 135, 137, 141, 142, 145, and 147 and, for qualified fractional ownership programs operating under part 91, subpart K. *See also* Fed. Aviation Admin., Aviation Safety Reporting Program, Advisory Circular 00-46D (Feb. 26, 1997).

4. Pursuant to 14 C.F.R Pt. 67, airmen must meet minimum medical standards for a First-, Second-, or Third-Class Medical Certificate. Each of the certificates requires a person to have 20/20 distant vision and near vision of 20/40 or better; to satisfy certain ear, nose, and throat equilibrium standards; to have no established medical history or clinical diagnosis of a personality disorder, a psychosis, a bipolar disorder, or substance dependence; to establish neurologic health and to rule-out epilepsy and other seizure disorders; to establish cardiovascular health; and to show a general medical condition that makes the person able to safely perform the duties or exercise the privileges of a particular airmen certificate (*e.g.*, no established medical history or clinical diagnosis of diabetes mellitus that requires insulin or any other hypoglycemic drug for control). *See*, *e.g.*, 14 C.F.R. §§ 67.101 to -.115; 14 C.F.R. §§67.201 to .215; and 14 C.F.R. §§ 67.301 to -.315.

In certain circumstances, medical officers of the Federal Aviation Administration ("FAA") (*e.g.*, the Federal Air Surgeon, Manager, Aerospace Medical Certification Division, or a Regional Flight Surgeon) recommend that an airman medical certificate be suspended or revoked, for example, when an airman does not meet the medical certification standards; there is a reasonable basis to question his or her qualifications; an airman fails to provide requested medical information, or provides intentionally false or incorrect information in support of medical certification. FAA Order 2150.3B, Compliance Enforcement Program, at 5-15 to 5-16.
See generally http://www.faa.gov/licenses_certificates/medical_certification/.

5. *Hughes v. State* (Fla. 3d DCA 2006), *supra*, represents a particularly public deviation from airmen regulations, specifically the "eight hours from bottle-to-throttle" rule under 14 C.F.R. § 91.17(a), which prohibits any person from acting or attempting to act as a crewmember of a civil aircraft within eight hours after the

consumption of any alcoholic beverage. Aviation authorities consider controlled substance violations and alcohol offenses so serious that "airmen" under 14 C.F.R. § 61.15(e) must advise the Federal Aviation Administration within sixty days of any conviction for operating a motor vehicle while intoxicated. Meanwhile, unwittingly, some airmen have even run afoul of applicable regulations by consuming over-the-counter medicines that contain slight alcohol content within the relevant pre-flight time period. *See* Fed. Aviation Admin., FAA Compliance and Enforcement Program, Order 2150.3B (Oct. 1, 2007). *See also* Denise Urzendowski Scofield, *Knowing When to Say When: Federal Regulation of Alcohol Consumption by Air Pilots*, 57 J. AIR L. & COM. 937 (1992).

6. The decision of *Baker v. Fed. Aviation Admin.* (7th Cir. 1990), *infra*, forecast the end of the "Age 60 Rule"—a regulation of dubious foundation that arguably forced accomplished and compliant pilots to retire prematurely. More recently, *Emory v. United Air Lines, Inc.* (D.D.C. 2013) considered the Fair Treatment for Experienced Pilots Act of 2007 through which Congress repealed the Federal Aviation Administration's ("FAA") long-contested "Age 60 Rule" and extended the maximum age for piloting commercial flights by five years to 65. FTEPA marked a significant victory for opponents of the old regime. Under the Act's nonretroactivity provision pilots who had turned 60 prior to FTEPA's enactment date and did not qualify for either one of two narrowly drawn statutory exceptions would be denied the benefits of the Age 65 Rule and, as was often the case, terminated. The *Emory* court explained:

> First implemented in 1959, The Federal Aviation Administration's ("FAA") so-called Age 60 Rule barred any person 60 years of age or older from serving as a pilot in flights conducted under Part 121 of the Federal Aviation Regulations. *See* 14 C.F.R. § 121.383(c) (2007).
>
> Although the Rule survived nearly a half-century's worth of challenges in federal courts, institutional support for the age 60 ceiling dwindled. In 2006, the International Civil Aviation Organization ("ICAO") revised the maximum age from 60 to 65 for certain pilots in international operations. The FAA responded by establishing the Age 60 Aviation Rulemaking Committee ("ARC") to make recommendations regarding the adoption of the ICAO standard, but the "polarized" Commission, with its 17 members "representing pilot unions, airlines, the aeromedical community, and the FAA," agreed on just one thing: "Any change to the Age 60 Rule should be prospective."

> Undeterred by the false start, FAA soldiered on. In January 2007, the agency announced it would amend the Age 60 Rule. Congress, however, preempted this rulemaking with the passage of FTEPA in December 2007. Among other changes, FTEPA abrogated the Age 60 Rule as of the Act's December 13, 2007, enactment date and replaced it with a new ceiling colloquially referred to as the "Age 65 Rule." Crucially, Congress gave the Age 65 Rule entirely prospective effect with just two exceptions. As codified in the Act's "Nonretroactivity" provision, an over–60 pilot that served as a "required flight deck crew member" ("RFDCM") on December 13, 2007, or was subsequently hired as a new pilot without seniority, could return to piloting Part 121 flights until age 65.

The "Age 60 Rule" was first scrutinized in *Air Line Pilots Ass'n Int'l v. Quesada* (2d Cir. 1960). There, the Air Line Pilots Association ("ALPA") sued for an injunction preventing enforcement of the Age 60 Rule and for a judicial declaration that the rule was null and void. However, a federal appellate court deferred to and upheld the conclusions of Federal Aviation Administrator Elwood R. ("Pete") Quesada that "older pilots because of their seniority under collective bargaining agreements often fly the newest, largest, and fastest planes [and] that available medical studies show that sudden incapacitation due to heart attacks or strokes becomes more frequent as men approach age sixty and present medical knowledge is such that it is impossible to predict with accuracy those individuals most likely to suffer attacks." Accordingly, ALPA—which subsequently and until recently supported the Age 60 Rule for almost three decades—lost its case.

The Age 60 Rule may have been more a product of economics and politics than medicine and law. It arose out of a labor dispute at American Airlines in the 1950s. That era began the jet age as the Boeing 707 and DC-8 replaced piston-driven airplanes. To save training costs, American Airlines Chief Executive Officer C.R. Smith preferred employing young pilots, including Korean-War veterans with jet experience. American Airlines (like Western Airlines and TWA) unilaterally set 60 as the age at which pilots would be required to retire. *See*, *e.g. Western Air Lines, Inc. v. Criswell* (1985). In large measure, that decision led to a 21-day walkout at American Airlines. Ultimately, American Airlines acceded to an arbitrator's ruling that it allow its over-60 pilots to fly.

Not to be defeated, C.R. Smith turned to his friend, the war-time commander for President Dwight D. Eisenhower and the first FAA Administrator—Pete Quesada. By letter dated February 5, 1959, Smith asked Quesada to establish 60 as a federally-mandated retirement age for pilots. Without any Congressional or FAA hearing to debate the matter, the Age 60 Rule was codified. Later, in 1962, Queseda retired from the FAA and was elected to the Board of Directors of American Airlines.

Given this history, opponents of the Age 60 Rule contend that the regulation is arbitrary, promoting business not safety. After all, airline pilots must pass flight physicals administered by an FAA-licensed examiner to retain their commercial license. Pilots must also pass semiannual simulator training and flight checks. Critics of the Age 60 Rule therefore suggest that these battery of proficiency requirements show why a rigid mandatory retirement law is unnecessary and unsubstantiated.

7. "Anecdotal evidence" relied upon in *Baker v. Fed. Aviation Admin.* (7th Cir. 1990), *infra*, merits attention. A 747 captain who safely landed a jet whose cargo door blew open in mid-air (*In re Air Disaster near Honolulu, Hawaii on Feb. 24, 1989* (N.D. Cal. 1990)) was probative of the advantage of pilot experience. Just five months later, on July 19, 1989, Captain Al Haynes, a 57 years old commercial pilot radioed trouble:

> Confirm we have no hydraulic fluid, which means we have no elevator control, almost none, and very little aileron control. I have serious doubts about making the airport. Have you got someplace near there, that we might be able to ditch? Unless we get control of this airplane, we're going to put it down wherever it happens to be.

Engine number two of United Airlines Flight 232, a DC-10 traveling from Denver to Chicago, exploded in-flight. A fatigued fan disk separated from the engine housing and pierced two of the aircraft's three hydraulic lines. Captain Haynes and his crew improvised for more than 40 minutes to maneuver their doomed airplane down for an emergency landing in Sioux City, Iowa. They did so by alternating power between the two remaining engines. Ultimately the 296 passengers aboard United Flight 232 cart wheeled wing-over-wing across airport asphalt and Iowa cornfields. That 185 passengers survived was miraculous. *See In re Air Crash Disaster at Sioux City, Iowa, on July 19, 1989* (N.D. Ill. 1990).

Later in 1989, two pilots made rookie mistakes aboard USAir Flight 5050. *See* David Fields, *Airlines, Agency to Study Link between Crews, Crashes*, WASH. TIMES, Jan. 1, 1990, at A8. The Boeing 737 overshot the end of a runway at LaGuardia Airport and skidded into New York's East River. The airplane was split in two and two passengers died. The pilot of Flight 5050, who had been trained on small commuter airplanes, had logged less than 150 hours of flying time as an aircraft commander.

These accidents all happened in 1989, a year in which more commercial airplane accidents occurred than in the preceding twenty years.That fact, combined with the record-setting pace of new pilot hires in that year, prompted federal and industry officials to investigate whether there was a link between an increase in commercial airplane disasters and the influx of pilots with limited experience. *See also* Bob Moos, *Don't Jettison Pilot Experience*, J. COMMERCE 8A (1989).

In fact, no study undertaken in connection with the Age 60 Rule between 1978 and 2005—including the National Academy of Science's Institute of Medicine Study (1978), the National Institute of Health Aging Report (1981), the Golaszewski Flight Time Study (1983), and the Civil Aeromedical Institute Hilton Systems Study (1984)—conclusively established that airline piloting becomes critical at any given age. While tentatively suggesting that 63 might be a good cut-off for mandatory pilot retirement, the Hilton Systems Study concluded that there was "no support for the hypothesis that pilots of scheduled air carriers had increased accident rates as they neared the age of 60." (*See, e.g., http://www.age60rule.com/docs/data_quality_ltr.html.*) Courts themselves have noticed "serious flaws" in the data underlying the Age 60 Rule, including the Golaszewski Flight Time Study in which "the accident rate for all pilots under age sixty is significantly understated compared to the rate for older pilots, whose accident rate is overstated." *See Baker, supra.*

The Age 60 Rule may be as the President of the Southwest Airlines Pilots' Association once described it, "a solution in search of a problem." Its political and scientific legitimacy was questioned for nearly 50 years and its economic impact cut particularly deep as bankrupt and financially distressed airlines with expensive defined-benefit pensions need pilots to retire while older pilots need to work longer to make up lost retirement funds. Meanwhile, application of the Age 60 Rule to domestic pilots was inconsistent with the waivers the FAA grants for over-60 pilots of foreign airlines. *See, e.g., Avera v. United Air Lines, Inc.*, 2010 WL 419400 (N.D. Fla. 2010); *Brooks v. Air Line Pilots Ass'n, Int'l* (D.D.C. 2009); *Adams v. Fed. Aviation Admin.* (D.C. Cir. 2008). *See generally* Nicholas D. O'Conner, *Too Experienced for the Flight Deck? Why the Age 65 Rule is Not Enough*, 17 ELDER L.J. 375 (2010).

8. After September 11th, hasty conclusions of terrorist activity frequently attach to aviation accidents and incidents. For example, post-9/11 airmen violations of operational regulations sometimes take on national security implications that go beyond aviation safety and the licensure of aviation professionals as when, in October 2009, Northwest Airlines Flight 188, an A320 with 144 passengers bound from San Diego to Minneapolis, overshot its destination by about 150 miles; the pilots were out of radio contact for more than an hour. The pilots initially claimed to have lost situational awareness because they were preoccupied with their laptop computers and/or immersed in conversation about airline policy. *See, e.g.*, Matthew L. Wald, *Flight Error on Northwest is the Focus on an Inquiry*, N.Y. TIMES, Oct. 23, 2009, at A19. Mindful of the September 11 hijackings, the Air National Guard had fighter jets on alert at two locations for an intercept mission. *E.g.*, Steve Karnowski, *Errant NWA Pilots Settle: Two Who Overshot MSP May Be Able to Fly in Future*, ST. PAUL PIONEER PRESS, Mar. 16, 2010, at A.13.

9. *United States v. Sabretech, Inc.* (11th Cir. 2001) represents a meeting point of aviation law, labor law, and criminal law (see also Chapter 5, *infra*), and highlights a growing trend by carriers to outsource responsibility for aircraft

maintenance, repair, and overhaul ("MRO"), *inter alia*. Should aviation accidents caused by the negligence of airline employees—or independent contractors—be criminalized? *See generally* Richard M. Dunn et al., *Criminalization in Aviation*, 38 SPG-BRIEF 10 (2009); Robert A. Brazener, Annotation, *Liability for Alleged Negligence of Independent Servicer or Repairer of Aircraft*, 41 A.L.R.3d 1320 (1972 & 2005 Supp.); L. Ronald Jorgensen, *The Defense of Aviation Mechanics and Repair Facilities from Enforcement Actions of the Federal Aviation Administration*, 54 J. AIR L. & COM. 349 (1988). *See http://www.airdisaster.com/reports/ntsb/AAR97-06.pdf* ("Aircraft Accident Report").

10. *Jifry v. Fed. Aviation Admin.* (D.C. Cir. 2004), and *Goodwin v. Ridge* (E.D. Ark. 2005), *supra*, center on core constitutional principles of due process of the law and the right to be free from discrimination on the basis of race. Do these decisions represent principled authorities that are owed deference in similar subsequent litigation under the rule of *stare decisis*? Or, are these decisions contextual and limited by the unique circumstances of September 11? *See, e.g.*, Linda L. Lane, *The Discoverability of Sensitive Security Information in Aviation Litigation*, 71 J. AIR L. & COM. 427 (2006); Justin Florence, Note, *Making the No Fly List Fly: A Due Process Model for Terrorist Watchlists*, 115 YALE L.J. 2148 (2006).

PROBLEM

On September 11, 2001, terrorists breached the nation's civil air transportation system. Masquerading as civilian air travelers, they carried box cutter knives aboard commercial airplanes without detection by airport security. They used the knives to hijack four commercial planes, three of which they managed to convert into guided missiles to attack New York City and Washington, D.C.

Two months later, on November 19, 2001, Congress enacted the Aviation and Transportation Security Act ("ATSA"), a legislative initiative designed to strengthen national security through the federalization of the civil transportation system. The cornerstone of the ATSA was the creation of the Transportation Security Administration ("TSA"), a federal agency charged with overseeing every aspect of civil transportation security in this country.

The most essential aspect of civil transportation security addressed by the ATSA, and for which TSA is accountable, is improving airport security to prevent a reprise of the tragic events of September 11, 2001. To that end, Congress directed TSA to recruit, employ, and train a sufficient number of federal airport security screeners to screen every passenger and all property aboard airplanes departing from United States airports within one year of the ATSA's passage.

To satisfy the airport security screening benchmarks established by the new law, TSA launched a "dynamic, high-pressure roll-out" of federally employed airport screeners in airports throughout the country. The TSA contracted a human resource services provider to aid in employee recruitment, which between March and November 2002 processed 2,198,505 on-line applications and assessed some 340,000 eligible candidates for screening positions. This resulted in the hiring of more than 62,000 screening personnel by TSA between April and December 2002. As a consequence of what must have been either haphazard or ill-planned deployment of personnel, approximately 400 airports were equipped with security screening staffs that were either too large so as to be unwieldy, or too small so as to be inadequate.

TSA therefore undertook to "right-size" the screener workforce in early 2003. Simultaneous to the right-sizing efforts, TSA was informed that it had to reduce its screening workforce by approximately ten percent due to budget constraints. Among the eight-hundred airport screeners laid off was an airport lead security screener at the Norfolk International Airport in Norfolk, Virginia from August 19, 2002 until his termination. He was a veteran of the United States Marine Corps, from which he received an honorable discharge after having served in Vietnam. He subsequently served in the Marine Corp Reserves for twelve years.

Upon his termination, the former lead security screener brought suit for violation of various provisions of the ATSA, the Veterans' Preference Act of 1944, the Administrative Procedure Act, and the United States Constitution. Defendant has filed a Motion to Dismiss or, in the Alternative, a Motion for Summary Judgment. How should the court rule? *See Springs v. Stone* (E.D. Va. 2005). Consider that, with respect to "private" airport security companies:

- Up to 80% of security workers were foreign nationals, in some cases even illegal aliens, and most of the companies were foreign owned.

- There were long-standing problems of employee security and the adequacy of background checks.

- Federal rules only required screeners to have twelve hours of classroom training, much of which was phony or faked, with spot tests showing that as many as 35% were not able to pass a "basic skills test."

- Tests revealed that "20 percent of the screeners accounted for 80 percent of the mistakes," but the planned test to screen screeners "was never put to use" by the FAA.

- Federal tests found that screeners manning carry-on baggage X-ray machines routinely missed one in five "obvious images of bombs or guns," and in the weeks following September 11, passengers made it through security with loaded guns, stun guns, knives, and Mace.

- The screening stations were manned by low-paid employees with no benefits and exceptionally high turnover rates.

- The companies became a "synonym for failure," impervious to substantive improvement and lacking managerial competence, without even a modicum of appreciation for public relations concerns.

In short, the baggage security system was run by companies that were "clueless" with respect to providing security against real terrorists, had been hired by airlines looking for the lowest price, and were regulated by government agencies that had only the most indirect influence and an indifferent sense of responsibility.

See also Phillip A. Karber, *Re-Constructing Global Aviation in an Era of the Civil Aircraft as a Weapon of Destruction*, 25 HARV. J.L. & PUB. POL'Y 781, 800-01 (2002).

B. LABOR RELATIONS— COLLECTIVE BARGAINING AND THE RAILWAY LABOR ACT

Crudely stated, airmen are employees and contractors who represent business costs. How carriers manage these costs and their relationships with labor is illustrated by the cases in this section and framed by the discussion of airline bankruptcies discussed in Chapter 3, Part B, *supra*. Consider that,

> [w]hile the bankruptcies of major competitors opened opportunities for Southwest Airlines, it also caused problems between the airline and its unions.
>
> The issue: Southwest saw its labor advantage erode as Delta Air Lines, United Airlines, American Airlines, US Airways and Northwest Airlines cut the wages and benefits of their employees and boosted productivity in bankruptcy court contracts.
>
> The result: Southwest unions have had to wait extraordinarily long times to gain new deals with the Dallas-based carrier. That wait has caused hard feelings and claims that Southwest management may have lost that loving feeling the company was built on.
>
> "We don't have that culture anymore. It's gone," said Greg Puriski, president of the union local that represents ramp workers. "I think we've pretty much accepted that it's

> gone, and that's not ever going to come back to the way it was."
>
> "The amount of good will on the part of the pilot group is much lower than I believe that it's ever been at Southwest Airlines," said Paul Jackson, president of the pilots union. "Again, can you point it at a particular executive? No. Can you point at a particular one event? No. It's an accumulation of blows."

Terry Maxon, *Southwest Airlines, Unions Struggle toward New Deals*, DALLAS MORNING NEWS, July 9, 2015, *http://www.dallasnews.com/business/airline-industry/20150708-southwest-airlines-unions-struggle-toward-new-deals.ece*.

Indeed, labor and employment is a hot button issue, raising important consumer protection and safety questions that implicate the welfare of airline passengers and the national commercial aviation system. The initial case below, *Baker v. Fed. Aviation Admin.*, presents what happens when an unusual rule arises from business rather than legal or policy considerations. (*See* Note 6, *infra.*) *Goodwin v. Ridge* and *Hawaiian Airlines v. Norris*, meanwhile, detail the intricate system by which employment discrimination and labor disputes are mediated and resolved under the Railway Labor Act. Finally, *Air Line Pilots Ass'n v. Eastern Air Lines* is an important decision that spotlights the key and elaborate procedural and substantive features of airline collective bargaining and the influence of bankruptcy law (*see* Chapter 3, Part B, *supra*) on those processes.

BAKER v. FED. AVIATION ADMIN.
917 F.2d 318 (7th Cir. 1990)

CUDAHY, Circuit Judge.

In 1988, this court decided *Aman v. Fed. Aviation Admin.* (7th Cir. 1988) ("*Aman I*"), in which current and former airline captains sought review under 49 U.S.C. § 1486(a) of a Federal Aviation Administration ("FAA") order denying a petition for exemptions from Federal Aviation Administration ("FAA") regulation § 121.383(c) ("age sixty rule"). The age sixty rule prohibits flights under Part 121 of FAA regulations, including commercial flights of aircraft seating more than thirty passengers, from taking off under the command of pilots age sixty or older. While the FAA is empowered to grant exemptions to this rule if it "finds that such action would be in the public interest," *see* 49 U.S.C. § 1421(c) (the public interest standard), no exemptions have ever been granted.

After recounting the age sixty rule's tortured thirty year history and establishing the appropriate "substantial evidence" standard of review, this court in *Aman I* carefully demarcated petitioners' two claims. The first was that pilots, age sixty or older, meeting petitioners' proposed battery of physical and psychological tests (the protocol), were no more likely to cause accidents due to sudden incapacitation or undetected deterioration of piloting skills than other pilots. The FAA rejected this claim, finding that it was not in the public interest to grant exemptions when petitioners' protocol did not surely reduce all incremental risks associated with the aging process. Although this court noted that it might well have concluded otherwise as a matter of first impression, it held that substantial evidence supported the FAA's finding.

Petitioners' second claim was that the flying experience gained by allowing pilots age sixty and older to fly offset any increased risk of accident due to sudden incapacitation or skill deterioration, and that granting limited exemptions effectively produced a net increase or, at least, no net decline in safety. The FAA summarily rejected this claim. Unsatisfied with the agency's cursory treatment, this court vacated the FAA order and remanded the matter to the agency for further proceedings.

On remand, the FAA again refused to grant exemptions, and an order to that effect is presently before us for review. After considering the FAA's new order and both parties' somewhat flawed evidence, we cannot justify a conclusion that, on average, experience sufficiently offsets possible age-related impairment of health or skills to clearly guarantee a net constancy or increase in safety. Accordingly, we affirm.

* * *

While substantial evidence must support the FAA's decision, petitioners have the burden of showing that circumstances justify exemptions from the age sixty rule, especially given the FAA's discretionary authority to act in this area. It is a heavy burden here involving obviously daunting problems of public safety. Age discrimination may form a dimension of the issue, but safety is the dominant and controlling consideration. The fact that it is apparently very difficult to demonstrate any clear conclusion with respect to the trade-off between experience and possible age-related impairment makes the task extremely onerous for the bearer of the burden of persuasion.

Petitioners have presented anecdotal evidence of superannuated pilots performing heroic deeds. Consider, for example, Captain David Cronin, who at age 59, on his second to last scheduled flight, heroically landed a Boeing 747 en route from Honolulu, Hawaii to Auckland, New Zealand after a forward cargo door blew open 17 minutes after take-off, opening a huge hole in the side of the plane. After two of the plane's four engines became disabled, Captain Cronin consulted emergency operating procedures which directed him to dive, reduce speed and drop the landing gear. However, 38 years of experience told him that, if that course were followed, the plane would lose too much altitude given its weight and multiple emergency situation. Captain Cronin instead operated many of the controls manually, constantly readjusting his speed and altitude calculations. With the exception of the nine passengers killed when the cargo door blew off, Cronin saved the lives of all passengers and crew aboard, safely landing the disabled plane at a much higher than normal speed.

In an appropriate context, we might give considerably more weight to the "anecdotal" evidence of pilots in their late fifties immediately before retirement performing amazing feats of airmanship than presumably would the FAA. As noted at oral argument, were the passengers of Flight 811 asked whether their Captain Cronin should be permitted to continue flying beyond the mandatory retirement age of sixty, few could doubt their answer. Nor are we in a position to say they would be incorrect. In the case before us, however, it is apparently not pilots who have performed aeronautical miracles who have sought exemptions, and we need not consider the arguable entitlement of such "special" pilots to exemptions from the age sixty rule.

While petitioners have thus made some suggestive anecdotal showings and presented impressive expert opinion evidence, they have been unable to develop a persuasive statistical record comparing average risks for pilots in various relevant age categories. Petitioners, relying on figures from the National Transportation Safety Board, presented evidence that pilots age sixty and older had a lower accident rate per 1,000 pilots than pilots in other age groups.

This evidence, however, failed to account for exposure to risk in terms of hours of flight time. Thus, a pilot who had flown only a relatively few hours in a year and therefore incurred only a reduced risk of accident would carry the same weight as a pilot who flew many hundreds of hours with their greater attendant risks. Such a study is, of course, of questionable value. In addition, no analysis indicated whether the difference in accident experience by age group was statistically significant, a sort of failure specifically criticized in *Aman I.* Petitioners also presented evidence that allowing pilots, sixty or older, to fly would increase crew experience on the average, but failed to show with any rigor that there was a significant lack of pilot experience in need of correction.

This is not to say that the FAA's evidence was any more persuasive. The agency relied heavily on an accident experience report by age category referred to as the Flight Time Study. Like petitioners' studies this report has serious flaws. Perhaps the Flight Time Study's greatest failing is that the data for pilots under age sixty include millions of relatively safe air carrier miles flown, miles which because of the age sixty rule were unavailable to pilots over sixty. In calculating the accident rate for pilots sixty and older, the Flight Time Study divides the number of general aviation accidents by general aviation flight time, the only category open to this group. But for pilots under age sixty, the study divides the number of general aviation accidents by general aviation flight time and, in addition, air carrier operations flight time.

Because miles flown in air carrier operations are nearly accident free, and millions of these extra miles are included in the figures for younger pilots but not for older ones, the accident rate for all pilots under age sixty is significantly understated compared to the rate for older pilots, whose accident rate is overstated. Indeed, looking at the Flight Time Study's chart of accident risk for Class I (airline transport) and Class II (commercial) pilots with greater than 5,000 hours total flight time, the jump in accidents at age sixty to sixty-nine from age fifty to fifty-nine simply looks too large to be credible. Even without correcting the Flight Time Study for this disparity in types of current flight hours, the FAA's own study on its face may in some aspects be construed to support the petitioners' claims, the raw data supporting a number of different possible conclusions.

Consider, for example, the data showing accident rates as a function of both total and recent flight time for Class III pilots (general aviation and student). These data indicate that pilots age 60-69 (even 70 and over) with more than 1,000 hours total flight time and more than 50 hours recent flight time apparently have two of the lowest accident rates of any age groups of pilots in Class III having various indicated combinations of total and recent flight time. These comparisons apply, of course, even with respect to younger pilots in their thirties and forties, whose safety qualifications are generally unquestioned. More than 1000 hours total flight time and more than 50 hours recent flight time might be a telling statistic if the FAA could, for example, condition exemptions on total and recent flight time. Safety would be advanced, presumably, if the FAA required pilots to have at least a total of 1,000 flight hours and at least 50 recent flight hours as a condition for exemption.

Another arguable flaw in the Flight Time Study is that all pilots in a ten-year age cohort are combined into a single statistic. Thus, a single point represents pilots aged sixty to sixty-nine. Presumably, more exemptions from the age sixty rule would likely be granted to pilots under, say, sixty-five than pilots over that age. Therefore, the cumulation of accidents caused by pilots in their late sixties with accidents caused by pilots in their early sixties may as a practical matter tend to skew the Study.

The FAA also presented evidence of automobile traffic accidents and fatalities related to age. The connection between automobile drivers and pilots itself seems tenuous given the pilots' training, demonstrated proficiency, medical fitness, etc. Some of the FAA's evidence does not reflect "exposure" and some of it attempts to relate the nonparallel categories of automobile fatalities and aircraft accidents. Because elderly people seem more likely to die as a result of traffic accidents than younger people, the probative value of this latter showing is diminished.

Along with a directive for a more complete consideration of petitioners' second claim on remand, the FAA was also requested to explain how it could rationally grant exemptions to younger pilots who had suffered from alcohol abuse, heart conditions and the like but not grant exemptions to apparently healthy and proficient pilots over age sixty.The agency's justification was that, where particular and identifiable health problems are shown, specific medical tests may be conducted to indicate whether the pilot in question can continue to perform. On the other hand, "[a]ssessing the risks associated with determining which pilots may fly beyond age 60 concerns detrimental conditions which are unknown." Exactly how this distinction applies as a practical matter is not entirely clear to us, but neither have the petitioners been able to demonstrate its invalidity either theoretically or practically. Nor have petitioners apparently yet been able to present to the FAA a totally reliable test or group of tests which would reveal with certainty any general deterioration of piloting skills associated with advancing age. For present purposes, we will not require more of the FAA with respect to the consistency of restoring stricken younger pilots to duty while barring oldsters whose records are impeccable.

* * *

Admittedly, petitioners in this case face a Catch-22: from one perspective they cannot get exemptions until they show they can fly large passenger aircraft safely, and they cannot show they can fly such planes safely until they get exemptions. Thus, a valid statistical demonstration of comparative safety records by age seems difficult to obtain unless all age groups are engaged in the same kinds of flying. Since the age sixty and over group may not pilot large passenger transport aircraft, statistical comparisons are suspect.

Nevertheless, it was the petitioners' burden to present persuasive evidence that granting exemptions would not impair safety. While we have seen no compelling evidence that granting exemptions would increase the risk of accident, neither have we seen strong evidence that the experience of the 60-and-over pilot clearly overbears the danger of deterioration of piloting skills (or of sudden incapacitation) associated with the aging process. Where crucial issues of public safety are at stake, we would look for such a showing. Were the FAA to grant exemptions, it (and we) would no doubt be better able to resolve the question before us, but, absent the requisite compelling evidence, we must defer in these circumstances to the expert agency.

We believe the agency's order is supported by substantial, albeit certainly not compelling, evidence. We reach this conclusion because of the obvious difficulty in attempting to balance on a statistical basis experience against reliable indicators of good health and ability to perform as age advances. Certainly the record abounds with testimonials by experts in both flying and medicine to the experience and judgment of the older aviator and the feasibility of assuring the good health and performance of this kind of pilot through frequent and sophisticated testing. We are certainly not in a position to say that the numerous supporters of the petitioners' case are wrong. And it is obvious that the FAA must continue and must enhance its efforts to accommodate their points of view. At this time, however, we are not prepared to overrule the agency in a matter of such immense sensitivity as this one. The FAA should not take this as a signal that the age sixty rule is sacrosanct and untouchable. Obviously, there is a great body of opinion that the time has come to move on. The agency must give serious attention to this opinion. Accordingly, the order of the Federal Aviation Administration is affirmed.

WILL, Senior District Judge, dissenting.

This court, in *Aman I*, reviewed the age 60 rule's "tortured history," majority established the appropriate "substantial evidence" standard of review, noted that while the FAA is theoretically empowered to grant exemptions from the rule, none has ever been granted, vacated the FAA's order and remanded the case to the agency for further proceedings and the presentation of further evidence that no airline pilot older than age 59, regardless of physical condition and experience, is qualified to fly a plane seating more than thirty passengers.

When the FAA adopted its age 60 and out rule some thirty-one years ago, in 1959, it justified the rule by stating

> that there is a progressive deterioration of certain important physiological and psychological functions with age, that significant medical defects attributable to the degenerative process occur at an increasing rate as age increases, and that sudden incapacity due to such medical defects becomes significantly more frequent in any group reaching age 60, and that such incapacity, due primarily to heart attacks and strokes, cannot be predicted accurately as to any specific individual on the basis of presently available scientific tests and criteria [so that] any attempt to be selective in predicting which individuals are likely to suffer an incapacitating attack would be futile under the circumstances and would not be medically sound.

24 Fed. Reg. 9767 (Dec. 5, 1959). At the same time, the FAA also found that:

> Other factors, even less susceptible to precise measurement [also] must be considered. These relate to loss of ability to perform highly skilled tasks rapidly, to resist fatigue, to maintain physical stamina, to perform, effectively in a complex and stressful environment, to apply experience, judgment and reasoning rapidly to new, changing and emergency situations, and to learn new techniques, skills and procedures. The progressive loss of these abilities ... even though they may be significant in themselves prior to age 60 ... assume greater significance at the older ages when coupled with medical defects leading to increased risk of sudden incapacitation.

Since 1959, numerous pilots, approaching or having celebrated their sixtieth birthdays, have petitioned for individual exemptions from the FAA's rigid enforcement of its age 60 and out rule. The agency, however, has never granted an exemption-to anyone, regardless of his or her physical qualifications or experience. Pilots with tens of thousands of hours of flight time and flawless records, and who pass every physical test with flying colors, suddenly are grounded on their sixtieth birthdays, even though the day before they were flying, without restrictions, and were acknowledged to be qualified and, ironically, are still deemed qualified to pilot planes with thirty passengers or less.

* * *

The FAA actually admits to a policy of uniformly denying all petitions for exemptions from the age 60 rule. It's not that the FAA pretends that no person over the age of 59 could ever safely pilot a Part 121 flight. In fact, the agency concedes that some over-59 captains would do just fine. Then why not grant exemptions to those pilots? Why does the FAA persist in refusing ever to exempt any pilot, no matter how able, from its 60 and out rule? And why does it refuse to issue meaningful standards and criteria for granting at least some exemptions? Because, says the FAA, although many pilots 60 and over would make safe captains, there is simply no way to tell the safe ones from the dangerous ones in advance.

In support of this position, the FAA advances, today, in 1990, the same kinds of justifications it originally offered thirty-one years ago, in 1959. And in 1990, just as in 1959, these justifications are of two types. The first starts from the proposition that "some psychomotor, emotional, intellectual and physical attributes necessary for enhanced flight crew performance deteriorate with age," resulting in a "sharp decline in physical and cognitive performance after age 60"; adds that there is no reliable way of measuring (or even necessarily detecting) the extent of an aging pilot's deterioration; and concludes that it is not scientifically possible to screen out safe 60-year-old pilots from dangerous ones without actually putting them up in the skies and letting them fly.

The FAA's second longstanding justification begins with the observation that at age 60 skills are not only deteriorating but beginning to do so at an increasing and increasingly unpredictable rate; adds that the dangers of their deteriorating to the point of sudden incapacitation (in flight, presumably) is significantly greater at age 60 and beyond than it was before; and finishes, again, with the assertion that there is no reliable way to tell a safe 60-year-old pilot, who won't suddenly collapse in flight, from a dangerous one, who will. "The aging process is largely unpredictable, and generally is not measurable. [T]here are no generally applicable medical tests that can, at this time, adequately determine which individual pilots are subject to incapacitation secondary to either acute cardiovascular or neurological events or to more subtle conditions related to cognitive functioning."

* * *

Two years ago, in *Aman I, supra*, the FAA, advancing both of its customary justifications, defended its original denial of many of the same petitions that are before us again on this appeal. At that time, this court partially upheld the logic of the FAA's customary justifications, finding what the FAA itself has repeatedly held in connection with every request for an exemption since 1959, *i.e.*, "substantial evidence [to] support[ ] ... rejection of the contention that the petitioners' protocol, combined with existing methods of operational testing, would screen out all increased risks of incapacitation or undetected skill deterioration among pilots older than sixty." The *Aman I* panel, however, ultimately vacated the FAA's denial and remanded for further proceedings, concluding that the FAA had "failed to set forth a sufficient factual or legal basis for its rejection of the petitioners' claim that older pilots' edge in experience offsets any undetected physical losses."

It is unclear to me just what the panel in *Aman I* meant for the FAA to do on remand. Given the number and variety of tests that are available and commonly used to measure the physical and cognitive powers of pilots-flight simulator tests, vision and depth perception tests, hearing tests, stress tests, blood tests, psychological workups, X-rays, angiograms and EKGs—I find it difficult to believe that there are skills or physical or cognitive abilities which the FAA can identify as necessary for safe flying but for which it either cannot or does not reliably test all pilots, including 60-year-olds and regardless of whether they pilot flights with more than thirty passengers or other flights with fewer passengers.

If it is true, however, that physical deterioration can't be tested and measured accurately, as the panel in *Aman I* found "substantial evidence" to show, then it baffles me how the FAA, on remand, was supposed to reconsider the relationship between physical skills and abilities, on the one hand, and experience on the other. For whether, if as a pilot grows older, experience lends an edge which offsets waning skills and abilities, necessarily depends on at least two things: (1) how much experience the pilot has and (2) how severely physical skills and abilities have "deteriorated." And if one of those things can't be reliably measured for risk, or even spotted—"[A] substantial body of medical opinion continues 'to doubt the feasibility'" of measuring the "incremental risk associated with ... undetected deterioration of skills among pilots over sixty,"—then balancing an intangible like experience against undetectable or unmeasurable deterioration would be some trick. The same problem, of course, must have faced the FAA on remand in trying to weigh the benefits of experience against its asserted concern about the allegedly unpredictable risks of "sudden incapacitation."

The more serious difficulty, however, with the FAA's continuing reliance on "sudden incapacitation"— the specter of a pilot in the cockpit, of no matter what age, suddenly stricken by a heart attack or a stroke—hasn't much to do with whether the incapacitated pilot, suddenly stricken, could by dint of experience avert a crash. At that point, the safety net obviously is not experience but the presence of one or two other qualified pilots in the cockpit. Instead, the troubling problem with the FAA's "sudden incapacitation" justification is its premise. The panel in *Aman I* found substantial evidence to support the FAA's conclusion that current medical science cannot determine which pilots over 60 will be most vulnerable to sudden and incapacitating disability.

But that should have been a follow-up inquiry, not the first one. The first inquiry should be whether there is substantial evidence, current and valid in 1990, to support the proposition that all pilots, age 60 and older, are significantly more prone to sudden medical catastrophe than other pilots. For the age 60 and out rule makes sense only if it screens for risks that are significantly higher for all 60-year-olds than for 30, 40 or 50-year-olds. Otherwise, the rule is simply an arbitrary, overly broad and outmoded presumption, smelling of age discrimination, about infirmities which do not uniformly afflict all pilots over 60 and should not be assumed to.

The panel in *Aman I* also remanded with instructions to the FAA to "make sense" of its increasing willingness to issue "special certificates" to younger pilots with records of heart disease, drug abuse and alcoholism—which conditions, like aging, can be progressive—in the face of its stubborn refusal ever to grant exemptions from the age 60 rule. In response, the FAA has now explained that "present tests can predict the expected course of a known medical deficiency" such as heart disease or alcoholism "with sufficient accuracy to allow valid, individualized judgments" but that "the same accuracy is not possible when assessing the decrements associated with the aging process."

The FAA, however, has not offered any evidence to support this distinction between the special certificates it grants to younger pilots and its refusal even to promulgate meaningful regulations and criteria for age exemptions for older pilots, much less to grant an age exemption to an older pilot. And there is no citation, either in the FAA's brief or its latest order, for the proposition that the symptoms of alcoholism, drug abuse and heart disease can be monitored more closely and reliably than the "decrements" of aging. We defer to agency expertise, where expertise has been demonstrated, but "deference should not be equated with a license to issue inconsistent determinations." The pilots have plausibly alleged that the FAA's distinctions and exemption practices are inconsistent. The FAA has only answered with unsupported and unconvincing assertions.

The majority acknowledges that "exactly how [the FAA's asserted] distinction [between aging and other conditions] applies as a practical matter is not entirely clear to us," but concludes that for present purposes, it will not require more of the FAA with respect to the consistency of restoring stricken younger (59 and under) pilots (suffering from alcohol abuse, drug abuse, heart conditions) to duty while grounding other pilots, 60 and over, whose records and physical condition are, by contrast, impeccable.

* * *

The FAA's record here is more than just "disappointing." The agency has relied on a seriously flawed Flight Time study even though, as the majority points out, "various experts, even some from the FAA, state that the study should not be relied on as determinative-or even probative on the question of the continued validity of the age sixty rule." In addition, as the majority also recognizes, "the FAA's own study on its face may in some aspects be construed to support the petitioners' claims." The FAA has also relied on evidence of automobile traffic accidents involving fatalities as related to age. But again, as the majority points out, "The connection between automobile drivers and pilots itself seems tenuous given the pilots' training, demonstrated proficiency, medical fitness, etc." and "attempts to relate nonparallel categories of automobile fatalities with aircraft accidents" does not reflect "exposure."

The petitioners, as the majority also concedes, face a Catch-22, if the FAA and this court require them to prove, with statistics that reflect actual flight time in large passenger transport planes with more than thirty passengers, that they can fly those planes as safely as pilots who are not yet 60. For until at least one exemption has been granted, none of the petitioners are eligible to pilot such flights and consequently no such statistics can be compiled. It is possible that statistics might be available for petitioners' flight time in the same large passenger aircraft but carrying thirty passengers or less or cargo. If such statistics are available, they have not been referred to by the FAA or the pilots.

In lieu of statistics, petitioners have presented impressive evidence of pilots on the brink of age 60 performing heroic deeds and saving lives where less experienced pilots might have failed. They have also presented what the majority concedes is "impressive expert opinion evidence" that at least some experienced pilots over age 60 are qualified to fly large commercial aircraft and may be even better qualified than younger, less experienced pilots. And, relying on figures from the National Transportation Safety Board, they have presented evidence that licensed pilots age 60 and older show a lower accident rate per 1,000 pilots than pilots in other age groups, although those statistics do not reflect the number of hours flown by members of each age group and we do not know, therefore, whether pilots age 60 and over fly more or fewer hours per year than pilots in other age groups.

The majority concludes, on the basis of the foregoing, that the FAA has presented "substantial evidence" in support of an absolute 60 and out rule, although it admits that it has seen "no compelling evidence that granting exemptions would increase the risk of accident ..." The majority also concludes that it has seen "no strong evidence that the experience of the 60-and-over pilot clearly overbears the danger of deterioration of piloting skills (or of sudden incapacitation) associated with the aging process."

Since the FAA has refused as a matter of policy to grant any exemptions, what the FAA and the majority are holding, in effect, is that every airline pilot, on his or her 60th birthday, and regardless of physical condition or experience, becomes a significantly greater safety hazard than before, even though, just one day before, he or she was FAA certified, qualified and safe. The evidence in this case does not warrant that conclusion. Nor does everyday, ordinary good old common sense.

* * *

Rather than again urging the FAA to recognize the need for keeping up with advanced technologies and accommodating other points of view, I would vacate the FAA's latest order and remand for action on three fronts.

I would remand, first, for consideration of the adoption of regulations establishing ascertainable and meaningful standards to govern the granting of at least some exemptions to the age 60 rule. The FAA's present regulations—which dangle the possibility of an exemption to a pilot who can show "why the exemption would not adversely affect safety" or why, at least, it "would provide a level of safety equal to that provided by the rule," 14 C.F.R. § 11.25(5)—do not sufficiently guide the agency in exercising its discretion and do not begin to provide adequate notice to pilots about the kind of showing that would justify an exemption. Moreover, in light of the agency's policy of never granting age 60 exemptions, its present regulations are a fraud.

I would also remand for a showing, by current and substantial evidence, that all pilots age 60 and over are significantly more prone to "sudden incapacitation" than all pilots under 60. The agency should re-examine the relevant data and articulate a satisfactory explanation, rationally connected to the facts, for its ongoing reliance on "sudden incapacitation" and for drawing a line at age 60. Finally, I would remand, yet again, for a reasoned and full explanation for treating requests for special medical certificates under 14 C.F.R. § 67.19 differently than petitions for exemptions from the age 60 and out rule. And in that connection, I would require the FAA to consider the possibility that obligating pilots 60 and older to undergo more frequent medical and skills examinations than other pilots—a technique the agency already uses to monitor the condition of pilots who have been granted "special issuances" under 14 C.F.R. § 67.19—might provide enough accurate and up-to-the-minute information about a pilot's health and skills to enable the agency to make individualized determinations about the risks of letting any particular captain, 60 or older, pilot a Part 121 flight, rather than arbitrarily and capriciously denying exemptions to all.

GOODWIN v. RIDGE

2005 WL 2176936 (E.D. Ark. 2005)

HOLMES, J.

This is an employment discrimination case. Kenny E. Goodwin, an African American male, brought a race discrimination claim pursuant to 42 U.S.C. § 2000e *et seq*. (Title VII of the Civil Rights Act of 1964) against Thomas J. Ridge in his official capacity as Secretary of the United States Department of Homeland Security. The defendant has moved for summary judgment. For the reasons stated below, this motion is granted.

I.

Following the terrorist attacks of September 11, 2001, Congress passed the Aviation and Transportation Security Act ("ATSA") and created the Transportation Security Administration ("TSA") to protect our nation's civil air transportation system. Section 110 of the ATSA requires the TSA to recruit and hire federal employees to provide security screening of passengers and cargo at commercial airports. Before the ATSA was passed, private firms performed airport security screening functions. Goodwin was employed by one of these private firms, Wackenhut, as an airport screener at the Little Rock National Airport. After the ATSA was enacted the TSA began the federalization process for airport security personnel.

To ensure the qualifications of security screeners, all applicants were required to meet specific job requirements and pass a series of tests. The minimum requirements were (1) a high school diploma, a GED, or equivalent, or (2) one year of work experience performing security work or as an aviation screener or x-ray technician. Applicants meeting these requirements were then required to complete an assessment process successfully.

In the assessment process, job candidates first took Phase I, a battery of computerized tests. Candidates who passed Phase I moved to Phase II, which consisted of a structured interview, physical performance tests, medical evaluations, and a background check. When candidates completed each portion of the assessment, the tester for that station initialed or checked off that the candidate had been to the station. These checklists did not indicate whether the candidate passed or failed that portion of the assessment.

All screener candidates were required to pass two physical performance tests, a luggage/box-lift test and a baggage-search test, which were separate and independent from any medical evaluations. Both physical performance tests were pass/fail tests intended to measure candidates' abilities to perform essential job functions. TSA standardized these tests by providing scripts for testers to use when giving instructions to candidates and conducting the tests. One of the physical performance tests, the baggage-search test, required candidates to put their hands in a covered box, identify objects by feeling them, and indicate the identified items on a preprinted answer sheet by circling them. The covered box contained 5 items, and the answer sheet listed 20 items. To pass the test, candidates had to correctly identify 4 of the 5 items in the box. All applicants were provided with the same instructions and completed the tests in the same exact manner.

Each candidate was given only one chance to take the physical performance portion of the assessment. Those who failed one or both of the physical performance tests were disqualified from consideration as a screener, and candidates were not informed which of the two tests they failed. None of the candidates was allowed to repeat these tests, and no candidate who failed either of the two physical performance tests was hired. TSA policy allows disqualified candidates to retest for a position after six months, however, if a vacancy is available.

In contrast, candidates who did not meet TSA's medical standards for vision and hearing were told what standards they did not meet and were allowed to attempt to obtain medical clearance by going to a private physician. Any applicant who passed both physical performance tests but did not demonstrate compliance with TSA medical standards at the assessment center could later submit documentation from a personal physician or specialist. Medical documentation demonstrating that a candidate satisfied TSA's medical standards was considered, and some applicants who had failed the medical evaluation at the assessment center were later hired after submitting such documentation.

Goodwin applied for a TSA position and attended a screener assessment. He passed Phase I and the structured interview component of Phase II but failed the baggage-search test in the physical performance portion of Phase II because he correctly identified only three items on the answer sheet. Goodwin was not hired as a TSA screener.

The defendant asserts that Goodwin was not hired because he failed the baggage-search test. Goodwin admits that he failed the baggage-search test, that none of the applicants at the assessment center was allowed to retake this test, and that no applicant who failed this test was hired by TSA as a screener. Goodwin argues, however, that he failed the baggage-search test because he was not wearing his eyeglasses and could not see the answer sheet. Goodwin further contends that he was not allowed to retake the baggage search test because of his race and that he was therefore not selected as a TSA screener due to racial discrimination.

* * *

Because there is no direct evidence of discriminatory intent, Goodwin's failure-to-hire claim is analyzed under the burden-shifting framework set out in *McDonnell Douglas Corp. v. Green* (1973), which means that a plaintiff typically must demonstrate the following four elements: (1) that he belonged to a protected class, (2) that he applied and met the minimum qualifications for the job, (3) that he was rejected, and (4) that after rejecting Goodwin the employer continued to seek applicants with Goodwin's qualifications.

The Supreme Court has recognized, however, that facts vary in Title VII cases and the *prima facie* proof required of a plaintiff may differ according to the situation. Accordingly, federal courts in some cases have held that, as an alternative to the fourth element stated above, the plaintiff may show that he was treated differently from similarly-situated members of the unprotected class. This element of disparate treatment in comparison to similarly-situated members of the unprotected class is most appropriate to apply under the circumstances of this case.

If the plaintiff establishes a *prima facie* case, a rebuttable presumption of discrimination is created. The employer may rebut this presumption by articulating one or more nondiscriminatory reasons for the employment decision. When the *prima facie* case has been successfully rebutted, the presumption of discrimination drops out of the picture, and the burden shifts back to the plaintiff to present evidence sufficient to support two findings. First, the plaintiff must present evidence that creates a fact issue as to whether the employer's proffered reasons are mere pretext. Second, he must present evidence that creates a reasonable inference that the adverse employment decision was an act of intentional discrimination based on race.

The parties in this case do not dispute the first and third elements: Goodwin is an African-American, a member of a protected class, and the TSA did not hire him. Goodwin asserts, however, that he was qualified for the screener job and that he was treated differently than other similarly-situated persons in the hiring process. Because Goodwin has failed to produce any evidence to establish that any material fact relevant to these issues is actually in dispute, he has not stated a *prima facie* case of racial discrimination.

Job Qualifications

As to the first issue, whether Goodwin was qualified for the job, he does not dispute that one of the job qualifications established by TSA was successful completion of the physical performance tests, including the baggage-search test. Goodwin does not dispute that he failed this test; rather, he contends that the test itself should be disregarded and that he was qualified for the job based on other factors not required by the TSA.

An employer is not required to hire an applicant who does not possess basic skills essential to performance of a particular job, regardless of the color of his skin. When the stated qualifications for the job at issue are objective, such as passing a certain test, the plaintiff must show that he meets the stated qualifications. An employer has wide discretion to establish its requirements and qualifications for particular positions, so long as these requirements do not discriminate based upon impermissible characteristics such as race. In the normal course of business, employers will hire the most qualified candidates, and an employer, not a federal court, is in the best position to identify those strengths that constitute the best qualifications. The Eighth Circuit has often noted that "'the employment-discrimination laws have not vested in the federal courts the authority to sit as super-personnel departments reviewing the wisdom or fairness of the business judgments made by employers, except to the extent that those judgments involve intentional discrimination.'"

The stated job qualifications in this case were both objective and nondiscriminatory. The purpose of the baggage-search test was to determine whether applicants could identify objects by feeling them, a job function relevant to the TSA screener positions. Goodwin admits that all applicants were provided with the same instructions and completed the test in the same exact manner. The activity of touching and identifying concealed objects would in no way directly discriminate between candidates of different races. Moreover, Goodwin has neither alleged nor offered any evidence to show that the test had a discriminatory impact upon African-Americans. Accordingly, TSA acted within its discretion as an employer in establishing the baggage-search test as a job qualification and rejecting applicants who failed the test.

Instead of offering any evidence or argument that the baggage-search test itself was racially discriminatory, Goodwin argues that he was qualified based upon other factors and that the test should be disregarded because it was poorly designed. Specifically, Goodwin states that he was qualified for the screener position because he had previously worked as a contract security screener, he continued to work as private contract screener until the federalization process of the airport security personnel was completed, he has an aviation management degree, and he is a veteran of the United States Army.

None of these factors was a qualification sought by the TSA for the airport screeners. Goodwin further argues that because job applicants had to read an answer sheet to indicate which items they had felt in the box, the test measured more than ability to tactually identify objects; it also measured an applicant's ability to see or read the answer sheet, *i.e.*, vision. Goodwin contends that he failed the test because he had forgotten his eyeglasses on the assessment day and could not see the answer sheet, not because he could not identify the objects by touch.

Even if Goodwin is correct that he possessed other job qualifications and that the baggage-search test had a design flaw, however, these facts are irrelevant. The TSA, as an employer, has the authority to establish its job qualifications, so long as its requirements do not discriminate based upon race or other improper factors. Goodwin, as a job applicant, is not at liberty to establish his own criteria for the TSA screener position and demand that TSA follow them.

Disparate Treatment

The remaining issue is whether Goodwin was treated differently than similarly-situated job candidates who were not members of the protected class. At the *prima facie* stage, a plaintiff's burden to show that he is similarly situated to other job applicants is not onerous. Goodwin admits that all screener candidates were required to successfully complete the assessment process and that no candidate who failed either of the two physical performance tests, which included the baggage-search test, was hired. Goodwin alleges that he received disparate treatment in the testing process, however, for two reasons.

First, Goodwin alleges that he informed the test proctors at the assessment center that he could not see the answer sheet but was denied the opportunity to either leave the center to get his eyeglasses and return to finish testing later or to retake the baggage-search test after failing it. Goodwin has shown no evidence that he was treated differently from any other job candidate in this regard. The TSA asserts that, to ensure the integrity of the assessment process, none of the job candidates was allowed to leave the assessment center after starting the physical performance tests and then return to complete them. Goodwin has produced no evidence to the contrary.

Instead, Goodwin complains that job candidates who failed the medical evaluations were later allowed to submit documentation from private physicians to establish that they met TSA's medical standards for vision and hearing. That candidates who failed the medical evaluation were permitted to submit later documentation to show that they met the qualifications while candidates who failed the baggage-search test were not in no way establishes disparate treatment based upon race.

The candidates who initially failed the medical evaluations were not similarly situated to Goodwin. He failed a proficiency test; they failed a medical evaluation. Goodwin has produced no evidence that TSA's different treatment of those who failed a proficiency test and those who failed a medical evaluation was a subterfuge for race discrimination. To the contrary, the undisputed evidence shows that both African-American and white applicants who initially failed the medical evaluations were later allowed to submit further medical documentation and were hired.

Goodwin complains that the baggage-search test was poorly designed and that his disqualification was unfair because some candidates who initially failed the medical vision tests were later hired. The wisdom or fairness of an employer's hiring practices is not subject to review by a federal court unless improper discrimination is involved. Although Goodwin insists that TSA's refusal to allow him to leave during the assessment to get his eyeglasses must have been due to some racial animus, he has produced no evidence to support that allegation. Bald allegations alone cannot create an issue of material fact to withstand a motion for summary judgment. There is no genuine issue of material fact. The defendant has established a *prima facie* case of entitlement to summary judgment. Goodwin has failed to meet proof with proof. The defendant's motion for summary judgment is granted.

HAWAIIAN AIRLINES, INC. v. NORRIS
512 U.S. 246 (1994)

Justice BLACKMUN delivered the opinion of the Court.

This action involves the scope of federal pre-emption under the Railway Labor Act (RLA), 45 U.S.C. § 151 *et seq*. The RLA, which was extended in 1936 to cover the airline industry, sets up a mandatory arbitral mechanism to handle disputes "growing out of grievances or out of the interpretation or application of agreements concerning rates of pay, rules, or working conditions," 45 U.S.C. § 153 First (i).

The question in this case is whether an aircraft mechanic who claims that he was discharged for refusing to certify the safety of a plane that he considered unsafe and for reporting his safety concerns to the Federal Aviation Administration may pursue available state-law remedies for wrongful discharge, or whether he may seek redress only through the RLA's arbitral mechanism. We hold that the RLA does not pre-empt his state-law causes of action.

* * *

Respondent Grant Norris is an aircraft mechanic licensed by the Federal Aviation Administration ("FAA"). His aircraft mechanic's license authorizes him to approve an airplane and return it to service after he has made, supervised, or inspected certain repairs performed on that plane. *See* Certification: Airmen Other Than Flight Crewmembers, 14 C.F.R. §§ 65.85 and 65.87 (1987). If he were to approve any aircraft on which the repairs did not conform to FAA safety regulations, the FAA could suspend or revoke his license. *See* Maintenance, Preventive Maintenance, Rebuilding and Alteration, 14 C.F.R. § 43.12 (1992).

On February 2, 1987, respondent was hired by petitioner Hawaiian Airlines, Inc. ("HAL"). Many of the terms of his employment were governed by a collective-bargaining agreement ("CBA") negotiated between the carrier and the International Association of Machinists and Aerospace Workers. Under the CBA, respondent's duties included inspecting and repairing all parts of a plane and its engine. On July 15, 1987, during a routine preflight inspection of a DC-9 plane, he noticed that one of the tires was worn. When he removed the wheel, respondent discovered that the axle sleeve, which should have been mirror smooth, was scarred and grooved. This damaged sleeve could cause the landing gear to fail.

Respondent recommended that the sleeve be replaced, but his supervisor ordered that it be sanded and returned to the plane. This was done, and the plane flew as scheduled. At the end of the shift, respondent refused to sign the maintenance record to certify that the repair had been performed satisfactorily and that the airplane was fit to fly. *See* 14 C.F.R. § 43.9(a) (1992). The supervisor immediately suspended him pending a termination hearing. Respondent immediately went home and called the FAA to report the problem with the sleeve. In response, the FAA initiated a comprehensive investigation, proposed a civil penalty of $964,000 against HAL, proposed the revocation of the license of the supervisor who terminated respondent, and ultimately settled all charges for a substantial fine.

Respondent then invoked the grievance procedure outlined in the CBA, and a "Step 1" grievance hearing was held on July 31, 1987. Petitioner HAL accused respondent of insubordination, claiming that his refusal to sign the record violated the CBA's provision that an aircraft mechanic "may be required to sign work records in connection with the work he performs." Respondent relied on the CBA's guarantees that an employee may not be discharged without just cause and may not be disciplined for refusing to perform work that is in violation of health or safety laws. The hearing officer terminated respondent for insubordination.

Still conforming to the CBA procedures, respondent appealed his termination, seeking a "Step 3" grievance hearing. Before this hearing took place, HAL offered to reduce respondent's punishment to suspension without pay, but warned him that "any further instance of failure to perform [his] duties in a responsible manner" could result in discharge. Respondent did not respond to this offer, nor, apparently, did he take further steps to pursue his grievance through the CBA procedures.

On December 18, 1987, respondent filed suit against HAL in Hawaii Circuit Court. His complaint included two wrongful-discharge torts—discharge in violation of the public policy expressed in the Federal Aviation Act of 1958 and implementing regulations, and discharge in violation of Hawaii's Whistleblower Protection Act.

The Hawaii Whistleblower Protection Act forbids an employer to "discharge, threaten, or otherwise discriminate against an employee ... because ... [t]he employee ... reports or is about to report to a public body ... a violation or a suspected violation of a law or rule adopted pursuant to law of this State, a political subdivision of this State, or the United States, unless the employee knows that the report is false." The Act authorizes an employee to file a civil action seeking injunctive relief and actual damages.

He also alleged that HAL had breached the CBA agreement. HAL removed the action to the United States District Court for the District of Hawaii, which dismissed the breach-of-contract claim as pre-empted by the RLA, and remanded the other claims to the state trial court. The trial court then dismissed respondent's claim of discharge in violation of public policy, holding that it, too, was pre-empted by the RLA's provision of exclusive arbitral procedures. The state court certified its order as final to permit respondent to take an immediate appeal.

In the meantime, respondent had filed a second lawsuit in state court, naming as defendants three of HAL's officers who allegedly directed, confirmed, or ratified the claimed retaliatory discharge. He again sought relief for, among other things, discharge in violation of public policy and of the Hawaii Whistleblower Protection Act. The Hawaii trial court dismissed these two counts as pre-empted by the RLA and certified the case for immediate appeal.

The Supreme Court of Hawaii reversed in both cases, concluding that the RLA did not pre-empt respondent's state tort actions. That court concluded that the plain language of § 153 First (i) does not support pre-emption of disputes independent of a labor agreement and interpreted the opinion in *Consolidated Rail Corporation (Conrail) v. Railway Labor Executives' Assn.* (1989), to limit RLA pre-emption to "disputes involving contractually defined rights."

The court rejected petitioners' argument that the retaliatory discharge claims were pre-empted because determining whether HAL discharged respondent for insubordination, and thus for just cause, required construing the CBA. The court pointed to *Lingle v. Norge Div. of Magic Chef, Inc.* (1988), a case involving § 301 of the Labor-Management Relations Act, 1947 ("LMRA"), in which the Court held that a claim of wrongful termination in retaliation for filing a state worker's compensation claim did not require interpretation of a CBA, but depended upon purely factual questions concerning the employee's conduct and the employer's motive. Because the same was true in this action, said the Supreme Court of Hawaii, respondent's state tort claims were not pre-empted. We granted *certiorari* in these consolidated cases.

* * *

Whether federal law pre-empts a state law establishing a cause of action is a question of congressional intent. Pre-emption of employment standards "within the traditional police power of the State" "should not be lightly inferred."

Congress' purpose in passing the RLA was to promote stability in labor-management relations by providing a comprehensive framework for resolving labor disputes. To realize this goal, the RLA establishes a mandatory arbitral mechanism for "the prompt and orderly settlement" of two classes of disputes.

The first class, those concerning "rates of pay, rules or working conditions," are deemed "major" disputes. Major disputes relate to "'the formation of collective [bargaining] agreements or efforts to secure them.'" *Conrail* (quoting *Elgin, J. & E.R. Co. v. Burley* (1945)). The second class of disputes, known as "minor" disputes, "gro[w] out of grievances or out of the interpretation or application of agreements covering rates of pay, rules, or working conditions." Minor disputes involve "controversies over the meaning of an existing collective bargaining agreement in a particular fact situation." Thus, "major disputes seek to create contractual rights, minor disputes to enforce them."

Petitioners contend that the conflict over respondent's firing is a minor dispute. If so, it must be resolved only through the RLA mechanisms, including the carrier's internal dispute-resolution processes and an adjustment board established by the employer and the unions. Thus, a determination that respondent's complaints constitute a minor dispute would pre-empt his state-law actions.

* * *

The Court's inquiry into the scope of minor disputes begins, of course, with the text of the statute. Petitioners point out that the statute defines minor disputes to include "disputes ... growing out of grievances, or out of the interpretation or application of [CBA's]." Petitioners argue that this disjunctive language must indicate that "grievances" means something other than labor-contract disputes, else the term "grievances" would be superfluous. Accordingly, petitioners suggest that "grievances" should be read to mean all employment-related disputes, including those based on statutory or common law.

Even if we were persuaded that the word "or" carried this weight, petitioners' interpretation produces an overlap not unlike the one it purports to avoid. Their expansive definition of "grievances" necessarily encompasses disputes growing out of "the interpretation or application" of CBA's. Thus, in attempting to save the term "grievances" from superfluity, petitioners would make the phrase after the "or" mere surplusage.

We think it more likely that "grievances," like disputes over "the interpretation or application" of CBA's, refers to disagreements over how to give effect to the bargained-for agreement. The use of "grievance" to refer to a claim arising out of a CBA is common in the labor-law context in general, and it has been understood in this way in the RLA context. *See* H.R. Rep. No. 1944, 73d Cong., 2d Sess., 2-3 (1934) (referring to RLA settlement of "minor disputes known as 'grievances,' which develop from the interpretation and/or application of the contracts between the labor unions and the carriers"). Significantly, too, the adjustment boards charged with administration of the minor-dispute provisions have understood these provisions as pertaining only to disputes invoking contract-based rights.

Accordingly, we believe that the most natural reading of the term "grievances" in this context is as a synonym for disputes involving the application or interpretation of a CBA. Nothing in the legislative history of the RLA or other sections of the statute undermines this conclusion. But even accepting that § 151a is susceptible of more than one interpretation, no proposed interpretation demonstrates a clear and manifest congressional purpose to create a regime that broadly pre-empts substantive protections extended by the States, independent of any negotiated labor agreement.

* * *

Our case law confirms that the category of minor disputes contemplated by § 151a are those that are grounded in the CBA. We have defined minor disputes as those involving the interpretation or application of existing labor agreements. *See e.g.*, Conrail ("The distinguishing feature of [a minor dispute] is that the dispute may be conclusively resolved by interpreting the existing [CBA]").

Moreover, we have held that the RLA's mechanism for resolving minor disputes does not pre-empt causes of action to enforce rights that are independent of the CBA. More than 60 years ago, the Court rejected a railroad's argument that the existence of the RLA arbitration scheme pre-empted a state statute regulating the number of workers required to operate certain equipment. Not long thereafter, the Court rejected a claim that the RLA pre-empted an order by the Illinois Commerce Commission requiring cabooses on all trains; the operative CBA required cabooses only on some of the trains. Although the Court assumed that a railroad adjustment board would have jurisdiction under the RLA over this dispute, it concluded that the state law was enforceable nonetheless:

> State laws have long regulated a great variety of conditions in transportation and industry, such as sanitary facilities and conditions, safety devices and protections, purity of water supply, fire protection, and innumerable others. Any of these matters might, be the subject of a demand by work[ers] for better protection and upon refusal might, we suppose, be the subject of a labor dispute which would have such effect on interstate commerce that federal agencies might be invoked to deal with some phase of it. But it cannot be said that the minimum requirements laid down by state authority are all set aside. We hold that the enactment by Congress of the [RLA] was not a preemption of the field of regulating working conditions themselves.

Thus, substantive protections provided by state law, independent of whatever labor agreement might govern, are not pre-empted under the RLA.

The Court has taken a consistent approach in the context of state actions for wrongful discharge. In *Andrews v. Louisville & Nashville R. Co.* (1972), the Court held that a state-law claim of wrongful termination was pre-empted, not because the RLA broadly pre-empts state-law claims based on discharge or discipline, but because the employee's claim was firmly rooted in a breach of the CBA itself. He asserted no right independent of that agreement:

> Here it is conceded by all that the only source of [Andrews'] right not to be discharged, and therefore to treat an alleged discharge as a 'wrongful' one that entitles him to damages, is the [CBA] ... [T]he disagreement turns on the

> extent of [the railroad's] obligation to restore [Andrews] to his regular duties following injury in an automobile accident. The existence and extent of such an obligation in a case such as this will depend on the interpretation of the [CBA]. Thus [Andrews'] claim, and [the railroad's] disallowance of it, stem from differing interpretations of the [CBA]. His claim is therefore subject to the Act's requirement that it be submitted to the Board for adjustment.

Here, in contrast, the CBA is not the "only source" of respondent's right not to be discharged wrongfully. In fact, the "only source" of the right respondent asserts in this action is state tort law. Wholly apart from any provision of the CBA, petitioners had a state-law obligation not to fire respondent in violation of public policy or in retaliation for whistle-blowing. The parties' obligation under the RLA to arbitrate disputes arising out of the application or interpretation of the CBA did not relieve petitioners of this duty.

* * *

The pre-emption standard—that a state-law cause of action is not pre-empted by the RLA if it involves rights and obligations that exist independent of the CBA—is virtually identical to the pre-emption standard the Court employs in cases involving § 301 of the LMRA.

In a case remarkably similar to the case before us now, this Court made clear that the existence of a potential CBA-based remedy did not deprive an employee of independent remedies available under state law. In *Lingle v. Norge Div. of Magic Chef, Inc.* (1988), an employee covered by a labor agreement was fired for filing an allegedly false worker's compensation claim. After filing a grievance pursuant to her CBA, which protected employees against discharge except for "proper" or "just" cause, she filed a complaint in state court, alleging that she had been discharged for exercising her rights under Illinois worker's compensation laws. The state court had held her state-law claim pre-empted because "the same analysis of the facts" was required in both the grievance proceeding and the state-court action. This Court reversed.

It recognized that where the resolution of a state-law claim depends on an interpretation of the CBA, the claim is pre-empted. It observed, however, that "purely factual questions" about an employee's conduct or an employer's conduct and motives do not "requir[e] a court to interpret any term of a collective-bargaining agreement." The state-law retaliatory discharge claim turned on just this sort of purely factual question: whether the employee was discharged or threatened with discharge, and, if so, whether the employer's motive in discharging her was to deter or interfere with her exercise of rights under Illinois worker's compensation law.

While recognizing that "the state-law analysis might well involve attention to the same factual considerations as the contractual determination of whether Lingle was fired for just cause," the Court disagreed that

> such parallelism render[ed] the state-law analysis dependent upon the contractual analysis. For while there may be instances in which the National Labor Relations Act pre-empts state law on the basis of the subject matter of the law in question, § 301 pre-emption merely ensures that federal law will be the basis for interpreting collective-bargaining agreements, and says nothing about the substantive rights a State may provide to workers when adjudication of those rights does not depend upon the interpretation of such agreements.
>
> In other words, even if dispute resolution pursuant to a collective-bargaining agreement, on the one hand, and state law, on the other, would require addressing precisely the same set of facts, as long as the state-law claim can be resolved without interpreting the agreement itself, the claim is "independent" of the agreement for § 301 pre-emption purposes.

We conclude that *Lingle* provides an appropriate framework for addressing pre-emption under the RLA, and we adopt the *Lingle* standard to resolve claims of RLA pre-emption.

The question under *Lingle* is whether respondent's state-law wrongful-discharge claims are independent of the CBA. Petitioners argue that resort to the CBA is necessary to determine whether respondent, in fact, was discharged. This argument is foreclosed by *Lingle* itself. *Lingle* teaches that the issue to be decided in this action—whether the employer's actions make out the element of discharge under Hawaii law—is a "purely factual questio[n]."

Nor are we persuaded by petitioners' contention that the state tort claims require a determination whether the discharge, if any, was justified by respondent's failure to sign the maintenance record, as the CBA required him to do. Although such a determination would be required with regard to respondent's separate allegation of discharge in violation of the CBA, the District Court dismissed that count as pre-empted by the RLA, and respondent does not challenge that dismissal. The state tort claims, by contrast, require only the purely factual inquiry into any retaliatory motive of the employer. Accordingly, we agree with the Supreme Court of Hawaii that respondent's claims for discharge in violation of public policy and in violation of the Hawaii Whistleblower Protection Act are not pre-empted by the RLA, and we affirm that court's judgment.

AIR LINE PILOTS ASS'N, INT'L. v. EASTERN AIR LINES
701 F. Supp. 865 (D.D.C. 1988)

BARRINGTON D. PARKER, Senior District Judge.

In separate verified complaints alleging violations of the Railway Labor Act ("RLA" or "Act"), the Air Line Pilots Association, International ("ALPA"), the International Machinists & Aerospace Workers ("IAM") and Local 553 Transport Workers Union of America ("TWU") have sued Eastern Air Lines, Inc. ("Eastern") and request both injunctive and declaratory relief.

In a joint motion for a preliminary injunction, filed on November 18, 1988, the three unions seek to halt the proposed sale of Eastern's Air Shuttle ("Shuttle") operations to Trump Shuttle, Inc. ("Trump Shuttle" or "Trump"). They claim that Eastern's proposed sale of the Shuttle to Trump violates both Eastern's *status quo* and collective bargaining obligations under the RLA, triggers a "major dispute" under the RLA because the proposed action was not based on any express or arguable contractual right or consistent past practice, and was undertaken with the express intent of undermining the unions and violates the statutory obligation to refrain from interfering with certified bargaining representatives. For the reasons stated below the Court determines that the sale of the Shuttle should not be halted. Accordingly, plaintiffs' motion for a preliminary injunction is denied.

I. FACTUAL FINDINGS

Plaintiffs serve as the certified collective bargaining representatives of Eastern's employees. ALPA is the representative for Eastern's pilots. The ALPA-Eastern collective bargaining agreement expired on July 1, 1988, and the parties are currently engaged in contract negotiations.

The IAM is the representative for Eastern's mechanics, baggage handlers, and other ground service personnel. The most recent IAM-Eastern agreement expired on December 31, 1987. Contract negotiations were started in October 1987, and for more than a year, the two have been engaged in negotiations for a new agreement before the National Mediation Board. ALPA and the IAM have been parties to successive collective bargaining agreements for more than 40 years.

Local 553 of TWU is the bargaining representative for Eastern's flight attendants. The Local and Eastern's management have had successive collective bargaining agreements for many years. Their current agreement remains in effect through this month. They exchanged formal notices of their intent to renegotiate the entire agreement in October 1988.

A.

Eastern is the nation's sixth largest air carrier and a wholly-owned subsidiary of the Texas Air Corporation ("Texas Air"). It provides scheduled passenger and cargo service out of hubs located in Atlanta, Miami, Philadelphia, and San Juan, Puerto Rico. It also operates passenger and other services extending through Central and South America.

Eastern operates a shuttle service, on an hourly basis, between LaGuardia Airport, New York City, and both Logan Airport, Boston, and National Airport, Washington, D.C. The Shuttle has operated for more than 25 years and is a well-established and profitable division of Eastern Air Lines. It provides employment for approximately 700 full-time employees, including 200 pilots, 146 machinists and approximately 250 flight attendants. It has no single permanent group of employees, rather, Eastern's workers bid for positions on basis of seniority. An employee's assignment to the Shuttle on a month-to-month basis depends upon the bids of more senior employees.

The Shuttle division employs 2.3% of Eastern's 30,500 employees, utilizes 6.7% of the company's 255 aircraft, accounts for approximately 1.5% of the company's total available seat miles ("ASM's"), and generates approximately 4.3% of the total operating revenue. The division accounts for approximately 2.9% of Eastern's total assets at net book value, and approximately 7% of its assets at fair market value.

The Shuttle's traffic is virtually limited to passengers who travel only between the three named cities. The passengers do not continue to other Eastern destinations. In recent years the Shuttle's market share has declined, primarily because of competition from Pan American which has penetrated the New York, Boston, and Washington shuttle market.

B.

In early 1988, Eastern sought to dispose of the Shuttle when it attempted to spin off the division to Air Shuttle, L.P., a newly formed subsidiary of Texas Air. The transaction was challenged by the IAM. The IAM sought relief and in March 1988, Judge Pratt of this Court found Eastern in contempt of an earlier July 1987 ruling. He enjoined the carrier from taking any steps to spin off the Shuttle operation, pending exhaustion of the dispute resolution procedures of the RLA. His ruling was subsequently vacated on procedural grounds. Meanwhile, Eastern withdrew its proposed plans.

This Memorandum Opinion involves Eastern's second attempt to dispose of the Shuttle when on October 12, 1988, Texas Air officials publicly announced a Purchase and Sale Agreement ("Agreement") between Eastern and Trump Shuttle, Inc. The Agreement provided for sale of the Shuttle division for $365 million in cash to be paid at the closing.

Trump Shuttle was formed in October 1988, by Donald J. Trump. He is the sole stockholder, board chairman and chief executive officer of Trump Shuttle which was formed to effect the purchase from Eastern. Mr. Trump is a successful entrepreneur engaged in real estate developments, hotel operations, and a variety of other enterprises.

C.

Plaintiffs do not contest the fairness of the $365 million sale price and it is estimated that the proceeds will provide Eastern with approximately $315 to $320 million net cash. The terms of the Agreement provide that Eastern sell its entire Shuttle division to Trump Shuttle. This includes all ground equipment, airport gate positions, 17 Boeing 727 aircraft, 92 airport landing and take-off slots, 14 airport gates, and related terminal facilities at LaGuardia, Logan, and National airports.

The Agreement provides that the Shuttle may not be resold to any of Eastern's six principal competitors (American, Delta, Northwest, United, USAir, or TWA) for a period of ten years. It also provides that for five years after the sale, Eastern will retain a right of first refusal if Trump decides to sell the Shuttle to those airlines, or if other potential purchasers attempt to buy it. The Agreement further provides that Trump Shuttle shall continue to participate in Eastern's OnePass, frequent flyer program for three years, and that for twelve years thereafter, Trump shall not participate in the frequent flyer program of any other airline.

Deposition testimony and declarations from various witnesses showed that following the sale, Eastern would continue to have substantial flight operations, assets and employees through the LaGuardia, Logan, and National airports. Expert witnesses, James F. Chadbourne and Daniel M. Kasper, agreed that the Shuttle sale would not have a significant impact on Eastern's non-shuttle operations.

Of great concern to plaintiffs is the impact of the Shuttle sale on Eastern's employees. Mr. Trump made it clear in his testimony on behalf of Trump Shuttle, that he extended to Eastern employees an opportunity to work for his company, that he would recognize the three unions, and support the present collective bargaining agreements.

The October 12 Agreement provides, *inter alia*, that Mr. Trump will offer guaranteed employment, in order of seniority, to Eastern's employees in the same numbers presently utilized, will establish wages and work rules identical to those in effect at Eastern—with full credit for seniority, and will not change existing wage rates and work rules without compliance with the Railway Labor Act. Employees would not be hired from any other source unless an insufficient number of Eastern's employees were willing to accept the employment offers. The Agreement also requires Trump to recognize Eastern's unions as the bargaining representative and as Captain John Bavis, an Eastern pilot and ranking ALPA official, testified to "assume as a successor" all rights and obligations of Eastern under any labor contract or the Railway Labor Act, "to the full extent permitted by law." No Eastern employee is required to accept the offer of employment; the choice is entirely optional.

Mr. Trump's job offers have been accepted by more than a sufficient number of Eastern employees to fully staff the Shuttle. Thus, no employee furloughs are likely as a result of the transaction. Employees who choose not to accept the employment option with Trump may remain with Eastern, employed and treated in accord with the seniority-based employment provisions of their respective collective bargaining agreement.

D.

The record shows that historically, Eastern has had a record of selling assets and eliminating services without prior bargaining with the unions. Such changes have taken place within the framework of the existing agreements. Captain John Bavis and others, whose deposition testimony or declarations are a part of this record, readily admitted that the following operations were terminated without union bargaining: The 1986 hub in Charlotte, North Carolina, the Moonlight Special between Houston and Chicago, operating between 1984-1987, the Military Airlift Command operations ("MAC flights") from 1974-1977, the Montreal, Canada-New York City shuttle operating in the mid-1970s, and the 1980-86 Contract Maintenance Center in Miami.

The Charlotte hub closing resulted in a substantial reduction of flights from 110 to 14 per day accompanied by a nearly 60% reduction within two months of the 176 IAM-represented employees. The Moonlight Special, a late night cargo service, commenced in Houston and was unilaterally transferred to Chicago and then unilaterally discontinued several months later. As a result of that decision IAM-represented employees, in addition to pilots and flight attendants, were displaced. While some of the employees preferred those work opportunities, Eastern did not bargain with the unions but made the unilateral decisions on its own. The MAC flights were chartered services for the United States military. Those non-scheduled operations carried premium pay together with seniority-based crew assignments for pilots and flight attendants. Between 1974 and 1977, there were high averages of MAC departures—38 per month. Since then the operations have been intermittent. In 1987, there were no operations and in 1988, there have been an average of only 11 per month. Again, Eastern's management alone made the decisions. As to the Miami Contract Maintenance Center, the deposition testimony of IAM representative, Charles Bryan showed that the operation was discontinued and employees' bumping and bidding rights were exercised in accordance with the IAM-Eastern collective bargaining agreement.

Several union witnesses testified that the above situations could be distinguished from the Shuttle sale since the Shuttle offered unique and unusual opportunities and personal conveniences for many. However, their testimony while interesting, did not alter the fact that past practices support a finding that significant changes affecting personnel and airline facilities have been made unilaterally by management without collective bargaining over such changes. Nor was their testimony sufficient to overcome the substantial corroboration of such practices otherwise found in the record, upon which the Court has relied.

The impact of the sale to Trump Shuttle pales in comparison to the impact of the September 1988 schedule change. The latter included the elimination and reduction of two major hub services, termination of all services to 14 cities, closure of a pilot domicile center, and disposition of more than 30 aircraft. But even more interesting, is the comparison between several particular items.

Elimination of the Shuttle involves approximately 700 employees, compared with the more than 3,000 affected by the fall schedule. The Shuttle sale results in a curtailment of only 62 departure flights per day from three cities, compared with a net curtailment of 143 daily flights under the fall schedule. Beyond the 62 departures, Eastern will continue its regular flight service to and from Boston, New York, and Washington, D.C., even though the Shuttle division is eliminated. Clearly, the fall schedule resulted in a reduction of far more services. Only 17 aircraft are eliminated by the Shuttle close down, compared to 30 from the fall schedule changes. Finally, there is a decrease of only 1.5% of total available seat miles as compared with the 15.4% decrease associated with the fall schedule.

Our Circuit Court recognized the fall schedule as changes consistent with past practices and consistent with the provisions of the Railway Labor Act. The changes resulting from the Trump sale are far less drastic than those resulting from the fall schedule. Several witnesses offered testimony presenting what they considered to be important distinctions from the Shuttle transaction. Their testimony, while not entirely discounted, is lacking and is insufficient to support a finding that the Railway Labor Act has been violated.

E.

As before, plaintiffs urge that the underlying reason and motive for the decision to sell the Shuttle is Eastern's bias or animus toward unions. After this Court found some merit in their position, our Circuit Court found otherwise and held that there were no forbidden purposes behind Eastern's decision and that there was no basis for a finding of union animus. That Court made its own judgment from a written record and without benefit of the witnesses' testimony.

Plaintiffs rely substantially on the showing in the earlier preliminary injunction proceedings to support a finding of bias and unlawful interference with union activity. However, they did attempt to strengthen their reliance on the 1987 "CHUNKS" memorandum. They claim that the memorandum was an overt manifestation of union bias, a deliberate plotting by Eastern management and Texas Air to block so-called "oppressive" demands of the IAM and ALPA. That claim, however, was based in large measure on hearsay testimony. After a careful review of plaintiffs' supporting testimony and documentation, the Court finds that their reliance on the CHUNKS memorandum is overdrawn and inconclusive. They have not made a sufficient showing beyond their original effort, which the Circuit Court rejected.

F.

The principal reason advanced by Eastern for the Shuttle sale is a critical and deteriorating financial condition which could prove fatal to the company's existence. The situation has been ongoing. Since the early 1980s Eastern has been faced with continual financial losses. In 1987, the company faced $194 million in losses before adjustments were made for the sale of certain assets. For the first half of 1988, losses approached $120 million. For the third quarter alone losses approached $349 million before capital gains were reported. More than $100 million in losses are anticipated for the present quarter.

The Eastern witnesses who testified clearly recognized that the company was experiencing a loss of cash and liquidity balances that impacted severely on the company's overall financial health, particularly its dwindling net worth. It is estimated that the Trump Shuttle sale will net at least $315 million after certain debt and expense obligations are discharged. Management maintains that the transaction will offset cash now absorbed by Eastern's large losses, allow it to remain in business, permit it to stem rumors of near insolvency, and stop the growing erosion of consumer confidence. Management testified that the net proceeds from the sale would serve to meet those problems. Eastern officials also testified that available alternatives to the sale were limited and uncertain. In their judgment, the sale would provide much needed liquidity with relatively little, if any, negative impact on the company's remaining core operations; the net cash acquired would allow consideration of long delayed preventive maintenance projects, modernization of operating assets, and improvement of the general quality of service. Absent such efforts, they felt that there was an increasing likelihood that Eastern would be unable to survive the competition which had been accelerated by the Air Line Deregulation Act of 1978 and the entry of Pan American in the shuttle market.

The testimony also showed that Eastern's core business was in dire need. The added cash assets would enable the company to develop its principal operations and generally, it would become a more profitable and upscale business.

Eastern officials were aware of the company's problems and recently undertook certain corrective measures. Current advertisements in the press rank the carrier as outstanding in on-time performance. Advertising budgets, in general, have been increased. Incentive programs to improve both customer service and market penetration have been introduced. New facilities and the upgrading of existing facilities in San Juan and Miami, respectively, have been accomplished. New flight kitchens have been considered and in fact, building operations are underway. With such improvements,

Eastern's management contends that it has made a thoughtful and prudent decision to employ the proceeds from the Shuttle sale in a manner that will allow them to continue those and other overdue changes.

G.

The unions challenge Eastern's claim that there is a critical need for cash and that the Shuttle sale would improve the company's cash position. The bottom line of their challenge, is that selling the Air Shuttle is simply not prudent. They claim that over the past several years, the Shuttle has returned sizable annual profits and that the indications are that it will continue to earn such profits. They also assert that any financial justification for the sale is belied by the fact that the company has failed to place in operation or even blueprint a well-defined recovery or profit improvement plan. Therefore, they claim, it is inconsistent for Eastern to argue that the sale will help the airline return to profitability when it has not even taken the fundamental planning steps. Based upon these considerations, the unions ask the Court to find that union animus and bias rather than the Company's financial condition serve as the impetus for the proposed sale.

After hearing hours of contradictory testimony by the "experts," the Court feels that Eastern has the better argument. There is no doubt that an ongoing struggle has and will continue to exist between Eastern and its certified bargaining representatives. However, the Court feels that equally plausible is the idea that management is seeking to rebuild the company and place it on a sound financial footing.

The unions claim that management is developing plans to liquidate the company and lead it into bankruptcy. If in fact Eastern is not committed to fighting its deferred maintenance problems but is only half-heartedly engaged in improving the core of its carrier system, then Eastern's executives are acting out a cruel hoax upon the legislative, executive, and judicial branches of our federal government and the general public as well. The passage of time should prove whether this is true.

II. CONCLUSIONS OF LAW

A. APPLICATION OF THE RAILWAY LABOR ACT MAJOR AND MINOR DISPUTES

The Railway Labor Act of 1926 was enacted in an effort to promote stability in labor management relations within the railroad industry. Since 1936, it has governed labor-management relations within the airline industry. The Act provides remedies for the resolution of employee disputes arising out of the interpretation of collective bargaining agreements and requires all parties to "exert every reasonable effort to make and maintain" collectively bargained agreements, and to abide by the terms of the most recent agreement until all the dispute resolution procedures have been exhausted. *See Detroit & Toledo Shore Line R.R. v. United Transp. Union* (1969) ("Shore Line").

The resolution procedures depend on whether the dispute is classified as "major" or "minor." A major dispute arises from the formation or change of collective agreements covering rates of pay, rules, or working conditions. *Elgin, J. & E.R. Co. v. Burley* (1945). The RLA establishes elaborate machinery for negotiation and mediation of major disputes. The exhaustive bargaining process is designed to force the parties into serious negotiation and to encourage compromise.

A minor dispute, on the other hand, arises from the interpretation or application of an existing agreement. "The dispute relates either to the meaning or proper application of a particular provision with reference to a specific situation or to an omitted case." Such a dispute is one that "arguably" can be covered by the existing collective bargaining agreement. *Maine Central R.R. Co. v. United Transp. Union* ("Maine Central"). Minor disputes are resolved through a formal grievance process that culminates in binding arbitration by the National Railroad Adjustment Board.

A major dispute triggers a *status quo* obligation. Both the carrier and the union must preserve the "actual, objective working conditions and practices, broadly conceived, which were in effect before the pending dispute arose and which are involved in or related to that dispute." Once a party proposes a change in the collective bargaining agreement, that party is required to serve notice of its intentions (a "section 6 notice"), and both parties must maintain the *status quo* until the bargaining processes have been exhausted. The Supreme Court has described those processes as "almost interminable." Once the process is exhausted without reaching agreement, the parties are released from their *status quo* obligations, and can resort to "self-help"-management may implement its proposed changes and the unions may strike.

In a minor dispute, however, the parties are not precluded from changing the *status quo*; management is free to implement its interpretation of the agreement and a union cannot make a minor dispute the subject of a strike. The changes made by management remain in effect unless declared invalid by the National Railroad Adjustment Board.

B. THE SHUTTLE SALE IS JUSTIFIED BY PAST AGREEMENTS AND PRACTICES

Whether the sale of the Shuttle is classified as a major or minor dispute depends on whether it involves "the acquisition of rights for the future," *Elgin*, or is "arguably comprehended within an already existing collective bargaining agreement." As our Circuit and other circuit courts have held, they look to the parties' settled past practices to determine whether disputed actions fall within a bargaining agreement.

1. *The Shuttle Sale is Contemplated by Past Agreements*

Eastern's collective bargaining agreement with Local 553 of the TWU clearly contemplates that Eastern may cut back or relocate its flight attendants. Obviously, one reason Eastern would implement such changes would be to reduce the number of flights or alter its schedule. The reason for the work reduction, whether the abandonment of a hub or the sale of an asset, is immaterial. As our Circuit held:

> [T]he [TWU-Eastern] contract's language is quite broad and evidences an awareness that work reductions might be necessary in the future; it does not specify what forces might cause such reductions.

As stated previously, the agreements between Eastern and ALPA and IAM have expired and the parties have exchanged section 6 notices. Our Circuit Court's recent decision refused to recognize the expiration of the agreements and the filing of section 6 notices as a major dispute. Rather, it looked to provisions in expired contracts as evidence of settled past practice.

The Eastern-ALPA collective bargaining agreement contemplates domicile closures, flight reductions, pilot displacements, and furloughs. Similarly, the Eastern-IAM agreement contains provisions dealing with reductions in force, employee furloughs, and transfers. These provisions not only "indicate that furloughs were contemplated by the parties," but also show that the unions recognized that their employees would be affected by domicile closings and flight reductions. It makes no difference that pilots, mechanics, and ground service personnel were laid off or relocated because planes were sold or because schedules were trimmed back. The collective bargaining agreements themselves serve as evidence of actual working conditions and practices. Because the sale of an asset, such as the Shuttle, is "arguably" within the labor contracts, the dispute may not be characterized as major.

2. *The Shuttle Sale is Consistent with Past Practices*

As discussed in this Court's findings, Eastern has a well-established history of selling airplanes and cutting back its flight operations. These past practices and working conditions may become part of a collective bargaining agreement even if the agreement is silent regarding the causes of work reductions and furloughs. While the agreements between Eastern and the unions fail to specify the procedures to be followed when assets are sold, the Supreme Court has recognized that it would be "virtually impossible to include all working conditions in a collective-bargaining agreement."

Courts must determine whether actions similar to a present disputed action had "occurred for a sufficient period of time with the knowledge and acquiescence of the employees to become in reality a part of the actual working conditions." The court is limited to determining whether the action is supported by past practice-it does not decide whether such action is prudent for the carrier's future:

> If [the carrier] presented instances of past practice accepted by the unions which, arguably, could support its contention, the court's inquiry must end; it is not for it to weigh, and decide who has the better of the argument. If the court did this, it overstepped its bounds and usurped the arbitrator's function.

Our Circuit Court recently held in *ALPA v. Eastern* that Eastern's past practices included the continued exercise of management rights to discontinue service, sell assets, and reassign or furlough employees. Prior to the Circuit's determination, this Court also found in its August 30, 1988 Memorandum Opinion that Eastern's practices of schedule changes, hub closures and asset sales were part of the actual, objective working conditions and practices followed by the airline. In that August 30, 1988 Memorandum Opinion, this Court held that Eastern's proposed September schedule changes were similar to past actions taken by the airline and concluded that "Eastern should be permitted to implement such changes without first bargaining with plaintiffs."

In reviewing Eastern's record, the Court is reminded that "[p]ast practice is ... not part of the total contract, unless it was accepted." Eastern has engaged in numerous sales or lease-outs of the same type of assets to be conveyed in the Shuttle sale. In addition, Eastern has frequently changed the size and scope of its operations, reassigned employees, and otherwise engaged in a wide range and variety of changes relating to personnel, facilities and services. Those decisions were not preceded by bargaining with plaintiff unions concerning the decisions or their effects, except as was provided in Eastern's pre-existing labor contracts.

Plaintiff unions have repeatedly tried to distinguish the facts of the Shuttle sale from previous sales or changes in service. They argue that the Shuttle provides unique employment opportunities and working conditions and that the transfer to Trump of a separate operating division is unprecedented. The Court is not persuaded by plaintiffs' attempt to differentiate the Trump deal from other business decisions of Eastern. Employment opportunities have been changed in the past; working conditions have frequently changed, arising from hub closures or discontinuance of service. Bumping and bidding rights have been frequently exercised by Eastern's employees, schedules have varied and the airlines' employees have adjusted and adapted. The unions have failed to identify any legal cognizable difference between the Shuttle sale and Eastern's repeated closures of principal hubs, elimination of discrete operating units, and sales of assets.

This Circuit has stated that "if the shuttle sale is analogous to the closing of a hub, the abandonment of a route or the sale of assets, then a question may be raised whether, under the parties' established bargaining tradition, the proposed action is subject to bargaining." After carefully examining Eastern's past practices, the Court holds that the proposed Shuttle sale is similar to prior actions in which the unions acquiesced; therefore, it falls within their bargaining agreements.

Since Eastern has no obligation to bargain with the plaintiff unions over its decision to sell the Shuttle, the proposed action does not create a major dispute. The collective bargaining provisions of the RLA do not prevent consummation of the Shuttle transaction. *See Japan Air Lines Co. v. IAM* (2d Cir. 1976) (no duty to bargain over decision to continue practice of subcontracting); *IAM v. Northeast Airlines, Inc.* (1st Cir. 1973) (no duty to bargain over decision to merge); *ALPA v. Transamerica Airlines, Inc.* (E.D.N.Y. 1986) (no obligation to bargain over decision to shut down airline and lease 12 aircraft to another carrier). The Supreme Court has consistently held that fundamental management decisions concerning the scope and direction of an employer's business fall outside the area of mandatory bargaining subjects.

The unions argue that Eastern must bargain over the effects of the proposed Shuttle sale before the airline can close the deal. The Court disagrees. First, Eastern's actions are "arguably comprehended" on the terms of its agreements with the plaintiffs; therefore, any dispute with respect to the impacts of the Shuttle sale upon employees must be considered minor. When this Court in its August 30, 1988 ruling instructed Eastern to "comply with the intricate RLA bargaining process" before it could furlough 4,000 employees in September 1988, this Circuit reversed, finding that the pre-existing provisions of Eastern's collective bargaining agreements contemplated work reductions even though they did not specify what forces might cause such reductions.

Secondly, while the Third Circuit in *Railway Labor Executive Ass'n v. Pittsburgh & Lake Erie R.R.* (3d Cir. 1988) held that a carrier must bargain over the effects of its business decisions before implementing any changes, this Circuit and others have disagreed. As our Circuit recently held, the agreements and the course of dealing contemplated the effects of such proposals. In *ALPA v. Transamerica Airlines, Inc.*, where the issue of effects bargaining was not even litigated, the Ninth Circuit recognized as a general principle that effects bargaining could continue after the carrier ceased operations. In *Northeast Airlines*, the First Circuit stated that "[w]here it is clear, as in the case of a merger, that bargaining about some effects of the decision would be ineffective unless the company could be required to renegotiate the merger, we believe that the duty to bargain about those effects does not arise at all."

In *Pittsburgh and Lake Erie R.R.*, the Third Circuit affirmed the district court's *status quo* injunction, enjoining the sale of the entire business only "to the extent that such sale does not include provisions for the maintenance of the *status quo* ..." In contrast to the present case, that court enjoined the sale because there was no past practice and the preexisting labor agreement did not provide for the effects of the transaction.

Finally, in *First National Maintenance*, the Supreme Court made it absolutely clear that a company need not secure the agreement of its unions or exhaust bargaining before it carries out a decision to close its business. The company's only obligation is to offer "meaningful bargaining at a meaningful time" over the effects of the decision. From the outset, Eastern has offered to bargain over its decision to sell the Shuttle to Donald Trump. When it announced the Trump deal, an Eastern executive wrote that the airline was "prepared to bargain about the effects of such decisions, as it has in the past, and to entertain any proposals the IAM might present on this subject." Eastern has never bargained over possible effects to its unions prior to closing a sale of assets or terminating flights. However, it has engaged in effects bargaining after the transactions and new schedules have been completed. These post-transaction negotiations have been "meaningful" as required by the Supreme Court. For example, Eastern initiated bargaining about the effects of the September 1988 schedule change, offering union members a new early-out option with pass privileges. Eastern reached agreement with the TWU on September 1, 1988, and the IAM on October 3, 1988, on extended leave programs to limit the employee impact of the downsizing.

3. *The Shuttle Sale is a Minor Dispute*

Eastern has met its "relatively light" burden of demonstrating that the Shuttle sale is a minor dispute. Eastern's position cannot be said to constitute the type of clear departure from its past practices necessary to trigger a finding of a major dispute under the RLA format.

Our Circuit's recent ruling holds true in this case:

> Given the express contractual terms and the similarity between the proposed [action by Eastern] and previous ones, the record compels a finding that Eastern's proposal [is] covered by the collective bargaining agreement and the course of dealing between the company and [its unions]. This [proposed action] is a minor dispute for purposes of resolution through the RLA, and the district court lack[s] jurisdiction to enjoin Eastern's [proposed action].

ALPA v. Eastern. The precedent clearly dictates that in a circumstance such as the present, this Court must deem the matter a minor dispute.

C. THE SHUTTLE SALE DOES NOT UNLAWFULLY INTERFERE WITH THE UNIONS

Plaintiffs contend that the sale of the Shuttle violates Sections 2 Third and Fourth of the RLA because it undermines the representative status of ALPA, IAM and Local 553 of TWU. They also claim that the sale is unlawful because its purpose is to discourage union activity at Eastern's remaining operations. Eastern counters that the unions have not shown that the airline's decision to sell the Shuttle was motivated by a desire to interfere with the unions. Eastern also contends that under the "mixed motive" *Wright Line* (1980, there is no labor law violation because Eastern has shown a compelling business need for selling the Shuttle.

Under the *Wright Line* test, plaintiff must make a *prima facie* showing sufficient to support the inference that the employer's anti-union bias was a "motivating factor." Once this is established, the burden shifts to the employer to demonstrate that it would have taken the same action even in the absence of union animus. This Circuit recently held in *ALPA v. Eastern*, that attacks on Eastern's flight reductions and employee furloughs as manifesting animus, are subject to analysis under *Wright Line*:

> We are persuaded that the Wright Line principle is applicable here ... Application of the Wright Line principle will provide full protection for the union activity protected by § 2 Third and Fourth and will avoid creating perverse incentives in either management or labor.

1. *New Evidence of Anti-Union Bias is Lacking*

Plaintiff unions cannot show a likelihood of success on their claim that Eastern's decision to sell the Shuttle was motivated by anti-union animus. In *ALPA v. Eastern*, our Court of Appeals recently ruled that the record provided little support for any finding that "forbidden purposes" controlled Eastern's decision. Because plaintiffs have failed to present new facts of union animus, the record has not changed since these parties were before this Court in August 1988. They have failed to make out a *prima facie* case in support of their allegations. They cannot satisfy their burden merely by proffering evidence of generalized anti-union bias. The unions have the burden of establishing a causal connection between the employer's hostility and the challenged action. Evidence of that causal connection is missing here.

It is not enough that the decision to sell the Shuttle may have an adverse impact on the unions. There must be a specific motive to chill unionism. The "CHUNKS" memorandum relied upon to prove that the decision to sell the Shuttle was part of a grand anti-union scheme was rejected by our Court of Appeals as evidence of labor law violations. The Circuit characterized the memorandum as evidence that management wanted to exert "economic pressure," which would not constitute unlawful interference with union rights. In view of these circumstances, this Court concludes that plaintiffs have not met their burden of proving unlawful motivation to pressure the unions.

2. *Eastern Has Shown a Financial Necessity to Sell Shuttle*

Even if there is some evidence that the Shuttle sale was motivated in part by a desire to undermine the unions' representative status, Eastern has met its burden by showing that it would have arranged to sell the Shuttle in the absence of union hostility. More than ten years ago, the Supreme Court held that once the plaintiff carried his burden of persuasion, the burden shifted to the employer to show by a preponderance of evidence that he would have reached the same decision even if, hypothetically, he had not been motivated by a desire to punish the plaintiff for exercising his rights. Since then the Court has applied this allocation of burdens of proof to labor law situations where anti-union sentiment was involved. In *NLRB v. Transportation Management Corp*. (1983), the Supreme Court held that an employer need only prove that "absent the improper motivation he would have acted in the same manner for wholly legitimate reasons."

As set forth in this Court's factual findings, there is credible testimony relating to Eastern's serious financial problems and desperate need for a cash infusion. Eastern's officials and several industry experts, claim that the airline needs several hundreds of million dollars in cash to stay in business. Because compelling business reasons exist for Eastern's sale of the Shuttle, this Court finds that regardless of anti-union bias, the Trump deal "would have occurred in any event and for valid reasons."

D. THE SHUTTLE SALE IS NOT A SALE OF "SUBSTANTIALLY ALL" OF EASTERN'S ASSETS AND DOES NOT VIOLATE IAM'S STOCK RIGHTS

The IAM claims that its members, as owners of certain preferred stock issued by Eastern under the 1984 Wage Investment Program ("WIP"), are entitled to vote on Eastern's decision to sell the Shuttle. Recognizing that the preferred stock requires a shareholder vote only on a sale of "all or substantially all" of Eastern's assets, the IAM contends that because the Shuttle is Eastern's only profitable operation, its sale amounts to the liquidation of the airline.

The IAM and the other unions have failed to show that the sale of the Shuttle constitutes a sale of "all or substantially all" of Eastern's assets. As the Court wrote in its findings, the Shuttle constitutes only 2.9% of Eastern's total assets at net book value (approximately 7.0% at fair market value), only 1.5% of Eastern's total operation, and only 4.3% of Eastern's total operating revenue. Clearly, the Shuttle cannot be considered "substantially all" of Eastern's assets.

Shareholder approval is not necessary in the ordinary course of business, nor is it usually mandatory in a major restructuring of a corporation. A leading case in this area explains that shareholder approval is not required "simply because an independent, important branch of a corporate business is sold." *Gimbel v. Signal Cos.* (Del. Ch. 1974). The Delaware court did state, however, that:

> If the sale is of assets quantitatively vital to the operation of the corporation and is out of the ordinary and substantially affects the existence and purpose of the operations, then it is beyond the power of the Board of Directors.

At this point, plaintiffs have failed to show that the Shuttle sale will substantially affect Eastern's corporate existence or purpose. There was evidence that after the sale, Eastern will remain a major airline, employing approximately 30,000 people and utilizing over 220 aircraft. The IAM has not established that the Shuttle transaction violates any provision of the WIP.

E. THE SHUTTLE SALE SHOULD NOT BE ENJOINED

Under the law of this Circuit, this Court does not have subject matter jurisdiction to enter an injunction in a minor dispute. The parties must attempt to negotiate their differences and if negotiations fail, the dispute must be submitted to an arbitration board for resolution. As our Circuit recently declared, "[T]he arbitration board's jurisdiction over minor disputes is exclusive; the courts do not have jurisdiction to issue *status quo* injunctions."

The First Circuit has repeatedly held that when disputes are classified as minor under the RLA, a district court does not have jurisdiction to enter *status quo* injunctions. That Circuit has pointed to the strong presumption that a minor dispute is the type of controversy mandated by Congress to be resolved outside the judicial system. The Supreme Court has addressed the policy against judicial involvement in labor disputes by way of injunctive relief: "An injunction does not settle a dispute-it simply disables one of the parties." Given this policy and the Circuit's recent decision, the Court finds itself without jurisdiction to issue equitable relief in this case.

III. CONCLUSION

Plaintiff unions have failed to meet their burden in this regard. In particular, they have failed to establish either by virtue of the facts or the law that they are likely to succeed on the merits. Further, the balance of equities weighs in favor of Eastern.

In issuing this opinion, the Court holds that the sale of the Shuttle to Donald Trump is a minor dispute under the Railway Labor Act. Under the law of this Circuit, the Court is deprived of the jurisdiction to enter a preliminary injunction. Accordingly, this conflict must be resolved through negotiation and arbitration. Hopefully, the management of Eastern will not see this decision as an invitation to undervalue the interests of its unions. In selling the airline's premier financial asset, Eastern management leaves itself a special obligation to provide a future for the company and its workers. If management is serious about rebuilding Eastern, now is a good time to start.

NOTES

1. Congress federalized the aviation security system after September 11, 2001. In addition to creating the Department of Homeland Security (of which the Transportation Security Administration is a part) in November, 2001, the government also assumed responsibility for screening passengers, a task historically managed by private airlines through independent contractors. As a result, all airport screeners now are federal employees. Aviation & Transportation Security Act, Pub. L. No. 107-071, 115 Stat. 597 (codified as amended in scattered sections of 49 U.S.C.). *See also* Andrew Hessick, *The Federalization of Airport Security: Privacy Implications*, 24 WHITTIER L. REV. 43-69 (2002-2003).

Whether to allow airport screeners to bargain collectively is a subject of great debate among federal lawmakers:

> Sen. Jim DeMint (R-S.C.) said that collective bargaining would "significantly undermine TSA's ability to respond to threats and protect the nation." Allowing airport screeners to bargain would have a "direct negative impact" on airport security, he said, because it would hamper the agency's 'ability to deploy people at any time.' DeMint said the FBI does not have collective bargaining.
>
> He did not mention that employees who do have collective bargaining include customs inspectors, border patrol agents, the Capitol Police, uniformed Secret Service officers and the Park Police in the federal service, according to the Federal Law Enforcement Officers Association. Many state and local police officers and firefighters also have such rights.

See Joe Davidson, *TSA Nominee is Urged to Reject Airport Screeners' Push for Collective Bargaining*, WASH. POST, June 11, 2010. Which viewpoint should prevail as the better policy?

2. Passenger misbehavior—or unlawful passenger interference with flight crews, as explored in Chapter 5.B, *infra*—does not arise in a vacuum and sometimes may be an unintended consequence of airline labor-management relations. Indeed, airline customers are a natural target for labor to manifest frustrations harbored toward carriers-employers. *See* Ina Paiva Cordle, *We're Not Asking for the World*, THE MIAMI HERALD, June 3, 2001, at 6E (quoting an American Airlines flight attendant, "When I see they are not willing to pacify us, and we're not asking for a huge chunk of change, it makes me ask: 'Do I want to do a good job for them?'").

Increasingly, passengers feel neglected or purposefully mistreated by the deregulated airlines, which appear unable or unwilling to both manage dense traffic patterns and provide quality service. *Airline Crews Demand More Action to Curb Passenger Rage*, THE MIAMI HERALD, July 7, 2001, at 2A (quoting a passenger, "It's air rage because the airlines aren't doing their jobs to secure those attendants ... If they would give out information in a timely manner, you wouldn't see air rage."). Passengers also analogize their air travel experiences to hostage situations while, reciprocally, flight crews regard passengers as "the enemy." Doug Gamble, *Remember the "Friendly Skies?*," SACRAMENTO BEE, Aug. 15, 1999, at I2 (stating that "there is no private-sector business with more open hostility between server and customer than that which exists with the airline industry.").

3. Face-to-face interaction between passengers and crews can be a source of conflict, yet ironically computers and automated technologies intended to improve airline service also contribute to passenger frustration by reducing the amount of personal contact between passengers and the airline corporate giants. *E.g.*, Ruwantissa Abeyratne, *E-Commerce and the Airline Passenger*, 66 J. AIR L. & COM. 1345 (2001). *See also* Marilyn Adams, *Tech Takes Bigger Role in Air Service*, USA TODAY, July 18, 2001, at 1B ("[t]oday, you can book a domestic flight, check in, upgrade from coach to business class, reserve a window or aisle seat, get a boarding pass and check luggage—all without speaking to a human.").

After September 11, 2001, the type of contact between airport personnel and passengers has raised privacy and vanity issues in the context of invasive airport security checks, which now include body-scanning machines, metal detection devices, pat-downs, and verbal interrogation. *See, e.g.*, Scott McCartney, *Airport Screeners Reveal Travelers' Surly Side*, WALL ST. J., June 9, 2010, at D1 (reporting that passenger "tried repeatedly to hold up his pants [while] a screener kept barking at him to keep his hands over his head, prisoner-style. That way the machine could get clear pictures of the whole body.").

4. Is an airline pilot required to clean and prepare and secure an airplane cabin before or after a flight? Can an airline unilaterally impose a comprehensive, mandatory drug testing program for its employees? While certain issues that arise between airline management and labor are answerable by reference to a controlling collective bargaining agreement, many aviation labor and employment disputes require judicial application of the Railway Labor Act, 45 U.S.C. § 151 *et seq*.

As shown by *Hawaiian Airlines, Inc. v. Norris* (1994) and *Air Line Pilots Ass'n, Int'l. v. Eastern Air Lines* (D.D.C. 1988), *supra*, courts are designed to play an extraordinarily limited role in aviation labor disputes in favor of extended rounds of alternative dispute resolution. Indeed, the forum for resolution depends upon the characterization of the dispute. The United States Supreme Court has differentiated "minor" and "major" disputes:

> [A] major dispute relates to disputes over formation of collective agreements or efforts to secure them. They arise when there is no such agreement or where it is sought to change the terms of one.
>
> [A] minor dispute contemplates the existence of a collective agreement already concluded or, at any rate, a situation in which no effort is made to bring about a formal change in terms or to create a new one. The dispute relates either to the meaning or proper allocation of a particular provision with reference to a specific situation or to an omitted case.

Elgin J & E.Ry. Co. v. Burley (1945). Stated another way, "'[m]ajor and 'minor' disputes do not necessarily refer to important and unimportant disputes, or significant and insignificant issues; rather, the terms refer to the bargaining context in which a dispute arises." *Int'l Brotherhood of Teamsters, Chauffers, Warehousemen & Helpers of America-Airline Division and Teamsters Local 19 v. Southwest Airlines Co.* (5th Cir. 1989).

5. In June, 2010, Spirit Airlines pilots declared a strike at 5 A.M. and walked-out on labor contract negotiations after more than three years of bargaining for better salaries and benefits. It was the first by pilots at a commercial U.S. carrier since 2001 and the first strike since Northwest Airlines mechanics walked out in 2005. *See, e.g.*, Jaclyn Giovis & Jerome Burdi, *Spirit Airlines Pilots Declare Strike and Walk Out on Negotiations*, S. FLA. SUN-SENTINEL, June 12, 2010, at 2010 WLNR 12001298. Disputes and negotiations between labor and management are carefully orchestrated and controlled by operation of law. Consider: On August 3, 1981, nearly 12,000 air traffic controllers—unionized through the Professional Air Traffic Controllers Organization ("PATCO")—walked off their jobs in a national protest of their employment agreement.

Forty-eight hours later, President Ronald Reagan fired every striking controller and replaced them—permanently—on the basis their strike was illegal and violated established federal law. *See* 5 U.S.C. § 7116(b)(7). The need for replacement air traffic controllers persists today as a result this watershed event. *See generally* Neil Fox, *PATCO and the Courts: Public Sector Labor Law as Ideology*, 1985 U. ILL. L. REV. 245 (1985); Bernard D. Meltzer & Cass R. Sunstein, *Public Employee Strikes, Executive Discretion, and the Air Traffic Controllers*, 50 U. CHI. L. REV. 731 (1983). For a discussion of the impact of labor-management strife after September 11th see generally Ross E. Davies, *Strike Season: Protecting Labor-Management Conflict in the Age of Terror*, 93 GEO. L.J. 1783 (2005).

The process for resolving "major disputes" follows statutorily-staged events:

1. Written notice of proposed changes in agreements affecting rates of pay, rules or working conditions ("Section 6 notices") must be given at least 30 days in advance.

2. Within ten days after receipt of the Section 6 notice, the parties shall agree to the time and place for the beginning of conferences;

3. The parties engage in direct negotiations in connection with the Section 6 notices;

4. If, during the course of direct negotiations, an agreement is reached, the parties are obliged to execute that agreement;

5. If no agreement is reached in direct negotiations and an "impasse" is reached, either party may request mediation by the National Mediation Board within ten days of termination of conferences (Section 5, First).

6. If mediation is invoked, the [National Mediation Board] is required to promptly put itself in communication with the parties and use its best efforts, by mediation, to bring them to agreement.

7. Whenever the Mediation Board concludes that an amicable settlement through mediation is not available, it proffers binding arbitration to the parties to resolve their disputes.

8. If arbitration is refused by one or both parties, the Board is required "at once" to notify both parties in writing that its mediation efforts have failed (the issuance of a "release") and advise the parties that for a period of 30 days thereafter, except in certain limited circumstances, the *status quo* must be maintained (the 30-day "cooling off period").

9. During the 30-day cooling off period, the President may, in his discretion, establish an Emergency Board to investigate and report regarding the dispute, and while the Emergency Board is in existence and for 30 days after its report to the President is issued, the parties are required to maintain the *status quo*.

10. At the end of the cooling off period, if no Emergency Board is established, the parties are free to engage in economic action to attempt to resolve the dispute. Congress may legislate a resolution of the dispute, which legislation is presumptively valid and

> constitutional. If such legislation includes binding arbitration of the dispute, normal standards of judicial review of the award will apply.

Roger H. Briton & Christopher Valentino, *Airline Collective Bargaining under the Railway Labor Act: The Management Perspective*, SR035 ALI-ABA 353 (2010).

6. *In re Ionosphere Clubs, Inc.* (2d Cir. 1990), in Chapter 3, *supra*, introduced the ubiquitous and critical consideration that unions can present for airline executives. As to its members, unions have a duty to represent fairly all employees subject to a collective bargaining agreement. This putatively clear directive creates dispute on occasion, however, particularly when carriers merge and their company seniority lists are merged into a single list. *See, e.g.*, *Addington v. U.S. Airlines Pilots Ass'n* (9th Cir. 2010) (evaluating when a duty of fair representation claim based on a union's representation becomes ripe). *See also Air Line Pilots Ass'n, Int'l v. O'Neill* (1991) (clarifying the standard that governs a claim that a union has breached its duty of fair representation in its negotiation of a back-to-work agreement terminating a strike, holding that (i) the rule that a union breaches its duty of fair representation if its actions are either "arbitrary, discriminatory, or in bad faith" applies to all union activity, including contract negotiation, and (ii) a union's actions are arbitrary only if, in light of the factual and legal landscape at the time of the union's actions, the union's behavior is so far outside a "wide range of reasonableness" as to be irrational).

Outsourcing, like consolidation of carriers, presents opportunities and challenges for contemporary airline management. Many major airlines feed their hub operations with passengers transported by partner or subsidiary regional carriers from mid- to small-sized markets, *e.g.*, American Airlines though American Eagle, which generally operates aircraft of 50 seats or fewer. As part of their collective bargaining agreement, airmen value "scope clauses," which limit how much flying the major carrier can outsource to the regional carriers. *See* Andrew Compart, *The Scope of Hope*, AVIATION WK. & SPACE TECH., May 24, 2010, at 46. *See also Air Line Pilots Ass'n v. Guilford Transp. Industries, Inc.* (1st Cir. 2005).

7. On May 11, 2010, the National Mediation Board formally announced its intention to amend the Railway Labor Act, 45 U.S.C. §§ 151 *et seq.*, to change the way unions are elected at airlines and rail lines. The Final Rule, making it easier for unions to win representation elections, states:

> As part of its ongoing efforts to further the statutory goals of the Railway Labor Act, the National Mediation Board (NMB or Board) is amending its Railway Labor Act rules to provide that, in representation disputes, a majority of valid ballots cast will determine the craft or class representative. This change to its election procedures will provide a more reliable measure/indicator of employee

> sentiment in representation disputes and provide employees with clear choices in representation matters.

75 Fed. Reg. 26,062 (May 11, 2010).

On May 17, 2010, the Air Transport Association of America ("ATA"), the trade organization for major airlines, brought suit in the United District Court for the District of Columbia, seeking to prevent changes to a 75-year-old rule that a union would be certified as the collective bargaining representative only if a majority of the total eligible employees in a relevant work group (*e.g.*, "class" or "craft") voted in favor of union representation—not just the votes cast. *Air Transport Ass'n of America, Inc. v. National Mediation Bd.*, Case No. 10-CV-804 (PLF). *See generally* Jennifer Michels, *Preceent-Setting Case*, AVIATION WK. & SPACE TECH., May 24, 2010, at 43.

8. As introduced in *Branche v. Airtran Airways, Inc.* (11th Cir. 2003), *supra*, the federal Whistleblower Protection Program ("WPP") was enacted as part of the Wendell H. Ford Aviation Investment and Reform Act for the 21st Century, Pub. L. No. 106-181, Title V, § 519(a), 114 Stat. 61, 145-49 (2000) ("AIR21"). In addition to state whistleblower statutes, the federal program was designed to "provide protection for airline employee whistleblowers by prohibiting the discharge or other discrimination against an employee who provides information to its employer or the Federal government about air safety or files or participates in a proceeding related to air safety." H.R. Rep. No. 106-167, pt. 1, at 100 (1999). Section 519 of AIR21prevents an airline from discriminating against an employee because he or she "provided ... to the employer or Federal Government information relating to any violation or alleged violation of any order, regulation, or standard of the [FAA] or any other provision of law relating to air carrier safety under [Title 49] or any other law of the United States ..." 49 U.S.C. § 42121(a). AIR21 thus was designed to protect not only those who report air safety violations to the government, but also those who make such reports to their employers. *See* 49 U.S.C. § 42121(a).

Consistent with this goal, the WPP established a detailed administrative scheme for the investigation and resolution of claims brought by airline employees. *See* 49 U.S.C. § 42121(b); 29 C.F.R. Part 1979. An aggrieved employee may file a complaint with the Secretary of Labor ("Secretary") within 90 days after the date on which a violation of the WPP occurs. Once an employee files a complaint and presents a *prima facie* case, the Secretary must conduct an investigation and issue a final order. *See id.* §§ 42121(b)(2)(A), (b)(3)(A). The statute explicitly provides for review of the Secretary's final order in the courts of appeal. In the event of non-compliance with the Secretary's final order, either the Secretary or the employee may bring a civil action in a federal district court to compel compliance with the Secretary's order.

9. As in any other industry, employment discrimination claims arise in airline operations. Several circuits have held that employment discrimination cases

brought against airlines are not preempted by the Airline Deregulation Act of 1978 (see Chapter 2, *supra*). *See, e.g., Wellons v. Northwest Airlines, Inc.* (6th Cir. 1999); *Parise v. Delta Airlines, Inc.*, (11th Cir. 1998); *Aloha Islandair v. Tseu* (9th Cir. 1997); *Abdu-Brisson v. Delta Airlines, Inc.* (2d Cir. 1997).

10. Federal law generally controls the number of hours employers may require employees to work over certain periods of time—including overtime, for example. Limits of the workload of pilots and air crew is as important as it may be wanting in the area of aviation employment and safety. On the evening of February 12, 2009, Colgan Air Flight 3407, a Bombardier DHC-8-400 operating as Continental Connection, crashed in icy conditions near Buffalo-Niagra International Airport, New York. The two pilots, twoflight attendants, and 45 passengers aboard the airplane were killed, one person on the ground was killed, and the airplane was destroyed by impact forces and a postcrash fire.

The National Transportation Safety Board "determine[d] that the probable cause of th[e] accident was the captain's inappropriate response to the activation of the stick shaker, which led to an aerodynamic stall from which the airplane did not recover. Contributing to the accident were (1) the flight crew's failure to monitor airspeed in relation to the rising position of the lowspeed cue, (2) the flight crew's failure to adhere to sterile cockpit procedures, (3) the captain's failure to effectively manage the flight, and (4) Colgan Air's inadequate procedures for airspeed selection and management during approaches in icing conditions." *See http://ntsb.gov/Publictn/2010/AAR1001.pdf.*

The Colgan accident focused attention on the demanding schedule of regional airline crews and the corresponding issue of pilot fatigue and workload management issues. *See, e.g.*, Michael Beebe, *Fatigue by Pilots an Issue in Probe*, BUFF. NEWS, May 11, 2009, at A1 ("... flying for a regional airline is often a grind, pilots say, one that makes them sometimes feel more like truck drivers than commercial pilots ... 'Fatigue is a scary, dangerous thing when it pertains to a crew member' ... Nobody is saying that pilot fatigue caused Flight 3407 to go down, but it's one of a number of possible explanations the [National Transportation Safety Board] has described pilot fatigue as widespread and has said the "laws, rules and regulations governing this aspect of transportation safety are archaic in many cases ... 'Pilots are routinely pushed into sacrificing needed rest to help their companies survive during economic downturns and bankruptcy,' John Prater, president of the Air Line Pilots Association, said.").

PROBLEM

After the tragic events of September 11, 2001, United Airlines suffered financial losses that caused the company to file for bankruptcy in December 2002. In 2003, United and the Air Line Pilots Association, International ("ALPA") negotiated a new labor agreement in which the pilots made significant concessions on wages, benefits and other issues, including a 40% wage reduction for the pilots. Over the next two years, as

United's financial condition deteriorated further, the pilots agreed to additional wage reductions and termination of a defined benefit pension plan. The parties agreed that they could modify the collective bargaining agreement ("CBA"), but neither side could unilaterally initiate negotiations until April 2009.

United and ALPA have a long history of contentious labor relations. In 1985, the pilots engaged in a month-long strike, during which United hired permanent replacements for the striking pilots. The pilots and the company negotiated a Back-to-Work Agreement at the end of the strike, with the pilots agreeing not to retaliate against the newly hired pilots or any pilots who crossed the picket line during the strike. In spite of the Back-to-Work Agreement, the pilots who worked during the strike were subjected to ostracism and harassment by the striking pilots for many years following the end of the strike. The harassment ranged from the juvenile (clicking a toy clicker when non-striking pilots entered a work area) to the petulant (refusing to shake hands with the non-striking pilots) to the repulsive (urinating or defecating in the flight bags of non-striking pilots). The striking pilots were both creative and persistent in their mistreatment of their non-striking counterparts, and some of the non-striking pilots eventually resigned their positions with United. The remaining United pilots came to believe that anyone who did not follow the majority position or ALPA's directives would be subjected to similar treatment.

After United exited bankruptcy in 2006, the company began to turn a profit. United recovered even more in 2007, earning approximately $1 billion in profit in that year. Beginning in December 2006, ALPA sought to reopen negotiations on the 2003 CBA even though it was not amendable until December 31, 2009. According to United, ALPA began to pressure United with a campaign that consisted of directives to pilots to engage in actions designed to cause flight delays and cancellations and to increase United's costs. United alleged that ALPA encouraged the pilots (a) to "fly the contract," that is, to adhere strictly to the terms of the 2003 CBA; (b) to refuse to voluntarily waive any section of the CBA, including provisions that were designated as waivable; (c) to refuse voluntary flight assignments known as "junior/senior manning"; (d) to increase fuel consumption; (e) to refuse to operate planes that had deferrable maintenance items; and (f) to take excessive amounts of time in pre-flight cockpit checks. United also alleged that, beginning in July 2008, ALPA coordinated a "sick-out" among United's junior pilots. The sick-out, in combination with the refusal to accept voluntary junior/senior manning assignments, caused several hundred flight cancellations, affecting approximately 30,000 United customers.

United Airlines sues for preliminary injunctive relief against ALPA. What result? *See United Air Lines, Inc. v. Air Line Pilots Ass'n, Int'l* (7th Cir. 2009).

C. UNMANNED AVIATION: "DRONES"

September 11th represented an intelligence failure—a failure to "connect the dots." As a consequence, lawmakers implemented different types of computerized profiling systems, many of which are detailed in Chapter 5, *infra*. Computers and automated technologies have long played an outsized role in aviation security, from X-rays to magnetometers in the 1960s to baggage screening systems more recently. But, the emergence of unmanned aerial systems ("UAS") as a weapon of first choice in the "war on terror" has been a particularly interesting development since September 11th.

The military dimensions of unmanned aerial vehicles—"drones"—grab most of the headlines as the innovation of autonomous and automated weapons raise unprecedented legal issues. But, the emergence of civil and commercial drone operations on an international scale offers an equally compelling storyline, too. The global appetite for drones in private and public spaces across a wide range of activities is enormous, from agriculture to search and rescue to sports videography to environmental conservation to anti-poaching and pizza delivery.

Worldwide interest in drones has as much to do with advances in miniaturization, engineering, and nano-technology as with a revolution in data collection and analytics. As transformational *information* devices, remotely piloted aircraft systems ("RPAS")—also known as "drones" or "unmanned aerial vehicles (UAV)" or "unmanned aerial system (UAS)"—are "smart" airborne platforms armed with ever-sophisticated sensor suites and software solutions. Now, using high resolution, multispectral, thermal, and hyperspectral sensors on drones, farmers use precision agriculture to assess yield and crop health from the air—a data-driven approach that is far more efficient than manual, ground-based processes reliant on the naked eye. Meanwhile, small drones offer journalists and law enforcement an asset whose agility is superior to that of traditional airplanes and rotorcraft, maximizing information gathering and surveillance capabilities while minimizing the human costs associated with low-altitude, close-proximity missions. Indeed, the abilities of drones to gather intelligence, surveillance, and reconnaissance ("ISR") is apparently limitless—constrained perhaps only by the law. But, so too is the technology's potential for invading and degrading longstanding legal principles protecting personal and societal privacy and property rights seemingly unbounded.

As ownership, operation, and interest in unmanned and optionally-manned aircraft increases in commercial spaces, a consistent and predictable regulatory framework is both needed and elusive. In some respects, the development of drone laws resembles the development of the common law with respect to manned aviation, as the cases below show.

Law and Technology

CALIFORNIA v. CIRAOLO
476 U.S. 207 (1985)

Chief Justice BURGER delivered the opinion of the Court.

We granted *certiorari* to determine whether the Fourth Amendment is violated by aerial observation without a warrant from an altitude of 1,000 feet of a fenced-in backyard within the curtilage of a home.

BACKGROUND

On September 2, 1982, Santa Clara Police received an anonymous telephone tip that marijuana was growing in respondent's backyard. Police were unable to observe the contents of respondent's yard from ground level because of a 6-foot outer fence and a 10-foot inner fence completely enclosing the yard. Later that day, Officer Shutz, who was assigned to investigate, secured a private plane and flew over respondent's house at an altitude of 1,000 feet, within navigable airspace; he was accompanied by Officer Rodriguez. Both officers were trained in marijuana identification. From the overflight, the officers readily identified marijuana plants 8 feet to 10 feet in height growing in a 15- by 25-foot plot in respondent's yard; they photographed the area with a standard 35mm camera.

On September 8, 1982, Officer Shutz obtained a search warrant on the basis of an affidavit describing the anonymous tip and their observations; a photograph depicting respondent's house, the backyard, and neighboring homes was attached to the affidavit as an exhibit. The warrant was executed the next day and 73 plants were seized; it is not disputed that these were marijuana.

After the trial court denied respondent's motion to suppress the evidence of the search, respondent pleaded guilty to a charge of cultivation of marijuana. The California Court of Appeal reversed, however, on the ground that the warrantless aerial observation of respondent's yard which led to the issuance of the warrant violated the Fourth Amendment. That court held first that respondent's backyard marijuana garden was within the "curtilage" of his home, under *Oliver v. United States* (1984). The court emphasized that the height and existence of the two fences constituted "objective criteria from which we may conclude he manifested a reasonable expectation of privacy by any standard."

Examining the particular method of surveillance undertaken, the court then found it "significant" that the flyover "was not the result of a routine patrol conducted for any other legitimate law enforcement or public safety objective, but was undertaken for the specific purpose of observing this particular enclosure within [respondent's] curtilage." It held this focused observation was "a direct and unauthorized intrusion into the sanctity of the home" which violated respondent's reasonable expectation of privacy. The California Supreme Court denied the State's petition for review. We granted the State's petition for *certiorari* and reverse.

The State argues that respondent has "knowingly exposed" his backyard to aerial observation, because all that was seen was visible to the naked eye from any aircraft flying overhead. The State analogizes its mode of observation to a knothole or opening in a fence: if there is an opening, the police may look.

The California Court of Appeal, as we noted earlier, accepted the analysis that unlike the casual observation of a private person flying overhead, this flight was focused specifically on a small suburban yard, and was not the result of any routine patrol overflight. Respondent contends he has done all that can reasonably be expected to tell the world he wishes to maintain the privacy of his garden within the curtilage without covering his yard. Such covering, he argues, would defeat its purpose as an outside living area; he asserts he has not "knowingly" exposed himself to aerial views.

DISCUSSION

The touchstone of Fourth Amendment analysis is whether a person has a "constitutionally protected reasonable expectation of privacy." *Katz v. United States* (1967) (Harlan, J., concurring). *Katz* posits a two-part inquiry: first, has the individual manifested a subjective expectation of privacy in the object of the challenged search? Second, is society willing to recognize that expectation as reasonable?

Clearly—and understandably—respondent has met the test of manifesting his own subjective intent and desire to maintain privacy as to his unlawful agricultural pursuits. However, we need not address that issue, for the State has not challenged the finding of the California Court of Appeal that respondent had such an expectation. It can reasonably be assumed that the 10-foot fence was placed to conceal the marijuana crop from at least street-level views. So far as the normal sidewalk traffic was concerned, this fence served that purpose, because respondent "took normal precautions to maintain his privacy." *Rawlings v. Kentucky* (1980).

Yet a 10-foot fence might not shield these plants from the eyes of a citizen or a policeman perched on the top of a truck or a two-level bus. Whether respondent therefore manifested a subjective expectation of privacy from all observations of his backyard, or whether instead he manifested merely a hope that no one would observe his unlawful gardening pursuits, is not entirely clear in these circumstances. Respondent appears to challenge the authority of government to observe his activity from any vantage point or place if the viewing is motivated by a law enforcement purpose, and not the result of a casual, accidental observation.

We turn, therefore, to the second inquiry under *Katz*, *i.e.*, whether that expectation is reasonable. In pursuing this inquiry, we must keep in mind that "[t]he test of legitimacy is not whether the individual chooses to conceal assertedly 'private' activity," but instead "whether the government's intrusion infringes upon the personal and societal values protected by the Fourth Amendment."

Respondent argues that because his yard was in the curtilage of his home, no governmental aerial observation is permissible under the Fourth Amendment without a warrant. The history and genesis of the curtilage doctrine are instructive. "At common law, the curtilage is the area to which extends the intimate activity associated with the 'sanctity of a man's home and the privacies of life.'" *Oliver*, *supra*. The protection afforded the curtilage is essentially a protection of families and personal privacy in an area intimately linked to the home, both physically and psychologically, where privacy expectations are most heightened. The claimed area here was immediately adjacent to a suburban home, surrounded by high double fences. This close nexus to the home would appear to encompass this small area within the curtilage. Accepting, as the State does, that this yard and its crop fall within the curtilage, the question remains whether naked-eye observation of the curtilage by police from an aircraft lawfully operating at an altitude of 1,000 feet violates an expectation of privacy that is reasonable.

That the area is within the curtilage does not itself bar all police observation. The Fourth Amendment protection of the home has never been extended to require law enforcement officers to shield their eyes when passing by a home on public thoroughfares. Nor does the mere fact that an individual has taken measures to restrict some views of his activities preclude an officer's observations from a public vantage point where he has a right to be and which renders the activities clearly visible. "What a person knowingly exposes to the public, even in his own home or office, is not a subject of Fourth Amendment protection." *Katz*, *supra*.

The observations by Officers Shutz and Rodriguez in this case took place within public navigable airspace in a physically nonintrusive manner; from this point they were able to observe plants readily discernible to the naked eye as marijuana. That the observation from aircraft was directed at identifying the plants and the officers were trained to recognize marijuana is irrelevant. Such observation is precisely what a judicial officer needs to provide a basis for a warrant. Any member of the public flying in this airspace who glanced down could have seen everything that these officers observed. On this record, we readily conclude that respondent's expectation that his garden was protected from such observation is unreasonable and is not an expectation that society is prepared to honor.

The dissent contends that the Court ignores Justice Harlan's warning in his concurrence in *Katz* that the Fourth Amendment should not be limited to proscribing only physical intrusions onto private property. But Justice Harlan's observations about future electronic developments and the potential for electronic interference with private communications were plainly not aimed at simple visual observations from a public place. Indeed, since *Katz* the Court has required warrants for electronic surveillance aimed at intercepting private conversations.

Justice Harlan made it crystal clear that he was resting on the reality that one who enters a telephone booth is entitled to assume that his conversation is not being intercepted. This does not translate readily into a rule of constitutional dimensions that one who grows illicit drugs in his backyard is "entitled to assume" his unlawful conduct will not be observed by a passing aircraft-or by a power company repair mechanic on a pole overlooking the yard. As Justice Harlan emphasized,

> a man's home is, for most purposes, a place where he expects privacy, but objects, activities, or statements that he exposes to the 'plain view' of outsiders are not 'protected' because no intention to keep them to himself has been exhibited. On the other hand, conversations in the open would not be protected against being overheard, for the expectation of privacy under the circumstances would be unreasonable.

One can reasonably doubt that in 1967 Justice Harlan considered an aircraft within the category of future "electronic" developments that could stealthily intrude upon an individual's privacy. In an age where private and commercial flight in the public airways is routine, it is unreasonable for respondent to expect that his marijuana plants were constitutionally protected from being observed with the naked eye from an altitude of 1,000 feet. The Fourth Amendment simply does not require the police traveling in the public airways at this altitude to obtain a warrant in order to observe what is visible to the naked eye.

Justice POWELL, with whom Justice BRENNAN, Justice MARSHALL, and Justice BLACKMUN join, dissenting.

Concurring in *Katz*, Justice Harlan warned that any decision to construe the Fourth Amendment as proscribing only physical intrusions by police onto private property "is, in the present day, bad physics as well as bad law, for reasonable expectations of privacy may be defeated by electronic as well as physical invasion." Because the Court today ignores that warning in an opinion that departs significantly from the standard developed in *Katz* for deciding when a Fourth Amendment violation has occurred, I dissent.

The Court concludes that Shutz could use an airplane—a product of modern technology—to intrude visually into respondent's yard. The Court argues that respondent had no reasonable expectation of privacy from aerial observation. It notes that Shutz was "within public navigable airspace," when he looked into and photographed respondent's yard. It then relies on the fact that the surveillance was not accompanied by a physical invasion of the curtilage. Reliance on the manner of surveillance is directly contrary to the standard of *Katz*, which identifies a constitutionally protected privacy right by focusing on the interests of the individual and of a free society. Since *Katz*, we have consistently held that the presence or absence of physical trespass by police is constitutionally irrelevant to the question whether society is prepared to recognize an asserted privacy interest as reasonable.

The Court's holding, therefore, must rest solely on the fact that members of the public fly in planes and may look down at homes as they fly over them. The Court does not explain why it finds this fact to be significant. One may assume that the Court believes that citizens bear the risk that air travelers will observe activities occurring within backyards that are open to the sun and air. This risk, the Court appears to hold, nullifies expectations of privacy in those yards even as to purposeful police surveillance from the air. The Court finds support for this conclusion in *United States v. Knotts* (1983).

This line of reasoning is flawed. First, the actual risk to privacy from commercial or pleasure aircraft is virtually nonexistent. Travelers on commercial flights, as well as private planes used for business or personal reasons, normally obtain at most a fleeting, anonymous, and nondiscriminating glimpse of the landscape and buildings over which they pass. The risk that a passenger on such a plane might observe private activities, and might connect those activities with particular people, is simply too trivial to protect against. It is no accident that, as a matter of common experience, many people build fences around their residential areas, but few build roofs over their backyards. Therefore, contrary to the Court's suggestion, people do not "'knowingly expos[e]'" their residential yards "'to the public' " merely by failing to build barriers that prevent aerial surveillance.

The Court's reliance on *Knotts* reveals the second problem with its analysis. The activities under surveillance in *Knotts* took place on public streets, not in private homes. Comings and goings on public streets are public matters, and the Constitution does not disable police from observing what every member of the public can see. The activity in this case, by contrast, took place within the private area immediately adjacent to a home. Yet the Court approves purposeful police surveillance of that activity and area similar to that approved in *Knotts* with respect to public activities and areas. The only possible basis for this holding is a judgment that the risk to privacy posed by the remote possibility that a private airplane passenger will notice outdoor activities is equivalent to the risk of official aerial surveillance.

But the Court fails to acknowledge the qualitative difference between police surveillance and other uses made of the airspace. Members of the public use the airspace for travel, business, or pleasure, not for the purpose of observing activities taking place within residential yards. Here, police conducted an overflight at low altitude solely for the purpose of discovering evidence of crime within a private enclave into which they were constitutionally forbidden to intrude at ground level without a warrant. It is not easy to believe that our society is prepared to force individuals to bear the risk of this type of warrantless police intrusion into their residential areas.

Since respondent had a reasonable expectation of privacy in his yard, aerial surveillance undertaken by the police for the purpose of discovering evidence of crime constituted a "search" within the meaning of the Fourth Amendment. "Warrantless searches are presumptively unreasonable, though the Court has recognized a few limited exceptions to this general rule."

This case presents no such exception. The indiscriminate nature of aerial surveillance, illustrated by Officer Shutz's photograph of respondent's home and enclosed yard as well as those of his neighbors, poses "far too serious a threat to privacy interests in the home to escape entirely some sort of Fourth Amendment oversight." Therefore, I would affirm the judgment of the California Court of Appeal ordering suppression of the marijuana plants.

Some may believe that this case, involving no physical intrusion on private property, presents "the obnoxious thing in its mildest and least repulsive form." But this Court recognized long ago that the essence of a Fourth Amendment violation is "not the breaking of [a person's] doors, and the rummaging of his drawers," but rather is "the invasion of his indefeasible right of personal security, personal liberty and private property."

Rapidly advancing technology now permits police to conduct surveillance in the home itself, an area where privacy interests are most cherished in our society, without any physical trespass. While the rule in *Katz* was designed to prevent silent and unseen invasions of Fourth Amendment privacy rights in a variety of settings, we have consistently afforded heightened protection to a person's right to be left alone in the privacy of his house. The Court fails to enforce that right or to give any weight to the longstanding presumption that warrantless intrusions into the home are unreasonable.

FLORIDA v. RILEY

488 U.S. 445 (1988)

Justice WHITE announced the judgment of the Court and delivered an opinion, in which THE CHIEF JUSTICE, Justice SCALIA, and Justice KENNEDY join.

On certification to it by a lower state court, the Florida Supreme Court addressed the following question: "Whether surveillance of the interior of a partially covered greenhouse in a residential backyard from the vantage point of a helicopter located 400 feet above the greenhouse constitutes a 'search' for which a warrant is required under the Fourth Amendment and Article I, § 12 of the Florida Constitution." The court answered the question in the affirmative, and we granted the State's petition for certiorari challenging that conclusion.

Respondent Riley lived in a mobile home located on five acres of rural property. A greenhouse was located 10 to 20 feet behind the mobile home. Two sides of the greenhouse were enclosed. The other two sides were not enclosed but the contents of the greenhouse were obscured from view from surrounding property by trees, shrubs, and the mobile home. The greenhouse was covered by corrugated roofing panels, some translucent and some opaque. At the time relevant to this case, two of the panels, amounting to approximately 10% of the roof area, were missing. A wire fence surrounded the mobile home and the greenhouse, and the property was posted with a "DO NOT ENTER" sign.

This case originated with an anonymous tip to the Pasco County Sheriff's office that marijuana was being grown on respondent's property. When an investigating officer discovered that he could not see the contents of the greenhouse from the road, he circled twice over respondent's property in a helicopter at the height of 400 feet. With his naked eye, he was able to see through the openings in the roof and one or more of the open sides of the greenhouse and to identify what he thought was marijuana growing in the structure. A warrant was obtained based on these observations, and the ensuing search revealed marijuana growing in the greenhouse.

Respondent was charged with possession of marijuana under Florida law. The trial court granted his motion to suppress; the Florida Court of Appeals reversed but certified the case to the Florida Supreme Court, which quashed the decision of the Court of Appeals and reinstated the trial court's suppression order.

We agree with the State's submission that our decision in *California v. Ciraolo* (1986) controls this case. There, acting on a tip, the police inspected the back-yard of a particular house while flying in a fixed-wing aircraft at 1,000 feet. With the naked eye the officers saw what they concluded was marijuana growing in the yard. A search warrant was obtained on the strength of this airborne inspection, and marijuana plants were found. The trial court refused to suppress this evidence, but a state appellate court held that the inspection violated the Fourth and Fourteenth Amendments to the United States Constitution, and that the warrant was therefore invalid. We in turn reversed, holding that the inspection was not a search subject to the Fourth Amendment.

We recognized that the yard was within the curtilage of the house, that a fence shielded the yard from observation from the street, and that the occupant had a subjective expectation of privacy. We held, however, that such an expectation was not reasonable and not one "that society is prepared to honor." Our reasoning was that the home and its curtilage are not necessarily protected from inspection that involves no physical invasion. "'What a person knowingly exposes to the public, even in his own home or office, is not a subject of Fourth Amendment protection.'"

As a general proposition, the police may see what may be seen "from a public vantage point where [they have] a right to be." Thus the police, like the public, would have been free to inspect the backyard garden from the street if their view had been unobstructed. They were likewise free to inspect the yard from the vantage point of an aircraft flying in the navigable airspace as this plane was. "In an age where private and commercial flight in the public airways is routine, it is unreasonable for respondent to expect that his marijuana plants were constitutionally protected from being observed with the naked eye from an altitude of 1,000 feet. The Fourth Amendment simply does not require the police traveling in the public airways at this altitude to obtain a warrant in order to observe what is visible to the naked eye."

We arrive at the same conclusion in the present case. In this case, as in *Ciraolo*, the property surveyed was within the curtilage of respondent's home. Riley no doubt intended and expected that his greenhouse would not be open to public inspection, and the precautions he took protected against ground-level observation. Because the sides and roof of his greenhouse were left partially open, however, what was growing in the greenhouse was subject to viewing from the air. Under the holding in *Ciraolo*, Riley could not reasonably have expected the contents of his greenhouse to be immune from examination by an officer seated in a fixed-wing aircraft flying in navigable airspace at an altitude of 1,000 feet or, as the Florida Supreme Court seemed to recognize, at an altitude of 500 feet, the lower limit of the navigable airspace for such an aircraft. Here, the inspection was made from a helicopter, but as is the case with fixed-wing planes, "private and commercial flight [by helicopter] in the public airways is routine" in this country, and there is no indication that such flights are unheard of in Pasco County, Florida. Riley could not reasonably have expected that his greenhouse was protected from public or official observation from a helicopter had it been flying within the navigable airspace for fixed-wing aircraft.

Nor on the facts before us, does it make a difference for Fourth Amendment purposes that the helicopter was flying at 400 feet when the officer saw what was growing in the greenhouse through the partially open roof and sides of the structure. We would have a different case if flying at that altitude had been contrary to law or regulation. But helicopters are not bound by the lower limits of the navigable airspace allowed to other aircraft.

Any member of the public could legally have been flying over Riley's property in a helicopter at the altitude of 400 feet and could have observed Riley's greenhouse. The police officer did no more. This is not to say that an inspection of the curtilage of a house from an aircraft will always pass muster under the Fourth Amendment simply because the plane is within the navigable airspace specified by law. But it is of obvious importance that the helicopter in this case was not violating the law, and there is nothing in the record or before us to suggest that helicopters flying at 400 feet are sufficiently rare in this country to lend substance to respondent's claim that he reasonably anticipated that his greenhouse would not be subject to observation from that altitude. Neither is there any intimation here that the helicopter interfered with respondent's normal use of the greenhouse or of other parts of the curtilage. As far as this record reveals, no intimate details connected with the use of the home or curtilage were observed, and there was no undue noise, and no wind, dust, or threat of injury. In these circumstances, there was no violation of the Fourth Amendment. The judgment of the Florida Supreme Court is accordingly reversed.

Justice O'CONNOR, concurring in the judgment.

I concur in the judgment reversing the Supreme Court of Florida because I agree that police observation of the greenhouse in Riley's curtilage from a helicopter passing at an altitude of 400 feet did not violate an expectation of privacy "that society is prepared to recognize as 'reasonable.'" *Katz v. United States* (1967) (Harlan, J., concurring). I write separately, however, to clarify the standard I believe follows from *California v. Ciraolo* (1986). In my view, the plurality's approach rests the scope of Fourth Amendment protection too heavily on compliance with FAA regulations whose purpose is to promote air safety, not to protect "[t]he right of the people to be secure in their persons, houses, papers, and effects, against unreasonable searches and seizures." U.S. CONST., AMDT. 4.

Ciraolo involved observation of curtilage by officers flying in an airplane at an altitude of 1,000 feet. In evaluating whether this observation constituted a search for which a warrant was required, we acknowledged the importance of curtilage in Fourth Amendment doctrine: "The protection afforded the curtilage is essentially a protection of families and personal privacy in an area intimately linked to the home, both physically and psychologically, where privacy expectations are most heightened." Although the curtilage is an area to which the private activities of the home extend, all police observation of the curtilage is not necessarily barred by the Fourth Amendment. As we observed: "The Fourth Amendment protection of the home has never been extended to require law enforcement officers to shield their eyes when passing by a home on public thoroughfares."

In *Ciraolo*, we likened observation from a plane traveling in "public navigable airspace" at 1,000 feet to observation by police "passing by a home on public thoroughfares." We held that "[i]n an age where private and commercial flight in the public airways is routine," it is unreasonable to expect the curtilage to be constitutionally protected from aerial observation with the naked eye from an altitude of 1,000 feet.

Ciraolo's expectation of privacy was unreasonable not because the airplane was operating where it had a "right to be," but because public air travel at 1,000 feet is a sufficiently routine part of modern life that it is unreasonable for persons on the ground to expect that their curtilage will not be observed from the air at that altitude. Although "helicopters are not bound by the lower limits of the navigable airspace allowed to other aircraft," there is no reason to assume that compliance with FAA regulations alone determines "'whether the government's intrusion infringes upon the personal and societal values protected by the Fourth Amendment.'" *Ciraolo, supra.* Because the FAA has decided that helicopters can lawfully operate at virtually any altitude so long as they pose no safety hazard, it does not follow that the expectations of privacy "society is prepared to recognize as 'reasonable' " simply mirror the FAA's safety concerns.

Observations of curtilage from helicopters at very low altitudes are not perfectly analogous to ground-level observations from public roads or sidewalks. While in both cases the police may have a legal right to occupy the physical space from which their observations are made, the two situations are not necessarily comparable in terms of whether expectations of privacy from such vantage points should be considered reasonable. Public roads, even those less traveled by, are clearly demarked public thoroughfares. Individuals who seek privacy can take precautions, tailored to the location of the road, to avoid disclosing private activities to those who pass by. They can build a tall fence, for example, and thus ensure private enjoyment of the curtilage without risking public observation from the road or sidewalk. If they do not take such precautions, they cannot reasonably expect privacy from public observation.

In contrast, even individuals who have taken effective precautions to ensure against ground-level observations cannot block off all conceivable aerial views of their outdoor patios and yards without entirely giving up their enjoyment of those areas. To require individuals to completely cover and enclose their curtilage is to demand more than the "precautions customarily taken by those seeking privacy." *Rakas v. Illinois* (1978) (Powell, J., concurring). The fact that a helicopter could conceivably observe the curtilage at virtually any altitude or angle, without violating FAA regulations, does not in itself mean that an individual has no reasonable expectation of privacy from such observation.

In determining whether Riley had a reasonable expectation of privacy from aerial observation, the relevant inquiry after *Ciraolo* is not whether the helicopter was where it had a right to be under FAA regulations. Rather, consistent with *Katz*, we must ask whether the helicopter was in the public airways at an altitude at which members of the public travel with sufficient regularity that Riley's expectation of privacy from aerial observation was not "one that society is prepared to recognize as 'reasonable.'" Thus, in determining "'whether the government's intrusion infringes upon the personal and societal values protected by the Fourth Amendment,'" it is not conclusive to observe, as the plurality does, that "[a]ny member of the public could legally have been flying over Riley's property in a helicopter at the altitude of 400 feet and could have observed Riley's greenhouse."

Nor is it conclusive that police helicopters may often fly at 400 feet. If the public rarely, if ever, travels overhead at such altitudes, the observation cannot be said to be from a vantage point generally used by the public and Riley cannot be said to have "knowingly expose[d]" his greenhouse to public view. However, if the public can generally be expected to travel over residential backyards at an altitude of 400 feet, Riley cannot reasonably expect his curtilage to be free from such aerial observation.

In my view, the defendant must bear the burden of proving that his expectation of privacy was a reasonable one, and thus that a "search" within the meaning of the Fourth Amendment even took place. Because there is reason to believe that there is considerable public use of airspace at altitudes of 400 feet and above, and because Riley introduced no evidence to the contrary before the Florida courts, I conclude that Riley's expectation that his curtilage was protected from naked-eye aerial observation from that altitude was not a reasonable one. However, public use of altitudes lower than that—particularly public observations from helicopters circling over the curtilage of a home—may be sufficiently rare that police surveillance from such altitudes would violate reasonable expectations of privacy, despite compliance with FAA air safety regulations.

Justice BRENNAN, with whom Justice MARSHALL and Justice STEVENS, join, dissenting.

The Court holds today that police officers need not obtain a warrant based on probable cause before circling in a helicopter 400 feet above a home in order to investigate what is taking place behind the walls of the curtilage. I cannot agree that the Fourth Amendment to the Constitution, which safeguards "[t]he right of the people to be secure in their persons, houses, papers, and effects, against unreasonable searches and seizures," tolerates such an intrusion on privacy and personal security.

* * *

The opinion for a plurality of the Court reads almost as if *Katz v. United States* (1967) had never been decided. Notwithstanding the disclaimers of its final paragraph, the opinion relies almost exclusively on the fact that the police officer conducted his surveillance from a vantage point where, under applicable Federal Aviation Administration regulations, he had a legal right to be. *Katz* teaches, however, that the relevant inquiry is whether the police surveillance "violated the privacy upon which [the defendant] justifiably relied,"—or, as Justice Harlan put it, whether the police violated an "expectation of privacy ... that society is prepared to recognize as 'reasonable.'" The result of that inquiry in any given case depends ultimately on the judgment "whether, if the particular form of surveillance practiced by the police is permitted to go unregulated by constitutional restraints, the amount of privacy and freedom remaining to citizens would be diminished to a compass inconsistent with the aims of a free and open society." Anthony G. Amsterdam, *Perspectives on the Fourth Amendment*, 58 MINN. L. REV. 349, 403 (1974).

The plurality undertakes no inquiry into whether low-level helicopter surveillance by the police of activities in an enclosed backyard is consistent with the "aims of a free and open society." Instead, it summarily concludes that Riley's expectation of privacy was unreasonable because "[a]ny member of the public could legally have been flying over Riley's property in a helicopter at the altitude of 400 feet and could have observed Riley's greenhouse." This observation is, in turn, based solely on the fact that the police helicopter was within the airspace within which such craft are allowed by federal safety regulations to fly.

I agree, of course, that "[w]hat a person knowingly exposes to the public ... is not a subject of Fourth Amendment protection." *Katz*. But I cannot agree that one "knowingly exposes [an area] to the public" solely because a helicopter may legally fly above it. Under the plurality's exceedingly grudging Fourth Amendment theory, the expectation of privacy is defeated if a single member of the public could conceivably position herself to see into the area in question without doing anything illegal. It is defeated whatever the difficulty a person would have in so positioning herself, and however infrequently anyone would in fact do so. In taking this view the plurality ignores the very essence of *Katz*.

The reason why there is no reasonable expectation of privacy in an area that is exposed to the public is that little diminution in "the amount of privacy and freedom remaining to citizens" will result from police surveillance of something that any passerby readily sees. To pretend, as the plurality opinion does, that the same is true when the police use a helicopter to peer over high fences is, at best, disingenuous. Notwithstanding the plurality's statistics about the number of helicopters registered in this country, can it seriously be questioned that Riley enjoyed virtually complete privacy in his backyard greenhouse, and that that privacy was invaded solely by police helicopter surveillance? Is the theoretical possibility that any member of the public (with sufficient means) could also have hired a helicopter and looked over Riley's fence of any relevance at all in determining whether Riley suffered a serious loss of privacy and personal security through the police action?

Seizing on a reference in *Ciraolo* to the fact that the police officer was in a position "where he ha[d] a right to be," today's plurality professes to find this case indistinguishable because FAA regulations do not impose a minimum altitude requirement on helicopter traffic; thus, the officer in this case too made his observations from a vantage point where he had a right to be.

It is a curious notion that the reach of the Fourth Amendment can be so largely defined by administrative regulations issued for purposes of flight safety. It is more curious still that the plurality relies to such an extent on the legality of the officer's act, when we have consistently refused to equate police violation of the law with infringement of the Fourth Amendment. But the plurality's willingness to end its inquiry when it finds that the officer was in a position he had a right to be in is misguided for an even more fundamental reason. Finding determinative the fact that the officer was where he had a right to be is, at bottom, an attempt to analogize surveillance from a helicopter to surveillance by a police officer standing on a public road and viewing evidence of crime through an open window or a gap in a fence. In such a situation, the occupant of the home may be said to lack any reasonable expectation of privacy in what can be seen from that road—even if, in fact, people rarely pass that way.

The police officer positioned 400 feet above Riley's backyard was not, however, standing on a public road. The vantage point he enjoyed was not one any citizen could readily share. His ability to see over Riley's fence depended on his use of a very expensive and sophisticated piece of machinery to which few ordinary citizens have access. In such circumstances it makes no more sense to rely on the legality of the officer's position in the skies than it would to judge the constitutionality of the wiretap in *Katz* by the legality of the officer's position outside the telephone booth. The simple inquiry whether the police officer had the legal right to be in the position from which he made his observations cannot suffice, for we cannot assume that Riley's curtilage was so open to the observations of passersby in the skies that he retained little privacy or personal security to be lost to police surveillance.

The question before us must be not whether the police were where they had a right to be, but whether public observation of Riley's curtilage was so commonplace that Riley's expectation of privacy in his backyard could not be considered reasonable. To say that an invasion of Riley's privacy from the skies was not impossible is most emphatically not the same as saying that his expectation of privacy within his enclosed curtilage was not "one that society is prepared to recognize as 'reasonable.'" *Katz*, *supra*. (Harlan, J., concurring).

While, as we held in *Ciraolo*, air traffic at elevations of 1,000 feet or more may be so common that whatever could be seen with the naked eye from that elevation is unprotected by the Fourth Amendment, it is a large step from there to say that the Amendment offers no protection against low-level helicopter surveillance of enclosed curtilage areas. To take this step is error enough. That the plurality does so with little analysis beyond its determination that the police complied with FAA regulations is particularly unfortunate.

* * *

Equally disconcerting is the lack of any meaningful limit to the plurality's holding. It is worth reiterating that the FAA regulations the plurality relies on as establishing that the officer was where he had a right to be set no minimum flight altitude for helicopters. It is difficult, therefore, to see what, if any, helicopter surveillance would run afoul of the plurality's rule that there exists no reasonable expectation of privacy as long as the helicopter is where it has a right to be.

Only in its final paragraph does the plurality opinion suggest that there might be some limits to police helicopter surveillance beyond those imposed by FAA regulations:

> Neither is there any intimation here that the helicopter interfered with respondent's normal use of the greenhouse or of other parts of the curtilage.

> As far as this record reveals, no intimate details connected with the use of the home or curtilage were observed, and there was no undue noise, and no wind, dust, or threat of injury. In these circumstances, there was no violation of the Fourth Amendment.

I will deal with the "intimate details" below. For the rest, one wonders what the plurality believes the purpose of the Fourth Amendment to be. If through noise, wind, dust, and threat of injury from helicopters the State "interfered with respondent's normal use of the greenhouse or of other parts of the curtilage," Riley might have a cause of action in inverse condemnation, but that is not what the Fourth Amendment is all about. Nowhere is this better stated than in Justice White's opinion for the Court in *Camara v. Municipal Court* (1967): "The basic purpose of this Amendment, as recognized in countless decisions of this Court, is to safeguard the privacy and security of individuals against arbitrary invasions by governmental officials."

If indeed the purpose of the restraints imposed by the Fourth Amendment is to "safeguard the privacy and security of individuals," then it is puzzling why it should be the helicopter's noise, wind, and dust that provides the measure of whether this constitutional safeguard has been infringed. Imagine a helicopter capable of hovering just above an enclosed courtyard or patio without generating any noise, wind, or dust at all—and, for good measure, without posing any threat of injury. Suppose the police employed this miraculous tool to discover not only what crops people were growing in their greenhouses, but also what books they were reading and who their dinner guests were. Suppose, finally, that the FAA regulations remained unchanged, so that the police were undeniably "where they had a right to be."

Would today's plurality continue to assert that "[t]he right of the people to be secure in their persons, houses, papers, and effects, against unreasonable searches and seizures" was not infringed by such surveillance? Yet that is the logical consequence of the plurality's rule that, so long as the police are where they have a right to be under air traffic regulations, the Fourth Amendment is offended only if the aerial surveillance interferes with the use of the backyard as a garden spot. Nor is there anything in the plurality's opinion to suggest that any different rule would apply were the police looking from their helicopter, not into the open curtilage, but through an open window into a room viewable only from the air.

* * *

Perhaps the most remarkable passage in the plurality opinion is its suggestion that the case might be a different one had any "intimate details connected with the use of the home or curtilage [been] observed." What, one wonders, is meant by "intimate details"? If the police had observed Riley embracing his wife in the backyard greenhouse, would we then say that his reasonable expectation of privacy had been infringed? Where in the Fourth Amendment or in our cases is there any warrant for imposing a requirement that the activity observed must be "intimate" in order to be protected by the Constitution?

It is difficult to avoid the conclusion that the plurality has allowed its analysis of Riley's expectation of privacy to be colored by its distaste for the activity in which he was engaged. It is indeed easy to forget, especially in view of current concern over drug trafficking, that the scope of the Fourth Amendment's protection does not turn on whether the activity disclosed by a search is illegal or innocuous. But we dismiss this as a "drug case" only at the peril of our own liberties. Justice Frankfurter once noted that "[i]t is a fair summary of history to say that the safeguards of liberty have frequently been forged in controversies involving not very nice people," *United States v. Rabinowitz* (1950) (dissenting opinion), and nowhere is this observation more apt than in the area of the Fourth Amendment, whose words have necessarily been given meaning largely through decisions suppressing evidence of criminal activity.

The principle enunciated in this case determines what limits the Fourth Amendment imposes on aerial surveillance of any person, for any reason. If the Constitution does not protect Riley's marijuana garden against such surveillance, it is hard to see how it will prohibit the government from aerial spying on the activities of a law-abiding citizen on her fully enclosed outdoor patio. As Professor Amsterdam has eloquently written: "The question is not whether you or I must draw the blinds before we commit a crime. It is whether you and I must discipline ourselves to draw the blinds every time we enter a room, under pain of surveillance if we do not."

* * *

I find little to disagree with Justice O'Connor's concurrence, apart from its closing paragraphs. A majority of the Court thus agrees that the fundamental inquiry is not whether the police were where they had a right to be under FAA regulations, but rather whether Riley's expectation of privacy was rendered illusory by the extent of 465
public observation of his backyard from aerial traffic at 400 feet.

What separates me from Justice O'Connor is essentially an empirical matter concerning the extent of public use of the airspace at that altitude, together with the question of how to resolve that issue. I do not think the constitutional claim should fail simply because "there is reason to believe" that there is "considerable" public flying this close to earth or because Riley "introduced no evidence to the contrary before the Florida courts." I should think that this might be an apt occasion for the application of Professor Davis' distinction between "adjudicative" and "legislative" facts. If so, I think we could take judicial notice that, while there may be an occasional privately owned helicopter that flies over populated areas at an altitude of 400 feet, such flights are a rarity and are almost entirely limited to approaching or leaving airports or to reporting traffic congestion near major roadways. And, as the concurrence agrees, the extent of police surveillance traffic cannot serve as a bootstrap to demonstrate public use of the airspace.

If, however, we are to resolve the issue by considering whether the appropriate party carried its burden of proof, I again think that Riley must prevail. Because the State has greater access to information concerning customary flight patterns and because the coercive power of the State ought not be brought to bear in cases in which it is unclear whether the prosecution is a product of an unconstitutional, warrantless search, the burden of proof properly rests with the State and *466 not with the individual defendant. The State quite clearly has not carried this burden.

* * *

The issue in this case is, ultimately, "how tightly the Fourth Amendment permits people to be driven back into the recesses of their lives by the risk of surveillance." The Court today approves warrantless helicopter surveillance from an altitude of 400 feet. While Justice O'Connor's opinion gives reason to hope that this altitude may constitute a lower limit, I find considerable cause for concern in the fact that a plurality of four Justices would remove virtually all constitutional barriers to police surveillance from the vantage point of helicopters. The Fourth Amendment demands that we temper our efforts to apprehend criminals with a concern for the impact on our fundamental liberties of the methods we use. I hope it will be a matter of concern to my colleagues that the police surveillance methods they would sanction were among those described 40 years ago in George Orwell's dread vision of life in the 1980's:

> The black-mustachio'd face gazed down from every commanding corner. There was one on the house front immediately opposite. BIG BROTHER IS WATCHING YOU, the caption said.... In the far distance a helicopter skimmed down between the roofs, hovered for an instant like a bluebottle, and darted away again with a curving flight. It was the Police Patrol, snooping into people's windows.

NINETEEN EIGHTY–FOUR 4 (1949). Who can read this passage without a shudder, and without the instinctive reaction that it depicts life in some country other than ours? I respectfully dissent.

Justice BLACKMUN, dissenting.

The question before the Court is whether the helicopter surveillance over Riley's property constituted a "search" within the meaning of the Fourth Amendment. I believe that answering this question depends upon whether Riley has a "reasonable expectation of privacy" that no such surveillance would occur, and does not depend upon the fact that the helicopter was flying at a lawful altitude under FAA regulations. A majority of this Court thus agrees to at least this much.

The inquiry then becomes how to determine whether Riley's expectation was a reasonable one. Justice Brennan, the two Justices who have joined him, and Justice O'Connor all believe that the reasonableness of Riley's expectation depends, in large measure, on the frequency of nonpolice helicopter flights at an altitude of 400 feet. Again, I agree.

How is this factual issue to be decided? Justice Brennan suggests that we may resolve it ourselves without any evidence in the record on this point. I am wary of this approach. While I, too, suspect that for most American communities it is a rare event when nonpolice helicopters fly over one's curtilage at an altitude of 400 feet, I am not convinced that we should establish a per se rule for the entire Nation based on judicial suspicion alone. But we need not abandon our judicial intuition entirely. The opinions of both Justice Brennan and Justice O'Connor implicitly recognize that none of our prior decisions tells us who has the burden of proving whether Riley's expectation of privacy was reasonable. In the absence of precedent on the point, it is appropriate for us to take into account our estimation of the frequency of nonpolice helicopter flights. Thus, because I believe that private helicopters rarely fly over curtilages at an altitude of 400 feet, I would impose upon the prosecution the burden of proving contrary facts necessary to show that Riley lacked a reasonable expectation of privacy. Indeed, I would establish this burden of proof for any helicopter surveillance case in which the flight occurred below 1,000 feet—in other words, for any aerial surveillance case not governed by the Court's decision in *California v. Ciraolo*.

In this case, the prosecution did not meet this burden of proof, as Justice Brennan notes. This failure should compel a finding that a Fourth Amendment search occurred. But because our prior cases gave the parties little guidance on the burden of proof issue, I would remand this case to allow the prosecution an opportunity to meet this burden.

The order of this Court, however, is not to remand the case in this manner. Rather, because Justice O'Connor would impose the burden of proof on Riley and because she would not allow Riley an opportunity to meet this burden, she joins the plurality's view that no Fourth Amendment search occurred. The judgment of the Court, therefore, is to reverse outright on the Fourth Amendment issue. Accordingly, for the reasons set forth above, I respectfully dissent.

KYLLO v. UNITED STATES

533 U.S. 227 (2001)

Justice SCALIA delivered the opinion of the Court.

This case presents the question whether the use of a thermal-imaging device aimed at a private home from a public street to detect relative amounts of heat within the home constitutes a "search" within the meaning of the Fourth Amendment.

In 1991 Agent William Elliott of the United States Department of the Interior came to suspect that marijuana was being grown in the home belonging to petitioner Danny Kyllo, part of a triplex on Rhododendron Drive in Florence, Oregon. Indoor marijuana growth typically requires high-intensity lamps. In order to determine whether an amount of heat was emanating from petitioner's home consistent with the use of such lamps, at 3:20 a.m. on January 16, 1992, Agent Elliott and Dan Haas used an Agema Thermovision 210 thermal imager to scan the triplex. Thermal imagers detect infrared radiation, which virtually all objects emit but which is not visible to the naked eye. The imager converts radiation into images based on relative warmth—black is cool, white is hot, shades of gray connote relative differences; in that respect, it operates somewhat like a video camera showing heat images.

I.

The scan of Kyllo's home took only a few minutes and was performed from the passenger seat of Agent Elliott's vehicle across the street from the front of the house and also from the street in back of the house. The scan showed that the roof over the garage and a side wall of petitioner's home were relatively hot compared to the rest of the home and substantially warmer than neighboring homes in the triplex. Agent Elliott concluded that petitioner was using halide lights to grow marijuana in his house, which indeed he was. Based on tips from informants, utility bills, and the thermal imaging, a Federal Magistrate Judge issued a warrant authorizing a search of petitioner's home, and the agents found an indoor growing operation involving more than 100 plants. Petitioner was indicted on one count of manufacturing marijuana. He unsuccessfully moved to suppress the evidence seized from his home and then entered a conditional guilty plea.

The Court of Appeals for the Ninth Circuit remanded the case for an evidentiary hearing regarding the intrusiveness of thermal imaging. On remand the District Court found that the Agema 210 "is a non-intrusive device which emits no rays or beams and shows a crude visual image of the heat being radiated from the outside of the house"; it "did not show any people or activity within the walls of the structure"; "[t]he device used cannot penetrate walls or windows to reveal conversations or human activities"; and "[n]o intimate details of the home were observed." Based on these findings, the District Court upheld the validity of the warrant that relied in part upon the thermal imaging, and reaffirmed its denial of the motion to suppress. A divided Court of Appeals initially reversed, but that opinion was withdrawn and the panel (after a change in composition) affirmed, with Judge Noonan dissenting. The court held that petitioner had shown no subjective expectation of privacy because he had made no attempt to conceal the heat escaping from his home, and even if he had, there was no objectively reasonable expectation of privacy because the imager "did not expose any intimate details of Kyllo's life," only "amorphous 'hot spots' on the roof and exterior wall." We granted certiorari.

II.

The Fourth Amendment provides that "[t]he right of the people to be secure in their persons, houses, papers, and effects, against unreasonable searches and seizures, shall not be violated." "At the very core" of the Fourth Amendment "stands the right of a man to retreat into his own home and there be free from unreasonable governmental intrusion." With few exceptions, the question whether a warrantless search of a home is reasonable and hence constitutional must be answered no.

On the other hand, the antecedent question whether or not a Fourth Amendment "search" has occurred is not so simple under our precedent. The permissibility of ordinary visual surveillance of a home used to be clear because, well into the 20th century, our Fourth Amendment jurisprudence was tied to common-law trespass. Visual surveillance was unquestionably lawful because "'the eye cannot by the laws of England be guilty of a trespass.'" *Boyd v. United States* (1886).We have since decoupled violation of a person's Fourth Amendment rights from trespassory violation of his property, but the lawfulness of warrantless visual surveillance of a home has still been preserved. As we observed in *California v. Ciraolo* (1986), "[t]he Fourth Amendment protection of the home has never been extended to require law enforcement officers to shield their eyes when passing by a home on public thoroughfares."

One might think that the new validating rationale would be that examining the portion of a house that is in plain public view, while it is a "search" despite the absence of trespass, is not an "unreasonable" one under the Fourth Amendment. But in fact we have held that visual observation is no "search" at all—perhaps in order to preserve somewhat more intact our doctrine that warrantless searches are presumptively unconstitutional. In assessing when a search is not a search, we have applied somewhat in reverse the principle first enunciated in *Katz v. United States* (1967).

Katz involved eavesdropping by means of an electronic listening device placed on the outside of a telephone booth—a location not within the catalog ("persons, houses, papers, and effects") that the Fourth Amendment protects against unreasonable searches. We held that the Fourth Amendment nonetheless protected Katz from the warrantless eavesdropping because he "justifiably relied" upon the privacy of the telephone booth. As Justice Harlan's oft-quoted concurrence described it, a Fourth Amendment search occurs when the government violates a subjective expectation of privacy that society recognizes as reasonable. We have subsequently applied this principle to hold that a Fourth

Amendment search does not occur—even when the explicitly protected location of a house is concerned—unless "the individual manifested a subjective expectation of privacy in the object of the challenged search," and "society [is] willing to recognize that expectation as reasonable." We have applied this test in holding that it is not a search for the police to use a pen register at the phone company to determine what numbers were dialed in a private home, and we have applied the test on two different occasions in holding that aerial surveillance of private homes and surrounding areas does not constitute a search..

The present case involves officers on a public street engaged in more than naked-eye surveillance of a home. We have previously reserved judgment as to how much technological enhancement of ordinary perception from such a vantage point, if any, is too much. While we upheld enhanced aerial photography of an industrial complex we noted that we found "it important that this is *not* an area immediately adjacent to a private home, where privacy expectations are most heightened."

III.

It would be foolish to contend that the degree of privacy secured to citizens by the Fourth Amendment has been entirely unaffected by the advance of technology. For example, as the cases discussed above make clear, the technology enabling human flight has exposed to public view (and hence, we have said, to official observation) uncovered portions of the house and its curtilage that once were private. The question we confront today is what limits there are upon this power of technology to shrink the realm of guaranteed privacy.

The *Katz* test—whether the individual has an expectation of privacy that society is prepared to recognize as reasonable—has often been criticized as circular, and hence subjective and unpredictable. While it may be difficult to refine *Katz* when the search of areas such as telephone booths, automobiles, or even the curtilage and uncovered portions of residences is at issue, in the case of the search of the interior of homes—the prototypical and hence most commonly litigated area of protected privacy—there is a ready criterion, with roots deep in the common law, of the minimal expectation of privacy that exists, and that is acknowledged to be reasonable. To withdraw protection of this minimum expectation would be to permit police technology to erode the privacy guaranteed by the Fourth Amendment. We think that obtaining by sense-enhancing technology any information regarding the interior of the home that could not otherwise have been obtained without physical "intrusion into a constitutionally protected area" constitutes a search—at least where (as here) the technology in question is not in general public use. This assures preservation of that degree of privacy against government that existed when the Fourth Amendment was adopted. On the basis of this criterion, the information obtained by the thermal imager in this case was the product of a search.

The Government maintains, however, that the thermal imaging must be upheld because it detected "only heat radiating from the external surface of the house." The dissent makes this its leading point, contending that there is a fundamental difference between what it calls "off-the-wall" observations and "through-the-wall surveillance." But just as a thermal imager captures only heat emanating from a house, so also a powerful directional microphone picks up only sound emanating from a house-and a satellite capable of scanning from many miles away would pick up only visible light emanating from a house.

We rejected such a mechanical interpretation of the Fourth Amendment in *Katz*, where the eavesdropping device picked up only sound waves that reached the exterior of the phone booth. Reversing that approach would leave the homeowner at the mercy of advancing technology—including imaging technology that could discern all human activity in the home. While the technology used in the present case was relatively crude, the rule we adopt must take account of more sophisticated systems that are already in use or in development.

The dissent's reliance on the distinction between "off-the-wall" and "through-the-wall" observation is entirely incompatible with the dissent's belief, which we discuss below, that thermal-imaging observations of the intimate details of a home are impermissible. The most sophisticated thermal-imaging devices continue to measure heat "off-the-wall" rather than "through-the-wall"; the dissent's disapproval of those more sophisticated thermal-imaging devices is an acknowledgement that there is no substance to this distinction. As for the dissent's extraordinary assertion that anything learned through "an inference" cannot be a search that would validate even the "through-the-wall" technologies that the dissent purports to disapprove. Surely the dissent does not believe that the through-the-wall radar or ultrasound technology produces an 8–by–10 Kodak glossy that needs no analysis (*i.e.*, the making of inferences). And, of course, the novel proposition that inference insulates a search is blatantly contrary to *United States v. Karo* (1984) where the police "inferred" from the activation of a beeper that a certain can of ether was in the home. The police activity was held to be a search, and the search was held unlawful.

The Government also contends that the thermal imaging was constitutional because it did not "detect private activities occurring in private areas." It points out that we observed that the enhanced aerial photography did not reveal any "intimate details" in *Dow Chemical Co. v. United States* (1986). *Dow Chemical*, however, involved enhanced aerial photography of an industrial complex, which does not share the Fourth Amendment sanctity of the home. The Fourth Amendment's protection of the home has never been tied to measurement of the quality or quantity of information obtained. In the home, our cases show, all details are intimate details, because the entire area is held safe from prying government eyes. Thus, in *Karo*, the only thing detected was a can of ether in the home; and in *Arizona v. Hicks* (1987), the only thing detected by a physical search that went beyond what officers lawfully present could observe in "plain view" was the registration number of a phonograph turntable. These were intimate details because they were details of the home, just as was the detail of how warm—or even how relatively warm—Kyllo was heating his residence.

Limiting the prohibition of thermal imaging to "intimate details" would not only be wrong in principle; it would be impractical in application, failing to provide "a workable accommodation between the needs of law enforcement and the interests protected by the Fourth Amendment," To begin with, there is no necessary connection between the sophistication of the surveillance equipment and the "intimacy" of the details that it observes—which means that one cannot say (and the police cannot be assured) that use of the relatively crude equipment at issue here will always be lawful.

The Agema Thermovision 210 might disclose, for example, at what hour each night the lady of the house takes her daily sauna and bath—a detail that many would consider "intimate"; and a much more sophisticated system might detect nothing more intimate than the fact that someone left a closet light on. We could not, in other words, develop a rule approving only that through-the-wall surveillance which identifies objects no smaller than 36 by 36 inches, but would have to develop a jurisprudence specifying which home activities are "intimate" and which are not. And even when (if ever) that jurisprudence were fully developed, no police officer would be able to know in advance whether his through-the-wall surveillance picks up "intimate" details—and thus would be unable to know in advance whether it is constitutional.

We have said that the Fourth Amendment draws "a firm line at the entrance to the house." That line, we think, must be not only firm but also bright—which requires clear specification of those methods of surveillance that require a warrant. While it is certainly possible to conclude from the videotape of the thermal imaging that occurred in this case that no "significant" compromise of the homeowner's privacy has occurred, we must take the long view, from the original meaning of the Fourth Amendment forward.

> The Fourth Amendment is to be construed in the light of what was deemed an unreasonable search and seizure when it was adopted, and in a manner which will conserve public interests as well as the interests and rights of individual citizens."

Carroll v. United States (1925).

Where, as here, the Government uses a device that is not in general public use, to explore details of the home that would previously have been unknowable without physical intrusion, the surveillance is a "search" and is presumptively unreasonable without a warrant.

Since we hold the Thermovision imaging to have been an unlawful search, it will remain for the District Court to determine whether, without the evidence it provided, the search warrant issued in this case was supported by probable cause—and if not, whether there is any other basis for supporting admission of the evidence that the search pursuant to the warrant produced. The judgment of the Court of Appeals is reversed; the case is remanded for further proceedings consistent with this opinion.

Justice STEVENS, with whom THE CHIEF JUSTICE, Justice O'CONNOR, and Justice KENNEDY join, dissenting.

There is, in my judgment, a distinction of constitutional magnitude between "through-the-wall surveillance" that gives the observer or listener direct access to information in a private area, on the one hand, and the thought processes used to draw inferences from information in the public domain, on the other hand. The Court has crafted a rule that purports to deal with direct observations of the inside of the home, but the case before us merely involves indirect deductions from "off-the-wall" surveillance, that is, observations of the exterior of the home. Those observations were made with a fairly primitive thermal imager that gathered data exposed on the outside of petitioner's home but did not invade any constitutionally protected interest in privacy. Moreover, I believe that the supposedly "bright-line" rule the Court has created in response to its concerns about future technological developments is unnecessary, unwise, and inconsistent with the Fourth Amendment.

I.

There is no need for the Court to craft a new rule to decide this case, as it is controlled by established principles from our Fourth Amendment jurisprudence. One of those core principles, of course, is that "searches and seizures *inside a home* without a warrant are presumptively unreasonable." *Payton v. New York* (1980). But it is equally well settled that searches and seizures of property in plain view are presumptively reasonable. Whether that property is residential or commercial, the basic principle is the same: "'What a person knowingly exposes to the public, even in his own home or office, is not a subject of Fourth Amendment protection.'" *California v. Ciraolo* (1986). That is the principle implicated here.

While the Court "take[s] the long view" and decides this case based largely on the potential of yet-to-be-developed technology that might allow "through-the-wall surveillance," this case involves nothing more than off-the-wall surveillance by law enforcement officers to gather information exposed to the general public from the outside of petitioner's home. All that the infrared camera did in this case was passively measure heat emitted from the exterior surfaces of petitioner's home; all that those measurements showed were relative differences in emission levels, vaguely indicating that some areas of the roof and outside walls were warmer than others. As still images from the infrared scans show, see Appendix, infra, no details regarding the interior of petitioner's home were revealed. Unlike an X-ray scan, or other possible "through-the-wall" techniques, the detection of infrared radiation emanating from the home did not accomplish "an unauthorized physical penetration into the premises," nor did it "obtain information that it could not have obtained by observation from outside the curtilage of the house,"

Indeed, the ordinary use of the senses might enable a neighbor or passerby to notice the heat emanating from a building, particularly if it is vented, as was the case here. Additionally, any member of the public might notice that one part of a house is warmer than another part or a nearby building if, for example, rainwater evaporates or snow melts at different rates across its surfaces. Such use of the senses would not convert into an unreasonable search if, instead, an adjoining neighbor allowed an officer onto her property to verify her perceptions with a sensitive thermometer. Nor, in my view, does such observation become an unreasonable search if made from a distance with the aid of a device that merely discloses that the exterior of one house, or one area of the house, is much warmer than another. Nothing more occurred in this case.

Thus, the notion that heat emissions from the outside of a dwelling are a private matter implicating the protections of the Fourth Amendment (the text of which guarantees the right of people "to be secure *in* their ... houses" against unreasonable searches and seizures is not only unprecedented but also quite difficult to take seriously. Heat waves, like aromas that are generated in a kitchen, or in a laboratory or opium den, enter the public domain if and when they leave a building. A subjective expectation that they would remain private is not only implausible but also surely not "one that society is prepared to recognize as 'reasonable.'" *Katz* (Harlan, J., concurring).

To be sure, the homeowner has a reasonable expectation of privacy concerning what takes place within the home, and the Fourth Amendment's protection against physical invasions of the home should apply to their functional equivalent. But the equipment in this case did not penetrate the walls of petitioner's home, and while it did pick up "details of the home" that were exposed to the public, it did not obtain "any information regarding the *interior* of the home." In the Court's own words, based on what the thermal imager "showed" regarding the outside of petitioner's home, the officers "concluded" that petitioner was engaging in illegal activity inside the home. It would be quite absurd to characterize their thought processes as "searches," regardless of whether they inferred (rightly) that petitioner was growing marijuana in his house, or (wrongly) that "the lady of the house [was taking] her daily sauna and bath." In either case, the only conclusions the officers reached concerning the interior of the home were at least as indirect as those that might have been inferred from the contents of discarded garbage or pen register data or, as in this case, subpoenaed utility records. For the first time in its history, the Court assumes that an inference can amount to a Fourth Amendment violation.

Notwithstanding the implications of today's decision, there is a strong public interest in avoiding constitutional litigation over the monitoring of emissions from homes, and over the inferences drawn from such monitoring. Just as "the police cannot reasonably be expected to avert their eyes from evidence of criminal activity that could have been observed by any member of the public," so too public officials should not have to avert their senses or their equipment from detecting emissions in the public domain such as excessive heat, traces of smoke, suspicious odors, odorless gases, airborne particulates, or radioactive emissions, any of which could identify hazards to the community. In my judgment, monitoring such emissions with "sense-enhancing technology," and drawing useful conclusions from such monitoring, is an entirely reasonable public service.

On the other hand, the countervailing privacy interest is at best trivial. After all, homes generally are insulated to keep heat in, rather than to prevent the detection of heat going out, and it does not seem to me that society will suffer from a rule requiring the rare homeowner who both intends to engage in uncommon activities that produce extraordinary amounts of heat, and wishes to conceal that production from outsiders, to make sure that the surrounding area is well insulated. The interest in concealing the heat escaping from one's house pales in significance to "the chief evil against which the wording of the Fourth Amendment is directed," the "physical entry of the home," and it is hard to believe that it is an interest the Framers sought to protect in our Constitution.

Since what was involved in this case was nothing more than drawing inferences from off-the-wall surveillance, rather than any "through-the-wall" surveillance, the officers' conduct did not amount to a search and was perfectly reasonable.

II.

Instead of trying to answer the question whether the use of the thermal imager in this case was even arguably unreasonable, the Court has fashioned a rule that is intended to provide essential guidance for the day when "more sophisticated systems" gain the "ability to 'see' through walls and other opaque barriers." The newly minted rule encompasses "obtaining [1] by sense-enhancing technology [2] any information regarding the interior of the home [3] that could not otherwise have been obtained without physical intrusion into a constitutionally protected area ... [4] at least where (as here) the technology in question is not in general public use."

In my judgment, the Court's new rule is at once too broad and too narrow, and is not justified by the Court's explanation for its adoption. As I have suggested, I would not erect a constitutional impediment to the use of sense-enhancing technology unless it provides its user with the functional equivalent of actual presence in the area being searched.

Despite the Court's attempt to draw a line that is "not only firm but also bright," the contours of its new rule are uncertain because its protection apparently dissipates as soon as the relevant technology is "in general public use." Yet how much use is general public use is not even hinted at by the Court's opinion, which makes the somewhat doubtful assumption that the thermal imager used in this case does not satisfy that criterion. In any event, putting aside its lack of clarity, this criterion is somewhat perverse because it seems likely that the threat to privacy will grow, rather than recede, as the use of intrusive equipment becomes more readily available.

It is clear, however, that the category of "sense-enhancing technology" covered by the new rule is far too broad. It would, for example, embrace potential mechanical substitutes for dogs trained to react when they sniff narcotics. But in *United States v. Place* (1983), we held that a dog sniff that "discloses only the presence or absence of narcotics" does "not constitute a 'search' within the meaning of the Fourth Amendment," and it must follow that sense-enhancing equipment that identifies nothing but illegal activity is not a search either. Nevertheless, the use of such a device would be unconstitutional under the Court's rule, as would the use of other new devices that might detect the odor of deadly bacteria or chemicals for making a new type of high explosive, even if the devices (like the dog sniffs) are "so limited both in the manner in which" they obtain information and "in the content of the information" they reveal. If nothing more than that sort of information could be obtained by using the devices in a public place to monitor emissions from a house, then their use would be no more objectionable than the use of the thermal imager in this case.

The application of the Court's new rule to "any information regarding the interior of the home," is also unnecessarily broad. If it takes sensitive equipment to detect an odor that identifies criminal conduct and nothing else, the fact that the odor emanates from the interior of a home should not provide it with constitutional protection. The criterion, moreover, is too sweeping in that information "regarding" the interior of a home apparently is not just information obtained through its walls, but also information concerning the outside of the building that could lead to (however many) inferences "regarding" what might be inside. Under that expansive view, I suppose, an officer using an infrared camera to observe a man silently entering the side door of a house at night carrying a pizza might conclude that its interior is now occupied by someone who likes pizza, and by doing so the officer would be guilty of conducting an unconstitutional "search" of the home.

Because the new rule applies to information regarding the "interior" of the home, it is too narrow as well as too broad. Clearly, a rule that is designed to protect individuals from the overly intrusive use of sense-enhancing equipment should not be limited to a home. If such equipment did provide its user with the functional equivalent of access to a private place—such as, for example, the telephone booth involved in *Katz*, or an office building—then the rule should apply to such an area as well as to a home. *See Katz* ("[T]he Fourth Amendment protects people, not places").

The final requirement of the Court's new rule, that the information "could not otherwise have been obtained without physical intrusion into a constitutionally protected area," also extends too far as the Court applies it. As noted, the Court effectively treats the mental process of analyzing data obtained from external sources as the equivalent of a physical intrusion into the home. As I have explained, however, the process of drawing inferences from data in the public domain should not be characterized as a search.

The two reasons advanced by the Court as justifications for the adoption of its new rule are both unpersuasive. First, the Court suggests that its rule is compelled by our holding in *Katz*, because in that case, as in this, the surveillance consisted of nothing more than the monitoring of waves emanating from a private area into the public domain. Yet there are critical differences between the cases.

In *Katz*, the electronic listening device attached to the outside of the phone booth allowed the officers to pick up the content of the conversation inside the booth, making them the functional equivalent of intruders because they gathered information that was otherwise available only to someone inside the private area; it would be as if, in this case, the thermal imager presented a view of the heat-generating activity inside petitioner's home. By contrast, the thermal imager here disclosed only the relative amounts of heat radiating from the house; it would be as if, in *Katz*, the listening device disclosed only the relative volume of sound leaving the booth, which presumably was discernible in the public domain. Surely, there is a significant difference between the general and well-settled expectation that strangers will not have direct access to the contents of private communications, on the one hand, and the rather theoretical expectation that an occasional homeowner would even care if anybody noticed the relative amounts of heat emanating from the walls of his house, on the other. It is pure hyperbole for the Court to suggest that refusing to extend the holding of *Katz* to this case would leave the homeowner at the mercy of "technology that could discern all human activity in the home."

Second, the Court argues that the permissibility of "through-the-wall surveillance" cannot depend on a distinction between observing "intimate details" such as "the lady of the house [taking] her daily sauna and bath," and noticing only "the nonintimate rug on the vestibule floor" or "objects no smaller than 36 by 36 inches." This entire argument assumes, of course, that the thermal imager in this case could or did perform "through-the-wall surveillance" that could identify any detail "that would previously have been unknowable without physical intrusion." In fact, the device could not,and did not, enable its user to identify either the lady of the house, the rug on the vestibule floor, or anything else inside the house, whether smaller or larger than 36 by 36 inches. Indeed, the vague thermal images of petitioner's home were submitted by him to the District Court as part of an expert report raising the question whether the device could even take "accurate, consistent infrared images" of the outside of his house. But even if the device could reliably show extraordinary differences in the amounts of heat leaving his home, drawing the inference that there was something suspicious occurring inside the residence—a conclusion that officers far less gifted than Sherlock Holmes would readily draw—does not qualify as "through-the-wall surveillance," much less a Fourth Amendment violation.

III.

Although the Court is properly and commendably concerned about the threats to privacy that may flow from advances in the technology available to the law enforcement profession, it has unfortunately failed to heed the tried and true counsel of judicial restraint. Instead of concentrating on the rather mundane issue that is actually presented by the case before it, the Court has endeavored to craft an all-encompassing rule for the future. It would be far wiser to give legislators an unimpeded opportunity to grapple with these emerging issues rather than to shackle them with prematurely devised constitutional constraints.

UNITED STATES v. JONES

132 S. Ct. 945 (2012)

Justice SCALIA delivered the opinion of the Court.

We decide whether the attachment of a Global–Positioning–System (GPS) tracking device to an individual's vehicle, and subsequent use of that device to monitor the vehicle's movements on public streets, constitutes a search or seizure within the meaning of the Fourth Amendment.

I.

In 2004 respondent Antoine Jones, owner and operator of a nightclub in the District of Columbia, came under suspicion of trafficking in narcotics and was made the target of an investigation by a joint FBI and Metropolitan Police Department task force. Officers employed various investigative techniques, including visual surveillance of the nightclub, installation of a camera focused on the front door of the club, and a pen register and wiretap covering Jones's cellular phone.

Based in part on information gathered from these sources, in 2005 the Government applied to the United States District Court for the District of Columbia for a warrant authorizing the use of an electronic tracking device on the Jeep Grand Cherokee registered to Jones's wife. A warrant issued, authorizing installation of the device in the District of Columbia and within 10 days.

On the 11th day, and not in the District of Columbia but in Maryland, agents installed a GPS tracking device on the undercarriage of the Jeep while it was parked in a public parking lot. Over the next 28 days, the Government used the device to track the vehicle's movements, and once had to replace the device's battery when the vehicle was parked in a different public lot in Maryland. By means of signals from multiple satellites, the device established the vehicle's location within 50 to 100 feet, and communicated that location by cellular phone to a Government computer. It relayed more than 2,000 pages of data over the 4–week period.

The Government ultimately obtained a multiple-count indictment charging Jones and several alleged co-conspirators with, as relevant here, conspiracy to distribute and possess with intent to distribute five kilograms or more of cocaine and 50 grams or more of cocaine base. Before trial, Jones filed a motion to suppress evidence obtained through the GPS device. The District Court granted the motion only in part, suppressing the data obtained while the vehicle was parked in the garage adjoining Jones's residence. It held the remaining data admissible, because "'[a] person traveling in an automobile on public thoroughfares has no reasonable expectation of privacy in his movements from one place to another.'" Jones's trial in October 2006 produced a hung jury on the conspiracy count.

In March 2007, a grand jury returned another indictment, charging Jones and others with the same conspiracy. The Government introduced at trial the same GPS-derived locational data admitted in the first trial, which connected Jones to the alleged conspirators' stash house that contained $850,000 in cash, 97 kilograms of cocaine, and 1 kilogram of cocaine base. The jury returned a guilty verdict, and the District Court sentenced Jones to life imprisonment.

The United States Court of Appeals for the District of Columbia Circuit reversed the conviction because of admission of the evidence obtained by warrantless use of the GPS device which, it said, violated the Fourth Amendment. The D.C. Circuit denied the Government's petition for rehearing *en banc*, with four judges dissenting. We granted certiorari.

* * *

The Fourth Amendment provides in relevant part that "[t]he right of the people to be secure in their persons, houses, papers, and effects, against unreasonable searches and seizures, shall not be violated." It is beyond dispute that a vehicle is an "effect" as that term is used in the Amendment. We hold that the Government's installation of a GPS device on a target's vehicle, and its use of that device to monitor the vehicle's movements, constitutes a "search."

It is important to be clear about what occurred in this case: The Government physically occupied private property for the purpose of obtaining information. We have no doubt that such a physical intrusion would have been considered a "search" within the meaning of the Fourth Amendment when it was adopted. *Entick v. Carrington*, 95 Eng. Rep. 807 (C.P. 1765), is a "case we have described as a 'monument of English freedom' 'undoubtedly familiar' to 'every American statesman' at the time the Constitution was adopted, and considered to be 'the true and ultimate expression of constitutional law' " with regard to search and seizure. In that case, Lord Camden expressed in plain terms the significance of property rights in search-and-seizure analysis:

> [O]ur law holds the property of every man so sacred, that no man can set his foot upon his neighbour's close without his leave; if he does he is a trespasser, though he does no damage at all; if he will tread upon his neighbour's ground, he must justify it by law.

Entick at 817. The text of the Fourth Amendment reflects its close connection to property, since otherwise it would have referred simply to "the right of the people to be secure against unreasonable searches and seizures"; the phrase "in their persons, houses, papers, and effects" would have been superfluous.

Consistent with this understanding, our Fourth Amendment jurisprudence was tied to common-law trespass, at least until the latter half of the 20th century. *Kyllo v. United States* (2001). Thus, in *Olmstead v. United States* (1928), we held that wiretaps attached to telephone wires on the public streets did not constitute a Fourth Amendment search because "[t]here was no entry of the houses or offices of the defendants."

Our later cases, of course, have deviated from that exclusively property-based approach. In *Katz v. United States* (1967), we said that "the Fourth Amendment protects people, not places," and found a violation in attachment of an eavesdropping device to a public telephone booth. Our later cases have applied the analysis of Justice Harlan's concurrence in that case, which said that a violation occurs when government officers violate a person's "reasonable expectation of privacy."

The Government contends that the Harlan standard shows that no search occurred here, since Jones had no "reasonable expectation of privacy" in the area of the Jeep accessed by Government agents (its underbody) and in the locations of the Jeep on the public roads, which were visible to all. But we need not address the Government's contentions, because Jones's Fourth Amendment rights do not rise or fall with the *Katz* formulation. At bottom, we must "assur[e] preservation of that degree of privacy against government that existed when the Fourth Amendment was adopted." *Kyllo*, *supra*. As explained, for most of our history the Fourth Amendment was understood to embody a particular concern for government trespass upon the areas ("persons, houses, papers, and effects") it enumerates.

Katz did not repudiate that understanding. Less than two years later the Court upheld defendants' contention that the Government could not introduce against them conversations between other people obtained by warrantless placement of electronic surveillance devices in their homes. The opinion rejected the dissent's contention that there was no Fourth Amendment violation "unless the conversational privacy of the homeowner himself is invaded." *Alderman v. United States* (1969). "[W]e [do not] believe that *Katz*, by holding that the Fourth Amendment protects persons and their private conversations, was intended to withdraw any of the protection which the Amendment extends to the home." *Id.*

More recently, in *Soldal v. Cook County* (1992), the Court unanimously rejected the argument that although a "seizure" had occurred "in a 'technical' sense" when a trailer home was forcibly removed, no Fourth Amendment violation occurred because law enforcement had not "invade[d] the [individuals'] privacy." *Katz* the Court explained, established that "property rights are not the sole measure of Fourth Amendment violations," but did not "snuf[f] out the previously recognized protection for property." As Justice Brennan explained in his concurrence in *United States v. Knotts* (1982), *Katz* did not erode the principle "that, when the Government does engage in physical intrusion of a constitutionally protected area in order to obtain information, that intrusion may constitute a violation of the Fourth Amendment." We have embodied that preservation of past rights in our very definition of "reasonable expectation of privacy" which we have said to be an expectation "that has a source outside of the Fourth Amendment, either by reference to concepts of real or personal property law or to understandings that are recognized and permitted by society." *Katz* did not narrow the Fourth Amendment's scope.

The Government contends that several of our post-*Katz* cases foreclose the conclusion that what occurred here constituted a search. It relies principally on two cases in which we rejected Fourth Amendment challenges to "beepers," electronic tracking devices that represent another form of electronic monitoring. The first case, *Knotts*, upheld against Fourth Amendment challenge the use of a "beeper" that had been placed in a container of chloroform, allowing law enforcement to monitor the location of the container. We said that there had been no infringement of Knotts' reasonable expectation of privacy since the information obtained—the location of the automobile carrying the container on public roads, and the location of the off-loaded container in open fields near Knotts' cabin—had been voluntarily conveyed to the public.

But as we have discussed, the *Katz* reasonable-expectation-of-privacy test has been added to, not substituted for, the common-law trespassory test. The holding in *Knotts* addressed only the former, since the latter was not at issue. The beeper had been placed in the container before it came into Knotts' possession, with the consent of the then-owner. Knotts did not challenge that installation, and we specifically declined to consider its effect on the Fourth Amendment analysis. *Knotts* would be relevant, perhaps, if the Government were making the argument that what would otherwise be an unconstitutional search is not such where it produces only public information. The Government does not make that argument, and we know of no case that would support it.

The second "beeper" case, *United States v. Karo* (1984), does not suggest a different conclusion. There we addressed the question left open by *Knotts*, whether the installation of a beeper in a container amounted to a search or seizure. As in *Knotts*, at the time the beeper was installed the container belonged to a third party, and it did not come into possession of the defendant until later. Thus, the specific question we considered was whether the installation "with the consent of the *original owner* constitute[d] a search or seizure ... when the container is delivered to a buyer having no knowledge of the presence of the beeper." We held not. The Government, we said, came into physical contact with the container only before it belonged to the defendant *Karo*; and the transfer of the container with the unmonitored beeper inside did not convey any information and thus did not invade Karo's privacy. That conclusion is perfectly consistent with the one we reach here. *Karo* accepted the container as it came to him, beeper and all, and was therefore not entitled to object to the beeper's presence, even though it was used to monitor the container's location. Jones, who possessed the Jeep at the time the Government trespassorily inserted the information-gathering device, is on much different footing.

* * *

The concurrence begins by accusing us of applying "18th-century tort law." That is a distortion. What we apply is an 18th-century guarantee against unreasonable searches, which we believe must provide at a minimum the degree of protection it afforded when it was adopted. The concurrence does not share that belief. It would apply exclusively *Katz's* reasonable-expectation-of-privacy test, even when that eliminates rights that previously existed.

The concurrence faults our approach for "present[ing] particularly vexing problems" in cases that do not involve physical contact, such as those that involve the transmission of electronic signals. We entirely fail to understand that point. For unlike the concurrence, which would make *Katz* the exclusive test, we do not make trespass the exclusive test. Situations involving merely the transmission of electronic signals without trespass would remain subject to *Katz* analysis.

In fact, it is the concurrence's insistence on the exclusivity of the *Katz* test that needlessly leads us into "particularly vexing problems" in the present case. This Court has to date not deviated from the understanding that mere visual observation does not constitute a search. We accordingly held in *Knotts* that "[a] person traveling in an automobile on public thoroughfares has no reasonable expectation of privacy in his movements from one place to another." Thus, even assuming that the concurrence is correct to say that "[t]raditional surveillance" of Jones for a 4–week period "would have required a large team of agents, multiple vehicles, and perhaps aerial assistance," our cases suggest that such visual observation is constitutionally permissible. It may be that achieving the same result through electronic means, without an accompanying trespass, is an unconstitutional invasion of privacy, but the present case does not require us to answer that question.

And answering it affirmatively leads us needlessly into additional thorny problems. The concurrence posits that "relatively short-term monitoring of a person's movements on public streets" is okay, but that "the use of longer term GPS monitoring in investigations of *most offenses*" is no good. That introduces yet another novelty into our jurisprudence. There is no precedent for the proposition that whether a search has occurred depends on the nature of the crime being investigated. And even accepting that novelty, it remains unexplained why a 4–week investigation is "surely" too long and why a drug-trafficking conspiracy involving substantial amounts of cash and narcotics is not an "extraordinary offens[e]" which may permit longer observation. What of a 2–day monitoring of a suspected purveyor of stolen electronics? Or of a 6–month monitoring of a suspected terrorist? We may have to grapple with these "vexing problems" in some future case where a classic trespassory search is not involved and resort must be had to *Katz* analysis; but there is no reason for rushing forward to resolve them here.

Justice SOTOMAYOR, concurring.

I join the Court's opinion because I agree that a search within the meaning of the Fourth Amendment occurs, at a minimum, "[w]here, as here, the Government obtains information by physically intruding on a constitutionally protected area." In this case, the Government installed a Global Positioning System (GPS) tracking device on respondent Antoine Jones' Jeep without a valid warrant and without Jones' consent, then used that device to monitor the Jeep's movements over the course of four weeks. The Government usurped Jones' property for the purpose of conducting surveillance on him, thereby invading privacy interests long afforded, and undoubtedly entitled to, Fourth Amendment protection.

Of course, the Fourth Amendment is not concerned only with trespassory intrusions on property. Rather, even in the absence of a trespass, "a Fourth Amendment search occurs when the government violates a subjective expectation of privacy that society recognizes as reasonable." In *Katz*, this Court enlarged its then-prevailing focus on property rights by announcing that the reach of the Fourth Amendment does not "turn upon the presence or absence of a physical intrusion." As the majority's opinion makes clear, however, *Katz*'s reasonable-expectation-of-privacy test augmented, but did not displace or diminish, the common-law trespassory test that preceded it. Thus, "when the Government does engage in physical intrusion of a constitutionally protected area in order to obtain information, that intrusion may constitute a violation of the Fourth Amendment."

Justice Alito's approach, which discounts altogether the constitutional relevance of the Government's physical intrusion on Jones' Jeep, erodes that longstanding protection for privacy expectations inherent in items of property that people possess or control. By contrast, the trespassory test applied in the majority's opinion reflects an irreducible constitutional minimum: When the Government physically invades personal property to gather information, a search occurs. The reaffirmation of that principle suffices to decide this case.

Nonetheless, as Justice Alito notes, physical intrusion is now unnecessary to many forms of surveillance. With increasing regularity, the Government will be capable of duplicating the monitoring undertaken in this case by enlisting factory- or owner-installed vehicle tracking devices or GPS-enabled smartphones. In cases of electronic or other novel modes of surveillance that do not depend upon a physical invasion on property, the majority opinion's trespassory test may provide little guidance. But "[s]ituations involving merely the transmission of electronic signals without trespass would remain subject to *Katz* analysis." As Justice Alito incisively observes, the same technological advances that have made possible nontrespassory surveillance techniques will also affect the *Katz* test by shaping the evolution of societal privacy expectations. Under that rubric, I agree with Justice Alito that, at the very least, "longer term GPS monitoring in investigations of most offenses impinges on expectations of privacy."

In cases involving even short-term monitoring, some unique attributes of GPS surveillance relevant to the *Katz* analysis will require particular attention. GPS monitoring generates a precise, comprehensive record of a person's public movements that reflects a wealth of detail about her familial, political, professional, religious, and sexual associations. The Government can store such records and efficiently mine them for information years into the future. And because GPS monitoring is cheap in comparison to conventional surveillance techniques and, by design, proceeds surreptitiously, it evades the ordinary checks that constrain abusive law enforcement practices: "limited police resources and community hostility."

Awareness that the Government may be watching chills associational and expressive freedoms. And the Government's unrestrained power to assemble data that reveal private aspects of identity is susceptible to abuse. The net result is that GPS monitoring—by making available at a relatively low cost such a substantial quantum of intimate information about any person whom the Government, in its unfettered discretion, chooses to track—may "alter the relationship between citizen and government in a way that is inimical to democratic society."

I would take these attributes of GPS monitoring into account when considering the existence of a reasonable societal expectation of privacy in the sum of one's public movements. I would ask whether people reasonably expect that their movements will be recorded and aggregated in a manner that enables the Government to ascertain, more or less at will, their political and religious beliefs, sexual habits, and so on. I do not regard as dispositive the fact that the Government might obtain the fruits of GPS monitoring through lawful conventional surveillance techniques. *See Kyllo* (leaving open the possibility that duplicating traditional surveillance "through electronic means, without an accompanying trespass, is an unconstitutional invasion of privacy"). I would also consider the appropriateness of entrusting to the Executive, in the absence of any oversight from a coordinate branch, a tool so amenable to misuse, especially in light of the Fourth Amendment's goal to curb arbitrary exercises of police power to and prevent "a too permeating police surveillance."

More fundamentally, it may be necessary to reconsider the premise that an individual has no reasonable expectation of privacy in information voluntarily disclosed to third parties. This approach is ill suited to the digital age, in which people reveal a great deal of information about themselves to third parties in the course of carrying out mundane tasks. People disclose the phone numbers that they dial or text to their cellular providers; the URLs that they visit and the e-mail addresses with which they correspond to their Internet service providers; and the books, groceries, and medications they purchase to online retailers. Perhaps, as Justice Alito notes, some people may find the "tradeoff" of privacy for convenience "worthwhile," or come to accept this "diminution of privacy" as "inevitable," and perhaps not. I for one doubt that people would accept without complaint the warrantless disclosure to the Government of a list of every Web site they had visited in the last week, or month, or year. But whatever the societal expectations, they can attain constitutionally protected status only if our Fourth Amendment jurisprudence ceases to treat secrecy as a prerequisite for privacy. I would not assume that all information voluntarily disclosed to some member of the public for a limited purpose is, for that reason alone, disentitled to Fourth Amendment protection.

Resolution of these difficult questions in this case is unnecessary, however, because the Government's physical intrusion on Jones' Jeep supplies a narrower basis for decision. I therefore join the majority's opinion.

Justice ALITO, with whom Justice GINSBURG, Justice BREYER, and Justice KAGAN join, concurring in the judgment.

This case requires us to apply the Fourth Amendment's prohibition of unreasonable searches and seizures to a 21st-century surveillance technique, the use of a Global Positioning System (GPS) device to monitor a vehicle's movements for an extended period of time. Ironically, the Court has chosen to decide this case based on 18th-century tort law. By attaching a small GPS device to the underside of the vehicle that respondent drove, the law enforcement officers in this case engaged in conduct that might have provided grounds in 1791 for a suit for trespass to chattels. And for this reason, the Court concludes, the installation and use of the GPS device constituted a search. This holding, in my judgment, is unwise. It strains the language of the Fourth Amendment; it has little if any support in current Fourth Amendment case law; and it is highly artificial. I would analyze the question presented in this case by asking whether respondent's reasonable expectations of privacy were violated by the long-term monitoring of the movements of the vehicle he drove.

* * *

The Fourth Amendment prohibits "unreasonable searches and seizures," and the Court makes very little effort to explain how the attachment or use of the GPS device fits within these terms. The Court does not contend that there was a seizure. A seizure of property occurs when there is "some meaningful interference with an individual's possessory interests in that property," and here there was none. Indeed, the success of the surveillance technique that the officers employed was dependent on the fact that the GPS did not interfere in any way with the operation of the vehicle, for if any such interference had been detected, the device might have been discovered.

The Court does claim that the installation and use of the GPS constituted a search, but this conclusion is dependent on the questionable proposition that these two procedures cannot be separated for purposes of Fourth Amendment analysis. If these two procedures are analyzed separately, it is not at all clear from the Court's opinion why either should be regarded as a search. It is clear that the attachment of the GPS device was not itself a search; if the device had not functioned or if the officers had not used it, no information would have been obtained. And the Court does not contend that the use of the device constituted a search either. On the contrary, the Court accepts the holding in *United States v. Knotts* (1983) that the use of a surreptitiously planted electronic device to monitor a vehicle's movements on public roads did not amount to a search.

The Court argues—and I agree—that "we must 'assur[e] preservation of that degree of privacy against government that existed when the Fourth Amendment was adopted.'" But it is almost impossible to think of late–18th-century situations that are analogous to what took place in this case. (Is it possible to imagine a case in which a constable secreted himself somewhere in a coach and remained there for a period of time in order to monitor the movements of the coach's owner?) The Court's theory seems to be that the concept of a search, as originally understood, comprehended any technical trespass that led to the gathering of evidence, but we know that this is incorrect. At common law, any unauthorized intrusion on private property was actionable, see Prosser & Keeton 75, but a trespass on open fields, as opposed to the "curtilage" of a home, does not fall within the scope of the Fourth Amendment because private property outside the curtilage is not part of a "hous[e]" within the meaning of the Fourth Amendment.

* * *

The Court's reasoning in this case is very similar to that in the Court's early decisions involving wiretapping and electronic eavesdropping, namely, that a technical trespass followed by the gathering of evidence constitutes a search. In the early electronic surveillance cases, the Court concluded that a Fourth Amendment search occurred when private conversations were monitored as a result of an "unauthorized physical penetration into the premises occupied" by the defendant. *Silverman v. United States* (1961). In *Silverman*, police officers listened to conversations in an attached home by inserting a "spike mike" through the wall that this house shared with the vacant house next door. This procedure was held to be a search because the mike made contact with a heating duct on the other side of the wall and thus "usurp[ed] ... an integral part of the premises."

By contrast, in cases in which there was no trespass, it was held that there was no search. Thus, in *Olmstead v. United States* (1928), the Court found that the Fourth Amendment did not apply because "[t]he taps from house lines were made in the streets near the houses." Similarly, the Court concluded that no search occurred in *Goldman v. United States* (1942), where a "detectaphone" was placed on the outer wall of defendant's office for the purpose of overhearing conversations held within the room.

This trespass-based rule was repeatedly criticized. In *Olmstead*, Justice Brandeis wrote that it was "immaterial where the physical connection with the telephone wires was made." Although a private conversation transmitted by wire did not fall within the literal words of the Fourth Amendment, he argued, the Amendment should be understood as prohibiting "every unjustifiable intrusion by the government upon the privacy of the individual." *See also, e.g.*, *Silverman* (Douglas, J., concurring) ("The concept of 'an unauthorized physical penetration into the premises,' on which the present decision rests seems to me beside the point. Was not the wrong ... done when the intimacies of the home were tapped, recorded, or revealed? The depth of the penetration of the electronic device—even the degree of its remoteness from the inside of the house—is not the measure of the injury"); *Goldman*, *supra*, (Murphy, J., dissenting) ("[T]he search of one's home or office no longer requires physical entry, for science has brought forth far more effective devices for the invasion of a person's privacy than the direct and obvious methods of oppression which were detested by our forebears and which inspired the Fourth Amendment").

Katz v. United States (1967) finally did away with the old approach, holding that a trespass was not required for a Fourth Amendment violation. *Katz* involved the use of a listening device that was attached to the outside of a public telephone booth and that allowed police officers to eavesdrop on one end of the target's phone conversation. This procedure did not physically intrude on the area occupied by the target, but the *Katz* Court, "repudiate[ed]" the old doctrine, and held that "[t]he fact that the electronic device employed ... did not happen to penetrate the wall of the booth can have no constitutional significance."

* * *

Disharmony with a substantial body of existing case law is only one of the problems with the Court's approach in this case. I will briefly note four others. First, the Court's reasoning largely disregards what is really important (the use of a GPS for the purpose of long-term tracking) and instead attaches great significance to something that most would view as relatively minor (attaching to the bottom of a car a small, light object that does not interfere in any way with the car's operation). Attaching such an object is generally regarded as so trivial that it does not provide a basis for recovery under modern tort law. But under the Court's reasoning, this conduct may violate the Fourth Amendment. By contrast, if long-term monitoring can be accomplished without committing a technical trespass—suppose, for example, that the Federal Government required or persuaded auto manufacturers to include a GPS tracking device in every car—the Court's theory would provide no protection.

Second, the Court's approach leads to incongruous results. If the police attach a GPS device to a car and use the device to follow the car for even a brief time, under the Court's theory, the Fourth Amendment applies. But if the police follow the same car for a much longer period using unmarked cars and aerial assistance, this tracking is not subject to any Fourth Amendment constraints.

In the present case, the Fourth Amendment applies, the Court concludes, because the officers installed the GPS device after respondent's wife, to whom the car was registered, turned it over to respondent for his exclusive use. But if the GPS had been attached prior to that time, the Court's theory would lead to a different result. The Court proceeds on the assumption that respondent "had at least the property rights of a bailee," but a bailee may sue for a trespass to chattel only if the injury occurs during the term of the bailment. So if the GPS device had been installed before respondent's wife gave him the keys, respondent would have no claim for trespass—and, presumably, no Fourth Amendment claim either.

Third, under the Court's theory, the coverage of the Fourth Amendment may vary from State to State. If the events at issue here had occurred in a community property State or a State that has adopted the Uniform Marital Property Act, respondent would likely be an owner of the vehicle, and it would not matter whether the GPS was installed before or after his wife turned over the keys. In non-community-property States, on the other hand, the registration of the vehicle in the name of respondent's wife would generally be regarded as presumptive evidence that she was the sole owner.

Fourth, the Court's reliance on the law of trespass will present particularly vexing problems in cases involving surveillance that is carried out by making electronic, as opposed to physical, contact with the item to be tracked. For example, suppose that the officers in the present case had followed respondent by surreptitiously activating a stolen vehicle detection system that came with the car when it was purchased. Would the sending of a radio signal to activate this system constitute a trespass to chattels? Trespass to chattels has traditionally required a physical touching of the property. In recent years, courts have wrestled with the application of this old tort in cases involving unwanted electronic contact with computer systems, and some have held that even the transmission of electrons that occurs when a communication is sent from one computer to another is enough. But may such decisions be followed in applying the Court's trespass theory? Assuming that what matters under the Court's theory is the law of trespass as it existed at the time of the adoption of the Fourth Amendment, do these recent decisions represent a change in the law or simply the application of the old tort to new situations?

* * *

The *Katz* expectation-of-privacy test avoids the problems and complications noted above, but it is not without its own difficulties. It involves a degree of circularity, and judges are apt to confuse their own expectations of privacy with those of the hypothetical reasonable person to which the *Katz* test looks. In addition, the *Katz* test rests on the assumption that this hypothetical reasonable person has a well-developed and stable set of privacy expectations. But technology can change those expectations. Dramatic technological change may lead to periods in which popular expectations are in flux and may ultimately produce significant changes in popular attitudes. New technology may provide increased convenience or security at the expense of privacy, and many people may find the tradeoff worthwhile. And even if the public does not welcome the diminution of privacy that new technology entails, they may eventually reconcile themselves to this development as inevitable.

On the other hand, concern about new intrusions on privacy may spur the enactment of legislation to protect against these intrusions. This is what ultimately happened with respect to wiretapping. After *Katz*, Congress did not leave it to the courts to develop a body of Fourth Amendment case law governing that complex subject. Instead, Congress promptly enacted a comprehensive statute and since that time, the regulation of wiretapping has been governed primarily by statute and not by case law. In an ironic sense, although *Katz* overruled *Olmstead*, Chief Justice Taft's suggestion in the latter case that the regulation of wiretapping was a matter better left for Congress has been borne out.

* * *

Recent years have seen the emergence of many new devices that permit the monitoring of a person's movements. In some locales, closed-circuit television video monitoring is becoming ubiquitous. On toll roads, automatic toll collection systems create a precise record of the movements of motorists who choose to make use of that convenience. Many motorists purchase cars that are equipped with devices that permit a central station to ascertain the car's location at any time so that roadside assistance may be provided if needed and the car may be found if it is stolen.

Perhaps most significant, cell phones and other wireless devices now permit wireless carriers to track and record the location of users—and as of June 2011, it has been reported, there were more than 322 million wireless devices in use in the United States. For older phones, the accuracy of the location information depends on the density of the tower network, but new "smart phones," which are equipped with a GPS device, permit more precise tracking. For example, when a user activates the GPS on such a phone, a provider is able to monitor the phone's location and speed of movement and can then report back real-time traffic conditions after combining ("crowdsourcing") the speed of all such phones on any particular road. Similarly, phone-location-tracking services are offered as "social" tools, allowing consumers to find (or to avoid) others who enroll in these services. The availability and use of these and other new devices will continue to shape the average person's expectations about the privacy of his or her daily movements.

In the pre-computer age, the greatest protections of privacy were neither constitutional nor statutory, but practical. Traditional surveillance for any extended period of time was difficult and costly and therefore rarely undertaken. The surveillance at issue in this case—constant monitoring of the location of a vehicle for four weeks—would have required a large team of agents, multiple vehicles, and perhaps aerial assistance. Only an investigation of unusual importance could have justified such an expenditure of law enforcement *964 resources. Devices like the one used in the present case, however, make long-term monitoring relatively easy and cheap. In circumstances involving dramatic technological change, the best solution to privacy concerns may be legislative. A legislative body is well situated to gauge changing public attitudes, to draw detailed lines, and to balance privacy and public safety in a comprehensive way. To date, however, Congress and most States have not enacted statutes regulating the use of GPS tracking technology for law enforcement purposes. The best that we can do in this case is to apply existing Fourth Amendment doctrine and to ask whether the use of GPS tracking in a particular case involved a degree of intrusion that a reasonable person would not have anticipated.

Under this approach, relatively short-term monitoring of a person's movements on public streets accords with expectations of privacy that our society has recognized as reasonable. But the use of longer term GPS monitoring in investigations of most offenses impinges on expectations of privacy. For such offenses, society's expectation has been that law enforcement agents and others would not—and indeed, in the main, simply could not—secretly monitor and catalogue every single movement of an individual's car for a very long period. In this case, for four weeks, law enforcement agents tracked every movement that respondent made in the vehicle he was driving. We need not identify with precision the point at which the tracking of this vehicle became a search, for the line was surely crossed before the 4–week mark. Other cases may present more difficult questions. But where uncertainty exists with respect to whether a certain period of GPS surveil lance is long enough to constitute a Fourth Amendment search, the police may always seek a warrant. We also need not consider whether prolonged GPS monitoring in the context of investigations involving extraordinary offenses would similarly intrude on a constitutionally protected sphere of privacy. In such cases, long-term tracking might have been mounted using previously available techniques.

For these reasons, I conclude that the lengthy monitoring that occurred in this case constituted a search under the Fourth Amendment. I therefore agree with the majority that the decision of the Court of Appeals must be affirmed.

Aviation Surveillance and Security

AMERICAN CIVIL LIBERTIES UNION v.
CENTRAL INTELLIGENCE AGENCY
2015 WL 3777275 (D.D.C. 2015)

ROSEMARY M. COLLYER, United States District Judge.

The Central Intelligence Agency ("CIA") engages in covert actions in foreign countries on behalf of the United States and, by necessity, practice, and statute, keeps its activities secret. The American Civil Liberties Union and the American Civil Liberties Union Foundation ("ACLU") are concerned about CIA activities overseas. Relying on the Freedom of Information Act ("FOIA"), ACLU requested all CIA records pertaining to the United States' use of drone strikes to carry out targeted killings of alleged Islamist terrorists overseas. CIA initially provided a Glomar response to ACLU, *i.e.*, it refused to confirm or deny that CIA had such records, which this Court approved. Thereafter various government officials made public statements about a U.S. operational role in drone strikes. The D.C. Circuit reversed and ordered CIA to begin the FOIA process anew.

On remand, ACLU narrowed its request, and CIA searched for and acknowledged the existence of twelve legal memoranda and thousands of classified intelligence products responsive to the narrowed request. CIA released a redacted version of a classified DOJ White Paper, but has withheld the other eleven legal memoranda and all of the intelligence products on the basis that disclosing these records would compromise classified, statutorily-protected, and privileged information. ACLU objects to CIA's response and asserts that some records must be released, specifically those records that (1) contain information that has already been officially acknowledged; (2) contain legal analysis or statistical or factual information that is not intertwined with classified intelligence information; and (3) have not been shown by CIA to be subject to a privilege.

Both parties move for summary judgment. For the reasons set forth below, the Court will grant CIA's Motion for Summary Judgment and deny ACLU's Cross–Motion for Summary Judgment.

I. FACTS

In September 2001, Congress authorized the use of military force against enemies of the United States. Authorization for Use of Military Force (AUMF), Pub.L. No. 107–40, 115 Stat. 224 (reprinted at 50 U.S.C. § 1541 note). Since that time, the United States and its allies have been engaged in a war with al-Qa'ida and its associated forces in Afghanistan, Pakistan and elsewhere. One of the recently-used weapons by the United States is an unmanned drone, which can deliver a missile strike against an enemy target with greater precision and less risk to innocent humans than a traditional bomb. ACLU has sued CIA over its refusal to release records concerning the United States' use of drones.

A. *Original FOIA Request*

In a January 13, 2010 letter, ACLU submitted a request for documents under the FOIA, 5 U.S.C. § 552, to CIA's Information and Privacy Coordinator seeking "records pertaining to the use of unmanned aerial vehicles ('UAVs')—commonly referred to as 'drones' and including the MQ–1 Predator and MQ–9 Reaper—by CIA and the Armed Forces for the purpose of killing targeted individuals." ACLU specifically requested records for certain categories of information:

- The "legal basis in domestic, foreign and international law upon which unmanned aerial vehicles" can be used to execute targeted killings, including who may be targeted with this weapon system, where and why;

- The "selection of human targets for drone strikes and any limits on who may be targeted by a drone strike;"

- "[C]ivilian casualties in drone strikes," including measures to limit civilian casualties;

- The "assessment or evaluation of individual drone strikes after the fact," including how the number and identities of victims are determined;

- "[G]eographical or territorial limits on the use of UAVs to kill targeted individuals;"

- The "number of drone strikes that have been executed for the purpose of killing human targets, the location of each such strike, and the agency of the government or branch of the military that undertook each such strike;"

- The "number, identity, status, and affiliation of individuals killed in drone strikes;"

- "[W]ho may pilot UAVs, who may cause weapons to be fired from UAVs, or who may otherwise be involved in the operation of UAVs for the purpose of executing targeted killings," including records pertaining to the involvement of CIA personnel, government contractors, or other non-military personnel, and;

- The "training, supervision, oversight, or discipline of UAV operators and others involved in the decision to execute a targeted killing" using a drone.

B. *Prior Proceedings*

CIA responded to the FOIA Request, stating that "the CIA [could] neither confirm nor deny the existence or nonexistence of records responsive to [ACLU's] request." CIA stated that the "fact of the existence or nonexistence of requested records is currently and properly classified and is intelligence sources and methods information that is protected from disclosure by section 6 of the CIA Act of 1949, as amended." ACLU filed an administrative appeal but then filed the Amended Complaint in this litigation (adding CIA as a defendant) and CIA closed the administrative file.

CIA moved for summary judgment, arguing that it could neither confirm nor deny the existence of responsive records. ACLU opposed, citing *inter alia,* a response to a question by then-CIA Director Leon J. Panetta after a speech, about the United States' use of drone strikes in Pakistan. Director Panetta responded:

> On the first issue, obviously because these are covert and secret operations I can't go into particulars. I think it does suffice to say that these operations have been very effective because they have been very precise in terms of the targeting and it involved a minimum of collateral damage. I know that some of the—sometimes the criticisms kind of sweep into other areas from either plane attacks or attacks from F–16s and others that go into these areas, which do involve a tremendous amount of collateral damage.
>
> And sometimes I've found in discussing this that all of this is kind of mixed together. But I can assure you that in terms of that particular area, it is very precise and it is very limited in terms of collateral damage and, very frankly, it's the only game in town in terms of confronting and trying to disrupt the al-Qaeda leadership.

This Court granted CIA's Motion for Summary Judgment, finding that CIA's Glomar response was justified under FOIA based on the nondisclosure provisions of the Central Intelligence Agency Act of 1949. With respect to Director Panetta's comments, the Court found that:

> [C]omments by Director Panetta did not officially disclose the CIA's involvement in the drone strike program.... Even if Director Panetta were speaking squarely on the issue of

> drone strikes, he never acknowledged the CIA's involvement in such program. That Director Panetta acknowledged that such a program exists and he had some knowledge of it, or that he was able to assess its success, is simply not tantamount to a specific acknowledgment of the CIA's involvement in such program, nor does it waive the CIA's ability to properly invoke Glomar.

This Court noted that "Plaintiffs seek exactly what is not publicly available—an official CIA acknowledgment of the fact that it is or is not involved in the drone strike program." This Court also ruled that CIA's Glomar response was independently authorized under a FOIA Exemption 1 based on Executive Order 13526, as well as the potential damage to national security that could occur by providing insight into CIA's foreign intelligence activities.

ACLU filed its notice of appeal, and thereafter, on January 30, 2012, President Obama appeared on a live internet video forum, and stated:

> I think that we have to be judicious in how we use drones. But understand that probably our ability to respect the sovereignty of other countries ... is enhanced by the fact that we are able to pinpoint-strike an al Qaeda operative in a place where the capacities of th[e] military in that country may not be able to get them. So obviously a lot of these strikes have been ... going after al Qaeda suspects who are up in very tough terrain along the border between Afghanistan and Pakistan.

On April 20, 2012, then-Assistant to the President for Homeland Security and Counterterrorism John Brennan remarked:

> So let me say it is as simply as I can. Yes, in full accordance with the law ... the United States Government conducts targeted strikes against specific al-Qaida terrorists, sometimes using remotely piloted aircraft, often referred to publicly as drones. And I'm here today because President Obama has instructed us to be more open with the American people about these efforts.

The D.C. Circuit reversed this Court, noting that ACLU's FOIA request was not limited to information about drones operated by CIA, but more broadly sought records pertaining to the use of drones by either CIA or the Armed Forces. The Circuit held that the Government had acknowledged officially that CIA has an "intelligence interest" in drone strikes.

Taking judicial notice of the statements made by President Obama and Mr. Brennan, the D.C. Circuit concluded that, "[g]iven these official acknowledgements ... it is neither logical nor plausible for the CIA to maintain that it would reveal anything not already in the public domain to say that the Agency 'at least has an intelligence interest' in such strikes."

The Circuit remanded for this Court to determine "'whether the contents—as distinguished from the existence—of the officially acknowledged records may be protected from disclosure by [FOIA] Exemptions.'" The Circuit instructed that, "with the failure of the CIA's broad Glomar response, the case must now proceed to the filing of a *Vaughn* index or other description of the kind of documents the Agency possesses, followed by litigation regarding whether the exemptions apply to those documents."

Since then, the Executive Branch continued to declassify and disclose previously-classified information. On May 22, 2013, Attorney General Eric Holder wrote to Senator Patrick J. Leahy, Chairman of the Senate Judiciary Committee, regarding counterterrorism operations. Attorney General Holder wrote:

> I am ... disclos[ing] to you certain information about the number of U.S. citizens who have been killed by U.S. counterterrorism operations outside of areas of active hostilities. Since 2009, the United States, in the conduct of U.S. counterterrorism operations against al-Qa'ida and its associated forces outside of areas of active hostilities, has specifically targeted and killed one U.S. citizen, Anwar al-Aulaqi.
>
> The United States is further aware of three other U.S. citizens who have been killed in such U.S. counterterrorism operations over that same time period: Samir Khan, 'Abd al-Rahman Anwar al-Aulaqi, and Jude Kenan Mohammed. These individuals were not specifically targeted by the United States.

Further, on May 23, 2013, President Obama himself disclosed that Anwar al-Aulaqi and three other U.S. citizens were killed in lethal drone operations overseas.

II. LEGAL STANDARDS

In a FOIA case, a district court decides de novo whether an agency properly withheld information under a claimed exemption. "The underlying facts are viewed in the light most favorable to the [FOIA] requester," and the exemptions are narrowly construed. The question here is whether ACLU can obtain certain legal memoranda concerning the U.S. Government's use of drone strikes and four type of records "routinely compiled by the CIA for analytical purposes containing charts or compilations about U.S. Government strikes sufficient to show" the detailed information requested on covert government actions.

CIA has invoked FOIA Exemptions 1, 3, and 5 to justify its withholding of records. ACLU maintains that CIA has improperly withheld information that has already been officially disclosed and that CIA has not justified any of the cited FOIA Exemptions.

A. *FOIA Exemption 1*

Under Exemption 1, FOIA does not require the production of records that are: "(A) specifically authorized under criteria established by an Executive order to be kept secret in the interest of national defense or foreign policy and (B) are in fact properly classified pursuant to such Executive order."

CIA argues that the withheld records fall into two of those categories: (1) "intelligence activities (including covert action), intelligence sources or methods, or cryptology" and (2) "foreign relations or foreign activities of the United States, including confidential sources." Specifically, CIA maintains that the legal memoranda, including the redacted portions of the DOJ White Paper, concern classified intelligence activities, sources, and methods, and that the redacted portions of the DOJ White Paper, which discuss a contemplated CIA operation in Yemen, and the intelligence products, which include information about U.S. government drone strikes, concern the foreign relations or foreign activities of the United States.

ACLU's objection is presented in three parts. First, ACLU contends that the legal analysis in the memoranda is not an intelligence activity, source or method, according to the ordinary use of those terms, and therefore cannot be withheld under Exemption 1 because it does not fall within a protected category listed in Section 1.4 of the Executive Order. Second, it argues that if CIA can justify withholding redacted portions of the DOJ White Paper simply because those portions implicate foreign activities, CIA's position is so expansive as to render CIA exempt from the FOIA altogether. Third, ACLU argues that CIA concedes that "strike metadata" is not itself an intelligence source or method based on the CIA's testimony that "[t]he information contained in these intelligence products would reveal the sources and methods of underlying intelligence collection."

Contrary to ACLU's argument, legal analysis need not constitute an intelligence activity, source, or method to be protected from disclosure under Exemption 1. Section 1.4 of the Executive Order directs that "[i]nformation shall not be considered for classification unless it ... *pertains to* ... intelligence activities (including covert action), intelligence sources or methods." For something to pertain to something else, it must be related or connected to such a thing. Thus, a legal analysis need not constitute an intelligence activity, source, or method by itself to warrant protection so long as it pertains to an intelligence activity, source, or method.

Here, CIA has withheld legal memoranda responsive to ACLU's request for legal memoranda that "concern[ ] the U.S. Government's use of armed drones to carry out premeditated killings." ACLU does not contend that drone strikes are not an intelligence activity or method (or possibly reveal sources), nor could it. Thus, it is entirely logical and plausible that the legal analyses in the withheld memoranda pertain to intelligence activities, sources, and methods.

ACLU insists that it only seeks "factual information" from the four kinds of intelligence products that contain charts or compilations of U.S. drone strikes, not anything that would reveal an intelligence activity, source, or method. To the contrary, ACLU seeks explicit details on U.S. drone strikes that would be "sufficient to show the identity of the intended targets, assessed number of people killed, dates, status of those killed, agencies involved, the location of each strike, and the identities of those killed if known." CIA Notice at 1. Such details could reveal the scope of the drone program, its successes and limitations, the "methodology behind the assessments and the priorities of the Agency" and more. The Court has no doubt that this kind of detail would reveal intelligence activities, sources, and methods and is properly protected under Exemption 1. The Court concludes that CIA has sustained its burden of showing that all the documents at issue were properly withheld from disclosure under FOIA Exemption 1.

B. *FOIA Exemption 5*

FOIA Exemption 5 protects from disclosure "inter-agency or intra-agency memoranda or letters which would not be available by law to a party other than an agency in litigation with the agency." This exemption encompasses material that is protected under the deliberative process privilege, the attorney-client privilege, and the presidential communications privilege.

The deliberative process privilege protects records "reflecting advisory opinions, recommendations and deliberations comprising part of a process by which governmental decisions and policies are formulated." It also covers "recommendations, draft documents, proposals, suggestions, and other subjective documents which reflect the personal opinions of the writer rather than the policy of the agency." To qualify for withholding, material must be both predecisional and deliberative:

> A document is predecisional if it was prepared in order to assist an agency decisionmaker in arriving at his decision, rather than to support a decision already made. Material is deliberative if it reflects the give-and-take of the consultative process. [The D.C. Circuit's] recent decisions on the deliberativeness inquiry have focused on whether

> disclosure of the requested material would tend to discourage candid discussion within an agency.

Petroleum Info. Corp. v. Dep't of Interior (D.C. Cir.1992). These documents are protected from release to promote "the quality of agency decisions by protecting open and frank discussion among those who make them within the Government."

The attorney-client privilege protects "confidential communications from clients to their attorneys, as well as communications from attorneys to their clients containing confidential information supplied by the client." The presidential communications privilege is a "presumptive privilege for [p]residential communications," *United States v. Nixon* (1974), that "preserves the President's ability to obtain candid and informed opinions from his advisors and to make decisions confidentially." The privilege protects those "documents or other materials that reflect presidential decision-making and deliberations and that the President believes should remain confidential," and, once the privilege is invoked, the documents become presumptively privileged. Further, unlike the deliberative process privilege, which is also encompassed under Exemption 5, the presidential communications privilege "applies to documents in their entirety, and covers final and post-decisional materials as well as pre-deliberative ones." Along with protecting communications that "directly involve" the President, the privilege also protects

> communications authored or solicited and received by those members of an immediate White House adviser's staff who have broad and significant responsibility for investigating and formulating the advice to be given the President on the particular matter to which the communications relate.

CIA justifies withholding the legal memoranda under the deliberative process, attorney-client, and presidential communication privileges. CIA testimony avers that "[a]ll of the material for which the deliberative process privilege was asserted reveals an interim stage in intra-agency and inter-agency discussions, which preceded a final decision of the CIA or other agency or component of the Executive Branch." CIA argues that attorney-client privilege protects "communications between the CIA and DOJ in connection with a request for the provision of legal advice as well as information provided by Agency personnel in furtherance of that advice." CIA affirms that "the confidentiality of these communications was maintained." Finally, CIA contends that the presidential communication privilege protects those documents which "reflect communications between Executive Branch agencies and presidential advisors for the purpose of presidential decision-making."

ACLU protests that CIA's Declaration fails to provide a foundation for invoking any of the cited privileges because it fails to explain how any of the claimed privileges actually applies to each of the legal memoranda for which they are invoked. However, the classified testimony, which was provided to the Court for *ex parte*, *in camera review*, provides fully detailed descriptions of the legal memoranda with more than sufficient information for this Court to determine the nature of each memo. In this respect, the Court finds that review of the memoranda themselves is unnecessary. As a result, the Court is fully satisfied that the cited privileges have been validly invoked and applied. Accordingly, the Court concludes that the contested legal memoranda, including the redacted portions of the DOJ White Paper, were properly withheld under Exemption 5 based on the applicable deliberative process, attorney-client, and presidential communication privileges.

C. *Official Acknowledgement*

When "information has been 'officially acknowledged,' its disclosure may be compelled even over an agency's otherwise valid exemption claim." To be officially acknowledged: "(1) the information requested must be as specific as the information previously released; (2) the information requested must match the information previously disclosed; and (3) the information requested must already have been made public through an official and documented disclosure."

The D.C. Circuit has cautioned that "'[p]rior disclosure of similar information does not suffice; instead, the specific information sought by the plaintiff must already be in the public domain by official disclosure. This insistence on exactitude recognizes the Government's vital interest in information relating to national security and foreign affairs.'" The fact that information is publicly available "does not necessarily mean that official disclosure will not cause harm cognizable under a FOIA exemption."

ACLU bears the burden of demonstrating that the information it seeks has been officially acknowledged. ACLU argues that the government has officially acknowledged basic facts about the drone program and information about the program's legal basis; therefore, ACLU concludes that some of the records CIA seeks to withhold must be released because the government has waived any FOIA exemptions with regard to such records. The CIA denies that any of the withheld records has been officially acknowledged and dismisses ACLU's argument as speculative.

The Court finds that none of the requested information is available through an official disclosure and, accordingly, CIA has not waived its validly invoked FOIA exemptions with respect to the withheld records. For the reasons set forth above, the Court will grant CIA's Motion for Summary Judgment and deny ACLU's Cross–Motion for Summary Judgment.

The White House
Office of Communications

PRESIDENTIAL MEMORANDUM: PROMOTING ECONOMIC COMPETITIVENESS WHILE SAFEGUARDING PRIVACY, CIVIL RIGHTS, AND CIVIL LIBERTIES IN DOMESTIC USE OF UNMANNED AIRCRAFT SYSTEMS

February 15, 2015
The White House

MEMORANDUM FOR THE HEADS OF
EXECUTIVE DEPARTMENTS AND AGENCIES

SUBJECT: PROMOTING ECONOMIC
COMPETITIVENESS WHILE SAFEGUARDING

PRIVACY, CIVIL RIGHTS, AND CIVIL LIBERTIES
IN DOMESTIC USE OF UNMANNED AIRCRAFT SYSTEMS

Unmanned Aircraft Systems (UAS) technology continues to improve rapidly, and increasingly UAS are able to perform a variety of missions with greater operational flexibility and at a lower cost than comparable manned aircraft. A wide spectrum of domestic users -- including industry, private citizens, and Federal, State, local, tribal, and territorial governments -- are using or expect to use these systems, which may play a transformative role in fields as diverse as urban infrastructure management, farming, public safety, coastal security, military training, search and rescue, and disaster response.

The Congress recognized the potential wide-ranging benefits of UAS operations within the United States in the FAA Modernization and Reform Act of 2012 (Public Law 112-95), which requires a plan to safely integrate civil UAS into the National Airspace System (NAS) by September 30, 2015. As compared to manned aircraft, UAS may provide lower-cost operation and augment existing capabilities while reducing risks to human life. Estimates suggest the positive economic impact to U.S. industry of the integration of UAS into the NAS could be substantial and likely will grow for the foreseeable future.

As UAS are integrated into the NAS, the Federal Government will take steps to ensure that the integration takes into account not only our economic competitiveness and public safety, but also the privacy, civil rights, and civil liberties concerns these systems may raise.

By the authority vested in me as President by the Constitution and the laws of the United States of America, and in order to establish transparent principles that govern the Federal Government's use of UAS in the NAS, and to promote the responsible use of this technology in the private and commercial sectors, it is hereby ordered as follows:

Section 1. ***UAS Policies and Procedures for Federal Government Use.***

The Federal Government currently operates UAS in the United States for several purposes, including to manage Federal lands, monitor wildfires, conduct scientific research, monitor our borders, support law enforcement, and effectively train our military. As with information collected by the Federal Government using any technology, where UAS is the platform for collection, information must be collected, used, retained, and disseminated consistent with the Constitution, Federal law, and other applicable regulations and policies. Agencies must, for example, comply with the Privacy Act of 1974 (5 U.S.C. 552a), which restricts the collection and dissemination of individuals' information that is maintained in systems of records, including personally identifiable information (PII), and permits individuals to seek access to and amendment of records.

(a) **Privacy Protections.**

Particularly in light of the diverse potential uses of UAS in the NAS, expected advancements in UAS technologies, and the anticipated increase in UAS use in the future, the Federal Government shall take steps to ensure that privacy protections and policies relative to UAS continue to keep pace with these developments. Accordingly, agencies shall, prior to deployment of new UAS technology and at least every 3 years, examine their existing UAS policies and procedures relating to the collection, use, retention, and dissemination of information obtained by UAS, to ensure that privacy, civil rights, and civil liberties are protected.

Agencies shall update their policies and procedures, or issue new policies and procedures, as necessary. In addition to requiring compliance with the Privacy Act in applicable circumstances, agencies that collect information through UAS in the NAS shall ensure that their policies and procedures with respect to such information incorporate the following requirements:

(i) **Collection and Use**. Agencies shall only collect information using UAS, or use UAS-collected information, to the extent that such collection or use is consistent with and relevant to an authorized purpose.

(ii) **Retention**. Information collected using UAS that may contain PII shall not be retained for more than 180 days unless retention of the information is determined to be necessary to an authorized mission of the retaining agency, is maintained in a system of records covered by the Privacy Act, or is required to be retained for a longer period by any other applicable law or regulation.

(iii) **Dissemination**. UAS-collected information that is not maintained in a system of records covered by the Privacy Act shall not be disseminated outside of the agency unless dissemination is required by law, or fulfills an authorized purpose and complies with agency requirements.

(b) **Civil Rights and Civil Liberties Protections**. To protect civil rights and civil liberties, agencies shall:

(i) ensure that policies are in place to prohibit the collection, use, retention, or dissemination of data in any manner that would violate the First Amendment or in any manner that would discriminate against persons based upon their ethnicity, race, gender, national origin, religion, sexual orientation, or gender identity, in violation of law;

(ii) ensure that UAS activities are performed in a manner consistent with the Constitution and applicable laws, Executive Orders, and other Presidential directives; and

(iii) ensure that adequate procedures are in place to receive, investigate, and address, as appropriate, privacy, civil rights, and civil liberties complaints.

(c) **Accountability**. To provide for effective oversight, agencies shall:

(i) ensure that oversight procedures for agencies' UAS use, including audits or assessments, comply with existing agency policies and regulations;

(ii) verify the existence of rules of conduct and training for Federal Government personnel and contractors who work on UAS programs, and procedures for reporting suspected cases of misuse or abuse of UAS technologies;

(iii) establish policies and procedures, or confirm that policies and procedures are in place, that provide meaningful oversight of individuals who have access to sensitive information (including any PII) collected using UAS;

(iv) ensure that any data-sharing agreements or policies, data use policies, and record management policies applicable to UAS conform to applicable laws, regulations, and policies;

(v) establish policies and procedures, or confirm that policies and procedures are in place, to authorize the use of UAS in response to a request for UAS assistance in support of Federal, State, local, tribal, or territorial government operations; and

(vi) require that State, local, tribal, and territorial government recipients of Federal grant funding for the purchase or use of UAS for their own operations have in place policies and procedures to safeguard individuals' privacy, civil rights, and civil liberties prior to expending such funds.

(d) **Transparency**. To promote transparency about their UAS activities within the NAS, agencies that use UAS shall, while not revealing information that could reasonably be expected to compromise law enforcement or national security: (i) provide notice to the public regarding where the agency's UAS are authorized to operate in the NAS; (ii) keep the public informed about the agency's UAS program as well as changes that would significantly affect privacy, civil rights, or civil liberties; and (iii) make available to the public, on an annual basis, a general summary of the agency's UAS operations during the previous fiscal year, to include a brief description of types or categories of missions flown, and the number of times the agency provided assistance to other agencies, or to State, local, tribal, or territorial governments.

(e) **Reports**. Within 180 days of the date of this memorandum, agencies shall provide the President with a status report on the implementation of this section. Within 1 year of the date of this memorandum, agencies shall publish information on how to access their publicly available policies and procedures implementing this section.

Sec. 2.
Multi-stakeholder Engagement Process.

In addition to the Federal uses of UAS described in section 1 of this memorandum, the combination of greater operational flexibility, lower capital requirements, and lower operating costs could allow UAS to be a transformative technology in the commercial and private sectors for fields as diverse as urban infrastructure management, farming, and disaster response. Although these opportunities will enhance American economic competitiveness, our Nation must be mindful of the potential implications for privacy, civil rights, and civil liberties. The Federal Government is committed to promoting the responsible use of this technology in a way that does not diminish rights and freedoms.

(a) There is hereby established a multi-stakeholder engagement process to develop and communicate best practices for privacy, accountability, and transparency issues regarding commercial and private UAS use in the NAS. The process will include stakeholders from the private sector.

(b) Within 90 days of the date of this memorandum, the Department of Commerce, through the National Telecommunications and Information Administration, and in consultation with other interested agencies, will initiate this multi-stakeholder engagement process to develop a framework regarding privacy, accountability, and transparency for commercial and private UAS use. For this process, commercial and private use includes the use of UAS for commercial purposes as civil aircraft, even if the use would qualify a UAS as a public aircraft under 49 U.S.C. 40102(a)(41) and 40125. The process shall not focus on law enforcement or other noncommercial governmental use.

Sec. 3.
Definitions.

As used in this memorandum:

(a) "**Agencies**" means executive departments and agencies of the Federal Government that conduct UAS operations in the NAS.

(b) "**Federal Government use**" means operations in which agencies operate UAS in the NAS. Federal Government use includes agency UAS operations on behalf of another agency or on behalf of a State, local, tribal, or territorial government, or when a nongovernmental entity operates UAS on behalf of an agency.

(c) "**National Airspace System**" means the common network of U.S. airspace; air navigation facilities, equipment, and services; airports or landing areas; aeronautical charts, information, and services; related rules, regulations, and procedures; technical information; and manpower and material. Included in this definition are system components shared jointly by the Departments of Defense, Transportation, and Homeland Security.

(d) "**Unmanned Aircraft System**" means an unmanned aircraft (an aircraft that is operated without direct human intervention from within or on the aircraft) and associated elements (including communication links and components that control the unmanned aircraft) that are required for the pilot or system operator in command to operate safely and efficiently in the NAS.

(e) "**Personally identifiable informat**ion" refers to information that can be used to distinguish or trace an individual's identity, either alone or when combined with other personal or identifying information that is linked or linkable to a specific individual, as set forth in Office of Management and Budget Memorandum M-07-16 (May 22, 2007) and Office of Management and Budget Memorandum M-10-23 (June 25, 2010).

Sec. 4.
General Provisions.

(a) This memorandum complements and is not intended to supersede existing laws and policies for UAS operations in the NAS, including the National Strategy for Aviation Security and its supporting plans, the FAA Modernization and Reform Act of 2012, the Federal Aviation Administration's (FAA's) Integration of Civil UAS in the NAS Roadmap, and the FAA's UAS Comprehensive Plan.

(b) This memorandum shall be implemented consistent with applicable law, and subject to the availability of appropriations.

(c) Nothing in this memorandum shall be construed to impair or otherwise affect: (i) the authority granted by law to an executive department, agency, or the head thereof; or (ii) the functions of the Director of the Office of Management and Budget relating to budgetary, administrative, or legislative proposals.

(d) Independent agencies are strongly encouraged to comply with this memorandum.

(e) This memorandum is not intended to, and does not, create any right or benefit, substantive or procedural, enforceable at law or in equity by any party against the United States, its departments, agencies, or entities, its officers, employees, or agents, or any other person.

(f) The Secretary of Commerce is hereby authorized and directed to publish this memorandum in the Federal Register.

BARACK OBAMA

FLA. STAT. § 934.50 SEARCHES AND SEIZURE USING A DRONE

(1) **SHORT TITLE**. This act may be cited as the "Freedom from Unwarranted Surveillance Act."

(2) **DEFINITIONS**.—As used in this act, the term:

(a) "Drone" means a powered, aerial vehicle that: (i) does not carry a human operator; (ii) uses aerodynamic forces to provide vehicle lift; (iii) can fly autonomously or be piloted remotely; (iv) can be expendable or recoverable; and (v) can carry a lethal or nonlethal payload.

(b) "Image" means a record of thermal, infrared, ultraviolet, visible light, or other electromagnetic waves; sound waves; odors; or other physical phenomena which captures conditions existing on or about real property or an individual located on that property.

(c) "Imaging device" means a mechanical, digital, or electronic viewing device; still camera; camcorder; motion picture camera; or any other instrument, equipment, or format capable of recording, storing, or transmitting an image.

(d) "Law enforcement agency" means a lawfully established state or local public agency that is responsible for the prevention and detection of crime, local government code enforcement, and the enforcement of penal, traffic, regulatory, game, or controlled substance laws.

(e) "Surveillance" means:

1. With respect to an owner, tenant, occupant, invitee, or licensee of privately owned real property, the observation of such persons with sufficient visual clarity to be able to obtain information about their identity, habits, conduct, movements, or whereabouts; or

2. With respect to privately owned real property, the observation of such property's physical improvements with sufficient visual clarity to be able to determine unique identifying features or its occupancy by one or more persons.

(3) **PROHIBITED USE OF DRONES**.

(a) A law enforcement agency may not use a drone to gather evidence or other information.

(b) A person, a state agency, or a political subdivision may not use a drone equipped with an imaging device to record an image of privately owned real property or of the owner, tenant, occupant, invitee, or licensee of such property with the intent to conduct surveillance on the individual or property captured in the image in violation of such person's reasonable expectation of privacy without his or her written consent. For purposes of this section, a person is presumed to have a reasonable expectation of privacy on his or her privately owned real property if he or she is not observable by persons located at ground level in a place where they have a legal right to be, regardless of whether he or she is observable from the air with the use of a drone.

(4) **EXCEPTIONS**. This section does not prohibit the use of a drone:

(a) To counter a high risk of a terrorist attack by a specific individual or organization if the United States Secretary of Homeland Security determines that credible intelligence indicates that there is such a risk.

(b) If the law enforcement agency first obtains a search warrant signed by a judge authorizing the use of a drone.

(c) If the law enforcement agency possesses reasonable suspicion that, under particular circumstances, swift action is needed to prevent imminent danger to life or serious damage to property, to forestall the imminent escape of a suspect or the destruction of evidence, or to achieve purposes including, but not limited to, facilitating the search for a missing person.

(d) By a person or an entity engaged in a business or profession licensed by the state, or by an agent, employee, or contractor thereof, if the drone is used only to perform reasonable tasks within the scope of practice or activities permitted under such person's or entity's license. However, this exception does not apply to a profession in which the licensee's authorized scope of practice includes obtaining information about the identity, habits, conduct, movements, whereabouts, affiliations, associations, transactions, reputation, or character of any society, person, or group of persons.

(e) By an employee or a contractor of a property appraiser who uses a drone solely for the purpose of assessing property for ad valorem taxation.

(f) To capture images by or for an electric, water, or natural gas utility:

1. For operations and maintenance of utility facilities, including facilities used in the generation, transmission, or distribution of electricity, gas, or water, for the purpose of maintaining utility system reliability and integrity;

2. For inspecting utility facilities, including pipelines, to determine construction, repair, maintenance, or replacement needs before, during, and after construction of such facilities;

3. For assessing vegetation growth for the purpose of maintaining clearances on utility rights-of-way;

4. For utility routing, siting, and permitting for the purpose of constructing utility facilities or providing utility service; or

5. For conducting environmental monitoring, as provided by federal, state, or local law, rule, or permit.

(g) For aerial mapping, if the person or entity using a drone for this purpose is operating in compliance with Federal Aviation Administration regulations.

(h) To deliver cargo, if the person or entity using a drone for this purpose is operating in compliance with Federal Aviation Administration regulations.

(i) To capture images necessary for the safe operation or navigation of a drone that is being used for a purpose allowed under federal or Florida law.

(5) **REMEDIES FOR VIOLATION**.

(a) An aggrieved party may initiate a civil action against a law enforcement agency to obtain all appropriate relief in order to prevent or remedy a violation of this section.

(b) The owner, tenant, occupant, invitee, or licensee of privately owned real property may initiate a civil action for compensatory damages for violations of this section and may seek injunctive relief to prevent future violations of this section against a person, state agency, or political subdivision that violates paragraph (3)(b). In such action, the prevailing party is entitled to recover reasonable attorney fees from the nonprevailing party based on the actual and reasonable time expended by his or her attorney billed at an appropriate hourly rate and, in cases in which the payment of such a fee is contingent on the outcome, without a multiplier, unless the action is tried to verdict, in which case a multiplier of up to twice the actual value of the time expended may be awarded in the discretion of the trial court.

(c) Punitive damages for a violation of paragraph (3)(b) may be sought against a person subject to other requirements and limitations of law, including, but not limited to, part II of chapter 768 and case law.

(d) The remedies provided for a violation of paragraph (3)(b) are cumulative to other existing remedies.

(6) **PROHIBITION ON USE OF EVIDENCE**. Evidence obtained or collected in violation of this act is not admissible as evidence in a criminal prosecution in any court of law in this state.

NOTES

1. Unmanned aircraft are known by a host of names in the United States, including remotely piloted vehicles ("RPVs"), drones, robot planes, and unmanned aerial vehicles ("UAVs). Fundamentally, they are aircraft that are operated without the possibility of direct human intervention from within or on the aircraft. Some UAVs are completely autonomous, functioning according to pre-programmed data or flight paths, while other UAVs are partially autonomous or automated in that they respond to commands from pilot-operated ground stations.

While unmanned aerial vehicles ("UAVs") are celebrated as a disruptive technology, they are not necessarily novel. In fact, notwithstanding recent and widespread attention (no doubt as a function of recent conflicts in Afghanistan, Iraq, and Kosovo), the history of unmanned aircraft dates backs to the early 1920s. For example, the United States tested (but never deployed) UAVs during World War I, and during World War II, a Hollywood actor and model airplane enthusiast, Reginald Denny, produced the "Dennymite" drone, which the U.S. Army used for gunnery practice in place of targets towed by piloted airplanes. *See* Charles Jarnot, *History in* INTRODUCTION TO UNMANNED AIRCRAFT SYSTEMS 1-15 (Richard K. Barnhart et al. eds. 2012). *See also* John Villasenor, *Observations from Above: Unmanned Aircraft Systems and Privacy*, 36 HARV. J.L. & PUB. POL'Y 457, 462 (2013) (tracing unmanned airplanes from Alphonse Penaud's rubber strand-powered models in the 1870s, through the British "Queen Bee" biplanes of the 1930s, to military assets of the United States, Russia, Canada, Israel, and Europe in the modern era). Later, in 1952, Denny's Radioplane Company was purchased by Northrop, maker of the twenty-first century Global Hawk RQ-4A that the U.S. Air Force and Navy use for surveillance.

2. The militarized context of UAVs frequently clouds public perception from a fuller understanding of unmanned aviation technology, including many civil and commercial uses in the arenas of insurance, natural gas pipeline monitoring, agriculture remote sensing, and aerial cinematography. *See, e.g.*, Kelsey D. Atherton, *Keeping up with the Droneses: The Week in Drones*, POPULAR SCI., *http://www.popsci.com/category/popsci-authors/kelsey-d-atherton*. Indeed, pejorative use of the term "drone" persists in public discussion about unmanned airplanes largely because of the technology's military origins. "Drones" are hunter-killer robots with scary names like "Predator" and "Reaper." They are scary "smart" with robust intelligence, reconnaissance, and surveillance ("ISR") capabilities. In the "war on terror"—an operation played out domestically as well as overseas—drones can stalk human beings with indefatigable persistence and kill them with "Hellfire" missiles.

UAVs optimize the political, business and human costs of "dull, dirty, and dangerous" activities in both marketplace and battlefield, however. Militarily, uses of drones include national defense, disaster response, homeland security and law enforcement, remote sensing, and ISR missions. In fact, the U.S. Air Force is training more unmanned aircraft pilots than manned ones. Meanwhile, civilian applications include traffic surveillance, weather monitoring, communications relay, border management, maritime patrol, crime prevention, forest fire monitoring, and drug interdiction. Similarly, in the commercial sector, UAVs can undertake fishery and agricultural management, freight, pipeline monitoring, aerial photography, and search and rescue tasks.

Do lawmakers have a role to play in shaping public perception of new technologies like drones? Alternatively, should lawmakers be blind to public perception in producing laws that govern drone operations and safety?

Consider that the Federal Aviation Administration is leading a public outreach campaign for the National Capital Region around Washington, D.C. to reinforce the message that the District of Columbia and cities and towns within a 15-mile radius of Ronald-Reagan Washington National Airport are a No Drone Zone. *See* Fed. Aviation Admin., *No Drone Zone*, *http://www.faa.gov/uas/no_drone_zone/.*

3. As detailed in the cases in this section, UAV intelligence and surveillance capabilities raise important constitutional considerations vis-à-vis civil liberties and privacy rights. For further commentary on this see Troy Roberts, *On the Radar: Government Unmanned Aerial Vehicles and Their Effect on Public Privacy Interests from Fourth Amendment Jurisprudence and Legislative Policy Perspectives*, 49 JURIMETRICS J. 291 (2009); Paul McBride, Comment, *Beyond Orwell: The Application of Unmanned Aircraft Systems in Domestic Surveillance Operations*, 74 J. AIR L. & COM. 627 (2009).

4. Under Title 14 of the Code of Federal Regulations, the Federal Aviation Administration has proposed to amend its regulations to adopt specific rules to allow the operation of small unmanned aircraft systems in the National Airspace System. These changes would address the operation of unmanned aircraft systems, certification of their operators, registration, and display of registration markings. The proposed rule would

also find that airworthiness certification is not required for small unmanned aircraft system operations that would be subject to this proposed rule. Lastly, the proposed rule would prohibit model aircraft from endangering the safety of the National Airspace System. The proposed rule is now open to public comment, with a final set of rules expected in 2017. Among the main points:

- The person actually flying a small UAS would be an "operator." An operator would have to be at least 17 years old, pass an aeronautical knowledge test and obtain an FAA UAS operator certificate. To maintain certification, the operator would have to pass the FAA knowledge tests every 24 months. A small UAS operator would not need any further private pilot certifications (i.e., a private pilot license or medical rating).

- The new rule also proposes operating limitations designed to minimize risks to other aircraft and people and property on the ground:

- A small UAS operator must always see and avoid manned aircraft. If there is a risk of collision, the UAS operator must be the first to maneuver away.

- The operator must discontinue the flight when continuing would pose a hazard to other aircraft, people or property.

- A small UAS operator must assess weather conditions, airspace restrictions and the location of people to lessen risks if he or she loses control of the UAS.

- A small UAS may not fly over people, except those directly involved with the flight.

- Flights should be limited to 500 feet altitude and no faster than 100 mph.

- Operators must stay out of airport flight paths and restricted airspace areas, and obey any FAA Temporary Flight Restrictions ("TFRs").

5. One scholar has resisted the suggestion that Congress should establish nationwide regulations to govern both law enforcement and civilian drone use, recommending instead "drone federalism: a state-based approach to privacy regulation that governs drone use by civilians, drawing on states' experience regulating other forms of civilian-on-civilian surveillance. This approach will allow necessary experimentation in how to best balance privacy concerns against First Amendment rights in the imminent era of drone-use democratization." *See* MARGOT E. KAMINSKI, *Drone Federalism: Civilian Drones and the Things They Carry*, 4 CAL. L. REV. CIRCUIT 57, 73-74. (2013).

Moreover:

> FAA regulation of small, low-flying drones does not preclude all state regulation. Congress has not created express statutory preemption of laws governing aerial surveillance, and has even expressly nodded to exceptions to federal preemption in the field of aviation. The original Federal Aviation Act had a savings clause explaining that "[n]othing contained in this Act shall in any way abridge or alter the remedies now existing at common law or by statute." In 1994, Congress amended this clause to explain that a "remedy under this part is in addition to any other remedies provided by law." Presumably, the 1994 revision still intends to exempt state tort laws, for example, from federal preemption.
>
> A number of courts have found federal preemption of state attempts to impose curfews on airports or enjoin flight patterns over certain areas. But federal aviation law does not preempt state common law tort claims for injuries suffered during crashes. Additionally, federal aviation law does not preempt a city's zoning power on land, because that power does not conflict with air use. However, aviation safety law impliedly preempts state schemes for regulating alcoholic beverages on board an aircraft.
>
> One interesting question will be whether the use of cameras on a drone is considered to fall under the regulatory power of the government in federal airspace, or under the state power to protect its citizens from privacy injuries on land. [T]here is no extensive system of privacy regulation on airplanes, [but] courts might find that airplane safety regulations impliedly preempt state regulation of cameras on planes, as they did the regulation of alcoholic beverages. (Another interesting question … is whether local governments in crowded cities might have additional authority to regulate drones at low altitude, owing to city-specific conditions such as wall-to-wall skyscrapers. Local regulation of drone altitude and traffic would have implications for drones' abilities to gather information.

6. What do drones have to do with the First Amendment? Considering that the core innovation of unmanned airplanes is not aeronautical science *per se*, but information technology, drones facilitate and produce many types of speech.

Harmonizing First Amendment speech rights with automated aerial technologies has proven difficult, however, particularly in the realm of journalism and media. *See Feds Concede Drone Filmmakers have First Amendment Rights*, available at *http://venturebeat.com/2015/04/14/feds-concede-drone-filmmakers-have-first-amendment-rights/. See also The FAA Tells the Media it Can't Use Drones for Journalism without Permission*, MOTHERBOARD, May 6, 2015, *http://motherboard.vice.com/read/the-faa-tells-the-media-it-cant-use-drones-for-journalism-without-permission.*

In fact, the FAA initially banned drone operations for media purposes. And, in a 2014 paper for the Mercatus Center at George Mason University, scholars Cynthia D. Love, Sean T. Lawson, and Avery E. Holton argued that the FAA's actions to prohibit drone use by the media infringed on core First Amendment protections:

> As UASs … have been put to a growing number of uses in domestic airspace, the Federal Aviation Administration has attempted to ban their commercial use. Efforts to enforce this ban have included sending dozens of cease-and-desist letters to UAS operators and even one attempt to levy a $10,000 fine. Most often, these UAS operators have been engaging in aerial photography, sometimes for news-gathering purposes.
>
> To date, little attention has been paid to the First Amendment implications of the ban. [We argue] that aerial photography with UASs, whether commercial or not, is protected First Amendment activity, particularly for news-gathering purposes. The FAA must take First Amendment–protected uses of this technology into account as it proceeds with meeting its congressional mandate to promulgate rules for domestic UASs.

Cynthia Love et al., *News from Above: First Amendment Implications of the Federal Aviation Administration Ban on Commercial Drones, Mercatus Working Paper*, September 2014, *available at http://mercatus.org/sites/default/files/Love-Commercial-Drone-Ban.pdf.* The paper also took the position that:

> Aerial photography and videography are protected under the First Amendment's free speech clause because they are part of the news-gathering process. The FAA's requirement that journalists obtain a permit to fly a drone to gather the same type of information a member of the general public could use a drone to obtain without a permit is inconsistent with the First Amendment. Journalists have the same rights

to access information as the general public, but the FAA's regulation treats them differently.

Moreover, the FAA's regulatory scheme is not content neutral and is an unconstitutional prior restraint on speech:

- *It concerns a public forum.* The airspace within a public forum, where drones can fly for news-gathering purposes, is itself a public forum, and the government may only restrict the journalistic use of drones with content-neutral regulations of time, place, and manner.

- *It bans on the basis of compensation.* The current FAA regulation does not stipulate when, where, or how a drone may be used, nor does it distinguish between types of drones. Instead, the FAA's ban focuses on whether compensation is involved. Given that journalists for traditional news media are often compensated—a significant incentive for news gathering under any conditions—the government cannot make this distinction a justification for prohibiting drone use.

- *It is not narrowly tailored.* The FAA's regulation of drones is not narrowly tailored to protect public safety—the receipt of compensation is wholly unrelated to the safety of drone use.

- *It is a prior restraint on speech.* When the government seeks to stop speech before it happens, it bears a heavy burden in justifying the restriction. In order to enforce a permitting scheme, the government must provide narrowly drawn, reasonable, and definite standards for officials to follow. The FAA has failed to create these standards.

The FAA's attempts to prohibit the use of drones for aerial photography and news gathering violate the First Amendment, because journalists have a constitutional right to access the same information as the general public, and the FAA's standards lack the rigorously defined, narrowly tailored restrictions the Supreme Court has required for restraints on speech.

The FAA can reverse course by focusing on specific time, place, and manner restrictions, as the First Amendment

> requires—allowing the news media the opportunity to innovate and improve reporting while saving money and lives.

7. With the number of UASs projected to be 15,000 by 2020, the prospect of accidents and mid-air collisions are not strictly hypothetical and in fact, recent events have aggravated the concern regulators have about UAS integration. In November, 2013, a malfunctioning UAV crashed into the USS Chancellorsville off the coast of Southern California, injuring two sailors. A remote controlled aircraft reportedly almost struck a US Airways flight about five miles from Tallahassee Regional Airport in Florida at an altitude of 2,300 feet a few months later.

Mishaps have occurred abroad, too. In 2014, the United Kingdom's Civil Aviation Authority prosecuted a man who flew his UAV in restricted airspace over a nuclear submarine facility, collecting an £800 fine and recouping £3,500 in legal costs. In Australia, a chartered aircraft preparing to land at Perth Airport missed an unmanned flying aircraft by 20 meters after taking evasive action. Three days later, a rescue helicopter with a crew of five nearly collided with a UAV hovering above a soccer stadium.

Measured against these events, the fervor to allow commercial UAS operations in the United States is rightly tempered by aviation regulators *See* Jack Nicas, *Increase in Drones Spotted Near Aircraft*, Wall St. J. Nov. 26, 2014, *http://www.wsj.com/articles/faa-reports-more-aircraft-drone-near-misses-1417025519*. *See also* Craig Whitlock, *Near-Collisions between Drones, Airliners Surge*, Nov. 26, 2014, WASH. POST, *https://www.washingtonpost.com/world/national-security/near-collisions-between-drones-airliners-surge-new-faa-reports-show/2014/11/26/9a8c1716-758c-11e4-bd1b-03009bd3e984_story.html*.

But, are drone collisions really an issue? In fact, according to an incident report of the Federal Aviation Administration, pilots of passenger airlines and other aircraft have reported 25 near-collisions with small drones across the United States since June 1, 2014. However, the difference between about five drone sightings a month at the beginning of 2014 and more recent reports of more frequent drone sightings may be the result of better reporting and record-keeping by pilots and controllers rather than a spike in careless or reckless UAV operations. In any event, despite an increase in amped-up reporting about drones buzzing passenger jets is an observation in commentary entitled "Birds of a Feather" by John Croft of Aviation Week & Space Technology. It raises the important consideration that "dangers to airlines from small UAVs may be more hype than substance."

> Rules or no rules, as the number of small, low-cost remotely piloted aircraft boom, the devices will undoubtedly come into conflict sooner or later with an air

> transport aircraft near an airport. The probability for harm when that happens is potentially no different from the risks already occurring from collisions with birds, and those are threats airlines fly with on a daily basis around the world. To mitigate the bird threat, the FAA and European certification standards require an airframe to handle the impact of a 4-lb. bird at high speeds and a windscreen to handle the same size bird without splintering the inner ply. The FAA also requires an aircraft's empennage to survive a collision with an 8-lb. bird at high speed. Both the FAA and Europe have stringent requirements for engines, which include ingesting single birds weighing 4-8 lb. and multiple birds weighing 1.9-2.5 lb., all while continuing to produce thrust at some level.

How should the law be designed to be a driver rather than an inhibitor of new technologies like drones, while at the same time deterring and punishing unscrupulous operators from operating carelessly or recklessly?

8. No approval is required from the FAA to fly a "model aircraft" for recreation. This policy balances the FAA's recognition that modelers are generally concerned about safety and exercise good judgment against the fact that "model aircraft can at times pose a hazard to full-scale aircraft in flight and to persons and property on the surface." As such, the FAA has proposed specific operating standards to reduce operational risks and "create a good neighbor environment with affected communities and airspace users."

In 1981, the FAA published Advisory Circular ("AC") 91-57, entitled "Model Aircraft Operating Standards," for the purpose of providing guidance to persons interested in flying model aircraft as a hobby or for recreational use. AC 91-57 focuses on site selection and recommends model airplane operations below 400 feet, three miles from an airport, and away from populated areas. *See* Fed. Aviation Admin, Advisory Circular 91-57, at ¶ 3(c). Specifically, AC 91-57 suggests that hobby-type airplanes not be flown higher than 400 feet above the surface that operators select an operating site that is of sufficient distance from populated and noise sensitive areas such as parks, schools, hospitals, and churches. To the extent flights occur within three miles of an airport, modelers are advised to notify the airport operator, or if applicable, control tower or flight service station. Moreover, hobbyists are advised not to fly in the presence of spectators until they are confident that the model aircraft has been flight tested and proven airworthy. Finally, the FAA expects that hobbyists will operate their recreational mode aircraft within visual line-of-sight ("VLOS"), giving way to, and avoiding flying in the proximity of full-scale aircraft.

Significantly, the model aircraft operating standards in AC 91-57 are not mandatory. Rather, it "encourages *voluntary* compliance." The voluntary nature of the FAA's guidance respecting model aircraft has presented confusion (or opportunity) for drone operators. This is so because the only apparent legal distinction between "drones" and "model aircraft" is operation or use. The FAA regards the flight of a model aircraft as illegal only when flown for commercial hire. Otherwise, no approval is required from the FAA to fly a "model aircraft" for recreation or hobby. Some operators have tried to operate "drones" under the FAA's model aircraft guidance statement, AC 91-57, as the basis for commercial UAV flight operations. This prompted the FAA to issue clarification in February 2007 concerning operations of unmanned aircraft in the National Airspace System. Unmanned Aircraft Operations in the National Airspace System, 72 Fed. Reg. 6689 (Feb. 13, 2007), *http://www.gpo.gov/fdsys/pkg/FR-2007-02-13/pdf/E7-2402.pdf.*

The chief message of the policy clarification was that "AC 91-57 only applies to modelers, and thus specifically excludes its use by persons or companies for business purposes." The FAA specifically stated:

> **Policy Statement**
>
> The FAA recognizes that people and companies other than modelers might be flying UAS with the mistaken understanding that they are legally operating under the authority of AC 91-57. AC 91-57 only applies to modelers, and thus specifically excludes its use by persons or companies for business purposes.
>
> The FAA has undertaken a safety review that will examine the feasibility of creating a different category of unmanned "vehicles" that may be defined by the operator's visual line of sight and are also small and slow enough to adequately mitigate hazards to other aircraft and persons on the ground. The end product of this analysis may be a new flight authorization instrument similar to AC 91-57, but focused on operations which do not qualify as sport and recreation, but also may not require a certificate of airworthiness. They will, however, require compliance with applicable FAA regulations and guidance developed for this category.

On September 2, 2015, however, the FAA cancelled 91-57, replacing with AC 91-57A, as follows, effectively tightening operational requirements on model aircraft operators.

9. Drone laws are emerging around the world, in which North America features some of the more robust drone policies and rules worldwide. On one end of the spectrum, Mexico implemented new rules in April 2015. Like other nations, Mexico ties operational freedoms with different weight classes with several classes of drones permitted to fly only in daylight.

Canada follows a European-type scheme for drones, segmenting aircraft by mass. For example, drones under 2 kg can be flown for any purpose without permission and without informing Transport Canada drones that weigh between 2.1kg and 25 kg can be flown if Transport Canada is informed of the type and location of flight. Drones being used for work or research that weigh more than 25 kg or recreational drones weighing over 35 kg can only be flown with a Special Flight Operations Certificate. All flights must stay below 90 meters, within line of site, far from airports, populated areas, and moving vehicles. "Work or research" drone operators must have $100,000 liability insurance, and all drones must give right-of-way to manned aircraft.

Meanwhile, while the United States Federal Aviation Administration generally allows hobby and recreational drone operators to fly within particular safety guidelines, commercial (*e.g.* for hire) drones are banned from operation unless exempted under Section 333 of the Federal Aviation Administration Modernization and Reform Act of 2012. As of October, 2015, the FAA had granted over 2,000 Certificates of Waiver or Authorization ("COA") and all Section 333 grants of exemption were automatically issued with a "blanket" 200-foot nationwide COA with certain restrictions around airports, restricted airspace, and other densely populated areas.

While it is true that U.S. airspace is among the busiest in the world, regulators have been criticized for their years-long delay in finalizing regulations for the integration of drones into the national airspace system. The intensity of the criticism is related to the permissible nature of both private and commercial drone operations in nearby Canada. In any case, a dedicated set of rules was announced by American regulators in 2015, and if implemented, would go into effect no earlier than 2017, likely providing that drones must be under 55lbs, operated within visual line of sight at a maximum speed of 87 knots and a maximum altitude 500 feet AGL. In the meantime, in October 2015, the FAA established a task force to recommend approaches to a registration system for all types of drones, hobby and recreational as well as commercial.

A comparison of proposed American and enacted Canadian regulations is useful; what explains the difference in regulatory approach? Are principled and understandable differences discernable?

COMPARISON OF CANADIAN RULES GOVERNING MICRO UAS CLASS WITH PROVISIONS OF PROPOSED PART 107 AND MICRO UAS SUB-CLASSIFICATION

Provision	Canada	Small UAS NPRM	Micro UAS Sub-classification
Definition of Small UAS	Up to 4.4 lbs (2 kg)	Up to 55 lbs (24 kg)	Up to 4.4 lbs (2 kg).
Maximum Altitude Above Ground	300 feet	500 feet	400 feet.
Airspace Limitations	Only within Class G airspace	Allowed within Class E in areas not designated for an airport. Otherwise, need ATC permission. Allowed within Class B, C and D with ATC permission. Allowed in Class G with no ATC permission.	Only within Class G airspace.
Distance from people and structures	100 feet laterally from any building, structure, vehicle, vessel or animal not associated with the operation and 100 feet from any person.	Simply prohibits UAS operations over any person not involved in the operations (unless under a covered structure).	Flying over any person is permitted.
Ability to extend operational area	No	Yes, from a waterborne vehicle	No.
Autonomous operations	No	Yes	No.
Aeronautical knowledge required	Yes; ground school	Yes; applicant would take knowledge test.	Yes; applicant would self-certify.
First person view permitted	No	Yes, provided operator is visually capable of seeing the small UAS.	No.
Operator training required	Yes, ground school	No	No.
Visual observer training required	Yes	No	No.
Operator certificate required	No	Yes (must pass basic UAS aeronautical test).	Yes (no knowledge test required).
Preflight safety assessment	Yes	Yes	Yes.
Operate within 5 miles of an airport	No	Yes	No.
Operate in a congested area	No	Yes	Yes.
Liability insurance	Yes, $100,000 CAN	No	No.
Daylight operations only	Yes	Yes	Yes.
Aircraft must be made out of frangible materials.	No	No	Yes.

10. Aviation amateurs and enthusiasts worldwide enjoy assembling and flying remote- and radio- controlled airplane models for education, leisure, or competitive sport racing. The law regards "RC" airplane operations as a hobby or recreational activities, though they can be serious undertakings involving risks to property and people.

In appearance and functionality, RC aircraft replicate all types of full-scale aircraft and helicopters in detail. They range from miniature and hand-held general aviation airplanes and helicopters to scaled-down F-16 fighter jets with military markings. A particularly impressive RC airplane is a 16-foot-long mock-up of a commercial jumbo-airliner, the Airbus A380, with a 2.6-gallon fuel tank and 17-foot wingspan. RC aircraft can be inexpensive, from models that are "ready-to-fly," electric-motor and "toy"-class airplanes to airplanes with balsa wood or Styrofoam bodies. At the other end of the RC spectrum are sophisticated and expensive (*e.g.*, $20,000) carbon fiber RC helicopters and aircraft (outfitted with retractable landing gear and dynamic flight control surfaces) that use first person view electronics (*e.g.*, "FPV"-cameras), autopilot, and stabilization systems to fly at speeds exceeding 200 miles per hour under the power of miniature internal combustion or jet engines. *See* Daniel Terdiman, *Incredible Remote-Control A380 Takes to the Skies,* CNET, Nov. 27, 2013, *http://www.cnet.com/news/incredible-remote-control-a380-takes-to-the-skies/*

Under the FAA Modernization and Reform Act of 2012, model aircraft must be flown strictly for hobby or recreational purposes—though the law does not elaborate on the intended meaning of "hobby or recreational purposes." As such, the FAA has applied accepted a dictionary definition of recreation where a "hobby" is a "pursuit outside one's regular occupation engaged in especially for relaxation" and a definition of recreation is "a refreshment of strength and spirits after work; a means of refreshment or diversion." These uses are consistent with the FAA's 2007 policy on model aircraft in which the [FAA] stated model aircraft operating guidelines did not apply to "persons or companies for business purposes." *See* 72 Fed. Reg. at 6690.

In this context, any operation not conducted strictly for hobby or recreation purposes could not be operated under the special rule for model aircraft, and clearly, commercial operations would not be hobby or recreation flights. Likewise, flights that are in furtherance of a business, or incidental to a person's business, would not be a hobby or recreation flight. Is the Federal Aviation Administration's distinction between hobby/recreation drones and commercial drones principled and rationale or reactionary and arbitrary? What is a better way forward?

Hobby or Recreation	***Not* Hobby or Recreation**
Flying a model aircraft at the local model aircraft club.	Receiving money for demonstrating aerobatics with a model aircraft
Taking photographs with a model aircraft for personal use.	A realtor using a model aircraft to photograph property that he is trying to sell and using the photos in the property's real estate listing. A person photographing a property or event and selling the photos to someone else.
Using a model aircraft to move a box from point to point without any kind of compensation.	Delivering packages to people for a fee.
Viewing a field to determine whether crops need water when they are grown for personal enjoyment.	Determining whether crops need to be watered that are grown as part of commercial farming operations.

PROBLEM

Consider the following from Alexis C. Madrigal, *If I Fly over My Neighbor's House, Is it Trespassing*, ATLANTIC, Oct. 10, 2012:

> My poor kitten, who my unfortunate Instagram contacts know too well, gets beat up every time he goes outside. There's a bully cat in the neighborhood who appears to relish in attacking cute, fluffy things as soon as they get out of human oversight. So, naturally, I bought a Parrot AR.Drone.2.0, a remote-controlled quadcopter with an HD camera attached, to see if I could spot where the punk bully cat hangs out.
>
> After some training runs in which I crashed the little UAV every fifteen seconds, I started to get the hang of where to push on my iPad to get the little AR.Drone to go the way I desired. And then, dodging trees and power lines, I sent the machine flying higher in the sky and scooted towards the fence, popped over it, and-terrified terrified of crashing in territory I didn't control—sped back across to the safety of my own backyard, and engaged the automatic landing sequence.
>
> Technically, I'd gone over the fence line, and if I'd done so on foot, intentionally, I would have nominally been guilty of trespassing. But if I were flying in a helicopter, a few hundred feet up, I would not have been guilty of trespassing. So, what about the air in between?

Should a dedicated altitude be created for drone operations? How should lawmakers incorporate new aviation technologies with common law concepts of trespass, privacy, and negligence, and Constitutional guarantees under the First, Fourth, and Tenth Amendments?

CHAPTER 5

AVIATION SECURITY

A. AIR PIRACY AND TERRORISM

On December 2, 2015, Syed Rizwan Farook, a religious Muslim and U.S. citizen, and his wife, Tashfeen Malik, a Pakistani from Saudi Arabia, massacred 14 people and wounded 21 in a shooting at a holiday party at a center for the disabled in San Bernardino, California, before they died in a shootout with authorities. Their motive was initially unknown, however law enforcement officials later suspected that the attackers were extremist sympathizers who had been radicalized and inspired by foreign terrorist organizations such as ISIS. "Terrorists have quickly adapted and evolved in order to carry out heinous plots since 9/11, and this tragedy reinforces the need for law enforcement to evolve its intelligence-gathering and investigative techniques," said U.S. Rep. Bob Goodlatte (R. Va.), chairman of the House Judiciary Committee, in reaction.

Though perhaps recent events such as the San Bernardino tragedy mark a new brand of terrorism, they find their origins in aviation disasters dating back at least 35 years. In many respects, the same type of actors involved in hijackings and air piracy in the 1980s are involved now, raising difficult and uncomfortable questions about whether and how U.S. lawmakers should profile passengers to mitigate against travel-related security risks (*see* Chapter 5, Part C, *infra*).

The opinions below detail how aviation security officials have long dealt—successfully and unsuccessfully—with terrorism. What precedential value do these authorities have for law enforcement going forward? In addition, in reading these cases, recognize the inherent limitations of courts to right monstrous wrongs. Recognize, too, the lack of even a uniform or generally accepted legal definition of terrorism. Title 18 of the United States Code distinguishes between "international" and "domestic" terrorism, for example. Moreover, while violence, political goals, and terror are shared concepts undergirding the term, more than 200 definitions of terrorism are scattered across the world. *See, e.g.*, JEFFREY D. SIMON, THE TERRORIST TRAP (Indiana University Press 1994). Historian Walter Laqueur has observed, "[i]n the real world, there is not one terrorism, but a variety of terrorisms. Any attempt to find a common denominator, a formula as suitable for Irish 19th-century terrorism as for narcoterrorism in Colombia or al Qaeda and Osama bin Laden, is bound to fail." *Categorizing Acts of Violence as Terrorism*, WALL. ST. J., Dec. 5-6, 2015, at A4.

STETHEM v. ISLAMIC REPUBLIC OF IRAN

201 F. Supp. 2d 78 (D.D.C. 2002)

JACKSON, District Judge.

On the morning of Friday, June 14, 1985, Trans World Airlines ("TWA") Flight No. 847, a Boeing 727, took off from Athens, Greece, bound for Rome, Italy, with a full complement of 143 passengers and a crew of eight. On board were U.S. citizens Robert Stethem, Kurt Carlson, Stuart Dahl, Jeffery Ingalls, Clinton Suggs, Tony Watson, and Kenneth Bowen. All were U.S. military personnel, enroute back to the United States from various assignments abroad and coincidentally aboard the same plane traveling in civilian dress.

Shortly after takeoff the plane was commandeered at gunpoint by at least two hijackers, also armed with hand grenades, who forced the plane to divert first to a landing for fuel in Beirut, then on to Algiers, and back once more to Beirut, finally landing dramatically at night in Beirut about 16 hours after the flight had commenced. During the journey several of the servicemen were brutally beaten by their captors. One was executed by gunshot to the head and his body shoved from the plane onto the tarmac at the Beirut airport. Eventually debarked from the plane as prisoners of a local militia in Beirut, the surviving servicemen were held captive by confederates of the hijackers until June 30, 1985, when they were released to Syrian military personnel and ultimately flown home. The airborne portion of their ordeal was characterized for some of them by excruciating pain from repeated beatings, and for all of them by stark terror in expectation of either an imminent violent death or prolonged captivity. While imprisoned in Beirut they were confined under execrable conditions, tormented with daily threats of torture and death, and vilified as citizens of a despised nation, all the while uncertain of their fate.

These two consolidated actions by the servicemen and their spouses, and by the personal representatives of the murder victim, seek to recover damages from the parties they hold ultimately responsible for these terrorist acts, the Islamic Republic of Iran and its Ministry of Information and Security, pursuant to the Foreign Sovereign Immunities Act ("FSIA"), 28 U.S.C. §§ 1602 *et seq*. Defaults were taken against defendants in both cases. Judgments will consequently be entered for plaintiffs.

BACKGROUND

Robert Dean Stethem (Deceased)

Robert Stethem, the murder victim, was identified by the hijackers early in the flight as a U.S. serviceman. He was, in fact, a 23-year-old U.S. Navy petty officer, trained as a diver and underwater construction specialist. In June, 1985, Stethem and fellow divers assigned to Underwater Construction Team No. 1 ("UCT1"), stationed in

Norfolk, Virginia, were aboard TWA 847 enroute back to the U.S. from Athens where they had spent several weeks repairing an underwater structure at a U.S. military installation nearby.

First thought to be a U.S. Marine by the hijackers (who never totally abandoned their suspicions), Stethem was taken to the front of the aircraft, his arms tightly bound, and beaten about the head and shoulders repeatedly with a pistol or an armrest wrenched from a passenger seat. He bled profusely. Although only semi-sensible, losing blood, and in obvious pain for much of the trip, he apparently never lost consciousness altogether. Upon the second landing in Beirut, Stethem was the hostage the hijackers selected for their first execution, partly to emphasize their insistence that their various demands be taken seriously, partly to manifest their hostility to Americans generally. The forward passenger door was thrown open, and one of the hijackers placed his gun to Stethem's head and fired a shot through his skull. As he was about to die he was heard to mutter an exclamation—"Oh, God"—indicating that he was aware of what was happening. His body was pushed from the open doorway to fall upon the pavement beneath the plane where it remained for several hours.

Stethem's survivors include his father and mother, Richard and Patricia Stethem; a sister, Sheryl (Stethem) Sierralta; and two brothers, Kenneth and Patrick Stethem. Although none were his dependents, the family is a remarkably close one. Filial and fraternal affection between Robert, his parents, and siblings was both mutual and intense.

The Stethems are a Navy family. Richard Stethem retired as a Senior Chief Petty Officer after a 25-year career, most of it on sea duty, and worked thereafter as a civilian employee of the Navy Department until 1995. Patricia met Richard while she herself was a sailor. Kenneth joined the Navy at age 19, became a SEAL, and retired in April, 2000, after 20 years. Patrick enlisted the day before TWA 847 was hijacked, followed his deceased brother into underwater construction, and remained a Navy diver for nearly 10 years.

The surviving Stethems last saw Robert at a family reunion in May, 1985, but were together again in June, 1985, to follow the saga of TWA 847 on CNN at the family home in Waldorf, Maryland, all the while besieged by an insatiable media horde at their doorstep. They first learned that Robert was the murdered U.S. serviceman thrown from the plane when Kenneth identified the distinctive shirt on the body on the tarmac shown on television as a shirt he had given his younger brother. All of the Stethem family have been diagnosed as suffering from post-traumatic stress syndrome. According to the psychologist who made the diagnosis, their grief at Robert's death remains unresolved to the present and will probably never subside.

Plaintiffs Richard Stethem and Patricia Stethem, as father and mother of Robert Stethem, are the duly appointed co-personal representatives of Robert's estate. Both are U.S. citizens, as are his brothers and sister. They bring this action in the nature of a wrongful death and survival action for such damages as may be recoverable from defendants under the FSIA by reason of Robert's false imprisonment as a hostage aboard TWA 847, his torture by beating prior to his death, and his extrajudicial killing that can only be characterized as an intentional, deliberate and premeditated act of murder. These damages include, as established by numerous prior decisions under the FSIA, the net economic loss to Robert's estate; compensation for his ante mortem pain and suffering; solatium for his immediate surviving kin; and punitive damages to chasten the perpetrators of these acts of terrorism and deter their repetition by others.

Kurt and Cheryl Carlson

Kurt and Cheryl Carlson are U.S. citizens, married since 1969, who reside in Illinois, where Kurt Carlson is a building contractor. In 1985, Carlson was a major in the U.S. Army Reserve, and he volunteered for an active duty assignment in Cairo, Egypt, to make a preliminary survey of facilities in preparation for forthcoming joint U.S.-Egyptian military exercises. On June 14, 1985, Carlson was enroute home from Egypt aboard TWA 847 when it landed in Athens where Robert Stethem and his companions boarded. (TWA 847 originated in Cairo.) Carlson, traveling alone, had acquired a standby seat in the first class cabin. Ten minutes into the flight the hijackers stormed the forward section of the plane, assaulted a flight attendant, and, brandishing both a pistol and hand grenades, shouted in English, "Americans come to die!"

Carlson surreptitiously slipped his military identification out of his pocket into the seat cushion, but was eventually discovered to be in the U.S. armed forces by the hijackers following an enforced passport collection in which the absence of a passport in his name was noted. (All U.S. military personnel were eventually identified, and as such treated with special hostility. Had they been U.S. Marines, they would all likely have been killed.) At first, however, he was forced into a seat in the aft cabin with all other passengers, and, like them, compelled to assume an excruciatingly uncomfortable position Carlson describes to this day as the "847 position"—hands behind head; head down, with elbows on knees—and to remain so, in total silence, whenever the plane was airborne.

Not until TWA 847 had landed in Algiers, some six hours into the flight, was Carlson singled out for special treatment. He and Stethem were marched at gunpoint to the forward cabin. His hands were bound behind him; he was blindfolded, and prodded to the cabin floor. He was then (as was Stethem) beaten at intervals about the head, shoulders, back and arms with a club. The hijackers intermittently shouted "one American must die," and they identified Carlson as the first who would do so if their demand that the plane be refueled was not complied with within successive 10- or 15-minute deadlines. Carlson fully expected to be killed. He was spared by the eventual arrival of a fuel truck, and TWA 847, once refueled, took off again for Beirut.

Following Stethem's death on the ground in Beirut, Carlson and all but one of the Navy divers were turned over to a contingent of local militia (known as Amal) who were confederated with the hijackers. They were held captive—and periodically tormented—for approximately two weeks in a filth-ridden basement dungeon in a combat zone somewhere in West Beirut.

Like most of the rest of the U.S. population, Cheryl Carlson followed the saga of TWA 847 on television, apprehensive that she would never see her husband again. When he did return she became aware of how profoundly the experience had affected him, and she has suffered with him through the manifestations of the post-traumatic stress syndrome with which he remains afflicted to the present—irrational fear, sleeplessness, nightmares, extreme irritability—and which has had a markedly deleterious effect on their marriage relationship.

Stuart and Martha Dahl

Stuart and Martha Dahl are U.S. citizens, have been married since 1974, and live in Virginia. Stuart Dahl retired from the U.S. Navy in 1997. In June of 1985 Stuart Dahl was the senior Navy petty officer and in charge of the diver detachment returning from Greece aboard TWA 847. Although he was never singled out for physical mistreatment by the hijackers (other than a blow to the head for breaking the "847 position"), he was aware that his shipmates Stethem and Suggs were being beaten, and overheard (from his "847 position") the sounds associated with Stethem's murder. While a captive in Beirut, as the senior enlisted man he maintained military discipline among his fellow prisoners who, under Kurt Carlson's command as the only commissioned officer present, governed themselves as if they were prisoners-of-war.

Tony and Pamala Watson

Tony and Pamala Watson have been married since 1975. Both are U.S. citizens and live in North Carolina. Tony Watson retired from a 20-year naval career in 1998 and owns a woodworking business. His experience was consistent with that of the other divers of UCT1, and Pamala Watson endured both the nationally televised vigil for the TWA 847 hostages, as did the other wives, and her husband's acute and chronic suffering at the memory of his ordeal once he returned home.

Kenneth and Vicki Bowen

The Bowens did not marry until 1988. Both are U.S. citizens. Kenneth Bowen left active duty with the Navy before the end of 1985, although he remained in the Reserve. He currently works as a bridge inspector for the U.S. Department of Transportation. Bowen was briefly confronted by one of the hijackers on the plane who accused him, with a gun to his forehead, of being a "U.S. Marine." Bowen demurred: "U.S. Navy." The hijacker said, "We kill Marines," and turned away.

Clinton Suggs and Chantal Gautier

Clinton Suggs, an American citizen, married Chantal Gautier, a Canadian, in 1982. He and Stethem were the closest of friends among the UCT1 divers, and were brought forward together by the hijackers to the first class cabin of TWA 847, and became the first to be bound, blindfolded, and beaten. Suggs overheard, at close range, the final moments of Stethem's life, including the fatal gunshot, and a hijacker's threat to execute another hostage in five minutes if his demands of the moment were not met. Suggs knew he would be next and resigned himself to die. Suggs and Gautier first separated in 1986 and ultimately divorced in 1991, a consequence they both attribute directly to the personality changes Suggs underwent as a result of the events of June, 1985.

Jeffrey Ingalls

Ingalls' identity was not discovered until after the other divers and Carlson had left the plane in Beirut. Consequently, he was separated from his shipmates and held captive elsewhere in the city, but only after being forced to lie on the ground and threatened with execution for having eluded earlier identification. He was confined in a 6 by 8 closet with three other American men—all Jewish civilians—for nine days. Ingalls remained in the Navy until 1998, retiring as a Master Chief Petty Officer and Master Diver. He now suffers from depression and lives as a recluse in New Hampshire.

Aside from the physical abuse inflicted upon some of them, each of the men aboard TWA 847 share a common memory of other particularly horrific details of the ordeal. They remember the acute discomfort associated with the "847 position" and the anticipation of a blow to the head if they changed posture or tried to communicate with another passenger. They recall the odor of overflowing lavatories covered with ordure; the ignominy of relieving themselves while being observed at gunpoint by a hijacker standing at the open door; the stifling heat while the plane sat motionless for hours, un-airconditioned, on a runway in the Algerian desert at midday; the virulent anti-American hatred spewed by the hijackers, especially at U.S. military personnel, and the brutality it provoked against certain of their companions. They remember expecting to die in a plane crash when the passengers were told by the pilot that the control tower at Beirut refused permission to land the second time and had darkened the runway.

Once off the plane in Beirut, they were herded into a line by their guards. Each remembers expecting an imminent execution by a firing squad. Then, imprisoned somewhere in the city, they recall their vermin-infested cells; the taunting guards who would awaken them at night for verbal abuse and would on occasion pretend to shoot them, then laugh at their discomfiture. The guards also proudly displayed photographs of the murdered Stethem's body lying beneath the plane. Another common memory is of being forced to witness the beating death of another unknown prisoner. They remember the spoiled food they were served, and the epidemic of dysentery that beset them all as a result. Each of them remembers, as do the wives, the onset and persistence of the symptoms of his own peculiar case of post-traumatic stress disorder: the constant anxiety and irritability; insomnia, followed by slumber with nightmares reprising the events of June, 1985; the unexpiated guilt at having survived, yet done nothing to prevent the murder of a shipmate whom they could not possibly have saved; the irrational idiosyncrasies each has developed, such as refusing to board planes with "Arabic-looking" co-passengers, carrying a tennis racket aboard a plane to be used as a weapon against any future hijackers, or sleeping on the floor, armed against nighttime intruders.

The hijackers—known only by the sobriquets "Crazy" and "Hitler" by the TWA passengers at the time—have been reliably identified as belonging to Hizballah, a radical Shi'ite paramilitary organization recruited, trained and financially supported by the Ministry of Information and Security ("MOIS") of the Islamic Republic of Iran. Originally affiliated with Amal, the Lebanese militia supported by Syria during the Lebanese civil war, and a frequent collaborator with Amal even after shifting allegiance to Iran following the Israeli invasion of Lebanon in 1982, Hizballah has been implicated in numerous acts of terrorism for which this district court has held its patron state Iran liable under the FSIA.

The record in this case contains extensive documentary evidence from U.S. intelligence sources connecting Hizballah to Iran and its Ministry of Information and Security. According to the testimony of U.S. Ambassador Robert Oakley who, as Director of Counterterrorism for the Department of State at the time, was directly involved in efforts to effect a military rescue or to induce the Lebanese or Algerian governments to secure the release of the passenger-hostages, the hijackers' initial demands—the release of prisoners in Israel and Kuwait—gave reason to believe they were agents of Amal. As later proved to be the case, however, Amal had employed Hizballah to undertake the actual hijacking, with support from Amal militia on the ground and in control of the Beirut airport. Further testimony from Robert McFarlane, U.S. National Security Advisor, established that his direct discussions with the leader of Amal (which had taken custody of all the hostage—save Ingalls—from the hijackers in Beirut) had been ineffectual in procuring their release. Not until approval had been given by Iranian President Rafsanjani from Tehran were they turned over to Syrian authorities in Damascus to be released.

DISCUSSION

While a foreign state is generally immune from the jurisdiction of the courts of the United States under the FSIA, *see* 28 U.S.C. § 1604, plaintiffs bring this action against defendants pursuant to section 1605(a)(7) of the Act. That section explicitly authorizes, as an exception to the general grant of sovereign immunity to foreign nations, suits against foreign states that sponsor terrorism for certain acts that cause personal injury or death if either the claimant or victim was a citizen of the United States at the time of the act. *See* 28 U.S.C. § 1605(a)(7).

In numerous suits preceding this action, private claimants have successfully invoked this statutory exception to establish a basis by which federal district courts may exercise subject matter jurisdiction over claims similar to those brought by plaintiffs here against these same defendants. Plaintiffs' causes of action in this case are predicated on the unlawful detention and torture of plaintiffs, and, in the case of Robert Stethem, his summary execution—acts which unequivocally beget claims eligible for relief under section 1605(a)(7).

The FSIA imposes two preconditions upon the exercise of subject matter jurisdiction by district courts over foreign states: the foreign state must have been designated a state sponsor of terrorism at the time the acts occurred, unless later so designated as a result of such act, and a plaintiff (either claimant or victim) must have been a United States citizen at the time of the incident. *See* 28 U.S.C. § 1605(a)(7)(A) and (B).

Both of these requirements are clearly satisfied here. Iran was designated as a state sponsor of terrorism pursuant to section 6(j) of the Export Administration Act of 1979 on January 19, 1984, and remains so designated today. The multiple plaintiffs bringing this action (except Chantal Gautier) have always been United States citizens. Accordingly, the Court finds that it has jurisdiction over the subject matter of this suit and the named defendants. And as the Court has previously found in so many similar cases before it, the evidence conclusively establishes that the Islamic Republic of Iran and its MOIS provided "material support or resources" to Hizballah, and Hizballah and its co-conspirator Amal were the perpetrators of these heinous acts of terrorism. Having concluded that defendants are liable for the tortious conduct alleged, the Court next considers the extent to which the plaintiffs should be compensated for the injuries they sustained as a result of their client organization's unconscionable behavior.

Consistent with its approach in previous FSIA cases involving claims for personal injury or death resulting from state-sponsored terrorism, this Court will evaluate plaintiffs' claims under the federal common law. While the Court will separately analyze the individual claims for compensatory damages brought by each plaintiff below, plaintiffs' claims for punitive damages will be dealt with in the aggregate.

Compensatory Damages—The Stethem Plaintiffs

Plaintiffs Richard and Patricia Stethem, in their own right, and as personal representatives of the Estate of Robert Dean Stethem, seek compensatory damages for Robert Stethem's wrongful death, his pain and suffering, and solatium for themselves and his surviving brothers and sister. Pursuant to their claim for wrongful death under federal common law, the Estate of Robert Stethem is entitled to monetary damages for funeral expenses and loss of prospective income if Robert's premature death was wrongful and proximately caused by an act of terrorism. As previously shown, agents of the defendants intentionally caused Robert's death. Moreover, it goes with saying that his summary execution was wrongful in that it was carried out by members of a terrorist organization with no legally cognizable basis for taking a life. Therefore, a calculation of the monetary damages actually suffered by Robert's estate is all that remains.

Loss of accretion damages are calculated by estimating a decedent's future earning potential based on the individual's work and education and adjusting that amount to account for inflation, rise in productivity, job advancement, and personal consumption. Dr. Herman Miller, an economic consultant, testified at trial that Robert's estate experienced economic losses of $904,665.00. In coming to this conclusion, Dr. Miller assumed that, following his service in the Navy, Robert would then attend and successfully complete college to become a civil engineer specializing in underwater construction. The Court finds these assumptions and Dr. Miller's corresponding estimation of accretion reasonable; therefore, it will enter an award for pecuniary loss in the amount of $904,665.00 in favor of the Estate of Robert Stethem.

As his personal representatives, the estate is also entitled to recover any damages Robert himself would have been entitled to for the extensive pain he suffered at the hands of the hijackers prior to and in the course of his death. The record is replete with evidence substantiating the Stethems' contention that Robert suffered excruciating pain while being viciously beaten and tortured over the course of fifteen hours. Known to those closest to him as an extremely virile and stoic young man who was able to endure pain without outwardly manifesting discomfort, witnesses testified that Robert cried out on several occasions throughout his ordeal. Particularly telling is the fact that Robert had to be dragged to the front of the plane by his tormentors because of his inability to walk just prior to his being shot in the back of the head. Even then, his suffering did not end. Based upon his finding at autopsy that Robert's lungs continued to function after he had been shot—significant quantities of blood were found to have been aspirated into his lungs—the forensic pathologist Dr. Michael Clark opined that Robert survived the gunshot wound for several minutes.

While pain and suffering is particularly difficult to quantify in terms of assessing damages, the Court can certainly award damages to Robert's estate commensurate with those awards for pain and suffering provided in prior FSIA cases. For purposes of comparison, Robert's suffering occurred in two distinct stages: (1) the pain he experienced from beatings prior to being shot in the head; and (2) the anguish of his final moments anticipating certain death and the pain he experienced after being shot while drowning in his own blood on the tarmac.

With respect to the former, this district court has typically compensated a plaintiff hostage (or his representative) in a FSIA case at a rate of $10,000 per day of captivity accompanied by physical torture. This formulaic approach has not precluded a greater or lesser award in a case where the evidence establishes that the victim of the maltreatment suffered more or less than the hostages in the preceding cases. Notwithstanding, the

$10,000 per diem amount serves as a useful benchmark for beginning the damages calculus in a manner that is both just and consistent with previous awards.

In this case, the Court finds that while the time in which Robert was tortured (*i.e.,* fifteen hours) was comparatively much shorter than that of other hostage victims previously considered by this district court, the sheer intensity and frequency of abuse caused Robert to experience a degree of suffering that exceeded that of previous hostages. The hijackers were both uncertain and insecure about their ability to control the volatile circumstances inherent in their hijacking of the plane. As a result, they chose to impose an inordinate amount of pain and suffering on Robert as an example to the other passengers should any have been contemplating resistance or revolt. As the uncertainty of the situation escalated, so did the intensity and frequency of the beatings to which Robert was subjected. The Court concludes that Robert's estate is entitled to $500,000.00 for the pain and suffering he endured prior to being singled out for execution.

With respect to the several minutes of anguish and pain Robert endured as and immediately after being shot by Hamadi and thrown from the plane, this district court has previously awarded the estates of terrorist victims suffering similarly brief yet intense pain an amount of $1,000,000. Likewise, this Court awards Robert's estate the sum of $1,000,000 for this terminal stage of his pain and suffering. In total, the Court will enter a judgment in favor of the Estate of Robert Stethem in the amount of $2,404,665.00.

The Stethem parents also seek loss of solatium damages on behalf of all the Stethems for the bereavement and grief attendant upon their loss of Robert's society and companionship. Because the District of Columbia does not recognize claims for loss of solatium, this Court has recognized this cause of action under the federal common law by relying upon the SECOND RESTATEMENT OF TORTS: "'[O]ne who by extreme and outrageous conduct intentionally or recklessly causes severe emotional distress to another is subject to liability for such emotional distress.'" All acts of terrorism are by their very definition extreme and outrageous and intended to cause the highest degree of emotional distress, literally, terror, in their targeted audience: The more extreme and outrageous, the greater the resulting distress. In this case, the agents of Hizballah and Amal engaged in conduct no less extreme than that of their fellow terrorists in earlier cases. Because the Stethems have consequently experienced grave emotional distress from having lost a beloved son and brother, they are entitled to damages for loss of solatium.

In calculating damages for loss of solatium in the case of a deceased family member, this district court has considered a variety of factors to include: (1) whether the decedent's death was sudden and unexpected; (2) whether the death was attributable to negligence or malice; (3) whether the claimants have sought medical treatment for depression and related disorders resulting from the decedent's death; (4) the nature (*i.e.*, closeness) of the relationship between the claimant and the decedent; and (5) the duration of the claimants' mental anguish in excess of that which would have been experienced following the decedent's natural death. Here, Robert's death was both sudden and unforeseen by his loved ones and the consequences of the terrorists' actions upon them all the more intense. While the Stethems have sought little in the way of professional help to assist them in coping with Robert's death, the enormity of their emotional distress remains evident even to this day.

There is no question based on the evidence presented at trial and the presence and testimony of members of the Stethem family in court that the Stethems have always enjoyed an extraordinarily close familial relationship. Each of the Stethems had a unique and special relationship with Robert and continues to mourn his death on a daily basis in his or her own way. Even 16 years later, the Stethems are unable, in many ways, to move beyond Robert's death. Indeed, the Court accepts Dr. Clark's conclusion that the Stethems will likely remain in the loss and loneliness stage of grief until their own deaths. Moreover, even were they to come to terms with Robert's death, continued media coverage of the events surrounding the hijacking from June 14-15, 1985 (most recently revived in connection with the events of September 11, 2001), serve as constant reminders of their loss.

Depending on the duration of captivity, this district court has on occasion awarded greater judgments for claims of loss of solatium to those family members of terrorism victims who were tortured over a prolonged period of time but not killed than to those family members of terrorist victims who expired relatively quickly (although usually suffering intense pain for several minutes) after a single deadly terrorist attack (*i.e.*, bombing, gunshot wound). The Stethems grieve not only the absence of Robert in their lives, but the knowledge that he suffered greatly prior to being executed. Their grief is tempered only by the knowledge that his suffering was of relatively brief duration, and that he died bravely. Accordingly, the Court will award the Stethem parents $5,000,000 each and the Stethem siblings $3,000,000 each for the loss of Robert's society and companionship.

Compensatory Damages—The Carlson plaintiffs

Plaintiffs Kurt Carlson, Stuart Dahl, Jeffery Ingalls, Clinton Suggs, Tony Watson, and Kenneth Bowen ("Carlson hostages") seek compensatory damages upon claims in the nature of kidnapping, false imprisonment, torture, assault, battery, intentional infliction of severe emotional distress, and violation of international human rights. Plaintiffs Cheryl Carlson, Martha Dahl, Chantal Gautier, and Pamala Watson ("Carlson spouses") seek compensatory damages for loss of consortium and solatium. As determined above, this Court holds the defendants responsible for the hijacking of TWA 847 and the attendant hostage taking and torture of the plaintiff hostages.

Although plaintiff hostages were detained for a period of days as opposed to months or years, they arguably remained captive under conditions entailing even more frequent physical and emotional trauma than that of some of the other plaintiff hostages to come before this Court. Indeed, because the hijackers felt compelled to assert and maintain complete control over the situation, they were tireless and unrelenting in their physical and emotional abuse of their hostages. As evidenced by the summary execution of Robert Stethem in their presence, many of the plaintiff hostages feared the imminent loss of their own lives and were themselves subjected to mock executions (*e.g.*, by firing squad or the dry firing of weapons pointed at their heads) several times during their detention. Even after being removed from the plane, the plaintiff hostages were held under armed guard in inhumane surroundings, witnessed acts of torture and brutality inflicted upon other prisoners, and lived in constant fear for their lives. Because of the terrifying intensity associated with the hijacking itself, as well as their subsequent detention, and the resulting permanent psychic damage they exhibit today, the Court concludes that a per diem calculation of damages is less appropriate than a lump sum award embracing the totality of their experience. Accordingly, this Court will award Kurt Carlson and Clinton Suggs $1,500,000.00 each, and Stuart Dahl, Jeffery Ingalls, Tony Watson, and Kenneth Bowen $1,000,000 apiece for injuries suffered at the hands of the agents of the defendants.

With regard to the claims for loss of consortium by the Carlson spouses, while they were without their husbands for a relatively short period of time, it is clear that the experience has had a detrimental and disturbing effect on their relationships. Their formerly healthy husbands returned estranged and incapable of participating in the marriage with the same physical and emotional warmth they previously displayed. To varying degrees, each of the plaintiff hostages continues to suffer from post-traumatic stress disorder and related behavioral disorders (*e.g.*, violent nightmares, hyper vigilance, uncontrollable tempers, impatience) that serve to interfere with their ability to function normally within any social relationship, including marriage. Therefore, this Court concludes that the Carlson spouses are entitled to damages for loss of consortium and solatium and will award them $200,000 each.

Punitive Damages

Plaintiffs also request an award of punitive damages against defendant MOIS for its role in providing support and resources to Hizballah and Amal. As in previous cases, the evidence clearly inculpates MOIS as the instigator and financier of terrorist acts by Hizballah and Amal in this case. The hostage taking, torture, and killing of innocent non-belligerents for political ends constitutes unconscionable conduct in any civilized society. Accordingly, the Court finds that not only are punitive damages authorized under the FSIA to punish the MOIS for its continued role in fomenting terrorist activity, and to the extent possible deter it from future criminal behavior, *see* 28 U.S.C. § 1606, but that the MOIS's role in sponsoring the agents responsible for the instant acts of terrorism warrants such an award. Consistent with this Court's prior experience and a calculation equivalent to approximately three times the estimated annual budget of MOIS for support of terrorism as testified to by Dr. Richard Clausen, the Court will assess punitive damages in the amount of $300,000,000 against the MOIS, to be awarded to all plaintiffs jointly and severally.

IN RE AIR DISASTER AT LOCKERBIE, SCOTLAND ON DEC. 21, 1988

37 F.3d 804 (2d Cir. 1994)

CARDAMONE, Circuit Judge.

Pan American World Airways, Inc. ("Pan Am") and Alert Management Systems, Inc. ("Alert") ("Pan Am," "defendants" or "appellants") appeal from final judgments entered on September 9, 1992 in the United States District Court for the Eastern District of New York in three cases arising out of the Pan Am Flight 103 terrorist bombing that occurred over Lockerbie, Scotland in December 1988. The trial was bifurcated into a liability phase, binding on all plaintiffs whose cases were consolidated in this multidistrict litigation, and a damages phase governing the cases of the three plaintiffs before us. The damages phase will also set the standards for damage awards in future cases resulting from this tragic disaster.

Few Americans have forgotten the bombing of Flight 103 over Lockerbie, Scotland a few days before Christmas in 1988. There were 259 Americans aboard Pan Am's plane from all walks of life. Among the passengers were business executives, entrepreneurs, airline employees, and college students—including 38 Syracuse University students returning home from study abroad. Although four years have passed since this tragedy occurred, it remains vivid in our national consciousness, standing as a reminder of our collective vulnerability to wanton terrorist acts.

The 13-week liability trial controlled all the consolidated cases that had been filed against Pan Am throughout the United States by the passengers' and the crews' survivors and representatives. Trial began April 27, 1992. The jurors heard lengthy testimony from 58 witnesses, much of which was introduced by the over 180 depositions obtained during massive discovery taken worldwide. At its close, the jury rendered a special verdict finding defendants guilty of willful misconduct that caused the explosion and the crash.

At the conclusion of the damages phase $9,225,000 was awarded to the Pagnucco family, $9,000,000 to the Bainbridge family, and $1,735,000 to the Porter family. Decedents Pagnucco and Bainbridge had been Pepsico attorneys, decedent Porter an electrician and part-time musician. The damage awards included damages for loss of society and damages for loss of parental care to adult children. No award for survival damages—sought by plaintiffs—was made because the jury found the passengers had suffered no conscious pain and suffering before their deaths. Pan Am and Alert appeal challenging the finding of liability and the damage awards.

BACKGROUND

On December 21, 1988 a bomb exploded on Pan Am Flight 103 causing it to crash over Lockerbie, Scotland. The 243 passengers and 16 crew members aboard the flight traveling from London to New York all perished. Numerous plaintiffs, including those in the cases before us, brought wrongful death actions against Pan Am and Alert, a Pan Am affiliate that provided security services in London and in Frankfurt, where Flight 103 originated. All those actions were consolidated for trial in the Eastern District of New York.

A single jury trial was conducted before Chief Judge Platt to try the liability issues common to the passenger cases. The parties agreed that the case was governed by the Warsaw Convention, formally named the Convention for the Unification of Certain Rules Relating to International Transportation by Air, done at Warsaw, Oct. 12, 1929, reprinted at 49 U.S.C. § 1502 (1988) [hereinafter "Warsaw Convention"]. Although the Warsaw Convention generally limits a carrier's liability for damages to $75,000 per passenger, Article 25 permits recovery of unlimited compensatory damages provided the carrier's "willful misconduct" caused the damages. An earlier decision of this Circuit established that punitive damages may not be collected under the Warsaw Convention. *In Re Air Disaster at Lockerbie, Scotland on December 21, 1988* ("*Lockerbie I*") (2d Cir. 1991).

On July 10, 1992 the jury found that the defendants engaged in willful misconduct that led to this fatal crash. The trial's liability phase centered on Pan Am's alleged noncompliance with Federal Aviation Administration ("FAA") directives concerning baggage inspection, particularly with regard to unaccompanied baggage that might contain explosives. Additional proof was introduced regarding other alleged misconduct on the air carrier's part. Plaintiffs contended that the bomb entered the flight on an unaccompanied bag that Pan Am, through its willful misconduct, failed to inspect and detect. Under plaintiffs' theory—detailed by several expert witnesses—the bomb was hidden inside a radio-cassette player packed in a bronze Samsonite suitcase. The suitcase supposedly traveled from Malta to Frankfurt on Air Malta Flight 180. There, the experts posited, it was transferred to the first leg of Flight 103 from Frankfurt to London, where it was then placed on Flight 103 bound for New York.

Although bags transferred from other flights to Flight 103 in Frankfurt were X-rayed, plaintiffs asserted the airline's X-ray procedure violated security requirements contained in an FAA regulation at issue in this case, Air Carrier Standard Security Program or ACSSP XV.C.1.(a), which ensured that bags matched passengers and that any unaccompanied bags be physically inspected. Pan Am unsuccessfully argued to the jury that its actions did not amount to willful misconduct, and that it was impossible to determine how the bomb was planted on Flight 103. To meet plaintiffs' claims of willful misconduct, Pan Am and Alert emphasized that the transferred bags had been examined using X-ray equipment, but that no bomb was discovered. They challenged plaintiffs' theory of causation and suggested that even if there were any misconduct on their part, it did not lead to the crash.

In finding defendants liable the jury rendered a special verdict. On the special verdict form, it indicated that it had specifically found (1) that "Pan Am (including Alert) engage[d] in willful misconduct," and (2) that the willful misconduct was "a substantial factor in causing the disaster." Following the liability phase, the jury then awarded compensatory damages in the three plaintiffs' cases. There are 207 other passenger cases pending, all awaiting the outcome of this appeal.

DISCUSSION

On appeal Pan Am rolls out a panoply of arguments, most involving evidence the district court excluded, and which, therefore, was not heard or considered by the jury. These contentions concern four broad areas: (I) the exclusion of evidence related to Pan Am and Alert's alleged noncompliance with ACSSP regulations concerning unaccompanied baggage; (II) the admission of evidence showing other alleged misconduct on appellants' part coupled with the disallowance of defense testimony concerning alternate theories of causation; (III) various other evidentiary rulings; and (IV) the legal bases for the damage awards. In the discussion that follows, we examine each of these four areas in order.

EXCLUDED EVIDENCE PAN AM AND ALERT ARGUE WOULD HAVE NEGATED ANY WILFUL MISCONDUCT ARISING FROM THEIR NONCOMPLIANCE WITH CERTAIN ACSSP REGULATIONS

Appellants insist the trial court committed reversible error in excluding several pieces of evidence that might have negated a finding of willful misconduct based on appellants' alleged failure to comply with FAA regulations concerning unaccompanied baggage. This first challenge centers on rulings excluding three lines of evidence that appellants believe were relevant to Pan Am and Alert's state of mind, that is, their willfulness. The main line of barred evidence purportedly demonstrated an oral waiver by the FAA, excusing Pan Am's compliance with relevant security regulations. The breach of those regulations was central to plaintiffs' case and, as a response, Pan Am and Alert sought to demonstrate that they thought they were complying with the FAA requirements.

The second piece of barred evidence was British regulations that did not require the observance of the same safety standards as did those of the FAA. Appellants sought to negate any inference of willfulness on their part by showing that X-raying baggage transferred from other airlines—the procedure Pan Am followed—complied with the British regulations. The third piece of evidence not entertained was proof that some experts believe the highest threat to airline safety is not posed by unaccompanied baggage. Each of these three lines of evidence, appellants urge, might have negated plaintiffs' showing of willful misconduct.

The standard of liability under the Warsaw Convention, as already noted, requires that a carrier have engaged in "willful misconduct" causing the claimed losses in order for plaintiffs to hold a carrier liable in an amount exceeding the Convention's $75,000 damage limit. *See* Warsaw Convention, art. 25. Willful misconduct under the Convention means that a carrier must have acted either (1) with knowledge that its actions would probably result in injury or death, or (2) in conscious or reckless disregard of the fact that death or injury would be the probable consequence of its actions. *See Ospina v. Trans World Airlines, Inc.*, (1993); *In re Korean Air Lines Disaster of September 1, 1983* (D.C. Cir. 1991).

The district court charged the jury under that standard and also charged it that the standard applied whether willful misconduct resulted from an act or failure to act by the carrier. Appellants do not challenge the district court's jury instruction as to willful misconduct. Instead, they focus on the just recited three different lines of proof they were not allowed to present to guide the jury's application of that standard, that is, the oral waiver, the British regulations, and expert testimony regarding the threat posed by unaccompanied baggage.

A. *The Alleged Oral Waiver*

We begin discussion by reference to the standard of review on appeal from an exclusion of evidence at trial. That standard establishes that the relevance and admissibility of proffered evidence rests in the sound discretion of the trial court. Defendants maintain that an FAA official granted them an oral waiver excusing strict compliance with certain FAA regulations, and that Chief Judge Platt abused his discretion when he disallowed their evidence purporting to demonstrate their belief in this waiver. Although Pan Am is imprecise as to the date of the purported waiver, it asserts it was given verbally to a Pan Am official. Virtually no written documentation supports it. Defendants' argument essentially is that this evidence would have shown that their X-ray inspection of interline bags complied with FAA requirements or that, regardless of FAA requirements, they did not act with conscious or reckless disregard of the probable consequences of their X-ray procedures since they thought the safety precautions they were following were permissible.

1. The Unambiguous Nature of ACSSP Regulation XV C.1.(a)

In support of this point, Pan Am points out that a regulation may be interpreted orally, and that the regulation at issue is ambiguous and therefore susceptible to such an interpretation. We are unable to accept appellants' premise that the supposed oral waiver was in fact an interpretation of an ambiguous regulation. As a matter of law the FAA regulation at issue here—ACSSP XV C.1.(a)—is not ambiguous, as the following discussion demonstrates.

In April 1986 the FAA established specific ACSSP regulations and mandated that they be followed at heightened security airports designated "extraordinary security" airports. Both Frankfurt and London's Heathrow airports were classified as "extraordinary security" airports. The central regulation at issue in this case, ACSSP regulation XV C.1.(a), concerns the detection of unaccompanied bags. It directs an air carrier operating out of an extraordinary security airport to

> [c]onduct a positive passenger/checked baggage match resulting in physical inspection or noncarriage of all unaccompanied bags. The carrier may use either physical match or administrative match, but, in either case, it should be done in a way that passengers are aware of the use of the procedures.

Air carriers like Pan Am, thus were required under the regulations first to do a physical or an administrative match to detect unaccompanied bags, and then to physically inspect any unaccompanied bags before they could be loaded. ACSSP XV C clearly ordered that an air carrier operating out of an extraordinary security airport "shall adopt and carry out the ... special procedures except where local conditions preclude and alternative measures have been approved by the FAA."

Under ACSSP XV C.1.(a) the positive match is designed to ensure that any unaccompanied bags definitely will be identified as such. The regulation permits the positive match to be done either as a "physical match," in which passengers identify their bags on the tarmac, or an "administrative match," in which the number of passengers boarding the aircraft and the number of bags checked are compared with the number of bags to be loaded.

Pan Am claimed that it conducted an administrative match. Plaintiffs averred that this administrative match did not comply with the regulations because it was incomplete and failed to identify all unaccompanied bags. Particularly, plaintiffs point out Pan Am's procedures did not identify the bags of interline passengers, *i.e.*, those passengers who had transferred to a Pan Am flight from another airline and whose bags had been checked with the other airline at the passengers' point of origin.

If a match conducted under the regulations revealed unaccompanied bags, the regulations expressly directed the airline to conduct the second step of the process, "physical inspection," before it could carry the bags. Plaintiffs demonstrated that Pan Am and Alert X-rayed all bags transferred from other carriers—so-called "interline" bags—but conducted no other inspection of such bags. Pan Am and Alert assert that physical inspection could be interpreted to mean an X-ray inspection. For several reasons, we think this a strained reading of the unambiguous regulation.

- First, the FAA promulgated “Physical Inspection Guidelines” in the ACSSP which specified that physical inspection involves opening and inspecting all compartments of baggage.The guidelines do not mention X-ray as an acceptable means of inspection.

- Second, the jury heard testimony from Pan Am’s own General Manager at Heathrow, and other witnesses as well, that physical inspection under the regulations involved opening up bags and that X-raying them did not satisfy the regulation.

- Third, ACSSP regulations applicable at other, lower security airports explicitly permitted X-ray or physical inspections.

Thus, it is plain that the regulations applicable at Frankfurt and London’s Heathrow were unambiguous: they did not permit X-ray inspections as a substitute for a physical inspection. We hold, therefore, that the district court did not err in refusing to allow witnesses—like the co-chair of the Pan Am Security Task Force, Richard Cozzi—to testify that they thought the regulations were ambiguous. As a matter of law, ACSSP XV C.1.(a) is not ambiguous in requiring a positive match and physical inspection of unaccompanied bags before they may be carried on board a departing plane. Introducing testimony to the contrary would have invaded the court’s function of determining the law and instructing the jury as to that law.

2. Proof of the Alleged Oral Waiver

Given that the FAA regulation in question is not ambiguous, Pan Am next asserts it obtained an oral waiver of the regulation from the FAA and that the district court erred in disallowing evidence of that waiver. Evidence showed that as of April 1986 Pan Am established procedures to ensure that unaccompanied interline bags were not carried on its airlines. However, the process for identifying unaccompanied interline bags proved too “cumbersome” and expensive. Pan Am therefore stopped performing a match for interline bags in London in February 1987 and in Frankfurt in July 1988. It also eliminated physical searches of unaccompanied interline bags. Thereafter bags were simply X-rayed and put on board, rather than matched against particular tickets. This was a violation of ACSSP XIV, which requires Pan Am to advise the FAA in writing if interline bag match has been discontinued.

It is apparent therefore from the record that Pan Am made no distinction on Flight 103 between interline accompanied versus interline unaccompanied bags. Most significantly, the Flight 103 pilot was not informed about the presence of unaccompanied interline bags, in violation of ACSSP XIII E. Pan Am managers allegedly instructed gate employees in London not to advise pilots of unaccompanied bags because it made crews “jittery.”

What remains central to appellants' defense is their reliance on X-ray alone to inspect interline bags transferred to Flight 103. They sought to introduce evidence that at 1986 and 1987 meetings, mostly with unidentified FAA officials, oral permission was purportedly given to Pan Am to allow it to deviate from the ACSSP regulations. Because of that waiver, they contend, they were in compliance with FAA requirements. They thus sought to show that their noncompliance from the letter of the regulations was excused by an exemption.

Yet, the relevant regulations expressly require a written application for a waiver and written FAA approval based on certain findings. The Director of the Office of Civil Aviation Security at the FAA at the time of the Pan Am bombing, Raymond Salazar, testified that in order to obtain an exemption from an ACSSP regulation an air carrier would have to file a written request and follow a specific procedure that was then in place. Salazar further denied ever granting an oral waiver to any Pan Am official or for that matter to any other air carrier. His predecessor at the FAA, Billie Vincent, testified to the same effect that written authorization and approval were required for exemption from ACSSP requirements.

Salazar was asked by plaintiffs to testify whether he had ever granted an oral waiver to a Pan Am official. The purpose of the question was to get an explanation of a statement contained in a Pan Am electronic mail ("e-mail") memorandum. Plaintiffs produced the e-mail message that Pan Am security officer Daniel Sonesen had sent to the regional Pan Am security representatives at Heathrow and Frankfurt. The e-mail message, dated March 28, 1988, stated in part, "the Dir. FAA R Salizar has granted X-ray as and [sic] alternative to searching pass. baggage." Salazar testified that that representation was inaccurate and a misrepresentation, and when pressed by counsel, characterized it as "a falsehood."

Despite requirements that exemptions be in writing, Pan Am offered no proof that it had ever applied for a written exemption from the provisions of ACSSP XV C.1.(a) at Heathrow or Frankfurt. There was evidence that Pan Am had made written applications on other occasions for exemptions from ACSSP XV C.1, 2, and 3, indicating that Pan Am was aware of the proper procedure for requesting a waiver. Further, Pan Am's Chairman, Thomas Plaskett, admitted the airline knew waivers had to be in writing.

Although the FAA regulations occupied a key role in the trial of this case, it must be kept in mind that Pan Am and Alert's compliance with them is not dispositive of the outcome. As appellants acknowledge in their brief, and as the court instructed the jury, proof of full compliance with the ACSSP would not necessarily provide appellants with a complete defense against a claim of willful misconduct. FAA regulations only establish minimum requirements for air carriers. A jury could conceivably find certain circumstances under which an air carrier had committed willful misconduct even though it followed FAA regulations to the letter. Similarly, noncompliance with ACSSP procedures will not necessarily lead to a per se finding of willful misconduct. A carrier might not have acted with willful misconduct, even were it to have failed to comply with an FAA regulation. The issue we are called upon to decide, thus, is whether evidence of Pan Am's alleged oral waiver should have been admitted by the trial court.

(a) Proposed Testimony

The excluded evidence concerning the oral waiver primarily involved the testimony of three witnesses. We are told that the first witness, Daniel Sonesen, would have testified that he approached the FAA in 1986 and received a verbal authorization for the X-ray-only inspection of interline bags, though he could not recall who gave this authorization. He would have testified further, so defendants state, that at an October 1987 meeting with Salazar and others he was advised that X-ray inspection would comply with ACSSP requirements.

Sonesen's pretrial deposition testimony was before the district court, but we are unable to find in the record an express offer of proof of what his testimony would have been. Moreover, our faith in the defendants' versions of Sonesen's testimony is not enhanced by the fact that Sonesen's 1990 deposition testimony is substantially inconsistent with the representations made by the defendants before us. Simply put, the defendants refused to put Sonesen on the stand for their own reasons, and yet want us to accept at face value representations not made under oath, not subject to cross-examination, and in fact inconsistent with prior testimony made under oath.

The second witness proffered by the defense was the former co-chair of the Pan Am Security Task Force, Richard Cozzi. Although Cozzi testified at trial, he was not permitted to testify as to Pan Am's purported verbal authorization from the FAA. Since his proposed testimony was preserved, we can see he would have testified that the Task Force in late 1986 wanted to find out if X-ray of interline bags would comply with the ACSSP, even though some members were doubtful it could comply; the Task Force instructed Sonesen to check with the FAA as to whether inspection by X-ray satisfied the ACSSP; and Sonesen reported back that he had done so and that the FAA said that X-ray inspection of interline bags would comply with the requirements. Even had Cozzi been permitted to testify on this issue, his statement respecting what Sonesen reported would have been inadmissible hearsay because it was offered for the truth of the matter asserted, to wit, that Salazar granted Pan Am a waiver of compliance with ACSSP XV C.1.(a). That Pan Am offered Cozzi's testimony for this purpose is clear from the record:

Mr. Shaughnessy: You talked about what Mr. Sonesen told you about his discussions with the FAA. Do you have an opinion as to whether Mr. Sonesen was telling the truth? ...

Mr. Cozzi: Yes. I certainly believed Mr. Sonesen was telling the truth. There was no reason for him not to.

The third witness was Pan Am's Chairman, Thomas Plaskett. Pan Am offered his testimony in an offer of proof, in which Plaskett stated that he did not recall having any conversations or information concerning whether the FAA had authorized Pan Am to use X-ray machines to examine luggage.

Additional evidence appellants sought, but were not allowed to introduce to show the supposed appropriateness of their procedures included testimony concerning a September 1988 FAA inspection at Heathrow at which Pan Am was not cited for violating ACSSP XV C.1.(a).

(b) Trial Court's Rulings

In a series of oral rulings repeated throughout the record, the trial judge stated that any testimony by defense witnesses as to the purported verbal authorization would be excluded. It treated the proffered evidence as an attempt to mount a so-called government authorization defense, the bounds of which will be discussed shortly. Chief Judge Platt believed that a government authorization defense may only be predicated on authorization from a government official with power to grant such authorization. He held the defense unavailable because anyone who might have given a verbal exemption at the FAA would have had no authority to do so. The trial court also observed that any evidence as to a verbal authorization would be irrelevant since Pan Am was charged with knowing the regulations, including those that stated amendments and exemptions to the regulations must be in writing.

Before analyzing the government authorization defense, we briefly discuss one of defendants' arguments for permitting the introduction of the verbal authorization defense: to rebut Salazar's statements concerning Sonesen's e-mail message, which plaintiffs had introduced into evidence. A trial court may in the interests of fairness allow otherwise inadmissible evidence on an issue when necessary to rebut a false impression left by inadmissible evidence introduced by an opposing party. But whether to entertain such sort of proof is left squarely in the trial judge's discretion since the presider at trial is in a better position to assess how to conduct it fairly than is an appellate court reading the record.

Here the district court did not abuse its discretion in declining to admit the evidence for this purpose. It directly offered Pan Am and Alert a curative instruction, stating, "[o]n the so-called verbal authorization, ... [i]f they want me to give the jury an instruction to disregard the testimony that came in at the outset of the case before I understood what the issue was, I will be glad to give that instruction." Since appellants refused to ask for that instruction, they waived any complaint as to harm they may have suffered due to Salazar's characterization of Sonesen's e-mail as inaccurate.

Nor is there merit in Pan Am's contention that it was an abuse of discretion to exclude testimony regarding a September 1988 FAA inspection at which Pan Am was not cited for violations relating to its X-ray procedure. Other evidence that was before the jury showed FAA inspections of Pan Am operations at Heathrow and Frankfurt had not resulted in any FAA citations.

Now turning to the substantive question of whether the district court erred in refusing to allow any evidence regarding the oral waiver, the plaintiffs' argue initially that Pan Am failed to make a proper offer of proof with respect to the evidence they sought to introduce. Assuming without deciding that defendants sufficiently preserved their objection does not change the result, as we demonstrate below. We note that the parties and the district court frame the legal issue they faced in different ways. Chief Judge Platt thought the offer of proof was an attempt by defendants to mount a government authorization defense. We believe the proffered proof also can be viewed as an attempt by defendants to invoke what is often referred to as a "mistake of law" defense. Defendants assert it was proof probative of defendants' states of mind.

(i) Government Authorization

Chief Judge Platt correctly ruled that a government authorization defense was not available to Pan Am and Alert. Such defense requires a demonstration of "legitimate reliance on an official interpretation of law." Under our case law, the official on whose interpretation the defendant allegedly relied must have actual authority.

Here all the evidence demonstrated that amendments to or exemptions from ACSSP XV C.1.(a) had to be made in writing by the FAA following written application. Both Salazar and Vincent testified that as Directors of the FAA Office of Civil Aviation Security they did not have the authority to alter the ACSSP orally. The regulations support this view, as did testimony of Pan Am's own witnesses. Pan Am's attempted government authorization defense was therefore properly precluded by the district court because the FAA officials allegedly contacted simply did not have the actual authority to grant any verbal authorization for Pan Am's X-ray-only inspection of interline bags.

(ii) Mistake of Law

Viewed as a mistake of law defense, defendants offered the oral waiver evidence to show they thought what they were doing was in accordance with the law and, even if they were mistaken, under such a circumstance they should not be held liable for willful misconduct. Yet, contrary to appellant's view, even were a mistake of law defense one that could be successfully interposed, it would not necessarily absolve Pan Am of liability in this Warsaw Convention case. The same standards governing the availability of mistake of law govern even when it might not supply a complete defense to liability—in this case, for example, the jury might have found that complying with the FAA minimum requirements was still inadequate under the circumstances on the ultimate issue of willful misconduct. The usual standards defining the permissibility of a mistake of law defense are as effective where the mistaken law is a regulation.

In any event, the oral waiver evidence was inadmissible for purposes of showing that Pan Am's violation of the FAA regulation was the result of a mistake of law. It has long been a maxim that "ignorance of the law is no excuse." The reason for this ancient rule is not because everyone knows the law, but because ignorance of it is a ready excuse easily raised and difficult to refute. We and the Supreme Court regularly acknowledge that a mistaken view of the law usually will not serve as an acceptable defense.

We see no reason that would prompt us to view heavily regulated air carriers—certified by the FAA and charged with knowledge of the relevant statutes and regulations under which they operate—the same as average citizens who face the daunting task of unraveling the complexities of the Internal Revenue Code. There is cause to be wary because of the ease with which air carriers could fabricate sham defenses and ignore with impunity safety regulations. Accordingly, when a law, rule or regulation that pertains to passenger and crew safety is clear, we hold that an air carrier—one of the handful of corporations in the business of transporting the public by air—may not claim ignorance of the law as an excuse.

Our holding is narrow. We reiterate it to emphasize its limitations: in a case brought under the Warsaw Convention involving violations of FAA regulations that pertain to the safety of those aboard an aircraft, against a defendant air carrier charged with knowing and following those regulations, that air carrier may not mount a mistake of law defense. In the instant case, therefore, the evidence offered by Pan Am regarding its mistaken view of what was required by the ACSSP was inadmissible for the purposes of mounting a mistake of law defense.

(iii) State of Mind

Notwithstanding the foregoing, appellants insist the oral waiver evidence was admissible on the question of their willful misconduct, which is of course the ultimate issue in this Warsaw Convention case.

Because the oral waiver evidence was so intertwined with the government authorization and mistake of law defenses, which as a matter of law were not available to defendants, we believe that admission of such evidence might well have been unnecessarily confusing and perhaps prejudicial so as to justify the trial court's refusal to allow its admission. Nonetheless, even were it an abuse of discretion to deny admission of the oral waiver evidence on the foregoing grounds, we hold that such an error was harmless.

The scope and nature of this evidence needs to be set forth in some detail. We begin in 1983 when a Pan Am flight leaving Rome, Italy for New York was the target of a bomb planted in an unaccompanied interline suitcase. Disaster was averted only when Turkish authorities conducted a passenger/bag match that uncovered the suitcase. Pan Am thus knew of this type of sabotage and that physical matches of suitcases were successful in averting such a terrorist act.

In 1985 a bomb hidden inside a radio and packed in an unaccompanied interline bag exploded on an Air India 747 over the North Atlantic, killing all aboard. The dangers of a bomb hidden inside radios packed in interline bags were well known to Pan Am and the airline industry. These two incidents not only led to the adoption of ACSSP XV.C.1(a), but they conveyed clear warnings that what actually happened at Lockerbie was a distinct possibility.

In September 1986 Pan Am received a report from a group of Israeli security experts commissioned to review Pan Am security at various airports, including Heathrow and Frankfurt. The security experts concluded that "under the present security system, Pan Am is highly vulnerable to most forms of terrorist attack. The fact that no major disaster has occurred to date is merely providential." The report specifically cautioned Pan Am on the use of X-ray machines as substitutes for physical searches, and the dangers of interline unaccompanied bags.

In October 1988 Alert Manager for Germany Ulrich Weber wrote a memo to New York headquarters citing the need for more personnel to remedy Frankfurt's security shortcomings. Only minimum efforts were made to remedy them.

In July 1988 the FAA issued a Security Bulletin warning of the high threat of a terrorist retaliatory attack because of the downing of an Iranian Jetliner. In November 1988 Pan Am received an FAA Security Bulletin warning that a raid on a terrorist group had uncovered a bomb built into a Toshiba radio cassette player ("Toshiba Warning"). The bulletin warned that the bomb was difficult to detect by the use of normal X-ray.

The most willful disregard of passenger safety, bordering on the outrageous, was in December 1988 when Pan Am received an FAA Security Bulletin advising that the United States Embassy in Helsinki had received a telephone warning that a Pan Am flight from Frankfurt to London and on to New York would be bombed ("Helsinki Warning"). The Helsinki Warning came just 14 days before the instant tragedy and specifically referred to the Toshiba Warning. Despite these warnings, Pan Am failed to conduct searches of unaccompanied interline luggage, and instead inspected such bags only by X-ray. Pan Am did not even alert X-ray technicians to watch for Toshiba radios. It violated FAA regulations by failing to match the bags with particular tickets without advising the FAA in writing that interline bag match had been discontinued. And it violated other FAA regulations by failing to warn pilots about the unaccompanied bags on board for fear that the crews might become "jittery." Additionally, Pan Am did not replace several members of its security team who were woefully under trained given their responsibility for thwarting terrorist attacks.

Moreover, the Helsinki Warning was deliberately placed under a pile of papers on the desk of the security officer who received the bulletin and was first discovered in the morning following the downing of Flight 103. There was also evidence that Weber, the security officer in charge, ordered the Pan Am employee who discovered the bulletin after the explosion to backdate the warning to give government investigators the impression that the warning was timely disseminated when received. The district court found that the backdating was evidence of consciousness of guilt on the part of Pan Am for its part in the wrongful causation of the crash.

This and other evidence overwhelmingly supported the jury's conclusion that but for Pan Am's wholly inadequate terrorist prevention techniques and its deliberate indifference and overt acts of willfulness, the bombing and the senseless loss of life would not have occurred. Even had Pan Am been permitted to present Sonesen's deposition testimony to the jury, the above recited proof, plus the additional fact that any waiver of FAA regulations had to be in writing, make it plain to us that it would not have affected the jury's finding that Pan Am was guilty of willful misconduct. Its exclusion was therefore harmless error.

Consequently, for all of the above reasons, the district court's refusal to permit the admission of Pan Am's oral waiver evidence—on government authorization, mistake of law, and state of mind grounds—does not constitute a sufficient basis for the granting of a new trial.

B. *British Regulations*

Appellants' second contention regarding wrongful exclusion of evidence concerning willful misconduct relates to British air safety regulations. Appellants sought to introduce British Department of Transportation documents and deposition testimony from James Jack, the Principal Aviation Security Advisor for the British Department of Transportation, in which he explained that Pan Am's reliance on X-raying interline bags would have complied with British security directives.

With respect to the exclusion of the documentary evidence there was no abuse of discretion. That evidence was proffered in the form of British Department of Transport documents and notably included circulars not having the force of law. In addition many of the documents were no longer in effect at the time of the accident. This proof was properly ruled inadmissible as irrelevant, vague, and remote.

The refusal to admit Jack's deposition is more problematic. The district court stated that it would not admit Jack's testimony about British regulations unless Pan Am and Alert stipulated that they had violated the ACSSP. Pan Am and Alert understandably refused to make such a potentially prejudicial stipulation. The trial court then suggested that Pan Am and Alert had to choose between claiming they followed the ACSSP or claiming that they violated it, but their willful misconduct should be judged by local security regulations.

We agree with Pan Am that it was error to force them to choose between alternate defenses. Alternate and inconsistent defenses are permitted in civil trials.

The district court had no authority to exclude evidence on the ground that it supported a defense not consistent with Pan Am and Alert's alternate theory. Nevertheless, though it was error to refuse to permit the few pages of Jack's deposition testimony to be read to the jury, it was harmless error. As we noted above, a ruling is harmless when we are fairly assured that admitting or refusing to admit certain proof had no substantial effect on the jury's verdict. Here the district court did permit Pan Am to adduce some testimony that its conduct comported with British regulations. The jury had that point before it. Further, plaintiffs' case rested principally on Pan Am and Alert's ACSSP violations, not on whether appellants violated British government's security regulations. The bulk of the evidence regarding the X-ray procedures concerned the issue of ACSSP violations, the importance of conducting a passenger/bag match, and appellants' purported knowing or reckless behavior in failing to follow FAA regulations.

Moreover, Pan Am and Alert presented a strong defense to the jury that even if they violated the ACSSP, their actions did not amount to willful misconduct. They insisted that a bomb contained in a suitcase would have been visible on X-ray. In fact, the parties stipulated to that fact. Appellants' counsel emphasized in closing argument and elsewhere the safety and expense of the X-ray technology purchased and employed by Pan Am, the fact that even an untrained person could spot a radio on one of their X-ray machines, and made the point that FAA inspections had shown Pan Am X-ray equipment to be in compliance with regulations. Dr. Grodzins, an MIT professor, testified regarding the effectiveness of X-ray examination of baggage. It simply cannot be supposed on the entirety of the voluminous record that Jack's several pages of deposition testimony would have substantially influenced the verdict, given the fact that the closely related defense that Pan Am presented failed to persuade the jury.

C. *"Highest Threat" Evidence*

The last of the three wrongfully excluded willful-misconduct-evidence assertions raised by Pan Am is the court's refusal to allow evidence that bombs in unaccompanied baggage did not pose the "highest threat" to airline safety. Appellants sought to introduce this evidence to refute the view of one of plaintiffs' experts that unaccompanied bags pose the greatest risk to airline security.

Pan Am and Alert sought to elicit testimony from their terrorism expert that unaccompanied bags do not pose the highest threat to airline safety; instead, unsuspecting couriers pose that threat. Plaintiffs' expert, Billie Vincent, had very briefly testified that the unaccompanied bag poses the "highest threat" to airline safety. The defense sought to rebut this position through their expert, Dr. Ariel Merari. They contend Vincent's testimony left a false impression as to Pan Am's degree of awareness of the probable consequences posed by unaccompanied baggage.

Although the district court did not admit the defense expert's testimony, it agreed to give an instruction that there was no evidence to show that unaccompanied bags posed the greatest security threat and that the jury should disregard any such opinion. Since such a curative instruction was given, any risk that Vincent's brief, qualitative testimony was improperly considered by the jury was removed. Thus, no abuse of discretion resulted from the exclusion of further testimony on this peripheral subject.

ADMISSION OF OTHER MISCONDUCT EVIDENCE BY PAN AM AND ALERT AND EXCLUSION OF THEIR ALTERNATIVE SUGGESTIONS OF CAUSATION

Pan Am and Alert's second major line of argument concerns what it thinks was an error in the trial court's admitting other evidence of misconduct on their part, while at the same time excluding the testimony of several of their witnesses who, they assert, would have presented alternative theories of causation. We examine each of these challenged rulings separately.

A. *Evidence of Appellants' Alleged Other Misconduct*

Appellants complain of evidence received to show other acts of alleged misconduct by the airline. This evidence of Pan Am's and Alert's other misconduct is divided into two categories—SECURITY VIOLATIONS ON FLIGHT 103 and THE "ALERT" SECURITY PROGRAM. With respect to the former alleged misconduct, the proof was as follows: (1) Ulrich Weber, the head of Alert in Frankfurt had been convicted in the U.S. of passing bad checks eight years before he was hired by Alert and had been fired after the disaster at Lockerbie for using a company credit card in a brothel; (2) the ramp around Flight 103 had been left unguarded in violation of ACSSP when the Alert employee assigned to guard it felt ill and went inside; (3) Alert employees were inadequately trained, particularly employee Sabine Fuchs who could not explain what a "selectee" was even though her job was to pick "selectees" out from passengers for further screening; one security agent for Flight 103 was an "alternate" who had only two to three hours of training and did not know what the ACSSP required. She thought someone else was monitoring the baggage; (4) Critical to this case is the fact that the X-ray technician for the flight, the only defense against the bomb, had been employed for only seven weeks, had no formal training, and had not been tested. He had never heard about the Toshiba warning.

The proof regarding THE "ALERT" SECURITY PROGRAM revealed first, that it was neither related to security, nor was it a program. Instituted by Pan Am in May 1986 during a period of sharp decline in international travel due to terrorist attacks, the program was a misleading public relations ploy designed to make would-be travelers feel more secure. An advertisement signed by Pan Am's chairman of the board and CEO was placed in the New York Times and other publications:

> Dear Air Traveler:
>
> On June 12, 1986, Pan Am will initiate one of the most far-reaching security programs in our industry, a program that will screen passengers, employees, airport facilities, baggage, and aircraft with unrelenting thoroughness.

The campaign also featured TV ads. As part of the program, Pan Am imposed a security surcharge on international passengers to pay for the promised additional security measures. The surcharge generated $18 million in annual revenue. The security surcharge was $5 each way on overseas tickets—many Flight 103 passengers paid the surcharge—but proceeds from the surcharge were not earmarked for security and instead were commingled with Pan Am's general funds. Alert's first president, Fred Ford, wrote a memo to Pan Am senior executives stating that the promised security program was not being put into effect and that passengers would complain "What do I get for my surcharge?"

The evidence revealed, second, that Alert added more guards during FAA inspections to make it appear that more guards were on duty than generally was the case; this included on one occasion having a guard from the front end of an airplane sent to the back when FAA inspectors come on board so that the inspectors would think that there was a guard at both places. Third, in 1986 Pan Am declined to adopt security recommendations made to it by the Israeli security consulting firm, KPI, which criticized Pan Am's reliance on X-ray and emphasized Pan Am's vulnerability to terrorist attack. Fourth, untrained sniffing dogs had been paraded in front of ticket counters at Kennedy airport to create an appearance of security which did not otherwise exist.

Appellants' motion to exclude proof not tied to the Air Malta theory of causation (that the bomb bag came from an interline transfer) was denied by the trial court. It observed that since appellants planned to contest the Air Malta theory, plaintiffs were entitled to present evidence of alleged other misconduct on defendants' parts. The trial judge reasoned that even if the Air Malta theory did not explain the bomb's presence on Flight 103, other pervasive and extensive willful misconduct by defendants must have accounted for the bomb's presence. Following this general ruling, no specific objections were made to the individual pieces of evidence listed above on any other grounds. Other objections that might have been raised were waived. Accordingly, we review this as a general ruling permitting the introduction of evidence showing prior misconduct, unrelated to the Air Malta theory.

This proof that Pan Am acted with willful misconduct through recklessly disregarding passenger safety in general, with knowledge of the probable consequences of that disregard, was properly received. Although Fed. R. Evid. 404(b) provides for the exclusion of prior misconduct evidence in order to show "character" or action "in conformity therewith," we follow the inclusionary approach to prior misconduct evidence that allows the admission of prior misconduct for any other relevant purpose.

Plaintiffs asserted that a contempt for security pervaded Pan Am from the highest to the lowest levels of the corporation, and that the totality of security failures would permit the jury to infer willful misconduct. We have approved consideration of the totality of a defendant's wrongdoing in determining whether willful misconduct existed.

Pan Am insists that causation was not established and that therefore the objected to willful misconduct evidence was speculative and unrelated as a cause of the crash. We think the question of whether it had a causative effect was, without objection or exception, properly submitted to the jury. We do not hold that as a matter of law the evidence in this case required the jury to agree with the plausibility of a theory that Pan Am and Alert's misconduct was so reckless it must have caused the bomb to go undetected. We say only that under the Warsaw Convention willful misconduct causing an accident may be established by inference from the totality of the circumstances.

This conclusion does not mean that any of the burden of proving causation was lifted from plaintiffs. It remained plaintiffs' duty to prove causation under whatever theory they pursued. In this connection, the district court carefully and in an extensive and well balanced charge instructed the jury that it must find not only willful misconduct, but also a causal connection between that misconduct and the passengers' deaths. Chief Judge Platt added that defendants' conduct would not be proximate cause of the accident if the accident would have occurred anyway, absent defendants' acts or omissions. Since the evidence introduced by the plaintiffs related to such a showing of causation, there was no error in its receipt.

B. *Evidence Challenging Plaintiffs' Causation Theory*

Various attempts by appellants to suggest other specific causation theories were then rebuffed by the trial court. Pan Am and Alert challenge the exclusion of the testimony of four defense witnesses: two offered as experts on terrorism, Noel Koch and Dr. Ariel Merari, and two offered as experts on terrorist bombings, Peter Gurney and John Horne of Scotland Yard. Pan Am also contends it was error to restrict its cross-examination of plaintiffs' experts, Billie Vincent and Rodney Wallis (the former Director of Security for the International Air Transport Association), with respect to other methods of bombing. The trial judge based his rulings largely on the fact that he found appellants had offered nothing to show there was any other specific bombing theory.

The trial court did not abuse its discretion in excluding the testimony of defense experts Koch and Merari because their conclusions as to more likely explanations for the bombing were speculative. Any testimony as to some other particular method of bombing—without any foundation that such method might explain the Flight 103 bombing—was clearly conjectural.

Further, appellants admit in their brief that they "did not undertake to prove what method the terrorists used to bomb the aircraft ... [but] contended that the method of bombing has not yet been established." Because there was no evidence presented with respect to other possible methods of causation that might explain how this tragic event occurred, and because appellants never sought to show that any other specific method of bombing could have caused it, any testimony relating to such other causes would necessarily be speculative. Although Dr. Merari and Noel Koch would also have provided general background information on terrorism, the determination whether or not this testimony would have been helpful to the jury rested squarely within the trial court's discretion.

Discretion was also properly exercised in limiting appellants' cross-examination of plaintiffs' experts to scenarios that had evidentiary support in the record. Cross-examination of plaintiffs' experts as to other causation theories—absent a good-faith basis to believe those theories had evidentiary support—was properly excluded. Trial courts possess wide discretion in limiting cross-examination and here the precluded questions could have drawn the jury into misleading conjecture. Pan Am and Alert were permitted lengthy cross-examination of plaintiffs' experts, and were only barred from suggesting, without basis, that other scenarios caused the bombing.

It was also not error to decline to receive the testimony of terrorist bombings experts Peter Gurney and John Horne. Their testimony as to the importance of X-rays would have been cumulative since similar testimony was adduced from other witnesses. Additionally, these witnesses' expertise as to X-rays was questionable. Both witnesses were explosives officers with Scotland Yard who specialized in street bombings. Neither had experience in aviation bombings or security. Moreover, neither had any background or knowledge concerning the Flight 103 bombing itself; the trial court found this rendered their proposed testimony unhelpful and largely irrelevant. This ruling was well within the trial court's Fed. R. Evid. 702 discretion.

Contrary to appellants' suggestions throughout their briefs, Pan Am and Alert were not thereby prevented from presenting a defense on causation. Pan Am and Alert's summation focused at length and in detail on criticizing plaintiffs' causation theory; this remained Pan Am and Alert's main theme throughout cross-examination and their defense case as well. They vigorously attacked major and minor pieces of evidence alike.

They were permitted to argue the possibility that a "rush-tag" bag, one by definition sent by the airline apart from its owner, was the unexplained, unaccompanied 13th interline bag X-rayed by operator Kurt Maier in Frankfurt. Importantly, appellants did not offer any fact witness to testify as to another method of bombing that might have caused Flight 103's crash.

Appellants admit that at trial they sought to argue that the method of bombing was not established and concede they were unable to suggest a specific alternate theory. They vigorously argued that the method of bombing was unclear, and accomplished this through extensive cross-examination of plaintiffs' experts. Pan Am and Alert also were not deterred from attacking plaintiffs' weaker theory that widespread misconduct on defendants part more likely than not caused the bomb to be loaded on Flight 103. In sum, Pan Am and Alert exercised the ample opportunities given them to undermine plaintiffs' causation theory. Thus, the rulings limiting cross-examination and expert testimony were unremarkable and without error.

OTHER EVIDENTIARY RULINGS

While appellants raise an array of objections to other evidentiary rulings—some of which patently involved judgment calls by the trial judge—none of them amount to reversible error.

A. *Plaintiffs' Experts' Testimony*

Appellants' first objection is to the testimony of plaintiffs' expert witnesses, Rodney Wallis and Billie Vincent. Wallis and Vincent gave their opinions relying on evidence adduced at trial, at times displaying for purposes of reference trial transcripts on a projection screen. Based on this testimony, for example, Wallis opined that Pan Am was operating under a commercial rather than security priority and that training requirements had been violated. Vincent stated—again based on other record testimony—that Pan Am had committed acts that violated ACSSP XV C.1.(a).

Pan Am insists the Wallis and Vincent testimony involved improper summaries of evidence. But the cases relied on for support are inapposite because they do not address experts' summarizing record evidence, but rather they address summaries of evidence of the sort covered under Fed. R. Evid. 1006.

The trial judge, therefore, properly ruled on the summary testimony under the federal rules governing expert testimony rather than under Rule 1006. Under those rules, expert testimony may be based on other testimony or evidence obtained at trial. *See* Fed. R. Evid. 703 ("The facts or data in the particular case upon which an expert bases an opinion or inference may be those perceived by or made known to the expert at or before the hearing."). No error occurred from the format of testimony summarizing the trial record or from the use of transparencies to highlight portions of the trial transcripts to which the witnesses referred when they were on the witness stand.

* * *

Pan Am's next contention has greater merit. It declares that plaintiffs' witnesses improperly offered legal opinions as to ACSSP violations. We agree that Vincent's statement as to his belief that Pan Am violated the ACSSP is dubious. While an expert witness may testify as to an ultimate fact issue the jury will decide, *see* Fed. R. Evid. 704, the general rule is that an expert may not testify as to what the law is, because such testimony would impinge on the trial court's function.

Thus, expert testimony expressing a legal conclusion should ordinarily be excluded because such testimony is not the way in which a legal standard should be communicated to the jury. Vincent's testimony that he had been lead to the conclusion "that Pan Am did indeed violate the ACSSP" embodied a legal conclusion that crossed the fine line between a permissible conclusion as to an ultimate issue of fact and an impermissible legal conclusion. Having said this much, we hasten to add that the introduction of Vincent's statement was not in our view a reversible error.

B. *Detective Constable Henderson's Testimony*

Scottish Detective Constable Derek Henderson provided deposition testimony as to his work in the Flight 103 investigation. He was assigned responsibility for matching certain bags—the ones that might have been placed in the flight container that was determined to have held the bag with the bomb—with passengers on the aircraft. Henderson prepared his report largely through compiling computerized records of bags. These computerized records had been set up to amass reports from passengers' and crew members' friends and relatives, and from evidence obtained at the scene of the crash.

Appellants object to the admission of the detective's testimony and his report. Based on his analysis of passenger records and information obtained from passengers' and crew members' friends and relatives, Henderson determined that the Samsonite bag containing the bomb was an unaccompanied bag from the Frankfurt flight. Defendants moved to exclude his reports as based on multiple layers of hearsay; Henderson had compiled his reports based upon other officers' reports of interviews they had conducted in this necessarily lengthy and involved investigation.

We believe the evidence was properly received under Fed. R. Evid. 803(8)(C), which provides an exception to the hearsay rule for reports of public agencies containing "factual findings resulting from an investigation made pursuant to authority granted by law, unless the sources of information or other circumstances indicate lack of trustworthiness."

The determination as to any lack of trustworthiness remains one properly left to the district court and its decision to admit a report under Fed. R. Evid. 803(8)(C) is one that we will uphold absent a manifest error. The investigation was timely, Henderson was an experienced and skilled investigator, and no bias may be presumed in the Scottish investigation. We cannot say the trial court abused its discretion in entertaining the report, particularly given its cautionary instructions to the jury concerning the report.

C. *X-ray Demonstration of Radio-Cassette Player*

Pan Am and Alert also sought to include an X-ray demonstration as part of their defense to show how clearly a radio-cassette player would appear on the screen. Such a demonstration was ultimately ruled irrelevant, given plaintiffs' offer to stipulate that a radio-cassette player would be visible on an X-ray screen. Pan Am and Alert nevertheless declare the demonstration would have generally supported Pan Am X-ray operator Kurt Maier's testimony that he X-rayed all the interline bags transferred to Flight 103 in Frankfurt.

The X-ray demonstration would not have either shaken or bolstered Maier's testimony since he said he could not remember whether any radios or cassette players appeared in any of the bags on Flight 103. More important, because plaintiffs stipulated that a radio cassette player would be clearly recognizable in an X-ray image the proffered demonstration would have been cumulative, and therefore inadmissible in the district court's discretion under Fed. R. Evid. 403.

DAMAGES FOR LOSS OF SOCIETY AND COMPANIONSHIP

Pan Am and Alert's last claims of error concern the damage awards. In each of the three cases whose damages phases were tried the jury was permitted to award compensatory damages to the decedent's spouse and children based on the loss of financial contributions, loss of services, loss of society and companionship, and loss of parental care. Appellants do not dispute the awards for the first two elements. But they contend that loss of society and companionship damages are not available under the Warsaw Convention, and that damages for the loss of parental care should not be available to adult children of crash victims.

As we noted in *Lockerbie I*, damages in a Warsaw Convention case are governed by federal common law principles consistent with the Convention's terms. Article 17 of the convention provides for recovery of compensatory damages. The first damages question to be analyzed is whether compensatory damages under the Convention include damages for loss of society and companionship.

In light of the broad language in the Warsaw Convention covering "damage sustained" and the lack of authority suggesting that the drafters wanted to limit compensatory damages to pecuniary loss, we are informed by general maritime law principles and hold the Warsaw Convention permits damage awards for loss of society and companionship.

We therefore affirm the loss of society awards to the Bainbridge and Porter families, since these families consisted of only spouses and dependant children. But the loss of society award to the Pagnucco family must be vacated since some of the family members were adult children and may or may not have been dependents. We remand this limited issue as it applies to the Pagnuccos to the district court for further proceedings consistent with this opinion.

On the issue of damages for lost parental care, we also must vacate and remand all three plaintiffs' cases to the district court because the district court erroneously instructed the jury on this issue. Damages for lost parental care are considered a pecuniary loss and are therefore recoverable. Appellants correctly contend the district court erred in declining to instruct the jury that damages for loss of fatherly care and guidance must be limited to the period of a child's minority, absent a showing of specific circumstances that the father's "guidance had a pecuniary value beyond the irreplaceable values of companionship and affection." Since no such limitation was charged to the jury on this damages issue, the jury awards for loss of parental care may not stand.

On remand, the district court should instruct the jury that it may take into consideration the care, attention, instruction, training, advice, and guidance the evidence shows the father might reasonably have been expected to give his children and to include the pecuniary value thereof in the damages it assesses. The damages for such loss must be limited to the period of a child's minority, absent a showing of specific circumstances that the father's guidance had a pecuniary value beyond that period.

CONCLUSION

The record of this trial is not a paradigm of a perfect trial. The critical question though is whether the trial was fair. Here we are satisfied upon an examination of the entire record that defendants received a fair trial. Accordingly, the jury verdicts as to liability are affirmed. However, the award for loss of society damages to the Pagnucco family is vacated as are the awards for loss of parental care in all three plaintiffs' cases. These cases are remanded to the district court for further proceedings on the outlined damage issues consistent with this opinion.

VAN GRAAFEILAND, Circuit Judge, dissenting.

As I said when writing my dissent to the original majority opinion, writing a dissenting opinion in the instant case is not a pleasant task. My name will be anathema to the hundreds of people who are seeking recoveries probably in excess of $1 billion, and my long-time friendship with Judge Platt may suffer some stress. However, because I am convinced that Pan Am did not receive a fair trial, I would be shirking my duties as a judge if I did not say so. Before undertaking the unpleasant task of discussing where I believe the district court erred, I find it necessary to undertake the even more unpleasant task of commenting briefly upon my colleagues' amended opinion, a substantial portion of which is devoted to a rebuttal of arguments that Pan Am never made.

Under the heading "The Alleged Oral Waiver" my colleagues state, "Defendants maintain that an FAA official granted them an oral waiver excusing strict compliance with certain FAA regulations, and that Chief Judge Platt abused his discretion when he disallowed their evidence purporting to demonstrate their belief in this waiver." The fact of the matter is that Pan Am made absolutely no claim of waiver. It argued, and offered testimony to prove, that what it sought and obtained from FAA officials was not a waiver, but an "interpretation" of what it deemed an ambiguous regulation. One of the tasks of Raymond Salazar, Director of Civil Aviation Security, and his staff was to promulgate regulations and thereafter to interpret them: "In that capacity we would—we, me, my staff would promulgate regulations, would provide interpretations."

Interpretations of regulations were not required to be in writing. Richard Cozzi, Pan Am's Director of Airport Security, described the practice as follows:

Q: Is it your understanding, sir, that before a change can be made to the ACSSP there has to be an application in writing to the FAA?

A: Yes.

Q: And that only when there is a written process of an application and an approval by the FAA, that the terms of the ACSSP can be changed?

A: That's true if an airline is requesting a waiver or something of that nature, yes. Not for an interpretation.

As will be discussed below, the district court clearly erred in rejecting all evidence offered by Pan Am in support of its contention that it received and relied upon an oral interpretation from Salazar. Although my colleagues devote seventeen pages of their amended opinion to a discussion of the "oral waiver," "government authorization," and "mistake of law" defenses, none of these defenses was asserted by Pan Am or is relevant to the pertinent issue herein.

* * *

Finally, my colleagues come to the question of the defendant's "State of Mind," which they acknowledge to be "the ultimate issue in this Warsaw Convention case." The following excerpt from Mr. Cozzi's excluded testimony demonstrates exactly how the "ultimate issue" was resolved and why the district court erred in not permitting the jury to hear the testimony:

Q: When did the discussions of the Security Task Force take place?

A: Discussions concerning the possibility of using X-ray to satisfy the ACSSP on interline baggage took place at the very first or at least second Security Task Force meeting.

The Security Task Force team was charged with writing sealed procedures, our developing manuals, and one of the very first things that Security Task Force needed to know is that did X-ray of interline baggage satisfy the ACSSP.

Q: And what was done in that respect?

A: That question was presented to Mr. Dan Sonesen, and I must say that his first reaction was doubtful.

However, we requested that he contact our PSI [FAA Principal Security Inspector] or whatever level was required within the FAA, and to report back to the task force as to whether X-ray met that intent.

At a subsequent meeting, Mr. Sonesen—

Pounian: Your Honor, I just want to note our objection on the record for hearsay from Mr. Sonesen.

Court: Yes. It's not admissible.

Shaughnessy: May I continue?

Court: Yes.

Q: Go ahead.

A: Mr. Sonesen reported back at the subsequent task force meeting that he had had conversation with the FAA and requested interpretation of intent and he came back and told us that, yes, X-ray did in fact satisfy that section of the ACSSP.

Q: Why did the task force seek this clarification?

Pounian: Objection to the question, as clarification, your Honor. I think that it's improper.

Court: That's the way they regard it, as a clarification of a statement that positive matching was required. That's their interpretation.

Mr. Pounian: I just think that it's leading, your Honor, in the context.

The Court: Sure, it is.

Q: Why did you seek this clarification, Mr. Cozzi?

A: We needed this clarification because the task force was charged with writing manuals and developing procedures, and we needed to know what direction those manuals and procedures were to take.

Q: And were you anxious to have X-ray approved under Section XV.C.1.A?

A: We were not anxious to have X-ray approved. We just needed to know what direction we were going in; if it had come back that it was not approved, then we would have developed procedures without utilizing X-ray.

As it turned out, we were told that it was approved, and we wrote the procedures accordingly.

Pounian: Your Honor, I'm going to have to move to strike that answer, based upon hearsay from Mr. Sonesen.

Court: None of this is, in my opinion, admissible either for hearsay reasons or for reasons you've indicated.

Pounian: I'm just saying for the purpose of presenting a record—

Court: That's his problem.

Pounian: I understand that, but I think Mr. Sonesen has to present the record, not Mr. Cozzi.

Court: Even if they called Mr. Sonesen, it would still be hearsay.

Shaughnessy: Your Honor, the state of mind is the issue here.

Court: It would still be hearsay.

Shaughnessy: Respectfully disagree, your Honor.

Court: You can't develop a unilateral state of mind.

Shaughnessy: It is not a unilateral state of mind. That's the point.

The district court's rulings on "hearsay" and "unilateral state of mind" will be commented upon below. Because, as in my dissent to the original majority opinion, I deem it necessary in the interest of uncontrovertible accuracy to quote at length from the record, I will not prolong this opinion by an extended counterstatement of the facts. Indeed, what is perhaps the most crucial fact has been established by stipulation, [Pan Am] insisted that a bomb contained in a suitcase would have been visible on X-ray. In fact, the parties stipulated to that fact.

It is worth noting, however, how this stipulation came into being. After Pan Am was satisfied that it could use X-ray examination of luggage, it purchased for the Frankfurt airport the most expensive up-to-date X-ray machine on the market, the Astrophysics Linescan X-ray Screening System.

Q: Does your company make a larger machine than this?

A: This is the largest machine we make.

Q: Does your company make a more expensive machine than this?

A: No, sir.

Q: At the time it was sold, was there a newer or more advanced state of the art machine than this?

A: No, sir.

Pan Am wanted the jury to see the machine and how it operated, and for this purpose it had the machine transported to the courthouse. For obvious reasons, plaintiffs' counsel did not want the jury to have the benefit of this first-hand observation, and he stipulated what an examination of the machine would have shown. Although Pan Am should not have been required to accept this stipulation in lieu of actual observation, the district court gave it no choice. At the district court's direction, the machine sat in the basement of the courthouse, alone and unobserved. The fact that plaintiffs' counsel objected to a jury inspection is evidence in and of itself that the district court erred in not permitting it.

Solely to demonstrate the danger of unquestioned reliance upon my colleagues' often-pejorative statement of facts, I address two excerpts from the majority opinion. [M]y colleagues say:

> The most willful disregard of passenger safety, bordering on the outrageous, was in December 1988 when Pan Am received an FAA Security Bulletin advising that the United States Embassy in Helsinki had received a telephone warning that a Pan Am flight from Frankfurt to London and on to New York would be bombed. (Helsinki Warning).
>
> In pertinent part, the Helsinki Warning, with letters substituted for names, read as follows:
>
> On December 5, 1988 an unidentified individual telephoned a U.S. diplomatic facility in Europe and stated that sometime within the next two weeks there would be a bombing attempt against a Pan American aircraft flying from Frankfurt, FRG to the U.S. An individual identified as "X", who allegedly is in Finland and a second individual identified only as "Y" and is in Frankfurt, are involved. According to the caller, "Y" will provide the device to "X" who will in turn provide it to an unidentified Finnish woman in Helsinki. The woman, would unwittingly take the device to Frankfurt and eventually onto the U.S. bound flight.

My colleagues' discussion of the Helsinki Warning is in the nature of a half-truth that calls for exposition. Pan Am's response to this warning, as described in the testimony of Wolfgang Schwab, a Pan Am supervisor at Frankfurt, was quite different than what my colleagues would have us believe:

Q: Prior to the Lockerbie disaster, had it been brought to your attention that there was a warning received by the United States Embassy in Helsinki to the effect that a Pan Am flight to the United States would be bombed?

A: Yes.

Q: Tell us, please, when and how that was brought to your attention?

A: I am not able to give you the exact point in time but it was certainly before Lockerbie, when we were told that a female Finnish passenger would try to smuggle a bomb aboard.

Q: Where were you when this came to your attention?

A: At the airport.

Q: Where in the airport?

A: On the job.

Q: Were you warned to pay particular attention to all female passengers or only Finnish female passengers?

A: Particularly to a female Finnish passenger.

Q: Did you ever issue any instructions to look out for Finnish women or to pay particular attention to Finnish women?

A: Yes, I did.

Q: When was that?

A: Before Lockerbie.

Q: What instructions or suggestions did you issue?

A: Now, I told the screeners and the staff that they were to pay particular attention to female Finnish passengers or woman [sic] coming from that region up there and I told them that one person would try to smuggle a bomb aboard a plane.

Q: Do you remember if you did it personally or if you asked someone else to do it?

A: I did it personally.

Perhaps even more troubling to me is my colleagues' statement of their opinion that the Helsinki Warning was "deliberately" placed under a pile of papers on the desk of a Pan Am security officer. Needless to say, no page citation to the record accompanied the word "deliberately." Because no changes made in a majority opinion can alter the immutable record of the trial court, I now direct my attention once again to what occurred below.

At one point near the end of the trial, Pan Am's counsel said to the court: "Now, Judge, I would tell you, on a scale of 1 to 10, doing what I want in this courtroom, I have been about a minus 2, or maybe imaginary numbers would be a better way to describe as the level to which I have gone." I have read the record dispassionately, and I completely agree with this observation. Plaintiffs' attorneys were permitted to range far and wide with prejudicial, irrelevant testimony, while Pan Am's counsel was precluded time and again from presenting relative and probative proof. Because I recognize that evidentiary rulings are largely discretionary, I will limit my discussion to what I deem the major reversible errors.

CONFLICT OF OPINION

At the outset, I want to state one clear and uncontrovertible fact: NO ONE KNOWS WHEN, WHERE OR HOW THE BOMB GOT ON THE PAN AM PLANE EXCEPT THE PERSON WHO PUT IT THERE.

The jury had to content itself with the expounding by plaintiffs' "experts" of what my colleagues correctly term "Plaintiffs' Causation Theory." The accuracy of the supposition that a suitcase carrying the bomb was sent unaccompanied from Malta to Frankfurt, was transferred there to a Pan Am plane in which it was flown to London, where it was transferred to the plane in which it subsequently exploded, was a crucial issue in the case, because "Plaintiffs' Causation Theory" was based upon Pan Am's allegedly deficient baggage checks during the two transfers. If there were no transfers, there could not have been any willfully deficient screenings. The district court permitted plaintiffs' experts to testify in support of the supposition but precluded any testimony by defendant's experts in opposition thereto. Having reviewed this proposed testimony of Pan Am's experts that the district court kept from the jury, I am convinced that had the jury been permitted to hear this evidence, there is a strong likelihood it would have rejected plaintiffs' contention that the bomb which exploded began its deadly journey in Malta.

The jurors who undoubtedly had suffered through the same experiences that many of us have, with missed planes and lost luggage during connecting airline flights, probably wondered how presumably clever and experienced terrorists reasonably could have expected an unaccompanied bag containing a bomb to travel from Malta to Frankfurt to London, through at least two sets of baggage checks, to be smuggled finally aboard Pan Am Flight 103 and explode only after the plane had left London. The jurors' willingness to accept the plaintiffs' theory undoubtedly would have been influenced in large measure by what Pan Am's witnesses said.

Refutation of plaintiffs' supposition was permitted from Wilfred Borg, the general manager of ground operations for Air Malta, one of the few witnesses produced by defendant whose testimony was admitted:

Q: Let me show you what we have marked as Exhibits HF-1 through HF-15 in evidence. (Handing.)

A: Thank you.

Q: Looking at those exhibits, Mr. Borg, have you ever seen them before?

A: Yes, I did.

Q: Would you tell the ladies and gentlemen what those documents are, the whole package?

A: That is the flight file or the ship's papers for Flight KM-180, destined to Frankfurt in Germany on the 21st of December 1988.

Q: When did you first see this particular flight file?

A: I saw this flight file, the first time, in February '89.

Q: What were the circumstances under which you saw the flight file at that time?

A: Our office in Germany had received a request from the German police requesting us whether we had any passengers or baggage connecting to Pan American flights out of Frankfurt.

They said they were investigating this, they wanted this information in view of the Lockerbie incident in December, '88.

Q: And what did you do with respect to their request?

A: The request was passed along to me by our office in Germany.

I requested the manager responsible to keep these records, to give me this relevant flight file. I went through it and gave the relevant replies to the German police.

Q: What were those replies?

A: We had no passengers connecting on the flights out of Frankfurt. We had no baggage destined to go in flights out of Frankfurt. And, we had no unaccompanied luggage on that flight.

* * *

Q: Now, sir, based upon everything that you've read and all the investigation that you did, are you able to tell this jury whether or not there was an unaccompanied bag on Flight 180?

A: No, there was no such bag.

Q: Were there any bags destined for Pan Am, any Pan Am flights?

A: No, there are no bags.

Q: Any passengers destined for any Pan Am flights?

Mr. Baumeister: Objection, leading.

Court: Sustained.

The following testimony of Dr. Ariel Merari of Tel Aviv University, an expert on terrorism and bombing, also would have shed unfavorable light on the Malta-origin "theory." However, this testimony was kept from the jury.

Q: Do you think, sir, that it is conjectural how the bomb got on board?

A: Could you please rephrase the question.

Q: Do you know how the bomb got on board?

A: No, I don't.

Q: Do you think any, based upon the readings you have done in this record, a fair-minded, honest, so-called expert, with a reasonable degree of professional certainty, could opine how the bomb got on board?

* * *

A: Well, of what I have read, including the trial transcripts, I cannot see how anybody can say with any degree of certainty how the bomb got on board.

Q: Do you have any level of familiarity with what our government has been saying with respect to the indictments of two Libyans?

A: Yes, I do.

Q: And have you had, to the extent you can discuss this in this forum, a conversation with any representatives of security or secret services of any governments on that subject?

A: Yes.

Q: Has whatever knowledge that has come to you through those discussions in any way changed your view that an honest and reasonable chap cannot say to a reasonable degree of professional certainty how this bomb got on board?

A: No. I still feel that I don't know how the bomb got on board and I don't think that at this particular stage, before more intelligence information comes in, which may be a long time after the incident, in some cases, I still feel that I don't know how the bomb got on board and I don't think anybody knows for sure or even in any degree of reasonable certainty how the bomb got on board at this time, except for the terrorists, of course.

* * *

Q: Is it possible that a bomb was smuggled on board Pan Am 103 by an unwitting courier?

A: I think it is.

Q: Has that possibility been widely discussed secretly in the intelligence community?

A: Yes, it has.

Even stronger refutation of the Malta theory was given by Peter Gurney, a Scotland Yard bomb expert, whose testimony also was kept from the jury:

Q: Let me ask you this: Do you have an opinion based upon your review of the data made available to you of the existence of the fire system that existed in that Neus Toshiba bomb B 453 radio cassette?

A: I do have an opinion.

Q: What is it?

A: I cannot see how such a device could have been used on a multi leg journey with one of the earlier legs being of longer duration than the flight on which the explosion took place.

* * *

Q: If you were a bomb designer wanting to blow up Pan Am 103 over the Atlantic Ocean on [sic] off the coast of the United Kingdom would you use the Air Malta routing suggested in this case?

A: I'm not a bomb designer. We often have to think like terrorist [sic] in order to combat them. I would think that that was very unlikely because air travel—there are many delays in air travel. Normally on the ground. So to work up the exact timing to get the thing to go off when you want it and not have it go off on the ground could be extremely difficult. This is used in a straightforward timer, sir.

Finally, the defense made an unsuccessful offer of proof of testimony by Noel Koch, a security consultant for the United States Department of Defense. If Koch had been permitted to testify on the subject, he would have said that the Air Malta theory is "widely at variance with *modus operandi* of Middle Eastern Terrorist attacks and specifically attacks on U.S. airlines," and that the "Air-Malta theory involves far too many variables to jibe with usual *modus operandi*." He also would have testified that the Pentagon relies on X-rays to scan baggage.

Admittedly, a district judge has wide discretion in determining whether to admit evidence. However, this discretion "may not be utilized to exclude the otherwise admissible opinion of a party's expert on a critical issue, while allowing the opinion of his adversary's expert on the same issue." The district judge's lack of even-handedness cannot be justified by his reliance on the indictment of two apprehended, unquestioned and unapproachable Middle Eastern terrorists:

> Court: And I must view the evidence that we're talking about in that light, not in the light of a criminal case, because we're not in a criminal case.
>
> Coddington: Exactly. And my submission to you is that you may not give any evidentiary weight to the fact of that indictment.
>
> Court: No. But I may give evidentiary weight, probable cause weight to the fact that a grand jury has returned the indictment. Not in a criminal case, but in the civil case, for purposes of, I may not so instruct the jury, but as a qualifier from my standpoint, I may give it that weight. In fact I must.

Neither can the lack of even-handedness be justified by the district court's treatment as "facts" of evidence that my colleagues correctly characterize as theory and supposition.

> Court: The narrow question for this jury is given the facts in this case—and we know it's a Toshiba radio and as to which there has been a specific warning and in which the bomb was, and there was a specific warning about the bomb being placed on a flight and so forth. Those specific warnings and not as to some other possible bomb, but as to that, how you handled it and how you handled it in Frankfurt and how you handled it in London Heathrow, the general lax procedures which they have described, if they find all of that to be willful misconduct which was the proximate cause of the crash, that's the issue for them to determine.

Needless to say, the "facts in this case" were to be determined by the jury, not the judge.

Because the house of cards to the effect that the bomb entered the stream of commerce in Malta was constructed entirely of opinion testimony introduced by plaintiffs, simple justice required that defendant's experts be given an opportunity to demolish it. Obviously any testimony concerning how the bomb got on the plane had to be conjectural. However, the burden of proof on this issue was on the plaintiffs, not the defendant. Pan Am nevertheless offered expert testimony to challenge plaintiffs' contentions, which the district court refused to receive.

If Pan Am's experts were correct in opining that no expert could testify with any degree of reasonable certainty how the bomb got on the plane, the district court's refusal to permit Pan Am's experts to so testify meant that the district court deprived Pan Am of all means of contesting the testimony of plaintiffs' experts on this important issue. The constitutional implications of such a result are obvious. "[T]he admission of a report containing 'conclusions' is subject to the ultimate safeguard—the opponent's right to present evidence tending to contradict or diminish the weight of those conclusions." *Beech Aircraft Corp. v. Rainey* (1988). Denial of this "ultimate safeguard" in the instant case was prejudicial reversible error.

WILFUL MISCONDUCT

A carrier covered by the Warsaw Convention cannot limit its liability to $75,000 if a plaintiff's damages were caused by the carrier's "willful misconduct." Willfulness as thus used involves the issue of intent, not an intent to violate an FAA regulation, but the intent to perform an act with knowledge that it probably will result in injury and with disregard of that probable consequence. The violation *vel non* of an FAA regulation, even if intentional, is not determinative of the issue of willful misconduct under the Convention. The issue of willfulness or wrongful intent is an issue of fact to be resolved by the jury. Because the issue of intent, or state of mind, is crucial in any determination of willful misconduct, the following generalizations concerning proof of intent will be helpful in the discussion that follows.

It cannot be gainsaid that resolution of the issue of willfulness involves consideration by the jury of the mental processes of Pan Am officials. [T]he state of mind of these officials was a fact question to be proved the same as any other fact, and the district judge had no right to reject testimony dealing with this fact because he deemed it incredible or unpersuasive. As the Supreme Court said in *Crawford v. United States* no material and proper evidence upon the issue of the defendant's intent should have been excluded, and the error committed by such exclusion was not harmless.

The record is clear that both the district court and plaintiffs' counsel had ample notice of Pan Am's intention to offer evidence of Sonesen's conversation with Salazar concerning the propriety of using X-ray screening. This intent was stated unambiguously in paragraphs 63-65 of the pretrial order:

> 63. In late 1986 or early 1987, Daniel Sonesen, System Director—Corporate Security and co-chairman of the Security Task Force, at the request of the other Security Task Force members, conferred with the FAA concerning the use of X-ray security screening of interline baggage at Pan Am European stations and whether the X-ray security screening of such baggage met the requirements of Section XV.C.1.(a) of the ACSSP.
>
> 64. At that time, the FAA permitted X-ray security screening of many items, and the FAA advised Mr. Sonesen that X-ray security screening of interline baggage met the requirements of Section XV.C.1.(a) of the ACSSP.
>
> 65. Mr. Sonesen reported back to the Security Task Force that the FAA had said that X-ray screening of interline baggage met the requirements of Section XV.C.1.(a) of the ACSSP.

Moreover, both the court and plaintiffs' counsel had copies of Sonesen's pretrial depositions in which he testified about his conversation with Salazar. Plaintiffs' counsel also had in his possession a copy of an E-mail message from Sonesen to Pan Am security officers that read as follows: PER MESSAGE OF 10 MAR-88 ANSWER: THE DIR. FAA R SALIZAR HAS GRANTED X-RAY AS AND [sic] ALTERNATE TO SEARCHING PASS. BAGGAGE.

Knowing what Sonesen's testimony would be, plaintiffs' counsel decided to meet the evidence head on by placing the E-mail message in evidence as part of his affirmative case. He then offered the following testimony from Salazar:

> Q: This document is something more than that, doesn't it, sir? It says that you granted X-ray as an alternative, doesn't it?
>
> A: Yes, that is what the document says.
>
> Q: You just said to me you never granted that to Mr. Sonesen?
>
> A: That's correct, I did not.
>
> Q: You had never even spoken to Mr. Sonesen, did you?

A: About this issue, I have no specific recollection of speaking to Mr. Sonesen about this issue.

Q: Therefore, sir, if you didn't grant permission to Mr. Sonesen, and he said in this document you did, isn't that a lie?

A: It is an improper interpretation.

Q: It is an improper interpretation. I am not talking interpretation now of the procedures, I am talking about the statement: R. Salazar granted.

Is that statement accurate?

A: No, it is false.

Q: So that statement, as it goes, R. Salazar has granted, is a lie.

A Voice: Objection.

A: Again, it is only what—I can say it is here. It is a misrepresentation. It is not an accurate depiction of the requirements for air carriers operating out of those stations.

Q: Can we agree that when Mr. Sonesen said that you had granted, in this phrase, that that was a falsehood?

A: That was a falsehood.

On the basis of Salazar's testimony, the district judge made a colossal blunder by a *sua sponte* ruling that was so contrary to established legal precedent and simple justice that it smacked of a due process and Seventh Amendment violation—he declared that he would receive no testimony from Sonesen or any other Pan Am employee in support of Sonesen's assertion of what Salazar had told him. Sonesen, whose proposed testimony was an important part of Pan Am's defense, was branded a liar, and the district judge precluded Pan Am from attempting to prove that he was not. So far as the jury knew, a substantial part of Pan Am's defense was built upon a lie, or as plaintiffs' counsel described it in summation, "a concocted piece of baloney."

The district court correctly charged the jury that "the violation of FAA regulations and safety standards ... would not necessarily constitute willful misconduct." However, because of the district court's erroneous exclusions of evidence, this portion of its charge became meaningless. The district judge treated this case as if Pan Am were being prosecuted for criminally violating a federal statute and, relying on his erroneous interpretation of criminal law, precluded every attempt by Pan Am to demonstrate that it did not know or believe that the probable result of its conduct would be injury to the plaintiffs.

> Court: This whole thing starts at page 65 and it goes right on through to page 78 and it leads up to the very question we have been discussing now for days, namely, the FAA, the alleged FAA verbal authorization.
>
> I don't see what this has got to do with the price of beans, what his understanding of the ACSSP procedures are. He's not in court here. The regulations speak for themselves.
>
> I don't see what basis this comes in under anyplace.
>
> Shaughnessy: Your Honor, this is a willful misconduct case.
>
> Court: I know it's a willful misconduct case, but willful misconduct is not excused by Sonesen's version of an oral permission which is not admissible in the FAA. It is not admissible. And that's all this is.
>
> * * *
>
> Court: Whether it be offered for the purpose of authority or willfulness or anything else, it is out.
>
> * * *
>
> Court: It just doesn't make any sense to me that anybody in his right mind would rely—would, in fact did rely on any such permission. It just didn't exist.
>
> * * *
>
> Shaughnessy: So I take it that all of the conversations among these people are out?
>
> Court: Obviously they're not objecting to it, but I'm going to sustain those three questions that he's objected to and I'm going to—you might as well know now

that I'm going to sustain the questions and answer on page 78.

Shaughnessy: I understand, your Honor.

Court: And anything else that they object to in between I'm going to sustain because I think it's irrelevant.

The district judge even precluded Pan Am from showing that FAA officials inspected Pan Am's operations both before and after the bombing and made no complaints of irregularities. The district judge's ruling on this issue is illustrative of his mind-set.

The Court: I'm satisfied, Mr. Shaughnessy, this is another back-door method of getting Mr. Sonesen's unilateral interpretation of his authority to bury the FAA regulations before this jury. I don't like you doing it.

I think the next time you attempt to do it you should alert the Court that this is what you're attempting to do. I have ruled upon it.

Had you gotten this before the jury before alerting me and one had been asleep, I probably would have had to declare a mistrial. We're six weeks into this trial.

The law has been stated by me to be that based upon two Second Circuit decisions, both of which went to the Supreme Court and certiorari was denied, you have promised me that you were going to show me the law was otherwise. You haven't.

You may not do this. I don't know how I can make myself clearer.

Shaughnessy: All I wanted was to ask the witness—

Court: You attempted to get this FAA report in before this jury with, knowing that this man was operating under this assumption, that what they were doing was correct and was in direct violation of the FAA regulations, and he was doing it on the basis of this

> verbal authorization of Mr. Sonesen who said he had reached him.
>
> According to FAA officials, testified he didn't have, and the regulations themselves say he couldn't have, and you can't do it.
>
> You do it again and I'm going to have to take appropriate action.

FAA's policy in looking for violations of its regulations is well known:

> ... [W]hen we feel there is a serious violation or serious numbers of violations that requires significant deterrent effect, we have been forced to go out and scrape up every possible violation of the Regulations that is appropriate in order to compute these large penalties.
>
> Testimony of Clark Onstad, Chief Counsel, FAA before the Subcommittee on Aviation of the Committee on Public Works and Transportation, House of Representatives, 96th Cong., 2d Sess. July 1, 1980, Record of Hearing on H.R. 7488 at 38.

A threat of contempt for attempting to introduce evidence that FAA officials who, after personally inspecting Pan Am's operations found no fault with them, is pretty strong medicine. However, it illustrates once again that the district judge was fully aware of what Sonesen's testimony would have been. For further evidence of this knowledge, see the following excerpts from the record:

Court: As I understood, your position is somebody in the FAA, I don't know who, told Sonesen or somebody in Pan Am verbally once they had the X-ray machine they didn't have to physically search a couple of bags.

Shaughnessy: That's correct.

Court: That is your position.

Shaughnessy: I understand.

* * *

Court: Mr. Sonesen's testimony was, as I recall it, and it's right here before us, Sonesen's testimony was that I got this verbal permission from Salazar, we discussed it up and down the hierarchy which would include these discussions here right up to what's his name.

* * *

Court: Salazar had the authority, but there has been nothing produced in writing and Sonesen said he got it orally and he acted on it orally and he told all of these people that he had the authority from the FAA and it's irrelevant what he told people in the Pan American organization on this subject, because he didn't have the authority.

I regret that my colleagues, in their zeal to support the outcome of an obviously unfair trial, advance the fallacious argument that a formal proffer of Sonesen's testimony was essential.

My colleagues go equally astray in arguing that Pan Am waived its objection to the district judge's erroneous exclusion of evidence by refusing to accept the following offer of the district court made after two months of trial:

> On the so-called verbal authorization, I didn't think they would be able to come up with any cases. Of course, they haven't come up with any cases, which changes the law in this circuit.
>
> If they want me to give the jury an instruction to disregard the testimony that came in at the outset of the case before I understood what the issue was, I will be glad to give that instruction.
>
> But I rather suspect they don't want me to highlight it at this point. But if they want me to, I will be glad to tell them that they are to disregard any such conversations between Salizar [sic] and they are to draw no inference one way or the other from it because it is irrelevant to this case, and Sorenson [sic]. But it is not admissible.

This offer was an obvious, but inevitably unsuccessful, attempt by the district court to mitigate its earlier blunder. The district court knew that plaintiffs' expert witness, Rodney Wallis, had the pertinent portions of Salazar's testimony recorded on acetate, which

Wallis displayed to the jury during what Pan Am's counsel accurately described as Wallis's pre-summation summation. In the course of this lengthy summation, a questionable practice at best, Wallis made the following comments concerning Salazar's testimony:

> And the reason I selected these was because I talked of violation, and this was showing me what the violation was. And I picked that out because, as I say, to me, it pointed me in a direction. It indicated what was the requirement. This was saying to me what the rules were, what the requirement was ... that was the message that I was getting from the Salazar testimony.

The above-quoted testimony, which constituted a "positive assessment of the trustworthiness and accuracy" of Salazar's testimony, clearly should not have been admitted. However, it was admitted, and neither the district court nor plaintiffs' counsel suggested that the jury might be instructed to disregard it. This was understandable, of course, because of the important role that Salazar's testimony played in Wallis's opinion.

Moreover, the suggested instruction that the jury disregard "any such conversations between Salazar and they are to draw no inference one way or the other from it because it is irrelevant to this case," followed by the statement that Sonesen's testimony remains inadmissible, simply demonstrates the district court's misunderstanding of the law. An instruction to the jury that the conversation between Sonesen and Salazar was irrelevant and should be disregarded would deprive Pan Am of one of its major defenses, *i.e.*, its lack of willfulness based on that very conversation. The undeniable fact is that the subjective proof of Sonesen's understanding was highly relevant, and Pan Am's counsel would have been foolish to stipulate otherwise. Pan Am's counsel's refusal to leap at the court's suggestion demonstrates that he had a better understanding of the applicable law than the district court or my colleagues have demonstrated.

Time and again, Pan Am's counsel explained his position to the district court, all to no avail:

> The meetings that are referred to there, testimony of Mr. Sonesen, I don't know whether Mr. Baumeister is going to read any of his deposition, was that there was a discussion at that meeting and that at that meeting Mr. Salazar said specifically that in connection with ICAO 514 and London Heathrow Airport in particular, that X-ray was a suitable alternative to the bag match.

> Now this is a willful misconduct case, your Honor, in which Mr. Sonesen, the plaintiffs are claiming they willfully disregarded this provision, 15C1(a). If the jury believes Mr. Salazar that in fact the discussion was limited to ICAO 514, they still could believe that Mr. Sonesen, based on the meeting and what was discussed, could have believed, legitimately believed, that X-ray was a suitable alternative and that Mr. Salazar had said that.
> This is a willful case, your Honor.

The district judge never budged from his misunderstanding of the law:

Court: The proposition before us is that Sonesen says—Sonesen not being Pan Am corporation, about whom we are talking, but only an employee of Pan Am. Sonesen says he got verbal permission from Salazar. The cases are quite clear, that that is inadmissible under the issue of lawfulness or otherwise, and I have never seen anything at the moment, recently, that casts any doubt on it.

* * *

Court: Ever heard the expression, an individual may not bind the government?

Coddington: Ever heard the expression that an individual may not bind the government? Yes, I have.

Court: The government enacted a regulation or promulgated a regulation, I may not take off my robe, I may not work until executive capacity authorizes to make that. United States against Sorenson [sic] regulates, while on this subject, said: Whoever had the authorization from the DIA and C.I.A. to smuggle guns to Russia, and so forth and so on, and the Second. Circuit upheld, may not do that verbally. That's the law.

This theory of yours, if you have verbal authorization from somebody to violate a regulation, I will have to charge the jury that an individual may not do that.

Coddington: Well, certainly I'm happy to brief that.

Court: Brief it all you want, because I sweated blood over this issue, because this was really quite serious. This was the business of taking armaments from this country and swapping it over from Russia, all on the okay of D.I.A. and C.I.A., and I wouldn't let them put that defense before the jury, and the Second. Circuit said I was right. I went through a tremendous amount of research and wrote an opinion on this, and it was published, United States versus Schwartz. You may not as an individual authorize somebody to do something against the regulation, whether you are high-ranking. I don't think the President may do it. I didn't have to decide.

* * *

Court: In any event, nobody approved this in writing. So the whole defense is a non-entity.

I know you don't want to get rid of it from your mind, but there it is. If you want to stop the trial and mandamus me to the Second Circuit and have your ears pinned back, fine.

But that's it, that's the ruling, you've got to live with it. You've got to stop trying to sneak it in through the back door or I'm going to have to take appropriate action.

* * *

Court: You might have some validity to it if—if there was any kind of an acknowledgment from Salazar that he—that he had any such conversation, but he emphatically denies it.

Everybody says it is not within anybody's power to give it or—and the regulation itself says you've got to have any modification in writing.

It just doesn't make any sense to me that anybody in his right mind would rely—would, in fact did rely on any such permission. It just didn't exist.

The cases of *United States v. Duggan* (2d Cir. 1984), *United States v. Schwartz* (2d Cir. 1991), and *United States v. Berg* (E.D.N.Y. 1987) so heavily relied upon by the district court and my colleagues, do not support their interpretation of the applicable law. Those cases involved alleged violations of criminal statutes, not the tort issue of whether the defendant willfully placed the decedents in a position of danger. Moreover, as we stated in *Duggan*, "[t]here is an exception [to the mistake of law rule] for legitimate reliance on an official interpretation of law. Finding in *Duggan* that the defendants had not received an "official interpretation of the law" we held that the defense of mistake of law was not available to them. We returned to that theme in *United States v. Schwartz*, *supra*, where we said, "Since *Schwartz* had no authority to authorize the crimes charged against them, Berg and Lisbona may not claim reliance on whatever account he might have given them." The authority of Raymond Salazar, Director of FAA Office of Civil Aviation Security, to interpret regulations which he and his staff had promulgated cannot be disputed.

* * *

We would be blinking reality if we did not hold that the district judge's erroneous rulings were prejudicial. Indeed, as disclosed by the following excerpt from the argument on appeal, plaintiffs' counsel admitted as much:

Judge Van Graafeiland:	Let me ask you this, Mr. Kreindler: If I read the record, I listen to your argument and I read the record, and I decide that Judge Platt said I'm not going to hear from Mr. Sonesen no matter what, would you concede that that is very prejudicial error in this case?
Mr. Kreindler:	Under those circumstances, yes. But that's not what happened. That's—
Judge Van Graafeiland:	I'm not asking you that. I'm asking you if I read this record and I decide that that is what happened—leave this offer of proof business out—if I decide that Judge Platt just simply said, I'm not going to hear Mr. Sonesen, that would be prejudicial error; wouldn't it, in this case?
Mr. Kreindler:	Your Honor, even—

Judge Van Graafeiland:	Counsel, wouldn't it be prejudicial error?
Mr. Kreindler:	Of course, if the judge were hearing—
Judge Van Graafeiland:	Of course, it would. Then we have got the issue: did he refuse to hear him, or didn't he?
Mr. Kreindler:	No.
Judge Van Graafeiland:	All right, that's the issue. I'll read the record very carefully, Mr. Kreindler.

Moreover, the district judge himself recognized the crucial importance of Sonesen's testimony when he said, "You're in trouble if this is your defense."

No one, I suggest, can dispute the proposition that even-handedness is the *sine qua non* of a fair trial. A trial is not a "game of blindman's buff." *United States v. Procter & Gamble Co.* (1958). It is a "search for the truth." 8 WRIGHT & MILLER, FEDERAL PRACTICE AND PROCEDURE § 2001, at 14. That search will succeed only if the trial court recognizes the right of each party to present its evidence and to rebut that of its opponent, a right that "is a fundamental element of due process of law." It is a rule as old as the proverbial hills that when a party opens a subject in its case in chief, its opponent is entitled to offer evidence on the same subject, *i.e.*, to explain, repel, counteract or disprove the evidence that the party introduced.

Even my colleagues concede that the district court erred in excluding evidence of British Airway regulations which, in the face of bombings by Irish terrorist organizations, permitted Pan Am and other carriers to X-ray unaccompanied baggage at Heathrow Airport. I regret that in my colleagues' apparent eagerness to affirm, they hold this error to be harmless. It was not harmless. It went squarely to a crucial issue in the case, *i.e.*, whether Pan Am knew that its use of X-ray screening probably would result in injury.

Evidence that, shortly after the Lockerbie accident the FAA amended its regulations so as to clarify the permissible use of X-ray screening, also went squarely to the issue of whether Pan Am should have anticipated danger in its pre-amendment use of X-rays. The district court's refusal to permit the jury to receive this evidence exacerbated all of the court's similar rulings that pervaded the trial. In short, it was another indication that the district court misunderstood the law. The issue was not whether Pan Am violated the regulation; it was whether Pan Am used X-ray screening with knowledge that its use would probably result in injury or in reckless disregard of the probable consequences.

DAMAGES

In my dissent to the original majority opinion, I expressed concern over my colleagues' handling of the question of damages. However, since my colleagues now agree that the cases must be returned to the district court for retrial on the issue of damages for loss of society and parental care, I will not repeat what I have already said.

CONCLUSION

Whenever, as here, an appellate court affirms a judgment based on opinion and conjecture, it faces the nagging possibility that someday the truth will out and prove the conjecture wrong. If the erroneous judgment was the culmination of a fair trial, the appellate court, although unhappy with its role in the error, need have no feeling of guilt or remorse. This would not be true if the errors below either were ignored or termed "harmless." Needless to say, I do not want someday to find myself in the latter unhappy situation.

If all of the irrelevant and prejudicial evidence dealing with such matters as television commercials and the private lives of Pan Am employees, together with the colloquies of court and counsel arising out of the district court's "425" erroneous rulings, were eliminated from this case, it could be retried in several weeks. My colleagues now agree that the case must be retried in part on the issue of damages. Particularly in view of the fact that the outcome in over two hundred claims hinges upon the judgment in the instant case, justice demands that the matter be remanded in its entirety so that it can be tried fairly. Except for the remand to the district court on the damages issue, I dissent.

STANFORD v. KUWAIT AIRWAYS CORP.

89 F.3d 117 (2d Cir. 1996)

McLAUGHLIN, Circuit Judge.

Four terrorists boarded Middle Eastern Airlines ("MEA") flight 426 in Beirut, Lebanon. The flight ended in Dubai, United Arab Emirates where the four terrorists disembarked, and connected with Kuwait Airways flight KU221, bound for Karachi, Pakistan. Three American diplomats, William Stanford, Charles Hegna, and Charles Kapar were also on board KU221. Shortly after take-off from Dubai, the terrorists hijacked KU221, forcing the pilot to turn north. The plane landed in Tehran, Iran and sat on the airport tarmac for days while the terrorists tortured the three American diplomats, finally murdering Hegna and Stanford.

Plaintiffs, Charles Kapar and the estates of the two deceased diplomats, brought this suit alleging that MEA's negligence was a proximate cause of the injuries and deaths occurring aboard KU221. After a jury trial in the United States District Court for the

Southern District of New York, the jury deadlocked, and the court declared a mistrial. MEA then filed a motion for judgment as a matter of law, arguing that MEA owed no duty to the three diplomats, and that MEA's actions (in Beirut) were not a proximate cause of the injuries and deaths aboard KU221 (in Tehran). The court granted MEA's motion.

Plaintiffs appeal, arguing that MEA owed them a duty to use due care to avoid the known risk of hijacking, MEA breached that duty by failing to screen passengers adequately in Beirut, and this breach was a proximate cause of their injuries. We reverse and remand for a new trial.

BACKGROUND

In the Fall of 1983, the Da'Wa, a group of Shiite extremists, was imprisoned in Kuwait for deadly attacks on the United States and French embassies in Beirut. A year later, the Shiite Muslim group Hezbollah, an Islamic terror organization based in Beirut, increased its violent opposition to the incarceration of the Da'Wa prisoners. With the first suicide car bombing of the American embassy in Beirut in 1983, Hezbollah embarked on large scale terrorist activities, kidnapping American journalists, diplomats and academics, and murdering scores of people in suicide car bombings. This Shiite Muslim terror group threatened continued attacks on Kuwaiti, French, and American citizens unless the Da'Wa prisoners were released.

In May, 1983, the International Air Transport Association ("IATA") held its 21st Security Advisory Committee meeting in Montreal, Canada to discuss security measures among member airlines. IATA, of which MEA is a member, is "a private organization of domestic and foreign air carriers engaged in scheduled international air transportation. One of IATA's major purposes set out in its Articles of Association is 'to provide means for collaboration among the air transport enterprises engaged directly or indirectly in international air transport services.'" *Stanford v. Kuwait Airways Corp.* (S.D.N.Y. 1986).

At this meeting, IATA discussed new techniques terror groups were using to circumvent airport security measures to infiltrate an airport or airline. The meeting discussed one particular method for terrorists to capitalize on the lax security at a "dirty" airport and board a plane bound for a more secure airport. Upon arrival at the more secure airport, the terrorists would transfer to a "target" airline and then hijack the target plane: "[T]he would be terrorist may well have traveled on the original Carrier without any intention of committing a terrorist act against that Carrier, but with the object of a transfer to another target Carrier." Minutes of the IATA 21st Security Advisory Committee Meeting, Montreal, May 4-5, 1983. IATA cautioned its members that "the only solution to this situation is to create circumstances where some degree of reliance can be placed on the security measures of other States."

MEA, Kuwait Airways, and other members of IATA, participated in a program of "interline" ticketing, a reciprocal arrangement whereby a single ticket written by one airline for a flight on that airline will also accommodate the same passenger's flight on a second airline with the revenues to be allocated *pro tanto* between the airlines. Passengers need only one ticket and one baggage check to travel on both airlines.

An MEA official admitted that he knew, in December 1984, that the security measures at Beirut airport were minimal. Specifically, MEA knew that X-ray machines for checking passengers' luggage were not operating and that metal detectors were apparently functioning but "locked" and not in use. In addition, MEA was aware or, in the exercise of reasonable prudence, should have been aware that many airlines had ceased all operations out of Beirut because of the threats of violence coming from Islamic militants in Beirut.

MEA maintained, however, that it was helpless to offer additional security measures because airport security was under the sole control of the Lebanese army. An MEA official testified that the military conducted searches of passengers and luggage by hand, but did not employ any more sophisticated forms of security screening. He also testified that MEA never asked the Lebanese military to strengthen the security measures at the Beirut airport.

MEA's employees at the Beirut airport were responsible for selling and examining passengers' tickets, checking the information on the tickets against visas and passports, and receiving baggage from the passengers. These employees were the first line of defense between hijackers who slipped through the ludicrous security at Beirut Airport and innocent passengers aboard MEA and connecting flights. Nevertheless, they did not perform any other searches, known as "secondary screening," of passengers or their bags. Also in place was a communications network within MEA, allowing MEA employees to relay information between its stations in Beirut and Dubai. There is no evidence, however, that MEA ever used this information network to contact its agents in Dubai to have them relay information to other IATA members about suspicious passengers; and its employees certainly did not do so in this case.

On December 2, 1984, in the eye of the political hurricane roaring through the Middle East, four Hezbollah hijackers purchased interline tickets for travel from Beirut to Bangkok, Thailand, via Dubai and Karachi. They began their journey by presenting their interline tickets to the MEA agents at the Beirut airport, where they boarded MEA flight 426 to Dubai.

The hijackers' tickets had a stench about them. They had been purchased on very short notice with cash, and the flight traced an outlandish route: the passengers were to fly on MEA from Beirut to Dubai, where they were then to connect with Kuwait Airways to Karachi, and from there continue on to Bangkok. This itinerary was bizarre because: (1) there were regularly scheduled direct flights between Beirut and Bangkok; (2) the four terrorists were the only passengers aboard MEA 426 to connect with a Kuwaiti airline—every other passenger aboard who happened to be traveling to Karachi connected in Dubai with a Pakistani International Airlines flight; and (3) there was another scheduled MEA flight from Beirut directly to Karachi on December 4th, a day after the hijackers' actual departure. If the hijackers had waited for this next flight, they would have avoided (a) the stop at Dubai, and (b) an unnecessary twenty-hour layover in Karachi while waiting for the same December 4th plane that would eventually take them to Bangkok. Still another suspicious feature of the journey was that the men were traveling one-way, a very long distance, without any checked baggage. None of this apparently raised the eyebrow of any MEA employee.

Upon arrival in Dubai, the hijackers alighted MEA flight 426 and headed for their target: Kuwait Airways flight KU221. KU221 had originated in Kuwait City, bound for Karachi with a fateful stop in Dubai. It carried William Stanford, Charles Hegna and Charles Kapar. The three were employed by the United States Department of State, Agency for International Development, and were en route from Kuwait City to their base of operations in Karachi. KU221 stopped in Dubai to refuel and to pick up additional passengers heading for Karachi. Passengers connecting to KU221 from other flights were required to take a bus on the tarmac to KU221 and climb a set of stairs to enter the jet through the forward door of the plane.

A Kuwait Airlines official placed a table at the top of the stairs leading to the forward door of flight KU221, where he checked connecting passengers' carry-on luggage as they boarded. One witness, Neil Beeston, testified that he saw three of the four hijackers standing on the tarmac near the unguarded—and not in use—rear stairs of the airplane during the boarding process. Other testimony established that the tarmac, in general, was poorly lit and not well guarded.

Once KU221 was airborne, and over the Gulf of Oman, two hijackers burst into the cockpit, pressed a grenade against the flight commander's neck and ordered him to fly the plane to Mehrabad Airport in Tehran. The flight crew complied, landing in Tehran in the early morning of December 4th.

The four hijackers were armed with pistols, explosives, and other weapons. They released the women and children passengers, but singled out Hegna, Stanford, Kapar and a fourth American, John Costa, and forced them into the first-class cabin. Over the next six days the hijackers murdered Hegna and Stanford and beat and tortured Kapar and Costa, using them as pawns to gain the release of the Da'Wa prisoners in Kuwait. Iranian commandos raided the aircraft on December 9th, rescued the remaining passengers, and captured the hijackers.

No one knows how the hijackers got their weapons on board flight KU221. There was no direct evidence that they had weapons in their possession on board MEA flight 426 or, later, when they boarded flight KU221. On the other hand, there was also no evidence that the weapons were already on board flight KU221 when the hijackers boarded. Plaintiffs showed that no weapons were found when KU221 was routinely cleaned at Dubai, that no passengers disembarked while the plane waited for about an hour on the tarmac at Dubai, and that all panels in the plane remained undisturbed. In addition, there was evidence that it was a common practice in the Middle East to allow one passenger to check in for a number of other passengers, thus allowing armed passengers to avoid contact with airline officials.

Plaintiffs brought this action against MEA, IATA, Kuwait Airways, Pan American World Airways, and Northwest Airlines. The claims against Kuwait Airways, Pan Am, and Northwest have been dismissed. The parties stipulated to the dismissal of claims against IATA.

The case against MEA went to trial but the jury was unable to reach a verdict. The court declared a mistrial. Later, MEA moved for judgment as a matter of law under Rule 50(b) of the Federal Rules of Civil Procedure, and the court granted the motion. The court reasoned that: (1) there was insufficient evidence for the jury to conclude that MEA owed plaintiffs a duty of care to avoid the risk of hijacking on another airline; (2) MEA's inaction was not a proximate cause of any of the injuries; and (3) the failure of (a) security at the Dubai airport and (b) Kuwait Airways's secondary screening measures were independent intervening acts breaking the causal chain that might have linked MEA's actions to the injury and deaths aboard flight KU221.

Plaintiffs appeal arguing that: (1) MEA had a duty to use due care to avoid the risk of hijacking within the interline system; (2) there was sufficient evidence for a jury to conclude that the failure of MEA to use due care was a proximate cause of the injuries; and (3) the foreseeable negligence of (a) the security officials at Dubai and (b) Kuwait Airways were not intervening acts breaking the causal link between MEA and the injuries and deaths. We reverse and remand the proceedings to the district court for a new trial.

DISCUSSION

Negligence

A. Duty

It is elementary that to find a party liable in negligence, there must have been a duty—a relationship between the two parties such that society imposes an obligation on one to protect the other from an unreasonable risk of harm. The question here is: did the circumstances in this case create a duty on the part of MEA to protect Kapar, Hegna, and Stanford? We think they did, and hold, as a matter of law, that MEA had a duty to protect the plaintiffs from unreasonable risk of foreseeable harm.

Duty is a relative concept. Whether an individual must protect another from the unreasonable risk of foreseeable harm depends on the nature of the risk and the particular level of knowledge of the alleged tortfeasor. Thus, "[t]he duty which one person may owe in a particular situation for the protection of another person is measured by the exigencies of the occasion." STUART M. SPEISER, ET AL., 2 THE AMERICAN LAW OF TORTS, § 9:4, at 1011 (1985). The alleged tortfeasor "must exercise such attention ... of the circumstances ... [and] knowledge of other pertinent matters, intelligence, and judgment as a 'reasonable person' would have—and, such superior attention ... knowledge, intelligence, and judgment as the actor himself happens to possess." 2 THE AMERICAN LAW OF TORTS, § 9:4, at 1012.

In determining whether a duty exists, a court should examine: (1) the relationship between the parties; and (2) the reasonable foreseeability of harm to the person injured.

1. *Relationship between MEA and the Victims*

Although the plaintiffs were not passengers on an MEA flight, it is too late in the day to suggest that contractual privity is a prerequisite to the existence of a duty. Indeed, "[t]he duty of vigilance to prevent injury has its source in the law applicable to human relations rather than in a narrow conception of privity." 57A AM. JUR. 2d *Negligence* § 93 (1989). Thus, even without contractual privity,

> [w]henever one person is by circumstances placed in such a position with regard to another that every one of ordinary sense who did think would at once recognize that if he did not use ordinary care and skill in his own conduct with regard to the circumstances he would cause danger of injury to the person or property of the other, a duty arises to use ordinary care and skill to avoid such danger.

Stagl v. Delta Airlines, Inc. (2d Cir. 1995).

Plaintiffs demonstrated that MEA joined an enterprise with interline airlines, including Kuwait Airways, to facilitate travel among the cooperating carriers. MEA's participation in interline arrangements with other IATA airlines was a lucrative venture. It expanded the reach of their routes, and facilitated inter-airline travel. Interline carriers shared the profits resulting from this cooperative endeavor.

In addition, based on evidence produced at trial, a jury could properly find that: as early as May, 1983, the Security Advisory Committee of IATA issued a warning that terrorists would board airlines at airports with poor security, and transfer to target airlines at other airports with tighter security. *See* Minutes of the IATA 21st Security Advisory Committee Meeting, Montreal, May 4-5, 1983. While it is unclear from the record to whom IATA issued the warning, MEA, as a member of IATA, knew or, in the exercise of reasonable care should have known, of the warning. In addition, MEA was fully aware of the poor security measures at the Beirut airport. MEA's Assistant Vice President at the Beirut station testified that he knew that the Lebanese military had, but did not use, metal detectors, that X-ray equipment was unavailable, and that security checks consisted only of personal searches over which MEA exercised no control.

IATA concluded that a critical way to protect passengers aboard target flights was to place increased reliance on security measures directed toward passengers upon their initial entry into the interline system. Thus, IATA implicitly recognized the principle that "[d]uty is largely grounded in the natural responsibilities of societal living and human relations, such as have the recognition of reasonable men." Accordingly, a jury could reasonably find that when MEA accepted interline passengers aboard its planes in Beirut, it knew or should have known that there was a danger that terrorists would try to board their airline only to transfer later to a vulnerable, interline target airplane. MEA operated out of Beirut airport, amidst heightened political tensions, an ongoing terrorist campaign that posed continuing threats against American and Kuwaiti citizens and establishments, and lax airport security. In addition, MEA was armed with information regarding unique terrorist hijacking tactics. Accepting interline passengers, while perhaps not normally a function implicating the safety of third parties, became such a function under the perilous circumstances existent at that time in Beirut.

If MEA, in the exercise of ordinary care, should have recognized that under these circumstances, knowing what it knew, there was an unreasonable risk of hijacking to passengers aboard its flight and other connecting flights, then the jury could find that MEA should have implemented secondary screening measures or warned other interline members of a possible threat of hijacking.

MEA argued that it could not put secondary screening measures in place because security was under the sole control of the Lebanese military. The district court concluded that plaintiffs failed to adduce proof that MEA could have conducted secondary screening procedures. This was an erroneous allocation of the burden of proof. It is not incumbent upon the plaintiff to disprove every possible defense to a negligence theory. If MEA's contention was that it had no duty because it was barred by the Lebanese military from instituting secondary screening procedures in Beirut, it was MEA's responsibility to prove this, not the plaintiffs' responsibility to disprove it. In any event, even if MEA's hands were tied by the Lebanese military, precluding secondary screening measures, nothing prevented MEA officials in Beirut from contacting connecting airlines to warn them of the danger of hijacking.

2. *The Reasonable Foreseeability of Harm to the Persons Injured*

In determining the existence of a duty, a court may examine the reasonable foreseeability of harm to the party injured. MEA argues that this erroneously conflates the concepts of duty and foreseeability. What MEA fails to recognize, however, is that there are two concepts of foreseeability, the one specific, the other general. The first concerns the foreseeability of the specific injury the plaintiff suffered, and focuses on whether the defendant's actions are a proximate cause of the harm. The second, and the one at issue here, concerns the general foreseeable risk which is crucial to determining the existence of a duty and helps to limit its scope.

In the second, or risk-defining sense, Judge Cardozo early recognized, "[t]he risk reasonably to be perceived defines the duty to be obeyed, and risk imports relation; it is risk to another or to others within the range of apprehension." *Palsgraf v. Long Island R.R. Co.* (N.Y. 1928). Hence,

> [t]he duty element of negligence focuses on whether the defendant's conduct foreseeably created a broader "zone of risk" that poses a general threat of harm to others ... The proximate causation element, on the other hand, is concerned with whether and to what extent the defendant's conduct foreseeably and substantially caused the specific injury that actually occurred ... As to duty, the proper inquiry for the reviewing appellate court is whether the defendant's conduct created a foreseeable zone of risk, not whether the defendant could foresee the specific injury that actually occurred.

McCain v. Florida Power Corp. (Fla. 1992).

There was evidence that MEA knew: (1) of the threatened attacks by Hezbollah terrorists; (2) that terrorists were boarding flights in dirty airports to infiltrate other airlines; (3) that the Beirut airport had extraordinarily poor security; and (4) that the four hijackers who boarded in Beirut had tickets which teemed with suspicion. A jury could reasonably find, under these circumstances, that if MEA did nothing, it would create a zone of risk that stretched at least as far as the innocent passengers aboard flights with which the four hijackers would eventually connect. It lay well within ordinary prudence for an airline to realize that persons at the dirty Beirut airport who purchased tickets on short notice with cash, checked no luggage for a flight from the Middle East to the Far East, and took a circuitous route aboard flights which (a) they did not have to take to reach their destination, (b) created inordinate delays and layovers, and (c) no other passenger aboard MEA flight 426 took, posed a hijacking threat.

In sum, the duty is dictated and measured by the exigencies of the situation, and the risk reasonably to be perceived defines the duty to be obeyed. We conclude that MEA, as a first leg interline carrier, had a duty to protect passengers on other interline connecting flights from unreasonable risk of harm through the use of reasonable precautions in the face of reasonably foreseeable risks. MEA was faced with a set of circumstances that a jury could reasonably find created a foreseeable risk, necessitating some action to protect others from an unreasonable threat of hijacking.

B. Breach

On the evidence presented a jury could reasonably find that MEA failed to take reasonable precautions in the face of foreseeable risks. This question should be left for the jury to decide on retrial.

C. Proximate Cause

The district court held that plaintiffs failed to prove that MEA's inaction was a proximate cause of the deaths of Hegna and Stanford, and the injuries sustained by Kapar. The court reasoned that: (1) there was no evidence of what the Lebanese military could have done if MEA had alerted them to the four suspicious men; (2) the evidence showed only that the weaponry emerged on board the Kuwait Airways plane, leaving open the possibility that the hijackers procured their weapons in Dubai; and (3) even if a causal link were established, the negligence of the Kuwait Airways employees and the Dubai airport security officials were intervening acts, breaking the chain of causation between MEA and the resultant harm.

We disagree with this analysis. Plaintiffs made at least a *prima facie* showing of causation, and this record does not present such an overwhelming amount of evidence that fair minded jurors "could not arrive at a verdict against [MEA]." Considering the evidence in the light most favorable to plaintiffs, and resolving all inferences that a jury might draw in their favor, it cannot be said that no rational juror could find in plaintiffs' favor.

The district court concluded that plaintiffs failed to establish proximate cause, in part, because "there [was] no evidence of what, if anything, the army would have done" if alerted by the MEA ticket agents of the threat posed by the four hijackers. We disagree.

First, as a practical matter, warning the Lebanese military was not the only option open to MEA. Even assuming that the Lebanese military, after receiving a warning of the possible threat, would do nothing, plaintiffs contend that MEA could have warned the connecting airlines on which MEA knew the hijackers had reservations. Consequently, the fact that there was no evidence of what, if anything, the military would have done, is not determinative. Second, the district court impermissibly substituted its judgment for that of the jury. We cannot say that the district court's doubts regarding the possible lack of concern of the Lebanese military amounts to such overwhelming evidence in favor of MEA that reasonable and fair-minded jurors would have to conclude that there was no causal link between MEA's inaction and the resultant injuries and deaths. The district court also noted that, even if MEA employees or the Lebanese military conducted a search, there was no evidence that they would have found the weapons used in the hijacking of KU221. The court concluded that it was possible that the hijackers did not get their weapons until they reached Dubai. Again, this is a case where reasonable minds can differ. The plaintiffs presented testimony and circumstantial evidence from which a reasonable person could infer that MEA's failure to act proximately caused Kapar's injuries and the deaths of Stanford and Hegna.

First, the plaintiffs offered the testimony of Neil Beeston, an engineer at Kuwait Airways and passenger aboard flight KU221, who witnessed three of the hijackers trying to use the unguarded rear stairs of the Kuwait Airways jet during the boarding process. Plaintiffs showed that it was common in the Middle East to allow one passenger to check in for several others, thus allowing armed cohorts to avoid detection. Also, the Kuwait Airways jet was cleaned at Dubai and no passengers were allowed to leave the aircraft. Furthermore, no passenger had access to any area of the plane, other than the toilets and overhead bins, where one could stash weapons. Plaintiffs showed that there was no evidence of tampering with any of the panels in the aircraft bathrooms. Finally, there was an IATA warning describing the *modus operandi* of some armed terrorists, who board airlines at dirty airports.

From this evidence a reasonable juror could conclude that the terrorists had the weapons in their possession at the very beginning of their journey in Beirut. One could reasonably conclude that the hijackers boarded the MEA flight armed (consistent with the *modus operandi* outlined in the IATA circular) and, once in Dubai, one "clean" hijacker checked in for the other three who attempted to bypass the Kuwait Airways official at the forward door by entering the rear stairwell. One could infer from the facts that (1) the cleaning crew discovered nothing, (2) no one left the plane, and (3) the plane's panels were not disturbed, that the weapons were not already aboard KU221 when it arrived in Dubai.

Plaintiffs were not required to prove causation beyond a reasonable doubt. It was sufficient to present evidence "from which reasonable persons may conclude that it [was] more probable that [the hijacking] was caused by [MEA] than that it was not." PROSSER AND KEATON, § 41, at 269. While reasonable minds could differ on this evidence, there is not such a dearth of proof on the issue of causation as to justify taking the matter away from the jury.

Finally, the district court concluded that plaintiffs failed to establish a proximate link between MEA and the injuries and deaths aboard flight KU221, because the negligence of the security officials and of the Kuwait Airways employees in Dubai were independent intervening acts breaking the causative chain. Again, we must disagree. The causative link is not broken by the negligent conduct of a third person when such conduct is normal or foreseeable under the circumstances. Questions regarding what is normal or foreseeable, like other questions of proximate cause, are generally issues for the trier of fact. Here, the evidence at trial, bathed in a light most favorable to plaintiffs, was sufficient to carry to the jury the issue of foreseeability of third party negligence. There was evidence that the airport at Dubai had poor tarmac security. Also, MEA had notice, from the IATA warning issued in May, 1983, that there were differing standards of security in airports across the Middle East, and that even those airports engaging in security measures were potentially lax due to the "delays in facilitation and escalating security costs ... [and the difficulty in meeting] the manning requirements for sufficient, trained personnel to operate a gate search system." Minutes of the IATA 21st Security Advisory Committee Meeting, Montreal, May 4-5, 1983.

Although it is arguable whether it was "foreseeable" that security measures would be insufficient in Dubai to respond to the heightened threat, such matters are properly left to the trier of fact. There was enough evidence to allow the jury to decide whether the actions of the Kuwait Airways employees and security officials in Dubai were "closely and reasonably associated with the immediate consequences of the defendant's act, and form a normal part of its aftermath ..." PROSSER & KEETON § 44, at 307. Just as a tortfeasor who negligently breaks a victim's leg must reasonably anticipate negligence on the part of the doctor setting that leg, so too an airline which does nothing to prevent potential hijackers from traveling aboard its aircraft may reasonably have to anticipate that other airlines will be lax in their security measures.

CONCLUSION

We recognize, as the district court did, that this is an "anguishingly distressing case." And we concede it is a close call. We conclude, however, that MEA was not so far removed from the actions aboard the ill-fated Kuwait Airways flight as to be entitled to judgment as a matter of law. MEA took on responsibilities in the clouded atmosphere of threatened terrorist attacks, with knowledge of terrorist hijacking tactics. With this awareness and knowledge it had a commensurate duty to protect those within a foreseeable scope of danger. Accordingly, we reverse the district court's grant of MEA's Rule 50(b) motion, and remand for a new trial.

ALEJANDRE v. REPUBLIC OF CUBA

996 F. Supp. 1239 (S.D. Fla. 1997)

JAMES LAWRENCE KING, District Judge.

I. INTRODUCTION

The government of Cuba, on February 24, 1996, in outrageous contempt for international law and basic human rights, murdered four human beings in international airspace over the Florida Straits. The victims were Brothers to the Rescue pilots, flying two civilian, unarmed planes on a routine humanitarian mission, searching for rafters in the waters between Cuba and the Florida Keys.

As the civilian planes flew over international waters, a Russian built MiG-29 of the Cuban Air Force, without warning, reason, or provocation, blasted the defenseless planes out of the sky with sophisticated air-to-air missiles in two separate attacks. The pilots and their aircraft disintegrated in the mid-air explosions following the impact of the missiles. The destruction was so complete that the four bodies were never recovered.

The personal representatives of three of the deceased instituted this action against the Republic of Cuba ("Cuba") and the Cuban Air Force to recover monetary damages for the killings. One of the victims was not a U.S. citizen and his family therefore could not join in the suit. This is the first lawsuit to rely on recent legislative enactments that strip foreign states of immunity for certain acts of terrorism. Neither Cuba nor the Cuban Air Force has defended this suit, asserting through a diplomatic note that this Court has no jurisdiction over Cuba or its political subdivisions. A default was thus entered against both Defendants on April 23, 1997 pursuant to Rule 55(a) of the Federal Rules of Civil Procedure. Because this is a lawsuit against a foreign state, however, the Court may not enter judgment by default. Rather, the claimants must establish their "claim or right to relief by evidence that is satisfactory to the Court." 28 U.S.C. § 1608(e) (1994).

The Congressional purpose behind this section was to protect foreign states from "unfounded default judgments rendered solely upon a procedural default." As detailed more fully below, the abundant evidence offered at trial more than satisfies the Court that Plaintiffs are entitled to relief. Moreover, it bears mention that Cuba's default has been willful, as evidenced by its diplomatic note rejecting this Court's jurisdiction, further bolstering the entry of a default judgment.

These three consolidated cases proceeded to trial on November 13, 14, and 20, 1997, on the issues of liability and damages. Because the Court finds that neither Cuba nor the Cuban Air Force is immune from suit for the killings, and because the facts amply prove both Defendants' liability and Plaintiffs' damages, the Court will enter judgment against Defendants.

II. FINDINGS OF FACT

At trial, Plaintiffs presented extensive testimonial and documentary evidence in support of their claims. Because Cuba has presented no defense, the Court will accept as true Plaintiffs' uncontroverted factual allegations.
The pertinent facts are as follows.

A. The Victims

Armando Alejandre was forty-five years old at the time of his death. Although born in Cuba, Alejandre made Miami, Florida his home at an early age and became a naturalized U.S. citizen. Alejandre served an active tour of duty for eight months in Vietnam, completed his college education at Florida International University, and worked as a consultant to the Metro-Dade Transit Authority at the time of his death. He is survived by his wife of twenty-one years, Marlene Alejandre, who serves as the Personal Representative of his estate, and his daughter Marlene, a college student. Both are Plaintiffs in this lawsuit.

Carlos Alberto Costa was born in the United States in 1966 and resided in Miami. He was only twenty-nine years old when the Cuban government ended his life. Always interested in aviation and hoping to someday oversee the operations of a major airport, Costa earned his bachelor's degree at Embry-Riddle Aeronautical University and worked as a Training Specialist for the Dade County Aviation Department. He is survived by his parents, Mirta Costa and Osvaldo Costa, and by his sister, Mirta Mendez, all of whom sue on his behalf.

Mario Mañuel De la Peña was also born in the United States and was a mere twenty-four years old at the time of his death. Working toward his goal of being an airline pilot, De la Peña was in his last semester at Embry-Riddle when he was killed. During that semester he had obtained a coveted and highly competitive internship with American Airlines. Embry-Riddle granted De la Peña a bachelor's degree in Professional Aeronautics posthumously. He is survived by a younger brother, Michael De La Peña, and his parents, Mario T. De la Peña and Miriam De la Peña, both of whom are Plaintiffs in this case.

B. The Shootdown

Alejandre, Costa, and De la Peña were all members of a Miami-based humanitarian organization known as Hermanos al Rescate, or Brothers to the Rescue. The organization's principal mission was to search the Florida Straits for rafters, Cuban refugees who had fled the island nation on precarious inner tubes or makeshift rafts, often perishing at sea. Brothers to the Rescue would locate the rafters and provide them with life-saving assistance by informing the U.S. Coast Guard of their location and condition.

On the morning of February 24, 1996, two of Brothers to the Rescue's civilian Cessna 337 aircraft departed from Opa Locka Airport in South Florida. (A third Brothers to the Rescue, Cessna 337 aircraft also departed on the mission. That plane returned safely to the United States.) Costa piloted one plane, accompanied by Pablo Morales, a Cuban national who had once been a rafter himself. De la Peña piloted the second plane, with Alejandre as his passenger. Before departing, the planes notified both Miami and Havana traffic controllers of their flight plans, which were to take them south of the 24th parallel. The 24th parallel, well north of Cuba's twelve-mile territorial sea, is the northernmost boundary of the Havana Flight Information Region. Commercial and civilian aircraft routinely fly in this area, and aviation practice requires that they notify Havana's traffic controllers when crossing south through the 24th parallel. Both Brothers to the Rescue planes complied with this custom by contacting Havana, identifying themselves, and stating their position and altitude.

While the two planes were still north of the 24th parallel, the Cuban Air Force launched two military aircraft, a MiG-29 and a MiG-23, operating under the control of Cuba's military ground station. The MiGs carried guns, close range missiles, bombs, and rockets and were piloted by members of the Cuban Air Force experienced in combat. Excerpts from radio communications between the MiG-29 and Havana Military Control detail what transpired next:

MiG-29: OK, the target is in sight; the target is in sight. It's a small aircraft. Copied, small aircraft in sight.

MiG-29: OK, we have it in sight, we have it in sight.

MiG-29: The target is in sight.

Military Control: Go ahead.

MiG-29: The target is in sight.

Military Control: Aircraft in sight.

MiG-29: Come again?

MiG-29: It's a small aircraft, a small aircraft.

MiG-29: It's white, white.

Military Control: Color and registration of the aircraft?

Military Control: Buddy.

MiG-29: Listen, the registration also?

Military Control: What kind and colour?

MiG-29: It's white and blue.

MiG-29: White and blue, at a low altitude, a small aircraft.

MiG-29: Give me some instructions.

MiG-29: Instructions!

MiG-29: Listen, authorize me ...

MiG-29: If we give it a pass, it will complicate things. We are going to give it a pass. Because some vessels are approaching there, I am going to give it a pass.

MiG-29	Talk, talk.
MiG-29:	I have it in lock-on, I have it in lock-on.
MiG-29:	We have it in lock-on. Give us authorization.
MiG-29:	It is a Cessna 337. That one. Give us authorization, damn it!
Military Control:	Fire.
MiG-29:	Give us authorization, damn it, we have it.
Military Control:	Authorized to destroy.
MiG-29:	I'm going to pass it.
Military Control:	Authorized to destroy.
MiG-29:	We already copied. We already copied.
Military Control:	Authorized to destroy.
MiG-29:	Understood, already received. Already received. Leave us alone for now.
Military Control:	Don't lose it.
MiG-29:	First launch.
MiG-29:	We hit him! Damn. We hit him! We hit him! We retired him!
MiG-29:	Wait to see where it fell.
MiG-29:	Come on in, come on in! Damn, we hit. F-----s!
MiG-29:	Mark the place where we took it out.
MiG-29:	We are over it. This one won't mess around anymore.
Military Control:	Congratulations to the two of you.
MiG-29:	Mark the spot.
MiG-29:	We're climbing and returning home.

Military Control:	Stand by there circling above.
MiG-29:	Over the target?
Military Control:	Correct.
MiG-29:	S-t, we did tell you, Buddy.
Military Control:	Correct, the target is marked.
MiG-29:	Go ahead.
Military Control:	OK, climb to 3200, 4000 meters above the destroyed target and maintain economical speed.
MiG-29:	Go ahead.
Military Control:	I need you to stand by ... there. What heading did the launch have?
MiG-29:	I have another aircraft in sight.
MiG-29:	We have another aircraft.
Military Control:	Follow it.
MiG-29:	Don't lose the other small aircraft.
MiG-29:	We have another aircraft in sight. It's in the area where (the first aircraft fell. It's in the area where it fell.
MiG-29:	We have the aircraft.
Military Control:	Stand by.
MiG-29:	Comrade, it's in the area of the event.
MiG-29:	Did you copy?
MiG-29:	OK, this aircraft is headed 90 degrees now.
MiG-29:	It's in the area of the event, where the target fell. They're going to have to authorize us.
MiG-29:	Hey, the SAR isn't needed. Nothing remains, nothing.

Military Control:	Correct, keep following the aircraft. You're going to stay above it.
MiG-29:	We're above it.
Military Control:	Correct …
MiG-29:	For what?
MiG-29:	Is the other authorized?
Military Control:	Correct.
MiG-29:	Great. Let's go Alberto.
MiG-29:	Understood; we are now going to destroy it.
Military Control:	Do you still have it in sight?
MiG-29:	We have it, we have it, we're working. Let us work.
MiG-29:	The other is destroyed; the other is destroyed. Fatherland or death, s—t! The other is down also.

The missiles disintegrated the Brothers to the Rescue planes, killing their occupants instantly and leaving almost no recoverable debris. Only a large oil slick marked the spot where the planes went down. The Cuban Air Force never notified or warned the civilian planes, never attempted other methods of interception, and never gave them the opportunity to land. The MiGs' first and only response was the intentional and malicious destruction of the Brothers to the Rescue planes and their four innocent occupants. Such behavior violated clearly established international norms requiring the exhaustion of all measures before resort to aggression against any aircraft and banning the use of force against civilian aircraft altogether.

These norms have been codified in various international instruments. *See, e.g.*, Convention on International Civil Aviation, Dec. 7, 1944, 61 Stat. 1180, 15 U.N.T.S. 295 (both the United States and Cuba are parties to the Convention). The proscription on using force against civilian planes attaches even if they penetrate foreign airspace. *See, e.g.*, Kay Hailbronner, *Freedom of the Air and the Convention on the Law of the Sea*, 77 AM. J. INT'L L. 490, 514 (1983) ("Even if an order to land is deliberately disregarded, a civil unarmed aircraft that intrudes into foreign airspace may not be fired upon."). Common sense dictates that the negligible threat civilian planes may pose does not justify the possible loss of life.

C. The International Reaction

The international community moved quickly and in unison to condemn the murders. The United Nations Security Council, the European Union, and the International Civil Aviation Organization ("ICAO") were among the many to issue statements deploring Cuba's excessive use of force. The French Ministry of Foreign Affairs stated that, "France regrets the use of such brutal methods which nothing can justify, regardless of the circumstances, toward aircraft presenting no threat to the safety of the population." Following an extensive investigation, the ICAO issued a report in June 1996 concluding that the planes were shot down over international waters. The ICAO also adopted a resolution reaffirming the prohibition of the use of weapons against civilian aircraft in flight and declaring such practices incompatible with elementary considerations of humanity and the dictates of customary international law.

The shootdown elicited a similar reaction from the United States and even precipitated the enactment of the Cuban Liberty and Democratic Solidarity ("LIBERTAD") Act of 1996, 22 U.S.C. §§ 6021-6091 (1997), which includes an entire section devoted to a condemnation of the Cuban attack. Among other findings, Congress characterized the shootdown as wholly disproportionate: "The response chosen by Fidel Castro, the use of lethal force, was completely inappropriate to the situation presented to the Cuban Government, making such actions a blatant and barbaric violation of international law and tantamount to cold-blooded murder." Finally, Congress concluded: "The Congress strongly condemns the act of terrorism by the Castro regime in shooting down the Brothers to the Rescue aircraft on February 24, 1996."

III. CONCLUSIONS OF LAW

A. Jurisdiction and Liability

District courts have original jurisdiction to hear suits, not barred by foreign sovereign immunity, that are brought against foreign states.

Under the Foreign Sovereign Immunities Act of 1976 ("FSIA"), 28 U.S.C. §§ 1602-1611, a federal court lacks subject matter jurisdiction to hear a claim against a foreign state unless the claim falls within one of the FSIA's enumerated exceptions. For example, if a foreign state commits a tortious act or engages in commercial activities in the United States, it may fall into one of the FSIA's exceptions and be stripped of immunity from suit in U.S. courts.

Most recently, Congress crafted an additional, narrow exception to foreign sovereign immunity through the Anti-Terrorism and Effective Death Penalty Act of 1996 ("AEDPA"), Pub. L. No. 104-132, § 221. AEDPA amended the FSIA to allow suits in U.S. courts against a foreign state that engages in acts of terrorism under certain specified circumstances. As a result, the FSIA now provides that a foreign state shall not be immune from the jurisdiction of U.S. courts in any case

> in which money damages are sought against a foreign state for personal injury or death that was caused by an act of torture, extrajudicial killing, aircraft sabotage, hostage taking, or the provision of material support or resources ... for such an act if such act or provision of material support is engaged in by an official, employee, or agent of such foreign state while acting within the scope of his or her office, employment, or agency.

In addition, section 1605(a)(7) imposes the following requirements: (1) the U.S. must have designated the foreign state as a state sponsor of terrorism pursuant to section 6(j) of the Export Administration Act of 1979; (2) the act must have occurred outside the foreign state; and (3) the claimants and victims must have been U.S. nationals at the time the acts occurred.

The record of this trial clearly establishes that all of these requirements have been met. First, the unprovoked firing of deadly rockets at defenseless, unarmed civilian aircraft undoubtedly comes within the statute's meaning of "extrajudicial killing." That term is defined in reference to its use in the Torture Victim Protection Act of 1991 ("TVPA"), which states that "the term 'extrajudicial killing' means a deliberated killing not authorized by a previous judgment pronounced by a regularly constituted court affording all the judicial guarantees which are recognized as indispensable by civilized peoples." 28 U.S.C. § 1350.

Cuba's actions in this case easily come within this definition. The occupants of the two civilian, unarmed planes received no warning whatsoever of their imminent destruction, much less the judicial process contemplated by the TVPA. *See Lafontant v. Aristide* (E.D.N.Y. 1994) (finding that assassination of political opponent fell within statute's definition of extrajudicial killing).

Second, the Cuban Air Force was acting as an agent of Cuba when it committed the killings. The Cuban Air Force is clearly an agent of the Cuban state, as it acts on Cuba's behalf and subject to Cuba's control. The evidence adduced at trial demonstrated how the pilots of the Cuban MiGs obtained authorization from state officials prior to the shootdown of each plane and hearty congratulations from those officials after the planes were destroyed.

Third, section 1605(a)(7)'s requirement that the foreign state have been designated as a state sponsor of terrorism has also been satisfied. Cuba was one of only seven states so designated at the time pursuant to the authority of the Export Administration Act of 1979.

Fourth, the act occurred outside of Cuban territory. Plaintiffs have presented undisputed and competent evidence that the planes were shot down over international waters. As discussed above, the ICAO Report concluded that the planes were over international waters when they were destroyed. Congress reached the same conclusion, finding that the first plane was "18 miles from the Cuban coast" when it was shot down, and that the second plane was "30.5 miles from the Cuban coast" when it was fired upon. These numbers place the planes well outside the twelve-mile territorial sea claimed by Cuba and permitted under international law. In addition, evidence from the crew and passengers on a nearby cruise ship, the Majesty of the Seas, and private fishing vessel, the Triliner, established beyond any doubt that the civilian aircraft were flying in international air space toward Florida (and away from Cuba) when the Defendants committed this brutal act of terrorism.

Finally, Plaintiffs and three of the four murdered pilots were U.S. citizens at the time of the shootdown. De la Peña and Costa were born in the United States, and Alejandre was a naturalized U.S. citizen. Plaintiffs were also U.S. citizens when the incident took place. Consequently, the facts of this case fall squarely within the requirements of section 1605(a)(7). Indeed, this is precisely the type of action for which Congress meant to provide redress by stripping terrorist states of immunity from the judgment of U.S. courts.

Having established an exception to foreign sovereign immunity, Plaintiffs base their substantive cause of action on a different statute, also enacted in 1996, entitled Civil Liability for Acts of State Sponsored Terrorism ("Civil Liability Act"). The Civil Liability Act creates a cause of action against agents of a foreign state that act under the conditions specified in FSIA section 1605(a)(7). It thus serves as an enforcement provision for acts described in section 1605(a)(7). If Plaintiffs prove an agent's liability under this Act, the foreign state employing the agent would also incur liability under the theory of *respondeat superior*.

Because, as detailed above, Plaintiffs have presented compelling evidence that all of the relevant statutory requirements have been met, the Court finds that both the Cuban Air Force and Cuba are liable for the murders of Alejandre, Costa, and De la Peña.

B. Damages

The amount of damages that Plaintiffs may recover in this case is specified in the Civil Liability Act. It provides that an agent of a foreign state who commits an extrajudicial killing as described in FSIA section 1605(a)(7) shall be liable for "money damages which may include economic damages, solatium, pain and suffering, and punitive damages." Thus, the Cuban Air Force is liable for both compensatory and punitive damages. Under the theory of *respondeat superior*, Cuba is liable for the same amount of damages as its agent, with the exception of punitive damages, which the FSIA prohibits against foreign states.

Section 1606 of the FSIA, which determines the extent of liability in suits against a foreign state, provides in pertinent part: "[T]he foreign state shall be liable in the same manner and to the same extent as a private individual under like circumstances; but a foreign state except for an agency or instrumentality thereof shall not be liable for punitive damages." Thus, although punitive damages may not be assessed against the Republic of Cuba, they may be assessed against the Cuban Air Force.

1. Compensatory Damages

To support their claim for compensatory damages, Plaintiffs presented the testimony of Dr. David Williams, an expert economist. Using widely-accepted methodology, Dr. Williams calculated the present value of De la Peña's and Costa's lost wages and benefits. He also calculated the present value of Alejandre's lost wages, benefits, and services to his family. The Court finds Dr. Williams's calculations to be reasonable and therefore adopts his figures for lost wages, benefits, and services.

In addition, Plaintiffs request damages for pain and suffering. The record is replete with testimony from Plaintiffs and other family members of the deceased, which attests in painful detail to the grief they have suffered as a result of the killings. The Court finds this evidence more than sufficient to justify the awards for pain and suffering that Plaintiffs request.

2. Punitive Damages

In addition to compensatory damages, punitive damages are explicitly permitted by the Civil Liability Act. The Court observes again that it may impose judgment and damages retroactively. First, Congress expressed its clear intent in AEDPA to allow suits against terrorist states for acts occurring before AEDPA's effective date. Second, the Civil Liability Act and AEDPA's amendments to the FSIA are jurisdictional provisions, and as the Supreme Court has explained, "We have regularly applied intervening statutes conferring or ousting jurisdiction, whether or not jurisdiction lay when the underlying conduct occurred or when the suit was filed." Finally, compensatory damages were already available against foreign states, and punitive damages were available against foreign governmental entities, long before changes to the FSIA made this suit possible.

Because this is the first case to proceed to trial under this Act, however, there is no precedent to guide the Court in determining whether punitive damages are appropriate in this particular case, and if so, in what amount. Thus, the Court will look both to the traditional purpose behind awarding punitive damages and to analogous federal court cases addressing the role of punitive damages in cases of egregious international human rights violations.

The purpose of punitive, or exemplary, damages has traditionally been twofold. First, they may serve as a tool to punish truly reprehensible conduct. In this way, the aggrieved plaintiff is given a socially acceptable avenue of retaliation, and, perhaps more importantly, the "punitive nature of exemplary awards also affords society a means of retribution for wrongs against the community interest." *See* Judith Camile Glasscock, *Emptying the Deep Pocket in Mass Tort Litigation*, 18 ST. MARY'S L.J. 977, 982 (1987). Punitive damages are also an appropriate remedy in international law. As the Supreme Court has observed, "[A]n attack from revenge and malignity, from gross abuse of power, and a settled purpose of mischief ... may be punished by all the penalties which the law of nations can properly administer."

The law also provides for awards of punitive damages upon the sound reasoning that they will deter others from committing similar acts. Courts reason that if a sizeable monetary sum over and above compensatory damages is assessed against the wrongdoer, he and others may be prevented from engaging in similar behavior in the future. As acknowledged in the RESTATEMENT (SECOND) OF TORTS, punitive damages are meant both "to punish [a defendant] for his outrageous conduct and to deter him and others like him from similar conduct in the future."

Most courts faced with gross violations of international human rights have employed the tool of punitive damages to achieve these dual purposes. By granting large exemplary awards, courts have both expressed their condemnation of human rights abuses and attempted to deter other international actors from engaging in similar practices. Most of these cases have been brought pursuant to the authority of the Alien Tort Claims Act ("ATCA"), 28 U.S.C. § 1350, which allows aliens to sue in U.S. federal court for torts that violate "the law of nations or a treaty of the United States," and the more recently enacted TVPA, which establishes a cause of action against individuals for torture.

Part of the reason why punitive damages have been extensively awarded in cases brought under the ATCA is that they serve to redress conduct so heinous that it has been condemned by the world community. Punitive damages help reinforce "the consensus of the community of humankind" that horrific abuses against the person will not be tolerated. Although, unlike claimants proceeding under the ATCA, Plaintiffs in this case do not have to prove a violation of international law in order to be entitled to damages, the Court finds that such an inquiry would be helpful in assessing the amount of punitive damages that should be awarded.

The practice of summary execution has been consistently condemned by the world community. A multitude of international agreements and declarations proclaim every individual's right not to be deprived of life wantonly and arbitrarily. So widespread is the consensus against extrajudicial killing that "every instrument or agreement that has attempted to define the scope of international human rights has 'recognized a right to life coupled with a right to due process to protect that right.'" The ban on extrajudicial killing thus rises to the level of *jus cogens*, a norm of international law so fundamental that it is binding on all members of the world community.

Cuba's extrajudicial killings of Mario T. De la Peña, Carlos Alberto Costa, and Armando Alejandre violated clearly established principles of international law. More importantly, they were inhumane acts against innocent civilians. The fact that the killings were premeditated and intentional, outside of Cuban territory, wholly disproportionate, and executed without warning or process makes this act unique in its brazen flouting of international norms. There appears to be no precedent for a military aircraft intentionally shooting down an unarmed, civilian plane.

The only conceivable parallel may be the shootdown of KAL Flight 007 by the former Soviet Union in 1983. That incident can be distinguished, however, by two keys facts: First, the Soviets were arguably under the impression that the KAL plane was a military aircraft, and, second, the plane had strayed into Soviet airspace. Neither of these facts is true in this case. Despite the fact that the KAL plane was in Soviet airspace, a commentator studying the incident concluded that the lethal use of force was completely inappropriate: "'Exclusive sovereignty' over airspace above a state was not enough to justify employing force." CRAIG A. MORGAN, THE SHOOTING OF KOREAN AIR LINES FLIGHT 007: RESPONSES TO UNAUTHORIZED AERIAL INCURSIONS, IN INTERNATIONAL INCIDENTS: THE LAW THAT COUNTS IN WORLD POLITICS, 202, 210 (W. Michael Reisman & Andrew R. Willard eds., 1988). International consensus is clear:

> [W]hen measures of force are employed to protect territorial sovereignty, whether on land, on sea, or in the air, their employment is subject to the duty to take into consideration the elementary obligations of humanity, and not to use a degree of force in excess of what is commensurate with the reality and gravity of the threat (if any).

The Court must therefore fashion a remedy consistent with the unprecedented nature of this act. The Court finds that Plaintiffs have proven their clear entitlement to punitive damages. Based upon this record, the Court would be shirking its duty were it to refrain from entering a substantial punitive damage award for the dual purpose of (1) expressing the strongest possible condemnation of the Cuban government for its responsibility for commission of this monstrous act, and (2) deterring Defendants from ever again committing other crimes of terrorism.

In addition to considerations of the heinousness of Cuba's act, the Court will follow the traditional approach of considering the Cuban Air Force's assets in its assessment of punitive damages. *See* RESTATEMENT (SECOND) OF TORTS § 908(2) (1977) ("In assessing punitive damages, the trier of fact can properly consider the character of the defendant's act, the nature and extent of the harm to the plaintiff that the defendant caused or intended to cause and the wealth of the defendant.").

Of course, it would be impossible for the Court to calculate precisely the assets of the Cuban Air Force. The record contains, however, testimony as to the value and number of the MiG fighter jets in the Cuban Air Force. Because this testimony is both uncontroverted and credible, the Court will accept it as true. The record reflects that each MiG is worth approximately $45 million, and that the Cuban Air Force owns approximately 102 MiGs. The total value of this fleet, which is undoubtedly only a fraction of the Cuban Air Force's total assets, is therefore approximately $4.59 billion. The Court finds that 1% of this total, or $45.9 million, should be assessed against the Cuban Air Force for each of the killings. This figure is dictated by the unparalleled nature of Cuba's actions and comports with similar judgments against individual, non-governmental defendants. Monetary damages, in whatever amount, can never adequately express the revulsion of this Court, and every civilized society, over these callous murders. Perhaps, however, this decision may serve in some small way as a deterrent to others in the future.

Accordingly, after a careful review of the record, and the Court being otherwise fully advised, it is ordered and adjudged that judgment is hereby entered on behalf of Plaintiffs and against Defendants the Republic of Cuba and the Cuban Air Force for total compensatory damages of $49,927,911. Further, judgment is hereby entered for Plaintiffs and against the Defendant the Cuban Air Force (only) as punitive damages, the sum of One Hundred Thirty Seven Million, Seven Hundred Thousand Dollars ($137,700,000).

The total compensatory and punitive damages herewith awarded to Plaintiffs are $187,627,911, for which sum execution may issue forthwith against the Defendants Cuba and the Cuban Air Force and against any of their assets wherever situated.

NOTES

1. Terrorism has always shadowed commercial airline travel. The first documented airline hijacking occurred as early as 1931, when Peruvian revolutionaries overtook a domestic flight to distribute propaganda. With behavior ranging from intimidation to homicide, hijackers have seized commercial airplanes typically to bargain for the exchange of political prisoners or to arrange escape to a particular destination like Cuba. For example, on September 14, 1980, a passenger aboard Eastern Airlines Flight 115 travelling from Tampa to Miami handed the flight attendant a note and asked that she give it to the captain:

> This is a request to take me to Cuba ... Now!
>
> This aircraft is in no danger. But don't take any chances. The life of many people is in your hands.
>
> A powerfull explosive device is set to go-off on pre-set time in a public location in Tampa. Many inocent people are goin to die—Any loss of life as a result of your haste and negligence and this airline management will be your responsibility. Copy of this note is in the mail to all major T-V networks news media, relatives and friends—They will know what happen in the ground and, who can help at the time Once in Cuba—Not Before. I will tell you exact location and how to disarm safely the device.
> Time is essential.
>
> THANKS-Carlos

United States v. Figueroa (11th Cir. 1982).

See also 4 Cuban Gunmen Hijack Airliner, N.Y. TIMES, Apr. 17, 1959, at 1 (reporting the hijacking of a Cuban domestic airliner by four individuals, who forced the pilot to fly them to Miami, Florida); *Youth Tries to Hijack Jetliner,* N.Y. TIMES, Nov. 18, 1965, at 1 (discussing an attempt by a 16-year-old to hijack a National Airlines flight, during which he attempted to shoot an aide to the federal space program); *Gunman Is Foiled in Jet Hijacking,* N.Y. TIMES, July 13, 1968, at 1 (recounting an attempt by a lone gunman to hijack a Delta Air Lines flight from Philadelphia, Pennsylvania, to fly to Cuba); *Arabs Hijack a Dutch Jet, With 288 Aboard, to Libya,* N.Y. TIMES, Nov. 26, 1973, at 1 (covering the hijacking of a KLM Air Lines flight over the Middle East); *2 Hijack Soviet Jet, Force It to Finland,* N.Y. TIMES, July 11, 1977, at 1; *German Jet Forced to Fly to Istanbul,* N.Y. TIMES, Mar. 27, 1985, at A11 (reporting the hijacking by a lone gunman of a Lufthansa flight from West Germany); *4 Injured as Crew on Cargo Jet Fights off Attempted Hijacking,* N.Y. TIMES, Apr. 7, 1994, at A12 (describing the attempted hijacking of a Federal Express airplane by a disgruntled employee).

On September 6, 1970 Pan American Flight 083, while on a regularly scheduled flight from Brussels to New York, was hijacked in the sky over London about 45 minutes after it had taken off from an intermediate stop in Amsterdam. Two men, Diop and Gueye, acting for the Popular Front for the Liberation of Palestine (the "PELP"), forced the crew of the aircraft to fly to Beirut, where a demolitions expert and explosives were put on board. The aircraft, a Boeing 747, was then flown to Egypt still under PFLP control. In Cairo, after the passengers were evacuated, the aircraft was totally destroyed. Is such aviation terrorism an insurable risk? *See Pan American World Airways, Inc. v. Aetna Cas. & Surety Co.*, 505 F.2d 989 (2d Cir. 1974).

2. *Stethem v. Islamic Republic of Iran* (D.D.C. 2002), *supra*, captures the fact that "[a]ll acts of terrorism are by their very definition extreme and outrageous and intended to cause the highest degree of emotional distress, literally, terror, in their targeted audience: The more extreme and outrageous, the greater the resulting distress." *See, e.g.*, BRUCE HOFFMAN, INSIDE TERRORISM (Columbia University Press 2006); R.I.R. Abeyratne, *The Effects of Unlawful Interference with Civil Aviation on World Peace and the Social Order*, 22 TRANSP. L.J. 449 (1995); Goeff Levitt, *Is Terrorism Worth Defining?*, 13 OHIO N.U. L. REV. 97 (1986); Walter Laqueur, *Reflections on Terrorism*, 64 FOREIGN AFF. 86 (1985); Richard Baxter, *A Skeptical Look at the Concept of Terrorism*, 7 AKRON L. REV. 380 (1974); John Dugard, *International Terrorism: Problems of Definition*, 50 INT'L AFF. 67 (1974). "Unfortunately, aviation terrorism is an activity with a huge terrorist advantage—with terrorists picking their spots while security authorities maintain continuous vigilance; with even operationally unsuccessful terrorist operations achieving at least some psychopolitical success through raising anxiety, distrust in leaders, and pressure towards visible and concurrently ineffective programs among population segments who believe that they are or might be under attack." *See Motivation and Aviation as a Terrorism Target*, INT'L BULL. POL. PSYCHOL., Nov. 5, 2003.

3. Terrorists generally have targeted international air travel because of aviation's global reach. That is, "[a]viation allows the U.S. and its allies to be accessible globally for attack without the need to infiltrate through the home territory of a target—be it government, business, or their representatives." *Motivation and Aviation as a Terrorism Target*, INT'L BULL. POL. PSYCHOL., Nov. 5, 2003. In this context, though Pan Am Airways was a private company and not a state-owned "flag carrier" of the United States, it was iconic of America; the destruction of Pan Am Flight 103 was a powerfully symbolic attack of the United States itself. *See In re Air Disaster at Lockerbie, Scotland on Dec. 21, 1988* (2d Cir. 1994), *supra*. So too were the targets of September 11th—the Pentagon, the World Trade Center Towers, and perhaps the White House or Capitol—selected for their representation of U.S. economic and military power.

The September 11th attacks were particularly significant in that they represented a direct attack on American soil. Moreover, the primary objective of the September 11th hijackers was to kill Americans, not to divert to a different destination or to leverage seized aircraft for negotiation purposes. One author suggests the first attempt "to convert a hijacked airplane into a flying bomb targeted on a symbol of international salience, and the only known prequel to September 11, was the Christmas Eve 1994 hijacking of a French Airbus by a four-man team from the Algerian terrorist movement GIA, who wanted to crash the plane into the Eiffel Tower." *See* Phillip A. Karber, *Re-Constructing Global Aviation in an Era of the Civil Aircraft as a Weapon of Destruction*, 25 HARV. J.L. PUB. POL'Y 781, 789 n.46 (2002-2003); Gary N. Horlick, *The Developing Law of Air Hijacking*, 12 HARV. INT'L L.J. 33 (1971). *But see Haas v. Gutierrez*, 2008 WL 2566634 (S.D.N.Y. 2008) (dismissing with prejudice complaints alleging the collapse of the World Trade Towers was a not a consequence of a terrorist hijacking but the result of being struck by the United States military's secret laser-like weaponry (*i.e.* "directed energy weapons")).

Pan Am 103 discussed in *In re Air Disaster at Lockerbie, Scotland on Dec. 21, 1988*, *supra*, represented a new type of international aviation terrorism because, unlike the events detailed in *Stethem v. Islamic Republic of Iran* (D.D.C. 2002), *supra*, and other previous hijackings, the culprits were nowhere to be seen. The 24-hour cable news cycle portrayed only images of thousands of scattered parts of a jumbo jet strewn across an empty open field. Is the political or psychological impact of aviation terrorism likely to subside given how routine airline travel is today? Or, is the effectiveness of airliner terrorism linked to something deeper, for example, an innate fear or concern about flight safety by the public generally?

See generally Ruwantissa Abeyratne, *Crisis Management Toward Restoring Confidence in Air Transport—Legal and Commercial Issues*, 67 J. AIR L. & COM. 595 (2002); Speedy Rice & Shana Fitzpatrick, *Terrorism and the Aviation Industry: Insights from the 1929 Warsaw Convention*, 78 N.D. L. REV. 713 (2002); Robert L. Rabin, *Indeterminate Future Harm in the Context of September 11*, 88 VA. L. REV. 1831 (2002); S.Z. Fuller, *Criminal Jurisdiction over Aircraft Hijacking*, 7 ISRAEL L. REV. 207 (1992); Sami Shubber, *Aircraft Hijacking under the Hague Convention*, 22 INT'L COMPL. L.Q. 687 (1973); Jerome L. Skinner, *An American Civil Law Response to International Terror*, 69 J. AIR L. & COM. 545 (2004); EDWARD MCWHINNEY, AERIAL PIRACY AND INTERNATIONAL TERRORISM: THE ILLEGAL DIVERSION OF AIRCRAFT AND INTERNATIONAL LAW (2d ed. 1987); S.K. GHOSH, AIRCARFT HIJACKING AND THE DEVELOPING LAW (1985); NANCY D. JOYNER, AERIAL HIJACKING AS AN INTERNATIONAL CRIME (1974); Alona E. Evans, *Aircraft Hijacking, What is Being Done?,* 67 AM. J. INT'L L. 641 (1973); Abraham Abramovsky, *The Constitutionality of the Anti-Hijacking Security System*, 22 BUFF. L. REV. 123 (1972).

4. As shown by *In re Air Disaster at Lockerbie, Scotland on Dec. 21, 1988* (2d Cir. 1994), *supra*, the Pan Am Flight 103 killings generated extensive litigation. The tragedy itself was a consequence of state-sponsored terrorism, giving rise to legal action against a sovereign foreign nation for wrongful death, battery, infliction of emotional distress, loss of consortium and violation of international law. Several claimants specifically alleged that Pan Am Flight 103 was the product of "[t]he actions of Libya in encouraging and sustaining [ ] private acts [of terrorism that] led to the deliberate and willful destruction of [the plane]." *See Smith v. Socialist People's Libyan Arab Jamahiriya* (E.D.N.Y. 1995). Similarly, *Stethem v. Islamic Republic of Iran* (D.D.C. 2002), and *Alejandre v. Republic of Cuba* (S.D. Fla. 1997), *supra*, represent judicial proceedings against identifiable states pursuant to the Foreign Services Immunities Act, 28 U.S.C. §§ 1602 *et seq*. In contrast, the modern era of aviation terrorism is typified by non-sovereign, rogue actors such as al-Qaeda. What is the role of international law and what role do courts have to serve, if any, in vindicating the rights of victims and meting out punishment for aviation crimes by such transient threats? *See generally* Shirlyce

Manning, *The United States' Response to International Air Safety*, 61 J. AIR L. & COM. 505 (1996); H.F. Van Panhuys, *Aircraft Hijacking and International Law*, 9 COLUM. J. TRANSNAT'L L.J. 1 (1970).

5. In 2007, the Supreme Court of the United States reformulated the standard by which to determine whether a federal complaint states a claim upon which relief can be granted under Fed. R. Civ. P. 12(b)(6). "To survive a motion to dismiss, a complaint must contain sufficient factual matter, accepted as true, to 'state a claim to relief that is plausible on its face.'" *Ashcroft v. Iqbal* (2009) (quoting *Bell Atl. Corp. v. Twombly* (2007)). Although this pleading standard "does not require 'detailed factual allegations,' ... it demands more than an unadorned, the-defendant-unlawfully-harmed me accusation." A pleading must contain "more than labels and conclusions, and a formulaic recitation of the elements of a cause of action will not do." Pleadings that "are no more than conclusions, are not entitled to assumption of truth. While legal conclusions can provide the framework of a complaint, they must be supported by factual allegations." Against this new "plausibility" standard, can cases alleging racial profiling be reconciled? Does this standard promote or stifle similar claims?

6. September 11th represents a failure by aviation security policymakers to "connect the dots" and recognize antecedent terrorist patterns. As a well-known former federal Department of Transportation Inspector General recounted:

> There was a plot ... to take four jetliners, maybe it was five, depending on if you count the plane that escaped. Anyway, there was a plot to take four jetliners. They hijacked them in a jihad to protest America's role in Israel. In this jihad, they would take the planes and crash them into something to do maximum harm to a nation and government at which they were very displeased. Sorry, but they would have casualties. They would not even give them a second thought ... You think I am talking about September Eleventh, don't you? I am not.
>
> I happen to be talking about September Twelfth, September 12, 1970. The same thing happened. The four planes were taken to the Middle East and blown up. In that case, they allowed the passengers—a very bizarre way that they did it, but they allowed the passengers to scramble to get off the plane.

See Mary Schiavo, *Flying Right: What it Takes to Make Aviation Safer and More Secure after 2001*, 14 DEPAUL BUS. L.J. 279, 294-95 (2001-2002). *Compare United States v. Mena* (1st Cir. 1991) (passenger dressed in a camouflage outfit and fatigue hat entered cockpit, clutching in one hand a tin can equipped with a wick and protruding brass contact and a cigarette lighter in his other hand, threatening to "blow up the aircraft" if he was not flown to Cuba) *with United States v. Reid* (D. Mass. 2002) (Richard Reid—the "shoe-bomber"—who tried to light and detonate the inner tongue of his sneaker aboard a Miami-to-Paris flight on December 22, 2001).

7. The explosive device that detonated aboard Pan Am 103 was "unaccompanied," leading to the institution of "bag-matching" programs designed to ensure that baggage aboard commercial airplanes corresponded to an enplaned passenger. *E.g.*, E. Aphrodite Thevos Tsairis, *Lesson of Lockerbie*, 22 SYRACUSE J. INT'L L. & COM. 31 (1996); R.I.R. Abeyrante, *Attempts at Ensuring Peace and Security in International Aviation*, 24 TRANSP. L.J. 27 (1996).

A former Director of the Office of Policy and Planning for Civil Aviation Security at the Federal Aviation Administration found a disturbing irony in the fact the bombing of Pan Am 103 over Lockerbie, Scotland in 1988 did not catalyze further significant upgrades to aviation security. Rather, an accident involving the explosion of Boeing 747 off the coast of New York in 1996, an event putatively unrelated to terrorism, did: "Several other events had come together at about the same time [as TWA Flight 800] to enable this tidal change to occur. First, several major terrorist events within the United States [occurred], beginning in 1993, includ[ing] the World Trade Center bombing, [ ] the murders at the headquarters of the Central Intelligence Agency, ... [and] the revelation in 1995 of the plot ... to destroy a large number of U.S. civil aircraft in Asia ..." Anthony Fainberg, *Aviation Security in the United States: Current and Future Trends*, 25 TRANSP. L.J. 195 (1998). *See also In re Air Crash off Long Island, New York, on July 17, 1996* (2d Cir. 2000), Chapter 6, *infra*. In fact, the explosion of TWA Flight 800 gave rise to federal anti-terrorism initiatives to profile airline passengers. *See* Chapter 5.C, *infra*.

8. On September 11, 2001, one of the four hijacked airplanes crashed in rural Pennsylvania after several passengers counter-attacked the hijackers onboard. JERE LONGMAN, AMONG THE HEROES: UNITED FLIGHT 93 AND THE PASSENGERS AND CREW WHO FOUGHT BACK (HarperCollins 2002); UNITED 93 (Sidney Kimmel Entertainment 2006). Indeed, airline passengers themselves have an important role to play in terms of securing commercial airplane travel.

In 2002, a company named Flight Watch America, Inc. offered $350 courses that would instruct not "self-defense or hand-to-hand combat, [but] ... awareness, preparation and just plain common sense" for airline passengers. Bob Keefe, *Class Teaches Passengers How to Combat Terrorism in the Air*, ATLANTA J.-CONST., Feb. 19, 2002, at 1D. After September 11, 2001, 82 percent of surveyed airline passengers said they would lead an attack to prevent terrorists from taking control of a plane. *Id.* Some commentators have argued that indeed "an individual, not bureaucracy, can ensure safety." Jamie L. Rhee, Comment, *Rational and Constitutional Approaches to Airline Safety in the Face of Terrorist Threats*, 49 DEPAUL L. REV. 847, 849 (2000). For example, one author suggests:

> [T]he air traveller represents an under-rated human factors issue in a system that has grown very fast and places a high degree of trust in regulatory and enforcement measures to solve many of its problems. The air traveller as an active participant in on-board safety has received little positive acknowledgment.
>
> * * *
>
> The airlines so far have failed to embrace passengers as important participants in maintaining a socially safe on-board environment. Passengers at large are treated as commodities.

Angela Dahlberg, *Airlines Need to Turn More of Their Attention to Passenger-Related Human Factors*, ICAO J., June 2001, at 15. Another author observes:

> The public will bear the additional expenses needed to improve aviation security, but is this where public responsibility ends? Do the passenger surcharges and user fees that characterize current transportation policy entitle the passenger to share in the security process itself? ... The idea still prevalent in our laws and policies—that the public will pay more, yet will remain uninvolved in the process—reflects the naivety of the "welfare state" policies of yesteryear. We are living a myth if we think that we can successfully avoid becoming involved, yet have aviation security improved. Government is not a bottomless pit of funds, nor has it shown itself to be an unbiased champion of our security interests.

N.J. Strantz, *From Technology to Teamwork: Aviation Security Reform since Pan Am Flight 103*, 3 ALB. L.J. SCI. & TECH. 235, 251 (1993).

9. In tracing the itinerary of the hijackers in *Stanford v. Kuwait Airways Corp.* (2d Cir. 1996), *supra*, the Court observed retrospectively:

> The hijackers' tickets had a stench about them. They had been purchased on very short notice with cash, and the flight traced an outlandish route: the passengers were to fly on MEA from Beirut to Dubai, where they were then to connect with Kuwait Airways to Karachi, and from there continue on to Bangkok.

> This itinerary was bizarre because: (1) there were regularly scheduled direct flights between Beirut and Bangkok; (2) the four terrorists were the only passengers aboard MEA 426 to connect with a Kuwaiti airline—every other passenger aboard who happened to be traveling to Karachi connected in Dubai with a Pakistani International Airlines flight; and (3) there was another scheduled MEA flight from Beirut directly to Karachi on December 4th, a day after the hijackers' actual departure.
>
> If the hijackers had waited for this next flight, they would have avoided (a) the stop at Dubai, and (b) an unnecessary twenty-hour layover in Karachi while waiting for the same December 4th plane that would eventually take them to Bangkok. Still another suspicious feature of the journey was that the men were traveling one-way, a very long distance, without any checked baggage. None of this apparently raised the eyebrow of any MEA employee.

Prospectively, is the profiling of airline passengers an effective technique to preempt aviation hijackings and terrorism? *See* Chapter 5.C, *infra*.

10. Airline passengers are business "invitees" of airlines and airports, to whom a legal duty is owed in certain circumstances. *See generally Dallas-Ft. Worth Intern. Airport Public Facility Imp. Corp. v. Banks* (Tx. Ct. App. 2010); *Jakobsen v. Massachusetts Port Authority* (1st Cir. 1975). In this context, airlines, as going concerns, want to avoid negative publicity and litigation. But, should airlines—rational actors who certainly would not destroy their aircraft or kill their passengers intentionally—be liable for terrorist events aboard or involving their airplanes? *See generally* Robert A. Brazener, *Annotation, Liability of Air Carrier for Damage or Injury Sustained by Passenger as a Result of Hijacking*, 72 A.L.R.3d 1299 (1976). To what degree, if any, do *In re Disaster at Lockerbie, Scotland on Dec. 21, 1988* (2d Cir. 1994), and *Stanford v. Kuwait Airways Corp.*, (2d Cir. 1996), *supra*, represent outcome-oriented decisions that place a premium on fashioning remedies instead of precisely identifying responsible parties? As a practical or perhaps political consideration, is it significant that all defendant airlines except Middle Eastern Airlines were dismissed in *Stanford, supra*?

PROBLEM

Ramzi Yousef entered Manila, the capital of the Philippines, under an assumed name. There, he devised a plan to attack United States airliners whereby five individuals would place bombs aboard twelve United States-flag aircraft that served routes in Southeast Asia. Conspirators would board an airliner in Southeast Asia, assemble a bomb on the plane, and then exit the plane during its first layover. As the planes continued on toward their next destinations, the time-bombs would detonate. Eleven of the twelve flights targeted were ultimately destined for cities in the United States.

Yousef and his co-conspirators performed several tests in preparation for the airline bombings. In December 1994, they placed one of the bombs they had constructed in a Manila movie theater. The bomb exploded, injuring several theater patrons. Ten days later, Yousef planted another test bomb under a passenger's seat during the first leg of a Philippine Airlines flight from Manila to Japan. Yousef disembarked from the plane during the stopover and then made his way back to Manila. During the second leg of the flight, the bomb exploded, killing one passenger and injuring others.

The plot to bomb the United States-flag airliners was uncovered in January 1995, only two weeks before the conspirators intended to carry it out. Yousef and a cohort were burning chemicals in their Manila apartment and accidentally caused a fire. An apartment security guard saw the smoke coming from the apartment and called the fire department. After the firemen left, the Philippine police arrived at the apartment, where they discovered chemicals and bomb components, a laptop computer on which Yousef had set forth the aircraft bombing plans, and other incriminating evidence. Yousef fled the country, but was captured in Pakistan the next month.

Does a United States court have jurisdiction over Yousef's extraterritorial conduct of attempting to damage or destroy aircraft in foreign air commerce pursuant to federal law? *See United States v. Yousef* (2d Cir. 2003).

B. INTERFERENCE WITH FLIGHT CREW

Federal law provides that an individual on an aircraft in the "special aircraft jurisdiction of the United States" who assaults or intimidates a flight crew member or flight attendant of the aircraft, or who interferes with the performance of the duties of the member or attendant or lessens the ability of the member or attendant to perform those duties, will be fined and/or imprisoned for up to 20 years, or both. However, if a dangerous weapon is used in assaulting or intimidating the member or attendant, the individual will be imprisoned for any term of years or for life.

Interestingly, the relationship between this statutory prohibition and terrorism is more attenuated than might be expected, as the very identity of violators is sometimes surprising. For example, crew members themselves have interfered with flight operations as when an American Airlines flight attendant began attacking her fellow crew members and U.S. marshals on both legs of an international flight from Charlotte, North Carolina in November 2015. According to affidavit testimony, the flight attendant slapped other flight attendants and shoved, punched, or kicked at marshals. *See* Michael Gordon, *Flight*

Attendant Accused of Attacking Own Crew, CHARLOTTE OBSERVER, Nov. 30, 2015, *http://www.charlotteobserver.com/news/local/crime/article47152575.html*.

Mental health issues, anxiety about flying, and alcohol frequently stoke and are at the center of such dangerous behavior. The following cases detail the limitations lawmakers and judges have in anticipating, preventing, and punishing such behavior.

UNITED STATES v. SPELLMAN

243 F. Supp. 2d 285 (E.D. Pa. 2003)

DALZELL, District Judge.

On January 7, 2003, defendant Alonzo Spellman pleaded guilty to interference with flight attendants and crew members and to two counts of simple assault on an aircraft, all arising from what can only be described as every air passenger's and crew member's nightmare on Delta Flight 2038 on July 23, 2002. At Spellman's sentencing yesterday, we were presented with the unusual coincidence of (a) the Government's motion for upward departure and (b) the defendant's motion for downward departure.

Factual Findings

It is undisputed that Alonzo Spellman is a veteran of the National Football League. After graduating from Ohio State University, where he was first-team AP All-Big Ten, Spellman starting in 1993 played with the Chicago Bears, where as a defensive end in 1995 he set a club record for sacks in consecutive games. He later signed with the Dallas Cowboys, and then played for the Detroit Lions until his release for tardiness at practices. As one might expect from his impressive career in football defense, Spellman is something of a man-mountain. Not only is he six feet, six inches tall, but he now weighs 330 pounds, and can be so formidable-looking that Philadelphia police officers were afraid to arrest him.

At the sentencing hearing, we heard the testimony of seven passengers and crew members who on July 23, 2002 shared the misfortune of flying on Delta Flight 2038 from Cincinnati, Ohio to Philadelphia, Pennsylvania. Shortly after sitting in Row 21 of the aircraft, Spellman began speaking loudly about a variety of subjects, including the plane crashing. He made remarks such as, "I hope we make it to Philadelphia before this plane crashes into a building." After the aircraft was airborne for about twenty minutes, Spellman added obscenities to his verbal barrage, including in a loud voice, "motherfucker," "fuck you," "shit," and "bitch."

When flight attendant Danielle Eller spoke to Spellman, he asked her if she was a Christian. Upon quietly answering in the affirmative, Spellman commanded her to say out loud that she was a Christian. Ms. Eller tried to ignore this behavior, and shortly thereafter she saw Spellman swinging his arms in the air and saying in a loud voice, "I'll smash your fucking head with my cleats, I will."

Flight attendants told Spellman that this kind of behavior was unacceptable, especially with families on the plane, and told him he was scaring many of the other over 130 passengers. Spellman ignored these requests. Ms. Eller reported that all of the passengers around Spellman remained frozen in their seats, frightened even to get up and go to the bathroom for fear of attracting Spellman's attention.

About a half hour into the flight, Karen Weaver, who sat in the seat in front of Spellman and who was traveling with her two small sons, turned around and requested that Spellman not use such vulgar language, explaining that she was traveling with small children. Spellman's response to Mrs. Weaver's polite request was, "Oh, you're going to tell me to mind my tongue, you Jew."

Although Mrs. Weaver tried to ignore Spellman, his verbal barrage continued with, "You hear me, Mom, now you're not going to talk to me." Commenting on Mrs. Weaver's skirt, he said, "Where do you get off wearing your miniskirt and showing your pussy to everyone?" He added that she "could show her body to everybody dressed like a whore in front of [her] kids." Spellman referred to Mrs. Weaver's two- and three-year-old sons as "sorry white boys." Mrs. Weaver remained quiet, but began crying. Her husband, Stephen, who was seated in a different row, tried to intervene. Spellman kept up his verbal assaults on Mrs. Weaver and taunted her husband, saying, "What are you going to do about it, Dad?"

Flight attendant Lane Stephens tried to accomplish what flight attendant Eller had failed to achieve, but Spellman immediately challenged her with loud and insulting comments about her appearance. When Ms. Stephens told Spellman that he couldn't use such language, and that police would meet the plane, Spellman responded that he didn't care and predicted that the police wouldn't do anything to him.

As Ms. Stephens was taking down the names of people in seats around Spellman as witnesses to give to the police, Spellman said to her, "You got a problem with me, you want me to take you down?" Since Spellman showed no signs of calming down, the flight attendants thrice advised the pilot, Captain Robert Freund, of what was happening. Captain Freund ultimately made an announcement requesting that the passenger stop his conduct and stating that it would result in his arrest. In response, Spellman yelled that he would "get off" because he was "bipolar."Spellman's conduct worsened after the Captain's admonition.

Passenger Arthur Daemmrich had the bad luck to sit next to Spellman. Mr. Daemmrich was so frightened that he spent much of the flight in the galley area without a seat (all other seats on the aircraft being occupied). Because he was so afraid, and notwithstanding Federal Aviation Administration regulations requiring all passengers to be seated and restrained by a seatbelt, flight attendant Anne Chase granted permission to Mr. Daemmrich to sit in the bathroom stall during the landing.

Perhaps most dramatic of all, several passengers reported that Spellman, according to the account of passenger John Liebenthal, "talked out loud about opening the door while in flight." Passenger Matthew Lynch, who testified that he takes about one hundred Delta flights per year, reported that he had "never experienced anything close to this," *i.e.*, statements about opening the door during flight. Passenger Carol McAdam recalled Spellman's words as, "Give me a parachute and I'll jump off this plane," and said that she believed, "This could be another incident similar to the hijackings that occurred on September 11." Passenger Sally Schulz reported that she "was particularly scared when Spellman said that he wanted to open the door so he could get out."

As a direct result of Spellman's conduct, Captain Freund contacted air traffic control at Philadelphia International Airport to request a "priority handling." The tower granted the Captain's request, and other planes that were ahead of Delta Flight 2038 were ordered to clear the way. Captain Freund testified that he had only "broken out" of an orderly landing pattern four times in his twenty-two years as a commercial airline pilot. He explained that this "hazardous procedure" created danger for the two aircraft ahead of Flight 2038 because in three to four seconds the planes automatically go at full power from a ten degree descending pitch to a thirty degree ascent, which is "very disconcerting for passengers—they scream out." Because his aircraft was landing before he and his crew could complete their normal protocol, Captain Freund also reported that there was "no tolerance for error" in his landing. Flight 2038 then landed ahead of the other planes.

Captain Freund directed all the passengers to remain seated until such time as Spellman was removed from the aircraft. But because of Mr. Weaver's fear for his children, as soon as the plane was on the ground, he "scooped up" his sons in each arm and ran up the narrow aisle to the galley while the aircraft taxied to the gate, a very dangerous act. Karen Weaver followed close behind.

Once the plane was near the gate, Captain Freund entered the passenger compartment to escort Spellman out of the plane. While the aft aircraft door was still closed and locked, Captain Freund approached Spellman and observed that it was "obvious" that the passengers around him "were terrified." On the Captain's approach, Spellman raised his hands to him and said, "You see this, I can feel the adrenaline rushing through my hands, I'm about to rip your throat out." Notwithstanding this ghastly and highly credible threat, (Captain Freund confessed that "I was shaking in my shoes. I was very, very scared.") Captain Freund continued to attempt to keep Spellman calm, but Spellman said that if the police came aboard, "they are going to carry me off in a body bag." The Captain testified that "I was certain people were going to be hurt."

At this point matters reached a level bordering on the surreal. When the Captain and Spellman finally got to the front of the plane, the aircraft door was not fully open.

Captain Freund asked why the ground crew had not opened the door and was informed that the Philadelphia police had told the ground personnel not to open the door until more police arrived. Not wanting to keep over 130 people hostage to this evident danger, the Captain commanded the crew to open the aircraft door.

When Spellman and his mother and sister left the aircraft, the armed Philadelphia police—perhaps as many as six of them—did nothing. At all times Spellman continued to act aggressively, cursing all the while and frightening everyone in his path. The passengers reported that when they complained to the Philadelphia police about their inaction, the officers, displaying indifference and abject cowardice, responded to them, "You want to help?"

After menacing about in the baggage area for upwards of forty-five minutes with the Philadelphia police at all times giving him a wide berth, Spellman eventually left the airport, unimpeded by local law enforcement. We believe that a sentence of eighteen months is on this record warranted. The government's motion is granted and the defendant's motion is denied.

ATLANTIC COAST AIRLINES v. COOK

857 N.E.2d 989 (Ind. 2006)

RUCKER, Justice.

In an action to recover damages for the negligent infliction of emotional distress, Indiana's modified impact rule requires a claimant to demonstrate a direct physical impact resulting from the negligence of another. Where the physical impact is slight, or the evidence of the physical impact is tenuous, we evaluate the alleged emotional distress to determine whether it is not likely speculative, exaggerated, fictitious, or unforeseeable. In this case, we conclude that the emotional distress or mental anguish allegedly suffered by the plaintiffs is speculative, and thus their claim for emotional distress damages must fail.

FACTS AND PROCEDURAL HISTORY

This case arises from a passenger's behavior onboard an aircraft five months after the September 11th terrorist hijackings of airplanes and less than two months after Richard Reid lit a match onboard a flight from Paris to Miami and attempted to detonate explosives hidden in his shoe. On February 8, 2002 Bryan and Jennifer Cook arrived at the Indianapolis International Airport for a direct flight to New York City. Delta Airlines handled ticket arrangements, and Atlantic Coast Airlines operated the flight. Globe Security Services, Inc. provided security for the airport. While passengers waited to board, a man later identified as French national Frederic Girard ran toward the gate and abruptly stopped. Mr. Cook observed that the unaccompanied Girard had two tickets in his possession for the flight and that airline security had detained Girard at the boarding gate before allowing him onto the airplane. He further noticed that Girard's face was red and his eyes were bloodshot and glassy.

While boarding the Fairchild Dornier 328, a small airplane with a capacity for thirty-two passengers, Girard ran up the steps and jumped inside. Rather than proceeding to his assigned seat, he attempted to sit in a seat nearest the cockpit but the flight attendant instructed him to sit in the back row. Girard took a seat in the rear of the aircraft but repeatedly pressed the attendant call button and light switch above his head. Prior to take-off, Mr. Cook approached the flight attendant and expressed concern that Girard was a possible security threat. The attendant acknowledged as much and explained that he had directed Girard to sit in the rear of the plane so he could keep an eye on him.

During take-off Girard disregarded instructions to remain seated with his seatbelt fastened. Then during the flight Girard lit a cigarette, disregarding directives from the flight attendant that smoking onboard was prohibited. Despite this admonition Girard was permitted to retain his lighter. Mr. Cook approached three male passengers and asked for their assistance in protecting the flight in the event Girard's behavior grew dangerous. Girard moved about the plane, sat in various empty seats and finally walked up the aisle toward the cockpit. Mr. Cook blocked his path and instructed him to sit. Without any physical contact with Mr. Cook, Girard returned to his seat and lit another cigarette.

The flight attendant again told him to extinguish the cigarette, and in response Girard stood and shouted, "Get back! Get back!" At this, Mr. Cook and other passengers approached Girard and ordered him to sit down. Instead Girard stomped his feet and shouted in French. Discernable to the Cooks were the words "World Trade Center," "Americans," and "New York City." Eventually a Delta Airlines employee convinced Girard to sit after speaking to him in French. The employee spent the remainder of the flight sitting across from Girard in the rear of the plane. Ultimately the pilot diverted the flight to Cleveland, Ohio where police placed Girard under arrest. The flight then continued to New York City.

Recalling the events of September 11th, and recalling also a passenger's attempt to detonate a shoe bomb aboard an airplane with the use of a match, the Cooks described their ordeal as one in which they "have never been so scared in their entire lives." The husband and wife filed a complaint in the Perry Township Small Claims Court in Marion County, Indiana, naming as defendants Delta Airlines, Atlantic Coast Airlines, and Globe Security Services, Inc. The Cooks pursued their claim on theories of negligence and breach of contract. They also sought damages for the negligent infliction of emotional distress.

The small claims court entered judgment against the Cooks, and they appealed to the Marion County Superior Court. After both sides conducted discovery, during which the trial court entered an order granting the Cooks' motion to compel discovery of

Atlantic Coast's passenger manifest, the defendants filed motions for summary judgment. Atlantic Coast alleged that it was entitled to judgment as a matter of law because the Cooks' negligence claim as well as their breach of contract claim was preempted by federal law, that the Cooks' complaint was barred for failure to file their appeal timely with the Marion Superior Court, and that the Cooks were not entitled to damages under Indiana's modified impact rule.

The trial court determined that the Cooks' complaint was not barred for failure to appeal timely to the Marion Superior Court, that neither Delta Airlines nor Atlantic Coast breached their contracts with the Cooks, that federal law did not preempt the Cooks' negligence claims, and that the Cooks' claims were not precluded under Indiana's modified impact rule. Delta Airlines and Atlantic Coast filed an interlocutory appeal and the Cooks cross-appealed.

On review the Court of Appeals affirmed in part and reversed in part the judgment of the trial court. The Court of Appeals held: (1) the trial court did not err when it concluded that the Cooks' appeal of the small claims court's decision was timely; (2) the Cooks' tort claims are not preempted by federal law; (3) the Cooks' claims for the negligent infliction of emotional distress are not precluded under Indiana's modified impact rule; (4) the trial court correctly granted the Cooks' motion to compel discovery; (5) there are genuine issues of material fact regarding whether Delta Airlines and Atlantic Coast breached their contracts with the Cooks; and (6) the Cooks waived appellate review of whether the trial court erred in entering summary judgment in favor of Delta Airlines on the Cooks' negligence claims.

Atlantic Coast sought rehearing complaining that the Court of Appeals' opinion abrogated the modified impact rule. In response, the court granted rehearing for the limited purpose of addressing this issue, but reaffirmed its opinion. Having previously granted Atlantic Coast's petition to transfer, we now affirm in part and reverse in part the judgment of the trial court.

DISCUSSION

Atlantic Coast makes three claims: (1) the Cooks' claim for emotional distress damages is precluded by Indiana's modified impact rule; (2) the Court of Appeals erred in reversing summary judgment in favor of Atlantic Coast on the Cooks' breach of contract claim because "[t]here is absolutely no evidence in the record what the exact contract was and exactly how Delta and [Atlantic Coast] breached their contract"; and (3) the Cooks' negligence claim is preempted by federal law.

* * *

Claims for the negligent infliction of mental or emotional distress have long been the subject of scholarly debate. Creating rules, formulating tests, and applying them to address such claims have proven a challenge for most courts. The majority of jurisdictions employ some variation or combination of the following common law limiting tests for evaluating these claims:

- the "physical injury" rule under which, generally speaking, the plaintiff's emotional distress must be accompanied by a physical injury or symptom;

- the "zone of danger" rule, under which recovery is limited to those plaintiffs who themselves were not physically injured but were placed in immediate risk of harm by a defendant's negligent conduct which injured another; and

- the "bystander" test, also sometimes called the "foreseeable bystander" test, which allows recovery to certain plaintiffs that witness the injury or death of a third party (who typically must be a close relative of the bystander) that is caused by the defendant's negligence.

The underlying policy reason binding together these judicially created approaches is that absent certain limitations, allowing recovery for mental or emotional distress will open the floodgates to spurious claims.

Before 1991 Indiana followed the rule that damages for mental or emotional distress were recoverable only when accompanied by and resulting from a physical injury. The underlying rationale for this rule was that "absent physical injury, mental anguish is speculative, subject to exaggeration, likely to lead to fictitious claims, and often so unforeseeable that there is no rational basis for awarding damages." But this court modified the rule in *Shuamber v. Henderson*. We held instead:

> When ... a plaintiff sustains a direct impact by the negligence of another and, by virtue of that direct involvement sustains an emotional trauma which is serious in nature and of a kind and extent normally expected to occur in a reasonable person, ... such a plaintiff is entitled to maintain an action to recover for that emotional trauma without regard to whether the emotional trauma arises out of or accompanies any physical injury to the plaintiff.

We further expounded upon the contours of what is now commonly referred to as the "modified impact rule."

The impact however does not need to cause physical injury to the plaintiff. Additionally the emotional trauma suffered by the plaintiff does not need to result from a physical injury caused by the impact. But how do we assess whether the degree of impact is sufficient to satisfy the requirement of the rule? We have answered this question as follows:

> [W]hen the courts have been satisfied that the facts of a particular case are such that the alleged mental anguish was not likely speculative, exaggerated, fictitious, or unforeseeable, then the claimant has been allowed to proceed with an emotional distress claim for damages even though the physical impact was slight, or the evidence of physical impact seemed to have been rather tenuous.

We acknowledge there have been calls to abandon the impact rule altogether. Among other things there are concerns that Indiana's impact rule, even as modified, may prohibit some litigants from recovering damages for bona fide emotional injury even though there has been no physical impact. These are respectable positions. But this jurisdiction is not alone in grappling with this area of the law for which there is no grand unified theory. We agree with the observations of the California Supreme Court:

> In order to avoid limitless liability out of all proportion to the degree of a defendant's negligence, and against which it is impossible to insure without imposing unacceptable costs on those among whom the risk is spread, the right to recover for negligently caused emotional distress must be limited ... [W]e balance the impact of arbitrary lines which deny recovery to some victims whose injury is very real against that of imposing liability out of proportion to culpability for negligent acts. We also weigh in the balance the importance to the administration of justice of clear guidelines under which litigants and trial courts may resolve disputes.

It is our view that the requirements under Indiana's rule are modest and that a less restrictive rule would raise the potential for a flood of trivial suits, pose the possibility of fraudulent claims that are difficult for judges and juries to detect, and result in unlimited and unpredictable liability. We therefore reaffirm that Indiana's impact rule continues to require a plaintiff to demonstrate a direct physical impact resulting from the negligence of another.

This Court has carved out an exception to the physical impact requirement for the negligent infliction of emotional distress. Mindful that the underlying rationale for direct impact is that "it provides clear and unambiguous evidence that the plaintiff was so directly involved in the incident giving rise to the emotional trauma that it is unlikely that the claim is merely spurious," we recognized that there may be circumstances under which a "plaintiff does not sustain a direct impact" but is nonetheless "sufficiently directly involved in the incident giving rise to the emotional trauma that we are able to distinguish legitimate claims from the mere spurious."

We thus adopted what is now commonly referred to as the bystander rule. "[W]here the direct impact test is not met, a bystander may nevertheless establish 'direct involvement' by proving that the plaintiff actually witnessed or came on the scene soon after the death or severe injury of a loved one with a relationship to the plaintiff analogous to a spouse, parent, child, grandparent, grandchild, or sibling caused by the defendant's negligent or otherwise tortious conduct." In sum, in order to recover damages for the negligent infliction emotional distress, a plaintiff must satisfy either the modified impact rule or the bystander rule. The elements for each are separate and distinct.

* * *

Turning to the case before us, the Cooks do not contend that the bystander rule applies to them. That is, the Cooks do not argue that they witnessed the death or severe injury of a loved one. Rather, their claim rises or falls on whether they suffered a direct physical impact from the alleged negligence of Atlantic Coast. The Cooks insist they did so and that the physical impact was both actual and constructive. According to the Cooks, breathing the smoke from Girard's lit cigarette and experiencing the vibrations from Girard's stomping feet caused an actual physical impact, and "constructive impact occurred by virtue of the physical effects on the [Cooks'] vital body functions in increased breathing, sweating, pulse, heart rate, adrenaline, and acuteness of the senses." We observe that neither this Court nor the Court of Appeals has ever addressed or adopted a theory of "constructive impact" as part of Indiana's impact rule, and we decline to do so today.

This leaves for our consideration whether smelling cigarette smoke and feeling floor vibrations satisfy the direct physical impact requirement of the rule. We first observe that at the very least this stretches the outer limits of the impact requirement. Indeed we doubt that most ordinary citizens would think of smelling cigarette smoke and feeling floor vibrations as physical impacts of any kind. But even assuming that in some theoretical sense these experiences may be characterized as physical impact, the impact was certainly very "slight" and "the evidence of physical impact seem[s] to have been rather tenuous." We thus explore whether the Cooks' alleged mental anguish is "not likely speculative, exaggerated, fictitious, or unforeseeable."

Mr. Cook acknowledges that neither he nor his spouse have sought medical or mental health treatment for their mental or emotional distress. In his deposition, Mr. Cook described his emotional state as being "shaken up ... anxious, just upset" and that he remained so "until [he and his wife] got to New York and got on the ground." Mr. Cook also testified that he was "distraught" and "probably didn't sleep well for at least a week and a half." He further asserted "whenever I get on a flight, I'm concerned that something could happen." According to Mr. Cook, "I will never view things the same as I did before February 8th, 02. I will never view things as—without the concern. I'm not saying it's going to ruin my life, but I will always be—I will always remember it, and I will always—if certain news stories come on, certain things are said, certain situations, when we have terror alerts, and so forth, I will—it will always trigger the memory, and I will always—it will always be in the back of my mind."

In her deposition, Mrs. Cook, who was seven months pregnant at the time of the incident, reported that after arriving in New York she "was just having lower abdominal pains. Could have been brought on by stress." Further, she reported that she started to feel better, "[o]nce we got home and I got back into my normal routine." Mrs. Cook also testified that she and her husband have traveled by air probably four times since this incident. On those flights Mrs. Cook described her emotional state as "I'm always nervous." When asked about the harm she incurred from the flight of February 8, 2002, Mrs. Cook said, "I feared for my life. I thought I was going to die." But she stopped having those fears "[w]hen we landed." According to Mrs. Cook, "It bothered me until we landed. It bothered me that it happened. It bothers me every time I get on a plane."

Apparently the alleged mental and emotional distress the Cooks experienced manifested itself in fear and anxiety at the time the events were unfolding. But this fear and anxiety were transitory, disappearing once the Cooks completed their flight. Since that time, in their own words, the Cooks have experienced feelings of being "bothered," "concerned," and "nervous." But these feelings about the world around us in general and air travel in particular is the plight of many citizens in this country, living as we do in a post-September 11 environment. As one treatise has explained:

> Complete emotional tranquility is seldom attainable in this world, and some degree of transient and trivial emotional distress is a part of the price of living among people. The law intervenes only where the distress inflicted is so severe that no reasonable [person] could be expected to endure it. The intensity and the duration of the distress are factors to be considered in determining its severity.

We do not suggest that the Cooks' fear and anxiety during the flight were trivial. But there was simply nothing before the trial court, and by extension before this Court, suggesting that the Cooks' fear and anxiety were anything other than temporary. And it is pure speculation to assume that the Cooks' later feelings of being bothered, concerned, and nervous are causally related to the events aboard the flight. Because the physical impact in this case was slight to nonexistent, allowing an emotional distress claim to proceed based on the Cooks' lingering mental anguish would essentially abrogate the requirements of Indiana's modified impact rule. In essence we view the alleged mental anguish here as speculative. Accordingly the trial court erred in denying Atlantic Coast's motion for summary judgment on this issue.

RUBIN v. UNITED AIR LINES, INC.

117 Cal. Rptr. 2d 109 (Cal. Ct. 2002)

JOHNSON, Acting P.J.

An airline passenger brought suit against an airline and others after Los Angeles Police Department officers removed her from a commercial flight about to depart for Hawaii. Her suit alleged causes of action for false arrest, false imprisonment, assault, battery and emotional distress. The airline claimed it was entitled to summary judgment as a matter of law because a provision of the Airline Deregulation Act of 1978 expressly preempted her state law tort claims. In the alternative, the airline claimed it was also entitled to judgment as a matter of law because it acted within its statutory discretion by refusing to transport a passenger it decided was, or might be, inimical to airline safety. The trial court granted summary judgment in favor of the airline.

We hold a passenger whom the airline believes is, or might become, inimical to the safety of the aircraft or its passengers may be ejected from a flight without subjecting the airline to tort liability if at the time airline personnel had a reasonable basis for believing the passenger presented a safety risk. We further conclude the airline's actions in this case were reasonable as a matter of law. Accordingly, we affirm the summary judgment.

FACTS AND PROCEEDINGS BELOW

Appellant, Ms. Adrienne Rubin, decided to join her husband, Stanford Rubin, a trusts and estates attorney who was then in Hawaii. She purchased an airline ticket from respondent United Airlines, Inc. ("United"). She paid for a coach ticket and upgraded the ticket to first class by using her husband's frequent flyer miles.

On October 28, 1998, Ms. Rubin arrived at the Los Angeles International Airport approximately an hour before the plane was scheduled to depart. She went directly to the gate with her bags. She waited in line a long time before she could present her ticket to the agent at the gate. Ms. Rubin had a first class itinerary card with a seat designation of 2F. However, the United computer showed no first-class reservation for her. The agent explained Ms. Rubin needed to surrender an additional 3,000 frequent flyer miles to qualify for a first class upgrade because, for some reason, 3,000 miles had been recredited to her husband's account. The agent directed Ms. Rubin to the customer service counter nearby.

Approximately 30 minutes remained before the flight for Hawaii was to depart. It took nearly 15 minutes for Ms. Rubin to reach the front of the line at the customer service counter. When the United agent finally located Ms. Rubin's frequent flyer account on the computer she discovered Ms. Rubin did not have the needed 3,000 miles in her account. Ms. Rubin told the agent to take the miles from her husband's account. Only 10 or so minutes remained before the plane was due to take off. The agent told Ms. Rubin to go to the gate while she continued to try to locate Mr. Rubin's frequent flyer account number.

Ms. Rubin went to the gate and told the gate agent she had a first class seat and wanted to board. The agent responded all first class seats on the flight had already been assigned. He explained the flight was very full but two or three seats were available in the coach section. The agent offered Ms. Rubin the option of taking one of the seats in coach or flying first class on a later flight. He apparently did not indicate a specific coach seat assignment. Ms. Rubin explained she had to leave on this flight because she and her husband had an engagement later in the day she did not want to miss. Ms. Rubin was adamant about wanting a first class seat, and on this particular flight. The gate agent notified the service director on board there was a person about to board who was insisting on leaving on this flight and insisting on a first class seat. The service director decided he would at least accommodate Ms. Rubin's wishes to leave on this flight.

The service director met Ms. Rubin in the jetway. Ms. Rubin told the service director she had a first class ticket, a seat assignment of 2F, and could not understand why the airline had given her seat away. Ms. Rubin told the service director she had to fly first class because she had a special diet. The director reiterated all first class seats were now assigned and occupied. He explained if she wanted to take this fight she would have to fly coach in seat 26B.

Ms. Rubin entered the plane. She did not go to seat 26B in coach. According to Ms. Rubin, the service director did not specify any particular seat but told her she could sit anywhere in coach. Instead, Ms. Rubin entered (or attempted to enter) the first class cabin to determine for herself whether seat 2F was in fact occupied. As the service director put it, "that's when the hair came up on the back of my neck, because, ... you're violating everything that it's about, because it was clearly stated to Mrs. Rubin that the first-class seats were full."

The purser of an aircraft has primary responsibility for the safety of the passengers and has ultimate authority over the other flight attendants. When she saw Ms. Rubin enter (or attempt to enter) the first class cabin, the purser, according to Ms. Rubin, "went ballistic." Ms. Rubin got into a lengthy and loud discussion with the purser. The service director intervened and again directed Ms. Rubin to take her seat in 26B. Instead, Ms. Rubin dropped her luggage in the doorway of the aircraft and took a bulkhead emergency row seat immediately behind the first class section. The service director told Ms. Rubin to store her bag. Ms. Rubin refused and told the director he could do it himself or have someone else store the bag if he wished. The service director and another stewardess repeatedly told Ms. Rubin she could not sit in row 9 either, both because she had been assigned seat 26B, and because she was not "emergency row qualified."

The service director left to consult with the purser. The purser, in the meantime, had already talked to the captain. The purser told the captain she had an irate passenger on board who refused to follow directions and who had attempted to make an unauthorized entry into the first class section. Based on the purser's representations, the captain agreed Ms. Rubin's demeanor and refusal to follow directions had the potential to create a safety problem in flight. The purser told the service director she would not fly if Ms. Rubin remained on board. The captain, purser and service director decided Ms. Rubin should be deplaned.

When the service director returned to the cabin Ms. Rubin was no longer sitting in row 9. She was instead sitting in another person's seat who had been in the lavatory. The person whose seat Ms. Rubin occupied was now sitting on the armrest of an aisle seat. The service director told Ms. Rubin she would have to deplane. In response, she instead finally took her assigned seat in 26B. By this time the flight was at least 15 minutes past schedule for takeoff. The other passengers were becoming impatient and unruly. Some yelled at United personnel suggesting they do something to regain control of the situation. A gate agent came on board to take Ms. Rubin off the plane. Ms. Rubin was talking loudly on her cell phone. She refused to acknowledge his presence or mission. He could not get Ms. Rubin to pay attention to him or to stop talking on the telephone. He left the plane in frustration. Now the flight was some 20 to 25 minutes past departure time. United personnel decided to call the Los Angeles Airport Police.

Passengers started applauding when the police officers boarded the plane. The Los Angeles police officers asked Ms. Rubin to leave the plane. Ms. Rubin kept interrupting to explain she believed she had a first class seat assignment and could not understand why United had given her seat away. The officers told Ms. Rubin the airplane was not going to take off with her on it. Ms. Rubin refused to leave the plane voluntarily. She refused to leave her seat, refused to stand up and refused to walk. The officers had to pick Ms. Rubin up out of her seat and carry her by her shoulders off the plane. As they proceeded in this fashion through the aisles passengers applauded and whistled. They also yelled and hurled wads of paper at Ms. Rubin.In the view of one officer, the situation on board was "a mob scene." He believed the other passengers were so frustrated and upset with Ms. Rubin because of the trouble and delay, he believed if United had permitted Ms. Rubin to stay on the flight "it could have gotten ugly."

The officers took Ms. Rubin off the plane. Her luggage was still where she had dropped it in the doorway. The service director removed her bag to the jetway. The officers detained Ms. Rubin at the police station for several hours. The officers contacted the Federal Aviation Administration and the Federal Bureau of Investigation as is required when investigating a potential federal charge of obstructing a flight crew. A representative from the Federal Aviation Administration arrived and interviewed Ms. Rubin, as did a sergeant from the Los Angeles Police Department. Ultimately, Ms. Rubin was not charged. The officers returned Ms. Rubin to the airport and she flew first class on the next flight to Hawaii.

Ms. Rubin filed suit against United, the City of Los Angeles, and the Los Angeles police officers who removed her from the plane. Her complaint alleged causes of action for false arrest, false imprisonment, unlawful search and seizure, assault, battery, and emotional distress. United moved for summary judgment claiming Ms. Rubin's state tort law causes of action were expressly preempted by the Airline Deregulation Act. In the alternative, United claimed it was entitled to judgment as a matter of law in any event, asserting it had acted within the broad discretion accorded airlines by federal law to decide when a passenger presents a security risk sufficient to be removed from a flight. United argued there were no material factual disputes and asserted it was thus entitled to judgment as a matter of law. The trial court granted United's motion and this appeal followed.

DISCUSSION

DECISIONAL LAW IS UNSETTLED, AND THUS INCONCLUSIVE, WHICH STATE LAW TORT CLAIMS ARE PREEMPTED BY FEDERAL LAW

The Airline Deregulation Act of 1978 ("ADA") prohibits states from "enact[ing] or enforc[ing] a law, regulation, or other provision having the force and effect of law related to a price, route, or service of an air carrier ..." This case concerns the scope of this preemptive provision as applied to a suit raising state tort law claims regarding, as United alleges, claims arising from its boarding procedures.

United claims "boarding procedures" are classified as a "service" and state claims challenging this airline service are expressly preempted by federal law. Ms. Rubin, by contrast, claims the airline gives a too all-encompassing reading to the term "service." She argues Congress used "service" in the public utility sense to only refer to the provision of air transportation to and from various markets at various times. She asserts her claims do not affect these services and thus are not preempted by the ADA.

We need not decide which of the competing definitions of "service" most accurately reflects Congress's intent in adopting section 41713. Regardless of the types of state claims which should be preempted under the rubric of "services" in the ADA, we conclude United properly exercised the discretion given it in section 44902 of the FAA to refuse Ms. Rubin passage in the circumstances presented in this case.

THE UNDISPUTED FACTS ESTABLISH AS A MATTER OF LAW UNITED HAD A REASONABLE BELIEF MS. RUBIN WAS OR COULD BE INIMICAL TO THE SAFETY OF THE FLIGHT WHICH JUSTIFIED UNITED IN REFUSING HER PASSAGE

Section 44902 of the FAA was originally enacted by Congress in 1961. This provision authorizes an airline to "refuse to transport a passenger or property the carrier decides is, or might be, inimical to safety." It provides:

> **(a)** ***Mandatory refusal.***
> The Administrator of the Federal Aviation Administration shall prescribe regulations requiring an air carrier, intrastate air carrier, or foreign air carrier to refuse to transport—(1) a passenger who does not consent to a search under section 44901(a) of this title establishing whether the passenger is carrying unlawfully a dangerous weapon, explosive, or other destructive substance; or (2) property of a passenger who does not consent to a search of the property establishing whether the property unlawfully contains a dangerous weapon, explosive, or other destructive substance.
>
> (b) ***Permissive refusal.***
> Subject to regulations of the Administrator, an air carrier, intrastate air carrier, or foreign air carrier may refuse to transport a passenger or property the carrier decides is, or might be, inimical to safety.
>
> (c) ***Agreeing to consent to search.***
> An agreement to carry passengers or property in air transportation or intrastate air transportation by an air carrier, intrastate air carrier, or foreign air carrier is deemed to include an agreement that the passenger or property will not be carried if consent to search the passenger or property for a purpose referred to in this section is not given.

Congress originally enacted this provision to help combat an air piracy problem. However, section 44902 is not, as Ms. Rubin suggests, reserved strictly for would-be terrorists and hijackers. Airlines have also invoked their discretion under this statute, as they have under common law, to exclude passengers in any number of circumstances.

As the Second Circuit noted in *Williams v. Trans World Airlines* (2d Cir. 1975), an airline's duty to perform its services with the highest possible degree of safety in the public interest has both a statutory and common law basis. All commercial airlines are common carriers, and as such, owe a duty of utmost care for their safety. On the other hand, although the discretion given an airline under this provision to refuse to transport a passenger for safety reasons is "decidedly expansive, [it] is not unfettered." *O'Carroll v. American Airlines, Inc.* (5th Cir. 1989). If an airline's refusal of transportation is arbitrary or capricious, its refusal can give rise to a claim by the offended passenger for damages. Stated another way, the decision to accept or refuse transport to a passenger based on considerations of safety and security "lies exclusively with the air carrier" and if such discretion is "exercised in good faith and for a rational reason" it will be upheld.

In the present case, the record evidence establishes as a matter of law Ms. Rubin presented a safety risk which justified United's decision to remove her from the plane. Unlike other situations, Ms. Rubin was not simply loudly belligerent about a non-safety matter. Also unlike other cases, this was not a case of misidentifying the objectionable passenger. Nor did Ms. Rubin present any evidence tending to suggest United ejected her from the flight simply to retaliate against her for arguing with the purser. Instead the evidence demonstrates Ms. Rubin committed what in the industry is considered a serious breach of security by making or attempting to make an unauthorized entry into the first class cabin. In addition, the evidence demonstrates Ms. Rubin deliberately and repeatedly refused to follow directions from any of the uniformed airline personnel regarding the safety issues of proper stowing of luggage and emergency row seating.

In his deposition testimony the service director explained airlines had developed a heightened sensitivity to safety issues after events such as the Gulf War, the Oklahoma City bombing, the bombing of the World Trade Towers, and the explosion of Pam Am flight 103 over Lockerbie, Scotland. As a result of these events airlines learned they had become potential targets, and at the direction of the Federal Aviation Administration, airlines and airports started taking safety issues much more seriously. According to the service director, it was for this reason the purser perceived Ms. Rubin's unauthorized intrusion, or attempted intrusion, into the first class area as a threatening act. All seats in first class were occupied thus all the purser knew was someone was attempting to enter the forward cabin who clearly had no business being there. The service director stated "the hair came up on the back of his neck" as he watched Ms. Rubin drop her bag and "run into" first class. Instead of leaving the area as directed Ms. Rubin argued loudly with the purser for several minutes and insisted she be permitted to fly in the fully occupied first class cabin. Even Ms. Rubin described the argument as a "confrontation."

Although the service director intervened in an attempt to accommodate Ms. Rubin she refused to follow his directions as well. She refused to stow her bag as directed, and in fact told the director if he did not want the bag in the doorway, he could stow it himself. The director told Ms. Rubin her assigned seat was 26B. Ms. Rubin refused to go to the back of the plane and instead sat in an empty seat immediately behind the first class cabin. United personnel told Ms. Rubin she could not sit in the emergency row bulkhead seat and repeatedly asked her to move. According to the service director, given her demonstrated unwillingness to follow directions, Ms. Rubin was not considered "emergency row qualified." It was only after much pleading Ms. Rubin finally moved. However, she still refused to follow orders to sit in seat 26B. She instead moved a bit further back and sat in someone's seat who was then in the lavatory. When the person returned from the lavatory, United personnel had to again request Ms. Rubin to leave the seat.

In the meantime the purser alerted the pilot who came out of the cockpit to assess the situation. The flight was already considerably delayed and many passengers were becoming upset and unruly. The pilot, purser and service director conferred and decided

Ms. Rubin should be removed from the flight. As the service director described the situation, "it was unacceptable behavior, it was unsafe behavior. I had a riot going on, just about, and this is where I draw the line."

Although a pilot necessarily relies in part on the purser and operations director in making the decision to deplane a passenger, a pilot has ultimate responsibility for the overall safety of the aircraft, its crew and passengers. *See* 14 C.F.R. § 121.537, subd. (d) (pilot has complete control over and responsibility for all passengers and crew "without limitation."). The Federal Aviation Administration has enacted numerous regulations granting considerable discretion to airlines and pilots to control dangerous or unruly behavior. For example, regulations grant authority (1) to the pilot and crew members to prohibit anyone from interfering, intimidating or threatening a crew member or interfering with his or her duties; (2) jointly to the pilot and director of operations for the initiation, continuation, diversion or termination of a flight; (3) to the pilot to ensure no flight crewmember is engaged in any activity which might distract the person from his or her duties during a critical phase of the flight. *See generally*, Tory A. Weigand, *Air Rage and Legal Pitfalls for State Based Claims Challenging Airline Regulation of Passenger Conduct During Flight*, 45 BOSTON. B.J. 10 (2001).

Ms. Rubin refused to comply with the gate agent's request to leave the plane voluntarily. In fact, she refused to stop talking on her cell phone long enough to even acknowledge his presence. The gate agent testified he thought Ms. Rubin could have been a danger to other passengers on the airplane because of her "aggressive behavior." The gate agent reasoned, "She wouldn't listen. She wouldn't listen to the uniform[ed] crew member[s], she wouldn't listen to the service director. She was very loud. And in her conversation on the phone, that was very loud, and completely ignoring my presence less than 20 inches from her, looking her dead in the eye ..."

United personnel then summoned the assistance of the Los Angeles Airport Police Department. Given the length of the delay of 20 to 25 minutes, and the volatile situation they discovered on board, the police officers were ready to arrest Ms. Rubin and file charges against her for obstructing a flight crew. The FAA makes it a criminal offense for a person to assault or intimidate a member of the flight crew in any way which interferes with his or her ability to perform his or her duties. 49 U.S.C. § 46504 provides:

> An individual on an aircraft in the special aircraft jurisdiction of the United States who, by assaulting or intimidating a flight crew member or flight attendant of the aircraft, interferes with the performance of the duties of the member or attendant or lessens the ability of the member or attendant to perform those duties, shall be fined under title 18, imprisoned for not more than 20 years, or both. However, if a dangerous weapon is used in assaulting or

> intimidating the member or attendant, the individual shall be imprisoned for any term of years or for life."

See also cases collected in William Mann, *All The (Air) Rage: Legal Implications Surrounding Airline and Government Bans on Unruly Passengers in the Sky*, 65 J. AIR. L. & COM. 857 (2000). Indeed, one of the officers believed because so many of the passengers were angry at Ms. Rubin her own personal safety would have been at risk had she remained on the flight.

In short, the undisputed evidence establishes Ms. Rubin did, or at least attempted to, make an unauthorized entry into the first class forward cabin area, which airline personnel consider a threatening act. Moreover, the undisputed evidence establishes Ms. Rubin repeatedly and deliberately refused to comply with any of the directions from any of the airline personnel regarding safety issues. This evidence in combination, coupled with the unruly and potentially dangerous situation she helped create on board, is sufficient as a matter of law to establish United when it made its decision had a reasonable basis for believing Ms. Rubin, was, "or might be, inimical to safety," which in turn justified removing her from this particular flight.

Ms. Rubin's allegedly triable issues of fact, for example, whether the flight was already somewhat delayed, whether the outraged purser unilaterally decided to have her ejected, or whether the passengers instead applauded because they were promised a free movie, are too immaterial to alter this conclusion. Accordingly, we further conclude the trial court correctly granted judgment in United's favor and dismissed the action. The judgment is affirmed.

SEDIGH v. DELTA AIRLINES, INC.

850 F. Supp. 197 (E.D.N.Y. 1994)

NICKERSON, District Judge.

Plaintiffs, Ali Sedigh ("Sedigh") and his wife Ezat Sedigh, brought this suit in New York State Supreme Court against defendant Delta Air Lines, a Delaware corporation, alleging unlawful imprisonment, assault, intentional infliction of emotional distress, slander, loss of comfort, and breach of contract. Plaintiffs seek over $4,000,000 in damages.

Defendant has moved for summary judgment. At oral argument the court determined that *pro bono* counsel should be appointed for plaintiffs, whose attorney had withdrawn from the action in February 1993. On March 1, 1994, over six months after oral argument and after several unsuccessful attempts to assign counsel, the court ordered that no further counsel should be assigned to plaintiffs.

I.

The complaint alleges, in pertinent part, the following: On March 25, 1992 Sedigh was a passenger on a Delta Air Lines flight from Germany to the United States. The flight made a stop-over at Frankfurt AM Main Airport. While at that airport, Sedigh made a comment to the effect, "So this is the country where so many [J]ews were killed." The flight captain then approached him, abused him verbally and physically, accused him of traveling with a false passport, and held him until the German Federal Police or Border Police arrived. At defendant's request the Police arrested Sedigh and charged him with crimes relating to the alteration of his United States Passport. He was held for three days in handcuffs, beaten by the German Police, and forced to pay a 3,000 Deutschmark fine for the alleged crime, which he claims he did not commit.

II.

Defendant's affidavits, exhibits, and unopposed statement of material facts pursuant to Local Rule 3(g) show the following: On March 24-25, 1992 Sedigh was traveling from the United States to Istanbul, Turkey. From John F. Kennedy International Airport he took Delta flight 106 to Frankfurt. There he was part of a group of connecting passengers who boarded Delta Flight 072. That flight was scheduled to leave for Istanbul at 12:05 P.M. but was delayed due to mechanical troubles with an air conditioning unit. He and the other connecting passengers boarded late, sometime after 12:05.

While the plane was on the ground Sedigh immediately attracted the attention of the flight attendants because he was agitated and acted nervously. He was seated in a non-smoking section but asked to move to a smoking section. After he moved one of the flight attendants saw him make two trips to the lavatory. On both occasions he stayed in for a long time but did not flush the toilet. During his second trip the smoke detector in the lavatory became activated.

While Sedigh was in the lavatory the second time the "Flight Attendant in Charge," Eva Durczak, went to the cockpit to report his behavior to the captain. She recounted his trips to the lavatory and the fact that, although the airplane was cool, he was sweating profusely. The captain told her to have the flight attendants keep him under surveillance. When Sedigh left the lavatory one of the flight attendants informed him that smoking in the lavatory was forbidden. He became more upset. Flight attendants and several passengers heard him muttering, "kill all the Jews," and vowing he was "going to get them."

Durczak reported Sedigh's increasing agitation and statements to the captain. The captain became concerned. He knew that on the plane were nine armed United States Federal Sky Marshals, assigned to flights deemed at greater risk of hijacking and sabotage. The captain asked the leader of that team of Marshals to come to the cockpit along with the Frankfurt Airport ground security coordinator, who was on the plane conducting a routine inspection. In the cockpit Durczak repeated her account to the Marshal and security coordinator.

The captain requested the Sky Marshals to evaluate the situation for security risk. The security coordinator directed the German police to bring some vehicles over to the plane. Two Sky Marshals then watched as Sedigh made a third trip to the lavatory. They searched the other lavatory and then waited for him to come out. At this time several passengers complained to the Marshals and flight attendant Iwona Zacharewecz that Sedigh had been heard saying "kill the Jews" and "Jews are to blame for world problems" before boarding, and that he had shouted "kill everyone" while on the plane. Durczak twice more returned to the cockpit to update the captain on the situation.

The captain again met with the leader of the Sky Marshals and the ground security coordinator. They reached a consensus that Sedigh posed a possible security risk. The captain recommended removing all of the passengers from the plane, ostensibly because of the continuing air conditioning malfunction, and then interviewing Sedigh in the airport terminal. The captain also said that law enforcement personnel should make any decision about him because the plane was still on the ground with its exterior doors open. The Sky Marshals' leader felt that he posed too great a risk to allow them to wait for buses to arrive to return the passengers to the terminal. The captain deferred to the Sky Marshal leader's judgment.

The Sky Marshals then met Sedigh as he exited the lavatory for the third time. They escorted him to the front of the plane. From there he was taken away by German police officers. The Federal Sky Marshals' report indicates that he went with no resistance. Bomb experts on the Sky Marshals team thereafter searched the cabin in and around where Sedigh had been seated and in the lavatory. They discovered that someone had tampered with the smoke detector in the lavatory, but they found no bomb. His baggage was removed from under the airplane and searched for explosives. Nothing was found. German authorities determined that the photograph on Sedigh's passport had been replaced. He was detained overnight and fined 3,000 Deutschmarks for attempting to travel through Germany with an altered passport. On March 26, 1992, the day after the events on Delta flight 072, he was returned to John F. Kennedy International Airport aboard Delta flight 107.

III.

Defendant moves for summary judgment, arguing that plaintiffs' state law tort and contract claims are preempted and that defendant's actions were a proper exercise

A. Preemption under Section 1305

The proper focus should be on whether or not the specific common law action addresses matters about which the airlines wish or are likely to compete. Viewed from that standpoint, Sedigh's claim should not be preempted. To decline to grant an exemption from his claim would hardly cause an airline to alter its competitive strategy in the slightest degree.

B. Discretionary Removal under Section 1511

The Federal Aviation Act provides another means of protecting airlines from suits such as this one. Section 1511 of title 49, appendix, sets the standard for an airline's refusal to transport a passenger who appears to pose a security threat. That section reads, in pertinent part:

> Subject to reasonable rules and regulations prescribed by the Secretary of Transportation, [a] carrier may also refuse transportation of a passenger or property when, in the opinion of the carrier, such transportation would or might be inimical to safety of flight.

The Court of Appeals for the Second Circuit has established criteria for determining whether an airline properly exercised its discretion to deny transport under this section.

> The test rests upon the facts and circumstances of the case as known to the airline at the time it formed its opinion and made its decision and whether or not the opinion and decision were rational and reasonable and not capricious or arbitrary in the light of those facts and circumstances. They are not to be tested by other facts later disclosed by hindsight.

Williams v. Trans World Airlines (2d Cir. 1975).

The court said that section 1511 is designed to prevent harm from hijacking and terrorism, the threat of which requires airlines to make decisions "within minutes ... of take-off." "The fact that the safety and well-being of many lives are dependent upon [the captain's] judgment necessarily means that the captain is vested with wide discretion." *Zervigon v. Piedmont Aviation, Inc* (S.D.N.Y. 1983).

On this motion for summary judgment the court draws all reasonable inferences in plaintiffs' favor. Plaintiff has not presented any evidence in opposition to defendant's motion. At oral argument Sedigh simply added that he is himself a Jew and that on the plane he had said, "This country kill[ed] the Jew[s]." In the months since the court ordered that no more counsel should be assigned, plaintiffs have not proceeded to prosecute the case or defend against the motion.

Drawing all reasonable inferences in plaintiffs' favor, this court finds the case one where at best a nervous passenger was muttering about the Germans having killed Jews. He was apparently understood by those around him to be expressing a desire to kill all the Jews. The airline's crew and various safety personnel made what appeared to them to be a reasonable safety decision not to permit him to remain on board. They then thought it appropriate to make a thorough search for bombs on the plane.

The captain and his crew proceeded in a careful and reasonable manner. The crew informed the captain of their concerns. The captain consulted with all available safety personnel. The airline was not obliged to make a more thorough investigation into Sedigh's background before making its determination that he posed a threat to the airplane. The court should not reject with the benefit of hindsight the consensus reached by those with responsibility to act. Defendant's motion for summary judgment is granted. The case is dismissed.

NOTES

1. In *United States v. Guest* (1966), the Supreme Court of the United States confirmed that the "freedom to travel throughout the United States has long been recognized as a basic right under the Constitution." How does this right—also articulated in *Kent v. Dulles* (1958) (Chapter 1.A, *supra*)—square with the legal rights of airlines relative to passengers deemed inimical to the safety of regular flight operations? *See generally* Kristine Cordier Karnezis, Annotation, *Propriety of Air Carrier's Refusal for Safety Reasons to Transport Person or Property Under 49 U.S.C. § 44902(B)*, 192 A.L.R. FED. 403 (2004).

2. "Road rage," "ground rage," and "air rage," represent a sampling of new terms in the modern transportation lexicon, expressing the sometimes antisocial reaction of travelers en route. *See generally* Joan Fleischman, *Miami Lawyer Yanked off Flight to Colorado*, THE MIAMI HERALD, Mar. 27, 2002, at 4A; Jo Bowman, *How 747 Pilot Knocked Out Drunken Pop Star*, SOUTH CHINA MORNING POST, Feb. 23, 2000, at 1; Complaint, Elabiad v. Schuller, No. 97-4907 (E.D.N.Y. 1997); Complaint, United States v. Robert Schuller, No. 97-1194M (E.D.N.Y. 1997) (alleging "Hour of Power" televangelist Reverend Robert Schuller placed a flight attendant in a head lock). In 2000, the Federal Aviation Administration reported 314 cases of "unruly passengers" while the airline industry contended over 4,000 air rage incidents occur per year. Marshall Wilson, *Airline Rage Policies Assailed, Unruly Passengers often Unprosecuted, Crews Say*, S.F. CHRON., July 7, 2001, at A13.

3. "Air rage" is a general intent crime defined and punishable by federal law:

> An individual on an aircraft in the special aircraft jurisdiction of the United States who, by assaulting or intimidating a flight crew member or flight attendant of the aircraft, interferes with the performance of the duties of the member or attendant or lessens the ability of the member or attendant to perform those duties, attempts or conspires to do such an act, shall be fined under title 18, imprisoned for not more than 20 years, or both.

49 U.S.C. § 46504. *See also* 14 C.F.R. §§ 91.11, 121.580, and 135.120. *See also* Nancy Lee Firak & Kimberly A. Schmaltz, *Air Rage: Choice of Law for Intentional Torts Occurring Over International Waters*, 63 ALB. L. REV. 1, 7 (1999) (defining air rage as "intentional acts that are highly disproportionate to motivating factors, which endanger the flight crew and/or other passengers and potentially jeopardize the safety of the aircraft itself.").

4. Air rage is not a phenomenon peculiar to airline travel within the United States. For example, before September 11, 2001, the United Kingdom's Civil Aviation Authority estimated that air rage incidents occurred an average of once out of every 870 flights. *Air Rage Incidents Four Times a Day*, BIRMINGHAM POST, Feb. 19, 2000, at 8. *See also Off-Duty SAA Steward Goes Berserk on Plane*, THE STAR (South Africa), Feb. 26, 2002 (reporting a drunk attendant on board a Bangkok to Johannesburg flight who, for thirty minutes, "tore down the aisles, swearing and taking swipes at passengers... biting some on their arms and hands... and forcing himself on a Chinese woman and kissing her," until restrained by fellow passengers).

5. Instances of air rage and interference with flight crew include:

- A passenger on a flight from London to Miami said to the passenger seated next to him, "If you give me a knife, I'll kill everyone on the plane." He then attempted to touch and kiss a female flight attendant and grabbed her arms several times and continued to try to kiss her before the Flight Service Manager told him to return to his seat. He then took several swings at the Flight Service Manager before the crew was able to get him to his seat. Before they got him in his seat, the passenger placed his hands on another female flight attendant and pushed her head to the side. Before two male flight attendants were able to restrain the passenger, he bit the first flight attendant on the arm. *United States v. Ahmed* (11th Cir. 2007);

- A banker on an international flight tried "to talk to the captain" by applying several "kung fu" kicks to the reinforced cockpit door.

Martin Merzer et al., *Crew's Ax Stops Cockpit Intruder*, THE MIAMI HERALD, Feb. 8, 2002, at 1A (reporting that the co-pilot subdued the panicked passenger by hitting him in the head with the blunt end of an ax);

- From August 1, 1993, until his arrest on September 22, 1993, a Virginia resident broadcast unauthorized radio messages to aircraft and air traffic controllers, pretending to be an air traffic controller at the Roanoke Regional Airport. Among other messages, he gave instructions to pilots who were preparing to land, including instructing incoming pilots to change frequencies, or to break off their approach. He told pilots they were not clear to land after they had been cleared to land by the tower, told pilots their runway was closed because of a disabled aircraft on the runway, and told landing pilots to hold short of a runway intersection. *United States v. Bocook* (4th Cir. 1995);

- A businessman defecated on an in-use service cart. Complaint, United States v. Gerard B. Finneran, No. 95-1744M (E.D.N.Y. 1995);

- Federal Express began investigating irregularities in the reporting of flight hours by one its flight engineers. One day before he was to appear at a company hearing, the engineer boarded a cargo plane flight in full flight gear and with carry-on items though he was not a member of the flight crew; he entered the cockpit and began adjusting instruments and controls. The real crew members arrived later, and assumed the engineer was a "jump-seater" (*i.e.,* an employee passenger). After the plane took off, the troubled engineer entered the cockpit and began attacking the crew with a hammer, spear gun, spear, claw hammers, and sledgehammers, severely injuring the crew. *United States v. Calloway* (6th Cir. 1997).

For more reading on unlawful airline passenger behavior see ANGELA DAHLBERG, AIR RAGE: THE UNDERESTIMATED SAFETY RISK (2001); Tory A. Weigand, *Air Rage and Legal Pitfalls for State-Based Claims Challenging Airline Regulation of Passenger Conduct During Flight*, BOSTON B. J., May/June 2001, at 10; *See generally* William Mann, Comment, *All the (Air) Rage: Legal Implications Surrounding Airline and Government Bans on Unruly Passengers in the Sky*, 65 J. AIR L. & COM. 857 (2000); John A. Glenn, Annotation, *Validity, Under Commerce Clause of Federal Constitution, of State Tolls or Taxes On, Or Affecting, Interstate or Foreign Air Carriers or Passengers*, 31 L. Ed. 2d 975 (1999). *See also* ELLIOTT HESTER, PLANE INSANITY: A FLIGHT ATTENDANT'S TALES OF SEX, RAGE AND QUEASINESS AT 30,000 FEET (St. Martin's Press 2002).

6. Consider a flight attendant's description of Southwest Airlines Flight 2466, bound for Ontario, California, from Las Vegas, Nevada:

> The cabin was total chaos, … when [a passenger] said "I have [a] bomb." I saw many of our male passengers unbuckle their seatbelts and they stood up and they—I remember seeing the people throwing punches and everybody, you know, they were all on top of Mr. Gonzalez … [The passenger] was hysterical and he was swinging and kicking and he was just—he was hitting and kicking passengers and the passengers were trying to take him down and hold him down.
>
> Many of the female passengers were screaming and yelling and crying. The cabin was total chaos. They were yelling, "We're going to die. We're going to crash. We're going down." And a lot of the women were hysterical. They were—they were thinking we were going to crash. Thinking they—when the passengers heard Mr. Gonzalez say, "I have a bomb," and at that point it was just all hell broke loose.

United States v. Gonzalez (9th Cir. 2007). Ultimately, FBI agents arrested the passenger, who told them that "he knew what he was doing was wrong but felt he had to do something to land the plane." At the change of plea hearing, Gonzalez acknowledged that, although he had used methamphetamine the day before the incident, he was aware of his actions and understood and knew what he was doing at the time of the incident.

Prior to the enactment of the "Uniting and Strengthening America by Providing Appropriate Tools Required to Intercept and Obstruct Terrorism Act of 2001" ("USA PATRIOT Act"), Pub. L. No. 107-56, 115 Stat. 272 (2001), referred to recklessly endangering the safety of the "aircraft *and passengers.*" Effective November 1, 2002, § 2A5.2(a)(2) was amended to refer to "endangering the safety of ... an airport or an aircraft; or … a mass transportation facility, a mass transportation vehicle, or a ferry." U.S.S.G. § 2A5.2(a)(2) (2003). Thus, sentencing now does not require a showing of endangerment to the passengers and even a threat to detonate an empty aircraft is punishable.

7. A bitter Internet culture exists with respect to airline customer service, *e.g.*, AirlinesSuck.com, AmericanAirlinesSucks.org, NorthWorstAir.org, Passengerrights.com, SkyRage.com, Ticked.com, TravelProblems.com and Untied.com. *See generally*, Marilyn Adams, *More Fliers Land on the Internet to Air Complaints*, USA TODAY, Apr. 18, 2000, at 12B. As illustrated in *United States v. Spellman*, (E.D. Pa. 2003), and *Rubin v. United Air Lines, Inc.* (Cal. Ct. 2002), *supra*, an airplane cabin

commingles passengers with different psychological impulses, travel phobias, and other propensities for inappropriate and threatening behavior—even without alcohol service.

8. Excessive alcohol misuse frequently is a contributor to passenger misconduct. *E.g.*, *United States v. Butt* (4th Cir. 1994); *United States v. Jenny*, (10th Cir. 1993). *See also* Keith L. Alexander, *Raising a Glass or Two—No More—To Safety in Flight*, WASH. POST, July 25, 2001, at E01 (discussing Senator Dianne Feinstein's (D-Cal.) letter to airline executives threatening to introduce legislation if the airlines did not "voluntarily" limit the number of alcoholic drinks served to passengers). *See also* Christian Giesecke, *Unruly Passengers: The Existing Legal System and Proposed Improvements*, 26 ANN. AIR & SPACE L. 45 (2001).

9. Aircraft piracy, which is a criminal offense under the Federal Aviation Act, should be distinguished from interference with flight crew. Pursuant to 49 U.S.C.§ 46502 (1996), "aircraft piracy"

> (A) means seizing or exercising control of an aircraft in the special aircraft jurisdiction of the United States by force, violence, threat of force or violence, or any form of intimidation, and with wrongful intent.
>
> (B) an attempt to commit aircraft piracy is in the special aircraft jurisdiction of the United States although the aircraft is not in flight at the time of the attempt if the aircraft would have been in the special aircraft jurisdiction of the United States had the aircraft piracy been completed.
>
> > (2) An individual committing or attempting or conspiring to commit aircraft piracy—(A) shall be imprisoned for at least 20 years; or (B) if the death of another individual results from the commission or attempt, shall be put to death.

See 14 C.F.R. Pt. 243. *See generally* William G. Phelps, *Validity, Construction, and Application of Provisions of Federal Aviation Act (49 U.S.C.A. Appx. §§ 1742 (i)(l), (n)), Punishing Air Piracy and Certain Acts Aboard Aircraft in Flight, or Boarding Aircraft*, 109 A.L.R. FED. 488 (1992). *See also United States v. Healy* (1964) (holding that a private airplane, like a commercial airliner, was an aircraft in flight in commerce subject to the anti-aircraft piracy law).

10. Did the security officials in *Sedigh v. Delta Air Lines, Inc.* (E.D.N.Y. 1994), *supra*, overreact? Consider that in 1985, Germany's parliament made it a crime to deny the Holocaust and the extermination of Jews. In 1994, the law was fortified even

further—anyone who publicly endorsed, denied or played down the genocide against Jews was subject to a maximum penalty of five years in jail and no less than the imposition of a fine. That said, Ali and Ezat Sedigh in fact were Jewish themselves. Are surnames a fair (if not reliable) indicator of who may or may not be a security threat to commercial aviation?

PROBLEM

Every fifteen minutes an announcement broadcasts over the public address system of North Carolina's Piedmont Trial Airport:

> May I have your attention, please. May I have your attention, please. Federal Aviation Administration security regulations require all passengers to maintain continual control of all carry-on luggage. Please do not leave any baggage unattended. All baggage is subject to inspection. Passengers are also cautioned not to accept any baggage, package or any items from persons unknown to you. If you are approached by any person asking you to accept any baggage, package or other items, immediately contact the nearest airplane representative, security screening personnel or airport authority police department. Thank you for your attention.

A little before 7:00 A.M. on Saturday, November 15, 1997, Mahmoud Hassouneh arrived at the Greensboro airport, intending to fly to Orlando, Florida to attend his cousin's wedding. At the AirTran ticket counter, Hassounch presented his ticket and driver's license. The airline employee then asked Hassouneh if any unknown person had asked him to carry anything on board the airplane. He responded, "Well, there were some either Iraqi or Irani[an] ... men outside who gave me a bomb to put in my bag." According to the airline employee, Hassouneh appeared "serious but kind of lighthearted," and was laughing and chuckling a little when he made the statement. Hassouneh was escorted over to a security area to run his bag through an X-ray machine during which he was informed that "it is a federal offense to make jokes about bombs in bags," to which Hassouneh allegedly replied, "You need to lighten up. It's just explosives."

Hassouneh is prosecuted under 18 U.S.C. § 35(b), a felony provision that requires the government to prove that an offender acted "willfully and maliciously, or with reckless disregard for the safety of human life." Is Hassouneh's reputation as a prankster or practical joker relevant with respect to the government's burden of proof? Is the airport public address announcement admissible as evidence? *United States v. Hassouneh* (4th Cir. 2000). What is the likely result after 9/11?

C. FOURTH AMENDMENT ISSUES: PROFILING AND "NO-FLY"

In December 2015, President Obama made a rare Oval Office address to the nation:

> Our nation has been at war with terrorists since al Qaeda killed nearly 3,000 Americans on 9/11. In the process, we've hardened our defenses -- from airports to financial centers, to other critical infrastructure. Intelligence and law enforcement agencies have disrupted countless plots here and overseas, and worked around the clock to keep us safe.
>
> Our military and counterterrorism professionals have relentlessly pursued terrorist networks overseas—disrupting safe havens in several different countries, killing Osama bin Laden, and decimating al Qaeda's leadership.
>
> Over the last few years, however, the terrorist threat has evolved into a new phase. As we've become better at preventing complex, multifaceted attacks like 9/11, terrorists turned to less complicated acts of violence like the mass shootings that are all too common in our society. It is this type of attack that we saw at Fort Hood in 2009; in Chattanooga earlier this year; and now in San Bernardino. And as groups like ISIL grew stronger amidst the chaos of war in Iraq and then Syria, and as the Internet erases the distance between countries, we see growing efforts by terrorists to poison the minds of people like the Boston Marathon bombers and the San Bernardino killers.
>
> * * *
>
> The threat from terrorism is real, but we will overcome it. We will destroy ISIL and any other organization that tries to harm us. Our success won't depend on tough talk, or abandoning our values, or giving into fear. That's what groups like ISIL are hoping for. Instead, we will prevail by being strong and smart, resilient and relentless, and by drawing upon every aspect of American power.
>
> * * *
>
> To begin with, Congress should act to make sure no one on a no-fly list is able to buy a gun. What could possibly be

> the argument for allowing a terrorist suspect to buy a semi-automatic weapon? This is a matter of national security.

Meanwhile, abroad, European Union interior ministers agreed to a Passenger Name Record deal whereby police looking for terrorism suspects would have access to names, personal details and credit-card information of air travelers on flights to, from, or within Europe. "Data would be kept for five years, and after six months, the names, addresses, and billing information of air passengers will be 'masked out,' meaning that policy will be able to get that information only with a court record." *See* Valentina Pop, *EU Agrees on Air Travelers Database*, WALL ST. J., Dec. 5-6, 2015, at A6.

Do these measures exact too high a cost to the First, Second, and Fourth Amendments of the Constitution, common law principles of privacy, and international affairs? The cases below demonstrate how courts contend with important issues of profiling and search and seizure. In many respects, what is happening at airports and on airplanes in terms of national security and anti-terrorism measures is reflective of broader legal and practical questions impacting about the health of American democracy and freedoms around the world.

UNITED STATES v. $124,570 U.S. CURRENCY

873 F.2d 1240 (9th Cir. 1989)

KOZINSKI, Circuit Judge.

Like more than a billion other airline passengers last year, Wayne G. Campbell passed through an airport security check on his way to a flight. During the course of the screening, the security officer discovered a large quantity of U.S. currency. Pursuant to an established arrangement, the officer notified agents of the United States Customs Service who paid her $250 for the tip. The tip led to Campbell's detention and confiscation of the currency.

Campbell challenges the legality of the search, raising fundamental questions about the extent to which law enforcement authorities may use airport security inspections to promote objectives unrelated to air safety.

I.

On January 5, 1987, Campbell placed his locked briefcase on a conveyor belt leading through an X-ray scanner operated by United Airlines at the Seattle International Airport. Picking up a dark mass on the X-ray screen, the Flight Terminal Security ("FTS") officer operating the scanner, Bonnie Boswell, asked Campbell to open the briefcase. First expressing reluctance, Campbell eventually agreed to do so privately, behind a screen. FTS officer Karen Kangas searched the case and found a very large quantity of currency. Kangas then questioned Campbell regarding his destination and eventually released him. Kangas returned the briefcase to Campbell, who proceeded to board United Airlines Flight 22 bound for Los Angeles.

FTS officers at the Seattle airport have a policy of reporting any sum of United States currency over $10,000 to the United States Customs Service and Airport Police. FTS officials are private law enforcement officers. Federal regulations require each airport and airplane operator to adopt and carry out a security program that meets federal standards. In discharging this responsibility, airports and airlines must train a corps of employees in special aviation security procedures, as well as in general law enforcement procedures consistent with the training standards set by the state and local jurisdictions in which the airport is located. These employees are then uniformed, armed with firearms and given arrest authority for violations of certain criminal laws.

Employees who report the discovery of such sums are paid $250 as a reward. Consistent with this policy, Kangas telephoned United States Customs Service Officer Steve Symms immediately after she released Campbell. Kangas gave Symms a description of Campbell, his briefcase and its contents, and his destination. Symms relayed this information to a customs agent at Los Angeles International Airport ("LAX"), who in turn informed Roger Guevarra, a Drug Enforcement Administration agent.

Acting on this information, Guevarra and a second DEA agent, Christopher Amato, met Campbell's flight and began following Campbell around the airport terminal building. After Campbell retrieved his suitcase and exited the building, the agents approached him and identified themselves as special agents of the DEA. In response to their questioning, Campbell admitted that he had $130,000 in his briefcase, but contended that the money belonged to a friend of his in Encino who had hired him to ransom a stolen painting. Campbell further explained that he had traveled to Seattle to read books and visit friends, and had stayed with friends there. He had taken the money to Seattle with him because he was afraid to leave it at home. Campbell would not give the name and telephone number of the friend for whom he was ransoming the painting.

Skeptical of this story, the agents decided to take the briefcase to a nearby DEA office for further investigation. They advised Campbell that he was not under arrest and was free to go, but that they would be detaining his briefcase. Campbell decided to follow the agents to the DEA office. Once there, Amato asked Campbell to open the briefcase and told him that, should he refuse, the agents would attempt to obtain a search warrant.

Campbell opened the briefcase revealing bundles of currency in denominations between five and one hundred dollars. The agents also found a substantial quantity of cigarette rolling papers, and a receipt from a Seattle hotel indicating that Campbell had stayed there from January 3 to January 5, 1987.

The DEA agents photocopied the papers and returned to Campbell everything except the currency. On January 6, 1987, DEA agents used Smoky, a narcotics-detecting dog, to test the currency for the odor of cocaine, heroin, marijuana and marijuana derivatives. Smoky's reaction to the currency indicated that one or more of these substances had come in contact with one or more of the bills.

The United States then filed this civil forfeiture action pursuant to 21 U.S.C. § 881(a)(6). Campbell filed a timely claim and answer, and moved to suppress the evidence uncovered by the search of his briefcase. The district court denied Campbell's motion to suppress and ruled that the currency was subject to forfeiture. Campbell appeals the district court's rulings.

II.

Commercial air travel, once a luxury, has become a staple of modern existence. For many Americans, boarding an airplane to travel across the state or across the country is as ordinary and commonplace an event as boarding a bus or train fifty years ago, or mounting a horse-drawn carriage around the turn of the century. Students going home for the holidays, corporate executives traveling on business, grandmothers visiting their grandchildren, federal judges riding circuit: Airplane travel has become the lifeblood of American society in the latter part of the twentieth century. According to the Federal Aviation Administration, in 1987 there were 1,095,600,000 airline passengers, an average of more than four trips for every man, woman and child in the United States. *See* OFFICE OF CIVIL AVIATION SECURITY, FEDERAL AVIATION ADMINISTRATION, SEMIANNUAL REPORT TO CONGRESS ON THE EFFECTIVENESS OF THE CIVIL AVIATION SECURITY PROGRAM JULY 1, 1987—DECEMBER 31, 1987 (1988); U.S. DEP'T OF COMMERCE, STATISTICAL ABSTRACT OF THE UNITED STATES 7 (1988).

Along with the good comes the bad. While airline travel provides unparalleled speed, comfort and convenience to travelers who must cross vast distances in a short time, it also gives terrorists and other criminals a unique opportunity for inflicting death and destruction. Airplanes are peculiarly vulnerable to hijacking, as well as to attacks with firearms and explosives; airports, where large numbers of people congregate, can be attractive targets for terrorism. Aware of these dangers, Congress passed the Air Transportation Security Act of 1974. The Act empowers the Administrator of the FAA to establish and monitor security procedures for preventing acts of criminal violence and aircraft piracy. The Administrator has promulgated regulations under the Act which, among other security measures, require all passengers and carry-on property to be screened by weapon-detecting security procedures.

On the basis of 14 years' experience, we can say with some confidence that the Air Transportation Security Act has been a success. Airline hijackings and similar incidents are a rarity in the United States. The security system set up at airports throughout the country processes millions of passengers every day with relatively little delay or inconvenience. Aware of the system's life-saving purpose, Americans submit to metal detectors and X-ray devices without a second thought. The intrusion into our privacy—and an intrusion it surely is—is accepted by most travelers with equanimity. The unavoidable consequence of this exhaustive search for weapons is that security personnel will become aware of many personal items that do not pose a danger to air safety. X-rays reveal, in outline, the contents of packages, often giving a good indication as to their inventory. When packages are opened, or when pockets are emptied, FTS agents will see many items that are considered private.

Normally, the intrusion is small. Materials other than weapons and explosives are usually ignored by FTS personnel; the disclosure has no permanent consequences and the passenger is able to regain his privacy in the anonymous throngs of a busy airport. Not so, however, when FTS officials single out a particular passenger on account of the contents of his pocket or briefcase. At that point the intrusion becomes more permanent, the invasion of privacy more severe. It is, moreover, an intrusion not automatically covered by the logic of the Air Transportation Safety Act.

While narrowly defined searches for guns and explosives are constitutional as justified by the need for air traffic safety, a generalized law enforcement search of all passengers as a condition for boarding a commercial aircraft would plainly be unconstitutional. Here we must consider whether the use of the airport security screening system to achieve ends unrelated to air safety violates the constitutional rights of commercial air travelers.

A.

We start with the fundamental proposition that "except in certain carefully defined classes of cases, a search of private property without proper consent is 'unreasonable' unless it has been authorized by a valid search warrant." *Camara v. Municipal Court* (1967). Among the "carefully defined classes of cases" for which no warrant is needed are administrative searches, that is, searches "conducted as part of a general regulatory scheme in furtherance of an administrative purpose, rather than as part of a criminal investigation to secure evidence of crime." *United States v. Davis* (9th Cir. 1973). In *Davis*, we approved warrantless airport security checks as administrative searches, relying on *Camara, United States v. Biswell* (1972), and *Wyman v. James* (1971). In approving the searches under this theory, we noted that the governmental interest in assuring air traffic safety is compelling while the intrusion into the privacy of passengers is as limited "as is consistent with the satisfaction of the administrative need that justifies it." *See Davis*.

Judge Browning's thoughtful and narrowly crafted opinion in *Davis* made it clear, however, that we were not placing our imprimatur on all airport searches, so long as they could colorably be classified as serving a security purpose. Quite the contrary. We recognized in *Davis* that administrative searches, like all other governmental searches, are subject to the Fourth Amendment's reasonableness requirement. To the extent that administrative searches are used for purposes other than those contemplated by the regulatory scheme, they may fall outside the rationale by virtue of which we have approved them. Specifically, in *Davis* we recognized the danger that "the screening of passengers and their carry-on luggage for weapons and explosives will be subverted into a general search for evidence of crime." Should that danger materialize, we noted, we would not hesitate to exclude the evidence so obtained.

The risk that administrative searches will be infected by general law enforcement objectives, and the concomitant need for the courts to maintain vigilance, is a recurrent theme in our cases and those of other courts. In *United States v. Schafer* (9th Cir. 1972), for example, we upheld the admission of evidence inadvertently discovered during a routine agricultural quarantine search, but were careful to note that "[n]othing in the record suggests that the administrative search in this case was 'employed as an instrument of criminal law enforcement to circumvent the latter's legal restrictions ...'"

The Supreme Court has repeatedly emphasized the importance of keeping criminal investigatory motives from coloring administrative searches. In *Camara*, the Supreme Court approved administrative searches as reasonable because "the inspections are neither personal in nature nor aimed at the discovery of evidence of crime, [and therefore] involve a relatively limited invasion of the urban citizen's privacy." In *Wyman*, the Court upheld the legality of a program requiring home visits by caseworkers as a condition for welfare assistance in part because "[t]he home visit is not a criminal investigation, does not equate with a criminal investigation, and ... is not in aid of any criminal proceeding." In *Abel v. United States* (1960), the Court held that evidence uncovered by a search incident to an arrest on an administrative warrant for deportation was admissible in court, but cautioned:

> We emphasize again that our view of the matter would be totally different had the evidence established ... that the administrative warrant was here employed as an instrument of criminal law enforcement to circumvent the latter's legal restrictions, rather than as a bona fide preliminary step in a deportation proceeding. The test is whether the decision to proceed administratively toward deportation was influenced by, and was carried out for, a purpose of amassing evidence in the prosecution for crime.

The concerns, expressed in this circuit and elsewhere, that administrative searches not become a tool for law enforcement, reflect the limited rationale supporting those searches. To sustain a warrantless search, a court must normally make a case-specific factual determination that an exception to the warrant requirement (*e.g.* exigent circumstances, plain view) is applicable. If the search is approved, the approval covers that case only.

An administrative search is different. By approving a warrantless search under this rationale, a court places its stamp of approval on an entire class of similar searches. Because it must consider the general, long-term implications of approving a new type of administrative search, the court will focus on legislative facts—those applicable to the entire class of cases—rather than adjudicative facts—those applicable only to the case before it. The court then relies on these legislative facts to make a dual determination: (1) that the search serves a narrow but compelling administrative objective; and (2) that the intrusion is as "limited ... as is consistent with satisfaction of the administrative need that justifies [it]." Once a type of search has been approved under this rationale, the court is freed from the need to make a specific factual inquiry in every subsequent case. In later cases, the search is deemed proper if it is covered by the approved rationale. By the same token, the court cannot sustain a subsequent search that differs in material respects from the search initially approved, as the same legislative facts may not be applicable.

In *Davis*, we approved airport security searches based on the understanding that they would be limited to searches for guns or explosives, and that they would be no more burdensome than necessary to achieve that objective. So long as the government officials conducting the searches pursue a single-minded objective—air safety—the rationale of *Davis* works well: the searches will, almost by definition, be no more intrusive than is necessary to achieve air safety. Not so where FTS officials have other objectives in mind. We can then no longer rely on the same legislative facts that underlay the search we approved in *Davis*.

The situation at Seattle Airport plainly falls outside the administrative search rationale approved in *Davis*. According to the agreed facts, there is an established working relationship between FTS personnel and other law enforcement officials at that airport. The FTS has a policy of encouraging agents to report the presence of "drugs and U.S. currency" to the U.S. Customs and Port Police and to "work hand-in-hand with [them] regarding detection and reporting of [such items]." The cooperation is made palpable by the fact that FTS officers are paid a substantial monetary reward for alerting law enforcement authorities of the identity of passengers carrying large sums of currency and, presumably, contraband or other evidence of crime.

This close working relationship between the FTS and law enforcement authorities has a significant distorting effect on airport searches as approved in *Davis*, materially altering the calculus by which we held such warrantless searches reasonable. The desire to cooperate with law enforcement authorities, encouraged by FTS policy and fueled by the hope for a reward, may well affect the actions of FTS agents in ways that were not contemplated or approved in *Davis*.

FTS officers have very broad latitude in deciding how deeply to probe in their search for weapons or explosives. For example, the officers must make the initial decision whether to manually search a piece of luggage after it has been scanned by X-rays. If the officers have only one objective—detecting firearms and explosives—we can safely defer to their judgment, as they would have no reason to open packages unless they contained something potentially dangerous. It is much different where the agents have a dual objective; the decision to open a particular briefcase may be motivated by the desire to comply with the FTS's cooperation policy. Particularly zealous FTS agents may choose to open packages more often, hoping to improve their chances of earning a reward. In short, the policy of "work[ing] hand-in-hand with U.S. Customs and Port Police regarding the detection and reporting of drugs and U.S. currency" will very likely influence FTS officers to conduct more searches, and more intrusive searches, than if they focus on air safety alone.

The case before us illustrates this point. After Campbell opened his briefcase and revealed the large quantity of currency, FTS agent Kangas "questioned [Campbell] and determined that he was taking a domestic flight to Los Angeles." Having found no weapons or explosives in Campbell's bag, agent Kangas's legitimate interest in Campbell's identity and destination were at an end; there was no further safety-related justification for detaining Campbell and prying into his affairs. Quite obviously, agent Kangas found herself hot on the trail of a reward and was doing what she could to help law enforcement authorities identify Campbell.

Aside from the direct effect on those passengers who are subject to the more intrusive searches, the cooperation between FTS personnel and law enforcement authorities may also have an adverse effect on other air travelers. To the extent FTS personnel devote time, energy and attention to achieving objectives other than air safety, their effectiveness in carrying out responsibilities under the Airport Transportation Security Act may be impaired.

Here, for example, even assuming that the decision to select Campbell for a manual inspection was legitimate, agents Boswell and Kangas spent more time dealing with him, and later with the customs agents, than if their interest had been limited to air safety. It is possible, of course, that in searching for contraband, FTS agents will find weapons or explosives. But this diversion of resources may also unnecessarily delay the flow of traffic through security checkpoints and distract FTS agents from the goals of the Air Transportation Security Act. We have no way of knowing the precise effect of the arrangement at the Seattle Airport on any particular search. And that's the problem: having determined that a material new variable has been introduced into the process, we can no longer rely on the legislative facts that underlay our approval of security checks as administrative searches in *Davis*.

We cannot fault law enforcement officials for focusing on airport security searches as a source of information regarding criminal activities.The task they face is enormous and important; a sieve through which pass the contents of billions of satchels, purses, briefcases and pockets will naturally strain out much that is of interest to law enforcement. But it is the very ubiquitousness of airport security checks that calls for the greatest vigilance on our part. Because these checks touch the lives of so many, because they have become such an accepted part of our existence, they are capable of great abuse. Liberty—the freedom from unwarranted intrusion by government—is as easily lost through insistent nibbles by government officials who seek to do their jobs too well as by those whose purpose it is to oppress; the piranha can be as deadly as the shark.

The accommodation reached between law enforcement authorities and FTS officials at the Seattle airport no doubt makes much sense from a law enforcement perspective. Too much sense. It effectively transforms a limited check for weapons and explosives into a general search for evidence of crime. This substantially erodes the privacy rights of passengers who travel through the system. "No one can serve two masters," we are told. MATTHEW 6:24. A limited administrative search cannot also serve unrelated law enforcement purposes. To the extent that Campbell was identified by FTS officials and reported to customs agents pursuant to an established policy of encouraging such reporting, the search can no longer be justified as an administrative search on the basis approved by us in *Davis*.

B.

Because we cannot uphold the search under the rationale of *Davis*, we must next consider whether it may be justified under any other exception to the warrant requirement.

We have already determined that an airport screening system cannot be justified as a limited search for weapons under *Terry v. Ohio* (1968). Nor can we uphold the search, as the government would have us do, on the basis of consent. There is some sense, we suppose, in which it could be said that Campbell consented to the search that led up to the discovery of the currency by FTS agents. But the scope of the consent is perforce limited by the nature of the search to which the subject submits. Passengers rushing to board a plane can fairly be said to have consented to a search for weapons and explosives; any such devices found in their possession are fair game for seizure. But passengers would be surprised to learn that they are also submitting to a more generalized search for contraband or, broader yet, things that are not in themselves illegal but merely look suspicious.

We are reluctant to hold that the consent given for airport security searches exceeds the rationale of those searches. Indeed, we doubt that the government could extract so broad a consent as a condition for boarding an airplane. As Professor LaFave notes, should the government decide to screen all passengers on trains, buses or cars, such a procedure could not be upheld on grounds of implied consent, in the absence of a constitutionally sufficient justification.

Any other conclusion "not only offends common sense, but flies in the face of the most fundamental Fourth Amendment principle that the government cannot 'avoid the restrictions of the Fourth Amendment by notifying the public that all telephone lines would be tapped or that all homes would be searched.'" 4 W. LAFAVE, SEARCH AND SEIZURE § 10.6(g) (2d ed. 1987). The true voluntariness of an airport search is doubtful in any event. As one commentator noted:

> A passenger is not, of course, compelled to travel by airplane, but many travelers would reasonably conclude that they had no realistic alternative. Instead of justifying passenger searches as consensual, we should candidly acknowledge the element of coercion and seek a rationale which justifies them, coercion notwithstanding.

Jay K. Wright, *Hijacking Risks and Airport Frisks: Reconciling Airline Security with the Fourth Amendment*, 9 CRIM. L. BULL. 491, 499-500 (1973). We have held that the "exercise of the constitutional right to travel may not be conditioned upon the relinquishment of another constitutional right (here, the Fourth Amendment right to be free of unreasonable search), absent a compelling state interest."

Because some compelling state interest must exist before the government can burden the constitutional right to travel, airport searches cannot be justified by consent alone. "At the minimum, governmental restrictions upon freedom to travel are to be weighed against the necessity advanced to justify them, and a restriction that burdens the right to travel 'too broadly and indiscriminately' cannot be sustained." We conclude, therefore, that the airport search established by the record in this case cannot be justified by consent. Nor are the exceptions to the warrant requirement established for exigent circumstances, inventory searches or border searches applicable. *See generally* Note, *The Constitutionality of Airport Searches*, 72 MICH. L. REV. 128 (1973).

Campbell raises a series of other objections to the procedures employed by the United States Customs Service in this case. He claims, for example, that his detention by customs agents at LAX violated the guidelines established by *United States v. Place*, 462 U.S. 696 (1983), and that the procedure for determining that the currency was used in connection with drug transactions was flawed. One or more of these contentions may well have merit. As we have resolved this case on other grounds, we need not reach these issues. Although we have serious doubt about the district court's ruling on the matter, we also need not reach Campbell's argument that there was not sufficient evidence to sustain a judgment of forfeiture. Thus, the order denying the motion to suppress is reversed. The order of forfeiture is vacated and the case is remanded for further proceedings consistent with this opinion.

UNITED STATES v. LOPEZ
328 F. Supp. 1077 (E.D.N.Y. 1971)

WEINSTEIN, District Judge.

Defendant is charged with concealing and facilitating the transportation of heroin and of conspiring to commit that crime. He has moved to suppress heroin taken from his person.

Presented is the question of whether the anti-hijacking system used at our airports is constitutional. For the reasons indicated below, we hold the system valid. Nevertheless, because in this particular case the elegant and objective method devised by the government to deter and apprehend hijackers was distorted in an irrational and prejudicial way by airlines personnel, defendant's motion must be granted.

FACTS

With his companion, Ernesto Perez Gonzalez, defendant, Frank Lorenzi Lopez, was apprehended on November 14, 1970 at John F. Kennedy International Airport as he was about to board a Pan American flight bound for Puerto Rico. Two Deputy United States Marshals had been called from a trailer adjacent to the Pan American premises where they were stationed in connection with the government's anti-hijacking program. An employee of Pan American had pointed out the two passengers as 'selectees'—persons whose 'profile' suggested a substantial likelihood that were potential hijackers; who had activated a magnetometer, a metal detection device; and who, upon request, had failed to produce identification.

The Marshals approached the two and asked if they would walk through the magnetometer installation again, first with, and then without, a small blue bag that Gonzalez was carrying. Each of them did so, activating the device on both trips. The Marshals again requested identification but none was produced. At this time Gonzalez identified himself by his proper name, indicating that the name Julio Lopez, which appeared on his ticket, was erroneous.

The two travelers were then asked to accompany the Marshals to a private area adjacent to the passenger boarding ramp where their outer clothing was patted down ('frisked') for weapons. A Marshal felt a hard object about 4 inches wide, 6 inches long, and three-quarters of an inch deep under Lopez's clothing. A tinfoil covered plastic envelope tightly packed with white powder had been discovered. Filed tested, the power proved positive for heroin. Gonzalez and Lopez were then arrested.

Both were charged with concealment and facilitating the transportation of the packet of narcotics found on Lopez and with conspiring to commit this crime. The government's evidence at the suppression hearing made it apparent that there was no case against Gonzalez, even if the heroin was admitted. Accordingly, a judgment of acquittal was granted after the government and Gonzalez waived a jury and agreed that the hearing testimony would be deemed received at the trial.

FEDERAL AERONAUTICS ADMINISTRATION SYSTEM FOR DISCOURAGING AND APPREHENDING POTENTIAL HIJACKERS

In October 1968 a Task Force was appointed to consider methods of combating the increasing number of airline hijackings. *Cf.* BIBLIOGRAPHY ON AIRPLANE HIJACKING, 26 THE RECORD OF THE ASSOC. OF THE BAR OF THE CITY OF NEW YORK, 325-332 (1971). A number of interested agencies including the Federal Aeronautics Administration, the Department of Justice and the Department of Commerce were represented. This Task Force included individuals trained in several disciplines including psychology, law, engineering and administration. Dr. John T. Dailey, a well-trained psychologist with a broad practical background in education and government personnel, took a leading role in developing and testing the Task Force ideas. At the hearing he testified at length and impressed the Court with his skill and honesty.

On the serious problems faced by the Task Force was that many millions of passengers use air transportation. Any practical procedure would have to permit maximum access to aircraft with minimal inconvenience and embarrassment to passengers and almost no delay in the operations of the airlines. Among the investigations undertaken by this group were a detailed study of the characteristics of all then known hijackers and of the air traveling public. Background investigations of hijackers as well as visual and photographic studies of boarding air passengers were relied upon. Among the findings were (1) hijackers were generally not highly motivated and resourceful and (2) they shared certain characteristics markedly distinguishing them from the general traveling public. In addition, engineering studies were undertaken of available weapon detection devices.

After thorough field testing of equipment and various screening techniques, the present anti-hijacking system was instituted. Although we are concerned primarily with the preflight apprehension aspect of the system its principal focus is on deterrence. Involved are the following elements:

1. **Heavy penalties**. A severe statute with possible death penalties for hijacking was adopted. There already were in force various regulations and statutes prohibiting the carrying on board of firearms and other weapons.

2. **Notice to the Public**. Signs in English and Spanish are posted at the boarding gates where passengers' tickets are checked reading as follows:

AVIATION SECURITY

AIRCRAFT HIJACKING IS A FEDERAL CRIME
PUNISHABLE BY DEATH

CARRYING CONCEALED WEAPONS ABOARD
AIRCRAFT IS PUNISHABLE BY PRISON SENTENCES
& FINES

PASSENGERS AND BAGGAGE
SUBJECT TO SEARCH

These signs are eleven by fourteen inches with half inch high letters. Warnings of the same or larger dimensions are conspicuously posted at other parts of the air terminal.

3. **Profile**. If a passenger meets a prescribed "profile" he is focused on by airline employees. The details of the profile and its use are set out below.

4. **Magnetometer**. A magnetometer is installed in the passageway leading to the plane so that all passengers must pass through it. It sets off a flash warning light when metal equal to or greater than an average 25 caliber gun in magnetic force deflecting power is carried by. This device is described in more detail below.

5. **Interview by Airlines Personnel**. A person who triggers the magnetometer and meets the profile requirements is 'interviewed' by airlines personnel. If he provides satisfactory identification, he is permitted to proceed unimpeded. Otherwise he is designated a "selectee" and is denied boarding until a Deputy United States Marshal is summoned.

6. **Interview by Marshal**. The Marshal again requests identification of those designated as "selectees." If satisfactory identification is not furnished it is suggested that the person go through the magnetometer once more. Before walking through, he is asked if he has any metal on his person or in any baggage he is carrying. If he replies in the negative and still sets off the magnetometer, a request is made that he submit to a "voluntary" search. It is explained that this search is part of an attempt by the government to prevent hijacking.

7. **Frisk**. The Marshal pats-down the external clothing of the subject in order to discover if he is carrying any weapons. Depending upon what is found as a result of the frisk, boarding is permitted or the person is detained.

The program is designed to speed passengers who are unlikely to present danger and to isolate, with the least possible discomforture or delay, those presenting a substantial probability of danger. At each successive screening state an attempt is made to permit as many as possible to complete boarding.

While no single screening technique can by itself completely protect the flying public—without creating an objectionable level of disturbance and inconvenience—probabilities are increased by combining several approaches, thus sufficiently reducing the size of the population which must untimately by physically interfered with to a practicable and socially acceptable level. *Cf. Rosado v. Wyman* (E.D.N.Y. 1970) (collecting authorities on use of mathematics in the law); Michael O. Finkelstein and William B. Fairley, *A Bayesian Approach to Identification Evidence*, 83 HARV. L. REV. 489 (1970).

The system seems to serve this purpose well. Whether because of it or for other reasons hijacking decreased in 1970 to approximately 50% of what it was in 1969. No flight fully protected by the program has been hijacked.

One sample consisting of 500,000 screened passengers showed that only 1,406 satisfied the profile—.28%. Approximately one-half of those were nevertheless permitted to board immediately after failing to activate the magnetometer, leaving 712, or .14% to be interviewed. Of those interviewed, 283, approximately one-third, were actually searched. Therefore, only .05% of the sample were ultimately subjected to a preventive weapons frisk. Twenty persons were denied boarding—approximately 1/15 of those searched and of these, 16 were arrested. In sum, almost everyone (99.86%) of the one-half million persons passed swiftly through the boarding process without even being asked a question and 99.95% boarded without being searched. In another sample of 226,000 screened passengers .57% were selected as meeting the profile; .28% were interviewed; and .13% were searched. It was reported that none were searched 'involuntarily' and only 24 were denied boarding.

Statistics for a number of covered airlines at the John F. Kennedy International Airport in December 1970 were produced. While the number of passengers using these airlines during this month is not shown, they carried a total of 2,645,000 passengers during the last six months of 1970—or on the average 441,000 each month. Three hundred and three reportedly met the profile and nine arrests were made. There were confiscations of 10 illegal knives, one tear gas pen, four hand guns, one gas gun and one pack of marijuana. The Kennedy statistics, insofar as they are affected by Pan American Airways figures, cannot now be relied upon, as discussed below.

That the risk of hijacking is greatly increased when a passenger possesses weapons can hardly be doubted. In the 80 hijacking incidents involving planes of United States registry up to June of 1970, there were 55 firearms, 20 knives, 14 alleged bombs, 3 razors or razor blades, 1 BB gun, 1 tear gas pen, and 1 broken bottle.

In camera testimony was persuasive that the characteristics of the potential hijackers chosen for the profile were well calculated to eliminate safe persons while isolating those likely to be dangerous. No one can be certain, of course, that anyone failing all the tests of the system will be a hijacker. In fact, approximately 14 out of every

15 people who were searched proved to have no weapons and were then permitted to proceed. Moreover, as the facts detailed below indicate, there is always the risk that a soundly designed process will be abused by ignorant, careless or malevolent personnel. As one commentator pointed out,

> permitting any use of certain mathematical methods entails a sufficiently high risk of misuse, or a risk of misuse sufficiently costly to avoid, that it would be irrational not to take such misuse into account when deciding whether to permit the methods to be employed at all.

Laurence Tribe, *Trial by Mathematics: Precision and Ritual in the Legal Process*, 84 HARV. L. REV. 1329, 1331 (1971). Measured against the air traveling population as a whole, the method is highly effective in narrowing the group which needs particular attention. Where the risks of hijacking to passengers and crew and to the viability of the entire industry are so great we cannot say on balance that use of the system is imprudent. Whether it meets the reasonableness test of the Constitution is an issue dealt with below.

Before turning to that problem there are two procedural difficulties that need to be resolved. One of them, the issue of in camera hearing, raises very serious questions. The other, acceptance of proof that the magnetometer did what it was purported to have done, is relatively simple. We turn to the simple issue first.

MAGNETOMETER

The electronic weapons detector—appropriately named "Friskem"—utilized in this case depends upon magnetic filed detectors called "flux-gate magnetometers." The unit was developed after conferences with representatives of the Task Force.

Its operation is based upon the physical fact that the earth is surrounded by a relatively constant magnetic field composed of lines of flux. Steel and other ferromagnetic metals are much better conductors than the air. When any such metal moves through an area, nearby magnetic lines of flux are distorted to some degree as they tend to converge and pass through the metal while seeking the path of least resistance. Such distortions occurring near a "fluxgate magnetometer" create a signal which can be amplified and calibrated to detect magnetic disturbances.

Though these scientific principals are not matters of common knowledge they may be readily and accurately determined, are verifiable to almost a certainty and are not disputed. The literature was placed in the Court file, notice was given to the parties that the Court intended to rely upon it, and there was no objection by either party. Under these circumstances the Court takes judicial notice of the scientific principles utilized in the design of the Friskem unit. The finds that such a machine, if properly constructed and operated, can perform in the manner described to the Court by testimony and manuals.

Since no opinion was brought to the Court's attention taking judicial notice of magnetometer capabilities, the Court also relied upon expert testimony adduced at the hearing. Such reliance is often the first step in a process that passes through judicial notice to acceptance on a theory of *stare decisis*. This has been the experience in connection with such scientific techniques as use of fingerprints, ballistic comparison and radar. Testimony and exhibits adduced at the hearing and trial indicated that the Friskem device was designed, in accordance with scientific principles already described, specifically to meet the requirements of the Task Force and that it was properly manufactured.

The model used in the instant case consists of a series of magnetometers in two vertical poles located 36 inches apart and amplification equipment and indicators contained in a console unit. As demonstrated in the Court, and as revealed in the various manuals, the operation of the equipment requires no understanding of its theory. Its calibration is easy and its adjustment can be assured by simple visual observations.

While the person who actually adjusted the machine at the airport was not available, it was proper to accept testimony with respect to the custom and practice of the enterprise. That practice demonstrated that the physical equipment was adjusted so that a light would flash when metal having the effect of a 25 caliber pistol passed through it.

The Friskmen unit will be activated by a variety of objects including a collection of ordinary belongings carried by passengers. In fact, somewhere in the order of 50% of the persons who pass through trigger it. Since, however, this is only one of a series of separating stages intended as much for deterrent value as for ability to ferret out metal objects, its usefulness is substantial.

IN CAMERA INVESTIGATION OF PROFILE

Were even one characteristic of the "profile" generally revealed, the system could be seriously undermined by hijackers fabricating an acceptable profile. Because of this serious danger, the Court excluded from the courtroom the public and the defendant—but not his attorney —when it took testimony which revealed the specific characteristics included in the profile and the findings which led to its adoption.

Defense counsel were permitted to hear all the testimony about the specific characteristics and were able to cross-examine witnesses. They were informed that should it be necessary to consult with their clients about any of this information they could make this known to the Court and it would then reconsider its decision to deny the information to the defendants. No such request was made.

The Court enjoined counsel not to reveal the profile and it has confidence that its injunction will be followed. Defendant argued that he be permitted to attend and be similarly enjoined but such an injunction could never be enforced. The evidence revealed that he was a narcotic addict or a dealer in narcotics or both who would feel no compunction about telling what he knew to all who would lend an ear in prison or out. Under these circumstances the Court had no choice but to exclude him. The testimony revealed that studies underlying the profile were thorough. Procedures followed in developing it were adequate. Appropriate statistical, sociological and psychological data and techniques were utilized. The profile is a highly effective procedure for isolating potential hijackers.

After studying known hijackers, the task force complied twenty-five to thirty characteristics in which hijackers differed significantly from the air-traveling public. By putting only a few of them together they could obtain a reliable combination sharply differentiating potential hijackers from non-hijackers.

During the testing period and shortly thereafter in 1969 the task force studied an additional sample of 30 new hijackers and found that over 90% of that group would have met the profile. There has been a continuous process of reevaluation in light of new hijackings and changes in trends of hijacking. Thus far the original profile has retained its validity. Those characteristics selected can be easily observed without exercising judgment. They do not discriminate against any group on the basis of religion, origin, political views, or race. They are precisely designed to select only those who present a high probability of being dangerous. Thus, they violate none of the traditional equal protection standards.

The constitutional issue raised by the decision to exclude the defendant from the inquiry on the profile, while permitting his counsel to attend and cross-examine witnesses, is obvious. Defendant has both a right to confront witnesses against him and to a public trial.

(a) Public Trial

American distrust for secret proceedings was roused by persecutions of the Inquisition and the Star Chamber; it has been nurtured by contemporary examples of abuse in a variety of repressive regimes. "The knowledge that every criminal trial is subject to contemporaneous review in the forum of public opinion is an effective restraint on possible abuse of judicial power." "Secret tribunals were effective instruments of oppression." *Estes v. Texas* (1965). This right to a public trial attaches at the suppression hearing—often the crucial stage.

Despite the important rights conferred on both the defendant and the public by the Constitution, exclusion of the public, or portions of it, for limited purposes and for short periods is sometimes justified in the public interest or in the interest of the defendant. Thus the risk of danger to witnesses or the need to preserve order warrants closed proceedings. The danger in revealing the profile is so great as to warrant the public's exclusion for a limited period. There was no violation of the right to a public trial.

(b) Right of confrontation

A much more difficult issue is presented by exclusion of the defendant himself. Normally vital to a fair trial is the Sixth Amendment right to confront witnesses. So, too, are the more general elements of fairness in due process. As in the case of the right to a public trial, a suppression hearing is considered part of the trial. The right is not absolute. It may be waived by acts or statements of the defendant. The Court may also exclude the defendant when necessary to preserve order and decorum in the courtroom.

It might be argued that exclusion of the defendant constitutes harmless error when his counsel was present and the defendant could not by his presence have contributed to his defense. In this case the only in camera testimony concerned revelation of the actual criteria contained in the profile which the defendant irrefutably satisfied. Defense counsel was present throughout the testimony any cross-examined the witnesses thoroughly. Arguably no prejudice resulted. The harmless error argument is, however, not sufficiently persuasive to justify the procedure adopted.

It is true that this defendant was in no position to assist his attorney with detailed knowledge of the events essential for a variety of tactical and other decisions in cross-examining, objecting and the like. But any defendant, if he is found guilty, should, as a matter of fundamental fairness and as part of the rehabilitative process, have the assurance, by reason of his direct observation, that justice was done. There could hardly be anything more rankling to a defendant and destructive of his morale and incentive to reform than to have the nagging suspicion that something was presented to the Court which should not have been.

In the case before us the testimony indicated that the airlines personnel at the boarding area act in close conjunction with the U.S. Marshals in a combined effort to thwart potential hijackers. While the Marshals ultimately perform the "frisk" it is the airline employees who have primary responsibility for applying the profile and designating "selectees." In fact, the uncontroverted testimony of the Marshals in this case was that they did not determine whether a passenger was a selectee but rather relied solely on the representation of the Pan American officials. In effect the system itself, communicating through the airline, acts as an informer providing information leading to interview and search. The reliability of that information depends upon the nature of the profile and on how well the airline employees have applied it.

The instant case presents a strong case for nondisclosure to the defendant because the informant is an objective system, not an individual who might be known to the defendant. He could not, by his presence, hope to impugn its credibility. Furthermore, since the level of probability required to justify a frisk is lower than 'probable cause' there is a corresponding lower necessity for disclosure. We turn our attention to the frisk issues.

FRISK

The Fourth Amendment requires "that the police must, whenever practicable, obtain advance judicial approval of searches and seizures through the warrant procedure." *Terry v. Ohio* (1968). No warrant was obtained for the search in this case, nor, as a practical matter could one have been expected.

The anti-hijacking system depends upon being able to swiftly sift out potential hijackers for closer scrutiny while permitting all passengers including "selectees" to board unless weapons are discovered. Exigencies of time precluded the Marshals from obtaining a warrant in this situation. The government has argued that continuing the boarding process after reading the posted and clearly observable signs which state "PASSENGERS AND BAGGAGE SUBJECT TO SEARCH" amounts to implied consent to searches such as occurred in this case. There was no evidence of express consent. Consent to a search involves a relinquishment of fundamental constitutional rights and should not be lightly inferred.

The government has failed to sustain its burden of establishing any sort of voluntary consent. The evidence shows only that the defendant did not resist or protest when the Marshals asked him to accompany them to the private area adjacent to the boarding ramp for a search. Such conduct by one who may think himself in custody (although actual custodial detention was not established) hardly amounts to an 'unequivocal, specific, and intelligently given' consent.

Nor can the government properly argue that it can condition the exercise of the defendant's constitutional right to travel on the voluntary relinquishment of his Fourth Amendment rights. Implied consent under such circumstances would be inherently coercive. The government's theory is further called into question by the testimony of the two Marshals who performed the searches in this case. They testified that the defendant was not free to go at any time after he had been interviewed by them. Thus, the defendant and others similarly situated could not vitiate the 'consent' by reversing a decision to board the aircraft.

The search cannot be justified as one "incident" to an arrest. Testimony of both Marshals revealed that the arrests were not made until after the frisk had been completed and the contraband seized. Similarly, there is no evidence of "hot pursuit" or danger of imminent destruction of any known evidence. No apparent offense was observed being committed in the presence of these officers which would have justified the search. The contraband was certainly not in "plain view." Thus, the only exception to the warrant rule under which the search of this defendant can be justified is the protective "frisk" for weapons authorized by *Terry*.

The anti-hijacking system is unusual in that it provides statistics showing the precise probabilities involved. Based upon the surveys available, out of every approximately 15 persons who are frisked one person is found with a weapon. Thus the probability that any person who is selected by the system to be frisked has a weapon is approximately 6%. We know that the frisk is conducted in private with as much courtesy as the circumstances permit and that those who are frisked and allowed to go on their way generally welcome the protective measures taken in their behalf rather than resent them. The substantial interest in preserving the integrity and safety of air travel by preventing hijacking is obvious. In light of the circumstances, a 6% danger of arms suffices to justify a frisk.

The statistics discussed earlier indicate that only somewhere on the order of 1/10 of 1% of all passengers screened are actually frisked and that included in that .1% are practically all of the potential hijackers. The procedure, as designed, operates on purely objective criteria independent of race, color, or creed. It is well calculated to winnow out potential hijackers while occasioning a bare minimum of inconvenience to a very small percentage of the flying public—an inconvenience which most subjects seem, in fact, to accept. A United States Marshall would be imprudent were he to refuse to heed the warning given to him by the system. A narrowly circumscribed protective weapons "pat-down" or "frisk" is constitutionally permissible under these circumstances.

We do not think it significant that frisks are normally intended to protect the officer against sudden assault during an interview of the suspect while the anti-hijacking frisk is utilized to protect passengers and the frisk takes place after preliminary questioning. It is not without significance that *Terry* repeatedly recognized that the policeman's frisk could be justified on the ground that it was needed to "protect himself and others from possible danger."

Mere statistical information such as that generated in this case does not, by itself, justify "frisks." If, for example reliable statistics were available that in a given community one person in fifteen (6%) regularly carried concealed weapons the police would not be justified in arbitrarily stopping and frisking anyone on the street. Such harassment by police without more objective evidence of criminal activity or a legitimate investigative purpose is proscribed by the Fourth Amendment. The Court is charged with the duty of balancing the competing interests of the individual and the society in each case presented. No single percentage figure can provide a test for constitutional legitimacy. Even in the hijacking situation, any intrusion by a Marshal beyond the legitimate scope of a weapons search is clearly unjustified and the fruits of such an excessive search would be inadmissible in a subsequent criminal proceeding.

In this case the location and size of the object and the fact that it was tightly packed and hard covered and that it was large enough to be a container for a pistol or even explosive material gave the Marshal ample cause to require removal from underneath defendant's clothing. Visual observation of the package covered with tinfoil would have increased the suspicion and apprehension of a reasonable officer. In fact, we find that the Marshal's conduct of this investigation was almost an exact model of the "frisk" approved in *Terry v. Ohio*.

SEIZURE OF CONTRABAND

We come now to the final Fourth Amendment issue before us and that is whether a frisk conducted in good faith to locate weapons believed to be present will justify the seizure of evidence of crimes other than those involved in boarding a plane with a weapon. The answer is yes. If a search is conducted in good faith to locate a weapon and if it does not go beyond the limits of what is required to uncover such an object then the officer need not close his eyes to evidence of other crimes which he may uncover.

We conclude that contraband seized as a result of a properly circumscribed investigatory frisk predicated on information generated by a well administrated federal anti-hijacking system is admissible in evidence. Such a seizure comports with established Fourth Amendment principles and were it not for the special circumstances of this case we would not hesitate to deny this motion to suppress.

DISQUIETING IMPLICATIONS OF SYSTEM

We reach this conclusion recognizing that the system used is disquieting. Employing a combination of psychological. sociological, and physical sciences to screen, inspect and categorize unsuspecting citizens raises visions of abuse in our increasingly technological society. Proposals based upon statistical research designed to predict who might commit crimes and giving them the special attention of law enforcement agencies is particularly disturbing. There is a basis for

> what anti-utopians like Huxley and Orwell have forecast—though these dismal despotisms will be far more stable and effective than their prophets have foreseen. For they will be equipped with techniques of inner-manipulation as unobtrusively fine as gossamer.

T. ROSZAK, THE MAKING OF A COUNTER CULTURE (1969).

Undoubtedly there are persons with objectively observable characteristics who provide a higher statistical probability of danger than the population as a whole. But our criminal law is based on the theory that we do not condemn people because they are potentially dangerous. We only prosecute illegal acts. Putting a group of potential violators in custody on the ground that this group contained all or nearly all of the people who would commit crimes in the future would raise the most serious constitutional issues. *But cf. Korematsu v. United States* (1944). The procedure before us accomplishes no such result and raising such spectors does not assist in a rational evaluation of the anti-hijacking program. This system does not constitute a first step along the road to preventive detention of potentially dangerous classes of persons.

We need not fear that approving use of the magnetometer to search by means of unseen electromagnetic lines of force foretells approval of more frightening systems: for example, one searching the brain waves of members of the public, as they unsuspectingly pass by check points, to determine if they are tense or frightened and thus, possibly, contemplating anti-social conduct. K.H. PRIBRAM, 2 BRAIN AND BEHAVIOR 47-49 (1969); David Cohen, *Magnetoencephalography: Evidence of Magnetic Fields Produced by Alpha-Rhythm Currents*, 161 SCIENCE 784 (1968); Berkhout, Walter and Adey, *Alterations of the Human Electroencephalogram Induced by Stressful Verbal Activity*, 27 ELECTROENCEPHALOGRAPHY AND CLINICAL NEUROPHYSIOLOGY 457 (1969). Such a use of technology might well raise serious problems of self-incrimination which are not present in this case.

Even the use of the magnetometer might be an objectionable intrusion were it not accompanied by an antecedent warning from the profile indicating a need to focus particular attention on the subject. We do not now decide whether, in the absence of some prior indication of danger, the government may validly require any citizen to pass through an electronic device which probes beneath his clothing and effects to reveal what he carries with him.

Finally, in the case before us, though electromagnetic waves are intercepted, the analogy to a clandestine wiretap is not valid since no communication—internal or external—of the subject is involved. *Cf. Katz v. United States* (1971). While candidly recognizing the disquieting possibilities suggested by the techniques of the anti-hijacking campaign, we are unpersuaded that the rights of air travelers generally have been or will be violated by the proper application of this system. We ought not be frightened out of taking sensible protective steps by the possibilities of misuse so long as our courts are in a position to prevent abuse should it arise.

SUPPRESSION IN THIS CASE

While evidence discovered during a frisk pursuant to this anti-hijacking procedure would normally be admissible, the special circumstances of the instant case require suppression. The Pan American Passenger Service Manager issued a memorandum on July 22, 1970 purporting to "update" the "profile" to be applied in the anti-hijacking screening procedure. This action was not authorized by Pan American Security Services, the United States Marshal Service, or the Federal Aeronautics Administration. It eliminated one criterion included in the official profile established by the Federal Aviation Administration and added two additional categories.

Both the government and Pan American disowned the memorandum and indicated that it had been withdrawn. Neither were able, however, to assure the Court that the boarding area personnel responsible for applying the profile to passengers on November 14, 1970 had not read the memorandum and were not following it. Under the circumstances, the Court must assume that the "updated" profile was, in fact, employed in selecting the defendant.

The one characteristic eliminated by this supplemental memorandum effectively excised from the screening procedure one of the fundamental characteristics of hijackers as described by Dr. Dailey during in camera testimony. One of the characteristics added introduced an ethnic element for which there is no experimental basis, thus raising serious equal protection problems. The second added criterion called for an act of individual judgment on the part of airline employees. The effect of these changes was to destroy the essential neutrality and objectivity of the approved profile.

In evaluating the constitutionality of the system that was actually in operation on the day in question we cannot now rely on the statistics presented to the Court since the properly conducted samplings utilized the official Task Force profile. These statistics were critical in our determination that this system was an appropriate method of protecting air travelers.

The procedure instituted to detect hijackers becomes unacceptable when abused in the manner described in this case. The approved system survives constitutional scrutiny only by its careful adherence to absolute objectivity and neutrality. When elements of discretion and prejudice are interjected it becomes constitutionally impermissible. While the abuse in this case was by airline officials, not the government, these employees were acting as government agents insofar as they designated "selectees" and alerted Marshals. The court's only effective means of controlling official excess is to refuse to admit in evidence the fruits of unconstitutional seizures.

The government may not institute a system such as this one and then deny responsibility for properly policing it. Continuous supervision and control of personnel who have the power to intrude on constitutional rights is essential. Any system and the dangers it poses must be evaluated in the light of the skills and the dedication of those who will operate it. We must sometimes recognize that, "[o]perating personnel simply are less disciplined, less dedicated, and less concerned about doing the job right (and there is) nothing in our contemporary culture which is likely to reverse the trend." W. K. Jones, *Regulation under Fire: Consumers, The Environment, The Economy, and The Impact of Change*, TWELFTH ANNUAL COLUMBIA LAW SYMPOSIUM (Mar. 20, 1971).

The anti-hijacking system can be a valuable and effective method of protecting millions of air travelers from the threat of violence and sudden death in the air. Properly supervised it is also constitutional. Abuses such as the one which occurred in this case must, however, be eliminated if evidence obtained in its operation is to be used in our Courts. As such, Defendant's motion to suppress evidence must be granted. Since without this evidence the government has no case, the indictment is dismissed.

MUSTAFA v. CITY OF CHICAGO

442 F.3d 544 (7th Cir. 2006)

WILLIAMS, Circuit Judge.

Anna Mustafa sued the defendant police officers for false arrest and violation of her civil rights following an incident at Chicago's O'Hare Airport. The district court granted summary judgment in favor of the defendants because it found that there was probable cause to arrest Mustafa, and even in the absence of probable cause, the defendants were protected by qualified immunity. Because we agree with the district court that the defendant officers acted upon probable cause and, in any event, acted within the scope of their immunity, we reject Mustafa's argument that summary judgment was improperly granted and affirm the district court's ruling.

BACKGROUND

Anna Mustafa is a 56-year-old American citizen of Palestinian descent and Muslim faith. On December 28, 2001, just three months after the attacks of September 11, Mustafa received word that her father had died in Israel. That afternoon, Mustafa arrived at the Swissair ticket counter at O'Hare, intending to fly to Tel Aviv by way of Zurich, Switzerland to attend her father's funeral. Mustafa was accompanied to the counter by nineteen members of her immediate family. Mustafa ordered a "Muslim" meal for the flight. Moments later, the Swissair clerk took Mustafa to a bomb-detection machine to have her two pieces of luggage inspected for weapons. Mustafa suspected that this was an instance of discriminatory religious or ethnic profiling.

Following the inspection, Mustafa complained about her treatment to a Swissair manager, Muhammad Qadeer, who offered to escort her to the gate because the screening was complete. During this exchange, Mustafa was screaming and the area was crowded. Mustafa realized that security personnel had failed to inspect her purse. She did not realize that carry-on bags would be screened at another checkpoint, and she was concerned that if Swissair later realized it had not checked the purse, she would be delayed and miss her flight. Mustafa tried to point out that her purse had not been inspected, saying, "You already checked my luggage. Maybe I have a bomb in my purse. Nobody has checked that." In response to the word "bomb," an employee working at a nearby United Airlines counter began to yell that she had heard the "B-word" and that security should be called. Another manager, Mauricio Penaranda, called the police to report an "unruly" passenger saying the word "bomb."

Within two to three minutes, defendant Officer Susan Schober arrived and observed what she later described as a "commotion." Qadeer informed her that Mustafa had made a statement like "Maybe I have a bomb in my purse." Officer Schober, Qadeer, Mustafa, and one of Mustafa's sons, Murad Mustafa, spent 20 to 30 minutes in conversation that focused on calming Mustafa down so that she could get on the flight to

Zurich. Following this conversation, defendants Sergeant Gawlik and Officer Burke arrived and asked Officer Schober if she had checked Mustafa's purse. Since the answer was no, the two new officers checked the purse, shouting abusively at Mustafa. Sergeant Gawlik placed Mustafa under arrest. Mustafa, her son Murad, and Sergeant Gawlik engaged in a screaming argument during which Sergeant Gawlik insulted Mustafa's family and made a racist reference to the September 11 terrorist attacks three months earlier.

Mustafa spent two days in jail before being released on $50,000 bond; she missed her father's funeral. Mustafa was indicted on a charge of Felony Disorderly Conduct — Bomb Threat pursuant to 720 Ill. Comp. Stat. 5/26-1(a)(3), but acquitted following a bench trial. The statute under which Mustafa was charged applies to any person who "Transmits or causes to be transmitted in any manner to another a false alarm to the effect that a bomb ... is concealed in such place that its explosion or release would endanger human life, knowing at the time of such transmission that there is no reasonable ground for believing that such bomb ... is concealed in such place."

After Mustafa was acquitted, she filed the instant suit against the City of Chicago and four police officers, which originally contained seven counts. A number of claims, including all those stated against the city, were dismissed. The defendant police officers moved for summary judgment on the surviving counts, false arrest and violation of Mustafa's right to equal protection under the law pursuant to 18 U.S.C. § 1983. The district court granted summary judgment for the defendants on both counts. This appeal followed.

II. ANALYSIS

A. There was Probable Cause to Arrest Mustafa

We review a district court's grant of summary judgment *de novo*, viewing the facts in the light most favorable to the non-moving party. Probable cause to arrest is an absolute defense to any claim under Section 1983 against police officers for wrongful arrest, false imprisonment, or malicious prosecution. This is so even where the defendant officers allegedly acted upon a malicious motive (such as the racism that Mustafa suggests motivated the defendants here).

Police officers have probable cause to arrest an individual when "the facts and circumstances within their knowledge and of which they have reasonably trustworthy information are sufficient to warrant a prudent person in believing that the suspect had committed" an offense. The court evaluates probable cause "not on the facts as an omniscient observer would perceive them," but rather "as they would have appeared to a reasonable person in the position of the arresting officer." *See Woods v. City of Chicago* (7th Cir. 2000).

Here, there were at least two separate facts that could have led a reasonable person to believe that a crime had been committed. First, the earliest arriving officer, Officer Schober, observed "commotion" and "agitation" in progress, with Mustafa at its center, at a crowded ticket counter at an international airport. *See* 720 Ill. Comp. Stat. 5/26-1(a)(1) ("A person commits disorderly conduct when he knowingly does any act in such an unreasonable manner as to alarm or disturb another and to provoke a breach of the peace"). Second, Qadeer, the Swissair manager, told the officers that the plaintiff had said, "Maybe I have a bomb." Once a reasonably credible witness informs an officer that a suspect has committed a crime, the police have probable cause to arrest the suspect. Qadeer's apparent credibility as a manager of Swissair at O'Hare has not been questioned here. Therefore, based on the undisputed facts, a prudent person might have believed that Mustafa committed the crime of making a false bomb threat.

Mustafa makes much of the fact that Qadeer never actually believed that Mustafa had a bomb in her purse. This argument misapprehends the focus of our review of the circumstances surrounding her arrest. The existence of probable cause does not depend on the actual truth of the complaint. The officers were entitled to take Qadeer at his word as to Mustafa's actions. Furthermore, the statute under which Mustafa was later charged applies categorically to all false bomb threats; it contains no element limiting its application to credible bomb threats or to those threats that convince the listener.

Likewise, the fact that Mustafa's statement was phrased conditionally, prefaced by the word "maybe," is irrelevant under the plain language of the statute, which forbids any "false alarm to the effect that a bomb ... is concealed." Particularly in light of the time and place of the event, which occurred in an international airport three months after the September 11 attacks, and the understandable sensitivity of air travelers and airport security personnel at that time, it was reasonable for the officers to conclude that Mustafa had committed disorderly conduct by stating that she might have a bomb in her purse.

Finally, Mustafa erroneously suggests that the defendant officers were derelict in their duty to investigate the circumstances surrounding the incident before arresting her. But police officers have no duty to investigate extenuating circumstances or search for exculpatory evidence once probable cause has been established via the accusation of a credible witness. They may simply arrest the accused suspect.

B. The Defendants were Protected by Qualified Immunity

Even if we were to find that there was insufficient probable cause to justify Mustafa's arrest, the doctrine of qualified immunity would nonetheless ensure a ruling in favor of the defendants.

Qualified immunity protects officers performing discretionary functions from civil liability so long as their conduct does not violate clearly established statutory or constitutional rights that a reasonable person would know about. A plaintiff seeking to defeat this defense in a Section 1983 action must show, first, that the plaintiff's rights were violated. Second, the plaintiff must show that the law concerning the plaintiff's asserted right was clearly established at the time the challenged conduct occurred. Finally, the court must determine whether a reasonably competent official would know that the conduct was unlawful in the situation he confronted. Here, Mustafa certainly had a right to be free from an arrest that lacked probable cause, and that right is clearly established, so the only remaining question is whether a reasonable officer could believe that it was lawful to arrest Mustafa.

As discussed above, Mustafa argues that it was unreasonable to believe she had committed a crime because her statement about a bomb was phrased as a possibility rather than a fact ("maybe I have a bomb in my purse"), because any reasonable person would have realized that she was not serious, and because she did not actually frighten or convince anyone that she had a real bomb. However, even if we accepted this argument, this would not disturb the defendants' qualified immunity defense.

As discussed above, the Illinois statute at issue applies to implausible and unconvincing bomb threats. *See People v. Barron* (Ill. Ct. 2004) (upholding the felony disorderly conduct conviction of an individual who joked about having a bomb in his shoe at Midway Airport, because the statute applies to false threats "regardless of the intention of the speaker or the effect the words have upon the person receiving them"). At the time of the arrest, prior to *Barron*, the application of the bomb threat statute to circumstances involving jokes, sarcasm, etc., was, perhaps, arguable; a court might theoretically read a limitation into the statute and apply it only to credible or convincing bomb threats. But where the law is open to interpretation, qualified immunity protects police officers who reasonably interpret an unclear statute. Reviewing courts must ask "whether X is a crime under the statute that the police arrested the plaintiff for violating. If the answer to that question was unclear when the arrest was made, the police are entitled to their immunity." *Northen v. City of Chicago* (7th Cir. 1997).

Here, the most Mustafa can plausibly claim is that the criminality of her conditional statement was unclear; no case clearly established that implausible threats fall outside of its reach. Furthermore, even if no reasonable person could have believed that Mustafa had made a genuine bomb threat, the officers might reasonably have believed that Mustafa had committed the closely related offense of nonspecific disorderly conduct under 720 Ill. Comp. Stat. 5/26-1(a)(1), which covers any unreasonable activity which alarms or disturbs another and provokes a breach of the peace. It is undisputed that Mustafa disturbed employees at the airport and that a noisy confrontation ensued. Officers may arrest individuals suspected of any crime; the fact that Mustafa was prosecuted under only the bomb threat section of the disorderly conduct statute does not mean that she could only properly be arrested under that section. Thus, the officers are protected by qualified immunity, and the district court's ruling in their favor is affirmed.

AL-WATAN v. AMERICAN AIRLINES, INC.

658 F. Supp. 2d 816 (E.D. Mich. 2009)

PAUL D. BORMAN, District Judge.

On August 28, 2007, Plaintiffs were scheduled to take Defendant's flight 590 from San Diego to Chicago. Plaintiffs, employees of DTC, a security contractor, were returning together from a training session with the United States military. Plaintiffs are all of Iraqi descent.

Prior to boarding the flight, a passenger on the flight, while still at the gate spoke to one of Defendant's customer service managers, Anne Grove, and to the police, to express her concern about four men, identified as Middle Eastern, who appeared to be acting suspiciously. Grove and the police officers spoke to the passenger, who complained that the men were speaking to each other in their native language. The police officers told the passenger that they had no reason to question or detain the men, as they had cleared security without incident and were not displaying any cause for intervention. Grove reported that everything appeared normal to her, and no other passengers complained.

Plaintiffs boarded the plane without incident, and took their seats. Plaintiffs were not assigned to sit together. Upon boarding, the passenger who complained at the gate decided that she did not want to take the flight, and asked to deplane. She told the flight attendant that one of the men she complained about at the gate glared at her and her children, then went to the lavatory, and when he returned to his seat, he put a blanket over his head. The passenger and her children deplaned.

Flight Attendants Ann Saltzman and Anthony Kotsonis also saw the man, Plaintiff Al-Watan, go to the lavatory at the rear of the plane shortly before departure. All of the three flight attendants on board, Saltzman, Kotsonis and Lead Flight Attendant Kenneth Koc, saw Al-Watan sitting in his seat with his head covered with a blanket. Koc testified "It looked to me like a mummy. It was over and down around the—it was just strange." Kotsonis also testified that the blanket completely covered Al-Watan's entire body and Kotsonis believed "he was hiding or appeared to be hiding." Al-Watan testified that he used the bathroom while passengers were still boarding the plane, and that he had covered his head with a blanket because he was exhausted and wanted to take a nap.

The flight attendants informed Captain Plummer about the passenger who deplaned, the reasons for her departure, and Al-Watan's actions. Thus, the flight captain was aware Al-Watan was of Middle Eastern descent. After a discussion, during which the captain asked the flight attendants whether they "felt comfortable with the situation at the time," and the flight attendants stated that they did not have a problem, the captain decided to proceed with the flight.

First Call to Captain Plummer

As the plane began to taxi, Lead Flight Attendant Koc called Captain Plummer and told him that during the safety demonstration, Plaintiff Al-Watan, the individual who had been previously sitting in his seat with his head covered by a blanket, had removed the blanket and now had leaned out into the aisle and stared directly at him. Koc testified, "I was startled as I looked down the aisle to see the passenger in 14D, who was now uncovered by the blanket, leaned over with his head out in the middle of the aisle staring intently at us."

Flight Attendant Saltzman also noticed Al-Watan leaning out into the aisle during the demonstration, and she "thought it was a little bit strange that we were being ... tracked with his eyes ... and the demeanor when we were getting the look, the evil eye, if you want to call it."

Second Call to Captain Plummer

Flight Attendant Koc called Captain Plummer a second time while the plane was taxiing and informed him that yet another man watched the flight attendants' safety demonstration in a way that disturbed the flight attendant. Flight attendant Anthony Kotsonis testified that during the demonstration he noted the passenger in seat 22F "glaring at [him] in a manner that actually scared me." Kotsonis stated that the passenger appeared agitated, flushed and was sweating. Kotsonis testified that the passenger glared at him—"agitated, mean facial expression." The passenger in 22F was Mr. Wessa Althwej, who is not a party in this case. Flight Attendant Kotsonis, who had observed Althwej directly, and had also heard about Al-Watan's actions, stated that when the flight attendants talked on the plane about the staring passengers, "[i]t was like each of those [Arabic] passengers had their assigned attendant."

Third Call to Captain Plummer

As the plane approached the runway, Captain Plummer received yet another call, this time from Flight Attendant Saltzman. Saltzman told the captain that a passenger, Paul Coslick, who identified himself as a Lieutenant in the U.S. Navy, told her that he was very concerned about the man sitting next to him because the man told him that he was traveling alone, while Coslick had seen the man with a group of other passengers, including Al-Watan, at the gate. Coslick testified that he noted that his seatmate came to the airport with five or six other men.

When Flight Attendant Saltzman was asked at her deposition why it alarmed her to learn that Coslick's seatmate was being inconsistent or untruthful about who he was traveling with, she testified:

> Well, because from past experience people—I mean, it's well-known now that a lot of terrorist groups are well-organized, they travel in groups and try to keep their identity hidden from other people by sitting in different parts of the aircraft, which is one of the things that we are aware of as flight attendants to be on the look out for.

The passenger to whom Coslick had spoken, the subject of his complaint, was Plaintiff Talal Cholagh. Cholagh told the San Diego Harbor Police that after he boarded the plane the passenger behind him, Coslick, "'asked about 50 questions' about his work, where he lived, where he was going, and who he was flying with." Cholagh also told the police that he felt uncomfortable answering the questions posed by the stranger, and did not want to give out too much information because Cholagh is a contractor for the military.

Captain Plummer Decides to Return to the Gate

After the third phone call, Captain Plummer decided to return the plane to the gate to "sort everything out." Captain Plummer testified that he decided to return to the gate because of the information he received in the multiple calls from the flight attendants. This included the fact that Plaintiff Al-Watan was Middle Eastern and appeared to be traveling with three other males.

Captain Plummer was processing the previously noted phone call information in the context of his 20 years of experience as a pilot. Captain Plummer testified that he decided to return to the gate out of safety concerns:

- "I needed to know if there was any connection with these people traveling as a group but saying they were traveling alone."

- Something this bad never happened to him in twenty years of being a pilot. "I would have to say return to the gate because of the unusual behavior that we were being exposed to that evening."

- He felt that the safety of the plane and its passengers was threatened, "[b]y the odd behavior of the passengers that I received these calls about."

- "Their unusual behavior and the fact that they said they were traveling alone but they were actually in a group."

- Captain Plummer recounted the unusual behavior: First, place a blanket over his head at his seat. Second, stare intently at a flight attendant—

gaze never left. Third, next to Coslick—not traveling with anyone. Coslick saw him with a group.

Once the plane returned to the gate, American Airlines Customer Service Manager Ann Grove called the police; either the first officer or the pilot or both had asked her to call the police. As all of the passengers exited the plane, the flight attendants pointed out the six Plaintiffs and one other man of Arabic descent on the flight, and the men were called over and talked to by the police. There is no evidence that Defendant's representatives or agents told the police to arrest the Plaintiffs.

The police officers questioned the men for up to two hours, after which they determined that no criminal activity had occurred, and released the men. Officer Adauto's report noted that Plaintiff Al-Watan "had red watery eyes and had the odor of an alcoholic beverage on his breath." The flight did not depart that evening because of a San Diego imposed late night curfew on flight activity. All passengers spent the night in San Diego. Flight Attendant Saltzman testified that the flight crew was "verbally accosted out at the front of the airport while we were waiting for our hotel pickup by man [Al-Watan] in 14D." Plaintiff Al-Watan was waiting in front of the airport for Fox News to show up for an interview. Flight 590 was rescheduled for the next morning. All of the Plaintiffs and the other passengers boarded the flight and flew to Chicago without incident.

On November 14, 2008, Defendant moved for summary judgment on the following grounds: (1) under 49 U.S.C. § 44902(b) it is immune from liability for the captain's decision to return the plane to the gate and remove Plaintiffs for questioning unless the captain's decision was arbitrary or capricious, and Plaintiffs cannot show that the captain's decision was arbitrary or capricious; (2) Plaintiffs' state law claims are based on the captain's decision; and therefore, are foreclosed because the captain's decision was not arbitrary or capricious; and (3) Plaintiff's state law claims are preempted by federal law.

III. ANALYSIS

A. Plaintiffs' Discrimination Claims

Plaintiffs allege that Defendant discriminated against them based on their race, color or national origin, in violation of 49 U.S.C. § 40127, prohibition on discrimination in air transportation and 42 U.S.C. § 2000a, prohibition against discrimination or segregation in places of public accommodation. Plaintiffs also allege that Defendant violated their civil rights, 42 U.S.C. § 1983, and denied them equal rights under the law, 42 U.S.C. § 1981, based on their race, color or national origin.

The Airline Deregulation Act, 49 U.S.C. 40101, *et seq.* contains a provision prohibiting discrimination in air transportation. The provision reads:

> (a) Persons in air transportation. An air carrier or foreign air carrier may not subject a person in air transportation to discrimination on the basis of race, color, national origin, religion, sex, or ancestry.

Defendant argues that it is not subject to liability for its employees' actions, pursuant to 49 U.S.C. § 44902(b), unless Plaintiffs show that the captain's decision to refuse to transport Plaintiffs was arbitrary and capricious. Title 49 U.S.C. § 44902(b) states: "Permissive refusal.—Subject to regulations of the Under Secretary, an air carrier, intrastate air carrier, or foreign air carrier may refuse to transport a passenger or property the carrier decides is, or might be, inimical to safety."

Plaintiffs do not allege a claim for refusal to transport; instead, Plaintiffs allege illegal and discriminatory activity after the passengers disembarked from the plane. The Court's analysis, however, must include the activity on the airplane, which triggered the activity after the Plaintiffs and the rest of the passengers disembarked. In their Complaint, Plaintiffs allege that "without any proper justification, Defendants feared Plaintiffs as a threat to security," and "[a]s a result of Defendants' discrimination and unjustified actions, the passengers of flight 590 were required to deplane."

Plaintiffs further allege that upon disembarking they were "pulled aside," physically separated from the other passengers, "detained and interrogated." Plaintiffs do not allege that Defendant refused to transport them. In fact, Plaintiffs acknowledge that they completed their travel plans the next day—with the same passengers, on that very same flight. However, Plaintiffs' Complaint relates to Defendant's refusal to transport them that night. Plaintiffs argue that the captain's decision to return to the gate, which they assert "may" be protected by § 44902, is unrelated to "summoning police and interrogating suspected terrorists." The Court finds that this ignores the totality of the circumstances relevant to the instant case.

Defendant argues, "Captain Plummer's decision to have Plaintiffs questioned by law enforcement in the gate area is inextricably intertwined with, and the logical extension of, his decision to return the aircraft to the gate." Plaintiff's counsel conceded this in his argument to the Court at a discovery hearing:

> What I want is documents that deal—that deal with the decision to return to the gate. That is the gravamen of this entire lawsuit. We say the decision to return to the gate was based off of racial discrimination; they say it was something else ... That's not that broad Judge, and it should be right in the heart of the case.

Plaintiffs ultimately were not refused transport, because all the passengers on the plane were required to deplane and wait overnight for the next flight because the airport curfew prevented a departure after the plane returned to the gate. The suspicious conduct involving some of the Plaintiffs was the reason Captain Plummer decided to return to the gate to further investigate the suspicious conduct.

* * *

The issues are, thus, two-fold: first, was the Captain's decision to return to the gate arbitrary and capricious; second, did Defendant's conduct upon returning to the gate violate the Plaintiffs' rights. The Court must separately evaluate Defendant's post-return conduct and the conduct of the police, unless there is evidence that Defendant controlled the police or ordered/requested the police to act in a specific manner that supports Plaintiffs' claims.

This Court's Opinion and Order Denying Defendant's Motion to Dismiss in the instant case adopted the arbitrary and capricious standard applied by the U.S. Court Appeals for the Second Circuit in *Williams v. Trans World Airlines* (2d Cir. 1975):

> The test of whether or not the airline properly exercised its power under [§ 44902] to refuse passage to an applicant or ticket-holder rests upon the facts and circumstances of the case as known to the airline at the time it formed its opinion and made its decision and whether or not the opinion and decision were rational and reasonable and not capricious or arbitrary in the light of those facts and circumstances. They are not to be tested by other facts later discovered by hindsight.

This Court's Opinion and Order denying Defendant's Motion to Dismiss adopted this test, and then, after noting that the Sixth Circuit has not ruled on this issue, quoted approvingly at length from the recent First Circuit opinion in *Cerqueira v. American Airlines, Inc.* (1st Cir. 2008). The Court's Opinion stated:

> The Sixth Circuit has not yet addressed the substantive analysis to be applied when a passenger alleges that an airline, citing security concerns, impermissibly removes him or her from an airplane on the base of race or national origin.
>
> In the recent case *Cerqueira v. American Airlines, Inc.* the First Circuit utilized the following analysis when evaluating a claim of discrimination under § 1981 when the airline asserts its statutory authority under § 44902(b):

> As a matter of federal policy, under the Federal Aviation Act, "assigning and maintaining safety [ranks] as the highest priority in air commerce." Thus, the highest priority is assigned to safety, even though the federal aviation statute also has a general prohibition on race and national origin discrimination."
>
> An air carrier may not subject a person in air transportation to discrimination on the basis of race, color, national origin, religion, sex or ancestry."

In 49 U.S.C. § 44902(a), which became effective in 1961, Congress mandated air carriers to refuse to transport passengers and property where a passenger does not consent to a search of his person or property for dangerous weapons, explosives, or destructive substances. In addition to mandating that some passengers be refused transport, Congress also authorized, at subsection (b), air carriers to engage in "permissive refusal":

> Subject to regulations of the Under Secretary, an air carrier, intrastate air carrier, or foreign air carrier may refuse to transport a passenger or property the carrier decides is, or might be, inimical to safety.

Thus Congress supplemented the discretion airlines already had under common law to exclude certain passengers, in light of their duty of utmost care to all passengers. It is obvious that § 44902(b) was enacted in furtherance of the first priority of safety in air traffic. The legislative history confirms this.

The permissive refusal authorization in § 44902(b) has several distinct components. The statute says the air carrier "may" refuse to transport, thus vesting discretion over the decision in the air carrier. That discretion is very broad. The carrier need not decide that the passenger or property is inimical to safety; the authorization extends to situations in which the carrier decides the passenger or property "might be" inimical to safety. The congressional authorization is granted to the air carrier to make the decision. The only limit contained in the statute on that discretion is that it be subject to regulations of the Under Secretary of Transportation for Security.

In turn, the Under Secretary has not promulgated regulations limiting the airline's discretion directly under 49 U.S.C. § 44902(b). However, one other regulation is directly pertinent, as it states that: "The pilot in command of an aircraft is directly responsible for, and is the final authority as to the operation of that aircraft." In other words, the pilot in command stands in the role of the air carrier for a decision to remove a passenger from a flight. The authorization in § 44902(b) also applies to decisions by others than the pilot not to rebook a passenger based on safety concerns. In this case, that decision was made by another person, based on information from the pilot.

While the statute refers to the air carrier's decision, the appropriate focus is on the actual decisionmaker: the pilot in command of the aircraft where the passenger is removed from the pilot's flight. That is so as a matter of law under 14 C.F.R. § 91.3. In practice in this context, it is not the air carrier that makes the decision to refuse transport to the passenger on the flight, but the pilot in command, who acts for the air carrier. Section 44902 itself does not provide for judicial review of decisions to refuse transportation by the pilot in command. Nonetheless, courts have entertained actions involving § 44902(b) brought under other general statutes which prohibit discrimination, such as § 1981and Title VI of the Civil Rights Act.

Accordingly, the parties have assumed that the protections of 49 U.S.C. § 44901 and the U.S. Department of Transportation administrative enforcement mechanisms to protect the rights of passengers, 49 U.S.C. §§ 46101, 46301, do not preclude the filing of actions under 42 U.S.C. §1981, and we will assume the same. It is clear that § 44902(b), being the more specific statute, applies to this case. Congress has, by statute, explicitly given safety the highest priority.

* * *

Some courts have described an air carrier's reliance on § 44902(b) as a defense in the nature of an immunity. In our view, § 44902(b) does not merely create a defense: the statute is an affirmative grant of permission to the air carrier. Congress specifically authorized permissive refusals by air carriers; Congress did not say § 44902 was merely creating a defense. It is the plaintiff who carries the burden to show that § 44902(b) is inapplicable.

The courts, by judicial construction of § 44902(b), have adopted a standard for liability for an airline's permissive refusal to transport decisions. This standard reconciles the primary priority of safety with other important policies, such as § 1981's prohibitions on racial discrimination. The standard most frequently articulated is that developed by the Second Circuit in *Williams*: that the air carrier's decision to refuse air transport must be shown to be arbitrary or capricious. We agree with *Williams* and hold that an air carrier's decisions to refuse transport under § 44902(b) are not subject to liability unless the decision is arbitrary or capricious.

We also agree with *Williams* that Congress did not intend the nondiscrimination provisions of the FAA or of § 1981 to limit or to render inoperative the refusal rights of the air carrier. Congress left decisions to refuse passage to the air carrier, and any review in the courts is limited to review for arbitrariness or capriciousness. Congress was also well aware that the air carriers' decisions to deny transport have to be made very quickly and based on limited information. Section 44902(b) must be interpreted in that light. Congress "did not contemplate that the flight would have to be held up or cancelled until certainty was achieved."

In applying 49 U.S.C. § 44902(b), this Court will utilize the arbitrary and capricious standard in deciding whether to grant Defendant's Motion for Summary Judgment. Thus, this Court must decide whether Plaintiffs have proffered sufficient evidence to create a genuine issue of material fact that Captain Plummer's decision, given the facts he knew at the time he made the decision to return to the gate, was arbitrary and capricious. A decision to refuse to transport a passenger that is motivated by the passenger's race is "inherently arbitrary and capricious." A refusal to transport "cannot give rise to a claim for damages under ... federal ... law unless the carrier's decision was arbitrary and capricious." *Schaeffer v. Cavallero*, 54 F. Supp. 2d 350, 351 (S.D.N.Y. 1999). In support of its argument that the captain's decision was not arbitrary and capricious, Defendant relies primarily on two cases: *Cerqueira*, *supra*, and *Dasrath v. Continental Airlines, Inc.* (D.N.J. 2006). In both cases, after reviewing the information relayed to the captain by the crew, the courts held that the captain's decision to refuse transport was not arbitrary and capricious.

In *Cerqueira* three passengers were removed from the plane for questioning by the state police (to a secured location away from the gate and apart from the other passengers and were questioned by one of the State Police troopers) based on the following facts: (1) one of the passengers approached the captain before the flight and asked him if he was the captain for the flight and asked the same question when he boarded the flight; (2) a different passenger had been hostile to a flight attendant about a seat change, and then he boarded the plane with the first class passengers, even though he was in coach, and immediately went to the bathroom for an extended period of time; (3) two of the three passengers were acting "very bizarrely and asking questions such as 'Is this how you want me to do it?'; (4) one of the passengers asked strange questions during the exit row safety briefing and laughed; (5) one of the passengers stared at a flight attendant during the general safety demonstration; and (6) the three passengers wished the other passengers "Happy New Year" in a "'very boisterous' manner."

The First Circuit concluded that "there is absolutely no evidence that the Captain himself or the [System Operations Control] manager had discriminatory animus, let alone that their decisions to refuse to transport a passenger, which were made under time pressure, were based on any discriminatory animus," and stated that the Captain's decision was justified given the safety concerns observed by the crew, which are recounted above. The First Circuit held:

> Review of a decision to refuse transport by the Captain is restricted to what information was actually known by the decisionmaker at the time of the decision. The test is not what the Captain reasonably should have known ... The

> Captain (or other decisionmaker) is entitled to accept at face value the representations made to him by other air carrier employees. Thus, even mistaken decisions are protected as long as they are not arbitrary or capricious.

The First Circuit further held that the burden is on the plaintiff to show the decision not to transport was arbitrary and capricious.

In *Dasrath*, a female passenger alerted the gate agent to suspicious behavior by the plaintiff and two other male passengers, specifically that three men who apparently knew each other were pretending not to know each other and doing "funny things, talking on cell phones." After one of the male passengers identified by the female passenger boarded the plane, he reached down and felt underneath a seat in first class.

He then moved to the rear of the plane where he removed his duffel bag from the overhead bin and placed it behind the exit row. Shortly thereafter, the captain saw the three men conversing; one of the men was perspiring heavily and would not stop looking at the captain.

The District Court in New Jersey held that the Captain acted reasonably when he removed the plaintiff, having removed the plaintiff only after being alerted to suspicious behavior that caused security concerns among the crew. The court concluded that "there were many events that would have led a reasonable person to believe that the three men ... were security risks." The court stated:

> [T]he undisputed facts as perceived by Captain Harris would preclude a jury from finding that he removed Mr. Dasarath from the aircraft for racial reasons or for any reasons other than concern for the security of the aircraft and the passengers.

The court in *Dasrath* also noted that it was reasonable to remove additional passengers as well as the suspiciously-acting passengers because they were known to be flying together.

Defendant also cited to four other cases in which passengers were removed from a plane due to safety concerns. In all of the cases cited by Defendant, there is one common fact: the passengers removed from the plane engaged in behavior that drew the attention of the flight attendants and justifiably alarmed them to the point that they contacted the pilot. Such is the case here. The flight attendants noticed the unusual and threatening behavior of plaintiffs Al-Watan and Cholagh, and non-party Wessa Althwej, who was seated in 22F, became concerned for the safety of the flight, and alerted Captain Plummer.

The flight attendants saw Al-Watan use the restroom, while the plane door was still open, return to his seat, put a blanket over his head, and then lean out into the aisle during the safety demonstration and stare at flight attendant Koc. Although use of the restroom is not a reason for concern, the placing of a blanket over the head before takeoff is a basis for concern, as is the leaning over into the aisle and staring menacingly at the flight attendant during safety instructions.

During post-boarding pre-flight, another passenger, Althwej, stared at a flight attendant to the point of distracting him. In addition, a passenger reported his concern about the passenger sitting next to him because when he asked whether the passenger was traveling alone, the man responded that he was, but the reporting passenger had seen his seatmate with a group in the terminal, including Al-Watan. What the pilot had on his "plate" was three calls from three different flight attendants, regarding suspicious or threatening behavior on board the aircraft even before it was off the ground.

All of these unusual actions by the passengers reasonably concerned the flight attendants, and justified their calls to the pilot. Nothing in their calls can be regarded as evidencing discrimination. Captain Plummer emphasized in his deposition that the fact that the flight attendants called him at all was unusual because the flight attendants are not supposed to call the pilot when the doors are closed and the airplane is moving. The fact that Captain Plummer received not one, but three calls, from the flight attendants raised red flags about the safety of continuing the flight. It was only after the third call that Captain Plummer returned the plane to the gate.

Based on the facts as Captain Plummer knew them to be when he decided to return the airplane to the gate, this Court holds that his decision was not arbitrary and capricious. There is no evidence that it was based on Plaintiffs' race or ethnicity. While Captain Plummer knew that Al-Watan was Middle Eastern, and he appeared to be traveling with at least three other men, the Plaintiffs' actions that impelled the three phone calls clearly establishes a reasonable basis for returning to the gate, and calling the police to find out information about the individuals. It is noteworthy that although Captain Plummer knew that a passenger [Leigh Williams] had an earlier negative interaction with Al-Watan at the gate, which was carried over on to the airplane, and that the passenger had deboarded with her children, that incident did not factor into his ultimate decision. Plummer relied on the subsequent information about the incidents on the plane that the flight attendants reported to him in the three phone calls.

The most significant suspicious uncontested information was that passenger Al-Watan had put a blanket over his head. The actions of Al-Watan, Cholagh and Althwej reasonably appeared as linked in a rapidly evolving situation. The totality of the circumstances supports Captain Plummer's decision to return to the gate out of safety concerns and request that the police talk to the individuals engaged in the suspicious activity, and other members of the group. That all of these individuals were of Arabic ancestry is a factual reality.

However, Plaintiff has not presented any evidence of racial bias by Defendant. Captain Plummer is entitled, and must be able, to implicitly rely on the information relayed to him by his flight crew, assuming it is reasonable and believable. The flight attendants are his eyes and ears in the passenger area of the airplane, while he is closeted in the cockpit. Plaintiffs have not set forth evidence of racial bias by any of the flight attendants or the captain.

* * *

The Court must now examine for racial discrimination Defendant's actions after the plane returned to the gate. Plaintiffs argue that the arbitrary and capricious standard in § 44902(b) does not extend to Captain Plummer's decision to call the police. This Court disagrees. As the court explained in *Ruta v. Delta Airlines* (S.D.N.Y. 2014), "if ... the Captain's decision to have Plaintiff removed was not arbitrary or capricious then it cannot have been arbitrary and capricious to call on law enforcement to enforce the Captain's decision." Indeed, in this case, there is even less activity by the Captain; Captain Plummer did not decide that Plaintiffs should be refused transport—just interviewed by police before reboarding, which turned out, for all passengers on the plane, to be the next morning.

Plaintiffs raised a related argument pointing to discrimination: the fact that all seven Arab men on the flight were identified by Defendant's employees for questioning by police, after the plane returned to the gate, even though only three men, Al-Watan, Cholagh and Althwej engaged in suspicious behavior. However, as noted before, there was evidence that the flight crew was aware that Plaintiffs were traveling together and this justified Defendant's identifying the group that included the suspicious individuals. Plaintiffs contend that Defendant's flight attendants identified individuals of Arabic descent to the police for questioning. Plaintiff Hasan Al-Zerej testified, "we were pointed at by the police and the flight attendants and separated from the rest [of the passengers]." Also, Al-Watan testified that an employee of Defendant pointed at him and, "delivered us to the police." The police proceeded to question the individuals.

This raises the issue of whether Defendant is responsible for conduct of the police, insofar as Plaintiffs allege that the police violated their rights. In addition, there is a question whether Defendant can be charged under 42 U.S.C. § 1983 as a state actor. There is no question that when a defendant reasonably believes that passengers have engaged in suspicious behavior, the passengers can be questioned by police.

The flight attendants' identification of a group of passengers they believed were traveling together raises the issue of whether the Defendant arbitrarily and capriciously identified all the Arab men on the flight for police questioning. To the extent that the six Plaintiffs were traveling together, there is no basis for finding the Defendant's decision to be arbitrary and capricious. As to the seventh individual of Arabic descent that was apparently identified to the police by Defendant, that individual was reported by the flight attendant to the captain as having exhibited strange and threatening behavior. There is no evidence supporting Plaintiffs' claim that Defendant acted in a discriminatory manner. Accordingly, this Court will enter summary judgment on Plaintiffs' discrimination claims.

B. Plaintiffs' Claim under 42 U.S.C. § 1983

Title 42 U.S.C. § 1983 only provides a remedy against persons acting under color of state law. Plaintiffs have not presented any evidence or argument that Defendant's refusal to transport them is attributable to a "state actor." Defendant made the decision to cancel the flight and call the police. Although Defendant pointed out Plaintiffs to the police, there is no evidence that Defendant directed the police officers to arrest Plaintiffs or otherwise directed the conduct of the police officers.

C. Plaintiffs' State Law Claims

Defendant argues that Plaintiffs' state law claims should also be dismissed because the Captain's decision was not arbitrary or capricious or, alternatively, because the state law claims are preempted by the Airline Deregulation Act, 49 U.S.C. § 41713(b). This Court holds that an airline's refusal to transport passengers cannot give rise to a claim for damages under either federal or state law unless the airline's decision was arbitrary and capricious. In this case, the Court finds that Defendant's action to return to the gate and call the police was not arbitrary and capricious; thus, Plaintiffs cannot prevail on their state law claims.

In addition, the Court agrees with the decision of the District Court in *Ruta*, that all of the state tort claims are preempted. Any alleged emotional and physical harm allegedly suffered by Plaintiffs was a direct result of the Captain's decision to remove them from the plane, as were the claims for negligence and intentional infliction of emotional distress.

There is no factual support for Plaintiffs' claim of false imprisonment. Defendant merely called the police to talk to Plaintiffs; there is no evidence that Defendant suggested that the police arrest Plaintiffs. This Court, therefore, enters summary judgment for Defendant on Plaintiffs' state law claims.

IV. CONCLUSION

The Court concludes that information provided to Captain Plummer regarding the highly suspicious onboard conduct supports his decision to return to the terminal and to call the police to investigate. Plaintiff Al-Watan's placing a blanket over his head "mummy-like" prior to takeoff, leaning out into the aisle and staring menacingly at flight attendants, and the other actions discussed above is cause for concern; Captain Plummer's decision was not arbitrary and capricious. Certainly, the suspicious conduct at issue was not, as Plaintiffs' counsel characterized it at oral argument, "innocent" or "completely silly."

There is no evidence that supports Plaintiffs' claim of discrimination by Captain Plummer. There is no evidence that Captain Plummer's action was race-based. The fact that the individuals who engaged in the suspicious conduct were of Middle Eastern/Iraqi descent does not support the conclusion that the decision to return to the gate was race-based rather than fact-based.

The three passengers of concern, based on their suspicious conduct, were Plaintiff Al-Watan, seat 14B; non-party Althwej in seat 22F; and Cholagh, the person seated next to Lieutenant Coslick in 31 B. The six Plaintiffs were traveling together. The police questioning, which occurred as a result of the justified suspicions of Captain Plummer, was tied to the question of whether to refuse passage to these men. Thus, the applicable standard to be applied in this case against Defendant, is whether Captain Plummer's conduct was arbitrary and capricious. What the Captain, and the Defendant airline did, was seek more information about the Plaintiffs, some of whom had engaged in highly suspicious activity.

Nevertheless, given that Defendant American Airlines did remove the Plaintiffs (and all the other passengers) from the plane, the analysis of Defendant's conduct comes under 49 U.S.C. § 44902(b) whether it properly exercised its discretion to remove a passenger based on the facts and circumstances known to the decision-maker at the time he or she made the decision. "The decision is not to be tested by other facts later disclosed by hindsight." *Sedigh v. Delta Airlines* (E.D.N.Y. 1994).

The Court further concludes that Plaintiffs' state claims: false imprisonment; intentional infliction of emotional distress; and negligence, must be dismissed because they are preempted by federal law. The Court finds that the same safety concerns that justified Captain Plummer's return to the gate, are the same concerns that caused him to request assistance of police to talk to the Plaintiffs. Captain Plummer's decision to return to the gate, based on the information he received provided to him by the crew, to seek more information about the suspicious situation was not arbitrary and capricious, and not discriminatory.

LATIF v. HOLDER

28 F. Supp. 3d 1134 (D. Ore. 2014)

BROWN, District Judge.

Plaintiffs are citizens and lawful permanent residents of the United States (including four veterans of the United States Armed Forces) who were not allowed to board flights to or from the United States or over United States airspace. Plaintiffs believe they were denied boarding because they are on the No–Fly List, a government terrorist watch list of individuals who are prohibited from boarding commercial flights that will pass through or over United States airspace. Federal and/or local government officials told some Plaintiffs that they are on the No–Fly List.

Each Plaintiff submitted applications for redress through the Department of Homeland Security Traveler Redress Inquiry Program ("DHS TRIP"). Despite Plaintiffs' requests to officials and agencies for explanations as to why they were not permitted to board flights, explanations have not been provided and Plaintiffs do not know whether they will be permitted to fly in the future. Plaintiffs now allege that Defendants have violated their Fifth Amendment right to procedural due process because Defendants have not given Plaintiffs any post-deprivation notice nor any meaningful opportunity to contest their continued inclusion on the No–Fly List. In Claim Three Plaintiffs assert Defendants' actions have been arbitrary and capricious and constitute "unlawful agency action" in violation of the APA.

FACTUAL BACKGROUND

I. The No–Fly List

The Federal Bureau of Investigation ("FBI"), which administers the Terrorist Screening Center ("TSC"), develops and maintains the federal government's consolidated Terrorist Screening Database ("TSDB" or sometimes referred to as "the watch list"). The No–Fly List is a subset of the TSDB.

TSC provides the No–Fly List to TSA, a component of the Department of Homeland Security (DHS), for use in pre-screening airline passengers, TSC receives nominations for inclusion in the TSDB and generally accepts those nominations on a showing of "reasonable suspicion" that the individuals are known or suspected terrorists based on the totality of the information. TSC defines its reasonable-suspicion standard as requiring "articulable facts which, taken together with rational inferences, reasonably warrant the determination that an individual 'is known or suspected to be, or has been engaged in conduct constituting, in preparation for, in aid of or related to, terrorism or terrorist activities.'"

The government also has its own "Watchlisting Guidance" for internal law-enforcement and intelligence use, and the No–Fly List has its own minimum substantive derogatory criteria. The government does not release these documents.

II. DHS TRIP Redress Process

DHS TRIP is the mechanism available for individuals to seek redress for any travel-related screening issues experienced at airports or while crossing United States borders; *i.e.*, denial of or delayed airline boarding, denial of or delayed entry into or exit from the United States, or continuous referral for additional (secondary) screening.

A. *Administrative Review*

Travelers who have faced such difficulties may submit a Traveler Inquiry Form to DHS TRIP online, by email, or by regular mail. The form prompts travelers to describe their complaint, to produce documentation relating to the issue, and to provide identification and their contact information. If the traveler is an exact or near match to an identity within the TSDB, DHS TRIP deems the complaint to be TSDB-related and forwards the traveler's complaint to TSC Redress for further review.

On receipt of the complaint, TSC Redress reviews the available information, including the information and documentation provided by the traveler, and determines (1) whether the traveler is an exact match to an identity in the TSDB and (2) whether the traveler should continue to be in the TSDB if the traveler is an exact match. When making this determination, TSC coordinates with the agency that originally nominated the individual to be included in the TSDB. If the traveler has been misidentified as someone who is an exact match to an identity in the TSDB, TSC Redress informs DHS of the misidentification. DHS, in conjunction with any other relevant agency, then addresses the misidentification by correcting information in the traveler's records or taking other appropriate action.

When DHS and/or TSC finish their review, DHS TRIP sends a determination letter advising the traveler that DHS TRIP has completed its review. A DHS TRIP determination letter neither confirms nor denies that the complainant is in the TSDB or on the No–Fly List and does not provide any further details about why the complainant may or may not be in the TSDB or on the No–Fly List. In some cases a DHS TRIP determination letter advises the recipient that he or she can pursue an administrative appeal of the determination letter with TSA or can seek judicial review in a United States court of appeals pursuant to 49 U.S.C. § 46110(a).

Determination letters, however, do not provide assurances about the complainant's ability to undertake future travel. In fact, DHS does not tell a complainant whether he or she is in the TSDB or a subset of the TSDB or give any explanation for inclusion on such a list at any point in the available administrative process. Thus, the complainant does not have an opportunity to contest or knowingly to offer corrections to the record on which any such determination may be based.

B. *Judicial Review*

When a final determination letter indicates the complainant may seek judicial review of the decisions represented in the letter, it does not advise whether the complainant is on the No–Fly List or provide the legal or factual basis for such inclusion.

If the complainant submits a petition for review to the appropriate court, the government furnishes the court (but not the petitioner) with the administrative record.

If the administrative DHS TRIP review of a petitioner's redress file resulted in a final determination that the petitioner is not on the No–Fly List, the administrative record will inform the court of that fact. If, on the other hand, the administrative DHS TRIP review of a petitioner's redress file resulted in a final determination that the petitioner is and should remain on the No–Fly List, the administrative record will include the information that the government relied on to maintain that listing. The government may have obtained this information from human sources, foreign governments, and/or "signals intelligence." The government may provide to the court ex parte and in camera information that is part of the administrative record and that the government has determined is classified, Sensitive Security Information, law-enforcement investigative information, and/or information otherwise privileged or protected from disclosure by statute or regulation.

The administrative record also includes any information that the petitioner submitted to the government as part of his or her DHS TRIP request, and the petitioner has access to that portion of the record. As noted, at no point during the judicial-review process does the government provide the petitioner with confirmation as to whether the petitioner is on the No–Fly List, set out the reasons for including petitioner's name on the List, or identify any information or evidence relied on to maintain the petitioner's name on the List.

For a petitioner who is on the No–Fly List, the court will review the administrative record submitted by the government in order to determine whether the government reasonably determined the petitioner satisfied the minimum substantive derogatory criteria for inclusion on the List. If after review the court determines the administrative record supports the petitioner's inclusion on the No–Fly List, it will deny the petition for review. If the court determines the administrative record contains insufficient evidence to satisfy the substantive derogatory criteria, however, the government takes the position that the court may remand the matter to the government for appropriate action.

III. Plaintiffs' Pertinent History

Plaintiffs are thirteen United States citizens who were denied boarding on flights over United States airspace after January 1, 2009, and who believe they are on the United States government's No–Fly List. Airline representatives, FBI agents, or other government officials told some Plaintiffs that they are on the No–Fly List. Each Plaintiff filed DHS TRIP complaints after being denied boarding and each received a determination letter that does not confirm or deny any Plaintiff's name is on any terrorist watch list nor provide a reason for any Plaintiff to be included in the TSDB or on the No–Fly List. Many of these Plaintiffs cannot travel overseas by any mode other than air because such journeys by boat or by land would be cost-prohibitive, would be time-consuming to a degree that Plaintiffs could not take the necessary time off from work, or would put Plaintiffs at risk of interrogation and detention by foreign authorities. In addition, some Plaintiffs are not physically well enough to endure such infeasible modes of travel.

While Plaintiffs' circumstances are similar in many ways, each of their experiences and difficulties relating to and arising from their alleged inclusion on the No–Fly List is unique as set forth in their Declarations filed in support of their Motion and summarized briefly below.

- ***Ayman Latif***: Latif is a United States Marine Corps veteran and lives in Stone Mountain, Georgia, with his wife and children. Between November 2008 and April 2010 Latif and his family were living in Egypt. When Latif and his family attempted to return to the United States in April 2010, Latif was not allowed to board the first leg of their flight from Cairo to Madrid. One month later Latif was questioned by FBI agents and told he was on the No–Fly List. Because he was unable to board a flight to the United States, Latif's United States veteran disability benefits were reduced from $899.00 per month to zero as the result of being unable to attend the scheduled evaluations required to keep his benefits. In August 2010 Latif returned home after the United States government granted him a "one-time waiver" to fly to the United States. Because the waiver was for "one time," Latif cannot fly again, and therefore, he is unable to travel from the United States to Egypt to resume studies or to Saudi Arabia to perform a hajj, a religious pilgrimage and Islamic obligation.

- ***Mohamed Sheikh Abdirahm Kariye***: Kariye lives in Portland, Oregon, with his wife and children. In March 2010 Kariye was not allowed to board a flight from Portland to Amsterdam, was surrounded in public by government officials at the airport, and was told by an airline employee that he was on a government watch list. Because Kariye is prohibited from boarding flights out of the United States, he could not fly to visit his daughter who was studying in Dubai and cannot travel to Saudi Arabia to accompany his mother on the hajj pilgrimage.

- ***Raymond Earl Knaeble IV***: Knaeble is a United States Army veteran and lives in Chicago, Illinois. In 2006 Knaeble was working in Kuwait. In March 2010 Knaeble flew from Kuwait to Bogota, Colombia, to marry his wife, a Colombian citizen, and to spend time with her family. On March 14, 2010, Knaeble was not allowed to board his flight from Bogota to Miami. Knaeble was subsequently questioned numerous times by FBI agents in Colombia. Because Knaeble was unable to fly home for a required medical examination, his employer rescinded its job offer for a position in Qatar. Knaeble attempted to return to the United States through Mexico where he was detained for over 15 hours, questioned, and forced to return to Bogota. Knaeble eventually returned to the United States in August 2010 by traveling for 12 days from Santa Marta, Colombia, to Panama City and then to Mexicali, California. United States and foreign authorities detained, interrogated, and searched Knaeble on numerous occasions during that journey.

- ***Faisal Nabin Kashem***: In January 2010 Kashem traveled from the United States to Saudi Arabia to attend a two-year Arabic language-certification program and eventually to enroll in a four-year Islamic studies program. In June 2010 Kashem attempted to fly from Jeddah, Saudi Arabia, to New York for summer vacation; was denied boarding; and was told by an airline employee that he was on the No–Fly List. FBI agents later questioned Kashem and told him that he was on the No–Fly List. After Kashem joined this lawsuit, the United States government offered him a "one-time waiver" to return to the United States, which he has so far declined because United States officials have refused to confirm that he will be able to return to Saudi Arabia to complete his studies.

- ***Elias Mustafa Mohamed***: In January 2010 Mohamed traveled from the United States to Saudi Arabia to attend a two-year Arabic language-certification program. In June 2010 Mohamed attempted to fly from Jeddah, Saudi Arabia, to his home in Seattle, Washington, via Washington, D.C., but he was not allowed to board his flight and was told by an airline employee that he was on the No–Fly List. FBI agents later questioned Mohamed and told him that he was on the No–Fly List. After joining this lawsuit, the United States government offered Mohamed a "one-time-waiver" to return to the United States, which he has so far declined because United States officials have refused to confirm that he will be able to return to Saudi Arabia to complete his studies.

- ***Steven William Washburn***: Washburn is a United States Air Force veteran and lives in New Mexico. In February 2010 Washburn was not allowed to board a flight from Ireland to Boston. He later attempted to fly from Dublin to London to Mexico City. Although he was allowed to board the flight from Dublin to London, on the London to Mexico City flight the aircraft turned around 3 ½ hours after takeoff and returned to London where Washburn was detained. On numerous later occasions FBI agents interrogated Washburn. In May 2010 Washburn returned to New Mexico by taking a series of five flights that eventually landed in Juarez, Mexico, where he crossed the United States border on foot. During this trip Mexican officials detained and interrogated Washburn. In June 2012 an FBI agent told Washburn that the agent would help remove Washburn's name from the No–Fly List if he agreed to speak to the FBI. Since May 2010 Washburn has been separated from his wife who is in Ireland because she has been unable to obtain a visa to come to the United States and Washburn is unable to fly to Ireland.

- ***Nagib Ali Ghaleb***: Ghaleb lives in Oakland, California. In February 2010 Ghaleb attempted to travel from Yemen where his wife and children were living to San Francisco via Frankfurt. Ghaleb was not allowed to board his flight from Frankfurt to San Francisco. FBI agents later interrogated Ghaleb and offered to arrange to fly him back to the United States if he agreed to tell them who the "bad guys" were in Yemen and San Francisco and to provide names of people from his mosque and community. The agents threatened to have Ghaleb imprisoned. In May 2010 Ghaleb again attempted to return to the United States. He was able to fly from Sana'a, Yemen, to Dubai, but he was not allowed to board his flight from Dubai to San Francisco. In July 2010 Ghaleb accepted a "one-time waiver" offered by the United States government to return to the United States. Because Ghaleb cannot fly, he cannot go to Yemen to be with his ill mother or to see his brothers or sisters.

- ***Abdullatif Muthanna***: Muthanna lives in Rochester, New York. In June 2009 Muthanna left Rochester to visit his wife and children who live in Yemen. In May 2010 Muthanna was to return to the United States on a flight from Aden, Yemen, to New York via Jeddah, Saudi Arabia, but he was not allowed to board his flight from Jeddah to New York. In September 2010 Muthanna accepted a "one-time waiver" offered by the United States government to return home. In June 2012 Muthanna wanted to be with his family and attempted to fly to Yemen, but he was not allowed to board a flight departing from New York. In August 2012 Muthanna attempted a journey of thirty-six days over land and by ship from Rochester to Yemen, but a ship captain refused to let Muthanna sail on a cargo freighter departing from Philadelphia on the recommendation of United States Customs and Border Protection. Muthanna was not allowed to board flights on four separate occasions before he finally boarded a flight from New York to Dubai in February 2013.

- ***Mashaal Rana***: Rana moved to Pakistan to pursue a master's degree in Islamic studies in 2009. In February 2010 Rana was not allowed to board a flight from Lahore, Pakistan, to New York. An FBI agent later interrogated Rana's brother, who lives in the United States. In October 2012 Rana was six-months pregnant and again attempted to return to New York to receive needed medical care and to deliver her child. Rana's brother worked with United States officials to clear Rana to fly. Rana received such clearance, but five hours before her flight was to depart she received notice that she would not be allowed to board. Rana was not able to find a safe alternative to travel to the United States before the birth of her child. In November 2010 the United States government offered Rana a "one-time waiver," which she has not used because she fears she would not be able to return to Pakistan to be with her husband.

- ***Ibraheim Y. Mashal***: Mashal is a United States Marine Corps veteran. Mashal was not allowed to board a flight from Chicago, Illinois, to Spokane, Washington, and was told by an airline representative that he was on the No–Fly List. FBI agents later questioned Mashal and told him that his name would be removed from the No–Fly List and he would receive compensation if he helped the FBI by serving as an informant. When Mashal asked to have his attorney present before answering the FBI's questions, the agents ended the meeting. Mashal owns a dog-training business. Because he is unable to fly, he has lost clients; had to turn down business; and has been prevented from attending his sister-in-law's graduation in Hawaii, the wedding of a close friend, the funeral of a close friend, and fundraising events for the nonprofit organization that he founded.

- ***Salah Ali Ahmed***: Ahmed lives in Norcross, Georgia. In July 2010 Ahmed attempted to travel from Atlanta to Yemen via Frankfurt and was not allowed to board the flight in Atlanta. FBI agents later questioned Ahmed. Because he is unable to fly, Ahmed was unable to travel to Yemen in 2012 when his brother died and is unable to travel to Yemen to visit his extended family and to manage property that he owns in Yemen.

- ***Amir Meshal***: Meshal lives in Minnesota. In June 2009 Meshal was not allowed to board a flight from Irvine, California, to Newark, New Jersey. FBI agents told Meshal that he was on a government list that prohibits him from flying. In October 2010 FBI agents offered Meshal the opportunity to serve as a government informant in exchange for assistance in removing his name from the No–Fly List. Because Meshal is unable to fly, he cannot visit his mother and extended family in Egypt.

- ***Stephen Durga Persaud***: Persaud lives in Irvine, California. In May 2010 Persaud was not allowed to board a flight from St. Thomas to Miami, An FBI agent told Persaud that he was on the No–Fly List, interrogated him, and told him the only way to get off the No–Fly List was to "talk to us." In June 2010 Persaud took a five-day boat trip from St. Thomas to Miami and a four-day train ride from Miami to Los Angeles so he could be home for the birth of his second child. Because he cannot fly, Persaud cannot travel to Saudi Arabia to perform the hajj pilgrimage.

DISCUSSION

I. Claim One: Procedural Due–Process

"Procedural due process imposes constraints on governmental decisions which deprive individuals of 'liberty' or 'property' interests within the meaning of the Due Process Clause of the Fifth or Fourteenth Amendment." *Mathews v. Eldridge* (1976). "The fundamental requirement of due process is the opportunity to be heard 'at a meaningful time and in a meaningful manner.'" Due process, however, "'is flexible and calls for such procedural protections as the particular situation demands.'"

The court must weigh three factors when evaluating the sufficiency of procedural protections: (1) "the private interest that will be affected by the official action"; (2) "the risk of an erroneous deprivation of such interest through the procedures used, and the probative value, if any, of additional or substitute procedural safeguards"; and (3) "the Government's interest, including the function involved and the fiscal and administrative burdens that the additional or substitute procedural requirement would entail,"

A. First Factor: Private Interest

Plaintiffs contend the first factor under *Mathews* weighs in their favor because Defendants' inclusion of Plaintiffs on the No–Fly List has deprived Plaintiffs of their constitutionally-protected liberty interests in travel and reputation.

1. *Right to Travel*

"The right to travel is a part of the 'liberty' of which the citizen cannot be deprived without due process of law under the Fifth Amendment." *Kent v. Dulles* (1958). "[T]he [Supreme] Court has consistently treated the right to International travel as a liberty interest that is protected by the Due Process Clause of the Fifth Amendment."

Relying primarily on *Gilmore v. Gonzales* (9th Cir. 2006), and *Green v. Transp. Sec. Admin.* (W.D. Wash. 2005), Defendants argue there is not a constitutional right to travel by airplane or by the most convenient form of travel. Defendants, therefore, contend Plaintiffs' rights to travel are not constitutionally burdened because the No–Fly List only prohibits travel by commercial aviation. Defendants argue there is not a constitutional right to travel by airplane or by the most convenient form of travel. Defendants, therefore, contend Plaintiffs' rights to travel are not constitutionally burdened because the No–Fly List only prohibits travel by commercial aviation.

Although there are viable alternatives to flying for domestic travel within the continental United States such as traveling by car or train, the Court disagrees with Defendants' contention that international air travel is a mere convenience in light of the realities of our modern world. Such an argument ignores the numerous reasons that an individual may have for wanting or needing to travel overseas quickly such as the birth of a child, the death of a loved one, a business opportunity, or a religious obligation. In *Ibrahim v. Department of Homeland Security* the court rejected an argument similar to the one that Defendants make in this case:

> While the Constitution does not ordinarily guarantee the right to travel by any particular form of transportation, given that other forms of travel usually remain possible, the fact remains that for *international* travel, air transport in these modern times is practically the only form of transportation, travel by ship being prohibitively expensive.... Decisions involving domestic air travel, such as the *Gilmore* case, are not on point.

Moreover, the burdens imposed by the restrictions on the plaintiffs in *Green* and *Gilmore* are far less than the alleged burdens in this matter. *Gilmore* involved the requirement that passengers present photo identification before boarding a commercial flight and *Green* involved passengers being subjected to enhanced security screening because they had been mistakenly identified as being on a terrorist watch list. Unlike the security-screening restrictions in *Green* and *Gilmore*, Plaintiffs' placement on the No–Fly List operates as a complete and indefinite ban on boarding commercial flights.

The Court also disagrees with Defendants' assertion that all modes of transportation must be foreclosed before any infringement of an individual's due-process right to international travel is triggered. In *DeNieva* the Ninth Circuit found the plaintiff's protected liberty interest in her right to international travel had been infringed in that "retention of [her] passport infringed upon her ability to travel internationally" because "[w]ithout her passport, she could travel internationally only *with great difficulty, if at all*." In other words, her protected liberty interest in international travel had been infringed even though she may not have been completely banned from traveling. As Plaintiffs' difficulties with international travel demonstrate, placement on the No–Fly List is a significant impediment to international travel. It is undisputed that inclusion on the No–Fly List completely bans listed persons from boarding commercial flights to or from the United States or over United States airspace. In addition, the realistic implications of being on the No–Fly List are far-reaching.

For example, TSC shares watch-list information with 22 foreign governments, and United States Customs and Border Protection makes recommendations to ship captains as to whether a passenger poses a risk to transportation security. Thus, having one's name on the watch list can also result in interference with an individual's ability to travel by means other than commercial airlines as evidenced by some Plaintiffs' experiences as they attempted to travel internationally or return to the United States by sea and by land. In addition, the ban on air travel has exposed some Plaintiffs to extensive detention and interrogation at the hands of foreign authorities. With perhaps the exception of travel to a small number of countries in North and Central America, a prohibition on flying turns routine international travel into an odyssey that imposes significant logistical, economic, and physical demands on travelers. Thus, while the nature of the deprivation in this case may be different from the retention of the plaintiff's passport in *DeNieva*, placement on the No–Fly List, as noted, results in an individual being able to "travel internationally only with great difficulty, if at all." Accordingly, the Court concludes on this record that Plaintiffs have constitutionally-protected liberty interests in traveling internationally by air, which are significantly affected by being placed on the No–Fly List.

The first step of the *Mathews* inquiry, however, does not end with mere recognition of a liberty interest. The Court must also weigh the liberty interest deprived against the other factors.

As noted, placement on the No–Fly List renders most international travel very difficult or impossible. One need not look beyond the hardships suffered by Plaintiffs to understand the significance of the deprivation of the right to travel internationally. Due to the major burden imposed by inclusion on the No–Fly List, Plaintiffs have suffered significantly including long-term separation from spouses and children; the inability to access desired medical and prenatal care; the inability to pursue an education of their choosing; the inability to participate in important religious rites; loss of employment opportunities; loss of government entitlements; the inability to visit family; and the inability to attend important personal and family events such as graduations, weddings, and funerals.

The Court concludes international travel is not a mere convenience or luxury in this modern world. Indeed, for many international travel is a necessary aspect of liberties sacred to members of a free society. Accordingly, on this record the Court concludes Plaintiffs' inclusion on the No–Fly List constitutes a significant deprivation of their liberty interests in international travel.

2. *Stigma–Plus—Reputation*

Plaintiffs also assert the first factor under *Mathews* has been satisfied because Plaintiffs have been stigmatized "in conjunction with their right to travel on the same terms as other travelers." Under the "stigma-plus" doctrine, the Supreme Court has recognized a constitutionally-protected interest in "a person's good name, reputation, honor, or integrity." "

To prevail on a claim under the stigma-plus doctrine, Plaintiffs must show (1) public disclosure of a stigmatizing statement by the government, the accuracy of which is contested; *plus* (2) the denial of some more tangible interest such as employment, or the alteration of a right or status recognized by state law." "'The plus must be a deprivation of a liberty or property interest by the state that directly affects the [Plaintiffs'] rights.'"

Under the "plus" prong, a plaintiff can show he has suffered a change of legal status if he "legally [cannot] do something that [he] could otherwise do."

Plaintiffs contend, and Defendants do not dispute, that placement on the No–Fly List satisfies the "stigma" prong because it carries with it the stigma of being a suspected terrorist that is publicly disclosed to airline employees and other travelers near the ticket counter. According to Defendants, however, Plaintiffs cannot meet the "plus" prong of the test because (1) Plaintiffs do not have a right to travel by commercial airline and (2) there is not a "connection" between the stigma and the "plus" in light of the fact that Plaintiffs have alternative means of travel.

As noted, the Court has concluded Plaintiffs have constitutionally-protected liberty interests in the right to travel internationally by air. In addition, the Court concludes Plaintiffs have satisfied the "plus" prong because being on the No–Fly List means Plaintiffs are legally barred from traveling by air at least to and from the United States and over United States airspace, which they would be able to do but for their inclusion on the No–Fly List. Thus, Plaintiffs have suffered a change in legal status because they "legally [cannot] do something that [they] otherwise could do." The Court, therefore, concludes on this record that Plaintiffs have constitutionally-protected liberty interests in their reputations. On the other hand, Plaintiffs' private interests at the heart of their stigma-plus claim are not as strong. Although placement on the No–Fly List carries with it the significant stigma of being a suspected terrorist and Defendants do not contest the fact that the public disclosure involved may be sufficient to satisfy the stigma-plus test, the Court notes the limited nature of the public disclosure in this case mitigates Plaintiffs' claims of injury to their reputations.

Because the No–Fly List is not released publicly, the "public" disclosure is limited to a relatively small group of individuals in the same area of the airport as the traveler when the traveler is denied boarding. Notwithstanding the fact that being denied boarding an airplane and, in some instances, being arrested or surrounded by security officials in an airport is doubtlessly stigmatizing, the Court notes the breadth and specificity of the public disclosure in this case is more limited than in the ordinary "stigma-plus" case.

On this record the Court concludes Plaintiffs' claims raise constitutionally-protected liberty interests both in international air travel and in reputation, and, therefore, the first factor under the Mathews test weighs heavily in Plaintiffs' favor.

B. Second Factor: Risk of Erroneous Deprivation

As noted, in the second *Mathews* factor the Court weighs "the risk of an erroneous deprivation of such interest through the procedures used, and the probative value, if any, of additional or substitute procedural safeguards."

1. *Risk of Erroneous Deprivation*

When considering the risk of erroneous deprivation, the Court considers both the substantive standard that the government uses to make its decision as well as the procedural processes in place.

As noted, nominations to the TSDB are generally accepted based on a "reasonable suspicion" that requires "articulable facts which, taken together with rational inferences, reasonably warrant the determination that an individual" meets the substantive derogatory criteria. This "reasonable suspicion" standard is the same as the traditional reasonable suspicion standard commonly applied by the courts. Although reasonable suspicion requires more than "a mere 'hunch,'" the evidence available "need not rise to the level required for probable cause, and ... falls considerably short of satisfying a preponderance of the evidence standard."

It is against the backdrop of this substantive standard that the Court considers the risk of erroneous deprivation of the protected interests; *i.e.*, the risk that travelers will be placed on the No–Fly List under Defendants' procedures despite not having a connection to terrorism or terrorist activities. Defendants argue there is little risk of erroneous deprivation because the TSC has implemented extensive quality controls to ensure that the TSDB includes only individuals who are properly placed there. Defendants point out that the TSDB is updated daily and audited for accuracy and currentness on a regular basis and that each entry into the TSDB receives individualized review if the individual files a DHS TRIP inquiry. Finally, Defendants argue judicial review of the DHS TRIP determination further diminishes the risk of erroneous deprivation.

Plaintiffs, in turn, cite a 2007 report by the United States Government Accountability Office and a 2009 report by the Department of Justice Office of the Inspector General that concludes the TSDB contains many errors and that the TSC has failed to take adequate steps to remove or to modify records in a timely manner even when necessary. In addition, Plaintiffs maintain the lack of notice of inclusion on the No–Fly List or the reasons therefor forces aggrieved travelers to guess about the evidence that they should submit in their defense and, by definition, creates a one-sided and insufficient record at both the administrative and judicial level that does not provide a genuine opportunity to present exculpatory evidence for the correction of errors.

Defendants point out that the information on which Plaintiffs rely to support their contention that the TSC has failed to modify adequately or to remove records when necessary is outdated and that the 2009 report indicated significant progress in maintenance of the TSDB. Although Defendants are correct that the TSC appears to have made improvements in ensuring the TSDB is current and accurate, Plaintiffs' contention that the TSDB carries with it a risk of error, nevertheless, carries significant weight.

This point was recently reinforced in *Ibrahim* where the plaintiff was nominated to the No–Fly List in 2004 as a consequence of human error despite the fact that she did not pose a threat to national security. Although Ibrahim was taken off the No–Fly List shortly after the 2004 listing, the mistake itself was not discovered until 2013 and Ibrahim continued to experience substantial difficulties through the date of the order in which Judge William Alsup ultimately ordered the government to purge references to the erroneous 2004 nomination in all of its databases. The fact that the TSDB could still contain erroneous information more than nine years after commission of the error belies Defendants' argument that the TSDB front-end safeguards substantially mitigate the risk of erroneous deprivation.

In any event, the DHS TRIP process suffers from an even more fundamental deficiency. As noted, the reasonable suspicion standard used to accept nominations to the TSDB is a low evidentiary threshold. This low standard is particularly significant in light of Defendants' refusal to reveal whether travelers who have been denied boarding and who submit DHS TRIP inquiries are on the No–Fly List and, if they are on the List, to provide the travelers with reasons for their inclusion on the List. "Without knowledge of a charge, even simple factual errors may go uncorrected despite potentially easy, ready, and persuasive explanations."

The availability of judicial review does little to cure this risk of error. While judicial review provides an independent examination of the existing administrative record, that review is of the same one-sided and potentially insufficient administrative record that TSC relied on in its listing decision without any additional meaningful opportunity for the aggrieved traveler to submit evidence intelligently in order to correct anticipated errors in the record.

Moreover, judicial review only extends to whether the government reasonably determined the traveler meets the minimum substantive derogatory criteria; i.e., the reasonable suspicion standard. Thus, the fundamental flaw at the administrative-review stage (the combination of a one-sided record and a low evidentiary standard) carries over to the judicial-review stage. Accordingly, on this record the Court concludes the DHS TRIP redress process, including the judicial review of DHS TRIP determinations, contains a high risk of erroneous deprivation of Plaintiffs' constitutionally-protected interests.

2. *Utility of Substitute Procedural Safeguards*

In its analysis of the second *Mathews* factor, the Court also considers the probative value of additional procedural safeguards. Plaintiffs contend due process requires Defendants to provide post-deprivation notice of their placement on the No–Fly List; notice of the reasons they have been placed on the List; and a post-deprivation, in-person hearing to permit Plaintiffs to present exculpatory evidence. Notably, Plaintiffs argue these additional safeguards are only necessary after a traveler has been denied boarding. Defendants, in turn, assert the current procedures are sufficient in light of the compelling government interests in national security and protection of classified information.

Clearly, additional procedural safeguards would provide significant probative value. In particular, notice of inclusion on the No–Fly List through the DHS TRIP process after a traveler has been denied boarding would permit the complainant to make an intelligent decision about whether to pursue an administrative or judicial appeal. In addition, notice of the reasons for inclusion on the No–Fly List as well as an opportunity to present exculpatory evidence would help ensure the accuracy and completeness of the record to be considered at both the administrative and judicial stages and, at the very least, would provide aggrieved travelers the opportunity to correct "simple factual errors" with "potentially easy, ready, and persuasive explanations." Thus, the Court concludes additional procedural safeguards would have significant probative value.

In summary, on this record the Court concludes the DHS TRIP process presently carries with it a high risk of erroneous deprivation in light of the low evidentiary standard required for placement on the No–Fly List together with the lack of a meaningful opportunity for individuals on the No–Fly List to provide exculpatory evidence in an effort to be taken off of the List. Moreover, the Court finds additional procedural safeguards would have significant probative value in ensuring that individuals are not erroneously deprived of their constitutionally-protected liberty interests. Accordingly, the Court concludes the second *Mathews* factor weighs heavily in favor of Plaintiffs.

C. The Government's Interest

When considering the third *Mathews* factor, the Court weighs "the Government's interest, including the function involved and the fiscal and administrative burdens that the additional or substitute procedural requirement would entail."

"[T]he Government's interest in combating terrorism is an urgent objective of the highest order." "It is 'obvious and unarguable' that no governmental interest is more compelling than the security of the Nation." *Haig v. Agee* (1981). "[T]he Constitution certainly does not require that the government take actions that would endanger national security" and obviously, the Court cannot and will not order Defendants to disclose classified information to Plaintiffs. On this record the Court concludes the governmental interests in combating terrorism and protecting classified information are particularly compelling, and, viewed in isolation, the third Mathews factor weighs heavily in Defendants' favor.

D. Balancing the *Mathews* Factors

Although balancing the Mathews factors is especially difficult in this case involving compelling interests on both sides, the Court, fortunately, does not have to paint on an empty canvass when balancing such interests. Indeed, several other courts have done so in circumstances that also required balancing a plaintiff's due-process right to contest the deprivation of important private interests with the government's interest in protecting national security and classified information.

In this context, the Court finds Plaintiffs here have significant protected liberty interests at stake. The adequacy of current procedures and potential additional procedures, however, affect the weight given to the governmental interest. Thus, while the government's interest in national security in this case weighs heavily, the sufficiency of the DHS TRIP redress process ultimately turns on the procedural protections provided to Plaintiffs.

Defendants' failure to provide any notice of the reasons for Plaintiffs' placement on the No–Fly List is especially important in light of the low evidentiary standard required to place an individual in the TSDB in the first place. When only an ex parte showing of reasonable suspicion supported by "articulable facts ... taken together with rational inferences" is necessary to place an individual in the TSDB, it is certainly possible, and probably likely, that "simple factual errors" with "potentially easy, ready, and persuasive explanations" could go uncorrected.

Thus, without proper notice and an opportunity to be heard, an individual could be doomed to indefinite placement on the No–Fly List. Moreover, there is nothing in the DHS TRIP administrative or judicial-review procedures that remedies this fundamental deficiency. The procedures afforded to Plaintiffs through the DHS TRIP process are wholly ineffective and, therefore, fall short of the "elementary and fundamental requirement of due process" to be afforded "notice reasonably calculated, under all the circumstances, to apprise interested parties of the pendency of the action and afford them an opportunity to present objections." Accordingly, on this record the Court concludes the absence of any meaningful procedures to afford Plaintiffs the opportunity to contest their placement on the No–Fly List violates Plaintiffs' rights to procedural due process.

And, although the Court holds Defendants must provide a new process that satisfies the constitutional requirements for due process, the Court concludes Defendants (and not the Court) must fashion new procedures that provide Plaintiffs with the requisite due process described herein without jeopardizing national security.

Because due process requires Defendants to provide Plaintiffs (who have all been denied boarding flights and who have submitted DHS TRIP inquiries without success) with notice regarding their status on the No–Fly List and the reasons for placement on that List, it follows that such notice must be reasonably calculated to permit each Plaintiff to submit evidence relevant to the reasons for their respective inclusions on the No–Fly List. In addition, Defendants must include any responsive evidence that Plaintiffs submit in the record to be considered at both the administrative and judicial stages of review. As noted, such procedures could include, but are not limited to, choosing to provide

Plaintiffs with unclassified summaries of the reasons for their respective placement on the No–Fly List or disclose the classified reasons to properly-cleared counsel.

Although this Court cannot foreclose the possibility that in some cases such disclosures may be limited or withheld altogether because any such disclosure would create an undue risk to national security, Defendants must make such a determination on a case-by-case basis including consideration of, at a minimum: (1) the nature and extent of the classified information, (2) the nature and extent of the threat to national security, and (3) the possible avenues available to allow the Plaintiff to respond more effectively to the charges. Such a determination must be reviewable by the relevant court.

II. Claim Three: Administrative Procedure Act

When prescreening passengers, Congress instructed the Executive to "establish a procedure to enable airline passengers, who are delayed or prohibited from boarding a flight because the advanced passenger prescreening system determined that they might pose a security threat, to appeal such determination and *correct information contained in the system*."

As discussed herein at length, the DHS TRIP process does not provide a meaningful mechanism for travelers who have been denied boarding to correct erroneous information in the government's terrorism databases. A traveler who has not been given any indication of the information that may be in the record does not have any way to correct that information. As a result, the DHS TRIP process "entirely fail[s] to consider an important aspect" of Congress's instructions with respect to travelers denied boarding because they are on the No–Fly List. Accordingly, on this record the Court concludes the DHS TRIP process violates § 706(2)(A) of the APA.

Additionally, because the Court has already concluded the DHS TRIP process violates Plaintiffs' procedural due-process rights, the Court also concludes the DHS TRIP process violates § 706(2)(B) of the APA.

NOTES

1. The September 11th hijackers—10 of 19 of whom were identified for further pre-flight security screening by a computer passenger profiling system—caused a cascade of damage by overtaking at least four jetliners with items not commonly regarded as weapons. In fact, their weapons were not guns and certainly were not the box cutters they used to gain cockpit access. Rather, the September 11th terrorists commandeered the entire commercial aviation system itself and vandalized existing infrastructure to exact death and disaster. In doing so, the September 11th terrorists exposed erroneous assumptions upon which national aviation security policy operated for decades. Thus,

> [t]he biggest challenge to preventing the civil aircraft from becoming a weapon of destruction is forty years of accumulated preconceptions that now need to be overcome. First and foremost, and emotionally toughest, is the recognition that the survival of the plane and its occupants is no longer the ultimate objective in a situation involving assailants attempting to seize control of the aircraft. Preventing terrorists from taking over the flight controls, and thus preventing them from turning the plane into a weapon of further destruction, takes precedence no matter what the danger to the plane.

See Phillip A. Karber, *Re-Constructing Global Aviation in an Era of the Civil Aircraft as a Weapon of Destruction*, 25 HARV. J.L. PUB. POL'Y 781, 793 (2002-2003).

2. A critical behind-the-scenes part of the "war on terror" following September 11th is the identification, tracking, and freezing of funds that could be funneled to terrorists for criminal purposes. Recall comments in the dissenting opinion in *Kent v. Dulles*, 357 U.S. 116 (1958), presented in Chapter 1.A, *supra,* that "[i]f an avowed communist is going abroad, it may be assumed that he will take counsel there with his fellows, will arrange for the steady flow of cash and information, and do his bit to promote the purpose of the 'conspiracy.'"

Is this assumption warranted in the modern global marketplace? Moreover, in this context, is searching for currency as an indicia of terrorist activity an appropriate national security objective? *See Kaminski v. Napolitano* N.D. Ill. 2009). If so, a core rationale of *United States v. $124,570 U.S. Currency* (9th Cir. 1989), *supra*—that there should be limits on the extent to which law enforcement authorities may use airport security inspections to promote objectives unrelated to air safety—is undercut after September 11th because it is not necessarily knowable what is or is not related to air safety today, right?

3. The court in *Stethem v. Islamic Republic of Iran* (D.D.C. 2002), in Chapter 5.A, *supra*, described the onset and persistence of post-traumatic stress disorders experienced by hijacking victims, including "irrational idiosyncrasies each has developed, such as refusing to board planes with 'Arabic-looking' co-passengers ..." Is that view an "irrational idiosyncrasy" and racist, or experience-based? Are the two mutually exclusive? Consider one appeal to common sense:

> Nobody is suggesting using ethnicity or religion as the only—or even the primary—factors in profiling terrorists. But it also makes no sense to take zero account of the fact that every suicide attack against U.S. aviation to date has been perpetrated by men of Muslim origin. While al Qaeda

> is no doubt seeking recruits who don't obviously display such characteristics, that doesn't mean we should ignore the likeliest candidates …
>
> The law on this is settled, and in the other direction. On multiple occasions the federal courts have upheld programs that treat groups differently when a "compelling" public interest can be identified: affirmative action, minority set-asides, composition of Congressional districts, and the all-male draft have all met that legal test. Yet the same people who allocate jobs, federal contracts and college admissions by race or ethnicity object to using them merely as one factor in deciding whom to inconvenience for a few minutes at an airline checkpoint. Surely aviation security is a far more compelling public interest than the allocation of federal set-asides.

The 'Profiling' Debate, WALL. ST. J., Aug. 19, 2006, at A10 (arguing that avoiding screening on the basis of ethnic and religious background has resulted in "a policy of random searches that focuses scarce screening resources as much on eight-year-old girls as on 22-year old men with Pakistani passports.").

See also Richard Lowry, *How to Deal with the Terrorist Threat—and How Not To*, NAT'L REV., Jan. 28, 2002, at 32 ("Arab-American groups still scream at any suggestion of commonsense security at airports, while the Bush administration still cowers at any association with 'racial profiling.' It has become clear in recent weeks that the pieties of American racial politics will remain unchanged – even after contributing to a mass murder."). *Contra* Debra J. Saunders, *Go Ahead, Search Granny*, S.F. CHRON., Aug. 17, 2006, at B7 ("Why … search little old white ladies when young Arab and Muslim men were behind the Sept. 11, 2001, attacks and other terrorist plots? The answer is: The feds should avoid racial profiling because it breeds discontent without enhancing security.")

Stated another way:

> The mathematical probability that a randomly chosen Arab passenger might attempt a mass-murder-suicide hijacking—while tiny—is considerably higher than the probability that a randomly chosen white, black, Hispanic, or Asian passenger might do the same. In constitutional-law parlance, while racial profiling may be presumptively unconstitutional, that presumption is overcome in the case of airline passengers, because the government has a compelling interest in preventing mass-murder-suicide

> hijackings, and because close scrutiny of Arab-looking people is narrowly tailored to protect that interest.

Stuart Taylor, Jr., *The Case for Using Racial Profiling at Airports*, NAT'L J., Sept. 22, 2001, at 2877. *Contra* Naureen Kamdar, *Muslim Americans are Americans, Too*, ATL. J.-CONST., Feb. 20, 2007, at A11 (editorial by American college student of Pakistani heritage selected for heightened airport screening: "I even understand that suspicion of Muslims is inevitable ... What I don't understand is why of any of that —beards or scarves included—allows bullying of American Muslims by airport security officials.").

4. The elements of the deterrence-promoting screening techniques of the Anti-Hijacking Profile discussed in *United States v. Lopez* (E.D.N.Y. 1977), *supra*, warrant attention. What characteristics of airline passengers are or might be significant for aviation anti-terrorism purposes? Consider what attributes or combination of attributes of the plaintiff in *Mustafa v. City of Chicago* (7th Cir. 2006), *supra*, are remarkable in composing a threat assessment: (i) name; (ii) gender; (iii) citizenship; (iv) ethnicity; (v) religion; (vi) travel origin-and-destination; (vii) number, gender, and composition of travel companions; (viii) nature of in-flight meal; (ix) purpose for travel; and (x) number of pieces of baggage. How does each feature rank in importance relative to the other features and why?

While controversial, profiling and discrimination are common, lawful features of economic life in America today. Businesses regularly segment customers on the basis of buying habits and patterns, where frequent customers can earn benefits such as gift cards or giveaways. Airlines profile and categorize their flight offerings through computer reservation ("CRS"), yield management systems, and frequent flyer reward programs. *See generally* Jane Kaufman & James R. Wrathall, *Who Owns the Customer? The Emerging Law of Commercial Transactions in Electronic Commerce Data*, 56 BUS. LAW. 213, 217 (2000) ("The regulation of the airline CRS system is an early example of the importance of data warehousing and customer profiling to competition in global markets."). *See also* Timothy M. Ravich, *Deregulation the Airline Computer Reservation Systems (CRS) Industry*, 69 J. AIR L. & COM. 387 (2004).

In state and federal courts across the nation lawyers profile potential jurors during *voir dire* and doing so is an important and permissible part of the judicial process on the condition jurors are not excluded on the basis of race, color, religion, sex, national origin or economic status. *See, e.g.*, 28 U.S.C. §§ 1862, 1870. *See, e.g.*, *Batson v. Kentucky* (1986). In another context, law enforcement officials themselves find drug courier profiles probative of drug trafficking operations. *See United States v. Slocum* (3d Cir. 1972). For example, in evaluating the lawfulness of the search and seizure of a drug trafficker, the Supreme Court of the United States, in *United States v. Mendendhall*, (1980), recognized use of a

> "drug courier profile"—an informally compiled abstract of characteristics thought typical of persons carrying illicit drugs. In this case the agents thought it relevant that (1) the respondent was arriving on a flight from Los Angeles, a city believed by the agents to be the place of origin for much of the heroin brought to Detroit; (2) the respondent was the last person to leave the plane, "appeared to be very nervous," and "completely scanned the whole area where [the agents] were standing"; (3) after leaving the plane the respondent proceeded past the baggage area without claiming any luggage; and (4) the respondent changed airlines for her flight out of Detroit.

The concurrence in *Mendenhall* also recognized the utility of behavioral observation:

> The relevant facts may be stated briefly. The respondent arrived at the Detroit Metropolitan Airport on a flight from Los Angeles. She was the last passenger to leave the aircraft. Two agents of the Drug Enforcement Administration watched the respondent enter the terminal, walk to the baggage area, then change directions and proceed to an Eastern Airlines ticket counter.
>
> After the respondent accepted a boarding pass for a flight to Pittsburgh, the two agents approached her. They identified themselves as federal officers, and requested some identification. The respondent gave them her driver's license and airline ticket. The agents asked the respondent several brief questions. The respondent accompanied the agents to an airport office where a body search conducted by a female police officer revealed two plastic bags of heroin.
>
> * * *
>
> The public has a compelling interest in detecting those who would traffic in deadly drugs for personal profit. Few problems affecting the health and welfare of our population, particularly our young, cause greater concern than the escalating use of controlled substances. Much of the drug traffic is highly organized and conducted by sophisticated criminal syndicates. The profits are enormous. And many drugs, including heroin, may be

easily concealed. As a result, the obstacles to detection of illegal conduct may be unmatched in any other area of law enforcement.

To meet this pressing concern, the Drug Enforcement Administration since 1974 has assigned highly skilled agents to the Detroit Airport as part of a nationwide program to intercept drug couriers transporting narcotics between major drug sources and distribution centers in the United States. Federal agents have developed "drug courier profiles" that describe the characteristics generally associated with narcotics traffickers. For example, because the Drug Enforcement Administration believes that most drugs enter Detroit from one of four "source" cites (Los Angeles, San Diego, Miami, or New York), agents pay particular attention to passengers who arrive from those places. During the first 18 months of the program, agents watching the Detroit Airport searched 141 persons in 96 encounters. They found controlled substances in 77 of the encounters and arrested 122 persons. When two of these agents stopped the respondent in February 1976, they were carrying out a highly specialized law enforcement operation designed to combat the serious societal threat posed by narcotics distribution.

* * *

The agents observed the respondent as she arrived in Detroit from Los Angeles. The respondent, who appeared very nervous, engaged in behavior that the agents believed was designed to evade detection. She deplaned only after all other passengers had left the aircraft. Agent Anderson testified that drug couriers often disembark last in order to have a clear view of the terminal so that they more easily can detect government agents. Once inside the terminal, the respondent scanned the entire gate area and walked "very, very slowly" toward the baggage area.

When she arrived there, she claimed no baggage. Instead, she asked a skycap for directions to the Eastern Airlines ticket counter located in a different terminal. Agent Anderson stood in line immediately behind the respondent at the ticket counter. Although she carried an American Airlines ticket for a flight from Detroit to Pittsburgh, she

> asked for an Eastern Airlines ticket. An airline employee gave her an Eastern Airlines boarding pass. Agent Anderson testified that drug couriers frequently travel without baggage and change flights en route to avoid surveillance. On the basis of these observations, the agents stopped and questioned the respondent.

See also Florida v. Royer (1983). Is the foregoing profiling appropriate with respect to aviation security? *See, e.g.*, Gregory T. Nojeim, *Aviation Security Profiling and Passengers' Civil Liberties*, 13-SUM. AIR & SPACE L. 3, 4 (1998).

For further discussion respecting profiling of airline passengers at airports see generally Ellen Baker, *Flying While Arab—Racial Profiling and Air Travel Security*, 67 J. AIR L. & COM. 1375 (2002); Charu A. Chandrasekhar, Comment, *Flying while Brown: Federal Civil Rights Remedies to Post-9/11 Airline Racial Profiling of South Asians*, 10 Asian L.J. 215 (2003). *See also* Raquel Aldana & Sylvia R. Lazos Vargas, *"Aliens" in Our Midst Post-9/11: Legislating Outsiderness within the Borders*, 38 U.C. DAVIS L. REV. 1683 (2005) (concluding "those regarded as undesirable foreigners are becoming more easily disembodied from their humanity"); Tracey Maclin, *"Voluntary" Interviews and Airport Searches of Middle Eastern Men: The Fourth Amendment in a Time of Terror*, 73 MISS. L.J. 471 (2003) (observing nearly unquestioned acceptance of profiling after September 11, 2001); Michael J. Whidden, Note, *Unequal Justice: Arabs in America and United States Terrorism Legislation*, 69 FORDHAM L. REV. 2825 (2001); Floyd D. Weatherspoon, *Racial Profiling of African-American Males: Stopped, Searched, and Stripped of Constitutional Protection*, 38 J. MARSHALL L. REV. 439 (2004); Amanda Main, *Racial Profiling in Places of Public Accommodation: Theories of Recovery and Relief*, 39 BRANDEIS L.J. 289 (2000); David A. Harris, *The Stories, the Statistics, and the Law: Why "Driving While Black" Matters*, 84 MINN. L. REV. 265 (1999).

5. A federal district court considered the ethnic constitution of domestic airline passengers. In reviewing whether the incidence of stopping minorities at an airport was disproportionate to that for whites when compared with the total number of travelers, the court noted that nationally, the racial and ethnic division of all airline travelers is 88 percent white, five percent African-American, one percent Asian, one percent Hispanic, and four percent "other." *United States v. Travis* (E.D. Ky. 1993). Is aviation national security an empirical or statistical matter such that counter-hijacking and -terrorism initiatives might be assisted meaningfully by use of computer-generated profiling systems?

6. Current airline passenger screening initiatives originated after July 17, 1996 when TWA Flight 800, a Boeing 747 from New York to Paris, exploded soon after take-off. A defective fuel tank caused the tragedy. Government officials initially thought

terrorists had destroyed the jumbojet, however. *See In re Air Crash off Long Island, New York, on July 17, 1996* (2d Cir. 2000), Chapter 6.B, *infra*.

In response, on August 22, 1996, President Bill Clinton announced the creation of the "White House Commission on Aviation Safety and Security." *See* Robert W. Hahn, *The Economics of Airline Safety and Security: An Analysis of the White House Commission's Recommendations*, 20 HARV. J.L. & PUB. POL'Y 791 (1997). The "Gore Commission" was charged with "develop[ing] and recommend[ing] to the President a strategy designed to improve aviation safety and security, both domestically and internationally." *See* Executive Order 13,015, 61 Fed. Reg. 43,937 (1996). On February 17, 1997, the Gore Commission issued its final report, making several security recommendations including the revitalization and reformulation of 1960s-era passenger profiling:

> First, FBI, CIA, and [Bureau of Alcohol, Tobacco, and Firearms] should evaluate and expand the research into known terrorists, hijackers, and bombers needed to develop the best possible profiling system. They should keep in mind that such a profile would be most useful to the airlines if it could be matched against automated passenger information which the airlines maintain. Second, the FBI and CIA should develop a system that would allow important intelligence information on known or suspected terrorists to be used in passenger profiling without compromising the integrity of the intelligence or its sources. Third, the Commission will establish an advisory board on civil liberties questions that arise from the development and use of profiling systems.

WHITE HOUSE COMMISSION ON AVIATION SAFETY AND SECURITY, FINAL REPORT, § 3.19.

The Federal Aviation Administration ("FAA") subsequently developed a computer-assisted passenger screening system through a grant to Northwest Airlines in 1996. *E.g.*, Bill Dedman, *FAA Looking to Expand System*, BOSTON GLOBE, Oct. 12, 2001, at A27. After testing a prototype, Northwest Airlines released the profiling software to other airlines through the FAA in December, 1997, and the profiling software operated through the internal computer reservation system of each airline and was known as the "Computer-Assisted Passenger Prescreening System" ("CAPPS"). *See Elec. Privacy Info. Ctr. v. Dep't of Homeland Sec.* (D.D.C. 2005); *Elec. Privacy Info. Ctr. v. Transp. Sec. Admin.* (D.D.C. 2006).

7. In *United States v. $124,570 U.S. Currency* (9th Cir. 1989), *supra*, the Ninth Circuit Court of Appeals cautioned that

> it is the very ubiquitousness of airport security checks that calls for the greatest vigilance on our part. Because these checks touch the lives of so many, because they have become such an accepted part of our existence, they are capable of great abuse. Liberty—the freedom from unwarranted intrusion by government" and as a right that "is as easily lost through insistent nibbles by government officials who seek to do their jobs too well as by those whose purpose it is to oppress; the piranha can be as deadly as the shark.

How does this liberty interest differ from the definition of liberty offered in *Kent v. Dulles* (1958), presented in Chapter 1.A, *supra*?

Are liberty and security mutually exclusive objectives in the context of air travel? *E.g.*, Daniel W. Sutherland, *Homeland Security and Civil Liberties: Protecting America's Way of Life*, 19 NOTRE DAME J.L. ETHICS & PUB. POL'Y 289, 302 (2005); Joseph Kubler, *U.S. Citizens as Enemy Combatants; Indication of a Roll-Back of Civil Liberties or a Sign of Our Jurisprudential Evolution*, 18 ST. JOHN'S J. LEGAL COMMENT. 631, 674 (2004); Diane P. Wood, *The Rule of Law in Times of Stress*, 70 U. CHI. L. REV. 455 (2003); Geoffrey Stone, *Civil Liberties in Wartime*, 28 J. S. CT. 215 (2003); Richard A. Posner, *Security Versus Civil Liberties*, ATLANTIC MONTHLY, at 46 (2001); WILLIAM H. REHNQUIST, ALL THE LAWS BUT ONE: CIVIL LIBERTIES IN WARTIME (1998). *See also* Frank Cerabino, *Hard-Won Freedoms Easily Lost, Groups Say*, PALM BEACH POST, Sept. 30, 2001, at 1A ("The fear and uncertainty of living among terrorists has made many Americans think that maybe Big Brother should be bigger—not smaller—and that hard-fought constitutional rights are negotiable in tough times."); *Compare* K. A. Taipale, *Technology, Security and Privacy: The Fear of Frankenstein, the Mythology of Privacy and the Lessons of King Ludd*, 7 YALE J.L. & TECH. 123 (2004-2005) ("Security and privacy are not a balancing act but rather dual obligations of a liberal democracy that present a wicked problem for policy makers.") *with* Darren W. Davis & Brian D. Silver, *Civil Liberties vs. Security: Public Opinion in the Context of the Terrorist Attacks on America*, 48 AM. J. POL. SCI. 28, 29 (2004) ("America's response to the terrorist attacks [of September 11, 2001] reveals a 'contestability of rights' ... and one cannot support both liberty and order at the same time ... as support for civil liberties increases, support for order and security decreases, and vice versa.").

8. Airlines collect information such as date of birth and gender through their reservations systems to confirm passenger identity for security purposes. With respect to the collection of such information, federal regulations require:

> (a) For covered flight segments, each covered airline shall:
>
> (1) Collect, or cause to be collected, the full name for each passenger who is a U.S. citizen. U.S.-citizen passengers for whom this information is not obtained shall not be boarded;
>
> (2) Solicit, or cause to be solicited, a name and telephone number of a contact from each passenger who is a U.S. citizen; and
>
> (3) Maintain a record of the information collected pursuant to this section.
>
> (b) The covered airline operating the flight segment shall be responsible for ensuring compliance with paragraph (a) of this section.

14 C.F.R. § 243.7.

As to the confidentiality of passenger data, applicable regulations provide:

> Covered airlines may use any method or procedure to collect, store and transmit the required information, subject to the following conditions:
>
> (a) Information on individual passengers shall be collected before each passenger boards the aircraft on a covered flight segment.
>
> (b) The information shall be kept until all passengers have disembarked from the covered flight segment.
>
> (c) The contact information collected pursuant to section 243.7(a)(2) of this part shall be kept confidential and released only to the U.S. Department of State, the National Transportation Safety Board (upon NTSB's request), and the U.S. Department of Transportation pursuant to oversight of this part. This paragraph does not preempt other governments or governmental agencies that have an independent, legal right to obtain this information.

> (d) The contact information collected pursuant to section 243.7(a)(2) of this part shall only be used by covered airlines for notification of family members or listed contacts following an aviation disaster. The information shall not be used for commercial or marketing purposes

14 C.F.R. § 243.9.

On May 1, 2010, Faisal Shahzad tried to bomb New York City's Time Square by abandoning an explosives-laden sports utility vehicle in the busy district. He was able to board a Dubai-bound flight at Kennedy International Airport undetected only hours later, raising serious questions about current security processes that require airlines to check the government's No-Fly list to make sure no one barred from commercial airplanes is a passenger. *See, e.g.*, Thomas Frank, *'No-Fly' List Flaws Seen in Boarding by Suspect*, USA TODAY, May 6, 2010, at 1A. To close this security hole, the Transportation Security Administration has called for implementation of "Secure Flight," the latest iteration of computer-assisted passenger screening systems. *See generally* Timothy M. Ravich, *Is Airline Passenger Profiling Necessary?*, 62 U. MIAMI L. REV. 1 (2007). *See, e.g.*, Stephen W. Dummer, Comment, *Secure Flight and Data Veillance, A New Type of Civil Liberties Erosion: Stripping Your Rights When You Don't Even Know It*, 75 MISS. L.J. 583 (2006); Leigh A. Kite, *Red-Flagging Civil Liberties and Due Process Rights in Airline Passengers: Will a Redesigned CAPPS II System Meet the Constitutional Challenge?*, 61 WASH. & LEE L. REV. 1385-1436 (2004).

9. As illustrated in *Mustafa v. City of Chicago*, 442 F.3d 544 (7th Cir. 2006), *supra*, the mere mention of the word "bomb" at an airport can be a serious violation of law itself. *See* Seena Foster, *Validity, Construction, and Application of Federal "Bomb Hoax Act" (18 U.S.C.A. §35)*, 168 A.L.R. FED. 551 (2001). *See also United States v. Hassouneh* (4th Cir. 2000). Yet, the passenger in *Mustafa* had no bomb or any criminal intentions and indeed it has been rare that actual wrongdoers so overtly make their intentions known. On the other hand, consider that on Christmas Day 2009, Umar Farouk Abdulmutallab, attempted to destroy an Amsterdam-Detroit flight by detonating plastic explosives hidden in his underwear. He was known to American intelligence analysts because his father, a banker in Nigeria, had reported him to the authorities, yet he had not been placed on the watch list. *E.g.*, Mike McIntire, *Ensnared by Error on Growing U.S. Watch List, With No Way Out*, N.Y. TIMES, Apr. 7, 2010, at A1. What threats should aviation security officials regard as creditable as opposed to incredible? Can practical considerations be harmonized with the law in this respect?

10. In *United States v. $124,570 U.S. Currency* (9th Cir. 1989), *supra*, the Ninth Circuit Court of Appeals opined that "airline hijackings and similar incidents are a rarity in the United States" thanks to the "life-saving purpose" of carry-on and weapon-detecting security procedures.

For aviation security purposes, however, are bombs more dangerous than people or vice-versa? *E.g.*, Michael A. Hiltzik, *How Did U.S. Airport Security Break Down?* L.A. TIMES, Sept. 23, 2001, at A1 ("For three decades, [aviation security] has been preoccupied with looking for guns and explosives rather than for dangerous people. ... That ... was its vulnerability ... U.S. Security efforts aim to catch the bomb, El Al's is to catch the bomber."). *See generally* Yvgenia S. Kleiner, Note, *Racial Profiling in the Name of National Security: Protecting Minority Travelers' Civil Liberties in the Age of Terrorism*, 30 B.C. THIRD WORLD L.J. 103 (2010); Sanford L. Dow, *Airport Security, Terrorism, and the Fourth Amendment: A Look Back and a Step Forward*, 58 J. AIR L. & COM. 1149 (1993); Humphrey G. Dawson, *Civil Aviation, Hijacking and International Terrorism: An Historical and Legal Review*, 15 INT'L BUS. LAW. 57 (1987).

In 2010, the government unveiled expensive full-body scanners. *See generally* Matthew L. Wald, *Air Security Gets Faster, but at Price of Privacy*, N.Y. TIMES, May 6, 2010, at F4. Should aviation security concerns trump personal privacy interests? *See All for It—and Completely Opposed*, AIR SAFETY WK., Oct. 11, 2004, at 2004 WL 61715487; Jennifer Babson, *False Alarm Diverts Delta Flight*, MIAMI HERALD, Dec. 27, 2004, at B1 (reporting diversion of 132-passenger flight from Colombia to Atlanta after the name of a passenger who was the victim of identity theft was mistakenly thought to be someone on a federal security watch list). Consider also this exchange on National Public Radio between a private citizen and a Transportation Security Administration spokesperson:

CALLER: I have been stopped 22 different times by the TSA, the FBI and the Secret Service. My name is similar to that of another person in Chicago, Illinois, who is apparently a financier of al-Qaeda. I have done everything possible to keep this from happening, and wanted to know if there's any advice you might be able to give me to get my name or my comparison name off this list.

TSA: . . . have you contacted the TSA Contact Center and gone through the process of submitting your name and filling out the form so that we can take a look at why that might be happening? I can't address what's causing your experiences with the FBI or the Secret Service, but as far as the airport security experience, if you're getting selected for secondary screening or being delayed before you're allowed to board, we're -- we've got the system set up . . .

CALLER: It's beyond secondary screening. I've been pulled off the tarmac in Denver and questioned by two

Secret Service agents; a very embarrassing issue. And, yes, I have been in contact with the TSA and I've really had no recourse other than to get every frequent-flier card I can and, again, to go one on one with a TSA agent as I'm getting ready to the board the plane.

TSA: . . . Secure Flight is a very clean-focused, well-defined program, and I think some of the references in that last exchange you had were to the predecessor, which was CAPPS II, which never really got off the ground and, in fact, it did grow beyond its original intent as a passenger prescreening system focused solely on aviation, and I think that was part of its demise. It just -- it started getting attachments, extra features. It got too heavy to take off.

NPR: Talk of the Nation: Interview: Mark Hatfield and Marcia Hoffman Talk About a New Screening System for the TSA (National Public Radio broadcast, Sept. 22, 2004). *See also* Matthew L. Wald & John Schwartz, *Airport Screening Program's Expansion Led to its Demise*, S. FLA. SUN-SENTINEL, Sept. 20, 2004, at 3A. *See also Green v. Transp. Sec. Admin.* (W.D. Wash. 2005).

PROBLEM

Daniel Farash was a ticketed passenger on a Continental Airlines flight from Miami-to-Newark. He was seated in an aisle seat of the bulkhead row in the first-class cabin. Shortly before departure, a flight attendant required Farash to move to another seat. The stated reason for moving him was that the airline needed to accommodate a father and his child aged twelve or younger. Farash believed the passenger in the seat adjacent to his new seat was a Continental Airlines executive or a federal air marshal and that the flight attendant profiled him based on his "Semitic looks and a middle eastern last name."

At some point during the flight, the flight attendant allegedly called the "air marshal" over to her, after which the marshal "engaged in several seconds of direct eye contact" with Farash. Aware that a federal air marshal had fatally shot a passenger on another flight that had departed from Miami only weeks earlier, "plaintiff was fearful and anxious of an investigation which would culminate in his being detained, scrutinized or worse." When the flight was over, another flight attendant reportedly apologized to Farash for the flight attendant's actions, but Farash's subsequent complaints to Continental's management met with nothing more than a statement that the airline assumed no responsibility. As a result of this conduct, Farash brought suit, alleging he suffered emotional distress, sleeplessness, shock, hypertension, reduced productivity, and a relapse of a post traumatic stress disorder he suffered three years ago.

Post-September 11th, do airlines have a duty, as a matter of tort law, to provide as stress free a flight environment as reasonably possible? *See Farash v. Continental Airlines, Inc.* (2d Cir. 2009). *See also Shqeirat v. U.S. Airways Group, Inc.* (D. Minn. 2009).

CHAPTER 6

ACCIDENT LITIGATION

A. Safety and Preemption

In July 2013 Asiana Airlines Flight 214 crash landed in San Francisco, California following a failed visual approach because its pilots reportedly were confused in working with autopilot systems. In March 2014, Malaysia Flight 370 mysteriously disappeared after somebody turned off the airplane's transponder. In February 2015, TransAsia Airways grounded most of its fleet after flight data indicated that pilots manually cut off fuel to the left engine in error after the right engine of a twin turboprop malfunctioned after takeoff. And, shockingly, these tragedies somehow pale in comparison to events of March 2015, when a Germanwings copilot locked himself in the flight deck of an airliner, which he programmed onto a crash course with the French Alps, killing all 150 people onboard.

These catastrophes make clear that few events more than aviation accidents invoke the legal term "mass torts." Indeed, to the extent a commercial aviation disaster might be attributed to negligence or intentional wrongdoing on the part of an operator or manufacturer, aviation accident litigation generates many complex administrative and substantive concerns for the judicial system, involving potentially dozens of parties, lawyers, governmental authorities, witnesses, experts, insurers, and airplane and component producers. This chapter overviews the main substantive, procedural, and ethical themes arising from catastrophic commercial airplane disasters as a leading example of mass tort litigation. September 11th, terrorism and air piracy discussed in Chapter 5, *supra*, color each of these issues.

VREELAND v. FERRER

71 So. 3d 70 (Fla. 2011)

LEWIS, J.

Danny Ferrer entered into an agreement to lease an airplane from Aerolease of America, Inc. ("Aerolease") for a period of one year. On January 14, 2005, after taking off from an airport in Lakeland, Florida, the plane crashed. The pilot, Donald Palas, and his passenger, Jose Martinez, were killed in the crash.

John Vreeland, in his capacity as administrator *ad litem* and personal representative of the Martinez estate, filed a wrongful death action against Aerolease. In support of the action, Vreeland first contended that Aerolease, as owner of the aircraft, was liable and responsible for the negligence of Palas in the operation and inspection of the aircraft. Second, Vreeland asserted that prior to the transfer of the aircraft to Ferrer, Aerolease negligently performed inspections and maintenance on the aircraft such that it was in a defective condition, which directly contributed to the crash. Lastly, Vreeland claimed that Aerolease published false information concerning the condition of the aircraft, which Ferrer relied upon. According to Vreeland, the actual condition of the aircraft significantly contributed to the crash.

Aerolease moved for summary final judgment, contending that a provision of federal law, 49 U.S.C. § 44112 ("Limitation of Liability"), preempted Florida law. The trial court held a hearing entered a summary final judgment in favor of Aerolease. The trial court noted that under Florida's "dangerous instrumentality" doctrine, the owner or lessor of an aircraft is vicariously liable for the negligent conduct of a pilot. However, the court concluded that 49 U.S.C. § 44112 preempted Florida law and, because Aerolease was not in actual possession or control of the aircraft at the time of the crash, the company was not responsible under the provisions of the federal statute. Vreeland filed a motion for reconsideration, asserting that the trial court's decision on vicarious liability effectively overruled the 1970 decision of the Florida Supreme Court in *Orefice v. Albert* (Fla. 1970). In *Orefice,* the Court held that an airplane was a dangerous instrumentality, and a wrongful death action could properly proceed against the co-owner of an airplane on the basis of vicarious liability.

Vreeland also asserted that Aerolease was in possession and control of the aircraft at the time of the alleged negligent maintenance and inspection and, therefore, federal law did not preempt this claim. The trial court denied reconsideration. On appeal, the Second District affirmed the decision of the trial court to the extent it held that the vicarious liability claim was preempted by federal law, but reversed the entry of the summary final judgment on the claim of negligent maintenance and inspection.

With regard to vicarious liability, the Second District examined the legislative history of the statutory predecessors to 49 U.S.C. § 44112, and concluded that the provision was enacted to shield an owner or lessor of a civil aircraft from vicarious liability under state law whenever the aircraft is not under his or her control. The Second District distinguished this Court's decision in *Orefice* on two bases.

First, the district court reasoned that the 1970 decision did not mention a predecessor statute to section 44112 that was in effect at the time that decision was issued. The absence of discussion concerning that predecessor statute, section 1404, in *Orefice* led the district court below to conclude that the parties failed to raise the issue of preemption before the Florida Supreme Court or the lower courts in *Orefice.* Second, the district court explained:

> The *Orefice* court's ruling that the dangerous instrumentality law imposed vicarious liability on owners of aircraft was based in part on its observation that Chapter

> 330, Florida Statutes (1970), reflected "a specific policy by the State of Florida to license and otherwise see after aircraft safety." The Florida statutes addressing aircraft safety have since been repealed.

With regard to the negligent inspection and maintenance claim, however, the Second District reversed the entry of the summary final judgment. The court below was of the opinion that the purpose of section 44112 was to shield an owner or lessor from the negligence of another when the aircraft is not in the possession or control of the owner or lessor. The statute was not intended to shield owners or lessors from negligence while in control or possession of the aircraft. The district court concluded that the claim that Aerolease was negligent with regard to maintenance and inspection while the aircraft was in its possession was not preempted by federal law and, therefore, the trial court erred when it entered summary final judgment on this claim. Vreeland filed a petition with this Court seeking review of the Second District's decision on the basis that it expressly and directly conflicts with the decision of this Court in *Orefice,* and we accepted review.

ANALYSIS

Florida Law—Dangerous Instrumentality Doctrine

The dangerous instrumentality doctrine has been a part of Florida common law for almost one hundred years. In 1920, the Florida Supreme Court considered whether a corporation could be held responsible for the negligence of an operator who injured another while driving an automobile owned by the corporation. *See Southern Cotton Oil Co. v. Anderson* (1920). In its analysis, the Court articulated what is now known as the dangerous instrumentality doctrine and concluded that the doctrine is applicable to motor vehicles:

> The principles of the common law do not permit the owner of an instrumentality that is not dangerous *per se*, but is peculiarly dangerous in its operation, to authorize another to use such instrumentality on the public highways without imposing upon such owner liability for negligent use. The liability grows out of the obligation of the owner to have the vehicle properly operated when it is by his authority on the public highway.
>
> An automobile being a dangerous machine, its owner should be responsible for the manner in which it is used; and his liability should extend to its use by any one with his consent. He may not deliver it over to any one he pleases and not be responsible for the consequences.

In a subsequent decision, this Court held that an individual who rented vehicles as part of a business was responsible for the negligence of the driver who rented the vehicle. In *Susco Car Rental System of Florida v. Leonard* (Fla. 1959), this Court determined that a car rental agency was responsible under the dangerous instrumentality doctrine for the operation of a motor vehicle where the vehicle was driven by a person not named in the rental contract, *even though* the individual who rented the car had agreed in the contract to be the sole driver.

Recently, the Fifth District Court of Appeal reiterated the concept and framework of the dangerous instrumentality doctrine and the purpose behind it:

> The doctrine imposes strict liability upon the owner of a motor vehicle by requiring that an owner who "gives authority to another to operate the owner's vehicle, by either express or implied consent, has a *nondelegable obligation to ensure that the vehicle is operated safely.*"
>
> The doctrine is intended to foster greater financial responsibility to pay for injuries caused by motor vehicles because the owner is in the best position to ensure that there are adequate resources to pay for damages caused by its misuse. The doctrine deters vehicle owners from entrusting their vehicles to drivers who are not responsible by making the owners strictly liable for any resulting loss.
>
> Liability of the owner is said to be "strict" because a plaintiff need not prove that an owner negligently entrusted the vehicle to its operator for liability to attach. However, the doctrine is distinguished from strict liability for ultra-hazardous activity, because the plaintiff must prove some fault, albeit on the part of the operator, which is then imputed to the owner under vicarious liability principles.

It was a federal court in 1951 that first applied Florida's dangerous instrumentality doctrine to aircraft. Specifically, in *Grain Dealers National Mutual Fire Insurance Co. v. Harrison* (5th Cir. 1951), an airplane passenger filed an action against the company that owned the aircraft for injuries suffered due to the negligence of the pilot. The Fifth Circuit Court of Appeals noted that there was no state decisional law that applied the doctrine to aircraft. However, the federal appellate court reviewed state judicial decisions that applied the dangerous instrumentality doctrine to motor vehicles and ultimately concluded:

> Our examination of these authorities and the reasoning underlying their pronouncements leave no room for doubt that, under Florida law, by which we are here governed, the airplane should be similarly classified with the automobile as "a dangerous agency when in operation."
>
> We can perceive no logical basis for any difference of classification which would authorize a holding that the rule of "dangerous agency" or "dangerous machine," which the Florida law applies to automobiles in operation, should be relaxed in the case of an airplane. This rule imposes liability upon the defendant for the acts and omissions of the pilot of its airplane which the jury was authorized to, and did, find constituted negligence.

Subsequently, this Court in *Orefice v. Albert* held that "an airplane, like an automobile, is a dangerous instrumentality when in operation." This Court concluded that the owner of an airplane who was not in control of the aircraft at the time of a crash that caused the death of a passenger could be held vicariously liable for the negligent conduct of the co-owner pilot. It is clear that the dangerous instrumentality doctrine applies to aircraft in Florida.

At issue in this case is whether the federal law currently codified at 49 U.S.C. § 44112 preempts Florida state law with regard to the liability of aircraft owners under the dangerous instrumentality doctrine and, if it does, how broadly the scope of that preemption covers.

49 U.S.C. § 44112 and its Legislative History

Title 49, section 44112, of the United States Code currently provides:

> § 44112. Limitation of liability
>
> (a) *Definitions*. In this section—
>
> (1) "lessor" means a person leasing for at least 30 days a civil aircraft, aircraft engine, or propeller.
>
> (2) "owner" means a person that owns a civil aircraft, aircraft engine, or propeller.
>
> (3) "secured party" means a person having a security interest in, or security title to, a civil

aircraft, aircraft engine, or propeller under a conditional sales contract, equipment trust contract, chattel or corporate mortgage, or similar instrument.

(b) *Liability*. A lessor, owner, or secured party is liable for personal injury, death, or property loss or damage on land or water only when a civil aircraft, aircraft engine, or propeller is in the actual possession or control of the lessor, owner, or secured party, and the personal injury, death, or property loss or damage occurs because of—

(1) the aircraft, engine, or propeller; or

(2) the flight of, or an object falling from, the aircraft, engine, or propeller.

There is *no* express preemption language within this clause. Therefore, if Florida law with regard to aircraft owner/lessor liability is preempted by section 44112, that preemption can only be implied because there is *no* express preemption.

In 1948, Congress enacted section 504 of the Civil Aeronautics Act, the original federal provision limiting the liability of aircraft owners and lessors. The reasons for enacting section 504 were articulated in great detail in the House Report that accompanied the legislation. Due to the importance of the report in the determination of Congressional intent, we must analyze its full text, which provides:

> This bill proposes to insert after section 503 of the Civil Aeronautics Act of 1938 a new section 504, as follows:
>
> Sec. 504.
>
> No person having a security interest in, or security title to, any civil aircraft under a contract of conditional sale, equipment trust, chattel or corporate mortgage, or other instrument of similar nature, and no lessor of any such aircraft under a bona fide lease of thirty days or more, shall be liable by reason of such interest or title, or by reason of his interest as lessor or owner of the aircraft so leased, for any injury to or death of persons, or damage to or loss of property, *on the surface of the earth (whether on land or water)* caused by such aircraft, or by the ascent, descent, or flight of such aircraft or by the dropping or falling of an

object therefrom, unless such aircraft is in the actual possession or control of such person at the time of such injury, death, damage, or loss.

Provisions of present Federal and State law might be construed to impose upon persons who are owners of aircraft *for security purposes only,* or who are lessors of aircraft, liability for damages caused by the operation of such aircraft even though they have no control over the operation of the aircraft. This bill would remove this doubt by providing clearly that such persons have no liability under such circumstances.The relief thus provided from potential unjust and discriminatory liability is necessary to encourage such persons to participate in the financing of aircraft purchases.

The provisions of present law above referred to are section 1(26) of the Civil Aeronautics Act of 1938 and section 5 of the Uniform Aeronautics Act. Section 1(26) of the Civil Aeronautics Act of 1938 reads as follows:

"operation of aircraft" or "operate aircraft" means the use of aircraft for the purpose of air navigation and includes the navigation of aircraft. Any person who causes or authorizes the operation of aircraft, whether with or without the right of legal control (in the capacity of owner, lessee, or otherwise) of the aircraft, shall be deemed to be engaged in the operation of aircraft within the meaning of this Act.

Section 5 of the Uniform Aeronautics Act is in force in at least 10 States and Hawaii. That section reads, in part, as follows:

The owner of every aircraft which is operated over the lands or the waters of this State is absolutely liable for *injuries to persons or property on the land or water beneath,* caused by the ascent, descent, or flight of the aircraft, or the dropping or falling of any object therefrom, whether such owner was negligent or not, unless the injury is caused in whole or in part by the negligence of the person injured, or of the owner or bailee of the property injured.

If the aircraft is leased at the time of the injury to persons or property, both owner and lessee shall be liable, and they

> may be sued jointly or either or both of them may be sued separately.
>
> This provision thus imposes absolute liability on owners of aircraft for damage caused *on the surface of the earth.* It is susceptible of a construction which would impose liability upon any person registered as owner, even though he holds title only as security under a mortgage or similar security instrument or as lessor under an equipment trust. If such interpretation were adopted, the security title holder could become liable for extensive damages *on the surface* caused by the operation of the aircraft.
>
> An owner in possession or control of aircraft, either personally or through an agent, should be liable for damages caused. A security owner not in possession or control of the aircraft, however, should not be liable for such damages. This bill would make it clear that this generally accepted rule applies and assures the security owner or lessee, that he would not be liable when he is not in possession or control of the aircraft.
>
> The limitation with respect to leases of 30 days or more, in case of lessors of aircraft, was included for the purpose of confining the section to leases executed as a part of some arrangement for financing purchases of aircraft. Any lease in connection with any such arrangement would almost certainly be for a period in excess of 30 days.

The language clearly references airplane owner/lessor liability for damages to persons and property that are *on the surface of the earth.*

In 1958, section 504 was incorporated into the newly enacted Federal Aviation Act. It was codified in the United States Code as 49 U.S.C. § 1404. In 1959, section 1404 was amended to broaden the protections of the provision to include not only owners or lessors of aircraft, but also owners and lessors of aircraft engines and propellers. Section 1404 then remained unchanged until 1994 when, as part of a revision of Title 49 of the United States Code, which governs transportation, it was merely reworded and recodified without substantive change as section 44112(b).

The House Report that accompanied the 1994 recodification specifically stated that the purpose of the revision to Title 49 was "to revise, codify, and enact *without substantive change* certain general and permanent laws related to transportation ... and to make other technical improvements in the Code." Given that the House Report expressly states that the revision of Title 49 was not intended to affect any substantive change, the Congressional intent behind the enactment of section 504 in 1948 still remains.

The Preemptive Scope of Section 44112

Every version of the owner/lessor liability federal statute since its enactment in 1948 has referenced injury, death, or property damage that has occurred *on land or water,* or *on the surface of the earth.* At no time has Congress removed this geographic requirement from the federal statute. With regard to statutory interpretation, the United States Supreme Court has stated that it is the duty of a court "to give effect, if possible, to every clause and word of a statute." To fulfill this directive, we must determine the Congressional intent embodied in this very specific geographic language.

The words "on land or water" or "on the surface of the earth" may be read to specify that the limitation on liability only applies to death, injury, or damage that is caused to people or property that are *physically* on the ground or in the water. Specifically, the limitation on liability would apply only to individuals and property that are underneath the aircraft during its flight, ascent, or descent.

Under this interpretation, Aerolease would not benefit from any limitation articulated by section 44112 because Martinez was not "on land or water" at the time of the crash—he was a passenger inside the aircraft.

To determine if such interpretation is consistent with Congressional intent, we return to the circumstances that led to the enactment of section 504 in 1948. The House Report that accompanied section 504 criticized a law in effect in multiple states that imposed "absolute liability on owners of aircraft for damage caused *on the surface of the earth.*" As previously stated, section 5 of the Uniform Aeronautics Act ("UAA") allowed absolute liability for "*injuries to persons or property on the land or water beneath.*" The specific language of the UAA that imposed absolute liability for injuries to people or property *beneath* the plane supports the more narrow interpretation of the phrase "on land or water" in current section 44112. Indeed, the title of section 5 of the UAA was "*Damage on Land.*"

Although Aerolease contends that Congress intended for section 44112 to cover *any* injuries, death, or damages caused by a plane striking the surface of the earth, Vreeland is correct that the Uniform Aeronautics Act contained a separate section that addressed injuries to airmen or passengers who were in the plane at the time of the incident. In fact, as demonstrated below, the UAA viewed the tort rights of individuals who were aboard the aircraft quite differently from those of people on the ground beneath the aircraft:

§ 4. **Lawfulness of flight**.—Flight in aircraft over the lands and waters of this State is lawful ... unless so conducted as to be imminently dangerous to *persons or property lawfully on the land or water beneath.*

§ 5. **Damage on land**.—The owner of *every aircraft which is operated over the lands or the waters of this State is absolutely liable for injuries to persons or property on the land or water beneath,* caused by the ascent, descent or flight of the aircraft, or the dropping or falling of any object therefrom, whether such owner was negligent or not, unless the injury is caused in whole or in part by the negligence of the person injured, or of the owner or bailee of the property injured.

If the aircraft is leased at the time of the injury to persons or property, both owner and lessee shall be liable, and they may be sued jointly or either or both of them may be sued separately. An aeronaut who is not the owner or lessee shall be liable only for the consequences of his own negligence. The injured person, or owner or bailee of the injured property, shall have a lien on the aircraft causing the injury to the extent of the damage caused by the aircraft or objects falling from it.

§ 6. **Collision of Aircraft**.—The liability of the owner of one aircraft to the owner of another aircraft, *or to aeronauts or passengers on either aircraft,* for damage caused by collision on land or in the air, shall be determined by the rules of law applicable to torts on land.

§ 7. **Jurisdiction Over Crimes and Torts**.—All crimes, torts, and other wrongs *committed by or against an aeronaut or passenger while in flight over this State* shall be governed by the laws of this State.

Unif. Aeronautics Act §§ 4–7, 11 U.L.A. 160–64 (1938). Thus, while the UAA imposed absolute liability for injury, death, or damage that occurred on the land or water beneath, the rights of airplane passengers and crew members were governed by the law of the state that adopted the UAA.

Congress was indisputably aware of the Uniform Aeronautics Act when it enacted section 504 in 1948. When Congress drafted language to limit the liability of airplane owners and lessors, it only addressed liability toward persons or property "on the surface of the earth." Section 504 did not expressly address airplane passengers or airmen, even though there were separate sections of the UAA that did so. Had Congress intended to preempt the provisions of the UAA that governed the tort rights of passengers and airmen, it could have easily modified the language of section 504 to not solely address injuries or damage that occur "on the surface of the earth (whether on land or water)." We conclude that by adopting a federal law that specifically referenced damages or injuries that occur *on the surface of the earth,* the 1948 Congress did not intend to preempt state law with regard to injuries to passengers or aircraft crew.

Further, section 1404/44112 is not the only federal aviation statute that references persons and property that are on the ground, *i.e.*, beneath the aircraft in the course of its ascent, descent, or flight. 49 U.S.C. § 40103 provides:

> (b) *Use of airspace.*—(1) The Administrator of the Federal Aviation Administration shall develop plans and policy for the use of the navigable airspace and assign by regulation or order the use of the airspace necessary to ensure the safety of aircraft and the efficient use of airspace. The Administrator may modify or revoke an assignment when required in the public interest.
>
> (2) The Administrator shall prescribe air traffic regulations on the flight of aircraft (including regulations on safe altitudes) for—(A) navigating, protecting, and identifying aircraft; (B) *protecting individuals and property on the ground;* (C) using the navigable airspace efficiently; and (D) preventing collision between aircraft, between aircraft and land or water vehicles, and between aircraft and airborne objects.

This provision was adapted from and enacted as part of the 1958 Federal Aviation Act. Thus, at a time when the airplane owner/lessor liability provision was incorporated into the FAA, Congress expressed an interest in protecting people and property on the ground. Hence, to not afford meaning to the words "on land or water" in current section 44112, this Court would not only be acting contrary to congressional intent, but would also be failing to give meaning to every word in section 44112. This would be completely contrary to the directive of the United States Supreme Court.

Decisional Law—Preemption

Decisions with regard to how section 44112/1404 should be interpreted are varied. Some cases narrowly hold that the enactment of the preemption provision in section 1404 did not demonstrate that Congress had preempted the entire field of aviation law. For example, in *Rogers v. Ray Gardner Flying Service, Inc.* (5th Cir. 1970), upon which Aerolease relies in support of its preemption claim, plaintiffs Mr. and Ms. Rogers filed a wrongful death action against Ray Gardner Flying Service for the death of their daughters in a plane crash. The plaintiffs conceded that no cause of action existed against the corporation for the alleged negligent conduct of the pilot under Oklahoma state law. However, the claimants asserted 49 U.S.C. § 1301(26) operated to *create a cause of action* for vicarious liability against the corporation under Oklahoma law. Section 1301(26) defined what constitutes the "operation of aircraft":

> (26) "Operation of aircraft" or "operate aircraft" means the use of aircraft, for the purpose of air navigation and includes the navigation of aircraft. Any person who causes or authorizes the operation of aircraft, whether with or without the right of legal control (in the capacity of owner, lessee, or otherwise) of the aircraft, shall be deemed to be engaged in the operation of aircraft within the meaning of this chapter.

The plaintiffs relied upon a provision in section 1404 to support their contention that section 1301(26) preempted state law and created a cause of action not authorized under Oklahoma state law. They asserted that "Congress purposefully considered the question of pre-empting state laws on bailment of airplanes and concluded that only those persons exempted by Section 1404 should not be held liable as operators."

The Fifth Circuit Court of Appeals disagreed with this reverse limitation/ cause of action assertion. The court concluded that, had Congress intended to preempt state tort law of bailments to broaden liability with regard to the operation of aircraft, "it was *fully capable of making that intent clear directly* and not by indirection requiring the circuitous reasoning plaintiffs find themselves driven to employ." The Fifth Circuit expressed "*disbelief,* in the absence of clearer evidence, that Congress would undertakc to alter the tort laws of numbers of states in such oblique fashion." The Fifth Circuit ultimately held that section 1301(26) did not preempt state tort law with regard to aircraft liability, and the plaintiffs' cause of action was governed strictly by Oklahoma state law.

Other courts have concluded that airplane owner/lessors are not responsible for *any* injuries if they are not in control or possession of the aircraft at the time of the incident. For example, in *Matei v. Cessna Aircraft Co.* (7th Cir. 1994), also relied upon by Aerolease, the Seventh Circuit Court of Appeals affirmed a trial court entry of a summary final judgment that held an aircraft owner who leased the aircraft to another company could not be held liable under either section 1404 or Illinois bailment law for the death of the pilot. However, in affirming the trial court decision, the Seventh Circuit provided a limited text of section 1404 as follows: "[N]o lessor of any [civil] aircraft ... under a bona fide lease of thirty days or more, shall be liable by reason of ... his interest as lessor or owner of the aircraft ... so leased, for any injury to or death of persons ... caused by such aircraft *unless such aircraft ... is in the actual possession or control of such person at the time of such injury, death, damage or loss.*" Thus, the Seventh Circuit in *Matei* relied upon an incomplete version of section 1404 that *omitted* any reference to the actual words of the statute, which stated injuries or damage that occur "on land or water," when it affirmed the determination of the district court that federal law exempted an owner/lessor from vicarious liability for the death of a pilot in a plane crash.

Finally, well-reasoned decisional law exists which expressly supports the limited preemption that we deem correct with regard to section 44112. In *Storie v. Southfield Leasing, Inc.* (1979), an aircraft owned by Southfield Leasing crashed and a passenger on the plane, Charles Storie, was killed. At the time of the crash, the aircraft was leased to Lebow Associates, for whom Storie worked. The administrator of Storie's estate filed a wrongful death action against Southfield. Southfield filed a motion for summary judgment contending that 49 U.S.C. § 1404 (1970) preempted Michigan state law with regard to a lessor's liability for airplane collisions.

The trial court entered summary final judgment on a different basis (the doctrine of *lex loci delecti*). The administrator appealed the summary judgment, and Southfield Leasing cross-appealed with regard to the failure of the trial court to grant summary judgment on the issue of preemption. The Michigan Appellate Court rejected Southfield Leasing's preemption argument and applied a reasoning which is consistent with our decision today:

> We do conclude that M.C.L. § 259.180a(1); M.S.A. § 10.280(1) does, in part, conflict with the provisions of 49 U.S.C. § 1404. The latter statute shields a lessor of an airplane from tort liability for any injury or loss suffered "on the surface of the earth." To the extent that M.C.L. § 259.180a(1); M.S.A. § 10.280(1) would impose liability for such an injury or loss upon the lessor of the airplane, the statute directly conflicts with Federal law and is preempted by it.
>
> A close reading of 49 U.S.C. § 1404 leads us to conclude, however, that the Federal statute is inapplicable to the situation presented under the circumstances of this case.
>
> *In the present case the injury occurred inside the aircraft and not upon the surface of the earth. We do not read 49 U.S.C. § 1404 as preventing the states from imposing liability upon the owners of airplanes in these circumstances.*
>
> Therefore, we conclude that M.C.L. § 259.180a(1); M.S.A. § 10.280(1) is not entirely preempted by the Federal legislation. As written, the Michigan statute imposes

> liability upon aircraft owners both for injuries incurred on the ground and those suffered inside the aircraft. Although liability for the former species of injury must yield to the Federal mandate, the liability imposed by the statute for the latter type of injury may be severed from the statute without doing injustice to the legislative intent.

The Michigan Supreme Court affirmed the lower court with little discussion directed to the holding of the Michigan appellate court with regard to federal preemption.

We conclude that the preemption analysis in *Storie* correctly tracks the legislative history of section 44112, and is also consistent with both the well-established presumption against federal preemption of state tort remedies and the savings clause that is now codified in section 40120(c) of the United States Code, which preserves "any other remedies provided by law." Therefore, we follow the reasoning of the Michigan Court of Appeals.

Application to this Case

Florida's dangerous instrumentality doctrine imposes vicarious liability upon owners and lessors of aircraft, even where the aircraft is not within their immediate control or possession at the time of the loss. To the extent that the doctrine applies to injuries, damages, or deaths that occur on the surface of the earth, the doctrine conflicts with, and is therefore preempted by, section 44112. However, because the death of Martinez occurred while he was a passenger in a plane that crashed—not on the ground beneath the plane—the wrongful death action filed by Vreeland is not preempted by section 44112. Rather, Florida's dangerous instrumentality doctrine applies, and the Second District erroneously affirmed the summary final judgment entered by the trial court in favor of Aerolease on the basis of federal preemption.

The dissent contends that our holding today "defies reality." Dissenting However, the dissent fails to provide any legal reasoning or precedent in support of this assertion other than the erroneous decision of the Second District below and completely disregards the fifty years of congressional history that surrounds this federal provision. Rather than presenting a basis for disagreement that is grounded in sound legal analysis and historical consideration, the dissent simply turns a blind eye to the well-documented creation and evolution of what is now section 44112 and the longstanding presumption against preemption of traditional state law remedies. It is certainly easy to proclaim that a legal analysis is absurd or nonsensical merely by pretending the extensive history in support of that analysis does not exist. If reality is defied in this case, the dissent is the culprit for willful blindness and a lack of cogent legal analysis.

POLSTON, J., dissenting.

I agree with the Second District that federal law preempts the application of Florida's dangerous instrumentality doctrine to Vreeland's claim that Aerolease, as the owner of the aircraft, is vicariously liable for the pilot's negligence.

The relevant portion of the Federal Aviation Act provides as follows:

> (b) Liability.—A lessor, owner, or secured party is liable for personal injury, death, or property loss or damage on land or water only when a civil aircraft, aircraft engine, or propeller is in the actual possession or control of the lessor, owner, or secured party, and the personal injury, death, or property loss or damage occurs because of—
>
> (1) the aircraft, engine, or propeller; or
>
> (2) the flight of, or an object falling from, the aircraft, engine, or propeller.

Based upon the plain meaning of this language, "the federal statute [shields] the owner or lessor of a civil aircraft from liability for the negligence of others committed when the aircraft was not in the owner's or lessor's possession or control." Therefore, like the Second District, I believe federal law preempts Florida's dangerous instrumentality doctrine here.

By narrowly construing the "on land or water" language of the statute, the majority holds that the federal statute only preempts Florida law when the loss of life occurs to someone on the ground beneath the aircraft. However, as the Second District noted, this reasoning does not "explain why an airplane crash does not cause an injury on the surface of the earth regardless of whether the injured person was in the airplane or standing on the ground." The majority's assertion that the federal statute does not apply because "Martinez was not 'on land or water' at the time of the crash—he was a passenger inside the aircraft" defies reality. Even though Martinez was in the aircraft when it hit land, his death occurred "on land," not in the aircraft prior to contact with land. The majority's view is inconsistent with the plain meaning of the statute, specifically the plain meaning of "on land." Therefore, I respectfully dissent.

* * *

GRAHAM v. TELEDYNE-CONTINENTAL MOTORS

805 F.2d 1386 (9th Cir. 1987)

KOZINSKI, Circuit Judge.

James Graham was the pilot of a twin engine Beechcraft Baron aircraft that crashed into the Sun Valley Mall in Concord, California on December 23, 1985. The accident resulted in five fatalities, numerous injuries and extensive property damage. Appellant Dorothy Graham, the executrix of James Graham's estate, has been named a defendant in several lawsuits arising from this event.

As charged by the Independent Safety Board Act of 1974, 49 U.S.C. §§ 1901 *et seq.* (1982), the National Transportation Safety Board ("NTSB") began an immediate investigation into the cause of the accident. To this end, the NTSB directed that the aircraft's two engines be shipped to their manufacturer, Teledyne Industries, Inc. ("Teledyne"). There the agency planned to conduct a complete teardown analysis. In accordance with NTSB practice, the proposed inspection and disassembly was to be conducted by Teledyne engineers working in conjunction with, and under the supervision of, NTSB officials.

The practice of disassembling airplane engines and other component parts on the premises of their manufacturer, with the assistance and participation of the manufacturer's personnel, grows out of the NTSB's belief that the manufacturer and its staff are best equipped to perform such functions. Each manufacturer uses somewhat different designs and specifications, requiring somewhat different tools and techniques for disassembly. The NTSB has determined that use of the manufacturer's facilities and personnel will maximize its ability to determine the cause of the accident while minimizing cost. Cost is minimized because this practice saves the NTSB from maintaining staff and facilities capable of disassembling every type of airplane component used in U.S. civil aviation.

On learning that the NTSB was shipping the engines to Teledyne for inspection and testing, appellant requested permission to have her technical representative participate in, or at least observe, the teardown inspection. Appellant asserted an interest because of the related civil litigation; she expressed fears about possible destructive testing and spoliation of evidence. The NTSB and Teledyne refused appellant's demands.

Appellant then brought this action seeking interlocutory and permanent injunctive relief. She alleged that the NTSB examination would cause irreparable harm due to the destruction of evidence, deprive her of due process by impairing her legal rights and remedies, and take her property (consisting of these rights) without just compensation. The district court denied a temporary restraining order, holding that the NTSB did not abuse its discretion under applicable statutes and regulations in deciding who shall participate in the accident investigation. In addition, the district court determined that appellant had failed to establish that any constitutional right would be violated by the pending engine examination. Graham immediately appealed, challenging the denial of the temporary restraining order. [T]his court enjoined appellees from conducting destructive testing pending resolution of the appeal.

STANDARD OF REVIEW

This is an appeal from the denial of a temporary restraining order ("TRO"). Generally, such an appeal is premature. In this case, however, the denial of the TRO effectively decided the merits of the case: should the NTSB and Teledyne proceed with the disassembly and inspection of the engines, appellant's claims will be rendered moot. Under these circumstances, the court will not require litigants to go through the futile act of reapplying for permanent relief and the denial of a TRO may be treated as a *de facto* denial of a permanent injunction.

Normally, an appeal from an order granting or denying interlocutory injunctive relief would be reviewed for abuse of discretion, and the inquiry would consider such factors as the balance of hardships and plaintiff's likelihood of success on the merits. However, in this case the only issue we need consider is whether the district court correctly applied the law. There are no facts in dispute, and, as noted, this appeal will effectively resolve the merits: if the district court correctly applied the law, the NTSB will proceed with its testing and the case will be rendered moot; if the district court erred, plaintiff will be entitled not merely to a TRO, but also to permanent injunctive relief. Therefore, we treat this as an appeal from a final judgment denying permanent injunctive relief and review the district court's interpretation of the applicable law *de novo*.

The NTSB argues that its decision to exclude appellant from the examination is one "committed to agency discretion by law" and is therefore immune from judicial review under 5 U.S.C. § 701(a). The agency has not established by the necessary "clear and convincing evidence" that the legislature intended to restrict access to judicial review in this area. Specifically, the NTSB must show that the statute in question provides "no meaningful standard" against which to judge the agency's action. The code sections authorizing the NTSB's investigation contain a variety of limitations on the agency's power. Nothing in the statutory language suggests that Congress intended to foreclose judicial consideration of claims that the agency exceeded those limits.

DISCUSSION

Appellant bases her claim for relief on two sources of authority. First, she argues that the regulations promulgated by the NTSB pursuant to the Independent Safety Board Act give her a right to participate in the inspection and disassembly procedures, or at least render it an abuse of discretion for the NTSB to refuse her request to participate. Second, she argues that the NTSB's refusal denies her the constitutionally guaranteed right to due process.

1. *The Regulations*

Appellant bases her claim on 49 C.F.R. §§ 831.9(a) & 831.10(a), which govern who will participate in the investigation and who may have access to the aircraft wreckage. However, neither of these sections gives appellant the rights she seeks.

Section 831.9(a) provides that NTSB's "investigator-in-charge may ... designate parties to participate in the field investigation." The section is written in the permissive. It gives no one a right to participate; it merely authorizes the investigator to designate parties to the investigation. Section 831.10(a) is even less helpful to appellant. That section restricts access to the wreckage to "the Board's accident investigation personnel and persons authorized ... to participate in any particular investigation, examination or testing." Since appellant's representative is not so authorized, he simply does not qualify under this regulation.

Appellant argues, however, that the NTSB's refusal to designate her representative as a participant in the investigation constitutes an abuse of discretion. In appellant's view, the NTSB was not entitled to exclude an entity with "legitimate interests" in the outcome of the investigation, while at the same time permitting Teledyne, a party with similar interests, to participate. Appellant argues quite plausibly that her interests are antithetical to those of Teledyne.

The plane crash was most likely caused either by mechanical failure or pilot error. Establishing one would tend to exclude the other. Graham believes that, by having its technical representatives present when the engines are torn down, Teledyne is given a substantial advantage in any subsequent adjudication of liability.

Appellant's attempt to impose upon the NTSB investigation rules of procedural fairness reflects a misconception of the Board's mission. The NTSB's authorizing statute provides that the Board shall "investigate or cause to be investigated (in such detail as it shall prescribe), and determine the facts, conditions, and circumstances and the cause or probable cause or causes of any ... aircraft accident." These investigations are not primarily for the purpose of determining civil liability; indeed, the Board has no authority to adjudicate the rights of private parties. The NTSB's function is "to promote transportation safety by conducting independent accident investigations and by formulating safety improvement recommendations."

We conclude that the NTSB did not abuse its discretion by deputizing Teledyne to participate in the investigation but refusing to accord Graham's representative the same status. Wherever the parties may stand with respect to each other under applicable tort law, they stand on much different footing vis-a-vis the NTSB's investigation. The use of Teledyne's facilities and expertise in disassembling its own engines could be indispensable in enabling the NTSB to carry out its mission.

By contrast, there is nothing unique appellant's expert could add to the investigation, or so the NTSB could rationally decide. The only one connected with appellant who might have had unique insight into what happened was James Graham, the pilot, who is dead. The NTSB did not abuse its discretion by determining that it did not require appellant's representative as a participant or observer in the teardown of the engines. [Moreover,] the district court determined, as an alternate ground for denying access to appellant, that Graham's representative also represented an insurance company. Under the regulations, this would render him entirely ineligible to participate in the investigation. *See* 49 C.F.R. § 831.9(c). Appellant contends this finding was clearly erroneous. Given our ruling, we need not reach this issue.

2. *The Constitution*

Appellant next argues that denying her access to the teardown inspection violates her right to due process. She contends that her right to contribution or indemnity from others involved in the accident is a property right that will be impaired if appellees are allowed to conduct destructive testing. Although appellant's interest in the investigation may be substantial, we conclude that her exclusion does not rise to the level of a due process violation.

Assuming appellant has a property interest in her contribution/indemnity cause of action, she will suffer no deprivation of that right. At most, appellant may be deprived of certain evidence that could assist her in litigation. Courts have consistently rejected arguments that deprivation of evidence constitutes a denial of due process. *See, e.g., Samuelson v. Susen* (3d Cir. 1978) (medical review committee privilege denying plaintiff information central to defamation action does not violate due process).

In addition, it is highly speculative whether appellant will in fact be deprived of any evidence. While having her representative present at the teardown is one way to ascertain what went wrong, other avenues are open to appellant to obtain substantially similar proof. Appellant will have access to the NTSB factual reports from the investigation. Moreover, although the expert testimony of Board employees is inadmissible, Graham may secure the testimony of NTSB investigators concerning the factual information they gathered during the course of the accident investigation. Finally, she will presumably have access to the physical evidence itself after the engines have been released by the NTSB.

Appellant has expressed concern that Teledyne may alter or destroy vital evidence. This case, however, is not much different from those where an adverse party retains possession of key elements of proof, *e.g.*, purloined trade secrets, documents proving fraud, or machinery involved in personal injury accidents. The presumptions and sanctions available to punish those who alter or destroy evidence must be considered sufficient to deter any misconduct and Teledyne is no doubt aware that its handling of the materials may come under intense scrutiny. In any case, as we understand the NTSB's procedures, the engines will be handled by Teledyne employees only under the supervision of NTSB investigators.

Graham's remaining claim for a taking of property is premature. If and when she suffers a deprivation, she may bring an inverse condemnation claim under the Tucker Act, 28 U.S.C. §§ 1346(a)(2), 1491. Such a suit, brought after the NTSB's investigation is completed, would avoid much of the speculation inherent in appellant's current action. It would also allow the NTSB to proceed with its investigation, unencumbered by concerns extraneous to—and inconsistent with—the important mission entrusted it by Congress.

Appellant is not the only one who can claim a legitimate interest in the NTSB's investigation; presumably the estates of others killed in the Sun Valley Mall crash, as well as those who were injured or suffered property damage, could assert that their rights will be impaired if their representatives are not allowed to observe the teardown. If appellant's claim were sustained on constitutional grounds, it would be difficult to exclude these others. The problem would be infinitely multiplied in a crash involving an airliner where literally hundreds of interested parties may be in the position of having some interest potentially affected by the NTSB's investigation. The NTSB would be rendered entirely ineffective in carrying out its mission if it were required to allow all of these parties access to every critical step of the investigation. The government must be allowed to carry out its responsibilities; if private property is taken in the process, the appropriate remedy is a suit for compensation.

ABDULLAH v. AMERICAN AIRLINES, INC.

181 F.3d 363 (3d Cir. 1998)

ROTH, Circuit Judge.

Plaintiffs Khaled Abdullah, Audrey James, Eardley James, and Velma George were passengers on American Airlines Flight 1473 from New York to San Juan, Puerto Rico, on August 28, 1991. En route, the aircraft encountered severe turbulence which caused serious injuries to a number of passengers, including the plaintiffs. The First Officer had noticed a weather system developing in the flight path and had illuminated the seatbelt sign. He had also gone to the back of the aircraft to warn the flight attendants that the ride could get choppy in ten minutes. None of the crew, however, alerted the passengers of the expected turbulence. Nor did the pilot change course in order to avoid the storm. Some of the injured passengers were wearing their seatbelts; some were not.

Plaintiffs filed two separate lawsuits against defendant American Airlines, Inc., alleging negligence on the part of the pilot and flight crew in failing to take reasonable precautions to avoid the turbulent conditions known to them and in failing to give warnings reasonably calculated to permit plaintiffs to take steps to protect themselves. A jury found American liable, found plaintiffs to be without any contributory fault, and awarded monetary damages aggregating more than two million dollars.

American filed a post-trial motion which requested dismissal and/or a new trial plus attorney's fees and costs. Among the grounds asserted was that the District Court had improperly used territorial common law to establish the standards of care for the pilots, flight attendants, and passengers. American argued that the FAA implicitly preempts the standards for airline safety. The District Court issued an Opinion, holding that the FAA impliedly preempts state and territorial regulation of aviation safety and standards of care for pilots, flight attendants, and passengers, but that plaintiffs may recover under state and territorial law for violation of federal standards. The District Court held that its error of law regarding preemption, which resulted in admission of evidence regarding standards other than the federal standards, warranted a new trial. Upon motion of the plaintiffs, the District Court certified this issue for interlocutory review. We granted interlocutory review.

DISCUSSION

The instant case concerns the species of preemption known as field preemption. Field preemption occurs if federal law "thoroughly occupies" the "legislative field" in question, *i.e.*, the field of aviation safety. Our finding of implied field preemption here is based on our conclusion that the FAA and relevant federal regulations establish complete and thorough safety standards for interstate and international air transportation that are not subject to supplementation by, or variation among, jurisdictions. While some courts have found federal law to preempt discrete aspects of air safety we hold that federal law establishes the applicable standards of care in the field of air safety, generally, thus preempting the entire field from state and territorial regulation.

Although the term "field preemption" suggests a broad scope, the scope of a field deemed preempted by federal law may be narrowly defined. For instance, we have held that federal regulation of nuclear safety preempted state tort law on the standard of care. Still, even though federal law controlled the standard of care, we held that the question whether causation and damages were federally preempted was a separate consideration. Similarly, in the instant case, we find that Congress, in enacting the FAA and relevant regulations, intended generally to preempt state and territorial regulation of aviation safety. Nevertheless, we find that plaintiffs may recover damages under state and territorial remedial schemes.

In coming to our answers to the certified question, we depart from the precedent established by a number of cases which hold that federal law does not preempt any aspect of air safety. As explained below, we find these cases to be unpersuasive, either because these courts presumed, without deciding through in-depth analysis, that the FAA did not preempt state or territorial air safety standards, or because these courts followed the preemption language of the Airline Deregulation Act ("ADA"), an economic deregulation statute that we find inapposite to resolving preemption questions relating to the safety of air operations. We conclude that Congress's intent to preempt state and territorial regulations of air safety is not affected by the language of the ADA.

A. *Federal Preemption of Air Safety Standards*

As the District Court set out in its thorough examination of the legislative history, the FAA was enacted in response to a series of "fatal air crashes between civil and military aircraft operating under separate flight rules." Congress's purpose in enacting the FAA was "to promote safety in aviation and thereby protect the lives of persons who travel on board aircraft." *In re Mexico City Aircrash of October 31, 1979* (9th Cir. 1983).

Congress found the creation of a single, uniform system of regulation vital to increasing air safety. By enacting the FAA, Congress intended to rest sole responsibility for supervising the aviation industry with the federal government:

> [A]viation is unique among transportation industries in its relation to the federal government—it is the only one whose operations are conducted almost wholly within federal jurisdiction, and are subject to little or no regulation by States or local authorities. Thus, the federal government bears virtually complete responsibility for the promotion and supervision of this industry in the public interest.

S. Rep. No. 1811, 85th Cong., 2d Sess. 5 (1958).

Similarly, the House Report accompanying the FAA indicates that one of the purposes of the Act is to give "[t]he Administrator of the new Federal Aviation Agency ... full responsibility and authority for the advancement and promulgation of civil aeronautics generally, including promulgation and enforcement of safety regulations." In addition, in a letter included as part of the House Report, the Airways Modernization Board Chairman wrote: "It is essential that one agency of government, and one agency alone, be responsible for issuing safety regulations if we are to have timely and effective guidelines for safety in aviation."

Thus, legislative history reveals that Congress intended the Administrator, on behalf of the Federal Aviation Administration, to exercise sole discretion in regulating air safety. And this is exactly what Congress accomplished through the FAA. Congress enacted Chapter 447, Safety Regulation, and directed the Administrator to "carry out this chapter in a way that best tends to reduce or eliminate the possibility or recurrence of accidents in air transportation."

To effectuate this broad authority to regulate air safety, the Administrator of the FAA has implemented a comprehensive system of rules and regulations, which promotes flight safety by regulating pilot certification, pilot pre-flight duties, pilot flight responsibilities, and flight rules. For example:

- 14 C.F.R. § 61.3 provides: "No person may act as pilot in command, or in any other capacity as a required pilot flight crew member of a civil aircraft of United States registry unless he has in his personal possession a current pilot certificate issued to him under this part."

- Before flight the pilot must review available information concerning the flight, 14 C.F.R. § 91.103, verify the aircraft's worthiness, 14 C.F.R. § 91.7, and ensure that passengers are briefed on the use of their seatbelts, 14 C.F.R. § 91.107.

- According to 14 C.F.R. § 91.13, "[n]o person may operate an aircraft in a careless or reckless manner so as to endanger the life or property of another."

- Furthermore 14 C.F.R. § 91.7 mandates that "[t]he pilot in command shall discontinue the flight when unairworthy mechanical, electrical, or structural conditions occur."

- And, 14 C.F.R. § 91.101 states: "This subpart prescribes flight rules governing the operation of aircraft within the United States and within 12 nautical miles from the coast of the United States."

The federal courts that adjudicated the first major cases involving the FAA interpreted its legislative history as evincing Congress's intent to exercise supremacy over the field of aviation safety. For instance, just after the passage of the FAA, the Second Circuit Court of Appeals remarked: "The Federal Aviation Act was passed by Congress for the purpose of centralizing in a single authority—indeed, in one administrator—the power to frame rules for the safe and efficient use of the nation's airspace." *Air Line Pilots Ass'n, Int'l v. Quesada* (2d Cir. 1960).

Because the legislative history of the FAA and its judicial interpretation indicate that Congress's intent was to federally regulate aviation safety, we find that any state or territorial standards of care relating to aviation safety are federally preempted. Our analysis is sustained by reference to the broad scope of the FAA, described above. It also is supported by decisions in which courts found federal preemption of discrete, safety-related matters, such as airspace management, flight operations, and aviation noise, because of the promulgation of specific federal regulations over those aspects of air safety. It follows from the evident intent of Congress that there be federal supervision of air safety and from the decisions in which courts have found federal preemption of discrete, safety-related matters, that federal law preempts the general field of aviation safety. Indeed, it would be illogical to conclude that, while federal law preempts state and territorial regulation of matters such as pilot licensing, it does not preempt regulations relating to the exercise of the specific skill for which licensing is necessary-pilots' operation of aircraft.

Moreover, our move from specific to general regulation is not without support in FAA regulations themselves. For example, 14 C.F.R. § 91.13(a), which governs "Careless or Reckless Operation," supplies a comprehensive standard of care to be exercised by pilots and flight crew. It provides, "No person may operate an aircraft in a careless or reckless manner so as to endanger the life or property of another." In a case then where there is no specific provision or regulation governing air safety, § 91.13(a) provides a general description of the standard required for the safe operation of aircraft.

Thus, in determining the standards of care in an aviation negligence action, a court must refer not only to specific regulations but also to the overall concept that aircraft may not be operated in a careless or reckless manner. The applicable standard of care is not limited to a particular regulation of a specific area; it expands to encompass the issue of whether the overall operation or conduct in question was careless or reckless. Moreover, when a jury is determining what constitutes careless or reckless operation of an aircraft, expert testimony on various aspects of aircraft safety may be helpful to the jury. In the present case, for example, the regulations on the use of seat belts and on the illumination of the "fasten seat belt" sign set the standard for determining both whether American operated the aircraft carelessly or recklessly and whether the passengers, who had not fastened their seatbelts, were contributorily negligent. In addition, expert testimony may help the jury to understand whether the way in which warnings of turbulence and/or illumination of seatbelt signs were conveyed to the passengers constituted careless or reckless operation.

We conclude, therefore, that because of the need for one, consistent means of regulating aviation safety, the standard applied in determining if there has been careless or reckless operation of an aircraft, should be federal; state or territorial regulation is preempted.

B. *Divergent Authority*

Despite the legislative history and interpreting authority which have informed our decision, many courts have held that the field of aviation safety is not federally preempted. We find, however, that the rationales, on which these courts have relied in reaching this conclusion, are unpersuasive. As explained below, either the courts have presumed, without any in-depth analysis, that the FAA does not preempt state or territorial air safety standards, or they have followed precedent involving the ADA, an economic deregulation statute which is inapposite to resolving preemption questions relating to the FAA and air safety. We will deal with these various rationales in turn.

a. *Expressio Unius Est Exclusio Alterius*

Expressio unius est exclusio alterius is a Latin maxim which means "to express one is to exclude the other." As with all easy answers, it should be taken with a grain of salt—or even better, with a grain of common sense. The maxim has been employed by some courts to justify a decision that air safety standards are not federally preempted. The main rationale for such a finding rests on Section 105(a)(1) of the ADA, which provides that the regulation of "rates, routes, and services" is expressly preempted. Based on the language of this section, some courts have observed that state tort law claims for personal injuries connected to airline operations are not preempted. *See, e.g., Hodges v. Delta Airlines, Inc.* (5th Cir. 1995); *see also American Airlines, Inc. v. Wolens*, (1995) (noting that the United States as Amicus Curiae had conceded that "[i]t is unlikely that [the ADA] preempts safety-related personal injury claims relating to airplane operations").

Such a result may not, of course, be inconsistent with our determination that even with federal preemption of standards of care, state tort remedies are preserved. A number of courts have, however, continued to use the state law standard of care, along with state remedies. They have concluded that the standards of care related to aviation safety by implication must not be preempted because *expressio unius est exclusio alterius*.

We agree with American that reliance on this maxim to determine whether safety standards are federally preempted is inappropriate. This maxim "stands on the faulty premise that all possible alternatives or supplemental provisions were necessarily considered and rejected by the legislative draftsmen." For that reason, it "can never override clear and contrary evidences of Congressional intent." As the District Court recognized in its comprehensive examination of the *exclusio unius maxim*, "the meaning of a statute is found in the evil which it is designed to remedy; and for this the court properly looks at contemporaneous events, the situation as it existed, and as it was pressed upon the attention of the legislative body." Thus, whether the maxim should be applied to the standards of care for pilots, flight attendants, and passengers depends on Congress's intent when it enacted the ADA-Congress's intent not only with respect to the ADA itself, but also regarding the ADA as it affected and interrelated with the earlier provisions of the FAA.

The ADA was enacted "[t]o ensure that the States would not undo federal deregulation with regulation of their own ... [by] prohibiting the States from enforcing any law 'relating to rates, routes, or services' of any air carrier." *Morales v. Trans World Airlines, Inc.* (1992). Airlines compete against one another by attracting passengers through the rates, routes, and services that they offer. Congress did not want the states to hamper this competition by their own regulation of these areas. Safe operations, however, are a necessity for all airlines. Whether or not to conform to safety standards is not an option for airlines in choosing a mode of competition. For this reason, safety of an airline's operations would not appear to fall within the ambit of the ADA and its pro-competition preemption clause. The ADA was enacted 20 years after the FAA. Under the circumstances then of Congress's intent in adopting both the FAA and the ADA, we do not find the *exclusio unius* maxim helpful on the issue of federal preemption of aviation safety standards.

b. *Absence of Federal-State Law Conflict*

Another rationale for finding that federal law does not preempt state and territorial safety standards rests upon the observation that Congress directed the Administrator to prescribe "minimum standards" to promote safety. 49 U.S.C. § 44701.Because the federal standards are "minimum," some courts have determined that a common law duty of safety may be owed beyond the FAA regulations. *See, e.g., In re Air Disaster at Lockerbie, Scotland* (2d Cir. 1994).

We have a problem with applying the type of analysis to determine that there is no federal preemption of aviation safety. First, there is no gap in the federal standards to fill with a state common law standard. The § 91.13(a) prohibition of "careless or reckless" operation of an aircraft occupies the apparent void beyond the specified "minimum" standards. Therefore, because the Administrator has provided both general and specific standards, there is no need to look to state or territorial law to provide standards beyond those established by the Administrator.

Moreover, in a federally preempted area, the question whether state or territorial law conflicts with federal law is a pointless inquiry. If Congress has preempted a field—whether it be expressly or by implication—state laws attempting to regulate within that field "will be invalidated no matter how well they comport with substantive federal policies." L. TRIBE, AMERICAN CONSTITUTIONAL LAW § 6-27 at 497 (2d ed. 1988).

c. *The Savings and Insurance Clauses*

The FAA's savings clause provides that, "[a] remedy under this part is in addition to any other remedies provided by law." 49 U.S.C. § 40120(c). The insurance clause requires that airlines maintain liability insurance "for bodily injury to, or death of, an individual ... resulting from the operation or maintenance of the aircraft." 49 U.S.C. § 41112(a). These two sections have been interpreted to mean that state safety standards are not preempted because Congress provided for compensation of injured persons.

These two sections do demonstrate that Congress intended to allow for compensation of persons who were injured in aviation mishaps. As we point out in our answer to the second part of the certified question, however, we do not find that state and territorial law remedies are preempted, only the standards of care for the safe operation of aircraft. For that reason, the inclusion of the savings and insurance clauses in the FAA is not inconsistent with our decision. Their inclusion as a part of the FAA is in fact compatible with our determination that state and territorial damage remedies are preserved.

d. *Reserved State Power*

Finally, as the District Court pointed out, some courts have found that federal law does not preempt state law in the field of aviation safety because they believe that states may regulate aviation safety under their traditional police powers. However, whether the states may invoke their police powers depends on whether the field is federally preempted. As a result, because we have found that the entire field of aviation safety is federally preempted, we need not consider whether the regulation of aviation safety falls within the traditional police powers of the states and territories.

C. No Federal Preemption of State and Territorial Remedies

Even though we have found federal preemption of the standards of aviation safety, we still conclude that the traditional state and territorial law remedies continue to exist for violation of those standards. Federal preemption of the standards of care can coexist with state and territorial tort remedies.

In the present case, we find no "irreconcilable conflict between federal and state standards." Nor do we find that "imposition of a [territorial] standard in a damages action would frustrate the objectives of the federal law." Quite to the contrary, it is evident in both the savings and the insurance clauses of the FAA that Congress found state damage remedies to be compatible with federal aviation safety standards. The savings clause provides that "a remedy under this part is in addition to any other remedies provided by law." Clearly, Congress did not intend to prohibit state damage remedies by this language. Moreover, the insurance clause requires airlines to maintain liability insurance "for bodily injury to, or death of, an individual ... resulting from the operation or maintenance of the aircraft." 49 U.S.C. § 41112(a). Congress could not have intended to abolish a damage remedy for injury or death if it required airlines to maintain insurance coverage to recompense injured persons. Furthermore, there is no federal remedy for personal injury or death caused by the operation or maintenance of aircraft to be found in the FAA itself. We must conclude, therefore, that the insurance proceeds are to be available as a remedy under state or territorial law.

CONCLUSION

Because we find Congress's intent to regulate interstate and international air safety to be unambiguous, we hold that state and territorial standards of care in aviation safety are federally preempted. Moreover, we find that state and territorial tort remedies can coexist with federal standards of care for air safety; thus, plaintiffs, who are injured during a flight as a result of the violation of federal air safety standards, may have a remedy in state or territorial law. We will remand this case to the District Court to evaluate whether the evidence on standards of care and the instructions given to the jury conformed to the federal aviation safety standards as we have described them, and for such further proceedings as it may deem necessary.

NOTES

1. Until only recently, Florida was one of few remaining jurisdictions to regard airplanes as "dangerous instrumentalities." *See Vreeland v. Ferrer* (Fla. 2011), *supra*. In fact, early aviation was seen as ultra-hazardous activity to which courts applied the doctrine of *res ipsa loquitur* to assess liability. *Compare Rochester Gas & Elec. Corp. v. Dunlop* (N.Y. Co. Ct. 1933) (finding strict liability for trespass and property damaged caused by airplane crash) *with Crist v. Civil Air Patrol* (N.Y. App. Div. 1967) (declining application of the strict liability doctrine of *res ipsa loquitur* in absence of showing of intent to crash airplane: "Technological advances and development, and the experiences of the last two decades have dissipated the universal early fears that flying was an ultrahazardous occupation."). *See also* Richard H. Gross, *Torts—Negligence—Applicability of Res Ipsa Loquitur to Airplane Accidents*—Parcell v. United States (S.D. W. Va. 1951), 31 TEX. L. REV. 606 (1953). Today,

> [t]he constant march of civilization and the amazing developments in all fields of human endeavor are ever changing the outward aspects of society and have made the life of the lawyer of today one of progressive experience and increasing responsibility. The things that are happening in the economic and social order should be, and are, reflected in the legal order. We who are heirs to the common law are coming more and more to realize that law is not the embodiment of inexorable scientific formulas and to understand the words of Mr. Justice Holmes: "The life of the law has not been logic; it has been experience."
>
> Since the art of flight had its first impact upon law forty years ago, the legal profession has been striving to bring our statutory and decisional law into line with social changes wrought by the airplane. The Conference of Commissioners on Uniform State Laws, the Committee on Aeronautical Law of the American Bar Association, the American Law Institute, the Air Transport Association, the National Association of State Aviation Officials, and numerous other voluntary and governmental groups—local, state, federal, and international—have endeavored to adapt the various branches of the law to the needs of the flying era.
>
> Uniform codes in relation to the right of flight, aviation tort liability, establishment and operation of airports, and other phases of aviation have been, from time to time, drafted

> and recommended to the states for adoption. The fact that some of these codes became outmoded before they had been extensively adopted is evidence of the dynamic character of the aviation industry and the exciting atmosphere in which aeronautical law is being developed.
>
> Aviation accidents may involve common carriers, contract carriers, or operators of private planes. They occur on the ground, at take-off or landing, or in mid-air. Claims are asserted in respect to passengers, shippers, employees, and third persons, and in respect to property damage as well as personal injury or death. The defendants may be manufacturers, vendors, and repairmen, as well as operators and third-party tort-feasors; and municipal, state, federal, and international laws and regulations are invoked on the questions of negligence, standard of care, and extent of liability. Thus, the decisions usually deal with familiar legal principles in unfamiliar settings. Senator McCarran … appropriately observes that "tort liability law in the field of aviation can best develop as a part of our general jurisprudence through judicial decisions based upon the great principles of justice found in thousands of cases decided by our courts."

E. Smythe Gambrell, *Aviation Accident Law*, 61 HARV. L. REV. 560 (1948).

2. On January 15, 2009, US Airways Flight 1549 departed New York for Charlotte. The airplane's windscreen turned dark brown after takeoff and a loud thud and burning smell confirmed what cockpit instruments indicated: both airplane engines struck and ingested large geese: "Aaah, this is Cactus 1549. We lost thrust in both engines. We are turning back toward LaGuardia … We're gonna be in the Hudson," Captain Chesley "Sully" Sullenberger radioed. In fact, Flight 1549 splashed down into the Hudson River and all of the approximately 155 passengers and crew evacuated the airplane safely in an event termed the "Miracle on the Hudson." *See generally* FAA Wildlife Strike Database, *at http://wildlife-mitigation.tc.faa.gov/wildlife/.*

Six months later, the world was reminded precisely why Flight 1549 was remarkable. On June 1, 2009, 228 souls perished when Air France Flight 447, encountered heavy turbulence over the Atlantic Ocean and plunged into the ocean below. While both events are unusual, as commercial airline travel is a matter of routine today and among the safest modes of transportation statistically, the vastly different endings of Flights 1549 and 447 illustrate the ubiquitous risks inherent in air travel. Aviation accidents are archetypical "mass torts." Accident litigation generates many complex administrative and substantive concerns for the judicial system, involving potentially dozens of parties, lawyers, governmental authorities, witnesses, experts, insurers, and airplane and component producers. *See, e.g.*, Robert W. Hahn, *The Economics of Airline Safety and Security: An Analysis of the White House Commission's Recommendations*, 20 HARV. J.L. & PUB. POL'Y 791, 804-06 (1997). Though frequently many parties are involved in aviation accidents, courts rarely certify class actions in mass aviation disaster lawsuits. *See, e.g.*, *Causey v. Pan Am. World Airways, Inc.* (E.D. Va. 1975); *Hobbs v. Northeast Airlines, Inc.* (E.D. Pa. 1970); *Marchesi v. Eastern Airlines, Inc.* (E.D.N.Y. 1975); *McDonnell Douglas Corp. v. U.S. Dist. Court for Cent. Dist. of California* (9th Cir. 1975).

3. Literally millions of people travel safely on a daily basis and this exceptional safety record is owed to the daring of early aviators for whom modern aeronautical technologies were unknown and yet-imagined. Airmail is the direct ancestor of the modern airline industry. Consider that "[a]n airmail pilot's life expectancy was four years, and thirty-one of the first forty pilots were killed before the service was turned over to private industry. While the Airmail Service was in operation, one in every six pilots was killed in a flying accident while delivering the mail." JEPPESEN, PRIVATE PILOT MANUAL 1-40 (2002).

On September 23, 1911, airmail service began on an experimental basis out of Long Island, New York. Over the next two decades, airmail gave rise to important aviation developments, including night flying, instrument flying, meteorological service, hard surface runways, radio communications, and multi-engine airplanes. By the late 1920s, airplane technology and airmail service were reliable as newly formed "airlines" bid competitively for contract airmail routes pursuant to the Airmail Act of 1925, Pub. L. No. 68-359, 43 Stat. 805 (1925) ("Kelly Act"), An Act to Encourage Commercial Aviation and to Authorize the Postmaster General to Contract for the Mail Service." Congress also passed the Air Commerce Act of 1926, Pub. L. No. 69-254, 44 Stat. 568 (1926), creating a substantial role for the federal government to promote air commerce and safety (*e.g.*, aircraft registration and licensing, and pilot medical certification).

In 1930, Congress enacted the Airmail Act of 1930 ("McNary-Watres Act"), which compensated airlines for airmail service on the basis of space instead of weight—an incentive that encouraged the use of aircraft suitable for commercial passenger purposes, not merely mail delivery. The 1930s legislation was favored by Postmaster General Walter Brown, a November 1928 political appointee of President Herbert Hoover. Brown aggressively sought the formation of a national, market-driven, federally regulated airline transportation system—precursor principles underlying the Airline Deregulation Act of 1978. Brown commanded great regulatory powers under the McNary-Watres Act through which

> [r]oute certificates were promptly issued on several routes; numerous extensions were granted; routes were consolidated; several carriers were required to carry

> passengers; new schedules were authorized, partly with an eye to passenger needs; and mail rates were increased to help meet the costs incurred in the transition to passenger service. An elaborate rate formula was established, providing for "variables" in rates, based primarily on amount of mail space reserved in the plane, and taking into account the flying conditions over the particular route, equipment used, and passenger capacity furnished.

See Frederick A. Ballard, *Federal Regulation of Aviation*, 60 HARV. L. REV. 1235, 1245-48 (1947). The "Great Depression" and the election of Franklin D. Roosevelt cast doubt on Brown's conduct, however.

A congressional committee led by Hugo Black, an Alabama Senator and future Justice of the Supreme Court of the United States, suggested that Brown and several airlines were colluding to end-run the competitive bidding process used to award airmail routes under then-applicable airmail and commerce laws. *See generally* Comment, *Merger and Monopoly in Domestic Aviation*, 62 COLUM. L. REV. 851, 854-55 (1962). In response, President Roosevelt ordered cancellation of all domestic airmail contracts and directed the army to transport airmail. *See* Exec. Order No. 6591, Feb. 9, 1934. In terms of aviation safety, the decision was disastrous:

> The airline pilots at the time of the cancellation were experienced even for a fledgling industry. Most of the pilots had over 4,000 hours of flying time and some had as much as 9,000 hours. They had day and night flying time and knew their routes well. They were used to the particular weather associated with the route and their aircraft were equipped with radio for air-to-ground communication.
>
> In contrast, the Army assigned open-cockpit airplanes to carry the airmail and their pilots had been restricted to flying 170 hours a year. The Army aircraft were not equipped for weather or night flying, and only 500 men were assigned to the entire operation, which had been handled by several thousand airline employees.
>
> The ill-prepared and poorly equipped Air Corps had tragic results in its efforts to carry out Farley's order. Three days before they were to take over the airmail routes three pilots were killed on their way to begin their assignment, and another crashed by escaped serious injury.

> The record for the first week's operations was equally tragic. Five Army pilots were killed and six more were seriously injured. Eight airplanes were ruined, and there was $300,000 worth of property damage. A few days later two more pilots were killed and one was critically injured.
>
> The needless slaughter went on into March of 1934. Finally, after 66 crashes, 12 deaths, and governmental costs of nearly $4 million, President Roosevelet ordered the Army to cease flying the airmail on June 1, 1934, after nearly six months' operation.

See, e.g., ROBERT M. KANE, AIR TRANSPORTATION 110-11 (13th ed. Kendall/Hunt Publishing Co. 1999); *Civil Aeronautics Board Policy: An Evaluation*, 57 YALE L.J. 1053 (1948).

Enactment of the Airmail Act of 1934 ("Black-McKellar Act"), 48 Stat. 933 (1934), reestablished private air carriage and a comprehensive system of federal aviation regulation was introduced soon thereafter through the Civil Aeronautics Act of 1938 ("McCarran-Lea Act"), 52 Stat. 973 (1938). By 1936, airline revenue from passenger traffic exceeded airmail income.

4. The Federal Aviation Act of 1958, Pub. L. No. 85-726, 72 Stat. 731 (1958), replaced the Civil Aeronautics Act of 1938. The laws were practically identical except for their coverage of air safety. Mid-air collisions gave rise to the new law by exposing the need for uniform air space management. *See generally* Justin T. Barkowski, Comment, *Managing Air Traffic Congestion through the Next Generation Air Transportation System: Satellite-Based Technology, Trajectories, and—Privatization?*, 37 PEPP. L. REV. 247, 259 (2010). Specifically, in 1956, a Kansas City-bound Trans World Airlines Constellation and a Chicago-bound United Airlines DC-7 departed within three minutes of each other from the same runway at Los Angeles International Airport; they collided over and fell into the Grand Canyon. In 1957, a Douglas Aircraft Company DC-7 and a United States Air Force F-89 collided near Sunland, California; the fighter plane crashed into nearby mountains while the DC-7 crashed into a junior high school playground, killing three students and injuring 70 others.

Mid-air collisions and "near-misses" (more accurately termed "near-hits") are rare but not unknown in modern aviation operations around the world. *See, e.g.*, *In re Air Crash near Peixoto de Azeveda, Brazil, on September 29, 2008* (E.D.N.Y. 2008) (evaluating doctrine of *forum non conveniens* in wrongful death action arising from the crash of a commercial airliner into the Amazon rainforest following a collision with a private jet). *See also* Alan Levin, *Some Say FAA Move Could Hide Midair Collision Risk*, USA TODAY, July 6, 2007, at 4A; *Fear of Flying*, BOSTON GLOBE, June 1, 1987, at 14.

Active private, general, and military aviation operations—including the emergence of "very light jets" and "unmanned aerial vehicles"—underscore the potential need for appropriate regulation or legal guidance to manage increased traffic in the national and international airspace. *See* 49 U.S.C. §§ 40103(b), 44502, and 44721. *See also* FED. AVIATION ADMIN., AFS-400 UAS Policy 05-01, UNMANNED AIRCRAFT SYSTEMS OPERATIONS IN THE U.S. NATIONAL AIRSPACE SYSTEM—INTERIM OPERATIONAL APPROVAL GUIDANCE (2005). *See also* Timothy M. Ravich, *The Integration of Unmanned Aerial Vehicles into the National Airspace*, 85 N.D. L. REV. 597 (2009); Douglas Marshall, *Unmanned Aerial Systems and International Civil Aviation Organization Regulations*, 85 N.D. L. REV. 693 (2009); Mark E. Peterson, *The UAV and the Current and Future Regulatory Construct for Integration into the National Airspace System*, 71 J. AIR L. & COM. 521 (2006).

5. The Air Commerce Act of 1926, Pub. L. No. 69-254, 44 Stat. 568 (1926), vested governmental authority over aviation operations in the President, Department of Commerce, Department of Defense, and the various states. In 1938, the Civil Aeronautics Act ("McCarran-Lea Act"), 52 Stat. 973 (1938), consolidated this diffuse regulatory responsibility in the Civil Aeronautics Authority. Later, the Civil Aeronautics Authority was split into the Civil Aeronautics Administration ("CAA") and Civil Aeronautics Board ("CAB"). The CAB regulated aviation economic operations (*e.g.*, airline fares and market entry) until 1985, and the CAA regulated safety. In 1958, Congress consolidated the CAA as the independent Federal Aviation Agency under the Federal Aviation Act, Pub. L. No. 85-726, 72 Stat. 731 (1958). On October 15, 1966, President Lyndon B. Johnson signed the act creating the modern United States Department of Transportation ("DOT"), combining the powers of the CAA and CAB in a newly named branch, the Federal Aviation Administration ("FAA"). Pub. L. No. 89-670, 80 Stat. 931 (1966). Both aviation economics and safety are core missions of the FAA:

> **(a) Economic regulation.** The Secretary of Transportation shall consider the following matters, among others, as being in the public interest and consistent with public convenience and necessity:
>
> (1) assigning and maintaining safety as the highest priority in air commerce.
>
> (2) before authorizing new air transportation services, evaluating the safety implications of those services.
>
> (3) preventing deterioration in established safety procedures, recognizing the clear intent, encouragement, and dedication of Congress to further the highest degree of safety in air transportation and air commerce, and to maintain the safety vigilance that has evolved in air transportation and air commerce

and has come to be expected by the traveling and shipping public.

(4) the availability of a variety of adequate, economic, efficient, and low-priced services without unreasonable discrimination or unfair or deceptive practices.

(5) coordinating transportation by, and improving relations among, air carriers, and encouraging fair wages and working conditions.

(6) placing maximum reliance on competitive market forces and on actual and potential competition—

(A) to provide the needed air transportation system; and

(B) to encourage efficient and well-managed air carriers to earn adequate profits and attract capital, considering any material differences between interstate air transportation and foreign air transportation.

(8) encouraging air transportation at major urban areas through secondary or satellite airports if consistent with regional airport plans of regional and local authorities, and if endorsed by appropriate State authorities—

(A) encouraging the transportation by air carriers that provide, in a specific market, transportation exclusively at those airports; and

(B) fostering an environment that allows those carriers to establish themselves and develop secondary or satellite airport services.

(9) preventing unfair, deceptive, predatory, or anticompetitive practices in air transportation.

(10) avoiding unreasonable industry concentration, excessive market domination, monopoly powers, and other conditions that would tend to allow at least one air carrier or foreign air carrier unreasonably to increase prices, reduce services, or exclude competition in air transportation.

(11) maintaining a complete and convenient system of continuous scheduled interstate air transportation for small communities and isolated areas with direct financial assistance

from the United States Government when appropriate.

(12) encouraging, developing, and maintaining an air transportation system relying on actual and potential competition—(A) to provide efficiency, innovation, and low prices; and (B) to decide on the variety and quality of, and determine prices for, air transportation services.

(13) encouraging entry into air transportation markets by new and existing air carriers and the continued strengthening of small air carriers to ensure a more effective and competitive airline industry.

(14) promoting, encouraging, and developing civil aeronautics and a viable, privately-owned United States air transport industry.

(15) strengthening the competitive position of air carriers to at least ensure equality with foreign air carriers, including the attainment of the opportunity for air carriers to maintain and increase their profitability in foreign air transportation.

(16) ensuring that consumers in all regions of the United States, including those in small communities and rural and remote areas, have access to affordable, regularly scheduled air service.

* * *

(d) Safety considerations in public interest.—In carrying out subpart III of this part and those provisions of subpart IV applicable in carrying out subpart III, the Administrator shall consider the following matters, among others, as being in the public interest:

(1) assigning, maintaining, and enhancing safety and security as the highest priorities in air commerce.

(2) regulating air commerce in a way that best promotes safety and fulfills national defense requirements.

(3) encouraging and developing civil aeronautics.

(4) controlling the use of the navigable airspace and regulating civil and military operations in that airspace in the interest of the safety and efficiency of both of those operations.

(5) consolidating research and development for air navigation facilities and the installation and operation of those facilities.

(6) developing and operating a common system of air traffic control and navigation for military and civil aircraft.

(7) providing assistance to law enforcement agencies in the enforcement of laws related to regulation of controlled substances, to the extent consistent with aviation safety.

Does the FAA's "dual mandate"—promoting aviation commerce and regulating safety—present a tolerable conflict of interest? *See generally* Mark C. Niles, *On the Hijacking of Agencies (and Airplanes): The Federal Aviation Administration, "Agency Capture," and Airline Security*, 10 AM. U. J. GENDER SOC. POL'Y & L. 381, 406-407 (2002); Lea Ann Carlisle, Comment, *The FAA v. the NTSB: Now that Congress Has Addressed the Federal Aviation Administration's "Dual Mandate," Has the FAA Begun Living Up to Its Amended Purpose of Making Air Travel Safer, or is the National Transportation Safety Board Still Doing its Job Alone?*, 66 J. AIR L. & COM. 741 (2001). *See also* MARY SCHIAVO, FLYING BLIND, FLYING SAFE (Avon 1998).

6. As introduced in *Graham v. Teledyne-Continental Motors* (9th Cir. 1987), and *Thomas Brooks Chartered v. Burnett* (10th Cir. 1990), *supra*, the National Transportation Safety Board ("NTSB") is an independent agency that determines the "probable cause" of aviation accidents and makes safety recommendations. In fact, the NTSB investigates accidents and incidents in all transportation categories—aviation, highway, marine, railroad, and pipeline and hazardous materials. *See* 49 C.F.R. Pts. 831, 835, and 845.

Consider that the NTSB has a "Most Wanted List" of safety issues to which it grades the FAA's response as "acceptable response, progressing in a timely manner," "acceptable response, progressing slowly," or "unacceptable response." In mid-2010, pilot proficiency, flying in icing conditions, and accidents and incidents caused by human fatigue were identified as issues to which the FAA had provided an "unacceptable response." *See http://www.ntsb.gov/Recs/mostwanted/aviation_issues.htm.* Should the Federal Aviation Administration be required to adopt and enforce the NTSB's "recommendations" as a matter of law? *See, e.g.*, Richard H. Fallon, Jr., *Enforcing Aviation Safety Regulations: The Case for Split-Enforcement Model of Agency Adjudication*, 4 ADMIN. L.J. 389 (1991).

7. As shown in *Bennett v. Southwest Airlines Co.* (7th Cir. 2007), ground operations and airports are a primarily important part of the aviation safety environment. Pursuant to the Airport and Airway Development Act of 1970, Pub. L. No. 91-258, 84 Stat. 219 (1970), the Federal Aviation Administration regulates certain airfields—particularly commercial airports—as to issues including number and type of firefighting

equipment vehicles at the airport, runway lighting, storage facilities for hazardous substances, runway paving, drainage, and so forth. Such decisions naturally give rise to litigation involving environmental rights. *See generally* 14 C.F.R. § 139. *See also* FAA Airport Safety, *http://www.faa.gov/airports/airport_safety/.*

For example, Logan Airport in Boston, Massachusetts—from which the September 11th terrorists began their attacks—is the largest airport in New England; it has a history of being one of the country's airports with the most delayed flights. In 2000, when 27.4 million passengers and 1 billion pounds of freight passed through the airport, Logan was ranked sixth nationally for airports with the most delays, even though it was ranked eleventh for overall number of takeoffs and landings and eighteenth for passenger volume. To ease this congestion, the relevant state transportation authority recommended building a new runway, realigning a taxiway, building a new centerfield taxiway, simplifying taxiway and runway crossings, and adding a surcharge for use of the airport during peak demand periods. Decisions of the FAA in this respect often invite environmental challenges by nearby communities, but generally are upheld unless "arbitrary and capricious." *See, e.g., Town of Winthrop v. Fed. Aviation Admin.* (1st Cir. 2008).

8. In addition to presenting the scope of events that might be considered aviation "accidents," ranging from personal injury to wrongful death actions, *Martin v. Midwest Express Holdings, Inc.* (9th Cir. 2009), *supra*, also features the topic of aviation product liability. Frequently, aviation plaintiff's counsel will seek punitive damages for injuries arising from a proven product defect. However, punitive damage awards are rare in such suits and case-specific. *But see In re Air Crash at Lexington, Kentucky, August 27, 2006* (E.D. Ky. June 6, 2008). *See also* LITIGATING THE AVIATION CASE: FROM PRE-TRIAL TO CLOSING ARGUMENT (Am. Bar Ass'n 3d ed. 2008).

9. The high profile of aviation litigation and its potential for significant damages can attract unscrupulous behavior, warranting mention of lawyer ethics and professionalism. Relatively few lawyers specialize in aviation law, including accident cases, but solicitation by unqualified lawyers has become commonplace, particularly in the Internet age, where a search of "aviation lawyer" may generate a list of lawyers who, other than listing "aviation" as a practice area, have had scant, if any, experience in the subject matter. *See generally* Wendell K. Smith, *The General Aviation Case*, UTAH B.J., Feb. 1999, at 17; Charles Maher, *Crashes & Disasters*, 5 CALIF. LAW. 39, 41 (1985). *See also Matter of Anis* (N.J. 1992). Lawyer referrals have also created problems:

> Sometimes the referring attorney has no preexisting relationship with the decedent or the claimants, but through advertising, publicity, or some other means has obtained several cases and wishes to refer them to an aviation specialist or involve such a specialist at some point. In this instance, the referring attorney usually insists on a portion

> of the total fee and may negotiate with one or more specialists to obtain the most profitable arrangement. Aviation specialists reported demands by such attorneys for as much as one-half the total fee.

JAMES S. KAKALIK ET AL., COSTS OF ASBESTOS LITIGATION 46 (1983) (plaintiffs received 37 percent of funds expended in asbestos litigation). To curb abuses, Congress enacted the Aviation Disaster Family Assistance Act of 1996 ("ADFAA"), prohibiting lawyers solicitation within 30 days of an aviation accident. In 2000, Congress expanded the ADFAA's "black out" period to 45 days. *See* 49 U.S.C. § 1136(g)(2) (2003). *See generally* Lester Brickman, *The Market for Contingent-Fee Financed Tort Litigation: Is It Price Competitive?*, 25 CARDOZO L. REV. 65, 107-08 (2003).

10. On July 25, 2000, a Continental Airlines DC-10 departed from Charles de Gaulle Airport in France. A 17-inch-long titanium wear strip was shed by the jumbo-jet and left on the runway. Air France Flight 4590—Concorde—departed next, bound for New York. The supersonic jet hit the strip, which punctured a tire, throwing rubber debris into the delta wing. A fuel tank ruptured and the airplane was ignited into a catastrophic fire. After a 90 second attempt to gain speed and altitude, the Concorde crashed into a nearby hotel, killing 113 people. In 2010, a French court tried Continental Airlines and two of its employees for manslaughter while prosecutors accused French officials of neglecting to fix known design defects in the airplane.

Should aviation accidents be criminalized? *See generally* Roderick D. van Dam, *Preserving Safety in Aviation: "Just Culture" and the Administration of Justice*, 22 AIR & SPACE LAW. 1 (2009); Richard M. Dunn et al., *Criminalization in Aviation*, 38-SPG BRIEF 10 (2009); Phillip J. Kolczynski, *The Criminal Liability of Aviators and Related Issues of Mixed Criminal-Civil Litigation: "A Venture in the Twilight Zone,"* 51 J. AIR L. & COM. 1 (1985); Pierre Sparaco, *An Icon on Trial*, AVIATION WK. & SPACE TECH., Mar. 29/Apr. 5, 2010, at 45. Pierre Sparaco, *Elusive Denouement*, AVIATION WK. & SPACE TECH., June 14/21, 2010, at 71 ("The trial ... further confirms that accident investigations and judiciary probes are largely incompatible."). *See also United States v. Sabretech, Inc.*, 271 F.3d 1018 (11th Cir. 2001), Chapter 4, *supra*.

PROBLEM

On October 11, 2006, New York Yankees pitcher Cory Lidle and his flight instructor, Tyler Stanger, flew a general aviation Cirrus aircraft northbound up the East River in a corridor of uncontrolled airspace around New York City. Approximately one mile north of the Queensboro Bridge, the aircraft attempted to execute a 180-degree turn to reverse its course and to avoid the controlled airspace surrounding LaGuardia Airport. The aircraft did not complete the turn successfully and crashed into an apartment building on East 72nd Street on Manhattan's Upper East Side, killing Lidle and Stanger. A wrongful death action ensued during which the principal dispute was whether the crash was due to a piloting error or to a malfunction of the aircraft's control system.

The airplane manufacturer, Cirrus, moved for summary judgment and asserted *Daubert* motions to strike expert testimony. Cirrus' briefs and memoranda refer to the "NTSB Blue Ribbon Report" and the "NTSB Aircraft Accident Brief." Cirrus' use of NTSB-related materials included references to the NTSB's determinations regarding the probable cause of the accident. Plaintiffs requested an order striking Cirrus' references to NTSB findings and conclusions. How should the court rule and why? *See Lidle v. Cirrus Design Corp.* (S.D.N.Y. Apr. 22, 2010).

B. CHOICE OF AVIATION LAW ADMIRALTY, DOSHA, FTCA, GARA

Deciding what law can or must apply to an aviation accident may be the most important preliminary issue in an aviation injury and wrongful death case, potentially representing the difference between multi-million-dollar and no recovery. As one respected authority stated, however, the process of deciding which among various and conflicting laws apply to a particular legal case is a "dismal swamp, filled with quaking quagmires, and inhabited by learned but eccentric professors who theorize about mysterious matters in a strange and incomprehensible jargon." William Prosser, *Interstate Publication*, 51 MICH. L. REV. 959, 971 (1953).

Indeed, the convergence of multiple parties, places, and issues in mass tort commercial airplane accident litigation underscores the need for competent counsel. The cases below present and evaluate the chief procedural, jurisdictional, and substantive laws that govern aviation safety in the United States. Not to be lost in reviewing these cases is the real and substantial psychological, emotional, and life costs that the victims and survivors of aviation tragedies pay. In this respect, the terrible consequences of aviation accidents, like other mass torts, may best be mitigated or avoided by ethical business leadership, quality-focused product research and development, regular training and compliance programs, and effective and appropriate government oversight in the first place—not necessarily by the threat of litigation and complex proceedings in courts of law around the world.

PIPER AIRCRAFT CO. v. REYNO
454 U.S. 235 (1981)

Justice MARSHALL delivered the opinion of the Court.

In July 1976, a small commercial aircraft crashed in the Scottish highlands during the course of a charter flight from Blackpool to Perth. The pilot and five passengers were killed instantly. The decedents were all Scottish subjects and residents, as are their heirs and next of kin. There were no eyewitnesses to the accident. At the time of the crash the plane was subject to Scottish air traffic control.

The aircraft, a twin-engine Piper Aztec, was manufactured in Pennsylvania by petitioner Piper Aircraft Co. ("Piper"). The propellers were manufactured in Ohio by petitioner Hartzell Propeller, Inc. ("Hartzell"). At the time of the crash the aircraft was registered in Great Britain and was owned and maintained by Air Navigation and Trading Co., Ltd. ("Air Navigation"). It was operated by McDonald Aviation, Ltd. ("McDonald"), a Scottish air taxi service. Both Air Navigation and McDonald were organized in the United Kingdom. The wreckage of the plane is now in a hangar in Farnsborough, England.

The British Department of Trade investigated the accident shortly after it occurred. A preliminary report found that the plane crashed after developing a spin, and suggested that mechanical failure in the plane or the propeller was responsible. At Hartzell's request, this report was reviewed by a three-member Review Board, which held a 9-day adversary hearing attended by all interested parties. The Review Board found no evidence of defective equipment and indicated that pilot error may have contributed to the accident. The pilot, who had obtained his commercial pilot's license only three months earlier, was flying over high ground at an altitude considerably lower than the minimum height required by his company's operations manual.

In July 1977, a California probate court appointed respondent Gaynell Reyno administratrix of the estates of the five passengers. Reyno is not related to and does not know any of the decedents or their survivors; she was a legal secretary to the attorney who filed this lawsuit. Several days after her appointment, Reyno commenced separate wrongful-death actions against Piper and Hartzell in the Superior Court of California, claiming negligence and strict liability. Air Navigation, McDonald, and the estate of the pilot are not parties to this litigation. The survivors of the five passengers whose estates are represented by Reyno filed a separate action in the United Kingdom against Air Navigation, McDonald, and the pilot's estate.

Reyno candidly admits that the action against Piper and Hartzell was filed in the United States because its laws regarding liability, capacity to sue, and damages are more favorable to her position than are those of Scotland. Scottish law does not recognize strict liability in tort. Moreover, it permits wrongful-death actions only when brought by a decedent's relatives. The relatives may sue only for "loss of support and society."

On petitioners' motion, the suit was removed to the United States District Court for the Central District of California. Piper then moved for transfer to the United States District Court for the Middle District of Pennsylvania, pursuant to 28 U.S.C. § 1404(a), which provides: "For the convenience of parties and witnesses, in the interest of justice, a district court may transfer any civil action to any other district or division where it might have been brought." Hartzell moved to dismiss for lack of personal jurisdiction, or in the alternative, to transfer. The District Court quashed service on Hartzell and transferred the case to the Middle District of Pennsylvania. Respondent then properly served process on Hartzell.

After the suit had been transferred, both Hartzell and Piper moved to dismiss the action on the ground of *forum non conveniens*. The District Court granted these motions, relying on the balancing test set forth by this Court in *Gulf Oil Corp. v. Gilbert* (1947), and its companion case, *Koster v. Lumbermens Mut. Cas. Co.* (1947).

In those decisions, the Court stated that a plaintiff's choice of forum should rarely be disturbed. However, when an alternative forum has jurisdiction to hear the case, and when trial in the chosen forum would "establish ... oppressiveness and vexation to a defendant ... out of all proportion to plaintiff's convenience," or when the "chosen forum [is] inappropriate because of considerations affecting the court's own administrative and legal problems," the court may, in the exercise of its sound discretion, dismiss the case. To guide trial court discretion, the Court provided a list of "private interest factors" affecting the convenience of the litigants, and a list of "public interest factors" affecting the convenience of the forum.

The factors pertaining to the private interests of the litigants included the "relative ease of access to sources of proof; availability of compulsory process for attendance of unwilling, and the cost of obtaining attendance of willing, witnesses; possibility of view of premises, if view would be appropriate to the action; and all other practical problems that make trial of a case easy, expeditious and inexpensive."

The public factors bearing on the question included the administrative difficulties flowing from court congestion; the "local interest in having localized controversies decided at home"; the interest in having the trial of a diversity case in a forum that is at home with the law that must govern the action; the avoidance of unnecessary problems in conflict of laws, or in the application of foreign law; and the unfairness of burdening citizens in an unrelated forum with jury duty.

After describing our decisions in *Gilbert* and *Koster*, the District Court analyzed the facts of these cases. It began by observing that an alternative forum existed in Scotland; Piper and Hartzell had agreed to submit to the jurisdiction of the Scottish courts and to waive any statute of limitations defense that might be available. It then stated that plaintiff's choice of forum was entitled to little weight. The court recognized that a plaintiff's choice ordinarily deserves substantial deference. It noted, however, that Reyno "is a representative of foreign citizens and residents seeking a forum in the United States because of the more liberal rules concerning products liability law," and that "the courts have been less solicitous when the plaintiff is not an American citizen or resident, and particularly when the foreign citizens seek to benefit from the more liberal tort rules provided for the protection of citizens and residents of the United States."

The District Court next examined several factors relating to the private interests of the litigants, and determined that these factors strongly pointed towards Scotland as the appropriate forum. Although evidence concerning the design, manufacture, and testing of the plane and propeller is located in the United States, the connections with Scotland are otherwise "overwhelming." The real parties in interest are citizens of Scotland, as were all the decedents. Witnesses who could testify regarding the maintenance of the aircraft, the training of the pilot, and the investigation of the accident—all essential to the defense—are in Great Britain. Moreover, all witnesses to damages are located in Scotland. Trial would be aided by familiarity with Scottish topography, and by easy access to the wreckage.

The District Court reasoned that because crucial witnesses and evidence were beyond the reach of compulsory process, and because the defendants would not be able to implead potential Scottish third-party defendants, it would be "unfair to make Piper and Hartzell proceed to trial in this forum." The survivors had brought separate actions in Scotland against the pilot, McDonald, and Air Navigation. "[I]t would be fairer to all parties and less costly if the entire case was presented to one jury with available testimony from all relevant witnesses." Although the court recognized that if trial were held in the United States, Piper and Hartzell could file indemnity or contribution actions against the Scottish defendants, it believed that there was a significant risk of inconsistent verdicts. The District Court explained that inconsistent verdicts might result if petitioners were held liable on the basis of strict liability here, and then required to prove negligence in an indemnity action in Scotland. Moreover, even if the same standard of liability applied, there was a danger that different juries would find different facts and produce inconsistent results.

The District Court concluded that the relevant public interests also pointed strongly towards dismissal. The court determined that Pennsylvania law would apply to Piper and Scottish law to Hartzell if the case were tried in the Middle District of Pennsylvania. As a result, "trial in this forum would be hopelessly complex and confusing for a jury." In addition, the court noted that it was unfamiliar with Scottish law and thus would have to rely upon experts from that country. The court also found that the trial would be enormously costly and time-consuming; that it would be unfair to burden citizens with jury duty when the Middle District of Pennsylvania has little connection with the controversy; and that Scotland has a substantial interest in the outcome of the litigation.

In opposing the motions to dismiss, respondent contended that dismissal would be unfair because Scottish law was less favorable. The District Court explicitly rejected this claim. It reasoned that the possibility that dismissal might lead to an unfavorable change in the law did not deserve significant weight; any deficiency in the foreign law was a "matter to be dealt with in the foreign forum."

* * *

On appeal, the United States Court of Appeals for the Third Circuit reversed and remanded for trial. The decision to reverse appears to be based on two alternative grounds. First, the Court held that the District Court abused its discretion in conducting the *Gilbert* analysis. Second, the Court held that dismissal is never appropriate where the law of the alternative forum is less favorable to the plaintiff.

The Court of Appeals began its review of the District Court's *Gilbert* analysis by noting that the plaintiff's choice of forum deserved substantial weight, even though the real parties in interest are nonresidents. It then rejected the District Court's balancing of the private interests. It found that Piper and Hartzell had failed adequately to support their claim that key witnesses would be unavailable if trial were held in the United States: they had never specified the witnesses they would call and the testimony these witnesses would provide. The Court of Appeals gave little weight to the fact that Piper and Hartzell would not be able to implead potential Scottish third-party defendants, reasoning that this difficulty would be "burdensome" but not "unfair." Finally, the court stated that resolution of the suit would not be significantly aided by familiarity with Scottish topography, or by viewing the wreckage.

The Court of Appeals also rejected the District Court's analysis of the public interest factors. It found that the District Court gave undue emphasis to the application of Scottish law: "'the mere fact that the court is called upon to determine and apply foreign law does not present a legal problem of the sort which would justify the dismissal of a case otherwise properly before the court.'" In any event, it believed that Scottish law need not be applied. After conducting its own choice-of-law analysis, the Court of Appeals determined that American law would govern the actions against both Piper and Hartzell. The same choice-of-law analysis apparently led it to conclude that Pennsylvania and Ohio, rather than Scotland, are the jurisdictions with the greatest policy interests in the dispute, and that all other public interest factors favored trial in the United States.

The Court of Appeals concluded as part of its choice-of-law analysis that the United States had the greatest policy interest in the dispute. It apparently believed that this conclusion necessarily implied that the *forum non conveniens* public interest factors pointed toward trial in the United States. In any event, it appears that the Court of Appeals would have reversed even if the District Court had properly balanced the public and private interests. The court stated:

> [I]t is apparent that the dismissal would work a change in the applicable law so that the plaintiff's strict liability claim would be eliminated from the case. But ... a dismissal for *forum non conveniens*, like a statutory transfer, "should not, despite its convenience, result in a change in the applicable law." Only when American law is not applicable, or when the foreign jurisdiction would, as a matter of its own choice

> of law, give the plaintiff the benefit of the claim to which she is entitled here, would dismissal be justified."

In other words, the court decided that dismissal is automatically barred if it would lead to a change in the applicable law unfavorable to the plaintiff.

We granted *certiorari* in these cases to consider the questions they raise concerning the proper application of the doctrine of *forum non conveniens*, specifically: (1) whether, in an action in federal district court brought by foreign plaintiffs against American defendants, the plaintiffs may defeat a motion to dismiss on the ground of *forum non conveniens* merely by showing that the substantive law that would be applied if the case were litigated in the district court is more favorable to them than the law that would be applied by the courts of their own nation, and (2) whether a motion to dismiss on grounds of *forum non conveniens* [should] be denied whenever the law of the alternate forum is less favorable to recovery than that which would be applied by the district court.

***

The Court of Appeals erred in holding that plaintiffs may defeat a motion to dismiss on the ground of *forum non conveniens* merely by showing that the substantive law that would be applied in the alternative forum is less favorable to the plaintiffs than that of the present forum. The possibility of a change in substantive law should ordinarily not be given conclusive or even substantial weight in the *forum non conveniens* inquiry.

We expressly rejected the position adopted by the Court of Appeals in our decision in *Canada Malting Co. v. Paterson Steamships, Ltd.* (1932). That case arose out of a collision between two vessels in American waters. The Canadian owners of cargo lost in the accident sued the Canadian owners of one of the vessels in Federal District Court. The cargo owners chose an American court in large part because the relevant American liability rules were more favorable than the Canadian rules. The District Court dismissed on grounds of *forum non conveniens*. The plaintiffs argued that dismissal was inappropriate because Canadian laws were less favorable to them. This Court nonetheless affirmed:

> We have no occasion to enquire by what law the rights of the parties are governed, as we are of the opinion that, under any view of that question, it lay within the discretion of the District Court to decline to assume jurisdiction over the controversy ... "[T]he court will not take cognizance of the case if justice would be as well done by remitting the parties to their home forum."

It is true that *Canada Malting* was decided before *Gilbert*, and that the doctrine of *forum non conveniens* was not fully crystallized until our decision in that case. However,

Gilbert in no way affects the validity of *Canada Malting*. Indeed, by holding that the central focus of the *forum non conveniens* inquiry is convenience, *Gilbert* implicitly recognized that dismissal may not be barred solely because of the possibility of an unfavorable change in law.

Under *Gilbert*, dismissal will ordinarily be appropriate where trial in the plaintiff's chosen forum imposes a heavy burden on the defendant or the court, and where the plaintiff is unable to offer any specific reasons of convenience supporting his choice. If substantial weight were given to the possibility of an unfavorable change in law, however, dismissal might be barred even where trial in the chosen forum was plainly inconvenient.

The Court of Appeals' decision is inconsistent with this Court's earlier *forum non conveniens* decisions in another respect. Those decisions have repeatedly emphasized the need to retain flexibility. In *Gilbert*, the Court refused to identify specific circumstances "which will justify or require either grant or denial of remedy." Similarly, in *Koster*, the Court rejected the contention that where a trial would involve inquiry into the internal affairs of a foreign corporation, dismissal was always appropriate. "That is one, but only one, factor which may show convenience." And in *Williams v. Green Bay & Western R. Co.*, we stated that we would not lay down a rigid rule to govern discretion, and that "[e]ach case turns on its facts." If central emphasis were placed on any one factor, the *forum non conveniens* doctrine would lose much of the very flexibility that makes it so valuable.

In fact, if conclusive or substantial weight were given to the possibility of a change in law, the *forum non conveniens* doctrine would become virtually useless. Jurisdiction and venue requirements are often easily satisfied. As a result, many plaintiffs are able to choose from among several forums. Ordinarily, these plaintiffs will select that forum whose choice-of-law rules are most advantageous. Thus, if the possibility of an unfavorable change in substantive law is given substantial weight in the *forum non conveniens* inquiry, dismissal would rarely be proper.

Except for the court below, every Federal Court of Appeals that has considered this question after *Gilbert* has held that dismissal on grounds of *forum non conveniens* may be granted even though the law applicable in the alternative forum is less favorable to the plaintiff's chance of recovery. Several courts have relied expressly on *Canada Malting* to hold that the possibility of an unfavorable change of law should not, by itself, bar dismissal.

The Court of Appeals' approach is not only inconsistent with the purpose of the *forum non conveniens* doctrine, but also poses substantial practical problems. If the possibility of a change in law were given substantial weight, deciding motions to dismiss on the ground of *forum non conveniens* would become quite difficult. Choice-of-law analysis would become extremely important, and the courts would frequently be required to interpret the law of foreign jurisdictions. First, the trial court would have to determine what law would apply if the case were tried in the chosen forum, and what law would apply if the case were tried in the alternative forum. It would then have to compare the rights, remedies, and procedures available under the law that would be applied in each forum. Dismissal would be appropriate only if the court concluded that the law applied by the alternative forum is as favorable to the plaintiff as that of the chosen forum.

The doctrine of *forum non conveniens*, however, is designed in part to help courts avoid conducting complex exercises in comparative law. As we stated in *Gilbert*, the public interest factors point towards dismissal where the court would be required to "untangle problems in conflict of laws, and in law foreign to itself."

Upholding the decision of the Court of Appeals would result in other practical problems. At least where the foreign plaintiff named an American manufacturer as defendant, a court could not dismiss the case on grounds of *forum non conveniens* where dismissal might lead to an unfavorable change in law. In fact, the defendant might not even have to be American. A foreign plaintiff seeking damages for an accident that occurred abroad might be able to obtain service of process on a foreign defendant who does business in the United States. Under the Court of Appeals' holding, dismissal would be barred if the law in the alternative forum were less favorable to the plaintiff—even though none of the parties are American, and even though there is absolutely no nexus between the subject matter of the litigation and the United States.

The American courts, which are already extremely attractive to foreign plaintiffs, would become even more attractive. First, all but 6 of the 50 American States—Delaware, Massachusetts, Michigan, North Carolina, Virginia, and Wyoming—offer strict liability. Rules roughly equivalent to American strict liability are effective in France, Belgium, and Luxembourg. West Germany and Japan have a strict liability statute for pharmaceuticals. However, strict liability remains primarily an American innovation. Second, the tort plaintiff may choose, at least potentially, from among 50 jurisdictions if he decides to file suit in the United States. Each of these jurisdictions applies its own set of malleable choice-of-law rules. Third, jury trials are almost always available in the United States, while they are never provided in civil law jurisdictions. Even in the United Kingdom, most civil actions are not tried before a jury. Fourth, unlike most foreign jurisdictions, American courts allow contingent attorney's fees, and do not tax losing parties with their opponents' attorney's fees. Fifth, discovery is more extensive in American than in foreign courts.

The flow of litigation into the United States would increase and further congest already crowded courts. In holding that the possibility of a change in law unfavorable to the plaintiff should not be given substantial weight, we also necessarily hold that the possibility of a change in law favorable to defendant should not be considered.

Respondent suggests that Piper and Hartzell filed the motion to dismiss, not simply because trial in the United States would be inconvenient, but also because they believe the laws of Scotland are more favorable. She argues that this should be taken into account in the analysis of the private interests. We recognize, of course, that Piper and Hartzell may be engaged in reverse forum-shopping. However, this possibility ordinarily should not enter into a trial court's analysis of the private interests. If the defendant is able to overcome the presumption in favor of plaintiff by showing that trial in the chosen forum would be unnecessarily burdensome, dismissal is appropriate—regardless of the fact that defendant may also be motivated by a desire to obtain a more favorable forum.

We do not hold that the possibility of an unfavorable change in law should never be a relevant consideration in a *forum non conveniens* inquiry. Of course, if the remedy provided by the alternative forum is so clearly inadequate or unsatisfactory that it is no remedy at all, the unfavorable change in law may be given substantial weight; the district court may conclude that dismissal would not be in the interests of justice. At the outset of any *forum non conveniens* inquiry, the court must determine whether there exists an alternative forum. Ordinarily, this requirement will be satisfied when the defendant is "amenable to process" in the other jurisdiction.

In rare circumstances, however, where the remedy offered by the other forum is clearly unsatisfactory, the other forum may not be an adequate alternative, and the initial requirement may not be satisfied. Thus, for example, dismissal would not be appropriate where the alternative forum does not permit litigation of the subject matter of the dispute. In these cases, however, the remedies that would be provided by the Scottish courts do not fall within this category. Although the relatives of the decedents may not be able to rely on a strict liability theory, and although their potential damages award may be smaller, there is no danger that they will be deprived of any remedy or treated unfairly.

* * *

The Court of Appeals also erred in rejecting the District Court's *Gilbert* analysis. The Court of Appeals stated that more weight should have been given to the plaintiff's choice of forum, and criticized the District Court's analysis of the private and public interests. However, the District Court's decision regarding the deference due plaintiff's choice of forum was appropriate. Furthermore, we do not believe that the District Court abused its discretion in weighing the private and public interests.

The District Court acknowledged that there is ordinarily a strong presumption in favor of the plaintiff's choice of forum, which may be overcome only when the private and public interest factors clearly point towards trial in the alternative forum. It held, however, that the presumption applies with less force when the plaintiff or real parties in interest are foreign. The District Court's distinction between resident or citizen plaintiffs and foreign plaintiffs is fully justified. In *Koster*, the Court indicated that a plaintiff's choice of forum is entitled to greater deference when the plaintiff has chosen the home forum. When the home forum has been chosen, it is reasonable to assume that this choice is convenient. When the plaintiff is foreign, however, this assumption is much less reasonable. Because the central purpose of any *forum non conveniens* inquiry is to ensure that the trial is convenient, a foreign plaintiff's choice deserves less deference.

Additionally, the *forum non conveniens* determination is committed to the sound discretion of the trial court. It may be reversed only when there has been a clear abuse of discretion; where the court has considered all relevant public and private interest factors, and where its balancing of these factors is reasonable, its decision deserves substantial deference. Here, the Court of Appeals expressly acknowledged that the standard of review was one of abuse of discretion. In examining the District Court's analysis of the public and private interests, however, the Court of Appeals seems to have lost sight of this rule, and substituted its own judgment for that of the District Court.

In analyzing the private interest factors, the District Court stated that the connections with Scotland are "overwhelming." This characterization may be somewhat exaggerated. Particularly with respect to the question of relative ease of access to sources of proof, the private interests point in both directions. As respondent emphasizes, records concerning the design, manufacture, and testing of the propeller and plane are located in the United States. She would have greater access to sources of proof relevant to her strict liability and negligence theories if trial were held here. However, the District Court did not act unreasonably in concluding that fewer evidentiary problems would be posed if the trial were held in Scotland. A large proportion of the relevant evidence is located in Great Britain.

The Court of Appeals found that the problems of proof could not be given any weight because Piper and Hartzell failed to describe with specificity the evidence they would not be able to obtain if trial were held in the United States. It suggested that defendants seeking *forum non conveniens* dismissal must submit affidavits identifying the witnesses they would call and the testimony these witnesses would provide if the trial were held in the alternative forum. Such detail is not necessary. Piper and Hartzell have moved for dismissal precisely because many crucial witnesses are located beyond the reach of compulsory process, and thus are difficult to identify or interview. Requiring extensive investigation would defeat the purpose of their motion. Of course, defendants must provide enough information to enable the District Court to balance the parties' interests. Our examination of the record convinces us that sufficient information was provided here. Both Piper and Hartzell submitted affidavits describing the evidentiary problems they would face if the trial were held in the United States.

The District Court correctly concluded that the problems posed by the inability to implead potential third-party defendants clearly supported holding the trial in Scotland. Joinder of the pilot's estate, Air Navigation, and McDonald is crucial to the presentation of petitioners' defense. If Piper and Hartzell can show that the accident was caused not by a design defect, but rather by the negligence of the pilot, the plane's owners, or the charter company, they will be relieved of all liability. It is true, of course, that if Hartzell and Piper were found liable after a trial in the United States, they could institute an action for indemnity or contribution against these parties in Scotland. It would be far more convenient, however, to resolve all claims in one trial. The Court of Appeals rejected this argument. Forcing petitioners to rely on actions for indemnity or contributions would be "burdensome" but not "unfair." Finding that trial in the plaintiff's chosen forum would be burdensome, however, is sufficient to support dismissal on grounds of *forum non conveniens*.

The District Court's review of the factors relating to the public interest was also reasonable. On the basis of its choice-of-law analysis, it concluded that if the case were tried in the Middle District of Pennsylvania, Pennsylvania law would apply to Piper and Scottish law to Hartzell. It stated that a trial involving two sets of laws would be confusing to the jury. It also noted its own lack of familiarity with Scottish law. Consideration of these problems was clearly appropriate under *Gilbert*; in that case we explicitly held that the need to apply foreign law pointed towards dismissal. The Court of Appeals found that the District Court's choice-of-law analysis was incorrect, and that American law would apply to both Hartzell and Piper. Thus, lack of familiarity with foreign law would not be a problem. Even if the Court of Appeals' conclusion is correct, however, all other public interest factors favored trial in Scotland.

Scotland has a very strong interest in this litigation. The accident occurred in its airspace. All of the decedents were Scottish. Apart from Piper and Hartzell, all potential plaintiffs and defendants are either Scottish or English. As we stated in *Gilbert*, there is "a local interest in having localized controversies decided at home." Respondent argues that American citizens have an interest in ensuring that American manufacturers are deterred from producing defective products, and that additional deterrence might be obtained if Piper and Hartzell were tried in the United States, where they could be sued on the basis of both negligence and strict liability. However, the incremental deterrence that would be gained if this trial were held in an American court is likely to be insignificant. The American interest in this accident is simply not sufficient to justify the enormous commitment of judicial time and resources that would inevitably be required if the case were to be tried here.

* * *

The Court of Appeals erred in holding that the possibility of an unfavorable change in law bars dismissal on the ground of *forum non conveniens*. It also erred in rejecting the District Court's *Gilbert* analysis. The District Court properly decided that the presumption in favor of the respondent's forum choice applied with less than maximum force because the real parties in interest are foreign. It did not act unreasonably in deciding that the private interests pointed towards trial in Scotland. Nor did it act unreasonably in deciding that the public interests favored trial in Scotland.

Justice STEVENS, with whom Justice BRENNAN joins, dissenting.

I would simply remand the case to the Court of Appeals for further consideration of the question whether the District Court correctly decided that Pennsylvania was not a convenient forum in which to litigate a claim against a Pennsylvania company that a plane was defectively designed and manufactured in Pennsylvania.

IN RE AIR CRASH NEAR CALI, COLOMBIA ON DECEMBER 20, 1995

24 F. Supp. 2d 1340 (S.D. Fla. 1998)

HIGHSMITH, District Judge.

This multidistrict litigation arises from the crash of American Airlines Flight 965 near Cali, Colombia, on December 20, 1995. One hundred and fifty one passengers and all six cabin crew members perished in the crash. Four passengers suffered non-fatal injuries.

In five passenger cases, American Airlines asserted third party claims for contribution and for "legal or equitable subrogation" against Honeywell, Inc. ("Honeywell") and Jeppesen Sanders, Inc. ("Jeppesen"). American Airlines predicates its claims on Honeywell's role as supplier of the Flight Management Computer ("FMC") used on Flight 965 and Jeppesen's role in furnishing the navigational database programmed into the FMC and the corresponding aviation charts. (American Airlines asserts claims for negligence, strict liability and breach of warranty against both Honeywell and Jeppesen.)

The Court notes that, on the approach to Cali, the pilots entered "R" into the FMC, anticipating (based on the aviation charts) that this cipher corresponded to a beacon designated as "Rozo." Instead, another beacon designated as "Romeo" was activated. This resulted in a change of the aircraft's heading to the east, over the Andes Mountains. When the pilots became aware of the aircraft's easterly swing, they turned back to the west, in the direction of the valley where the Cali airport is located. Sadly, since the aircraft had been descending during these directional changes, Flight 965 never made it back to the valley. It crashed into the side of a mountain.

DISCUSSION

Honeywell and Jeppesen predicate their motions for summary judgment on the trial court's legal conclusion that the conduct of the pilots constitutes willful misconduct under the Warsaw Convention and the operation of the Uniform Contribution among Tortfeasors Act ("UCATA") upon said conclusion. Specifically, the trial judge concluded "that the undisputed facts, and the many points conceded by American, simply leave no room for a reasonable jury to find that the pilots' deliberate decision to continue to descend the aircraft from an off course position at night, in an environment known for high terrain, and despite the unequivocal warning of their training that 'most of the aircraft that have hit the mountains in Latin America did so because the crew apparently did not know where they were' was anything other than an act of willful misconduct-whether we examine the state of mind of the pilots or simply the myriad clues that told them just how far, and how dangerously, off course Flight 965 had traveled."

Honeywell and Jeppesen differ, however, with regard to the UCATA version that should be applied as to each of them. Honeywell advocates application of the Act as adopted by Arizona, while Jeppesen argues for consideration of Colorado's version. American Airlines, in turn, argues that "federal common law" should apply to uphold its contribution claims against both third party defendants. In the alternative, American Airlines seeks application of Florida law, a state that has also adopted UCATA. In light of these divergent postures, the Court must address at the outset the issue of what law should apply.

1. "Federal Common Law"

First, the Court considers American Airlines' argument that it may pursue its contribution claims "under the applicable federal common law." There are serious flaws with American Airlines' posture. Suffice it to say, however, that the "applicable federal common law" invoked by American Airlines is essentially derived from a single case, *Kohr v. Allegheny Airlines, Inc.* (7th Cir. 1974).

In *Kohr*, the Seventh Circuit declared a need for "a federal rule of contribution and indemnity governing mid-air collisions," such as the one giving rise to the litigation before it. The case involved a small airplane which collided with Allegheny's aircraft over Indiana airspace, while the larger craft was under the direction of federal traffic controllers out of Indianapolis' airport. All eighty-two occupants of the Allegheny plane, as well as the pilot of the small craft, perished. Wrongful death actions were commenced on behalf of almost all of the decedents. The named defendants were Allegheny, the corporate owners of the small craft, the estate of the small craft's pilot and the United States. The claims against the latter were brought pursuant to the Federal Tort Claims Act, due to the involvement of the traffic controllers, who were employed by the Federal Aviation Administration. The trial court had applied Indiana's absolute bar against contribution and indemnification among joint tortfeasors to dismiss the cross-claims and third-party complaints for contribution and indemnity brought by Allegheny and the United States against the corporate owners of the small craft and against the estate of the small craft's pilot.

Given this factual scenario, the *Kohr* court deemed it desirable that a federal rule of contribution and indemnity be applied. The court perceived a "predominant, indeed almost exclusive, interest of the federal government in regulating the affairs of the nation's airways" as justification for adopting such a rule. A second benefit would be the elimination of "inconsistency of result in similar collision occurrences as well as within the same occurrence due to the application of differing state laws on contribution and indemnity." Having determined the need for establishing a "federal rule of contribution and indemnity," the court went on to formulate such a rule by basing contribution and indemnity on comparative negligence. In so doing, the *Kohr* court rejected "as being outmoded and entirely unsatisfactory, the contention that the federal rule should be one of no contribution." The court explained:

> We agree that "there is an obvious lack of sense and justice in a rule which permits the entire burden of a loss, for which two defendants were equally, unintentionally responsible, to be shouldered on to one alone, according to the accident of a successful levy of execution, the existence of liability insurance, the plaintiff['s] whim or spite, or his collusion with the other wrongdoer, while the latter goes scot free."

As discussed later in this opinion, these sentiments had been expressed by other courts when carving out exceptions to the common law's "no contribution" rule. Indeed, a similar rationale pervades the Uniform Contribution among Tortfeasors Act and its adoption by numerous jurisdictions. However, the *Kohr* court's perceived need for creating a uniform body of federal law governing contribution and indemnity in aviation cases has not been echoed by other federal courts.

In *Overseas Nat'l Airways, Inc. v. United States* (2d Cir. 1985) for example, the Second Circuit rejected the United States' request for the creation and application of "a federal common law rule of decision that would govern whenever the United States seeks contribution from a joint tortfeasor in an aircraft accident case." The *Overseas* court found the arguments of the United States persuasive but concluded that it was not free to create such a federal rule of contribution in light of the provisions of the Federal Tort Claims Act and applicable Supreme Court precedent.

Specifically, the *Overseas* court cited *Executive Jet Aviation, Inc. v. City of Cleveland* (1972), for the proposition that "the Supreme Court warned that federal courts must be extremely cautious in creating federal law that preempts traditional state law causes of action." Heeding this warning, this Court declines American Airlines' invitation to apply "federal common law" to the contribution claims in this litigation and to rely upon *Kohr v. Allegheny* as the source of the "applicable federal common law."

* * *

3. The Uniform Contribution among Tortfeasors Act

a. A historical perspective

In 1799, the common law principle that there is no right of contribution as between joint tortfeasors was established. The rule was articulated as, "*in pari delicto potior est conditio defendentis*." In modern day terms the rule means, "Where the fault is mutual, the law will leave the case as it finds it." BLACK'S LAW DICTIONARY 791 (6th ed. 1990). Over time, this harsh rule was softened in a number of jurisdictions by permitting contribution among joint tortfeasors "so long as their negligent acts were not characterizable, because of the degree of negligence involved, as intentional wrongs, and so long as the joint tortfeasors share[d] a common liability to the injured person." ANNOTATION, CONTRIBUTION BETWEEN NEGLIGENT TORTFEASORS AT COMMON LAW, 60 A.L.R.2d at 1371.

At least one jurisdiction that applied the exception to the common law rule also considered situations involving vicariously liable tortfeasors. In *George's Radio v. Capital Transit Co.*, (D.C. Cir. 1942), the United States Court of Appeals for the District of Columbia considered the question "whether-in the District of Columbia-a right of contribution exists and should be declared between two persons liable for a tort in the absence, on the part of either, of any personal participation, personal culpability, fraud, or moral wrong." The case arose from a three-way traffic accident involving a Capital Transit Company bus, an automobile operated by an agent of George's Radio, Inc. and an individual, Oisboid, who sued both businesses for damages. Upon prevailing in the underlying action against both defendants, Oisboid demanded payment of the judgment in full by George's Radio, Inc. and refused to take enforcement actions against the Transit Company. George's Radio, Inc. then brought a suit in equity for contribution against the Transit Company.

Abandoning its earlier absolute rule barring contribution, the court stated, "We are, therefore, of opinion that the rule denying contribution in favor of unintentional or negligent tortfeasors is wrong to the same extent that it would be wrong to enforce contribution in the case of willful wrongdoers or those guilty of flagrantly wrongful conduct." After citing with approval recent cases applying these more equitable concepts, the court concluded, "The sum and substance of the ruling in all is that, where the parties are not intentional and willful wrongdoers, but are made such by legal inference or intendment, contribution may be enforced." Thus, the court allowed the contribution claim to proceed.

Some years later, in *Knell v. Feltman* (D.C. Cir. 1949), the same court considered whether the fact that one tortfeasor "had personally participated in the commission of the tort" would take the case "out of the ruling of the George's Radio case where both wrongdoers were 'vicariously' negligent." After commenting on the widespread revulsion against the strict common law rule and noting that "many courts have riddled it with exceptions," the court articulated one such exception as: "contribution may be enforced among concurrent tort-feasors who are only vicariously negligent." The court went on to explain, "Obviously the creation of this exception was a differentiation from the *Merryweather* situation where the wrongdoers were deliberately such, and so was a recognition, perhaps unconscious, of the true *Merryweather* rule. Thus went the reasoning: if the tort-feasors were not personally present and had not directed their agents to commit the tort, they could not have intentionally done wrong and, therefore, the harsh rule of no contribution should be relaxed in their favor." The court concluded, "No reason appears for denying the same favorable treatment to the unintentionally negligent, even though he personally committed the tortious act."

b. Florida law

Florida applied the strict rule of no contribution until 1975. Yet, as early as 1849, the Florida Supreme Court allowed contribution in an action of *assumpsit*, stating, "The principal (sic) of contribution does not seem to have sprung from contract, but is based on a principle of justice and equity, that one person should not be singled out by the creator to pay the whole demand; and where this occurs, the law intervenes and places sureties relatively to each other in a state of equality as to the amount paid, and gives the party paying a remedy by action for contribution." *Love v. Gibson* (Fla. 1849).

In *Lincenberg v. Issen* (Fla. 1975), the Florida Supreme Court receded from the common law rule of no contribution in tort cases, noting, "The rationale for this change of view is generally explained that principles of justice require that in the case of a common obligation, the discharge of it by one of the obligors without proportionate payment from the others, gives the latter an advantage to which he is not equitably entitled." Among the cases cited by the *Lincenberg* court in support of this proposition is the previously discussed *George's Radio*. One of the factors considered by the Florida Supreme Court for abandoning the rule of no contribution was Florida's adoption of a comparative negligence rule. Taking this development into consideration, the Florida Supreme Court reasoned that "it would be undesirable for this Court to retain a rule that under a system based on fault, casts the entire burden of a loss for which several may be responsible upon only one of those at fault."

As noted by the Supreme Court, during the pendency of the *Lincenberg* appeal, Florida adopted the Uniform Contribution among Tortfeasors Act, which became effective on June 13, 1975 and applied to all causes of action pending as of that date. Rather than rely on the newly enacted statute, however, the Supreme Court independently rejected the common law rule.

As adopted by Florida (Fla. Stat. § 768.31), the Uniform Contribution among Tortfeasors Act ("UCATA") provides, in pertinent part:

(2)(a) Except as otherwise provided in this act, when two or more persons become jointly or severally liable in tort for the same injury to person or property, or for the same wrongful death, there is a right of contribution among them even though judgment has not been recovered against all or any of them.

(2)(b) The right of contribution exists only in favor of a tortfeasor who has paid more than her or his *pro rata* share of the common liability, and the tortfeasor's total recovery is limited to the amount paid by her or him in excess of her or his *pro rata* share. No tortfeasor is compelled to make contribution beyond her or his own *pro rata* share of the entire liability.

(2)(c) There is no right of contribution in favor of any tortfeasor who has intentionally (willfully or wantonly) caused or contributed to the injury or wrongful death.

* * *

(3) In determining the *pro rata* shares of tortfeasors in the entire liability: (a) their relative degrees of fault shall be the basis for allocation of liability; (b) if equity requires, the collective liability of some as a group shall constitute a single share; (c) principles of equity applicable to contribution generally shall apply.

It is significant to note that, unlike Florida's version, the model statute encloses the words "willfully or wantonly" in brackets rather than parentheses. Specifically, the model Act provides: "There is no right of contribution in favor of any tortfeasor who has intentionally [willfully or wantonly] caused or contributed to the injury or wrongful death." According to the comments accompanying the 1955 Revised Act:

> The substance of this provision is found in a few of the existing statutes, usually in rather vague language. Kentucky and Virginia, for example, provide that there must be no "moral turpitude." The 1939 Act was silent on the matter. The policy here followed is that of the original rule as to contribution, that the court will not aid an intentional wrongdoer in a cause of action which is founded on his own wrong. In cases of concerted battery, for example, there appears to be little reason to shift any part of the liability to another.

> Two valid reasons exist for extending the exclusion to willful and wanton acts causing or contributing to the injury.
>
> In the first place willful and wanton acts seem naturally to belong in the same class with intentional wrongs and to imply moral turpitude on the part of the wrongdoer. The policy of the section as drafted adopts the law of those states which do not recognize classification of negligence into degrees. It is intended to convey the idea that there is a difference between negligence and willful or wanton misconduct.
>
> In the second place, by excluding willful and wanton actors from the right to contribution, we eliminate most of the arguments urged for a rule allocating the shares of liability on the basis of relative degrees of fault.
>
> In many states "gross and wanton negligence" in guest statutes is construed to mean willful and wanton conduct. This is the rule which should be applied in determining the right of contribution under this act.
>
> Brackets have been placed around "willfully or wantonly" so they may be omitted in those states where they mean something less than they imply and where by including them the bar of the remedy would be too broad.

Another significant difference between the model Act and Florida's version is found in the determination of *pro rata* shares. Florida's statute dictates that, "In determining the *pro rata* shares of tortfeasors in the entire liability: their relative degrees of fault shall be the basis for allocation of liability." The model Act provides that, "In determining the *pro rata* shares of tortfeasors in the entire liability their relative degrees of fault shall not be considered." The comment to this section states:

> This section in positive terms resolves several difficult questions of policy.
>
> First, it recognizes and registers the lack of need for a comparative negligence or degree of fault rule in contribution cases. As stated in the comments on subsection 1(c) the exclusion of intentional, willful and wanton actors from the right to contribution eliminates the better

arguments for a relative degree of fault rule.

Florida adopted the remainder of the *pro rata* share provision verbatim from the model Act: "If equity requires, the collective liability of some as a group shall constitute a single share. Principles of equity applicable to contribution generally shall apply." Fla. Stat. § 768.31(3)(b)-(c). The comments of the model statute's drafters with regard to collective liability provide:

> Second [this section] invokes the rule of equity which requires class liability, including the common liability arising from vicarious relationships, to be treated as a single share. For instance the liability of a master and servant for the wrong of the servant should in fairness be treated as a single share.

It appears from the foregoing commentary, that the drafters of the model Act intended for a state to either keep the terms "willfully or wantonly," thereby barring contribution where a tortfeasors' conduct met either the "intentionally" or the "willfully or wantonly" standards, or to eliminate the optional "willfully or wantonly" language, thereby making the contribution remedy broader. It also appears that the drafters of the model Act did not anticipate Florida's decision to import the words "willfully or wantonly," albeit in parentheses, while computing *pro rata* shares on the basis of degrees of fault, rather than on simple proportion based on the number of joint tortfeasors. Finally, it is noteworthy that the drafters considered as equitable the treatment of vicariously liable and actual tortfeasors as a single entity for purposes of determining the number of *pro rata* shares.

Florida's decision to prorate shares on the basis of degrees of fault is logical when considering the contribution statute *in pari materia* with the comparative fault statute. Indeed, the Florida Supreme Court in *Lincenberg*, made it plain that the two go hand in hand when it observed, "it would be undesirable for this Court to retain a rule that under a system based on fault, casts the entire burden of a loss for which several may be responsible upon only one of those at fault." Interestingly, Florida's comparative fault statute "applies to negligence cases" and "does not apply ... to any action based upon an intentional tort." Thus, the Florida legislature's decision to include the words "willfully or wantonly" in the contribution statute, but in parentheses, might be interpreted as merely defining the word "intentionally," the only level of conduct that explicitly bars a tortfeasor from the benefits of the comparative fault statute.

c. Analysis

With these underlying principles in mind, the Court next considers the applicability of Florida's UCATA as a bar to American Airlines' contribution claims. As previously stated, Honeywell and Jeppesen rely on Judge Marcus' determination that the

Flight 965 pilots engaged in "willful misconduct" to invoke UCATA's denial of a right of contribution to "any tortfeasor who has intentionally (willfully or wantonly) caused or contributed to the injury or wrongful death." Given the statutory ambiguities discussed above, it is not surprising that a review of Florida cases provides little guidance.

In *Diaz v. Sears, Roebuck & Co.*, (Fla. 3d DCA 1985), the Third District Court of Appeals flatly stated that the contribution bar "applies only to intentional tortfeasors." In an earlier opinion, however, the Third District remanded a case to the trial court for consideration of various issues, including whether a joint tortfeasor "was guilty of wanton conduct causing or contributing to the injury, such as to preclude him from recovering contribution." *Johnson v. Ludwig*, (Fla. 3d DCA 1976). Moreover, the case upon which both Honeywell and Jeppesen rely does not completely dispose of the issue.

In *Nesbitt v. Auto-Owners Ins. Co.*, (Fla. 5th DCA 1980), a special verdict form posed the question, "Did Earl I. Tillman [Auto-Owners Ins. Co.'s insured] intentionally (willfully and wantonly) or with reckless indifference to the rights of others, cause or contribute to the injuries to Ethel Nesbitt?," to which the jury answered "yes," underlining the words "reckless indifference" and "rights of others." Acknowledging that the contribution statute does not include the words "or with reckless indifference to the rights of others," the Fifth District reasoned:

> [W]illful or wanton conduct or conduct which displays a reckless indifference to the rights of others is tantamount to intentional conduct for the purposes of this statute. It is understandable there may be a lack of proof that a tortfeasor formed a specific intent to injure another, but his conduct may be of such a willful, wanton or reckless degree as to amount to the "intention" mentioned in the statute. In this case the evidence showed the appellee's insured was driving while under the influence of alcohol. Although that in itself may be dangerous or even reckless and come up to the standard intended by the statute and the jury instruction, it does not necessarily do so. It depends upon the facts of the case, the degree of the "influence" and that ultimately is a jury question.

For purposes of applying the *Nesbitt* court's interpretation of Florida's UCATA to this litigation, the undersigned adopts Judge Marcus' legal conclusion, that the pilots of Flight 965 engaged in "willful misconduct" under the meaning of the Warsaw Convention, as the law of the case. In reaching this conclusion, Judge Marcus applied the test enunciated by the Eleventh Circuit in *Butler v. Aeromexico* (11th Cir. 1985), under which "willful misconduct may be proved in one of three ways: by showing the intentional performance of an act with (1) knowledge that the act will probably result in injury or damage; (2) with reckless disregard of the consequences; or (3) a deliberate purpose not to discharge some duty necessary to safety." Judge Marcus analyzed the conduct of the pilots in light of the first two prongs of the Butler test and concluded that no reasonable juror could find that such conduct "did not constitute the intentional performance of an act with knowledge that the act will probably result in injury or damage or an act performed in reckless disregard of the consequences." In reaching this conclusion, Judge Marcus examined the pilots' conduct from the point of view of "objective recklessness" as well as by considering their state of mind. In addition to accepting Judge Marcus' legal conclusion regarding "willful misconduct" as the law of the case, the undersigned further assumes, for purposes of Honeywell's and Jeppesen's motions, that said conclusion translates to "recklessness" under Florida law. However, the *Nesbitt* case does not stand for the proposition that all "reckless" conduct bars contribution as a matter of law. Therefore, the Court concludes that Honeywell and Jeppesen are not entitled to summary judgment of non-liability on American Airlines' contribution claims.

d. Vicarious liability

American Airlines' posture as a vicariously liable tortfeasor also militates against barring its contribution claims against Honeywell and Jeppesen as a matter of law. As discussed in the historical perspective section of this opinion, the development of exceptions to the common law bar against contribution included equitable considerations with regard to vicariously liable defendants.

With particular reference to Florida's adoption of UCATA, the Court finds further support for allowing a vicariously liable tortfeasor's contribution claim to proceed in Florida, in the state's scheme for awarding punitive damages. Under Florida law, "a plaintiff must (a) establish that the conduct of the employee was willful and wanton and (b) establish some fault on the part of a corporate employer in order to support a claim of vicarious liability against the corporate employer for punitive damages." Thus, Florida has articulated a policy of not punishing employers by way of imposition of punitive damages absent a showing that the employer itself was at fault, even if such fault amounts only to ordinary negligence. Nothing in the record of this litigation supports even an inference that American Airlines' liability is predicated on any fault of its own. Thus, barring American Airlines' contribution claims would contravene Florida's explicit policy regarding vicariously liable tortfeasors in the area of punitive damages.

Another relevant consideration is the fact that Article 25, Section 2, of the Warsaw Convention, which eliminates the cap on damages for "willful misconduct" specifically states that "the carrier shall not be entitled to avail himself of [the provisions of the Convention], if the damage is caused under the same circumstances by any agent of the carrier acting within the scope of his employment." Judge Marcus's attribution of liability to American Airlines is wholly predicated on Section 2 of Article 25. It is interesting to note that the drafters of the Warsaw Convention took the trouble to specifically include vicarious liability as an alternative means of lifting the cap on the damages limitation imposed by the Convention. The silence of Florida's legislature on this issue in enacting UCATA might be interpreted, in light of the common law developments, as a presumption that vicariously liable tortfeasors are not subject to the statutory bar. In conclusion, Third Party Defendants Jeppesen Sanderson, Inc.'s and Honeywell, Inc.'s respective motions for summary judgment are denied.

EXECUTIVE JET AVIATION, INC. v. CITY OF CLEVELAND, OHIO

409 U.S. 249 (1972)

Mr. Justice STEWART delivered the opinion for a unanimous Court.

On July 28, 1968, a jet aircraft, owned and operated by the petitioners, struck a flock of seagulls as it was taking off from Burke Lakefront Airport in Cleveland, Ohio, adjacent to Lake Erie. As a result, the plane lost its power, crashed, and ultimately sank in the navigable waters of Lake Erie, a short distance from the airport. The question before us is whether the petitioner's suit for property damage to the aircraft, allegedly caused by the respondents' negligence, lies within federal admiralty jurisdiction.

When the crash occurred, the plane was manned by a pilot, a co-pilot, and a stewardess, and was departing Cleveland on a charter flight to Portland, Maine, where it was to pick up passengers and then continue to White Plains, New York. After being cleared for takeoff by the respondent Dicken, who was the federal air traffic controller at the airport, the plane took off, becoming airborne at about half the distance down the runway. The takeoff flushed the seagulls on the runway, and they rose into the airspace directly ahead of the ascending plane. Ingestion of the birds into the plane's jet engines caused an almost total loss of power. Descending back toward the runway in a semi-stalled condition, the plane veered slightly to the left, struck a portion of the airport perimeter fence and the top of a nearby pickup truck, and then settled in Lake Erie just off the end of the runway and less than one-fifth of a statute mile offshore. There were no injuries to the crew, but the aircraft soon sank and became a total loss.

Invoking federal admiralty jurisdiction under 28 U.S.C. § 1333(1), the petitioners brought this suit for damages in the District Court for the Northern District of Ohio against Dicken and the other respondents alleging that the crash had been caused by the respondents' negligent failure to keep the runway free of the birds or to give adequate warning of their presence. The District Court, in an unreported opinion, held that the suit was not cognizable in admiralty and dismissed the complaint for lack of subject matter jurisdiction.

Relying primarily on the Sixth Circuit precedent of *Chapman v. City of Grosse Pointe Farms* (6th Cir. 1967), the District Court held that admiralty jurisdiction over torts may properly be invoked only when two criteria are met: (1) the locality where the alleged tortious wrong occurred must have been on navigable waters; and (2) there must have been a relationship between the wrong and some maritime service, navigation, or commerce on navigable waters.

The District Court found that the allegations of the petitioners' complaint satisfied neither of these criteria. With respect to the locality of the alleged wrong, the court stated that "the alleged negligence became operative upon the aircraft while it was over the land; and in this sense the 'impact' of the alleged negligence occurred with the gulls disabled the plane's engines (over the land) ... From this point on the plane was disabled and was caused to fall. Whether it came down upon land or upon water was largely fortuitous." Alternatively, the court concluded that the wrong bore no relationship to maritime service, navigation, or commerce:

> Assuming that air commerce bears some relationship to maritime commerce when the former is carried out over navigable waters, the relevant circumstances here were unconnected with the maritime facets of air commerce.
>
> The claimed 'wrong' in this case was the alleged failure to keep the runway free of birds and the failure to adequately warn the pilots of their presence upon the end of the runway. When the alleged negligence occurred, and when it became operative upon the aircraft, all the parties were engaged in functions common to all air commerce, whether over land or over sea.
>
> Thus, the conclusion here must be that the operative facts of the claim in this case are concerned with the land-connected aspects of air-commerce, namely, the maintenance and operation of an airport located on the land and the dangers encountered by an aircraft when using its runways for take-off.

The Court of Appeals for the Sixth Circuit affirmed on the ground that "the alleged tort in this case occurred on land before the aircraft reached Lake Erie ..." Hence, that court found it "not necessary to consider the question of maritime relationship or nexus discussed by this court in (*Chapman*)." We granted *certiorari* to consider a seemingly important question affecting the jurisdiction of the federal courts.

I.

Determination of the question whether a tort is "maritime" and thus within the admiralty jurisdiction of the federal courts has traditionally depended upon the locality of the wrong. If the wrong occurred on navigable waters, the action is within admiralty jurisdiction; if the wrong occurred on land, it is not.

As early as 1813, in *Thomas v. Lane* (C.C. Me.), Mr. Justice Story, on Circuit, stated this general principle:

> In regard to torts I have always understood, that the jurisdiction of the admiralty is exclusively dependent upon the locality of the act. The admiralty has not, and never (I believe) deliberately claimed to have any jurisdiction over torts, except such as are maritime torts, that is, such as are committed on the high seas, or on waters within the ebb and flow of the tide.

In *The Plymouth* (1866), the Court essayed a definition of when a tort is "located" on navigable waters:

> The wrong and injury complained of must have been committed wholly upon the high seas or navigable waters, or, at least, the substance and consummation of the same must have taken place upon these waters to be within the admiralty jurisdiction.
>
> The jurisdiction of the admiralty over maritime torts does not depend upon the wrong having been committed on board the vessel, but upon its having been committed on the high seas or other navigable waters.
>
> Every species of tort, however occurring, and whether on board a vessel or not, if upon the high seas or navigable waters, is of admiralty cognizance.

The Court has often reiterated this rule of locality. As recently as last Term, in *Victory Carries, Inc. v. Law* (1971), we repeated that, "(t)he historic view of this Court has been that the maritime tort jurisdiction of the federal courts is determined by the locality of the accident and that maritime law governs only those torts occurring on the navigable waters of the United States."

This locality test, of course, was established and grew up in an era when it was difficult to conceive of a tortious occurrence on navigable waters other than in connection with a waterborne vessel. Indeed, for the traditional types of maritime torts, the traditional test has worked quite satisfactorily. As a leading admiralty text has put the matter:

> It should be stressed that the important cases in admiralty are not the borderline cases on jurisdiction; these may exercise a perverse fascination in the occasion they afford

> for elaborate casuistry, but the main business of the (admiralty) court involves claims for cargo damage, collision, seamen's injuries and the like-all well and comfortably within the circle, and far from the penumbra.

G. GILMORE & C. BLACK, THE LAW OF ADMIRALTY 24 n.88 (1957). But it is the perverse and casuistic borderline situations that have demonstrated some of the problems with the locality test of maritime tort jurisdiction.

In *Smith & Son v. Taylor* (1928), for instance, a longshoreman unloading a vessel was standing on the pier when he was struck by a cargo laden sling from the ship and knocked into the water where he was later found dead. This Court held that there was no admiralty jurisdiction in that case, despite the fact that the longshoreman was knocked into the water, because the blow by the sling was what gave rise to the cause of action, and it took effect on the land. Hence, the Court concluded, "(t)he substance and consummation of the occurrence which gave rise to the cause of action took place on land." In the converse factual setting, however, where a longshoreman working on the deck of a vessel was struck by a hoist and knocked onto the pier, the Court upheld admiralty jurisdiction because the cause of action arose on the vessel. *Minnie v. Port Huron Terminal Co.* (1935). *See also The Admiral People* (1935).

Other serious difficulties with the locality test are illustrated by cases where the maritime locality of the tort is clear, but where the invocation of admiralty jurisdiction seems almost absurd. If a swimmer at a public beach is injured by another swimmer or by a submerged object on the bottom, or if a piece of machinery sustains water damage from being dropped into a harbor by a land-based crane, a literal application of the locality test invokes not only the jurisdiction of the federal courts, but the full panoply of the substantive admiralty law as well. In cases such as these, some courts have adhered to a mechanical application of the strict locality rule and have sustained admiralty jurisdiction despite and lack of any connection between the wrong and traditional forms of maritime commerce and navigation. Other courts, however, have held in such situations that a maritime locality is not sufficient to bring the tort within federal admiralty jurisdiction, but that there must also be a maritime nexus—some relationship between the tort and traditional maritime activities, involving navigation or commerce on navigable waters.

The Court of Appeals for the Sixth Circuit, for instance, in the *Chapman* case, where a swimmer at a public beach was injured, held that

> (a)bsent such a relationship, admiralty jurisdiction would depend entirely upon the fact that a tort occurred on navigable waters; a fact which in and of itself, in light of the historical justification for federal admiralty jurisdiction, are quite immaterial to any meaningful invocation of the jurisdiction of admiralty courts.

As early as 1850, admiralty scholars began to suggest that a traditional maritime activity, as well as a maritime locality, is necessary to invoke admiralty jurisdiction over torts. In that year, Judge Benedict expressed his "celebrated doubt" as to whether such jurisdiction did not depend, in addition to a maritime locality, upon some "relation of the parties to a ship or vessel, embracing only those tortious violation(s) of maritime right and duty which occur in vessels to which the Admiralty jurisdiction, in cases of contracts, applies." E. BENEDICT, THE AMERICAN ADMIRALTY 173 (1850). More recently, commentators have actively criticized the rule of locality as the sole criterion for admiralty jurisdiction, and have recommended adoption of a maritime relationship requirement as well. *See* 7A J. MOORE, FEDERAL PRACTICE, ADMIRALTY, .325(3) and .325(5) (2d ed. 1972).

In 1969, the American Law Institute's Study of the Division of Jurisdiction Between State and Federal Courts ("ALI STUDY") also made that recommendation, stating:

> It is hard to think of any reason why access to federal court should be allowed without regard to amount in controversy or citizenship of the parties merely because of the fortuity that a tort occurred on navigable waters, rather than on other waters or on land. The federal courts should not be burdened with every case of an injured swimmer.

Despite the broad language of cases like *The Plymouth*, the fact is that this Court has never explicitly held that a maritime locality is the sole test of admiralty tort jurisdiction. The last time the Court considered the matter, the question was left open. *Atlantic Transport Co. of West Virginia v. Imbrovek* (1914). In that case, a stevedore brought suit for injuries sustained on board a vessel while loading and stowing copper. The petitioner admitted the maritime locality of the tort, but contended that no maritime relationship was present. The Court sustained federal admiralty jurisdiction, but found that it was not necessary to decide whether locality alone is sufficient:

> Even if it be assumed that the requirement as to locality in tort cases, while indispensable, is not necessarily exclusive, still in the present case the wrong which was the subject of the suit was, we think, of a maritime nature and hence the District Court, from any point of view, and jurisdiction.
>
> If more is required than the locality of the wrong in order to give the court jurisdiction, the relation of the wrong to maritime service, to navigation and to commerce on navigable waters, was quite sufficient.

Since the time of that decision the Court has not squarely dealt with the question left open there, although opinions in several cases have discussed the maritime or non-maritime nature of the tort and its relationship to maritime navigation.

In *Rodrigue v. Aetna Cas. & Surety Co.* (1969), for instance, we held that admiralty had no jurisdiction of wrongful-death actions under the Death on the High Seas Act, 46 U.S.C. § 761 *et seq*., arising out of accidents on artificial island drilling rigs in the Gulf of Mexico more than a marine league offshore. We relied in that case on the fact that the accidents bore no relation to any navigational function:

> The accidents in question here involved no collision with a vessel, and the structures were not navigational aids. They were islands, albeit artificial ones ... and the accidents had no more connection with the ordinary stuff of admiralty than do accidents on piers.

Apart from the difficulties involved in trying to apply the locality rule as the sole test of admiralty tort jurisdiction, another indictment of that test is to be found in the number of times the federal courts and the Congress, in the interests of justice, have had to create exceptions to it in the converse situation, *i.e.*, when the tort has no maritime locality, but does bear a relationship to maritime service, commerce, or navigation. For example, in *O'Donnell v. Great Lakes Dredge & Dock Co.* (1943), the Court sustained the application of the Jones Act, 46 U.S.C. § 688, to injuries to a seaman on land, because of the seaman's connection with maritime commerce. We relied in that case on an analogy to maintenance and cure:

> (T)he maritime law, as recognized in the federal courts, has not in general allowed recovery for personal injuries occurring on land. But there is an important exception to this generalization in the case of maintenance and cure. From its dawn, the maritime law has recognized the seaman's right to maintenance and cure for injuries suffered in the course of his service to his vessel, whether occurring on sea or on land.

Similarly, the doctrine of unseaworthiness has been extended to permit a seaman or a longshoreman to recover from a ship owner for injuries sustained wholly on land, so long as those injuries were caused by defects in the ship or its gear.

Congress, too, has extended admiralty jurisdiction predicated on the relation of the wrong to maritime activities, regardless of the locality of the tort. In the Extension of Admiralty Jurisdiction Act, 46 U.S.C. § 740, enacted in 1948, Congress provided:

> The admiralty and maritime jurisdiction of the United States shall extend to and include all cases of damage or injury, to person or property, caused by a vessel on navigable water, notwithstanding that such damage or injury be done or consummated on land.

This Act was passed specifically to overrule cases, such as *The Plymouth*, *supra*, holding that admiralty does not provide a remedy for damage done to land structures by ships on navigable waters.

In sum, there has existed over the years a judicial, legislative, and scholarly recognition that, in determining whether there is admiralty jurisdiction over a particular tort or class of torts, reliance on the relationship of the wrong to traditional maritime activity is often more sensible and consonant with the purposes of maritime law than a purely mechanical application of the locality test.

II.

One area in which locality as the exclusive test of admiralty tort jurisdiction has given rise to serious problems in application is that of aviation. For the reasons discussed above and those to be discussed, we have concluded that maritime locality alone is not a sufficient predicate for admiralty jurisdiction in aviation tort cases.

In one of the earliest aircraft cases brought in admiralty, *The Crawford Bros., No.* 2 (W.D. Wash. 1914), in which a libel *in rem* for repairs was brought against an airplane that had crashed into Puget Sound, the federal court declined to assume jurisdiction, reasoning that an airplane could not be characterized as a maritime vessel. *The Crawford Bros*. was followed by a number of cases dealing with seaplanes, in which the courts restricted admiralty jurisdiction to occurrences involving planes that were afloat on navigable waters.

Continuing doubt as to the applicability of admiralty law to aircraft was illustrated by cases in the 1930's and 1940's holding that aircraft owners could not invoke the benefits of the maritime doctrine of limitation of liability, and that crimes committed on board aircraft flying over international waters were not punishable under criminal statutes proscribing acts committed on the high seas. Moreover, Congress exempted all aircraft from conformity with United States navigation and shipping laws under the Federal Aviation Act of 1958.

In 1952, however, Congress amended the criminal jurisdiction of admiralty to include crimes committed aboard aircraft while in flight over the high seas or any other waters within the admiralty jurisdiction of the United States except waters within the territorial jurisdiction of any State. The first major extension of admiralty jurisdiction to land-based aircraft came in wrongful-death actions arising out of aircraft crashes at sea and brought under the Death on the High Seas Act, 46 U.S.C. § 761 *et seq*. The federal courts took jurisdiction of such cases because the literal provisions of that statute appeared to be clearly applicable.

The Death on the High Seas Act, enacted in 1920, provides:

> Whenever the death of a person shall be caused by wrongful act, neglect, or default occurring on the high seas beyond a marine league from the shore of any State, or the District of Columbia, or the Territories or dependencies of the United States, the personal representative of the decedent may maintain a suit for damages in the district courts of the United States, in admiralty.

The first aviation case brought pursuant to the Death on the High Seas Act was apparently *Choy v. Pan American Airways Co.* (S.D.N.Y. 1941), where death was caused by the crash of a seaplane into the Pacific Ocean during a transoceanic flight. The District Court upheld admiralty jurisdiction on the ground that the language of the Act was broad and made no reference to surface vessels. According to the court:

> The statute certainly includes the phrase 'on the high seas' but there is no reason why this should make the law operable only on a horizontal plane. The very next phrase 'beyond a marine league from the shore of any State' may be said to include a vertical sense and another dimension.

Since *Choy*, many actions for wrongful death arising out of aircraft crashes into the high seas beyond one marine league from shore have been brought under the Death on the High Seas Act, and federal jurisdiction has consistently been sustained in those cases. Indeed, it may be considered as settled today that this specific federal statute gives the federal admiralty courts jurisdiction of such wrongful-death actions.

In recent years, however, some federal courts have been persuaded in aviation cases to extend their admiralty jurisdiction beyond the statutory coverage of the Death on the High Seas Act. Several cases have held that actions for personal injuries arising out of aircraft crashes into the high seas more than one league off shore or arising out of aircraft accidents in the airspace over the high seas were cognizable in admiralty because of their maritime locality, although they were not within the scope of the Death on the High Seas Act or any other federal legislation.

These cases, as well as most of those brought under the Death on the High Seas Act, involved torts both with a maritime locality, in that the alleged negligence became operative while the aircraft was on or over navigable waters, and also with some relationship to maritime commerce, at least insofar as the aircraft was beyond state territorial waters and performing a function-transoceanic crossing-that previously would have been performed by waterborne vessels. (Whether this type of relationship to maritime commerce is a sufficient maritime nexus to justify admiralty jurisdiction over airplane accidents is discussed *infra*. We do not decide that question in this case.)

But a further extension of admiralty jurisdiction was created when courts began to sustain that jurisdiction in situations such as the one now before us—when the claim arose out of an aircraft accident that occurred on or over navigable waters within state territorial limits, and when the aircraft was not on a transoceanic flight. Apparently, the first such case grew out of a 1960 crash of a commercial jet, bound from Boston to Philadelphia, that collided with a flock of birds over the airport runway and crashed into Boston Harbor within one minute after takeoff. *See Weinstein v. Eastern Airlines, Inc.* (3d Cir. 1963). In deciding that a wrongful-death action arising from this crash was within admiralty jurisdiction, the Court of Appeals for the Third Circuit applied the strict locality rule and found that the tort had a maritime locality. The court further justified the invocation of admiralty jurisdiction in that case by an analogy to the Death on the High Seas Act:

> If, as it has been held, a tort claim arising out of the crash of an airplane beyond the one marine league line is within the jurisdiction of admiralty, then a fortiori a crash of an aircraft just short of that line but still within the navigable waters is within that jurisdiction as well.

There have been a few subsequent cases to like effect. To the contrary, of course, is the decision of the Court of Appeals for the Sixth Circuit in the present case.

III.

These latter cases graphically demonstrate the problems involved in applying a locality-alone test of admiralty tort jurisdiction to the crashes of aircraft. Airplanes, unlike waterborne vessels, are not limited by physical boundaries and can and do operate over both land and navigable bodies of water. As Professor Moore and his colleague Professor Pelaez have stated, "In both death and injury cases ... it is evident that while distinctions based on locality often are in fact quite relevant where water vessels are concerned, they entirely lose their significance where aircraft, which are not geographically restrained, are concerned." 7A J. MOORE, FEDERAL PRACTICE, ADMIRALTY, .330(5), at 3772-73.

In flights within the continental United States, which are principally over land, the fact that an aircraft happens to fall in navigable waters, rather than on land, is wholly fortuitous. The ALI STUDY, in criticizing the *Weinstein* decision, observed:

> If a plane takes off from Boston's Logan Airport bound for Philadelphia, and crashes on takeoff, it makes little sense that the next of kin of the passengers killed should be left to their usual remedies, ordinarily in state court, if the plane crashes on land, but that they have access to a federal court, and the distinctive substantive law of admiralty applies, if the wrecked plane ends up in the waters of Boston Harbor.

Moreover, not only is the locality test in such cases wholly adventitious, but it is sometimes almost impossible to apply with any degree of certainty. Under the locality test, the tort "occurs" where the alleged negligence took effect, and in the case of aircraft that locus is often most difficult to determine.

The case before us provides a good example of these difficulties. The petitioners contend that since their aircraft crashed into the navigable waters of Lake Erie and was totally destroyed when it sank in those waters, the locality of the tort, or the place where the alleged negligence took effect, was there. The fact that the major damage to their plane would not have occurred if it had not landed in the lake indicates, they say, that the substance and consummation of the wrong took place in navigable waters.

The respondents, on the other hand, argue that the alleged negligence took effect when the plane collided with the birds-over land. Relying on cases such as *Smith & Son v. Taylor*, *supra*, where admiralty jurisdiction was denied in the case of a longshoreman struck by a ship's sling while standing on a pier, and knocked into the water, the respondents contend that a tort "occurs" at the point of first impact of the alleged negligence. Here, they say, the cause of action arose as soon as the plane struck the birds; from then on, the plane was destined to fall, and whether it came down on land or water should not affect "the locality of the act."

In the view we take of the question before us, we need not decide who has the better of this dispute. It is enough to note that either position gives rise to the problems inherent in applying the strict locality test of admiralty tort jurisdiction in aviation accident cases. The petitioners' argument, if accepted, would make jurisdiction depend on where the plane ended up—a circumstance that could be wholly fortuitous and completely unrelated to the tort itself.

The anomaly is well illustrated by the hypothetical case of two aircraft colliding at a high altitude, with one crashing on land and the other in a navigable river. If, on the other hand, the respondents' position were adopted, jurisdiction would depend on whether the plane happened to be flying over land or water when the original impact of the alleged negligence occurred. This circumstance, too, could be totally fortuitous. If the plane in the present case struck the birds over Cleveland's Lakefront Airport, admiralty jurisdiction would not lie; but if the plane had just crossed the shoreline when it struck the birds, admiralty jurisdiction would attach, even if the plane were then able to make it back to the airport and crash land there. These are hardly the types of distinctions with which admiralty law was designed to deal.

All these and other difficulties that can arise in attempting to apply the locality test of admiralty jurisdiction to aeronautical torts are, of course, attributable to the inherent nature of aircraft. Unlike waterborne vessels, they are not restrained by one—dimensional geographic and physical boundaries. For this elementary reason, we conclude that the mere fact that the alleged wrong "occurs" or "is located" on or over navigable waters—whatever that means in an aviation context-is not of itself sufficient to turn an airplane negligence case into a "maritime tort." It is far more consistent with the history and purpose of admiralty to require also that the wrong bear a significant relationship to traditional maritime activity. We hold that unless such a relationship exists, claims arising from airplane accidents are not cognizable in admiralty in the absence of legislation to the contrary.

IV.

This conclusion, however, does not end our inquiry, for there remains the question of what constitutes, in the context of aviation, a significant relationship to traditional maritime activity. The petitioners argue that any aircraft falling into navigable waters has a sufficient relationship to maritime activity to satisfy the test. The relevant analogy, they say, is not between flying aircraft and sailing ships, but between a downed plane and a sinking ship. Quoting from the *Weinstein* opinion, they contend: "When an aircraft crashes into navigable waters, the dangers to persons and property are much the same as those arising out of the sinking of a ship or a collision between two vessels." The dissenting opinion in the Court of Appeals in the present case made the same argument:

> I believe that there are many comparisons between the problems of aircraft over navigable waters and those of the ships which the aircraft are rapidly replacing.
>
> Problems posed for aircraft landing on, crashing on, or sinking into navigable waters differ markedly from landings upon land. In such instances, wind and wave and water, the normal problems of the mariner, become the approach or survival problems of the pilot and his passengers. What I would hold is that tort cases arising out of aircraft crashes into navigable waters are cognizable in admiralty jurisdiction even if the negligent conduct is alleged to have happened wholly on land.

We cannot accept that definition of traditional maritime activity. It is true that in a literal sense there may be some similarities between the problems posed for a plane downed on water and those faced by a sinking ship. But the differences between the two modes of transportation are far greater, in terms of their basic qualities and traditions and consequently in terms of the conceptual expertise of the law to be applied. Moreover, if the mere happenstance that an aircraft falls into navigable waters creates a maritime relationship because of the maritime dangers to a sinking plane, then the maritime relationship test would be the same as the petitioners' view of the maritime-locality test, with the same inherent fortuity.

The law of admiralty has evolved over many centuries, designed and molded to handle problems of vessels relegated to ply the waterways of the world, beyond whose shores they cannot go. That law deals with navigational rules-rules that govern the manner and direction those vessels may rightly move upon the waters. When a collision occurs or a ship founders at sea, the law of admiralty looks to those rules to determine fault, liability, and all other questions that may arise from such a catastrophe. Through long experience, the law of the sea knows how to determine whether a particular ship is seaworthy, and it knows the nature of maintenance and cure. It is concerned with maritime liens, the general average, captures and prizes, limitation of liability, cargo damage, and claims for salvage.

Rules and concepts such as these are wholly alien to air commerce, whose vehicles operate in a totally different element, unhindered by geographical boundaries and exempt from the navigational rules of the maritime road. The matters with which admiralty is basically concerned have no conceivable bearing on the operation of aircraft, whether over land or water. Indeed, in contexts other than tort, Congress and the courts have recognized that, because of these differences, aircraft are not subject to maritime law. Although dangers of wind and wave faced by a plane that has crashed on navigable waters may be superficially similar to those encountered by a sinking ship, the plane's unexpected descent will almost invariably have been attributable to a cause unrelated to the sea—be it pilot error, defective design or manufacture of airframe or engine, error of a traffic controller at an airport, or some other cause; and the determination of liability will thus be based on factual and conceptual inquiries unfamiliar to the law of admiralty. It is clear, therefore, that neither the fact that a plane goes down on navigable waters nor the fact that the negligence "occurs" while a plane is flying over such waters is enough to create such a relationship to traditional maritime activity as to justify the invocation of admiralty jurisdiction.

We need not decide today whether an aviation tort can ever, under any circumstances bear a sufficient relationship to traditional maritime activity to come within admiralty jurisdiction in the absence of legislation. But, one commentator has posited:

> What possible rational basis is there in holding that the personal representative of a passenger killed in the crash of an airplane traveling from Shannon, Ireland to Logan Field in Boston has a cause of action within the admiralty

> jurisdiction if the plane goes down three miles from shore; may have a cause of action within the admiralty jurisdiction if the plane goes down within an area circumscribed by the shore and the three-mile limit; and will not have a cause of action within the admiralty jurisdiction if the plane managed to remain airborne until reaching the Massachusetts coast? And this notwithstanding that the plane may have developed engine trouble or been the victim of pilot error at an identical site far out over the Atlantic.

It could be argued, for instance, that if a plane flying from New York to London crashed in the mid-Atlantic, there would be admiralty jurisdiction over resulting tort claims even absent a specific statute. An aircraft in that situation might be thought to bear a significant relationship to traditional maritime activity because it would be performing a function traditionally performed by waterborne vessels. Apart from transoceanic flights, the Government's brief suggests that another example where admiralty jurisdiction might properly be invoked in an airplane accident case on the ground that the plane was performing a function traditionally performed by waterborne vessels, is shown in *Hornsby v. Fish Meal Co.* (5th Cir. 1970), which involved the mid-air collision of two light aircraft used in spotting schools of fish and the crash of those aircraft into the Gulf of Mexico within one marine league of the Louisiana shore.

Moreover, other factors might come into play in the area of international air commerce-choice-of-forum problems, choice of law problems, international-law problems, problems involving multi-nation conventions and treaties, and so on In such a situation, it has been stated: "Were the maritime law not applicable, it is argued that the recovery would depend upon a confusing consideration of what substantive law to apply, *i.e.*, the law of the forum, the law of the place where each decedent (or injured party) purchased his ticket, the law of the place where the plane took off, or, perhaps, the law of the point of destination."

But none of these considerations is of concern in the case before us. The flight of the petitioners' land-based aircraft was to be from Cleveland to Portland, Maine, and thence to White Plains, New York—a flight that would have been almost entirely over land was within the continental United States. After it struck the flock of seagulls over the runway, the plane descended the settled in Lake Erie within the territorial waters of Ohio. We can find no significant relationship between such an even befalling a land-based plane flying from one point in the continental United States to another, and traditional maritime activity involving navigation and commerce on navigable waters.

In the situation before us, which is only fortuitously and incidentally connected to navigable waters and which bears no relationship to traditional maritime activity, the Ohio courts could plainly exercise jurisdiction over the suit, (there is no diversity of citizenship between petitioners and the City of Cleveland) and could plainly apply familiar concepts of Ohio tort law without any effect on maritime endeavors. The possibility that the petitioners would have to litigate the same claim in two forums is the same possibility that would exist if their plane had stopped on the shore of the lake, instead of going into the water, and is the same possibility that exists every time a plane goes down on land, negligence of the federal air traffic controller is alleged, and there is no diversity of citizenship. This problem cannot be solved merely by upholding admiralty jurisdiction in cases where the plane happens to fall on navigable waters.

It may be, as the petitioners argue, that aviation tort cases should be governed by uniform substantive and procedural laws and that such actions should be heard in the federal courts so as to avoid divergent results and duplicitous litigation in multi-party cases. But for this Court to uphold federal admiralty jurisdiction in a few wholly fortuitous aircraft cases would be a most quixotic way of approaching that goal. If federal uniformity is the desired goal with respect to claims arising from aviation accidents, Congress is free under the Commerce Clause to enact legislation applicable to all such accidents, whether occurring on land or water, and adapted to the specific characteristics of air commerce.

For the reasons stated in this opinion we hold that, in the absence of legislation to the contrary, there is no federal admiralty jurisdiction over aviation tort claims arising from flights by land-based aircraft between points within the continental United States. (Some such flights, *e.g.*, New York City to Miami, Florida, no doubt involve passage over "the high seas beyond a marine league from the shore of any State." To the extent that the terms of the Death on the High Seas Act become applicable to such flights, that Act, of course, is "legislation to the contrary.") The judgment is affirmed.

IN RE AIR CRASH OFF LONG ISLAND, NEW YORK, ON JULY 17, 1996

209 F.3d 200 (2d Cir. 2000)

FEINBERG, Circuit Judge.

The appeal arises out of the crash of TWA Flight 800, which departed from John F. Kennedy International Airport in New York on July 17, 1996, for Paris, France and Rome, Italy. Shortly after takeoff, the plane appears to have exploded in midair and crashed. According to the National Transportation Safety Board, the crash occurred approximately eight nautical miles south of the shore of Long Island, New York. All 230 persons on board perished.

Plaintiffs are relatives and estate representatives of 213 passengers and crew members who died in the crash. Defendant Trans World Airlines owned and operated the aircraft. Defendant The Boeing Company manufactured the aircraft, and defendant Hydro-Aire, Inc., manufactured the aircraft's fuel pumps.

DISCUSSION

The appeal primarily concerns the interpretation of § 1 of the Death on the High Seas Act, 46 U.S.C. §§ 761-767 ("DOHSA") provides for a right of action:

> Whenever the death of a person shall be caused by wrongful act, neglect, or default occurring on the high seas beyond a marine league from the shore of any State, or the District of Columbia, or the Territories or dependencies of the United States.

The parties agree that the crash occurred eight nautical miles off the coast of Long Island, which is "beyond a marine league from the shore of any State." However, the parties differ as to the meaning of "high seas."

Plaintiffs argue that "high seas" refers to those waters beyond the territorial waters of the United States. Under Presidential Proclamation No. 5928, issued in 1988 by President Reagan, the territorial waters of the United States extend 12 miles from the shore of the United States.[1] As the crash occurred eight miles off the coast of Long Island, plaintiffs maintain it occurred in United States territorial waters, rather than on the high seas, and thus DOHSA does not apply.

Defendants contend that the term "high seas" means all waters beyond the low-water mark, *e.g.*, "the shoreline of a sea marking the edge of the water at the lowest point of the ordinary ebb tide." BLACK'S LAW DICTIONARY 1586 (7th ed. 1999). Defendants conclude that because the crash occurred both beyond the low-water mark and more than a marine league from the shore of Long Island, DOHSA applies. (Our dissenting colleague advocates a third position, that "high seas" means all waters beyond a marine league from the shore.)

The question whether DOHSA applies is significant because § 2 of DOHSA limits recovery to "a fair and just compensation for the pecuniary loss sustained by the persons for whose benefit the suit is brought." If DOHSA does not apply, however, plaintiffs claim they are entitled to nonpecuniary damages, *e.g.*, for pre-death pain and suffering and survivor's grief.

---

[1] On August 2, 1999, President Clinton extended the boundaries of the contiguous zone of the United States, a zone of waters "contiguous to the territorial sea of the United States," to 24 nautical miles. See Presidential Proclamation No. 7219, 64 Fed. Reg. 48,701 (Aug. 2, 1999). Because this crash predated President Clinton's Proclamation, we have no occasion to consider its effect.

A. *Background of the Death on the High Seas Act*

The Death on the High Seas Act provided a remedy for wrongful death at sea where none had clearly existed before. The federal courts initially recognized a right of action for wrongful death in general maritime law, based largely on humanitarian considerations: "[C]ertainly it better becomes the humane and liberal character of proceedings in admiralty to give than to withhold the remedy, when not required to withhold it by established and inflexible rules." *The Sea Gull* (C.C. Md. 1865) (No. 12,578) (Chase, C.J.).

The Supreme Court took a more restrictive approach, however, in *The Harrisburg*, 119 U.S. 199 (1886). In that case, a steamer collided with a schooner in waters between the coast of Massachusetts and the islands of Martha's Vineyard and Nantucket, killing the first officer of the schooner. Because the decedent's widow and child did not bring suit within the applicable state statutes of limitations, they sought to recover under general maritime law. The Supreme Court held that as there was no common-law remedy for wrongful death on land, there would be none at sea. Plaintiffs were thus entitled to no relief in the absence of a statute.

The Harrisburg was ultimately overruled in *Moragne v. States Marine Lines, Inc.* (1970), which established a remedy for wrongful death under general maritime law in a "meticulously reasoned" and "remarkably far-ranging" opinion by Justice Harlan for a unanimous Court. The *Moragne* Court explained that *The Harrisburg* assumed, wrongly, that the United States followed British common law, under which there was no wrongful death action because the penalty for all intentional or negligent homicide was death and forfeiture of the felon's property to the Crown, leaving nothing to recover in a civil suit. In any event, "the wholesale abandonment" of the prohibition on wrongful death actions in England and in the United States justified overruling *The Harrisburg*.

Judicial efforts to counteract the harshness of the rule of *The Harrisburg*, by expanding existing statutes to provide for recovery, complicated matters. The Supreme Court held in *The Hamilton* (1907), for example, that one citizen of Delaware could bring suit in admiralty against another under Delaware's wrongful death statute, even though the death had occurred on the high seas, seven miles off the coast of Virginia. Justice Holmes, writing for the Court, reasoned that Delaware law defined the obligations of the parties, "even when personally on the high seas." Similarly, in *La Bourgogne* (1908), the Court applied French law to an accident between French and British ships because the collision occurred on the high seas. The tension between the logic of *The Harrisburg* and *The Hamilton* "created jurisdictional fictions and serious problems in choice of law that sometimes denied recovery altogether." *Offshore Logistics v. Tallentire* (1986). Dismayed by these cases, the Maritime Law Association ("MLA") began drafting the bill that became the Death on the High Seas Act.

B. *The Drafting of the Death on the High Seas Act*

Congress initially sought to create a uniform remedy for wrongful death, but gradually refined the scope of DOHSA so as not to displace preexisting state remedies. Although the phrase "high seas" was rarely the focus of debate, the legislative history provides some indication of how that phrase should be interpreted to effectuate the purposes of DOHSA. The first priority was to draft a statute allowing recovery for wrongful death on the high seas. Critics of *The Harrisburg* maintained that the rule of that case had been rejected by "(e)very country of western Europe," and was a "disgrace to a civilized people." The MLA drafted a bill that would achieve uniformity in maritime remedies, displacing the patchwork of state statutory remedies that raised difficult choice of law issues. From 1909 through 1915, therefore, the proposed legislation provided a remedy "on the high seas, the Great Lakes, or any navigable waters of the United States." The rest of DOHSA's legislative history concerns the narrowing of this provision. In the 1914 congressional debates on DOHSA, conducted in the wake of litigation growing out of the Titanic disaster in 1912, objections arose that the bill would oust state jurisdiction over wrongful death and substitute an inadequate federal remedy. In response to opposition from members of Congress and local practitioners, the MLA abandoned its effort to draft a uniform remedy. Instead, it submitted a new bill in 1916 that "does not interfere with the law in force ... It simply covers waters that are not now covered."

The 1916 version of DOHSA preserved state remedies in three significant ways. First, the drafters changed "any navigable waters of the United States" to "any navigable waters of the Panama Canal Zone, the District of Columbia, or the Territories or dependencies of the United States," eliminating DOHSA's reach over navigable waters within state jurisdiction. Second, the drafters added a section, which became § 7 of DOHSA, that provided that the act would not affect state wrongful death remedies for deaths in state territorial waters. This provision also exempted the Great Lakes or "any waters within the territorial limits of any State" from DOHSA's scope. Finally, the later drafts added the words "beyond a marine league" to § 1, so that the proposed act covered deaths "on the high seas beyond a marine league from the shore of any State." This version of DOHSA was narrowed further when the Secretary of War requested that Congress avoid legislating in the Panama Canal Zone. The Panama Canal Zone reference was moved to § 7, which lists certain waters excluded from DOHSA's scope.

The statute that Congress passed in 1920 created a remedy for wrongful death "occurring on the high seas beyond a marine league from the shore of any State, or the District of Columbia, or the Territories or dependencies of the United States." The parties agree that the phrase "beyond a marine league" excludes from DOHSA's reach state territorial waters, which traditionally lay within three nautical miles from shore.[2]

---

[2] The territorial waters of Texas and Florida, however, extended three leagues seaward (roughly 10 miles), based on the boundaries extant when Texas was admitted, and Florida readmitted, into the Union.

C. *The Meaning of "High Seas"*

We believe that plaintiffs' understanding of "high seas" is superior to defendants, because it rests on the Supreme Court's definition of "high seas" at the time DOHSA was enacted, a definition that the Supreme Court and this court have reiterated in the decades following DOHSA. Furthermore, no post-DOHSA authority supports defendants' definition of "high seas" as "beyond the low-water mark."

1. The Supreme Court's Understanding of "High Seas" at the Time of DOHSA's Enactment

Although the boundary of this country's territorial sea at roughly three miles remained constant for almost two centuries, this limit was set on an *ad hoc* basis. In 1793, seeking to remain neutral in the war between France, Britain and Spain in the Atlantic Ocean, Secretary of State Thomas Jefferson claimed the "smallest distance" for the extent of American territorial seas. Relying on "the utmost range of a cannon ball, usually stated at one sea league," Jefferson made a claim for three nautical miles.

Although Jefferson reserved "the ultimate extent" of the claim "for future deliberation," and noted that a case could be made for 20 miles, the scope of our territorial sea remained constant until 1988.

By the time DOHSA was enacted in 1920, the Supreme Court generally interpreted "high seas" to mean international or non-sovereign waters, most notably in the cases upon which the authors and supporters of DOHSA relied. In 1881, for example, the Supreme Court described the "high seas" as "where the law of no particular State has exclusive force, but all are equal." *The Scotland* (1881). In the years DOHSA was pending before Congress, Justice Holmes characterized the "high seas" as "outside the territory, in a place belonging to no other sovereign."

These decisions, which interpreted "high seas" to mean "non-territorial waters," shaped the terms of the debate over DOHSA. The House and Senate Judiciary Committee Reports largely consisted of letters from supporters of DOHSA. These DOHSA proponents repeatedly invoked *The Hamilton* and *The Scotland* in the course of describing the purpose and meaning of DOHSA. Under the Supreme Court's analysis, the consistent reliance on these decisions in setting the terms of the debate over DOHSA strongly suggests that Congress understood "high seas" to mean what these cases said it did, that is, international waters.

In support of their interpretation, defendants rely heavily on the statements of Congressman Bryan of Washington, an opponent of DOHSA, who argued in 1914 that the "high seas" would include the waters of Puget Sound. Yet "it is well established that speeches by opponents of legislation are entitled to relatively little weight in determining the meaning of the Act in question."

The Supreme Court continued to define "high seas" as "international waters" in the years immediately following DOHSA. In *Cunard S.S. Co. v. Mellon* (1923), the Court ruled that a Prohibition statute could be enforced only within the territorial limits of the United States. The Court rejected the argument that the Prohibition Amendment covered ships "outside the waters of the United States, whether on the high seas or in foreign waters," because "on the high seas ... there is no territorial sovereign."

It is true that the Court has not provided a consistent definition of "high seas" throughout the past two centuries. Defendants' understanding of the "high seas" as those seas beyond the low-water mark appears to have been shared by Justice Story, who characterized the high seas as "the open, uninclosed ocean, or that portion of the sea, which is without the *fauces terrae* on the sea coast." Yet Justice Story's definition was not the authoritative definition of "high seas." In the early nineteenth century, Justices Thompson and Baldwin, sitting in district court cases, interpreted "high seas" to mean non-sovereign waters.

Because defendants' definition of high seas as "beyond the low-water mark" was neither the dominant definition of "high seas," nor the definition used in those Supreme Court cases that shaped the congressional debate over DOHSA, nor, as discussed below, is it used in modern decisions concerning DOHSA, we reject it.

2. The Structure and Purpose of DOHSA

An analysis of the structure and purpose of DOHSA also supports plaintiffs' understanding of "high seas." We should interpret both "high seas" and "beyond a marine league" to have independent meaning. Defendants' definition violates this canon of statutory construction because it renders "high seas" superfluous. Defendants provide no examples in which the low-water mark is not well within a marine league, that is, three nautical miles, of the coast. We do not see why Congress would have retained two geographical boundaries in the statute when one-beyond a marine league-subsumes the other.

Plaintiffs' interpretation, however, defines "beyond a marine league" as a geographical boundary and "high seas" as a political boundary subject to change. While the geographical and political boundaries were coterminous in 1920, there was no reason to think that would always be the case. At the time DOHSA was enacted, the "minimum limit of the territorial jurisdiction of a nation" was a marine league. "The void that existed in maritime law up until 1920 was the absence of any remedy for wrongful death on the high seas. Congress, in acting to fill that void, legislated only to the three-mile limit because that was the extent of the problem."

Furthermore, the legislative history of DOHSA shows that while "high seas" was always part of the statutory language, "beyond a marine league" was not added until later drafts, to preserve state remedies. Congress added this section at the same time it dropped "any navigable waters of the United States." Defendants do not explain why Congress did not also drop "high seas" at that point in the drafting process; under defendants' interpretation that high seas means those waters beyond the low-water mark, the phrase "beyond a marine league" would by itself exclude state territorial waters. Congress's decision to retain the phrase "high seas" strongly supports plaintiffs' claim that "high seas" has a different independent meaning: it denotes international waters beyond both state and federal territorial waters.

Not only did Congress retain the phrase "high seas" in § 1, but also Congress inserted another provision in the 1919 drafts of the statute that used the phrase "high seas." Section 4 provides that, "[w]henever a right of action is granted by the law of any foreign State on account of death by wrongful act, neglect, or fault, occurring upon the high seas, such right may be maintained in an appropriate action in admiralty in the courts of the United States." By suggesting that foreign nations may well have legislated their own wrongful death remedies for the "high seas," § 4 indicates that "high seas" lay outside the sole jurisdiction of the United States. Thus § 4's reference to "high seas" indicates international waters, "a place belonging to no other sovereign" in Justice Holmes's phrase in *The Hamilton*. Congress's use of "high seas" as international waters in § 4 strongly suggests that it used "high seas" to mean international waters in § 1.

Plaintiffs' interpretation of "high seas" as international, that is, nonterritorial, waters is also consistent with § 7 of DOHSA, which states:

> The provisions of any State statute giving or regulating rights of action or remedies for death shall not be affected by this chapter. Nor shall this chapter apply to the Great Lakes or to any waters within the territorial limits of any State, or to any navigable waters in the Panama Canal Zone.

Defendants argue that § 7 lists waters excluded from DOHSA's scope, so that this section would be devoid of meaning if plaintiffs' definition of "high seas" as nonterritorial waters were correct, because none of the waters listed in § 7 are nonterritorial waters. This argument ignores that the drafters of DOHSA were forced to expressly disclaim any ouster of state remedies for wrongful death. On the floor of the House of Representatives, there were objections that § 7 was "superfluous" because § 1 clearly limited the scope of DOHSA to the high seas. One of DOHSA's supporters responded that § 7 was added "out of an abundant caution, to calm the minds" of DOHSA's opponents. Section 7 was inserted to clarify that state waters were not subject to DOHSA. As Judge Sweet pointed out, the aim of § 7 is not to set forth all waters that are beyond the scope of DOHSA, because it makes no mention of the territorial waters referred to in § 1 that are not within the scope of DOHSA (waters within a marine league of the shore of "the District of Columbia, or the Territories or dependencies of the United States").

Finally, applying DOHSA to federal territorial waters would subvert DOHSA's purpose of creating a remedy where none existed before, rather than displacing preexisting state or federal remedies. The legislative history "indicates that Congress intended to ensure the continued availability of a remedy, historically provided by the States, for deaths in territorial waters." Congress intended to exclude federal territorial waters from the scope of DOHSA because federal and state common-law remedies already existed for deaths in those waters.

It would be particularly inappropriate to displace preexisting state or federal remedies where, as here, recovery could be more generous than under DOHSA. As the Supreme Court noted in *Moragne*, "the state remedies that were left undisturbed not only were familiar but also may actually have been more generous than the remedy provided by the new Act." The Supreme Court has frequently reiterated Chief Justice Chase's admonition that, "the humane and liberal character of proceedings in admiralty" advises in favor of more generous recovery.

The statute and legislative history demonstrate that in DOHSA, Congress prioritized the preservation of preexisting remedies over securing uniformity in admiralty law. Because defendants' interpretation of the critical language in DOHSA would oust preexisting remedies for deaths in territorial waters, which may prove to be more generous than recovery under DOHSA, we reject that interpretation as inconsistent with the purpose of the statute.

3. The Meaning of "High Seas"—1920-1988

For most of the century there was no band of United States territorial waters between state territorial waters and the high seas similar to that created by Proclamation 5928, which in 1988 extended United States territorial waters from three to 12 miles. It was not inaccurate to say that the high seas effectively began at a marine league, *i.e.*, three nautical miles from the shore of any state. Thus, as was the case with defendants' definition of "high seas" as "beyond the low-water mark," there is some support for the claim that "high seas" equals "beyond a marine league." There is scant authority, however, for the claim that even in light of Proclamation 5928, the high seas still begin at one marine league, rather than at the 12-mile boundary the Proclamation established.

In the years following DOHSA, the dominant understanding of "high seas" remained "beyond United States territorial waters." In *United States v. Louisiana* (1969) ["*Louisiana I*"], which concerned the scope of the Submerged Lands Act, the Supreme Court provided a jurisdictional map of the seas:

> Under generally accepted principles of international law, the navigable sea is divided into three zones ... Nearest to the nation's shores are its inland, or internal waters. These are subject to the complete sovereignty of the nation ...

> Beyond the inland waters, and measured from their seaward edge, is a belt known as the marginal, or territorial sea. Within it the coastal nation may exercise extensive control but cannot deny the right of innocent passage to foreign nations. *Outside the territorial sea are the high seas, which are international waters not subject to the dominion of any single nation.*

In setting forth this scheme, the Court relied on the United States Convention on the High Seas, which states that, "[t]he term 'high seas' means all parts of the sea that are not included in the territorial sea or in the internal waters of a State."

The Supreme Court has frequently considered the extent and nature of wrongful-death remedies under general maritime law. From DOHSA (enacted in 1920) to *Moragne* (decided in 1970), DOHSA provided the remedy for deaths on the high seas, while state wrongful death statutes provided the remedy for deaths in territorial waters. After *Moragne* overruled *The Harrisburg* and established a remedy for wrongful death under general maritime law, subsequent cases set forth the elements of a *Moragne*-type remedy. Where the death occurs on the high seas, however, the Court has made clear that DOHSA is the exclusive remedy. Where the death did not occur on the high seas, but in territorial waters, DOHSA does not oust state remedies. In a recent discussion of DOHSA, the Supreme Court unanimously concluded that § 7 of DOHSA "stops DOHSA from displacing state law in territorial waters." Because the Court was obliged to "preserve the application of state statutes to deaths within territorial waters," it rejected a claim that DOHSA was the remedy for a death that occurred in the waters of Puerto Rico, a territory of the United States.

This court has generally interpreted "high seas" to mean international waters. In 1924, for example, we characterized the "high seas" as "'where the law of no particular state has exclusive force, but all are equal.'" *The Buenos Aires* (2d Cir. 1924). Similarly, in *Cove Tankers Corp. v. United Ship Repair, Inc.* (2d Cir. 1982), we noted that "the Supreme Court's definition of high seas" was "'international waters not subject to the dominion of any single nation.'" We have also explicitly relied on the boundary between territorial and international waters in setting the scope of DOHSA, explaining that the purpose of DOHSA "was to create a uniform cause of action where none existed before and which arose beyond the territorial limits of the United States or any State thereof." *D'Aleman v. Pan American World Airways* (2d Cir. 1958).

Defendants rely heavily on statements of this court that the high seas begin where state territorial waters end. This argument overlooks that when those cases were decided, there were no federal territorial waters that lay between state territorial waters and the high seas. Thus the boundary between the high seas and state waters was the same as the boundary between the high seas and federal waters. Where federal territorial waters do exist, however, the high seas begin where those federal territorial waters end.

4. The Application of DOHSA to Foreign Territorial Waters

Defendants rely on a line of cases applying DOHSA to the territorial waters of a foreign state to suggest that the scope of DOHSA is not coextensive with international waters. In *In re Air Crash Disaster Near Bombay, India on January 1, 1978* (W.D. Wash. 1982), for example, the court ruled that because the remedy created by DOHSA should be broadly construed, DOHSA applied within the territorial waters of India. In *Jennings v. Boeing Co.* (E.D. Pa. 1987), the court applied DOHSA to a plane crash two and a half miles off the coast of the Shetland Islands, Scotland. The application of DOHSA to foreign territorial waters has produced somewhat unusual results, such as the extension of DOHSA to a river in Peru and a lake in Venezuela.

Obviously, we are not faced here with a wrongful death claim arising out of an accident in the territorial waters of a foreign nation. We take no position on what courts should do when faced with the difficult question of whether to apply DOHSA in foreign territorial waters, where plaintiffs might otherwise be left with only foreign remedies in foreign courts. The decisions applying DOHSA to foreign territorial waters seek to provide a remedy in federal court for survivors of those killed in maritime accidents. These decisions do not require—or even suggest—the application of DOHSA to the territorial waters of the United States, where plaintiffs already have a state or federal remedy. Furthermore, none of these cases support defendants' interpretation of the relevant statutory language in DOHSA.

D. *The Effect of Presidential Proclamation No. 5928*

The parties do not dispute that had the crash occurred before Presidential Proclamation No. 5928 was issued in 1988, the crash would have occurred beyond United States territorial waters so that DOHSA would apply. The issue, therefore, is whether after issuance of the Proclamation, DOHSA applied to the waters between three and 12 miles from the shore. The Proclamation, issued by President Reagan, provides for:

> the extension of the territorial sea of the United States of America, the Commonwealth of Puerto Rico, Guam, American Samoa, the United States Virgin Islands, the Commonwealth of the Northern Mariana Islands, and any other territory or possession over which the United States exercises sovereignty.
>
> The territorial sea of the United States henceforth extends to 12 nautical miles from the baselines of the United States determined in accordance with international law.

As United States District Judge Robert W. Sweet noted in the case below, "The President also expressly stated that the Proclamation is consistent with international law. The

President's exercise of constitutional power over foreign affairs is therefore consistent with international law."

The Proclamation thus alters the three-mile boundary that had historically defined the territorial sea. Concluding that "Congress intended DOHSA's application to depend on the border between United States and international territory," Judge Sweet here explained that the Proclamation effectively moved the starting point of DOHSA from three to 12 miles offshore. As the crash occurred eight miles off the coast of Long Island, it occurred within the territorial waters of the United States and DOHSA did not apply.

Defendants note that the Proclamation includes a provision that states as follows: "Nothing in this Proclamation extends or otherwise alters existing Federal or State law or other jurisdiction, rights, legal interests or obligations derived therefrom." Defendants argue that the district court imputed an effect to the Proclamation that it explicitly disclaimed.

Commenting on the effect of the Proclamation, the Office of Legal Counsel of the United States Department of Justice explained: "The issue is whether Congress intended for the jurisdiction of any existing statute to include an expanded territorial sea. Thus, the question is one of legislative intent." Therefore, the impact of the Proclamation must be assessed on a statute-by-statute basis. Based on our analysis of Congress's intent in enacting DOHSA, we decline to adopt defendants' view of the effect of the Proclamation.

The background and legislative history of DOHSA demonstrate Congress's intent to exclude all state and federal territorial waters from its scope. Nothing in DOHSA's history or purpose provides a persuasive reason to fix immutably the scope of the statute to the boundary between United States territorial waters and nonterritorial waters as it existed in 1920. Thus, plaintiffs are correct in concluding that the effect of the Proclamation is to move the starting point of the application of DOHSA from three to 12 miles from the coast.

Plaintiffs' interpretation of the Proclamation does not change DOHSA, but designates certain additional waters to which DOHSA does not apply. If Congress in 1920 had included a definition of "high seas" as "waters outside United States or state territorial waters, where no nation is sovereign," as we believe it essentially did, the Proclamation would not change this definition. Indeed, if the Proclamation is construed to create a zone of federal territorial waters subject to DOHSA, then this would violate the disclaimer. DOHSA would effectively be amended by excluding federal territorial waters up to three miles from its coverage, but including federal territorial waters between three and 12 miles. Such an effect would be inconsistent with Congress's intent to exclude all federal territorial waters from the scope of DOHSA. In sum, once the United States or any state or territory thereof has asserted sovereignty over certain waters, DOHSA does not govern the remedies available in those waters.

E. *Remedies in Federal Territorial Waters*

Finally, defendants object that the district court created a "no-man's land" between three and 12 miles from the shore of the coastal states. As our discussion of DOHSA's history and purpose makes clear, the district court's decision did not create a "no-man's land," but recognized that the Proclamation created a larger zone of federal territorial waters. This zone of waters is governed by the same remedies that have traditionally governed federal territorial waters. Defendants insist that exempting the federal territorial waters affected by the Proclamation from DOHSA creates inconsistency and undermines uniformity. But it would be more inconsistent, and more arbitrary, to impose one remedial scheme over certain federal territorial waters (up to three miles) and a different remedial scheme over other federal territorial waters (from three to 12 miles).

The core purpose of DOHSA was to provide a remedy where one did not exist before, not to oust either a *Moragne*-type remedy or state law remedies. The remedies available to plaintiffs for wrongful death in the federal territorial waters in which the crash occurred may prove better suited to this case than DOHSA's statutory requirements. As the Supreme Court has said, we leave for the district court to resolve the conflict of law questions in determining which remedies are available. We hold only that the Death on the High Seas does not apply to federal territorial waters and conclude, for the reasons stated above, that plaintiffs' interpretation of the relevant statutory language better reflects the meaning and purpose of the Death on the High Seas Act.

SOTOMAYOR, Circuit Judge, dissenting.

In an understandable desire to provide the relatives and estate representatives of the 213 victims of the TWA Flight 800 crash with a "more generous" recovery, the majority fails to give proper effect to the limiting language of Proclamation 5982; to DOHSA's language, legislative history, and purpose; and to a wealth of case law since DOHSA's passage, all of which support the inexorable conclusion that DOHSA applies to all deaths occurring "beyond a marine league [three nautical miles] from the shore of any State," and not only to deaths occurring beyond the U.S. territorial sea.

By its explicit terms, the Proclamation changed the meaning of the U.S. territorial sea—and thus its complement the "high seas"—for international, but not domestic, law purposes. The majority nevertheless applies the territorial boundaries set forth in the Proclamation to DOHSA, even though the meaning of "high seas" for the purposes of DOHSA is a question purely of domestic law. Moreover, the majority's application of the Proclamation to DOHSA is grounded almost entirely on its interpretation of what Congress probably thought the term "high seas" meant at the time of DOHSA's passage, *i.e.*, "waters ... where no nation is sovereign," and the majority's assumption that Congress viewed the three nautical mile line at which the high seas commenced as a "political boundary line subject to change." Based on this reasoning, the majority concludes that the Proclamation's expansion of the boundary line of the U.S. territorial sea from three to twelve nautical miles necessarily excluded DOHSA's application in this nine mile zone.

The majority's focus on Congress' understanding of the term "high seas" in 1920 is misplaced. The majority ignores that the DOHSA Congress, by using the phrase "high seas beyond one marine league from the shore of any State," intended both to define and to indicate the geographical boundary line at which the high seas began—three nautical miles from the U.S. coast—because that boundary line coincided with the outer border of the states' territorial seas. Congress wished to preserve state remedies in state waters, and to provide a separate remedy, *i.e.*, DOHSA, to waters subject only to federal jurisdiction, *i.e.*, "the high seas beyond a marine league." Simply stated, it is irrelevant whether Congress shared the international legal understanding of "high seas" as "non-sovereign waters," because its only concern at the time of DOHSA's passage was state, and not federal, boundaries. Nothing in DOHSA's language or legislative history supports the majority's conclusion that Congress intended "high seas" to be a variable term "subject to change" because of evolving international concepts.

The majority's conclusion is also contrary to the holdings and dicta of every other court that has considered this issue, and cannot be reconciled with a long line of cases from at least four other circuits applying DOHSA to deaths occurring in foreign territorial waters—in other words, waters indisputably subject to foreign sovereigns. I do not believe that the Proclamation replaced DOHSA with general federal maritime law in the zone of waters lying between three and twelve nautical miles seaward of the U.S. coast (the "disputed zone"). I therefore respectfully dissent.

Congress—and the President—have the opportunity to amend DOHSA to incorporate a more generous remedial scheme, just as they have the opportunity, if so inclined, to preclude DOHSA's application in the disputed zone. I have no desire to pre-empt the legislative process by reading DOHSA more broadly than the Proclamation dictates or than the DOHSA Congress intended. The appropriate remedial scheme for deaths occurring off the United States coast is clearly a legislative policy choice, which should not be made by the courts.

UNITED STATES v. S.A. EMPRESA DE VIACO O AEREA RIO GRANDENSE (VARIG AIRLINES)

467 U.S. 797 (1984)

Chief Justice BURGER delivered the opinion of the Court.

We granted *certiorari* in these two cases to determine whether the United States may be held liable under the Federal Tort Claims Act, for the negligence of the Federal Aviation Administration in certificating certain aircraft for use in commercial aviation.

I.

A. NO. 82-1349

On July 11, 1973, a commercial jet aircraft owned by respondent S.A. Empresa De Viacao Aerea Rio Grandense ("Varig Airlines") was flying from Rio de Janeiro to Paris when a fire broke out in one of the aft lavatories. The fire produced a thick black smoke, which quickly filled the cabin and cockpit. Despite the pilots' successful effort to land the plane, 124 of the 135 persons on board died from asphyxiation or the effects of toxic gases produced by the fire. Most of the plane's fuselage was consumed by a post-impact fire.

Before introducing a new type of aircraft, a manufacturer must first obtain from the FAA a type certificate signifying that the basic design of the aircraft meets the minimum criteria specified in the safety regulations promulgated by the Federal Aviation Administration ("FAA"). When applying for a type certificate, the manufacturer must supply the FAA with detailed plans, data, and documentation illustrating the aircraft design and demonstrating its compliance with FAA regulations. FAA employees or private employees who represent the FAA then examine the manufacturer's submission for conformity with the regulations.

The aircraft involved in this accident was a Boeing 707, a product of the Boeing Co. In 1958 the Civil Aeronautics Agency, a predecessor of the FAA, had issued a type certificate for the Boeing 707, certifying that its designs, plans, specifications, and performance data had been shown to be in conformity with minimum safety standards. Seaboard Airlines originally purchased this particular plane for domestic use; in 1969 Seaboard sold the plane to respondent Varig Airlines, a Brazilian air carrier, which used the plane commercially from 1969 to 1973.

After the accident respondent Varig Airlines brought an action against the United States under the Federal Tort Claims Act seeking damages for the destroyed aircraft. The families and personal representatives of many of the passengers, also respondents here, brought a separate suit under the Act pressing claims for wrongful death. The two actions were consolidated in the United States District Court for the Central District of California.

Respondents asserted that the fire originated in the towel disposal area located below the sink unit in one of the lavatories and alleged that the towel disposal area was not capable of containing fire. In support of their argument, respondents pointed to an air safety regulation requiring that waste receptacles be made of fire-resistant materials and incorporate covers or other provisions for containing possible fires. Respondents claimed that the CAA had been negligent when it inspected the Boeing 707 and issued a type certificate to an aircraft that did not comply with CAA fire protection standards. The District Court granted summary judgment for the United States on the ground that California law does not recognize an actionable tort duty for inspection and certification activities. The District Court also found that, even if respondents had stated a cause of action in tort, recovery against the United States was barred by two exceptions to the Act: the discretionary function exception and the misrepresentation exception.

The United States Court of Appeals for the Ninth Circuit reversed, reasoning that a private person inspecting and certificating aircraft for airworthiness would be liable for negligent inspection under the California "Good Samaritan" rule, and concluding that the United States should be judged by the same rule. The Court of Appeals rejected the Government's argument that respondents' actions were barred by 28 U.S.C. § 2680(h), which provides that the United States is not subject to liability for any claim arising out of misrepresentation. Interpreting respondents' claims as arising from the negligence of the CAA inspection rather than from any implicit misrepresentation in the resultant certificate, the Court of Appeals held that the misrepresentation exception did not apply.

Finally, the Court of Appeals addressed the Government's reliance upon the discretionary function exception to the Act, which exempts the United States from liability for claims "based upon the exercise or performance or the failure to exercise or perform a discretionary function or duty ..." The Court of Appeals viewed the inspection of aircraft for compliance with air safety regulations as a function not entailing the sort of policymaking discretion contemplated by the discretionary function exception.

B. NO. 82-1350

In October 1968, a DeHavilland Dove aircraft owned by respondent John Dowdle and used in the operation of an air taxi service caught fire in midair, crashed, and burned near Las Vegas, Nev. The pilot, copilot, and two passengers were killed. The cause of the crash was an in-flight fire in the forward baggage compartment of the aircraft.

The DeHavilland Dove airplane was manufactured in the United Kingdom in 1951 and then purchased by Air Wisconsin, another air taxi operator. In 1965 Air Wisconsin contracted with Aerodyne Engineering Corp. to install a gasoline-burning cabin heater in the airplane. Aerodyne applied for, and was granted, a supplemental type certificate from the FAA authorizing the installation of the heater. Any person who alters an aircraft by introducing a major change in the type design must obtain from the FAA a supplemental type certificate. In order to obtain such a certificate, the applicant must supply the FAA with drawings, plans, and other data sufficient to establish that the altered aircraft meets all applicable airworthiness requirements. Aerodyne then installed the heater pursuant to its contract with Air Wisconsin. In 1966, relying in part upon the supplemental type certificate as an indication of the airplane's airworthiness, respondent Dowdle purchased the DeHavilland Dove from Air Wisconsin.

In the aftermath of the crash, respondent Dowdle filed this action for property damage against the United States under the Federal Tort Claims Act. Respondent insurance companies also filed suit under the Act, seeking reimbursement for moneys paid for liability coverage on behalf of Dowdle. The United States District Court for the Southern District of California found that the crash resulted from defects in the installation of the gasoline line leading to the cabin heater. The District Court concluded that the installation did not comply with the applicable FAA regulations and held that the Government was negligent in certifying an installation that did not comply with those safety requirements, and accordingly, entered judgment for respondents.

On appeal, the United States Court of Appeals for the Ninth Circuit reversed and remanded for the District Court to consider whether the California courts would impose a duty of due care upon the Government by applying the "Good Samaritan" doctrine of §§ 323 and 324A of the RESTATEMENT (SECOND) OF TORTS. The Court of Appeals also requested the District Court to determine whether, under the facts of this case, the California courts would find such a duty breached if a private person had issued the supplemental type certificate in question here. On remand, the District Court again entered judgment for respondents, finding that the California "Good Samaritan" rule would apply in this case and would give rise to liability on these facts. On the Government's second appeal, the Ninth Circuit affirmed the judgment of the District Court. In so holding, the Court of Appeals followed reasoning nearly identical to that employed in its decision in No. 82-1349, decided the same day. We granted *certiorari* and we now reverse.

II.

In the Federal Aviation Act of 1958 Congress directed the Secretary of Transportation to promote the safety of flight of civil aircraft in air commerce by establishing minimum standards for aircraft design, materials, workmanship, construction, and performance. Congress also granted the Secretary the discretion to prescribe reasonable rules and regulations governing the inspection of aircraft, including the manner in which such inspections should be made. Congress emphasized, however, that air carriers themselves retained certain responsibilities to promote the public interest in air safety: the duty to perform their services with the highest possible degree of safety, the duty to make or cause to be made every inspection required by the Secretary, and the duty to observe and comply with all other administrative requirements established by him.

In 1958, when the type certificate for the Boeing 707 aircraft owned by respondent Varig Airlines was issued, the Civil Aeronautics Act of 1938, was the governing statute. As originally enacted, the Federal Aviation Act vested in the Federal Aviation Agency all regulatory authority over aviation safety. This agency was later renamed the Federal Aviation Administration and placed in the Department of Transportation. All the functions, powers, and duties of the Federal Aviation Agency were then transferred to the Secretary of Transportation. Congress also established a multistep certification process to monitor the aviation industry's compliance with the requirements developed by the Secretary. Acting as the Secretary's designee, the FAA has promulgated a comprehensive set of regulations delineating the minimum safety standards with which the designers and manufacturers of aircraft must comply before marketing their products.

At each step in the certification process, FAA employees or their representatives evaluate materials submitted by aircraft manufacturers to determine whether the manufacturer has satisfied these regulatory requirements. Upon a showing by the manufacturer that the prescribed safety standards have been met, the FAA issues an appropriate certificate permitting the manufacturer to continue with production and marketing. The first stage of the FAA compliance review is type certification. A manufacturer wishing to introduce a new type of aircraft must first obtain FAA approval of the plane's basic design in the form of a type certificate. After receiving an application for a type certificate, the Secretary must "make, or require the applicant to make, such tests during manufacture and upon completion as the Secretary ... deems reasonably necessary in the interest of safety." 49 U.S.C. § 1423(a)(2). By regulation, the FAA has made the applicant itself responsible for conducting all inspections and tests necessary to determine that the aircraft comports with FAA airworthiness requirements. The applicant submits to the FAA the designs, drawings, test reports, and computations necessary to show that the aircraft sought to be certificated satisfies FAA regulations.

One major manufacturer of commercial aircraft estimated that in the course of obtaining a type certificate for a new wide-body aircraft it would submit to the FAA approximately 300,000 engineering drawings and changes, 2,000 engineering reports, and 200 other reports. In addition, it would subject the aircraft to about 80 major ground tests and 1,600 hours of flight tests. In the course of the type certification process, the manufacturer produces a prototype of the new aircraft and conducts both ground and flight tests. FAA employees or their representatives then review the data submitted by the applicant and make such inspections or tests as they deem necessary to ascertain compliance with the regulations. If the FAA finds that the proposed aircraft design comports with minimum safety standards, it signifies its approval by issuing a type certificate.

Production may not begin, however, until a production certificate authorizing the manufacture of duplicates of the prototype is issued. To obtain a production certificate, the manufacturer must prove to the FAA that it has established and can maintain a quality control system to assure that each aircraft will meet the design provisions of the type certificate. When it is satisfied that duplicate aircraft will conform to the approved type design, the FAA issues a production certificate, and the manufacturer may begin mass production of the approved aircraft. Before any aircraft may be placed into service, however, its owner must obtain from the FAA an airworthiness certificate, which denotes that the particular aircraft in question conforms to the type certificate and is in condition for safe operation. It is unlawful for any person to operate an aircraft in air commerce without a valid airworthiness certificate.

An additional certificate is required when an aircraft is altered by the introduction of a major change in its type design. To obtain this supplemental type certificate, the applicant must show the FAA that the altered aircraft meets all applicable airworthiness requirements. The applicant is responsible for conducting the inspections and tests necessary to demonstrate that each change in the type design complies with the regulations. The methods used by FAA employees or their representatives to determine an applicant's compliance with minimum safety standards are generally the same as those employed for basic type certification. FAA Order 8110.4, Type Certification 32 (1967) (hereinafter "FAA Order 8110.4"); CAA MANUAL OF PROCEDURE, FLIGHT OPERATIONS AND AIRWORTHINESS, *Type Certification* § .5106(a) (1957) (hereinafter "CAA MANUAL OF PROCEDURE").

With fewer than 400 engineers, the FAA obviously cannot complete this elaborate compliance review process alone. Accordingly, 49 U.S.C. § 1355 authorizes the Secretary to delegate certain inspection and certification responsibilities to properly qualified private persons. By regulation, the Secretary has provided for the appointment of private individuals to serve as designated engineering representatives to assist in the FAA certification process. These representatives are typically employees of aircraft manufacturers who possess detailed knowledge of an aircraft's design based upon their day-to-day involvement in its development. The representatives act as surrogates of the FAA in examining, inspecting, and testing aircraft for purposes of certification. In determining whether an aircraft complies with FAA regulations, they are guided by the same requirements, instructions, and procedures as FAA employees. FAA employees may briefly review the reports and other data submitted by representatives before certificating a subject aircraft.

III.

The Federal Tort Claims Act, 28 U.S.C. § 1346(b), authorizes suits against the United States for damages

> for injury or loss of property, or personal injury or death caused by the negligent or wrongful act or omission of any employee of the Government while acting within the scope of his office or employment, under circumstances where the United States, if a private person, would be liable to the claimant in accordance with the law of the place where the act or omission occurred.

The Act further provides that the United States shall be liable with respect to tort claims "in the same manner and to the same extent as a private individual under like circumstances." The Act did not waive the sovereign immunity of the United States in all respects, however; Congress was careful to except from the Act's broad waiver of immunity several important classes of tort claims. Of particular relevance here, 28 U.S.C.

§ 2680(a) provides that the Act shall not apply to

> [a]ny claim based upon an act or omission of an employee of the Government, exercising due care, in the execution of a statute or regulation, whether or not such statute or regulation be valid, or based *upon the exercise or performance or the failure to exercise or perform a discretionary function or duty on the part of a federal agency or an employee of the Government, whether or not the discretion involved be abused.*

The discretionary function exception, embodied in the second clause of § 2680(a), marks the boundary between Congress' willingness to impose tort liability upon the United States and its desire to protect certain governmental activities from exposure to suit by private individuals. The legislative materials of the 77th Congress illustrate most clearly Congress' purpose in fashioning the discretionary function exception. A Government spokesman appearing before the House Committee on the Judiciary described the discretionary function exception as a "highly important exception"—

> [It is] designed to preclude application of the act to a claim based upon an alleged abuse of discretionary authority by a regulatory or licensing agency—for example, the Federal Trade Commission, the Securities and Exchange Commission, the Foreign Funds Control Office of the Treasury, or others.
>
> It is neither desirable nor intended that the constitutionality of legislation, the legality of regulations, or the propriety of a discretionary administrative act should be tested through the medium of a damage suit for tort. The same holds true of other administrative action not of a regulatory nature, such as the expenditure of Federal funds, the execution of a Federal project, and the like. On the other hand, the common law torts of employees of regulatory agencies, as well as of all other Federal agencies, would be included within the scope of the bill.

It was believed that claims of the kind embraced by the discretionary function exception would have been exempted from the waiver of sovereign immunity by judicial construction; nevertheless, the specific exception was added to make clear that the Act was not to be extended into the realm of the validity of legislation or discretionary administrative action.

While it is unnecessary—and indeed impossible—to define with precision every contour of the discretionary function exception, from the legislative and judicial materials, it is possible to isolate several factors useful in determining when the acts of a Government employee are protected from liability. First, it is the nature of the conduct, rather than the status of the actor, that governs whether the discretionary function exception applies in a given case. Thus, the basic inquiry concerning the application of the discretionary function exception is whether the challenged acts of a Government employee—whatever his or her rank—are of the nature and quality that Congress intended to shield from tort liability. Second, whatever else the discretionary function exception may include, it plainly was intended to encompass the discretionary acts of the Government acting in its role as a regulator of the conduct of private individuals.

IV.

We now consider whether the discretionary function exception immunizes from tort liability the FAA certification process involved in these cases. Respondents in No. 82-1349 argue that the CAA was negligent in issuing a type certificate for the Boeing 707 aircraft in 1958 because the lavatory trash receptacle did not satisfy applicable safety regulations. Similarly, respondents in No. 82-1350 claim negligence in the FAA's issuance of a supplemental type certificate in 1965 for the DeHavilland Dove aircraft; they assert that the installation of the fuel line leading to the cabin heater violated FAA airworthiness standards. From the records in these cases there is no indication that either the Boeing 707 trash receptacle or the DeHavilland Dove cabin heater was actually inspected or reviewed by an FAA inspector or representative. Respondents thus argue in effect that the negligent failure of the FAA to inspect certain aspects of aircraft type design in the process of certification gives rise to a cause of action against the United States under the Act.

The Government, on the other hand, urges that the basic responsibility for satisfying FAA air safety standards rests with the manufacturer, not with the FAA. The role of the FAA, the Government says, is merely to police the conduct of private individuals by monitoring their compliance with FAA regulations. According to the Government, the FAA accomplishes its monitoring function by means of a "spot-check" program designed to encourage manufacturers and operators to comply fully with minimum safety requirements. Such regulatory activity, the Government argues, is the sort of governmental conduct protected by the discretionary function exception to the Act. We agree that the discretionary function exception precludes a tort action based upon the conduct of the FAA in certificating these aircraft for use in commercial aviation.

As noted *supra*, the Secretary of Transportation has the duty to promote safety in air transportation by promulgating reasonable rules and regulations governing the inspection, servicing, and overhaul of civil aircraft. In her discretion, the Secretary may also prescribe

> the periods for, and *the manner in, which such inspection, servicing, and overhaul shall be made*, including provision for examinations and reports by properly qualified private persons whose examinations or reports the Secretary of Transportation may accept in lieu of those made by its officers and employees."

Thus, Congress specifically empowered the Secretary to establish and implement a mechanism for enforcing compliance with minimum safety standards according to her "judgment of the best course."

In the exercise of this discretion, the FAA, as the Secretary's designee, has devised a system of compliance review that involves certification of aircraft design and manufacture at several stages of production. The FAA certification process is founded upon a relatively simple notion: the duty to ensure that an aircraft conforms to FAA safety regulations lies with the manufacturer and operator, while the FAA retains the responsibility for policing compliance. This premise finds ample support in the statute and regulations. *See, e.g.*, 49 U.S.C. § 1421(b) (duty rests on air carriers to perform their services with highest possible degree of safety); § 1425(a) (air carrier has duty to make or cause to be made inspections required by Secretary and duty to comply with regulations); 14 C.F.R. § 21.17 (1983) (applicant for type certificate must show that aircraft meets applicable requirements); § 21.33 (applicant for type certificate must conduct all tests and inspections necessary to determine compliance); § 21.35 (specifying tests that must be made by applicants for type certificates).

Thus, the manufacturer is required to develop the plans and specifications and perform the inspections and tests necessary to establish that an aircraft design comports with the applicable regulations; the FAA then reviews the data for conformity purposes by conducting a "spot check" of the manufacturer's work. The operation of this "spot-check" system is outlined in detail in the handbooks and manuals developed by the CAA and FAA for the use of their employees. For example, the CAA MANUAL OF PROCEDURE for type certification in effect at the time of the certification of the Boeing 707 provided:

> Conformity determination may be varied depending upon circumstances. *A manufacturer's policies, quality control procedures, experience, inspection personnel, equipment, and facilities will dictate the extent of conformity inspection to be conducted or witnessed by [CAA employees]*.
>
> Differences between manufacturers require that the conformity program be adjusted to fit existing conditions. In the case of an inexperienced manufacturer whose ability is unknown, it may be necessary to conduct a high percentage of conformity inspections until such time as the

> [CAA] inspector feels he can safely rely to a greater degree upon the company inspectors. *He may then gradually reduce his own inspection or witnessing accordingly.*
>
> Experienced manufacturers having previously demonstrated the acceptability of their quality control and inspection competence ... should benefit by greater [CAA] confidence.
>
> *In such cases, conformity determination may be made through a planned system of spot-checking critical parts and assemblies and by reviewing inspection records and materials review dispositions ... It is not intended that the inspector personally conduct a complete conformity inspection of each part he records on a [CAA] form.*
>
> He should, however, visually inspect and witness the manufacturer's inspection of the critical characteristics ... In a program of this type, increased confidence in the manufacturer, plus a planned program of spot-checking by [CAA employees], should result in obtaining increased knowledge of conformity of the end product.
>
> Regardless of the manufacturer's experience, it is the [CAA] inspector's responsibility to assure that a complete conformity inspection has been performed by the manufacturer and that the results of this inspection are properly recorded and reported.

CAA MANUAL OF PROCEDURE § .330. (Emphasis added.) *See also* FAA Order 8110.4.

As to the engineering review of an application for a type certificate, the CAA materials note that only a "relatively small number of engineers" are available to evaluate for compliance with air safety regulations the data submitted by applicants. Accordingly, the Manual states:

> *It is obvious that complete detailed checking of data is not possible. Instead, an overriding check method should be used* [which] is predicated on the fact that the applicant has completely checked all data presented for examination. These data are to be examined in turn by the [CAA] engineer for method and completeness, and *with sufficient spot-checking to ascertain that the design complies with the minimum airworthiness requirements.*

CAA MANUAL OF PROCEDURE § .41. *See also* FAA Order 8110.4, p. 60. In a recent report, the National Academy of Sciences recognized that because "FAA engineers cannot review each of the thousands of drawings, calculations, reports, and tests involved in the type certification process," the agency must place great reliance on the manufacturer. The report also noted that "in most cases the FAA staff performs only a cursory review of the substance of th[e] overwhelming volume of documents" submitted for its approval.

The procedure for supplemental type certification is much the same. According to the Manual of Procedure applicable to the supplemental type certification of the DeHavilland Dove, an applicant must submit to the FAA data describing the proposed change in type design, which may be accompanied by drawings or photographs of the suggested alteration. The methods for determining compliance with applicable safety regulations are generally the same as those used for basic type certification. Physical inspections of the proposed modification in type design are required when compliance with the applicable regulations "cannot be determined adequately from an evaluation of the technical data." CAA MANUAL OF PROCEDURE § 5106(b). Moreover, FAA representatives are authorized to approve data covering major changes in type design and obtain supplemental type certifications without prior review by the FAA.

Respondents' contention that the FAA was negligent in failing to inspect certain elements of aircraft design before certificating the Boeing 707 and DeHavilland Dove necessarily challenges two aspects of the certification procedure: the FAA's decision to implement the "spot-check" system of compliance review, and the application of that "spot-check" system to the particular aircraft involved in these cases. In our view, both components of respondents' claim are barred by the discretionary function exception to the Act.

The FAA's implementation of a mechanism for compliance review is plainly discretionary activity of the "nature and quality" protected by § 2680(a). When an agency determines the extent to which it will supervise the safety procedures of private individuals, it is exercising discretionary regulatory authority of the most basic kind. Decisions as to the manner of enforcing regulations directly affect the feasibility and practicality of the Government's regulatory program; such decisions require the agency to establish priorities for the accomplishment of its policy objectives by balancing the objectives sought to be obtained against such practical considerations as staffing and funding.

Here, the FAA has determined that a program of "spot-checking" manufacturers' compliance with minimum safety standards best accommodates the goal of air transportation safety and the reality of finite agency resources. Judicial intervention in such decision-making through private tort suits would require the courts to "second-guess" the political, social, and economic judgments of an agency exercising its regulatory function. It was precisely this sort of judicial intervention in policymaking that the discretionary function exception was designed to prevent.

It follows that the acts of FAA employees in executing the "spot-check" program in accordance with agency directives are protected by the discretionary function exception as well. The FAA employees who conducted compliance reviews of the aircraft involved in this case were specifically empowered to make policy judgments regarding the degree of confidence that might reasonably be placed in a given manufacturer, the need to maximize compliance with FAA regulations, and the efficient allocation of agency resources. In administering the "spot-check" program, these FAA engineers and inspectors necessarily took certain calculated risks, but those risks were encountered for the advancement of a governmental purpose and pursuant to the specific grant of authority in the regulations and operating manuals. Under such circumstances, the FAA's alleged negligence in failing to check certain specific items in the course of certificating a particular aircraft falls squarely within the discretionary function exception.

V.

In rendering the United States amenable to some suits in tort, Congress could not have intended to impose liability for the regulatory enforcement activities of the FAA challenged in this case. The FAA has a statutory duty to promote safety in air transportation, not to insure it. We hold that these actions against the FAA for its alleged negligence in certificating aircraft for use in commercial aviation are barred by the discretionary function exception of the Federal Tort Claims Act. Accordingly, the judgments of the United States Court of Appeals for the Ninth Circuit are reversed.

NOTES

1. On March 27, 1977, almost 600 people died when two Boeing 747 jumbo-jets collided on a runway in Tenerife in the Canary Islands. It was the worst aviation disaster prior to September 11, 2001. In litigation arising out of the tragedy, Dutch plaintiffs sued U.S.-based Pan American Airways and two of its New York-based crew members in American courts. Because all of the evidence was located in the Netherlands and Dutch civil law applied, the case was dismissed from an American court on grounds of *forum non conveniens*. *Bouvy-Loggers v. Pan American World Airways, Inc.* (S.D.N.Y. 1978). The case epitomizes the fact that United States courts are attractive forums for non-U.S. plaintiffs to try aviation cases for accidents occurring outside the United States.

American juries generally award higher damages awards—including punitive damages—than fact finders in foreign jurisdictions. Additionally, plaintiffs are advantaged by the liberal discovery regime, availability of legal theories including strict liability, and contingency fee arrangements permitted under federal and state rules of civil procedure. *See generally* Lory Barsdate Easton, *Getting out of Dodge: Defense Pointers on Jurisdictional Issues in Aviation Torts Litigation*, 20-WTR Air & Space Law. 9, 9 (2006). When considering whether to move for dismissal on grounds of *forum non conveniens*, therefore, aviation defense counsel consider

> the causes of action available to plaintiff, potential ranges of damages awards, the civil procedure and appeal process, the typical time from filing to disposition of a complex civil action, local attitudes toward U.S. corporate defendants, the availability of documents and witnesses, the procedures (if any) for nonparty discovery, the viability of contribution or indemnity claims against other potentially responsible parties, the methods for enforcement of judgments and risks of asset seizure, and any potential for criminal prosecution arising from torts liability claims.

Id. See also Ronald A. Brand, *Comparative Forum Non Conveniens and the Hague Convention on Jurisdiction and Judgments*, 37 TEX. INT'L L.J. 467 (2002); James L. Baudino, Comment, *Venue Issues against Negligent Carriers—International and Domestic Travel; The Plaintiff's Choice?*, 61 J. AIR L. & COM. 163 (1996); Alexander Reus, *Judicial Discretion: A Comparative View of the Doctrine of Forum Non Conveniens in the United States, the United Kingdom, and Germany*, 16 LOY. L.A. INT'L & COMP. L.J. 455 (1994).

2. Choice-of-law is a threshold issue in aviation cases, as demonstrated by *Piper Aircraft Co. v. Reyno* (1981), and *In re Air Crash near Cali, Columbia on December 20, 1995* (S.D. Fla. 1998), *supra.* It may be the most important preliminary issue in aviation litigation, potentially representing the difference between multi-million-dollar and no recovery. As one authority stated, however, the law of conflicts generally is a "dismal swamp, filled with quaking quagmires, and inhabited by learned but eccentric professors who theorize about mysterious matters in a strange and incomprehensible jargon." William Prosser, *Interstate Publication*, 51 MICH. L. REV. 959, 971 (1953).

Federal courts apply the choice-of-law rules of the forum state, and in multi-district litigation, the transferee court must apply the choice-of-law rules from the jurisdiction from which the case was transferred. Aviation practitioners must master several choice-of-law approaches, including the traditional *lex loci delicti* doctrine of the FIRST RESTATEMENT OF CONFLICT OF LAW (*e.g.*, where the wrong or tort was committed), the *lex fori* doctrine (*e.g.*, applying the forum's law absent an overwhelming or rational reason to the contrary), the "most significant contacts" of the Second Restatement, (*e.g.*, focusing upon the factual contacts alone), the "better law" theory (allowing judges to subjectively determine the "better law"), and the "combined modern" approach (applying mixed choice-of-law methodologies).

Differing burdens and presumptions also impact choice-of-law determinations in aviation cases. In diversity actions, "unless the parties argue otherwise, it is assumed that the law of the forum and the laws of the applicable jurisdictions are in substance the same." *National Ass'n of Sporting Goods Wholesalers, Inc. v. F.T.L. Marketing Corp.* (7th Cir. 1985). When another state's law is asserted, courts evaluate the forum's choice-of-law rules, but

> [i]n cases involving aircraft accidents, the general rule is that little weight is given to the place of injury in choice-of-law determinations. The usual explanation is that, given an airplane's mobility, the location of an unexpected event such as an airplane crash is almost always fortuitous.

Wert v. McDonnell Douglas Corp. (E.D. Mo. 1986). "When certain contacts involving a tort are located in two or more states with identical local law rules on the same issue in question, the case will be treated for choice-of-law purposes as if those contacts were grouped in a single state." RESTATEMENT (SECOND) OF CONFLICT OF LAWS (1971), at § 146, Comment h.

3. Consider:

> Eighteen years before 9/11, there was 9/1—a Cold War event so tragic and catastrophic that, like the attacks on the World Trade Center and the Pentagon by Arab fanatics in the new millennium, it seared itself into the consciousness of three nations. On August 31, 1983, a Boeing 747 aircraft, operated by Korean Air Lines (KAL) and carrying 269 passengers, departed New York City at approximately 11:50 P.M. After a fuel stop in Anchorage, Alaska, the flight would proceed to its final destination, Seoul, Korea, where it would land on September 1, 1983.
>
> The pilots, however, inadvertently failed to program the aircraft's inertial navigation system properly. Flying in the dark over the North Pacific at 35,000 feet, the aircraft slowly drifted off course, until it entered Soviet airspace near Sakhalin Island. With the belief that a spy plane was approaching, the Soviet air force scrambled three fighter jets to intercept the wayward aircraft.
>
> Within minutes, and without warning, the Soviet jets fired heat-seeking missiles at the aircraft. The exploding missiles damaged the aircraft's hydraulic systems, and shrapnel penetrated the cabin, causing a rapid decompression. The

> crippled aircraft entered a long, spiraling descent before it slammed into the Sea of Japan and was destroyed. All 269 passengers and crew on board the aircraft perished, including 105 Koreans, 28 Japanese, and 62 Americans.
>
> Although it was impossible to foresee at the time, the KAL Flight 007 disaster would permanently change the body of jurisprudence under the federal maritime wrongful death statute, The Death on the High Seas Act (DOHSA). Not only did the disaster have a significant impact on Cold War relations between the United States and the Soviet Union, it spawned two decisions by the U.S. Supreme Court that swept away recovery of non-pecuniary damages in DOHSA cases.
>
> Those decisions were handed down in the mid-1990s against the backdrop of another noteworthy mass airline disaster: TWA Flight 800. In response to an outpouring of sympathy for the families of the victims of TWA Flight 800, Congress took up the question of compensation for non-pecuniary damages in cases governed by DOHSA. The result was an amendment to DOHSA known as the "Commercial Aviation Exception," which allows recovery of loss of society damages in actions arising from a "commercial aviation accident."

Stephen R. Ginger & Will S. Skinner, *DOHSA's Commercial Aviation Exception: How Mass Airline Disasters Influenced Congress on Compensation for Deaths on the High Seas*, 75 J. AIR L. & COM. 137, 137-38 (2010).

In re Air Crash off Long Island, New York, on July 17, 1996 (2d Cir. 2000) arose from the TWA Flight 800 disaster and implicated the Death on the High Seas Act ("DOHSA"), a federal statute creating a private cause of action for wrongful death on the high seas where no legal remedy otherwise would exist. The DOHSA provides:

> When the death of an individual is caused by wrongful act, neglect, or default occurring on the high seas beyond 3 nautical miles from the shore of the United States, the personal representative of the decedent may bring a civil action in admiralty against the person or vessel responsible. The action shall be for the exclusive benefit of the decedent's spouse, parent, child, or dependent relative.

46 U.S.C. § 30302 (2006). *See also Dooley v. Korean Air Lines Co.* (1998); *Zicherman v. Korean Air Lines Co.* (1996).

The panel majority *In re Air Crash off Long Island, New York, on July 17, 1996,* held that although the crash occurred beyond a marine league—approximately three miles—from shore, the DOHSA did not apply (and thus the plaintiffs could recover for non-pecuniary damages) because the crash did not occur on the "high seas," which it defined as "international waters beyond both state and federal territorial waters. *See also Eberli v. Cirrus Design Corp.* (S.D. Fla. 2009) (evaluating post-TWA Flight 800 amendments to the DOHSA, 46 U.S.C. § 30307(b).)

Judge Sonia Sotomayor dissented from the panel majority holding, reasoning the DOHSA "applies to all deaths occurring 'beyond a marine league [three nautical miles] from the shore of any State,' and not only to deaths occurring beyond the U.S. territorial sea." Judge Sotomayor emphasized that Congress in 1920 had enacted the DOHSA to "preserve state remedies in state waters, and to provide a separate remedy … to waters subject only to federal jurisdiction." She explained that when the DOHSA was enacted, the "high seas" started at the three-mile mark, and that this did not change when President Ronald Reagan signed a 1988 Proclamation that extended the U.S. territorial waters to twelve nautical miles. Judge Sotomayor acknowledged that the majority's holding will create "a more generous remedial scheme" for the victims' families, but countered that "[t]he appropriate remedial scheme for deaths occurring off the United States coast is clearly a legislative policy choice, which should not be made by the courts." *See generally* Amy Howe, *Judge Sotomayor's Civil Opinions, http://www.scotusblog.com/2009/05/judge-sotomayor%e2%80%99s-civil-opinions-part-iv/.*

Appointed by President Barack Obama, Judge Sotomayor joined the Supreme Court of the United States as an Associate Justice in August 2009. What might Justice Sotomayor's presence on the Supreme Court signify, if anything, with respect to the future of DOHSA legislation and jurisprudence?

4. While the "locality test" may not be sufficient for admiralty jurisdiction to attach to aviation accident litigation, the "significant relationship test" presented in the seminal case of *Executive Jet Aviation, Inc. v. City of Cleveland* (1972), *supra*, the impact of an aviation incident, if any, on maritime commerce is an appropriate consideration. In that context, courts have found that the sinking of an aircraft in navigable waters creates a "potentially disruptive impact on maritime commerce" such that admiralty jurisdiction generally applies. *E.g.*, *In re Air Crash at Belle Harbor New York on November 12, 2001* (S.D.N.Y. 2006). *See also Anderson v. United States* (11th Cir. 2003) (applying admiralty jurisdiction upon finding that an aircraft on a Navy aircraft carrier was an "appurtenance" of the vessel causing plaintiff's injuries).

The Extension of Admiralty Jurisdiction Act ("AEA"), 46 U.S.C. § 30101 (2006), originally enacted in 1948, extends the admiralty and maritime jurisdiction of the United States "to include all cases of damage or injury, to person or property, caused by a vessel on navigable water, notwithstanding that such damage or injury be done or consummated on land." The AEA was designed to "end the concern over the sometimes confusing line between land and water" by affording litigants a potential remedy in "all cases" in which a vessel causes an injury. *E.g.*, *Gutierrez v. Waterman S.S. Corp.* (1963) (finding vessel liable in admiralty for injuries to longshoremen who slipped on beans spilled on pier while cargo was being unloaded). The AEA will apply only to damage or injury that is caused by a "vessel on navigable water." *E.g.*, *Pearson v. Northeast Airlines, Inc.* (S.D.N.Y. 1961) (declining to apply AEA to an airplane crash occurring on an island, where the decedent "[s]ustained no injury of any kind contributing to his death while the airplane was in flight over the sea.").

For example, in considering whether a crane on a barge afloat in navigable waters could be a vessel under the AEA, the United Supreme Court considered a "connection test," *e.g.*, (1) whether the "general features" of an incident had "a potentially disruptive impact on maritime commerce," and (2) whether "the general character" of the "activity giving rise to the incident" showed a "substantial relationship to traditional maritime activity." *Jermoe B. Grubart, Inc. v. Great Lakes Dredge & Dock Co.* (1995).

5. Application of admiralty jurisdiction is important to aviation practitioners because damages computations often turn on that initial determination. Admiralty jurisdiction generally disallows non-pecuniary damages in personal injury suits in admiralty (*e.g.*, *Miles v. Apex Marine Corp.* (1990)). Under the choice of law doctrine of *dépeçage*, moreover, courts determine which state has the most significant interest in the application of its law to the issue of damages, including punitive damages. Section 145 of the RESTATEMENT (SECOND) provides that "[t]he rights and liabilities of the parties with respect to an issue in tort are determined by the local law of the state which, with respect to that issue, has the most significant relationship to the occurrence and the parties." Thus, for example, reducing a plaintiff's future economic damages to present value is a matter of state substantive law. *Ageloff v. Delta Airlines, Inc.* (11th Cir. 1988).

Similarly, the DOHSA's admiralty jurisdiction means that juries are not available. *E.g., Krop v. Douglas Aircraft Co.* (E.D.N.Y. 1971); *Harris v. United Airlines, Inc.* (S.D. Iowa 1967). As to damages, the DOHSA provides for "fair and just compensation for the pecuniary loss sustained by the individuals for whose benefit the action is brought, … apportion[ed] … among those individuals in proportion to the loss each has sustained." *See* 46 U.S.C. § 30303. The usual factors applied in DOHSA actions include the deceased's age; earning capacity; surviving beneficiaries and their ages; contributions to beneficiaries; condition of health; and prospects for advancement. *E.g.*, *In re Air Crash Near Nantucket Island, Massachusetts, on October 31, 1999* (E.D.N.Y. 2006).

Damages under the DOHSA are reduced to present value through the use of a discount rate, and while prejudgment interest generally is available under DOHSA, punitive damages are not. "[C]ontributory negligence of the decedent is not a bar to recovery" under the DOHSA, and courts must "consider the degree of negligence of the decedent and reduce the recovery accordingly." *See* 46 U.S.C. § 30304.

6. The federal government plays a significant and wide-spanning role in promoting and ensuring safety in commercial airline operations (see Chapter 6.A., *supra*), through the Federal Aviation Administration, National Transportation Safety Board, and National Aeronautics and Space Association. For example, almost all air traffic controllers are federal employees and some lawsuits involve allegations against flight service stations or air traffic controllers for failure to provide accurate or complete weather information, negligence in facility staffing, or defects in the placement, use, and training associated with radar equipment. *E.g.*, *Spurgin-Dienst v. United States* (7th Cir. 2004); *Airplanes of Boca, Inc. v. United States* (S.D. Fla. 2003); *Alinsky v. United States* (7th Cir. 2006). Whether, where, and in what amount the government can be sued in such circumstances is governed by the Federal Tort Claims Act, 28 U.S.C. § 1346(b) ("FTCA"). *See generally* Rodney Patton, *Sisyphus, the Boulder, and the Choice-of-Law Hill: The Analytical Framework for Resolving the Unusual and Complex Choice-of-Law Issues that Can Arise when the United States is a Party in an Aviation Case*, 71 J. AIR L. & COM. 471 (2006).

While the federal government and its political subdivisions generally are insulated from lawsuits under the doctrine of sovereign immunity, the United States government may be legally accountable in certain circumstances, as seen in *United States v. S.A. Empresa de Viaco Aerea Rio Grandense (Varig Airlines)*, *supra*. Indeed, suits against the United States arise under the FTCA, pursuant to which federal district courts have exclusive jurisdiction of civil actions on claims against the United States for money damages, for injury or loss of property, or personal injury or death caused by the negligent or wrongful act or omission of any government employee acting within the scope of his office or employment of the government, if a private person would be liable to the claimant in accordance with the law of the place where the act or omission occurred.

7. The Federal Tort Claims Act, 28 U.S.C. § 1346(b) ("FTCA"), imposes strict administrative conditions precedent to claims under the FTCA. In order to seek legal redress against the United States, a claimant first must present the claim to the appropriate federal agency and have that claim finally denied by the agency in writing, by certified or registered mail. Only until the applicable federal agency expressly denies a claim or does not make a final disposition of the claim within six (6) months after the claim is filed (the so-called "stale complaint" rule) can a claimant consider its claim finally denied and proceed with litigation. Even then, aviation counsel or claimants must take care that any lawsuit ultimately filed does not seek damages in an amount greater than the amount presented to the federal agency, unless an increase in the damages

sought is based upon newly discovered evidence not reasonably discoverable at the time the claim was presented.

Attorneys' fees are available under the FTCA, meanwhile, but the FTCA prohibits the charge, demand, receipt, or collection of attorney's fees that are in excess of 25 percent of any judgment rendered or settlement reached under the FTCA.

8. The FTCA does not exonerate the United States under the doctrine of sovereign immunity in all circumstances and significant litigation centers on the "discretionary function" exception to the Federal Tort Claims Act ("FTCA"). Rather, the "discretionary function" exception provides that the government is immune from a claim based on a government employee's act or omission, exercising due care, in the execution of a statute of regulation, whether or not the statute or regulation is valid, or based upon the exercise or performance or the failure to exercise or perform a discretionary function or duty on the part of the federal agency or a government employee.

The discretionary function exception consists of a two-part test: first, the challenged conduct must "involve an element of judgment or choice" and second, the "'judgment [must be] of the kind that the discretionary function exception was designed to shield.'" *E.g.*, *Bollinger v. United States* (E.D. Wash. Nov. 20, 2006). The Supreme Court of the United States has reasoned that "[t]he discretionary function exception, embodied in the second clause of § 2680(a), marks the boundary between Congress' willingness to impose tort liability upon the United States and its desire to protect certain governmental activities from exposure to suit by private individuals." *United States v. S.A. Empresa de Viacao Aerea Rio Grandense (Varig Airlines)* (1984), *supra.*

The "discretionary function" exception has been asserted in the post-September 11, 2001 commercial aviation environment. For example, in *Barnes v. United States* (E.D. Tenn. July 18, 2006), an airline passenger sued the United States under the FTCA for damages due to a wrist injury she sustained when preparing to enter airport security. She claimed that Transportation Safety Administration ("TSA") security officers required her to remove her shoes before walking through a metal detector and that because no chair was provided, she lost her balance and fell. The trial court entered summary judgment in the TSA's favor because there was no duty to provide plaintiff with a chair, and no evidence either that the cause in fact of the passenger's injuries was the absence of a chair or that the absence of a chair proximately caused plaintiff's injuries. The *Barnes* court concluded that the TSA bore no duty to provide the plaintiff-passenger with a chair to help her to remove her shows because it was not reasonably foreseeable that passengers would fall and injure themselves while trying to remove shoes at security checkpoints.

9. *Castillo v. Cessna Aircraft Co.* (S.D. Fla. Apr. 26, 2010) introduces the topic of "general" aviation. General aviation aircraft may be defined as airplanes having a maximum seating capacity of fewer than twenty passengers that are not engaged in

regularly scheduled airline operations. General Aviation Revitalization Act of 1994, Pub. L. No. 103-298, § 2(c), 108 Stat. 1552, 1553 (codified at 49 U.S.C. §40101 (2006)). There were 231,607 such aircraft in active use in 2007. *See, e.g.,* GEN. AVIATION MFRS. ASS'N, 2008 GENERAL AVIATION STATISTICAL DATABOOK & INDUSTRY OUTLOOK 28 (2008). In 2008, general aviation aircraft accounted for approximately forty-four percent of all aviation fatalities in the United States. *See* NAT'L TRANSP. SAFETY BD., AVIATION ACCIDENT STATISTICS, at tbl.1, *http://www.ntsb.gov/aviation/stats.htm. See also* A. Mitchell Polinsky & Steven Shavell, *The Uneasy Case for Product Liability*, 123 HARV. L. REV. 1437, 1455-56 & n.68 (2010).

In November 2009, automobile industry executives appeared before Congress to request taxpayer bailout money to survive the Great Recession that began manifested in 2008. They flew to Washington, D.C. in corporate jets, drawing the ire of politicians and citizens alike by perpetuating the perception that equates general aviation with wealth and luxury. To blunt this perception, the National Business Aviation Association ("NBAA") emphasized that "[t]he vast majority of the passengers who fly on a business airplane are salespeople, engineers, technicians, and other mid-level employees." *See generally* Ed Bolen, *Business Aviation is Essential to Local Economies and the National Interest*, Jan. 28, 2009, *http://www.nbaa.org/advocacy/issues/essential/20090128-business-aviation-makes-sense.php. See also Fay Vincent, Corporate Jets and Congress*, WALL ST. J., Nov. 26, 2008, at A13.

10. The General Aviation Revitalization Act ("GARA") discussed in *Castillo v. Cessna Aircraft Co.* (S.D. Fla. Apr. 26, 2010) is the product of many competing business, political, procedural, and equitable considerations. GARA was implemented to rejuvenate the general aviation market in light of litigation costs arising from product liability lawsuits. *See, e.g.*, William J. Woodward, Jr., *The Third Way: Mediation of Products Claims in the Piper Aircraft Trust*, 17 AM. BANKR. INST. L. REV. 463 (2009).

In considering GARA legislation, the United States Senate noted that "[t]he rationale for this time limitation is that general aviation manufacturers should not be exposed to liability for harm caused by their products for an unlimited period of time ... Accidents involving general aviation aircraft which have been in use, for example, 25 years or more, are not likely to be due to any defect in the design or manufacture of the product because the product has operated safely for a long period of time." S. Rep. No. 202, 103d Cong. 1st Sess. (1993).

More specifically, in the mid-1990s Congress was deeply concerned about staggering product liability costs that United States manufacturers of general aviation aircraft confronted. Lawmakers believed that manufacturers were being "driven to the wall," among other things, because of the long tail of liability attached to those aircraft, which could be used for decades after they were first manufactured and sold. *See* H.R. Rep. No. 103-525, pt. I, at 1-4 (1994), *reprinted in* 1994 U.S.C.C.A.N. 1638, 1638-41. In other words, general aviation manufacturers could be sued today for airplanes made many years ago. Accordingly, Congress enacted GARA, which formally is a federal statute of repose that prescribes an 18-year limitation on claims against general aviation aircraft manufacturers of any new component, system, subassembly, or other part of the aircraft, from the time of the first delivery of the airplane, with certain exceptions discussed below.

Four circumstances exist in which GARA's 18-year statute of repose will not bar a claim against a general aviation manufacturer:

- **Misrepresentation.** A claimant will avoid GARA's time-bar upon pleading and proving injuries causally related to a manufacturer's knowing misrepresentation, concealment, or withholding of information that is material and relevant to the performance, maintenance, or operation of an aircraft.

- **Medical or Emergency Treatment.** Under the "air ambulance" exception, a "patient" will not be barred from bringing a claim for injuries sustained while the claimant was a passenger aboard an aircraft while receiving treatment for a medical or "other emergency."

- **Aboard the Aircraft**. GARA will not apply to claimants who were *not* aboard the aircraft at the time of the accident. For example, GARA does not apply to accidents resulting in injury or death to persons on the ground or aboard other aircraft in the event of a mid-air collision.

- **Written Warranty.** Courts will give effect to a written manufacturer's warranty of a product for a definite period of time beyond 18 years from delivery.

PROBLEM

On November 20, 2006, an American Airlines flight attendant was scheduled to work on Flight 1857 departing from Newark Liberty International Airport in New Jersey. She passed through the walk-through magnetometer, but "set it off." After removing her jewelry, the flight attendant passed through the walk-through magnetometer a second time, and again set it off. She was then directed to undergo an individual inspection performed by a Transportation Security Administration ("TSA") employee with a handheld magnetometer, or hand-wand.

An employee of the TSA performed the individual inspection in what the flight attendant described as a "physically invasive, abusive and harassing" manner. Specifically, she alleged that the TSA employee:

1. Placed her hands along Ms. Coulter's breasts with the palm of her hand, with significant pressure;

2. Instructed Ms. Coulter to undo her belt;

3. Placed her hands inside the waistband of Ms. Coulter's skirt and against her stomach;

4. Asked Ms. Coulter to put one foot forward, in essentially a lunge position, and then placed the hand-wand directly on Ms. Coulter's skin, starting at her ankle, with great force; and

5. Gradually moved the hand-wand up against Ms. Coulter's body, forcefully all the way up her leg, and then forcefully shoved the hand-wand into Ms. Coulter's groin/private area.

In February, 2007, the flight attendant's attorney sent to the TSA a Claim of Damage, Injury or Death form, describing the incident and demanding $50,000 to settle the claim. Ms. Coulter initiated a lawsuit against the TSA and its employee over six months later for sexual harassment, sexual assault, assault, and battery, together with common law causes of action for intentional infliction of emotional distress, and negligent infliction of emotional distress. The TSA moved to dismiss the lawsuit. Should the motion be denied and, if so, upon what grounds? *See Coulter v. United States* (D.N.J. Sept. 24, 2008).

C. INTERNATIONAL LIABILITY TREATIES

In the early days of commercial airline travel, nations around the world created a system to limit airline accident liability in order to allow the extremely fragile industry to grow. Specifically, in 1929, the United States signed the international treaty known as the Warsaw Convention to create a uniform body of rules governing international air liability. The Warsaw Convention generally favored commercial airline interests. However, as commercial international air travel became more routine, the need to ensure the protection of consumers in international travel by air and for equitable compensation based on the principles of restitution increased. Accordingly, in 1999, the Montreal Convention was adopted (including in the United States several years later). The cases and materials below explore the claims and defenses available under international treatises generally applicable to international aviation accidents.

EL AL ISRAEL AIRLINES, LTD. v. TSENG

525 U.S. 155 (1999)

Justice GINSBURG delivered the opinion of the Court.

Plaintiff-respondent Tsui Yuan Tseng was subjected to an intrusive security search at John F. Kennedy International Airport in New York before she boarded an El Al Israel Airlines May 22, 1993 flight to Tel Aviv. Tseng seeks tort damages from El Al for this occurrence.

The episode-in-suit does not qualify as an "accident" within the meaning of the treaty popularly known as the Warsaw Convention, which governs air carrier liability for "all international transportation." Convention for the Unification of Certain Rules Relating to International Transportation by Air, Oct. 12, 1929. Tseng alleges psychic or psychosomatic injuries, but no "bodily injury," as that term is used in the Convention. Her case presents a question of the Convention's exclusivity: When the Convention allows no recovery for the episode-in-suit, does it correspondingly preclude the passenger from maintaining an action for damages under another source of law, in this case, New York tort law?

The exclusivity question before us has been settled prospectively in a Warsaw Convention protocol (Montreal Protocol No. 4) recently ratified by the Senate. Montreal Protocol No. 4 to Amend the Convention for the Unification of Certain Rules Relating to International Carriage By Air, signed at Warsaw on October 12, 1929, as amended by the Protocol Done at the Hague on September 8, 1955 ("Montreal Protocol No. 4"), *reprinted in* S. Exec. Rep. No. 105-20, pp. 21-32 (1998). In accord with the protocol, Tseng concedes, a passenger whose injury is not compensable under the Convention (because it entails no "bodily injury" or was not the result of an "accident") will have no recourse to an alternate remedy. We conclude that the protocol, to which the United States has now subscribed, clarifies, but does not change, the Convention's exclusivity domain. We therefore hold that recovery for a personal injury suffered "on board [an] aircraft or in the course of any of the operations of embarking or disembarking," Art. 17, 49 Stat. 3018, if not allowed under the Convention, is not available at all.

I.

At the outset, we highlight key provisions of the treaty we are interpreting. Chapter I of the Warsaw Convention, entitled "SCOPE-DEFINITIONS," declares in Article 1(1) that the "[C]onvention shall apply to all international transportation of persons, baggage, or goods performed by aircraft for hire." Chapter III, entitled "LIABILITY OF THE CARRIER," defines in Articles 17, 18, and 19 the three kinds of liability for which the Convention provides. Article 17 establishes the conditions of liability for personal injury to passengers:

> The carrier shall be liable for damage sustained in the event of the death or wounding of a passenger or any other bodily injury suffered by a passenger, if the accident which caused the damage so sustained took place on board the aircraft or in the course of any of the operations of embarking or disembarking.

Article 18 establishes the conditions of liability for damage to baggage or goods. Article 18 provides, in relevant part:

> The carrier shall be liable for damage sustained in the event of the destruction or loss of, or of damage to, any checked baggage or any goods, if the occurrence which caused the damage so sustained took place during the transportation by air.

Article 19 establishes the conditions of liability for damage caused by delay. *Id.* Article 19 provides, "[t]he carrier shall be liable for damage occasioned by delay in the transportation by air of passengers, baggage, or goods." Article 24, referring back to Articles 17, 18, and 19, instructs:

> In the cases covered by articles 18 and 19 any action for damages, however founded, can only be brought subject to the conditions and limits set out in this convention.
>
> In the cases covered by article 17 the provisions of the preceding paragraph shall also apply, without prejudice to the questions as to who are the persons who have the right to bring suit and what are their respective rights.

Chapter III of the Convention sets forth a number of other rules governing air carrier liability. Among these, Article 20 relieves a carrier of liability if it has "taken all necessary measures to avoid the damage." Article 22 sets monetary limits on a carrier's liability for harm to passengers and baggage. Article 23 invalidates "[a]ny [contract] provision tending to relieve the carrier of liability or to fix a lower limit than that which is laid down in th[e] [C]onvention." Article 25(1) renders the Convention's limits on liability inapplicable if the damage is caused by a carrier's "willful misconduct."

II.

On May 22, 1993, Tsui Yuan Tseng arrived at John F. Kennedy International Airport ("JFK") to board an El Al Israel Airlines flight to Tel Aviv. In conformity with standard El Al preboarding procedures, a security guard questioned Tseng about her destination and travel plans. The guard considered Tseng's responses "illogical," and ranked her as a "high risk" passenger. Tseng was taken to a private security room where her baggage and person were searched for explosives and detonating devices. She was told to remove her shoes, jacket, and sweater, and to lower her blue jeans to midhip. A female security guard searched Tseng's body outside her clothes by hand with an electronic security wand.

After the search, which lasted 15 minutes, El Al personnel decided that Tseng did not pose a security threat and allowed her to board the flight. Tseng later testified that she "was really sick and very upset" during the flight, that she was "emotionally traumatized and disturbed" during her month-long trip in Israel, and that, upon her return, she underwent medical and psychiatric treatment for the lingering effects of the body search.

Tseng filed suit against El Al in 1994 in a New York state court of first instance. Her complaint alleged a state-law personal injury claim based on the May 22, 1993 episode at JFK. Tseng's pleading charged, inter alia, assault and false imprisonment, but alleged no bodily injury.

III.

We accept it as given that El Al's search of Tseng was not an "accident" within the meaning of Article 17, for the parties do not place that Court of Appeals conclusion at issue. We also accept, again only for purposes of this decision, that El Al's actions did not constitute "willful misconduct"; accordingly, we confront no issue under Article 25 of the Convention. The parties do not dispute that the episode-in-suit occurred in international transportation in the course of embarking.

Our inquiry begins with the text of Article 24, which prescribes the exclusivity of the Convention's provisions for air carrier liability. "[I]t is our responsibility to give the specific words of the treaty a meaning consistent with the shared expectations of the contracting parties." "Because a treaty ratified by the United States is not only the law of this land, *see* U.S. Const., Art. II, § 2, but also an agreement among sovereign powers, we have traditionally considered as aids to its interpretation the negotiating and drafting history (travaux préparatoires) and the postratification understanding of the contracting parties."

Article 24 provides that "cases covered by article 17"—or in the governing French text, "les cas prévus à l'àrticle 17"—may "only be brought subject to the conditions and limits set out in th[e] [C]onvention." That prescription is not a model of the clear drafter's art. We recognize that the words lend themselves to divergent interpretation. In Tseng's view, and in the view of the Court of Appeals, "les cas prévus à l'àrticle 17" means those cases in which a passenger could actually maintain a claim for relief under Article 17. So read, Article 24 would permit any passenger whose personal injury suit did not satisfy the liability conditions of Article 17 to pursue the claim under local law.

In El Al's view, on the other hand, and in the view of the United States as *amicus curiae*, "les cas prévus à l'àrticle 17" refers generically to all personal injury cases stemming from occurrences on board an aircraft or in embarking or disembarking, and simply distinguishes that class of cases (Article 17 cases) from cases involving damaged luggage or goods, or delay (which Articles 18 and 19 address). So read, Article 24 would preclude a passenger from asserting any air transit personal injury claims under local law, including claims that failed to satisfy Article 17's liability conditions, notably, because the injury did not result from an "accident," or because the "accident" did not result in physical injury or physical manifestation of injury.

Respect is ordinarily due the reasonable views of the Executive Branch concerning the meaning of an international treaty. We conclude that the Government's construction of Article 24 is most faithful to the Convention's text, purpose, and overall structure.

A.

The cardinal purpose of the Warsaw Convention is to "achiev[e] uniformity of rules governing claims arising from international air transportation." The Convention signatories, in the treaty's preamble, specifically "recognized the advantage of regulating in a uniform manner the conditions of ... the liability of the carrier." To provide the desired uniformity, Chapter III of the Convention sets out an array of liability rules which, the treaty declares, "apply to all international transportation of persons, baggage, or goods performed by aircraft."

In that Chapter, the Convention describes and defines the three areas of air carrier liability (personal injuries in Article 17, baggage or goods loss, destruction, or damage in Article 18, and damage occasioned by delay in Article 19), the conditions exempting air carriers from liability (Article 20), the monetary limits of liability (Article 22), and the circumstances in which air carriers may not limit liability (Articles 23 and 25). Given the Convention's comprehensive scheme of liability rules and its textual emphasis on uniformity, we would be hard put to conclude that the delegates at Warsaw meant to subject air carriers to the distinct, non-uniform liability rules of the individual signatory nations.

A complementary purpose of the Convention is to accommodate or balance the interests of passengers seeking recovery for personal injuries, and the interests of air carriers seeking to limit potential liability. Before the Warsaw accord, injured passengers could file suits for damages, subject only to the limitations of the forum's laws, including the forum's choice-of-law regime. This exposure inhibited the growth of the then-fledgling international airline industry. Many international air carriers at that time endeavored to require passengers, as a condition of air travel, to relieve or reduce the carrier's liability in case of injury. The Convention drafters designed Articles 17, 22, and 24 of the Convention as a compromise between the interests of air carriers and their customers worldwide. In Article 17 of the Convention, carriers are denied the contractual prerogative to exclude or limit their liability for personal injury. In Articles 22 and 24, passengers are limited in the amount of damages they may recover, and are restricted in the claims they may pursue by the conditions and limits set out in the Convention.

Construing the Convention to allow passengers to pursue claims under local law when the Convention does not permit recovery could produce several anomalies. Carriers might be exposed to unlimited liability under diverse legal regimes, but would be prevented, under the treaty, from contracting out of such liability. Passengers injured physically in an emergency landing might be subject to the liability caps of the Convention, while those merely traumatized in the same mishap would be free to sue outside of the Convention for potentially unlimited damages.

B.

The drafting history of Article 17 is consistent with our understanding of the preemptive effect of the Convention. The preliminary draft of the Convention submitted to the conference at Warsaw made air carriers liable "in the case of death, wounding, or any other bodily injury suffered by a traveler." In the later draft that prescribed what is now Article 17, airline liability was narrowed to encompass only bodily injury caused by an "accident." It is improbable that, at the same time the drafters narrowed the conditions of air carrier liability in Article 17, they intended, in Article 24, to permit passengers to skirt those conditions by pursuing claims under local law. Sir Alfred Dennis of Great Britain stated at the Warsaw Conference that Article 24 is "a very important stipulation which touches the very substance of the Convention, because [it] excludes recourse to common law."

C.

Montreal Protocol No. 4, ratified by the Senate on September 28, 1998, amends Article 24 to read, in relevant part: "In the carriage of passengers and baggage, any action for damages, however founded, can only be brought subject to the conditions and limits set out in this Convention." Article 24, as amended by Montreal Protocol No. 4, provides:

> In the carriage of passengers and baggage, any action for damages, however founded, can only be brought subject to the conditions and limits set out in this Convention, without prejudice to the question as to who are the persons who have the right to bring suit and what are their respective rights.
>
> In the carriage of cargo, any action for damages, however founded, whether under this Convention or in contract or in tort or otherwise, can only be brought subject to the

> conditions and limits of liability set out in this Convention without prejudice to the question as to who are the persons who have the right to bring suit and what are their respective rights.
>
> Such limits of liability constitute maximum limits and may not be exceeded whatever the circumstances which gave rise to the liability.

Both parties agree that, under the amended Article 24, the Convention's preemptive effect is clear: The treaty precludes passengers from bringing actions under local law when they cannot establish air carrier liability under the treaty. Revised Article 24, El Al urges and we agree, merely clarifies, it does not alter, the Convention's rule of exclusivity. Supporting the position that revised Article 24 provides for preemption not earlier established, Tseng urges that federal preemption of state law is disfavored generally, and particularly when matters of health and safety are at stake. Tseng overlooks in this regard that the nation-state, not subdivisions within one nation, is the focus of the Convention and the perspective of our treaty partners. Our home-centered preemption analysis, therefore, should not be applied, mechanically, in construing our international obligations.

Decisions of the courts of other Convention signatories corroborate our understanding of the Convention's preemptive effect. The British House of Lords considered and decided the very question we now face concerning the Convention's exclusivity when a passenger alleges psychological damages, but no physical injury, resulting from an occurrence that is not an "accident" under Article 17.

Reviewing the text, structure, and drafting history of the Convention, the Lords concluded that the Convention was designed to "ensure that, in all questions relating to the carrier's liability, it is the provisions of the [C]onvention which apply and that the passenger does not have access to any other remedies, whether under the common law or otherwise, which may be available within the particular country where he chooses to raise his action." Courts of other nations bound by the Convention have also recognized the treaty's encompassing preemptive effect. The "opinions of our sister signatories," we have observed, are "entitled to considerable weight." The text, drafting history, and underlying purpose of the Convention, in sum, counsel us to adhere to a view of the treaty's exclusivity shared by our treaty partners.

For the reasons stated, we hold that the Warsaw Convention precludes a passenger from maintaining an action for personal injury damages under local law when her claim does not satisfy the conditions for liability under the Convention.

Justice STEVENS, dissenting.

I agree with the Court that the drafters of the Convention intended that the treaty largely supplant local law. The Convention, however, does not preempt local law in cases arising out of "willful misconduct." Article 25 expressly provides that a carrier shall not be entitled to avail itself of the provisions of the Convention that "exclude or limit" its liability if its misconduct is willful. Moreover, the question whether the carrier's wrongful act "is considered to be equivalent to willful misconduct" is determined by "the law of the court to which the case is submitted." Accordingly, the vast majority of the potential claims by passengers against international air carriers are either preempted by Article 24 or unequivocally governed by local law under Article 25.

Putting these cases aside, we are left with a narrow sliver of incidents involving personal injury that arise neither from an accident nor willful misconduct. Although the drafters of the treaty may not have realized that any such cases might arise, our construction of the term "accident" in *Air France v. Saks* had the effect of either recognizing or creating this narrow band of cases. Frankly, I am not persuaded that this case belongs in this interstitial niche because I believe it should have been resolved by determining that petitioner's alleged misconduct was either an accident within the meaning of Article 17, or involved willfulness as a matter of local law. Be that as it may, the parties have insisted that we decide the case on the assumption that it belongs in the sliver about which the treaty is silent.

The interest in uniformity would not be significantly impaired if the number of cases not preempted, like those involving willful misconduct, was slightly enlarged to encompass those relatively rare cases in which the injury resulted from neither an accident nor a willful wrong. That the interest in uniformity is accommodated in one category of cases but not the other simply raises, without resolving, the question whether the drafters of the treaty intended to treat personal injury non-accident cases as though they involved accidents. A plaintiff in such a case, unlike those injured by an accident, receives no benefit from the treaty, and normally should not have a claim that is valid under local law preempted, unless the treaty expressly requires that result.

Everyone agrees that the literal text of the treaty does not preempt claims of personal injury that do not arise out of an accident. It is equally clear that nothing in the drafting history requires that result. On the contrary, the amendment to the title of the Convention made in response to the proposal advanced by the Czechoslovak delegation suggests that the parties assumed that local law would apply to all nonaccident cases. I agree with the Court that that inference is not strong enough, in itself, to require that the ambiguity be resolved in the plaintiff's favor. It suffices for me, however, that the history is just as ambiguous as the text. I firmly believe that a treaty, like an Act of Congress, should not be construed to preempt state law unless its intent to do so is clear. For this reason, I respectfully dissent.

AIR FRANCE v. SAKS

470 U.S. 1338 (1985)

Justice O'CONNOR delivered the opinion of the Court.

Article 17 of the Warsaw Convention makes air carriers liable for injuries sustained by a passenger "if the accident which caused the damage so sustained took place on board the aircraft or in the course of any of the operations of embarking or disembarking." We granted *certiorari* to resolve a conflict among the Courts of Appeals as to the proper definition of the word "accident" as used in this international air carriage treaty.

I.

On November 16, 1980, respondent Valerie Saks boarded an Air France jetliner in Paris for a 12-hour flight to Los Angeles. The flight went smoothly in all respects until, as the aircraft descended to Los Angeles, Saks felt severe pressure and pain in her left ear. The pain continued after the plane landed, but Saks disembarked without informing any Air France crew member or employee of her ailment. Five days later, Saks consulted a doctor who concluded that she had become permanently deaf in her left ear.

Saks filed suit against Air France in California state court, alleging that her hearing loss was caused by negligent maintenance and operation of the jetliner's pressurization system. The case was removed to the United States District Court for the Central District of California. After extensive discovery, Air France moved for summary judgment on the ground that respondent could not prove that her injury was caused by an "accident" within the meaning of the Warsaw Convention.

The term "accident," according to Air France, means an "abnormal, unusual or unexpected occurrence aboard the aircraft." All the available evidence, including the post-flight reports, pilot's affidavit, and passenger testimony, indicated that the aircraft's pressurization system had operated in the usual manner. Accordingly, the airline contended that the suit should be dismissed because the only alleged cause of respondent's injury—normal operation of a pressurization system—could not qualify as an "accident." In her opposition to the summary judgment motion, Saks acknowledged that "[t]he sole question of law presented ... by the parties is whether a loss of hearing proximately caused by normal operation of the aircraft's pressurization system is an "accident" within the meaning of Article 17 of the Warsaw Convention ..." She argued that "accident" should be defined as a "hazard of air travel," and that her injury had indeed been caused by such a hazard.

Relying on precedent which defines the term "accident" in Article 17 as an "unusual or unexpected" happening, the District Court granted summary judgment to Air France. A divided panel of the Court of Appeals for the Ninth Circuit reversed. The appellate court reviewed the history of the Warsaw Convention and its modification by the 1966 Montreal Agreement, a private agreement among airlines that has been approved by the United States Government. The court concluded that the language, history, and policy of the Warsaw Convention and the Montreal Agreement impose absolute liability on airlines for injuries proximately caused by the risks inherent in air travel. The court found a definition of "accident" consistent with this history and policy in Annex 13 to the Convention on International Civil Aviation: "an occurrence associated with the operation of an aircraft which takes place between the time any person boards the aircraft with the intention of flight and all such persons have disembarked." Normal cabin pressure changes qualify as an "accident" under this definition. A dissent agreed with the District Court that "accident" should be defined as an unusual or unexpected occurrence. We disagree with the definition of "accident" adopted by the Court of Appeals, and we reverse.

II.

Air France is liable to a passenger under the terms of the Warsaw Convention only if the passenger proves that an "accident" was the cause of her injury. The narrow issue presented is whether respondent can meet this burden by showing that her injury was caused by the normal operation of the aircraft's pressurization system. The proper answer turns on interpretation of a clause in an international treaty to which the United States is a party. "[T]reaties are construed more liberally than private agreements, and to ascertain their meaning we may look beyond the written words to the history of the treaty, the negotiations, and the practical construction adopted by the parties." The analysis must begin, however, with the text of the treaty and the context in which the written words are used.

A.

Article 17 of the Warsaw Convention establishes the liability of international air carriers for harm to passengers. Article 18 contains parallel provisions regarding liability for damage to baggage. The governing text of the Convention is in the French language.

Two significant features of these provisions stand out in both the French and the English texts. First, Article 17 imposes liability for injuries to passengers caused by an "accident" whereas Article 18 imposes liability for destruction or loss of baggage caused by an "occurrence." This difference in the parallel language of Articles 17 and 18 implies that the drafters of the Convention understood the word "accident" to mean something different than the word "occurrence," for they otherwise logically would have used the same word in each article. The language of the Convention accordingly renders suspect the opinion of the Court of Appeals that "accident" means "occurrence."

Second, the text of Article 17 refers to an accident which caused the passenger's injury, and not to an accident which is the passenger's injury. In light of the many senses in which the word "accident" can be used, this distinction is significant. As Lord Lindley observed in 1903:

> The word "accident" is not a technical legal term with a clearly defined meaning. Speaking generally, but with reference to legal liabilities, an accident means any unintended and unexpected occurrence which produces hurt or loss. But it is often used to denote any unintended and unexpected loss or hurt apart from its cause; and if the cause is not known the loss or hurt itself would certainly be called an accident. The word "accident" is also often used to denote both the cause and the effect, no attempt being made to discriminate between them."

In Article 17, the drafters of the Warsaw Convention apparently did make an attempt to discriminate between "the cause and the effect"; they specified that air carriers would be liable if an accident caused the passenger's injury. The text of the Convention thus implies that, however we define "accident," it is the cause of the injury that must satisfy the definition rather than the occurrence of the injury alone. American jurisprudence has long recognized this distinction between an accident that is the cause of an injury and an injury that is itself an accident.

While the text of the Convention gives these two clues to the meaning of "accident," it does not define the term. Nor is the context in which the term is used illuminating. To determine the meaning of the term "accident" in Article 17 we must consider its French legal meaning. This is true not because "we are forever chained to French law" by the Convention, *see Rosman v. Trans World Airlines, Inc.* (N.Y. Ct. App. 1974), but because it is our responsibility to give the specific words of the treaty a meaning consistent with the shared expectations of the contracting parties. We look to the French legal meaning for guidance as to these expectations because the Warsaw Convention was drafted in French by continental jurists.

A survey of French cases and dictionaries indicates that the French legal meaning of the term "accident" differs little from the meaning of the term in Great Britain, Germany, or the United States. Thus, while the word "accident" is often used to refer to the event of a person's injury, it is also sometimes used to describe a cause of injury, and when the word is used in this latter sense, it is usually defined as a fortuitous, unexpected, unusual, or unintended event. This parallels British and American jurisprudence. The text of the Convention consequently suggests that the passenger's injury must be caused by an unexpected or unusual event.

B.

This interpretation of Article 17 is consistent with the negotiating history of the Convention, the conduct of the parties to the Convention, and the weight of precedent in foreign and American courts. In interpreting a treaty it is proper, of course, to refer to the records of its drafting and negotiation. In part because the "travaux preparatoires" of the Warsaw Convention are published and generally available to litigants, courts frequently refer to these materials to resolve ambiguities in the text.

The treaty that became the Warsaw Convention was first drafted at an international conference in Paris in 1925. The protocol resulting from the Parish Conference contained an article specifying: "The carrier is liable for accidents, losses, breakdowns, and delays. It is not liable if it can prove that it has taken reasonable measures designed to pre-empt damage ..." The protocol drafted at Paris was revised several times by a committee of experts on air law, and then submitted to a second international conference that convened in Warsaw in 1929. The draft submitted to the conference stated:

> The carrier shall be liable for damage sustained during carriage: (a) in the case of death, wounding, or any other bodily injury suffered by a traveler; (b) in the case of destruction, loss, or damage to goods or baggage; (c) in the case of delay suffered by a traveler, goods, or baggage.

Article 22 of this draft, like the original Paris draft, permitted the carrier to avoid liability by proving it had taken reasonable measures to avoid the damage. None of the early drafts required that an accident cause the passenger's injury.

At Warsaw, delegates from several nations objected to the application of identical liability rules to both passenger injuries and damage to baggage, and the German delegation proposed separate liability rules for passengers and baggage. The need for separate rules arose primarily because delegates thought that liability for baggage should commence upon delivery to the carrier, whereas liability for passengers should commence when the passengers later embark upon the aircraft. The Reporter on the Preliminary Draft of the Convention argued it would be too difficult to draft language specifying this distinction, and that such a distinction would be unnecessary because "Article 22 establishes a very mitigated system of liability for the carrier, and from the moment that the carrier has taken the reasonable measures, he does not answer for the risks, nor for the accidents occur[r]ing to people by the fault of third parties, nor for accidents occur [r]ing for any other cause." The delegates were unpersuaded, and a majority voted to have a drafting committee rework the liability provisions for passengers and baggage.

A few days later, the drafting committee proposed the liability provisions that became Articles 17 and 18 of the Convention. Article 20(1) of the final draft contains the "necessary measures" language which the Reporter believed would shield the carrier from liability for "the accidents occur[r]ing to people by the fault of third parties" and for "accidents occur[r]ing for any other cause." Nevertheless, the redrafted Article 17 also required as a prerequisite to liability that an accident cause the passenger's injury, whereas the redrafted Article 18 required only that an occurrence cause the damage to baggage.

Although Article 17 and Article 18 as redrafted were approved with little discussion, the President of the drafting committee observed that "given that there are entirely different liability cases: death or wounding, disappearance of goods, delay, we have deemed that it would be better to begin by setting out the causes of liability for persons, then for goods and baggage, and finally liability in the case of delay." This comment at least implies that the addition of language of causation to Articles 17 and 18 had a broader purpose than specification of the time at which liability commenced. It further suggests that the causes of liability for persons were intended to be different from the causes of liability for baggage. The records of the negotiation of the Convention accordingly support what is evident from its text: "A passenger's injury must be caused by an accident, and an accident must mean something different than an 'occurrence' on the plane." Like the text of the Convention, however, the records of its negotiation offer no precise definition of "accident." Reference to the conduct of the parties to the Convention and the subsequent interpretations of the signatories helps clarify the meaning of the term.

At a Guatemala City International Conference on Air Law in 1971, representatives of many of the Warsaw signatories approved an amendment to Article 17 which would impose liability on the carrier for an "event which caused the death or injury" rather than for an "accident which caused" the passenger's injury, but would exempt the carrier from liability if the death or injury resulted "solely from the state of health of the passenger." The Guatemala City Protocol of 1971 and the Montreal Protocols Nos. 3 and 4 of 1975 include this amendment, but have yet to be ratified by the Senate, and therefore do not govern the disposition of this case. The statements of the delegates at Guatemala City indicate that they viewed the switch from "accident" to "event" as expanding the scope of carrier liability to passengers. The Swedish Delegate, for example, in referring to the choice between the words "accident" and "event," emphasized that the word "accident" is too narrow because a carrier might be found liable for "other acts which could not be considered as accidents."

In determining precisely what causes can be considered accidents, we "find the opinions of our sister signatories to be entitled to considerable weight." *Benjamins v. British European Airways* (2d Cir. 1979). While few decisions are precisely on point, we note that, in *Air France v. Haddad*, Judgment of June 19, 1979, Cour d'appel de Paris, Première Chambre Civile, 1979 Revue Francaise de Droit Aérien, at 328, a French court observed that the term "accident" in Article 17 of the Warsaw Convention embraces causes of injuries that are fortuitous or unpredictable.

European legal scholars have generally construed the word "accident" in Article 17 to require that the passenger's injury be caused by a sudden or unexpected event other than the normal operation of the plane. *See, e.g.*, O. RIESE & LACOUR, PRÉCIS DE DROIT AÉRIEN 264 (1951) (noting that Swiss and German law require that the damage be caused by an accident, and arguing that an accident should be construed as an event which is sudden and independent of the will of the carrier); 1 C. SHAWCROSS & K. BEAUMONT, AIR LAW ¶ VII(148) (4th ed. 1984) (noting that the Court of Appeals for the Third Circuit's definition of accident accords with some English definitions and "might well commend itself to an English court"). These observations are in accord with American decisions which, while interpreting the term "accident" broadly nevertheless refuse to extend the term to cover routine travel procedures that produce an injury due to the peculiar internal condition of a passenger.

III.

We conclude that liability under Article 17 of the Warsaw Convention arises only if a passenger's injury is caused by an unexpected or unusual event or happening that is external to the passenger. This definition should be flexibly applied after assessment of all the circumstances surrounding a passenger's injuries. For example, lower courts in this country have interpreted Article 17 broadly enough to encompass torts committed by terrorists or fellow passengers. In cases where there is contradictory evidence, it is for the trier of fact to decide whether an "accident" as here defined caused the passenger's injury. But when the injury indisputably results from the passenger's own internal reaction to the usual, normal, and expected operation of the aircraft, it has not been caused by an accident, and Article 17 of the Warsaw Convention cannot apply. The judgment of the Court of Appeals in this case must accordingly be reversed. We recognize that any standard requiring courts to distinguish causes that are "accidents" from causes that are "occurrences" requires drawing a line, and we realize that "reasonable [people] may differ widely as to the place where the line should fall."

We draw this line today only because the language of Articles 17 and 18 requires it, and not because of any desire to plunge into the "Serbonian bog" that accompanies attempts to distinguish between causes that are accidents and injuries that are accidents. Any injury is the product of a chain of causes, and we require only that the passenger be able to prove that some link in the chain was an unusual or unexpected event external to the passenger. Until Article 17 of the Warsaw Convention is changed by the signatories, it cannot be stretched to impose carrier liability for injuries that are not caused by accidents. It remains "[o]ur duty ...to enforce the ...treaties of the United States, whatever they might be, and ...the Warsaw Convention remains the supreme law of the land." The judgment of the Court of Appeals is reversed, and the case is remanded for further proceedings consistent with this opinion.

OLYMPIC AIRWAYS v. HUSAIN

540 U.S. 644 (2003)

Justice THOMAS delivered the opinion of the Court.

Article 17 of the Warsaw Convention ("Convention") imposes liability on an air carrier for a passenger's death or bodily injury caused by an "accident" that occurred in connection with an international flight. In *Air France v. Saks* (1985), the Court explained that the term "accident" in the Convention refers to an "unexpected or unusual event or happening that is external to the passenger," and not to "the passenger's own internal reaction to the usual, normal, and expected operation of the aircraft. The issue we must decide is whether the "accident" condition precedent to air carrier liability under Article 17 is satisfied when the carrier's unusual and unexpected refusal to assist a passenger is a link in a chain of causation resulting in a passenger's pre-existing medical condition being aggravated by exposure to a normal condition in the aircraft cabin. We conclude that it is.

I.

In December 1997, Dr. Abid Hanson and his wife, Rubina Husain (hereinafter respondent), traveled with their children and another family from San Francisco to Athens and Cairo for a family vacation. During a stopover in New York, Dr. Hanson learned for the first time that petitioner allowed its passengers to smoke on international flights. Because Dr. Hanson had suffered from asthma and was sensitive to secondhand smoke, respondent requested and obtained seats away from the smoking section. Dr. Hanson experienced no problems on the flights to Cairo.

For the return flights, Dr. Hanson and respondent arrived early at the Cairo airport in order to request nonsmoking seats. Respondent showed the check-in agent a physician's letter explaining that Dr. Hanson "has [a] history of recurrent anaphylactic reactions," and asked the agent to ensure that their seats were in the nonsmoking section. The flight to Athens was uneventful. After boarding the plane for the flight to San Francisco, Dr. Hanson and respondent discovered that their seats were located only three rows in front of the economy-class smoking section. Respondent advised Maria Leptourgou, a flight attendant for petitioner, that Dr. Hanson could not sit in a smoking area, and said, "'You have to move him.'" The flight attendant told her to "'have a seat.'" After all the passengers had boarded but prior to takeoff, respondent again asked Ms. Leptourgou to move Dr. Hanson, explaining that he was "'allergic to smoke.'" Ms. Leptourgou replied that she could not reseat Dr. Hanson because the plane was "'totally full'" and she was "too busy" to help.

Shortly after takeoff, passengers in the smoking section began to smoke, and Dr. Hanson was soon surrounded by ambient cigarette smoke. Respondent spoke with Ms. Leptourgou a third time, stating, "'You have to move my husband from here.'" Ms.

Leptourgou again refused, stating that the plane was full. Ms. Leptourgou told respondent that Dr. Hanson could switch seats with another passenger, but that respondent would have to ask other passengers herself, without the flight crew's assistance. Respondent told Ms. Leptourgou that Dr. Hanson had to move even if the only available seat was in the cockpit or in business class, but Ms. Leptourgou refused to provide any assistance. Dr. Hanson and respondent did not know at the time that, despite Ms. Leptourgou's representations, the flight was actually not full. There were 11 unoccupied passenger seats, most of which were in economy class, and 28 "non-revenue passengers," 15 of whom were seated in economy class rows farther away from the smoking section than Dr. Hanson's seat.

About two hours into the flight, the smoking noticeably increased in the rows behind Dr. Hanson. Dr. Hanson asked respondent for a new inhaler because the one he had been using was empty. Dr. Hanson then moved toward the front of the plane to get some fresher air. While he was leaning against a chair near the galley area, Dr. Hanson gestured to respondent to get his emergency kit. Respondent returned with it and gave him a shot of epinephrine. She then awoke Dr. Umesh Sabharwal, an allergist, with whom Dr. Hanson and respondent had been traveling. Dr. Sabharwal gave Dr. Hanson another shot of epinephrine and began to administer CPR and oxygen. Dr. Hanson died shortly thereafter. (For religious reasons, no autopsy was performed to determine the cause of death.)

Respondents filed a wrongful-death suit in California state court. Petitioner removed the case to federal court, and the District Court found petitioner liable for Dr. Hanson's death. The District Court held that Ms. Leptourgou's refusal to reseat Dr. Hanson constituted an "accident" within the meaning of Article 17. Applying *Saks*' definition of that term, the court reasoned that the flight attendant's conduct was external to Dr. Hanson and, because it was in "blatant disregard of industry standards and airline policies," was not expected or usual. The Ninth Circuit affirmed. Applying *Saks'* definition of "accident," the Ninth Circuit agreed that the flight attendant's refusal to reseat Dr. Hanson "was clearly external to Dr. Hanson, and it was unexpected and unusual in light of industry standards, Olympic policy, and the simple nature of Dr. Hanson's requested accommodation." We granted *certiorari* and now affirm.

II.

A.

We begin with the language of Article 17 of the Convention, which provides:

> The carrier shall be liable for damage sustained in the event of the death or wounding of a passenger or any other bodily injury suffered by a passenger, if the accident which caused the damage so sustained took place on board the aircraft or

> in the course of any of the operations of embarking or disembarking.

The Warsaw Convention's governing text is in French. We cite to the official English translation of the Convention, which was before the Senate when it consented to ratification of the Convention in 1934.

After a plaintiff has established a *prima facie* case of liability under Article 17 by showing that the injury was caused by an "accident," the air carrier has the opportunity to prove under Article 20 that it took "all necessary measures to avoid the damage or that it was impossible for [the airline] to take such measures." Thus, Article 17 creates a presumption of air carrier liability and shifts the burden to the air carrier to prove lack of negligence under Article 20. Article 22(1) caps the amount recoverable under Article 17 in the event of death or bodily injury, and Article 25(1) removes the cap if the damage is caused by the "willful misconduct" of the airline or its agent, acting within the scope of his employment. Additionally, Article 21 enables an air carrier to avoid or reduce its liability if it can prove the passenger's comparative negligence.

In *Saks*, the Court recognized that the text of the Convention does not define the term "accident" and that the context in which it is used is not "illuminating." The Court nevertheless discerned the meaning of the term "accident" from the Convention's text, structure, and history as well as from the subsequent conduct of the parties to the Convention.

Neither party here contests *Saks'* definition of the term "accident" under Article 17 of the Convention. Rather, the parties differ as to which event should be the focus of the "accident" inquiry. The Court's reasoning in *Saks* sheds light on whether the flight attendant's refusal to assist a passenger in a medical crisis is the proper focus of the "accident" inquiry. In *Saks*, the Court addressed whether a passenger's "'loss of hearing proximately caused by normal operation of the aircraft's pressurization system'" was an "'accident.'" The Court concluded that it was not, because the injury was her "own internal reaction" to the normal pressurization of the aircraft's cabin. The Court noted two textual clues to the meaning of the term "accident."

First, the Convention distinguishes between liability under Article 17 for death or injuries to passengers caused by an "accident" and liability under Article 18 for destruction or loss of baggage caused by an "occurrence." The difference in these provisions implies that the meaning of the term "accident" is different from that of "occurrence."

Second, the Court found significant the fact that Article 17 focuses on the "accident which caused" the passenger's injury and not an accident that is the passenger's injury. The Court explained that it is the cause of the injury-rather than the occurrence of the injury-that must satisfy the definition of "accident." And recognizing the Court's responsibility to read the treaty in a manner "consistent with the shared expectations of the contracting parties," the Court also looked to the French legal meaning of the term "accident," which when used to describe the cause of an injury, is usually defined as a "fortuitous, unexpected, unusual, or unintended event." Accordingly, the Court held in *Saks* that an "accident" under Article 17 is "an unexpected or unusual event or happening that is external to the passenger," and not "the passenger's own internal reaction to the usual, normal, and expected operation of the aircraft."

The Court emphasized that the definition of "accident" "should be flexibly applied after assessment of all the circumstances surrounding a passenger's injuries." The Court further contemplated that intentional conduct could fall within the "accident" definition under Article 17, an interpretation that comports with another provision of the Convention. As such, *Saks* correctly characterized the term "accident" as encompassing more than unintentional conduct. The term "accident" has at least two plausible yet distinct definitions. On the one hand, as noted in *Saks*, "accident" may be defined as an unintended event. *See* WEBSTER'S NEW WORLD COLLEGE DICTIONARY 8 (4th ed. 999) ("a happening that is not ... intended"); *see also* AMERICAN HERITAGE DICTIONARY 10 (4th ed. 2000) ("[l]ack of intention; chance").

On the other hand, as noted in *Saks*, the term "accident" may be defined as an event that is "unusual" or "unexpected," whether the result of intentional action or not. *See* BLACK'S LAW DICTIONARY 15 (6th ed.1990) ("an unusual, fortuitous, unexpected, unforeseen, or unlooked for event, happening or occurrence" and "if happening wholly or partly through human agency, an event which under the circumstances is unusual and unexpected by the person to whom it happens"); *see also* AMERICAN HERITAGE DICTIONARY, *supra*, at 10 ("[a]n unexpected and undesirable event," "[a]n unforeseen incident"). Although either definition of "accident" is at first glance plausible, neither party contests the definition adopted by the Court in *Saks*, which after careful examination discerned the meaning of "accident" under Article 17 of the Convention as an "unexpected or unusual event or happening that is external to the passenger."

The Court focused its analysis on determining "what causes can be considered accidents," and observed that Article 17 "embraces causes of injuries" that are "unexpected or unusual." The Court did not suggest that only one event could constitute the "accident," recognizing that "[a]ny injury is the product of a chain of causes." Thus, for purposes of the "accident" inquiry, the Court stated that a plaintiff need only be able to prove that "some link in the chain was an unusual or unexpected event external to the passenger."

B.

Petitioner argues that the "accident" inquiry should focus on the "injury producing event," which, according to petitioner, was the presence of ambient cigarette smoke in the aircraft's cabin. Because petitioner's policies permitted smoking on international flights, petitioner contends that Dr. Hanson's death resulted from his own internal reaction-namely, an asthma attack-to the normal operation of the aircraft. Petitioner also argues that the flight attendant's failure to move Dr. Hanson was inaction, whereas Article 17 requires an action that causes the injury.

We disagree. As an initial matter, we note that petitioner did not challenge in the Court of Appeals the District Court's finding that the flight attendant's conduct in three times refusing to move Dr. Hanson was unusual or unexpected in light of the relevant industry standard or petitioner's own company policy. Petitioner instead argued that the flight attendant's conduct was irrelevant for purposes of the "accident" inquiry and that the only relevant event was the presence of the ambient cigarette smoke in the aircraft's cabin. Consequently, we need not dispositively determine whether the flight attendant's conduct qualified as "unusual or unexpected" under *Saks*, but may assume that it was for purposes of this opinion.

Petitioner's focus on the ambient cigarette smoke as the injury producing event is misplaced. We do not doubt that the presence of ambient cigarette smoke in the aircraft's cabin during an international flight might have been "normal" at the time of the flight in question. But petitioner's "injury producing event" inquiry—which looks to "the precise factual 'event' that caused the injury"—neglects the reality that there are often multiple interrelated factual events that combine to cause any given injury. In *Saks*, the Court recognized that any one of these factual events or happenings may be a link in the chain of causes and—so long as it is unusual or unexpected—could constitute an "accident" under Article 17. Indeed, the very fact that multiple events will necessarily combine and interrelate to cause any particular injury makes it difficult to define, in any coherent or non-question-begging way, any single event as the "injury producing event."

Petitioner's only claim to the contrary here is to say: "Looking to the purely factual description of relevant events, the aggravating event was Dr. Hanson remaining in his assigned non-smoking seat and being exposed to ambient smoke, which allegedly aggravated his pre-existing asthmatic condition leading to his death," and that the "injury producing event" was "not the flight attendant's failure to act or violation of industry standards." Petitioner ignores the fact that the flight attendant's refusal on three separate occasions to move Dr. Hanson was also a "factual 'event,'" that the District Court correctly found to be a "'link in the chain'" of causes that led to Dr. Hanson's death, Petitioner's statement that the flight attendant's failure to reseat Dr. Hanson was not the "injury producing event" is nothing more than a bald assertion, unsupported by any law or argument.

An example illustrates why petitioner's emphasis on the ambient cigarette smoke as the "injury producing event" is misplaced. Suppose that petitioner mistakenly assigns respondent and her husband to seats in the middle of the smoking section, and that respondent and her husband do not notice that they are in the smoking section until after the flight has departed. Suppose further that, as here, the flight attendant refused to assist respondent and her husband despite repeated requests to move. In this hypothetical case, it would appear that, "[l]ooking to the purely factual description of relevant events, the aggravating event was [the passenger] remaining in his assigned seat and being exposed to ambient smoke, which allegedly aggravated his pre-existing asthmatic condition leading to his death." To argue otherwise, petitioner would have to suggest that the misassignment to the smoking section was the "injury producing event," but this would simply beg the question.

The fact is, the exposure to smoke, the misassignment to the smoking section, and the refusal to move the passenger would all be factual events contributing to the death of the passenger. In the instant case, the same can be said: The exposure to the smoke and the refusal to assist the passenger are happenings that both contributed to the passenger's death.

And petitioner's argument that the flight attendant's failure to act cannot constitute an "accident" because only affirmative acts are "event[s] or happening[s]" under *Saks* is unavailing. The distinction between action and inaction, as petitioner uses these terms, would perhaps be relevant were this a tort law negligence case. But respondents do not advocate, and petitioner vigorously rejects, that a negligence regime applies under Article 17 of the Convention. The relevant "accident" inquiry under *Saks* is whether there is "an unexpected or unusual event or happening." The rejection of an explicit request for assistance would be an "event" or "happening" under the ordinary and usual definitions of these terms. *See* AMERICAN HERITAGE DICTIONARY 635 (3d ed. 1992) ("event": "[s]omething that takes place; an occurrence"); BLACK'S LAW DICTIONARY 554-55 (6th ed. 1990) ("event": "Something that happens"); WEBSTER'S NEW INTERNATIONAL DICTIONARY 885 (2d ed. 1949) ("event": "The fact of taking place or occurring; occurrence" or "[t]hat which comes, arrives, or happens").

The dissent cites two cases from our sister signatories England and Australia—*Deep Vein Thrombosis and Air Travel Group Litigation*, [2004] Q.B. 234, and *Qantas Ltd. v. Povey*, [2003] VSCA 227, ¶ 17, ¶ 17 (Dec. 23, 2003), respectively—and suggests that we should simply defer to their judgment on the matter. But our conclusion is not inconsistent with *Deep Vein Thrombosis and Air Travel Group Litigation*, where the England and Wales Court of Appeals commented on the District Court and Court of Appeal opinions in this case, and agreed that Dr. Hanson's death had resulted from an accident. The English court reasoned: "The refusal of the flight attendant to move Dr. Hanson cannot properly be considered as mere inertia, or a non-event. It was a refusal to provide an alternative seat which formed part of a more complex incident, whereby Dr. Hanson was exposed to smoke in circumstances that can properly be described as unusual and unexpected."

To the extent that the precise reasoning used by the courts in *Deep Vein Thrombosis and Air Travel Group Litigation* is inconsistent with our reasoning, we reject the analysis of those cases for the reasons stated in the body of this opinion. In such a circumstance, we are hesitant to "follo[w]" the opinions of intermediate appellate courts of our sister signatories, post, at 1231 (SCALIA, J., dissenting). This is especially true where there are substantial factual distinctions between these cases or to advise on precautions which would avoid or minimise that risk and where the respective courts of last resort—the House of Lords and High Court of Australia—have yet to speak.

Moreover, the fallacy of petitioner's position that an "accident" cannot take the form of inaction is illustrated by the following example. Suppose that a passenger on a flight inexplicably collapses and stops breathing and that a medical doctor informs the flight crew that the passenger's life could be saved only if the plane lands within one hour. Suppose further that it is industry standard and airline policy to divert a flight to the nearest airport when a passenger otherwise faces imminent death. If the plane is within 30 minutes of a suitable airport, but the crew chooses to continue its cross-country flight, "[t]he notion that this is not an unusual event is staggering."

We do not suggest—as the dissent erroneously contends—that liability must lie because otherwise "harsh results," (opinion of SCALIA, J.), would ensue. This hypothetical merely illustrates that the failure of an airline crew to take certain necessary vital steps could quite naturally and, in routine usage of the language, be an "event or happening."

Confirming this interpretation, other provisions of the Convention suggest that there is often no distinction between action and inaction on the issue of ultimate liability. For example, Article 25 provides that Article 22's liability cap does not apply in the event of "willful misconduct or ... such default on [the carrier's] part as, in accordance with the law of the court to which the case is submitted, is considered to be equivalent to willful misconduct." The Montreal Protocol No. 4 to Amend the Convention for the Unification of Certain Rules relating to International Carriage by Air (1975) amends Article 25 by replacing "willful misconduct" with the language "done with intent to cause damage or recklessly and with knowledge that damage would probably result," as long as the airline's employee or agent was acting "within the scope of his employment." In 1998, the United States gave its advice and consent to ratification of the protocol, and it entered into force in the United States on March 4, 1999. Because the facts here took place in 1997-1998, Montreal Protocol No. 4 does not apply.

Because liability can be imposed for death or bodily injury only in the case of an Article 17 "accident" and Article 25 only lifts the caps once liability has been found, these provisions read together tend to show that inaction can give rise to liability. Moreover, Article 20(1) makes clear that the "due care" defense is unavailable when a carrier has failed to take "all necessary measures to avoid the damage." These provisions suggest that an air carrier's inaction can be the basis for liability.

Finally, petitioner contends that the Ninth Circuit improperly created a negligence-based "accident" standard under Article 17 by focusing on the flight crew's negligence as the "accident." The Ninth Circuit stated: "The failure to act in the face of a known, serious risk satisfies the meaning of 'accident' within Article 17 so long as reasonable alternatives exist that would substantially minimize the risk and implementing these alternatives would not unreasonably interfere with the normal, expected operation of the airplane." Admittedly, this language does seem to approve of a negligence-based approach. However, no party disputes the Ninth Circuit's holding that the flight attendant's conduct was "unexpected and unusual," which is the operative language under *Saks* and the correct Article 17 analysis. For the foregoing reasons, we conclude that the conduct here constitutes an "accident" under Article 17 of the Warsaw Convention. Accordingly, the judgment of the Court of Appeals is affirmed.

Justice BREYER took no part in the consideration or decision of this case.

Justice SCALIA, with whom Justice O'CONNOR join and dissent, in part.

When we interpret a treaty, we accord the judgments of our sister signatories "'considerable weight.'" True to that canon, our previous Warsaw Convention opinions have carefully considered foreign case law. Today's decision stands out for its failure to give any serious consideration to how the courts of our treaty partners have resolved the legal issues before us.

This sudden insularity is striking, since the Court in recent years has canvassed the prevailing law in other nations (at least Western European nations) to determine the meaning of an American Constitution that those nations had no part in framing and that those nations' courts have no role in enforcing. One would have thought that foreign courts' interpretations of a treaty that their governments adopted jointly with ours, and that they have an actual role in applying, would be (to put it mildly) all the more relevant.

The Court's new abstemiousness with regard to foreign fare is not without consequence: Within the past year, appellate courts in both England and Australia have rendered decisions squarely at odds with today's holding. Because the Court offers no convincing explanation why these cases should not be followed, I respectfully dissent.

I.

The Court holds that an airline's mere inaction can constitute an "accident" within the meaning of the Warsaw Convention. It derives this principle from our definition of "accident" in *Saks* as "an unexpected or unusual event or happening that is external to the passenger." The Court says this definition encompasses failures to act like the flight attendant's refusal to reseat Hanson in the face of a request for assistance.

That is far from clear. The word "accident" is used in two distinct senses. One refers to something that is unintentional, not "on purpose"—as in, "the hundred typing monkeys' verbatim reproduction of War and Peace was an accident." The other refers to an unusual and unexpected event, intentional or not: One may say he has been involved in a "train accident," for example, whether or not the derailment was intentionally caused. As the Court notes, *Saks* adopted the latter definition rather than the former. That distinction is crucial because, while there is no doubt that inaction can be an accident in the former sense ("I accidentally left the stove on"), whether it can be so in the latter sense is questionable.

Two of our sister signatories have concluded that it cannot. In *Deep Vein Thrombosis and Air Travel Group Litigation*, [2004] Q.B. 234, England's Court of Appeal, in an opinion by the Master of the Rolls that relied heavily on *Abramson v. Japan Airlines Co.* (3d Cir. 1984), and analyzed more than a half-dozen other non-English decisions, held as follows:

> A critical issue in this appeal is whether a failure to act, or an omission, can constitute an accident for the purposes of article 17. Often a failure to act results in an accident, or forms part of a series of acts and omissions which together constitute an accident. In such circumstances it may not be easy to distinguish between acts and omissions. I cannot see, however, how inaction itself can ever properly be described as an accident. It is not an event; it is a non-event. Inaction is the antithesis of an accident.

Six months later, the appellate division of the Supreme Court of Victoria, Australia, in an opinion that likewise gave extensive consideration to American and other foreign decisions, agreed:

> The allegations in substance do no more than state a failure to do something, and this cannot be characterised as an event or happening, whatever be the concomitant background to that failure to warn or advise. That is not to say that a failure to take a specific required step in the course of flying an aircraft, or in picking up or setting down passengers, cannot lead to an event or happening of the requisite unusual or unexpected kind and thus be an accident for the purpose of the article.
>
> A failure by a pilot to use some device in the expected and correct manner, such as a failure to let down the landing wheels or a chance omission to adjust the level of pressurisation, may lead, as has been held, to an accident contemplated by Article 17, but I would venture to suggest that it is not the failure to take the step which is properly to be characterised as an accident but rather its immediate and

> disastrous consequence whether that be the dangerous landing on the belly of the aircraft or an immediate unexpected and dangerous drop in pressurisation.

Qantas Ltd. v. Povey, [2003] VSCA 227, ¶ 17 (Dec. 23, 2003).

We can, and should, look to decisions of other signatories when we interpret treaty provisions. Foreign constructions are evidence of the original shared understanding of the contracting parties. Moreover, it is reasonable to impute to the parties an intent that their respective courts strive to interpret the treaty consistently. (The Warsaw Convention's preamble specifically acknowledges "the advantage of regulating in a uniform manner the conditions of ... the liability of the carrier.") Finally, even if we disagree, we surely owe the conclusions reached by appellate courts of other signatories the courtesy of respectful consideration.

The Court nonetheless dismisses *Deep Vein Thrombosis* and *Povey* in a footnote responding to this dissent. As to the former, it claims (choosing its words carefully) that the "conclusion "it reaches is "not inconsistent" with that case. The reader should not think this to be a contention that the Master of the Rolls' opinion might be read to agree with today's holding that inaction can constitute an "accident." (To repeat the conclusion of that opinion: "Inaction is the antithesis of an accident." [2004] Q.B., at 247, ¶ 25.) What it refers to is the fact that the Master of the Rolls distinguished the Court of Appeals' judgment below (announced in an opinion that assumed inaction was involved, but did not at all discuss the action-inaction distinction) on the ground that action was involved —namely, "insistence that [Hanson] remain seated in the area exposed to smoke." The Court quotes only part of the relevant discussion.

Here is what the Master of the Rolls said about our case in full:

> I have no difficulty with the result in this case but, with respect, I question the reasoning of the judge in both events. The refusal of the flight attendant to move Dr. Hanson cannot properly be considered as mere inertia, or a non-event. It was a refusal to provide an alternative seat which formed part of a more complex incident, whereby Dr. Hanson was exposed to smoke in circumstances that can properly be described as unusual and unexpected. The existence of the non-smoking zone provided the opportunity for Dr. Hanson, if suitably placed within it, to avoid exposure to the smoke that threatened his health and, as it proved, his life.
>
> The direct cause of his death was the unnecessary exposure to the smoke. The refusal of the attendant to move him

> could be described as insistence that he remain seated in the area exposed to smoke. The exposure to smoke in these circumstances could, in my view, properly be described as an unusual or unexpected event.

Deep Vein Thrombosis and Air Travel Group Litigation, [2004] Q.B. 234.

As I explain below, that theory does not quite work because, in fact, the flight attendant did not insist that Hanson remain seated. But we can ignore this detail for the time being. The point is that the English court thought Husain could recover, not because the action-inaction distinction was irrelevant, but because, even though action was indispensable, it had in fact occurred.

The Court charts our course in exactly the opposite direction, spending three pages explaining why the action-*inaction* distinction is irrelevant. If the Court agrees with the Master of the Rolls that this case involves action, why does it needlessly place us in conflict with the courts of other signatories by deciding the then-irrelevant issue of whether inaction can constitute an accident? It would suffice to hold that our case involves action and end the analysis there. Whether inaction can constitute an accident under the Warsaw Convention is a significant issue on which international consensus is important; whether Husain can recover for her husband's death in this one case is not. As they stand, however, the core holdings of this case and Deep Vein Thrombosis—their *rationes decidendi*—are not only not "not inconsistent"; they are completely opposite.

To the extent the Court implies that *Deep Vein Thrombosis* and *Povey* merit only slight consideration because they were not decided by courts of last resort, I note that our prior Warsaw Convention cases have looked to decisions of intermediate appellate foreign courts as well as supreme courts. Moreover, *Deep Vein Thrombosis* was no ordinary decision. It was *authored* by the Master of the Rolls, the chief judge of England's civil appellate court—a position thought by many to be even more influential than that of a Law Lord.

That there are "substantial factual distinctions" between the cases, is surely beside the point. A legal rule may arise in different contexts, but the differences are relevant only if the logic of the rule makes them so. *Deep Vein Thrombosis* and *Povey* hold in no uncertain terms that inaction cannot be an accident; not that inaction consisting of failure to warn of deep vein thrombosis cannot be an accident. Maintaining a coherent international body of treaty law requires us to give deference to the legal rules our treaty partners adopt. It is not enough to avoid inconsistent decisions on factually identical cases.

I would follow the holdings of *Deep Vein Thrombosis* and *Povey*, since the Court's analysis today is no more convincing than theirs. Merely pointing to dictionaries that define "'event'" as an "'occurrence'" or "'[s]omething that happens,'" hardly resolves the problem; it only reformulates one question (whether "accident" includes nonevents) into an equivalent one (whether "accident" includes nonoccurrences and nonhappenings).

Equally unavailing is the reliance, on Article 25 of the Warsaw Convention (which lifts liability caps for injury caused by a "default" of the airline equivalent to willful misconduct) and Article 20 (which precludes the airline's due-care defense if it fails to take "all necessary measures" to avoid the injury). The Court's analytical error in invoking these provisions is to assume that the inaction these provisions contemplate is the accident itself. The treaty imposes no such requirement. If a pilot negligently forgets to lower the landing gear, causing the plane to crash and killing all passengers on board, then recovery is presumptively available (because the crash that caused the deaths is an accident), and the due-care defense is inapplicable (because the pilot's negligent omission also caused the deaths), even though the omission is not the accident. Similarly, if a flight attendant fails to prevent the boarding of an individual whom she knows to be a terrorist, and who later shoots a passenger, the damages cap might be lifted even though the accident (the shooting) and the default (the failure to prevent boarding) do not coincide. Without the invented restriction that the Article 20 or 25 default be the accident itself, the Court's argument based on those provisions loses all force.

As for the Court's hypothetical of the crew that refuses to divert after a passenger collapses: This would be more persuasive as a *reductio ad absurdum* if the Eleventh Circuit had not already ruled out Article 17 liability in substantially these very circumstances. A legal construction is not fallacious merely because it has harsh results. The Convention denies a remedy, even when outrageous conduct and grievous injury have occurred, unless there has been an "accident." Whatever that term means, it certainly does not equate to "outrageous conduct that causes grievous injury." It is a mistake to assume that the Convention must provide relief whenever traditional tort law would do so.

To the contrary, a principal object of the Convention was to promote the growth of the fledgling airline industry by limiting the circumstances under which passengers could sue. Unless there has been an accident, there is no liability, whether the claim is trivial, *cf. Lee v. American Airlines Inc.* (5th Cir. 2004) (suit for "loss of a 'refreshing, memorable vacation'"), or cries out for redress.

Were we confronting the issue in the first instance, perhaps the Court could persuade me to its view. But courts in two other countries have already rejected it, and their reasoning is no less compelling than the Court's. I would follow *Deep Vein Thrombosis* and *Povey* and hold that mere inaction cannot be an "accident" under Article 17.

II.

Respondents argue that, even if the Convention distinguishes action from inaction, this case involves sufficient elements of action to support recovery. That argument is not implausible; as noted earlier, the court in *Deep Vein Thrombosis* suggested that "[t]he refusal of the attendant to move [Hanson] could be described as insistence that he remain seated in the area exposed to smoke." I cannot agree with this analysis, however, because it miscomprehends the facts of this case. That the flight attendant explicitly refused Husain's pleas for help after the third request, rather than simply ignoring them, does not transform her inaction into action. The refusal acknowledged her inaction, but it was the inaction, not the acknowledgment, that caused Hanson's death. Unlike the previous responses, the third was a mere refusal to assist, and so cannot be the basis for liability under Article 17.

But even if the flight attendant's insistence that Hanson remain seated before takeoff was unusual or unexpected, and hence an accident, it was not a compensable cause of Hanson's death. It was perhaps a but for cause (had the flight attendant allowed him to move before takeoff, he might have lived, just as he might have lived if he had taken a different flight); but it was not a proximate cause, which is surely a predicate for recovery. Any early insistence that Hanson remain seated became moot once the attendant later told Husain and her husband they were free to move about.

There is, however, one complication, which I think requires us to remand this case to the District Court: Although the flight attendant, once the plane was aloft, invited Husain to find another passenger willing to switch seats, she did not invite Husain to find an empty seat, but to the contrary affirmatively represented that the plane was full. If such a misrepresentation is unusual and unexpected; and (the more difficult question) if it can reasonably be said that it caused Hanson's death—*i.e.*, that Husain would have searched for and found an empty seat, although unwilling to ask another passenger to move-then a cause of action might lie. I would remand so that the District Court could consider in the first instance whether the flight attendant's misrepresentation about the plane's being full, independent of any failure to reseat, was an accident that caused Hanson's death. Tragic though Dr. Hanson's death may have been, it does not justify the Court's putting us in needless conflict with other signatories to the Warsaw Convention. I respectfully dissent.

* * *

AZIZ V. AIR INDIA LTD.

658 F. Supp. 2d 1144 (C.D. Cal. 2009)

STEPHEN G. LARSON, District Judge.

This case involves the tragic story of a passenger suffering cardiac arrest on-board a lengthy international flight and later being pronounced dead by paramedics at the arrival gate. The question before the Court is whether the airline's failure to have onboard an automated external defibrillator ("AED") renders it liable for the passenger's death under international law, as established by treaty. For the reasons set forth below, the Court holds that, under the law governing this case, the aircraft is not required to have such a device in place and, therefore, awards summary judgment in favor of the airline.

I. UNDISPUTED FACTS

Air India Limited, d/b/a Air India ("Air India"), is a foreign air carrier, organized under the laws of and with its principal place of business in India, that operates aircraft in the United States pursuant to a certificate issued under Part 129 of the Federal Aviation Regulations.

On June 27, 2007, Ramazan Aziz was a passenger on board Air India Flight 137 from Frankfurt, Germany, to Los Angeles, California, traveling on a round-trip ticket on Air India originating in Los Angeles. After landing at Los Angeles International Airport, and while the airplane was still in the process of taxiing to the gate, a passenger seated next to Aziz noticed that he had collapsed and was not breathing. The passenger called the flight attendant and alerted her to Aziz's condition. Another passenger seated nearby reported to the flight attendant that, an hour earlier, she had spoken to Aziz, and that after that conversation the passenger presumed Aziz had fallen asleep.

Air India's procedures for assisting medically ill passengers are as follows: (1) The In-Flight Supervisor ("IFS") shall be informed; (2) a suitable announcement shall be made requesting the help of a qualified medical practitioner; (3) the cabin crew shall render every assistance to the doctor treating the sick passenger by ensuring that the doctor has privacy to conduct the examination and that a bed is prepared if necessary; (4) the IFS or Flight Purser shall indicate in the flight report the doctor's name, address, registration number, seat number, and the sector on which assistance was sought; (5) if a doctor is not available on board and the passenger's condition appears serious, the IFS shall inform the Commander so that a message can be sent for a doctor to meet the flight at the next port of call; and (6) the Commander shall be informed in all cases where the passenger's illness appears serious.

When Air India Flight 137's flight crew was alerted to Aziz's condition, the flight attendant immediately summoned an on-board doctor, a passenger who identified himself as Dr. Gautam Mittal, and then notified the IFS and the plane's captain. Dr. Mittal examined Aziz and took his vital signs. Dr. Mittal found that Aziz was not breathing, did not have a pulse, and was very pale. As Dr. Mittal was treating Aziz, the flight crew contacted the airport for paramedics and requested that they respond to the aircraft at the arrival gate. The flight crew initially provided Dr. Mittal with a stethoscope and a blood pressure apparatus. Later, a flight attendant also brought him an oxygen mask and tank. Dr. Mittal had another passenger standing nearby administer oxygen to Aziz while the doctor performed CPR on Aziz. At no time did Dr. Mittal ask the flight crew for a defibrillator or any other equipment or medicine. Paramedics boarded the aircraft after it arrived at the gate fifteen minutes later and the door was opened. Upon entering the aircraft the paramedics spotted Aziz lying in his seat, (and for reasons never explained) unattended and with no medical services being provided by anyone.

Although the paramedics found that Aziz was not breathing and had no pulse, they noted that he was not yet asystolic (no heart contractions) and their EKG monitor initially showed that he did emulate ventricular fibrillation ("V-fib") waves. The paramedics attempted CPR and employed an AED to administer a defibrillation shock on Aziz. Thereafter, the monitor showed that Aziz became asystolic. Epinephrine and Atrophine were administered intravenously at which point Aziz's heart temporarily resumed ventricular fibrillation waves on the monitor. Continuing attempts to revive Aziz's heart were unsuccessful and Aziz thereafter remained asystolic. Aziz was pronounced dead on board the airplane at 5:45 P.M. No autopsy of Aziz's body was performed.

Aziz's wife and his four children eventually filed suit against Air India alleging a state law tort claim of wrongful death based on the contention that, if the aircraft was equipped with an AED, Aziz would have survived.

II. ANALAYSIS

Neither party disputes that the Montreal Convention applies to the allegations leveled by the Aziz family, and thereby preempts their state common law wrongful death claim. Aziz's round-trip international flight unquestionably constitutes "international carriage" as that phrase is defined in the Montreal Convention, and therefore "any action for damages" arising from such a "carriage of passengers[,] ... however founded, whether ... in contract or in tort or otherwise, can only be brought subject to the conditions and such limits of liability as are set out in" the convention.

The question, then, is whether the Aziz family can establish a viable claim against Air India under the framework set forth in the Montreal Convention. The circumstances under which an airline carrier may be liable for injury to a passenger during an international flight are set forth in Article 17 of the Montreal Convention:

> The carrier shall be liable for damage sustained in the event of the death or wounding of a passenger or any other bodily injury suffered by a passenger, if the accident which caused the damage so sustained took place on board the aircraft or in the course of any of the operations of embarking or disembarking.

The United States Supreme Court has interpreted this treaty language as requiring that, for a passenger to hold an airline carrier liable for any injury he or she sustains, the passenger must establish that (1) there has been an "accident," (2) that caused the passenger's injury, and (3) that said accident occurred while on board the aircraft or in the course of embarking or disembarking the aircraft. Here, the parties' spar over whether an "accident" occurred and, if it did, whether such an accident "caused" Aziz's death.

Nowhere does the convention define the term "accident," but the United States Supreme Court later supplied meaning to the term (as it was used in the predecessor to the present convention—the Warsaw Convention) in the case of *Air France v. Saks* (1985). There, the court held that "accident" means "an unexpected or unusual event or happening that is external to the passenger." As explained by the court, although "this definition should be flexibly applied after assessment of all the circumstances surrounding a passenger's injuries," at its core, "when the injury indisputably results from the passenger's own internal reaction to the usual, normal, and expected operation of the aircraft, it has not been caused by an accident." Questions of negligence are not implicated or even relevant; instead the focus of the inquiry is on "the nature of the event which caused the injury rather than the care taken by the airline to avert the injury." Thus, for there to have been an "accident", the Aziz family must show that the asserted act or omission was unexpected or an unusual event that was external to Aziz, and that actually caused his death.

A. *Whether the Occurrence was "External" to the Passenger*

Air India takes the position that, because Aziz's heart attack was nothing more than his own "internal" reaction to an otherwise uneventful, routine flight (as opposed to being something "external" to him), it cannot form the basis for an "accident" under the Montreal Convention. The airline reads the Aziz family's complaint too narrowly. Their complaint is not with simply their husband and father suffering a medical emergency while onboard the aircraft; instead their complaint is directed at the airline's failure to stock a particular medical device on the plane, characterizing that failure as the "event" which was the "unusual or unexpected" occurrence that "caused" his death. No serious argument can be advanced that the airline's decision on whether to stock its aircraft with AEDs was something external to Aziz.

The Supreme Court has held that a flight attendant's repeated refusal to honor a request to reseat a passenger who was severely allergic to tobacco smoke further away from the plane's smoking section was external to the passenger, see *Olympic Airways v. Husain* (2004); in much the same way an airline's decision on what medical equipment to place onboard its aircraft is external to the passenger. Indeed, in nearly all the cases cited to by Air India in support of its legal proposition regarding externality, the courts have simply held that the fact of a passenger suffering a heart attack or some other physical ailment, by itself, was not an "external" occurrence under the convention.

Here, however, the Aziz family is arguing that there was something more that caused his death separate and apart from the heart attack itself, namely, Air India's failure to stock an AED on its aircraft. That something else was "external" to Aziz and thus could qualify as an "accident" under the Montreal Convention depending upon whether the other requirements are met.

B. *Whether Failure to have AED Onboard Airplane was an "Event"*

With respect to the failure to have an AED onboard, Air India argues that such an omission was not an "event" as defined in the Montreal Convention. Air India makes the argument that, without a specific plea made to flight attendants for an AED by the on-board doctor, any inaction on its or the flight crew's part (or in this case, the affirmative decision not to stock the plane with said AED) was simply an act of omission for which no liability may attach. In Air India's view, only a failure to act in the face of either explicit requests by the passenger (or a doctor in his or her stead if the passenger is unconscious), or regulatory requirements to provide certain aid or provisions, can constitute an "event" for which it can be held liable. Using this reading, Air India notes that no event occurred here, as the airline followed all of its own internal procedures and Dr. Mittal did not make a request for an AED during the incident in question on Flight 137.

Here, there is no dispute that Aziz did not make a "specific health based request" for an AED; a result that is not surprising given that he was comatose and suffering from a heart attack at the time. Nor did the physician who treated him onboard the plane, Dr. Mittal, make such a request. However, in a later interview with private investigators, Dr. Mittal downplayed the significance of his failure to ask for an AED, explaining that "his whole attention was on the cardiac massage and CPR efforts," not making requests for particular items of medical equipment. Indeed, from the interview with Dr. Mittal, it appears that at no point did he make a request for any of the medical equipment that was onboard the airplane and that he did in fact use to treat Aziz; instead, flight attendants simply brought, unsolicited, such equipment to him. Thus, it would appear that if an AED was onboard Flight 137 the flight attendant would have brought it to Dr. Mittal unsolicited. Nonetheless, the Court agrees that there is, in fact, no evidence of a request for an AED being made.

This then leaves the question as to whether having an AED onboard an international flight was either required by a public agency or was an industry standard at the time.

For its part, Air India labels the Aziz family's call for the provision of an AED onboard international flights as asking for the airline to do something more than what Dr. Mittal sought, and states that the Ninth Circuit rejected such a basis for liability. That court did provide that "[a]ttributing liability to an air carrier for failing to do all it can to prevent an injury that is inherent in air travel ... improperly shifts the focus of the inquiry from the nature of the event which caused the injury to the alleged failure of the air carrier to avert the same." On that basis, Air India labels the Aziz family as seeking to impose liability on account of the "risk inherent in air travel" where there are "limited resources available to respond to medical emergencies." This contention, however, assumes that there was no legal requirement that airlines carry AEDs on board international flights or an industry standard for the same, an assumption to which the Court now turns.

The Aziz family points to FAA regulations which state that, "for treatment of injuries, medical events or minor accidents that might occur during flight time [,] each airplane must have the following equipment[:] ... in airplanes for which a flight attendant is required and with a maximum payload capacity of more than 7,500 pounds, an approved automated external defibrillator as of April 12, 2004." *See* 14 C.F.R. § 121.803. The Aziz family also note that the Office of the Director of Civil Aviation for the Indian government promulgated a regulation in 2002 that mirrors the requirements contained in the FAA regulation quoted above. Specifically, the Indian regulation provided that, effective April 12, 2004, "all scheduled airlines operating transport category aircraft capable of carrying more than 30 passengers including crew when engaged in commercial flights shall carry one approved automated external defibrillators to provide the option to treat any serious medical events during flight time." Air India responds by arguing that both regulations cited to by the Aziz family are irrelevant to international flights.

Insofar as the FAA regulation is concerned, Air India notes that the cited provisions only apply to domestic U.S. air carriers. A separate section to the FAA regulations contained in the Code of Federal Regulations—part 129 of Title 14 of the C.F.R. (as opposed to part 121 cited to by the Aziz family)—applies to foreign air carriers. Indeed, Air India operates aircraft in the United States pursuant to a certificate issued under part 129 of the Federal Aviation Regulations. Section 129.11 of part 129 of the regulations, in contrast, provides that "each foreign air carrier shall conduct its operations within the United States in accordance with operations specifications issued by the Administrator under this part and in accordance with the Standards and Recommended Practices contained in part I (International Commercial Air Transport) of Annex 6 (Operation of Aircraft) to the Convention on International Civil Aviation Organization ("ICAO")." *See* 14 C.F.R. § 129.11. There are no operation specifications under part 129 (as opposed to those found in part 121 for domestic carriers) requiring foreign air carriers to equip their aircraft with AEDs. This the Aziz family does not contest.

Nor, at the time of the incident in question, Air India argues was there any requirement for onboard AEDs found in part I of Annex 6 to the ICAO. On this point, the Aziz family takes exception. They note that section 6.2.2 to Part I Annex 6 of the ICAO requires (using the word "shall") that airplanes be "equipped with a) accessible and adequate medical supplies appropriate to the number of passengers the aeroplane is authorized to carry" and recommends that such "medical supplies" consist of "one or more first-aid kits, and a medical kit, for the use of medical doctors or other qualified persons in treating in-flight medical emergencies for aeroplanes authorized to carry more than 250 passengers." According to the Aziz family, such a requirement may have compelled that an AED be onboard an international flight "in order for [the] medical supplies onboard to be adequate."

Air India responds that the same provision requiring "adequate medical supplies" also notes that "[g]uidance on the types, number, location and contents of the medical supplies is given in Attachment B," and then provides that attachment. An AED is not among the list of required medical supplies and equipment in Attachment B to the ICAO. Indeed, that attachment contains a specific statement regarding AEDs and their presence on international flights:

> Based on the limited available evidence, only a very small number of passengers are likely to benefit from the carriage of ... AED on aeroplanes. However, many operators carry them because they offer the only effective treatment for cardiac fibrillation. The likelihood of use, and therefore of potential benefit to a passenger, is greatest in aircraft carrying a large number of passengers, over long duration sector lengths. The carriage of AEDs should be determined by operators on the basis of a risk assessment taking into account the particular needs of the operation.

Although this statement would appear to strongly recommend that an AED be carried onboard a long flight such as that which occurred here (noting that the dangers inherent in failing to have such a device onboard are for flights "carrying a large number of passengers over a long duration sector lengths"), as explained above, the Ninth Circuit has made plain that failure to heed recommendations or suggestions made by governmental or international agencies is not enough to constitute an "event" under the Montreal Convention. Given that this "recommendation" is all that the ICAO provides with regards to AEDs, the Court holds that Air India's failure to heed the ICAO's suggestion is insufficient to constitute an "event" as understood under the Montreal Convention.

As far as the requirement of the Indian government cited to by the Aziz family, Air India represents that, on November 12, 2003, (after the regulation's effective date), the Indian government expressly retracted its directive for Air India to carry an AED on board its domestic passenger flights. The letter in question from the Director of Airworthiness for the Indian Director General of Civil Aviation begins by noting the requirements cited to by the Aziz family, and then observes that "[s]ome of the scheduled airlines had expressed reservations about installation of such equipment on the aircraft with the plea that cabin crew need to be trained for use of such equipment and there are chances that airline may be sued in the court for negligence in case of any death of passenger."

The letter also observed that, outside of the United States FAA regulations mandating AEDs onboard domestic flights, no other governmental agency had made the presence of such equipment "mandatory." In light of these concerns, the letter concluded that "this requirement [for the provision of AEDs onboard aircraft] would be deferred until the JAA makes it mandatory to European operators." Neither side has submitted any evidence as to whether the JAA has ever mandated that European operators of aircraft carry AEDs onboard. Thus, the Court is in no position to ignore the import from the Indian government's decision to suspend its requirement that an AED be placed onboard domestic flights.

On this point, all that the Aziz family argues is that they "cannot at this moment ascertain the propriety of the letter['s]" effect on abrogating what would otherwise be the clear mandate contained in the regulation. As expressed by their counsel, "it seems utterly impracticable that a letter from the government of India to the airline wholly owned by the government of India, can suffice as a rescission of an obligation of a law." What is missing, however, is any evidence or argument (other than the personal supposition of counsel) that the letter cannot do as it proclaims—to suspend an airline regulation issued earlier by the Indian government. In the absence of such proof, and without any other evidence on the question, the Court takes the letter on its face as accomplishing what it claims to have done. Thus, as with the ICAO's suggestion, the Court finds this failure to comply with a rescinded regulation insufficient to constitute an event under the Montreal Convention.

C. *Was Lack of AED Onboard Airplane was Unexpected or Unusual*

Air India further argues that, even were the Court to find that an "event" did occur, the lack of an AED onboard an international flight was not an "unexpected or unusual" occurrence. Thus, the question of industry standards vis-a-vis whether an "event" occurred bleeds into resolution of the "unexpected or unusual" occurrence question as well.

Air India asserts that conformity with its own policies and compliance with applicable laws and regulations is sufficient, foreclosing any contention that the occurrence at issue was unusual or unexpected. In essence, Air India seeks for a court to shy away from reference to industry standards in establishing whether an occurrence is unusual or unexpected. There is case law outside the Ninth Circuit to support such an approach; the Fifth Circuit in *Blansett v. Continental Airlines, Inc.* (5th Cir. 2004), held that an airline's decision to merely cleave to the requirements of a public agency (as opposed to conforming to industry standards) was not an unusual or unexpected occurrence.

Although such an approach is consistent with the analysis that failure to conform to regulatory recommendations—which are akin to industry standards—is not sufficient to constitute an "event," this Court is of the view that applying such a rationale to what is to be expected from an airline carrier goes beyond the boundaries of what the phrase "unusual or unexpected" is ordinarily understood to mean.

Nevertheless, the Court need not resolve this question, as the Aziz family has failed to proffer any evidence establishing that there was in fact an industry standard to provide such AED devices on board international flights. In this regard, Air India correctly observes that the Aziz family has "presented ... no evidence that an industry standard among foreign airlines regarding onboard AEDs exist," that no evidence has been presented showing "that any governing body recommended or required AEDs," and there has been no showing that "at least one of the many other foreign or international airlines carried onboard AEDs at the time of the incident."

Air India not only correctly identifies what the Aziz family has failed to proffer, but also that the missing evidence would be of the type needed to establish an industry standard. This does not mean that such evidence does not in fact exist to substantiate each of those points, but the duty to provide such evidence rests with the Aziz family, and it is a burden they have not met.

Indeed, certain periodicals would appear to address some of the factual deficits pointed to by Air India. *See* MEDICAL GUIDELINES FOR AIRLINE TRAVEL, SECOND EDITION, AEROSPACE MEDICAL ASSOCIATION MEDICAL GUIDELINES TASK FORCE, Vol. 74, No. 5, section II (May 2003 supplement) (noting "[m]any of the world's airlines have greatly increased their capacity for providing medical care to passengers in-flight by enhancing their onboard emergency medical kits (EMKs). One of the more significant changes is the greater availability of automatic external defibrillators (AEDs)" and that "[t]he European Joint Aviation Authority already mandates similar requirements"). None of this evidence was ever offered, much less submitted, to the Court. Moreover, the Court cannot analyze the import (or lack thereof) of such information contained in a periodical.

The Aziz family seeks to reframe the point, arguing that the domestic requirements in both the United States and India to have AEDs onboard was instructive of a "shift" in industry standards "towards implementing AEDs," which thereby demonstrates that Air India Flight 137 taking off from Frankfurt, Germany, without such equipment onboard was unusual or unexpected. Even assuming that domestic regulatory requirements could be considered in establishing an international norm, a growing shift toward something is not the same as an established standard to provide the same.

In the absence of such proof, the Court finds that there is insufficient evidence to establish that there is an industry standard upon which a showing of an "unusual or unexpected" occurrence can be made regarding the lack of an AED onboard Air India Flight 137. Thus, in the final analysis, the Aziz family cannot show that their husband and father's death was a result of an "accident" as that term is understood under the Montreal Convention.

III. CONCLUSION

Accordingly, the Court denies the Aziz family's motion for summary judgment and grants Air India's motion for summary judgment, finding that Aziz's death onboard Flight 137 was neither an "event" nor an "unusual or unexpected" occurrence in light of the lack of evidence on industry standards regarding the latter, and the affirmative proof by Air India that provision of such AED devices was neither requested by Dr. Mittal nor was it required by governmental or international regulatory agencies at the relevant time for international flights.

Insofar as whether the lack of such a device "caused" Aziz's death, the Court finds that there is a disputed issue of fact (one even obliquely conceded by Air India's medical expert, Dr. Ilan Kedan, on the point given the paramedics finding that Aziz was systolic at the time when they first examined him and had V-fib waves when initially hooked up to their EKG monitor. The exception taken by Air India to the lack of an autopsy does nothing to dampen the factual dispute arising from the EKG monitor's results upon the paramedics first arriving at the gate. That is sufficient to send the issue of causation to a jury.

* * *

CONVENTION FOR THE UNIFICATION OF CERTAIN RULES FOR INTERNATIONAL CARRIAGE BY AIR

S. Treaty Doc. No. 106-45, 1999 WL 33292734

THE STATES PARTIES TO THIS CONVENTION

RECOGNIZING the significant contribution of the Convention for the Unification of Certain Rules Relating to International Carriage by Air signed in Warsaw on 12 October 1929, hereinafter referred to as the "Warsaw Convention," and other related instruments to the harmonization of private international air law;

RECOGNIZING the need to modernize and consolidate the Warsaw Convention and related instruments;

RECOGNIZING the importance of ensuring protection of the interests of consumers in international carriage by air and the need for equitable compensation based on the principle of restitution;

REAFFIRMING the desirability of an orderly development of international air transport operations and the smooth flow of passengers, baggage and cargo in accordance with the principles and objectives of the Convention on International Civil Aviation, done at Chicago on 7 December 1944;

CONVINCED that collective State action for further harmonization and codification of certain rules governing international carriage by air through a new Convention is the most adequate means of achieving an equitable balance of interests;

HAVE AGREED AS FOLLOWS:

CHAPTER I

GENERAL PROVISIONS

ARTICLE 1
SCOPE OF APPLICATION

1. This Convention applies to all international carriage of persons, baggage or cargo performed by aircraft for reward. It applies equally to gratuitous carriage by aircraft performed by an air transport undertaking.

2. For the purposes of this Convention, the expression international carriage means any carriage in which, according to the agreement between the parties, the place of departure and the place of destination, whether or not there be a break in the carriage or a transhipment, are situated either within the territories of two States Parties, or within the

territory of a single State Party if there is an agreed stopping place within the territory of another State, even if that State is not a State Party. Carriage between two points within the territory of a single State Party without an agreed stopping place within the territory of another State is not international carriage for the purposes of this Convention.

3. Carriage to be performed by several successive carriers is deemed, for the purposes of this Convention, to be one undivided carriage if it has been regarded by the parties as a single operation, whether it had been agreed upon under the form of a single contract or of a series of contracts, and it does not lose its international character merely because one contract or a series of contracts is to be performed entirely within the territory of the same State.

4. This Convention applies also to carriage as set out in Chapter V, subject to the terms contained therein.

ARTICLE 2
CARRIAGE PERFORMED BY STATE AND CARRIAGE OF POSTAL ITEMS

1. This Convention applies to carriage performed by the State or by legally constituted public bodies provided it falls within the conditions laid down in Article 1.

2. In the carriage of postal items, the carrier shall be liable only to the relevant postal administration in accordance with the rules applicable to the relationship between the carriers and the postal administrations.

3. Except as provided in paragraph 2 of this Article, the provisions of this Convention shall not apply to the carriage of postal items.

CHAPTER II

DOCUMENTATION AND DUTIES OF THE PARTIES RELATING TO THE CARRIAGE OF PASSENGERS, BAGGAGE AND CARGO

ARTICLE 3
PASSENGERS AND BAGGAGE

1. In respect of carriage of passengers, an individual or collective document of carriage shall be delivered containing:

(a) an indication of the places of departure and destination;

(b) if the places of departure and destination are within the territory of a single State Party, one or more agreed stopping places being within the territory of another State, an indication of at least one such stopping place.

2. Any other means which preserves the information indicated in paragraph 1 may be substituted for the delivery of the document referred to in that paragraph. If any such other means is used, the carrier shall offer to deliver to the passenger a written statement of the information so preserved.

3. The carrier shall deliver to the passenger a baggage identification tag for each piece of checked baggage.

4. The passenger shall be given written notice to the effect that where this Convention is applicable it governs and may limit the liability of carriers in respect of death or injury and for destruction or loss of, or damage to, baggage, and for delay.

5. Non-compliance with the provisions of the foregoing paragraphs shall not affect the existence or the validity of the contract of carriage, which shall, nonetheless, be subject to the rules of this Convention including those relating to limitation of liability.

ARTICLE 4
CARGO

1. In respect of the carriage of cargo, an air waybill shall be delivered.

2. Any other means which preserves a record of the carriage to be performed may be substituted for the delivery of an air waybill. If such other means are used, the carrier shall, if so requested by the consignor, deliver to the consignor a cargo receipt permitting identification of the consignment and access to the information contained in the record preserved by such other means.

ARTICLE 5
CONTENTS OF AIR WAYBILL OR CARGO RECEIPT

The air waybill or the cargo receipt shall include: (a) an indication of the places of departure and destination; (b) if the places of departure and destination are within the territory of a single State Party, one or more agreed stopping places being within the territory of another State, an indication of at least one such stopping place; and (c) an indication of the weight of the consignment.

ARTICLE 6
DOCUMENT RELATING TO THE NATURE OF THE CARGO

The consignor may be required, if necessary to meet the formalities of customs, police and similar public authorities, to deliver a document indicating the nature of the cargo. This provision creates for the carrier no duty, obligation or liability resulting therefrom.

ARTICLE 7
DESCRIPTION OF AIR WAYBILL

1. The air waybill shall be made out by the consignor in three original parts.

2. The first part shall be marked "for the carrier"; it shall be signed by the consignor. The second part shall be marked "for the consignee"; it shall be signed by the consignor and by the carrier. The third part shall be signed by the carrier who shall hand it to the consignor after the cargo has been accepted.

3. The signature of the carrier and that of the consignor may be printed or stamped.

4. If, at the request of the consignor, the carrier makes out the air waybill, the carrier shall be deemed, subject to proof to the contrary, to have done so on behalf of the consignor.

ARTICLE 8
DOCUMENTATION FOR MULTIPLE PACKAGES

When there is more than one package: (a) the carrier of cargo has the right to require the consignor to make out separate air waybills; (b) the consignor has the right to require the carrier to deliver separate cargo receipts when the other means referred to in paragraph 2 of Article 4 are used.

ARTICLE 9
NON-COMPLIANCE WITH DOCUMENTARY REQUIREMENTS

Non-compliance with the provisions of Articles 4 to 8 shall not affect the existence or the validity of the contract of carriage, which shall, nonetheless, be subject to the rules of this Convention including those relating to limitation of liability.

ARTICLE 10
RESPONSIBILITY FOR PARTICULARS OF DOCUMENTATION

1. The consignor is responsible for the correctness of the particulars and statements relating to the cargo inserted by it or on its behalf in the air waybill or furnished by it or on its behalf to the carrier for insertion in the cargo receipt or for insertion in the record preserved by the other means referred to in paragraph 2 of Article 4. The foregoing shall also apply where the person acting on behalf of the consignor is also the agent of the carrier.

2. The consignor shall indemnify the carrier against all damage suffered by it, or by any other person to whom the carrier is liable, by reason of the irregularity,

incorrectness or incompleteness of the particulars and statements furnished by the consignor or on its behalf.

3. Subject to the provisions of paragraphs 1 and 2 of this Article, the carrier shall indemnify the consignor against all damage suffered by it, or by any other person to whom the consignor is liable, by reason of the irregularity, incorrectness or incompleteness of the particulars and statements inserted by the carrier or on its behalf in the cargo receipt or in the record preserved by the other means referred to in paragraph 2 of Article 4.

ARTICLE 11
EVIDENTIARY VALUE OF DOCUMENTATION

1. The air waybill or the cargo receipt is prima facie evidence of the conclusion of the contract, of the acceptance of the cargo and of the conditions of carriage mentioned therein.

2. Any statements in the air waybill or the cargo receipt relating to the weight, dimensions and packing of the cargo, as well as those relating to the number of packages, are prima facie evidence of the facts stated; those relating to the quantity, volume and condition of the cargo do not constitute evidence against the carrier except so far as they both have been, and are stated in the air waybill or the cargo receipt to have been, checked by it in the presence of the consignor, or relate to the apparent condition of the cargo.

ARTICLE 12
RIGHT OF DISPOSITION OF CARGO

1. Subject to its liability to carry out all its obligations under the contract of carriage, the consignor has the right to dispose of the cargo by withdrawing it at the airport of departure or destination, or by stopping it in the course of the journey on any landing, or by calling for it to be delivered at the place of destination or in the course of the journey to a person other than the consignee originally designated, or by requiring it to be returned to the airport of departure. The consignor must not exercise this right of disposition in such a way as to prejudice the carrier or other consignors and must reimburse any expenses occasioned by the exercise of this right.

2. If it is impossible to carry out the instructions of the consignor, the carrier must so inform the consignor forthwith.

3. If the carrier carries out the instructions of the consignor for the disposition of the cargo without requiring the production of the part of the air waybill or the cargo receipt delivered to the latter, the carrier will be liable, without prejudice to its right of recovery from the consignor, for any damage which may be caused thereby to

any person who is lawfully in possession of that part of the air waybill or the cargo receipt.

4. The right conferred on the consignor ceases at the moment when that of the consignee begins in accordance with Article 13. Nevertheless, if the consignee declines to accept the cargo, or cannot be communicated with, the consignor resumes its right of disposition.

ARTICLE 13
DELIVERY OF THE CARGO

1. Except when the consignor has exercised its right under Article 12, the consignee is entitled, on arrival of the cargo at the place of destination, to require the carrier to deliver the cargo to it, on payment of the charges due and on complying with the conditions of carriage.

2. Unless it is otherwise agreed, it is the duty of the carrier to give notice to the consignee as soon as the cargo arrives.

3. If the carrier admits the loss of the cargo, or if the cargo has not arrived at the expiration of seven days after the date on which it ought to have arrived, the consignee is entitled to enforce against the carrier the rights which flow from the contract of carriage.

ARTICLE 14
ENFORCEMENT OF THE RIGHTS OF CONSIGNOR AND CONSIGNEE

The consignor and the consignee can respectively enforce all the rights given to them by Articles 12 and 13, each in its own name, whether it is acting in its own interest or in the interest of another, provided that it carries out the obligations imposed by the contract of carriage.

ARTICLE 15
RELATIONS OF CONSIGNOR AND CONSIGNEE OR MUTUAL RELATIONS OF THIRD PARTIES

1. Articles 12, 13 and 14 do not affect either the relations of the consignor and the consignee with each other or the mutual relations of third parties whose rights are derived either from the consignor or from the consignee.

2. The provisions of Articles 12, 13 and 14 can only be varied by express provision in the air waybill or the cargo receipt.

ARTICLE 16
FORMALITIES OF CUSTOMS, POLICE OR OTHER PUBLIC AUTHORITIES

1. The consignor must furnish such information and such documents as are necessary to meet the formalities of customs, police and any other public authorities before the cargo can be delivered to the consignee. The consignor is liable to the carrier for any damage occasioned by the absence, insufficiency or irregularity of any such information or documents, unless the damage is due to the fault of the carrier, its servants or agents.

2. The carrier is under no obligation to enquire into the correctness or sufficiency of such information or documents.

CHAPTER III

LIABILITY OF THE CARRIER AND EXTENT OF COMPENSATION FOR DAMAGE

ARTICLE 17
DEATH AND INJURY OF PASSENGERS—DAMAGE TO BAGGAGE

1. The carrier is liable for damage sustained in case of death or bodily injury of a passenger upon condition only that the accident which caused the death or injury took place on board the aircraft or in the course of any of the operations of embarking or disembarking.

2. The carrier is liable for damage sustained in case of destruction or loss of, or of damage to, checked baggage upon condition only that the event which caused the destruction, loss or damage took place on board the aircraft or during any period within which the checked baggage was in the charge of the carrier. However, the carrier is not liable if and to the extent that the damage resulted from the inherent defect, quality or vice of the baggage. In the case of unchecked baggage, including personal items, the carrier is liable if the damage resulted from its fault or that of its servants or agents.

3. If the carrier admits the loss of the checked baggage, or if the checked baggage has not arrived at the expiration of twenty-one days after the date on which it ought to have arrived, the passenger is entitled to enforce against the carrier the rights which flow from the contract of carriage.

4. Unless otherwise specified, in this Convention the term "baggage" means both checked baggage and unchecked baggage.

ARTICLE 18
DAMAGE TO CARGO

1. The carrier is liable for damage sustained in the event of the destruction or loss of, or damage to, cargo upon condition only that the event which caused the damage so sustained took place during the carriage by air.

2. However, the carrier is not liable if and to the extent it proves that the destruction, or loss of, or damage to, the cargo resulted from one or more of the following:

(a) inherent defect, quality or vice of that cargo;

(b) defective packing of that cargo performed by a person other than the carrier or its servants or agents;

(c) an act of war or an armed conflict;

(d) an act of public authority carried out in connection with the entry, exit or transit of the cargo.

3. The carriage by air within the meaning of paragraph 1 of this Article comprises the period during which the cargo is in the charge of the carrier.

4. The period of the carriage by air does not extend to any carriage by land, by sea or by inland waterway performed outside an airport. If, however, such carriage takes place in the performance of a contract for carriage by air, for the purpose of loading, delivery or transhipment, any damage is presumed, subject to proof to the contrary, to have been the result of an event which took place during the carriage by air. If a carrier, without the consent of the consignor, substitutes carriage by another mode of transport for the whole or part of a carriage intended by the agreement between the parties to be carriage by air, such carriage by another mode of transport is deemed to be within the period of carriage by air.

ARTICLE 19
DELAY

The carrier is liable for damage occasioned by delay in the carriage by air of passengers, baggage or cargo. Nevertheless, the carrier shall not be liable for damage occasioned by delay if it proves that it and its servants and agents took all measures that could reasonably be required to avoid the damage or that it was impossible for it or them to take such measures.

ARTICLE 20
EXONERATION

If the carrier proves that the damage was caused or contributed to by the negligence or other wrongful act or omission of the person claiming compensation, or the person from whom he or she derives his or her rights, the carrier shall be wholly or partly exonerated from its liability to the claimant to the extent that such negligence or wrongful act or omission caused or contributed to the damage. When by reason of death or injury of a passenger compensation is claimed by a person other than the passenger, the carrier shall likewise be wholly or partly exonerated from its liability to the extent that it proves that the damage was caused or contributed to by the negligence or other wrongful act or omission of that passenger. This Article applies to all the liability provisions in this Convention, including paragraph 1 of Article 21.

ARTICLE 21
COMPENSATION IN CASE OF DEATH OR INJURY OF PASSENGERS

1. For damages arising under paragraph 1 of Article 17 not exceeding 100,000 Special Drawing Rights for each passenger, the carrier shall not be able to exclude or limit its liability.

2. The carrier shall not be liable for damages arising under paragraph 1 of Article 17 to the extent that they exceed for each passenger 100,000 Special Drawing Rights if the carrier proves that: (a) such damage was not due to the negligence or other wrongful act or omission of the carrier or its servants or agents; or (b) such damage was solely due to the negligence or other wrongful act or omission of a third party.

ARTICLE 22
LIMITS OF LIABILITY IN RELATION TO DELAY, BAGGAGE AND CARGO

1. In the case of damage caused by delay as specified in Article 19 in the carriage of persons, the liability of the carrier for each passenger is limited to 4,150 Special Drawing Rights.

2. In the carriage of baggage, the liability of the carrier in the case of destruction, loss, damage or delay is limited to 1,000 Special Drawing Rights for each passenger unless the passenger has made, at the time when the checked baggage was handed over to the carrier, a special declaration of interest in delivery at destination and has paid a supplementary sum if the case so requires. In that case the carrier will be liable to pay a sum not exceeding the declared sum, unless it proves that the sum is greater than the passenger's actual interest in delivery at destination.

3. In the carriage of cargo, the liability of the carrier in the case of destruction, loss, damage or delay is limited to a sum of 17 Special Drawing Rights per kilogramme, unless the consignor has made, at the time when the package was handed

over to the carrier, a special declaration of interest in delivery at destination and has paid a supplementary sum if the case so requires. In that case the carrier will be liable to pay a sum not exceeding the declared sum, unless it proves that the sum is greater than the consignor's actual interest in delivery at destination.

4. In the case of destruction, loss, damage or delay of part of the cargo, or of any object contained therein, the weight to be taken into consideration in determining the amount to which the carrier's liability is limited shall be only the total weight of the package or packages concerned. Nevertheless, when the destruction, loss, damage or delay of a part of the cargo, or of an object contained therein, affects the value of other packages covered by the same air waybill, or the same receipt or, if they were not issued, by the same record preserved by the other means referred to in paragraph 2 of Article 4, the total weight of such package or packages shall also be taken into consideration in determining the limit of liability.

5. The foregoing provisions of paragraphs 1 and 2 of this Article shall not apply if it is proved that the damage resulted from an act or omission of the carrier, its servants or agents, done with intent to cause damage or recklessly and with knowledge that damage would probably result; provided that, in the case of such act or omission of a servant or agent, it is also proved that such servant or agent was acting within the scope of its employment.

6. The limits prescribed in Article 21 and in this Article shall not prevent the court from awarding, in accordance with its own law, in addition, the whole or part of the court costs and of the other expenses of the litigation incurred by the plaintiff, including interest. The foregoing provision shall not apply if the amount of the damages awarded, excluding court costs and other expenses of the litigation, does not exceed the sum which the carrier has offered in writing to the plaintiff within a period of six months from the date of the occurrence causing the damage, or before the commencement of the action, if that is later.

ARTICLE 23
CONVERSION OF MONETARY UNITS

1. The sums mentioned in terms of Special Drawing Right in this Convention shall be deemed to refer to the Special Drawing Right as defined by the International Monetary Fund. Conversion of the sums into national currencies shall, in case of judicial proceedings, be made according to the value of such currencies in terms of the Special Drawing Right at the date of the judgment. The value of a national currency, in terms of the Special Drawing Right, of a State Party which is a Member of the International Monetary Fund, shall be calculated in accordance with the method of valuation applied by the International Monetary Fund, in effect at the date of the judgment, for its operations and transactions. The value of a national currency, in terms of the Special Drawing Right, of a State Party which is not a Member of the International Monetary Fund, shall be calculated in a manner determined by that State.

2. Nevertheless, those States which are not Members of the International Monetary Fund and whose law does not permit the application of the provisions of paragraph 1 of this Article may, at the time of ratification or accession or at any time thereafter, declare that the limit of liability of the carrier prescribed in Article 21 is fixed at a sum of 1,500,000 monetary units per passenger in judicial proceedings in their territories; 62,500 monetary units per passenger with respect to paragraph 1 of Article 22; 15,000 monetary units per passenger with respect to paragraph 2 of Article 22; and 250 monetary units per kilogramme with respect to paragraph 3 of Article 22. This monetary unit corresponds to sixty-five and a half milligrammes of gold of millesimal fineness nine hundred. These sums may be converted into the national currency concerned in round figures. The conversion of these sums into national currency shall be made according to the law of the State concerned.

3. The calculation mentioned in the last sentence of paragraph 1 of this Article and the conversion method mentioned in paragraph 2 of this Article shall be made in such manner as to express in the national currency of the State Party as far as possible the same real value for the amounts in Articles 21 and 22 as would result from the application of the first three sentences of paragraph 1 of this Article. States Parties shall communicate to the depositary the manner of calculation pursuant to paragraph 1 of this Article, or the result of the conversion in paragraph 2 of this Article as the case may be, when depositing an instrument of ratification, acceptance, approval of or accession to this Convention and whenever there is a change in either.

ARTICLE 24
REVIEW OF LIMITS

1. Without prejudice to the provisions of Article 25 of this Convention and subject to paragraph 2 below, the limits of liability prescribed in Articles 21, 22 and 23 shall be reviewed by the Depositary at five-year intervals, the first such review to take place at the end of the fifth year following the date of entry into force of this Convention, or if the Convention does not enter into force within five years of the date it is first open for signature, within the first year of its entry into force, by reference to an inflation factor which corresponds to the accumulated rate of inflation since the previous revision or in the first instance since the date of entry into force of the Convention. The measure of the rate of inflation to be used in determining the inflation factor shall be the weighted average of the annual rates of increase or decrease in the Consumer Price Indices of the States whose currencies comprise the Special Drawing Right mentioned in paragraph 1 of Article 23.

2. If the review referred to in the preceding paragraph concludes that the inflation factor has exceeded 10 per cent, the Depositary shall notify States Parties of a revision of the limits of liability. Any such revision shall become effective six months after its notification to the States Parties. If within three months after its notification to the States Parties a majority of the States Parties register their disapproval, the revision shall not become effective and the Depositary shall refer the matter to a meeting of the

States Parties. The Depositary shall immediately notify all States Parties of the coming into force of any revision.

3. Notwithstanding paragraph 1 of this Article, the procedure referred to in paragraph 2 of this Article shall be applied at any time provided that one-third of the States Parties express a desire to that effect and upon condition that the inflation factor referred to in paragraph 1 has exceeded 30 per cent since the previous revision or since the date of entry into force of this Convention if there has been no previous revision. Subsequent reviews using the procedure described in paragraph 1 of this Article will take place at five-year intervals starting at the end of the fifth year following the date of the reviews under the present paragraph.

ARTICLE 25
STIPULATION ON LIMITS

A carrier may stipulate that the contract of carriage shall be subject to higher limits of liability than those provided for in this Convention or to no limits of liability whatsoever.

ARTICLE 26
INVALIDITY OF CONTRACTUAL PROVISIONS

Any provision tending to relieve the carrier of liability or to fix a lower limit than that which is laid down in this Convention shall be null and void, but the nullity of any such provision does not involve the nullity of the whole contract, which shall remain subject to the provisions of this Convention.

ARTICLE 27
FREEDOM TO CONTRACT

Nothing contained in this Convention shall prevent the carrier from refusing to enter into any contract of carriage, from waiving any defences available under the Convention, or from laying down conditions which do not conflict with the provisions of this Convention.

ARTICLE 28
ADVANCE PAYMENTS

In the case of aircraft accidents resulting in death or injury of passengers, the carrier shall, if required by its national law, make advance payments without delay to a natural person or persons who are entitled to claim compensation in order to meet the immediate economic needs of such persons. Such advance payments shall not constitute a recognition of liability and may be offset against any amounts subsequently paid as damages by the carrier.

ARTICLE 29
BASIS OF CLAIMS

In the carriage of passengers, baggage and cargo, any action for damages, however founded, whether under this Convention or in contract or in tort or otherwise, can only be brought subject to the conditions and such limits of liability as are set out in this Convention without prejudice to the question as to who are the persons who have the right to bring suit and what are their respective rights. In any such action, punitive, exemplary or any other non-compensatory damages shall not be recoverable.

ARTICLE 30
SERVANTS, AGENTS—AGGREGATION OF CLAIMS

1. If an action is brought against a servant or agent of the carrier arising out of damage to which the Convention relates, such servant or agent, if they prove that they acted within the scope of their employment, shall be entitled to avail themselves of the conditions and limits of liability which the carrier itself is entitled to invoke under this Convention.

2. The aggregate of the amounts recoverable from the carrier, its servants and agents, in that case, shall not exceed the said limits.

3. Save in respect of the carriage of cargo, the provisions of paragraphs 1 and 2 of this Article shall not apply if it is proved that the damage resulted from an act or omission of the servant or agent done with intent to cause damage or recklessly and with knowledge that damage would probably result.

ARTICLE 31
TIMELY NOTICE OF COMPLAINTS

1. Receipt by the person entitled to delivery of checked baggage or cargo without complaint is prima facie evidence that the same has been delivered in good condition and in accordance with the document of carriage or with the record preserved by the other means referred to in paragraph 2 of Article 3 and paragraph 2 of Article 4.

2. In the case of damage, the person entitled to delivery must complain to the carrier forthwith after the discovery of the damage, and, at the latest, within seven days from the date of receipt in the case of checked baggage and fourteen days from the date of receipt in the case of cargo. In the case of delay, the complaint must be made at the latest within twenty-one days from the date on which the baggage or cargo have been placed at his or her disposal.

3. Every complaint must be made in writing and given or dispatched within the times aforesaid.

4. If no complaint is made within the times aforesaid, no action shall lie against the carrier, save in the case of fraud on its part.

ARTICLE 32
DEATH OF PERSON LIABLE

In the case of the death of the person liable, an action for damages lies in accordance with the terms of this Convention against those legally representing his or her estate.

ARTICLE 33
JURISDICTION

1. An action for damages must be brought, at the option of the plaintiff, in the territory of one of the States Parties, either before the court of the domicile of the carrier or of its principal place of business, or where it has a place of business through which the contract has been made or before the court at the place of destination.

2. In respect of damage resulting from the death or injury of a passenger, an action may be brought before one of the courts mentioned in paragraph 1 of this Article, or in the territory of a State Party in which at the time of the accident the passenger has his or her principal and permanent residence and to or from which the carrier operates services for the carriage of passengers by air, either on its own aircraft, or on another carrier's aircraft pursuant to a commercial agreement, and in which that carrier conducts its business of carriage of passengers by air from premises leased or owned by the carrier itself or by another carrier with which it has a commercial agreement.

3. For the purposes of paragraph 2, (a) "commercial agreement" means an agreement, other than an agency agreement, made between carriers and relating to the provision of their joint services for carriage of passengers by air; (b) "principal and permanent residence" means the one fixed and permanent abode of the passenger at the time of the accident. The nationality of the passenger shall not be the determining factor in this regard.

4. Questions of procedure shall be governed by the law of the court seised of the case.

ARTICLE 34
ARBITRATION

1. Subject to the provisions of this Article, the parties to the contract of carriage for cargo may stipulate that any dispute relating to the liability of the carrier under this Convention shall be settled by arbitration. Such agreement shall be in writing.

2. The arbitration proceedings shall, at the option of the claimant, take place within one of the jurisdictions referred to in Article 33.

3. The arbitrator or arbitration tribunal shall apply the provisions of this Convention.

4. The provisions of paragraphs 2 and 3 of this Article shall be deemed to be part of every arbitration clause or agreement, and any term of such clause or agreement which is inconsistent therewith shall be null and void.

ARTICLE 35
LIMITATION OF ACTIONS

1. The right to damages shall be extinguished if an action is not brought within a period of two years, reckoned from the date of arrival at the destination, or from the date on which the aircraft ought to have arrived, or from the date on which the carriage stopped.

2. The method of calculating that period shall be determined by the law of the court seised of the case.

ARTICLE 36
SUCCESSIVE CARRIAGE

1. In the case of carriage to be performed by various successive carriers and falling within the definition set out in paragraph 3 of Article 1, each carrier which accepts passengers, baggage or cargo is subject to the rules set out in this Convention and is deemed to be one of the parties to the contract of carriage in so far as the contract deals with that part of the carriage which is performed under its supervision.

2. In the case of carriage of this nature, the passenger or any person entitled to compensation in respect of him or her can take action only against the carrier which performed the carriage during which the accident or the delay occurred, save in the case where, by express agreement, the first carrier has assumed liability for the whole journey.

3. As regards baggage or cargo, the passenger or consignor will have a right of action against the first carrier, and the passenger or consignee who is entitled to delivery will have a right of action against the last carrier, and further, each may take action against the carrier which performed the carriage during which the destruction, loss, damage or delay took place. These carriers will be jointly and severally liable to the passenger or to the consignor or consignee.

ARTICLE 37
RIGHT OF RECOURSE AGAINST THIRD PARTIES

Nothing in this Convention shall prejudice the question whether a person liable for damage in accordance with its provisions has a right of recourse against any other person.

CHAPTER IV

COMBINED CARRIAGE

ARTICLE 38
COMBINED CARRIAGE

1. In the case of combined carriage performed partly by air and partly by any other mode of carriage, the provisions of this Convention shall, subject to paragraph 4 of Article 18, apply only to the carriage by air, provided that the carriage by air falls within the terms of Article 1.

2. Nothing in this Convention shall prevent the parties in the case of combined carriage from inserting in the document of air carriage conditions relating to other modes of carriage, provided that the provisions of this Convention are observed as regards the carriage by air.

CHAPTER V

CARRIAGE BY AIR PERFORMED BY A PERSON OTHER THAN THE CONTRACTING CARRIER

ARTICLE 39
CONTRACTING CARRIER—ACTUAL CARRIER

The provisions of this Chapter apply when a person (hereinafter referred to as "the contracting carrier") as a principal makes a contract of carriage governed by this Convention with a passenger or consignor or with a person acting on behalf of the passenger or consignor, and another person (hereinafter referred to as "the actual carrier") performs, by virtue of authority from the contracting carrier, the whole or part of the carriage, but is not with respect to such part a successive carrier within the meaning of this Convention. Such authority shall be presumed in the absence of proof to the contrary.

ARTICLE 40
RESPECTIVE LIABILITY OF CONTRACTING AND ACTUAL CARRIERS

If an actual carrier performs the whole or part of carriage which, according to the contract referred to in Article 39, is governed by this Convention, both the contracting carrier and the actual carrier shall, except as otherwise provided in this Chapter, be subject to the rules of this Convention, the former for the whole of the carriage contemplated in the contract, the latter solely for the carriage which it performs.

ARTICLE 41
MUTUAL LIABILITY

1. The acts and omissions of the actual carrier and of its servants and agents acting within the scope of their employment shall, in relation to the carriage performed by the actual carrier, be deemed to be also those of the contracting carrier.

2. The acts and omissions of the contracting carrier and of its servants and agents acting within the scope of their employment shall, in relation to the carriage performed by the actual carrier, be deemed to be also those of the actual carrier. Nevertheless, no such act or omission shall subject the actual carrier to liability exceeding the amounts referred to in Articles 21, 22, 23 and 24. Any special agreement under which the contracting carrier assumes obligations not imposed by this Convention or any waiver of rights or defences conferred by this Convention or any special declaration of interest in delivery at destination contemplated in Article 22 shall not affect the actual carrier unless agreed to by it.

ARTICLE 42
ADDRESSEE OF COMPLAINTS AND INSTRUCTIONS

Any complaint to be made or instruction to be given under this Convention to the carrier shall have the same effect whether addressed to the contracting carrier or to the actual carrier. Nevertheless, instructions referred to in Article 12 shall only be effective if addressed to the contracting carrier.

ARTICLE 43
SERVANTS AND AGENTS

In relation to the carriage performed by the actual carrier, any servant or agent of that carrier or of the contracting carrier shall, if they prove that they acted within the scope of their employment, be entitled to avail themselves of the conditions and limits of liability which are applicable under this Convention to the carrier whose servant or agent they are, unless it is proved that they acted in a manner that prevents the limits of liability from being invoked.

ARTICLE 44
AGGREGATION OF DAMAGES

In relation to the carriage performed by the actual carrier, the aggregate of the amounts recoverable from that carrier and the contracting carrier, and from their servants and agents acting within the scope of their employment, shall not exceed the highest amount which could be awarded against either the contracting carrier or the actual carrier under this Convention, but none of the persons mentioned shall be liable for a sum in excess of the limit applicable to that person.

ARTICLE 45
ADDRESSEE OF CLAIMS

In relation to the carriage performed by the actual carrier, an action for damages may be brought, at the option of the plaintiff, against that carrier or the contracting carrier, or against both together or separately. If the action is brought against only one of those carriers, that carrier shall have the right to require the other carrier to be joined in the proceedings, the procedure and effects being governed by the law of the court seised of the case.

ARTICLE 46
ADDITIONAL JURISDICTION

Any action for damages contemplated in Article 45 must be brought, at the option of the plaintiff, in the territory of one of the States Parties, either before a court in which an action may be brought against the contracting carrier, as provided in Article 33, or before the court having jurisdiction at the place where the actual carrier has its domicile or its principal place of business.

ARTICLE 47
INVALIDITY OF CONTRACTUAL PROVISIONS

Any contractual provision tending to relieve the contracting carrier or the actual carrier of liability under this Chapter or to fix a lower limit than that which is applicable according to this Chapter shall be null and void, but the nullity of any such provision does not involve the nullity of the whole contract, which shall remain subject to the provisions of this Chapter.

ARTICLE 48
MUTUAL RELATIONS OF CONTRACTING AND ACTUAL CARRIERS

Except as provided in Article 45, nothing in this Chapter shall affect the rights and obligations of the carriers between themselves, including any right of recourse or indemnification.

CHAPTER VI

OTHER PROVISIONS

ARTICLE 49
MANDATORY APPLICATION

Any clause contained in the contract of carriage and all special agreements entered into before the damage occurred by which the parties purport to infringe the rules laid down by this Convention, whether by deciding the law to be applied, or by altering the rules as to jurisdiction, shall be null and void.

ARTICLE 50
INSURANCE

States Parties shall require their carriers to maintain adequate insurance covering their liability under this Convention. A carrier may be required by the State Party into which it operates to furnish evidence that it maintains adequate insurance covering its liability under this Convention.

ARTICLE 51
CARRIAGE PERFORMED IN EXTRAORDINARY CIRCUMSTANCES

The provisions of Articles 3 to 5, 7 and 8 relating to the documentation of carriage shall not apply in the case of carriage performed in extraordinary circumstances outside the normal scope of a carrier business.

ARTICLE 52
DEFINITION OF DAYS

The expression "days" when used in this Convention means calendar days, not working days.

CHAPTER VII

FINAL CLAUSES

ARTICLE 53
SIGNATURE, RATIFICATION AND ENTRY INTO FORCE

1. This Convention shall be open for signature in Montreal on 28 May 1999 by States participating in the International Conference on Air Law held at Montreal from 10 to 28 May 1999. After 28 May 1999, the Convention shall be open to all States for signature at the Headquarters of the International Civil Aviation Organization in Montreal until it enters into force in accordance with paragraph 6 of this Article.

2. This Convention shall similarly be open for signature by Regional Economic Integration Organisations. For the purpose of this Convention, a "Regional Economic Integration Organisation" means any organisation which is constituted by sovereign States of a given region which has competence in respect of certain matters governed by this Convention and has been duly authorized to sign and to ratify, accept, approve or accede to this Convention.

A reference to a "State Party" or "States Parties" in this Convention, otherwise than in paragraph 2 of Article 1, paragraph 1(b) of Article 3, paragraph (b) of Article 5, Articles 23, 33, 46 and paragraph (b) of Article 57, applies equally to a Regional Economic Integration Organisation. For the purpose of Article 24, the references to "a majority of the States Parties" and "one-third of the States Parties" shall not apply to a Regional Economic Integration Organisation.

3. This Convention shall be subject to ratification by States and by Regional Economic Integration Organisations which have signed it.

4. Any State or Regional Economic Integration Organisation which does not sign this Convention may accept, approve or accede to it at any time.

5. Instruments of ratification, acceptance, approval or accession shall be deposited with the International Civil Aviation Organization, which is hereby designated the Depositary.

6. This Convention shall enter into force on the sixtieth day following the date of deposit of the thirtieth instrument of ratification, acceptance, approval or accession with the Depositary between the States which have deposited such instrument. An instrument deposited by a Regional Economic Integration Organisation shall not be counted for the purpose of this paragraph.

7. For other States and for other Regional Economic Integration Organisations, this Convention shall take effect sixty days following the date of deposit of the instrument of ratification, acceptance, approval or accession.

8. The Depositary shall promptly notify all signatories and States Parties of: (a) each signature of this Convention and date thereof; (b) each deposit of an instrument of ratification, acceptance, approval or accession and date thereof; (c) the date of entry into force of this Convention; (d) the date of the coming into force of any revision of the limits of liability established under this Convention; (e) any denunciation under Article 54.

ARTICLE 54
DENUNCIATION

1. Any State Party may denounce this Convention by written notification to the Depositary.

2. Denunciation shall take effect one hundred and eighty days following the date on which notification is received by the Depositary.

ARTICLE 55
RELATIONSHIP WITH OTHER WARSAW CONVENTION INSTRUMENTS

This Convention shall prevail over any rules which apply to international carriage by air:

1. Between States Parties to this Convention by virtue of those States commonly being Party to:

(a) the Convention for the Unification of Certain Rules Relating to International Carriage by Air Signed at Warsaw on 12 October 1929 (hereinafter called the Warsaw Convention);

(b) the Protocol to Amend the Convention for the Unification of Certain Rules Relating to International Carriage by Air Signed at Warsaw on 12 October 1929, Done at The Hague on 28 September 1955 (hereinafter called The Hague Protocol);

(c) the Convention, Supplementary to the Warsaw Convention, for the Unification of Certain Rules Relating to International Carriage by Air Performed by a Person Other than the Contracting Carrier, signed at Guadalajara on 18 September 1961 (hereinafter called the Guadalajara Convention);

(d) the Protocol to Amend the Convention for the Unification of Certain Rules Relating to International Carriage by Air Signed at Warsaw on 12 October 1929 as Amended by the Protocol Done at The Hague on 28 September 1955 Signed at Guatemala City on 8 March 1971 (hereinafter called the Guatemala City Protocol);

(e) Additional Protocol Nos. 1 to 3 and Montreal Protocol No. 4 to amend the Warsaw Convention as amended by The Hague Protocol or the Warsaw Convention as amended by both The Hague Protocol and the Guatemala City Protocol Signed at Montreal on 25 September 1975 (hereinafter called the Montreal Protocols); or

2. within the territory of any single State Party to this Convention by virtue of that State being Party to one or more of the instruments referred to in sub-paragraphs (a) to (e) above.

ARTICLE 56
STATES WITH MORE THAN ONE SYSTEM OF LAW

1. If a State has two or more territorial units in which different systems of law are applicable in relation to matters dealt with in this Convention, it may at the time of signature, ratification, acceptance, approval or accession declare that this Convention shall extend to all its territorial units or only to one or more of them and may modify this declaration by submitting another declaration at any time.

2. Any such declaration shall be notified to the Depositary and shall state expressly the territorial units to which the Convention applies.

3. In relation to a State Party which has made such a declaration: (a) references in Article 23 to "national currency" shall be construed as referring to the currency of the relevant territorial unit of that State; and (b) the reference in Article 28 to "national law" shall be construed as referring to the law of the relevant territorial unit of that State.

ARTICLE 57
RESERVATIONS

No reservation may be made to this Convention except that a State Party may at any time declare by a notification addressed to the Depositary that this Convention shall not apply to: (a) international carriage by air performed and operated directly by that State Party for non-commercial purposes in respect to its functions and duties as a sovereign State; and/or (b) the carriage of persons, cargo and baggage for its military authorities on aircraft registered in or leased by that State Party, the whole capacity of which has been reserved by or on behalf of such authorities.

IN WITNESS WHEREOF the undersigned Plenipotentiaries, having been duly authorized, have signed this Convention.

DONE at Montreal on the 28th day of May of the year one thousand nine hundred and ninety-nine in the English, Arabic, Chinese, French, Russian and Spanish languages, all texts being equally authentic. This Convention shall remain deposited in the archives of the International Civil Aviation Organization, and certified copies thereof shall be transmitted by the Depositary to all States Parties to this Convention, as well as to all States Parties to the Warsaw Convention, The Hague Protocol, the Guadalajara Convention, the Guatemala City Protocol, and the Montreal Protocols.

NOTES

1. The Montreal Convention is the product of a meeting sponsored by the United Nations in 1999 of delegates from 121 different states via the International Civil Aviation Organization—ICAO. *See http://www.icao.int/*. The Montreal Convention has been ratified by more than 95 nations to date. The United States adopted the treaty in November, 2003, as a replacement to the Warsaw Convention. *See* Convention for the Unification of Certain Rules for International Carriage by Air, *http://www.state.gov/e/eeb/rls/othr/ata/114157.htm*. *See also Ehrlich v. American Airlines* (2d Cir. 2004).

What law applies to an international aviation accident that occurred prior to ratification of the Montreal Convention by a particular state, *e.g.*, an accident involving an American passenger pre-2003? To what law should courts look in resolving disputes arising out of international transportation involving nations that ratified neither the Warsaw nor the Montreal Convention? What treaty applies where one nation applies the Warsaw Convention and another nation employs the Montreal Convention? The scenarios are numerous. *See, e.g.,* Thomas J. Whalen, *Guidance on the Application of Liability Regimes to Claims* (Sept. 2006), *http://www.eckertseamans.com/file/pdf/alerts/j1023668.pdf*.

2. The Montreal Convention—like its predecessor, the Warsaw Convention—applies only to "international carriage," meaning

> any carriage in which, according to the agreement between the parties, the place of departure and the place of destination, whether there be a break in carriage or transhipment, are situated either within the territories of two States Parties, or within the territory of a single State Party if there is an agreed stopping place within the territory of another State, even if that State is not a State Party.

See, e.g., Coyle v. P.T. Garuda Indonesia (9th Cir. 2004). Importantly, if a passenger is traveling internationally, the Montreal Convention preempts all other laws and is the exclusive remedy for injury or death in international aviation accident cases, see *El Al Israeli Airlines, Ltd. v. Tsui Yuan Tseng* (1999), and "[a] passenger whose injuries fall within the scope of the Convention is either entitled to recovery under the Convention or not at all." *Magan v. Lufthansa German Airlines* (2d Cir. 2003).

Whether a claimant under the Montreal Convention was traveling internationally is not always obvious. For example, the Montreal Convention may apply to a domestic flight that is but a part of an international itinerary (*e.g.*, Illinois to New York to Ireland). Consider:

> *Single Operation.* A Denver-to-Chicago flight was "international transportation" under the Warsaw Convention where the passenger-plaintiff's layover in Denver was to make a connection after a flight from London, tickets were sold by the same travel agent, and the parties had knowledge of the trip as a single operation. *See Robertson v. American Airlines, Inc.* (D.C. Cir. 2005).

> *"Domestic" Operations.* A domestic flight constitutes international transportation if it is part of an international itinerary regarded by the parties—the passenger and the carrier—as a single operation. Art. 1(2)-(3). *See Haldimann v. Delta Airlines, Inc.* (D.C. Cir. 1999).

The intent of the parties is a critical consideration in determining the international character of air carriage, therefore. Does a stop-over in a foreign country qualify as international carriage under the Montreal Convention? *See, e.g., Gustafson v. American Airlines, Inc.* (D. Mass. 2009). *See also Jones v. USA 3000 Airlines* (E.D. Mo. Feb. 9, 2009) ("for round-trip international travel, the place of destination is the same as the place of departure.").

3. The definition of "accident" under both the Warsaw Convention and its successor, the Montreal Convention, has generated a substantial body of decisional law. An "accident" under either treaty has been defined generally as an "unexpected or unusual event that is external to the passenger" occurring during the embarking or disembarking of an aircraft, but its application has been case-specific. *See, e.g., Olympic Airways v. Husain* (2004), and *Air France v. Saks* (1985), *supra*. *See also Watts v. Am. Airlines, Inc.* (S.D. Ind. Oct. 10, 2007) (holding that where an international passenger died in flight from a heart attack, the airline's failure to respond to that medical emergency constituted an "accident.")

One federal district court has noted that, "as the causal balance shifts towards acts and conditions that are independent of the knowledge or will of the carrier, or not associated with the operation of the aircraft or airline nor arising from risks characteristic of air travel, and instead are more unique to the passenger alleging injury, the lesser the claimant's probability of recovery." *Fulop v. Malev Hungarian Airlines*, (S.D.N.Y. 2001). *See generally Sethy v. Malev-Hungarian Airlines, Inc.* (S.D.N.Y. Aug. 31, 2000); *Curley v. American Airlines, Inc.* (S.D.N.Y. 1994); *Price v. British Airways* (S.D.N.Y. July 7, 1992); *Margrave v. British Airways* (S.D.N.Y. 1986); *Warshaw v. Trans World Airlines, Inc.* (E.D. Pa. 1977); *Potter v. Delta Air Lines, Inc.* (5th Cir. 1996) (no "accident" where the alleged injury arose from an altercation between two passengers without any involvement of flight crew); *Stone v. Continental Airlines, Inc.*, (D. Haw. 1995) (same); *Tsevas v. Delta Air Lines, Inc.* (N.D. Ill. Dec. 1, 1997) (finding injuries were caused by an "accident" where assault by one passenger on another occurred after the flight attendant excessively served drinks to the attacker and refused to intervene or to change plaintiff's seat assignments). *See also Schneider v. Swiss Air Transp. Co., Ltd.* (D. Me. 1988) (finding "accident" where plaintiff was injured in moving from her seat when another passenger refused to put his seat upright and flight crew denied assistance).

Some courts have construed "accident" quite narrowly, finding no liability in situations where the circumstances indicate no causal involvement or relationship of the carrier in the events constituting the alleged accident, as demonstrated by the absence of evidence of any abnormal aircraft operations; departures from recognized industry standards, carrier policies or procedures; or aberrant conduct of employees in some way related to the operation of the aircraft or airline. In those situations, courts seem to emphasize occurrences outside the airline's control or ability to prevent, or that are not related to hazards inherently associated with aviation, but rather are risks incident to "living in a world such as ours," may not be classified as accidents under the Convention. *Martinez Hernandez v. Air France* (1st Cir. 1976) (rejecting an argument that a terrorist attack within an airport was a "characteristic of air travel" to which Article 17 liability should apply). *See, e.g., Maxwell v. Aer Lingus Ltd.* (D. Mass. 2000); *Gotz v. Delta Airlines, Inc.* (D. Mass. 1998) (finding no accident where a passenger was injured by another engaged in removing an overhead bag, where there was no failure by the flight attendant to intervene and no request for assistance); *Price v. British Airways* (S.D.N.Y. July 7, 1992). *But cf. Pittman v. Grayson* (S.D.N.Y.1994) (finding no accident, because the events did not constitute risks inherent in air travel, even though plaintiff alleged that airline personnel had assisted in smuggling and transporting a passenger on a flight out of the country in violation of a court order); *Curley v. American Airlines, Inc.*, (S.D.N.Y.1994) (no accident even where plaintiff claimed that the flight captain falsely identified him to Mexican police officials as having smoked marijuana while aboard the aircraft, resulting in plaintiff's alleged injuries from detention and search by the Mexican police; the court concluded that being suspected and falsely accused of smoking marijuana in the airplane's lavatory was not a risk inherent in air travel).

4. Jurisdiction is a primary concern of any lawsuit, and it can be a complex substantive and procedural matter for courts and practitioners in aviation accident cases given the international character of commercial airline travel. In 2002, Congress enacted the Multiparty, Multiforum Trial Jurisdiction Act ("MMTJA"), 28 U.S.C. § 1369, granting federal district courts original jurisdiction over civil actions arising from a single accident involving at least 75 fatalities, where minimal diversity exists on the adverse parties, as follows:

> The district courts shall have original jurisdiction of any civil action involving minimal diversity between adverse parties that arises from a single accident, where at least 75 natural persons have died in the accident at a discrete location, if—

(1) a defendant resides in a State and a substantial part of the accident took place in another State or other location, regardless of whether that defendant is also a resident of the State where a substantial part of the accident took place;

(2) any two defendants reside in different States, regardless of whether such defendants are also residents of the same State or States; or

(3) substantial parts of the accident took place in different States.

In 2010, the Supreme Court of the United States decided *Hertz Corp. v. Friend* (2010), holding that a corporation's principal place of business for diversity purposes, is its "nerve center." Could a corporate aviation defendant successfully remove an accident case under the MMTJA in order to set up a subsequent move for dismissal under the doctrine of *forum non conveniens* through *Hertz Corp.*? *See, e.g.*, *Vivas v. The Boeing Co.* (Ill. App. Ct. 2009).

5. Subject to a two-year repose period, the Montreal Convention permits lawsuits against carriers for damages resulting in the death or injury of passengers in international transportation in several forums, including: (i) the carrier's domicile; (ii) the carrier's principal place of business; (iii) the place of business where the contract was made; and (iv) the passenger's destination. Significantly, Article 33 of the Montreal Convention adds a "fifth jurisdiction," namely the country in which a passenger has his or her "principal and permanent residence" at the time of the accident. The Montreal Convention specifically defines this residence as "the one fixed and permanent abode of the passenger at the time of the accident." Because "[t]he nationality of the passenger shall not be the determining factor in this regard," it is now possible for American citizens to seek relief in United States courts for international carriage arising under the Montreal Convention.) Article 33(4) of the Montreal Convention also provides that "[q]uestions of procedure shall be governed by the law of the court seised of the case."

6. The text of the Warsaw Convention is silent on the availability of the doctrine of *forum non conveniens*. With respect to jurisdiction and procedure, Article 28 provides:

(1) An action for damages must be brought, at the option of the plaintiff, in the territory of one of the High Contracting States, either before the court of the domicile of the carrier or of his principal place of business, of where he has a place of business

through which the contract has been made, or before the court at the place of destination.

(2) Questions of procedure shall be governed by the law of the court to which the case is submitted.

See Convention for the Unification of Certain Rules Relating to International Transportation by Air, Oct. 12, 1929, 49 Stat. 3000, 3020-21, T.S. No. 876 (1934), note following 49 U.S.C. § 40105. Does this mean that the doctrine of *forum non conveniens* applies in cases involving international aviation disputes under the Montreal Convention? *E.g.*, *Pierre-Louis v. Newvac Corp.* (11th Cir. 2009).

7. Damages are a significant part of aviation accident litigation. Commentators have noted that, "there is virtually always someone who is liable for an aviation accident … [t]ypically, the defendants either agree among themselves about how to divide expenditures for compensation and litigation, or they agree to let the outcome of one trial decide the division of liability." JAMES S. KAKALIK ET AL., COSTS AND COMPENSATION PAID IN AVIATION ACCIDENT LITIGATION 88 (1988). Moreover, aviation mass torts are notably efficient. Where mass tort plaintiffs generally receive about 50 percent of funds expended, that figure reaches 71 percent in aviation torts. *Compare id.* at 93-94 *with* JAMES S. KAKALIK ET AL., COSTS OF ASBETOS LITIGATION 39-40 (1983) (plaintiffs received 37 percent of funds expended in asbestos litigation). *See also* R. Daniel Truitt, *Hints of Uneven Playing Field in Aviation Torts: Is There Proof?*, 61 J. AIR L. & COM. 577 (1996).

Aviation litigation can be more lucrative than most mass tort litigation. Aviation settlements generally can average in the $1 million range. Eric S. Roth, Note, *Confronting Solicitation of Mass Disaster Victims*, 2 GEO. J. LEGAL ETHICS 967, 976, n.46 (1989). In 1996-97, the median jury verdicts in aviation cases in federal district court was $937,000, far higher than the median for "product liability" cases, and 43.8 percent of the verdicts were $1 million or more. *See* BUREAU OF JUSTICE STATISTICS, BULLETIN: FEDERAL TORT TRIALS AND VERDICTS, 1996-97 5 (1999), *http://www.ojp.usdoj.gov/bjs/pub/pdf/fttv97.pdf.*

While courts construing the Montreal Convention routinely rely on Warsaw Convention precedent to interpret similar provisions, see *Weiss v. El Al Israeli Airlines, Ltd.* (S.D.N.Y. 2006), a distinguishing feature of the Montreal Convention is its two-tier liability system, which is more liberal to plaintiff passengers than the Warsaw Convention it replaced. *See* Convention for the Unification of Certain Rules for International Carriage by Air, Oct. 12, 1929, 49 Stat. 3000, 137 L.N.T.S. 11, *reprinted in* 49 U.S.C. § 40105 (1994). Under Article 21 of the Montreal Convention, carriers may be strictly liable to each passenger up to 113,100.00 Special Drawing Rights ("SDRs") for provable damages (approximately US $147,596.00, where US $1 exchanges for .723977 SDR, in 2015). *http://www.imf.org/external/np/fin/data/rms_sdrv.aspx*. Liability (not strict) beyond that amount is not limited, but subject to certain defenses. Non-strict liability exists only if damage is (1) due to carrier negligence or other wrongful act or omission; or (2) solely due to the negligence or other wrongful act or omission of a third party.

8. As a policy matter, should mental injuries, unassociated from bodily injury, be recoverable under the Montreal Convention? *See, e.g.*, McKay Cunningham, *The Montreal Convention: Can Passengers Finally Recover for Mental Injuries?*, 41 VAND. J. TRANSNAT'L L. 1043 (2008). *See also Eastern Airlines, Inc. v. Floyd* (1991).

9. Strategic alliances, long a marketing tool in the tourism and hospitality industries, have gained prominence in today's airline business. The number of airline flights that are operated by one airline but sold by one or more other airlines—"code-sharing"—has grown exponentially in the last decade. Code-sharing is a driving force of both domestic and international airline alliances. *See In re Air Crash at Taipei, Taiwan* (C.D. Cal. 2002). However, passengers sometimes are unclear about the practical and legal operation of such arrangements.

Federal law defines "code-sharing" to mean "an arrangement whereby a carrier's designator code is used to identify a flight operated by another carrier." *See* 14 C.F.R. § 257.3(c)). (A "designator code," in turn, is a multiple letter character code that identifies a particular flight, *e.g.*, UA123 for United Airlines Flight 123.) Airline economics support code-sharing arrangements because they offer consumers what they want, namely "online" as opposed to "interline" connections. An interline itinerary involves travel on one airline from point A to point B and on a different airline from point B to point C. Code-sharing provides passengers one-stop shopping by allowing different airlines to offer one-stop service from point A to point C, with each airline independently setting the price for service between cities that it otherwise would not have served.

Under the Warsaw Convention, only the airline that actually transports the injured passenger could be held liable as the responsible "carrier." The Montreal Convention similarly addresses several different arrangements between or among interline carriers, including "contracting," "actual," and "successive" carriers under Articles 36, 39, 40, and 41. Are code-share carriers alter egos of each other for purposes of determining liability under the international aviation treaties? *See, e.g., Best v. BWIA West Indies Airways, Ltd.* (E.D.N.Y. 2008).

10. Historically, courts have considered whether terrorist activity falls within the "unexpected or unusual happening" test under the Warsaw Convention. For example, on August 5, 1973, at Hellenikon Airport in Athens, Greece, two Palestinian terrorists hurled three grenades and unleashed a salvo of small-arms fire into a line of passengers preparing to board TWA Flight 881 to New York. Three people died and more than forty others were injured. The United States Court of Appeals for the Second Circuit affirmed a federal trial court's decision to hold TWA responsible for indemnification for the

deaths and injuries sustained at Athens given the Warsaw Convention's provision that an airline was absolutely liable up to a maximum $75,000 for bodily injury sustained "in the course of any of the operations of embarking." *See Day v. Trans World Airlines, Inc.* (2d Cir. 1975). Even presuming an act of terrorism is "unexpected or unusual," what then is the definition of "terrorism." *See, e.g.*, Aviv Cohen, *Cyberterrorism: Are We Legally Ready?*, 9 J. INT'L BUS. & L. 1 (2010); Harold Caplan, *Who Should Pay for Aerial Terrorism?*, 21 NO. 3 AIR & SPACE L. 11 (2007).

PROBLEM

On September 11, 2001, five terrorists hijacked American Airlines Flight 77 en route from Washington Dulles International Airport to Los Angeles International Airport, and crashed it into the Pentagon, killing themselves, 53 passengers and the six-person crew. Leslie Ann Whittington and Sandra D. Teague were two of the unfortunate passengers. They had purchased tickets for onward travel from Los Angeles to Sydney, Australia.

The personal representative of the decedents' respective estates brought suit against American Airlines and others under the Air Transportation Safety and System Stabilization Act of 2001, alleging claims under the Warsaw Convention and on various other grounds. Plaintiffs ultimately moved for summary judgment, arguing that the Warsaw Convention, defendant American Airlines, Inc. is strictly liable for the documented injuries and that the carrier cannot sustain an affirmative defense under Article 20 of the Warsaw Convention that the carrier and its agents had "taken all necessary measures to avoid the damage or that it was impossible for them to take such measures." American Airlines opposed the motion.

What result should obtain? *In re September 11 Litigation* (S.D.N.Y. 2007). Does the Montreal Convention dictate a different result?

INDEX

www.ingramcontent.com/pod-product-compliance
Lightning Source LLC
LaVergne TN
LVHW080057220926
848484LV00007BA/1798